www.letsgo.com

EUROPE

Researcher-Writers
Ian Armstrong
Serena Booth
Heather Buffo
Adeline Byrne
Kevin Friel
Reina Gattuso
Christopher Holthouse
Christine Ann Hurd
Angie Jo
William Locke
Lynn Miao
Rodrigo Andrés Murillo
Anna Papp
Anthony Ramicone
Uliana Savostenko
Priyanka Sen
Chris Xu

Editorial Director
Claire McLaughlin

Research Manager
Christopher Holthouse

Associate Editor
Mackenzie Dolginow

Staff Writers
Powell Eddins
Sarah Fellay
Hai-Li Kong
Devi Lockwood
Anna Papp
Sonali Salgado
Colton Welch

D0061778

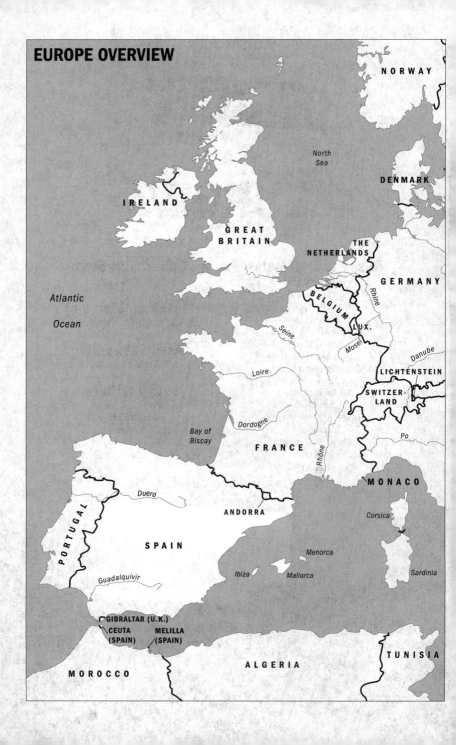

FINLAND

SWEDEN

ESTONIA

RUSSIA

LATVIA

LITHUANIA

RUSSIA

BELARUS

Vistula

Elbe

POLAND

Oder

UKRAINE

CZECH
REPUBLIC

SLOVAKIA

MOLDOVA

AUSTRIA

HUNGARY

SLOVENIA

ROMANIA

CROATIA

Danube

Black
Sea

SAN
MARINO

BOSNIA
&
HERZ.

SERBIA

BULGARIA

Adriatic
Sea

MONT.

KOS.

ALBANIA

MACEDONIA

ITALY

TURKEY

Tyrrhenian
Sea

Aegean

GREECE

Sea

Ionian
Sea

Sicily

Rhodes

Crete

MALTA

Mediterranean
Sea

N

LG

0   200 kilometers

0   200 miles

CONTENTS

RESEARCHER-WRITERS

IAN ARMSTRONG. Though he never left the Iberian Peninsula, Ian hopped deftly from culture to culture and language to language. Between Castile, Asturias, Basque Country, Catalonia, Valencia, Andalucía, and Gibraltar (UK), Ian conquered the peninsula more thoroughly than anyone since the Umayyads, and grew a beard that would make Hemingway cry little-girl tears.

SERENA BOOTH: Serena made Germany her home—even bringing along a bread pot to do some cooking while she penned notes on Berlin's many museums. Wielding a mighty sword of opinion, she put German culture to the test: judging by her high marks for *schnitzel*, opera, and most palaces, we're sure it passed with flying colors.

HEATHER BUFFO. Armed with a few choice French phrases ("Bonjour!" "Merde!"), Heather ran a marathon sprint through Paris, Brussels, and the south of France. With a trusty traveling gnome at her side, Heather briefly joined the ranks of France's Most Wanted and befriended some shockingly deceptive bartenders. She eventually wound up on a paradisiacal beach, tan and scheming how to smuggle Nutella crepes back into the US.

ADELINE BYRNE. Addie, driven by wanderlust and an unmatched enthusiasm for Irish spirits, traversed the Emerald Isle and made it her own. Always living on the edge, she progressed from dodging junkies in Northside to teetering on cliffs at the end of the earth, and is probably still where we left her: bellowing drinking songs with old Irish men in a forgotten pub.

KEVIN FRIEL: Hailing from the sunny shores of southern California, Kevin brought his laid-back vibe to Amsterdam. On bikes, gondolas, and sheer determination, he powered through endless cheese sandwiches and daunting Dutch spelling while still saving time to grow a luscious Euro-beard. Thankfully, despite his nearby accommodation, Kevin resisted the red lights and committed himself to kick-butt copy.

REINA GATTUSO. Carrying only a sundress and a Virginia Wolfe novel, Reina followed the scent of jasmine through northern Italy. With politics and silly faces as her only weapons, Reina gathered a gang of Korean hostel owners and old Italian professors and set out to conquer every museum in Italy. As she wandered the Cinque Terre, she contemplated starting an international campaign for art appreciation but decided that Italy was so *bella*, it wasn't really necessary.

CHRISTOPHER HOLTHOUSE. From Padua to Palermo, Chris train-hopped over 600 miles down the coast of Italy. Though his attempts to become a monk were shamelessly rejected, Chris put 7 years of Latin training to good use when he cried and waxed poetic at Virgil's grave. On a one-man mission to become the next Ansel Adams, Chris spent the rest of his route eating snacks, climbing intrepidly to the tops of things, and narrowly avoiding lightning.

CHRISTINE ANN HURD: A beloved Let's Go's veterans, Christine returned to Europe this summer, taking her wit and droll humor to Great Britain, the country that invented them. After researching Austria and Hungary in 2012, Christine traded palinka for Pimm's and *wiener schnitzel* for fish 'n' chips in the UK. Christine also found time to stalk Benedict Cumberbatch and pay a requisite visits to 221B Baker St. and the BBC Headquarters.

ANGIE JO: Angie took her passion and poetry to the Golden Horn this summer, enveloping herself in the history, culture, and hospitality of Istanbul. In the midst of skirting protests in Taksim Square and eating plenty of *pide*, Angie befriended a wizard on the way to Çanakkale, spent time in quiet reflection at the soldiers' graves in Gallipoli, and watched some slicked-down Turkish men compete at Edirne's Oil Wrestling Festival.

WILLIAM LOCKE. Will learned many things on his northern European adventure: one can go to Glasgow and live to tell about it, Copenhagen's Little Mermaid statue is a serious let-down, and "sandwich" is a really hard word to spell. From exotic Scandinavia to his old stomping grounds of Oxford, Cambridge, and the British Isles, Will's prose informs the reader—then leaves him or her in an existential breakdown.

LYNN MIAO: In eight short weeks, Lynn championed the behemoth that is Paris. A fast master of the Vélib' system, she biked her way up many a hill and across the cities 20 *arrondissements*, scouting out new establishments at every turn. After climbing the steps of Montmartre, storming the streets of the city on Bastille Day, and trekking out to Chartres and Versailles, Lynn spent the last days of her route relaxing in Lyon with a big bottle of well-deserved wine.

RODRIGO ANDRÉS MURILLO: From the raging streets of El Raval to the stunning mosaics of Park Guell, Andrés discovered both the unparalleled beauty and the unsettling underbelly of Barcelona this summer. Taking aggressive prostitutes and lost wallets in stride, he immersed himself thoroughly in Spanish culture, churned out an epic amount of copy, and even managed to squeeze in some babysitting on the side.

ANNA PAPP: Undeterred by inclement weather, Anna took to her route with enough enthusiasm to power a small rocket ship—though who wouldn't do the same with all that delicious beer? Tapping her European roots, she settled into the local life, expertly reporting on famous defenestrations, babies scaling TV towers, and the majesty of cabbage soup.

ANTHONY RAMICONE. Upon arriving in Portugal, Anthony was out of his country but hardly out of his element. He took to the welcoming Portuguese culture like a fish to water—or, perhaps, a *sardinha* to a grill. During his travels he found the hippest hostels, the cheapest drinks, the sweetest eats, and a chapel made of bones—hardcore. Or maybe post hardcore.

ULIANA SAVOSTENKO: A native of Russia and a natural globetrotter, Uliana tackled yet another language while researching in Florence, Tuscany, and northern Italy. Over eight weeks, she climbed the endless stairs of the Duomo and the Leaning Tower, grew tired of Italy's excessive nudes, and spent her birthday relaxing at the beach, all while taking precious care of Svindel, the office gnome.

PRIYANKA SEN: From the Temple of Jupiter to an audience with the pope, Priyanka's journey through Rome featured all things divine. "Researching" perfect pastries, pistachio gelato, and phallic-shaped pasta, she connected with her classical brethren as she traveled the Via Appia and ventured to the foot of Vesuvius. With copy that was raunchy at times and hilarious always, Priyanka took this years coverage *ad astra*.

CHRIS XU: With nothing more than a backpack and a duffel, Chris took a break from rowing the Charles River to explore Madrid and the Spanish countryside. After some crazy nights of cervesas and *flamenco*, Chris relished the simple life: churros for breakfast and trekking through ancient fortresses.

DISCOVER

EUROPE

Everyone you know—parents, friends, and especially random old men in parks—probably has a few stories that start, "When I was in Europe..." For all the shenanigans that ensue, these tales might as well begin with, "Once upon a time..." Still, for the most part, they're true stories. A kindly matriarch will cook you dinner and insist on setting you up with one of her children; a shop owner will convince you to buy mooncakes before you figure out what's really in them; you'll spend all night trying to dodge a neighborhood's worth of stray cats who seem to think you're their king; you'll meet a princess disguised as a pixie-haired commoner and fall in love over Vespa rides and one hilarious prank at the Bocca della Verità. Wait, that last one was *Roman Holiday*—but you get the point.

The unifying theme of this guide is adventure. Not geography, not sights, not history. Europe has been the stomping ground of students for generations, precisely because of the opportunities for escapes and escapades it provides. It has the whole gamut of architectural periods and incredible renovations, brogues and rolling r's, and residents who drink alcohol like water. And you're always in the good company of fellow travelers, both young and old, out on adventures like you. Give Europe a chance, think outside of the box, and you can make your trip something worth bragging about. Who knows? Maybe *Roman Holiday* was based on a true story.

when to go

Summer is the busiest time to travel in Europe. The season's many festivals can jack up prices, but it might be worth it to catch Avignon's Festival or London's Proms. Late spring and early autumn bring fewer tourists and cheaper airfares—meaning they're good times to go, if you can get the days off. Winter travel is great for those looking to hit the ski ranges around the mountains, but not the best time to take a walking tour through Prague. Plus, you'll find that some hotels, restaurants, and sights have limited hours or are on vacation—from you.

what to do

MY HOSTEL OR YOURS?

Not loving the exchange rate on the euro? Hostels are a great option, particularly in more affordable places like the Netherlands, Portugal, and Eastern Europe.

- **ALL CENTRAL HOSTEL (BUDAPEST, HUNGARY):** The name says it all—never miss a piece of the action at this hostel, where your bed is only minutes from the city's best sightseeing and eateries. (p. 422)

- **2G04 HOSTEL (BRUSSELS, BELGIUM):** Are you a solo traveler looking to meet fellow back-packers with no strings attached? 2G04's "no large groups" policy means lots of opportunities to meet new people without feeling left out. (p. 60)

- **BELIEVE-IT-OR-NOT HOSTEL (VIENNA, AUSTRIA):** This inexpensive and spunky hostel made believers out of us. (p. 16)

- **SAMAY SEVILLA HOSTAL (SEVILLA, SPAIN):** Walking and tapas tours, flamenco and discoteca outings—is this a hostel or a dream come true? (p. 795)

- **OOPS! (PARIS, FRANCE):** Meet droves of young travelers looking for a lively night out at this hostel in Montparnasse. Staying here definitely won't be a mistake. (p. 124)

FOOD FOR THOUGHT

From French *patisseries* to Italian *pizzerie*, the sheer wealth of cuisine options across Europe could keep your palate entertained for several lifetimes. It's a miracle that all travelers don't return home 50lb. heavier and desperately in need of a larger pant size.

- **CIP CIAP (VENICE, ITALY).** The crispy crust. Gooey, melted cheese. The smell of tomatoes and basil...we think it's the best pizza and Venice, and we're hungry just thinking about it. (p. 556)

- **EL SOBRINO DE BOTÍN (MADRID, SPAIN):** If reading *The Sun Also Rises* made you think, "Gee, I'd like to eat that suckling pig Hemingway mentioned," you're weird. You should also go to this upscale restaurant. (p. 731)

- **AUGUSTINERKELLER BEERHALL AND RESTAURANT (MUNICH, GERMANY):** Sausages, sauerkraut, and beer. What did you think you would eat in Munich? (p. 311)

- **RESTAURANT 3FC (PARIS, FRANCE):** Once you've eaten your weight in bread, cheese, and pastries, leave France for North Africa for an irresistible kebab from Restaurant 3FC. (p. 147)

- **SUR OCAKBAŞI (ISTANBUL, TURKEY):** We can't stress it enough: this will likely be the best meal you eat in Istanbul. Just breathe, dive in, and enjoy the foodgasm. (p. 852)

- **PIEMINISTER (LONDON, GREAT BRITAIN):** You've likely heard not-too-great things about British food. These pies will certainly change your mind. (p. 349)

- **MOST BLING:** The Pope's crib (a.k.a. Vatican City, p. 497), where you'll find the sickest frescoes and some Swiss guards in tricked out uniforms.

- **WORST MUSEUM TO VISIT WITH YOUR FAMILY (ESPECIALLY CREEPY UNCLE NICK):** The Amsterdam Sex Museum (p. 658).

- **BEST WAY TO GET SO FRESH AND SO CLEAN:** Getting pummelled by a nearly naked hairy Turkish guy in one of Istanbul's hamams is actually a lot more relaxing than you'd think (p. 860).

- **BEST OPPORTUNITY TO ASK SOMEONE TO SLEEP WITH YOU WITHOUT GETTING SLAPPED:** Paris's Moulin Rouge (p. 165). Thanks, Christina Aguilera!

- **BEST WAY TO CONTRACT EARLY-ONSET DIABETES:** Cologne's Schokoladenmuseum (p. 282), where gold fountains spurt out samples of sweet, sweet, chocolate goodness.

THE GREAT INDOORS

Let's get real: you didn't come to Europe for the trees—except the ones in the background of the *Mona Lisa*. Each of these museums could keep you distracted for a lifetime or four.

- **THE LOUVRE (PARIS, FRANCE):** We promise it was famous before *The Da Vinci Code.* (p. 125)

- **THE BRITISH MUSEUM, THE NATIONAL GALLERY, THE TATE MODERN, AND THE VICTORIA AND ALBERT MUSEUM (LONDON, UK):** We couldn't pick just one—nor should you, because they're all free! (p. 336).

- **UFFIZI GALLERY (FLORENCE, ITALY):** Venus's flowing locks, a swan-like depiction of Mary with Jesus, and 43 other rooms full of art are waiting for you (and thousands of other sightseers) to appreciate their magnificence (p. 589)

- **MOSTEIRO DOS JERÓNIMOS (LISBON, PORTUGAL):** Okay, so it's more of a church than a museum. But it's remained in near-perfect condition for over 500 years, so if you want to party (maybe pray is more appropriate) like it's 1502, this is the place. (p. 692)

- **DOX (PRAGUE, CZECH REPUBLIC):** If you're in Europe for more than 10min., you're bound to see something from (a) Antiquity or (b) the Renaissance. DOX and its constantly rotating contemporary art exhibits are a welcome and insightful reprieve. (p. 91)

- **VERZETSMUSEUM (AMSTERDAM, THE NETHERLANDS):** Learn about World War II and its effects in the Netherlands from a different perspective at the Dutch Resistence Museum. (p. 662)

- **FUNDACIÓ MIRÓ (BARCELONA, SPAIN):** Do you like bright colors, abstract shapes, and staring slightly puzzled to fully understand a piece of art? You'll love Joan Miró and this collection of his works and others inspired by him. (p. 823)

BEYOND TOURISM

Get off the tourist bus, put down your camera, and realize that Europe has even more to offer than priceless art and heavenly gelato. Take a class, volunteer, or get a job while abroad—you'll still have time for museum hopping, don't worry.

- **WWOOF, WWOOF!:** No, this isn't about dog walking. WWOOF (World Wide Opportunities on Organic Farms) lets you channel your inner dirty hippie and work on Europe's organic farms.

what to do

top 5 places to see dead people

5. STEPHANSDOM AND GRABEN (VIENNA, AUSTRIA): A great view upstairs, a catacomb of plague skeletons downstairs. (p. 15)

4. BASILICA DI SANTA CROCE (FLORENCE, ITALY): Italy's best and brightest—Dante, Michelangelo, Galileo, Machiavelli, and Rossini—rest here. (p. 594)

3. PANTEÃ NACIONAL (LISBON, PORTUGAL): See the tombs of Salazar's opponents at the National Pantheon, which took over 250 years to finally be completed. (p. 691)

2. WESTERKERK CHURCH (AMSTERDAM, THE NETHERLANDS): Try to find Rembrandt's burying place—even if the sanctuary's keepers don't know where he's hiding. (p. 660)

1. SAINT PETER'S BASILICA (ROME, ITALY): Don't be too creeped out by the mummified popes on display in Vatican City. (p. 497)

Give it a try across the continent, from Portugal (p. 713) to the Netherlands (p. 683) to the Czech Republic (p. 111).

- **DOGS TRUST.** This one *does* actually involve puppies. Specifically, walking, playing with, and generally basking in the cuteness of dogs in the UK. (p. 413)

- **SNACKST DU INGELSCH?** Don't understand what that means? You will after an intensive German-language program. (p. 321)

- **TURKISH DELIGHTS.** Spend time with adorable children against the backdrop of one of Istanbul's poorer, more residential neighborhoods with Mavi Kalem. (p. 873)

- **MEI I HELP YOU?** Marketing English in Ireland (MEI) is great for those with TEFL certification—they work with over 55 language institutions and help you find placement. (p. 481)

suggested itineraries

THE GRAND TOUR *(6 weeks)*

Brace yourself. This is one serious trip, but it's absolutely worth it. We recommend you tackle it with the help of budget airlines or a railpass (p. 879).

LONDON (4 DAYS): Load up on history, tweed, and tea. Make every attempt to serendipitously run into William, Kate, and baby George.

AMSTERDAM (3 DAYS): Amsterdam has it all: imperial history, artistic pedigree, great music. Plus, coffeeshops and legalized prostitution! You might not want to write home to mom about this leg of the trip.

BRUSSELS (2 DAYS): Go beyond the waffles, the chocolate, and the beer to find...a peeing statue. Well, that's something.

PARIS (4 DAYS): The quintessential European city will have you singing of *la vie en rose* in no time.

NICE (2 DAYS): The best of the Riviera is hiding somewhere between tourist flocks.

BARCELONA (3 DAYS): Stroll through the medieval streets of Barri Gótic in search of damsels to rescue and 🐉**dragons** to slay.

LISBON (2 DAYS): Sip *vinho do porto* while gazing at the sunset over the Rio Tejo.

MADRID (2 DAYS): Eat dinner at midnight, go out until dawn, and explore the city between siestas.

discover

ROME (4 DAYS): Get the best of the old—the Colosseum owes a lot to facelifts—and the new—bars in the Centro Storico and clubs in Testaccio—in the Eternal City.

FLORENCE (3 DAYS): Throw yourself into the Renaissance, which seems to live on in every Florentine building.

VENICE (2 DAYS): You don't have to ride gondolas to enjoy the nooks and crannies of this lagoon island. They're overpriced anyway.

PRAGUE (3 DAYS): During the day, the Charles Bridge is overrun with tourists and vendors, but there's nothing quite so magical at night.

MUNICH (2 DAYS): Oktoberfest will leave you wishing for some January- through December-fests.

BERLIN (3 DAYS): Look out for horn-rimmed glasses and cardigans among Friedrichshain's nightclubs, which are housed in former DDR buildings.

ISTANBUL (3 DAYS): Experience the city that has been fought over for millennia. Europe-d out? Asia is a cheap ferry ride away.

VENI, VIDI, VICI

You've got the ruins of ancient Greece and Rome, the art and architecture of the Middle Ages and Renaissance, masterpieces of the Impressionists, and reminders of Europe's oft-troubled political and religious history. Sounds corny, but it's true: traveling in Europe brings all the things you failed to learn in history class (the papacy, German unification, Protestant Reformation, World War II—to name a few) to life.

MADRID, SPAIN: There's a lot of history within the Museo del Prado's walls, even with only one-tenth of the collection on display at any time.

VERSAILLES, FRANCE: The Sun King had it pretty sweet—at least for a while.

ROME, ITALY: It's got a bloody history, but you'll be bloody impressed.

ISTANBUL, TURKEY: This city has more history in its name than most do in their entirety.

BERLIN, GERMANY: Check out the East Side Gallery to learn more about the Cold War and its impact on the people caught on either side of the wall.

STOP AND SMELL THE ROSES

In case you didn't know: you're going to spend a lot of time in Europe inside (with good reason—see "The Great Indoors" a few pages back). But that doesn't mean you shouldn't get a little fresh air, since Europe is packed with as many parks and gardens as it is with museums and cathedrals.

SEVILLA, SPAIN: You didn't think you'd be getting a safari in Europe, did you? You can—though you'll see forests, swamps, and dunes instead of giraffes on the savannah—at the Parque Nacional de Doñana.

VIENNA, AUSTRIA: Roam the gardens of the Hapsburgs at the Belvedere and pretend for an afternoon that you'll ever live in such lavish opulence.

EDINBURGH, UK: Sometimes flowers and trees aren't just for aesthetic beauty. Visit the Royal Botanic Gardens a scientific plant experience.

PARIS, FRANCE: If you're looking to see green, you've come to the right place. There's certainly no shortage of grassy knolls in this city.

PRAGUE, CZECH REPUBLIC: The walk up to Petřín Hill won't exactly be relaxing, but the views and sights throughout the tree-topped area is worth the hike.

THE ULTIMATE PUB CRAWL

Partying is as legitimate a reason to go to Europe as any other. Drinking customs say a lot about a city's culture, and... who are we kidding? It's fun. Don't be ashamed!

DUBLIN, IRELAND: Perhaps, more aptly, Publin?

OXFORD, UK: Party with the best and brighest in this university town.

AMSTERDAM, THE NETHERLANDS: We recommend the GLBT nightlife. Other activities are yours to choose.

COLOGNE, GERMANY: This city has some of the best of Germany's party scene.

BUDAPEST, HUNGARY. Down pálinka in the city's many ruin pubs.

PRAGUE, CZECH REPUBLIC: The beer is cheaper than water!

MUNICH, GERMANY: This is the birthplace of Oktoberfest and the beer garden.

BORDEAUX, FRANCE: We get it, too much beer. Welcome to wine country!

ROME, ITALY. Casually sip wine on the Spanish Steps. Classic.

BARCELONA, SPAIN: Every good night ends with a beautiful sunrise. Well done.

discover

how to use this book

CHAPTERS

Conquering the great continent of Europe is no easy task. Many have tried—from Julius Caesar to Napoleon—and all have failed. That's why you've come to us. We've been criss-crossing the continent for 54 years, smelling out the sightliest sights and the homiest hostels, and now, dear reader, we will pass on all of our knowledge to you. Let's get this show on the road with the travel coverage chapters—the meat of any *Let's Go* book.

We'll start off with Austria, where you can embark on your own Alpine adventure, à la *The Sound of Music*. From there, we trek on over to feast on *frites* in Belgium, then take in the old-world magic of the Czech Republic. In France we explore fine art and finer dining, and meet Beethoven and Berliners in Germany. We cross the Channel to get our fill of Beefeaters and double-decker buses in Britain, head back east to Hungary's thermal baths, and return to the Emerald Isle to drink Guinness over Joyce. We give you the lowdown on Italy's artistic treatures, the best museums in the Netherlands, and where to find Portugal's finest port, then finish our grand tour with the sun-drenched beaches of Spain and the continent-spanning ancient wonders of Turkey.

But that's not all, folks. We also have a few extra chapters for you to peruse:

CHAPTER	DESCRIPTION
Discover Europe	Discover tells you what to do, when to do it, and where to go for it. The absolute coolest things about any destination get highlighted in this chapter at the front of all *Let's Go* books.
Essentials	Essentials contains the practical info you need before, during, and after your trip—visas, regional transportation, health and safety, phrasebooks, and more.

BEYOND TOURISM

As student travelers ourselves, we at *Let's Go* encourage fellow globetrotters to see the world beyond the tour bus. We encourage people to try alternative forms of travel that let them engage with a community, immerse themselves a foreign culture, and get an even more enriching abroad experience. At the end of each chapter in this book, we offer suggestions for studying, volunteering, and working in a given country; we hope these suggestions let you get even more out of your trip.

ACCOMMODATIONS

In this book, we've listed our favorite hostels, hotels, B&Bs, and guest houses, along with helpful information about navigating the accommodations market, in the "Get a Room!" boxes in every destination. Our full list of reviews—along with our hotel and hostel booking engine powered by ⬛Hostelworld—can be found at **www.letsgo.com**.

LISTINGS

Listings—a.k.a. reviews of individual establishments—constitute a majority of *Let's Go* coverage. Our Researcher-Writers list establishments in order from **best to worst value**—not necessarily quality. (Obviously a five-star hotel is nicer than a hostel, but it would probably be ranked lower because it's not as good a value.) Listings pack in a lot of information, but it's easy to digest if you know how they're constructed:

ESTABLISHMENT NAME   TYPE OF ESTABLISHMENT $-$$$$

Address   ☎phone number   website

Editorial review goes here.

i Directions to the establishment. Other practical information about the establishment, like age restrictions at a club or whether breakfast is included at a hostel. Prices for goods or services. ◩ Hours or schedules.

ICONS

First things first: places and things that we absolutely love, sappily cherish, generally obsess over, and wholeheartedly endorse are denoted by the all-empowering ✍**Let's Go thumbs-up.** In addition, the icons scattered at the end of a listing (as you saw in the sample above) can serve as visual cues to help you navigate each listing:

✍	Let's Go recommends	☎	Phone numbers
i	General information	⏰	Hours

PRICE DIVERSITY

A final set of icons corresponds to what we call our "price diversity" scale, which approximates how much money you can expect to spend at a given establishment. For **accommodations,** we base our range on the cheapest price for which a single traveler can stay for one night. For **food,** we estimate the average amount one traveler will spend in one sitting. The table below tells you what you'll *typically* find in Europe at the corresponding price range, but keep in mind that no scale can allow for the quirks of all individual establishments.

ACCOMMODATIONS	WHAT YOU'RE LIKELY TO FIND
$	Campgrounds and dorm rooms, both in hostels and actual universities, as well as some convents in Italy. Expect bunk beds and a communal bath. You may have to provide or rent towels and sheets.
$$	Upper-end hostels and lower-end hotels. You may have a private bathroom, or a sink in your room with a communal shower in the hall.
$$$	A small room with a private bath. Should have some amenities, such as phone and TV. Breakfast may be included.
$$$$	Large hotels, chains, and fancy boutiques. If it doesn't have the perks you want (and more), you've paid too much.

FOOD	WHAT YOU'RE LIKELY TO FIND
$	Street food, fast-food joints, university cafeterias, and bakeries (yum). Usually takeout, but you may have the option of sitting down.
$$	Sandwiches, pizza, low-priced entrees, ethnic eateries, and bar grub. Either takeout or sit-down service with slightly classier decor.
$$$	A somewhat fancy restaurant. Entrees tend to be heartier or more elaborate, but you're really paying for decor and ambience. Few restaurants in this range have a dress code, but some may look down on T-shirts and sandals.
$$$$	Your meal might cost more than your room, but there's a reason—it's something fabulous, famous, or both. Slacks and dress shirts may be expected.

discover

AUSTRIA

The Seine has its lovers' trysts. The Thames has its bridges. The Tiber has Romulus and Remus. The Danube has—well, put on the Blue Danube and lace up your waltzing shoes, traveler, because this river will have you dancing. For joy, that is. This area has been inspiring troubled writers, wacky musicians, and singing families for centuries, but it's still hard to pinpoint exactly what is special about Austria and its iconic waterway. Maybe it's that Austria has maintained much of the charming 17th- and 18th-century architecture built along the river, resulting in a picturesque scene whether you stay in Vienna or venture into von Trapp territory in Salzburg. Or you can experience Austria's second-largest but often overlooked city, Graz, whose local university makes it a haven for students. Or maybe it's that the Viennese really do dance the waltz en masse on New Year's Eve. We haven't found one, all-encompassing answer yet (though not for lack of trying). We challenge you to find it, one cup of Viennese coffee and Danube backdrop at a time.

greatest hits

- **ROYAL DIGS.** Wander around Schloβ Schönbrunn (p. 20), an imperial summer residence with a French garden that brings Versailles to mind.
- **ONE-NIGHT STAND.** Buy a €5 standing-room ticket to Mozart's Don Giovanni at the gorgeous Staatsoper (p. 32).
- **DRINK LIKE THE LOCALS.** Rub elbows with village denizens while sipping home-grown Austrian wine at Heuriger Hirt (p. 25), just outside of Vienna.
- **THE HILLS ARE ALIVE.** Let your inner Von Trapp child sing as you stroll through **Salzburg** (p. 38), where you can see nearly endless renditions of the musical.

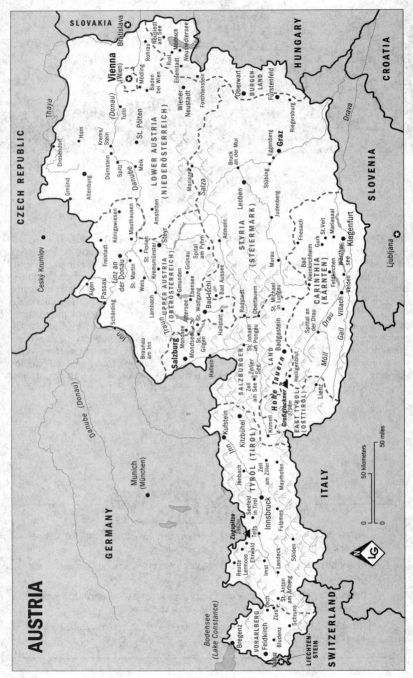

AUSTRIA

austria

SLOVAKIA Bratislava

CZECH REPUBLIC

GERMANY

HUNGARY

CROATIA

SLOVENIA

ITALY

SWITZERLAND

LIECHTEN-STEIN

Vienna (Wien)

Český Krumlov

Drosendorf

Gmünd

Altenburg

Horn

Krems/Stein

Dürnstein

Spitz

Melk

St. Pölten

Tulln

(Donau)

Thaya

Rohrau

Neusiedl am See

Mörbisch

Neusiedlersee

Rust

Eisenstadt

Baden bei Wien

Mödling

Wiener Neustadt

Forchtenstein

Oberwart

BURGEN-LAND

Fürstenfeld

Riegersburg

LOWER AUSTRIA (NIEDERÖSTERREICH)

Mariazell

Salza

Bruck an der Mur

Eggenberg

Stübing

Graz

Danube

Königswiesen

Mauthausen

Amstetten

Steyr

Freistadt

Linz an der Donau

St. Martin

St. Florian

Kremsmünster

Spital am Pyhrn

Grünau

Admont

Leoben

Judenberg

Murau

Friesach

Gurk

St. Veit

Mariasaal

STYRIA (STEIERMARK)

Wels

Lambach

Welz

UPPER AUSTRIA (OBERÖSTERREICH)

Gmunden

Altersee

Ebensee

Bad-Ischl

Radstadt

St. Michael in Lungau

Bad Kleinkirchheim

Feldkirchen

CARINTHIA (KÄRNTEN)

Velden

Wörther see

Klagenfurt

Schärding

Passau

Augen

Braunau am Inn

Mondsee

Mondsee

St. Gilgen

St. Wolfgang

Hallein

Hallstatt

Bad Aussee

Obertauern

Spittal an der Drau

Villach

Traun

Salzburg

Zell am See

SALZBURGER

Zeller See

St. Johann in Pongau

Badgastein

LAND

Hohe Tauern

Heiligenblut

Lienz

Großglockner 3798m

Gail

Drava

Ljubljana

Krimml

EAST TYROL (OSTTIROL)

Möll

Drau

Munich (München)

Kufstein

Kitzbühel

Jenbach

Zell am Ziller

Mayrhofen

Fulpmes

TYROL (TIROL)

Inn

Zugspitze 962m

Seefeld in Tirol

Telfs

Ehrwald

Innsbruck

Sölden

Reutte

Lermoos

Imst

Landeck

Lech

Zürs

St. Anton am Arlberg

Schruns

VORARLBERG

Bregenz

Feldkirch

Bludenz

Bludenz

Bodensee (Lake Constance)

Danube (Donau)

Inn

0 50 kilometers
0 50 miles

N
LG

Vienna serves as the center of student life in Austria and has the bargains and culture to match. Leave your hostel in Mariahilf or Neubau and grab a bargain breakfast at **Naschmarkt**—an open-air market stocked with delicious ingredients and prepared meals alike. After refueling, split from the Core Districts, and head for the Inner City to people-watch at Franziskanerplatz with a cappuccino from **Kleines Cafe**. When the sun sets, head to **First Floor** for some drinks with other Viennese youth, or get your culture on at Staatsoper, where standing room tickets start at just €2.50.

Though Salzburg is home to its own eponymous university, the city's identity as a tourist town is not especially conducive to bargains or even student discounts. Your best opportunity to ogle other young things will be at **Monkeys cafe.bar** or the **Shamrock Irish Pub,** which offers .5L glasses of Guinness for €4.50.

vienna

It's difficult to believe that Sigmund Freud concocted his very cynical portrayal of the human psyche in a city as beautiful as Vienna. What must have gone through his mind as he passed through the cobblestone streets? As he gazed up at the creviced hollows of Stephansdom, whose majesty subtly suggests that there must be a God, did Freud find his super-ego? Did he hear the soft laughs of those imbibing in the wine fields north of Vienna and discover his id?

But surely, Herr Freud, Vienna was a city of dreams, too. Just look to the dreams of the opulent Hapsburgs, constructing castles and palaces as if they would be residing in them for millennia. See the dreams of Gustav Klimt and Egon Schiele, brushing aside coffee and cigarettes while wildly sketching away. Then there are the dreams of Mozart, Strauss, and Beethoven that still play as whispers from the bodies of freshly-hewn violins. All these centuries of Vienna's dreams are remembered, interpreted, and celebrated in the city's dozens of museums devoted to this collective conscience of culture and art.

While it may be easy to dream in Vienna, it is much harder to sleep. Despite its devotion to a powerful past, the city has kept in step with the rest of Europe, which means the trademark combination of languorous, late-night dinners, later-night clubs, and latest-night kebab stands. Even if your heart does not tend toward nostalgia, there will surely be enough to keep you occupied. However, if you do long for a taste of a place that has transcended the word "city" to instead embody an Old World Mecca, Vienna will subtly, completely, and utterly grab your knock-kneed heart.

ORIENTATION

The heart of Vienna is the **Inner City,** which includes everything encircled by the Ringstrasse and can be conflated with District I. In the center of the Inner City is the U-Bahn stop of all U-Bahn stops: **Stephansplatz,** which is overshadowed by the giant cathedral, **Stephansdom.** Around the bulls eye of the Inner City lie the **Core Districts** (II-IX), which start with Leopoldstadt in the north and circling around to the hospital district, Alsergrund (here's to hoping you don't find yourself there!). The **Outer Districts** (X-XXIII), as one might surmise, border the Core Districts, starting at Favoriten in the south and generally circling clockwise to the Liesing.

Note: while other river-based cities, such as Budapest, can be navigated by plotting points against the location of the river, don't be surprised if you never even see

vienna

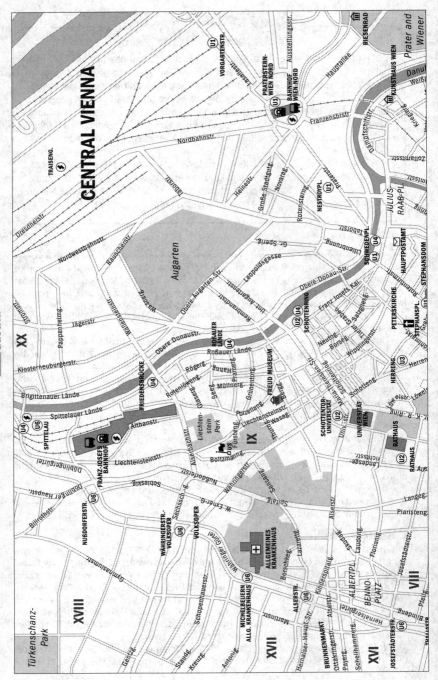

CENTRAL VIENNA

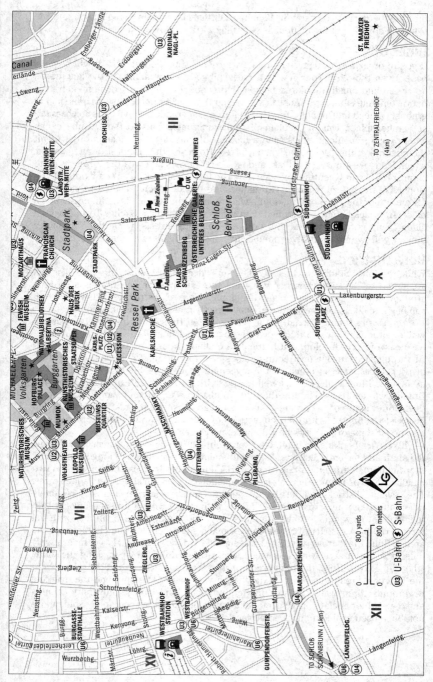

vienna

the Danube during your stay in Vienna. Plan instead on using Stephanspl. and the towering spires of Stephansdom as your major orientation points.

Inner City

If you're breezing through Vienna on a whirlwind trip, the Inner Stadt will be your base. Even though its purview is a mere 1.4 sq. mi. contained by the **Ringstrasse,** its cream and mustard-colored façades hide enough museums to commemorate a nation ten times the size of Austria. As a general rule, if it's not a museum or an incongruously placed McDonald's, then it's a church, the grandest of which is **Stephansdom** at Stephensplatz. Out of Stephenspl., **Rotenturmstrasse** runs to the Danube canal, where young Viennese locals (and a handful of tourists) disappear in order to hit the nightlife of the "Bermuda Triangle" area. However, the grandest of all is **Graben,** which leads west out of the Platz and is where tourists and wealthy locals come to shop at H&M and Valentino, respectively. The Inner Stadt provides some other diversions, like the opera, where performances are broadcast on a giant screen outside for a tenth of the price of an indoor seat. In reality, the whole of the Inner Stadt is a museum of aesthetics: cafes filled with writers and the best Sacher Torte (they all claim theirs is the best) spill out onto the gleaming streets, while the Stadtpark's bowing willow trees and silver ponds carry the drifting lilt of a Viennese accent.

Core Districts

While the Inner Stadt is technically the center district of Vienna, the Core Districts are home to the city's heart. Away from the camera-snapping hordes swarming around Stephansdom, Versace, and the stained glass of District I, it is here that you can begin to see a clearer picture of what exactly it means to live in Vienna.

Across the Danube canal to the east is the gritty second district, **Leopoldstadt,** which, although home to the overly photographed Prater Riesenrad and Augarten, has not won its redevelopment battle. In a C-shape around the Inner Stadt, districts III through IX fan out in a counter-clockwise formation. To the south, the third district, **Landstrasse,** is home to the sweeping grounds of Schloss Belvedere and its famous Klimt collection as well as the quirky, color-crazy Kunsthaus Wien and Hundertwasser Haus. The fourth and fifth districts, **Weiden** and **Margareten,** respectively, offer some of the greatest gastronomical pleasures; the tasty **Naschmarkt** and **Gumpendorfer Strasse,** with their collections of cafes, restaurants, and coffeehouses, also boast some of the city's best dining experiences.

If you are booking a hostel, it's likely you will be staying in **Mariahilf,** or **Neubau,** the sixth and seventh districts. Mariahilf is named after the city's longest shopping thoroughfare, Mariahilferstr., with more H&M branches than can be counted on two hands as well as many other international chains, ice cream shops, and shoe stores. The seventh district stretches west from the Museumsquartier and is refreshingly non-mainstream next to Mariahilf. Many of the city's young artisans have set up high-end jewelry and clothing boutiques here, and the nightlife is vibrant, with the former red light district of Spittelberg bringing some cobblestone character to the area. Behind the **Rathaus** (City Hall), the eighth district of **Josefstadt** is a comparatively quiet residential area, with the exception of the nightlife hotspot along the **Gürtel** (the Belt Road). Here, the bars are built into the structure of the **Stadtbahn,** where the U6 runs, creating a funky underground vibe where DJs spin and the drinking never ends. **Alsergrund,** the ninth district, is mainly home to the university campus and a wealthier enclave. The spectacular spires of **Votivkirche** accompany some more notable museums, including the **Liechtenstein.**

austria

Outer Districts

The Outer Districts (numbers X-XXIII) encircle the Core Districts in a clockwise direction, starting from the south, and include far fewer sights and way more locals. By far the most popular draws for tourists in the Outer Districts are the grounds and imperial rooms of **Schloss Schönbrunn** in the 13th district, one of the most spectacular sights in the whole city. In the 14th, Otto Wagner's **Kirche am Steinhof** glistens before a backdrop of green hillside in one of the city's wealthier districts, **Hietzing**.

Just beyond the **Gürtel** (which separates the Core Districts from the Outer Districts in the west) in the 15th and 16th districts, a number of additional hostels lie along and around the top portion of Mariahilferstr., around the Westbahhof. With the exception of the commercial Mariahilferstr., this area tends to feel either industrial or strictly residential, and even dining options become more limited. The southernmost districts, **Simmering (XI), Favoriten (X),** and **Meidling (XII),** are not terribly interesting and are generally avoided by tourists, with the exception of those visiting the Central Cemetery. The 15th, **Rudolfsheim-Fünfhaus,** houses much of the immigrant population, including Turks and Serbs, and can feel a bit unsafe at night due to the strange habits of loiterers and "women of the night."

A gem of the Outer Districts is **Dobling (XIX)** and, in particular, the *heurigers* (wine taverns) in **Grinzing**, where you can spend an evening dining (and drinking) along cobblestone streets and lush, green avenues. While some of these have bowed to the tourist influx and have started to embody a more Epcot-version of what Austria should be like, there are still some authentic *heurigers* that overlook wine fields and the elusive Danube River.

SIGHTS

Inner City

🏛 STEPHANSDOM
CHURCH

Stephanspl.   ☎01 515 52 35 26 www.stephanskirche.at

In its Gothic, melancholic splendor, Stephansdom dwarfs its eponymous plaza with a presence that could only be deemed monolithic. Inside the hallowed halls of this cathedral, built in 1147, tourists can venture below into the catacombs or visit the ornate stone pulpit (try to spot the pulpit's creator, Anton Pilgrim, peeking out from under the stairs in what must be the most awesome signature ever). For those in search of some great panoramic shots, either whisk up an elevator to the north tower (Nordturm) or climb the 343 steps to the taller Hochturm for an even more stunning view.

i U1 or U3: Stephanspl. Church admission €3, with audio guide €5. Catacomb tour €4.50, children €1.50. Tower and bell €4.50/1.50. M-Sa 6am-10pm, Su 7am-10pm. Bell and tower open daily 8:15am-4:30pm. Tours M-Sa 9-11:30am and 1-4:30pm, Su 1-4:30pm. 🕐 Church open

🏛 ALBERTINA
MUSEUM, STATEROOMS

Albertinapl. 1   ☎01 53 48 30 www.albertina.at

Vienna's contemporary complement to the older works of the Kunsthistorisches Museum, the Albertina houses several floors of generally more modern art as well as a set of Hapsburg state rooms (which are less-traversed and more opulent than their Hofburg brethren). On the fine art side, don't miss the top floor's permanent art collection, which features Degas, Picasso, Miro, and Kandinsky. The remaining exhibits rotate every few months, and temporary exhibits on Gottfried Heinwein, Max Ernst, and the Dutch Masters are expected to run in 2013.

i U1 or U3: Stephanspl. Or U1, U2, or U4: Karlspl. €11, seniors and Vienna card holders €9, under 19 free. Audio guide €4. 10am-9pm, Th-Su 10am-6pm. 🕐 Open M-Tu 10am-6pm, W

get a room!

Compared to other European cities, Vienna is admittedly expensive when it comes to finding accommodations. However, if you don't mind residing a ways from the heart of the city, there are definitely some gems in the city's outlying districts that are also conveniently located on the invaluable public transportation lines. If you'd like to avoid the hostel scene, try a pension—the German version of what we know as slightly upscale B&Bs. And if you insist on Hapsburg opulence, there are hotels in the center of the city that would make Franz Josef very happy indeed (okay, no servants, but this is the 21st century.) Below are a few of our favorites; you can find the full list of our recommendations on **www.letsgo.com**.

BELIEVE-IT-OR-NOT HOSTEL   HOSTEL $$$
Myrthengasse 10, apt. 14   ☎676 55 000 55 www.believe-it-or-not-vienna.at
While the entrance might look a bit dilapidated, the interior of this small hostel is one of the most beautiful and crisp styles we've ever seen. Sit down on one of the comfy white couches, use one of three netbooks for free (actually, everything in this hostel, from snacks to laundry to shampoo, is complimentary) or chill with a bottle of wine over a soccer game.
i Bus 48A. 8-bed dorms with shared bath €25; 4-bed dorms with private bath €29. ☼ Reception 8am-noon, 24hr. availability over intercom.

HOSTELRUTHENSTEINER   HOSTEL $$
Robert Hamerlinggasse 24   ☎01 89 342 02 www.hostelruthensteiner.com
If you have come to Vienna to channel the arts à la Owen Wilson in *Midnight in Paris*, this hostel is perfect for you. Bedecked with Klimt and Hundertwasser and stocked with a bar to liquify your burgeoning talent within, Ruthensteiner also directly encourages the arts with a cadre of musical instruments free for youto use. The only downside is its location in the Outer Districts, but artists thrive in solitude, do they not?
i U3 or U6: Westbahnhof. Walk down Mariahilferstr. away from the train station and turn left onto Haidmannsgasse. Take the 1st right onto Robert Hamerlinggasse, and there is a sign for the hostel. Free Wi-Fi. Lockers included. Book exchange and musical instruments available. Credit card surcharge 3%. 8- to 10-bed dorms €18-21; singles €40-64. ☼ Reception 24hr.

NATIONALBIBLIOTHEK/STATE HALL   LIBRARY
Josefpl. 1   ☎01 53 41 03 94 www.onb.ac.at
Hermione would have spent all of her time in this stunning library, probably the grandest pantheon to literature you'll ever see. Commissioned by Emperor Charles VI, the library has double-story bookcases, marble statues, and pastel ceiling frescoes that stretch to every corner. After just a few minutes inside, it becomes clear that Austria has its priorities straight. The library also features two literary exhibits each year, but we recommend spending most of your time just being bitter that your school's library doesn't even have a working printer most of the time.
i U1, U2, or U4: Karlspl. Or U3: Herrengasse. €7, students €4.50. ☼ Open Tu-W 10am-6pm, Th 10am-9pm, F-Su 10am-6pm.

HOFBURG PALACE   MUSEUM, IMPERIAL APARTMENTS
Heldenpl.   ☎01 533 75 70 www.hofburg-wien.at
A visit inside the Hofburg consists of three parts: the Imperial Silver Collection, a museum about Empress Elisabeth, and the Imperial Apartments where Franz Joseph and Elisabeth lived. The Silver Collection is basically case after case of cutlery and dishes, and the handy audio guide provides a complement to what

would otherwise just be a Crate&Barrel showroom. The Sisi Museum delves into the life of Empress Elisabeth Sisi, from her childhood to her tragic assassination, with artifacts and stunning replicas of her gowns and jewels. Finally, in the Imperial Apartments, you can see how Franz and Elizabeth ate, slept, and bathed in elegance. Be sure to take a guided tour to hear fun tidbits, like Elizabeth's impressive imperative to learn Hungarian in the hours it took for her hair to be properly coiffed each day.

i *U3: Herrengasse. Or, U2 or U3: Volkstheater, then tram 1 or 2. Audio guide free with entrance ticket. Tickets for each sight €10.50, students €9.50, ages 6-18 €6.50. Sisi Ticket (entrance to all 3 Hofburg venues plus the Furniture Collection and Schönbrunn Palace) €23.50, students €21.50, ages 6-18 €14. Jul-Aug 9am-6pm, Sept-Jun 9am-5:30pm. ☼ Open daily*

KUNSTHISTORISCHES MUSEUM
Maria-Theresien-Platz

MUSEUM
☎01 52 52 40 www.khm.at

As you walk up the main staircase inside the Kunsthistorisches Museum, the first sign that you're in a legitimate house of art is a towering, pearly statue of Theseus lunging at a fallen centaur (Theseus's *Kampf mit den Kentaurenkönig Eurython*). This museum houses Vienna's largest collection of art, including ancient Egyptian, Greek, and Roman antiquities as well as a slew of paintings from the 15th to 19th centuries. The paintings are truly special, so feast upon Rembrandt's self-portraits and Peter Bruegel's *Hunters in the Snow*.

i *U2 or U3: Volkstheater. Or tram 1, 2. €12, with Vienna card €11, students under 27 €9, under 19 free. 10am-6pm. ☼ Open Tu-W 10am-6pm, Th 10am-9pm, F-Su*

STADTPARK
Main entrance from Johannesgasse

PARK
☎

Nestled into the Ringstr., this large green space is an idyllic place for you to enjoy your gelato or your Goethe. Statues of dignitaries and musicians (10 points to Ravenclaw for finding the gilded Johann Strauss) beckon to all on summer afternoons. If you're into self-denial, drool from afar at Vienna's most acclaimed restaurant, Steierereck, where a meal will set you back over €100, and avoid the Kursalon, whose nightly dinner-music deals ooze tourist tackiness.

i *U4: Stadtpark or U3: Stubentor. Or tram 1 or 2. Free. ☼ Open 24hr.*

MAK (MUSEUM FUR ANGEWANDTE KUNST)
Stubenring 5

MUSEUM
☎01 71 13 60 www.mak.at

The MAK is what would happen if a design shop had its own museum. Vases, intricately carved cabinets, sleek cutlery, and an absurd number of chairs are displayed from every artistic movement, whether it be Baroque, Art Deco, or Roccoco. However, the best part of this applied arts museum when we visited was the "Design for Change" exhibit, which featured new forms of design and technology like Smartcars, biofeedback iPhone apps, and ergonomic furniture that would make any technology nerd drool.

i *U3: Stubentor; tram 1 or 2. €8, students €5.50, children and under 19 free, family €11. Free for all Sa. Tours €2. W-Su 10am-6pm. English tours Su at noon. ☼ Open Tu 10am-midnight,*

SECESSION
Friedrichstr. 12

EXHIBITION HALL
☎01 587 53 07 www.secession.at

This square building with a golden, laurel-leaf dome will certainly catch your eye as you wander through the Naschmarkt and Karlspl. area. Built to house the works of the Vienna Secession movement at the turn of the 20th century, the interior spaces are currently used for rotating modern art exhibits (check the current program online).However, most people go just to see the basement room that houses Gustav Klimt's *Beethoven Frieze*. Said to be an interpretation of Beethoven's *Symphony No. 9*, it depicts mankind's search for happiness on three walls of the rectangular room.

i *U1, U2, or U4: Karlspl. €8.50, students and seniors €5. Tours €1.50. ☼ Open Tu-Su 10am-6pm.*

vienna

HAUS DER MUSIK   MUSEUM

Seilerstätte 30   ☎01 513 48 50 www.hdm.at

The four floors of this interactive world of music could take five hours to fully explore, but if you're marching to the tune of *Flight of the Bumblebee*, spend most of your time on the third floor in the "Great Composers" section. Focusing on Haydn, Mozart, Beethoven, and Mahler, this area has a machine where you type your name and have Mozart compose a song for you, or you can conduct the Vienna Philharmonic with a baton that functions like a Wii remote. If the science of sound is more your style, the second floor, with its sci-fi-like tunnels and darkened rooms, offers great experiments that the kid in you will love.

i U1, U2, or U4: Karlspl. €10, students €8.50, ages 3-12 €5.50. Combined ticket with Mozarthaus €15, children €7. ⧖ Open daily 10am-10pm.

JÜDISCHES MUSEUM (JEWISH MUSEUM)   HISTORY MUSEUM

Dorotheergasse 11   ☎01 535 04 31 www.jmv.at

While the wide collection of prayer books, scrolls, Torah, curtains, and other artifacts on display at the Jewish Museum are quite beautiful, the lengthy historical explanations might be a bit dry for those who aren't obsessed with the past. However, the rotating exhibits that focus on the work of Jewish artists will likely fascinate a wider audience. Most notably, the museum has initiated a new Q&A program, and the atrium has been dedicated to a visual presentation of questions (and answers) about Judaism displayed on the wall.

i U1 or U3: Stephanspl. Walk down Graben, then turn left onto Dorotheergasse. €6.50, students €4. ⧖ Open M-F 10am-6pm, Su 10am-6pm.

PETERSKIRCHE   CHURCH

Peterspl.   ☎01 533 64 33 www.peterskirche.at

Standing on the site of a 4th-century Roman church and supported by the Opus Dei (*Da Vinci Code*, anyone?), Peterskirche's turquoise dome glows eerily, especially when illuminated at night. The soft beige-rose marble walls make for a soft, easily photographable sight (a nice contrast from the endless dark naves of Stephansdom). If you have time, stop by for a free organ concert, as the acoustics are one of the church's best features.

i U1 or U3: Stephanspl. Head down Grabenon the left. Free. ⧖ Open M-F 7am-8pm, Sa-Su 9am-9pm. Free organ concerts M-F 3pm, Sa-Su 8pm.

MOZARTHAUS   MUSEUM

Domgasse 5   ☎01 512 17 91 www.mozarthausvienna.at

This apartment is the only surviving Mozart house and is where the musical genius composed *The Marriage of Figaro* at the height of his wealth and fame. The first floor of the museum speculates how Mozart lived during his time here (plaques read "Guest room?" and "Dining Room?").The second and third floors focus more on the historical period in Vienna; don't miss the hologram (not just for Tupac, guys) of *The Magic Flute* being performed. Unfortunately, many of the other displays don't do the composer or his music justice.

i U1 or U3: Stephanspl. Walk down Singerstr. and turn left onto Blutgasse. Audio tour in English included with ticket price. €9, students and seniors €7. Combined ticket with Haus der Musik €15, children €7. ⧖ Open daily 10am-7pm.

NATURHISTORISCHES MUSEUM   NATURAL HISTORY MUSEUM

Burgring 7   ☎01 52 17 70 www.nhm-wien.ac.at

A visitor could be tempted to pass this museum by, as natural history museums tend to become repetitive (yes, we know, the dinosaurs went extinct). However, the Naturhistorisches boasts a positively breathtaking gem collection in Room IV that is heralded as the most valuable on the continent, including a topaz weighing 250lb. For those less interested in shiny things, the museum also holds

austria

the world-famous *Venus von Wollendorf*—a tiny, well-endowed woman who was carved almost 30,000 ago.

i *U2 or U3: Volkstheater; tram 1 or 2;bus 2A, 48A. €10, seniors €8, students €5, under 19 free. Guided tours €2.50. Scientific tours €6.50. M 9am-6:30pm, W 9am-9pm, Th-Su 9am-6:30pm. Tours to roof Su 3pm.* 🗓 *Open*

Core Districts

🏛 BELVEDERE
MUSEUM, PALACE GARDENS

Prinz Eugen Str. 27 (Upper), Rennweg 6 (Lower)   ☎01 795 570 www.belvedere.at

Just in case you needed another reminder of the Hapsburgs's obscene wealth, the Belvedere palace complex is happy to provide one. Yes, this is where you'll find a fountain every ten steps, a garden that resembles a hedge maze, and statues of Greek gods holding up the pillars of Oberes (Upper) Belvedere and Unteres (Lower) Belvedere (which are now, unsurprisingly, museums). While it may seem as though every single museum and souvenir shop in Vienna has some relic of Gustav Klimt's artistry, Oberes Belvedere actually possesses the most famous of Klimt's paintings—*The Kiss*. Along with that gilded, swooning woman, Oberes Belvedere also contains a large collection of Viennese landscapes, Anselm Feuerbach's *Orpheus Leading Eurydice Out of the Underworld*, and a collection of remarkable, well-preserved Gothic statues. Meanwhile, Unteres Belvedere, across the expanse of palace gardens, is privy to rotating exhibits in two halls connected by some equally opulent palace rooms.

i *Tram D, O, or 71. Unteres (Lower) Belvedere €9.50, seniors €7.50, students €7, under 18 free. Combined tickets (Unteres and Oberes) €14/11/10/free.* 🗓 *Upper Belvedere open daily 10am-6pm. Lower Beldevere open M-Tu 10am-6pm, W 10am-9pm, Th-Su 10am-6pm.*

🏛 KUNST HAUS WIEN
MUSEUM

Untere Weißgerberstr. 13   ☎01 712 04 91 www.kunsthauswien.com

From an early age, school teachers noticed Friedensreich Hundertwasser's "unusual sense of color and form," currently apparent in the building of the Kunst Haus Wien and all its works within. The floor and pipes curve, and the stairs are stacked with bright tiles and bits of mirror that make the Kunst Haus a cartoonish, magical land appropriate for a Dr. Seuss book. The first two floors of the museum contain Hundertwasser's spectacular sketches, with titles including *Stokes, Splotches, and Heads* and *Who Has Eaten All My Windows?*, while the third floor is used for rotating exhibits.

i *U1 or U4: Schwedenpl. Tram 1: Radetzkypl. €10, students €8, ages 11-18 €5.* 🗓 *Open daily 10am-7pm.*

LEOPOLD MUSEUM
ART MUSEUM

Museumspl. 1   ☎01 525 70 www.leopoldmuseum.org

The Leopold collection focuses on Viennese artists of the 19th and 20th century, and as befits a modern gallery, form follows function. The glistening white walls and large airy rooms provide a cheery sort of Danish modernist setting in which to view some of the incredibly dark works of Egon Schiele, on whom the collection has a particular focus. For a particularly interesting journey, sift through the inter-war part of the collection and cock your head at the sometimes baffling works of Albin Egger-Lienz and Anton Kolig.

i *U2: Museumsquartier. Or U2 or U3: Volkstheater. €12, students €8.* 🗓 *Open year-round M 10am-6pm, W 10am-6pm, Th 10am-9pm, F-Su 10am-6pm. Open in the summer Tu 10am-6pm.*

ST. MARXER FRIEDHOF
CEMETERY

III, Leberstr. 6-8   ☎01 4000 80 42

Closed in the 19th century, this Romantic-style cemetery lies near-abandoned in the third district. However, with its wild trees and weedy plots, this resting place is one of the calmest green spaces in the city. If you feel the incessant need to

vienna

do something touristy, Mozart's grave and its nicely manicured flowers are at your service.

i Tram 71: St. Marx. Bus 74A. Free. ☼ Open daily 7am-dusk.

MUMOK (MUSEUM MODERNER KUNST STIFTUNG LUDWIG WIEN)   MUSEUM

Museumspl. 1   ☎01 525 000 www.mumok.at

This modern art museum seems to be hit-or-miss depending on the exhibits that rotate every two to three months. The events range from displays of prominent modern art to more unconventional genres, such as fashion and architecture. As befitting a modern museum, the space itself is a gray, square warehouse with glass elevators to swiftly guide you through the museum's five floors.

i U2 or U3: Volkstheater. Or U2: Museumsquartier. €9, students under 27 €6.50. ☼ Open M 2-7pm, Tu-W 10am-7pm, Th 10am-9pm, F-Su 10am-7pm.

KARLSKIRCHE   CHURCH

Karlspl.   ☎01 504 61 87 www.karlskirche.at

Karlskirche offers something a bit different from the other churches in Vienna: 100ft. of scaffolding. However, the elevator and stainless steel stairs aren't for construction workers, but rather for visitors who want to stand among the angels. Well, angels in frescoes. If you feel that you'd like to reenact the Tower of Babel, climb an additional five flights of stairs to reach the very top of the dome for an unimpressive view (behind a chain fence and thick glass) of the city.

i U1, U2, or U4: Karlspl. €6, students €4, under 11 free. Groups of 6 or more €5 per person. Audio tour €2. ☼ Open M-Sa 9am-12:30pm and 1-6pm, Su 1-6pm.

Outer Districts

austria

☒ SCHLOSS SCHÖNBRUNN   PALACE, GARDENS, IMPERIAL APARTMENTS

Schönbrunner Schloßstr. 47   ☎01 811 130 www.schoenbrunn.at

If you have been to Versailles at a time that was not the French Revolution, you will probably agree that it's a nice place. This is the Hapsburgs' take on obscene royal wealth, but the tropes are the same: statues of Greek gods, expensively furnished rooms, and "grounds." The magic lies in the maze of wooded paths and walkways that you can enjoy for free; meander your way around the Fountain of Neptune and up to the Gloriette on the hill. For those who like navel-gazing at once-awesome royals, there are two tours for your desires: the Imperial Tour and the larger, Grand Tour that features the most expensive room in the palace, with rare rosewood paneling.

i U4, Tram 10 or 58, or Bus 10A:Schonbrunn. Walk in the direction the train is heading and Schönbrunn is on the left. Admission to gardens and grounds free. Imperial Tour (22 rooms) €10.50, students €9.50, with Vienna Card €10.50. Grand Tour (40 rooms) €13.50, students and with Vienna Card €12.20. 8:30am-6:30pm; Sept-Oct 8:30am-5:30pm; Nov-Mar 8:30am-5pm. ☼ Open daily Apr-Jun 8:30am-5:30pm; Jul-Aug

KIRCHE AM STEINHOF   CHURCH

Baumgartner Höhe 1   ☎01 910 601 12 04

Kirche am Steinhof, built by Otto Wagner in 1907, is a shining (literally) example of the Jugendstil art movement and one of the most important Art Nouveau churches in the world. The copper dome is blindingly bright against the otherwise green hillside where the church resides. The surrounding park was formerly a Nazi psychiatry center (for people who the Nazis thought were crazy, not crazy Nazis) but is now worth a visit, as golden meadows are set in front of the hilly horizon. Four angels stand guard at the entrance to the church, while ornate mosaics, creamy white walls, and stained-glass windows illuminate the interior.

i U3: Ottakring. From the stop, take 48A: Psychiatrisches Zentrum. Tours (50min.) €8, students and children €4. Art Nouveau tour (1½hr.) €12, students €6. Art Nouveau tour runs Apr-Sept every W at 2pm. ☼ Free viewing Sa 4-5pm. Mass Su and holidays 9:30am.

ZENTRALFRIEDHOF   CEMETERY
Simmeringer Haupstr. 234   ☎01 760 410 www.friedhoefewien.at
Stone cherubim, crosses, and pillars decorate over 2.5million tombs in Vienna's
Central Cemetery. From the main entrance (Gate II), a straight walk down the
central aisle will bring you to the resting ground's most musically-gifted inhabitants, including Beethoven, Brahms, and Schubert, as well as a fake tomb for
Mozart (the real one is in St. Marx). The cemetery is nearly deserted during the
day, as many of its sections have been closed for decades, and the romantic-style
layout is like a beautifully messy version of Schönbrunn.

i Tram 71: Zentralfriedhof; the 2ndZentralfriedhof stop is the main entrance. Free. Cars €2.20.
7am-6pm; Nov-Feb 8am-5pm; Mar 7am-6pm; Apr 7am-7pm. ⊡ Open daily May-Aug 7am-8pm;
Sept 7am-7pm; Oct 7am-6pm; Nov-Feb 8am-5pm; Mar 7am-6pm; Apr 7am-7pm.

FOOD

Inner City

▨ KLEINES CAFÉ   CAFE $$
Franziskanerpl. 3
This is what you came to Vienna for. While the more famous establishments
ensnare tourists with their "Freud smoked here" and "Beethoven croaked here"
claims, the winding inn-like interior of Kleines is filled with all the requirements
for an outstanding cafe: great coffee, patrons in tweed jackets, and waiters that
haven't yet been jaded. Drink your *melange* outside on the terrace overlooking
the church or stay inside to share in the artsy sentiment of those within.

i U1 or U3: Stephanspl. Coffee €2-4. Entrees €5.50-10. ⊡ Open M-Sa 10am-2am, Su 1pm-2am.

GASTHAUS PÖSCHL   TRADITIONAL $$
Weihburggasse 17   ☎01 513 52 88
Right near the Franciscan Church, this traditional Vienneserestaurant skips
the shock and awe that is Figlmüller and goes right to well-portioned local
cuisine with an international twist. It's also owned by actor Hanno Pöschl, who
occasionally helps out as a waiter during his off-hours. Try strawberries in sour
cream or sip a *melange* amid the close chatter of customers.

i Tram D. Salads €7-13. Entrees €9-19. ⊡ Open daily noon-midnight.

FIGLMÜLLER   TRADITIONAL $$$
Wollzeile 5   ☎01 51 26 17 77 www.figlmueller.at
For a wiener schnitzel larger than the 12in. plate it rests on, look no further
than this alleyway icon. The restaurant gives off a vibe similar to southern US
restaurants that advertise 72oz. burgers no one can finish, complete with waiters
asking the patrons if they've "given up yet." But for those with smaller stomachs,
Figlmüller also accepts the notion of taking leftovers home.

i U1 or U3: Stephanspl. Additional location at Backerstr. 6. English menu available. Entrees €10-
15. 11am-10:30pm. ⊡ Open daily 11am-10:30pm.

TRZESNIEWSKI   SANDWICHES $
Dorotheerg 1   ☎01 512 32 91
While its origins are Polish, this sandwich shop has won its place in the hearts of
the Viennese with its insanely cheap pitch: a mini-sandwich for €1. With dozens
of topping choices, including fiery-hot paprika, subtle smoked salmon, and the
daring chicken liver spread, Trzesniewski is a perfect place to grab some sandwiches to go while exploring the Inner City. And it doesn't even matter if you
can't pronounce the name—your mouth will probably be full anyway.

i U1 or U3: Stephanspl. Walk down Grabenand look for the signs on the left, about 3 blocks down.
Brotchen €1. 9am-5pm. ⊡ Open M-F 8:30am-7:30pm, Sa 9am-5pm.

EISSALON TUCHLAUBEN

GELATO $

Tuchlauben 15 ☎01 533 25 53 www.eissalon-tuchlauben.at

After you spend entirely too much time snapping photos on the mammoth asphalt of Stephanspl., head over to this *gelateria* for a gleaming, apricot-colored diner decor and a delicious apricot-flavored dessert. While most tourists are drawn to more flashy establishments in the square, the low hedges surrounding Tuchlauben afford a much desired degree of privacy.

i *U1 or U3: Stephanspl. Cups and cones €1.20-4.30. 11am-8pm.* ⌚ *Open Apr-Sept M-Sa 10am-11:30pm, Su 11am-11:30pm; Oct M-Sa 10am-8pm, Su 11am-8pm.*

DEMEL

CAFE $$

Kohlmarkt 14 ☎01 53 51 71 70 www.demel.at

Demel once produced the chocolates for the Imperial Palace, and now it produces every sweet imaginable for an imperious public. While the confectionary-filled first room would be enough for us to recommend this restaurant, Demel's strongest point is the cafe upstairs, complete with twinkling chandeliers and light streaming through the soft linen curtains. Order a hot chocolate and compare the difference between Demel's Sacher Torte recipe and Hotel Sacher's, two recipes that have been a point of contention for decades.

i *U1 or U3: Stephanspl. Or U3:Herrengasse. Coffee €3-7.80. Soups and entrees €6.20-21. Desserts €6.40-8. 9am-7pm.* ⌚ *Open daily 9am-7pm.*

CAFE DIGLAS

CAFE $$

Wollzeile 10 ☎01 512 57 65 www.diglas.at

The popularity of this plush *kaffeehaus* has grown over the years, evident now by the menu offered in every language imaginable. While the crystal chandeliers, velvet booths, and marble tables may feel like a step back in time, inflation has continued to march on regardless, so don't get too optimistic—a coffee and dessert alone can set you back close to €10. However, we suppose that the delightful ambience of a cafe filled with chatter and laughter is included in the price.

i *U1 or U3: Stephanspl. Teas €3.30. Breakfast €4.20-9.20. Entrees €7.50-15.50. Desserts €4.50.* ⌚ *Open daily 7am-midnight.*

LIMES

MEDITERRANEAN $$$

Hoher Markt 10 ☎01 90 58 00 www.restaurant-limes.at

Limes serves up fresh salads, pastas, and other Mediterranean fare in its urban chic interior or out on the patio at the edge of Hoher Market. While the inside can seem a bit dark despite its white furniture, the outdoor patio, with cushioned benches and shaded tables, is a lovely place to try some *Saltimbocca* (€16) while snatching bits of conversation from passersby.

i *U1 or U3: Stephanspl. Or U1 or U4: Schwedenpl. Credit card min. €15. Entrees €6.50-20.50. 10am-midnight.* ⌚ *Open M-F 11am-midnight, Sa 10am-midnight*

1516 BREWING COMPANY

PUB $$

Schwarzenbergstr. 2 ☎01 961 15 16 www.1516brewingcompany.com

Although America wasn't even a sparkle in the pilgrims' eyes in 1516, this pub has all the classic American favorites, from burgers to sandwiches to salads that don't include cabbage. Try the specialty beer that's brewed on site, and pick something that seems small, such as the toasted rye bread with mozzarella and tomato (€5.50), so you can go for seconds on the delicious lager.

i *U1, U2, or U4: Karlpl. Entrees €8-13. Sandwiches and burgers €5.50-9.20. until 2am.* ⌚ *Open M-Th 10am-2am, F 10am-3am, Sa 11am-3am, Su 11am-2am. Kitchen open until 2am.*

ÖSTERREICHER IM MAK

CAFE, BAR $$$

Stubenring 5 ☎01 714 01 21 www.oesterreicherimmak.at

Serving up modern and traditional Viennese cuisine, Österreicher im MAK has all the appropriate design elements to rival its neighboring museum (unsurprisingly called "The MAK")—mostly in its combination of oddly-shaped high and

austria

low bar tables, which create a weird sense of space inside. During lunch, if the weather is suitable, most patrons flock outdoors and take advantage of the daily lunch bargain special (€9.80).

i *U3 to Stubentor; Tram 1 or 2.Coffee €3-5. Entrees €13-22. Wine by the glass €3.50-6. 6-11pm.* ✆ *Open daily 11:30am-3pm and*

Core Districts

⊠ NASCHMARKT MARKET $$
Wienzeile ✆
Snuggled between Linke Wienzeile and Reche Wienzeile, this seemingly endless open-air market can provide hours of diversion as you wander through an assortment of fruits, nuts, meats, cheeses, scarves, sadly predictable "I Love Vienna" bags, and enough people drinking beer to fuel a Guinness commercial. If you happen to swing by on a Saturday, you can focus more on dry goods, as a flea market takes place in the morning and afternoon.

i *U1, U2, or U4: Karlspl.* ✆ *Market stalls open M-F 6am-7:30pm, Sa 6am-5pm. Flea market open Sa 6:30am-4pm.*

⊠ RA'MIEN VIETNAMESE $$
Gumpendorfer Str. 9 ✆01 585 47 98 www.ramien.at
With a relatively simple decor of white tables and skinny-legged metal chairs, this Vietnamese restaurant emphasizes complex and spicy ingredient combinations. With lo mein, pho, and rice bowls for the taking (well, you have to pay obviously), we recommend that you try the rice bowl with halibut and ginger (€8.80). Rice bowls are also accompanied by a small salad and slice of fruit to prepare and cleanse your palate.

i *U2: Museumsquartier. Credit card min. €10. Entrees €7-14.* ✆ *Open Tu-Su 11am-midnight.*

GASTHAUS WICKERL VIENNESE $$
Porzellangasse 24A ✆01 317 74 89
While a lot of District II establishments feature diverse, international cuisine to appease the local student population, Gasthaus Wickerl provides reliable Viennese favorites for a slightly older clientele. We would tell you to try the schnitzel, but hopefully you will have realized by now that that's an unspoken imperative. Sit on the outside terrace or head inside to enjoy that old-fashioned, homey decor that many other traditional restaurants attempt but fail to achieve.

i *Tram D. Salads €5-7. Entrees €9-16.* ✆ *Open M-F 9am-midnight, Sa 10am-midnight, Su 11am-11pm.*

DER WIENER DEEWAN PAKISTANI, HALAL
Liechtensteinstr. 10 ✆01 925 1185 www.deewan.at
Well loved by both the media and the local student population, this Pakistani buffet lives by the motto, "Eat what you want, pay what you wish." Serving an array of Pakistani meat and vegetarian dishes, this place also has the exceptional quality of being one of the only halal restaurants in the area. Overshadowed by absurdly colorful walls, the booths are always packed with eager guests, so come during less busy hours to ensure that you get a table.

i *U2: Schottentor. Or bus #40A: Bergasse.* ✆ *Open M-Sa 11am-11pm.*

HALLE CAFE $$
Museumspl. 1 ✆01 523 70 01 www.motto.at
While restaurants in the Museumsquartier are often packed with hipsters wearing dark jeans and something between a smirk and a sneer, this trendy, light cafe serves unparalleled breakfasts (€6.50-9.80) that will banish away the artistic blues. If you'd rather spend your time sleeping than enjoying croissants, Halle

vienna

also boasts a bar tucked right next to MUMOK. Perhaps under the influence, the stark modern art museum will look less imposing.

i U2: Museumsquartier. Alternatively, U2 or U3: Volkstheater. Entrees €8-19. Sandwiches €8. ✍ Open daily 10am-2am.

CAFE SPERL   CAFE $$
Gumpendorfer Str. 11-13   ☎01 586 41 58 www.cafesperl.at

As the faint buzz of German floats through the crowd of patrons smoking on the terrace, it is easy to realize that this is your traditional coffeehouse removed from the tourist slalom that is the Inner City. Buoyed by a traditional, mustard yellow exterior that is typical of Vienna, you can take your coffee indoors and eat among globed lamps or sit outside on the terrace overlooking Gumpendorfer Str. Apparently, Archduke Franz Ferdinand dined at this establishment (founded in 1880), so take yourself out and make sure your love doesn't burn this city.

i U2: Museumsquartier. Bus #57A: Station Köstlergasse. Coffee from €2.60. Small entrees €3.20-6.80. ✍ Open M-Sa 7am-11pm, Su 11am-8pm.

YAK AND YETI   NEPALESE $$
Hofmühlgasse 21   ☎01 595 54 52 www.yakundyeti.at

Take your taste buds on a journey east for some traditional Nepalese cuisine in a colorful courtyard removed from the somewhat bleak sixth district. Thursdays is "*Momo* Day," so you can sample all the sauces and fillings in an all-you-can-eat *momo* (Himalayan dumpling) buffet (€12). Or, on Tuesdays, eat *Dal Bhaat* (a rice, lentil, meat, and veggie meal) with your fingers in the traditional style (all you can eat; €10).

i U4: Pilgramgasse. Or bus #13A: Esterhazygasse. Appetizers €3-4.75. Entrees €6-18. Desserts €3.50-5.50. ✍ Open M-F 11:30am-2:30pm and 6-10:30pm, Sa 11:30am-10:30pm.

GASTHAUS UBL   VIENNESE $$$
Presgasse 26   ☎01 587 64 37

Just down the street from the Naschmarkt, this Viennese *beisel* holds its own culinary clout against the string of endless restaurants nearby. The traditional Austrian dishes, often with slight influences from other cuisines, have garnered this establishment much acclaim throughout the years. Enjoy your *schweins-braten, schnitzel,* or *semmelknodel* on the terrace, which is shielded from the street by a thick line of trees.

i U4 or bus #59A: Kettenbruckengasse. Reservations recommended. Entrees €8.50-18. ✍ Open daily noon-2pm and 6-10pm.

LUCKY NOODLES   ASIAN $
Mariahilferstr. 77

If you are in the mood for fast and easy takeout after a day of shopping on the fantastically crowded Mariahilferstr., you can't go wrong with a steaming box of Lucky Noodles—go for the vegetables, chicken, or both. As Lucky Noodles serves a steady stream of customers from a stand built into the wall and the nearby seating area is pretty small, it's best to grab a box and run.

i U3: Zeiglergasse. Noodles €3-4. ✍ Open daily 10:30am-11:30pm.

FRESCO GRILL   MEXICAN $$
Liechtensteinstr. 10   ☎01 660 467 89 83 www.frescogrill.at

This is as close to a Tex-Mex joint as you're going to find in a schnitzel-loving city. Fresco Grill offers burritos as well as a selection of tacos and spicy chili dishes. For such a small place, there are a startling number of seats on a smaller first floor and outside on Liechtensteinstr. Enjoy your Americana amid shockingly neon paintings of watermelons and rainbow stairs.

i U2: Schottentor. 30min. of free Wi-Fi access for customers; can create student account for a 5% discount. Tacos €5.40-8. Chili €3.50-7.20. ✍ Open M-F 11:30am-10pm, Sa 5:30-10pm.

austria

NICE RICE
VEGETARIAN, INDIAN $$

Mariahilferstr. 45, im Raimundhof 49   ☎1 586 28 39 www.nicerice.at

While you might think that Nice Rice would be similar to nearby Lucky Noodles with its friendly, adjective-grain name construction, this small Indian restaurant provides patrons with more of a sit-down cuisine experience. Head down the cobblestone alley to this place, where you can sip a cold *Ingwar-Orangentee* and munch on the Nice Rice Salad (hummus, tomatoes, cheese, black olives; €2.90).

i *U3: Neubaugasse or U2: Museumsquartier. The restaurant is down an alleyway off Mariahilferstr. Entrees €4-15. Lunch menu €8. ◘ Open M-Sa 10am-7pm.*

ELEFANT CASTLE
INDIAN, CAFE $

Neubaugasse 45   ☎0699 192 084 59 www.elefantcastle.at

While this cafe is about the size of a kitchen, Elefant Castle makes up for its size with creativity. Most of the food has an Indian-inspired theme, but some of the sandwiches, such as the Charlie Brown (peanut butter, bacon, tomatoes, and avocado) are just deliciously bizarre. If you crave something heartier, try one of the curry dishes, which come with a side of rice.

i *U3: Neubaugasse. Sandwiches €4. Curries €7. ◘ Open M-F 11:30am-3:30pm.*

Outer Districts

▓ HEURIGER HIRT
WINE, TAVERN $$

Eisernenhandgasse 165   ☎01 318 9641 www.zurschildkrot.com

Finally, a place in Vienna that can be called traditional without centering their business model around *wiener schnitzel*. Vienna has a thriving wine business, and this wine tavern nestled in the hills of nearby village Kahlenbergerdorf is the perfect poster boy for the wine's cool and crisp undertones. This would be a good time to bring out the Deutsch, as its somewhat-remote location precludes an entirely local clientele; or, if the somewhat-strenuous climb up the hill has wiped your *Erinnerung*, simply point. Rehydrate with a glass of white wine and gaze down upon the Danube from your shaded picnic bench.

i *Bus #239: Verein Kahlenbergerdorf. Walkthrough the small town to your left and up Eisernenhandgasse. It's about a 15min. walk up the hill. The place is popular with locals, so if you plan to come around 7:30 or 8pm, make a reservation. Pay as you go. Meat portions €3-6. Salad portion €2-4. Slices of bread or garnishes €0.40 each. F-Su noon-11pm. ◘ Open Apr-Oct W-F 3pm-11pm, Sa-Su noon-11pm; Nov-Mar*

▓ OBERLAA-DOMMAYER
VIENNESE $$

Auhofstr. 2   ☎01 877 546 50 www.dommayer.at

The grandeur of nearby Schönbrunn must have seeped into this delightful coffeehouse hidden only a few blocks away. But despite the waiters garbed in dress shirts and black vests, Cafe Dommayer does not require patrons to don absurd *My Fair Lady* hats or diamond cuff links: rather, the vine-enswathed courtyard plays host to scruffy crossword solvers and the haute bourgeoisie alike. If you insist on classing it up, try the smoked salmon toast with horseradish cream (€12.90) and a Maria Theresa (coffee, apricot liqueur, milk) with your pinky finger at attention.

i *U4: Hietzing. Entrees €4.80-12. Coffee €2.30-6. Torte €3.60. ◘ Open daily 7am-10pm.*

FRANCESCO
ITALIAN, BIERGARTEN $$$

Grinzinger Str. 50   ☎01 369 23 11 www.francesco.at

Given Austria's proximity to Italy, you'd expect some culinary influences to make their way across the alpine border; and for your cheese-craving taste buds, Francesco delivers. Well, they don't actually deliver to your door, but they do have a creative selection of relatively cheap pizza as well as some ritzier meat and fish dishes. While the food is solidly Italian (no mozzarella with schnitzel

vienna

combinations), the decor is a hybrid of classical statues and dark wooden walls reminiscent of a Viennese hunting lodge.

i Bus #38A from U4 Heiligenstadt. Get off at the Neugebauer stop and walk a bit further on Grinzinger Str. The restaurant is on the left. Entrees €6.50-24. ☼ Open daily 11:30am-midnight.

KENT TURKISH $$
Brunnengasse 67 ☎01 405 91 73 www.kentrestaurant.at

Right off of the busy market street of Brunnengasse, this Turkish restaurant provides succulent kebabs that put the thousands of kebab stands in Vienna to shame. Along with offering joy on a stick, this restaurant also has a strong vegetarian menu. After ordering your dish from the glass case where all of the specialties are on display, take a seat in the long hall filled with spirited banter in both German and Turkish (a multiculturalism that is reflected in the hybrid menu listings as well).

i U6: Josefstädter Str. Go west onto Gaullachergasse and turn right onto Brunnengasse. The restaurant is on the left. Entrees €7-13. 10am-10pm. ☼ Open daily

MAYER AM PFARRPLATZ WINE TAVERN $$$
Eroicagasse 4 ☎01 370 12 87 www.pfarrplatz.at

Alle Menschen werden Brüder ("all menare brothers") in the ivy-veiled courtyard of Mayer am Pfarrplatz. Beethoven himself lived right nearby and composed his sixth symphony (the pastoral one, which makes sense given the delectable calm that pervades the area) during his stay. This *heuriger* has thus become somewhat of a landmark but still keeps things local with an emphasis on meat served buffet-style and, of course, the nectar of the grapevine. Enjoy a glass of wine (or sample all 20 off the rotating list if you're as ambitious as Ludwig) in the secluded outdoor terrace that positively deafens you to the outside world.

i Bus 38A leaves from Heiligenstadt U4 toHeiligenstadt Fernsprachamt. Walk down Grinzinger Str. and turn right onto Nestelbachgasse. The restaurant is on the right on the corner of Nestelbachgasse and Eroicagasse. Menu and buffet from €11 from 7pm. ☼ Open M-F 8:30am-midnight, Sa-Su from noon. Music

10ER MARIE WINE TAVERN $$
Ottakringer Str. 222-224 ☎01 489 46 47 www.fuhrgassl-huber.at

We assume that the logic behind naming this wine tavern is a tribute to a particularly well-hydrated woman. However, men and women alike (with heavy representation from the senior citizen crowd) gather at this tavern's emerald green picnic benches in order to enjoy spritzer after spritzer after wine after spritzer. Because this is a *heuriger* and not a restaurant, the food merely serves as an anchor so you don't float away with all that bubbly. Come in the afternoon for some relaxed sipping or later in the day when the usual crowd starts floating in.

i U3: Ottakring. Turn left onto Thaliastr., then turn right onto Johannes Krawarik. Spritzers and wines €1.80-2. Buffet from €1.30. M-Sa 3pm-midnight. ☼ Open

STRANDGASTHAUS BIRNER'S VIENNESE $$
An der Oberen Alten Donau 47 ☎01 271 53 36 www.gasthausbirner.at

If you've been wondering where the Danube actually is in Vienna, there is no better introduction than this eatery on the northern bank of that wonderful blue stream. From its three tiers of seating, you can gaze upon splash-happy children and tenacious boaters while enjoying traditional Viennese fare without the somewhat-fake gingham flair that accompanies more touristy joints. Birner's does have indoor seating, but the view is the pinnacle of the place, so enjoy one of their ice cream treats among nature.

i U6: Neue Donau. Go down the stairs and follow the U-Bahn toward Florisdorf on the pedestrian walkway across the river. Turn right after you cross it and walk for about 5min. The restaurant is on the right (on the water!). Entrees €8-15. Lunch special €5.90 from 11am-3pm. 9am-11pm. ☼ Open daily

SAIGON   VIETNAMESE $$
Neulerchenfelderstr. 37   ☎01 408 74 36 www.saigon.at
This Vietnamese restaurant is the real deal—from the crispy, light egg rolls with dipping sauce and mint leaves to the large bowls of noodle soup (pho). The dishes are artistically arranged and garnished with cucumber and tomato slices and a flower-shaped radish, and while you generally shouldn't judge a pho by its photo, luckily the meals taste as good as they look. The ambience of Saigon is also oddly calming; the aquarium and dark-palette decor create a relaxed atmosphere that encourage you to enjoy your meal instead of scarfing it down.
i U6: Josefstädter Str. Go a smidge south of the U-Bahn stop and turn west onto Neulerchenfelderstr. The restaurant is on the left past the Brunnengasse Markt. Entrees €9-18. Open daily 11:30am-11pm. Sometimes closed on M in Jul and Aug; check website beforehand.

FIGL'S   VIENNESE, BIERGARTEN $$$
Grinzinger Str. 55   ☎01 320 42 57 www.figls.at
Figl's avoids the somewhat-contrived traditional atmosphere and instead opts for a strange identity that mixes "normal" cuisine and Viennese. The menu wouldn't look out of place in the German Biergarten at Disney World's Epcot, with the gratuitous wiener schnitzel along with an American burger to shut up the kids after a three hour wait for Space Mountain. That being said, while Walt Disney's tourist trap has been shanghai'ing people for decades, foreigners are almost nonexistent at Figl's, a major selling point for what otherwise would be just another schnitzel-based establishment.
i Bus #38A from U4 Heiligenstadt. Get off at the Neugebauer stop and walk a bit farther on Grinzinger Str. The restaurant is on the right. Entrees €8-23. 11:30am-4pm. 🍴 Open daily 11:30am-midnight. Lunch menu served M-F

NIGHTLIFE
Inner City

▩ FIRST FLOOR   BAR
Seitenstettengasse 5   ☎01 533 78 66
With Sinatra crooning in the background and waiters who will light your cigarette for you, this classic bar in District I is a haven secluded from the louder, flashier bars on Seitenstettengasse. With paneling and molding from the 1930s mixed with a modern aquarium running the length of the bar, the jazzy music and smoky velvet of this bar's interior gives it plenty of good ambience. On an off night, the friendly bartenders might even drop in a free pisco sour for your troubles.
i U1 or U4: Schwedenpl. Mixed drinks €7-10. 🍴 Open M-Sa 7pm-4am, Su 7pm-3am.

FLEX   CLUB, BAR
Am Donaukanal   ☎01 533 75 25 www.flex.at
Located in a gritty, unused subway tunnel, Flex's industrial space has hosted some world-famous DJs (and no wonder, as their sound system is the best in the country). In 2003, Spex magazine voted Flex the best club in the German-speaking world, and though 2003 is actually quite a while ago, casually-dressed party-goers still flood this alternative venue (although it has had some trouble keeping out the under-18 crowd). From the club's grinding dance floor to the attached cafe, the best part of Flex remains its cheap alcohol.
i U2 or U4: Schottenring; Tram 1 or 31: Schottenring. Free entrance to Flex Cafe. Club cover €4-12. 🍴 Open daily 6pm-4am.

vienna

VOLKSGARTEN DISCO   CLUB, BAR
Burgring 1, Volksgarten   ☎01 532 42 41 www.volksgarten.at
Located on the edge of the Volksgarten green space, this popular club is for
those who are tired of the gritty slurp-and-jostle bars of youth. With a smooth,
modern decor and gently pulsing multi-colored lights, you could almost fall
asleep if it weren't for the throbbing electronic that urges patrons to dance until
their hearts can take it no longer. Dress a bit more conscientiously if you deign;
however, you can always escape to the outdoor pavilion if the scene inside is
making you feel self-conscious.
*i U2 or U3: Volkstheater. Cover up to €20 depending on event. ☼ Open F-Sa 11pm-late; some-
times open during the week for special events.*

DICK MACK'S   IRISH PUB
Marc-Aurel-Str. 7   ☎01 67 67 06 81 24 www.paddysco.at/dickmack
Just beyond Schwedenpl.'s Bermuda Triangle and its pricey beers, Dick Mack's
is the Irish pub that all the local university students swear by. The decor is
nothing special, mostly consisting of long benches that look like Lord of the
Rings set pieces, but the beers are the cheapest in the land. A quick tip: if you
don't immediately see a table, never fear, and keep going down to the basement,
where room after room unfurls with additional seating.
i U1 or U4: Schwedenpl. Beer €2.20. Mixed drinks €2.80. ☼ Open M-Sa 8pm-4am.

ONYX   BAR
Stephanspl. 12   ☎01 535 39 69 www.doco.com
With an unparalleled view of Stephansdom through this bar's floor-to-ceiling
windows, you would not be remiss to take someone you want to impress to this
high-falutin' establishment. Fruity drinks, especially the Frozen Blackberry with
vodka and lemon, draw smitten couples and Vienna's young business crowd
to Onyx's sleek couches and stools while lounge music drifts pleasantly in the
background.
i U1 or U3: Stephanspl. Mixed drinks €9-14. ☼ Open daily 9am-2am.

PLANTER'S CLUB   BAR
Zelinkagasse 4   ☎01 533 33 93 15 www.plantersclub.com
Low red-leather chairs, small coffee tables, and palm fronds adorn this colo-
nial-style bar with enough bottles behind it to make an entire nation tipsy. Be
prepared to stay a while because the cocktail menu is at least 20 pages long, and
for spirit aficionados, there are over 450 types to fire up your throat. If you're
tired of the concept of the pub crawl and want to plant yourself in one place for
the night, the bar gets crowded around 10pm with a slightly older crowd than the
neighboring club scene, so come early to snag a seat.
*i U2 or U4: Schottenring. Mixed drinks €7-15. ☼ Open M-W 5pm-2am, Th-Sa 5pm-4am, Su
5pm-2am.*

Core Districts

🏖 **STRANDBAR HERRMANN**   BAR
Herrmannpark   ☎0688 866 60 36 www.strandbarherrmann.at
This classy, canal-side venue is as close to a beach bar as you're going to find in
Vienna. *Let's Go* does not recommend swimming in the canal, but there are plenty of deck chairs to repose upon during the day (and strategically placed sand
to increase the illusion). While this place is in the vicinity of dance club central,
the mood here more befits a langorous evening with live music and a cold brew.
*i U1 or U4: Schwedenpl., exit to Urania. Or U3, Tram 1, 2, or 2A: Stubentor. Beer from €3.50. ☼
Open daily 2pm-2am.*

austria

CHELSEA   BAR, CLUB, MUSIC VENUE
Lerchenfelder Gürtel/Stadtbahnbögen 29-30   ☎01 407 93 09 www.chelsea.co.at
Chelsea opened in the Stadtbahnbögen back when this area was a red light district and soon came to revolutionize the Gürtel nightlife scene. While many other bars on the Gürtel strip look like Howard Roark creations with more glass than sense, the only glass in Chelsea are the shot and beer glasses patrons are knocking back with gusto. With rock, Britpop, and funk blaring within its brick walls, Chelsea attracts down-to-earth patrons who arrive ready to drink. Come early because this place gets pretty packed.
i *U6, Tram 46, or bus #48A: Thaliastr. Cover from free to €12.* 🕖 *Open daily 6pm-4am.*

BABU   BAR, CLUB
Stadtbahnbögen 181-184   ☎699 11 75 40 72 www.babu.at
This large restaurant-cum-club expands over four archways of the Gürtel underneath the U6 tracks. Past its dark glass façade, it's more glass and air, with a split-level design and crisp white seats. From the top floor, you can look out the windows onto the Gürtel. If you like being watched instead, put on your best ice queen expression and join your gussied-up bretheren on the lower level.
i *U6: Nußdorfer Str.* 🕖 *Open daily 5pm-late.*

CHARLIE P'S   IRISH PUB
Währinger Str. 3   ☎01 409 79 23 www.charlieps-irishpub.at
Like **Dick Mack's** (p. 28), this Irish pub boasts cheap drinks and a young, penny-pinching student crowd that wants to drink a lot without spending too much. Nevertheless, Charlie P's still manages to maintain an atmosphere of well-mannered frivolity and doesn't let things get too rowdy. The upstairs area has big tables and benches where patrons can sit and talk with a large group of friends; otherwise, you can head to the cellar where there is an additional bar, some high tables, and the always-popular karaoke on Rock 'n' Roll Mondays.
i *U2: Schottentor.* 🕖 *Open M-Th 2pm-2am, F 2pm-3am, Sa 1pm-3am, Su 1pm-1am.*

PRATERSAUNA   CLUB
Waldsteingartenstr. 135   ☎01 72 919 27 www.pratersauna.tv
One of the newest clubs in Vienna's "in" scene, Pratersauna is a former sauna converted into a club. A deck and lawn with chairs encircle the pool, which looks temptingly lit up on warm summer evenings. However, this is not Los Angeles, and unfortunately it's not open when the club is in full swing. The alternative, warehouse-style dance floors reflect the minimalist drum and bass lines that are played, so it's going to take a number of drinks before you feel like you can dance to the beats here. The high entrance price is mostly due to hype; spend willingly, but don't be surprised if you are a bit underwhelmed, especially if you show up before 2am.
i *U2: Messe. Or Tram 1: Prater Hauptallee. Cover from free to €15. 1-9pm.* 🕖 *Open May-Sept W-Sa 9pm-6am; Sept-Apr 11pm-6am. Pool open W-Sa*

B72   BAR, MUSIC VENUE
Hernalser Gürtel, Stadtbahnbögen 72   ☎01 409 21 28 www.b72.at
Part of the growing Gürtel nightlife scene (under the railway arches), this small venue regularly hosts national and international DJs and bands, though it's particularly well known within the Austrian alternative music world. Come on Saturdays when there is no cover as well as a tribute to indie pop that seems to please the crowd greatly. The venue is cleverly split over two floors; the two bars and stage reside on the ground level, while on the first level there are tables and chairs with views down onto the stage.
i *U6 or Tram 43: Alser Str. Cover from free to €15.* 🕖 *Open M-Th 8pm-4am, F-Sa 8pm-6am, Su 8pm-4am.*

vienna

Q[KJU:] BAR, CLUB
Währinger Gürtel, Stadtbahnbögen 142-144   ☎01 804 50 55 www.kju-bar.at
Frequented by a young, party-going crowd, Q[kju:] is another club venue on the
Gürtel nightlife scene that caters to a rowdy, dance-happy clientele. The bar is
decked-out with pomp, and a giant chandelier hangs from a brick archway while
neon lights flash from the walls. While the clientele is happy to look a bit less
composed while dancing, the sartorial scene here is still dressy, so don't expect
Street Dance.
i U6: Währinger Str., Volksoper. 🕐 Open M-Sa 8pm-4am.

PRATERDOME CLUB
Riesenradpl. 7   ☎908 119 29 00 www.praterdome.at
The largest club in Vienna, Praterdome fulfills every raver's fantasy with four
dance floors playing every type of music imaginable, from techno to house
to R&B to '80s hits, and 12 bars to help you with your dance moves. While the
Starburst laser lights and neon colors are admittedly cool, the clientele often
takes this as permission to dance maniacally (which usually just ends up a bit
trashy instead). Mentally prepare yourself for a long night out and bring a very,
very large group of friends—it's likely you will lose a few in this massive party
complex.
i U1: Praterstern. Cover from free to €10. 🕐 Open Th-Sa 10pm-late.

CAFE STEIN BAR
Währinger Str. 6-8   ☎01 319 72 41 www.cafe-stein.com
In the warm weather, Cafe Stein's outdoor deck is the best place to enjoy a quiet
beer or wine and close conversation with friends. The views of Votivkirche lit
up at night provide a nice backdrop for discussions about the philosophical
tropes that Viennese university students love. During the cooler seasons, the
three floors inside offer a more lively night out as students come to forget their
academic and existential woes.
i U2, Tram 37, 38, 40, 41, 42, 43, 44, orbus #1A: Schottentor. 🕐 Open M-Sa 8am-1am, Su
9am-1am.

HALBESTADT BAR
Währinger Gürtel, Stadtbahnbögen 155   ☎01 319 47 35 www.halbestadt.at
This intimate, tiny cocktail bar is practically hidden in a single archway of the
Stadtbahnbogen. The bar stretches along one side, while on the other side, a
single leather bench runs the length of the room. Sit with one or two friends for
a quiet drink or watch a spirited soccer game and view the Gürtel through the
large windows at either end of the bar. Then, when the alcohol has worked its
magic, hit up the crazier clubs nearby if you so desire.
i U6, Tram 40, 41, 42, or bus #40A: Währinger Str., Volksoper. Weekend reservations required. 🕐
Open M-Th 7pm-2am, F-Sa 7pm-4am.

LUTZ BAR AND CLUB BAR, CAFE, CLUB
Mariahilfer Str. 3   ☎01 585 36 46 www.lutz-bar.at, www.lutz-club.at
This is one of those venues that transitions from day tonight seamlessly, shifting
from a cafe to a popular bar and club as evening sets in. A red carpet leads you
into the building, and the bar is only a few steps away as a dressed-to-kill party
crowd rolls in. The downstairs club, complete with laser neon lights and a dance
floor, is a welcome anomaly in the normally-quiet Museumsquartier area, and
every night is a different event, such as "Tipsy Tuesdays."
i U2: Museumsquartier. 🕐 Bar and cafe open M-F 8am-late, Sa 9am-late, Su 10am-late. Club
open daily 9:30pm-late.

austria

RHIZ   BAR, CLUB, MUSIC VENUE
Lerchenfelder Gürtel, Stadtbahnbögen 37-38   ☎01 409 25 05 www.rhiz.org
This casual and cramped music venue particularly appeals to people with a
love for electronic music. Ten years ago, Rhiz was the place for experimental
electronic sounds that pushed the boundaries of the music world, while today,
live international acts ranging from electronic to rock play regularly to packed
houses. A brief word of warning: the acoustics of the tunnel combined with the
music can be a bit rough on sensitive ears.
i U6, Tram 2 or 33: Josefstädter Str. Cover from free to €10. 6pm-late. DJs start at about 9pm.
🕿 *Open daily*

Outer Districts

U4   CLUB
Schonbrunner Str. 222   ☎01 817 11 92 www.u-4.at
While U2 hasn't yet made an appearance at U4, this underground nightclub has
boasted appearances by star-man David Bowie and the blissful Nirvana throughout its 30 years of business. While its District XII location means it's removed
from the rest of the nightlife in Vienna, this only encourages the stay-until-the-
sun-rises attitude you'll find here. Choose one of the dance floors (one smoking,
one non-smoking) and enjoy rainbow strobe lights and an eclectic mix of hard
rock, electronica, and'80s hits.
*i U4: Meidlinger Hauptstrasse. The club is directly behind the station on Schönbrunner Str. pre-
cise dates and headliners. 🕿 Open M-Sa 10pm-6am or later. Check schedule on the website for
more*

ARTS AND CULTURE

Theater

TANZQUARTIER WIEN   CORE DISTRICTS
Museumspl. 1   ☎01 581 35 91 www.tqw.at
This theater balances a somewhat ambitious schedule of dance premieres with
workshops open to the public for a small fee, and if one thing is guaranteed, you
will not be bored. The pieces range from exploration of the elements of fashion
to one-woman shows that carry enough drama for an ensemble.
*i U2: Museumspl. Or U2 or U3: Volkstheater. In Museumsquartier, walk beyond the Leopold Mu-
seum and turn right. Tickets €11-18, students €7.50-12.50. Rush tickets available for students
15min. before the performance, €7. Open dance classes (professional level) €7-10.50. 🕿 Box
office and information office open M-F 9am-8pm, Sa 10am-8pm.*

THEATER AN DER WIEN   CORE DISTRICTS
Linke Wienzeile 6   ☎01 588 85 www.theater-wien.at
One of Vienna's youngest opera houses (it opened in2006), Theater an der Wien's
shows keep running in July and August when the regular opera season stops,
making it a primary opera destination. The venue itself is done up in an old-fashioned style, with a main orchestra seating section as well as curved balconies.
While many theaters have more blind spots than a Hummer, you should be able
to see most of the action no matter what the price of your ticket.
*i U1, U2, or U4: Karlspl. Walk along the north side of the park onto Friedrichstr. and continue
along the road as it turns into Linke Wienzeille. The theater is on the right. Tickets €12-160. Student
rush operas €15, concerts €10. Standing-room tickets €7. 🕿 Box office open daily10am-7pm.
Student rush tickets available 30min. before curtain. Standing room (based on availability) can be
purchased 1hr. before show time.*

VIENNA'S ENGLISH THEATER

Josefsgasse 12   ☎01 402 126 00 www.englishtheatre.at

Vienna's English Theater was established in 1963 as a summer theater for tourists (who didn't know German, mainly), but its popularity enabled it to expand into the traditional theater season for locals who speak English. In 2004, it was awarded the Nestroy Prize for 40 years of achievement, with appearances by the likes of Judi Dench and Leslie Nielsen, and has continued its high-profile season with visits from Chicago-based Second City and performances of popular plays such as *Boeing Boeing*.

i U2 and U3: Volkstheater. Or Tram 1 or D: Parliament; Tram 2: Rathaus; or Bus #13A: Piaristengasse. Tickets €22-42, students and under 18 20% off. Standby tickets €9. ◨ Box office open on performance days M-F10am-7:30pm, Sa 5pm-7:30pm; on non-performance days M-F 10am-5pm. Limited number of standby tickets available 15min. before curtain.

Film

ENGLISH CINEMA HAYDN

Mariahilferstr. 57   ☎01 587 22 62 www.haydnkino.at

If you're desperate for the latest Marvel movie or Johnny Depp's newest attempt at being eccentric, this cinema is one of the few in the city that presents English-language films without subtitles and in a venue that has—gasp—stadium seating. With four theaters, Haydn can probably provide you with at least one new release (and perhaps one that you haven't gotten around to seeing yet).

i U3: Neubaugasse. Walk northeast on Mariahilferstr. Tickets €6.50-9. Check online for times and specific prices. ◨ Box office opens 15min.before 1st show and closes 15min. after beginning of last show.

BURG KINO

Opernring 19   ☎01 587 84 06 www.burgkino.at

Right down the street from the Vienna Philharmonic, Burg Kino provides tourist-voyeurism with screenings of Orson Welles's masterpiece, *The Third Man*, set in Vienna. One screen is reserved for big-picture blockbusters while the other, smaller screen rotates a cadre of smaller, indie films and documentaries that we think you probably haven't seen yet.

i U1, U2, U4, Tram 1, 2, or D: Karlspl. Follow Wiener Str. along the north edge of the park and turn left onto Getreidemarkt. Turn left onto Gumpendorfer Str., then take the 1st right and turn immediately right again onto Opernring. Tickets M-Th €5, F-Su €6. ◨ Box office opens 30min. before 1st showing.

ARTIS INTERNATIONAL

Schultergasse 5   ☎01 535 65 70 www.cineplexx.at

Tucked away off the main drag near Stephanspl., this Inner City cinema manages to still give off that old-timey vibe while only showing recent Hollywood flicks in English (and generally without those annoying subtitles.) If you balk at smaller theaters that seat about 70 or so without a stadium style, then make sure you pick a show in Room 1, which offers the largest screen and seating options.

i U1 or U3: Stephanspl. Walk with traffic on Rotenturmstr., then turn left onto Hoher Markt. Take the 4th right onto Schultergasse. Tickets €6-10. Check online for specific pricing and show times. ◨ Box office opens15-30min. before 1st showing.

Music

▨ STAATSOPER (STATE OPERA)

Opernring 2   ☎514 44 22 50 www.wiener-staatsoper.at

For many visitors, seeing an opera in the gorgeous, gilded Staatsoper is a highlight of a trip to Vienna. In the 2012-2013 season, Johann Strauss's *Die Fledermaus*, Mozart's *Die Zäuberflöte* and *Le nozze di Figaro*, Puccini's *Madame Butterfly*

austria

and *Tosca*, and Verdi's *Aida* are just six of the productions on a program that also includes more obscure operas and ballet performances. The opera season runs from September to June, but during the summer months, operas are shown on a 50 sq. m screen in the plaza in front of the Opera House for free.

i U1, U2, U4, Trams 1, 2, D, J, 62, 65: Karlspl. Walk north on Kämtner Str. and turn left onto Opernring. Tickets €8-225. Tours €6.50, students and children €3.50, seniors €5.50. ⚄ Box office (Operngasse 2514 44 78 80) open M-F 8am-6pm, Sa-Su 9am-noon. Tours of the Opera House vary based on show schedule, but usually 1-3 per day in the afternoon; check website ahead of time. Tickets include entrance to Opera Museum (except on M). Standing-room tickets are available 80min. before curtains.

WIENER PHILHARMONIC ORCHESTRA
INNER CITY

Ticket and Ball Office, Kärntner Ring 12 ☎01 505 65 25 www.wienerphilharmoniker.at

The Wiener Philharmonic Orchestra embodies the musical spirit of Vienna. Strauss, Mahler, Bruckner, and Wagner are some of the famous names that have been associated with the orchestra over the years, which is perhaps why season subscriptions often sell out years in advance. If you happen to be in Vienna in early June, the orchestra gives a free concert at Schönbrunn Palace, which metamorphoses into Vienna's equivalent of a football game, with fried food stands, beer, and teenagers dancing ironically to "The Blue Danube."

i U1, U2, U4, Tram 1, 2, or D: Karlspl. Walk north on Kämtner Str. and turn right onto Kärntner Ring. Prices vary. ⚄ Box office open M-F 9:30am-3:30pm, and 1hr. before the subscription concerts and end-of-year concerts.

WIENER STADTHALLE
OUTER DISTRICTS

Vogelweidpl. 14 ☎01 98 100 www.stadthalle.com

The Stadthalle presents the greatest variety of music, entertainment, and artistic acts of any Vienna venue as well as some sports and even kids' musicals. Although it lacks Old World opera house charm (the building resembles a spaceship), it has hosted big-name musicians including Guns'n'Roses and the Red Hot Chili Peppers.

i U6: Burgasse. From the U-Bahn, walk down Hüttledorfer Str., then turn right onto Vogelweidpl. The Stadthalle is on the right. Ticket prices vary based on event. ⚄ Box office (between Hall D and Hall F) open M-Sa 10am-8pm.

Festivals

🎇 DONAUINSEL FEST (DANUBE ISLAND FESTIVAL)
DANUBE ISLAND

Danube Island www.donauinselfest.at

The Donauinsel Fest is really the only festival that gets this island much attention from tourists in Vienna, but boy does it feel like a star for this one weekend in June. Two million locals and visitors flock to the green space for the closest thing the city can produce to a State Fair, with amusement park rides, free music, and beer-laden enthusiasts who often dress up in group costumes with their friends for fun.

i U1: Donauinsel or U6: Handelskai. Concerts and music free. Food, drink, and rides vary. ⚄ Jun; check website for specific dates.

VIENNALE
INNER CITY

Siebensterngasse 2 ☎01 526 59 47 www.viennale.at

If you find yourself in Vienna in late October, then the city will make you an offer you cannot refuse. The Viennale film festival plays 300 of the freshest international documentaries, shorts, and experimental shorts for those who love the smell of new film in the morning. Over the past few years, the festival selections have gained more diversity than a box of chocolates and over 90,000 visitors (and not all of them insane film buffs) attend screenings, film discussions, and the annual tribute to a recognized actor (who is sometimes a headliner, such as

vienna

Tilda Swinton in 2009). This calm introduction to a film festival that is a contender with Cannes could be the beginning of a beautiful friendship.

i Cinemas throughout the Inner Stadt. ⌚ Festival runs every Oct.

RAINBOW PARADE   INNER CITY, CORE DISTRICTS
Ringstr.   ☎01 216 66 04 www.regenbogenparade.at

Only begun in 1996, the gay pride parade has now become one of Vienna's largest events, sweeping the Ringstr. with all the customary celebratory articles: glitter, rainbows, and drag queens that give "fierce" a new definition. The parade culminates in a free concert with multiple acts, food, drink stands on the streets, and a generally exuberant atmosphere that might seem unexpected in this city where the big event is usually a somber requiem in Stephansdom. Be on the lookout for the blow-up, rainbow-colored balloons shaped like male genitalia.

i U4: Stadtpark. From Stadtpark to Schwarzenbergerpl. Parade and concert free. ⌚ Early in Jul.

SHOPPING

Clothing

MOTMOT   CORE DISTRICTS
Kirchengasse 36   ☎01 924 27 19 www.motmotshop.com

If you're one of those people who is obsessed with whales, mustaches, bicycles, and other hipster paraphernalia—wait, are you Zooey Deschanel? Never mind. This place is teeming with T-shirts that come in every color of the rainbow and simple, quirky prints. If you don't want to advertise yourself as a hipster (and you know that the real ones don't), then try a button with the same images available.

i U3: Volkstheater. Walk down Burggasse and turn left onto Kirchengasse. The store is on the left. T-shirts from €34. Buttons €1. ⌚ Open Tu-F noon-7pm, Sa noon-5pm.

BE A GOOD GIRL   CORE DISTRICTS
Westbahnstr. 5A   ☎01 524 47 28 www.beagoodgirl.at

While part of this shop is a hair salon (chic, obviously), the other half has interesting concept bags, wallets, fedoras, and shoes for sale as part of a "top to toe" style manifesto. There is also an interesting selection of design and art books laid out on coffee tables make this akin to someone's living room rather than a hair cuttery or boutique shop.

i U3: Neubaugasse. Walk down Neubaugasse and turn left onto Westbahnstr. Haircuts €65. Fedora priceless. ⌚ Open Tu-F 10am-7pm, Sa 10am-4pm.

Music

SCOUT RECORDS   CORE DISTRICTS
Capistrangasse 3

Stepping into this record store is like venturing into a music collector's basement, diverse enough to make Atticus Finch proud. Shelves, filing bins, and even cardboard boxes are all overflowing with vinyl, CDs, and DVDs; only the staff are able to find anything in this chaotic system.

i U3: Neubaugasse. Walk toward the city on Mariahilferstr. and turn right onto Capistrangasse. CDs from €3. Vinyl records up to €40. ⌚ Open M-F 2-7pm, Sa 10am-2pm.

SUBSTANCE   CORE DISTRICTS
Westbahnstr. 16   ☎01 523 67 57 www.substance-store.com

The pristine rows of CDs and vinyl records here are shiny and expensive, making this music store the place to buy new music. However, among the electronica and alternative, there are also a few throwbacks like Johnny Cash and Jimi Hendrix thrown in for some legitimacy. A great bonus is the listening stations right by the window, so that you can indeed show everyone walking past your undying love for music.

austria

i U3 or Tram 49: Neubaugasse. Walk north on Neubaugasse and turn left onto Westbahnstr. The store is on the right. ☒ Open M-F 11am-7:30pm, Sa 10am-6pm.

AUDIAMO
OUTER DISTRICTS

Kaiserstr. 70   ☎01 699 95 31 90 www.audiamo.com

You don't have to go to the ends of the earth or be Sherlock Holmes to find this audiobook store hawking its wares. If you're like us and feel like you have to experience atonement for the lack of reading during vacation, then definitely pay a visit to this well-organized specialty shop whose traditional English selection makes War Horse look positively French. No tinkering or tailoring is required; just soldier on over to the cafe and spy on fellow patrons as you sip your coffee to an intellectual soundtrack almost as great as a damn good shag.

i U6 or Tram 5: Burggasse. Walk north on Neubaugürtel and turn right onto Kandlgasse. Kaiserstr. is the 2nd left. Audiobooks from €8. ☒ Open M-F 9am-7pm, Sa 10am-5pm.

Books

▓ SHAKESPEARE AND CO. BOOKSELLERS
CORE DISTRICTS

Sterngasse 2   ☎01 535 50 35 www.shakespeare.co.at

This store's motto is "Let yourself be found by a book," and there really is no better place to do just that than here, where you will find a random assortment of philosophy, travel literature, and fiction. Located in a nook in one of the oldest parts of the Inner Stadt, Shakespeare and Co. "arranges" its books artfully on wooden bookshelves that stretch from floor to ceiling—and the best part is that there are hardly any multiple copies, making each purchase seem weirdly precious.

i U1 or U4: Schwedenpl. Walk along the river and turn left onto Judengasse. Turn right onto Sterrgasse. Used books from €3. New books from €8. ☒ Open 6 days a week 9am-9pm; call ahead for weekly schedule.

BUCHLANDUNG
CORE DISTRICTS

Internal Mariahilferstr. 123   ☎01 595 01 02 60 www.buchlandung.at

If you are a bit tired of the limited selection carried by small, independent bookstores, then look no further than BuchLandung's Mariahilferstr. location, where the selection is large (and the books come at hardly any charge). While it is primarily devoted to German-language books, the glass walls of this megalith store also carry a number of cheap English selections. Pick one up on your way to Schönbrunn on the U6 and read guilt-free.

i U3: Westbahnhof. Exit on Innere Mariahilferstr. The shop is on the right side of the plaza. Novels from €5. ☒ Open M-F 9am-7:30pm, Sa 9am-6pm.

LOMOGRAPHY
CORE DISTRICTS

Museumspl. 1   ☎01 524 02 20 www.kunsthallewien.at/en/shop

If you think "Candle in the Wind" every time you hear "Diana," you're not alone. But at Lomography, Diana is a type of camera; this store is happy to provide slightly expensive cameras for all of your museum-stomping needs. Along with the photography focus, it also carries witty postcards for when the artistic blues have got you down.

i U2: Musemspl. Or U2 or U3: Volkstheater. In Museumsquartier, the shop is beneath the stairs of the MUMOK. Cameras €100. Postcards from €1.20. ☒ Open daily 11am-7pm.

ESSENTIALS

Practicalities

• **TOURIST OFFICES: Albertinaplatz.** (☎01 24 555 www.vienna.info *i* Located in the Inner City, across from the Albertina Museum and behind the Opera House ☒ Open daily 9am-7pm.)

vienna

- **EMBASSIES:** Australia (Mattiellistr. 2-4 ☎01 506 740 www.australian-embassy.at ☒ Open M-F 8:30am-4:30pm.) Canada (Laurenzerberg 2, 3rd fl. ☎01 531 38 30 00 www.kanada.at ☒ Open M-F 8:30am-12:30pm and 1:30-3:30pm.) UK (Jauresgasse 12 ☎01 716 130 www. britishembassy.at ☒ Open M-F 9am-1pm and 2-5pm.) US (Boltzmanngasse 16 ☎01 313 390 www.usembassy.atm ☒ Open M-F 8-11:30am.)
- **INTERNET CAFES: Künstlerhauskino Wien Internetcafe.** (Karlspl. 5 ☎587 96 63 19 *i* €2 per 30min. ☒ Open daily 11am-9pm.) **Surfland.c@fe.** (Krugerstr. 10 ☎512 77 01 *i* €1.50 base fee and an additional €0.09 per min. ☒ Open M-F 10am-8:30pm, Sa-Su 11am-8:30pm.)
- **POST OFFICE: Hauptpotamt** is the city's main post office and is located in the Inner City. (Fleischmarkt 19 ☎0577 677 10 10 *i* Other branches are located throughout the city; look for the yellow signs and post boxes. ☒ Open M-F 7am-10pm, Sa-Su 9am-10pm.)
- **POSTAL CODES:** 1010 (Inner City) through 1023 (District XXIII).

Emergency

- **POLICE:** ☎133
- **AMBULANCE:** ☎144
- **FIRE:** ☎122
- **PHYSICIAN:** ☎141
- **PHYSICIANS HOTLINE FOR VISITORS:** ☎513 9595 (☒ 24hr.)
- **EMERGENCY DENTAL:** ☎512 20 78 (☒ Service on nights and weekends.)
- **PHARMACY:** ☎15 50 (☒ Open on nights and weekends.)

Getting There

By Plane

Vienna is centrally located in Europe and is quite easy to reach via plane. **Vienna-Schwechat Airport** (Wien-Schwechat Flughafen ☎7007 222 33 www.viennaairport. at) is home to **Austrian Airlines** (www.austrian.com), which runs non-stop flights from most major cities in Europe to Vienna multiple times a day. Other airlines that fly to Vienna include **British Airways** (www.britishairways.com), **easyJet** (www.easyjet.com), **Aer Lingus** (www.aerlingus.com), **Lufthansa** (www.lufthansa.com), **KLM** (www.klm. com), **Air France** (www.airfrance.com), and **United Airlines** (www.united.com).

One of the least stressful ways to reach the city center after a long flight is via the **City Airport Train** (CAT, www.cityairporttrain.com). It will drop you off at **Wien Mitte** in a mere 16min.; you can then connect to the U4 underground line at Landstrasse. The CAT runs every 30min. (☒ From the airport to the city daily 5:38am-11:38pm. From the city to the airport daily 6:05am-12:05am. *i* 1-way €11, round-trip €17; with Vienna Card €10/16; under 15 free. On board tickets €12.)

In addition to the CAT, the **Schellbahn** (S-7 or S-8) runs into the city, though it's a bit trickier to navigate. Look for the trains going to the city that read "*Wien Mitte,*" "*Wien Nord,*" or "*Florisdorf,*" while the train to the airport should have a "*Flughafen*" or "*Wolfsthal*" sign (1-way tickets €5.40.)

Airport Express Buses also shuttle between various places in the city center and the airport and take about 20min. (www.postbus.at ☎1 7007 323 00 or 517 17 *i* 1-way €8, children €4, with Vienna Card €7. ☒ Every 30min., 5am-midnight.)

By Train

There are a number of train stations located throughout the city that serve as major hubs for both local and international trains.

If you were wondering where the **Südbahnhof** went, it is gone. But don't freak out just yet. Since 2009, the Südbahnhof has been under construction, and the shiny, new **Vienna Central Station** will take the place of this now defunct station, with trains beginning to run in December 2012. The VCS is scheduled for completion in 2015 and will take over international travel from Westbahnhof and Wien Meidling. During construction, the eastern portion of Südbahnhof (Ostbahn) will remain running, taking east-bound trains to destinations like Bratislava.

The **Westbahnhof** was recently renovated into a shopping-mall-cum-train-station. If you're planning to travel to other parts of Austria or international destinations including Budapest, Munich, Hamburg, Berlin, or Zurich, then this is your train station. When the Vienna Central Station is completed, however, the Westbahnhof will only be used for travel within Austria. The airport buses and taxis still drop off at and pick up from the station, and you can easily connect to the U3 or U6 underground lines as well as tram lines 5, 6, 9, 18, 52, and 58.

In Vienna's District XII, **Wien Meidling** lies at the end of Meidlinger Haupstr. and serves international destinations in the Czech Republic, Poland, and Germany. It has taken over all the local arrivals and departures that previously used the Südbahnhof and also connects to the U6 Station Philadelphiabrücke, tram 62, bus lines 7A, 7B, 8A, 9A, 15A, 59A, and 62A, and S-Bahn lines S1, S2, S3, S4, S5, S6, S9, and S15. Wien Meidling has taxi stands, luggage lockers, ticket machines, an ÖBB Travel Centre, and an information desk.

The **City Airport Train** arrives at Wien Mitte, where you can easily connect to the U3 and U4 underground lines and multiple S-Bahn lines.

Getting Around

By Wiener Linien

Vienna's public transportation system, the Wiener Linien (www.wienerlinien.at), is extensive, reliable, and safe. It consists of the **U-Bahn** (underground), **trams** (above ground), and **buses**. The **Vienna Card** (available in hotels, at the tourist information center on Albertinapl., and at the airport for €19.90) gives you 72hr. of unlimited transportation access within the city as well as discounts on over 200 of the city's sights. Other useful transportation tickets include the 24hr. season ticket (€6.70), 48hr. season ticket (€11.70), 72hr. season ticket (€14.50), and monthly ticket (€45). A single ride costs €2. For the U-Bahn, buy your ticket at the multilingual machines and stamp it at the little blue boxes to validate it before reaching the platforms. Single tickets for trams and buses can be purchased on board for €2.20, coins only. The five U-Bahn lines run on weekdays from 5am to midnight (they're easy to spot due to the large blue signs with a "U" emblazoned on them), while the buses and trams stop running a bit earlier (look for Strassenbahn and Autobus signs on the street). Check the Wiener Linien website for exact schedules of specific lines. In September 2010, the U-Bahn lines started to run all night on Fridays and Saturdays in addition to the night buses that already cover a large portion of the city.

Nearly every sight can be easily reached using the U-Bahn, which transverses the city in six, über-punctual lines. If you plan on jumping around the city and hitting just the main sights, the U3 line that connects the Westbahnhof to Stephanspl. is your new best friend, with stops that include Stephansdom, Hofburg Palace (Herrengasse), the Museum District (Volkstheater), the shopping Mecca that is Mariahilferstrasse (Neubaugasse, Zieglergasse), and the Westbahnhof, where you can catch an international train to your next destination. For those wanting to explore nightlife, the U6 line toward Florisdorf follows the **Gürtel,** which boasts dozens of pubs built into the brick underneath the train tracks.

By Taxi

Because the public transportation system is so extensive, taxis are not entirely necessary, but they come in handy when the night bus is elusive from Sunday through Thursday. Some taxi numbers include ☎4000 011 11, ☎4000 010 00 (Inner City), ☎601

60, ☎401 00, and ☎313 00, although the best bet is to pick one up on the street (all accredited taxis in the city are known to be reliable.) In the Inner City, taxis cluster on **Rotenturmstrasse** and **Schwedenplatz** near the nightlife, but they also wait outside other well-known clubs in the Core and Outer Districts. Taxis have set rates for the airport, and some are exclusively airport taxis: **C and K** (☎444 44) and **Airportdriver** (☎22 8 22) run €35-48, depending on the number of passengers. An Austria-wide taxi number is ☎1718.

By Bike

Because of Vienna's manageable size, bikes are extremely common on warmer spring days and during the summer; there are over 1100km of safe bike paths throughout the city. **City Bike** is a public bike rental system with over 60 stands located around Vienna, usually near public transportation hubs (From €5 per hr., €4 for students). To rent a bike, you will need a City Bike tourist card (unless you somehow have a MasterCard or Visa associated with an Austrian bank). **Royal Tours** (Herrengasse 1-3) and **Pedal Power** (Ausstellunstr. 3) offer the cards for €2 per day, but it's worth asking your hostel or hotel as well.

By Suburban Train

The suburban train network **Austrian Federal Railways, ÖBB** is extensive and provides swift and easy access to Vienna's surrounding towns and countryside. If you're itching to explore Salzburg, Graz, or even some of the smaller, more provincial towns, then you'll probably be catching a train at the Westbahnhof (U3, U6) or Wien Meidling on the Philidelphia Brücke stop (U6). These trains require different tickets than the inner-city public transport, but all the stations have multilingual machines or ticket counters. Single rides start at €3.60 for nearby towns, such as Mödling.

salzburg

Salzburg has gone soft. What used to be the site of pillaging and burning, churches falling into piles of divine rubble, and Mozart clawing around the edges of truth sonata after sonata is now perfectly content to orient most of the typical tourist experience around an admittedly well-shot but absurdly plotted movie starring Julie Andrews and Christopher Plummer. Alas, all cities cannot retain their crusading kick-assery, and it's probably a good thing for Salzburg's architecture, considering everything in the city has been destroyed and rebuilt multiple times. But then again, you would be remiss to define Salzburg solely by mountain-twirling and wistful singing about Edelweiss. For one thing, the definitive symbol of Salzburg is a fortress **(Festung Hohensalzburg)** that has never once been conquered. If you fancy yourself an ascetic or devotee more than a war-buff, Salzburg boasts a dozen more-famous-than-the-next cathedrals (the **Dom**), abbeys **(Nonnberg Abbey)**, churches **(Franziskaner Kirche)**, and monasteries (the **Augustinian Monastery**) and then there's the shopping. **Getreidsgasse** is the Diagon Alley of Europe; its hundreds of stores are packed along the street, each with a classy metal banner hanging outside the front

ORIENTATION

Salzburg is divided into East and West Salzburg by the blue-green river Salzach. On the west side lies most of the **Old Town**, a maze of plazas and alleyways and, yes, Catholic cathedrals. The dominant feature of this side of town is the looming **Festung Hohensalzburg**, the large white fortress that spits out a small train car every 10min. to bring weary sightseers back to ground level after carrying them up to enjoy the view. The fun extends to the north of the area with Mönchsberg, the long, narrow mountain upon which the fortress sits. Four bridges connect the older part of the city to East Salzburg, which has a more open, boulevard city layout. More than likely, you'll be entering this part of the city through the Hauptbahnhof.

East Salzburg

East Salzburg is a series of shady lanes, wide streets, and some of the city's newer sights. The main place to visit is the **Mirabell Palace and Gardens,** which lies just east of the river Salzach and has a fabulous view of the **Festung Hohensalzburg** opposite the fast-flowing stream. Most of the main attractions lie within the ring of **Franz-Josef-Straße** that encircles the part of the Old Town that bleeds into East Salzburg and runs between the Salzach and the Kapuzinerberg Hill. Unless you're looking for something specific, there really is no reason to go north of the Hauptbahnhof, as this area is mostly industrial and corporate, offering little in the way of sightseeing joys.

West Salzburg

West Salzburg is where all of the tourists dwell. The streets are charming and nestled between sights more famous than the next, and every business has a small metal plaque outside to satisfy foreign curiosity. Once you enter the city proper, the main thoroughfare is **Getreidegasse,** along which every international store and chain restaurant (as well as some choice local places and Mozart's birthplace) lies. Between Getreidegasse and the blockade of Mönchsberg are huge open plazas that crop up one after the other, as is the case with Mozartpl., Residenzpl., and Dompl. The pedestrian area extends throughout this whole area, reaching an eastern boundary at Nonntaler Hauptstr. Past this point, the area again becomes commercialized, and there isn't much to see. Working in from the river, the nightlife area is concentrated around **Rudolfskai,** which lies along the river banks south of the Staatsbrücke.

SIGHTS

East Salzburg

⬛ EAGLE'S NEST (KEHLSTEIN)   VIEW
Kehlstein, Germany   ☎490 86 52 29 69 www.kehlsteinhaus.de

When der Führer reached his 50th birthday, you can imagine there was a bit of a scramble to pick a present for his special day. The answer? A super-high lookout point in the Bavarian mountains. The lookout point now hosts a restaurant that tries not to dwell upon what happened here 70 years ago. However, tourists still shoot up in a 40-story elevator to view the Octagonal Room (where Hitler entertained dignitaries) and the Pine Room (Eva Braun's favorite) as well as for the tremendous views of the mountains themselves. Be advised that visiting the Eagle's Nest involves crossing the border into Germany; there are rarely border controls, but bring your passport just in case.

i Salzburg Hauptbahnhof to Berchtesgaden Hauptbahnhof. Take bus #838 and get off at the Dokumentation stop. You'll have to pay to take the special shuttles up to the top; otherwise you can take the 2-3hr. hike on the clearly marked path for free. Bus and lift return trip €15.50, children under 14 €9. Fun Fact: At the end of The Sound of the Music, when the von Trapp family climbs over the mountains, they are actually crossing over into Germany and would have been in the line of sight of Kehlstein. ⌚ Open May 17-Oct 8:20am-5pm.

⬛ MIRABELL PALACE   PALACE, GARDENS
Mirabellpl. 4   ☎66 28 07 20

Are those drag queens? Yes. A man playing "Kalinka" on the accordion? Yes. Is that a string quartet playing Mozart? Of course. Is there any reason why you should not visit the Mirabell Gardens? No. The Pegasus statue and rainbow explosion of flower formations define Austrian aesthetics in one fell swoop: a love of mythology and outrageous beauty. The drag queens are a bit outside of

get a room!

Below are a few of our favorite accommodations in Salzburg; you can find the full list of our recommendations on **www.letsgo.com**.

☒ YOHO INTERNATIONAL YOUTH HOSTEL   HOSTEL $$

Paracelsusstr. 9   ☎662 87 96 49 www.yoho.at

No pirates to be found here, but you will discover pretty much every other treasure a traveler could want—including Wi-Fi, a bar, breakfast, a Nintendo Wii, and the requisite The Sound of Music nightly screening—at this large hostel. All rooms have decor that shies away from institutional metal bunks in favor of light wood and buttercup-yellow sheets. The hostel bar serves €3.50 mojitos and usually ends up packed with a cheery, somewhat-raucous crowd watching the soccer game.

i Bus #22 to Wirtschaftskammer. Walk east along Lasserstr. and turn right onto Paracelsusstr. 4- and 6-bed dorms (male, female, and mixed) €20-23; singles €40. Linens and keycard €5 deposit. ☒ Reception 24hr.

☒ HAUS CHRISTINE   B&B $$

Panoramaweg 3   ☎662 45 67 73 www.haus-christine.org

If you and a friend or two came to Austria to experience the bright, scenic side of the alpine country, then this B&B nestled in the hills will be perfect to feast your eyes upon. The rooms are done up in light pastels, with a breakfast room that looks out into the surrounding forest. It's a blessing and curse that the location is so beautiful, as it is a bit more of a hassle to get into the city than at other hostels, but the view comes at a price that's worth paying.

i Bus #21 to Werner-von-Siemens-Platz. Go east on Söllheimer Straße and turn left onto Bergstr. Haus Christine is clearly marked on the left. Breakfast included. Doubles €40; triples €57; quads €72. ☒ Reception flexible depending on guests' schedule.

☒ GASTHAUS HINTERBRÜHL   GUESTHOUSE $$$

Schanzlgasse 12   ☎662 84 67 98 www.gasthaus-hinterbruehl.at

With its pine-carved headboards, you'd think that this hotel was pulled straight from the Laura Ingalls Wilder prairie. Bizarrely enough, it's only a 2min. walk from the Old Town and is a good bet for those who want old-fashioned Austrian charm (the building is 800 years old) as opposed to the über-modern spaceship style that most chain hotels favor. The best part is the garden and the views of the Dom against a mountain backdrop.

i Bus #5 or 25 to Justizgebäude. Walk away from the river and turn right onto Schanzlgasse. Breakfast included. Singles €42; doubles €66; triples €79. ☒ Call ahead if arriving on Sunday.

this purview, but you might still find them dressed up in traditional Austrian garb and willing to take pictures with confused tourists.

i Bus #1, 2, 3, 5, 6, 25, or 32 to Mirabellpl. (Schloss). Gardens free. ☒ Palace open M 8am-4pm, Tu 1-4pm, W-Th 8am-4pm, F 1-4pm. Gardens open daily 6am-dusk.

SALT MINES   MINES

Bergwerkstr. 83, Germany   ☎49 (0)86 52 60 02 20 www.salzzeitreise.de

If we were to time travel, the number one commodity we would take with us to fifth-century Salzburg would be salt itself (a pound of which in die gute alte Zeit costs as much as a pound of gold). The Reichenbach mines are now in Germany after the principality of Salzburg was cut down to size in the 19th century, and they're still churning out good ol' NaCl to this day. The tour is a bit like a mining

austria

amusement park tour, with a train that brings you to the center, a series of slides from one part of the cave to the other, and a boat ride across a lake complete with technicolor lighting effects. Be advised that visiting the Salt Mines involves crossing the border into Germany; there are rarely border controls, but it is advised that you bring your passport.

i Take the ÖBB rail to Berchtesgaden Hauptbahnhof. Take bus #840 from the Bahnhof Berchtesgaden. Get off at the Salzbergwerk. €15, with Salzburg card €12. ☼ Open daily May-Oct 9am-5pm; Nov-Apr 11am-3pm.

CAPUCHIN MONASTERY   HIKING, VIEW
Kapuzinerberg 6   ☎662 87 35 63 0

If you want The Passion of the Christ without all of the crazy Mel Gibson Aramaic, then the Capuchin monks have something for you. The monastery is a place of pilgrimage due to its stunning, 17th-century Baroque Stations of the Cross running up the side of the hill that overlooks all of East Salzburg. An expansive parking garage now lies under the mountain, but ignore that and use your own two feet for a mini-climb up the city's most accessible mountain.

i Bus #4 to Hofwirt. Walk along Linzergasse and turn left onto Kapuzinberg. Climb the mountain. Free. ☼ Open M-Sa 6am-6pm, Su 8am-6pm.

West Salzburg

FESTUNG HOHENSALZBURG   FORTRESS
Mönchsberg 34   ☎662 84 24 30 11 www.salzburg-burgen.at

The only thing that has ever invaded this millennium-old fortress are tourists streaming from either the funicular that runs up the mountain or the perilous footpath (by which you literally have to pass through die Höllenpforte—"The Gates of Hell"). Overlooking the rest of the city, the castle provides the requisite beautiful view along with a series of eccentric attractions, such as a torture chamber and a marionette museum. (We know that, somewhere, Chuckie is proud). The best way to attack the castle is by avoiding the pricey souvenir gambits; instead, work your way down the castle from the top parapet that the on-site maps recommend as the second stop.

i Bus #3, 5, 6, 8, 20, 25, or 28 to Rathaus. Enter the Old Town by walking south along the river and head toward the Dom (with the green domes). Go toward the mountain behind it until you get to Festungsgasse. The sign for the funicular is large. If you want to walk up the footpath, turn right and continue along the road uphill until you reach the entrance. Fortress via Festungbahn €11, via footpath €7.80. Ticket includes admission to all museums in the fortress as well as an audio guide. ☼ Open daily Jan-Apr 9:30am-5pm; May-Sept 9am-7pm; Oct-Dec 9:30am-5pm.

DOM   CATHEDRAL
Dompl.   ☎662 84 41 89 www.salzburger-dom.at

If the Salzburg Dom represents anything, it's the utter absurdity of war and religious feuds. In 1167, the whole shebang was burned down because pyromaniac Frederick Barbarossa refused to acknowledge the "anti-Pope" Paschal. Like seemingly everything in Western Europe, the church was also destroyed in 1944 when an American bomb collapsed the cathedral completely. Despite all the trials and tribulations, the organ is still in good condition, and frequent concerts emphasize the visual delight with auditory stimuli.

i Bus #3, 5, 6, 8, 20, 25, or 28 to Rathaus. From the stop, go into the Old Town and turn left onto Getreidegasse until you come out onto the huge Residenepl. The cathedral is on the opposite side of the plaza. Donations encouraged. ☼ Open Jan-Feb M-Sa 8am-5pm, Su 1-5pm; Mar-Apr M-Sa 9am-6pm, Su 1-6pm; May-Sept M-Sa 8am-7pm, Su 1-7pm; Oct M-Sa 8am-6pm, Su 1-6pm, Nov M-Sa 8am-5pm, Su 1-5pm; Dec M-Sa 8am-6pm, Su 1-6pm.

MOZART'S BIRTHPLACE
MUSEUM

Getreidegasse 9 ☎662 84 43 13

While Vienna tries to emphasize that it's the city Mozart actually wanted to live in, Salzburg is indeed where the prodigious story began. This museum provides a startlingly cumulative portrait of what it was like to dwell among the 16,000 Salzburg residents of Mozart's time and also houses the master's own tiny violin and dozens upon dozens of original works. The museum is a study in romanticizing Mozart's life, and as a particularly apt plaque for the boy-turned-man-wonder states: "In the Romantic era, Mozart's allegedly tragic life circumstances corresponded to the romantic image of the unappreciated genius who had do die at such an early age."

i Bus #3, 5, 6, 8, 20, 25, or 28 to Rathaus. Walk away from the river into the Old Town and turn right onto Getreidegasse. The museum is on the left in a bright yellow building. €7. ☑ Open daily 9am-5:30pm.

ST. PETER'S ABBEY
MONASTERY, CHURCH, CEMETERY

St. Peter Bezirk 1/2 ☎662 84 45 76 0 www.erzabtei.at

If you happen to be the sibling of a famous German-speaking musician, you're probably buried in St. Peter's Friedhof along with Mozart's sister, Haydn's brother, and a litany of other notables-by-connection. The monastery and church date back to the eighth century, making the complex the oldest monastery in the German-speaking world. The cool and somewhat creepy icing on the abbey's cake are the catacombs, which you can experience in a Hunchback of Notre Dame fashion for a small fee.

i Bus #3, 5, 6, 8, 20, 25, or 28 to Rathaus. From the stop, walk away from the river into the Old Town and turn left onto Getreidegasse until you come out onto the huge Residenepl. Go past the cathedral; the abbey is located up against the mountain. Catacombs €1.50, students €1. ☑ Church open daily 8am-noon and 2:30-6:30pm. Cemetery open daily 6:30am-dusk. Catacombs open May-Sept Tu-Su 10:30am-5pm; Oct-Apr W-Th 10:30am-3:30pm, F-Sa 10:30am-4pm.

NONNBERG ABBEY
ABBEY

Nonnberggasse 2 ☎662 84 16 07

This would be the point where we start bursting into "Climb Every Mountain," but alas, there's only one mountain you need to climb (and sadly no streams to ford). Nestled under Festung Hohensalzburg, this abbey has hosted nuns for almost a millennium. In the olden days, the abbey was actually the site of some gender parity when an archbishop decreed the abbess of Nonnberg equal to the abbot of St. Peter's in 1241. It has retained its quiet, royal beatitude with a darkened, romantic chapel and well-groomed graves outside.

i Bus #3, 5, 6, 8, 20, 25, or 28 to Rathaus. Enter the Old Town and walk toward the Dom (with the green domes). Go toward the mountain behind it until you get to Festungsgasse. Walk left along the mountain on this street and turn right when you get to the building with the onion dome. Free. ☑ Open daily 7am-dusk.

ROYAL PALACE RESIDENCES
STATE ROOMS

Residenzpl. 1 ☎662 80 42 26 90 www.salzburg-burgen.at

In a world where IKEA holds a monopoly on our lives and our collective goal is a sofa unit with green stripes, these state rooms serve as a comforting reminder that the consumers of years past were 100 times worse than us. The Royal Palace Residences not only boast the requisite giant crystal chandeliers but are also home to the room that hosted a six-year-old Mozart sawing away on his tiny violin.

i Bus #3, 5, 6, 8, 20, 25, or 28 to Rathaus. Walk away from the river into the Old Town and walk toward the Dom. You'll come out onto Residenzpl.; the residence is on the right. €9. ☑ Open daily 10am-5pm; check website as dates vary.

austria

MUSEUM OF NATURAL HISTORY AND TECHNOLOGY   MUSEUM
Museumspl. 5   ☎662 84 26 530 www.hausdernatur.at
With everything in Salzburg clocking in at hundreds upon hundreds of years
old, this museum is perfect for those more excited about the Higgs boson
than hellacious stories of power-driven priests. The aquarium is the highlight
of the complex, with thousands of fish streaming in between carefully placed
barnacles; the interactive part of the museum is worth checking out as well. The
museum can't completely escape its Salzburg location, though, and one of the
coolest exhibits is the "walk-in violin."
    i Bus #20, 24, or 28 to Ferdinand Hanusch Platz (Franz-Josef-Kai). Walk with traffic along Franz
Josef Kai and turn left onto Museumspl. €7.50, students €5. ⚄ Open daily 9am-5pm.

HELLBRUNN PALACE   PALACE, FOUNTAINS
Fürstenweg 37   ☎662 82 03 72 0 www.hellbrunn.at
It's no wonder this place starts with "Hell," as the devil surely lives in the trick
fountains that dot this massive palatial complex. The Austrians are crazy about
commissioning palaces for themselves, and Hellbrunn was the brainchild of
Prince Archbishop in 1612 (talk about separation of church and state). The
trick fountains are definitely the best part, as jets of water suddenly shoot out
at random passersby to great giggles and some grimaces. The folklore museum
will satisfy the less spontaneous with beautiful examples of traditional costume
as well as a number of relics.
    i Bus #25 to Fürstenweg. There are clear signs to the entrance. Guided tour of fountains, palace,
and folklore museum €9.50; students €6.50. Park free. ⚄ Open daily Apr 9am-4:30pm; May-Jun
9am-5:30pm; Jul-Aug 9am-6pm; Sept 9am-5:30pm; Oct 9am-4:30pm.

AUGUSTINIAN BREWERY   BREWERY
Augustinergasse 4   ☎662 43 12 46 www.augustinerbier.at
Tourists come from hundreds of miles around to taste the purest beer on earth.
While we really don't ask what's in the beers of today, the brewery here still
follows the Purity Law of 1516, which, despite what it sounds like, has nothing
to do with virgins. It's all about ingredients, and the beers here are guaranteed to
contain only hops, water, malt, and yeast.
    i Bus #7, 8, 20, 21, 27, or 28 to Bärenwirt. Walk north on Müllner Hauptstr and turn left onto
Augustinergasse. Tokens for beer €3. ⚄ Open M-F 3-11pm, Sa-Su 2:30-11pm.

FOOD
East Salzburg
▨ **CAFE SHAKESPEARE**   CAFE $$
Hubert-Sattler-Gasse 3   ☎650 77 35 357 www.shakespeare.at
Cafe Shakespeare is a cafe and bar named after the Bard, with a healthy dose of
anti-American alternative art for good measure. The outdoor terrace has a clear
view of the Mirabell Palace, while the interior has comforting wood paneling
that's overlooked by a distressed bald eagle and a choice four-letter word to
describe patriotism. The bar is where the youth gather to smoke and drink white
beer after white beer, but the menu has some special items—the Hausgemachtes
toast is a small but simple step in your pursuit of happiness.
    i Bus #1, 2, 3, 5, 6, 25, or 32 to Mirabellpl. (Schloß). It's on the left side of the church. Entrees
€8.50-12.40. Dessert €3.20-4.20. ⚄ Open M-F 10am-1am, Sa 4pm-2am, Su 4pm-midnight.

RiSTORANTE DA ALBERTO   ITALIAN $$
Franz-Josef-Straße 37   ☎662 88 10 81
Occasionally, it's nice when the menu is in eight different languages or tries to
attempt three different cuisines, but most of the time, it ends up feeling like a
bad trip to Disney World. Fortunately, Alberto is full-and-out Italian—none of

salzburg

those shenanigans of overly deferential cuisine to suit the capricious whims of English speakers. The restaurant is secluded in a quieter part of the New Town, and the pizza is crispy, delicious, and cheaper than what it'll cost you to enter most museums in the city. And who's to say that a good pizza isn't a comparable form of art?

i Bus #2 or 4 to Wolf-Diestrich-Straße. Walk in the direction the bus came in and turn right onto Franz-Josef-Straße. Pizza €8-11. Pasta €9-12. ◻ Open daily 11:30am-2:30pm and 5:30-10pm.

CAFE BAZAR   CAFE $$
Schwarzstr. 3   ☎662 87 42 78

It's a bit bizarre that you might be sitting in the same seat that Marlene Dietriech once lounged in. However, the only angels you'll be seeing presently are the fantastically down-to-earth waiters and waitresses at this classiest of cafes in the New Town. The menu is the typical toast, soup, and occasional entree that so defines the Salzburg scene, but the hanging newspapers, free-standing coat hangers, and wood-and-gold decor give the guests an easier time of imagining what the cafe was like in its heyday as the center of artistic thought.

i Bus #27 to Landestheater. Walk down Schwarzstr.; the cafe is on the left. Small eats €4-12. Coffee €2.70-6. ◻ Open M-Sa 7:30am-11pm, Su 9am-6pm.

West Salzburg

▨ EISGROTTE   GELATO $
Getreidegasse 40   ☎662 84 31 57 www.eisgrotte.at

The name means "Ice Cave," but the theme of this gelato joint is more '50s diner, with neon signs and the svelte red leather seats we've come to associate with soda fountains. During the day, the servers dole out scoops like mad to clamoring tourists, but if you go during slower hours, after the nearby shops have closed around 6pm, you'll have a chance to breathe and enjoy your ice cream in your own personal cave of happiness.

i Bus #3, 5, 6, 8, 20, 25, or 28 to Rathaus. Walk away from the river into the Old Town and turn right onto Getreidegasse. The store is on the right. 1-scoop cone €1. ◻ Open daily 9am-midnight.

CAFE PAMINA   CAFE $$
Judengasse 17   ☎662 84 23 38

Cafes and bakeries are like rabbits in Salzburg—they multiply like crazy and their food is super-light. Pamina is what you could call an antithetical hearty cafe, with some of the best ice cream variations around (try the eponymous, big-as-your-face Pamina with frozen yogurt, strawberry ice cream, strawberries, and whipped cream). The location on the quiet Judengasse is ideal for enjoying Salzburg without feeling rushed by tourists waiting outside.

i Bus #3, 5, 6, 8, 20, 25, or 28 to Rathaus. Walk away from the river and into the Old Town. Turn left onto Getreidegasse, which becomes Judengasse. Ice cream €3-7. ◻ Open M-Sa 9am-6pm.

CARPE DIEM   RESTAURANT $$$$
Getreidegasse 50   ☎662 84 88 00 www.carpediemfinestfingerfood.com

Carpe Diem takes its name seriously, making delicious gourmet food available for the seizing at every price range. If you live by a YOLO philosophy (carpe diem for stupid people), find a friend and order the €98 menu for two. If you're not insane, you can order something nice like strawberries with white chocolate and basil (€13.50) or one of the many finger food options for under €10. The best part about a restaurant that goes from €10-100 is that the decor has to suit the people paying €100, so relish the classy, super-modern black leather furnishings.

i Bus #3, 5, 6, 8, 20, 25, or 28 to Rathaus. Walk away from the river into the Old Town and turn right onto Getreidegasse. The restaurant is on the right. 3-course lunch menu €19.50. Desserts €11.50-13.50. A la carte €5.40-10.90. ◻ Open daily from 8:30am-midnight.

REPUBLIC CAFE $$

Anton-Neumayr-Platz 2 ☎662 84 16 13

Republic, conveniently, is more like its own little republic than a cafe. The sprawling, orange-themed cafe takes up most of Anton-Neumayr-Platz and publishes its own magazine, has a radio channel, bar, restaurant, and club. Packed at all hours, it's great if you want to have large chunks of time to people-watch, as the waiters aren't rushing to get you out of your seat despite the teeming crowds.

i *Bus #3, 5, 6, 8, 20, 25, or 28 to Rathaus. Walk away from the river into the Old Town and turn right onto Getreidegasse. Walk all the way down and turn right once you hit the mountain. Republic is in the plaza. Sandwiches €4-13. Meat entrees €14-19.60* ⏰ *Open M-Th 8am-1am, F-Sa 8am-4am, Su 8am-1am.*

NIGHTLIFE

East Salzburg

⚓ PEPE COCKTAIL BAR BAR

Steingasse 3 ☎662 87 36 62 www.pepe-cocktailbar.at

It's nice when you find a place that doesn't serve only 10 variations of beer to a rowdy crowd. Pepe definitely caters well to its ZARA-clad crowd as they throw back cocktail after cocktail in this remarkably chic bar. While most of the drinks are tropical-themed, with daiquiris given ample advertisement, we recommend the Schwermatrose (rum, kahlua, lime, and lemon) for a fresh beginning to a pub crawl along Steingasse.

i *Bus #3, 5, 6, 8, 20, 25, or 28 to Rathaus. Cross the bridge into East Salzburg and take a quick right onto Steingasse. The bar is on the left.* ⏰ *Open Tu-Sa 7pm-3am.*

⚓ MONKEYS CAFE.BAR BAR

Imbergstr. 2A ☎662 87 66 52 www.monkeys-salzburg.at

In between two streets along the Salzach, this bar seemingly contains all of the city's young students and tourists in its laser-lighted interior. The inside is modern without being too yuppie and caters to its international clientele by hosting Latin disco nights as well as City of the Week events on Friday evenings. During the winter, the bar also becomes a thriving cafe.

i *Bus #3, 5, 6, 8, 20, 25, or 28 to Rathaus. Cross the bridge over into East Salzburg and take a quick right onto Giselakai, which turns into Imbergstr.* ⏰ *Open M-Th 11:30am-2am, F-Sa 11:30am-4am, Su 11:30am-2am.*

SAITENSPRUNG PUB, BAR

Steingasse 11 ☎662 88 13 77 www.shamrocksalzburg.com

This youth-oriented club's back wall is dug straight out of the side of Kapuzinerberg Hill. The music is the latest Top 40 hits, and the martinis are a particularly popular option for the under-25 crowd. The best part of this place, however, is just sitting in the bar feeling serene in the understated, natural decor.

i *Bus #3, 5, 6, 8, 20, 25, or 28 to Rathaus. Cross into East Salzburg and turn right onto Steingasse. The bar is on the left.* ⏰ *Open daily 9pm-4am.*

CHEZ ROLAND MUSIC, BAR

Giselakai 15 ☎662 87 43 35 www.chez-roland.com

Since Salzburg doesn't have in much in the way of dive bars, it is best to remain in the realm of the classy with Chez Roland. Around since the '70s, the archway-dominated bar has been a rotating door for luminaries of the Salzburg Festival scene. Don't go crazy on the liquor here—instead, blend in and order a nice Austrian wine for only €3 a glass.

i *Bus #3, 5, 6, 8, 20, 25, or 28 to Rathaus. Cross over to east Salzburg and turn right onto Giselakai.* ⏰ *Open daily 7:30pm-late.*

salzburg

West Salzburg

MURPHY'S LAW IRISH PUB
IRISH, PUB

Gstättengasse 33 ☎662 84 28 82

Murphy's Law reminds us that "if anything can go wrong, it will." We suppose that this Irish pub adds the corollary, "When it does indeed go wrong, drink up!" The spirit of this place is infectious, with riotous laughter and sometimes unintelligible jabber between friends filling the air. The bonhomie extends to betting pools and trips to see games that are organized to keep the patrons coming back.

i Bus #1, 4, 5, 7, 8, 20, 21, 22, 24, 27, or 28 to Mönchsbergaufzug. Take a quick left onto Griesgasse until you reach the end; cross the street onto Gstättengasse. The bar is on the left. ☑ Open M-F 2pm-2am, Sa-Su 11am-2am.

SODA CLUB
ELECTRONIC MUSIC, BAR

Gstättengasse 21 ☎650 91 68 787 www.sodaclub.cc

What better place to lose yourself in electronic beats and dubstep drops than a bar built into the side of a mountain (even if it once was filled with monks)? Exposed cave walls put exposed brick to shame as a decor option, and the drinks are surprisingly cheap given the upscale vibe.

i Bus #1, 4, 5, 7, 8, 20, 21, 22, 24, 27, or 28 to Mönchsbergaufzug. Take a quick left onto Griesgasse and continue until you reach the end; cross the street onto Gstättengasse. The bar is on the left. ☑ Open Tu 9pm-4am, W-Sa 9pm-5am.

SHAMROCK IRISH PUB
PUB, BAR

Rudolfskai 12 ☎662 84 16 10 www.shamrocksalzburg.com

Shamrock gets a little bit too into the Irish campiness (the first indicator is the sign that says "Irish Food! Irish Staff! Irish Music!"). Regardless, the place is packed with Austrian and international students watching soccer and kicking back cider after beer after Guinness. The decor reminds us inextricably of the Prancing Pony of The Lord of the Rings fame, with thick, dark wooden benches and a general sense of camaraderie, until the Ringwraith called morning comes.

i Bus #3, 5, 6, 8, 20, 25, or 28 to Rathaus. Walk with traffic along Rudolfskai. .5L Guinness €4.50. ☑ Open M-W noon-3am, Th-Sa noon-4am, Su noon-2am.

VIS A VIS
MUSIC, PUB

Rudolfskai 24 ☎662 84 12 90 www.visavis-bar.at

VisÁ Vis caters to an under-30 crowd that doesn't feel as sporty as the football-salivating group at the nearby Irish pubs. The emphasis here is a bit on excess, as the bar pushes groups to buy bottles of Absolut with four Red Bulls to wash it down. Nothing gets too out of hand under the exposed brick archway, which has enough lights to provoke an awed comment of "double rainbow" every now and then. Each night has a different theme, but it's worth it to go on Wednesdays when the cocktails (the bar's specialty) are under €4 before midnight.

i Bus #3, 5, 6, 8, 20, 25, or 28 to Rathaus. Walk with traffic on Rudolfskai; the bar is on the left. ☑ Open daily 8pm-4am.

ARTS AND CULTURE

LANDESTHEATER
THEATER

Schwarzstr. 22 ☎662 87 15 120 www.salzburger-landestheater.at

The Landestheater is the premier Salzburg option for those looking for a warm glass of Deutsche Kultur. The opera performances tend to stick to Wagner and cartoon villain soundtracks, while the non-musical theater side sports an ambitious line-up of Chekhov, Frisch, Schiller, Mann, and everyone's favorite—Kafka. While the theater's regular season isn't open until the fall, the theater also hosts some Salzburg Festival events.

i Bus #27 to Landestheater. Ticket price varies according to performance. Check website during *the season for details.* ⏲ *Late Aug-Jun M-F 10am-1pm and 2-4pm.*

MARIONETTEN THEATER

THEATER

Schwarzstr. 24 ☎662 87 24 06 www.marionetten.at

We're not a fan of beating the dead horse that is *The Sound of Music*, but a scene along the lines of "The Lonely Goatherd," with preciously floating marionettes, is what you can expect from this summer theater. The performances tend to go straight for the German classics, with The Magic Flute, Hansel and Gretel, and Die Fledermaus among the repertoire. This place also stands out from other Austrian theaters with its English subtitles. Even if you think puppets are a bit juvenile, you might revise your opinion after seeing a blow-out rendition of Don Giovanni.

i Bus #27 to Landestheater. The Marionnetten Theater is just past the Landestheater on the side of the street opposite the river. €18-35, students €18. ⏲ *Open May-Sept 9am-1pm and 2hr. before each performance.*

MOZARTEUM

MUSIC

Theatergasse 2 ☎662 87 44 54 www.mozarteum.at

The students of Salzburg's Mozarteum frequently branch out to play Mendelssohn quartets in the nearby Mirabell Gardens, but the graded performances can be viewed by the public as well. The university has a full orchestra and smaller chamber music groups that give performances throughout the year. A special schedule run during the festival month is also played by students of the summer academy. Tickets can be purchased through the Mozart Foundation.

i Bus #1, 3, 4, 5, 6, 21, 22, 25, or 27. Prices vary by event. Check website before ordering tickets. ⏲ *Open Sept-Jun M-F 9am-5pm, Sa 9am-noon.*

SALZBURG FESTIVAL

FESTIVAL

Herbert-von-Karajan-Platz 11 ☎662 80 45 500 www.salzburgerfestspiele.at

For a brief moment, the tourist trap of Julie Andrews is forgotten in favor of an aspect of Salzburg culture that was, interestingly enough, featured in The Sound of Music: the Salzburg Festival. Operas, concerts, and other performances play continuously for days upon days upon days as a blow-out approach to the arts that will make you never want to hear Mozart again. As a bonus, the Salzburg Festival actually has some English events that will leave you feeling künstlerisch instead of künstlich (artistic, not artificial).

i The festival takes place at many different venues throughout the city. Tickets vary greatly depending on performance. Check website for details. ⏲ *Late Jul-early Sept.*

SHOPPING

🏛 RED BULL WORLD

CLOTHING

Getreidegasse 34 ☎662 84 36 05 www.redbullworld.at

The flagship Red Bull store will give you wings—for a price. If you want to be the Icarus of credit cards, by all means, max out your limit on Red Bull-emblazoned paraphernalia. For those less in love with labels, the store also sells a variety of merely kick-ass effects, such as AWOLNATION CDs.

i Bus #3, 5, 6, 8, 20, 25, or 28 to Rathaus. Walk away from the river into the Old Town and turn right onto Getreidegasse. The store is on the left. Shirt €35. CDs around €15. ⏲ *Open M-F 9:30am-6pm, Sa 9:30am-5pm.*

🏛 HÖLLRIGL

BOOKS

Sigmund-Haffnergasse 10 ☎662 84 11 460

Unlike Salzburg's oldest cathedral and fortress, there are reasons other than fire and acid rain that there aren't any millennia-old bookstores in town. Mainly, no one back then was literate. Höllrigl, however, is the oldest bookstore you'll find in Austria (founded in 1519) and operates on an indie-style set-up, with recom-

salzburg

mendations by staff members, dim lighting, and not much room between the shelves. Needless to say, you can lose hours in here.

i Bus #3, 5, 6, 8, 20, 25, or 28 to Rathaus. Walk away from the river into the Old Town, turn left when you hit Getreidegasse and Judengasse, then take a quick right onto Sigmund-Haffnergasse. Paperbacks from €9. ☺ Open M-F 9am-6:30pm, Sa 9am-6pm.

ESSENTIALS
Practicalities

- **SALZBURG TOURIST OFFICE:** Mozartpl. 5 (☎662 88 98 73 30 www.salzburg.info ☺ Open daily June-Aug 9am-7pm; Sept-May 9am-6pm.) Other tourist offices located at the airport (Innsbrucker Buddesstr. 95) and the train station (Südtiroler Platz. 1).

- **INTERNET:** Salzburg has recently begun a free Wi-Fi program in the city, with coverage around the Salzach river from 5am-midnight. Coverage includes Mozartpl., Volksgarten, Mirabell Palace, and Max-Reinhardt-Platz.

- **GLBT:** Austria is considered a conservative country. While same-sex partnerships have been recently legalized, the country's strong Catholicism has stood in the way of complete equality. **HOSI (Homosexual Initiative)** provides a list of GLBT-friendly establishments in Salzburg. (Gabelsbergerstr. 26 ☎662 43 59 27 www.hosi.or.at/english ☺ Open M-W 10am-5pm, F 10am-5pm.)

Emergency

- **AMBULANCE:** ☎112

- **FIRE DEPARTMENT:** ☎144

- **POLICE:** ☎133

- **DENTIST ON CALL:** ☎662 87 34 66

- **DOCTOR ON CALL:** ☎662 87 13 27

Getting There
By Plane

To fly into Salzburg, travelers will pass through the **W.A. Mozart International Airport** (Innsbrucker Bundesstr. 95 ☎662 85 80 79 11). Many places fly directly from other European cities to Salzburg, but those who are traveling overseas might find it easier to fly into Flughafen München in southern Germany and take the airport shuttle to Ostbahnhof, then a DB or ÖBB train to Salzburg Hauptbahnhof (€24). To get to the city center from the Salzburg airport, take bus #2 (☺ Every 10-20min., M-F 5:30am-10:30pm, Sa 6am-11pm, Su 6:30am-11pm) to the Hauptbahnhof train station, from which you can take a number of buses to various locations in the city.

By Train

The **Salzburg Hauptbahnhof** receives a large number of international trains, including trains to and from Zürich (€51 ☺ 6hr.), Munich (€25 ☺ 2hr.), Budapest (€44 ☺ 5½hr.), and Frankfurt (€107 ☺ 5hr.) as well as trains to and from Vienna (€50 ☺ 3hr.) and Innsbruck (€41 ☺ 2hr.). There is reduced coverage on Sundays, so check the ÖBB website at www.oebb.at, where you can reserve your tickets ahead of time. If traveling within Austria, simply buy a ticket at the offices in each major train station.

Getting Around
By Foot

The best way to see most of the Old Town is by walking, as even bicycles have a hard time navigating these pedestrian-crowded streets.

By Bike

If you're planning to spend an extended period of time in Salzburg, renting or buying a bike will probably be your best bet. Because the public transportation system relies on buses, traffic can build up around the Old Town. For shorter stays, **TopBike** provides bike rentals. (Staatsbrücke, Franz-Josef-Kai www.topbike.at *i* €7 per hour, €20 per day. ☑ Open daily Apr-June 10am-5pm, July-Aug 9am-7pm, Sept-Oct 10am-5pm.)

By Car

If you consider yourself the outdoorsy sort, then a car might come in handy to explore the surrounding Bavarian Alps and other mountaineering options. The downside is that many rental companies have a 3-day minimum rental period; nevertheless try **AutoEurope** if you're interested. (12 Gniglerstrasse ☎1 866 16 51 From €150 for 3 days.)

By Bus

Bus fares cost €2.10 per trip, €5 for a 24hr. pass, and €13.10 for a week-long pass. If you purchase the **Salzburg Card,** you have access to all public transportation (including the funicular to the top of Festungs Hohensalzburg and the Mönchsberg Elevator) for free. (Mozartpl. 5 ☎3662 88 98 70 www.salzburg.info *i* Includes admission to all sights in Vienna and use of public transportation network. 24hr. card €25, under 15 €12.50; 48hr. €34/17; 72hr. card €40/20.)

austria essentials

MONEY
Tipping and Bargaining

Service staff is paid by the hour, but a service charge is not usually included in an item's unit price. Cheap customers typically just round up to the nearest whole euro, but it's customary and polite to tip 10-15% if you are satisfied with the service. If the service was poor, you don't have to tip at all. To tip, tell the waiter the total of the bill with the tip included. Do not leave the tip on the table; hand it directly to the server. It is standard to tip a taxi driver at least €1, housekeepers €1-2 per day, and public toilet attendants around €0.50.

Taxes

Most goods in Austria are subject to a value added tax (VAT) of 20% (a reduced tax of 10% is applied to accommodations, certain foods, and some passenger transportation). Non-EU visitors who are taking these goods home unused may be refunded this tax for purchases totaling over €75 per store. When making purchases, request a VAT form and present it at a Tax Free Shopping Office, found at most airports, road borders, and ferry stations, or by mail. Refunds must be claimed within six months.

SAFETY AND HEALTH
Local Laws and Police

Certain regulations might seem harsh and unusual (e.g. jaywalking is a €5 fine), but abide by all local laws while in Austria; your embassy will not necessarily get you off the hook. Always be sure to carry a valid passport, as police have the right to ask for identification.

Drugs and Alcohol

The drinking age in Austria is 16 for beer and wine and 18 for spirits. The maximum blood alcohol content level for drivers is 0.05%. Avoid public drunkenness; it can jeopardize your safety and earn the disdain of locals. While possession of marijuana or hashish is illegal, possession of small quantities for personal consumption is decriminalized in Austria. Each region has interpreted "small quantities" differently (anywhere from 5 to 30g). Carrying drugs across an international border—considered to be drug trafficking—is a serious offense that could land you in prison.

austria 101

HISTORY

The first known settlers in Austria were nomadic hunter-gatherers who arrived in approximately 80,000 BCE. These rovers, possibly called by a sound of music, began settling and mining salt, farming, and domesticating livestock, while glaciers (possibly repelled by said music) crawled north, carving out the Alpine alleys of postcard fame today and making room for greater habitation of Austrian lands. In 500 BCE, the Celts took control of the salt mines and established the kingdom of Noricum, which developed a relatively affluent economy based on a thriving salt and iron trade. In turn, the Romans conquered their Austrian neighbors to secure the Danube frontier against marauding Germanic tribes in 15 BCE. Not until the fifth century CE did Germanic raids finally force the Romans to retreat from Noricum. Over the next three centuries, various people, including the Huns, Ostrogoths, and Lombards, roamed through the Austrian territories, but none established a lasting settlement.

From 800 to 1740, the Holy Roman Empire and the Hapsburg family from Switzerland fought for control over Austrian territory. It was a rocky road, filled with treaties, wars, more treaties, a Napoleon, and an Otto. In 1866, said Otto (von Bismarck) led Prussia in defeating Austria. In 1867, the Hungarian parliament voted to end the Austrian Empire and form the dual Austro-Hungarian Empire. Non-German speakers were marginalized in the new empire until 1907, when the government ceded basic rights to all peoples in the Empire and accepted universal male suffrage. However, many of the concessions to the Slavic peoples came too late, causing the burgeoning of nationalist sentiments and the severe divisions within the empire.

An even more severe consequence was the assassination of Franz Ferdinand, heir to the imperial throne, and his wife by a young Serbian nationalist in Sarajevo in 1914. Franz Josef cited this as a reason to attack the Serbs, beginning the Domino effect that would culminate in World War I. The war ended in 1918 but saw the end of the Hapsburg dynasty with the creation of the first Republic of Austria. World War II followed on the heels of the First Republic's rocky existence and the welcoming of the Nazis into Germany and the ensuing unification of the two countries. While WWII raged, Nazis directed the construction of concentration camps and an estimated 150,000 Jews, along with leading intellectuals, dissidents, handicapped persons, Gypsies, and homosexuals, were systematically tortured and murdered. One-third of the Jewish population was purged, and most others fled the country.

In 1945, Soviet troops brutally "liberated" and split Austria into four zones of occupation to re-establish an Austrian government. By April of the same year a provisional government was established with 75-year-old Karl Renner as president. In November, the National Assembly declared Austria's independence from Germany. With Joseph Stalin's death in 1955, Austria signed the State Treaty, under which the four powers granted Austria complete sovereignty on the condition that it remain neutral. The State Treaty, along with the Federal Constitution of the First Republic, which was restored in 1945, formed the basis of the Second Republic., today's acting government. During the 1990s, Austria was accepted into the European Union. It also joined the Economic and Monetary Union and replaced its currency, the Austrian Schilling, with the euro in 2002.

FOOD AND DRINK

Traditional Austrian food is a cardiologist's nightmare, which means it has to taste good. Most meals are hearty and focus on Schweinefleisch (pork), Kalbsfleisch (veal), Wurst (sausage), Eier (eggs), Käse (cheese), Brot (bread), and Karoffeln or Erdapfeln (potatoes). Most vegetarian options include mushrooms, like Steinpilze or Eierschwammerl. If you can't stand fungi, Spätzle (homemade noodles often serve with melted cheese) is an available traditional dish. Breakfast options include yogurt and Müsli (soaked granola). Austrians are known for their desserts, like torte in various fruit flavors and dessert dumplings and pancakes, all of which can be paired with Austrian coffee, like a mélange (Viennese coffee with cream and cinnamon).

The most famous Austrian wine is probably Gumpoldskirchen from Lower Austria. Another good bet is the Klosterneuburger. If beer is your alcoholic beverage of choice, you'll find fantastic choices like Ottakringer, Gold Fassl, and Zipfer.

MUSIC

Classical Era

Late 18th-century Vienna was a happening music scene. In fact, composers hung out in salons, making fun of each other and listening to themselves play music they wrote in the style now called "Viennese Classicism." The first master composer of Viennese Classicism was Josef Haydn (1732-1890), who wrote 52 piano sonatas, 24 piano and organ concertos, 104 symphonies, and 83 string quartets. Wolfgang Amadeus Mozart (1756-1791) represents the pinnacle of this era. Born in Salzburg, Mozart left his hometown for Vienna, where he produced his first mature concerti, his most famous Italian operas (like Le Nozze di Figaro), and the beloved string showpiece, Eine kleine Nachtmusik. Ludwig van Beethoven (1770-1827) followed in Mozart's footsteps as a transplant to Vienna and as one of the most famous musicians of the time. His music is often placed between Viennese Classicism and Romanticism.

Romantic Era and Late 19th Century

The music of Franz Schubert (1797-1828) is the lifeblood of Romanticism, a movement characterized by swelling emotion, larger orchestras, interest in the natural world, and storytelling. Born in the suburb of Lichtenthal, Schubert began his career as a chorister in the imperial Hofkapelle and later made his living teaching music. Mainly self-taught, he composed the Unfinished Symphony and the Symphony in C Major, which are now considered masterpieces but were virtually unknown during his lifetime. His lyrical genius was more readily recognized in his Lieder, a musical setting of poems by Goethe, Schiller, and Heine. These song cycles were made famous during musical soirées called Schubertiaden, which spawned a new trend of social gatherings in Biedermeier Vienna, featuring chamber music, readings, and alcohol.

Like Beethoven, Johannes Brahms (1833-1897) straddled musical traditions. In his home near the Karlskirche in Vienna, Brahms composed his Hungarian Dances, piano concerti, and numerous symphonies, all of which were first performed by the Vienna Philharmonic. Despite his own Romantic compositions, Brahms is often regarded as a Classicist who used his status and position in the Viennese Musikverein to oppose Romanticism and the musical experiments of his archrival, Richard Wagner.

austria 101

If you want to soak in all of Austria's rich culture without doing the touristy, "5-days-and-we're-out" (or the Before Sunrise-y "1-magical-night-and-we're-out"), you've come to the right place. The following study, volunteer, and work opportunities are as carefully curated as any exhibit that you'd find in the Museumsquartier.

STUDYING

- **EMORY IN VIENNA:** Emory's summer program in Vienna focuses on German language as well as music and cultural history. (http://german.emory.edu/home/abroad/vienna/index.html)

- **MACALESTER GERMAN STUDY ABROAD PROGRAM:** A semester-long program split between Berlin's Goethe Institute (two months) and the University of Vienna (four months). Participants must have studied German for at least four semesters. (www.macalester.edu/academics/german/studyabroad)

- **UNIVERSITY OF WASHINGTON:** This study abroad program takes place during the spring semester in Vienna and involves language classes, visits to famous sites and museums, and a seminar on contemporary Austrian culture and society. (http://germanics.washington.edu/study-abroad/spring-vienna)

- **UNIVERSITY OF INNSBRUCK:** The University of Innsbruck is located in the Alps and is a strong research institution. (www.uibk.ac.at/index.html.en)

- **IES:** IES offers two semester-long Vienna programs, one focused on musicand the other on European society and culture. (www.iesabroad.org)

- **KRAMETERHOF:** This research station and educational farm on the slopes of Mt. Schwarzenberg is where Sepp Holzer developed the branch of permaculture known as Holzer Permaculture. There are courses and tours offered here throughout the year. (www.krameterhof.at)

VOLUNTEERING

- **GOABROAD:** New projects are listed here all the time. (www.goabroad.com)

- **GEOVISIONS:** Conservation Corps Austria is GeoVisions' one- to three-month program where you live with a host family and work as a private language tutor for 15 hours per week in exchange for room and board. (www.geovisions.org)

- **VOLUNTEERS FOR PEACE:** Volunteer opportunities are updated all the time and include things like homestays, environmental studies, archaeology, or native cultural studies. The program fee includes room and board. (www.vfp.org)

- **ZILLERTAL ALPS HIGH MOUNTAIN NATURE PARK:** The park currently offers two volunteer opportunities, one on the Protected Forest Project and the other on the Protecting Mountain Meadows Project. (www.zillertal.at)

- **THE BELVEDERE:** A world-class art museum, the Belvedere is always looking for volunteers to help out. (www.belvedere.at/en/freunde-support/members/volunteering)

- **PLATFORM FOR INTERNATIONAL COOPERATION ON UNDOCUMENTED MIGRANTS (PICUM):** PICUM is an NGO that "aims to promote respect for the human rights of undocumented migrants within Europe." It also provides the contact information of many organizations in Austria that are working toward the same goal, such as Diakonie (counseling services) or Aids Hilfe Wien (testing and treatment for HIV-positive patients). Check out these organizations for places to potentially volunteer. (http://picum.org/en/resources/contacts-of-organisations/links-to-organisations-austria)

WORKING

- **VIRTUAL VIENNA:** A site aimed at expats that provides job and internship information and postings. (http://virtualvienna.net)

- **AU PAIR AUSTRIA:** An au pair agency based in Vienna and an International Au Pair Association member, this agency provides free placements, an emergency hotline, au pair excursions, and contacts for other au pairs in Austria. (www.aupairaustria.at/english.aspx)

- **BERLITZ:** With the slogan "A Global Education Company," a job teaching English with Berlitz in Vienna is one way to ensure you have some spending money. (www.berlitz.com/Careers/33)

- **CEF LANGUAGE INSTITUTE:** A sprachschulen (language school) with locations all over Austria, this is another option to try if you're going down the English-teaching route in your job search. (www.cef.at)

- **WWOOF AUSTRIA:** Join WWOOF Austria to get access to more than 200 farm listings. Choose an organic farm that you want to work on in exchange for room and board. (www.wwoof.at/en)

- **SKI RESORTS:** During Austria's winter, consider being a ski bum at one of the myriad resorts scattered throughout the country. There are jobs as hotel employees, drivers, lift operators, babysitters, etc.

Orchestral music had mass appeal as well. Beginning with Johan Strauss the Elder (1804-1849), the Strauss family kept Vienna dancing for much of the 19th century. Largely responsible for the "Viennese Waltz," Johann Strauss the Younger (1825-1899) wrote the Blue Danube and Tales of the Vienna Woods, the two most recognized waltzes of all time. Strauss also produced popular operas, like Die Fledermaus. Gustav Mahler's (1860-1911) music, as a direct precursor to the Second Viennese experiments of Arnold Schöneberg, incorporated fragments and deliberately inconclusive musical segments. Mahler employed unusual instrumentation and startling harmonic juxtaposition, and his music formed an integral part of the fin de siècle Viennese avant-garde.

Modern Era

While Mahler destabilized the conventions of composition, Arnold Schöneberg (1874-1951) broke away from traditional harmony altogether. Originally a devotee of Richard Wagner, Schöneberg rejected compositional rules that require music to be set in a tonal key and, with his 12-tone system, pursued what is generally called atonality. His students Anton von Webern and Alban Berg expanded and modified Schöneberg's 12-tone system to create masterpieces of their own.

BELGIUM

Belgium may not rank near the top of most people's lists of must-see European vacation spots. Next to the Netherlands or Greece, Belgium doesn't scream party central, and it doesn't have famous sights like you can find in Italy and France. But many people spend a whole Eurotrip searching for, and failing to find, the kind of small-town charm that is this entire country's specialty. Shift your vacation into a different gear and indulge in Belgium's own version of whimsy. Plus, Belgian cuisine revolves around fries, waffles, chocolate, and beer. It's basically the best Sunday brunch you've ever had, and it never ends.

If you have a penchant for public urination, you'll probably enjoy yourself in Brussels. Peeing statues aplenty await you; it's hard to turn the corner without seeing something taking a leak. It's cute when you're made out of bronze, but Let's Go doesn't recommend trying it yourself—indecent exposure charges don't make good souvenirs. While you're avoiding criminal charges, you might want to swing by the European Quarter, where you'll find more ambassadors and Eurocrats than you can shake a roll of red tape at. Brussels is also home to dozens of museums, art galleries, and theaters for the cultural traveler in you. And don't forget Bruges, one of Europe's most charmingly preserved medieval cities. It's not just small-town charm you'll find in Belgium; this is the place for small-country charm.

greatest hits

- **MELT IN YOUR MOUTH.** Belgian chocolate is famous for a reason. Head to the Musée du Cacao et du Chocolat in the Grand Palace to stare at more than you could ever possibly eat (p. 59).

- **2001: A BEER ODYSSEY.** With over 2000 beers available (and counting), **Delirium** (p. 65) will quickly become your favorite nighttime hangout in Brussels.

- **IN BRUGES.** Climb the **Belfort** (p. 69) or sample tradition Belgian fare at **Pas Partout** (p. 70). Maybe you'll even run into Colin Farrell. (You probably won't.)

In a country with this much beer, chocolate, and French fries, it's not surprising that there's a group of students on every corner. Any bar you visit in Brussel's **Lower Town** is pretty much guaranteed to be packed with students on the weekends. Once you've cured your hangover, Brussels still has a lot to offer: Fashion-forward youth pass the daylight hours shopping at rue Neuve or lounging in the outdoor bars and cafes just west of the Bourse. If high culture gives you that drunk slap-happy feeling, BOZAR offers tremendous student discounts on everything from art exhibitions to classical music concerts. Edgy concerts at the Botanique will force you into close contact (literally) with other students who pile in to listen to little-known bands. Northern **Bruges** is far from a student town, but it attracts a surprisingly large number of young backpackers, who gather in its excellent hostels. Bruges's most famous sights—its churches, windmills, and canals—are all free to the explorer who's willing to walk.

brussels

ORIENTATION

The center of Brussels is roughly split between **Upper Town,** on the hill, and **Lower Town,** at the foot of that hill. These neighborhoods bleed into each other a bit, but the clear heart of the city is the **Grand Place** in Lower Town. These two areas are encircled by a guitar-pick shaped loop of main roads and part of the metro. The biggest metro stops that serve this area are **Gare du Nord** in the north, Arts-Loi in the east, Place Louise in the south, **Gare du Midi** in the southwest, and Comte de Flandre in the west, with **Gare Centrale** smack-dab in the middle. Going east of Arts-Loi will take you to **Place Schuman,** the neighborhood that houses the EU and its parliamentary big-wigs along with the grand Parc du Cinquantenaire/Jubelpark and some of the city's coolest museums. South of the city center is **Louise,** best known for its shopping, and Place Flagey, where a picturesque pond is dotted with funky bars. These four areas—Upper and Lower Town in the center, Place Schuman in the east, and Louise in the south—make up the meat of Brussels. A bit farther northwest, at the end of the metro, is **Heysel,** where you will find some of Brussels's more concentrated tourist traps, including the Atomium (which, however tourist trappy, you should still see).

Lower Town

Brussels is not a huge tourist destination, but those who do visit tend to stay near the **Grand Place,** or "Grand Plaza," where the **Musée de la Ville** (city museum) and the **Hôtel de Ville** (town hall) are located. The busy Grand Place is the heart of Brussels, where you will find the best of the city's waffles, chocolate, and tourists, but venturing away from this center and through the smaller, winding streets will allow you to really experience the city. **Manneken Pis** is a straight shot from the Grand Place down **rue de L'Etuve;** going farther east and south will lead you into the Upper Town. Northwest of the Grand Place, **boulevard Anspach,** accessible by metro stop Bourse, is a diagonal that bisects the city where you will find basic needs like ATMs, pharmacies, and *alimentations.* Farther west of the Bourse and bd Anspach is **Place Saint-Géry,** home to most of Brussels's night owls. To the north is **rue Neuve,** a central shopping district filled with clothing outlets and fast food. Rue Neuve is flanked to the west by the

belgium

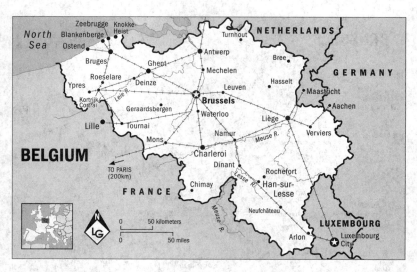

beautiful neighborhood of **Sainte Catherine,** which is a bit pricey but still a welcome respite from the noise of the Grand Place.

Upper Town

Upper Town is divided into a number of smaller neighborhoods that wrap around the eastern and southern ends of Lower Town, each of which maintains a distinct personality despite rather blurred borders. These areas are home to Brussels's best museums and some fancy shopping—great places to spend the day before heading to the city center for an evening beer.

Broad, traffic-laden streets and long city blocks make Upper Town difficult to navigate by foot, so take advantage of the metro and tram lines. Use the **Mont des Arts** and the **Place Royale** as your central anchors when navigating Upper Town. From there, the **rue Royale** will take you past the **Parc de Bruxelles** and many of the Upper Town's museums, galleries, and grand palaces, not to mention the Belgian Parliament. Be careful going much farther north near La Botanique, especially at night; this area is unofficially known as Brussels's red light district. South of Place Royale are **boulevard de Waterloo** and **avenue de la Toison d'Or,** which hug the eastern edge of Upper Town and extend down to shopaholic heaven, **avenue Louise.**

Place Schuman and Heysel

Venturing outside the loose bounds of Upper and Lower Towns will take a few metro stops, but it's worth leaving the busy city center for a day. Place Schuman (which typically refers to the metro stop and its surrounding buildings) is just east of the city center and home to the **European Commission** and **European Parliament.** The area is much nicer than central Brussels but consequently is populated almost entirely by Eurocrats and doesn't really cater to the student crowd or the student budget. Parc du Cinquantenaire Jubelpark is a few steps farther east of Place Schuman and houses the **Musée Royal de l'Armée et d'Histoire Militaire** and **Autoworld,** which are definitely worth visiting after a picnic in the big park. To the south of Place Schuman is the European Parliament and Place du Luxembourg (or P'Lux), which feeds and waters all the tired politicians.

On the opposite side of town, northeast of the city center, is **Heysel,** the last major stop on the Brussels metro. It seems far but only takes 20min. to reach and is worth

brussels

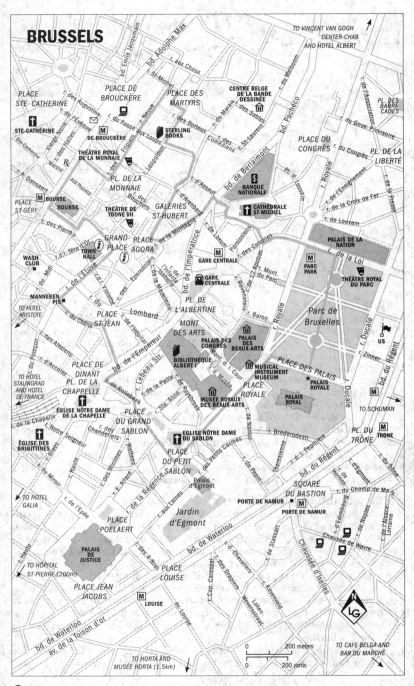

BRUSSELS

TO VINCENT VAN GOGH
CENTER-CHAB
AND HOTEL ALBERT

the ride if only to see the **Atomium,** the signature structure from the 1958 World Expo. **Mini-Europe** is a fun little excursion if you're feeling the need to get in touch with your inner child.

SIGHTS

Brussels is definitely underrated in the things-to-see category. Aside from its notorious and unusual statues and the **Grand Place,** Brussels has a diverse array of museums and several lovely city parks that are worth your time. Parc Leopold and the Square Marie Louise Plein are beautiful respites from the city noise. So while you definitely shouldn't miss everyone's favorite urinating boy, don't let anyone fool you into thinking that's all there is to see in Brussels.

Lower Town

The Lower Town has most of Brussels' famous sights.

◪ MANNEKEN PIS   STATUE
Intersection of rue de l'Étuve and rue du Chêne

Prepare to be both amused and underwhelmed by the icon of Brussels—a 2ft. tall statue of a little boy peeing into a pond. Don't ask us what it means (his actual origins are unknown); all we know is that he is continually swamped with giggling tourists and that he likes to celebrate certain national holidays and events.

i Head southwest from the Grand Place along rue de l'Étuve. The Manneken is 3 blocks down. Check the vendor's calendar to see what the Manneken Pis will be wearing and when.

GRAND PLACE   SQUARE
Grand Place

The historic center of Brussels is a grand place known, naturally, as the Grand Place. Many of the tourists are too focused on what's in front of them to look up—that's a mistake, as the really worthwhile, intricate architecture is actually above you. Make sure to return once the sun goes down, when the famous Guildhall buildings, including the Hôtel de Ville and the Maison de Roi, are dramatically illuminated.

i ⓂBourse. Head straight down rue de la Bourse, which leads to the northeast corner of the square.

MUSÉE DU CACAO ET DU CHOCOLAT   MUSEUM
9-11 rue de la Tête d'Or   ☎02 514 20 48 www.mucc.be

What's more Belgian than peeing statues? Chocolate, that's what. Opened in 1998 by Jo Draps, the daughter of one of the founders of Godiva, the Musée du Cacao et du Chocolat is a chocoholic's dream (or worst nightmare, if it's Lent). Fresh milk chocolate is churned in the entrance, and the backroom allows you to watch a chocolate chef work his magic.

i ⓂBourse. Head straight down rue de la Bourse, which leads to the northeast corner of the Grand Place. The museum is just south of the Grand Place. €5.50; students, seniors, and ages 12-16 €4.50; under 12 free with parent. ⚄ Open Tu-Su 10am-4:30pm.

MUSÉE DE LA VILLE DE BRUXELLES (LA MAISON DU ROI)   MUSEUM
Grand Place   ☎02 279 43 50 www.bruxelles.be

The dignified building that houses the Musée de la Ville de Bruxelles is arguably a bigger deal than the museum itself. La Maison du Roi (King's House) was built in the 13th century to both demonstrate the power of the Belgian prince and serve as an economic center for the city. Make sure to check out the stone remains from the original building on the first floor and the room with model replicas of 13th-century Brussels.

i In the northeast corner of Grand Place €4; students, seniors, and groups €3; children €2. Under 18 free on weekends. ⚄ Open Tu-W 10am-5pm, Th 10am-8pm, F-Su 10am-5pm.

brussels

get a room!

Accommodations in Brussels fill up quickly. The EU Parliament attracts Europe's elite and the pricey, bougie hotels that come with them. Most student-friendly accommodations are located slightly north of the **Grand Place** and are within walking distance of Lower Town. Hotels will get more expensive in Upper Town, and the neighborhoods will generally get more unsafe for solo travelers the further south you get. There is no clearly defined high or low season in Brussels, although prices drop significantly in July and August, when Parliament is on vacation. For more recommendations, visit **www.letsgo.com.**

2GO4 HOSTEL
HOSTEL $$

99 bd Emile Jacqmain ☎02 219 30 19 www.2go4.be

2go4 is a haven for young solo travelers thanks to its strict no-large-groups policy. Shared spaces like the funky common room and the well-trafficked communal kitchen make for good opportunities to meet your fellow travelers. Amenities like individual reading lights and power outlets, plus the convenient location, make up for the sub-standard showers.

i Ⓜ*Rogier. Follow bd d'Anvers and turn left onto bd Emile Jacqmain. Linens included. Towels available for rent. Max. 6 people per group. Free Wi-Fi. Computers available. Dorms €21-29; singles €50-55.* ⏰ *Reception 7am-1pm and 4-10pm.*

SLEEP WELL
HOSTEL, HOTEL $$

23 rue du Damier ☎02 218 50 50 www.sleepwell.be

Sleep Well has hostel and hotel components. Both are bright, cheerful, and cheap, and they share huge common areas and a popular bar. The hostel, though, has an inconvenient lockout between 11am and 3pm.

i Ⓜ*Rogier. Follow rue Neuve and turn left onto rue de la Blanchisserie. Rue du Damier is on your right. Breakfast and linens included. Towels available for rent. Wi-Fi €1 per 30min. Dorms €20-24; singles €36; doubles €54.* ⏰ *Reception 24hr. Lockout 11am-3pm.*

JACQUES BREL
HOSTEL $$

30 rue de la Sablonnière ☎02 218 01 87 www.laj.be

Surprisingly lively, Jacques Brel provides a modern bar and lounge in its reception area. Rooms are comfortable, priced for budget travelers, and not nearly as boring as the exterior suggests. The hostel is conveniently located right at a 20min. walk from the Grand Place.

i Ⓜ*Botanique. Head south down rue Royale (away from Botanique) and take the 1st left. Breakfast and linens included. Reserve 4 weeks in advance. Free Wi-Fi and computer access. 6- to 8-bed dorms €21; 3- to 5-bed dorms €23; singles €36. Over age 25 add €2.* ⏰ *Reception daily 7am-midnight. Lockout 10am-3pm.*

JEANNEKE PIS
STATUE

Off rue des Bouchers

The poor lonely sister of Manneken Pis is locked away behind bars (albeit pretty ones) down a tiny alleyway and isn't even listed by the Tourist Office in its official guides—where are women's rights activists when you need them? Jeanneke Pis shows no shame as she squats down to do her business in a small pond. Conceived by Denis Adrien Debourvrie in 1985, the statue doesn't actually urinate anymore, but local lore has it that if you toss a coin in Jeanneke's puddle, the little girl will bring you luck. So throw a penny in the pond for good fortune and feminism.

i Ⓜ*Bourse. Just off rue des Bouchers. Take a right after Chez Léon.*

Upper Town

▨ MAGRITTE MUSEUM   MUSEUM
3 rue de la Régence   ☎02 508 32 11 www.musee-magritte-museum.be

René Magritte may not be the most famous painter in the Musées Royaux des Beaux-Arts collection, but he's certainly one of the most interesting. The paintings of this master of Surrealism question the relationship between words, images, and reality. Start your tour at the glass elevator, where Magritte paintings on the opposite wall blur together eerily as the elevator rushes by. Make sure to check out the collection of hand-drawn images—compiled by Magritte, Scutenaire, Hamoir, and Nougé—in which each of the friends took turns drawing a different limb or cross-section of the human form without looking at what their colleagues had previously drawn.

i ⓂParc. Walk south down rue Royale. €8, seniors €5, students €2, under 19 and 1st W of each month after 1pm free. Audio tour €4. Combined ticket with Musées Royeaux des Beaux-Arts €13, students €3. ☼ Open Tu 10am-5pm, W 10am-8pm, Th-Su 10am-5pm.

▨ CATHÉDRALE DES SAINTS MICHEL ET GUDULE   CATHEDRAL
15 rue du Bois Sauvage   ☎02 217 85 45 www.cathedralestmichel.be

Perhaps the grandest cathedral in Brussels, Saint Michel et Gudule expects respectful silence from all its visitors. Blabbermouths have no fear: when you hear the grand organ mysteriously playing from the lofty stretches above, you'll have no problem shutting up. 11th-century architecture snobs didn't like its original design, so the church was rebuilt in the Gothic style over the next three centuries. As you wander through the splendor of the Catholic cathedral, gaze up to the saintly statues guarding the walls.

i ⓂGare Centrale. Free. Crypt €1. Free choir concerts throughout the year. ☼ Open M-F 7:30am-6pm, Sa-Su 8:30am-6pm. Mass in French Su 10, 11:30am, and 12:30pm.

MUSICAL INSTRUMENTS MUSEUM (MIM)   MUSEUM
2 montagne de la Cour   ☎02 545 01 30 www.musicalinstrumentsmuseum.be

If you have the slightest interest in music, the history of instruments, or just cool art deco buildings, you should get yourself on down to MIM. This museum just celebrated its 10th anniversary, and the 10 floors of its collection feature impressive interactive exhibits, though not every floor has something to look at. A large glass elevator leads to the top floors and the rooftop restaurant, which boasts a panoramic view of the city. The most ingenious part of the museum is the audio tour, which, instead of being vocal, is just music.

i ⓂParc. Permanent collection free 1st W of each month after 1pm. €5, under 26 and over 64 €4, under 13 free. Audio guide free with admission. ☼ Open Tu-F 9:30am-5pm, Sa-Su 10am-5pm. Last tickets sold 4:15pm.

CENTRE BELGE DE LA BANDE DESINÉE   MUSEUM
20 rue des Sables   ☎02 219 19 80 www.cbbd.be

Don't expect to find Marvel or DC on the shelves of this comic book museum, dedicated to the likes of Tintin and Boulle and Bill. Real comic book nerds head downstairs to the library, where you can read as many comics as you want, or pop next door to the bookshop where you can purchase your own to take home with you.

i ⓂRogier. ☼ Open Tu-Su 10am-6pm. Reception closes at 5:30pm.

MUSÉES ROYAUX DES BEAUX-ARTS   MUSEUM
3 rue de la Régence   ☎02 508 32 11 www.fine-arts-museum.be

The Musées Royaux des Beaux-Arts, attached to the Magritte Museum, holds a vast collection split between modern and ancient works. The modern arts section displays mind-boggling works from the 19th through 21st centuries, including provocative paintings and sculptures that will either fascinate you or make you wonder why you bought a ticket.

i Ⓜ*Parc. Walk south down rue Royale. €8, students €5, under 18 and 1st W of each month after 1pm free. Combined ticket with Magritte Museum €13, students €3.* Ⓧ *Open Tu-Su 10am-5pm. Last entry 4pm.*

Place Schuman and Heysel

▨ MUSÉE ROYAL DE L'ARMÉE ET D'HISTOIRE MILITAIRE

MUSEUM

3 Parc du Cinquantenaire ☎02 737 78 33 www.klm-mra.be

This grand museum is absolutely massive, and you can easily get lost among the weapons and swords on display here. The aviation hall is the largest part of the museum; you'll spend most of your time here, where light aircraft from WWI and WWII abound. History buffs and war nerds could easily spend a couple of hours here, but those of you who aren't impressed by generations of war technology may want to just do a quick in-and-out while at the nearby park.

i Ⓜ*Schuman. Head through the Arcade du Cinquantenaire; the museum is on the left, through the parking lot and across from Autoworld. Free. Audio guides €2-3.* Ⓧ *Open Tu-Su 9am-noon and 1-4:45pm. Aviation hall open Tu-Su 9am-4:45pm. Sky Cafe open 11am-4pm.*

▨ PARC DU CINQUANTENAIRE

PARK

This park's Arcade Cinquantenaire looks like a cross between the Arc de Triomphe and the Brandenburg Gate, so take some pictures of it and try to convince your gullible/clueless friends that you went to Paris or Berlin (for bonus points, use two different photos of it and convince them you went to both).

i Ⓜ*Schuman. At the end of rue de la Loi.*

ATOMIUM

MONUMENT

Sq. de l'Atomium ☎02 475 47 77 www.atomium.be

For some, the Atomium is a horrific eyesore in the Brussels skyline; for others, it's a stroke of architectural genius. Built for the 1958 World Expo, André Waterkeyn designed this monument to resemble the atom of an iron crystal—just 165 billion times bigger. The top of the Atomium offers a panoramic view of the city, as well as a restaurant and cafe, and a permanent exhibition on the '58 Expo and the Atomium's construction.

i Ⓜ*Heysel €11, students and ages 12-18 €8, ages 6-11 €4, under 6 free. Audio tour €2.* Ⓧ *Open daily 10am-6pm. Last entry 30min. before close.*

FOOD

Even though it's the capital of the EU, Brussels does not have capital prices. With *friteries* and waffle joints on every other corner, in addition to the traditionally meat-and-potato heavy Flemish diet, don't expect to tighten the notches on your belt any time soon. ost restaurants have outdoor terraces, and the weather is almost always pleasant enough to enjoy the fresh air.

Lower Town

The Lower Town offers some of the best places to get all your artery-clogging cravings met. There are also plenty of touristy rip-offs, most of which are centered on the **rue des Bouchers.** For late-night munchies or a meal on the run, try the **rue du Marché aux Fromages,** just off the Grand Place—it's sometimes called the "rue des pittas" or "kebab street."

▨ FRITLAND

FRITERIE $

49 rue Henri Maus ☎02 514 06 27

Forget about arteries: we'll gladly wash down as many fistfuls of creamy, mayonnaise-dipped French fries with as many cans of blonde Belgian beer as we like, merci beaucoup. Especially when the whole thing only costs €5 per round (seriously, €3 for a mountain of fries and sauce, €2 for the beer).

i Ⓜ*De Brouckere. Head northwest on rue de l'Evêque and turn left onto bd Anspach. Turn left onto rue des Pierres; Fritland is on the left. Beer €2. Fries €3. Chicken kebab €3.* ⓐ *Open M-Th 11am-1am, F-Sa 11am until dawn, Su 11am-1am.*

▨ MOKAFE
CAFE $

9 Galerie du Roi ☎02 511 78 70

Tucked inside the fancy (and expensive) Galerie du Roi is the charming Mokafe, a cafe specializing in waffles—not the €1 sugar balls sold around Manneken Pis, but the proper Belgian kind, served on a real plate with powdered sugar on top. You'll be dining with locals, a few tourists, and the biggest waffle snobs of them all: little old Belgian ladies.

i From the Grand Place, take the rue de la Colline on the eastern side to reach the Galerie du Roi. It looks like a shopping center inside a palace. Sandwiches €2-4. Waffles €3-5. ⓐ *Open daily 7am-8pm, but hours are flexible.*

▨ IN'T SPINNEKOPKE
TRADITIONAL, BELGIAN $$$

1 pl. Jardin aux Fleurs ☎02 511 86 95 www.spinnekopke.be

Spinnekopke (that's "spider's head" in Flemish) might not sound like an appetizing name for a restaurant. But once you take in this rustic tavern's candlelit tables and crowds of locals, you'll know that you've stumbled across something very exciting. Green-aproned waiters will attend to your table with the utmost attention. For a really tasty meal, try one of the many sauces available for their steak (steak €17.50, with sauce €3), including a brilliant cheese, lambik beer, and cream sauce.

i Ⓜ*Bourse. Head down rue Orts and turn left onto rue des Charteux, which leads to pl. du Jardin aux Fleurs. English menus available.* ⓐ *Open M-F noon-3pm and 6-11pm, Sa-Su 24hr.*

FIN DE SIÈCLE
BELGIAN $$

9 rue des Charteux ☎2 513 51 23

Don't let the borderline pornographic prints of greased up hands caressing female lady parts turn you off (or on). Aside from the uncomfortable choice of wall art, Fin de Siècle is a perfect gem. With a small patio, a deep interior, and high ceilings, Fin de Siècle caters to a relaxed, intimate crowd of regulars looking to enjoy a respite from the rowdy bar scene of nearby pl. St Géry.

i Ⓜ*Bourse. Head down rue Auguste Orts and take a left onto rue des Charteux. Plats €12-19.* ⓐ *Open daily in the evening until late.*

Upper Town

If you're near the **Place de la Liberté,** a number of convenience stores carry snacks and sandwich fixings for a picnic in the **Parc de Bruxelles.** In the southern part of Upper Town, the area around **Place Flagey**—though far from the city center—boasts a number of interesting and moderately priced eateries.

▨ EAT PARADE
SANDWICHES $$

87 rue de Namur ☎02 511 11 95

The only procession here is the line of Brussels's businessmen stretching out the door, and if you can make it past the packed crowd to the counter of this cozy lunchtime joint, you'll see why they're eager to be part of the spectacle. Do as the locals do and take your chef d'œuvre to the nearby Parc de Bruxelles for the perfect summer picnic in front of the Royal Palace.

i Ⓜ*Port de Namur. Walk northwest on rue du Namur; Eat Parade is on the next corner after the big intersection. Sandwiches €4.* ⓐ *Open M-F 7am-3:45pm, Sa 9:30am-4pm.*

brussels

LE PERROQUET
SALADS AND PITA $$

31 rue Watteeu
☎02 512 99 22

If you're starting to feel weighed down by all those fries and waffles drowned in chocolate, head to Le Perroquet for a vegetable cleanse. The menu was created in collaboration with a dietician, and the servings, are healthy enough to keep your cardiologist at bay. Butterfly chairs make the quiet terrace a great place to enjoy a drink with your health-conscious significant other.

i ⓂLouise. *Head northwest on av. de la Toison d'Or; at the roundabout, take the 3rd exit onto rue des Quatre Bras; continue onto pl. Poelaert. At the next roundabout, take the 2nd exit onto rue de la Régence and turn left onto rue Van Moer. Continue onto rue Watteeu; Le Perroquet is on the left. €12 min. credit cards.* ☒ *Open M noon-11:30pm, Tu-W noon-midnight, Th-Sa noon-1am, Su noon-11:30pm.*

THE MERCEDES HOUSE
BRASSERIE $$$

22-24 rue Bodenbroek
☎02 400 42 63

Looking for a way to combine your love of cars with some fine Belgian dining? This brasserie is part of the Mercedes House, which showcases Mercedes-Benz cars, and is an ideal location for a coffee or light lunch. Hot drinks are available and can be enjoyed on the terrace outside, where you can also admire the shop's crop of shiny cars. At lunchtime, you can sample traditional dishes that won't drive away with your money, but if you want to take a different kind of spin, order a bottle of champagne at €50 a pop.

i ⓂParc. *Entrées €11.50-15.50. Plats €15.50-24.* ☒ *Open M-F 11:30am-3pm.*

Place Schuman and Heysel

ANTOINE'S
FRITERIE $

1 pl. Jourdan

Around lunchtime, crowds of businessmen, children, students, and tourists descend on Brussels's oldest friterie for large, piping-hot portions of some of the city's best frites. Many people head to grassy Parc Léopold to enjoy their fries alfresco.

i ⓂSchuman. *Pl. Jourdan is just off rue Froissart. Frites €2-2.20. Sauce €0.50.* ☒ *Open M-Th 11:30am-1am, F-Sa 11:30am-2am, Su 11:30am-1am.*

CHEZ MOI
PIZZERIA, BAR $

66 rue du Luxembourg
☎02 280 26 66

Avoid the expensive eateries in and around the EU area and join the young workers devouring their delicious (and dirt-cheap) pizza slices on the grass of pl. du Luxembourg. Chez Moi offers a daily menu of classic flavors (mushroom, pepperoni, etc.).

i ⓂMaelbeek. *Turn left onto rue de la Loi after exiting the station. Take the 1st left onto rue de Trèves, walk 4 blocks, then turn right onto pl. du Luxembourg. Head right across the square to get to rue du Luxembourg. Takeout and delivery available. Slices €2-3.50.* ☒ *Open M-W 11am-11pm, Th-F 11am-midnight.*

CAFÉ PARC AVENUE
CAFE $$$$

50 av. d'Auderghem
☎02 742 28 10 www.parc-avenue.be

Eating out in the EU area can be expensive. Fortunately, this upscale cafe has €16 lunch special that includes the entrée and plat of the day. It may not sound like much, but after mounds of greasy fries and sweet waffles, this meal will leave you feeling as satisfied and as slick as the suits lunching next to you.

i ⓂSchuman. *Walk toward the park and to the right; the cafe is on the corner of rue Belliard and av. d'Auderghem. Entrees €8-12. Salads €12-14. Plats €16-34.* ☒ *Open M-F 11am-2:30pm and 6:30-11pm.*

NIGHTLIFE

We encourage you to sample as many **good Belgian brews** as humanly possible, but remember: the metro stops at midnight. The cheapest and most popular bars are in Lower Town, which features a decent mix of tourist traps and well-kept local secrets. Upper Town nightlife is less vibrant and more expensive, with bars and lounges full of 30-somethings in abundance but fewer options for students.

Lower Town

The Lower Town has the liveliest nightlife in Brussels.

DELIRIUM   BAR

4A Impasse de la Fidélité   ☎02 514 44 34 www.deliriumcafe.be

If you want to party hard in Brussels, Delirium is the place to do it. While its immense popularity means that all of the drunkest tourists (and Belgians) will be here, Delirium is a large enough place that you won't mind. Shenanigans and revelry abound, and with a selection of more than 2000 beers, this bar provides the opportunity to get drunk on new brews every night. Beware: these beers are strong (10% alcohol), so exercise some caution when you go out—it's not called Delirium for nothing.

i ⓂDe Brouchere. Walk south on bd Anspach 1 block, turn left onto rue Grétry, and continue about 2 blocks; the bar is on the left. Beer €2-6. ☼ Open daily 10am-4am.

L'ESTAMINET TOONE   PUB

Impasse Schuddeveld 6   ☎02 511 71 37 www.toone.be

You are likely to run into a chill, older crowd at l'Estaminet Toone, but occasional live music, marionettes dangling from the ceiling, and laughter keep this place light-hearted and young. This tavern neighbors le Royal Théâtre Toone, where you can enjoy an evening marionette show before heading down to the bar for some brews. The bar is accessed through a long tunnel, so although it may get a bit noisy inside, the hubbub from rue des Bouchers is (thankfully) drowned out.

i ⓂDe Brouckère. Walk 1 block south on bd Anspach to rue Grétry and turn left. Continue down rue des Brouchers; a big sign over the road points to Toone, on the right. Cash only. Beers €2.50-6.50. ☼ Open Tu-Su noon-midnight.

BONNEFOOI   BAR

8 rue des Pierres   ☎048 762 22 31 www.bonnefooi.be

Bonnefooi is one of Brussels's most pleasant bars, and it attracts a steady stream of young tourists to its unobtrusive side street near Bourse. It's not as wild as its 8am closing time might suggest, but it is a great place to relax at the end of a night of partying.

i ⓂBourse. Just off of bd Anspach. Beer €2-4. Mixed drinks €7. ☼ Open daily 6pm-8am.

GOUPIL LE FOL   BAR

22 rue de la Violette   ☎02 511 13 96

This eclectic estaminet is one of the Lower Town's best finds. A sign outside explains that the bar will not serve Coca-Cola to its patrons (except as a vehicle for alcohol). Step inside and you'll be enveloped in a world of revolution, literature, and art. Goupil le Fol is packed with an intellectual crowd of alternative students and older art-lovers, and the owner, Abel, counts the Princes of Spain and Belgium among his patrons.

i ⓂBourse. From the Grand Place, head down rue des Chapeliers and turn left onto rue de la Violette. Beer €3-6. ☼ Open daily 6pm-6am.

Upper Town

Apart from one of the city's best clubs, Upper Town nightlife tends to be less vibrant and more expensive than in the Lower Town.

brussels

FUSE
CLUB

208 rue Blaes ☎02 511 97 89 www.fuse.be

Fuse proudly proclaims itself "Best Belgian Club Ever." That might be overdoing it, but it is one of Brussels's biggest and liveliest clubs, with pounding music and drinks that will make even the worst dancing excusable.

i ⓂPort de Hal. Head north on bd du Midi, then turn right onto rue Blaes. Cover Sa before midnight €6, after midnight €11. Drinks €4-10. ☼ Open on club nights Th-Sa 11pm-late.

LA FLEUR EN PAPIER DORÉ
PUB

55 rue des Alexiens ☎02 511 16 59 www.lafleurenpapierdore.be

A mix of older locals and young artsy types crowd this historic pub just off of the Sablon area. Now protected by the Belgian government, it counts the artist Magritte and Tintin author Hergé among its former clientele. Temporary art exhibits fill the kooky space, making for a nice break from the monotonous profusion of Irish pubs and dark taverns.

i ⓂGare du Midi. Beer €2-7. ☼ Open Tu-Sa 11am-midnight, Su 11am-7pm.

Place Schuman and Heysel

JAMES JOYCE
IRISH PUB

34 rue Archimède ☎04 7162 05 80

If you show up to James Joyce solo, never fear—you will surely depart among (new) friends. This pub caters a bit more to the middle-aged crowd than the student scene, but as some travelers might say, every hour is happy hour here. The only Brussels bar with a full dartboard, a smoke room, and a reading corner with books that include (you guessed it) Ulysses, James Joyce ensures that there will be no shortage of conversation topics.

i ⓂSchuman. Walk north on rue Archimède 1½ blocks. James Joyce is on the left just past the Hairy Canary. Bartenders will make mixed drinks on request but no fancy mixed drinks. Live music 1st Th of each month. ☼ Open M-Th 5pm-late, F 5pm-7am, Sa noon-7am, Su noon-late.

SOHO
CLUB

47 bd du Triomphe ☎02 649 35 00 www.soho-club.be

Soho is one of Brussels's liveliest clubs, despite being situated near the EU district. The 20-something crowd on the gigantic dance floor is a welcome break from the older Eurocrats found in the area. Expect a wide variety of music and theme nights.

i ⓂHankar. Head west on Chaussée de Wavre and turn left onto rue de la Chasse Royale, then right onto bd du Triomphe. The Hankar stop is serviced by the night bus. Cover €10. Drinks €5-10. ☼ Open Th-Sa 11pm-late.

ARTS AND CULTURE

BEURSSCHOUWBURG
THEATER

20-28 rue Auguste Orts ☎02 550 03 50 www.beursschouwburg.be

A haven for up-and-coming artists, the Beursschouwburg hosts modern theater productions along with film and documentary screenings, dance performances, and temporary art installations. On Wednesdays, they host a free, student-oriented show with the superb title SHOW, which stands for "Shit Happens on Wednesday."

i ⓂBourse €12, students €10. ☼ Box office open M-F 10am-6pm.

LE BOTANIQUE
CONCERTS

bd du Jardin. 29-31 Botanique ☎02 218 37 32 www.botanique.be

The Botanical Gardens make for a beautiful stroll during the day, but things get a little raunchier at night, when the grand building that towers above the gardens hosts some of the best concerts in the city. Three different stages provide an

belgium

intimate performance space for artists from the UK, continental Europe, and on occasion the US; past heavyweight performers include Ellie Goulding, Marina and the Diamonds, and Kate Nash. Brussels's student crowd can't get enough of Le Botanique, and in recent years it has become the city's most popular venue for live music.

i ⓂBotanique. Buy tickets online. Some tickets available at the door. Prices vary by show. ⓏBox office open daily 10am-6pm.

THÉÂTRE ROYAL DU PARC
THEATER

3 rue de la Loi ☎02 505 30 30 www.theatreduparc.be

If you're game for a laugh, then get yourself down to the Parc and pick up a ticket to see a variety of performances. The early 2013 season included Sherlock Holmes, Around the World in 80 Days, Oedipus, and Les Misérables.

i ⓂTroon. Walk toward the park and to the left; the theater is in the corner of the park. Ticket €5-30. Student tickets €9.50. ⓏBox office open Sept-May M-Sa 11am-6pm, Su 11am-5pm; Jun and Aug Tu-F 11am-6pm. Closed all of Jul.

ESSENTIALS
Practicalities

- **TOURIST OFFICES:** 🖳**Use-it** makes maps especially for student travelers that are available for free at many hostels as well as at their office and on their website. The office staff can give advice on nightlife, food, shopping, GLBT life, and more. They also provide a list of festivals and events, have free internet (computers available), and free coffee. (8 Steenkoolkaai www.use-it. be ⓂSte-Catherine. Ⓩ Open M-Sa 10am-1pm and 2-6pm.) The **central tourist office,** in the east corner of the Grand Place (ⓂBourse), sells the **Brussels Card,** which includes free public transport, a city map, free museum access, and discounts at a few shops and restaurants for one, two, or three days (€24/34/40). There is also a second, less central office (2-4 rue Royale) and another at the central concourse of Gare du Midi (open daily 9am-6pm). (☎02 513 89 40 www.brusselsinternational.be Ⓩ Open daily 10am-6pm.)

- **CURRENCY EXCHANGE: CBC Automatic Change ATMs.** (7 Grand Place ☎02 546 12 11 Ⓩ Open 24hr. Also at ⓂDe Brouckere and ⓂGare du Midi.)

- **INTERNET: CyberCafés.** (86 bd Émile Jacqmain *i* €1,50 per 30min. Ⓩ Open daily 9am-10pm.) Free Wi-Fi is available at **McDonald's, Exki,** and **Quick** on rue Neuve.

- **POST OFFICES: Central Office.** (1 bd Anspach ☎02 201 23 45 *i* ⓂDe Brouckère. Belgium €0.75, EU €1.09, other countries €1.29. Ⓩ Open M-F 8:30am-6pm, Sa 10am-4pm.)

- **POSTAL CODE:** 1000.

Emergency

- **EMERGENCY:** For police, ambulance, or fire, call ☎100 or ☎101.

- **POLICE: Police headquarters** are located at 30 rue du Marché au Charbon. (☎02 279 77 11 *i* ⓂBourse. From the Grand Place, follow rue du Marché au Charbon from the northwest corner of the square. Ⓩ Open 24hr.)

- **LATE-NIGHT PHARMACIES:** Pharmacies in Brussels rotate hours, so there will always be one reasonably close to you that's open late. Pharmacies will usually display hours on a sign. **Pharmacie Fripiers** is closest to the Grand Place. (24B rue des Fripiers ☎02 218 04 91 Ⓩ Open M-F 9am-7pm, Sa 9:30am-7pm.) To find one open near you, visit www.servicedegarde. be or call ☎0800 20 600.

- **HOSPITALS/MEDICAL SERVICES:** The Saint-Pierre University Hospital has two locations. **Saint-Pierre University Hospital–Site César de Paepe** is a 10min. walk from the Grand Place. (11 rue des Alexiens ☎02 506 71 11 www.stpierre-bru.be *i* ⓂBourges. From the Grand

brussels

Place, exit through the southernmost corner of the square and turn left onto rue des Alexiens.) **Saint-Pierre University Hospital (International Patients Service)** is to the south. (322 rue Haute ☎02 535 33 17 www.stpierre-bru.be *i* Tram #3, 4, 33, or 51 to Ⓜ️Porte de Hal. Head south on rue Haute. 🕒 Open 24hr.)

Getting There

BY PLANE

The **Brussels airport** (BRU ☎090 07 00 00 www.brusselsairport.be) is 14km from the city center. Trains run between the airport and Gare du Midi every 20min. (€6-7 max; 5am-midnight). STIB bus #12 runs until 8pm, later on weekends and public holidays; bus #21 runs every 30min. (🕒 5am-11pm, until midnight during the summer). **Brussels South Charleroi Airport** (CRL ☎090 20 24 90 www.charleroi-airport.com) is a budget airline hub 45km south of Brussels. A shuttle runs from the airport to Gare du Midi. (€13, round-trip €22. 🕒 Every 30min.)

BY TRAIN

Brussels has three main train stations: **Gare du Midi, Gare Centrale,** and **Gare du Nord.** All international trains stop at Gare du Midi, and most stop at Gare Centrale and Gare du Nord as well. Gare Centrale is the closest to the center and the Grand Place. Gare du Nord is in the north just past Botanique. Gare du Midi is in the southwest on bd du Midi. Brussels can be reached from Bruges (€12 🕒 30min.), Amsterdam (€43 🕒 3hr.), and Paris (€55-86 🕒 1hr. from Ⓜ️Midi); trains also run from London (www.eurostar.com €60-240 🕒 2hr.). There are also normal commuter trains that run between Amsterdam and Brussels that you can board without advance booking, but you can (and probably should) book in advance.

Getting Around

Getting around Brussels is cheap and simple on foot, especially in Lower Town. With skinny, winding streets that change names often (and often have two names to begin with), it's easy to get lost. Luckily, it's also easy to get found: look for tall signposts around Lower Town and the major museum districts of Upper Town. These will point you in the direction of major attractions and metro stations and will even suggest whether to walk or take the metro based on how far your destination may be. Cars rule the roads in Brussels, so bikes are only advisable for the truly brave. If you want to bike around Brussels, there are **villo** (bike rental) points located at key locations throughout the city; the first 30min. is free, but you pay incrementally for each 30min. thereafter (www.villo.be).

BY PUBLIC TRANSPORTATION

The metro system rings the city, with a main **tram** running vertically through the middle and two other lines running east to west. There are 18 trams in total. The **bus** and tram system connects the various quarters of the city, and night buses service major stops on Friday and Saturday nights every 30min. until 3am. All public transport in Brussels is run by the **Société des Transports Intercommunaux Bruxellois (STIB).** (☎07 023 20 00 www.stib.be 🕒 System operates daily 5am-midnight.) The **metro**, tram, and bus all use the same tickets. (€2, purchased inside vehicle €2.50; round-trip €3.50; day pass €6; 10-trip ticket €13.) It's a good idea to pick up a copy of the metro map, which also contains information about transfers and night buses. The map is free and available at ticket counters and at the Gare du Midi.

BY TAXI

After the metro stops running, you can call **Taxi Bleus** (☎02 268 00 00), **Taxi Verts** (☎02 349 49 49), **Taxis Oranges** (☎02 349 43 43), **Autolux** (☎02 411 41 42), or **CNTU** (☎02 374 20 20). Official taxi signs are yellow and black. Taxi prices are calculated by distance (€1.66-2.70 per km), plus a fixed base charge (€2.40, at night €4.40). **Collecto** is a

shared taxi system that has 200 pickup points in Brussels (☎02 800 36 36 www.
collecto.org *i* €6. ☼11pm-6am. Call 20min. or more in advance).

bruges

There's a reason you'll meet cute old couples on second honeymoons in Bruges: with
its picturesque canals and narrow old houses, it looks a little like a fairy-tale land.
The cobbled streets are often clogged with tourists wearing fanny packs and toting
cameras; most congregate around the museums, which range from the history of the
frite to Flemish art. Put in a little extra effort, and locals will happily share with you
all of Bruges's ghost stories, weird secrets, and small-town charm.

ORIENTATION

Thanks to its small size, Bruges is very easy to navigate. Getting lost in the city is
more fun than worrying, since it takes only 10min. to get back on track. Bruges is
surrounded by a canal which cuts through the center of the city, so if you do get
lost, just follow the water. **The Markt** is the center of town, and is recognizable by the
large **belfry tower,** which can be seen from almost any part of town. Four of Bruges's
main roads emanate from the Markt: **St-Jakobstraat** to the northwest, **Vlamingstraat** to
the northeast, **Wollestraat** to the southeast, and **Steenstraat** to the southwest. East of
the Markt along Breidelstraat is **the Burg,** Bruges's other main square, which boasts
the Town Hall and Holy Blood Chapel. **Hoogstraat** runs east from the Burg, while
Blezelstraat runs south. You can easily find all destinations in Bruges from the Markt
and the Burg.

SIGHTS

Bruges loves young people, leading to huge discounts for those under 26.

BELFORT
7 Markt
TOWER
☎050 44 87 78   www.museabrugge.be

If you've bribed the weather gods into giving Beligum a cloudless day, the gorgeous view from the Belfort can extend all the way to the North Sea. Keep in
mind that the 83m structure was built centuries before the age of elevators so
you'll have to climb a lot of stairs to get that photo-op. But the panoramic view
over the entire city is well worth the huffing and puffing.

i Grand Markt. €8, under 26 €6, seniors €6. ☼ Open daily 9:30am-5pm.

HOLY BLOOD CHAPEL
10 Burg
CHURCH
☎050 33 67 92

This small church has one main draw which brings religious visitors and tourists
by the thousands every year: a vial containing what the church claims to be the
blood of Christ. The prized possession is displayed every day from 2-4pm; head
up the flight of stairs and pay your respects (or even kiss!) the glass container
containing one of Christianity's most prized possessions. In mid-May, the city of
Bruges holds the annual Holy Blood Procession, a tradition dating back to the
14th century.

i In the southwest corner of the Burg. Free. Tickets must be purchased in advance at www.tick-
etsbrugge.be. ☼ Open daily Apr-Sept 9:30am-noon and 2-5pm; Oct-Mar 10am-noon and 2-5pm.

GROENINGE MUSEUM
12 Dijver
MUSEUM
☎050 44 87 43   www.museabrugge.be

The Groeninge Museum houses Bruges's best collection of Flemish and Belgian
artists from the 15th-20th centuries. As you move through the rooms, you'll
begin to appreciate the talent that went into some of these obscure religious
paintings, particularly Provost's various intriguing depictions of the life of Saint

Nicolas. However we also particularly enjoyed the more modern interpretation of the Last Supper by Gustave van de Woestyne. The ticket also gets you access to the temporary exhibition in the Arentshuis as well as The Forum, which is Bruges center for contemporary art.

i *From the Markt, head south along Wollestraat and cross the bridge. Take a right onto Dijver and through the archway on your left €8. ☼ Open Tu-Su 9:30am-5pm.*

FOOD

Bruges is brimming with restaurants—unfortunately, the local specialty is pawning small portions of overpriced food off on unsuspecting tourists. These places cluster around the Markt, but you know better than to fall into these traps. Instead, head a little farther out from the Markt to find a quality place, which will leave neither your wallet nor your stomach empty.

🍴 PAS PARTOUT   TRADITIONAL $
1 Jeruzalemstraat   ☎050 33 51 16 srpaspartout@busmail.net

This restaurant used to be a three-star Michelin restaurant where it cost a fortune just to look at the menu, but a few years ago it was taken over and turned into a social service project, in an attempt to serve high quality food to those who wouldn't normally be able to afford it. Now the older locals of Bruges come to Pas Partout to have cheap meals (under €10) of the highest quality in the area. Besides the food not much matches the restaurants origins for in many ways the place kinda feels like a cafeteria, but not in a bad way it is just plain and with a nondescript atmosphere. Do not let this stop you from coming here though for you will not regret taking your lunch at this hidden treasure.

i *From the Burg, head along Hoogstraat to the east, cross the bridge and continue onto Molenmeers. Turn left onto Jeruzalemstraat just past the laundrette and continue to the end of the road. Meal €7.30-10.75. ☼ Open M-Sa 11:45am-2:15pm.*

MÉDARD   TRADITIONAL $
18 Sint Ammandstraat   ☎050 34 86 84

Médrad has a history which goes back all the way to the 1930s, when the current owner's grandparents first opened their first little restaurant in Bruges. Food has been in the family for generations, and in 2003 the current owner moved back into what was once her parents' house to reopen the doors of Médrad. Locals started flocking back almost immediately, and after a look at the menu we can see why. The specialty spaghetti (€6.50) comes with cheese, vegetables, and plenty of ground beef—and this is just one of the small dishes. If you're really hungry try the large dishes, if you dare.

i *Just off of the Markt. Reservations recommended. Meals €6.50. Sandwiches €3-5. ☼ Open Tu-Sa noon-3pm and 6:30-7:30pm. Closed in the evenings on W and Su.*

GRAND KAFFEE DE PASSAGE   TRADITIONAL $$
26-28 Dweerstraat   ☎050 34 01 40 www.passagebruges.com

The Grand Kaffee is deeply traditional, and proud of it. Portraits of family members spanning the generations hang on the walls, but this doesn't make the place feel like some sort of creepy memorial, for even these pics have character to them as they are all different sizes and housed in different style frames. The large interior matches by carrying a dim and classic feel to it that is exactly what you will want when enjoying the traditional Flemish cuisine offered here. Even the menu looks like a storybook, and the intricate writing is translated into English to make choosing even easier.

i *From the Markt, head down Steenstraat which leads into Zuidzandstraat. Dweerstraat is on the right. Meal €9-16. ☼ Open daily 6-10pm.*

Bruges draws a fair amount of young backpackers, so hostels are plentiful in the city center and just outside the city walls. Visit **www.letsgo.com** for more hostel and hotel recommendations.

CHARLIE ROCKETS
HOSTEL $

19 Hoogstraat   ☎050 33 06 60   www.charlierockets.com

It's all American at Charlie Rockets, so you'll feel right at home in this hostel off of Bruges's main square. The large dorm rooms are spacious and the bathrooms are clean and modern, but Charlie is really out of this world compared to its competition due to its rocking bar, which is actually one of the highlights of a night out in Bruges. Save yourself the trouble and literally live at the bar.

i Hoogstraat runs southeast from the Burg. Free Wi-Fi. Breakfast and sheets included. 6- to 8-bed dorm €19-21. Doubles €43-55 ☑ Reception open 6am-4am.

NIGHTLIFE

Nightlife in Bruges is pretty easy-going; the only things that stay open until 7am are the *frites* stands. Locals enjoy a quiet drink in some hidden spots, while the tourists congregate near the Markt to down pricey pints. For a more authentically Belgian experience, head to one of the bars below. This is a place to drink slowly and strike up conversations with the locals.

▧ LUCIFERNUM
BAR

8 Twijnstraat

Ring the bell here on a Saturday night, and the doors of Lucifernum swing open, unleashing a series of the weird and wonderful. The scaffolding is a piece of permanent artwork that Willy Restin, the owner of the bar and a local Mephistopheles (in a good way), refuses to take down. During the summer months, the crowds head outside to lounge in Willy's garden, which feels more like the backyard of someone's house. Locals consider this to be one of the hidden gems of Bruges, so don't turn up expecting to down shots and stumble out wasted. Pay Willy and his friends some respect and treat this treasure for what it is: an absolutely fantastic venue for you to channel your inner Oscar Wilde. Keep in mind that Willy doesn't let his place fill up passed capacity, so don't arrive too late if you want to get in.

i From The Burg, head along Hoogstraat. Take a left up Kelkstraat and turn right onto Twijnstraat. Ring the doorbell (indicated with a sign). Entry to either bar includes a free drink. No official dress code, but leave your sneakers at the hostel. Rum Bar cove €5; includes 1 free drink. Absinthe Bar cover €6; includes 1 drink. Drinks €5-6. ☑ Open Su 6:30pm-2am.

▧ 'T POATERSGAT
BAR

82 Vlamingstraat

The owner of this bar bought the underground passage which connects the church above with the outside world. The owner claims that the monks that used to live in the church used the passage to sneak out, change into civilian clothes, and head down to the brothel at the end of the road. Nowadays the brothel no longer exists, but the underground passage is home to 't Poatersgat and still keeps the locals of Bruges pretty happy. Those who aren't in the know often miss the rabbit hole of an entrance; the door is embedded in the wall of the church, very low down, and many say the only way to find it is to "stumble down the steps by chance." (Be careful not to hit your head if you've had a few drinks already.) Once inside you will discover an elegant and rather cozy bar, fit

bruges

with plenty of seating and plenty of young locals filling up those seats. Definitely a highlight of the Bruges nightlife.

i *Vlamingstraat is just off the Markt. Free Wi-Fi. Beer €2.50-5. ⏰ Open daily 5pm-late.*

DE GARRE PUB

1 De Garre ☎050 34 10 29

They say no one just stumbles across De Garre—if you manage to find it, you were destined to visit. That's because De Garre is one of Bruges's best hidden pubs. Located down a small alleyway between the Markt and the Burg, De Garre is the only place to sample the smooth and tasty De Garre beer (€4). This 11.5% beer is a strong brew, so strong that the pub only allows you to have three in one sitting. Inside, the two-story house-like seating area is very typical of Belgian watering holes, and the cheese which comes with every beer helps the drinks along nicely.

i *De Garre is just off of Breydelstraat, in between the Markt and the Burg. Bee €2-3.50. ⏰ Open M-F noon-midnight, Sa 11am-1am, Su noon-midnight.*

ESSENTIALS

Practicalities

- **TOURIST OFFICES: In and Uit Brugge.** (Concertgebouw 34 't Zand ☎050 44 46 46 www. bruges.be/tourism ⏰ Open daily 10am-6pm.) A smaller branch is in the train station, **Stationsplein.** (⏰ Open M-F 10am-5pm, Sa-Su 10am-2pm.)

- **ATMS:** In the **Markt,** on **Vlamingstraat,** and in **Simosteviplein.**

- **INTERNET:** There's free Wi-Fi at the train station, at the bars of central hostels, and at a few bars like **'t Poatersgat** (see **Nightlife**).

- **POST OFFICES:** The central post office is at **5 Markt.** (☎050 33 14 11 www.depost.be ⏰ Open M-F 9am-6pm, Sa 9am-3pm.)

- **POSTAL CODE:** 8000.

Emergency

- **POLICE:** The police headquarters are at **7 Hauwerstraat.** (☎050 44 88 44 From the Markt, exit on the northwest side and turn left onto Geldmuntstraat, which becomes Noordzandstraat. Turn left onto Vrijdagmarkt, then right onto Hauwerstraat.)

- **LATE-NIGHT PHARMACIES:** Call the 24hr. pharmacy hotline. (☎0900 10 500 ⏰ Operates 10pm-9am.)

- **HOSPITALS/MEDICAL SERVICES: Hospital AZ St-Jan.** (Riddershove 10 ☎050 45 21 11 www.azbrugge.be Bus #13 to AZ Sint-Jan AV.)

Getting There

Bruges is really only reachable by train, but its train station has services that run to several Belgian and international cities and the three stations in Brussels. (€13. ⏰ 50min.) To reach Bruges from other major European cities, you will have to change at Brussels Midi/Zuid or Brussels Nord. (⏰ Ticket office open June-Aug M-Sa 10am-7pm, Su 10am-7pm; Sept-May M-Sa 10am-6pm, Su 10am-7pm.)

Getting Around

Bruges is a rather simple city for tourists to navigate, thanks to the abundance of pedestrian walkways and bike lanes; in fact, you'll find more bikes on the road than you will cars, especially in the center. Most visitors tackle the city by foot, heading from the station into the center and exploring the cobbled streets and densely clustered sights. If you're hoping to explore further afield, or if you have more time to spend in

belgium

Bruges, then renting a bike may be a good idea. Try Ropellier Bikes at 26 Mariastraat. (☎050 34 32 62 *i* €4 per hr., €8 per 4hr., €12 per day. ② Open daily 9am-7pm.) Bruges Bike Rental offers a student discount on single-day rentals. (17 Desparsstraat ☎050 61 61 08 *i* €4 per hr.; €6 per 2hr.; €8 per 4hr.; €12 per day, students €8. ② Open daily 10am-10pm.)

The bus system in Bruges is run by De Lijn, whose office is at the train station (Stationsplein. ☎070 220 200; €0.30 per min. wwww.delijn.be). Buses #1, 6, and 11 go from the station into the town center. Buses #58 and 62 stop at Memling Campsite (see p. 178). Bus #2 stops at Europa HI Youth Hostel. Tickets are valid for 1hr. (€1.20 if bought at the station booth, €2 if bought on board.)

belgium essentials

MONEY

Tipping

In Belgium, service charges are included in the bill at restaurants. Waiters do not depend on tips for their livelihood, so there is no need to feel guilty about not leaving a tip. Still, leaving 5-10% extra will certainly be appreciated. Higher than that is just showing off. Tips in bars are very unusual; cab drivers are normally tipped about 10%.

Taxes

The quoted price of goods in Belgium includes value added tax (VAT). This tax on goods is generally levied at 21% in Belgium, although some goods are subject to lower rates. Non-EU visitors who are taking these goods home unused may be refunded this tax for purchases totaling over €125 per store. When making purchases, request a VAT form and present it at a Tax Free Shopping Office, found at most airports, road borders, and ferry stations, or by mail. Refunds must be claimed within six months.

SAFETY AND HEALTH

Drugs and Alcohol

Belgium has fairly liberal attitudes regarding alcohol, with no legal drinking age. You have to be 16 to buy your own alcohol (18 for spirits), but it's perfectly legal for someone else to buy alcohol and pass it to someone under 16. Public drunkenness, however, is frowned upon.

Belgium's attitude toward even soft drugs is traditional and conservative. Marijuana is illegal and not tolerated. Coffeeshops in Belgium are just that.

belgium 101

HISTORY

Belgium Is Born (1815-1945)

The 1815 Congress of Vienna awarded Belgium to the Netherlands in an attempt to create a stable buffer state to the north of France. The Belgians revolted against the arrangement in 1830, and their country's independence was recognized the following year. Faced with both the weakness and strategic importance of Belgium, the other

If you just can't get enough of the fabulous chocolate, beer, and waffle shops in Belgium, this section has some suggestions for ways to extend your stay through volunteer, study, and work opportunities.

STUDY

Most universities in Belgium can be divided into two categories: French-speaking or Dutch-speaking. Pick a side and stick with it.

- **UNIVERSITÉ LIBRE DE BRUXELLES:** One of the two schools whose name is translated to English as "Free University of Brussels," this one is mostly French-speaking. (www.ulbruxelles. be/ulb/presentation/uk.html)

- **VRIJE UNIVERSITEIT BRUSSEL:** The second of the two schools translated to "Free University of Brussels," this one is mostly Dutch-speaking. (www.vub.ac.be/en)

- **AMERICAN UNIVERSITY'S BRUSSELS CENTER:** American University's Brussels Center offers two summer programs and one term-time program (repeated fall and spring) in the home of the EU. (www.aub.be)

- **UNIVERSITY OF LEUVEN (KU LEUVEN):** KU Leuven is a Dutch-speaking university in Flanders. (www.kuleuven.be/english)

- **UNIVERSITY OF LIEGE:** If you want to be able to say you've got Walloon pride, check out this public French-speaking university in Wallonia. (www.ulg.ac.be)

- **VESALIUS COLLEGE:** Established by VUB and Boston University, Vesalius is an American-style college that offers an undergraduate education in English. (www.vesalius.edu)

VOLUNTEER

Belgium is home to many NGOs and many international diplomatic entities, so take advantage of the vibrant international atmosphere and bury yourself in a volunteer opportunity.

- **OXFAM:** Oxfam's stated mission is to end poverty and injustice by protecting human rights. Oxfam has three different options for Belgium volunteers, depending on the language you speak. (www.oxfam.org/en/getinvolved/volunteer)

- **WEP INTERNATIONAL:** If you are a high school student who wants to spend time abroad in Belgium, or if you are slightly older and want to be set up with a farm stay, a home stay, or a language buddy in Belgium, then this is the program for you. (http://wepinternational.org)

- **COMMUNITY HELP SERVICE (CHS):** Volunteer your time manning a CHS help line; CHS's stated mission is to provide information, support, and mental health services in English in Belgium. (www.chsbelgium.org/volunteers.htm)

- **AUSCHWITZ FOUNDATION:** The Auschwitz Foundation, founded by former political prisoners who ended up in Belgium after World War II, is aimed at research and remembrance of the Holocaust. (www.auschwitz.be)

- **EDUCATIONAL PROGRAMMES ABROAD (EPA INTERNSHIPS):** EPA Internships can set you up with internships in Brussels or courses at Vesalius College, an English language college. This is not a program for the faint of heart or the empty of pocket. (www.epa-internships.org/programs/brussels)

- **GREENPEACE:** Volunteer to work toward a better environment with Greenpeace in Belgium. (www.greenpeace.org/belgium)

- **NATIONAL BOTANIC GARDEN OF BELGIUM:** Help conserve biodiversity and spread knowledge of plants and horticulture at the National Botanic Garden. (www.br.fgov.be)

WORK

Working in Belgium as a foreigner requires a fair amount of paperwork and red tape but isn't impossible.

- **WORLD WIDE OPPORTUNITIES ON ORGANIC FARMS (WWOOF):** Working on a farm in Belgium in exchange for room and board (and occasional pocket money) sounds like paradise to some. If it does to you, check out WWOOF Belgium. (www.wwoof.net)

- **GREATAUPAIR:** An au pair program that works internationally and has placements for au pairs in Belgium. (www.greataupair.com)

- **THE BEST AU PAIR:** If great isn't good enough, this au pair program also works internationally and has placements in Belgium. (www.thebestaupair.com)

- **AU PAIR BELGIUM:** For those looking for a smaller, more local au pair agency, check out Au Pair Belgium. (www.aupairbelgium.be)

- **ENGLISH ACADEMY:** Most positions teaching or tutoring English require certification and training of some sort. If you have relevant teaching experience, it's worth applying. (www.englishacademy.be/eng-jobs-new.asp)

European powers agreed to recognize and protect its neutrality. It ended up being one of the key causes of WWI.

Germany's invasion of neutral Belgium at the start of World War One escalated the conflict by forcing Britain to honor its commitment to defend Belgium from foreign attack. King Albert I and his army spent four years in the trenches fighting to repel the invaders, and some of the Western Front's most tragic battles were fought in Belgium. The country was decimated by the war, and, when the Germans again invaded in 1940, Leopold III surrendered almost immediately—provoking criticism from his allies but saving the country from the worst of the destruction.

If You Don't Want to Be invaded By 'Em, Join 'Em (1945-present)

Belgium shed its former neutrality after the war by joining NATO, which is head-quartered in Brussels, and the Benelux economic union with the Netherlands and Luxembourg. More influence came in the 1960s, when Brussels became the political center of the European Economic Community, the predecessor of the European Union. The influx of bureaucrats filled Brussels with a household necessity that remains in vogue today: red tape. Relations between the French- and Flemish-speaking regions are strained, and political debates are often defined by language. Many people believe the country should split in two, although ending 180 years of Belgian unity would be a dramatic step to take, and is not likely in the immediate future.

FOOD AND DRINK

Street Cart/Calorie Chart?

What would the American diner be like without the influence of Belgium? A visit to Brussels reveals that Americana may not be so, well, American after all. Throughout Belgium, vendors with small carts sell frites—despite their American name, the Belgians invented the French fry first. Unlike the hometown drive-thru, these fries are always crispy and piping hot, because Belgians cook them twice, including right before they are served.

Chocolat, Chocolat, Chocolat

Brussels is likely home to more than a few slightly mad chocolatiers. It certainly has a number of chocolate factories and quaint sweet shops. In his Brussels kitchen in 1912, Jean Neuhaus invented the praline, the quintessential Belgian chocolate, when he filled chocolate shells with cream and nut pastes.

Beer!

Need we say more? It's the de facto national drink of Belgium—8700 different varieties are produced in the country. Nowhere will you find more brews than in the bars and cafes of the cosmopolitan Belgian capital. Ordering wine at a Brussels brasserie is basically like ordering beer in Napa Valley. Brussels bars serve beer in all colors (a Flemish red, anyone?) and flavors (do raspberry and peach beer sound appealing?).

CZECH REPUBLIC

Throughout the Czech Republic, the vestiges of Bohemian glory and communist rule can be found on the same block. More recently, the '90s sparked the transformation of this country into an alternative, electrifying country. Döner kebabs, bockwurst, and Czech cheeses are peddled side by side. Freewheeling youth and a relentless drive toward the modern mean endless streets of hip hangouts and vehemently chill attitudes, making Czech cities, especially Prague, some of the best student destinations in Europe. And even though the locals might be too cool for school they do appreciate a tenacity to learn, evident from all the Czechs who cheer your blatantly wrong attempts at their language. Whether they're dishing heapings of local cuisine onto your plate, sharing beers with you at a low-key Prague pub, or inviting you to a local party, the citizens will open their arms to you.

greatest hits

- **ART NOUVEAU'S POSTER BOY.** Get the full picture of the artist at the **Alfons Mucha Museum** (p. 82), which features original posters as well as other designs.

- **VITUS IS VITAL.** A trip to the Czech capital would not be complete without a visit to Prague Castle, in particular **St. Vitus Cathedral** (p. 89).

- **DRINK DRINK.** In case you had doubts, they named it twice: **Bar Bar** (p. 96) is one of the best spots in the city for nighttime drinks and international cuisine. Yum yum.

student life

Prague's university is Univerzita Karlova v Praze (Charles University), founded in 1348. Its campus is spread across the city, but you're bound to run into students if you frequent the right bars, such as **Bunkr Parukářka** or **Matrix.** If you're looking to find the study-abroad crowd, **Roxy** is a good club option and is always packed with foreign youth. And if you're just dying to be in an indie film, snoop around **FAMU: Filmová a televizní fakulta Akademie múzických umění v Praze,** a film school located in Nové Město that is known to bring all the alternative boys to its yard.

prague

At the end of the day, Prague is a city of magic. Prague isn't sterile the way most Western European capitals are, but it's not a post-communist wreck either—it's caught in the middle, somewhere in between daily reality and the realm of legends. And we don't just mean "legend" legends, like the one about the Golem of Prague. We mean the legends of people—these cobblestone streets were once walked upon by Franz Kafka, after all. There's also the legend of Charles IV, the ambitious Czech king who dreamed up Prague the way it looks today (aside from the fast food restaurants, those came later). And then there's the far more recent specter of communism, which left the entire country in a hangover that still hasn't ended. Speaking of hangovers, we haven't even told you about the beer which is cheaper than water, about the cafés which teem with easy-going locals, and about the art, which creeps around in all forms, from the subtlest of jazz melodies to the heaviest of modern sculptures. There will be moments in between, when all you see are other tourists breathing at your neck, Western shops turning the city into just another European capital, and the Czechs either not speaking English or speaking it in an offensive way, but it's the moments of magic for which you came here. For these, the entire trip is worth it.

ORIENTATION

Nové Město

The New Town is dominated by two enormous squares. **Wenceslas Square** (Václavské náměstí), a former horse market, is now occupied by Western-style shops, sausage hawkers, and the equestrian statue of St. Wenceslas, while **Charles Square** (Karlovo náměstí), a former cattle market, is today covered by a somewhat-unkempt park. **Národní třída** is a major street that separates the Old Town from the New; here you'll find the impressive **National Theater.** Fast-food joints litter **I.P. Pavlova,** a square on the border of Nové Město and Vinohrady.

Staré Město

Old Town Square (Staroměstské náměstí) is the heart of Staré Město. Some of Prague's most famous landmarks—the **Astronomical Clock** and **Church of Our Lady before Týn**—are located here. To the west is the iconic **Charles Bridge,** while the streets to the east lead to **Municipal House** and ⓜNáměstí Míru. To the north is Josefov, a small historic Jewish neighborhood completely enveloped by the river, and Staré Město. Finally, streets to the south (Melantrichova, Jilská) connect Old Town Square with **Wenceslas Square** and **Národní Třída,** which mark the beginning of Nové Město. Trams and the metro don't go directly through Staré Město but rather skirt its edges; walking is the preferred mode of transportation.

Josefov

Josefov is a historically Jewish district of Prague whose main attractions are five **synagogues** and the **Old Jewish Cemetery.** It may seem surprising that such a district survives in post-WWII Europe—in fact, during the Nazi occupation, Hitler demarcated the area as a future museum of the soon-to-be extinct Jewish people. Aside from the surviving synagogues, most of the buildings in the area were demolished in the late 19th century and replaced with Art Nouveau architecture. The area is also famous for its connection to the writer **Franz Kafka,** who was born nearby, and whose name is now plastered on every other souvenir sold here. The synagogues here are certainly worth a visit, but the neighborhood is also one of the biggest tourist traps in Prague, with over-priced restaurants (think mussels and lobster), high-end fashion boutiques, and souvenir peddlers.

Malá Strana

Malá Strana, literally "Lesser Town," got the name because of its placement below the castle, but we see nothing "lesser" about it. Squeezed between Prague Castle and the Vltava and stretching up Petřín Hill, Malá Strana is the stomping ground for more established, better-known artists. To the north, Malá Strana merges smoothly into Hradčany, while to the south you'll find the neighborhood of **Smíchov,** best known for its large shopping mall and the Smíchov train station. **Malostranské náměstí** is Malá Strana's main square and **Újezd** is its main street, snaking from north to south along Petřín Park. Malá Strana's only metro stop is **Malostranská** (on the A line), but it can also be conquered on foot or by **tram** (12, 20, 22).

Hradčany

A visit to Hradčany is a must—the neighborhood is home to the **Prague Castle,** which contains such well-known sights as **Saint Vitus Cathedral** and the **Golden Lane.** Outside of the castle, don't miss **Strahov Monastery's** collection of natural oddities (the remains of a dodo bird, a narwhal tusk, etc.) and **Loreta,** one of the most important pilgrimage destinations in the Czech Republic. Most of the surrounding establishments are unabashed tourist traps, but this doesn't detract from Hradčany's real charms—sloping cobblestone streets and some of the best panoramic views of Prague. Located just

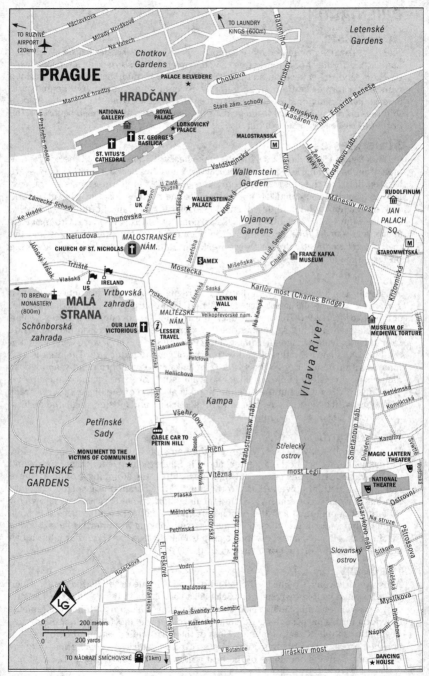

PRAGUE

HRADČANY

Chotkov Gardens

Letenské Gardens

TO RUZYNĚ AIRPORT (20km)

TO LAUNDRY KINGS (600m)

Václavkova
Milady Horákové
Na Valech
Mariánské hradby
U Prašného mostu

PALACE BELVEDERE ★

Chotkova

Staré zám. schody

Badeniho
Brusko

nábř. Edvarda Beneše

NATIONAL GALLERY 🏛
ROYAL PALACE ★
LOBKOVICKÝ PALACE ★
ST. GEORGE'S BASILICA 🏛
ST. VITUS'S CATHEDRAL ✝

U Bruských kasáren

MALOSTRANSKÁ Ⓜ

U železná lávky
Klárov
Kosařkovo nábř.

Zámecké Schody
Ke Hradu
Thunovská

UK 🏴

U Zlaté Studně
Sněmovni
Tomášská
Valdštejnská

WALLENSTEIN PALACE

Wallenstein Garden

Letenská

Mánesův most

RUDOLFINUM 🏛
JAN PALACH SQ.

Nerudova
CHURCH OF ST. NICHOLAS ✝

MALOSTRANSKÉ NÁM.

Josefska
Vojanovy Gardens
U Luž Semináře

STAROMĚSTSKÁ Ⓜ

Tržiště
Vlašská
US 🏴
IRELAND 🏴

SAMEX ✝
Mostecká
Mišeňská
Cihelná

FRANZ KAFKA MUSEUM 🏛

Křižovnická

TO BREŇOV MONASTERY (800m)

MALÁ STRANA

Vrtbovská zahrada

Prokopská
Lázeňská
Saská

Karlův most (Charles Bridge)

Na Kampě

Schönborská zahrada

OUR LADY VICTORIOUS ✝

MALTÉZSKÉ NÁM.
ⓘ LESSER TRAVEL

LENNON WALL ★
Velkopřevorské nám.

Maltézská
Nosticova
Harantova
Pelclova

MUSEUM OF MEDIEVAL TORTURE 🏛

Vitava River

Hellichova

Kampa

Betlémská
Konviktská

Petřínské Sady

Všehrdova
Úvoz
Jánská

CABLE CAR TO PETRIN HILL

Smetanovo nábř.
Divadelní
Karoliny
Seminářská
Voršilská

MAGIC LANTERN THEATER 🎭

MONUMENT TO THE VICTIMS OF COMMUNISM ★

Říční
Seříkova
Vítězná

Malostransk.nábř.

Střelecký ostrov

most Legii

NATIONAL THEATRE 🎭

PETŘINSKÉ GARDENS

Plaská
Mělnická
Petřínská

Zborovská
Janáčkovo nábř.

Masarykovo nábř.
Na struze

Ostrovní

Holečkova
Preslova
El. Peškové
Štefánikova

Vodní
Malátova
Pavla Švandy Ze Semčic
Kořenského
V Botanice

Slovanský ostrov

Šitkova

Pštrossova
Vojtěšská
Myslíkova
Dittrichova
Náplavní

N LG

0   200 meters
0   200 yards

TO NÁDRAŽÍ SMÍCHOVSKÉ 🚉 (1km) ↓

Jiráskův most

DANCING HOUSE ★

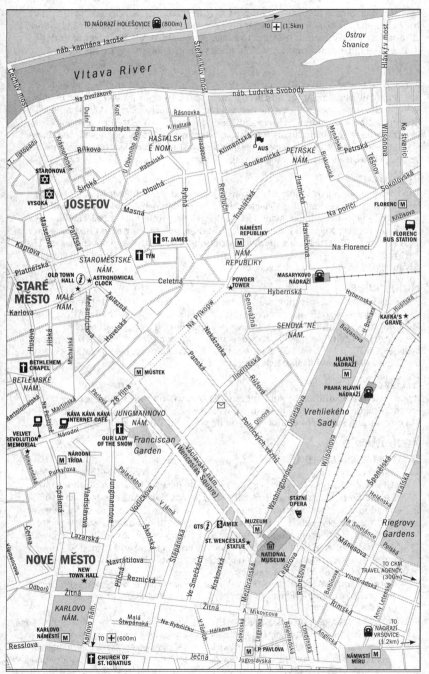

north of Malá Strana and west of **Letenské sady,** Hradčany is also a good place to start your hike up to Petřín Tower, or your dive down the hill toward Malá Strana's more affordable establishments. To get to Hradčany, take metro A to **Malostranská** and then walk up the hill, or take **tram 22,** which drops you off right above the castle.

Žižkov

In Žižkov there's no street that doesn't slope, no wall safe from graffiti, and no block without a pub or a bar. At the northern border of Žižkov there's **Vítkov Hill** and the **statue of Jan Žižka,** the one-eyed Hussite general for whom the neighborhood is named. To the south Žižkov borders Riegrovy sady and Vinohrady, while to the east it includes two big cemeteries, including **New Jewish Cemetery,** where Franz Kafka is buried. **Trams** 5, 9, 11, and 26 are the best way of getting to and from Žižkov, as the nearest metro station, **Jířho z Poděbrad,** is in neighboring Vinohrady.

Vinohrady

The western border of Vinohrady is roughly denoted by Ⓜ**I.P. Pavlova.** The neighborhood then stretches east along **Vinohradská,** all the way to ⓂŽelivského. **Náměstí Míru** is located just a few blocks away from I.P. Pavlova, while **Jiřího z Poděbrad** is close to Žižkov. **Riegrovy sady** and Žižkov border Vinohrady to the north and **Havlíčkovy sady** is to the south. **Vyšehrad** is a separate district, just one metro stop southwest of I.P. Pavlova. Walking in Vinohrady is an option, but if you want to save time, you can take advantage of the frequent tram service.

Holešovice

Holešovice used to be an industrial suburb, but today, thanks to steady gentrification, it's turning into one of Prague's most exciting neighborhoods. Situated north of Staré Město at a bend in the Vltava, Holešovice is split in two by railroad tracks. It's not as pedestrian-friendly a neighborhood as many others in Prague, so we recommend **trams** 1, 3, 5, 12, 14, 17, and 25 to get around. The two closest metro stations are on the C line: **Vltavská** and **Nádraží Holešovice.**

SIGHTS

If you visit Prague during the summer months, you will be viewing the historical sites around Prague Castle and Old Town Sq. with thousands of other people. You'll miss the crowds and save a lot of money if you do your Old Town sightseeing at night.

Nové Město

⬛ ALFONS MUCHA MUSEUM   MUSEUM

Panská 7   ☎224 216 415 www.mucha.cz

Alfons Mucha rose to fame overnight when he designed a poster on short notice for the French actress Sarah Bernhardt. The Art Nouveau artist was and still is a national hero, so it is no wonder that you can now find copies of his posters of gorgeous semi-nude women anywhere. Sure, the famous Parisian posters (with Ms. Bernhardt) are here, but be sure to pay equal attention to the Czech posters, photos of Paul Gauguin playing the artist's piano and of models dressed up as Greek Orthodox monks, and Mucha's sketchbooks, along with his window design for the St. Vitus Cathedral.

i A or B: Můstek. Walk up Václavské náměstí in the direction of the St. Wenceslas statue. Turn left onto Jindřišská and left again onto Panská. The museum is on the left. 180Kč, students 120Kč. ☒ Open daily 10am-6pm.

WENCESLAS SQUARE (VÁCLAVSKÉ NÁMĚSTÍ)   SQUARE

Once a horse market, Václavské náměstí now sells everything on the two sides of the beautiful green hedges and wide pedestrian walkways. American-style department stores and historic hotels compete for attention, with vendors ped-

get a room!

Prague has accommodations to suit every budget. In general, Staré Město costs more and offers less, while Nové Město costs less and offers more. There are several great hostels in Holešovice, Vinohrady, and Malá Strana, but these may require a metro or a tram ride to visit sights. There's also a network of student dorms that function as hostels during the summer (www.czechcampus.com) that tend to be cheaper than most hostels.

⬛ MOSAIC HOUSE   HOTEL, HOSTEL $$
Odborů 4   ☎246 008 324 www.mosaichouse.com

Although there are four-star hotel rooms available, most people seem to be young and ready to party. Mosaic House also has an epic 26-bed female dorm, which, despite what you'd think, is quite fun and comfortable. Plus, it uses renewable energy sources and a water recycling system.

i *B: Karlovo náměstí. Head north along the western edge of the square. Take a left onto Odborů at the northwest corner. Free Wi-Fi. Computer use 50Kč per hr. Breakfast 150Kč. Key deposit 50Kč. Towels included for hotel guests, with dorms 30Kč. Lockers included. Women's dorm available. Dorms 300-625Kč; doubles 1440Kč.* ⟳ *Reception 24hr.*

⬛ SIR TOBY'S HOSTEL   HOSTEL $$
Dělnická 24   ☎246 032 610 www.sirtobys.com

From rooms with outlandish names (Opa's Girlfriend, Paprika Palace) to events like beer and crepe tastings, Sir Toby's does everything with a dose of personality. Before heading out, grab one of the custom maps of the area or ask one of the receptionists about the old family photos on the wall to hear some hilarious, sketchy, and probably made-up stories.

i *C: Vltavská. Take tram 1, 3, 5, or 25 or walk along the tram tracks for 3 stops to Dělnická. Turn left onto Dělnická; the hostel is on the left. Free Wi-Fi and computer use. Breakfast 100Kč. Dinner 90-110Kč. Lockers included. Towels 15Kč with a 200Kč deposit; included with private rooms. Laundry 100Kč. Dorms 150-600Kč; doubles 900-1000Kč. 5% discount for ISIC holders who reserve online.* ⟳ *Reception 24hr.*

⬛ HOSTEL ONE PRAGUE   HOSTEL $$
Cimburkova 8   ☎222 221 423 www.hosteloneprague.com

Žižkov's vibe and Prague's famous monuments are equally represented in the graffiti-esque paintings that decorate Hostel One. The private doubles feel like apartments, and the 10-room dorms have their own bathrooms. The staff organizes free trips to some of Prague's best nightlife spots.

i *Trams 5, 9, or 26: Lipanská. Walk uphill on Seifertova, past the big church, then turn right onto Cimburkova. The hostel is on the right. Free Wi-Fi. Computers available for use. Linens included. Laundry 200Kč. Towels 20Kč. Dorms 290-690Kč; private rooms 590-790Kč per person.* ⟳ *Reception open 7:30am-12:30am. Garden closes at 10pm.*

dling up to six different types of sausage. The square is dominated by the **National Museum**, which began a five-year renovation in 2011. Some of the exhibits have been moved to the modern building next door (Vinohradská 1, www.nm.cz *i* 100Kč, students 70Kč). Don't miss the statue of St. Wenceslas, where the proclamation of Czechoslovakia's independence was read in 1918. Artist David Černý's hilarious parody of this statue can be found inside the Lucerna complex on Vodičková and involves an upside-down hanging horse.

i *A or B: Můstek, or A or C: Muzeum. Free.*

DANCING HOUSE
LANDMARK

Rašínovo nábřeží 80

The Dancing House supposedly shows a woman and a man dancing together, which is why it was originally dubbed "Fred and Ginger" after the famous dancing duo. Some complain that the masterpiece does not fit with the beautiful Baroque and Art Nouveau buildings nearby; others say that American architects such as Frank Gehry should not invade the well-preserved architecture of central European cities. However, we think that the modern building (a collaboration between Gehry and Vlado Milunić) is a new gem in the old city. Its symbolic location—on a lot leveled after the Bombing of Prague—and deconstructivist architecture remind visitors of the horrors of the past century, while the charming playfulness of the angles and materials symbolize the hopeful future.

i B: Karlovo náměstí. From the metro, walk down Resslova toward the river. The building is on the left. Coffee 45-70Kč. Beer 40-90Kč.

SAINT HENRY TOWER (JINDŘIŠSKÁ VĚŽ)
BELFRY

Jindřišská ulice ☎224 232 429 www.jindrisskavez.cz

Dating back to 1455, this tower was ingeniously converted so that most of its floors serve different roles. From the bottom up: whiskey bar (1-2 fl.), gallery (3 fl.), Prague Tower museum (4 fl.), toilets (5 fl.), museum (6 fl.), restaurant (7-9 fl.), and observation deck (10 fl.). As you can probably guess from the fact that the bathrooms take up an entire level, the floors are rather small. However, the price of the ticket allows you to see everything inside, so take the elevator to the top and then work your way down. The view from the top may be "average" compared to others in the city, but even an average view of Prague is breathtaking.

i A or B: Můstek. From the metro, walk up Václavské náměstí in the direction of the St. Wenceslas statue. Turn left onto Jindřišská and continue to the end of the street. 90Kč, students 60Kč. Cash only. ⚉ Open daily Apr-Sept 10am-7pm; Oct-Mar 10am-6pm.

NEW TOWN HALL (NOVOMĚSTSKÁ RADNICE)
TOWNHALL

Karlovo náměstí 1/23 ☎224 948 225 www.nrpraha.cz

Luckily, strong wires protect the lovely view of Charles Square from the observation deck of New Town Hall. Why luckily? Well, it was here that the First Defenestration of Prague took place in 1419, when a mob of Hussites stormed the town hall and tossed some 15 councilors and other dignitaries out the window. Later on, the building functioned as a prison, and executions took place in the town hall's courtyard as recently as the Nazi occupation. Other than its interesting history, the tower is a lot like the many other tall structures in the city: it has a bunch (221) of steps, small exhibits, and often plays host to weddings.

i B: Karlovo náměstí. From the metro, look for the giant tower on the northern end of the square. 500Kč, students 30Kč. Cash only. ⚉ Open Apr-Oct Tu-Su 10am-6pm.

Staré Město

🏛 CHARLES BRIDGE
BRIDGE

Charles the IV commissioned the most famous of the 17 bridges crossing the Vltava River in Prague and laid down the first stone on July 9, 1357. Weather gods have been less kind to the 30 statues added between 1600 and 1800, and the city removed and replaced original statues of characters such as the Czech martyr St. John of Nepomuk and Algerian St. Augustine. If you want to escape the hordes of tourists, admire the sight from the banks of the river around sunset or climb up the stairs of the **Old Town Bridge Tower** for a gorgeous view of Old Town, Lesser Town, and the other bridges of Prague.

i A: Staroměstská. Facing the river, turn left onto Křížovnická. Continue straight; the bridge is on the right. Tower 75Kč, students 55Kč. ⚉ Open daily Nov-Dec 10am-8pm; Apr-Oct 10am-10pm; Dec-Mar 10am-6pm.

ASTRONOMICAL CLOCK TOWER AND OLD TOWN HALL (STAROMĚSTSKÁ RADNICE)   BELFRY

Staroměstské náměstí   ☎724 911 556

At the ripe age of just over 600-years-old, this mysterious machine is divided into three parts that contain much more info than your smartphone's clock app. On the hour, the top of the clock always puts on a little show: 12 apostles poke their heads out, a rooster crows, and the crowd of tourists below goes bananas. The human hand, sun, moon, and little star dials of the astronomical clock below reveal Babylonian, Old Bohemian, German, and Sidereal time and Zodiac information. The clock can also tell you whether it is dawn, day, dusk, or night (in case you need a clock for that) and the position of the moon. The calendar dial, divided into 365 parts, tells you the day and symbolic representations for each month. For a breathtaking view of the city and a very cozy bonding experience with dozens of other tourists thanks to the modern elevator planted in the medieval building, head to the top of the tower.

i A: Staroměstská. Walk on Kaprova away from the river, turn left onto Malé Náměstí, and turn left after the street ends. Exhibition hall 100Kč, students 80Kč. Tower 100/80Kč. ◙ Hall open M 11am-6pm, Tu-Su 9am-6pm. Last tour 5pm. Tower open M 11am-10pm, Tu-Su 9am-10pm.

CHURCH OF OUR LADY BEFORE TÝN (MATKY BOŽÍ PŘED TÝNEM)   CHURCH

Staroměstské náměstí   www.tyn.cz

The two enormous Gothic spires of Our Lady before Týn dominate the skyline of the otherwise Baroque buildings of Old Town Square. It houses Prague's oldest organ but, more importantly, contains the remains of the astronomer Tycho Brahe, who revolutionized astronomy and allegedly peed himself to death. As the story goes, in 1601 Brahe was at Emperor Rudolf's for dinner and, in the name of decorum, refused to leave the dinner table to relieve himself, to the point that his poor bladder burst. On your way out, see if the sign on the door still eloquently reads "Draw up to oneself," instead of a good ol' "Pull."

i A: Staroměstská. Walk on Kaprova away from the river, turn left onto Malé Náměstí, and turn left after the street ends. The church is across Old Town Square. Free. ◙ Open Tu-Sa 10am-1pm and 3-5pm, Su 10am-noon.

MUNICIPAL HOUSE (OBECNÍ DŮM)   CONCERT HALL

Naměstí Republiky 5   ☎222 002 101 www.obecnidum.cz

The Municipal House was built in 1912, when a wave of nationalism swept over the Czech people. It is therefore no wonder that the beautiful concert and meeting hall proudly uses symbols of Czech history in its large and small details: the marbles are red and white (the national colors), the intricate floor and door handle details emphasize the talents of the Czech people, and the **Smetana Hall** (home of the Czech Philharmonic Orchestra) is named after one of the most important Czech composers. It was here that Czechoslovakia declared independence in 1918 and here that the Communist Party held the first meetings with Václav Havel and other leaders of the Civic Form in 1989.

i B: Náměstí Republiky. From Old Town Square, walk east on Celetná all the way to Náměstí Republiky; the Municipal House is on the left. Tours in Czech and English. Tickets must be purchased on the day of your visit at the ticket office, located in the Municipal House. Guided tours 290Kč, students 240Kč, families 500Kč. ◙ Open daily 10am-7pm. Tour times vary by week and month; check the online calendar for details.

SAINT JAMES CATHEDRAL (KOSTOL SVATÉHO JAKUBA VĚTŠÍHO)   CHURCH

Malá Štupartská 6

We would warn all superstitious travelers to stay away from this cathedral of gory legends if it weren't for the monumental Baroque interior with red- and cream- colored marble pilasters and a stunning organ with 8277 pipes. One of the legends is that a thief tried to steal the necklace off a Virgin Mary statue that came to life, grabbed the thief's arm, and refused to let it go. He had to cut off his arm *127 Hours*-style, and, to this day, a mummified arm hangs near the entrance of the church.

i *From Old Town Square, head down Týnska (with Our Lady before Týn on the left) and continue straight through the courtyards as it turns into Týn. The courtyard lets out at Malá Štupartská, where you should take a left. Free. ☼ Open M-Th 9:30am-noon, F 2-4pm, Sa 9:30am-noon and 2-3:30pm, Su 2-4pm.*

Josefov

A **joint ticket** grants admission to all synagogues (aside from Staronová Synagoga) and the Old Jewish Cemetery, while another joint ticket includes the Staronová Synagoge. (*i* Audio tours inside Pinkas Synagogue for 250Kč, students 200Kč. Joint ticket 300Kč, students 200Kč. All sights 480Kč, students 320Kč. ☼ Open in summer M-F 9am-6pm, Su 9am-6pm; in winter M-F 9am-4:30pm, Su 9am-4:30pm. Closed on Jewish holidays.) There are at least five ticket offices, so if a particular line seems to be advancing at a glacial pace, skip to the next one.

PINKAS SYNAGOGUE (PINKASOVA SYNAGOGA)   SYNAGOGUE
Široká 23/3   ☎222 317 191 www.jewishmuseum.cz

A trip to this nearly 500-year-old synagogue is most powerful when you come early in the morning and are one of the only ones to walk through the bare walls covered with the names, birth dates, and death dates of almost 80,000 Czech Jews who were murdered during the Holocaust. The upper floor contains a small but incredibly heartbreaking exhibit of drawings and collages by children during their time in Terezín.

i *A: Staroměstská. Walk toward the river 1 block, then turn right onto Valentinská. The synagogue is at the end of the street.*

OLD JEWISH CEMETERY (STARÝ ŽIDOVSKÝ HŘBITOV)   CEMETERY
U starého hřbitova 243/3a   ☎222 317 191 www.jewishmuseum.cz

This cemetery may remind one of a shark's mouth—the eroded and broken tombstones jut out at unexpected angles, one over another, since the graves were dug in layers. Over time, since the earliest grave was laid around 1439, the earth settled so that stones from the lower layers were pushed to the surface. Make sure to notice the little stones on the tombstones—traditionally, these are used instead of flowers, adding to the beautiful, gray-and-green simplicity of the cemetery. There are also many prominent gravestones, including those of Rabbi Low, the supposed creator of the mythical Golem, and David Gans, a Renaissance scholar, historian, mathematician, and astronomer.

i *Enter through Pinkas Synagogue. Camera permit 50Kč.*

OLD-NEW SYNAGOGUE (STARONOVÁ SYNAGOGA)   SYNAGOGUE
Maiselova   ☎222 318 664 www.synagogue.cz

The Old-New Synagogue is the oldest synagogue in all of Europe and the oldest working synagogue outside Israel. There are a few legends attached to the place. First, the remains of Golem are said to be hidden in the synagogue's attic. Second, the synagogue is supposedly protected from fire by angels (this would account for its longevity). Inside, there's also a replica of the flag flown by the congregation in 1496, when Ladislaus Jagiellon first allowed the Jews to fly their own city flag. The Old-New Synagogue is still the center of Prague's Jewish community. Just south of the Old-New synagogue is the **Jewish Town Hall,** which is not accessible to the public but whose clock tower has a timekeeper that ticks counterclockwise (just in case you needed to see one of those before you die).

i *A: Staroměstská. Walk away from the river on Kaprova, then turn left onto Maiselova. Continue after the Maisel Synagogue. The synagogue is on the right. Men must cover their heads (yarmulkes free). Services reserved for practicing members of the Jewish community. 200Kč, students 140Kč. Free guides in several languages.*

Malá Strana

⬛ PETŘÍN TOWER (PETŘÍNSKÁ ROZHLEDNA)   TOWER
Petřín Hill

If the Petřín lookout tower seems like a shameless knockoff of the Eiffel Tower, that's because it is. The Eiffel Tower debuted at the 1889 World's Fair, and this shorter, fatter cousin popped up two years later at the Czech Jubilee Exposition. It's at the top of **Petřín Hill,** and from the lookout 299 steps up, you can see a 360-degree panorama of the brick rooftops of Prague and the Czech countryside. If you're lazy and have money, you can pay extra to take the elevator (55Kč),but the clever double-staircase means that climbers don't have to awkwardly go around the tired tourists descending the tower. If you go on a clear day, you can even see Snezka, the highest mountain in the Czech Republic (about 150km away). The hilltop around the tower also has a number of worthwhile sights, including the **mirror labyrinth** (built for the 1891 Jubilee Exposition) and the **Memorial to the Victims of Communism,** a haunting and conceptually fascinating monument near the Újezd tram station.

i *Walk up Petřín hill or take the funicular from Újezd (all public transportation tickets valid, 24Kč for 30min. ticket). After getting off the funicular, turn right and continue along the wall until you see the tower. There's also a path that leads here from Strahov Monastery. 105Kč, students 55Kč, family 260Kč. Elevator 55Kč. Mirror labyrinth 70Kč, students 50Kč. Cash only. ☒ Open daily 10am-10pm. Mirror labyrinth open daily 10am-10pm.*

CHURCH OF SAINT NICHOLAS   CHURCH
Malostranské náměstí 1   ☎257 534 215 www.psalterium.cz

If you've spent any time in Europe, you've likely seen a church or two (or 50) by now. But this ain't no ordinary house of the Lord. Boldly colored celestial scenes play out on an enormous fresco that spans the length of the towering ceiling. Floating above it all, like the magical cherry on this holy sundae, sits the behemoth dome. Built by a team of three generations (father, son, and son-in-law) over 100 years in the 17th century, St. Nicholas is considered to be the most beautiful example of High Baroque architecture in Central Europe and was influential in defining the style throughout the continent. Don't forget to climb upstairs and see the 19th-century graffiti on the wooden handrail.

i *A: Malostranská. Follow Letenská to Malostranské náměstí or take tram 12, 20, or 22 for 1 stop. 70Kč, students 50Kč. Free entry for prayer daily 8:30-9am. Cash only. ☒ Open daily Apr-Oct 9am-4:45pm; Nov-Mar 9am-3:45pm. Tours every day. Holy Mass Su 8:30am.*

JOHN LENNON WALL   MURAL
Velkopřevorské náměstí

The John Lennon Wall is the property of the Knights of Malta, who have given up whitewashing the graffiti in this quiet, relaxing area. Western songs were banned during the Communist years, so when someone painted John Lennon's face on this wall after the iconic singer was shot in 1980, it was an act of defiance against the regime. Since then, the wall has been an ever-changing communal work of art—graffiti is layered over more graffiti, almost all of which celebrates peace, freedom, and other things Mr. Lennon stood for. The original drawing is long gone, but there will always be at least one Lennon face for you to pose with. Better yet, draw your own while you listen to "Imagine."

i *From the Charles Bridge, take a left onto Lázeňská soon after the bridge ends. Stay on it as it curves around into Velkopřevorské náměstí. Free. ☒ Open 24hr.*

FRANZ KAFKA MUSEUM   MUSEUM
Cihelná 2b   ☎221 451 400 www.kafkamuseum.cz

You'll probably notice David Černý's sculpture of pissing statues first, so we'll start our description of the Franz Kafka Museum with them. Recognize the shape of the pool that the two guys are standing in? It's the Czech Republic. Once you walk past the statues and into the museum, you'll just become more confused. In an attempt to be as disorienting as Kafka's writing, this museum goes crazy with shadowy video projections, the sound of dripping water, and dramatic lighting. The actual exhibit is a bit less dramatic; it's mostly facsimiles of Kafka's written documents and some old photographs.

i A: Malostranská. Go down Klárov along the river, veering left at the fork between U Lužické Semináře and Cihelná. The museum is on the left. 180Kč, students 120Kč, family 490Kč. ⚄ Open daily 10am-6pm.

MUSEUM KAMPA   MUSEUM
U Sovových mlýnů 2   ☎257 286 147 www.museumkampa.cz
The cost of admission may be a bit high, but modern art enthusiasts should not miss this riverside museum. The collection focuses on sculptures and paintings by Central European artists, most of whom were persecuted under Communism. At the end, climb the stairs to the observation deck, which has a great view over the Vltava (and feels as though it's about to keel over into it).

i A: Malostranská. From the metro, walk south along the river to Kampa Island. The museum is on the east side of the island at the edge of the river. Look for a giant chair or 3 enormous babies. 280Kč, students 140Kč. ⚄ Open daily 10am-6pm.

Hradčany

The following sights are only a small sampling of what the castle complex has to offer. **Saint George's Basilica** dates back to 920 CE and is also part of a short tour of the area. Next door, **Saint George's Convent** now functions as a museum of 19th-century Bohemian art and sculpture. The **Powder Tower** houses a small exhibit on the castle guards. Admission to the latter two comes with the long tour ticket.

▨ PRAGUE CASTLE (PRAŽSKÝ HRAD)   CASTLE
                                                        ☎224 372 423 www.hrad.cz
The "Prague Castle" refers to the entire, almost 70,000 sq. m complex of many different buildings, streets, and gardens surrounded by tall walls and steep stairs. The Castle should be almost as crucial to your trip to Prague as the buildings have been to the city's history (read: very important). The Prague Castle has been the seat of the Bohemian government since its construction over a millennium ago. It was home to such legendary kings as Charles IV and Rudolph II as well as the first Czechoslovak president, Tomáš Garrigue Masaryk. During World War II, Reinhard Heydrich, the Nazi-appointed protector of the city and notorious "Butcher of Prague," used the castle as his headquarters. It is said that whoever unlawfully wore the crown jewels would die within a year—Heydrich supposedly wore the jewels and, as predicted, was assassinated less than a year later. The Castle may be packed with tourists, but it's definitely worth the extra time to wander around and explore. Arrive on the hour to catch the changing of the guard—the ceremony at noon also includes fanfare. Bonus points: without breaking the law, try to make one of the guards on duty move. We weren't able to do it, but there must be a way.

i Tram 22: Pražský hrad. From the stop, go down U Prašného Mostu, past the Royal Gardens, and into the Second Courtyard. Alternatively, hike up Nerudova. Ticket office and info center located opposite St. Vitus Cathedral, inside the castle walls. Short tour covers admission to everything important; long tour includes everything important and other—rather uninteresting—sights. These are not guided tours, just combined tickets to different buildings. Tickets are valid for 2 consecutive days. Short tour 250Kč, students 125Kč. Long tour 350/175Kč. Photo permit for interiors 50Kč. ⚄ Ticket office and historical monuments open daily Apr-Oct 9am-5pm; Nov-Mar 9am-4pm. Castle grounds open daily Apr-Oct 5am-midnight; Nov-Mar 6am-11pm.

ST. VITUS CATHEDRAL (KATEDRÁLA SV. VÍTA) CHURCH

St. Vitus is the protector of actors, dancers, and comedians and is said to shield you against lightning storms as well as oversleeping (the latter is probably more useful). However, the young Christian—he was only about 15 when he died—managed not only to become a saint but had this gorgeous Gothic cathedral named after him. The cathedral is an architectural masterpiece, complete with three magnificent towers and more flying buttresses than it knows what to do with (no wonder it took almost 600 years to complete). Don't miss the beautiful window above the entrance and the Wenceslas Chapel *(Svatováclavská kaple)*, which has walls lined with precious stones and paintings. Despite their old look, the window mosaics were all made in the 1940s, and some even contain sponsorship messages (including those for an insurance company). Some of the most important Czech kings are buried here, including Charles IV (plus his four wives), Jiří z Poděbrad, and Wenceslas IV. The silver tomb next to the altar belongs to St. John Nepomuk, who supposedly had his tongue torn out and was then thrown off the Charles Bridge because he refused to tell Wenceslas IV what the king's wife had confessed. The Bohemian crown jewels are kept in a room with seven locks, the keys to which are kept in the hands of seven different Czech leaders, both secular and religious. There's also a reliquary (not accessible to the public) that contains the skulls of various saints and some brain matter of John Nepomuk. For a great view, climb the 287 steps of the Great South Tower.

i The Cathedral is the enormous church on the eastern part of the castle complex. Some parts of the Cathedral are accessible without a ticket, but the rest is included in the short and long tour tickets. "Treasure of St. Vitus Cathedral" exhibition 300Kč, students 150Kč.

GOLDEN LANE AND DALIBOR TOWER STREET, TOWER

The authorities' decision to make the formerly free Golden Lane accessible only with a paid ticket caused an uproar among Czech citizens a few years ago. This legendary street lined with hobbit-size houses once belonged to the castle's artillerymen and artisans. Some of the houses are furnished as they would have looked hundreds of years ago; the tiny home of the herbalist is full of dried-up plants, while the house of the seamstress is one of the biggest. Franz Kafka spent a year living in the blue house (#22); today, it's a disappointing gift shop full of copies of "A Country Doctor," the novel that Kafka wrote in the itsy-bitsy dwelling. At the end of the street, you'll come to the base of Dalibor Tower, a former prison whose most famous resident was the knight Dalibor. Dalibor is the subject of the imprecise Czech adage "Necessity taught Dalibor how to play the fiddle"—indeed, the only "fiddle" that Dalibor encountered in the prison was the torture instrument designed to get prisoners to confess by stretching them like horsehair on a fiddle bow. The tower exhibits a variety of torture and execution implements, including "Spanish boots" (designed to crush legs and feet) and an executioner's axe. The most jarring, however, is the "body cage" hanging in the middle of the small basement room. We're not sure that placing a skull in the head part was necessary; it looks uncomfortable enough without it.

i To the right of the basilica, follow Jiřská halfway down and take a left onto Zlatá ulička, or "Golden Lane."

Žižkov

JEWISH CEMETERY CEMETERY
Fibichova Street www.jewishmuseum.cz

Known as the First Jewish Cemetery of Olsany, this quiet cemetery is the resting place of more than 40,000 members of the Jewish community of Prague, many the victims of plague epidemics. Even though the tombstones of many notable rabbis and Jewish scholars can be found here, the cemetery was not cared for throughout most of the last few decades, especially during the construction of the neighboring TV Tower, and many gravestones are now damaged. Today, the cemetery continues to be a perplexingly beautiful ground of wild ivy and grass climbing over the closely packed tombstones covered in Hebrew scripts. As the site is not well known, you will most likely be one of few visitors. Walk through the small paths and reflect on the strange proximity of the ugly Žižkov TV Tower.

i A: Jiřího z Poděbrad. Walk toward the TV Tower on Milešovská, then take a left onto Ondříčkova, then an almost immediate right onto Fibichova. The cemetery is on the right, after the TV Tower. 60Kč. Open M 11am-3pm, W 11am-3pm, F 9am-1pm.

ŽIŽKOV TELEVISION TOWER
TOWER
Mahlerovy sady 1 ☎724 251 286 www.praguerocket.com

Although from a distance the Žižkov TV Tower looks like a Soviet launch missile that never left Earth, it is no more comprehensible from far away than it is from its base. Unlike most of Prague's other towers, this 216m (709ft.) giant is not decorated with gargoyles, cherubs, or saints, but rather enormous crawling babies. These nine babies are the brainchildren of controversial Czech artist David Černý, who permanently attached them to the tower in 2001 (perhaps as a reference to the earlier paranoia that the radio transmissions would hurt infants around the area). This wasn't the only worry of the Czechs, though; many suspected that the tower was actually built to jam signals from Western TV and radio programs. Even though the three observation decks provide a magnificent 360-degree view of the entire city (from fun hanging chairs in one observation deck), the tower seems less concerned with tourists than hosting business conferences. So if you are eager to take the elevator to the top (sorry, no stairs), check the schedule before visiting unless you want to be redirected to the restaurant.

i A: Jiřího z Poděbrad. Walk toward the TV Tower on Milešovská, then take a left onto Ondříčkova, then take an immediate right onto Fibichova. You won't miss it. 150Kč, students and seniors 100Kč, families 350Kč. Observation deck open daily 8am-midnight.

Vinohrady

Aside from Vyšehrad, Vinohrady is also home to some of Prague's nicer parks and greenery. **Riegrovysady** is a hilly park north of Náměstí Míru, with grassy slopes from which you can see the castle and much of Prague. Do as the young locals do: buy a plastic cup of beer from one of the nearby beer gardens, sit on the grass, and take in the view. The vine-covered **Havlíčkovy sady**, to the southeast of Náměstí Míru, is a posher setting; visit its wine bar, **Viniční Altán,** where you can sample many varieties of wine (www.vinicni-altan.cz *i* Wine from 30Kč. Open daily 11am-11pm).

VYŠEHRAD
MONUMENT
V Pevnosti 5B ☎241 410 348 www.praha-vysehrad.cz

Overlooking the hills of Prague next to the beautiful Vltava, Vyšehrad served as the royal residence of the Czech kings until 1140, when they moved to Hradčany. Though not much remains from the castle once founded by Princess Libuše (who supposedly foresaw the greatness of Prague before it became, well, great), the park is raised by the tall walls of Vyšehrad's fortifications and delivers one of the best views of the city. The complex also contains a number of interesting sites. There's the towering neo-Gothic **Church of St. Peter and St. Paul,** whose interior looks like a colorful codex and reflects the many times that the basilica has been rebuilt over the last 1000 years. Next to the church is the **Vyšehrad cemetery,** where some of the most prominent Czech artists (including painter Alphonse Mucha, composer Antonin Dvorak, and writer Karel Čapek) are buried. There's also a snoozefest of an archeological exhibition in the **Gothic Cellar,** while the **Vyšehrad Gallery** exhibits work by Czech painters. If you're interested in seeing

czech republic

six of the statues that were originally part of the Charles Bridge, you can go on a short guided tour of casemates and Gorlice. Finally, make sure you check out the view of the city from Vyšehrad's fortifications—it's one of the best in Prague.

i C: Vyšehrad. From the metro, head toward "Kongresové Centrum" and walk across this conference complex, keeping right. At the end, turn right and head down a staircase, then turn left and cross a parking lot. To the right there is a cobblestone road that leads to Vyšehrad. Guided tours of the casemate leave on the hour 10am-5pm. Park admission free. English map and guide 35Kč, cemetery guide 50Kč. Church of St. Peter and St. Paul 30Kč. Casemate 50Kč. Vyšehrad Gallery 20Kč. Gothic Cellar 50Kč. Cash only. ⌚ Exhibitions open daily Nov-Mar 9:30am-5pm; Apr-Oct 9:30am-6pm. St. Peter and St. Paul open M-W 10am-6pm, Tu-Th 10am-5:30pm, F-Sa 10am-6pm, Su 10:30am-6pm.

Holešovice

DOX
CONTEMPORARY ART
Poupětova 1   ☎774 145 434 www.doxprague.org

DOX is at the cutting edge of Prague's contemporary art scene; this should be obvious from the turquoise and orange paintings that adorn the modern building of the gallery that was transformed from an old wagon factory. We can't predict what show will be up when you visit, but the large floors and varying rooms of DOX can hold up to eight exhibitions, a cool arts library, and a design and book shop. Past programs include David Černy's controversial "Entropa" as well as an extensive exhibition called "Disabled by Normality," which questioned the meaning of the words "normal" and "disabled."

i C: Nádraží Holešovice. Take tram 5 or 12 or walk along the tram tracks to Ortenovo náměstí. From here, continue along the tracks on Komunardů and take the 1st right onto Poupětova. DOX is on the right. 180Kč; students 90Kč; art history, art, design, or architecture students 40Kč. ⌚ Open M 10am-6pm, W-F 11am-7pm, Sa-Su 10am-6pm.

LETENSKÉ SADY
PARK
The gigantic metronome is the tourist highlight of this sprawling, wooded park above the banks of the Vltava. The metronome, which continues to be Prague's heartbeat, was installed in 1991 on the spot where a statue of Joseph Stalin (the world's largest statue at the time) once stood. He sure had a view he didn't deserve. The gorgeous panorama supplemented with graffiti is now popular among skateboarding teenagers, friends and couples sharing a drink, and appreciative tourists. Toward the east side of the park, you can find the sometimes-functioning oldest carousel in Europe. There are also a few cheap beer gardens where you can enjoy a cold one while looking over Prague's rooftops. Finally, there's the famous Hanavský Pavilon, an expensive restaurant in a beautiful Art Nouveau château that was constructed for the Jubilee Exhibition in 1891.

i B: Hradčanská. From the station, walk to the other side of the building and head southeast. You'll run into the enormous park. Or take metro C to Vltavská and head west.

VELETRŽNÍ PALÁC / NÁRODNÍ GALERIE (NATIONAL GALLERY)
MUSEUM
Dukelských hrdinů 47   ☎224 301 111 www.ngprague.cz

Veletržní Palác is Prague's MoMA. There are five enormous floors with U-shaped galleries packed with Czech and international modern art. The building's exterior stands out both in terms of its modern look and size, but it is only while walking around inside that you'll realize how immense this gallery is. Although the permanent international collection is more than impressive, with entire rooms of Picassos and Gauguins and many interesting pieces by Klimt, Miró, and Lichtenstein, Veletržní Palác is most interesting thanks to its Czech art. The hallways full of Czech sculptures, designs, and architecture are very unique and definitely worth a visit. And if for nothing else, you must go to the museum for Mucha's "Slav Epic," 20 enormous scenes from the history of the Slavic people.

i C: Nádraží Holešovice. From the station take tram 12, 14, or 17 or walk along the tram tracks (passing the Exhibition Ground) for 2 stops to Veletržní. The museum is at the tram stop. 240Kč, students 120Kč. Audio tour 30Kč. ☑ Open Tu-Su 10am-6pm.

FOOD

Nové Město

◪ POTREFENÁ HUSA   CZECH $$

Resslova 1   ☎224 918 691 www.staropramen.cz/husa

Potrefená Husa was launched by Prague's Staropramen brewery in order to "improve the beer culture in Czech Republic" (which is kind of like somebody aiming to improve the cocaine culture in Colombia). Nevertheless, the three rooms of the underground restaurant have nifty details such as brick walls full of beer bottles, flip-through menus, and TVs hanging from the ceiling. The food, from cabbage soup to barbecued ribs, is well above average, and the restaurant's own brewer has a badass name (Mr. Jaroslav Svoboda). You could go for any brew you want, but we have to recommend Staropramen, especially the delicious lager, Staropramen Granát, that the restaurant serves in 0.4L cups for the same price as 0.3L of other beers. Locals and tourists alike visit Potrefená Husa for a delicious, filling, and out-of-the-ordinary meal.

i B: Karlovo náměstí. From the station, head down Resslova, toward the river. The restaurant is on the right. Entrees 145-285Kč. Desserts 25-109Kč. Beer 27-37Kč. ☑ Open M-W 11am-midnight, Th-Sa 11am-1am, Su 11am-11pm.

◪ LIBEŘSKÉ LAHŮDKY   BAKERY $

Vodičkova 9   ☎222 540 828 www.liberskelahudky.cz

This is not a restaurant. You won't have to go through the trouble of getting a table, guessing what will taste good based on a couple of words, or even being nice to your waiter. Instead, the entire establishment is one U-shaped counter overflowing with small sandwiches, cakes, cold salads, baguettes, meats, and, of course, liters of alcohol in the background. The open-faced sandwiches (*chlebíčky*) are artistic creations that come packed with eggs, ham, salami, and more. The bite-sized "mini desserts" (only 9Kč) are all enticing, and if you suck at making decisions about food, you can order 10 and have a feast in the nearby Karlovo náměstí for the price of one small cake somewhere else. There's no seating, so don't plan to stay for hours, but definitely check out this place before you skip town.

i B: Karlovo náměstí. From the metro, head north past the New Town Hall, staying right on Vodičkova when it forks. The restaurant is on the left. Baguettes 35-45Kč. Cakes 12-36Kč. Sandwiches from 17Kč. Cash only. ☑ Open M-F 7am-7pm, Sa-Su 8am-6pm.

RESTAURACE V CÍPU   CZECH $$

V Cípu   ☎607 177 107 www.vcipu.cz

Even though it's right in the center of the city, this little restaurant remains a secret to most foreigners. With wooden benches that often need to be shared between locals and some rustic signs and posters on the pale walls, V Cípu feels unpretentious and inviting. Locals come here for cheap Czech classics and for the bitter, strong, and golden brown Zlatopramen tank beer, which you can't get from the tap anywhere else in the country. Try the delicious and cheap soups, excellent fried cheese, or the duck.

i A or B: Můstek. From the metro, walk northeast on Na Příkopě and take the 1st right onto Panská. Take the 1st right onto V Cípu, opposite the Alfons Mucha Museum. Pub food 35-60Kč. Meat entrees 118-153Kč. Lunch menu 73-94Kč. Beer 19-33Kč. ☑ Open daily 11am-midnight.

czech republic

GLOBE CAFÉ
AMERICAN $$
Pštrossova 6   ☎224 934 203 www.globebookstore.cz

Part bookstore, part cafe, part cultural center, Globe is one of the best-known American outposts in Prague. Even though the American expat community has dwindled considerably in recent years and the clientele is starting to lean toward locals, Globe still offers some cultural comfort. There are up to 10,000 English-language books in the entrance room, in front of the main cafe room with enormous red walls full of colorful Botero-esque paintings. There is a full American brunch on the weekends, refillable drip coffee, and a menu of burgers, sandwiches, and other Western food every day. During happy hour (M-F 5-7pm), cocktails are super cheap, and cultural events, mostly in English (free film screenings, author readings, live music), take place almost every night.

i B: *Karlovo náměstí. From the metro, take Resslova toward the river and turn right onto Na Zderaze, which becomes Pštrossova; the cafe is on the right. Sandwiches and burgers 140-180Kč. Desserts 65-80Kč. Beer 20-40Kč. Internet access 60Kč per hr. Open M-Th 9:30am-midnight, F-Su 9:30am-1am (or later). Kitchen open until 11pm. Bookstore open daily 9:30am-11pm.*

PIZZERIA KMOTRA
PIZZA $$
V Jirchářích 12   ☎224 934 100 www.kmotra.cz

Kmotra ("the godmother") is known for its quality pizza and low prices. Supposedly the oldest pizza house in Prague, Kmotra sports a cozy downstairs cellar, with multiple rooms filled with warm hanging lamps, wooden tables, flat screen TVs, and plenty of local families and friends. There are more than 30 kinds of pizza here, all of which come with thin crusts and generous toppings, but the other options, such as the tomato soup, are almost equally satisfying. If you're after slightly less traditional toppings, try Špenátová II, which is topped with spinach, bacon, and a sizzling egg.

i B: *Národní třída. From the metro, head down Ostrovní toward the river. Take the 2nd left onto Voršilská. Starters 40-99Kč. Pizzas 115-165Kč. Pasta 99-150Kč.* ☒ *Open daily 11am-midnight.*

CAFÉ SLAVIA
CAFE $$
Smetanovo nábřeží 2   ☎224 218 493 www.cafeslavia.cz

Perhaps the best-known cafe in all of Prague, Slavia was historically the haunt of artists, intellectuals, and dissidents, including Renaissance man Václav Havel. Today, it's a large and bustling tourist attraction on a busy corner across from the beautiful National Theater and the Vltava, which means you can people watch the passing citizens comfortably from your bourgeois coffee perch. Slavia sends customers back in time with nightly piano music, a restored 1930s Art Deco interior with black and white photos, and waiters in bow ties. The food, although expensive, is great.

i B: *Národní třída. From the metro, walk north on Spálená and then turn left onto Národní. The restaurant is at the end of the street, across from the National Theater. Czech dishes 139-198Kč. Desserts 45-109Kč. Coffee 39-85Kč.* ☒ *Open M-F 8am-midnight, Sa-Su 9am-midnight.*

MAMACOFFEE
COFFEE $
Vodičkova 6   ☎773 337 309 www.mamacoffee.cz

Mamacoffee's name isn't the only adorable aspect of this coffee place. The two levels of the cafe are decorated with pretty cursive letters on blackboards, the espresso comes in cute blue and white porcelain, and there are entire bottles of melted cane sugar to flavor your iced coffee. The organic, fair trade beans come from all corners of the world, and the entire brewing process (from three spoonfuls of coffee beans to steaming cup) takes place before your eyes. Have your cup to go, or even better, enjoy it while working or reading on the upper level.

i B: *Karlovo náměstí. From the metro, head north past the New Town Hall. Stay to the right on Vodičkova when it forks; the cafe is on the right. 2nd location in Vinohrady. Coffee 35-67Kč.* ☒ *Open M-F 8am-10pm, Sa-Su 10am-10pm.*

LEMON LEAF   THAI $$
Myslíkova 14   ☎224 919 056 www.lemon.cz

The tall, yellowish interior of Lemon Leaf provides a fitting backdrop for the delicious Thai food you'll find here. It's cheap, too, especially on weekdays during lunchtime (11am-3pm) and happy hour (3:30-6pm, 20% discount on all meals). You won't have much time to admire the enormous sunset-like photos of Asian fields or the masks hanging on the walls, as your attention will be diverted by the delicious rolls and butter that arrive at your table right away. The drinks (such as the refreshing cucumber lemonade) come in large cups and are perfect partners for the big bowls of pasta. On a beautiful day, you can also join the many locals sitting outside.

i B: Karlovo náměstí. From the square, take Resslova toward the river and then take a right onto Na Zderaze. Continue to the intersection of Na Zderaze and Myslíkova. Curries 159-189Kč. Entrees 139-199Kč. Lunch menu 89-149Kč. ✪ Open M-Th 11am-11pm, F 11am-midnight, Sa noon-midnight, Su noon-11pm.

ANGELATO   ICE CREAM $
Rytířská 27   ☎224 235 123 www.angelato.cz

Word on the street is that this is the best ice cream place in all of Prague. We're inclined to agree—the taste is smooth, creamy, and downright surprising. The Mozart ice cream may be the best idea that mankind ever had since the Mozartkugel itself. Intrigued? Then don't take our word for it; go find out for yourself. Ice cream heaven is only 30Kč away.

i A or B: Můstek. From the metro, walk up Na Můstku toward the Old Town. The shop is on the left. 1 scoop 30Kč; 2 scoops 55Kč. Cash only. ✪ Open daily 11am-10pm.

Staré Město

▨ HAVELSKÁ KORUNA   CZECH $
Havelská 21   ☎224 228 769

Havelská Koruna may be a bit intimidating at first when the employee at the entrance places a piece of paper in your hand and points you toward a stack of trays that might remind you of your college dining hall days. But this self-service restaurant is as authentic as anything you may find in Staré Město. This is a place full of real food for real people, and you'll find it pleasantly packed with locals and tourists who chow down amid the standing and seating options sprinkled around characteristically Central European wooden columns. You can't go wrong when you order bread for only 3Kč with a delicious soup before you move on to traditional Czech dishes such as Moravian sparrow or roast beef on mushrooms. If you're in the market for an enormous dessert, try one of their sweet meals, such as mini-cakes with vanilla cream, a favorite of adults and kids alike.

i A or B: Můstek. From the station, head north on Na Můstku and continue as it turns onto Melantrichova. Take a right onto Havelská. The restaurant is on the left. Sides 13-26Kč. Soups 22-44Kč. Entrees 55-85Kč. Beer 20-36 Kč. Cash only. ✪ Open daily 10am-8pm.

▨ GRAND CAFÉ ORIENT   CAFE $$
Ovocný trh 19   ☎224 224 240 www.grandcafeorient.cz

Don't be ashamed if you feel a little tipsy from the Bacardi rum and Kahlua in your Coffee Grand Orient while gazing at the green and gold details of what is supposedly the world's only Cubist cafe, located on the second floor of the Black Madonna House. Imagine that there are Czech Cubists very critically admiring the nearby buildings from the small balcony that is now packed with tourists enjoying delicious cheesecakes. If the small sandwiches, salads, and plethora of pancake options are not persuading enough, just stop by to check

czech republic

out the incredibly cool coat hangers near the entrance (beauty, after all, is in the details).

i B: Náměstí Republiky. From Old Town Square, walk toward Church of Our Lady before Týn. Keep the church on your right and continue down Celetná. The cafe is at the fork of Celetná and Ovocný trh, on the 2nd fl. Crepes 105-150Kč. Desserts 30-150Kč.Coffee 45-85Kč. Cash only. ☼ Open M-F 9am-10pm, Sa-Su 10am-10pm.

BEAS VEGETARIAN DHABA INDIAN, VEGETARIAN $
Týnská   ☎608 035 727

This small but colorful vegetarian buffet, tucked away in a little courtyard, is about as good a deal as you can get in Old Town. This is evident from lonely locals who come here to enjoy the savory smell of Indian food and large plates of the daily special. You'll also find free jugs of water on every table under the large, vibrant paintings and photographs that adorn the walls. The selection changes daily, but you can always count on basmati rice, two kinds of *daal*, samosas, healthy juices, teas, and *lassi*, an Indian yogurt-based drink.

i B: Náměstí Republiky. From Old Town Square, walk toward Church of Our Lady before Týn, pass it on the left, and continue down Týnska. After you pass the church, keep left on Týnska—don't go straight. Turn left into a small courtyard; Beas Vegetarian Dhaba is to the left of Hostel Týn. Self-service food 20Kč per 100g. Lassi 24-26Kč. Coffee 35Kč. Other locations at Vlastislavova 24 (Ⓜ Národní Třída), Sokolovská 93 (Ⓜ Křižikova), Bělehradská 90 (Ⓜ I.P. Pavlova) ☼ Open M-F 11am-8pm, Sa noon-8pm, Su noon-6pm.

LOKÁL CZECH $$
Dlouhá 33   ☎222 316 265 www.ambi.cz

Let this place be your introduction to a uniquely Czech way of treating beer—the "tank system." The beer skips pasteurization and is instead stored in giant tanks (not kegs), where it remains cut off from oxygen. The beer's first meeting with air is when it is poured; your first meeting with thebeer is when it is delivered to your table, where you can refresh yourself in the relaxed yet elegant arched hallway that is as long as a street block. The menu, which changes daily, includes traditional Czech dishes that promise meals full of fresh ingredients and top-quality smoked meats made in the restaurant's own butcher shop. Lokál is packed with locals, so it's a good idea to make a reservation.

i B: Náměstí Republiky. Walk toward the river on Revoluční and turn left onto Dlouhá. Lokál is on the right. Starters 65-105Kč. Soups 39Kč. Sides 35-45Kč. Entrees 99-159Kč. Desserts 35-59Kč. Beer 31-42Kč. ☼ Open M-F 11am-1am, Sa noon-1am, Su noon-10pm. Kitchen open M-F 11am-9:45pm, Sa noon-9:45pm, Su noon-8:45pm.

LEHKÁ HLAVA VEGETARIAN $$
Boršov 2   ☎222 220 665 www.lehkahlava.cz

Even alpha-wolf carnivores should consider this intriguing restaurant, whose name means "Clear Mind." If you've been having any muddled thoughts about the virtues of vegetarian cuisine, the information about the sources of plant-based protein at the back of the menu might help to clear things up. Three Czech designers transformed the interior of a more than 500-year-old building by creating cozy salons for private parties, along with larger rooms for bigger gatherings. Unlike many vegetarian restaurants, this one seeks to make the world a better place through big plates of great food. The Kimchi probiotic salad promises you will look and feel better while the egg-free cheesecake makes vegan couples with matching tattoos and elegant ladies equally happy.

i A: Staroměstská. Walk south on Smetanovo nábřeží, turn slightly left onto Karoliny Světlé. Turn left onto Boršov (a tiny street). Reservations recommended. Starters 80-105Kč. Salads 105-145Kč. Entrees 130-210Kč. Desserts 70-80Kč. ☼ Open M-F 11:30am-11:30pm, Sa-Su noon-11:30pm. Lunch menu until 3:30pm. Between 3:30-5pm, only drinks, cold appetizers, and desserts served. Brunch served 1st Su of the month 10:30am-2pm.

prague

DUENDE CAFE, BAR $

Karolíny Světlé 30 ☎775 186 077 www.barduende.cz

One of the many small bars clustered around this area, Duende has plenty of personality—so much that it could be mistaken for a junk shop. Buoys hang next to leaping tigers, old guitars, a chandelier of small plastic heads, Arabic signs, and Christian posters. If you have nobody to talk to, try to engage one of the artsy students brooding over their diaries or just hopelessly stare at the bartender smoking cigarettes and singing along to Pink Floyd. Drinks are cheap, and there is a small menu of snacks to accompany your unrequited pining.

i A: Staroměstská. Walk south on Smetanovo nábřeží, then turn slightly left onto Karoliny Světlé. Duende is on the left. Beer 20-45Kč. Coffee 35-55Kč. Snacks 35-77Kč. Cash only. ⊠ Open M-F 1pm-midnight, Sa 3pm-midnight, Su 4pm-midnight.

Josefov

⊠ KOLKOVNA CZECH $$$

V Kolkovně 8 ☎224 819 701 www.kolkovna-restaurant.cz

Kolkovna, one of the best places in Josefov, looks a lot like the Czech restaurants aimed mostly at tourists, but this one is actually worth your time. The interior is enormous (and boasts a non-smoking section underground), with dark green walls, vintage posters, and large bars that serve Pilsner from the tank. If you come for the great lunch menu or delicious soups (some served with salty pretzels) around noon, you will probably be one of a few customers, but dinnertime is a different story. Consider yourself lucky if you get a spot at one of the large wooden tables that are perfect for drinking beer with your generously portioned and delicious meal.

i A: Staroměstská. Facing away from the river, turn left onto Žatecka, then right onto Široka. The restaurant is in the square with the Franz Kafka statue. Soups 45-78Kč. Salads 105-185Kč. Czech specialties 175-350Kč. Beer 34-52Kč. ⊠ Open daily 11am-midnight.

Malá Strana

⊠ BAR BAR RESTAURANT, BAR $$

Všehrdova 17 ☎257 312 246 www.bar-bar.cz

The menu at Bar Bar is full of lean meats and veggies but never compromises flavor; the delicious blend of local and exotic flavors results in a surprisingly unique dining experience. We recommend that you share the candlelight, a large jug of lemonade, and the degustation menu with someone special. Bar Bar is also twice as fun as your regular bar at night, so don't hesitate to come by for a drink in the company of brooding poets and painters.

i A: Malostranská. From the station, walk south or take tram 12, 20, or 22 to Hellichova. Continue walking south on Újezd, then turn left onto Všehrdova. The restaurant is on the right. Entrees 139-298Kč. Desserts 119-139Kč. Beer 29-42Kč. Cocktails 90-175Kč. ⊠ Open M-Sa noon-midnight, Su noon-6pm.

DOBRÁ TRAFIKA CAFE, WINE BAR $

Újezd 37 ☎257 320 188 www.dobratrafika.cz

If you make your way through the unremarkable store in front, you'll discover an excellent cafe in the back, popular with artists, musicians, and other tea-drinking types. Speaking of tea, this place has a four-page menu dedicated to the stuff, in addition to coffee from 20 different countries and rare, dark, and sweet Primátor beer on tap. If you're hungry, try the weirdest pita bread you've ever seen: fillings range from banana to Georgian eggplant. The courtyard is a lovely place to enjoy any beverage, and there's also a small wine bar downstairs.

i A: Malostranská. From the metro, walk south or take tram 12, 20, or 22 south to Hellichova. Continue walking south on Újezd; the specialty store is on the right. Pitas 29-78Kč. Beer 29-32Kč. Coffee 27-85Kč. Cash only. ⊠ Open M-F 7:30am-11pm, Sa 8am- 11pm, Su 9am-11pm.

TLUSTÁ MYŠ   CZECH $$
Všehrdova 19   ☎605 282 506 www.tlustamys.cz
Tlustá Myš ("Fat Mouse"), next door to Bar Bar, has similarly awesome food
and prices but a completely different aura. Judging by the Pilsner Urquell, Be-
cherovka, and other alcohol posters that cover the brick walls around the wood-
en tables, Fat Mouse could be any old Czech pub or restaurant. But perhaps
because of the cute mouse drawings on the menu, the wooden mouse sculpture,
and the Little Mole lollipops at the bar, Tlustá Myš's charm helps it stand out.
We recommend the steak California (chicken cutlet with cheese and peaches),
which, name aside, is a traditional Czech meal.
   i A: Malostranská. From the metro, walk south or take tram 12, 20, or 22 to Hellichova. Continue
walking south on Újezd and turn left onto Všehrdova. The restaurant is on the right. Starters 55-
99Kč. Entrees 119-165Kč. Desserts 49-59Kč. Beer 16-36Kč. 20% discount daily noon-2pm. Cash
only. ☼ Open M-F 11:30am-midnight, Sa noon-midnight, Su noon-10pm.

Hradčany

When it comes to most restaurants in Hradčany, we'll quote Admiral Ackbar: "It's
a (tourist) trap!" For a cheap bite to eat, try the fast-food hole-in-the-wall near the
intersection of Pohořelec and Úvoz (hot dogs 25Kč, cheeseburgers 50Kč) or the
Žabka market across the street.

▦ U ZAVĚŠENÝHO KAFE   CZECH $$
Úvoz 6   ☎605 294 595 www.uzavesenyhokafe.com
The inner courtyard of U Zavěšenýho Kafe is probably one of the nicest (and
most affordable) places to enjoy a coffee, dessert, or enormous plate of duck
meat around the Prague Castle. The restaurant is a favorite of not only travelers
but also loyal locals, many of whom send back snapshots of themselves (and
their babies) wearing "U Zavěšenýho Kafe" T-shirts from locations such as the
Galápagos Islands, Himalayas, and Brazil. The abacus near the counter shows
the number of "hanging coffees"—coffees purchased in advance by local patrons for the benefit of people without money to pay.
   i Tram 22: Malostranské náměstí. From the tram stop, walk uphill on Nerudova and continue as
it becomes Úvoz. The restaurant is on the right. Entrees 85-175Kč. Desserts 22-65Kč. Cash only.
☼ Open daily 10am-11pm.

BELLAVISTA   CZECH $$$
Strahovské nádvoří 1   ☎220 517 274 www.bella-vista.cz
It doesn't take a genius to figure out that the reason people come here is the
Čajovna (pretty view). And although we would have to be idiots to deny the
restaurant of this claim (the view really is gorgeous), we still recommend that
you enjoy the view for free, one level below the long lane of the open-air restau-
rant. However, if you don't mind spending about twice as much for everything,
then do join the many other tourists here for a cold beer, nice wine, or a big
plate of fancy and delicious meals; this could mean anything from veal burgers
to marinated arugula.
   i The restaurant is below Strahov Monastery. Facing the monastery, turn left and continue until
you reach a sloping path leading to the restaurant. Entrees 195-565Kč. Desserts 120-135Kč.
Small beer 65-69Kč. ☼ Open daily 11am-midnight.

Žižkov

U SADU   CZECH $$
Škroupovo náměstí 5   ☎222 727 072 www.usadu.cz
This may be one of Žižkov's best-known restaurants among locals and tourists
alike. On most nights, the patio seating and dining room are full, the latter both
with people and an entire antique shop of typewriters, cameras, and chande-
lier-like lamps dangling from the ceiling. But the coolest part of the restaurant is

U Sadu's smoky cellar; a spiral staircase behind the gambling machines leads to a foosball table and several small rooms filled with younger people. Food comes with baskets of bread and utensils, although you will need the strength of your teeth (and stomach) for the almost two pounds of smoked ribs with mustard and horseradish (we are pretty sure this is meant for an entire group of hungry backpackers).

i A: Jiřího z Poděbrad. From the metro, cross diagonally through the park (pass in front of the church), then walk north on Laubova. U Sadu is at the northern side of the square with the round-about. Snacks 55-95Kč. Meat entrees 125-195Kč. Beer 35-89Kč. Beer snacks 95-455Kč. ☼ Open M-W 9am-2am, Th-Sa 9am-4am, Su 9am-2am. Kitchen open until 2am.

U VYSTRELENÝHO VOKA   PUB $
U Božích bojovníků 3   ☎222 540 465 www.uvoka.cz

The title of this place means "at the shot-out eye," and over the last 19 years, this pub has become something of a cult establishment. The menu is the opposite of fussy—the only two categories you can choose from are "cold food" and "warm food." Try the inexpensive Danube sausage (35Kč) or, if you want to splurge, the fried cheese (80Kč). The cascading terraces above the pub actually belong to a different establishment, **Kavárna U Voka** (*i* Beer 26-33Kč ☼ Open M-F 3-10pm, Sa-Su 2-10pm), which is an equally great place to grab a drink. Oh, and if you ask the staff what the name means, you'll get a 30min. lecture on the history ofŽižkov. Short answer: it refers to the one-eyed Jan Žižka, a famous Hussite general.

i Tram 5, 9, or 26: Husinecká. Walk uphill on Seifertova, then turn left onto Blahníkova and continue as it turns into Jeronýmova. When you reach Husitská, take a right and then the 1st left into a little alley marked U Božích bojovníků. Cold food 30-44Kč. Warm food 35-89Kč. ☼ Open daily 4:30pm-1am.

VEGAN CITY BISTRO   VEGAN $
Husitská 45   ☎420 607 987 516 www.vegancity.cz

Fortunately, Vegan City Bistro's food is infinitely more tasteful than its interior and website designs. As you can probably guess from the name, fake flowers, fake bamboo columns, and plastic chairs, this establishment specializes in fast food. However, this is not a reason to turn away from the interesting vegan dishes that range from cheap sushi, rolls, and soups such as "Thai goulash" as well as the heap self-service food bar. Stop by for a quick lunch if you are tired of meat-heavy Czech dishes.

i Bus 133, 175, 207, 509. Continue walking away from the train station. The restaurant is on the left. Self-service 19Kč per 100g. Entrees 7-119Kč. ☼ Open M-F 10am-9pm, Sa 11am-9pm.

Vinohrady

▨ VINÁRNA U PALEČKA   CZECH $$
Nitranská 22   ☎224 250 626 www.vinarnaupalecka.cz

If you're after some great traditional Czech cuisine served between cool brick walls and wooden columns, this is the place. You don't have to have this specific wish, though—just come to enjoy the amazing and fattening Czech food. The menu is longer and more varied than the ones you'll find in most Czech restaurants—it even makes a few attempts at Mexican cuisine and kebabs, although we suggest sticking to the tried and true. Try the "Old Prague" mix for those filling Czech meats or one of the many options with Hungarian sausage (but only if your journey doesn't take you to Budapest later).

i A: Jiřího z Poděbrad. From the station, head south on Nitranská; the restaurant is on the left. Free Wi-Fi. Starters 40-330Kč. Soup 35-40Kč. Entrees 80-230Kč. Beer 25-35Kč. Lunch 65-75Kč. ☼ Open daily 11am-midnight. Lunch menu 11am-4pm.

czech republic

CAFÉ ŠLÁGR   CAFE **$**

Francouzská 72   ☎607 277 688 www.kavarnaslagr.cz

True to the spirit of the First Czechoslovak Republic (1918-38), a sign on the wall of this traditional cafe prohibits "all left-wing political discussions." So skip the politics and enjoy the desserts, coffees, and affordable brunch options. The marzipan cakes are almost as beautiful as the mosaic floors, elaborate railings, antique posters, and high ceilings of the cafe. If you're unfamiliar with Czech sweets, choose the overflowing *veternik* or the cream-filled *kremrole*. Take your desserts and coffee to the comfy back room for a more intimate setting.

i A: Náměstí Míru or tram 4 or 22: Krymská. From the station, walk southeast along Francouzská. The cafe is on the right. Baked goods 17-40Kč. Brunch 49-79Kč. Coffee 39-75Kč. Cash only. ☼ Open daily 10am-10pm. Brunch served 10am-2pm.

LAS ADELITAS   MEXICAN **$$**

Americká 8   ☎222 542 031 www.lasadelitas.cz

The Aztec Soup alone contains everything that many consider to be the hallmarks of Mexican food: chili, avocado, sour cream sauce, chicken, tons of cheese, and tortilla croutons. However, Las Adelitas is more than that. It definitely trumps several would-be Mexican restaurants, maybe not in size of the portions but definitely in authenticity. The chefs and owners are from Mexico, the music is Mexican, the photos on the wall are Mexican, and the tables and utensil holders below the low, arched ceilings are beautifully decorated with blue and yellow tiles. And we haven't even mentioned the Corona. Thirsty amigos who drink too much of this rather pricey beverage might not make it to the end of the meal.

i A: Náměstí Míru. From the station, walk down Americká. The restaurant is on the left, past the square with the dinosaur fountain. Soup 59Kč. Tacos 185-245Kč. Burritos 165-209Kč. Enchiladas 179-185Kč. Beer 29-75Kč. ☼ Open M-F 11am-1am, Sa-Su noon-1am. Kitchen open until 10pm.

Holešovice

OUKY DOUKY   CAFE **$**

Janovského 14   ☎266 711 531 www.oukydouky.cz

Ouky Douky is a merry corner of crammed boxes and shelves of used books. If you venture here, you'll also find deliciously filling breakfasts (the Mexican breakfast and Hugo's Holešovice breakfast served until 1pm are great), chatting locals, and intellectual events such as book discussions. Enjoy one of the crunchy baguettes while using the computers to translate some of the most confusing titles from the bargain book section.

i C: Vltavská. From the metro, take tram 1 or 25 or walk along the tracks on Bubenské for 1 stop to Strossmayerovo náměstí. Facing the church, take a left onto Janovského. The cafe is on the right. Breakfast 98-148Kč. Sandwiches 86-126Kč. Coffee 29-39Kč. Internet 15Kč per 10 minutes. Cash only. ☼ Open daily 8am-midnight. Breakfast daily 8am-1pm.

LA CRÊPERIE   CREPES **$**

Janovského 4   ☎220 878 040 www.lacreperie.cz

Many cafes in Prague will fix you a crepe, but here, they are the specialty. The adorably illustrated menu has almost 50 kinds of savory galettes and sweet crepes. You can even design your own crepe-monster: add ice cream or chocolate sauce to your lemon or chestnut cream crepes. Although French music plays in the underground rooms and the walls are covered with black-and-white photos of Paris and nautical-themed drawings, La Crêperie is cozy and unpretentious.

i C: Vltavská. From the metro, take tram 1 or 25 or walk along the tracks for 1 stop to Strossmayerovo náměstí. Turn left just past St. Antonín Church and walk past the tea shop. La Crêperie is on the left. Crepes 35-79Kč. Galettes 42-134Kč. Coffee 33-98Kč. Cash only. ☼ Open daily 9am-11pm.

prague

ZLATÁ KOVADLINA CZECH, BOWLING $$
Komunardů 36 ☎246 005 313 www.zlatakovadlina.com

Bowling and eating, two pastimes of the wise and lazy man, are ingeniously combined in this underground restaurant filled with locals. The cuisine is mostly traditional Czech, so you can nibble on your pork fillet covered in delicious tomato sauce while taking advantage of one of the four bowling lanes. The cheap lunch menu sometimes includes meals such as Szechuan chicken (although we're not sure how that tastes with Pilsner).

i *C: Vltavská. From the station, take tram 1, 3, 5, or 25 or walk along the tram tracks for 3 stops to Dělnická. Continue 1½ blocks; the restaurant is on the right. Entrees 79-199Kč. Beer 17-32Kč. Bowling 260-360Kč per person per hr. ◑ Open M-Th 11am-11pm, F 11am-midnight, Sa noon-midnight, Su noon-10pm. Lanes open daily 2pm-midnight.*

NIGHTLIFE

Although Prague has one of the greatest clubs in Europe (Cross Club) and a few genuinely amazing bars, most of the nightlife centers on the *hospoda* (pub) scene. Pubs stay open late (W until midnight, Th-Sa until 2-4am, Su until midnight), while clubs stay open until 4am or later. All outdoor terraces have to close at 10pm, after which most guests head indoors.

Nové Město

U SUDU BAR
Vodičkova 10 ☎222 232 207 www.usudu.cz

From the street, the pub under the Pilsner Urquell sign that reads "Sudu" might look pretty tame—four tables, a small bar, and subtle photographs. But head inside, and you'll become Alice in Wonderland, at least for a little while. The stairs lead down into a large underground room, then a tunnel to a different room, rinse, and repeat: U Sudu's cellar is a labyrinth of drinking spaces, all with a slightly different ambiance of green lights and brick walls. There's a room for watching sports and one for foosball and still another with live DJs. Aside from regular drinks, U Sudu also has 18-proof Master beer on tap. If you come during the day, you can also sit outside in the small courtyard.

i *B: Karlovo náměstí. From the metro, head north on Vodičkova past New Town Hall. The bar is on the right. DJs W-Sa 10pm-close. Snacks 16-55Kč. Beer 24-55Kč. Cash only. ◑ Open M-Th 9am-4am, F 9am-5am, Sa 10am-5am, Su 10am-3am.*

ROCK CAFÉ CLUB, MUSIC VENUE
Národní 20 ☎224 933 947 www.rockcafe.cz

Loud and raw and with equal amounts of beer in plastic cups and splashed across the floor, Rock Café remains one of Prague's best known music venues. Aside from live music, Rock Café also hosts film screenings and plays. The bands that play here tend to have weird, unfamiliar names, but lots of people seem to go crazy in front of the stage regardless.

i *B: Národní třída. From the metro, walk north on Spálená and then turn left onto Národní. The music club is on the left. Cover 50-150Kč; Tu free. Beer 27-59Kč. Liquor 30-115Kč. Cash only. ◑ Open M-F 10am-3am, Sa 5pm-3am, Su 5pm-1am.*

JÁMA (THE HOLLOW) PUB
V Jámě 7 ☎224 222 383 www.jamapub.cz

Jáma is one of those places where you either feel extremely epic for knowing basically every important band in the history of music whose posters are represented on the brick walls, or you just quietly order the largest Tex-Mex meal with extra guacamole and tell yourself you're just too young to associate any tunes with the famous names. Nevertheless, we suggest you enjoy your time here over one of the 12 great beers here that feature some secret wonders of microbreweries. Jáma's large interior and lively atmosphere make it a great place to hang out, and many English-speaking foreigners and locals do just that.

i *A or B: Můstek. From the metro, walk down Wenceslas Square and then turn right onto Vodičkova. Take the 1st left onto V Jámě; the pub is on the left. Beer 29-45Kč. Tex-Mex meals 99-265Kč. Lunch menu 85-135Kč. 10% off with Citibank card.* ☼ *Open daily 11am-1am.*

REDUTA JAZZ CLUB JAZZ CLUB
Národní 20 ☎224 933 487 www.redutajazzclub.cz

Reduta Jazz Club is perfect for a sexy and relaxing evening. When you sit in the long red sofas—surrounded by black and white photographs of the most famous stars of the genre—the smooth live jazz and a nice drink in your hand will take all your troubles away for the night. Founded in 1958, Prague's first jazz club has jazz, both Czech and international, on the menu every night. In the '90s, Bill Clinton visited the venue and hopped on stage to jam with the band, an event that was recorded and released on CD. Check out the "saxophone bar" downstairs, where tap beer is pumped out of a saxophone-shaped spigot.

i *B: Národní třída. From the metro, walk north on Spálená and turn left onto Národní. Reduta is on the left. Cover 285Kč, students 240Kč. Beer 30-50Kč. Wine 50Kč. Liquor 50-100Kč.* ☼ *Open daily 7pm-midnight. Music 9:30pm-midnight.*

Staré Město

CHAPEAU ROUGE BAR, CLUB
Jakubská 2 ☎222 316 328 www.chapeaurouge.cz

The fiery red interior of Chapeau Rouge is packed with mostly tourists and edgy decorations that adorn the walls and the windows (think toy babies and spinning, Madonna-like statues). Although you will have to share your table with other couples, groups of beer-chugging gentlemen, and maybe even some locals if you stay at the street-level bar, people-watching or drinking with your friends is still worth the experience at Chapeau Rouge. The two smokier and darker underground dance floors can be anything from rather empty to rather loud. The bar, established in 1919, is old and narrow, but you'll still be pleased to find two flat screen TVs here.

i *B: Náměstí Republiky. Head toward Old Town Square on Králodvorská. Turn right onto Rybná, then left onto Jakubská. The bar is on the left. Downstairs is often free; if not, cover may be 50-100Kč. Beer 28-40Kč. Shots 65Kč. Cocktails 85-115Kč. Cash only.* ☼ *Bar open M-Th noon-3am, F noon-4am, Sa 4pm-4am, Su 4pm-2am. Club open M-Th 9pm-4am, F-Sa 9pm-6am, Su 9pm-4am. Underground concerts usually start at 8pm.*

PROPAGANDA PUB (IRON CURTAIN) PUB
Michalská 12 ☎776 858 333 www.propagandapub.cz

Propaganda Pub has become a popular place for tourists since its entrepreneurial creator, who also dreamed up Bohemia Bagel and the Museum of Communism, endeavored to establish a club with more than 200 original artifacts from Prague's time behind the Iron Curtain. The large, underground place accommodates everything from Latin Parties and Funkshui Radio Nights to DJs, rock-reggae-jazz fusion bands, and quiet conversations in the cozy Red Library (which, unsurprisingly, is full of socialist literature). The beers from the first keg cost only 12Kč on Monday nights, and ladies get two cocktails for the price of one on "Wasted Wednesdays." As drinks and choices from the grill are relatively cheap, consider dropping some of your change in the cup labeled "People who tip have better sex" before leaving to continue your night somewhere else.

i *A or B: Můstek. Turn left onto 28 října, then turn right onto Perlová. Continue as it becomes Michalská. The pub is on the right. Not to be confused with Propaganda Café on Pštrossova 29. Beer 25-35Kč.* ☼ *Open daily 6pm-late. Kitchen open until midnight.*

ROXY/NOD
Dlouhá 33

CLUB, GALLERY
www.roxy.cz

Roxy is an enormous nightclub with a vaguely industrial feel, big name DJs, and all genres of Czech and international performers. Free Monday nights at Roxy are popular with locals. The circular bars supply reasonably priced drinks and views of the revelers below, but if you're interested in something more relaxed and creative, you should consider stopping by the art gallery on the first floor. You can start the night by sipping cocktails while walking through the innovative works in the galleries; on some nights, you can even cheer for the new Picassos of Prague while they battle and display their talents in events such as timed art competitions.

i B: Náměstí Republiky. Walk north on Revoluční, then turn onto Dlouhá. Roxy is on the right. Most concerts 100Kč. Beer 39Kč. Shots 39-70Kč. Cocktails 85-189Kč. Cash only. ◙ Club open daily 10pm-5am.

Malá Strana

▩ **JAZZ DOCK**
Janáčkovo nábřeží 2

JAZZ CLUB
☎774 058 838 www.jazzdock.cz

This new jazz club has been making waves—and not just because it's on the water. Jazz Dock swings hard during live performances every night of the week. The gig here is serious; there are double shows five days per week, children's theater on Saturday, and a Dixieland program on Sunday. Due to its genius acoustic design, live music can play until 4am without prompting noise complaints.

i B: Anděl. From the metro, head toward the river on Lidická. At the river, take a left and continue for 6 blocks. Jazz Dock is down some stairs on the right. Jam session Sa 1am. Guests who visit the club 3 times are entitled to a 10% discount on future club transactions. Cover 120-450Kč, under 25 or over 65 90Kč. Beer 23-43Kč. Cocktails 135-155Kč. Meals 125-225Kč. ◙ Open M-Th 3pm-4am, F-Sa 1pm-4am, Su 1pm-2am. Concerts daily Jan-Jun 7 and 10pm; Jul-Aug 10pm; Sept-Dec 7 and 10pm.

KLUB ÚJEZD
Újezd 18

BAR
☎251 510 873 www.klubujezd.cz

The only thing wilder than Klub Újezd's guests is its decor: although the yellow walls themselves are nothing special, the bathroom doors show monsters doing their business, and a giant leviathan snaps above the bar. The clientele isn't exactly monstrous, but the three floors can cater to three very different scenes. The upstairs cafe is secluded and smoky, the basement is dungeon-like, with a DJ spinning on a mini stage for the 20 people who can squeeze in, and the main bar is filled with all kinds of people who just like to sit and drink.

i A: Malostranská. From the metro, walk south or take tram 12, 20, or 22 to Újezd. Beer 23-70Kč. Cocktails 59-149Kč. Cash only. ◙ Bar open daily 2pm-4am. Cafe open daily 6pm-4am. Club open daily 6pm-4am.

BLUE LIGHT BAR
Josefská 1

BAR
☎257 533 126 www.bluelightbar.cz

The scratched up walls plastered with posters, chandeliers made from green beer bottles, candles on the rocky tables, and the mysterious reddish hue will make you want buy drinks and stick around a while at this great bar. The intimate scene is a well-known hangout for Czech politicians, artists, and singers, and it's a frequent location for parties. If Czech heavyweights don't impress you, checkout Daniel Craig's signature right above the bar. While the odds that you'll brush shoulders with *007* are slim, you can still pretend your life is shaken, not stirred.

i A: Malostranská. From the metro, head down Letenská toward Malostranské náměstí. Turn left into Josefská before you reach the square. The bar is on the right. Beer 35-85Kč. Cocktails 105-175Kč. Coffee 55-100Kč. Cash only. ◙ Open daily 6pm-3am.

czech republic

Žižkov

⬛ BIG LEBOWSKI
BAR

Slavíkova 16   ☎774 722 276 www.biglebowski.cz

There aren't many places in the world where you can come in, order a drink, and pay whatever price you want. This is such a place, created by the late owner, Mr. Lebowski. If you don't speak Czech, the employees and customers will laughingly discuss their guesses about how much you would spend on a delightful glass of beer (30Kč is a fair price, according to some locals). The bar seems tiny at first, but there's an upper level with two rooms filled with snapshots of cult films like *The Godfather* and *Pulp Fiction;* head here for lively discussions or games of chess, poker, Scrabble.

i A: Jiřího z Poděbrad. From the metro, walk north on Slavíkova. The bar is on the right. Pay as much as you want. ⏱ Open daily 6pm-midnight (or later).

BUKOWSKI'S
BAR

Bořivojova 86

Simply calling Bukowski's a "designer cocktail bar" would undermine the dark yet intellectual aura (accented by red candles) of this famous but not too touristy bar. After what some call Prague's best cocktails (including The Dorian Gray, The Naked Lunch, and chocolate martinis), your tipsy feet will enjoy a fully carpeted floor while you read (or attempt to read) the books on the maze of bookshelves that covers an entire wall.

i Trams 5, 9, or 26: Husinecká. From the tram, take Seifertova east, turn right onto Víta Nejedlého, then right onto Bořivojova. Beer 30-45Kč. Cocktails 85-130Kč. Cash only. ⏱ Open daily 7pm-3am.

Vinohrady

Vinohrady is full of small bars and clubs and is home to Prague's gay bars.

RADOST FX
CLUB

Bělehradská 120   ☎224 254 776 www.radostfx.cz

The painted Coke bottles seem symbolic: Radost FX, the "home of extravagant parties," opened in 1992 and was among the first to bring Western-style clubbing to the newly democratic country. Not that you care—you're just here to dance. Well, you've come to the right place. Fancy wallpaper, metal walls, and weird chandeliers add up to an edgy atmosphere (to stay fresh, the interior design changes every year). When you tire of dancing, head upstairs to the lounge and soak up the alcohol with pricey vegetarian food. You must try one of the following drinks: Cosmic Granny, Lesbian Joy, or Sex with an Alien (just don't combine any of them).

i C: I.P. Pavlova. From the station, head east on Jugoslávská for a little more than 1 block. When you reach Bělehradská, the club is on the left. Hip hop Th. House F. R&B Sa. Cover 100-150Kč; women free 10pm-midnight. Beer 35-95Kč. Cocktails 110-145Kč. ⏱ Open Th-Sa 10pm-5am.

SOKOOL
BAR

Polská 1   ☎222 210 528 www.sokool.cz

We won't make a joke about SoKool being "so cool," as the bar's name actually comes from the word *sokolovna* (gym). With an interior full of posters, signs, stuffed eagles, wooden tables, and other typical pub stuff, SoKool is beloved by both young and not-so-young locals. It serves beer in 1L glasses *(tupláky)*, and it's right next to Riegrovy sady (a popular student hangout; grab a plastic cup of beer and sit on the grassy slope that overlooks the city). SoKool also has one of the world's best cabbage soups (just our opinion). Don't expect any dancing, though; SoKool is more about drinking and bonding.

i A: Náměstí Míru. From the station, walk east on Korunní, then turn left onto Budečská. Continue to the end and head up the stairs. Beer 17-64Kč. Beer snacks 49-139Kč. Shots 30-60Kč. Cash only. ⏱ Open M-F 11am-midnight, Sa noon-midnight, Su noon-11pm.

prague

PIANO BAR

Milešovská 10   ☎775 727 496 www.pianobar.sweb.cz

Some say that this low-key gay bar that seems popular with mostly local men is like every other gay bar outside of touristy Prague, but we say that this place is perfect for experiencing real Czech nightlife. The interior is smoky and full of quirky hanging decorations (clocks, rainbow-colored flip-flops) and plenty of wooden tables. There's no dance floor and no light rigs—just a jukebox. And if you play the piano, you might end up being "live music" for the night. The prices are very friendly, but we would suggest that you bring a couple of Czech phrases with you, as they may come in handy when you order.

i A: Jiřího z Poděbrad. From the station, head east on Vinohradská, then take a left onto Milešovská. Beer 19-30Kč. Shots 37-57Kč. Cash only. ⏰ Open daily 5pm-5am.

Holešovice

◙ CROSS CLUB

Plynární 23   ☎736 535 010 www.crossclub.cz

This is about the coolest club you'll ever set foot in. Affectionately dubbed "Optimus Prime's Ass" by some, the place is decorated with the most amazing assortment of neon-lit industrial steel you'll find outside a junk yard (or anywhere at all). Cross exists on five levels, with a three-floor outdoor patio and maze of rooms downstairs. There are two sections: the upstairs cafe and patio are free for everyone, while access to the underground club requires a cover that varies widely. The descent into the club is surreal, as each room has its own quirks: one is just tall enough to sit in, while another is illuminated by lamps made from car engines. The upstairs cafe hosts cultural events, such as free film screenings on Wednesdays that showcase works by young Czech filmmakers as well as established directors.

i C: Nádraží Holešovice. From the metro, walk east on Plynární, past the bus bay and parallel to the tram tracks. Cross Club is the tall yellow building with metal sculptures out front. Cover 40-270Kč. Beer 19-37Kč. Cash only. ⏰ Cafe open daily 2pm-2am. Club open daily 6pm-late (anywhere between 2-6am).

SASAZU

Bubenské nábřeží 306   ☎284 097 444 www.sasazu.com

The location of SaSaZu is sort of bizarre: not only is the building a former slaughterhouse, but the club is also located in an enormous open-market filled with hundreds of knock-off bags during the daylight and some fancy cars at night. But this is the only way the enormous dance floor of SaSaZu, which is flanked by six bars. The DJ's saucer-shaped outpost hovers over the dancing crowds. There is also an über-stylish restaurant in the complex (your outfit should aim for just as über-stylish if you want to compete with others).

i C: Vltavská. From the metro, take tram 1, 3, 5, or 25 or walk along the tracks on Bubenské nábřeží for 1 stop to Pražská Tržnice (Prague Market) and enter the Prague Market grounds. SaSaZu is to the left, in front of a big parking lot. No open-toed shoes for men. Cover 100-200Kč; no cover for womenbefore midnight. Cocktails 145-185Kč. Beer 49-75Kč. Entrees 130-485Kč. ⏰ Restaurant open daily noon-midnight. Club hours depend on events; check the website.

ARTS AND CULTURE

While Prague has incredible shows, art, and concerts, there are also tons of god-awful tourist shows that cost inexcusable sums. Use this rule of thumb: if it costs more than 200Kč after a student discount, it's probably not worth the money.

NATIONAL THEATER (NÁRODNÍ DIVADLO)

NOVÉ MĚSTO

Národní třída 4 ☎224 901 638 www.narodni-divadlo.cz

The gorgeous and historic Neo-Renaissance building of the National Theater, located on the bank of the Vltava, is considered the Czech Republic's most important cultural institution. The program includes ballet, opera, and Czech-language drama. The theater opened in 1881, though various fires and other setbacks have caused alterations since then. The venue closes for the summer, but smaller, open-air productions often grace its inner courtyard.

i B: Národní třída. From the station, walk north to Národní třída and turn left toward the river. Tickets 30-1100Kč. 🕐 Open daily 10am-6pm. Evening box office opens 45min. before curtain.

STATE OPERA (STÁTNÍ OPERA PRAHA)

NOVÉ MĚSTO

Legerova 75 ☎296 117 111 www.opera.cz

Thanks to the State Opera's student-rush program, travelers can see a fully staged opera for less than the price of a sausage at the nearby Wenceslas Sq. Presenting more than a dozen operas every month, the State Opera sticks with favorites; works by Tchaikovsky, Mozart, Puccini, and Verdi are most frequently produced, with some other names occasionally mixed in.

i A or C: Muzeum. From the station, head past the National Museum. The State Opera is before the train station. Operas have Czech and English supertitles. Formal attire encouraged. Tickets 150-1200Kč. Up to 50% student discounts. 🕐 Open daily 10am-6:00pm. Evening box office opens 1hr. before curtain.

ESTATES THEATER

STARÉ MĚSTO

Železná 11 ☎224 228 503 www.stavovskedivadlo.cz

If it's not enough for you to walk by the famous theater where Mozart premiered *Don Giovanni*, buy a ticket to one of the performances. These days, the tourist-friendly Estates puts on mostly operatic hits like *Carmen, The Marriage of Figaro,* and—you guessed it—*Don Giovanni.* If you walk by during the day, you will often see people handing out flyers about performances. Getting a "place to stand" ticket (only 50Kč) is a great idea if you only want to see the beautiful interior and a half hour or so from an opera.

i A or B: Můstek. From Old Town Sq. walk south on Železná; the theater is on the left. Tickets 50-1340Kč. 🕐 Open daily 10am-6:00pm. Evening box office opens 1hr. before curtain. Performances usually at 5 or 7pm.

RUDOLFINUM

CONCERT HALL

Alšovo nábřeži 12 ☎227 059 227 www.ceskafilharmonie.cz

The gorgeous riverfront location of the Neo-Renaissance Rudolfinum alone makes it a perfect concert venue. The big stage, complete with an impressive organ, has been the home of the Czech Philharmonic Orchestra since 1896. The first concert that took place in this building was conducted by none other than the composer Antonín Dvořák, who was the orchestra's first conductor. The matinees and afternoon concerts tend to be cheaper than those in the evening, and with a student discount on top of that, hearing the Czech Republic's top symphony orchestra will cost practically nothing.

i B: Staroměstská. From the metro, walk toward the river. Rudolfinum is the big building to the right. The box office is on the side facing away from the river. Tickets 110-600Kč. 50% student discount. 🕐 Box office open M-F 10am-6pm; closed in summer.

ESSENTIALS
Practicalities

- **TOURIST OFFICES:** Prague Information Service. (Staroměstské náměstí 1. ☎221 714 444 www.praguewelcome.cz *i* On the ground floor of Old Town Hall, to the left of the Astronomical Clock. 🕐 Open daily Apr-Oct 9am-8pm; Nov-Mar 9am-7pm.) Other branches: Rytířská 31,

Malostranská mostecká věž (Malá Strana Bridge Tower), Hlavní nádraží (main train station), and Letiště Praha Ruzyně (Prague airport, terminal 2).

- **TOURS:** 🖳**New Europe Tours** offers free tours of the city center. (www.newpraguetours.com *i* Tours depart the Starbucks in Old Town Sq. 🕐 3hr., 11am and 2pm.) **Prague Royal Walk** offers walking tours of the city center. (www.discover-prague.com *i* Free. 🕐 2½hr., 11am and 2pm.)

- **LUGGAGE STORAGE:** At the **main train station** (Hlavní nádraží) in either self-service lockers (☎777 082 226 *i* Max. 24hr. 60-90Kč per day 🕐 Open daily 3:10am-12:50am) or in the storage room (*i* Max. 30 days, 60-100Kč per day. 🕐 Open daily 6am-11pm). Florenc bus station. (35Kč per day. 🕐 Open daily 5am-midnight.)

- **POST OFFICE:** Jindřišská 14. ☎221 131 111 www.ceskaposta.cz. ⓂMůstek. 🕐 Open daily 7:30am-8pm.

- **INTERNET CAFES:** Many cafes and restaurants offer free Wi-Fi. Computer use in internet cafes usually costs around 60Kč per hr. **Bohemia Bagel.** (Masná 2 ☎224 812 560 *i* Internet 2Kč per min. 🕐 Open daily 8am-9:30pm.)

Emergency

- **EMERGENCY NUMBERS:** ☎112 (operators speak Czech, English, and German). **Medical Emergencies:** ☎155. **Fire:** ☎150.

- **PHARMACIES: Lékárna Palackého.** (Palackého 5 ☎224 946 982 ⓂMůstek. 🕐 24hr.) **Lékárna u Svaté Ludmily.** (Belgická 37. ☎222 519 731 ⓂNáměstí Míru. 🕐 24hr.)

- **MEDICAL SERVICES: Na Homolce.** (Roentgenova 2 ☎257 272 144 www.homolka.cz *i* Tram 22 or 36 to Vypich. 🕐 Emergency room open 24hr. Foreign department open M-F 7:30am-4:30pm, but foreigners can get help anytime.) **Doctor Health Centre Prague.** (Vodičkova 28 ☎603 433 833 www.doctor-prague.cz. ⓂMůstek 🕐 Open M-F 8am-4:30pm. Hotline 24hr.)

Getting There

By Plane

Ruzyně Airport (☎220 111 888 www.prg.aero) is some 10km west of the city center. The cheapest way to get to the center is to take bus **#119** to ⓂDejvická (26Kč 🕐 24min.) or **#110** to ⓂZličín (26Kč 🕐 18min.) and then change to the metro. **Airport Express** buses go directly to the main train station. (Hlavní nádraží. *i* 50Kč. 🕐 35min., every 30min. 6:30am-10pm.) **Student Agency** go to the Florenc bus station. (60Kč. 🕐 Every hr. 6am-9pm.)

By Train

Prague has three major train stations: the main one is **Hlavní nádraží** in Prague 2; the others are **Smíchovské nádraží** in Smíchov and **Nádraží Holešovice** in Holšovice. Trains are operated by **Česká Doprava** (☎840 112 113 www.cd.cz). International destinations include: **Berlin** (1425Kč. 🕐 5hr., 8 per day.); **Bratislava** (643Kč. 🕐 4hr., 8 per day.); **Budapest** (1430Kč. 🕐 7hr., 6 per day.); **Krakow** (1025Kč. 🕐 8hr., 3 per day.); Moscow (3628Kč. 🕐 33hr., 1 per day.); **Munich** (1385Kč. 🕐 6hr., 4 per day.); **Vienna** (1010Kč. 🕐 5hr., 8 per day.); and **Warsaw** (1300Kč. 🕐 9-12hr., 3 per day.)

By Bus

Florenc ÚAN (☎900 144 444) is Prague's main bus terminal. To search bus schedules, visit www.jizdnirady.idnes.cz/autobusy/spojeni. **Eurolines** (☎245 005 245 www.euro-lines.cz) runs international buses to some 20 European countries and a few domestic destinations. **Student Agency** (☎841 101 101 www.studentagency.cz) runs domestic and international buses with discounted prices for ISIC holders and travelers under 26.

Getting Around

By Public Transportation

Prague's tram system alone could sufficiently serve this pocket-sized city, but Prague also has a metro, a bus system, a horde of taxis, a funicular, and some ferries. Dopravní Podnik Prahy (☎296 191 817 www.dpp.cz) runs the public transportation system. Tickets can be used for trams, the metro, buses, the funicular, and some ferries. The limited ticket (18Kč) is valid for 20min. or five metro stations, while the **basic ticket** (26Kč) is valid for 75min. and unlimited transfers. One-, three-, and five-day tickets are also available (100/330/500Kč), while a **monthly pass** (670Kč) can be purchased only at certain DPP centers. Tickets are available at ticket machines and convenience stores and must be validated when you enter a vehicle or the metro platform; unstamped tickets are not valid. **Ticket inspections** are more frequent on the metro than on trams and buses; the fine for not having a validated ticket is 800Kč. There are three metro lines (A is green, B is yellow, C is red); they run M-Th from 5am-midnight, F-Sa from 5am-1am, and Su from 5am-midnight. Aside from walking, trams are probably the best way to get around the city. **Tram #22** connects some of the most important parts of Prague. Travelers should beware of pickpockets on crowded vehicles. It is customary to let seniors sit in your seat if there are no empty seats. Locals are nearly silent on public transportation—don't make an ass of yourself.

czech republic essentials

MONEY

Tipping and Bargaining

Like most European cities, Prague's policy on tipping is pretty relaxed: most locals will just round up. Aim for around 5-10% if you're satisfied with your service. Touristy restaurants in the center of town will expect a 15-20% tip, but it's best to avoid those places anyway. Bargaining is only done in open-air markets or antique shops.

SAFETY AND HEALTH

Local Laws and Police

You should not hesitate to contact the police in the Czech Republic. Be sure to carry a valid passport, as police have the right to ask for identification. Police can sometimes be unhelpful if you are the victim of a currency exchange scam; in that case, you might be better off seeking advice from your embassy or consulate.

Drugs and Alcohol

If you carry insulin, syringes, or any prescription drugs on your person, you must also carry a copy of the prescriptions and a doctor's note. The drinking age in the Czech Republic is 18. Avoid public drunkenness, as it will jeopardize your safety. The possession of small quantities of marijuana (less than 15g) was decriminalized in 2009. Carrying drugs across an international border—drug trafficking—is a serious offense that could land you in prison.

Smoking is incredibly popular in the Czech Republic. If you are sensitive to cigarette smoke, ask for a non-smoking room in a hotel or hostel or to be seated in the non-smoking area of restaurants.

SPECIFIC CONCERNS

Petty Crime and Scams

Scams and petty theft are unfortunately common in the Czech Republic. An especially common scam in bars and nightclubs involves a local woman inviting a traveler to buy her drinks, which end up costing exorbitant prices; the proprietors of the establishment (in cahoots with the scam artist) may then use force to ensure that the bill is paid. Travelers should always check the prices of drinks before ordering. Another common scam involves a team of con artists posing as metro clerks and demanding that you pay large fines because your ticket is invalid. Credit card fraud is also common in Eastern Europe. Travelers who have lost credit cards or fear that the security of their accounts has been compromised should contact their credit card companies immediately.

Con artists often work in groups and may involve children. Beware of certain classics: sob stories that require money, rolls of bills "found" on the street, mustard spilled (or saliva spit) onto your shoulder to distract you while they snatch your bag. **Never let your passport or your bags out of your sight.** Hostel workers will sometimes stand at bus and train arrival points to recruit tired and disoriented travelers to their hostel; never believe strangers who tell you that theirs is the only hostel open. Beware of **pickpockets** in large crowds, especially on public transportation.

Visitors to Prague should never enter a taxi containing anyone in addition to the driver and should never split rides with strangers. While traveling by train, it may be preferable to travel in cheaper "cattle-car" type seating arrangements; the large number of witnesses makes such carriages safer than seating in individual compartments. Travelers should avoid riding on night buses or trains, where the risk of robbery or assault is particularly high. *Let's Go* does not recommend hitchhiking and picking up hitchhikers.

czech republic 101

HISTORY

The land that is now the Czech Republic has been home to human settlements since the Neolithic Era. Celts settled the Vltava River basin around 200 BCE; they were followed by Germanic tribes and, later, by Slavic peoples who swept in from the east. Prague, founded in the eighth century CE, served as the seat of the Kingdom of Bohemia, which was part of the Holy Roman Empire. The Czechs beat back a Mongol invasion of Europe in 1235, and extended their own territory as far as Poland and the Adriatic. Charles IV (who reigned 1346-1378) presided over a Czech "Golden Age," building Prague into an imperial capital and founding central Europe's first university there.

Defenestration is the New Reformation (1401-1800)

Bohemia's prosperity was imperiled by the viral Reformation bug then spreading across Europe. The passionate sermons of reformer Jan Hus turned Czech parishioners against Catholicism, until the church fought back (with fire) and burned Hus at the stake. His followers, known as the Hussites, carried on his message of religious reform and, taking the whole "overthrow the Church" thing a bit literally, threw 15 town officials out of a window in the First Defenestration of Prague (spoiler: there's another one coming up). The Hussites eventually became the majority religion in the region and defended themselves against a series of anti-Protestant crusades, known as the Hussite Wars. But the ascension of the Catholic Hapsburg Dynasty to the head of the Holy Roman Empire brought new enemies to Protestantism. Returning to tried-and-true methods, Praguers sent the Catholic-friendly regents of Bohemia flying out the window in the Second Defenestration of 1618 (the regents' survival has been variously attributed to divine intervention and the large pile of horse manure in which they landed). This set off the bloody Thirty Years' War, which ended in the consolidation of Hapsburg control. The next two centuries were marked by the forced conversion and expulsion of Protestants; invasions by Ottomans, Saxons, and Swedes; and several plagues and famines.

Nationalism Czechs In (1801-1945)

Bohemia remained an imperial possession of the Austrians, and then became part of the Austro-Hungarian Empire. Czech nationalism grew into a potent political force throughout the 19th century. In 1848, workers and students took to the streets against their Austrian overlords, and in the next decades, Prague developed a reputation for liberal politics and cultural cachet. 150,000 Czech soldiers gave their lives in WWI, but when the Austro-Hungarian Empire collapsed at the war's close, the Czechs finally achieved independence in the new nation-state of Czechoslovakia. Nazi Germany cut this growth short, first by stripping the Sudetenland from Czechoslovakia in the Munich Agreement and then by invading the rest of the country in 1939. Czech freedom fighters evicted theNazis with the help of the Red Army in the 1945 Prague Uprising.

Springtime for Stalin (1946-1989)

The Communists gained a plurality of the vote in the first free post-war elections, held in 1946, but took complete control of the country in a Moscow-backed coup two years later. Political repression and censorship followed as the Iron Curtain was drawn across Czechoslovakia. In 1968, economic troubles and student demonstrations led to the political reforms and de-Stalinization of the Prague Spring. Feeling threatened, the Soviet Union led an invasion of 200,000 Warsaw Pact troops to halt what it perceived as the inevitable democratization of Czechoslovakia. Citizens tore down Prague street signs so the invaders would get lost, but their resistance was no match for Soviet tanks, and the country was dragged back into Moscow's orbit for another two decades. During the 41 years of the Communist dictatorship, more than 250,000 Czechoslovaks were imprisoned by the Communist regime, and many more fled.

Velvet Underground (1989-today)

In 1989, peaceful demonstrators faced off against the Communist apparatchiks in what became known as the Velvet Revolution. Huge protests and a country-wide strike forced Communist Party leaders to step down. Václav Havel, a famous playwright and dissident, was elected president in December, and free elections were held in June of the next year. Three years later, the Czech Republic and Slovakia split apart (both insist that the decision was mutual). The Czech Republic went on to join NATO in 1999 and the EU in 2004. Today, the Czech Republic is consistently ranked as one of the healthiest, safest, and most democratic nations in Europe.

CUSTOMS AND ETIQUETTE

Czechs tend to smile only when genuinely pleased, so don't be surprised at their indifference to your witticisms. Keep in mind that a serious demeanor is a show of respect. It's polite to say hello (dobrý den) and goodbye (na shledanou) to people you meet, even complete strangers. If you find yourself invited to someone's home, remember to remove your shoes. Finally, shouting, drunkenly singing, or even just speaking to your friends on the subway or tram is a surefire way to identify yourself as a foreigner; you'll notice that natives are silent on their commutes.

The Czech Republic is the exciting misfit of Europe—the country fought off communism from the East, but it doesn't exactly conform to the polished vibe of the West. From musical covers of the Velvet Underground to the Velvet Revolution, counterculture runs through this country's gritty history. But don't be unnerved by the idea of crossing into Eastern Europe. In fact, the Czech Republic is up-to-date, fashionable, and intellectual, putting the Czechs on par with the most hip of hipsters—even the ones who wear tinted Ray Bans on cloudy days. Surrounded with savvy bohemians—the Czech Republic makes for a great place for the burgeoning student to learn, work, and grow.

STUDY

- **SCHOOL FOR INTERNATIONAL TRAINING (SIT):** For the creative artists, the SIT program in Prague focuses on how visual, performing, and literary artists thrived and impacted social and political life in the post-socialist era. (www.sit.edu/studyabroad/ssa_czr.cfm)

- **CHARLES UNIVERSITY:** As a part of its Czech Summer School program, Charles University in Prague offers an intensive summer language program that focus on written language, spoken communication, reading abilities, and listening skills. No previous knowledge of Czech is required, and classes are offered at levels ranging from beginner to highly-advanced. (www.studyabroadineurope.com)

- **PCFE FILM SCHOOL:** PCFE Film School in Prague hosts a summer workshop for aspiring filmmakers. Courses on screenwriting, directing, and editing are taught by Oscar and Cannes award winners. Each student must shoot, direct, write, and edit a short film of his or her own. (www.filmstudies.cz/film-schools-programs/summer-workshops)
- **UNIVERSITY STUDIES ABROAD CONSORTIUM:** The University Studies Abroad Consortium has a study abroad program that focuses on the medieval aspects of Prague. Excursions to local castles and historical sites are included. (http://usac.unr.edu/study-abroad-programs/czech-republic/prague)

VOLUNTEER

- **EARTHWATCH WORLDWIDE:** Volunteer to be a part of Dr. Krecek and Dr. Horicka's long-term research project in the Jizera Mountains; their program aims to identify strategies that can help rehabilitate the environment of North Bohemia. Duties include testing pH, collecting water samples, and sampling aquatic organisms. (www.earthwatch.org/europe/expeditions/exped_research_focus/rd_czech.html)
- **INTERNATIONAL PROGRAMS:** International Programs offers semester study abroad programs with the unique value of having the option to volunteer while you learn. There are a multitude of one-day activities and a list of semester-long opportunities, like editing personal memoirs about life under Nazism. (www.international-programs.com/spring-semester-study-abroad-program-with-volunteer-option-in-prague-at-charles-university)
- **WWOOF:** Learn about organic farming lifestyles as you till the land in romantic and rural hamlets registered with Czech Republic's national World Wide Opportunities on Organic Farms organization. (www.wwoof.cz/ll)
- **FOOTBALL FOR DEVELOPMENT:** Volunteer for Football for Development, an event that brings Kenyan and Czech soccer players together every June in the Czech Republic. This organization looks for creative youth who are willing to get involved in development cooperation by writing articles or compiling photo reports. (www.fotbalprorozvoj.org/index.php/zapojte-se/jako-do-brovolnik)

WORK

- **CIEE:** The CIEE study abroad program offers pre-screened internship positions that qualified students can choose from as an alternative option to taking certain courses. Opportunities involve working with education, human rights, and film NGOs. (www.ciee.org/study-abroad/czech-republic/prague/central-european-studies)
- **GLOBAL PLAYERS:** Global Players offers internship opportunities in Prague for student-athletes only. This program offers both part-time and full-time internships that you can partake in while continuing your training. (www.playtheglobe.org/intern-abroad)
- **GAP MEDICS:** In large hospital in the picturesque town of Liberec, partake in shadowing projects and complete a pre-med, pre-nursing, or pre-dentistry internship. 1-866-922-8539 http://www.gapmedics.com/destinations/central-europe
- **FIFTY FIVE REAL ESTATE:** Fifty Five Real Estate is an organization in Prague that is searching for students willing to learn about viral marketing, social networking, and website design in an internship setting. (www.fiftyfive.cz/jobs-en)

BEYOND TOURISM
www.letsgo.com
LET'S GO

FOOD AND DRINK

Although Czech writer Pavel Eisner once described his country's food as "quite deleterious to the soul," the Czech Republic's heavy meat and potatoes diet is a good way to line your stomach for a night of pivo. For Czechs, oběd (lunch) is traditionally the main meal of the day. In urban Prague they're more likely to go for a quick fix of klobása (smoked sausage), from stands such as those that line Wenceslas Sq.

For those with carnivorous urges, menus are conveniently organized by category of meat. Pork, the most popular, comes in sausages, goulash, and, for the more adventurous, pig offal. As for vegetarians, the joke goes that there are two vegetarian options—green cabbage and red cabbage. Although somewhat of an exaggeration (there's often frozen spinach!), traditional non-meat dishes extend little beyond salat (salad), smažený sýr (fried cheese), and bramboráky (potato pancakes). Filling knedlíky (dumplings) come as side dishes or desserts, in an uninspiring set of flavors: potato, fruit, and even bread. If visions of pierogi or Chinese dumplings are dancing in your head, think again: these guys are more like matzah meal rolled into a loaf and sliced.

If you don't immediately take to Czech cuisine, fear not: almost everything tastes better with beer (or at least after you've had a few). Czechs are some of the world's heaviest beer drinkers, with each person knocking back five half liters in an average sitting, which computes to a stunning average of 287 pints per person per year. Even under Communist rule, beer was subsidized. The Czechs recognize only two types of beer: světlé (light) and černé (dark). Darker beers are rich and taste like cake. The local degree system tells you how much malt extract was used in brewing: the higher the degree, the more malt and the greater the alcohol content. Twelve-degree beer is about four- to five-percent alcohol, and most taverns serve 10- or 12-degree beer. The most common Czech beer is Pilsner, named after the town Plzen outside of Prague.

FRANCE

Think of a famous idea. Any famous idea. Or for that matter any brushstroke, article of clothing, architectural style, camera technique, great thinker that should have been medicated, or hip reason to brew a Molotov cocktail. If that idea is Western, then it is probably French (or at least hotly contested and contributed to a French intellectual movement). Your first walk around Paris will be defined by a paralyzing level of excitement. Your first party in Monaco might result in a Hangover-esque situation. It's no secret that young Americans "backpack" through France to lose their virginity and construct their identity at a safe distance from their parents. The successes of James Baldwin, Gertrude Stein, and Ernest Hemingway suggest that we couldn't have chosen a better spot; there is a pervading sense in France that everything is here.

Students might go to France to be fashionably disaffected artists in boho-chic corner cafes, but this isn't the land of berets and baguettes anymore: it's the land of sustainable energy and the 35hr. work week. As France wrestles with the economic and cultural ramifications of a globalized world, this is also, increasingly, the country of parkour and veil bans, sprawling Chinatowns and the Marie Leonie case of 2004. Nowhere is the cognitive dissonance of these cultural collisions more evident than in Marseille, whose burgeoning Little Algeria encroaches upon the city's Old World streets. In the midst of these transitions, the most sacred of French traditions remain gloriously preserved—you might eat a lot of kebabs while you're here, but you can still riot against The Man in the morning and commit adultery by noon.

greatest hits

- **WE'LL ALWAYS HAVE PARIS.** From the "metal asparagus" of the **Eiffel Tower** (p. 130) to the bars of **St-Germain** (p. 156), you'll have plenty to do in France's capital.

- **THAT'LL DO NICELY. Nice** might be the best city on the Côte d'Azur for backpackers, and it's definitely the cheapest (p. 207).

FRANCE

North Sea

BRITAIN

Manchester

Amsterdam

NETHERLANDS

Münster

Rotterdam

Düsseldorf

Bristol

London

BELGIUM

GERMANY

Folkestone

Dover

Dunkerque

Antwerp

Brussels

Plymouth

Portsmouth

Calais

Boulogne-sur-Mer

Lille

Mainz

Channel Islands

English Channel (La Manche)

Somme R.

Arras

LUX.

Metz

Amiens

Cherbourg

Le Havre

Rouen

Reims

Bayeux

Caen

Seine R.

Marne R.

Épernay

Nancy

Strasbourg

Roscoff

St-Malo

Paris

Sélestat

Brest

Dinan

Mont-St-Michel

Chartres

Troyes

Colmar

Quimper

Rennes

Le Mans

Orléans

Fontainebleau

Mulhouse

Angers

Blois

Besançon

Belle Île

Nantes

Saumur

Tours

Amboise

Loire R.

Indre R.

Bourges

Nevers

Dijon

Pontarlier

SWITZ.

Bern

Île d'Yeu

Poitiers

Beaune

Haut-Jura Mts.

ATLANTIC OCEAN

Vichy

Cluny

Lake Geneva

Geneva

ALPS

La Rochelle

Limoges

Clermont-Ferrand

Lyon

Annecy

Chamonix

Cognac

Angoulême

Le-Mont-Dore

Mont Blanc 4810m

Gironde R.

Montignac

Les Eyzies-de-Tayac

Le Puy de Sancy

Grenoble

ITALY

Bay of Biscay

Sarlat

Cévennes Mts.

Rhône R.

Bordeaux

Dordogne R.

Castelnaud-la-Chapelle

TGV Line

Garonne R.

MONACO

Menton

Avignon

Nice

Adour R.

Nîmes

Aix-en-Provence

Antibes

Cannes

Biarritz

Bayonne

Toulouse

Montpellier

Arles

St-Raphaël

CÔTE D'AZUR

Bilbao

St-Jean-Pied-de-Port

Carcassonne

Marseille

St-Tropez

Lourdes

Cauterets

Perpignan

Golfe du Lion

Toulon

PYRENEES

Aude R.

TO CORSICA

Burgos

ANDORRA

SPAIN

Zaragoza

Barcelona

Mediterranean Sea

N

0   150 kilometers

0   150 miles

Valencia

Cap Corse

Bastia

Calvi

CORSICA

Corte

Ajaccio

Porto-Vecchio

Bonifacio

SARDINIA (ITALY)

france

France is famous for the birth of analytical geometry, angsty existentialism, and keepin' it real. These philosphical movements didn't come from nowhere—with over 80 public universities and the elite Grandes Écoles, France isn't lacking in young intellect and imagination. Home to the famous Sorbonne, the second oldest academic institution in the world, **Paris's** Latin Quarter is teeming with students of all nationalities. Many of the cheap bars sprinkled throughout the Latin Quarter offer student happy hours or English trivia nights. Students flee from the tourist-heavy areas of the Champs-Élysées and Châtelet-Les Halles to the cheap brasseries and restaurants of Montparnasse and Southern Paris.

Though you could probably spend several satisfied lifetimes in Paris, we encourage you to backpack your way through the rest of the country. Needless to say, **Bordeaux** is the perfect destination for *vin*-loving students; the place de la Victoire is where the local college denizens head once the sun has set. If you're there on the first Sunday of the month, all the city's museums are free to enter. Heading down south to France's Mediterranean coast, you'll likely end up in **Nice.** And with a centrally located youth hostel and a variety of both historical and alcoholic forms of entertainment, it will quickly move to the top of your destination list.

paris

Paris leaves an impression on everyone, from students perfecting their *langue française* to tourists who wonder why the French don't pronounce half the consonants in each word. This city has been home to countless films, daydreams, and kings named Louis, and it easily destroys all diets with its arsenal of buttery croissants and delicate pastries. Nearly everyone in the world idealizes Paris, whether it's for the Eiffel Tower, the intellectual literary cafes, or the impossibly chic and be-scarfed denizens of the city. But don't let yourself be disillusioned by ideals—yes, everyone is in love with Paris, but this place can be rough, and that waiter over there? Yeah, he's judging you. When you get Englished for the first time (when your mangled French inquiry is interrupted with an English response), you'll start to realize that your Converse won't cut it after all and that maybe you should have paid more attention in French class. Parifs will charm and bitchslap you with equal gusto, but don't get too le tired—think of it as a gentle form of Parisian hazing. Once you learn your way around the narrow, cobblestoned streets and nail down your *merci, beaucoup*, Paris will be more spectacular than ever. Some tiny corner of it will be yours in memory and experience, whether it's admiring a painting in an empty room at the Louvre (they exist), listening to the bells of Notre Dame chime as you sit by the Seine, sunbathing in the gorgeous Jardin du Luxembourg, or biting into your first Nutella banana crêpe. Slow down and don't worry about how well you're fitting in—this city is big and captivating enough for everyone to claim their little slice.

ORIENTATION

Despite all the invasions, revolutions, and riots throughout French history, Paris was still meticulously planned. The Seine River flows from east to west through the middle of the city, splitting it into two sections. The *Rive Gauche* (Left Bank) to the south is known as the intellectual heart of Paris, while the *Rive Droite* (Right Bank) to the north is famous for fashion, art, and commerce. The two islands in the middle

paris

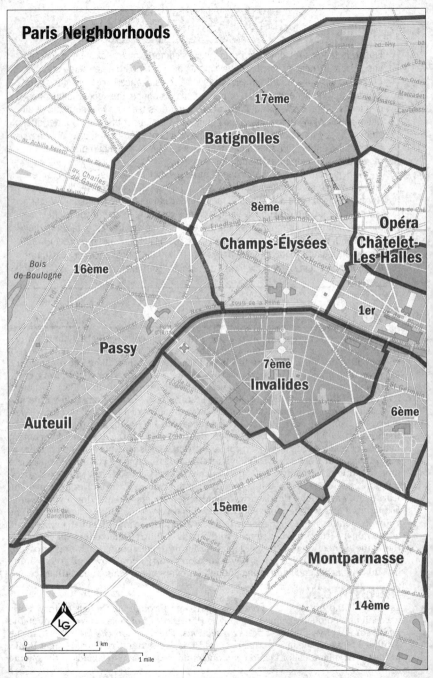

Paris Neighborhoods

17ème

Batignolles

8ème

Champs-Élysées

Opéra
Châtelet-
Les Halles

Bois
de Boulogne

16ème

Passy

1er

7ème

Invalides

6ème

Auteuil

15ème

Montparnasse

14ème

0   1 km

0   1 mile

france

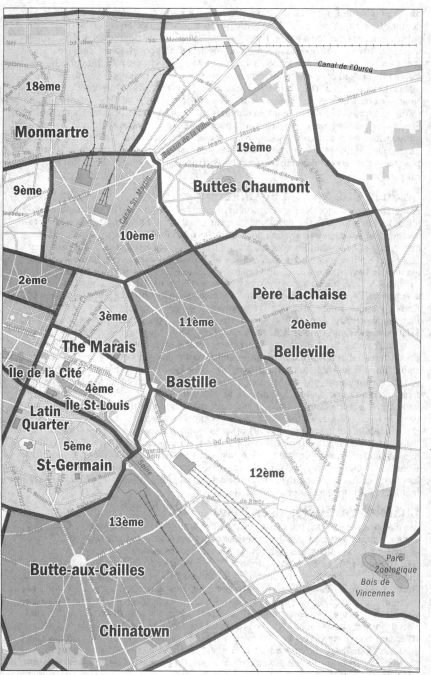

of the Seine, the Île de la Cité and Île St-Louis, are the geographical and historical center of the city. The rest of Paris is divided into 20 *arrondissements* (districts) that spiral outward from the islands. These *arrondissements* are numbered; for example, the Eiffel Tower is located in *le septième* (the seventh), abbreviated 7ème.

If the simplicity of this layout sounds too good to be true, it is. Neighborhoods frequently spread over multiple *arrondissements* and are often referred to by name rather than number. The Marais, for example, is in both the 3ème and the 4ème. Neighborhood names are based on major connecting hubs of the Métro or train (Montparnasse, Bastille) or major landmarks and roads (Champs-Élysées, Invalides). Streets are marked on every corner, and numerous signs point toward train stations, landmarks, and certain *triomphant* roundabouts. You can try to walk through it all, but the size of the city is deceiving. So when your feet start to fall off, remember that buses and the subway go almost everywhere in the city, and your hostel is just a short ride away.

Île de la Cité and Île St-Louis

Some 2000 years ago, the French monarchy claimed Les Îles as the geographic center of its kingdom and the royal and governmental seat of power. The islands were perfectly located and easily defendable in the middle of the Seine—think castles, drawbridges, fire-breathing **dragons**, and then don't because you're probably thinking of a bad *Shrek* sequel. Today, you can see how Paris grew outward, both physically expanding beyond the islands and politically distancing itself from the monarchy.

Île de la Cité, the larger of the two islands, is still considered the city's center and is home to Paris's *kilomètre zéro*, from which distances are measured and where France's major roads originate. Trigger-happy tourists congregate on two streets that cut vertically through the island: the Boulevard du Palais, where you'll find **Sainte-Chappelle** and the **Palais du Justice**, and rue de la Cité, the next street over that runs in front of **Notre Dame**. Unsurprisingly, most of the restaurants here are less than interested in fair prices and authenticity, particularly as you get closer to Notre Dame, but it is possible to find worthy spots tucked in the nooks and crannies of this island. Although the physical center of the city sounds like an ideal place to stay, most accommodations are overpriced, and once the tourist traffic clears out after sunset, the islands tend to become uncomfortably quiet, with the exception of the plaza in front of Notre Dame. Île St-Louis, the quiet younger sister of the two islands, sits peacefully beside its impressive big brother and provides a welcome escape from the crowds and bustle across the way. The restaurants and shops here are smaller in scale and are mostly located on **rue Saint-Louis en l'Île.** The only Métro stop on the islands is Ⓜ**Cité**, between bd du Palais and rue de la Cité, but several other stops are located just across the bridges that connect the islands to the mainland of the city, including Paris's largest stop, Ⓜ**Châtelet.**

Châtelet-Les Halles (1er, 2ème)

Les Îles are the geographic center of the city, but, with the exception of the Eiffel Tower, Paris's 1er and 2ème arrondissements are the fountainhead from which everything flows. Most famously, the **Louvre** and **Les Halles** marketplace draw crowds from far and wide to Paris's bellybutton. Naturally, this area is tourist-heavy during the daytime, especially in the summer. Unfortunately, Les Halles and the Jardin des Halles have been under serious renovation and reconstruction since 2011 and are currently an unsightly block of cranes and concrete; the project is expected to be finished in bits and pieces through 2016. Ⓜ**Châtelet-Les Halles** is the city's main transportation hub and is located in the southeast corner of these neighborhoods; three RER and five Métro lines can be accessed between here and the two connecting stations, Ⓜ**Châtelet** and Ⓜ**Les Halles.** The Ⓜ**Opéra** stop is a prominent point in the northwest corner of the neighborhood, topped off by **boulevard Haussmann/Montmar-**

tre/**Poissonnière** and hugged in the east by **boulevard de Sébastopol.** The closer you are to the Louvre, the more likely prices are to be unnecessarily high, so make the effort to go a few blocks farther north, east, or west to get away from the loud crowds and equally annoying prices. **Rue St-Denis** runs parallel to bd de Sébastopol and is generally a dependable strip for good but pricey nightlife and more reasonable food and accommodation options.

The Marais (3ème, 4ème)

The Marais embodies the ultimate ugly duckling tale. Originally a bog (*marais* means "marsh"), the area became livable in the 13th century when monks drained the land to build the **Right Bank.** When Henri IV constructed the glorious **place des Vosges** in the early 17th century, the area suddenly became the city's center of fashionable living, and luxury and scandal soon took hold. Royal haunts gave way to slums and tenements during the Revolution, and many of the grand *hôtels particuliers* fell into ruin or disrepair. In the 1950s, the Marais was revived and declared a historic neighborhood; since then, decades of gentrification and renovation have restored the Marais to its pre-Revolutionary glory. Once palatial mansions have become exquisite museums, and the tiny, twisting streets are crowded with hip bars, avant-garde galleries, and one-of-a-kind boutiques.

   Boulevard de Sébastopol divides the Marais from Les Halles in the west, and the **Centre Pompidou** anchors down the southwest portion of the neighborhood. The Métro 1 runs along the rue de Rivoli, which marks the southern border. The northern and eastern borders are defined by the **Boulevard Saint-Martin** and the **Plaza République,** and bd Beaumarchais, which runs along the Métro 8, forms a quarter-circle border around the Marais. The quickest way to go north-south is to take the Métro 11 beginning from the **Hôtel de Ville** along the rue de Beaubourg. Today, the Marais is known as a center of Parisian diversity. **Rue des Rosiers,** in the heart of the 4ème, is the center of Paris's Jewish population, though the steady influx of hyper-hip clothing and rising rents have led to a significant loss of Jewish establishments. But the Marais remains lively on Sunday and quieter on Saturday, the Jewish day of rest. The neighborhood is also unquestionably the GLBT center of Paris, with the community's hub at the intersection of **rue Sainte-Croix de la Brettonerie** and **rue Vieille du Temple.** Though the steady stream of tourists has begun to wear on the Marais's eclectic personality, the district continues to be a distinctive mix of old and new, queer and straight, cheap and chic.

Latin Quarter and St-Germain (5ème, 6ème)

The Latin Quarter and St-Germain are two of Paris's primary tourist neighborhoods, second only to the areas around the Louvre, Notre Dame, and the Hôtel de Ville. The Latin Quarter, however, got its name from the many institutions of higher learning in the area, including the famous **Sorbonne,** where Latin scriptures and studies were more prevalent than kissing couples along the Seine. To this day, these neighborhoods—the Latin Quarter in particular—are the student hubs of Paris, mixing overpriced tourist traps with budget-friendly student hangouts. **Boulevard St-Michel** divides the two areas, with St-Germain to the west and the Latin Quarter to the east. Meanwhile, **Boulevard du Montparnasse** and **Boulevard de Port Royal** separate both areas from southern Paris, with the **Jardin du Luxembourg** and the **Panthéon** being the central icons of each *arrondissement*. As tempted as you may be to shell out your money in St-Germain-des-Prés, your wallet will thank you if you head to the 5ème and roam **rue Monge** and **rue Mouffetard** for affordable food, nightlife, and accommodations.

paris

Invalides (7ème)

If Paris was Jay-Z, then the **Eiffel Tower** would be his Beyoncé—both are icons in their own right, and together, they are absolute magic. Everyone that comes to Paris will want to see the world's greatest power couple, so prep yourself for the higher prices and overeager tourists who are crazy in love with snapping pics left and right. The Eiffel Tower(s) over the 7ème, but the rest of Destiny's Child is nearby and have more than made it on their own. Starting from the west, the **Champs de Mars** stretches southeast in front of the Eiffel Tower, with Ⓜ**École Militaire** at its feet. In the middle of the neighborhood is the **Esplanade of Les Invalides**, topped off in the north with Ⓜ**Invalides** and to the south with the **Musée de l'Armée**. Continue east to find the **Musée d'Orsay** (and its long lines) on the banks of the Seine. The **Quai d'Orsay, rue de l'Université**, and **rue St-Dominique** run West to East through the neighborhood and make for great strolls past the brasseries and cafés. And if you don't want to walk, the RER C chugs along the Seine and will conveniently drop you off right in front of the biggest attractions, but for a scenic route, take the 69 bus, which travels from the Eiffel Tower all the way to the Musée d'Orsay.

Champs-Élysées (8ème)

The Champs-Élysées is a whole other kind of Paris, where even the Métro stops seem to sparkle with glamor. This is the Paris where the daughters of American millionaires throw their bachelorette parties and where fashion moguls wipe their you-know-whats with only the finest of handwoven silks. It's a fun place to window shop and daydream about the finer things in life, but the buck stops there.

Avenue des Champs-Elysées is the heart of this area, pumping life from the **Arc de Triomphe** through the rows of designer shops and out-of-this-world expensive restaurants and nightclubs. If you want to continue to immerse yourself in all the beautiful things you will probably never have, head for **Avenue Montaigne, rue du Faubourg St-Honoré**, or the side streets around **La Madeleine**. The #2 Métro line separates the 8ème from the 16ème in the north, but the closer you get to this area, the fewer tourists you will find.

Opéra (9ème) and Canal St-Martin (10ème)

Although they follow the spiral pattern from the center of the city along with the other *arrondissements*, the 9ème and 10ème feel a bit ambiguously plopped in the middle of the *Rive Droite*. The 9ème can be particularly difficult to navigate, especially since its namesake Métro stop and tourist site, the Paris Opéra, is positioned at its southern tip rather than at the center. The 9ème is roughly surrounded by the #2 Métro line in the north along bd de Clichy, Gare St-Lazare in the west, and Ⓜ Opéra in the south. Navigating the Opéra neighborhood by rail will generally mean traveling in the east-west directions: The #8 and #9 Métro runs along bd Haussmann in the south and conveniently begins at **Opéra Garnier** and will drop you off at Ⓜ**République**, near the Canal St-Martin. To the north, the #2 runs along bd Clichy and intersects with the #12, which actually cuts vertically through the neighborhood to reach **Notre Dame de Lorette** and eventually Gare St. Lazare. Finally, the #7 runs diagonally from the southwest corner of the *arrondissement* from Ⓜ Opéra to the northeast corner of the Canal St-Martin neighborhood.

Right next to the 9ème, the 10ème is known (and named for) the **Canal Saint-Martin**, which runs along the eastern border of the *arrondissement*. Stray too far from this "mini-Seine" (i.e., anywhere west of bd Magenta), and you'll find yourself smack in the middle of the sketchy area that surrounds the **Gare du Nord** and **Gare de l'Est**. If the gun armories and cash-for-gold stores didn't give you a hint, we'll tell you now: stay clear of this area at night.

Bastille (11ème, 12ème)

The Bastille is home to the famous prison where the French Revolution kicked things off with a bang on July 14, 1789. A few centuries later, Parisians still storm this neighborhood nightly in search of the latest cocktails, culinary innovations, and up-and-coming musicians in the city. Five Métro lines converge at Ⓜ**République** and Ⓜ**Nation,** and three lines at Ⓜ**Bastille,** making this district a busy transport hub. Although the area is still a bit worn around the edges, Bastille is a neighborhood that is well known for its cheap food, red-hot nightlife, and uncrowded stores for those in search of stress-free shopping. The highest concentration of all three is in the area between **rue de Charenton,** in the south of the 11ème, and **rue de la Roquette,** running northeast away from the Bastille. Late-night cheap eats, youth hostels, and bars where memories are made and forgotten line the streets east of République and particularly along **rue Oberkampf.** The Algerian community offers countless dining options at the **Marché d'Aligre,** where the weekly outdoor market sets up. The **Viaduc des Arts** and the gorgeous **Promenade Plantée** (see **Sights,** p. 135) will lead you toward the more expensive shops and galleries in the 12ème.

Montparnasse and Southern Paris (13ème, 14ème, 15ème)

These three *arrondissements*, which make up nearly one-sixth of Paris, lack the photo-ops and famous sights that attract tourists elsewhere in the city. They do, however, tend to comprise Paris's so-called better half, where locals dominate the tourists and the pace of life is more relaxed. The neighborhoods spread east to west in ascending order, with Montparnasse somewhere in between the 14ème and 15ème in the area immediately surrounding the **Montparnasse Tower** and the **Cimetière du Montparnasse** in the 14ème. Your best mode of transportation between here will be the #6 Métro line, which runs aboveground along bd du Grenelle and bd Garibaldi on the northern edge of the 15ème, then cuts a bit farther down into the 14ème and 13ème along bd St-Jacques and bd Vincent. The 15ème and 14ème are divided by the train tracks that stem from the SNCF station behind the Montparnasse Tower, and **rue de la Santé** roughly divides the 14ème and the 13ème. The 13ème has a strange combination of characters thanks to **Chinatown,** nestled south of rue de Tolbiac, and the small hippie enclave surrounding **rue de la Butte aux Cailles,** which avoids the capitalist drive to overcharge for meals or entertainment. The bank of the River Seine along the 13ème is home to a series of floating bars and restaurants, especially opposite the Parc de Bercy, though many travelers don't make it this far south or east.

Auteuil, Passy & Batignolles (16ème, 17ème)

The 16ème and 17ème are almost devoid of tourists. More residential, these neighborhoods are home to ladies who lunch, their beautiful children, and their overworked husbands. The 16ème is frequented by Parisian elites who have money and are willing to spend it in the expensive boutiques and cafe lounges lining the main roads around Ⓜ**Trocadéro.** The 17ème, meanwhile, is far more relaxed in terms of its residents and prices. Its sheer size and lack of notable sights make this area a retreat for working class citizens and overly earnest teenagers who take leisurely strolls or sit in the many cafes.

The 16ème covers the area west of the 8ème, where the Seine dives sharply south. Auteuil and Passy are loosely defined, if at all, but Auteuil generally covers the southern half of the *arrondissement*, while Passy makes up the northern half (although you probably won't hear many Parisians refer specifically to either one). Most tourist traffic converges at Ⓜ Trocadéro at the **Palais de Chaillot;** many major sights are scattered about the banks of the river, especially near Ⓜ**Passy** (between the **Musée du Vin** and **Maison de Radio France**), where you can find some of the best views of the Eiffel Tower. The northern border of this area is generally marked by the **Arc de Triomphe.**

The 17ème consists of the area directly north of the Arc de Triomphe and the 8ème. Batignolles tends to refer just to the eastern corner of this *arrondissement*, around the **Square des Batignolles.** It is in and around the square that most of the best bars and restaurants in the neighborhood can be found, especially along and just off **rue des Dames.** Pl. du Maréchal Juin anchors the other side of town and is connected to bd des Batignolles and bd de Courcelles by av. de Villiers.

Montmartre (18ème)

Montmartre is easily the most eccentric of Paris's *arrondissements*, with religious landmarks like the **Basilique du Sacré-Cœur** looming over the infamous **Moulin Rouge** and the land of the scantily-clad **Red Light District.** Half the fun around here is bumbling about the cobblestone streets and posing next to the street art and graffiti as you huff and puff your way up and down the stairs. There's a super-touristy area on **rue de Steinkerque** if you want to pick up some postcards, but please, stay away from the corny berets and the overpriced food around these parts. The 18ème has recently exploded with youth hostels that keep bars full at night but also attract pickpockets. The neighborhood sits on top of a huge hill that is a bit of a hike, so plan your sightseeing accordingly. The bottom of the hill is lined by **boulevard de Clichy** and **boulevard de Rochechouart,** under which the #2 Métro line runs and where you can find a lot of great bars. **Boulevard Barbès** roughly borders the eastern end of this area, and the Cimetière de Montmartre borders it to the west.

Buttes-Chaumont & Belleville (19ème, 20ème)

The Buttes-Chaumont and Belleville neighborhoods cover a huge area, but several well-placed Métro lines make them easy to navigate. Even though this corner of Paris may be a bit far, in a city where green space comes at a premium, these neighborhoods have more than their fair share of beautiful parks—**Parc de Belleville** comes with sweeping views of the Parisian skyline. At night, the bars in this area come alive with artsy locals who love to kick back cheap booze or dance the night away at **Rosa Bonheur** or **La Bellevilloise.** Running along the northern edge of the 19ème is av. Jean Jaurès and the #5 Métro, which lead straight to Parc de la Villette. To the west, the #2 Métro runs straight down bd de la Villette and stops near the Parc de Belleville, Père-Lachaise Cemetery, and nearly every main street from the 19ème to the 20ème. The #9, #3, and #11 Métros run horizontally through the area, and the #11 runs through rue de Belleville, which is home to Paris's second largest Chinatown and host to a number of cheap eateries. While this area is full of goodies, it can also be a little rough around the edges when the sun sets, so we advise caution after dark.

SIGHTS

Seeing everything in Paris is exhausting if not impossible (even we struggled a bit). For a short trip, visiting the main attractions can mean waiting in lines, feeling the urge to add the annoying couple in front of you to the body count at the Catacombs, and becoming completely desensitized to some of mankind's greatest feats of engineering and art. Give yourself a break. Before heading off to see something because you saw it on a postcard, check this section for what's really worth it. Some of Paris's most interesting sights are devoid of tourists.

Île de la Cité and Île St-Louis

NOTRE DAME CATHEDRAL

Île de la Cité ☎01 42 34 56 10 www.notredameparis.fr

If you've read this far, stay with us for a little longer. Here is what you need to see and do when visiting Notre Dame. First, as you enter, notice the headless figures above the doors. Revolutionaries thought that the King of Judah was somehow related to the French monarch (he's not) and decapitated him. From the entrance, you'll see massive crowds. Keep to the right and follow the arrows past Joan of Arc to the Treasury, where you can see Napoleon's sweet emperor cloak as well as relics like St. Louis's tunic. Jesus's thorny crown rests here too, but it's only revealed on the first Friday of the month at 3pm. The *crème de la crème* is the 13-ton bell in the South Tower that requires eight men—or one hunchback—to ring.

i Ⓜ*Cité. Walk down the street away from the quai onto rue de la Cité. Free. Audio tour €5, includes treasury visit. Towers €8.50, reduced €5.50, under 18 and EU citizens under 26 free. ☒ Cathedral open daily 8am-6:45pm. Towers open daily Apr-Sept 10am-6:30pm; Oct-Mar 10am-5:30pm. Last entry 4:45pm. Free tours in French M-F 2 and 3pm, Sa-Su 2:30pm; English W-Th 2pm, Sa 2:30pm. Treasury open M-F 9:30am-6pm, Sa 9:30am-6:30pm, Su 1:30-6:30pm; last entry 15min. before close. Su Mass 8:30am (French), 10am (Gregorian Chants), 11:30am (easy French with some English thrown in), 12:45pm, and 6:30pm.*

SAINTE-CHAPELLE
CHURCH

6 bd du Palais ☎01 53 40 60 80 www.monuments-nationaux.fr

Everybody needs the occasional diversion to get through a service. Take the 13th-century equivalent of TVs in church: the stunning floor-to-ceiling stained glass windows in the **Upper Chapel** of Sainte-Chapelle, illuminating dreamscapes of no fewer than 1113 individual Biblical stories. They really tried, but you just can't squeeze that many depictions onto stained glass and make it understandable without a priest (or tour guide) explaining each one. The easiest to make out is the Passion of the Christ, located at the apex of the chapel. The **Lower Chapel** has a blue, vaulted ceiling dotted with the golden symbol of the French monarchy, the *fleurs-de-lis*, and contains a few "treasures" (i.e., platter-sized portraits of saints). This was where mortals served God, while royalty got to get a little closer in the Upper Chapel.

i Ⓜ*Cité. Walk away from the quai, turn right onto the sidewalk, and turn left onto bd du Palais. Within Palais de la Cité. €8.50, ages 18-25 €5.50, under 18 and EU citizens under 25 free. Audio guide €4.50. Twin ticket with Conciergerie €12.50, ages 18-25 €8.50, under 18 free. ☒ Open daily Mar-Oct 9:30am-6pm; Nov-Feb 9am-5pm. Last entry 30min. before close. Open W evenings May 15-Sept 15, last entry 9pm.*

CONCIERGERIE
PALACE, PRISON

2 bd du Palais ☎01 53 40 60 80 www.monuments-nationaux.fr

It can't compete with Versailles in grandeur, but the Conciergerie has hosted over four centuries worth of French royalty and functioned as the administrative headquarters for the city for much longer. Perhaps most famously, the Conciergerie is best known for its other function: a prison where revolutionary celebrities like Robespierre and the unforgettable Queen Marie Antoinette were put behind bars. During the Reign of Terror, over 2000 executions took place over the course of a single year—if you have a common French last name, check the list of executed prisoners to see if you have any long-lost guillotined relatives.

i Ⓜ*Cité. Walk toward the quai, then turn left onto bd du Palais. The entrance is on the right. €8.50, students €5.50, EU citizens ages 18-25 and under 18 free. Combined ticket with Sainte-Chapelle €12.50, students €8.50, under 18 and EU citizens ages 18-25 free. ☒ Open daily 9:30am-6pm, last entry 5:30pm.*

PONT NEUF
BRIDGE

Though its name might suggest otherwise, the bridge cutting through the western tip of Île de la Cité is the oldest in Paris. Completed in 1607, it was the center of Paris until the end of the 18th century—street performers, pickpockets, traders, and curious members of the bourgeoisie would congregate around this bustling

get a room!

Budget accommodations (or budget anything, for that matter) can be difficult to find in Paris. But there are still deals for savvy travelers who know where to look. Expect to pay about €40-60 for the best budget hotels, which can be very quirky or forgettable but are always clean and more peaceful than the alternatives. If you're doing Paris on the cheap, be warned that you can't always count on having your own bathroom or shower, even if you shell out for a single. For more recommendations, visit **www.letsgo.com**.

CENTRE INTERNATIONALE DE PARIS (BVJ): PARIS LOUVRE   HOSTEL $$
20 rue Jean-Jacques Rousseau   ☎01 53 00 90 90 www.bvjhotel.com

With 240 beds, this hostel knows how to run a clean and efficient enterprise, with bare bones but spacious dormitories of four to 10 beds. In the summer, it's packed with international youths and backpackers looking to capitalize on the cheap prices and prime location.

i Ⓜ*Louvre-Rivoli. Walk north on rue du Louvre and turn left onto rue St-Honoré. Turn right onto rue Jean-Jacques Rousseau. 3-night max. stay; extensions can be arranged upon arrival. Breakfast included. Dorms €30; doubles €70. Cash only.* ⏰ *Reception 24hr.*

HÔTEL JEANNE D'ARC   HOTEL $$$
3 rue de Jarente   ☎01 48 87 62 11 www.lesvoixdejeanne.com

Hotel Jeanne d'Arc will brighten up any traveler's day with fun and artistic decor in the lobby and common area. And best of all, it's a cheaper option than most of the hotels in the area and only a few steps away from the Métro. A deal this good fills up quickly during the summer, so be sure to book ahead.

i Ⓜ*St-Paul. Walk against traffic onto rue de Rivoli; turn left onto rue de Sévigné, then right onto rue de Jarente. Breakfast €8. Reserve 2-3 months in advance (earlier for stays in Sept-Oct). Singles €65; 1-bed doubles €81-96; 2-bed doubles €119.*

YOUNG AND HAPPY HOSTEL   HOSTEL $$
80 rue Mouffetard   ☎01 47 07 47 07 www.youngandhappy.fr

A funky, lively hostel with 21 clean rooms, some with showers and toilets, Young and Happy Hostel is where you want to stay in the 5ème, if not in all of Paris. It's a great option if you're young, fun, and on a budget. Light sleepers, however, should consider staying elsewhere—rue Mouffetard gets quite noisy at night. While impromptu, their reception doubles as a bar and serves drinks if you ask for them.

i Ⓜ*Place Monge. From rue Monge, walk behind the pl. Monge on rue Ortolan and turn left onto rue Mouffetard. The hostel is on the righ. Breakfast included. Twins €30-45; 3- and 5-person dorms €22-38; 10-person €19-33.* ⏰ *Reception 24hr. Lockout 11am-4pm.*

OOPS!   HOSTEL $$
50 av. des Gobelins   ☎01 47 07 47 00 www.oops-paris.com

It's easy to see why young backpackers flock to this hostel in droves: from the fun patterns in the rooms to the lists of clubs and parties in the lobby to the fast Wi-Fi, Oops! is designed for the young, wild, and free. Top it all off with cheap prices and ensuite bathrooms (so clutch), it's understandable that you have to book in advance.

i Ⓜ*Les Gobelins. Walk south on av. des Gobelins toward pl. d'Italie. The hostel is 3 blocks from the Métro, on the right. Cash only. Breakfast included. Lobby computers available. Reserve online. Mar-Oct dorms €30-42, private rooms €70-115; Nov-Feb dorms €23-28, private rooms €60-80.* ⏰ *Reception 24hr. Lockout 11am-4pm.*

france

bridge. The occasional gargoyle and a statue of Henri IV are all that Pont Neuf has to offer nowadays.

i ⓂPont Neuf.

CRYPTE ARCHEOLOGIQUE   MUSEUM
7 arvis Notre-Dame, pl. Jean-Paul II   ☎01 55 42 50 10 www.crypte.paris.fr

Hidden beneath feet of countless tourists traipsing about the plaza in front of the Notre Dame lies the Crypte Archeologique. This museum displays the excavations of 2000-year-old archaeological layers, from the fortified walls from the 4th century to the foundations of medieval homes to ancient bath houses. The museum is rather small and dimly lit, and while the museum does its best to explain the various ruins, the remains of the ancient city are quite underwhelming—it's difficult to make out any structures when everything looks like various piles of eroded gray stones.

i ⓂCité. Walk down the street away from the quai onto rue de la Cité. There is a set of stairs at the end of the plaza in front of Notre Dame that looks like an entrance to the Métro. €5, seniors €3.50, ages 14-26 €2.50, under 14 free. Audio guide €3. ☒ Open Tu-Su 10am-6pm, last entry 5:30pm.

Châtelet-Les Halles

Châtelet-Les Halles is perhaps Paris's densest tourist area, and that's saying something.

▨ MUSÉE DU LOUVRE   MUSEUM
rue de Rivoli   ☎01 40 20 53 17 www.louvre.fr

On the **second floor,** only Sully and Richelieu are accessible. In Sully, all of the rooms are filled with French paintings that typically require some background study in art history to fully appreciate. Richelieu is filled with student groups and more obscure tours checking out the remaining Belgian, Dutch, German, Russian, and Scandinavian works. These are pretty to look at, but you may be better off spending a little more time getting friendly with your favorites from earlier. Unless you're planning on bunking up next to the *Venus de Milo*, seeing everything at the Louvre is impossible. Just getting a glimpse of what's in front of you, though, is a pretty good start.

i ⓂPalais Royal-Musée du Louvre. Follow the crowds. Walk past the rue de Rivoli with the flow of traffic on rue de Rohan. All-day access, access to Musée Delacroix included. The Carte Louvre Jeunes entitles the owner to 1-year unlimited access without waiting in line and free access for the owner and a guest on W and F after 6pm. €11, under 18 and EU citizens ages 18-25 free. Special exhibits €12. Combined ticket €15. Carte Louvre Jeunes ages 26-29 €35, 18-25 €15. 1st Su of every month (does not include special exhibits) free. F after 6pm free for under 26 of all nationalities. Audio tour €5, under 18 €3. ☒ Open M 9am-6pm, W 9am-9:45pm, Th 9am-6pm, F 9am-10pm, Sa-Su 9am-6pm. Last entry 45min. before close; rooms begin to close 30min. before museum.

▨ JARDIN DES TUILERIES   GARDEN
pl. de la Concorde, rue de Rivoli

Covering the distance from the Louvre to the pl. de la Concorde, the Tuileries and their colorful green chairs are a favorite of tourists during the summer and with Parisians who like to drag them off and sit with them alone (chairs, not tourists). As with the gardens of Versailles and the Palais du Luxembourg, something as fabulous as the Louvre requires a massive complex of hedges, trees, and a very large fountain. The gardens grew as each successive king added something to call his own. Today, the Tuileries are filled with food stands, merry-go-rounds, and a huge Ferris wheel near the rue de Rivoli entrance, rendering it all quite different from the Tuscan sanctuary Henry originally intended.

i ⓂTuileries. Between pl. de la Concorde and Musée Louvre. Free. ☒ Open daily Jun-Aug 7am-11pm; Sept 7am-9pm; Oct-Mar 7:30am-7:30pm; Apr-May 7am-9pm. Amusement park open Jun-mid-Aug.

paris

MUSÉE DE L'ORANGERIE
MUSEUM

Jardin des Tuileries   ☎01 44 77 80 07 www.musee-orangerie.fr

Although this was once the greenhouse of the Jardin des Tuileries, the only flowers that the Musée de l'Orangerie holds now are Monet's *Water Lilies*, which remains a surprisingly serene exhibit despite the crowds. The museum displays primarily works by Impressionist and post-Impressionist painters such as Monet, Picasso, and Renoir and received the collection of renowne dart collector Paul Guillaume in the 1960s. Show up at 9am or on free Sundays (the first Sunday of every month) if you don't want to roast in the sun for most of the day.

i Ⓜ*Concorde. Walk down pl. de la Concorde along the Tuileries Gardens to its main entrance and turn right immediately; the museum is in front. €7.50, students and after 5pm €5. Combined ticket with Musée d'Orsay €16. Free 1st Su every month.* ☼ *Open M 9am-6pm, W-Su 9am-6pm. Last entry 5:30pm, rooms cleared at 5:45pm.*

MUSÉE DES ARTS DÉCORATIFS
MUSEUM

107 rue de Rivoli   ☎01 44 55 57 50 www.lesartsdecoratifs.fr

Fashion-conscious Francophiles and lovers of pretty things could easily spend a full day perusing the Musée des Arts Decoratifs. Spanning 10 floors, this enormous museum complex is comprised of three different collections, in addition to many smaller exhibits. **Arts Décoratifs** (Interior Design), **Mode et Textile** (Fashion and Fabric), and **Publicité** (Advertisement) are all dedicated to *haute couture* designs that the average tourist has probably never experienced. The Arts Décoratifs have exhibits on interior design, from period rooms of the Middle Ages to part of Jeanne Lanvin's house to some groovy, Proust-inspired furniture from the '70s. The Mode et Textile has exhibits on the evolution of fashion from the '70s to the '90s and features small exhibits on prominent fashion designers, including Yves Saint Laurent. The jewelry collection, **Galerie des Bijoux,** will make anyone's engagement ring look embarrassing.

i Ⓜ*Palais Royal-Musée du Louvre. Walk with the traffic on rue de Rivoli; the museum is on the left. Free audio tour. All 3 museums €9.50, ages 18-25 €7.50, under 18 and EU citizens 18-25 free.* ☼ *Open Tu-Su 11am-6pm, temporary exhibitions have extended hours Th until 9pm. Last entry 30min. before close.*

ÉGLISE SAINT-EUSTACHE
CHURCH

2 rue du Jour   ☎01 42 36 31 05 www.saint-eustache.org

With so many cathedrals in Paris, it can quickly seem like a competition of "Whose is bigger?" And while size doesn't matter to God, Église St-Eustache probably never worried about pleasing Jesus. The Romanesque church boasts incredibly tall, 34m vaulted ceilings, the largest pipe organ in France, its fair share of stained glass, paintings by Rubens, and a silver sculpture dedicated to the victims of the AIDS epidemic.

i Ⓜ*Les Halles. Walk up Allée André Breton and turn left onto rue Rambuteau; the church is on the right. Audio tours available in English, ID required. Free. Audio tour suggested donation €3.* ☼ *Open M-F 9:30am-7pm, Sa 10am-7pm, Su 9am-7pm. Mass Sa 6pm; Su 9:30am, 11am, 6pm.*

PALAIS-ROYAL
PALACE

25 rue de Valois   ☎01 49 27 09 09

This palace has a history plagued with abandonment, debauchery, and low funding. Louis XIV lived here as a child before moving on to bigger and better digs at Versailles. Henrietta Maria, the wife of the deposed English king Charles I, called the palace home after being kicked out of her own country for being Catholic. (The French reaction to her showing up was apparently, "You're Catholic? Move into this palace!") In the 18th century, Louise Henrietta de Bourbon moved in, and the palace was the site of her numerous debaucheries and extramarital affairs—at least a palace is far classier than a motel room. Finally, in 1781, the broke Duke of Orléans had to rent out the space to raise money. Today, the palace is a government building and closed to the public, but you can still see the impressive façade facing the Louvre and visit the Cour d'Honneur and the inner courtyard, which contains artist Daniel Buren's *Les Colonnes de Buren*. The gardens are nowhere near as nice as the nearby Tuileries, and the famous arcades are priced exclusively for window shopping.

i ⓂPalais Royal-Musée du Louvre. Cour d'Honneur accessible from entrance on rue St-Honoré at the front of the palace. Free. ⓩ Fountain, galleries, and garden open Jun-Aug daily 7am-11pm; Sept 7am-9:30pm; Oct-Mar 7:30am-8:30pm; Apr-May 7am-10:15pm.

The Marais

▨ **CENTRE POMPIDOU**   MUSEUM, LIBRARY

pl. Georges Pompidou, rue Beaubourg   ☎01 44 78 12 33 www.centrepompidou.fr

The exterior of the Pompidou is a crazed network of yellow electrical tubes, green water pipes, and blue ventilation ducts, leaving plenty of space inside for all the good stuff. The center's functions are as varied as its colors; it serves as a cultural theme park of ultra-modern exhibition, performance, and research space. It is home to Europe's largest modern art museum, **Musée National d'Art Moderne**, which occupies the fourth, fifth, and sixth floors with a collection of over 60,000 works dating from 1905. Be sure to check out Duchamp's infamous *Fountain*, which is just a urinal that he signed "R. Mutt," because, hey, it's modern art. Temporary exhibits on international modern art fill the sixth floor. Other parts of the complex to explore include **Salle Garance**, which runs an adventurous film series; **Bibliothèque Publique d'Information**, a free library; **Institut de la Recherche de la Coordination Acoustique/Musique (IRCAM)**, an institute and laboratory for the development of new technology; and the rooftop restaurant, **Georges**.

i ⓂRambuteau or Hôtel de Ville. From ⓂRambuteau, walk down rue Beaubourg with the flow of traffic, turn right onto rue Rambuteau, then left at the plaza; the entrance is on the left. From ⓂHôtel de Ville, walk up rue de Renard against the flow of traffic, turn left onto rue St-Merri, then right into the plaza; the entrance is on the right. Free Wi-Fi. Museum €13, under 26 €11, under 18 and EU citizens ages 18-25 free. 1st Su of the month free. Library and forum free. ⓩ Center open M 11am-10pm, W-Su 11am-10pm. Museum open M 11am-9pm, W-Su 11am-9pm. Last tickets sold at 8pm. Library open M noon-10pm, W-F noon-10pm, Sa-Su 11am-10pm.

▨ **MUSÉE CARNAVALET**   MUSEUM

23 rue de Sévigné   ☎01 44 59 58 58 www.carnavalet.paris.fr

Located in Mme. de Sévigné's beautiful, 16th-century *hôtel particulier* and the neighboring Hôtel Le Peletier de St-Fargeau, this meticulously arranged and engaging museum traces Paris's history from its origins to Napoleon III. The history of Paris is long, and this museum is pretty large, so we recommend grabbing a map and taking your time as you stroll through ornate 18th-century apartments. The city's urban development is conveyed through small-scale models, paintings (expect to see a lot of portraits), antique furniture, and sculptural fragments. Highlights include the famous *The Tennis Court Oath*, Marcel Proust's fully reconstructed bedroom, and a piece of the Bastille prison wall. (We tried, but shouting *"Vive la Revolution!"* doesn't entitle you to touch it.)

i ⓂChemin Vert. Take rue St-Gilles, which becomes rue du Parc Royal, and turn left onto rue de Sévigné. Free. Audio tour €5. ⓩ Open Tu-Su 10am-6pm. Last entry 5:15pm.

▨ **MUSÉE DE LA CHASSE ET DE LA NATURE**   MUSEUM

62 rue des Archives   ☎01 48 87 40 36 www.chassenature.org

Yes, yes, we all love animals, but please save your horror for PETA meetings. This eclectic museum isn't just about bloodshed—it displays hunting-themed arts, weaponry, and stuffed animals that explore man's relationship with nature through the history and practices of hunting. The museum's interior is reminiscent of the sumptuous living rooms in a hunting lodge and contains a variety of cabinets for animals like the owls, boars, and stags, with drawers you can pull out to see their droppings. By far the most impressive room is the Trophy Room, with a stuffed polar bear on its hind legs, cheetahs in a glass case, heads of a rhinoceros, lion, tiger, moose, deer, boars, etc.

i ⓂRambuteau. *Walk against traffic on rue Beaubourg, turn right onto rue Michel le Comte, then left onto rue des Archives €6, ages 18-25 and seniors €4.50, under 18 free. 1st Su of each month free.* ⓩ *Open Tu-Su 11am-6pm.*

🏛 PLACE DES VOSGES   PARK

Paris's oldest and perhaps snootiest public square has served many generations of residents, from the knights who clashed swords in medieval tournaments to the hipsters who tan and swap bottles during picnics today. All 36 buildings that line the square were constructed by Baptiste du Cerceau in the same architectural style; look for pink brick, slate roofs, and street-level arcades. The quaint atmosphere attracted **Cardinal Richelieu** (who lived at no. 21 when he wasn't busy mad-dogging musketeers), writer **Alphonse Daudet** (who lived at no. 8), and **Victor Hugo**(no. 6). It was also the venue for one of seven-year-old prodigy **Mozart's** concerts, inspiring every "My Child is an Honor Student" bumper sticker that has been printed since. Come here to people watch, sunbathe, nap in the grass, and wish you were friends with Molière or Voltaire.

i ⓂSt-Paul or Bastille. *Follow rue St-Antoine and turn onto rue de Birague. Free Wi-Fi.*

MAISON DE VICTOR HUGO   MUSEUM
6 pl. des Vosges   ☎01 42 72 10 16 www.musee-hugo.paris.fr

Dedicated to the father of French Romanticism and housed in the building where he lived from 1832 to 1848, this museum displays memorabilia from his pre-exile, exile, and post-exile days, including his family's little-known paintings and the desk where he wrote standing up. On the first floor, the collection reveals paintings of scenes from *Les Misérables* and other works. On your way up, don't miss the caricatures of good ol' Hugo by André Gill. Upstairs, you'll find Hugo's apartments, a recreation of the bedroom where he died, and the *chambre chinoise*, which reveals his flamboyant interior decorating skills and just how romantic he really was.

i ⓂSt-Paul or Bastille. *Follow rue St-Antoine and turn onto rue de Birague. Free. Special exhibit €5, students and under 26 €2.50. Audio tour €5.* ⓩ *Open Tu-Su 10am-6pm. Last entry 5:40pm.*

GALERIE THULLIER   GALLERY
13 rue de Thorigny   ☎01 42 77 33 23 www.galeriethuillier.com

One of Paris's most active galleries, Galerie Thullier has exhibits that rotate every two weeks, which means that there's always something new to see when you visit. The art displayed here ranges across all styles, and the gallery exhibits a number of different artists at any given time. Although there is no real permanent collection, some artists have close relationships with the gallery and show their work here as often as possible.

i ⓂSt-Sébastien-Froissart. *Walk down rue du Pont aux Choux and turn left onto rue de Turenne, then right onto rue de Thorigny.* ⓩ *Open Tu-Sa 1-7pm.*

Latin Quarter and St-Germain

🏛 PANTHÉON   HISTORICAL MONUMENT, CRYPT
pl. du Panthéon   ☎01 44 32 18 04 http://pantheon.monuments-nationaux.fr

If there's one building that doesn't know the meaning of antidisestablishmentarianism, it's the Panthéon. Because the Neoclassical building went back and forth between a church and a "secular mausoleum" over the years, it contains some surprising eternal residents. Within the crypt, tombs alternate between Christian heroes, such as St. Louis, and Enlightenment thinkers like Voltaire, Rousseau, and Descartes (who would probably object to being placed so close to icons

france

of church dogma). What's worse, both Foucault's pendulum and revolutionary statues lie above the remains of Joan of Arc and Ste. Geneviève. Other famous graves include those of Victor Hugo, Émile Zola, and Marie Curie, the only female resident. The trip up the dome has three stops, with 360-degree views of the Marais and the Latin Quarter, and you can meander the colonnade at the top for the allotted 10min. before being herded back down.

i Ⓜ*Cardinal Lemoine. Head away from the river on rue du Cardinal Lemoine and turn right onto rue Clovis. Walk until you reach pl. du Panthéon. Dome visits Apr-Oct in Dutch, English, French, German, Russian, and Spanish. €7.50, ages 18-25 €4.50, under 18 and EU citizens under 26 free. ☒ Open daily Apr-Sept 10am-6:30pm, Oct-Mar 10am-6pm. Last entry 45min. before close.*

LE JARDIN DU LUXEMBOURG   GARDEN
Main entrance on bd St-Michel   www.senat.fr/visite/jardin

As with most ornate things in Paris, these gardens and the Palais du Luxembourg used to be exclusively for royalty until the revolutions began in 1789. Today, the park is a favorite among Parisians, who love to hole up with a book on a bench by the apple orchards or snag a colorful aluminum chair and bask in the sun during their lunch break. Children run around this park like they own it, and with a carousel, numerous playgrounds, and 1920s wooden sailboats by the Grand Bassin Pond, the kiddos are definitely getting the most out of it. Don't get too excited about picnicking, though—perfectly manicured lawns like these are off-limits, and the one patch of grass that is open is unsurprisingly crowded. The Palais, which now houses the Sénat, is still off-limits, but the best and most sought-after spot in the garden is the **Fontaine des Médicis,** a vine-covered grotto east of the Palais that features a murky fish pond and Baroque fountain sculptures.

i Ⓜ*Odéon or RER B: Luxembourg. Guided tours in French Apr-Oct 1st W of each month 9:30am. Tours start at pl. André Honorat behind the observatory. Free. ☒ Open daily in summer 7:30am-1hr. before sunset; in winter 8am-1hr. before sunset.*

SHAKESPEARE AND CO. BOOKSTORE   BOOKSTORE
37 rue de la Bûcherie   ☎01 43 25 40 93 www.shakespeareandcompany.com

Sylvia Beach's original Shakespeare and Co. at 8 rue Dupuytren (later at 12 rue de l'Odéon) is legendary among Parisian Anglophones and American literature nerds alike. An alcoholic crew of expat writers gathered here in the '20s, and Hemingway described the bookstore in *A Moveable Feast.* After closing during World War II, George Whitman—no relation to Walt—opened the current ragtag bookstore on the shores of the Seine in 1951, dubbing it "a socialist utopia masquerading as a bookstore." This certainly isn't your run-of-the-mill, money-making Barnes&Noble; they're in it for the love of the game at Shakespeare and Co. Grab a book off the shelves and head to the quiet library overlooking the Seine on the second floor.

i Ⓜ*St-Michel. Take quai de Montebello toward Notre Dame and turn right onto rue St-Jacques. Rue de la Bûcherie is on the left. ☒ Open M-F 10am-11pm, Sa-Su 11am-11pm.*

MUSÉE ZADKINE   MUSEUM
100B rue d'Assas   ☎01 55 42 77 20 www.zadkine.paris.fr

Installed in the former house and studio of Russian sculptor Ossip Zadkine (1890-1967), this pleasantly tourist-free museum houses a terrific collection of his extensive work in a minimalist, modern setting of clean-cut white walls. While most artists tend to stick to one area, Zadkine worked in 12 different styles, from Primitivism to Neoclassicism to Cubism, and the museum's collection includes all of his creative periods. Visitors can pore over his classical masterpiece, *L'hommage à Apollinaire,* then immerse themselves in his more modern and strikingly disembodied *Le Torse de la Ville Détruite.* The tiny forested garden, realized by landscape painter Gilles Clément, is a welcome retreat from the busier northern part of the 6ème. Don't forget to indulge in a free cup of hot tea, served in a bamboo cup on your way out.

i Ⓜ*Vavin. At the intersection, turn left onto rue de la Grande Chaumière, then right onto rue Notre-Dame des Champs. Turn left onto rue Joseph Bara, then left onto rue d'Assas. Guided tours available by reservation. Permanent exhibit free; temporary exhibits vary.* ☒ *Open daily 10am-6pm.*

ARÈNES DE LUTÈCE
PARK, HISTORIC MONUMENT

49 rue Monge

Back in the days of the Romans in the first and second centuries, this amphitheater was used for spectacles like **gladiator battles** and animal fights attended by as many as 15,000 people. Tamer audiences came for the plays and comedies, but we bet the place only really filled up for the bloodbaths. In the 13th century, the amphitheater, long out of use, was completely filled in and remained undiscovered until 1869. Today, the seating around the amphitheater has been restored and opened to the public. Occasionally, there are summertime performances that feature music, comedy, theater, and dance, but this circular sandpit is generally used for pick-up soccer games and various other forms of public folly (some things never change). Around the amphitheater are some small walking paths and dense foliage that provides some much-needed shade during the hot summer.

i Ⓜ*Place Monge. At the intersection of rue de Navarre and rue des Arènes; the Métro stop is beneath it. Occasionally hosts outdoor performances.* ☒ *Closing times vary during the year, open M-F 8am, Sa-Su 9am. Open May-Aug M-F 8am-9:30pm, Sa-Su 9am-9:30pm.*

Invalides

🏛 EIFFEL TOWER
TOWER

Champs de Mars ☎08 92 70 12 39 www.tour-eiffel.fr

At 324m—just a tad shorter than New York City's Chrysler Building—the tower is a tremendous feat of design and engineering, though wind does cause it to occasionally sway 6 to 7cm (nobody's perfect). The lines are unsurprisingly long, but the unparalleled view from the top floor deserves a visit. The cheapest way to ascend the tower is by burning off those *pain au chocolat* calories on the world's most iconic Stairmaster, although the third floor is only accessible by elevator. Waiting until nightfall to make your ascent cuts down the line and ups the glamour; buying your ticket online can also save you hours—we mean that literally. At the top, captioned aerial photographs help you locate other famous landmarks; on a clear day it is possible to see Chartres, 88km away. From dusk until 2am (Sept-May 1am) the tower sparkles with light for 10min. on the hour.

i Ⓜ*Bir-Hakeim,* Ⓜ*Trocadéro, or* Ⓜ*École Militaire. From* Ⓜ*Bir-Hakeim, walk toward the Seine, turn right onto quai de Grenelle, and the Eiffel Tower is on the right. From* Ⓜ*École Militaire, walk up av. de la Bourdonnais against traffic. Elevator to 2nd fl. €8.50, ages 12-24 €7, ages 4-11 and handicapped €4, under 4 free; elevator to top €14.50/13/10/free; stair entrance to 2nd fl. €5/3.50/3/ free. Buy your ticket online and pick your time to climb in order to cut down the wait.* ☒ *Elevator open daily Jun 15-Sept 1 9am-12:45am; rest of year 9:30am-11:45pm. Last entry 45min. before close. Stairs open daily Jun 15-Sept 1 9am-12:45am, last entry midnight; rest of year 9:30am-6:30pm, last entry 6pm.*

🏛 MUSÉE D'ORSAY
MUSEUM

62 rue de Lille ☎01 40 49 48 14 www.musee-orsay.com

Aesthetic taste is fickle. When a handful of artists were rejected from the Louvre salon in the 19th century, they opened an exhibition across the way, prompting both the scorn of stick-up-their-arses *académiciens* and the rise of Impressionism. Today, people line up at the Musée d'Orsay to see this collection of groundbreaking rejects. Originally a train station, the museum is fairly large and is best seen over several visits so you don't become art-ed out. The first and second floors contain pre-Impressionist works and lesser-known artists, with all the big names and famous works of Impressionist and Post-Impressionist art on the more crowded top floor. Everything at the museum is practically a must see, but if you're really crunched for time, limit yourself to Van Gogh's portraits and *Starry Night*, Degas's ballerinas, Cézanne's *Apples and Oranges* and other still lifes, and Seurat and Signac's Pointillism. Avoid the long lines by buying a ticket beforehand and hopping over to Entrance C.

i ⓂSolférino. Access at entrance A off the square at 1 rue de la Légion d'Honneur. €9, ages 18-25 €6.50, under 18 and EU citizens 18-26 free, joint ticket with Musée Rodin €15. ⓞ Open Tu-W 9:30am-6pm, Th 9:30am-9:45pm, F-Su 9:30am-6pm. Visitors asked to leave 30min. before close.

▧ MUSÉE DE L'ARMÉE   MUSEUM
129 rue de Grenelle   ☎08 10 11 33 99 www.musee-armee.fr

Americans in favor of the Second Amendment, European empire enthusiasts, and war buffs will all find a visit to the Musée de l'Armée a surefire good time. Housed inside the grand Hôtel des Invalides and built by Louis XIV for his war veterans, the museum is comprised of six main parts. The impressive **Église du Dôme** is the most recognizable part of the museum and holds the **tomb of Napoleon** surrounded by sculptures and inscriptions celebrating our favorite *petit* emperor. The dome and the Saint-Louis des Invalides chapel are flanked by the Charles de Gaulle historical exhibit and collections covering Louis XIV to Napoleon III in the East Wing and the fantastic World War I and World War II exhibit and ancient armor and arms collections in the West Wing. Even for those who aren't crazy about ordnance will find something fascinating here. Whether it's the shiny street taxi used to shuttle soldiers in WWI, animated maps of major battles and conquests, or the collection of armor for children (both terrifying and strangely cute), the museum covers quite a bit of ground.

i ⓂInvalides or ⓂLa Tour-Maubourg. The museum is located in the center of the park. Admission to all museum €9.50, students under 26 €7.50, EU citizens and under 18 free; €7.50 after 5pm in the summer, after 4pm in the winter, and late on Tu. Temporary exhibits €8.50; entrance to both permanent and temporary €12. Audio tour €6, under 26 €4. ⓞ Open daily Apr-Oct 10am-6pm; Nov-Mar 10am-5pm. Dome Church and Modern Department are open Apr-Sept until 9pm; Jul-Aug until 7pm. Except Jul-Sept, 1st M of every month only Dome Church and artillery trail are open. Charles de Gaulle Monument closed every M.

▧ MUSÉE RODIN   MUSEUM
79 rue de Varenne   ☎01 44 18 61 10 www.musee-rodin.fr

After Auguste Rodin (1840-1917) was rejected by the most prestigious art school in Paris, he rejected the idealized styles and themes in sculpture to create works of vivid realism. Living well is the best revenge—today the art world considers him the father of modern sculpture. This museum houses three of Rodin's most famous sculptures, *Le Penseur* (The Thinker), *La Porte de L'Enfer*, and *Le Baiser*. For one of the best photo ops of all time, strike a pose like *Le Penseur* contemplating *Le Penseur*—so meta. Meanwhile, *The Gates of Hell* is a bronze mess of lustful pairs swirling in the violent turbulence of the second ring of Hell from Dante's *Divine Comedy*. Rodin's lesser-known sculptures are inside the Hôtel Biron, the 18th-century building where he lived and worked.

i ⓂVarenne. Temporary exhibits housed in the chapel, to the right as you enter. Museum €9, ages 18-25 €5, under 18 and EU citizens under 26 free; garden €1/1/free; joint ticket with Musee d'Orsay €15. 1st Su of the month free. Audio tours in 6 languages €4 each for permanent and temporary exhibits, combined ticket €6. ⓞ Open Tu-Su 10am-5:45pm, last entry 5:15pm.

▧ CHAMPS DE MARS   PARK
Lined with more lovers than trees, the expansive lawn that stretches from the École Militaire to the Eiffel Tower is called the Champs de Mars (Field of Mars). Close to the neighborhood's military monuments and museums, it has

paris

historically lived up to the Roman god of war for whom it was named. The open field has been used for military boot camp and as a convenient place for violent demonstrations, including but not limited to a slew of civilian massacres during the Revolution. At the end of the Champs de Mars, toward the Military School, is the "Wall of Peace," a glass structure that has 32 languages' worth of the word "peace" inscribed on its walls in an attempt to make up for the field's bloody past. For a picnic with a view, head over to rue Cler to buy some baguettes and charcuterie from the open-air markets as you watch the sun set behind the Eiffel Tower.

i Ⓜ*La Motte Picquet-Grenelle or* Ⓜ*École Militaire.*

MUSÉE DE LÉGION D'HONNEUR   MUSEUM
2 rue de la Légion-d'Honneur   ☎01 40 62 84 25 www.musee-legiondhonneur.fr

This museum is worth a brief (and free) visit when you're all art-ed out by the Musée d'Orsay across the street. It showcases France's highest honors, decorations, and orders—in other words, there are some very ornate pendants, medallions, and insignias on display here. The most famous and prestigious items here are the royal collars of the Legion of Honor, a national order established in 1802 by Napoleon, who understood the importance of shiny objects when he famously declared, "It is with such baubles that men are led." Other must-sees here are the foreign orders from countries such as Madagascar to Japan and the enormous black velvet royal capes.

i RER *Musée d'Orsay or* Ⓜ*Solférino. Across the street from Musée d'Orsay. Handicapped entrance at 1 rue de Solférino. Free entrance and audio tour.* 🕐 *Open W-Su 1-6pm.*

MUSÉE MAILLOL   MUSEUM
61 rue de Grenelle   ☎01 42 22 59 58 www.museemaillol.com

The museum was founded by Aristide Maillol's muse, Dina Vierny, who was 15 when she met the French sculptor. Unlike Georgia O'Keefe's ambiguous "lady" flower images, the work of Maillol is pretty straightforward. Nude sculptures and paintings form the backbone of this museum's permanent collection on the upper levels, although the first and second floors are dominated by detailed and well-curated temporary exhibits that range from art from Pompeii to work by Murano glass makers.

i Ⓜ*Rue du Bac. Walk down rue de Bac along the flow of traffic and turn left onto rue de Grenelle. The museum is on the right €11; ages 11-25, unemployed, and handicapped €9; under 11 free. Audio tour €5.* 🕐 *Open daily 10:30am-7pm, last entry 45min. before close.*

MUSÉE DU QUAI BRANLY   MUSEUM
37 quai Branly   ☎01 56 61 70 00 www.quaibranly.fr

Museums can get old real quick, but before you can even think about how tired your feet are, this time machine/museum of natural history will shower you with its theatricality—every which way you turn will be a new video about Indian shadow puppets, a collection of wooden Polynesian ancestral poles, or a group of noisy school children (no, they're not on display, but they're essentially permanent fixtures here). The museum doesn't have any rooms, which creates some rather abrupt transitions from the four organized regions (Africa, Asia, the Americas, and Oceania). In case you can't tell the difference between a Nepalese tunic and an African one, look at the floor: the color under your feet corresponds to what section of the world you are in. Be sure to sit in one of the many hidden sound caves to take in some tribal noises in solitude, but beware of local high school students using the dark spaces as personal make-out rooms.

i Ⓜ*Alma-Marceau. Cross Pont de l'Alma and follow quai Branly toward the Eiffel Tower. €8.50, under 18 and EU citizens 18-25 free. Temporary exhibit €7. Joint ticket €10. Audio tour €5.* 🕐 *Open Tu-W 11am-7pm, Th-Sa 11am-9pm, Su 11am-7pm.*

Champs-Élysées

ARC DE TRIOMPHE
HISTORIC MONUMENT

pl. Charles de Gaulle-Étoile
www.arc-de-triomphe.monuments-nationaux.fr

Probably the second most iconic structure in the whole city, the Arc de Triomphe dominates the Champs-Élysées and remains strikingly powerful even when viewed from a distance. The original architect imagined an unparalleled tribute to France's military prowess in the form of a giant, bejeweled elephant. Fortunately, Napoleon had the more restrained idea of building an arch. You could probably pull together an exhibition of French history since the arch's 1836 completion based purely on photos of the Arc's use in ceremonial celebrations. It stands both as a tribute to French military triumphs and as a memorial to those who have fallen in battle. The Tomb of the Unknown Soldier, added in 1920, lies under the arch. Every day at 6:30pm, the tomb's eternal flame is re-lit in a ceremony. The Arc is spectacular to look at, and it returns the favor by being spectacular to look from. The observation deck offers a brilliant view of the Historic Axis, which stretches from the Louvre to the Grande Arche de la Défense.

i ⓜCharles de Gaulle-l'Étoile. *You will die (and face a hefty fine) if you try to dodge the 10-lane merry-go-round of cars around the arch, so use the pedestrian underpass on the right side of the Champs-Élysées, facing the arch. Expect long waits, although you can escape the crowds if you go before noon. Buy tickets in the pedestrian underpass. €9.50, ages 18-25 €6, under 18 and EU citizens 18-25 free.* ⏰ *Open daily Apr-Sept 10am-11pm; Oct-Mar 10am-10:30pm. Last entry 45min. before close.*

PINACOTHÈQUE
MUSEUM

28 pl. de la Madeleine
☎01 42 68 02 01 www.pinacotheque.com

A young contender in Paris's competitive museum scene, Pinacothèque has held its own since it opened in 2007. When director Marc Restellini, a little-known art scholar not backed by any large foundation, decided to open up his own museum, the museum world refused to take him seriously. To their great surprise (and chagrin), temporary exhibits on Edvard Munch, Jackson Pollock, and the terracotta warriors from China drew round-the-block visitors. Unbeholden to any higher powers, this museum runs entirely on gift shop and ticket sales, so it can afford to be a little more experimental in its exhibitions—the permanent collection contains startling juxtapositions, with works by Picasso next to pieces by 17th-century Dutch painter Frans Hals next to one of Warhol's stereographs of Marilyn Monroe. The permanent collection is worth a visit, although the stars here are the more extensive temporary exhibits.

i ⓜMadeleine. *Facing the front of the church, turn around to the right, and the ticket office is located on the corner of rue Vignon and rue de Sèze. Audio tours available for download online. Permanent collection €8, ages 12-25 and students €6, under 12 free; temporary collections €12/10; combined tickets €18-22.* ⏰ *Open M-Tu 10:30am-6:30pm, W 10:30am-9pm, Th 10:30am-6:30pm, F 10:30am-9pm, Sa-Su 10:30am-6:30pm. Last entry 45min. before close.*

AVENUE DES CHAMPS-ÉLYSÉES
SHOPPING DISTRICT

From pl. Charles de Gaulle-Étoile to pl. de la Concorde

There's a reason we included it here and not in **Shopping**—you can't afford it. The Champs-Élysées seems to be a magnificent celebration of the elite's pomp and fortuitous circumstance, but it's mostly filled with flashy cars, expensive cafes packed with rich foreigners, and kitschy shops. On the plus side, it does offer some of the best people watching in Europe. The avenue also hosts most major French events: on **Bastille Day,** the largest parade in Europe takes place here, as does the final stretch of the **Tour de France.** Huge national celebrations, like FIFA World Cup championships and political demonstrations, also love to clog up this commercial artery. While the Champs itself may be deteriorating in class (with

paris

the invasion of chain stores), many of its side streets, like **Avenue Montaigne,** have picked up the slack and ooze sophistication.

i ⓂCharles de Gaulle-l'Étoile, ⓂGeorge V, ⓂFranklin D. Roosevelt, or ⓂChamps-Élysées-Clemenceau stops all along the avenue.

PLACE DE LA CONCORDE
PLAZA

pl. de la Concorde

Constructed by Louis XV in honor of himself, the Place de la Concorde quickly became ground zero for all public grievances against the monarchy. During the Reign of Terror, the complex of buildings was renamed Place de la Révolution, and 1343 aristocrats were guillotined here in less than the span of one year. Louis XVI met his end near the statue that symbolizes the French town of Brest, and the obelisk marks the spot where Marie Antoinette, Charlotte Corday (Marat's assassin), Lavoisier, Danton, and Robespierre lost their heads. Flanking either side of Concorde's intersection with the wide **Champs-Élysées** are reproductions of Guillaume Coustou's **Chevaux de Marly;** also known as *Africans Mastering the Numidian Horses*, the original sculptures are now in the Louvre to protect them from pollution. At night, the Concorde's dynamic ambiance begins to soften, and the obelisk, fountains, and lamps are dramatically illuminated. On **Bastille Day,** a military parade led by the President of the Republic marches through the Concorde (usually around 10am) and down the Champs-Élysées to the Arc de Triomphe, and an impressive fireworks display lights up the sky over the plaza at night. At the end of July, the **Tour de France** finalists pull through the Concorde and into the home stretch on the Champs-Élysées. Tourists be warned: between the Concorde's monumental scale, lack of crosswalks, and heavy traffic, crossing the street here is impossible at best and fatal at worst. Unless you want to see the obelisk up close, it's best to admire it from afar and then circle around the plaza to get to Madeleine or the Champs-Élysées, rather than cross the plaza directly.

i ⓂConcorde.

OBÉLISQUE DE LUXOR
HISTORIC MONUMENT

pl. de la Concorde

In the center of Paris's largest and most infamous public square, the 3300-year-old Obélisque de Luxor stands at a monumental 72ft. The spot was originally occupied by a statue of Louis XV (after whom the square was originally named) that was destroyed in 1748 by an angry mob. King Louis-Philippe, anxious to avoid revolutionary rancor, opted for a less contentious symbol: the 220-ton, red granite, hieroglyphic-covered obelisk presented to Charles X from the Viceroy of Egypt in 1829. The obelisk, which dates back to the 13th century BCE, recalls the royal accomplishments of Ramses II and wasn't erected until 1836. Today, it forms the axis of what many refer to as the "royal perspective"—a spectacular view of Paris from the Louvre, in which the Place de la Concorde, the Arc de Triomphe, and the Grande Arche de la Défense appear to form a straight line through the center of the city. The view serves as a physical timeline of Paris's history, from the reign of Louis XIV all the way to the celebration of modern commerce.

i ⓂConcorde.

GRAND PALAIS
PALACE

3 av. du Général Eisenhower ☎01 44 13 17 17 www.grandpalais.fr

Designed for the 1900 World's Fair, the Grand Palais and the accompanying Petit Palais across the street were lauded as exemplary works of Art Nouveau architecture. Today, the Grand Palais is used as a concert venue and an exhibition space for wildly popular temporary installations on artists such as Klimt and Monet. It is also well known as the annual host of Chanel's elaborate fashion shows. For the temporary exhibits, it's best to buy a ticket in advance and skip the lines. Otherwise, most of the building's beauty can be admired outside for free, especially at night, when the 6000 metric ton glass ceiling glows, lighting up the French flag that flies above it.

i Ⓜ*Champs-Élysées-Clemenceau. Prices vary depending on exhibitions. €8-16, ages 18-26 €6-10. ☾ Hours vary widely based on the exhibition. Closed Tu.*

Bastille

▨ VIADUC DES ARTS AND PROMENADE PLANTÉE   PARK, SHOPPING STRIP
1-129 av. Daumesnil   ☎01 44 75 80 66 www.viaducdesarts.fr

An oft-overlooked sight, the elevated Promenade Plantée runs along the old Vincennes railway line and was the inspiration for New York City's High Line. The 4.5km pathway and its fragrant flowers make for a terrific afternoon stroll, or at least a greener alternative to the busy streets below. If you're short on time, the Jardin de Reuilly is a much larger, beautiful place for a picnic before you have to scramble back down to the concrete streets when the sun sets. Below the Promenade on av. Daumesnil, Paris's contemporary artists occupy the shops under the heavy archways of the **Viaduc des Arts.** You can find everything from flashy *haute couture* to workshops that use leather, wood, copper, and glass to create trendy art collections that scream, "Look at me! I'm artistic!" from the windows.

i Ⓜ*Bastille. Promenade runs from the Bois de Vincennes to the rue de Lyon. The Viaduc des Arts runs along av. Daumesnil from rue de Lyon to rue de Charenton. Entrances to the Promenade are at Ledru Rollin, Hector Malot, and bd Diderot. ☾ Park opens M-F 8am, Sa-Su 9am. Closing hours vary, around 5:45pm in winter, 9:30pm in summer. Stores open M-Sa; hours vary, with many taking a 2hr. lunch break at noon.*

BASTILLE PRISON   HISTORIC SITE
Visitors to the prison subsist on symbolic value alone—it's one of the most popular sights in Paris that doesn't actually exist. On July 14, 1789, an angry Parisian mob stormed this bastion of royal tyranny, sparking the French Revolution. They only liberated seven prisoners, but who's counting? Two days later, the Assemblée Nationale ordered the prison to be demolished. Today, all that remains is the fortress's ground plan, still visible as a line of paving stones in the pl. de la Bastille. But it was hardly the hell hole that the Revolutionaries who tore it down imagined it to be. Bastille's elite inmates were allowed to furnish their suites, use fresh linens, bring their own servants, and receive guests; the Cardinal de Rohan famously held a dinner party for 20 in his cell. Notable prisoners included the **Man in the Iron Mask** (made famous by writer Alexandre Dumas), the Comte de Mirabeau, Voltaire (twice), and the Marquis de Sade. The anniversary of the storming is celebrated every year on July 14 and (much like a certain celebration 10 days earlier across the Atlantic) is a time of glorious fireworks and copious amounts of alcohol, with festivities concentrated around pl. de la Bastille (but note that the fireworks are over the Eiffel Tower).

i Ⓜ*Bastille.*

MALHIA KENT   FASHION
19 av. Daumesnil   ☎01 53 44 76 76 www.malhia.com

Fulfilling every *Project Runway* fantasy, this workshop gives an up-close, behind-the-scenes look at fashion. High-end fabrics made out of colorful threads of glitter, lace, and feathers will delight any aspiring seamstress, but for those who don't know how to make it work with a sewing machine, there's not much to see other than a ton of really expensive, shiny pieces of cloth. Maybe they would make fancy, albeit rough, hand towels? Or place mats?

i Ⓜ*Bastille. In the Viaduc des Arts. Items usually run from €75-300. ☾ Open Tu-F 10am-7pm, Sa 11am-7pm.*

Montparnasse and Southern Paris

CATACOMBS
HISTORIC LANDMARK

1 av. du Colonel Henri Roi-Tanguy   ☎01 43 22 47 63   www.catacombes-de-paris.fr

The Catacombs were the original site of Paris's quarries, but they were converted into an ossuary in 1785 to help alleviate the stench rising from overcrowded cemeteries—somehow, burying six million people at once seemed like a better idea. Not for the claustrophobic or faint of heart, this 45min. excursion leads visitors down a winding spiral staircase to a welcoming sign: "Stop! Here is the Empire of Death." Stacks of skulls and femurs line the walls, with the highlight being the barrel-shaped arrangement of skulls and shinbones. Try to arrive before the opening at 10am; hordes of tourists form extremely long lines hoping to escape the pressing sun. The visitors' passage is well marked, so don't worry about getting lost. Try trailing behind the group a little for the ultimate creepy experience—you won't be disappointed.

i Ⓜ*Denfert Rochereau. Cross av. du Colonel Henri Roi-Tanguy with the lion on the left. Audio tour €3. €8, over 60 €6, ages 14-26 €4, under 14 free. ☒ Open Tu-Su 10am-5pm. Last entry 4pm.*

TOUR MONTPARNASSE
TOWER

33 av. du Maine   ☎01 45 38 52 56   www.tourmontparnasse56.com

Everyone loves a great panorama of Paris, but the perennial problem is that no matter how many stairs your climb or elevators you take, you can't see the landmark you're standing on. Tour Montparnasse solves this problem with a 196m vantage point over the city and a terrific view of nearly all of Paris's famous landmarks, all without forcing you to see the stark and monolithic tower itself. The elevator is allegedly the fastest in Europe (moving at 19ft. per second—not a lot of time to clear the pressure in your ears) and spits you out at a mandatory photo line on the 56th floor. After being shoved in front of a fake city skyline and forced to smile for a picture that you probably don't want, you're finally allowed up to the 59th floor to take in the beauty and meticulous planning of Paris's historic streets. Thankfully, the city ruled that similar eyesores could not be constructed in Paris's downtown shortly after this one was built.

i Ⓜ*Montparnasse-Bienvenue. Entrance on rue de l'Arrivée. €13.50, students and under 20 €7, under 15 €8, under 7 free. ☒ Open Apr-Sept daily 9:30am-11:30pm, Oct-Mar M-Th 9:30am-10:30pm, F-Sa 9:30am-11pm, Su 9:30am-10:30pm. Last entry 30min. before close.*

MÉMORIAL DE LA LIBÉRATION DE PARIS
MEMORIAL, MUSEUM

23 allée de la 2ème DB, Jardin Atlantique   ☎01 40 64 39 44   www.ml-leclerc-moulin.paris.fr

Opened in 1994 for the 50th anniversary of the liberation of Paris from Nazi control, this memorial is composed of the **Mémorial du Maréchal LeClerc** and the **Musée Jean Moulin,** named for two celebrated World War II heroes. French hero Jean Moulin organized and unified the French resistance before his arrest, interrogation, and death under the Gestapo. The whole memorial is located above the SNCF station, where LeClerc set up his command post in 1944, and in the neighborhood where Moulin lived under the artist guise *Romanin* prior to his military success. The two galleries are symbolically connected by the Liberation Gallery, which is meant to represent the remarkable unification of resistance forces to fight the Nazi regime and liberate France. The galleries contain an impressive array of 13 screens that play a harrowing series of video footage chronicling the tragedies and victories Paris experienced over the course of Nazi occupation and liberation.

i Ⓜ*Montparnasse-Bienvenue. Follow signs for the Memorial Leclerc from the Métro stop to the Memorial; the museum is on top of the SNCF terminal. Permanent collection free. Audio tour €5. Rotating exhibits vary, usually €5, ages 14-26 €2. ☒ Open Tu-Su 10am-6pm.*

france

Auteuil, Passy & Batignolles

🖼 PALAIS DE TOKYO
MUSEUM

13 av. du President Wilson ☎01 81 97 35 88 www.palaisdetokyo.com

The Palais de Tokyo rejects the label "museum," and prefers to call itself a site "devoted to contemporary creativity." The artistic creations of future Duchamps, Basquiats, and Harings are featured here in all forms imaginable, from paintings and sculpture to projections, videos, dance, and fashion. If the world of art, with all of its hallowed names and iconic images, seems a bit stuffy and staid to you, you'll be glad to know that very little at this site is permanent—exhibitions are only up for a few months. Although the stuff here may seem ridiculous and esoteric (someone explain to us how trapezoids count as modern art), the museum's unpretentious attitude toward art and its anti-museum stance make it a liberating and surprisingly personal visit.

i Ⓜléna €10, under 26 and seniors €8, under 18 free. When there are no exhibits, the Palais is open for free. 🕐 Open M noon-midnight, W-Su noon-midnight. We told you this wasn't your typical museum.

🖼 PALAIS DE CHAILLOT
MUSEUMS, HISTORIC BUILDING

1 pl. du Trocadéro

To prep for the 1937 World's Fair, the French government tore down the old Palais du Trocadéro and built the current Palais de Chaillot. With its stellar view of the Eiffel Tower from across the Pont d'Iéna, the Palais has attracted its share of visitors, from Adolf Hitler to the UN General Assembly (to make up for the former). In 1948 they adopted the Universal Declaration of Human Rights at the Palais, and today the wide esplanade between the two wings is known as the "Esplanade of Human Rights." On either side of the esplanade are the arching wings of the Palais. The southern wing houses the Musée National de la Marine (The National Navy Museum) and the Musée de l'Homme (Museum of Man). The eastern wing contains the **Cité de l'Architecture** and Théatre National de Chaillot. For those who don't want to pay to enter the museums, the esplanade and the view are free, although the food stands nearby are not.

i Open M 11am-6pm, W-F 11am-6pm, Sa-Su 11am-7pm. Musée de l'Homme closed for renovations until 2015.

🖼 MUSÉE D'ART MODERNE DE LA VILLE DE PARIS
MUSEUM

11 av. du President Wilson ☎01 53 67 40 00 www.mam.paris.fr

If the Centre Pompidou is too high a price to pay for modern art, the free permanent collection at this museum features works by major figures like Picasso, Duchamp, and Matisse and is every bit as wonky. The highlight of this museum is usually the well-attended and excellent temporary exhibitions. Most recently, the museum did a retrospective on Keith Haring with a focus on his political artwork, which is essentially all of his work. During the summer, the museum cafe opens up to a gorgeous terrace with a river view.

i Ⓜléna. Cross the street to av. du President Wilson and walk with the Seine to your right. Permanent collection free. Temporary exhibits €10, students €5. 🕐 Permanent collection open Tu-Su 10am-6pm. Last entry 5:45pm. Special exhibits open Tu-W 10am-6pm, Th 10am-10pm, F-Su 10am-6pm.

🖼 LA GRANDE ARCHE DE LA DEFENSE
MONUMENT

1 parvis de la Défense ☎01 49 07 27 55 www.grandearche.com

When French President François Mitterand created an international design competition for Paris's newest monument, those who entered the artistic fray faced some intimidating predecessors—who wanted to compete with Gustave Eiffel? Danish architect Johan Otto Von Spreckelsen took the plunge in 1983 and submitted his design for an arch that matches the glassy skyscrapers of this ultramodern business district and has become one of Paris's defining monuments. Made of 300,000 tons of white marble and standing taller than the Notre Dame, the arch was inaugurated on July 14, 1989, on the bicentennial of the French Revolution. It lies on the same boulevard as the Arc de Triomphe, and on a clear day, you can take the stairs to the top and see the Louvre. Since 2010, however, the elevator to the roof has been shut down, along with the museums that were located on the roof. The stairs remain open, and the plaza still offers a great view of the boulevard and the Arc de Triomphe in the distance.

i Ⓜ*La Défense.*

MUSÉE MARMOTTAN MONET   MUSEUM
2 rue Louis-Boilly   ☎01 44 96 50 33 www.marmottan.com

For those who want some breathing room while appreciating Impressionist art—kisses to the Musée d'Orsay, but the Musée Marmottan Monet is free from crowds and filled with over 100 Impressionist and Post-Impressionist paintings, from Claude Monet's *Water Lilies* and other pieces from his personal collection. If you tire of Manet, Degas, or Gauguin, you can admire the grandiose collection of Napoleonic furniture (including Napoleon's bed, which is unsurprisingly *petit*). Be sure to pay a visit to the exhibit on illuminated manuscripts and medieval artwork, which is surprisingly captivating—this is probably the closest you'll ever get to stained glass from a 13th-century cathedral.

i Ⓜ*La Muette. Walk with traffic on av. Mozart, turn left onto Chaussée de la Muette, walk through the Jardin de Ranelagh on av. Jardin de Ranelagh, turn right onto av. Raphael, then left onto rue Louis-Boilly; the museum is on the right. €10, under 18 and students under 26 €5. Audio guides €3.* 🕙 *Open Tu-W 10am-6pm, Th 10am-8pm, F-Su 10am-6pm. Last entry 30min. before close.*

MUSÉE DE LA MODE ET DU COSTUME   MUSEUM
10 av. Pierre 1er de Serbie   ☎01 56 52 86 00 www.galliera.paris.fr

There's no denying it—the French dress to impress. This museum elegantly displays the history of fashion from the 18th to the 20th century. With 30,000 outfits, 70,000 accessories, and not much space in which to display them, the museum organizes its exhibits by century and rotates them more swiftly than a Lady Gaga costume change.

i Ⓜ*Iéna. Walk down av. Pierre 1er de Serbice. Entrance is on the right side of the street. Entrance on pl. Rochambeau. €7, students and seniors €5.50.* 🕙 *Open Tu-Su 10am-6pm. Last entry 5:30pm.*

MUSÉE DU VIN   MUSEUM
5 sq Charles Dickens   ☎01 45 25 63 26 www.museeduvinparis.com

A wine museum in Paris has so much potential, but you would need to pregame the Musée du Vin to make it interesting. The museum is located in the underground tunnels of limestone quarries and contains various displays of many highly technical tools such as "bunghole openers" and "tasting pliers," with confusing and terse explanations of their functions. The creepily lifelike figures in the museum don't help much with the explanation of the winemaking process, and the bulletins are almost completely in French. At the end of your tour of the museum, there is a tasting of a glass of rosé, white, or red wine—but for €12, you may be better off just buying a bottle elsewhere.

i Ⓜ*Passy. Go down the stairs, turn right onto pl. Albioni, then right onto rue des Eaux; the museum is tucked away at the end of the street. Self-guided tour and 1 glass of wine €12; students, seniors, and visitors with disabilities €10.* 🕙 *Open Tu-Su 10am-6pm.*

STATUE OF LIBERTY   STATUE
Pont de Grenelle

Most things in Paris are done with flourish and a sense of grandeur—this, however, is more of an afterthought. Not even 40ft. tall, this replica of France's famous gift to the US is not worth your precious time. But you know what is?

The man-made island it sits on. The Île aux Cygnes floats in the middle of the Seine and offers great views of Paris and the Eiffel Tower, while the leafy trees provide welcome shade for a pleasant picnic.

i Ⓜ*Javel or* Ⓜ*Passy. From* Ⓜ*Javel walk toward the Seine, turn right onto quai André Citroen, turn left onto Pont Grenelle, and take stairs down to the Île aux Cygnes. From* Ⓜ*Passy walk down rue d'Albioni toward the Seine and cross av. du President Kennedy to the Pont Bir-Hakeim; turn right onto Île aux Cygnes and walk all the way down.*

Montmartre

🔲 BASILIQUE DU SACRÉ-CŒUR
CHURCH

35 rue du Chevalier-de-la-Barre ☎01 53 41 89 00 www.sacre-coeur-montmartre.fr

Situated 129m above sea level, this splendid basilica was first planned in 1870 to serve as a spiritual bulwark for France and the Catholic Church, which were facing an imminent military defeat and German occupation. The basilica was commissioned by the National Assembly and was initially meant to be an assertion of conservative Catholic power, but the only people that assert themselves on the steps today are the scammers offering "free" bracelets, so keep your wits about you after you reach the top of the exhausting climb. Inside, the basilica's dome is dominated by an image of Jesus Christ with his arms outspread, and if you're up for more stairs, climb up to the dome for an even better (and still free) view of the Parisian rooftops. Return to the steps of the basilica at night to watch the Eiffel Tower light up and sparkle.

i Ⓜ*Lamarck-Caulaincourt. Take rue Caulaincourt and turn right onto rue Lamrack. Follow rue Lamrack until you reach the basilica. Free. ⏰ Basilica open daily 6am-10:30pm. Dome open daily Mar-Nov 9am-7pm; Dec-Feb 9am-6pm. Mass M-F 11:15am, 6:30pm, 10pm; Sa 10pm; Su 11am, 6pm, 10pm.*

Buttes-Chaumont & Belleville

🔲 PARC DE BELLEVILLE
PARK

27 rue Piat

Parc de Belleville is the place to get lost. Get lost in a book. Get lost in a meal of baguettes, cheese, apples, and wine. Get lost in a game of badminton. Or get lost just wandering about the terraces and smelling the endless colorful flowers. The park is located on a slope, resulting in gorgeous views from the top of Parisian landmarks like the Eiffel Tower and the Panthéon. Come at sundown, when you can see the reds and yellows of the sky above the Parisian skyline. Gently bubbling fountains decorate different parts of the park and add a pleasant ambient soundtrack to the landscape. The park is divided into terraces and different grassy areas that are used for pick-up soccer games or picnics. Be sure to check out the summer schedule of the public amphitheater for concerts and festivals. Although Parc de Belleville closes after dark and many patrons clear out by late evening, fences are low and often breached by bored teenagers looking for a place to rendezvous after hours. (*Let's Go* does not recommend hopping fences like a hoodlum).

i Ⓜ*Pyrénées. Walk west on rue de Belleville, then turn left onto rue Piat. Entrances on rue Piat, rue des Couronnes, rue Bisson, and rue Jouye-Rouve. Free. ⏰ Open daily dawn to dusk.*

🔲 CITÉ DE LA MUSIQUE
MUSEUM

221 av. Jean Jaurès ☎01 44 84 44 84 www.citedelamusique.fr

The Cité de la Musique is an institution that offers concerts, practice rooms, a media library, and workshops, although the highlight is the Musée de la Musique. The museum takes visitors on a tour of music from prehistoric times, with flutes and mammoth tusk horns, to ornate 16th-century Venetian pianos (a must-see) to early 20th-century radios. With over a thousand instruments and a fantastic free audio tour with music clips (we wouldn't expect anything less), the museum

paris

shows you how wonderful the world sounded pre-Autotune. Highlights include instruments formerly owned by greats like Frédéric Chopin, Stradivarius violins, gilded baroque-style harpsichords, and a small collection of world instruments. Temporary exhibits hit the museum's lower levels twice a year and cover a range of musical styles and time periods; a recent exhibit was dedicated entirely to Bob Dylan.

i Ⓜ*Porte de Pantin. Extra charges may apply for temporary exhibits. Concert €8-41, 50% discount under 16, under 26 €9 if tickets are available. Museum €7, under 26 free; joint with temporary exhibits €9/5. ☒ Info center open Tu-Sa noon-6pm, Su 10am-6pm. Musée de la Musique open Tu-Sa noon-6pm, Su 10am-6pm. Last entry 5:15pm.*

▨ PARC DES BUTTES-CHAUMONT   PARK

Not your average Parisian park, the Buttes-Chaumont was modeled after Hyde Park in London, but it seems more like Pandora from *Avatar*. In the 13th century, this area was the site of a gibbet (an iron cage filled with the rotting corpses of criminals), a dumping ground for dead horses, a haven for worms, and a gypsum quarry (the origin of the term "plaster of Paris"). Thankfully, it's come a long way since then. Around the park and walkways, a barrier of trees provides shade, but there is more than enough sun for a picnic or laying out on the steep grassy slopes that overlook the high cliff. Bridges lead over the surrounding lake to the top, where designer Adolphe Alphand decided (why? we don't know) to build a small Roman temple. For some solitary ambling and a rare moment of peace and greenery, mosey along one of the many narrow footpaths.

i Ⓜ*Buttes-Chaumont. Free. ☒ Open daily Apr 7am-9pm; May-Aug 7am-10pm; Sept 7am-9pm; Oct-Mar 7am-8pm.*

FOOD

Say goodbye to foot-long subs and that sticky pre-sliced cheese they sell at Costco; you're not in Kansas anymore. Food is an integral part of French life—while world-famous chefs and their three-star prices are valued Parisian institutions, you don't have to break the bank for excellent cuisine, especially if you come at lunchtime (when prices are nearly half what they are at dinner). Brasseries are even more casual and foster a lively and irreverent atmosphere. The least expensive option is usually a creperie, which specialize in thin Breton pancakes filled with meat, vegetables, cheeses, chocolate, or fruits. Creperies might conjure images of yuppie brunches and awkward first dates for Americans, but here in Paris, you can often eat a crepe for less than you'd pay for a patty at the great Golden Arches. Specialty food shops, including *boulangeries* (bakeries), *patisseries* (pastry shops), and *chocolatiers* (chocolate shops), provide delicious and inexpensive picnic supplies. A number of cheap kebab and falafel stands around town also serve quick, cheap fare. *Bon appétit!*

Île de la Cité and Île St-Louis

▨ CAFÉ MED   RESTAURANT, CREPERIE $$
77 rue St-Louis-en-l'Île   ☎01 43 29 73 17

On an island dominated by tourists, Café Med is a welcoming and surprisingly affordable spot for lunch and dinner. This usually packed cafe has prix-fixe meals for under 10 euro and enormous, crispy crepes. Colorful Moulin Rouge posters decorate the walls, but this small cafe has a much more laid-back and casual vibe thanks to the French locals and experienced travelers who chatter away over hot apple tarts.

i Ⓜ*Pont Marie. Cross Pont Marie, turn right onto quai de Bourbon, left onto rue le Regrattier, then right onto rue St-Louis-en-l'Île. Café Med is on the left. Prix-fixe menus from €9.90-19.90. ☒ Open daily 11:45am-3:15pm and 6:45pm-10:30pm.*

france

MA SALLEÀ MANGER
RESTAURANT, COCKTAIL BAR $$

26 pl. Dauphine ☎01 43 29 52 34 www.masalleamanger.com

If a cafe is located in the quiet pl. Dauphine, why not make the plaza your dining room? Seat yourself outside at Ma Salle à Manger, a tiny restaurant featuring food from the southwest region of France. Feast on their Basque specialties like the celebrated Basque pâté surrounded by vintage posters from the Bayonne festivals and red-and-white checkered aprons hanging on the walls.

i Ⓜ*Cité or* Ⓜ*Pont Neuf. From Pont Neuf, cross the bridge and turn left into the square. Plats €15-18. Prix-fixe menu (entrée and plat or plat and dessert) for lunch €19.50, dinner €22.50. ☼ Open daily from 9:30am-10:30pm.*

LE PETIT PLATEAU
CAFE $$

1 quai aux Fleurs ☎01 44 07 61 86

With beautiful views of the Seine and a nice breeze to boot, this affordable cafe fills up quickly at lunchtime. Le Petit Plateau is located around the corner from the main street but is close enough to the foot traffic for some excellent people watching in relative peace and quiet. The stars of the show here are the quiches, which are made fresh every day, although the establishment also has its share of quality salads (the one with goat cheese is a popular choice).

i Ⓜ*Cité. Walk toward the Seine, turn right onto quai de la Corse, then walk until Pont Saint-Louis; the cafe is on the right, next to Esmeralda. Quiches from €8.50. Salads €10.5-11.50. Sandwiches €5-15. Lunch €12.50-16.50. ☼ Open daily 10am-6pm.*

LA RÉSERVE DE QUASIMODO
CAFE $$

4 rue de la Colombe ☎01 46 34 67 67

Conversations flow freely here, just as they have for the last seven centuries. The food here is as good as that of the next French cafe, but this establishment operates a small wine cellar to pair perfect selections with each dish (or with an assortment of cheese or charcuterie if you're not feeling too hungry). This restaurant also offers sandwiches and the cheapest takeaway crepes on the island—don't be fooled into paying more than 3 euro for a Nutella crepe!

i Ⓜ*Cité. Walk toward the Seine, turn right onto quai de la Corse, then left onto rue de la Colombe; Quasimodo is on the left. Plats €11-13. Salads €6.5-11. Sandwiches €4-7. Entrées €5. Lunch special €16. ☼ Open M-Sa noon-11pm. Kitchen open until 10 pm.*

The Marais

L'AS DU FALLAFEL
FALAFEL $

34 rue des Rosiers ☎01 48 87 63 60

L'As du Fallafel has become a landmark, and with good reason. Get a view into the kitchen, and you'll see giant tubs of freshly cut veggies and the chef frying falafel as fast as it's ordered. Patrons line up outside for the famous "falafel special"—we think of it as more of a magic trick, because we still don't know how they managed to fit everything into that pita. With greasy fried eggplant, hummus, pickled cabbage, cucumber, and, of course, plenty of crunchy falafel balls, it's huge, and it's especially fun to watch everyone try to eat it as neatly as possible. Avoid this place during dinner hours, as the wait can reach 30min.

i Ⓜ*St-Paul. Take rue Pavée and turn left onto rue des Rosiers. Falafel special €5.50. Shawarma €8. Eat-in falafel €8. ☼ Open M-Th 11am-midnight, F 11am-5pm, Su 11am-midnight.*

BREIZH CAFÉ
CAFE $$

109 rue Vieille du Temple ☎01 42 72 13 77 http://breizhcafe.com

The crepes here are easy, Breizh-y, beautiful. The galettes are made with organic eggs and flour from Brittany, and Breizh Café also serves fancy shmancy hand-made Bordier butter to smear on your crepe. Quality is king here, and nearly everything is made from some sort of premium product that melts foodies right then and there. Those on a budget will doubly appreciate the prices, with numerous options that easily ring in to under €10. Complete your meal with one of nearly 20 different ciders to wash it all down.

i Ⓜ*St-Sébastien-Froissart. Walk down rue du Pont aux Choux with the traffic and turn left onto rue Vieille du Temple; Breizh Café is on the right. Savory crepes €4.50-11.80. Sweet crepes €3.80-7.50. Ciders €3.50. Ⓩ Open W-Sa 11:30am-11pm, Su 11:30am-10pm.*

🏠 PAIN VIN FROMAGE   TRADITIONAL $$$
3 rue Geoffrey L'Angevin   ☎01 42 74 07 52 www.painvinfromage.com

Gee, wonder what they serve here? Perhaps, bread, wine, and cheese? Nobody does the Holy Trinity of French cuisine quite as well as this rustic Parisian gem. If you can handle the rich, ripe smell of cheese and hot fondue for an evening, it will be worth it. With a selection of fine cheeses from seven different regions in France and the perfect wine selection to pair them with, the gentlemen might as well twist their handle-bar mustaches with a *hoh hoh hoh* while the ladies puff on their long cigarette handles with an *ooh là là!* For a more romantic experience—you're in Paris, make the most of it—head downstairs to the quieter, dimmed, and intimate stone basement.

i Ⓜ*Rambuteau or* Ⓜ*Hôtel de Ville. Reservations recommended. Entrées €4-9.50. Charcuterie platters €8.50-10. Fondue €14-16.50. Regional cheese platters €18. Ⓩ Open daily 7-11:30pm. Closed Jul 15-Aug 15.*

Latin Quarter and St-Germain

🏠 AU P'TIT GREC   CREPERIE $
62 rue Mouffetard   ☎01 43 36 45 06

Forget about all the other crepes you've eaten—the *crepes salées* (savory crepes) at Au P'tit Grec laugh at the other crepes you've eaten. You think you've had crepes? Think again. Filled with anything from chorizo to chèvre to mushrooms to bacon, these enormous crepes are stuffed to their physical limit with everything you've ever wanted and combinations you didn't even know you desired. Be sure to add in salad, tomatoes, and onions at no extra charge. This takeout joint has a few bar stools if you can snag a seat, but on a busy day, expect quite a crowd outside of its blue doorway, with everyone clamoring for the cheap crepes before hitting up the nearby bars.

i Ⓜ*Place Monge. Walk down rue Monge, turn right onto rue Ortolan, then left onto rue Mouffe-tard. Au P'tit Grec is on the right. Crepes salées €3-5.80, crepes sucrées €1.50-4.50. Ⓩ Open daily 11am-midnight.*

🏠 HUÎTRERIE RÉGIS   OYSTERS $$$
3 rue de Montfaucon   ☎01 44 41 10 07 http://huitrerieregis.com

Oysters are the only child at Huîtrerie Régis and are showered with the utmost care and affection of the restaurant, which is dedicated entirely to the dish. The oysters are undeniably the stars of the restaurant, and Huîtrerie Régis is arguably the gem of Paris's oyster bars. The tiny, whitewashed dining room with sky blue plates feels like a Mediterranean cottage and is usually packed for dinner. If the restaurant is too crowded, Huîtrerie Régis also sells shucked oysters to go, and with oysters this good, not too much preparation is needed for a delicious meal at home.

i Ⓜ*Saint-Germain-des-Prés or Mabillon. From Saint-Germain, walk down bd Saint-Germain in the direction of the traffic, turn right onto rue du Four, then left onto rue de Montfaucon; Huîtrerie is on the left. From Mabillon, walk up rue du Four in the direction of traffic, turn right onto rue de Montfacon; Huîtrerie is on the left. Dozen oysters €18.50-59, to-go €15-37. Ⓩ Open Tu-Su noon-2:30pm and 6:30-10:30pm.*

PATISSERIE VIENNOISE

CAFE $

8 rue de l'École de Médecine   ☎01 43 26 60 48

Competition is justly fierce when it comes to patisseries in Paris, but Patisserie Viennoise takes the cake, pun fully intended. This tiny shop and small, two-room *salon de thé* is famous among Paris locals for their sumptuous hot chocolate and *café viennois*, a piping hot espresso with a very generous serving of whipped cream (Cholesterol? What's that?). Their pastries are also pretty good, but puts you in grave danger of a sugar coma when coupled with one of their hot drinks.

i ⓂOdeon or Cluny-La Sorbonne. From Odeon, walk down bd Saint-Germain in the direction of traffic for 1 block, turn right onto rue Hautefeuille, then left onto rue de l'École de Médecine; Patisserie is on the left. From Cluny-La Sorbonne, walk up bd Saint-Germain against traffic, turn left onto bd Saint-Michel and right onto rue de l'École de Médecine; Patisserie is on the right. Cafe €2. Hot chocolate €3-3.50. Café viennois €3.50-4. ☒ Open M-F 9am-7pm.

LA BOTTEGA DI PASTAVINO

ITALIAN, EPICERIE $

18 rue de Buci   ☎01 44 07 09 56

Every boulangerie in Paris sells panini, but at Pastavino, the sandwiches seem to come straight from the Italian motherland. Served on hot, thick focaccia, with mozzarella so good you'll wonder which country really knows its cheeses, the panini are the main draw of this tiny establishment and are a great deal in this expensive area. Pastavino also doubles as an Italian *épicerie*—sorry, we mean *bottega*—filled with specialty pastas, cannoli, antipasti, gnocchi, and a slew of sauces.

i ⓂMabillon. Walk up rue du Four, past bd Saint-Germain, onto rue de Buci. Pastavino is on the left. Panini €4.50-6. ☒ Open M-Sa 9:30am-8:15pm.

DE CLERQ

BELGIAN FRIES $

184 rue Saint-Jacques   ☎01 43 54 24 20

Everybody, from students from the nearby Sorbonne to professionals in sharp suits to policemen, gets in line at De Clerq for the excellent and cheap Belgian fries. The potatoes are hand-peeled, imported fresh daily, and dipped twice in beef grease before being drizzled in house sauces. The fries are the main draw here, although the burgers and the *liège* waffles are quite popular as well. This is a takeaway joint, so grab your meal and head to the Jardin du Luxembourg to munch away.

i RER Luxembourg. Walk up the bd Saint-Michel toward the Jardin du Luxembourg, turn right onto rue le Goff, right onto rue Gay-Lussac, left onto rue Royer-Collard, left onto rue Saint-Jacques, and walk 1 block; De Clerq is on the left. Fries €2.50-4.50. Burgers €3.50-5.80. Waffles €2.50. ☒ Open M-Th 11am-10pm, F-Sa 11am-midnight, Su 6:30-10pm.

LES PAPILLES

TRADITIONAL, WINE BAR $$$$

30 rue Gay Lussac   ☎01 43 25 20 79 www.lespapillesparis.fr

Part wine shop, part épicerie, part restaurant, and all delicious, Les Papilles ranks as a top choice of food critics and is always packed during dinner. The small restaurant has an old-world charm, with tiny tables, a zinc bar, a colorful mosaic floor, and an entire wall of neatly arranged bottles of wine. Although there is a fair share of tourists in this restaurant, the food remains faithful to French cuisine, and the prix-fixe, four-course menu (the only option in the house) is always expertly prepared. If you're looking to splurge for a meal, this is the place to do it.

i RER Luxembourg. Walk up the bd Saint-Michel toward the Jardin du Luxembourg, turn right onto rue le Goff, and right onto rue Gay-Lussac; Les Papilles is up the block on the right. Reservations recommended €7 corkage fee. Prix-fixe meals €35. ☒ Open Tu-Sa noon-2pm and 7-10pm.

paris

LE CAFÉ DE LA NOUVELLE MAIRIE
19 rue des Fossés Saint-Jacques

CAFE, WINE BAR $$$
☎01 44 07 04 41

After hipsters go through their rough, transitional 20s, the successful survivors morph into incredibly self-assured, unpretentious, and impeccably styled 30-somethings, and those 30-somethings come to this cafe. Here, they sip espressos as they read the latest novel and swap literary criticism over glasses of fine wine excellently paired with the small plates of French dishes. Those that aren't huddled over a two-person table are at the bar or are holding hands with their partners on the peaceful terrace outside.

i *RER Luxembourg. Walk toward the Jardin du Luxembourg, turn right onto rue le Goff, right onto rue Gay-Lussac, left onto rue Royer-Collard, left onto rue Saint-Jacques, and right onto rue des Fossés Saint-Jacques; the cafe is on the left. Wine €5-7 per glass. Entrées €5-12. plats €9-15. Dessert €6-8. Cash only ☒ Open M-F 8am-midnight.*

Invalides

The chic 7ème is low on budget options, but there are a number of quality restaurants here that are worth the extra euro.

⊠ BARTHÉLÉMY
51 rue de Grenelle

FROMAGERIE $
☎01 45 48 56 75

The French go hard on cheese, and every square inch of this famous fromagerie is packed with every type of (expensive) cheese imaginable. This store is frequently filled with older French customers who know their brie and hang tight with Madame Barthélémy. Barthélémy is quite small and crowded, so the staff may not be able to give those without a cheese palate the low-down on the goods—it's best to know your preferences before you go. The limiting factors here are your wallet and how long you can endure the sharp, pungent scent of ripening cheese.

i Ⓜ*Rue de Bac. Walk south down bd Raspail and turn right onto rue de Grenelle; the shop is on the right, just before the next corner. Cheese from €3-12. ☒ Open M-F 8:30am-1:30pm and 4-7pm, Sa 8:30am-1:30pm and 3-7pm.*

⊠ CHEZ LUCIE
15 rue Augereau

CREOLE $$
☎01 45 55 08 74 www.restuarant-chez-lucie.fr

You've been working that French scowl to perfection, but at this creole hole-in-the-wall, it's actually okay to grin and chat up the owner, who regularly shoots the breeze with his customers and will gladly show you pictures of his wife. Specializing in dishes from Martinique, Chez Lucie has options you won't normally see in Paris, from fish in coconut milk to spicy catfish to the more adventurous shark toufée. The portions are enormous for such a low price, and the *ti'ponch* (rum punch) will knock you on your ass.

i Ⓜ*École Militaire. Walk toward the Eiffel Tower on av. de la Bourdonnais, turn right onto rue de Grenelle, and take an immediate left onto rue Augereau. The restaurant is on the right (with a bright yellow awning). Entrées €7. plats €13-20. 3-course lunch special €16. Dinner menu with entrée, plat, and dessert €26. ☒ Open daily noon-2pm and 7-11pm.*

LE SACÀ DOS
47 rue de Bourgogne

TRADITIONAL $$$
☎01 45 55 15 35 www.le-sac-a-dos.fr

This restaurant is near some of Paris's biggest attractions, but its location on a quiet street saves it from mobs of tourists. Le Sac à Dos is a small, unassuming French restaurant that buys ingredients fresh every morning from local markets. For budget travelers, this place is on the pricier end, but you're paying for some peace to go with your *foie gras* and *mousse au chocolat* (served in a cookie bowl).

i Ⓜ*Varenne. Walk away from Pont d'Alexandre III on bd des Invalides and turn left onto rue de Varenne. Walk 1 block, past the Musée-Rodin, to rue de Bourgogne and turn left. The restaurant is on the right. Prix-fixe dinner €20. Plats €12-18. Desserts €6. ☒ Open M-Sa 11am-2:30pm and 6:30-11pm.*

france

DEBAUVE&GALLAIS   CHOCOLATIER $

30 rue des Saints-Pères   ☎01 45 48 54 67 www.debauve-et-gallais.com

Around here, DG isn't short for a fashion house—cue Debauve&Gallais, former royal chocolate suppliers for the rulers of France. Sulpice Debauve, chemist-turned-chocolatier, landed his cushy gig when Marie Antoinette complained that her medicine tasted bad, and Debauve, unlike parents worldwide who would ignore these complaints, created *pistoles* (chocolate coins) for her. Debauve later took in his nephew, Gallais, and today the family-owned chocolate shop continues to sell its renowned and pricey currency alongside a variety of nougats, ganaches, and other assorted bonbons.

i Ⓜ*St-Germain-des-Prés. Walk west on bd St-Germain and turn right onto rue des Saints-Pères. Boite de Pistoles de Marie-Antoinette €34.* ☺ *Open M-Sa 9am-7pm.*

Champs-Élysées

◪ **TY YANN**   CREPERIE $

10 rue de Constantinople   ☎01 40 08 00 17

The ever-smiling Breton chef and owner, M. Yann, cheerfully prepares outstanding and relatively inexpensive *galettes* (€7.50-11) and crepes in this tiny, unassuming restaurant, where the walls are decorated with his mother's pastoral paintings. Many of the crepes here are expertly flambéed for meals that are too hot to handle, and some creative concoctions include La Vannetaise (sausage sauteed in cognac, Emmental cheese, and onions; €10). The *galettes* will more than fill you for a meal, so come with a friend and split a sweet crepe for dessert—we recommend the honey almond lemon. Wash it all down with a bowl of cider in an adorable ceramic mug.

i Ⓜ*Europe. Walk up rue de Rome with the train tracks on the right and turn left onto rue de Constantinople; Ty Yann is on the right. Crepe €7.50-11. Credit card min. €12.* ☺ *Open M noon-2:30pm, Tu-F noon-2:30pm and 7:30-10:30pm, Sa 7:30-10:30pm.*

◪ **LADURÉE**   TEA HOUSE $

18 rue Royale   ☎01 49 60 21 79 www.laduree.com

Opened in 1862, Ladurée started off as a modest bakery. It has since become so famous that a *Gossip Girl* employee was flown here to buy macaroons so Chuck could properly offer his heart to Blair. On a more typical day the rococo decor of this tea salon—the original location of a franchise that now extends to 13 countries—attracts a jarring mix of well-groomed shoppers and tourists in sneakers. Along with the infamous mini macaroons arranged in pyramids in the window (beware: the rose flavor tastes like bathroom freshener), most items here are liable to induce a diabetic coma. Ladurée also sells other pastries, but save your money for their expensive macaroons. Dine in the salon or queue up for a culinary orgasm to go.

i Ⓜ*Concorde. Walk up rue Royale toward the Church Madeleine, away from the pl. de Concorde. Ladurée is on right. Other locations at 75 av. des Champs-Elysées, 21 rue Bonaparte, and 64 bd Haussmann. Box of 6 mini macaroons €15.80.* ☺ *Open M-Th 8am-7:30pm, F-Sa 8am-8pm, Su 10am-7pm.*

AMOUR DE BURGER   BURGERS $$

7 rue Godot de Mauroy   ☎01 53 30 09 72 www.amourdeburger.com

Amour de Burger will have you falling in love with burgers all over again. Set up like an American greasy spoon, this affordable French burger joint still maintains a European air, with most patrons sipping on white wine or watching a soccer match on the TV above the bar. Like all French bread, the brioche buns rank better than their American counterparts, and the patties are a bit thicker and stockier than those from American diners. The portions, however, are not quite as French and will leave you both stuffed and head-over-heels in love with this Parisian anomaly. Pescetarians and vegetarians should spring for the salmon or veggie burgers, and those who want a French twist can order a burger foie gras.

i ⓂMadeleine. *Facing the church, turn around to the left, toward Pinacotheque; pass Pinacotheque and take the 1st left. Amour de Burger is on the left. Burger €12-18.50. Dinner menu €10 and 13.* ☒ *Open M noon-3pm, Tu-F noon-3pm and 7-11:30pm.*

Opéra and Canal St-Martin

▨ CHARTIER   TRADITIONAL $$
7 rue du Faubourg Montmartre   ☎01 47 70 86 29 www.restaurant-chartier.com

Even with the swift-footed waiters and the two huge floors packed with Parisians and tourists, there just isn't enough Chartier to go around. On a busy night, you'll just have to wait your turn to eat in the famous restaurant's glam, art deco interior. Chartier has been in business for over 100 years, and with its fame, it could easily charge out the you-know-what for its menu, but thankfully for budget travelers, it has held true to its original purpose of hearty French meals at decent prices. Its popularity, however, means that efficiency is prized here, so don't expect an intimate, drawn-out meal. Seat, order, food, check, and don't even try to pull any funny business with special requests.

i ⓂGrands Boulevards. *Walk with traffic down bd Poissonnière and turn right onto rue du Faubourg Montmartre. Reservations recommended for larger groups. Menu €18. Entrées €2-7. plats €8.50-13.50. Cheese plates €2-2.60. Desserts €2.20-4.* ☒ *Open daily 11:30am-10pm.*

▨ SUPERNATURE   BRUNCH, ORGANIC $
12 rue de Trévise   ☎01 47 70 21 03 www.super-nature.fr

After all that cheese and wine, it's time to feel good about your life choices, and Supernature is here to help. The restaurant serves up quite a few delicious healthy options, with a few non-vegetarian choices tossed in—this is France after all. Expect to see and hear buzzwords like "local" and "organic" around here and a packed crowd at the incredible Sunday brunch. For those looking for a cheaper meal, get in line with the Parisians at the takeout joint down the block, with its generous *formules* for €7.60.

i ⓂGrands Boulevards. *Walk against the traffic on bd Poissonnière, turn left onto rue Rougemont, then right onto rue Bergère, then left onto rue de Trévise. Supernature on right. Reservations recommended for Su brunch. Brunch €20. Lunch menu €16-20. Takeout formules €7.60-8.60.* ☒ *Open M-F noon-4pm, Su 11:30am-4pm.*

▨ BOB'S JUICE BAR   SMOOTHIES, BAGELS $
15 rue Lucien Sampaix   ☎09 50 06 36 18

This juice bar wouldn't raise an eyebrow in Brooklyn, but its vegetarian fare (read: not just salads) and health-food focus make it stand out in Paris. The communal table at this small, hippie, eco-conscious smoothie and lunchtime spot is usually filled with backpackers and locals alike. Those looking to detox with veggies and superfoods will find more than enough acai and quinoa salad in the house, although Bob's also serves homemade pastries for those with a sweet tooth.

i ⓂJacques Bonsergent. *Walk up bd Magenta toward Gare du Nord and turn right onto rue Lucien Sampaix. Juice Bar is ½ a block up on the left. Smoothies €6. Bagel sandwiches €6.* ☒ *Open M-F 7:30am-3pm.*

▨ CHEZ MAURICE   BISTRO $$
26 rue des Vinaigriers   ☎01 46 07 07 91

Finally, a real, dirt cheap French meal. While the inside may seem standard for a bistro—think red-checkered tablecloths and curtains, dark wood interiors, and framed, vintage-y posters—the *escargot* and steak tartare here make it a favorite of young locals with scruffy beards. Hold out for the desserts, where you'll be hard-pressed to choose between crème brûlée or chocolate fondue.

i ⓜJacques Bonsergent. *Walk up bd Magenta toward Gare du Nord and turn right onto rue Lucien Sampaix. Walk 1 block to rue des Vinaigriers and turn right. The restaurant is on the right. Menu formule €11-18.* ⏰ *Open M-F noon-3pm and 6:30-11pm, Sa 6:30-11pm.*

Bastille

▨ RESTAURANT 3FC
KEBABS, ALGERIAN $

16 rue d'Aligre
☎01 43 46 07 73

If you're starving, only have a meager supply of coins jangling in your pocket, and don't want to eat out of the garbage, hit 3FC. Not only is the food cheaper than dirt (€0.70 per kebab—we estimate that the current market price for dirt is at least €0.90 per handful), but it's bangin' delicious. Choose from a selection of raw kebabs in the front freezer, take them to the kitchen, and wait for the fresh-grilled meat to be brought back to your seat. This place is packed on a nightly basis (note: kebabs are particularly popular among the drunk-munchies crowd), but the beauty of food on a stick is that it's just as mobile as you are.

i ⓜLedru-Rollin. *Walk east on rue du Faubourg St-Antoine away from Bastille, take the 3rd right onto rue du Cotte, and turn left onto rue d'Aligre. Kebab €0.70-2. Sandwiches with fries €4. Cous-cous €7. Entrées €3.50. plats €6.* ⏰ *Open Sept-Jun daily 11am-midnight.*

▨ WEST COUNTRY GIRL
CREPERIE $$

6 passage St-Ambroise
☎01 47 00 72 54 www.westcountrygirl.com

West Country Girl is where Parisians take their lucky visiting friends for an excellent taste of the city's quintessential dish. This small creperie is tucked into a quiet side street in Bastille, and its simple wooden furniture, large open windows, and white walls with flecks of pink paint make the place feel like someone's extended dining room. The galettes here are simple, and the menu is short and filled with classics, like goat cheese and spinach and ham, cheese, and eggs. To top it all off, the lunch menu is unbeatable, ringing in at €10.50 for a savory and dessert crepe with a glass of Breton cider. Be sure to order the melt-in-your-mouth house specialty, a homemade salted caramel butter crepe.

i Parmentier. *Walk down av. Parmentier toward rue Oberkampf, turn left onto rue Lechevin, then left onto Passage St-Ambroise; West Country Girl is on the left. Lunch menu €10.50. Savory crepes €4-8, sweet €2.60-7.50.* ⏰ *Open Tu-Sa noon-2pm and 7:30-10pm.*

▨ AUGUSTE
SANDWICHES $

10 rue St-Sabin
☎01 47 00 77 84 www.augusteparis.com

Shame on all the other *sandwicheries* when AUGUSTE sells 'em at €2-3 apiece (with organic ingredients!) without breaking a sweat. Nothing too fancy here, just the good old staples that you can wash down with their freshly made smoothie of the day. Pinch some pennies with trendy adults and students in this sparsely designed, stone-walled spot and marvel at the deal you're getting.

i ⓜBréguet-Sabin. *Walk against the traffic on bd Richard-Lenoir and continue down rue St-Sabin against the traffic; AUGUSTE is on the left. Sandwiches €2-4. Soups €3-5. Smoothies €3-5. Cash only.* ⏰ *Open Sept-Jun M-Sa noon-2:30pm and 5pm-1am; Jul-Aug noon-2:30pm.*

▨ LE GOYAVIER
CREOLE $$$

4 rue St-Bernard
☎01 43 79 61 41

Hailing from the Réunion Island in the Indian Ocean, the chef here knows how to cook up a real South Asian meal and cooks it damn well. The place doesn't hide behind any fancy, ornamental decor—the sign out front is plain and the tables are unremarkable. The only complaint around here is about the prices, with each dish coming in at €20 and over. If you're willing to splurge, though, the

paris

generous servings and superb *rougail* sausages straight from the pot are worth your while.

i Ⓜ*Ledru Rollin. Walk east on rue du Fauberge St-Antoine and turn left onto rue St-Bernard. The restaurant is on the right behind the scaffolding. Reservations recommended. Entrées €6-10. plats €20-22. House punch €6. Cash or check only. ☪ Open M-Tu and Th-Su 8pm-midnight.*

CANNIBALE CAFÉ   TRADITIONAL $$

93 rue Jean-Pierre Timbaud   ☎01 49 29 00 40 http://cannibalecafe.com

Don't be turned off by the name—believe it or not, this restaurant has a decent list of vegetarian options, and its Rococo bar and creative and stylish clientele are leagues beyond any cannibalistic barbarianism. Intellectuals and artistes frequent this bar during the day to loiter over coffee and the free Wi-Fi. Come dinnertime, classier friends turned off by the hedonism of Oberkampf pop over for a late night drink or a dish of rich tuna rilletes or duck confit.

i Ⓜ*Couronnes. Walk down rue Jean-Pierre Timbaud; Cannibale is on the right. Weekday lunch menu €9.90-13.90. Entrées €6.50-9.50. plats €13-23. Platters €14. Desserts €7-9. ☪ Open daily 8am-2am.*

PAUSE CAFE   CAFE $$

41 rue de Charonne   ☎01 48 06 80 33

Hipster glasses are an unofficial prerequisite for working here. People climb over themselves to get a seat on the large outdoor terrace to peruse the straight-forward menu of salads, beer, tartare, and honey-glazed duck breast. French people adore this place and chatter away all day on the terrace devoid of any Anglophones. This place is so hip that it was featured in the '90s hit film, *Chacun Cherche Son Chat*, which we suspect is the main reason people come here.

i Ⓜ*Ledru-Rollin. Take av. Ledru-Rollin north and turn left onto rue de Charonne. Entrée €6-11. plats €12-15.80. Desserts €5.50-6. Brunch €19.50. ☪ Open M-Sa 7am-2am, Su 7am-8pm.*

Montparnasse and Southern Paris

▨ CHEZ GLADINES   BASQUE $$

30 rue des 5 Diamants   ☎01 45 80 70 10

Chez Gladines has the exposed brick walls and red-checkered tablecloth of any other French bistro, but the jam-packed restaurant and prominent Basque flag tells a different story. This joint and its enormous salads are hugely popular with customers, who will gladly wait for an hour for a table during dinner rush. Dishes are relatively cheap for the amount of food you get, making it a great place to share dishes.

i Ⓜ*Place d'Italie. Take bd Auguste Blanqui away from pl. d'Italie and turn left onto rue des 5 Diamants. Salads €7-11. plats €10-15. Wine €2.40-3 per glass. Cash only. ☪ Open M-F noon-3pm and 5pm-midnight, Sa-Su noon-4pm and 5pm-1am.*

▨ PHO 14   VIETNAMESE $

129 av. de Choisy   ☎01 45 83 61 15

If you're hankering for good *pho*, there's no need to fly to Vietnam—make it Pho 14. A local favorite that draws starving students and penny-pinching barmen, Pho 14 (not to be confused with Pho 13 next door) serves huge bowls of *pho* beef (flank steak in spicy soup with rice) for reasonable prices. The hot meals and crowded tables make for a steamy restaurant during the summer, but you can cool down with red bean, coconut milk, and cane sugar drink. This restaurant usually has a line out the door at night and during the lunch rush, so try to arrive on the early or late side of dinner.

i Ⓜ*Tolbiac. Walk east on rue de Tolbiac and turn left onto av. de Choisy. Pho €7-8.50. Drinks €3.60. ☪ Open daily 9am-11pm.*

LE DRAPEAU DE LA FIDELITÉ

21 rue Copreaux

TRADITIONAL, VIETNAMESE $

☎01 45 66 73 82 http://phamconquan.free.fr

The owner is a former philosophy professor from Saigon University who decided to switch things up and opened this hole-in-the-wall dive that serves up delicious bowls of *pho*, *beef bourguignon*, and other goodies at €6 a plate. The university air still lingers in the reams of books on the wall, the crowds of students, and the prices: for his students, whom he affectionately calls his "*chouchous du quartier,*" or "favorites of the neighborhood," the price drops to €5. Don't forget to drink some beer for €2—the cheerful red font outside reminds you to "Drink a little bit. It's pleasant." We couldn't agree more.

i ⓜVolontaires. *Walk against the traffic on rue de Vaugirard, turn right onto rue Copreaux; Le Drapeau is on the right. plat €6, students €5. Coffee €1. Beer €2-2.50. Wine €2-2.60. Cash only.* ⓩ *Open daily 11:30am-10pm. Kitchen open 11:30am-8:30pm.*

KHAI TRI

93 av. d'Ivry

BANH MI $

☎01 45 82 96 81

You think you know cheap? Your local banh mi joint at home is probably pricier, and less delicious, than Khai Tri. At €3.20 for a half-baguette bursting with all the usual goodies of sliced pork, pâté, and pickled carrots, the banh mi here is simply unbeatable. With only three different types of sandwiches and not much else on the menu, this tiny sandwich shop is wildly popular with customers, who frequently line up outside for a cheap lunchtime sandwich.

i ⓜTolbiac. *Walk down rue de Tolbiac toward av. de Choisy Banh, away from the McDonald's. Walk 1 block, turn right onto av. d'Ivry; Khai Tri is on the right. Banh mi €2.90-3.20.* ⓩ *Open Tu-Sa 9:40am-5:40pm, Su 10am-5:30pm.*

CREPERIE JOSSELIN

67 rue du Montparnasse

CREPERIE $$

☎01 43 20 93 50

In a city where you can't walk two blocks without passing a crepe stand and on a block teeming with creperies, Josselin still manages to stand out thanks to its delicious dedication to the culinary craft of crepe-making. Miniature violins, lace window curtains, and little porcelain teacups decorate the wooden interior of this cozy, grandmotherly restaurant. The edges of the Breton crepes here are thin, crisp, and dainty, and the pocket inside is full of terrific combinations, like warm goat cheese drizzled with honey or banana and chocolate flambéed with rum. The wait can be long for dinner, so come for the lunch special (€12 for a savory crepe, a dessert crepe, and a drink).

i ⓜEdgar Quinet. *Walk up rue du Montparnasse with traffic; Crêperie Josselin is on the right. Savory crepes €5-9.80. Sweet crepes €5-7.80. Cash only.* ⓩ *Open Tu-F 11:30am-3pm and 6-11:30pm, Sa noon-midnight, Su noon-11pm.*

LE TEMPS DES CERISES

18 rue de la Butte aux Cailles

TRADITIONAL $$

☎01 45 89 69 48

Not only is this place an excellent French bistro, but in line with the hipster-activist background of the neighborhood, Le Temps is an anti-cellphone (turn it off!) worker's cooperative since 1976. Their history may give them major street cred, but this place is popular with locals and students for the quality of its food and lively atmosphere during the dinner hours. It's location at the heart of Quarter Butte-aux-Cailles also makes it a perfect jumping off point for drinks later in the night.

i ⓜCorvisart. *Walk toward rue Corvisart away from Pizza Hut on the same side of bd Auguste-Blanqui as Pizza Hut. Turn left onto a passageway and take the stairs through Jardin Brassai, pass rue des 5 Diamants, turn right onto rue Gérard, turn left onto rue de la Butte aux Cailles; Le Temps is on the left. plat du jour €11. Lunch menu M-F, Su €12-15. Dinner menu €19.50-24.50. Entrées €4.5-15. plats €11-20. Wine €3-5.* ⓩ *Open daily 11:45am-2:30pm and 7:15-11:45pm.*

paris

ATELIER AUBRAC

51 bd Garibaldi

TRADITIONAL $$$$

☎01 45 66 96 78 http://www.atelieraubrac.com/

This cool, traditional French restaurant is a carnivorous cavern. With hefty plates full of the kind of meat you'd expect a lumberjack or quarterback to enjoy, Atelier Aubrac is a place you want to come to with an empty stomach. If you're not sure what to order, have a chat with the gregarious chef, although it'd be hard to go wrong with a 10oz. rib eye steak or a 7oz. rump steak. Lunchtime tends to bring in a professional crowd, but the clientele gets more diverse at dinner.

i ⓂSèvres-Lecourbe. Walk northwest on bd Garibaldi; the restaurant is on the right. Lunch menu €16-19. Dinner menu €23.50-27.50. Entrées €7-13. plats €14-29. 🕐 Open M-F 12:30-2:15pm and 7:30-10:15pm, Sa 7-10:15pm.

Auteuil, Passy & Batignolles

BATIGNOLLES ORGANIC PRODUCE MARKET

bd de Batignolles

MARKET $

There are only two organic markets of note in Paris, and in comparison to the larger, more crowded market at bd Raspail, the one at Batignolles is smaller, less chaotic, and, as a result, much more fun. Stretching across bd de Batignolles every Saturday morning, the Batignolles Organic Produce Market is a delectable jumble of singing shoppers, hats, flowers, bottles of apple cider, honey, textiles, loaves of bread, and obscenely large hunks of cheese, not to mention gorgeous, organic fruits and vegetables. You can buy a crêpe here, nibble on samples as you stroll through, or construct a gourmet picnic with ease and schlep it to the nearby Square des Batignolles.

i ⓂRome. On the traffic divider along bd des Batignolles, at the border of the 8ème and 17ème. 🕐 Open Sa 9am-2pm.

3 PIÈCES CUISINE

25 rue de Chéroy

BRUNCH, TRADITIONAL $$

☎01 44 90 85 10

3 Pièces Cuisine keeps things casual with (surprise!) just three spacious rooms and a bar that comes alive at night. The one-page menu is equally simple, with a variety of burgers, tartines, sandwiches, and salads. The restaurant's bright red, green, purple, and yellow colors match the lively clientele, who pack 3PC on Sundays for the ultra-cheap brunch (€11) and at night for the mojitos before heading out into the night.

i ⓂVilliers. Head east down bd de Batignolles (which is bd de Courcelles in the other direction) and take a left onto rue de Chéroy. The restaurant is on the next corner on the left. Brunch €11. Prix fixe menus €10-15. Plats €7.50. Cocktails €5-7. 🕐 Open daily 8:30am-1:30am.

LE CLUB DES 5

57 rue des Batignolles

TRADITIONAL $$

☎01 53 04 94 73 www.leclubdes5.fr

The five friends who founded this fun restaurant wanted to bring the vibe of their childhood in the '80s to the place. Le Club des 5 is a combination of nostalgia and hipster, with street signs and cartoon characters decorating the walls of this casual restaurant and one entire section plastered with colorful magazine cutouts. The menu contains grown-up dishes, such as rotisserie chicken and hanger steak, alongside the ones for the kid in you, like the Megacheeseburger and Oreo cheesecake.

i ⓂPl. de Clichy. With your back to Montmartre, walk 3 blocks down bd des Batignolles and turn right onto rue des Batignolles. The cafe is 2 blocks down on the left. Lunch plat €11; entrée and plat €14; entrée, plat, and dessert €17. Dinner plats €16-20. Brunch €26. 🕐 Open M 7:30-11pm, Tu-Su noon-2:30pm and 7:30-11pm. Brunch served Sa-Su noon-4pm.

LE PATIO PROVENÇAL   TRADITIONAL $$$
116 rue des Dames   ☎01 42 93 73 73 www.patioprovencal.fr

Those in the market for an intimate meal–couples and double daters alike–
should head to Le Patio Provençal for expertly done French dining. A wonderful
skylight brightens the seating in the middle of the restaurant, while several
wooden booths allow for more private dining. In the background, Norah Jones
serenades your indoor garden dinner to round out the relaxed vibe. The menu
may not be exotic for Paris, but you won't hear any complaints about their duck
confit and lamb chops, and vegetarians rejoice at their options at this restaurant.
Be sure to leave enough room for all three courses—you won't want to miss out.

i ⓂVilliers. *Follow rue de Levis away from the intersection and turn right onto rue des Dames.
Lunch men €17. Dinner menu from €24, weekends €28. Entrées €9. plats €17-20. Desserts €8.* ⏲
Open M-Sa noon-2:30pm and 7-10:30pm.

Montmartre

Montmartre has tons of great food options at relatively reasonable prices, especially
considering how popular the area is with tourists.

LE CAFÉ LOMI   CAFE $
3 Rue Marcadet   ☎09 80 39 56 24 www.cafelomi.com

This isn't a cafe that you just "happen" upon—this coffee shop is a bit far flung,
which saves it from the hordes of tourists who would drink up all the carefully
crafted *noisettes* and the hipsters who would take up all the comfortable leather
chairs and couches. Le Café Lomi used to just be in the business of hand-se-
lecting coffees from all over the world and expertly roasting it on site, but
thankfully for us, it now also serves espressos made from the roasted beans to
neighborhood patrons.

i ⓂMarcadet Poissonniers. *Walk down rue Ordener, past bd Ornano, 4 blocks. The cafe is on the
right. Espresso €2-2.40. Cappuccino €3.90-4.30.* ⏲ *Open W-Su 10am-7pm.*

LE POTAGER DU PÈRE THIERRY   TRADITIONAL $$
16 rue Trois Frères   ☎01 53 28 26 20

Almost as soon as this tiny bistro opens its doors, couples and friends swoop
in, grab a coveted table, and settle in for a somewhat cramped but masterfully
prepared dinner. The red-checkered napkins and smooth stone walls set the
scene for a traditional French bistro experience, but the light fixtures made
from colanders and the shiny wooden tables add a more modern twist to this
restaurant. The specialty of the house is undoubtedly the *l'œuf cocottes au foie
gras* (eggs baked in foie gras; €7), although the catch of the day and the filet
mignon are also standouts on the menu.

i ⓂAbsesses. *Walk down rue Yvonne le Tac, turn left onto rue des Trois Frères; Le Potager is on
the right. Reservations recommended. Entrées €6-7. plats €12-16. Dessert €6-8.* ⏲ *Open daily
8pm-midnight.*

LE BAL CAFÉ   BRUNCH $$$
6 Impasse de la Défense   ☎01 44 70 75 51 www.le-bal.fr

Nobody does brunch quite like the British, and with the stellar combination of
truly exceptional coffee (none of that overpriced instant stuff found in Parisian
cafes) and former chefs from Rose Bakery running the kitchen, Le Bal Café has
become quite the darling of food critics. Throw in an art exhibition space in a
former ballroom next to the minimalist dining space, and you've got yourself a
bona fide hipster hangout.

i ⓂPlace de Clichy. *Walk up av. de Clichy away from the roundabout for 2 blocks, turn right onto
Impasse de la Défense; the cafe is on the right. Reservations recommended for brunch. Entrées
€6-8. plats €13-16. Dessert €6.* ⏲ *Open W-F noon-2:30pm and 8-10:30pm, Sa 11am-3pm and
8-10:30pm, Su 11am-4pm.*

paris

Buttes-Chaumont & Belleville

LA BOULANGERIE PAR VÉRONIQUE MAUCLERC   BOULANGERIE, PATISSERIE

83 rue de Crimée   ☎01 42 40 64 55

Baking its divine bread in one of only four remaining wood-fired ovens in France, this *boulangerie* uses only organic ingredients in its creations. Run by Véronique herself, the bakers here begin mixing their mythical, organic dough at 2am. She doesn't even use yeast—instead, *levain*, a natural riser, is added to the bread, which is then left for up to 15hr. to rise. While on the outside this *boulangerie* may seem similar to all the other ones you'll come across in Paris, don't make the mistake of walking blithely by. People make the pilgrimage here for the bread, so for once, skip the croissant (gasp!). Trust us—the pistachio, almond, hazelnut bread is worth your precious cash. If you don't want to buy a whole loaf, ask for a *tranche* (slice) instead. Be sure to stop by the *salon de thé* tucked in the back for a spoil-me-rotten Sunday brunch.

i ⓂLaumière. Walk northeast on av. Jean Jaurès, then turn right onto rue de Crimée; the boulangerie is near the end of the block on the right. Chocolate chip cookies €2.10. Chocolate tarts €3.80. Lemon meringue tarts €4.10. ⌚ Boulangerie open Tu-F 9am-2pm and 3:30-8pm, Sa-Su 8am-8pm. Salon de thé open Tu-Sa 9am-5:30pm.

L'ATLANTIDE   NORTH AFRICAN $$$

7 av. Laumière   ☎01 42 45 09 81 www.latlantide.fr

Moroccan food is all the rage in Paris, but for L'Atlantide, it's more than a trend. Cough up a pretty penny because this Berber restaurant knows what it's doing and isn't afraid to charge top dollar for its tajines and couscous dishes. Traditional North African rugs hang from the ceiling, and wood carvings and driftwood room dividers create a decidedly Moroccan air. Even though "As Time Goes By" may not be playing in the background, with all the dim lighting and imported North African wine, we bet that a meal here could be the start of many beautiful friendships.

i ⓂLaumière. Walk south down av. de Laumière toward the park. L'Atlantide is near the end of the road on the right. Entrées €6-10. Couscous €13-19.50. Tajines €14-19.50. ⌚ Open M-F 7-10:30pm, Sa-Su noon-2:30pm and 7-10:30pm.

NIGHTLIFE

You may have told your parents, professors, and prospective employers that you've traveled to Paris to compare the works of Monet and Manet (hint: it's not just one letter), but after more than 50 years in the business, we at *Let's Go* know it isn't just art that draws the young and the restless to Europe. If you're traveling to drink and mingle, Paris will not disappoint. Nightlife here is debaucherous, and there's something for everyone. Bars are either chic cafes bursting with people watching potential, party joints all about rock and teen angst, or laid-back local spots that double as havens for English-speakers. Clubbing in Paris is less about hip DJs and cutting-edge beats than it is about dressing up and being seen. Drinks are expensive, so Parisians usually stick to the ones included with the cover. Many clubs accept reservations, which means there's no available seating on busy nights. It's best to be confident (but not aggressive) about getting in. Bars in the 5ème and 6ème draw international students, while Châtelet-Les Halles attracts a slightly older set. The Marais is the center of Parisian GLBT nightlife.

france

Île de la Cité and Île St-Louis

Far from a party spot, the islands are a bit of a nightlife wasteland. If you're looking for a quiet terrace on which to share a beer and conversation, this is your spot.
Tourists tend to clear out of les Îles after dark, so the pace is comfortably slower
here.

LE SOLEIL D'OR
15 bd du Palais

BRASSERIE

☎01 43 54 22 22

This place is a tourist magnet during the day thanks to its location at a busy
intersection, faux-modern seating, and Berthillon ice cream. You may not
want to stay here all night, but come get schwasty during happy hour, with
pints of beer and cocktails for €6 until 9pm.

i Ⓜ*Cité. Turn left down bd du Palais from the Métro; the brasserie is on the corner. Happy hour
3-9pm. Beer €6-8. Cocktails €6-9. Happy hour drinks €6. ☒ Open daily 6:15am-10pm.*

Châtelet-Les Halles

The bars in Châtelet are close together and easy to find. This neighborhood has its
fair share of GLBT bars (though it's no Marais) and smaller establishments that are
packed until dawn.

📧 BANANA CAFÉ
13 rue de la Ferronerie

BAR, CLUB,GLBT

☎01 42 33 35 31 www.bananacafeparis.com

Situated in the heart of Châtelet, Banana Café is the GLBT capital outside of
the Marais. The club suits a wide clientele that ranges from the young crowds
taking advantage of the cheap happy hour on the terrace to the erotic dancers stationed outside. Head downstairs after midnight for a lively piano bar
and more dance space before hopping out at dawn to catch the Métro back
home. There are weekly themed nights that take place Th-Sa from midnight
to dawn.

i Ⓜ*Châtelet. Walk 3 blocks down rue St-Denis and turn right onto rue de la Ferronerie. Cover F-Sa
€10; includes 1 drink. Beer €5.50. Cocktails €11. Happy hour pints €3; cocktails €4-5. ☒ Open
daily 6pm-6am. Happy hour 6-11pm.*

📧 LES CARIATIDES
3 rue de Palestro

BAR, CONCERT VENUE

☎01 42 36 19 72 www.lescariatides.com

Clearly this bar's signs about moderate drinking are less than effective,
and the only thing that's louder than the music here is the sound of drunk
partiers trying to sing along. Downstairs in the basement, Les Cariatides has
gigs playing anything from rock to pop to indie nearly every night, and it
quickly becomes full on the weekends. For some fresh air, wrangle your way
to the bar and order some decently priced tapas before heading back down
to dance the night away.

i Ⓜ*Etienne Marcel. Walk up rue de Turbigo against the flow of traffic, turn left onto rue de Palstre;
Les Cariatides is on the left. Shot €4. Pint of beer €6-8. Tapas €10 for 5. Happy hour pint €4-5;
cocktails €6. Extra €1 on all drinks after 1am. ☒ Open M-Sa 6pm-4am, Su 2-4pm. Happy hour
M-Sa 6-9pm.*

The Marais

There are about as many bars and clubs in the Marais as there are people, and the
establishments you'll find here are just as diverse as the crowds.

📧 CANDELARIA
52 rue de Saintonge

BAR, TACOS

☎01 42 74 41 28 www.candelariaparis.com

This bar takes hole-in-the-wall to a completely new level. Fronted by a greasy
tacos joint, Candelaria is easy to miss and just looks like an oddly popular
bougie dive where you can get some good guac. But wiggle past the crowds
(and there are always crowds), and you will happen upon a small, unmarked

door—make your way inside and fall through the proverbial rabbit hole into one of Paris's most popular bars. This hidden, stone-walled bar is much larger than the tapas joint outside and is even more crowded. The dim bar is usually standing room only and is quite popular with the locals, hipsters, and intellectuals, with a healthy presence of Anglophone students thrown in. The house punch, made with cognac and spiced wine, is pricey but a must, and their cocktails are absolutely delicious.

i *Filles du Calvaires. Walk down rue des Filles du Calvaire with traffic, turn right onto rue de Bretagne, then right onto rue de Saintonge; Candelaria is on the right. House punch €54 for 4-6 people. Cocktails €12. Guac and chips €5.50. ⏰ Kitchen in front open W 12:30-11pm, Th-Sa 12:30pm-midnight, Su 12:30-11pm. Bar open daily 6pm-2am.*

RAIDD BAR
BAR, CLUB, GLBT

23 rue Vieille du Temple   ☎01 42 77 04 88

If you want a penis, or just want to see one, come here. Sparkling disco balls light up Raidd Bar, as do the muscular, tank-topped torsos of the sexy male bartenders. After 11pm, performers strip down in the glass shower built into the wall and begin to rub themselves clean while your mind gets dirty. There's a notoriously strict door policy: women aren't allowed unless they are outnumbered by (gorgeous) men, and since this place has no cover, prepare for a long wait on the weekends.

i Ⓜ*Hôtel de Ville. Walk up rue du Renard, turn right onto rue de la Verrerie, then left onto rue du Temple; Raidd Bar is on the left. Beer €6.50. Mixed drinks €8.70, €6 before 9pm. Cocktails €8.70-11, €6-8 before 9pm. Happy hour beer €4.20. ⏰ Open M-Th 5pm-4am, F-Su 5pm-5am. Happy hour 5-11pm.*

LE BARAV
WINE BAR

6 rue Charles François Dupuis   ☎01 48 04 57 59 www.lebarav.fr

Even the staunchest, frown-iest Parisians manage to have a good time at this *très* popular wine bar. Old hipsters, young hipsters, students, and professionals—everyone makes the trek to the northern reaches of the Marais to dine at this dimly lit, wooden bar for the delicious tapenades, large antipasti, charcuterie platters, and perfectly paired cheap glasses of wine from the cave next door. Reservations are recommended in the evening unless you want to be unceremoniously bounced from your table when your time is up.

i Ⓜ*Temple. Head down Passage Sainte-Elisabeth with the traffic, turn right onto rue du Temple, left onto rue Dupetit-Thouars, then left onto rue Charles-François Dupuis; Le Barav is on the right. Reservations recommended. Lunch menu €10. Entrées €5.50. plats €11.50-12.50. Salads €10.50. Platters €5.50-16. Glass of wine €5. Pint €6. ⏰ Open M noon-3pm, Tu-F noon-3pm and 6pm-12:30am, Sa 6pm-12:30am.*

LE KOMPTOIR
BAR

27 rue Quincampoix   ☎01 42 77 75 35 www.lekomptoir.fr

Head to this tapas bar for some of the cheapest happy hour pints and cocktails in the Marais. Le Komptoir's distinctive backwards "K" in its name hints at its backwards (but awesome) behavior of offering cheap drinks, free entry to concerts, and a surprisingly long food menu, complete with paella (€13). There are plenty of tables on the ground floor and in the basement, making this a great bar for groups.

i Ⓜ*Hôtel de Ville. In the pl. Michelet. Walk up rue du Renard, turn right onto rue St-Merri, then left onto rue Quincampoix. Jazz concerts Th 9pm. No cover, but must buy a drink. Beer €6.20-6.80. Cocktails €7.50-8.50. Tapas €7.50-13. Happy hour pints €4.40-4.80; cocktails 2 for 1. ⏰ Open Tu-Su 10am-2am. Happy hour 5:30-8:30pm.*

france

STOLLY'S
BAR

16 rue Cloche Percé   ☎01 42 76 06 76 www.cheapblonde.com

This small Anglophone hangout takes the sketchy out of the dive bar but leaves the attitude. Older, non-trendy locals in tattoos and strict black attire kick back pitchers of cheap blonde beer (€12) to ensure that the bar lives up to its motto: "Hangovers installed and serviced here." Come inside, have a pint, and shout at the TV with the regulars that stake out a seat at a sticky table before the place fills up at night.

i ⓂSt-Paul. From the Métro, turn right onto rue Pavée, then left onto rue du Roi de Sicile. Turn left onto rue Cloche Percé. Shooters €3-6. Beer pints €5-6; pitcher of blond beer €12. Cocktails €7-8. Happy hour pints and cocktails €6. ⓧ Open daily 4:30pm-2am. Happy hour 4-8pm. Terrace open until midnight.

LE YONO
BAR, CLUB

37 rue Vieille du Temple   ☎01 42 74 31 65 www.leyono.fr

It's easy to walk past Le Yono, as it's set back from the street through a stone corridor that makes for a grand entrance (and later a perfect smoker's getaway) to this cave-like club. The bar area is big and open and makes a great space for chatting on weekdays under the translucent ceilings, but on weekends, the real party is downstairs. The mosaics on the walls light up a dance floor packed with students dancing along with DJs that rock the house with electronic beats.

i ⓂHôtel de Ville. Walk against traffic on rue de Rivoli and turn left. Or from ⓂSt-Paul, walk with traffic on rue de Rivoli and turn right. Live music 2-3 times per week. Downstairs open F-Sa. Cocktails €10-12. Happy hour cocktails €5.50, pint of Heineken €5.50. Mojitos 10-12. Pint of beer €7-8. Tapas Th-Sa €5-9. ⓧ Open Tu-Sa 6pm-2am.

O'SULLIVAN'S REBEL BAR
BAR

http://chatelet.osullivans-pubs.com   ☎01 42 71 42 72

A tattooed take on an Irish bar, O'Sullivan's Rebel Bar makes Paris's chain bars look like classy English tea rooms. The walls are covered with graffiti, the menus are unapologetically sticky, and the place can get pretty crowded on a game night. The patrons, complete with piercings and shaved heads, couldn't care less about noise levels or their livers and make this place a riot almost as soon as it opens.

i ⓂHôtel de Ville. Walk up rue du Renard and turn left onto rue de la Verrerie, which becomes rue des Lombards. M all-night happy hour. Pints €6-7. Shots €5-9. Cocktails €7-16. Happy hour pints €4; cocktails €5.50. ⓧ Open M-Th 5pm-2am, F 5pm-5am, Sa 2pm-5am, Su 2pm-2am. Happy hour 5-9pm.

L'ART BRUT
BAR

78 rue Quincampoix   ☎01 42 72 17 36 www.artbrutbistrot.fr

In case the crowds didn't tip you off, this bar is a favorite in the neighborhood. Young locals come here in groups and easily fill up this small, narrow bar and spill out onto the street during the warmer months. Changing art installations hang on the walls of wood and stone, giving this place a hipster-artsy vibe, just in case the low prices didn't attract enough attention and adoration. Sip some organic wine a €3.50 a pop as you nod along to the rock and Balkan folk music and fill yourself with cheap dishes of charcuterie and cheese platters.

i ⓂRambuteau or ⓂEtienne-Marcel. From Rambuteau, walk down rue Beaubourg with traffic, turn right onto rue Rambuteau, then right onto rue Qincampoix; L'Art Brut is on the right. From Etienne-Marcel, walk down rue-aux-Ours and turn right onto rue Quincampoix; L'Art Brut is on the left. Organic wine €3.50 per glass. Pints of beer €4.50-6.50. Cocktails €6-9. Platters €9.50. ⓧ Open daily 4pm-2am.

paris

L'ATTIRAIL   BAR

9 rue au Maire   ☎01 42 72 44 42 www.lattirail.fr

On a street filled with subpar Asian *traiteurs* and seemingly nothing else, L'Attirail shines through like a cabin in the woods, a light through the expensive darkness, an oasis in the midst of €10 cocktails. Here, 20-somethings and students clink glasses and swap stories on the warm terrace or inside the bar, where the walls are covered with passport photos of past patrons. Drinks here are cheap, and happy hour starts early, making this a great place to get schwasty before hitting up more active venues later on in the night.

i ⓂArts et Métiers. Walk down rue Réamur with traffic, turn right onto rue Volta, then left onto rue au Maire; L'Attirail is on the left. Salads €9.50. plats €9.50-12. Drinks €4.50-5.50. ⓧ Open M-Sa 10:30am-2am, Su 5pm-2am. Happy hour 3:30-8pm.

Latin Quarter and St-Germain

The neighborhoods are where you'll find the majority of Paris's students spending their intellectual (or not so intellectual) nights out.

L'ANTIDOTE   BAR

45 rue Descartes   ☎01 43 54 69 78 www.lantidote-paris.com

If you've got problems, alcohol is not the answer, but hey, if you're just having a poisonously boring weekend and want a morerambunctious night out, L'Antidote may be your answer. During the week, the two enormous television screens make this place more of a sports bar, but come weekend, crowds of young Parisians and backpackers from nearby hostels flock to this bar to shake it like a Polaroid picture on the sweaty, stone-vaulted dance floor. Drinks flow freely thanks to the superb happy hour, and the prime location on rue Mouffetard makes it easy to bar hop, though we doubt you'll want to leave.

i ⓂPlace Monge. Walk down rue Lacépède, turn right onto rue Mouffetard, and walk 1 block; L'Antidote is on the right. Happy hour pint of beer €3-5.50; cocktails €5.50-7.50. Shots €25 for 10, €3 for 1. Pint of beer €4.80-6.80. Cocktails €7-8.50. ⓧ Open daily 5pm-2am. Happy hour 5pm-9pm.

LE PANTALON   BAR

7 rue Royer-Collard   ☎01 40 51 85 85

If there was ever such a thing as a takeaway beer and cocktail bar, this is it. Packed to the gills with laid-back Sorbonne students and recent college grads in suits, this narrow bar is a student epicenter, drawing crowds on the weekends with its cheap drinks and specialty shots. It can sometimes be a bit claustrophobic inside, and the tap by the window and the extra cents it costs to drink indoors directs a lot of traffic onto the streets. On the cobblestoned sidewalk, patrons mill about in their T-shirts and take long draws from cigarettes after a long day. Grab a group of friends, or just work on your tolerance and order the 10 shots for €5 deal to start (or end) your night with a schwasty bang.

i RER Luxembourg. Walk toward the Jardin du Luxembourg, turn right onto rue le Goff, right onto rue Gay-Lussac, and left onto rue Royer-Collard; Le Pantalon is on the right. Bee €2.50-7. Cocktails €7. Shots €2.50, €10 for 5. Cash only. ⓧ Open daily 3pm-2am. Happy hour 5:30pm-7:30pm.

LE PIANO VACHE   DIVE BAR

8 rue Làplace   ☎01 46 33 75 03 http://lepianovache.fr

Le Piano Vache is all about vintage rock and has remained largely unchanged since opening in 1969. Plastered with old posters and filled with equally ancient couches, this bar looks like it was decorated by a tipsy, nostalgic rockstar. This dive oozes 1970s underground cool, and the live music, themed nights, and ter-

france

rific happy hour specials attract a mélange of regulars and students who spread out at the large wooden tables.

i ⓂMaubert-Mutualité. Walk down rue des Carmes against the flow of traffic 4 blocks, turn left onto rue Làplace; Le Piano Vache is on the left. M live jazz 9:30pm-1:30am, Tu '80s night 9:30pm-2am, W Goth music DJ 9pm-2am, Th discounted prices all night, F rock DJ 9pm-2am, Sa DJ 9pm-2am. Coffee €1. Beer €4-7. Cocktails €7-8. M night pints €7; cocktails €10. Th night pints €5; cocktails €5; tapas €5. ⓩ Open M-Sa noon-2am; during school holidays 6pm-2am.

▨ L'ACADÉMIE DE LA BIÈRE
BAR
88 bd de Port-Royal ☎01 43 54 66 65 www.academie-biere.com

With 12 beers on tap and 150 bottled varieties, L'Académie de la Bière is as serious about its brews as Parisians are about their wine. Popular with students looking to unwind on the weekend, the bar itself is minuscule, but the extensive patio (which is covered and sometimes heated, depending on the weather) is filled end-to-end with those spirit-seeking students. Most drinkers come to L'Académie to study the brews, but any smart student knows not to drink on an empty stomach—the steaming hot plates of mussels and German sausages alone are worth a visit to this restaurant.

i ⓂVavin. Walk southeast on bd du Montparnasse as it turns into bd du Port-Royal. The bar is on the left. Beer €6-8. Mussels €8-9. Sausages €8-14. ⓩ Open M-Th 10am-2am, F-Sa 10am-3am, Su 10am-2am. Happy hour daily 3:30-7:30pm.

LE 10 BAR
BAR
10 rue de l'Odéon ☎01 43 26 66 83 http://10bar.pagesperso-orange.fr

Founded in 1955, Le 10 Bar has become quite the silver fox as it ages gracefully while retaining its 1950s charm—even Clooney could take some pointers. The itsy bar is a bit musty smelling, and the posters from 1950s plays are fading fast, but the antique woodwork and jukebox that croons Édith Piaf and Aretha Franklin will take you on your own *Midnight in Paris* field trip. This bar is for the nostalgic and those who fancy themselves intellectuals or artists with a penchant for sangria. At 9pm, head downstairs to the basement where Ernest Hemingway used to write inspired tales after amorous encounters with his mistress who lived above the bar. Although we don't recommend trespassing above the bar in search of a lover, you may still feel literary love in the air at Le Bar 10; memorize a few lines of French poetry and flirt the night away.

i ⓂOdéon. Walk south to where the road splits into 3 forks and take the middle fork; Le 10 Bar is on the right. Sangria €3.50 per glass. Beer €4-5.50. Cash only. ⓩ Open daily 6pm-2am. Basement opens at 9pm.

LE VIOLON DINGUE
BAR, CLUB
46 rue de la Montagne Ste-Geneviève ☎01 43 25 79 93

Known as "le VD" to locals, this bar has some of the cheapest happy hour drinks around, and it's open the latest. The upstairs feels like a pub with a strong American influence, complete with football from the US. After 1am, though, the place floods with young French students and American tourists who swarm to get into the downstairs club, where the latest top 40 hits blast against the vaulted stone ceilings until 5am.

i ⓂCardinal Lemoine. Walk uphill on rue du Cardinal Lemoine and turn right onto rue Clovis. Walk 1 block and turn right onto rue Descartes. When you hit the plaza, the bar is on the left. Beer €6. Cocktails €7-10. Happy hour beer €3-4; cocktails €5-6; jagerbombs €5. Prices increase €1 after 1:30am. ⓩ Open Tu-Sa 8pm-5am. Club open Tu-Sa midnight-5am. Happy hour Tu-Sa 7-10pm.

Invalides

LE CONCORDE ATLANTIQUE
CLUB

23 quai Anatole France   ☎01 40 56 02 82   www.bateauconcordeatlantique.com

Take a three-story club with half thought-out themed *soirées,* add copious amounts of booze deals, and transform it into a boat right on the Seine. You have just imagined Le Concorde Atlantique. On Friday and Saturday nights there's usually a line to enter this club, where the party can start as early as 10pm and keeps going until 5am. Expect to find a healthy number of tourists here in the packed crowd, although there are no swim trunks or flippy-floppies in sight—only well-dressed 20-somethings who are less interested in keeping it classy and more interested in making it nasty. Keep an eye out during the summer for the Terrassa parties, with a series of locally famous DJs. *Soirées* are shamelessly promoted, often with cover charges that include free drinks and the occasional ladies' night. The deals don't end there: the website **www.parisbouge. com** is an invaluable resource here, giving out cheap tickets and drink passes that can save travelers as much as 50%.

i Ⓜ*Assemblée Nationale, right on the Seine in between Pont de la Concorde and walking bridge Solferino. Cover from €10-20, includes (sometimes up to 5) free drinks. Some nights men pay extra €5-10. ⏰ Open Tu-Sa 8pm-5am.*

Champs-Élysées

Glam is the name of the game at the trendy, expensive bars and clubs of the 8ème. Dress up and bring some attractive friends or a fat wallet—it's going to be a pricey night out.

🏳️ LE QUEEN
CLUB

102 av. des Champs-Élysées   ☎01 53 89 08 90   www.queen.fr

Le Queen is a renowned Parisian institution where drag queens, superstars, tourists, and go-go boys get down and dirty to the mainstream rhythms of a 10,000-gigawatt sound system. Open all night, every night, Le Queen has *soirées* for just about every party demographic you can think of, although the hot-mess and perennially-drunk crowd is well attended here. Be prepared to show ID to gain entrance to this flashy disco with a light-up dance floor, which features theme nights that include the occasional gay *soirée.*

i Ⓜ*Georges V. Disco on M. Ladies night on W; no cover for women 11:30pm-1am. Live DJ on F. Cove €20, includes 1 drink. Drinks €15. ⏰ Open daily 11:30pm-6am.*

LE SHOWCASE
CLUB

Under Pont Alexandre III, Port des Champs Elysées   ☎01 45 61 25 43   www.showcase.fr

One of the most popular clubs with the bohemian bourgeoisie in Paris (kids with money), Le Showcase's limited operation days and even more limited entrance make it nearly impossible to get in without some good-looking friends. Every Friday and Saturday night, live international DJs spin techno and electro beats for the well-heeled crowds in this super-dim club. To be sure you'll make it in, get on the "guest list" by registering your name for free online, then dance 'til dawn in this dungeon-esque club.

i Ⓜ*Champs-Elysées-Clemenceau. Entry typically free before midnight. Register for free on their website or Facebook page to be added to the guest list. Cover €10-15. Beer €9. Cocktails €15. ⏰ Open F-Sa 11pm-dawn.*

THE FREEDOM
BAR

8 rue de Berri   ☎01 53 75 25 50   www.maydayinns.com/the-freedom.html

To hear some English and catch a game or two, visit The Freedom and hang out with the regulars here. This pub is more low-key than the usual English joint and is more of a watering hole for local Anglophones than a buzzing joint at which

france

to start the night—although the cheap drinks on student nights make it worth a quick stop.

i Ⓜ*George V. Walk away from the Arc de Triomphe and turn left down rue de Berri. Student Night on Th; pint €4, vodka shots €2.50. DJs F-Sa. Ladies night F-Sa; cocktail and vodka shots €6. Beer €6-7.* Ⓩ *Open M-W 11:30am-2am, Th 11:30am-4am, F-Sa 11:30am-5am, Su 11:30am-2am.*

LE SENS UNIQUE
WINE BAR

47 rue de Ponthieu   ☎01 43 59 76 77

In an area writhing with girls who don't know how to walk in their 5in. stilettos and guys who spend as much time on their hair as their outfits, Le Sens Unique manages to keep it classy—and we mean really classy. Silver couches, a wine bar with dried vines wrapped over the bar, a brick interior, and street signs decorating the walls, this mellow local hideout is almost entirely devoid of tourists. The gentle owner welcomes everyone with open arms to sample hand-selected fine wines from Périgord, in the Bourdeaux region of southern France. Although the wines here aren't super cheap and only a few are sold by the glass, the quality of the drinks and the relaxing atmosphere are well worth the price. Those with a little more than $20 in their pockets should splurge on the foodie-approved dishes here, too.

i Ⓜ*Franklin D. Roosevelt. Walk up the Champs-Élysées toward the Arc de Triomphe, turn right onto rue La Boétie, then left onto rue de Ponthieu. Or* Ⓜ*George V. Walk down the Champs-Élysées away from the Arc de Triomphe, turn left onto rue de Berri and right onto rue de Ponthieu. Beaujoulais Nouveau 3-day wine tasting event starts 3rd Th in Nov. Wine €4.50-6.* Ⓩ *Open M-Sa noon-11pm.*

Opéra and Canal St-Martin

▨ LE VERRE VOLÉ
RESTAURANT, BAR

67 rue Lancry   ☎01 48 03 17 34 www.leverrevole.fr

This restaurant is tiny, but that's not the only reason why you'll need a reservation here for lunch and dinner. This unassuming wine bar and restaurant has developed quite the cult following by food critics and bobos who pine after the generous dishes paired with the organic and natural wines. While you won't hang out here all night, this great location on the canal is the perfect spot to mingle with young Parisian hipsters over a glass of one of the restaurant's many wines.

i Ⓜ*Jacques Bonsergent. Walk down bd de Magenta and turn left onto rue de Lancry; it's just before the canal. Wine from €5.50 per glass. Corkage fee €7. Entrées €6.50-9. plats €11-13.* Ⓩ *Open Tu-Su noon-3:30pm and 6:30-11:30pm.*

▨ CHEZ PRUNE
CAFE, BAR

36 rue Beaurepaire   ☎01 42 49 89 19

In case the colorful graffiti didn't tip you off, this neighborhood is artsy. And in case the fedora-ed, scruffed-up clientele didn't tip you off, Chez Prune is the water cooler for all the young bohemians in this neighborhood. The cafe has a spacious terrace that is nearly always full of groups of friends sharing the terrific charcuterie and cheese platters or couples chowing down on zucchini pancakes. Located along the canal and various bike and footpaths, Chez Prune is the place to see the trendy folk of Paris pass by on their bikes or with a cigarette in hand. At night, you can cozy up next to the canal with a *vin chaud*, as this bar fills up with 20-somethings looking to get tipsy off a few cheap drinks.

i Ⓜ*Jacques Bonsergent. Walk up rue de Lancry with the flow of traffic, turn right onto quai de Valmy, and Chez Prune is on right. Cocktails €8.50. plats €14.* Ⓩ *Open M-F 8am-2am, Su 10am-2am.*

CORCORAN'S
IRISH PUB, CLUB

23 bd Poissonnière   ☎01 40 39 00 16 www.corcorans.fr

During the day, this Irish pub serves up all the greasy Anglo-Saxon goods, like fish and chips and Irish stew for the few customers that come through. At night,

Corcoran's comes alive as a hoppin' nightclub Th-Sa nights. A flurry of French and English speakers alternately populate the dance floor, so if you're looking to play it smooth in your native tongue, throw back a Guinness and party like a rockstar at Corcoran's, where you'll find the best of both worlds. Don't show up too sloshed if you want the bouncers to let you in.

i ⓜGrands Boulevards. Upon exiting the Métro, look for the green awning. Other locations in the Bastille, St-Michel, and Clichy areas. Happy hour M-F 5-9pm. Karaoke Th 9pm. Live music 4 times a week. Su 3pm traditional Irish music and step dancing. Shots €4. Beer €6.50-7. Mixed drinks €8. Happy hour mixed drinks €6, pints €5. ⓩ Open daily 10am-dawn.

LE BRÉBANT   CAFE, BAR

32 bd Poissonnière   ☎01 47 70 01 02 www.cafelebrebantparis.com

Of all the bars in this concentrated nook around ⓜGrands Boulevards, Le Brebant has the privilege of occupying the largest corner of the intersection, thereby outdoing all its neighbors in size and noise. Open late into the night, this cafe has an impressive selection of seafood, though the non-happy hour drinks are quite pricey. The art deco interior makes for a pretty sight, although we recommend people watching the plastered partiers exiting from Corcoran's across the street.

i ⓜGrands Boulevards. Across from Corcoran's. Free Wi-Fi. Happy hour mixed drinks and beer €6. ⓩ Open daily 7pm-6am.

Bastille

Nightlife in the 11ème has long consisted of Anglophones who drink too much and rockers and hipsters who intend to stay out until the Métro starts up again.

▧ LE BARON ROUGE   WINE BAR

1 rue Théophile Roussel   ☎01 43 43 14 32

This wine bar is doing it right with a 45 bottle selection of reds and whites that start from as low as €1.50 a glass, leaving you with plenty of money left over for a rich *assiette* of charcuterie, cheese, or oysters. The pros and regulars bring their own bottles and fill them up straight from the barrels before taking their drinks outside to the pavement. If you're lucky, you can nab an impromptu barrel table surface for you drink. With booze this good and this cheap, the crowd really doesn't need much to keep the conversation and laughter going.

i ⓜLedru-Rollin. Walk south with traffic on av. Ladru-Rollin, then turn left onto rue de Prague. Turn left with traffic onto rue Traversière. Wine €1.50-3.60. Platters €7-16. ⓩ Open Tu-F10am-2pm and 5-11pm, Sa 10am-10pm, Su 10am-4pm.

▧ UFO   BAR

49 rue Jean-Pierre Timbaud   ☎06 09 81 93 59

UFO's pricing is out of this world, with happy hour pints for €3.50 and pastis for €1.50. The super-scuffed and worn furniture also looks like it's been through a wormhole and back. Cheap drinks and a short happy hour means that the student and young rockers here down their drinks at inhuman speeds before dancing to garage rock, punk, and funk. Weekend DJs make this dive bar a prime destination for an invasion.

i Parmentier. Walk up av. Parmentier toward the brasserie Le Plein Soleil, turn right onto rue Jean-Pierre Timbaud; UFO is on the left. Cocktails €5-10. Beers €4-7. Happy hour pints €3.50, glass of wine €1.50, pastis €1.50. ⓩ Open daily 6pm-2am. Happy hour daily 6-8pm.

Montparnasse and Southern Paris

The central area around the Montparnasse Tower and the train station is mostly filled with generic, somewhat inauthentic cafes, but the farther you wander from this area, the more likely you are to find some local spots.

BATOFAR

Across from 11 quai Francois Mauriac ☎01 53 60 17 00 www.batofar.org

You might feel like T-Pain at this nightclub, which occupies the lowest level of a boat and leads a quadruple life as a nightclub, concert venue, restaurant, and bar. Ideally located on the quiet eastern end of the Seine, the Batofar brings the area alive at night with its live concerts and bangin' DJs. If you're not interested in sweaty dancing, singing, and bumpin' and grinding, hit the bar on the breezy top level of the boat. You can also head for the shore and relax on the patio, also known as *La Plage*, where you can enjoy fresh rum punch made with pineapples, oranges, mangoes, or cranberries. Locals love this increasingly popular locale as much as the savvy backpackers who know it exists.

i Ⓜ*Quai de la Gare. Go to the Seine and head down the stairs to the riverbank, then turn right so the river is on your left. Walk about 5min. DJ every night and after concerts. Tickets can be bought at the door, usually €3-25. White sangria €5. Punch €6. Cocktails €10. Tapas €5. ☼ Open daily noon-late. Patio on the bank (La Plage) open May-Sept noon-1am; brunch on Su. Terrace on the boat open daily 6pm-midnight. Happy hour Oct-Apr 6-8pm; May-Sept 5-7pm. Restaurant open Tu-Sa noon-2:30pm and 7:30-11:30pm. Concerts usually start 7pm or later.*

LA FOLIE EN TÊTE

33 rue de la Butte-aux-Cailles ☎01 45 80 65 99 http://lafolieentete.wix.com/lesite

Decorated with musical instruments, street signs, and newspaper clippings announcing Bob Marley concerts, this bar loves its reggae, rock, and world music. This bar has one of the cheapest happy hours in the neighborhood and is well known for its strong ti' punch and excellent mojitos. Hipsters, poets, musicians, broke students, and the occasional suit and tie keep it packed and steamy until closing.

i Ⓜ*Place d'Italie. From pl. d'Italie, follow rue Bobillot. Turn right onto rue de la Butte-aux-Cailles and follow it as it turns right. Beer €5-6. Cocktails €7.50. Happy hour cocktails €5, pints €3-3.50. ☼ Open M-Sa 5pm-2am, Su 6pm-midnight. Happy hour daily 5-8pm.*

LE MERLE MOQUER

11 rue de la Butte aux Cailles ☎01 45 65 12 43

Capturing the spirit of the neighborhood with its eclectic mix of color block walls, uneven stools, spray-painted doors, '80s music, and a rather random selection of art, this bar is a little funky and not at all fussy. The naked lady and her pig friend painted near the door are here to offer you a plastic patio chair and a selection of over 20 different types of rum.

i Ⓜ*Corvisart. Follow the signs to Butteaux Cailles, south of the Métro stop. Drinks €4-6. Happy hour pints €3, rum punch €5. ☼ Open daily 5pm-1:30am. Happy hour 5-8pm.*

CAFE OZ: DENFERT ROCHEREAU

3 pl. Denfert-Rochereau ☎01 47 38 76 77 www.cafe-oz.com

Opened in May 2011, the newest and largest iteration of this Australian chain is rumored to have the largest terraces in Paris. The view from the terrace in front of the bar is more likely to be of hurried travelers lugging suitcases than of a chic Parisian sidewalk, so we recommend heading to the other terrace in the back. After midnight, the older crowd vacates, and the massive interior becomes packed with young bodies dancing on tables, stairs, and wherever there's room. Things are kept cool thanks to the drafty, 30ft. ceilings. Despite Oz's size, the giant kangaroo out front and walls covered in boomerangs still make you feel like you're in a packed hut on a beach in Queensland.

i Ⓜ*Denfert-Rochereau, behind the RER station. Cover charg €15 with drink, depending on the night. Shooters €5. Beer €7-8. Cocktails €10. Happy hour cocktails €7. Bar snacks €6-9. ☼ Kitchen open M-Sa noon-4pm. Bar open M noon-2am, Tu-W noon-3am, Th-Sa noon-5am. Snacks served W-Sa 5pm-9pm. Happy hour M 5pm-midnight, Tu-Sa 5-8pm, Su 5pm-midnight.*

paris

Auteuil, Passy & Batignolles

Just like the food, the nightlife in these *arrondissements* tends to be cheaper, younger, and chiller in the 17ème than in the 16ème, where you'll find a bevy of overpriced bars and nightclubs.

LES CAVES POPULAIRES   BAR
22 rue des Dames   ☎01 53 04 08 32

For some cheap drinks, bohemian company, and some good cheese and charcuterie platters, Les Caves Populaires is the bar of choice. The bar stands out from the relatively quiet rue des Dames with its noise—this place is full even in the afternoon—and with its red mosaic exterior and whitewashed stone walls. In a place where the coffee is organic, served with a stick of cinnamon, and only €1, it only makes sense that the groups of friends here have rosy cheeks from laughter (although the cheap glasses of wine can't hurt).

i Ⓜ*Place de Clichy. Walk down bd des Batignolles with the flow of traffic (away from the traffic circle). Turn right onto rue Lecluse, turn left onto rue des Dames; Les Caves is on the right. Wine from €2 per glass. Shot €3-4. Cocktails €3-12.* ☼ *Open M-Sa 8am-1am, Su 11am-1am.*

FROG XVI   BAR
110 bis av. Kleber   ☎01 47 27 88 88 www.frogpubs.com

One of several English Frog pubs across Paris, Frog XVI is the trendier cousin of the more traditional Frog and Rosbif. With two levels, rock music, large comfortable leather seats, and the microbreweries downstairs in full view, this is the place to loosen up and hang out with old friends or make new ones over a quality beer. The crowd here is a healthy mix of young locals and tourists, which means this place can fill up quickly, so plan your arrival accordingly, especially on a game day.

i Ⓜ*Trocadéro. Free Wi-Fi. DJ Th-Sa. Brunch Sa-Su noon-4pm. Happy hour M-F 5:30-8pm. Lunch menu M-F €12.50. Pints €5. Beer €7.* ☼ *Open daily noon-2am.*

LE BLOC   CAFE, BAR
21 rue Brochant   ☎01 53 11 02 37

Formerly a warehouse, this cafe was updated with a super modern, minimalist exterior, with clean cut lines and an enormous window for the first floor. The walls of this multi-level cafe are decorated with photographs, and there's a nook under the stairs with a cramped but comfortable array of lounge chairs, including a creatively redesigned shopping cart (yes, it is somehow comfortable). Parisians who want to associate themselves with chicness—or who are actually chic—park it here for a decent meal, and in the evenings lo-fi electro music plays in the background as the Parisians get ready for the rest of the night.

i Ⓜ*Brochant. From the Métro, walk straight onto rue Brochant. Free Wi-Fi. Half beer €2.70. Cocktails €7. Salads €8-11.50. Daily specials for €10.* ☼ *Open daily 8:30am-2am.*

DUPLEX   CLUB
2 bis av. Foch   ☎01 45 00 45 00 www.leduplex.com

Stories of this late-night disco make their way around Paris, and we mean that in an infamous way. The three-story subterranean club has several rooms with different music playing, but you can expect to hear the usual techno, house, top 40, and some throwback hip hop. Women in heels and snappy looking men pack this club and don't stop until 6am—just in time to go home on the Métro.

i Ⓜ*Charles de Gaulle-Étoile. Half block from the Circe. Cover (includes 1 drink) M-Th €15, F-Sa €20, Su €15. Drinks M €8, Tu-Th €9, F-Sa €11, Su €9.* ☼ *Open daily midnight to 6am.*

L'ENDROIT   BAR, CAFE
67 place du Dr Félix Lobligeois   ☎01 42 29 50 00

L'Endroit is French for "the place," and this is definitely the place to be. The Parisians who gather here suck down pint-sized mojitos and laugh carelessly

france

over a shared pack of cigarettes. When the sun's out, chowing down on massive burgers accompanied by even more massive salads seems to be a popular activity. Once darkness strikes, so do those midnight munchies, and with L'Endroit closing shop on the weekends at 5am, there's nothing like a pre-dawn meal.

i Open M-Th 11am-2am, F-Sa 11am-5am, Su 11am-2am.

Montmartre

With sex shops and strippers galore, Montmartre can be sketchy at night, with some loud drunkards making quite a scene and pickpockets eyeing the tipsy tourists.

▨ MARLUSSE ET LAPIN
BAR

14 rue Germain Pilon ☎01 42 59 17 97

Even in a neighborhood teeming with sex shops and cabarets, a place like Marlusse et Lapin stands out for its weirdness. In the back of this tiny bar is "Grandma's Chamber," with flowery wallpaper, a sewing machine, a bed that now functions as seating, and black and white photos of grandparents. In case this scene isn't bizarre enough for you, order a glass of authentic absinthe for a truly down-the-rabbit-hole experience. In case wormwood isn't your thing, this place also serves up popular flavored shots for €3 if you can elbow your way to the bar.

i ⓂPigalle or Abbsesses. From Pigalle, facing the rounded plaza, turn right and walk down bd de Clichy, then turn right onto rue Germain Pilon; Marlusse is on the right. From Abbsesses, facing the church, head right on rue des Absesses, then left onto rue Germain Pilon; Marlusse is on the left. Shot €3. Half pint beers €2.80. Cocktails €5-7. Absinthe €6-9. Happy hour beer €3-4; mixed drinks €4.50. Ⓩ Open daily 4pm-2am. Happy hour 4-8pm.

Buttes-Chaumont & Belleville

Instead of clubs and dirty dancing, the loud, artsy bars in 19ème and 20ème are the centers of nightlife around here and attract mostly the hipster locals.

▨ ROSA BONHEUR
BAR, GLBT

2 av. de la Cascade ☎01 42 00 00 45 www.rosabonheur.fr

Nestled in the Parc des Buttes Chaumont, Rosa Bonheur has arguably the best setting in all of Paris. As it gets dark, the mystery of the forest and the fading colors of the sunset infect all the young people here with a romanticism reminiscent of *A Midsummer Night's Dream*—left and right, everyone is dancing, fumbling, laughing, and locking lips. Groups of friends settle down at tables outside or stand around barrels to polish off bottles of wine, while couples dance and grind about indoors on the crowded dance floor. In addition to all this laid-back hedonism, Rosa has a conscientious heart: this restaurant also hosts a lot of community service and charity events for GLBT rights and environmental awareness, along with Paris's *Silence de Danse*, an event where you put on headphones, dance, and look really funny.

i ⓂBotzaris. Entrance at the gates facing 74 Botzaris. Tapa €5-8. Sangria €4. Pints €5. Mojitos €8. ⓏOpen W-Su noon-midnight. Last entry 11pm.

▨ LES PÈRES POPULAIRES
BAR

46 rue Buzenval ☎01 43 48 49 22

"Père" means "father" in French, and we wish our dads were this cool. This bar is filled with 20-somethings unchained to any commitments, much less fatherhood, who gather here to drink cheap beer or sip €1 espressos at the mismatched tables, cozy couches, or the bright green bar. And when shots are €3 and beer is €2.60, it's no wonder that the booze flows freely and the Parisians (you won't find a single tourist here) become uncharacteristically loud. Les Pères has no sign on the outside, and it doesn't need one—it's the loudest, happiest place on the block.

i ⓂBuzenval. Walk down rue Buzenval against the flow of traffic; the bar is on the left. Coffee €1. Shots €3. Beer €2.60-6.50. Wine €2.70-9. Sandwiches €3.90. ⓏOpen M-F 8am-2am, Sa-Su 10am-2am.

paris

LA BELLEVILLOISE
BAR, CONCERT

19-21 rue Boyer ☎0146 36 07 07 www.labellevilloise.com

La Bellevilloise is the multi-tasking, effortlessly cool older sister you always wish you were. A hugely popular institution in Paris, this establishment is a restaurant, bar, and club in one. Whether or not you want a delicious brunch with live jazz, a night of electro-swing music by an up-and-coming band, or a chance to admire some contemporary art as you take a break from swinging to Creole beats, La Bellevilloise has you covered. Even though it may be far from the center of the city, Parisians from *arrondissements* all over venture here for the music and the food, so be sure to make a reservation for meals and be prepared to share some personal space as you shake about.

i Ⓜ*Ménilmontant. Walk along rue de Ménilmontant with traffic until rue Boyer. Turn right onto rue Boyer; La Bellevilloise is on the right. Concerts and club 19+, some events 21+. Live music in the restaurant 4-5 times per week. Su brunch with live jazz. Reservations recommended for dinner and brunch. Concerts €10-15. Wine €4. Beer €4-9. Shots €5. Cocktails €9. ☺ Open W-F 7pm-2am, Sa 11am-2am, Su brunch 11am-4:30pm.*

O' PARIS
CAFE, BAR

1 rue des Envierges ☎01 43 66 38 54 www.le-o-paris.com

For one of the best terraces in all Paris, come to O' Paris. Located at the top of steep slope, this cafe/bar overlooks the gorgeous Parc de Belleville, with the Eiffel Tower and the Parisian rooftops all at your feet. With a view this great, it's no wonder that this cafe is the spot of choice for the fashionable denizens of the 20ème and bobos from all over Paris. And as if the view wasn't enough, the €2 coffee and €10 lunch menu make it hard to find a seat on the packed street corner when the sun's out. The dinner menu here is a little pricey, and it's the view that's most important, so save your evening dining money for elsewhere or, better yet, pack a picnic and tan in the park right in front of you. During the evening, O' Paris is buzzing with patrons who refuse to budge from their seats and stay for drinks and a relaxed and beautiful midnight in Paris.

i Ⓜ*Pyrénées. Facing McDonald's, head left and walk up rue de Belleville, then turn left onto rue Piat; O' Paris is on the left. Lunch menu €10. Brunch €17-22. ☺ Open M-W 10:30am-2am, Th-Su 10am-2am.*

AUX FOLIES
BAR

8 rue de Belleville ☎01 46 36 65 98

If you ever need to feel cool or, damn, if you just are cool, you should be at this bar. Frequented by everyone from suave and collected older men to young, frenetic locals to graffiti artists who have tagged the nearby alleyways, Aux Folies is nearly always packed with an artsier crowd that doesn't mind a little dirt, drinks their coffee black, and likes their booze cheap (beers start at €2). This bar was once a mini-theater where Edith Piaf used to sing, and the unchanged decor and neon lights help maintain an old-school vibe. The terrace gets a rare bit of sunlight on this crowded, narrow street, but just be prepared to elbow your way into a seat.

i Ⓜ*Belleville. Walk up rue de Belleville; Aux Folies is on the left. Beer €2-4. Wine €3 per glass. Cocktails €4.50. ☺ Open M-Sa 6am-2am, Su 7am-1am.*

ARTS AND CULTURE

A trip to the Opéra Garnier, comic relief at the Odéon Théâtre, or late-night wining and dining at the Moulin Rouge are all possibilities for total cultural immersion and will leave you with more memories than that one night on the Mouffetard. If this sounds boring to you (hopefully it doesn't, but we cater to all tastes), you'll be pleased to know that Paris's concerts get just as rowdy as its clubs. Whether you have a solid grasp of French or are a novice who's just laughing because everyone else is, you'll definitely leave feeling a bit more *je ne sais quoi*.

Theater

◪ ODÉON THÉÂTRE DE L'EUROPE

LATIN QUARTER AND ST-GERMAIN

2 rue Corneille   ☎01 44 85 40 40 www.theatre-odeon.fr

The Odéon is a classically beautiful theater: gold lines the mezzanine and muted red upholstery covers the chairs. Many plays at this national theater are performed in foreign languages, with French translations shown above on a screen, which can make if frustrating if you don't *parler* the language. If you do, though, or if you just don't mind, the prices here are stunningly reasonable, and standing tickets are dirt cheap. The under-26 crowd can score the luxury of a seat for the same price, so save your young legs—watching foreign performances of *As You Like It* or *Platonov* takes enough energy already.

i Ⓜ*Odéon. Limited number of rush tickets available 2hr. before the start of the show. Shows €10-36, under 26 €6-18. Rush tickets €6. ☒ Performances generally M-Sa 8pm, Su 3pm.*

◪ THÉÂTRE DE LA VILLE

CHÂTELET-LES HALLES

2 pl. du Châtelet   ☎01 42 74 22 77 www.theatredelaville-paris.com

Since the'80s, the Théâtre de la Ville has become a major outlet for avant-garde theater, dance, and music for those who aren't afraid to go far out in performances titled "Disabled Theater" and "The Pornography of Souls." The theater is a bit more traditional and puts on classics by the likes of Shakespeare and Balzac, along with more contemporary German, Japanese, and American playwrights.

i Ⓜ*Châtelet. Walk down rue de Rivoli toward Hôtel de Ville. Tickets €19-25, under 30 €9-20. ☒ Box office open M 11am-7pm, Tu-Sa11am-8pm.*

Cabaret

◪ AU LAPIN AGILE

MONTMARTRE

22 rue des Saules   ☎01 46 06 85 87 www.au-lapin-agile.com

Halfway up a steep, cobblestoned hill that American tourists describe as "just like San Francisco," Au Lapin Agile has been providing savvy Parisians and tourists with traditional music, dance, and theater since the late 19th century. The performers present old French songs, ballads, lively sing-alongs, and guitar performances that last well into the night. The tiny theater was a popular spot for the 20th-century bohemian art scene—Picasso, Utrillo, and Max Jacob are on the list of people who cabareted here.

i Ⓜ*Lamarck-Coulaincourt. Follow rue St-Vincen to rue des Saules. Tickets €24, students under 26 €17. Tu-F and Su cover includes 1 drink. Drinks €6-7. ☒ Shows Tu-Su 9pm-1am.*

BAL DU MOULIN ROUGE

MONTMARTRE

82 bd de Clichy   ☎01 53 09 82 82 www.moulin-rouge.com

The Moulin Rouge promises to be as trippy and over-the-top as Baz Luhrmann's film, but at €99 a show, the famed glam and glitz just isn't worth it. The world-famous home of the can-can opened in 1889 and has hosted international superstars like Ella Fitzgerald and Johnny Rey, and it now welcomes a fair crowd of tourists for an evening of sequins, tassels, and skin. The shows remain risqué, and the late show is cheaper, but be prepared to stand if it's a busy night.

i Ⓜ*Blanche Sarl. Elegant attire required; no shorts, sneakers, or sportswear. 9 and 11pm show €99, with ½-bottle of champagne €109. 7pm dinner and 9pm show €180-210. Occasional lunch shows €100-130; call for more info. ☒ Dinner daily 7pm. Shows daily 9 and 11pm.*

Cinema

▨ L'ARLEQUIN
LATIN QUARTER AND ST-GERMAIN

76 rue de Rennes   ☎01 45 44 28 80

A proud revival theater, L'Arlequin mixes modern French films with artsy selections from a pool of international award-winners. Four films are featured each week, undoubtedly decreasing the prevalence of adolescent movie-hopping. Some films are in English, but the vast majority are in French.

i Ⓜ*St-Sulpice. Walk down rue de Rennes toward the Café de Métro; L'Arlequinon is on the right. €9.60; students, under 18, and over 60 €7.10.*

CINÉMATHÈQUE FRANÇAISE
BASTILLE

51 rue de Bercy   ☎01 71 19 33 33 www.cinematheque.fr

Though it's had some problems settling down (it's moved over five times, most recently in 2005), the Cinémathèque Française is dedicated to all things film. On the upper levels, the excellent Musée du Cinéma showcases old projectors and photographic plates alongside grand costumes and set pieces from movies like *Psycho* and *Métropolis*. The well-curated temporary exhibits on periods of film history and cinematic icons like Bette Davis, Tim Burton, and Jacques Demy draw a crowd of devoted cinephiles and casual moviegoers. And of course, the center screens multiple classics, near-classics, or soon-to-be classics per day; foreign selections are usually subtitled in French. Films by directors like Hitchcock, Fellini, Clément, and Matarazzo might be hard to understand in French, but hey, the picture's worth a thousand words.

i Ⓜ*Bercy. Musée du Cinéma €5, ages 18-26 and seniors €4, under 18 €2.50, Su 10am-1pm free; temporary exhibition €10/8/5; films €6.50/5.50/3. Joint ticket Musée with temporary exhibition €12, Musée and film €7. ☼ Musée open M-Sa noon-7pm, Su 10am-8pm. Temporary exhibition M 10am-8pm, W 10am-8pm, Th 10am-10pm, F-Su 10am-8pm. Ticket window open M noon-last showing, W-Sa noon-last showing, Su 10am-last showing.*

ACTION CHRISTINE
LATIN QUARTER AND ST-GERMAIN

4 rue Christine   ☎01 43 33 85 78 www.actioncinemas.com

This small theater plays restored American flicks from the 1930s through the '70s, like *African Queen, Bedlam,* and (of course) *King Kong.* This is a nice way to escape the heat, and the films are voiced over with French subtitles for Anglophone enjoyment.

i Ⓜ*Odéon. Follow rue de L'Éperon and turn right onto rue St-André des Arts. Turn right onto rue Grands Augustins, then left onto rue Christine. Films in English with French subtitles. €8, under 20 and students €6. ☼ Shows 2-10pm.*

Music

▨ POINT EPHÉMÈRE
OPÉRA AND CANAL ST-MARTIN

200 quai de Valmy   ☎01 40 34 02 48 www.pointephemere.org

Located in the bobo Canal St-Martin area, Point Ephémère is a mecca for hipsters who smoke to be ironic and artistes who probably know cooler bands than you do. Bringing in lesser-known rock bands from France, Belgium, the UK, the US, and elsewhere, this concert hall is crowded with young people four or five days a week. And as if hosting urban gospel rock and psychedelic bands didn't give it enough street cred, outside the concert hall is a bar, restaurant, and art expo space with artists' residences upstairs.

i Ⓜ*Louis Blanc. Walk down rue Louis Blanc toward the canal. Entrance is on the canal side, not the street. Buy tickets at the box office inside Point Ephémère in advance, online, or at the door, cheaper in advance. Be careful after dark. Concerts €15-20. Lunch menus €11.50-14.50. Brunch €16. Dinner à la carte. ☼ Bar open M-Sa noon-2am, Su noon-9pm. Restaurant open M-F 12:30-2:30pm and 8-11:15pm, Sa 12:30-2:30pm, Su noon-4:30pm. Brunch Su, in the summer Sa-Su. Snacks daily noon-1am.*

france

LE BATACLAN   BASTILLE
50 bd Voltaire   ☎01 43 14 00 30 www.le-bataclan.com

In French, *bataclan* is slang for "stuff" or "junk." In French music culture, Bataclan means a packed, 1500-person Chinese pagoda that hosts alternative and indie rock, synthetic pop, hip hop, reggae, and folk acts like Local Natives, Bastille, and Fabolous. The craziest venue in Bastille, Le Bataclan attracts a more local crowd, since the French love their more obscure bands (who are usually cheaper than those playing at La Cigale). Be sure to pregame with Capri Sun for their themed '80s or '90s parties that easily go until 6am.

i ⓂOberkampf. Tickets €15-50. ⌚ Shows start at 7:30pm.

Opera and Dance

PALAIS GARNIER (OPÉRA GARNIER)   OPÉRA AND CANAL ST-MARTIN
pl. de l'Opéra   ☎08 92 89 90 90 www.operadeparis.fr

You can tour it during the day, but going at night is a whole different ball game. The chandeliers dim, the stage lights up, and you are thrown back to the *fin de siècle* with ballet performances ranging from *Orpheus and Eurydice* to the *Bolshoi Ballet*. Although the Opéra Garnier confusingly no longer performs operas, its ballets, recitals, chamber music concerts, and choral performances still draw crowds of older adults and the lucky holders of youth rush tickets who are interested in more than the ornate architecture of the building.

i ⓂOpéra. Tickets usually available 2 weeks before the show. Tickets generally €10-110. Under 28 rush tickets sold 1hr. before show starts based on availability, operas €25, ballets €15, concerts €10. ⌚ Box office open M-Sa 11:30am-6:30pm.

OPÉRA BASTILLE   BASTILLE
pl. de la Bastille   ☎08 92 89 90 90 www.operadeparis.fr

Although considered Opéra Garnier's "ugly" other half, the Opéra Bastille has been the primary home of the Paris Opera since 1989. Matching its tiered glass exterior and geometric interior, the Opéra Bastille puts on classical pieces with a modern spin. There may not be gilded columns, but the breathtaking performances more than compensate.

i ⓂBastille. Tickets can be purchased online, by mail, by phone, or in person. Tickets €5-140. Under 28 rush tickets sold 1hr. before show starts based on availability, operas €25, ballets €15, concerts €10. 32 spots are reserved for €5 each and are sold 1½hr. before performance. ⌚ Box office open M-Sa 2:30-6:30pm.

SHOPPING

"Shopping" and "Paris" are almost synonymous. But the excessive wealth of the Champs-Élysées and Île St-Louis are not for the faint of heart—they're for the rich. Indeed, the many antiques, rare books, and tempting tourist trappings you'll find across the city could easily empty pockets. No one likes credit card debt, so we recommend the vintage shops and quirky boutiques in the youthful Marais and Bastille neighborhoods.

Books

SHAKESPEARE AND CO.   LATIN QUARTER AND ST-GERMAIN
37 rue de la Bûcherie   ☎01 43 25 40 93 www.shakespeareandcompany.com

This is more than just a bookstore. See **Sights** (p. 129).

i ⓂSt-Michel. Take quai de Montebello toward Notre Dame and turn right onto rue St-Jacques. Rue de la Bûcherie is on the left. ⌚ Open daily 10am-11pm.

paris

GIBERT JEUNE

pl. St-Michel ☎01 56 81 22 www.gibertjeune.fr

If you're studying abroad in Paris, this is probably where you'll want to buy your textbooks—Gibert Jeune carries over 300,000 titles, and with this many books, the store has multiple locations within walking distance for different genres. Buy a book and get the Gibert Jeune bag to blend in with the rest of Paris's literary crowd. Bonus: it's air-conditioned, which makes for a cool, intellectual getaway on a hot summer day.

i Ⓜ St-Michel. *Multiple locations along quai St-Michel, pl. Saint-Michel, and rue de la Huchette.* ⏰ *Open M-Sa 9:30am-7:30pm.*

SAN FRANCISCO BOOK CO.

17 rue Monsieur le Prince ☎01 43 29 15 70 www.sanfranciscobooksparis.com

San Francisco Book Co. is a quaint little English-language bookshop filled floor to ceiling with used books. If you're running low on cash, you can rummage through the €1-3 books outside or sell or trade your own books here. Find some summer fiction or mysteries on your own, or ask the gentle owner from Lincoln, Nebraska, about his more rare finds. You may not guess that among the Jodi Picoult novels and Michelin travel guides lie first edition copies of James Joyce's *Ulysses* or prints of Latin classics from the 17th century.

i Ⓜ Odéon. *From the intersection, walk down rue Dupuytren. Turn left at the end of the street onto rue Monsieur le Prince.* ⏰ *Open M-Sa 11am-9pm, Su 2-7:30pm.*

POP CULTURE SHOP

23 rue Keller ☎01 43 55 34 68 www.myspace.com/popcultureshop

Pop Culture Shop is focused on a specific kind of pop culture: comic books and superhero memorabilia. Shelves upon shelves of comic books make this a geek's gold mine in Bastille's shopping district. The shop is only a few years old, but the owner's collection has been in the works for many more. Find all your Batman and Green Lantern classics as well as some less mainstream names. In the back you can browse a decent collection of vinyls and figurines.

i Ⓜ Bastille. *Walk down rue de la Roquette and turn right onto rue Keller. Comic book €5-10. Vinyls €12-24.* ⏰ *Open Sept-Jun M 2-7:30pm, Tu-Sa 11am-7:30pm; Jul-Aug M-W 2-7:30pm, Th-Sa 11:30-7:30pm.*

LES MOTSÀ LA BOUCHE

6 rue Ste-Croix de la Bretonnerie ☎01 42 78 88 30 www.motsbouche.com

Logically located in the Marais, this two-story bookstore offers mostly GLBT literature, photography, magazines, and art, with everything from Proust to guides on lesbian lovemaking. Straight guys could probably learn a few pointers from that last one, too. And right next to the gay pornzines are some works by Foucault and Arendt because, you know, it's all interchangeable. Most books are in French, but there is an English section with books by David Sedaris and, of course, *Brokeback Mountain*. Head downstairs for the international DVD collection (€7-25); titles range from the artistic to the pornographic.

i Ⓜ Hôtel de Ville. *Take a left onto rue Vieille du Temple and a left onto rue Ste-Croix de la Bretonnerie. Books €8-21.* ⏰ *Open M-Sa 11am-11pm, Su1-9pm.*

Clothing

Parisians know how to dress well. It's in their blood. If you want to dress like them, you don't have to drain your bank account—or as they say in French, *"fais chauffer ta carte bleu"* ("heat up your credit card"). **Galeries Lafayette** is the French equivalent of Macy's and will save you time and money, not to mention the embarrassing experience of being asked to leave Louis V. For everything vintage, from pre-World War II garb to totally radical Jeff Spicoli get-ups, head to the Marais and Bastille. **Les Halles**

france

are also a mega complex of stores that sell everything from clothing to music and provide all that your average supermall has to offer.

◙ FREE'P' STAR
MARAIS

8 rue Ste-Croix de la Bretonnerie   ☎01 42 76 03 72 www.freepstar.com

Enter as Plain Jane and leave as Madonna—from the '80s or '90s, that is. Choose from a wide selection of vintage dresses (€20), velvet blazers (€40), boots (€30), and military-style jackets (€5) that all seem like a good idea when surrounded by other antiquated pieces but require some gumption to be worn out in the open—maybe shoulder pads are making a comeback? Dig around the €10 denim pile and €3 bin for ripped jeans that died out with Kurt Cobain.

i Ⓜ*Hôtel de Ville. Follow rue de Renard and turn right onto rue St-Merri, which becomes rue Ste-Croix de la Bretonnerie. There are 2 other locations at 61 rue de la Verrerie (01 42 78 076) and 20 rue de Rivoli. Credit card min €20. ⌚ Open M-F 11am-9pm, Sa-Su noon-9pm.*

SOBRAL
LES ÎLES

79 rue St-Louis-en-l'Île   ☎01 43 25 80 10 www.sobraldesign.fr

Brazilian artist Sobral is inspired by nature and makes all of his products with natural elements. Tiny Eiffel Towers, bangle bracelets, and elaborate necklaces are all made from natural resin infused with colors and objects in patterns reminiscent of tie-dye. The prices here may be fairly expensive, but it's a fun place to window shop. After all, Sobral only has three locations outside of Brazil, and this is one of them.

i Ⓜ*Pont Marie. Walk across the bridge and continue straight, then turn right onto rue St-Louis-en-l'Île. Rings €35. Bracelets €28-56. Earrings €18-40. Necklaces €78-120. Mirrors from €110.* ⌚ *Open daily 11am-7:30pm.*

Vintage

◙ COME ON EILEEN
BASTILLE

16-18 rue des Taillandiers   ☎01 43 38 12 11

Forget tacky vintage blazers and enormous shoulder pads—this vintage paradise is full of timeless designer goods, thank you. From Vanessa Bruno dresses to Marc Jacobs heels, your finds will leave you dying to brag to your friends about what a savvy thrift shopper you are. Look Faye Dunaway-chic in your Lanvin flats and not Bill Cosby-itchy in those, ahem, memorable sweaters.

i Ⓜ*Voltaire or*Ⓜ*Bastille. Walk up rue de la Roquette; rue des Taillandiers is about halfway between the 2 stops. Items from €30-80.* ⌚ *Open M 11am-8:30pm, Tu 3-8:30pm, W-F 11am-8:30pm, Su 2-8pm. Store opens at 2pm in Aug; closes at 5pm in winter.*

◙ MAMIE SHOP
OPÉRA

73 rue de Rochechouart   ☎01 42 82 09 98

Right next door to Mamie Blue, Mamie Shop offers a bigger selection and a little more flair than its sister store. The shop feels a bit like Willy Wonka's version of a clothing store, with spaces narrow enough for just one person to fit at a time, but with so many rooms and clothing, you could easily get lost. Sadly, there are no glass elevators for sale, just some interesting articles of clothing. Mamie Blue specializes in clothing from the 1920s to the 1970s, with flowery dresses and Mad Men-esque blouses, although we're thinking the prices might be a little over-adjusted for inflation.

i Ⓜ*Anvers or Barbès. From bd de Rochechouart, turn onto rue de Rochechouart, which is located between the 2 Métro stops. Tailoring available. Men's jackets from €30. Dresses €40-175.* ⌚ *Open M 3-6pm, Tu-Sa 11am-12:30pm and 3-6pm.*

paris

Specialty

🔖 PALAIS DES THÉS

MARAIS

64 rue Vieille du Temple ☎01 48 87 80 60 www.palaisdesthes.com

Le Palais des Thés lives up to its name with a grand, handpicked selection of teas. Tea experts travel to 20 countries in Asia, Africa, and South America to find the highest quality supplies. By personally traveling to each tea estate, the owners are able to ensure fair trade and labor practices and keep an eye on local environmental issues, so you can steep your organic jasmine tea with a clean conscience. Teas can be as inexpensive as €3-4 or as pricey as €100 for 100g. Describe your preferences and tastes to the welcoming staff, and they will point you in the direction of the tea that best fits your needs (and your pocketbook).

i Ⓜ*St-Paul. Walk up rue Malher as it turns into rue Payenne. Turn left onto rue des Francs Bourgeois, then turn right onto rue Vieille du Temple. 4 other locations around the city. Most tea €3.50-17 per 100g. ☼ Open M-Sa 10am-8pm.*

🔖 CAILLES DE LUXE

BASTILLE

15 rue Keller ☎09 53 02 65 22 www.caillesdeluxe.com

When the owners of this glam little shop decided they were fed up with quality jewelry costing a fortune, they decided to go into the business themselves. Bright colors and simple geometric shapes mark the staples of this shop and make for fantastic statement pieces. Go a notch or two above with some of the more unusual items, like necklaces with Scrabble ornaments or fun Ghostbusters earrings. This is definitely a place for the ladies, so guys might want to find a nice place to sit for a while.

i Ⓜ*Voltaire. Walk southwest on rue de la Roquette and turn left onto rue Keller; the store is about halfway down on the left. Earrings from €9. Rings from €5. ☼ Open Tu-Sa 11am-8pm.*

🔖 LE MARCHÉ AUX FLEURS

ÎLE DE LA CITÉ AND ÎLE ST-LOUIS

pl. Louis-Lépine

The flower market at the center of Île de la Cité brings a welcome scene of green and freshness to the city streets. Go traditional and buy your sweetheart a dozen roses or a wild orchid. Or go rogue and opt for a birdhouse, seeds for an herb garden, or a rare tree from Madagascar.

i Ⓜ*Cité. Flowers from €5. ☼ Open M 10am-6:30pm, W-Su 10am-6:30pm.*

ESSENTIALS

Practicalities

- **TOURIST OFFICES: Bureau Central d'Accueil** provides maps and tour information and books accommodations. (25 rue des Pyramides ☎01 49 52 42 63 www.parisinfo.com *i* Pyramides.☼ Open daily May-Oct 9am-7pm; Nov-Apr 10am-7pm.) Also located at Gare de Lyon (☎01 43 33 24 ☼ Open M-Sa 8am-6pm); Gare du Nord (☎01 45 26 94 82 ☼ Open daily 8am-6pm); Gare de L'est (☼ Open M-Sa 8am-7pm); Anvers facing 72 bd Rochechouart (☼ Open daily 10am-6pm). **Tourist kiosks** at Ⓜ ChampsÉlysées-Clemenceau, Ⓜ Cité in front of Notre Dame, Ⓜ Hôtel de Ville inside the Hôtel de Ville, Ⓜ Anvers, and Ⓜ Bastille. All offices and kiosks have tourist maps; Métro, bus, and RER maps; and walking guides to Paris produced by the Paris Convention and Visitors Bureau. Most hotels and hostels also offer these resources for free.

- **TOURS: Bateaux-Mouches** offers boat tours along the Seine. (Port de la Conférence, Pont de l'Alma ☎01 42 25 02 28 www.bateaux-mouches.fr *i* Ⓜ Alma-Marceau or Ⓜ Franklin Roosevelt. Tours in English €12.50, under 12 €5.50, under 4 free. ☼ Cruise about 70min. Apr-Sept M-F every 20-30min. 10:15am-10:30pm; Oct-Mar M-F every 11am-9pm, Sa-Su 10:15am-9pm every 45-60min.)

- **GLBT RESOURCES: Paris Gay Village.** (61-63 rue Beaubourg ☎01 77 15 89 42 www. parisgayvillage.com *i* ⓂRambuteau. English spoken. ☑ Open M 6-8pm, Tu-Th 3:30-8pm, F 1-8pm, Sa 1-7pm.) Recommends GLBT accommodations, listings, and networking. SKOPIK map can be found at most tourist offices. Map of GLBT friendly establishments throughout Paris. **Centre Gay et Lesbien** (63 rue Beaubourg ☎01 43 57 21 47 www.centrelgbtparis.org *i* ⓂRambuteau. English spoken. Provides legal assistance, networking. ☑ Open M 6-8pm, Tu 3-8pm, W 12:30-8pm, Th 3-8pm, F-Sa 12:30-8pm, Su 4-7pm.

- **STUDENT RESOURCES: Centre d'Information et de Documentation pour la Jeunesse** provides information on temporary work, job placement, tourism info, and housing for students studying in Paris. (101 quai Branly ☎01 44 49 12 00 www.cidj.com *i* ⓂBir-Hakeim. ☑ Open Tu-F 1-6pm, Sa 1-5pm.)

- **TICKET AGENCIES: FNAC.** (74 av. des Champs-Élysées ☎08 25 02 00 20 www.fnacspec-tacles.com *i* ⓂFranklin D. Roosevelt.ⓂChâtelet/Les Halles. Various other FNAC stores throughout Paris; check the website for more locations. ☑ Open M-Sa 10am-11:45pm, Su noon-11:45pm.)

- **INTERNET: American Library in Paris** has computers and internet access for members or guests with day passes. (10 rue du Général Camou ☎01 53 59 12 60 www.americanlibrary-inparis.org *i* ⓂÉcole Militaire. ☑ Open Tu-Sa10am-7pm, Su 1-7pm; Jul-Aug Tu-F 1-7pm, Sa 10am-4pm.) There is also free Wi-Fi at **Centre Pompidou** and in its **Bibliothèque Publique d'Information.** (pl. Georges Pompidou, rue Beaubourg 8 ⓂRambuteau or ⓂHôtel de Ville. ☑ Center open M 11am-9pm, W-Su 11am-9pm. Library open M noon-10pm, W-F noon-10pm, Sa-Su 11am-10pm.) There is also always free Wi-Fi at McDonald's, Starbucks, and shaky Wi-Fi in public parks.

- **POST OFFICES: La Poste** runs the French postal system (www.laposte.fr). There are many post offices in Paris that are generally open M-F 8am-7pm and Sa 8am-noon. The most centrally located post offices are in **Saint-Germain** (118 bd St-Germain *i* ⓂOdéon. ☑ Open M-F 8am-8pm, Sa 9am-5pm) and **Châtelet-Les Halles.** (1 rue Pierre Lescot *i* ⓂLes-Halles. ☑ Open M-F 8am-6:30pm, Sa 9am-1pm.) The **Paris Louvre** post office is also easily accessible. (52 rue du Louvre *i* ⓂLouvre-Rivoli. ☑ Open 7:30am-6pm.)

Emergency

- **POLICE:** 17. **Préfecture de la Police.** (9 bd Palais ☎01 53 71 53 71 *i* ⓂCité. Across the street from the Palais de Justice. ☑ Open 24hr.)

- **CRISIS LINE: SOS Help!** is an emergency hotline for English speakers. (☎01 46 21 46 46)

- **DOCTORS:** ☎36 24, Dentist: ☎01 43 37 51 00. (☑ Available daily 3-11pm.) Ambulance (SAMU): ☎15. Fire: ☎18.

- **LATE-NIGHT PHARMACIES: Pharmacie Les Champs.** (84 av. des Champs-Élysées ☎01 45 62 02 41 *i* ⓂFranklin Roosevelt. ☑ Open daily 24hr.) **Grande Pharmacie Daumesnil.** (6 pl. Félix Eboué ☎01 43 43 19 03 *i* ⓂDaumesnil. ☑ Open daily 8:30am-10pm.) **Pharmacie européenne.** (6 pl. de Clichy ☎01 48 74 65 18 *i* ⓂPl. de Clichy. ☑ Open daily 24hr.) **Pharmacie Première.** (24 bd de Sébastopol ☎01 48 87 62 30 *i* ⓂChatelet. ☑ Open daily 8am-midnight.)

- **HOSPITALS/MEDICAL SERVICES: American Hospital of Paris.** (Pedestrian entrance at 63 bd Victor Hugo, vehicle entrance at 84 bd de la Saussaye. ☎01 46 41 25 25 www.ameri-can-hospital.org *i* ⓂPort Maillot, then bus 82 to last stop Hôpital Américain. Or ⓂPonte de Neuilly, then bus #93 to Hôpital Américan. Or ⓂPont de Levallois-Bécon, walk down rue Anatole France, turn right onto rue Baudin, walk 4 blocks, continue down rue Greffulhe and rue de Villiers, turn right onto bd du Château, walk 1 block, and turn right onto bd Victor Hugo; Hospital is on the left.) **Hôpital Bichat.** (46 rue Henri Huchard ☎01 40 25 80 80 *i* ⓂPorte de St-Ouen.)

paris

Getting There

How you arrive in Paris will be dictated by where you are traveling from. Those flying across the Atlantic will most likely end up at **Paris-Charles de Gaulle,** one of Europe's main international hubs. If flying from within Europe on a budget airline, you'll probably fly into **Orly.** Though it hardly counts as arriving in Paris, flying into **Beauvais** from other European cities will often save you a lot of money even with the €16, 75min. shuttle ride into the Porte Maillot station in Paris. RER lines, buses, and shuttles run regularly from all three airports to Paris; however, time and price vary with each airport. With its confusingly endless number of train stations, Paris offers options for both those coming from within France and those who are traveling by train from elsewhere in Europe.

BY PLANE

PARIS-CHARLES DE GAULLE (CDG)

Roissy-en-France, 23km northeast of Paris | from landline in Paris ☎3950
from abroad ☎01 70 36 39 50 www.adp.fr.

Most transatlantic flights land at Aéroport Paris-CDG. The two cheapest and fastest ways to get into the city from Paris-CDG are by RER and by bus. The RER train services Terminals 1, 2, and 3. The RER B (€9.50, includes Métro transport when you get off the RER) will take you to central Paris. To transfer to the Métro, get off at Gare du Nord, Châtelet-Les Halles, or St-Michel. The **Roissybus** (☎01 49 25 61 87 *i* €10 ⏱45-60min., every 15-20min. during day; 20-30min. at night. Departures from Opéra 5:45am-11pm, from CDG 6am-11pm.) departs from Terminals 1,2 and 3 and arrives at Opéra. **Les Cars Air France** (☎08 92 35 08 20) departs from Terminals 1, 2, and 3 and connects to Étoile and Porte Maillot (Line 2) or Gare de Lyon and Gare Montparnasse (Line 4).

ORLY (ORY)

Orly, 18km south of Paris | ☎01 49 15 15 15 www.adp.fr.

Aéroport d'Orly is used by charters and many continental flights. From Orly Sud Gate G or Gate I, platform 1, or Orly Ouest level G, Gate F, take the **Orly-Rail** shuttle bus to the Pont de Rungis/Aéroport d'Orly train station, where you can board the RER C for a number of destinations in Paris, including Châtelet, St-Michel, Invalides, and Gare d'Austerlitz (RER C). Another option is the RATP 🚇**Orlybus** (☎08 36 68 77 14 *i* €7.20 ⏱ 30min., every 15-20min.), which runs between Métro and RER stop Denfert-Rochereau and Orly's south and west terminal. RATP also runs **Orlyval** (☎01 69 93 53 00 *i* VAL ticket €8.40, VAL-RER ticket €11.30), a combination Métro, RER, and VAL rail shuttle. The VAL shuttle goes from Antony (RER B) to Orly Ouest and Sud. Buy tickets at any RATP booth in the city or from the Orlyval agencies at Orly Ouest, Orly Sud, and Antony. See www.aeroportsdeparis.fr for maps of transportation between Orly and different locations in Paris. **Les Cars Air France** (☎08 92 35 08 20) connects from Orly Sud and Ouest terminals to Gare Montparnasse, Invalides, and Étoile (Line 1).

BY TRAIN

SNCF (www.sncf.com) sells train tickets for travel within France and abroad and offers *la Carte 12-27*, which guarantees reduced prices of up to 60% after you pay a one-time €50 fee. **Rail Europe** (www.raileurope.com) also sells tickets for travel within France and abroad, but prices for US residents tend to be higher than those offered by SNCF. There are several major train stations in Paris: **Gare d'Austerlitz** services southwest France, Spain, Portugal; **Gare de l'Est** for eastern France, Germany, Switzerland, eastern Europe; **Gare de Lyon** for southeast France, Italy; **Gare de Nord** for northern France, Germany, Belgium, Netherlands, UK. From Gare de Lyon, there are trains to Lyon (2hr., €25-92), Marseilles (3-4hr., €25-120), and Nice (5hr. 30min., €25-125). For London and the UK, book up to 120 days in advance with **www.eurostar.com**

(€42-183, 2hr. 30min. to London from Gare du Nord). For Brussels (1hr. 30min., €29-99) and Amsterdam (3hr. 15min., €35-130) from Gare du Nord, use **www.thalys.com**. For Switzerland from Gare de Lyon to Geneva, book through www.sncf.com (3-4hr., €25-130). For Italy, trains depart from Gare de Lyon; for overnight sleepers, book with **www.thello.com** (Milan, 10hr. €35-220; Rome, 15hr., €100-275). For Spain, book through www.sncf.com; overnights from Gare d'Austerlitz (Barcelona, 11hr. 30min., €96-211); daytime trains from Gare de Lyon (Barcelona, 6hr. 30min., €106-175). For Germany, book through www.sncf.com (Cologne, 3-4hr. direct, €99-120; Frankfurt, 4hr. direct, €89-119) for overnights and daytime trains.

Thalys.com offers reduced prices for those under 26. **Gare du Nord** (112 rue de Maubeuge) is the arrival point for trains from northern France and Germany as well as Amsterdam (From €65, 3½hr.), Brussels (From €50, 1hr.), and London €50-120, 2½hr.). **Gare de l'Est** (78 bd de Strasbourg) receives trains from eastern France and southern Germany, Austria, Hungary, Munich, (€125-163, 9-10½hr.), and Prague (€118-172, 12-15hr.). **Gare de Lyon** (20 bd Diderot) has trains from Florence (€135-170, 9-12hr.), Lyon (€60-70, 2hr.), Marseille (€45-70, 3-4hr.), Nice (€100, 5½hr.), and Rome (€177-200, 12-15hr.). **Gare d'Austerlitz** (85 quai d'Austerlitz) services the Loire Valley and the Iberian peninsula, including Barcelona (€135-170, 7-12hr.) and Madrid (€220-300, 12-13hr.). **Gare St-Lazare** (13 rue d'Amsterdam) will welcome you from northern France, while **Gare Montparnasse** (17 bd Vaugirard) is the destination of trains from northeastern and southwestern France.

Getting Around

BY Métro

In general, the Métro is easy to navigate, and trains run swiftly and frequently. Most of Paris lies within zones 1-2, so don't worry about the suburbs in zones 3-5. Pick up a colorful map at any station. Métro stations themselves are a distinctive part of the city's landscape and are marked with an "M" or with *"Métropolitain,"* but along the Champs-Élysées, they are unmarked stairs leading underground. The earliest trains start running around 5:30am, and the last ones leave the end-of-the-line stations (the *portes de Paris*) at about 12:15am during the week and at 2:15am on Friday and Saturday. In general, be at the Métro by 1am if you want to take it home at night. Connections to other lines are indicated by *correspondance* signs, and exits are marked by blue *sortie* signs. Transfers are free if made within a station, but it's not always possible to reverse direction on the same line without exiting. Hold onto your ticket until you exit the Métro and pass the point marked **Limite de Validité des Billets**; a uniformed RATP *contrôleur* (inspector) may request to see it on any train. If you're caught without a ticket, you will have to pay a €30 fine on the spot. It's a good idea to carry one more ticket than you need, although most, but not all, stations have ticket machines that now accept both bills and coins. Tickets cost €1.70 per journey, although it's much more useful to buy a *carnet* of 10 tickets for €13.30. You can also buy unlimited Métro passes for 1 day (€6.60), and on the weekend, young'uns under 26 can buy a day pass for €3.65. For longer visits, you can buy a week- or month-long (€19.80/65.10) **Navigo Découverte Pass**, which costs an additional €5 and requires a passport photo to attach to the card. Month-long passes begin the 1st day of the month, and week-long passes begin on Monday. You can also buy a *Paris Visite* pass (meant for tourists) for unlimited travel for 1-5 days with rather meager discounts (1-day pass €10.55; 2-day €17.15; 3-day €23.40; 5-day €33.70.)

When it's getting really late, your best chance of getting the train you want is heading to the biggest stations, like Gare du Nord, Gare de l'Est, and Châtelet-Les Halles. However, these stations are often full of tourists and pickpockets, so stay alert when traveling at night or avoid it altogether. If you must travel by public trans-

paris

port late at night, get to know the Noctilien bus (see below). When in doubt, take a taxi.

BY RER

The **RER** *(Réseau Express Régional)* is the RATP's suburban train system, which passes through central Paris and travels much faster than the Métro. There are five RER lines, marked A-E, with different branches designated by a number. The newest line, E, is called the Eole *(Est-Ouest Liaison Express)* and links Gare Magenta to Gare St-Lazare. Within central Paris, the RER works just like the Métro and requires the same ticket for the same price (if you have to transfer from the RER to the Métro or vice versa, however, you will need another ticket). The principal stops within the city that link the RER to the Métro are Gare du Nord, Nation, Charles de Gaulle-Étoile, Gare de Lyon, Châtelet-Les Halles, St-Michel, and Denfert-Rochereau. The electric signs next to each track list all the possible stops for trains running on that track. Be sure that the little square next to your destination is lit up. Trips to the suburbs require more expensive tickets that can also be bought at the automatic booths where you purchase Métro tickets. You must know what zone you're going to in order to buy the proper ticket. In order to exit the RER station, insert your ticket just as you did to enter and pass through. Like the Métro, the RER runs 5:30am-12:30am on weekdays and until 2:30am on weekends, but never wait until 2:30am to get to the Métro or RER. Again, if you must travel by public transportation late at night, get to know the Noctilien bus.

BY BUS

Although slower than the Métro, a bus ride can be a cheap sightseeing tour and a helpful introduction to the city's layout. Bus tickets are the same as those used for the Métro and can be purchased in Métro stations or from bus drivers (€1.70). Enter the bus through the front door and punch your ticket by pushing it into the machine next to the driver's seat. Inspectors may ask to see your ticket, so hold on to it until you get off. When you want to get off, press the red button so the *arrêt demandé* (stop requested) sign lights up. Most buses run daily 7am-8:30pm, although those marked **Autobus du nuit** continue until 1:30am. The **Noctilien** runs all night (daily 12:30am-5:30am) and services more than 45 routes throughout the city. If you plan to use this frequently, get a map of the routes from a Métro station and study it. Hard. Look for bus stops marked with a moon sign. Check out www.noctilien.fr or inquire at a major Métro station or Gare de l'Est for more information on Noctilien buses. Complete bus route maps are posted at the bus stops, while individual lines only give out maps of their own routes. Noctilien #2 runs to all the major train stations along the periphery of the city, while #12 and #13 run between Châtelet and Gare de Montparnasse.

BY TAXI

Traveling by taxi in Paris can be intimidating. Parisian taxis usually have three fares that change based on the time of day and day of the week. Rush hours and early morning hours on the weekends are the priciest, while morning to midday fares on weekdays are the cheapest. Fares are measured out by the kilometer and only switch to waiting time if a trip is over an hour. The pick-up base charge is €2.40, and minimum fare is €6.40. Each additional person after three passengers costs €3, and each additional piece of luggage after the first costs €1. A typical 20min. taxi ride costs €12-20, and a 40min. ride can be as much as €50. Taxis are easily hailed from any major boulevard or avenue, but stands are often outside major Métro intersections. If the taxi's green light is on, it is available. From the airport, prices skyrocket and begin at €50. It's never a bad idea to ask for a receipt at the end of your trip in case of dispute or lost property.

BY BIKE

If just don't feel like walking or gambling with timetables, bike rentals may be for you. There are many **Vélib'** stations around the city where you can rent a public bike for prices ranging from €1.70 for the day, €8 for the week, and €29 for the year. Each time you take it out, the first 30min. are free, the next 30min. are €1, 2nd additional 30min. are €2, and each additional 30min. thereafter €4. You can return the bike at any Vélib' station. If you arrive at a station and there are no open spots, go to the machine, punch in your number, and receive an additional 15min. to find another open station. Stations at the top of hills are generally open, and those at the bottom are typically not; spots near major tourist destinations and the quais are often a safe bet. If you want to rent on the spot, you must have a credit card with a chip on it to use the automatic booths where you can rent a bike; otherwise, you can rent from www.velib.fr to receive a subscription code. **Paris Bike Tour** also offers bike rentals for €20 for a 24hr. period; each extra day costs €10 (13 rue Brantôme ☎01 42 74 22 14 ☑ Open daily 9:30am-6:30pm). The bad news is they also require €250 deposit and a copy of your photo ID.

versailles

Less than a 30min. train ride (or a 15min. death commute by scooter) from the center of Paris is a town famous for a single house. "House" might be an understatement. Your history books will tell you that this palace was hated just as much as the Bastille, but thankfully its beauty (and we can only assume massive tourism potential) saved it from the raging mob. Versailles is about as modest as the man who built it—the ultimate arrogant Frenchman, the "Sun King," Louis XIV. He had plenty of time to pimp his 580m-long crib, too, over his 72-year rule. The city surrounding the château mainly serves as another suburb for wealthy Parisian families. Some things never change.

ORIENTATION

Versailles is a blessing for the navigationally challenged. In the middle of the **place d'Armes** sits the massive **Château de Versailles,** with **avenue de Paris** extending from the center. Crossing av. de Paris is **avenue de l'Europe,** which leads to the train stations Rive Droite and Rive Gauche (corresponding to the terminus locations in Paris). Av. de l'Europe also crosses through **place de Notre Dame,** where you can find your banks, large open-air market, and cheap creperies. For a daytrip, you won't need to go beyond the two avenues, whose intersection is home to the tourist office.

SIGHTS

▨ CHÂTEAU

☎01 30 83 78 89 www.chateauversailles.fr

The **Queen's Bedchamber** (which cannot be rented out; keep holding out for the Lincoln Bedroom), where royal births were public events to prove the legitimacy of heirs, is much less ornate than the king's but almost exactly as the queen left it on October 6, 1789. Not to worry though; from what we could tell, they changed the sheets.

i €15, under 18 and EU residents 18-25 free; includes audio tour. €6 for the château for everyone after 4pm from Apr 16-Jun 30. "Passport" €18, under 18 and EU residents 18-25 free; allows entry to the château, Trianon palace, and Marie-Antoinette's Estate. ☑ Château open Tu-Su Apr-Oct 9am-6:30pm, last entry 6pm; Nov-Mar 9am-5:30pm, last entry 4:50pm.

versailles

GARDENS

When you have a big-ass house, you need a big-ass garden to go with it—otherwise it just looks silly. The château gardens are an impressive 800 hectares (if you aren't fluent in hectares, just know that they're huge) and are filled with fountains and row upon row of hedges. The price of admission to the château includes this visit, so go look at the pretty shrubbery and the numerous statues (and lip-locked couples) hidden in the groves. Make sure you bring a hat, sunglasses, and sunblock because the shrubs and exposed boulevards don't offer much in the way of shade—you don't want to end up as red as Louis XIV's heels. During **Les Grandes Eaux Musicales,** almost all the fountains are turned on at the same time, and chamber music booms from among the groves, but you'll have to pay extra to experience that.

i Free. Grandes Eaux Musicale €8, under 18 €6, under 6 free. ☒ Gardens open daily Apr-Oct 8am-8:30pm; Nov-Mar 8am-6pm. Grandes Eaux Musicales Apr-Oct Sa-Su 11am-noon and 3:30-5:30pm.

ESSENTIALS
Practicalities

- **TOURIST OFFICES:** Get maps, hotel and market information, and a complete city guide (even though you're probably just going to the château). Also provides travel advice for visitors with disabilities. (2 bis av. de Paris ☎01 39 24 88 88 www.versailles-tourimse.com *i* Corner of av. de Paris and av. de l'Europe. ☒ Open Apr-Sept M 10am-6pm, Tu-Su 9am-7pm; Oct-Mar M 11am-5pm, Tu-Sa 9am-6pm, Su 11am-5pm.)

- **PHARMACIES:** English spoken with Dr. Elizabeth Kennedy. (rue de la Pourvoirerie ☎01 39 50 09 23 *i* Corner of rue Maréchal Foch and rue de la Pourvoirerie ☒ Open M 10am-7:30pm, Tu-Sa 9am-7:30pm.)

- **ATMS: HSBC.** (18 rue du Maréchal Foch ☒ Open 24hr.)

Getting There

RER trains beginning with "V" run from St-Michel Notre Dame to the **Versailles Rive Gauche station.** From **Gare St-Lazare,** trains run to **Gare Versailles Rive Droite,** which is on the opposite side of the town and equidistant from the château as the other train station. From Montparnasse, trains arrive at **Gare de Chantiers,** which is the farthest from the château. Buy your RER ticket before going through the turnstile to the platform; when purchasing from a machine, look for the **Île-de-France ticket** option. While a Métro ticket will get you through these turnstiles, it won't get you through RER turnstiles at the other end and could ultimately result in a significant fine. (*i* Round-trip €4.10, with Navigo Decouverte €3.20. ☒ 30-40min., every 20min. from 4:50am-12:15am.)

Getting Around

Versailles is entirely walkable for what you want to see; it's almost like they anticipated the tourists when they built it. Any bus that goes to the city center will stop next to the château, but you can walk to and from most points of interest in 10min. The area in front of the château is called the **Place d'Armes** and faces toward the château. The diagonal street on the right, **av. de St-Cloud,** has a number of decently priced eateries, and if you continue and turn left onto rue du Maréchal Foch, there are even cheaper options.

chartres

Were it not for a holy scrap of fabric, Chartres might still be a sleepy hamlet. But the cloth that the Virgin Mary supposedly wore when she gave birth to Jesus somehow ended up here, making Chartres a major medieval pilgrimage center. The majestic, Gothic cathedral towering over the city and the magnificent stained glass aren't the only reason to visit; the *vieille ville* (Old Town) is also a masterpiece of medieval architecture, which almost makes you forget the zooming highways that have encroached upon it.

ORIENTATION

To reach the **Cathédrale** from the train station, walk straight ahead down **avenue Jehan de Beauce,** cut diagonally across **place de Châtelet** to reach the mini roundabout, continue straight on rue Saint-Même, turn left onto rue du Cheval Blanc, continue right onto rue de l'Étroit Degré,and the cathedral is on the left. Upon seeing the cathedral and the **place de la Cathédrale,** you'll quickly begin to comprehend that the church isn't the only show in town. Don't make the mistake of asking a local where the cathedral is; you'll get laughed at or severely snarked. The **Musée des Beaux-Arts** and other prominent sights are located behind the cathedral. **La Maison Picassiette** is a little farther out, about 10min. away from the *vieille ville* by taxi or 20min. by Filibus. Chartres's medieval tangle of streets can be confusing, but getting lost is enjoyable, and with a city this small and spires that prominent, you'll never be lost for long.

SIGHTS

◪ La Cathédrale Notre-Dame de Chartres

LA CATHÉDRALE CHURCH

18 cloître Notre-Dame ☎02 37 21 75 02 www.cathedrale-chartres.org

Other must-sees include the 176 stained glass windows that date from the 13th century. They were preserved through both World Wars by the heroic and extremely savvy town authorities, who carefully dismantled all the windows and stored them in Dordogne until the fighting was over. The glass designs are characterized by a stunning color known as "Chartres blue," which has not been successfully reproduced in modern times. The windows of Chartres often distract visitors from the treasure below their feet: a winding labyrinth pattern that is carved into the floor in the rear of the nave. The labyrinth originally served as a pilgrimage substitute—by following this pattern on their hands and knees, the devout would enact a symbolic voyage to Jerusalem and still have time to be home by dinner.

i *In pl. de la Cathédrale. Free. English tours begin outside the gift shop in the cathedral. 1hr. English audio tours available at the gift shop require ID. English tours €10, students and children €5. Audio tours for cathedral €4.20; for choir loft €3.20; for both €6.20. ☒ Open daily 8:30am-7:30pm; open until 10pm Tu, F, and Su Jul-Aug. English tours Easter-Oct M-Sa noon and 2:45pm; Nov-Easter M-Sa noon.*

TOUR JEHAN-DE-BEAUCE TOWER

☎02 37 21 22 07

Only the physically fit and non-claustrophobic can climb the narrow, 300-step staircase to the cathedral's north tower, but those who do shall receive a stellar view of the city. The panorama and chance to see the cathedral from a new angle is quite astonishing. If you can't make it all the way to the top, the first viewing platform offers a slightly obstructed but still impressive panorama.

i *€7.50, non-EU citizens ages 18-25 €4.50. 1st Su of the month, EU citizens 18-25 and under 18 free. ☒ Open May-Aug M-Sa 9:30am-12:30pm and 2-6pm, Su 2-6pm; Sept-Apr M-Sa 9:30am-12:30pm and 2-5pm, Su 2-5pm. Last entry 30min. before close.*

chartres

LA CRYPTE

CRYPT

Visitors may enter the 110m subterranean crypt only as part of a guided tour. Highlights include the original statues from the façade and the scarily deep ninth-century well, in which Vikings tossed the bodies of their victims during raids. Other than that, though, the various small chapels alternate between Gothic and Romanesque styles and are much less impressive than the cathedral itself, so make time for this attraction only if you've got time to kill before your train leaves.

i 30min. tours leave from the store opposite the cathedral's south entrance at 18 cloître Notre-Dame. English leaflets are available at La Crypte store. €3, students €2.40, under 7 free. ☼ Tours Apr-Oct M-Sa 11am, 2:15pm, 3:30pm, and 4:30pm; Su 2:15pm, 3:30pm, and 4:30pm. Tours Nov-Mar M-Sa 11am and 4:15pm; Su 4:15pm. Additional 5:15pm tour Jun 22-Sept 21.

Other Sights

◪ MAISON PICASSIETTE

MUSEUM

22 rue du Repos ☎02 37 34 10 78

Most people are satisfied just remodeling their home after buying it, but Raymond Isidore has outdone any HGTV show. Over the course of 24 years, Isidore decorated his home with extraordinary, intricate mosaics crafted from pieces of broken and discarded glass and pottery that he found. His nickname was Picassiette, from the words *piquer* ("to steal") and *assiette* ("plate"). Everything from the doghouse to the stove to the watering can is covered in mosaics of cathedral and Biblical themes, with the occasional Mona Lisa thrown for good fun. Although this sight is a bit far from Chartres, its weirdness and incredible intricacy make for quite the memorable visit and an entirely new understanding of hot glue that will shame every macaroni art project your mother ever put up on the fridge.

i From the train station, take the #4 Filibus toward Madeleine to the Picassiette stop. From the bus stop, walk back the way you came to rue du Repos, turn right, and Maison Picassiette is on the left. Buses every 15-20 min. €1.10 bus fare each way. €5.40, students and under 26 €2.70, under 18 free; combined ticket with Musée des Beaux-Arts €7.30/3.65. ☼ Open M 10am-6pm, W-Sa 10am-6pm. Last entry 15min. before close.

MUSÉE DES BEAUX-ARTS

MUSEUM

29 cloître Notre-Dame ☎02 37 90 45 80

The former Bishop's Palace, the beautiful and creaky building which is now home to this museum is a little more impressive than the collection itself. The museum deals with the medieval history of Chartres and displays 15th- through 19th-century European paintings, 17th- and 18th-century harpsichords, suits of armor, and a sword collection.

i Across the street from the cathedral. Permanent collection €3.40, students €1.70; permanent collection and temporary exhibits €5.40/2.70; combined ticket with Maison Picassiette €7.30/3.65. Free for under 18, 1st Su Sept-Jun. ☼ Open May-Oct W 10am-noon and 2-6pm, Sa 10am-noon and 2-6pm, Su 2-6pm; Nov-Apr M 10am-noon and 2-5pm, Sa 10am-noon and 2-5pm, Su 2-5pm. Last entry 30min. before close.

CENTRE INTERNATIONAL DU VITRAIL

MUSEUM

5 rue du Cardinal Pie ☎02 37 21 65 72 www.centre-vitrail.org

With 176 stained glass windows in the cathedral, it only makes sense that there's a museum dedicated to stained glass, although it's not clear why it's held in a 12th-century medieval tithe barn. The museum is mostly in French, with exhibits explaining the process of creating the windows and the evolution of the craft from the Middle Ages to the modern day. Downstairs, you'll find an impressive exhibit on modern stained glass art, although it's mostly abstract and lacking in images of archangels slaying **dragons.**

i Across the street from the cathedral. €5.50, students and under 18 €4, under 16 free. ☼ Open

france

M-F 9:30am-12:30pm and 1:30-6pm, Sa 10am-12:30pm and 2:30-6pm, Su 2:30-6pm. Last entry 15min. before close.

FOOD

Food in Chartres really only caters to the tourist population, so falling into a pricey tourist trap is inevitable. While your cheapest option is always to picnic in the Jardins de l'Évech, there are some calmer joints that don't attract the hordes of pilgrims.

ÉPICERIE DE LA PLACE BILLARD
GROCERY $
19 rue des Changes   ☎02 37 21 00 25

Épicerie de la Place Billard is a friendly, inexpensive grocery store that sells all the picnic basics, plus some: pick up some goat cheese-flavored chips and speculoos-flavored cookies to go with all those Kinder bars you'll be gorging on. Take your loot to the Jardins de l'Éveché for a terrific view of Chartres.

i From rue Cloître Notre Dame, turn left onto rue des Changes and walk 3 blocks; Épicerie is on the right. From there to the Jardins de l'Éveché, walk back to rue Cloître Notre Dame, turn right, and fork left to the northeast face of the church to see Jardins and the view in front of you. ☉ Open daily 5am-7:30pm.

LE PARVIS
CAFE, TRADITIONAL $$
13 place de la Cathédrale   ☎02 37 21 12 12 www.le-parvis-chartres.fr

If you're going to eat out or sit down for coffee anywhere in this touristy town, make it here. With free Wi-Fi, a terrace in the shadow of the cathedral, and set menus starting at €12, Le Parvis should be the pilgrimage site for budget travelers. Come on a Friday or Saturday night for the live jazz before heading back home.

i From rue Cloître Notre Dame, head toward the spires of the cathedral and continue around the church; Parvis is on the left. Free Wi-Fi. Live jazz Sept-Jun F-Sa 9:30pm-12:30am; Jul-Aug 7:30pm-12:30am. Menu fixed €10-15. Entrées €8.50-15. plats €11-16.50. Dessert €4.50-7.50 ☉ Open daily 10am-10:30pm.

ESSENTIALS

Practicalities

- **TOURIST OFFICES:** The **Office de Tourisme de Chartres** provides maps and books accommodations. (pl. de la Cathédrale ☎02 37 18 26 26 www.chartres-tourisme.com ☉ Open M-F 9am-1pm and 2-6pm, Sa 10am-1pm and 2-6pm.)
- **TOURS:** English-language walking tours are available at the tourist office. (€6, under 12 €4. ☉ 1hr., Jul-Aug Tu 2:30pm.) Audio tours of the *vieille ville* are also available. (€5.50, 2 for €8.50. ☉ 1hr.)
- **CURRENCY EXCHANGE: Currency Exchange Office.** (Parvis de la Cathédrale ☎02 37 36 42 33 ☉ Open Mar-Oct M-Sa 9am-5pm.)

Emergency

- **POLICE: Hôtel de Police.** (57 rue du Docteur Maunoury ☎02 37 23 42 84 *i* Follow rue Collin d'Harleville to pl. des Épars and continue onto rue du Docteur Maunoury.)
- **LATE-NIGHT PHARMACIES: Pharmacie Desprez Buis.** (49 rue Soleil d'Or ☎02 37 36 ☎02 63 ☉ Open 24hr.)
- **HOSPITALS/MEDICAL SERVICES: Louis Pasteur Hospital.** (4 rue Claude Bernard ☎02 37 30 30 30 English-speaking doctors.) For a closer but French-speaking hospital, go to 34 rue du Docteur Maunoury, near the police station.

chartres

Getting There

Chartres is accessible by frequent **trains** from Gare Montparnasse, on the Nogent-le-Rotrou line. There are two SNCF trains per hour during the summer; pick up a schedule ahead of time, as times are often irregular. Trains take an hour and cost €30 (ages 12-24 and seniors €22, under 12 €5). The train station in Chartres is located at pl. Pierre Sémard (☎02 37 84 61 50).

Getting Around

Chartres is a very walkable city, with most of its worthwhile sights clustered around the cathedral. The Maison Picassiette is the main exception and is most accessible by **taxi**. We suggest **Taxi 2000** (pl. Pierre Sémard ☎02 37 36 00 00). If you ever get lost, look up—the cathedral is visible from almost everywhere in the town, so you can easily find your way back to the center.

lyon

Cleaner, smaller, and with twice the waterfront to enjoy, Lyon (Lee-ohn) is more relaxed than Paris and can claim a few more centuries of history. Its location along the road that connected Italy to the Atlantic and at the confluence of the Rhône and Saône rivers made Lyon the obvious choice to serve as the Roman Empire's only major city west of Italy. The city may have gone downhill in the ensuing centuries, but it has recently shed its long-standing reputation as a gritty industrial city and now emphasizes its beautiful parks, history as a center for silk manufacturing, well-preserved Renaissance quarter, and modern financial sector.

ORIENTATION

Like Paris, Lyon is split into *arrondissements* that are often referred to by number (1er, 2ème, etc). Unlike Paris, most of Lyon is quite walkable and fairly hilly—good for some gluteal action to go with your sightseeing. The city is split in three by the **Rhône** and **Saône rivers. Vieux Lyon,** the oldest and most picturesque part of the city, is to the west of the Saône and is one of Europe's largest Renaissance neighborhoods. Walk along the cobblestoned street and explore its covered pathways, called *traboules,* which were once used by silk workers to get between their homes and shops (maps available at www.lyontraboules.net). The Métro stop Ⓜ**Vieux Lyon** is at the center of the old town, and funiculars will take you up the hill from there. Between the rivers lies modern Lyon's center, **Presqu'île,** which is itself centered on pl. Bellecour. Here you'll find the tourist office and lots of restaurants and stores. As a rule of thumb, Presqu'île is out to get your money. North of Presqu'île is **Terreaux,** one of the most diverse parts of the city and home to the breathtaking buildings of the Hôtel de Ville and the terrific Musée des Beaux-Arts. **Croix-Rousse** is perched on top of a very large hill to the north of the city. Head here for some wonderful views of Lyon and to check out its own extensive system of *traboules* on your own or with a guided tour. East of the Rhône is the **Parc de la Tête d'Or,** an enormous English garden with a zoo, summer boating, and plenty of walking and jogging paths. The main train station, **Gare Part-Dieu,** also lies east of the Rhône.

SIGHTS

🏛 BASILIQUE NOTRE DAME DE FOURVIÈRE CHURCH
8 pl. de Fourvière   ☎04 78 25 86 19 www.fourviere.org

From cholera outbreaks to scurvy epidemics, Lyon has quite a (literally) plagued past, and since 1638, the people of Lyon have made offerings at Fourvière to the Virgin Mary in exchange for protection. In 1872, the Archbishop pledged to erect a church if the town was spared from war. The result was this basilica, known in English as Our Lady of Fourvière, which has been the crown jewel of Lyon's skyline since its completion in 1897. Locals call it *un éléphant renversé*, since it looks a bit like Dumbo fell over at the top of the hill. If climbing up Fourvière wasn't tough enough, the Tour de l'Observatoire offers a fantastic panorama of the city, although you can only go up on a guided tour. For a free view, you can just head to the back of the basilica and gaze at Lyon sprawling below. Descend from there via the Jardins des Rosaires for a peaceful walk.

i Ⓜ*Vieux Lyon. Climb the hill, or take the funicular from Vieux Lyon to Fourvière. Free. Basilica tour suggested donation. Tour de l'Observatoire €6, under 12 €3.* Ⓩ *Open daily 8am-7pm. Chapel open daily 7am-7pm. 1¼ Tour de l'Observatoire daily 2:30 and 4pm; Jun-Sept additional tour M-Sa 11am. Basilica tours M-Sa 9am-noon and 2-6pm, Su 2-6pm.*

🏛 MUSEÉ DES BEAUX-ARTS   MUSEUM
20 pl. des Terreaux   ☎04 72 10 17 40 www.mba-lyon.fr
Nothing can rival the Louvre, but it says something when Lyon's Musée des Beaux-Arts instantly inspires comparisons. Housed in a former ornate convent, Palais St-Pierre, the museum's exhibits range from Egyptian mummies to paintings by Braque, Chagall, and Picasso to Neoclassical sculptures by Rodin, Maillol, and Zadkine. A doorway from Ptolemy IV's temple anchors the antiquities section, and a gruesome 17th-century tapestry shows the Trojan queen Hecuba ripping out her captor's eyes. It's not all serious business, though—Vincenzo Campi's *Les mangeurs de ricotta* shows a group of portly peasants munching on a piece of cheese, nicely garnished with a fly. The best part? Little grasshoppers under 26 get in free. Just beware of scammers masquerading as UNICEF workers in front of the museum.

i Ⓜ*Hôtel de Ville. Walk north on rue de la République, turn left onto rue Joseph Serlin; the museum is on the left. €7, under 26 free. Audio tour free.* Ⓩ *Open M 10am-6pm, W-Th 10am-6pm, F 10:30am-6pm, Sa-Su 10am-6pm.; partial closing 12:30-2pm. Garden open in summer 7:30am-7pm; in winter 7:30am-6pm.*

🏛 MUSÉE GALLO-ROMAINS AND ARCHEOLOGICAL SITE   MUSEUM, RUINS
17 rue Cléberg   ☎04 72 38 49 30 www.musees-gallo-romains.com
As if conquering Gaul wasn't already enough, the Romans decided to hike all the way up this steep hill to build their capital. One of the most important cities in the Empire, Lugunum, as it was known 2000 years ago, was a political and cultural hub with amphitheaters, temples, and council chambers. Locals now clamber over these ruins for a peaceful break and great views of the city and basilica. The two ancient theaters (Grand Théâtre and the Odéon) host big-name acts during the summer that draw legions of audiences, while the museum at the top holds enough relics, stone blocks, and beautiful mosaics to recreate the old Roman city. Look for the impressive Fish Mosaic, complete with shrimp, ducks, and sea monsters.

i Ⓜ*Vieux Lyon. Climb the hill and take a right at the Archéologique. Audio tour free. Archaeological site free. Museum €4, students €2.50, under 18 free; during exposition period €7/4.50/free. Th free entry.* Ⓩ *Ruins open Apr 15-Sept 15 daily 7am-9pm; Sept 16-April 14 7am-7pm. Close at 6pm during the Nuits de Fourvière festival in Jul. Museum open Tu-Su 10am-6pm; last entry 30min. before close.*

INSTITUT LUMIÈRE   MUSEUM
25 rue du 1er Film   ☎04 78 78 18 95 www.institut-lumiere.org
In the early 1900s, brothers Auguste and Louis Lumière transformed cinema and helped spread the new medium across the world with inventions ranging from film perforations to color film. Although this museum, housed in the old Lumière family villa, can get tediously technical, it makes up for it with an impressive garden room with enormous windows, cool displays on early 3D technology,

lyon

and panoramic films. The institute also hosts movie screenings, festivals, and outdoor summer film showings.

i Ⓜ*Monplaisir Lumière. The museum is in the square. €6.50, under 18 and students €5.50. Audio tours €3.* ⏰ *Open Tu-Su 10am-6:30pm.*

LA MAISON DES CANUTS   MUSEUM
10-12 rue d'Ivry   ☎04 78 28 62 04 www.maisondescanuts.com

Literally at the top of the Croix-Rousse area (if the steep stairs intimidate you, take the Métro), this museum is dedicated to Lyon's days at the top of the European silk industry. If you're already in the neighborhood, the free exhibit on the history of the city's silk industry makes for a quick and informative detour, although the place is more of a vehicle for the adjoining silk store. The items here are exclusively Lyonnais and unsurprisingly expensive.

i Ⓜ*Croix-Rousse. Cross pl. de la Croix-Rousse and walk north up Grande rue de la Croix-Rousse, then take the 1st right. Free. Tours of museu €6.50, students and under 26 €3.50, under 12 free; joint ticket for museum and traboules tours €11/6.* ⏰ *Open M-Sa 10am-6:30pm. Guided tours M-Sa 11am and 3:30pm. Tours of the museum last 50min.Tours of the traboules Sa and during school vacations, additional 1½hr. after 2:30pm museum tour.*

FOOD

🍴 LE VIEUX LYON   LYONNAIS $$
44 rue St-Jean   ☎04 78 42 48 89

The cobblestoned street of rue St-Jean runs right through Vieux Lyon, attracting crowds of tourists and tourists traps. Many of the traditional *bouchons Lyonnais* on this street are fairly pricey and are essentially all more or less the same experience. For the cheapest meal on the block, Le Vieux Lyon serves up a three-course meal for €13 that's every bit as good as the pricier *bouchons* surrounding it. Be sure to order the traditional *Lyonnais* dish, the *andouillete Lyonnaise* with mustard sauce and a side of cheesy potatoes. Then grab a seat outside to count the number of fanny packs you see.

i *Men €13-24. plats €13-22.* ⏰ *Open Tu-Sa noon-2pm and 6-10pm, Su noon-2pm.*

🍴 CAFÉ 203   TRADITIONAL $$
9 rue du Garet   ☎04 78 28 66 65

Like any responsible adult, you know better than to drink on an empty stomach. Avoid any unwelcome bodily reactions by starting your night off with a cheap meal at Café 203, the hangout of Lyon's cool kids before they start bar hopping. The restaurant sprawls over a narrow pedestrian area, covering it with elevated wooden platforms, dark stools, and small tables topped with precariously balanced plates. The generous charcuterie platters easily feed two to three people, and the burgers come with all-you-can-eat fries. Seal the deal with a liter of mojitos for €16.50 to start your night off right.

i *From pl. des Terreaux, walk past the Hôtel de Ville to the right, onto rue Joseph Serlin, and continue for 2 blocks, then turn right onto rue du Garet; Café 203 is on the left. Charcuterie platters €13.70-21.40. Burgers with all-you-can-eat fries €12.90-15.80. 1L mojitos €16.50. Weekday lunch menu noon-3pm €9.50-16.70.* ⏰ *Open daily 7am-1:30am.*

LE PETIT GLOUTON   CREPERIE $$
56 rue St-Jean   ☎04 78 37 30 10

This little restaurant is one of many *bouchons Lyonnais* on rue St-Jean, only it charges a bit more for a three-course meal than some cheaper *bouchons* nearby. If you are going to eat here, the specialty dishes of this restaurant include the house beef fondue and roasted lamb with thyme, which come in at €15.

i Ⓜ*Vieux Lyon. Walk north through pl. St-Jean onto rue St-Jean. Crepe €3.15-5.75. Prix-fixe meals €10.80-30.* ⏰ *Open daily 11:30am-2pm and 6-11:30pm.*

Charmingly quaint singles in Lyon's city center can cost as little as €40, and the areas around place Ampère and Gare de Perrache offer more budget hotels. Below are a few recommendations; for more, visit **www.letsgo.com**

AJ DE VIEUX LYON (HI)
HOSTEL $

41-45 Montée du Chemin Neuf ☎04 78 15 05 50 www.fuaj.org

As this is the only hostel in town, it's full of budget travelers—students, backpackers, elderly people, even entire families—and can fill up fast. The breakfast might not be much, but request a room with a view of the city, and that won't matter much.

i Ⓜ*Vieux Lyon. Walk up the hill, or take the St-Just funicular to Minimes. Turn left at the stop, and walk downhill onto Montée du Chemin Neuf. 6-night max. stay. €11 HI membership. 6-bed dorms €24. ☒ Reception open 9pm-1pm and 2-8pm. Lockout 10am-2pm.*

HÔTEL LE BOULEVARDIER
HOTEL $$$

5 rue de la Fromagerie ☎04 78 28 48 22 www.leboulevardier.fr

If you forgot to reserve a dorm at AJ, don't worry—you won't have to go to the Radisson that looms threateningly across the Rhône. Check into this hotel for an interesting and (relatively) affordable stay in Lyon. Rooms have very tall ceilings, brand new bathrooms, and a whole lot of space. Be sure to call ahead if you're arriving in the afternoon.

i Ⓜ*Cordeliers. Walk down rue Grenette against the flow of traffic, turn right onto rue du Président Édouard Herriot, then left onto rue de la Fromagerie; the hotel is on the right. Free Wi-Fi. Breakfast €6. Singles €56-66; doubles €59-69; triples €72-82 ☒ Reception open 7am-12:30pm and 5-8pm.*

HÔTEL IRIS
HOTEL $$$

36 rue de l'Arbre Sec ☎04 78 39 93 80 www.hoteliris.fr

While getting to a nunnery may make you feel a little like Ophelia, the only thing rotten at this convent-turned-hotel are the stairs (which are in dire need of a paint job). Otherwise, the sizable rooms here have high-vaulted ceilings and giant, colorful armchairs.Late-summer travelers beware: this hotel is closed for the last two weeks of August.

i Ⓜ*Hôtel de Ville. Walk south on rue de la République and turn left onto rue de l'Arbre Sec. Iris is 2 blocks down on the right. Breakfast €6. Singles €60; doubles €65-80. ☒ Reception open 7am-noon and 4:30-8pm.Hotel closed last 2 weeks of Aug.*

lyon

NIGHTLIFE

AYERS ROCK
BAR, CLUB

Boat 17 quai Augagneur ☎08 20 32 02 03 www.ayersrockcafe.com

With music so loud that you have to shout to order a drink, Ayers Rock really isn't the place to come for a chat. It is, however, the place to come if you're in the mood for a night of dancing, excited barmen, and Australian fun—just don't expect anyone to get here until 10pm. Fake kangaroos abound, there's not a word of French on the menu, and various screens display rugby matches as people get down (under) on the crowded dance floor. The 700-person Ayers Rock Boat is a popular summer club and has a more expensive drink menu.

i *Cafe: From pl. des Terreaux, head uphill onto rue Romarin and take the 1st right. Boat:* Ⓜ*Cordeliers. Cross Pont Lafayette, turn right, and walk along the waterfront, a little past Pont Wilson. Student night on Tu with happy hour prices. Shooter €3. Beer €5.50-5.80. Cocktails €7. Mixed drinks €7-8. Happy hour cocktails and pints €3.50. Cover for boat €8, with 1 drink. ☒ Open M-Sa during term-time 8pm-3am; during vacations 8pm-1am. Happy hour (cafe only) 8-10pm.*

🐌 THE BEERS   BAR
3 place Saint-Paul   ☎04 72 00 23 60

Rebellious youngsters buck the oppressive dominance of wine in France by
heading to the Beers to sample one of its 50 different types of beers. The huge
terrace is absolutely packed with young Lyonnais chattering loudly, sipping
their Belgian beers, and chopping up their own charcuterie by the waters of
the Saône. Popular at all hours and only a few minutes away from the nearby
Auberge, this is where you want to take your new hostel friends before heading
out for more action across the Saône.

*i From pl. des Terreaux, head down rue Constantine with the flow of traffic and cross the bridge;
the Beers is immediately to the left. Free Wi-Fi. Pint €5-7. Cocktails €7.50-8. Platters €5-10. Happy
hour pints of Duvel €4. ☉ Open M-Th 5pm-1am, F-Sa 3pm-3am, Su 5pm-1am. Happy hour 6-9pm.*

LA TAVERNE DU PERROQUET BOURRÉ   BAR
18 rue Ste-Catherine   ☎06 68 68 03 12 www.perroquet-bourre.com

Yo ho ho, and many bottles of rum. After tasting the 40 different varieties, you
too will be stumbling around like a *perroquet bourré* (drunken parrot). Come
on the later end of the night and watch the dancing barmen chuck, throw, and
toss cocktails to the music. This bar is decked-out like a ship's brig (if a ship had
red, blue, and ultraviolet lighting), and the "Jack Sparrow"—white rum, vanilla
rum, cocoa cream, banana, and cane sugar—will set you sailing for a sequel (or
three) in no time.

*i From pl. des Terreaux, head uphill onto rue Romarin and take the 1st left. Beer €2. Flaming shots
€4. Pint €5. Mixed drinks €6.50-7. Cocktails €7-8. Rum €3-10. Buy 1 cocktail, get 1 free during
happy hour. W €5 daiquiri special. ☉ Open M-W 7:30pm-1am, Th-Sa 7:30pm-3am, Su 7:30pm-
1am. Happy hour 6-9:30pm.*

ARTS AND CULTURE

If you know French, Lyon can be a hilarious city, with killer comedy clubs like Le
Complexe du Rire and Les Tontons Flingueurs above pl. des Terreaux. It's also home
to the famous *guignol* puppet, a character based on the city's silk workers (though
the shows are aimed at children). For English shows, your best bet is the Opéra
de Lyon (pl. de la Comédie ☎04 69 85 54 54 www.opera-lyon.com ⓂHôtel de Ville.
Box office open Tu-Sa noon-6pm), which hosts operas, dance shows, and concerts
starting at €10. The building mixes sleek modern design with a 19th-century façade
and houses a terrace with a jazz cafe that gets crowded in the summer. Each summer,
Lyon hosts Les Nuits de Fourvière,an international music and dance festival held at
the ancient Roman amphitheater. Tickets sell for around €40, and the festival attracts
big-name acts like Woody Allen, Patti Smith, Sinead O'Connor, and the Byrds to the
Vieux Lyon hill. (☎04 72 32 00 00 www.nuitsdefourviere.com)

ESSENTIALS
Practicalities

- **TOURIST OFFICES:** The tourist office offers free accommodation bookings, a free public transportation map, and the 🐌 Lyon City Card (1 day €24, 2 days €31, 3 days €41), which gets you
free entry into Lyon's 22 museums, free public transport, unlimited bike rentals with Vélo'v, a
city tour, a boat tour (Apr-Oct), and discounts at select establishments, including the National
Opera and bicycle tours. Student pricing for the card is available upon request (€17/25/33).
The office is located in the Tourist Office Pavillion. (pl. Bellecour, 2ème ☎04 72 77 69 69 www.
lyon-france.com. ☉ Open daily 9am-6pm.)

- **TOURS:** The tourist office offers guided English tours of various parts of the city, from the
traboules to the backstage of the Opéra to City Hall. (€10-12, students and ages 8-18 €5,
under 8 free.)

- **CONSULATES:** US. (1 quai Jules Courmant, 2ème ☎04 78 38 36 88 ⏰ Open M-F 10am-noon, and by appointment 2-5pm) Canada. (17 rue Bourgelat, 2ème ☎04 72 77 64 07)

- **CURRENCY EXCHANGE:** Goldfinger SARL offers no-commission exchanges. (81 rue de la République ☎04 72 40 06 00 ⏰ Open M-Sa 9:30am-6:15pm.)

- **ATMS:** 24hr. ATMs line pl. Bellecour and rue Victor Hugo, which runs to the south from the square. An HSBC bank is located at 18 pl. Bellecour. (☎04 78 92 31 00 ⏰ Open M-F 8:45am-12:15pm and 2-5pm.)

- **LAUNDROMATS:** 19 rue Ste-Hélène, 2ème. (*i* Wash €4 per 7kg; dry €1 per 10min.; detergent €0.90. ⏰ Open daily 7:30am-8:30pm.)

- **INTERNET:** The library at Vieux-Lyon has free internet, rue Romarin by pl. des Terreaux is lined with cyber-cafes, and bookstore-cafe Raconte Moi la Terre has Wi-Fi and internet access. (14 rue du *plat* ☎04 78 92 60 22 www.racontemoilaterre.com *i* €4 per hr. ⏰ Open M noon-7:30pm, Tu-Sa 10am-7:30pm.)

- **POST OFFICES:** Pl. Antonin Poncet, next to pl. Bellecour in the 2ème. (⏰ Open Jan-Jul M-F 9am-7pm, Sa 9am-12:30pm and 2-5pm; limited hours during Aug.)

- **POSTAL CODES:** 69001-69009; last digit corresponds to *arrondissement*.

Emergency

- **POLICE:** Commissariat 2ème, 47 rue de la Charité (☎04 78 42 26 56).

- **LATE-NIGHT PHARMACIES:** Pharmacies stay open overnight on a rotating basis. Call ☎3237 or check www.3237.fr for information on what's open. *i* On Sundays and holidays, there's a €4 pharmacy surcharge. The Blanchet des Cordeliers pharmacy is frequently open overnight. (5 pl. des Cordeliers, 2ème ☎04 78 42 12 42 ⏰ Open daily 8pm-7am.)

- **HOSPITAL:** Hôpital St-Joseph St-Luc. (20 quai Claude Bernard, 7ème ☎04 78 61 81 81, emergency ☎04 78 61 80 00 www.ch-stjoseph-stluc-lyon.fr) The central hospital line has information about other general and specialist hospitals in the city. (☎08 20 08 20 69)

Getting There

BY PLANE

Lyon's main airport is **Aéroport Lyon-Saint-Exupéry** (LYS). You can reach the city proper from the airport by trains run by **Rhônexpress,** which stops at the Lyon Part-Dieu, Vaulx-en-Velin La Soie, and Meyzieu ZI stations. (www.rhonexpress.fr *i* €13.50, round-trip €24.50; under 26 €12.50/22. ⏰ 30min. duration, buses every 30min. from 5-6am and 9pm-12:40am, every 15min. from 6am-9pm.) Tickets can be bought online in advance at a discount.

BY TRAIN

Lyon is served by two main train stations. The main station is **Gare de Lyon Part-Dieu,** where all national and international trains arrive. (5 pl. Charles Béraudier, 3ème ⓜPart-Dieu. ⏰ Station open daily 4:50am-12:45am. Info desk open daily 5am-12:45am. Ticket window open M-W 5:10am-8:45pm, Th-F 5:15am-9:45pm, Sa 5:10am-8:45pm, Su 6:45-9:45pm). **Gare de Perrache** is the final stop of most Lyon-bound trains. (14 cours de Verdun, 2ème. ⏰ Station open M-Sa 4:45am-12:30am, Su 4:45am-1:30am. Info desk open M-Sa 4:45am-12:30am, Su 4:45am-1:30am. Ticket office open M-Th 5:30am-8:30pm, F 5:30am-9:30pm, Sa 6am-8:30pm, Su 9:30am-9:30pm). Trains arrive at both stations from Marseille (€20-106 ⏰ 2hr., every hr.), Nice (€32-92 ⏰ 4hr. 30min., every hr.), Paris (€30-92 ⏰ 2hr., every hr.), Strasbourg (€25-163 ⏰ 3-4hr., every hr.)

lyon

Getting Around

Lyon can easily be tackled by foot, but there's a solid public transportation system available for longer journeys.

BY PUBLIC TRANSPORTATION

All public transportation in Lyon is run by **TCL** (☎04 26 10 12 12 www.tcl.fr). There are information offices at the bus and train stations, Part-Dieu and Perrache, as well as at major Métro stations. Useful maps of the city and its bus routes are available from the tourist office and info centers. All tickets (€1.70) are valid for one-way travel on the Métro, bus, and tram and are good for changes for 1hr. You get a discount when you buy 10 tickets (€14.70, students €12.90). There are 26 major bus lines, which run daily 5am-midnight. The T1 Tramway line connects the two train stations directly. Two funicular lines climb to the top of Fourvière (€2.60). One runs from ⓂVieux Lyon to Fourvière (🕑 Daily 6am-10pm) and another from ⓂVieux Lyon to St-Just, through Minimes (🕑 Daily 5:23am-midnight).

BY BIKE

Vélo'v (☎08 00 08 35 68 www.velov.grandlyon.com) makes renting a bike easy by having rental spots all around the city center. You'll need a credit card with a smart chip (most American cards don't have one) to rent from a docking station, or you can rent one online. You also need at least €150 in debit or credit for the hold they put on your account. A day card costs €1.50, and a 7-day card costs €5. You take a bike from any docking station, then return it to any other station when you're done; you're then charged for the time you had the bike out. The first 30min. is free, the second 30min. is €1, and every 30min. after that costs €2. Just remember that Lyon can be a hilly place, and if you intend to go up to Croix-Rousse or Vieux Lyon, you should be in good physical shape.

France already takes its wine seriously, but Bordeaux kicks it up a notch or three. The world-renowned region has been producing wine since the 1st century, and in 2007 UNESCO listed the entire city as a world heritage site. Today, college students and hipsters hang out at pl. de la Victoire in the student quarter, children splash in the waters of the Miroir d'Eau, and young lovers take in the grand 18th-century architecture and stain their mouths purple at the legendary vineyards of St-Émilion, Médoc, Sauternes, and Graves. Come to Bordeaux for the viticulture and vineyards, but spend a day admiring the impressive architecture, first-rate wine bars, and sophisticated arts scene.

france

bordeaux

Bordeaux may well be the wine capital of the world. College students and hipsters hang out at pl. de la Victoire in the student quarter, children splash in the waters of the Miroir d'Eau, and young lovers take in the grand 18th-century architecture while tourists stain their mouths purple at the legendary vineyards of St-Émilion, Médoc, Sauternes, and Graves. Come to Bordeaux for the viticulture, but stay for the panoramic views, sophisticated arts scene, and vibrant nightlife.

ORIENTATION

Bordeaux sits on the west bank of the Garonne River, which flows south to north into the Biscay. The Gare St-Jean train station is at the southern end of the city, a 30 minute hike from the centre-ville. To get to town, walk past the kebab joints and sex shops on cours de la Marne until you reach pl. de la Victoire, the student nightlife quarter. From here, turn right under the arch onto the pedestrian street rue Ste-Catherine. The centre-ville is a straight shot ahead. (You can also take tram

C or bus #16 from the train station and get off at pl. de la Bourse.) The heart of the *centre-ville* is pl. de la Comédie, instantly recognizable for its opulent Grand Théâtre. Rue Ste-Catherine then turns into cours du XXX Juillet (that's the number, not a sex shop), where you'll find the main tourist office right before the tree-filled Esplanade des Quinconces, a large plaza and important public-transportation hub. Back at pl. de la Comédie, you can get to pl. Gambetta, another one of Bordeaux's centers, by walking west for a short distance along cours de l'Intendance. Rue de la Porte Dijeaux (which turns into rue St-Rémi) runs from the archway at the southeast corner of pl. Gambetta to pl. dela Bourse, across the street from Bordeaux's iconic public art installation, the Miroir d'Eau, by the river.

get a room!

For more recommendations, visit **www.letsgo.com**.

🏨 AUBERGE DE LA JEUNESSE BARBEY
HOSTEL $

22 cours Barbey ☎05 56 33 00 70 http://www.auberge-jeunesse-bordeaux.com
The newly renovated hostel is close to Gare St-Jean and is by far the closest hostel to the center of Bordeaux even though you'll still be 30 min. away on foot. The Wi-Fi is speedy, breakfast is decent, and the bathrooms are clean, but this colorful, color-blocked has poor ventilation, transforming the 4-6 person dorms into veritable steam rooms during the summer.
i From Gare St-Jean, walk on rue Charles Domercq towards the curve in the street and continue on cours de la Marne for 4 blocks, turn left on cours Barbey, hostel on left. Breakfast and linens included. Rooms separated by gender. 1 lobby computer. Kitchen available. 3 night maximum stay. Dorm €23. ☒ Lockout 11am-4pm. Hostel closed 2-5am. Reception closed from 11am-2pm and 9-9:45pm.

🏨 HOTEL STUDIO
HOTEL $

26 rue Huguerie ☎05 56 48 00 14 www.hotel-studio-bordeaux.fr
A long-time Let's Go favorite, Hotel Studio is worlds better than the nearby youth hostel at just a fraction more of the price. The rooms are decked out in bright colors and bathed in plenty of sunlight from the large windows—maybe a bit too much in the during the hot summers. The hotel is also located in thecity center, saving you the 30 min. walk or €1.40 bus ride to the centre-ville.
i From Pl. Gambetta, walk along cours Georges Clémenceau then turn left onto rue Huguerie just before the statue and traffic circle at pl. de Tourny. Breakfast €5. Free Wi-Fi. Singles €30-35; doubles €32-40; twin beds €46; triples €54; quads €70. ☒ Reception M-F 7am-8:30pm, Sa-Su 8am-8pm.

HOTEL CHIC DE LYON
HOTEL $$

31 rue des Remparts ☎05 56 81 34 38
In the heart of the *centre-ville*, this hotel absolutely shines, from the crisp white sheets to the bare white walls to the large windows with lace curtains. Rooms here are unexpectedly affordable and an even better deal if you're traveling as a couple or a twosome comfortable with their sexuality. Only downside is the lack of AC or fans.
i From Ⓜ Ste-Catherine, head east down cours d'Alsace Lorraine, turn right onto pl. Pley Berland, then right onto rue des Remparts. Breakfast €5. Singles €35-45; doubles €45-59; triples €69-75. ☒ Reception 7am-11pm.

bordeaux

SIGHTS

⬛ MIROIR D'EAU
pl. de la Bourse

PUBLIC ART

Accessible from the grand buildings of pl. de la Bourse and beside the banks of the Garonne River, the Miroir d'Eau (Water Mirror) is a spectacular public art installation and an icon of modern Bordeaux. Designed by the Parisian fontainier Jean-Max Llorca and installed in 2006, it's the biggest reflecting mirror on earth—2cm of water transform 3500 sq. m of black granite into a stunning panoramic reflection of the old city. In the summer months though, the kids splashing around transform this reflecting pool to a communal puddle, so join them and take off your shoes, or bring your camera or sketchpad, especially around sunset.

i Tram C to pl. de la Bourse. Free. ☑ Water and fog display cycles daily 10am-10pm.

⬛ MAISON DU VIN
1 cours du XXX Juillet

WINE SCHOOL, BAR
☎05 56 00 43 47

Gone are your days of cluelessly throwing around words like *terroir* and *appellation*. Cultivate your knowledge of grapes and press it into good use at la Maison du Vin, headquarters of Bordeaux's winemaking industry. Its elegant Bar à Vin serves carefully curated selections of the region's best at surprisingly low prices with free Wi-Fi and AC, making this the perfect pit stop on a hot day of sightseeing. But if you don't have the guts (or nose) to face the cellars yet, the 2hr. introductory course at l'École du Vin will set you on the path to becoming a master sommelier.

i Directly across from the main tourist office. Tram B or C to Quinconces. Tickets for the course can be purchased at the Maison du Vin or at the tourist office. Wine-tasting cours €35, students €15. Bar à Vin €2-8 per glass of wine. ☑ Courses offered Jul-Sept M-Sa 10am in English and 3pm in French. Barà Vin open M-Sa 11am-10pm.

TOUR PEY-BERLAND
pl. Pey-Berland

TOWER, PANORAMIC VIEWS
☎05 56 81 26 25

It may be 231 steps to the top of this tower, but we promise that it'll go by quicker than you think. Offering the best views of Bordeaux and the Cathédrale St-André, this bell tower was built apart from the church to protect it from the vibrations of the bell. (Though the tower was completed in 1440, it had to wait another 413 years to get its four bells). The climb, with its ever-narrowing walls, is definitely not for the claustrophobic, and the way down is quite dizzying, but the two terraces provide great vistas of the city, and helpful plaques point out landmarks and give a little of the city's history. Just 19 people are allowed at a time in the tower, so watch out for student groups, otherwise you might be facing a long, hot wait.

i Tram A or B to Hôtel de Ville. Behind the cathedral. €5.5, under 18 and EU citizens ages 18-25 free. ☑ Open daily Jun-Sept 10am-1:15pm and 2-6pm; Oct-May Tu-Su 10am-12:30pm and 2-5:30pm.

FOOD

⬛ LE PETIT COMMERCE
22 rue du Parlement St Pierre

SEAFOOD $$$
☎05 56 79 76 58

Bordeaux is going to take your budget and tear it to pieces, but guess what? You'll love it. Fine dining here comes at a pretty penny, but if you're willing to shell out €20 for a meal, do it for the incredibly fresh seafood at Le Petit Commerce, easily one of the culinary highlights of this seaside city. The tables on the pedestrian sidewalk in front of this restaurant are nearly always packed, drawing a healthy mix of savvy tourist and local foodies with its generous tapas

france

and perfectly paired wines. Don't miss the flavorful grilled squid or the enormous platter of grilled prawns.

i From pl. de la Bourse, walk down rue Fernand Philippart, turn left on rue des Caperans, turn left on rue du Parlement St Pierre, Le Petit Commerce on right. Free Wi-Fi. Tapa €7-28, plats €17-32. ☑ Open daily 11:30am-3pm and 6pm-midnight, bar until 2am.

LA PAPAYE
CREOLE $$
14 rue Fernand Philippart   ☎05 56 44 76 88 www.lapapaye.populus.org

Spicy, salty, fruity, and sometimes everything at once, La Papaye serves up specialties from Madagascar, Réunion, and the Antilles. The richly seasoned meats and vegetables come with small sides of white rice, fresh veggies, and marinated salads. If you're worried about straying too far from France, you'll be relieved to know that the *plats* still go down well with a glass of Bordeaux.

i From Pl. de la Bourse, with your back to the 3 Graces Fountain and the Garonne River, take the left fork ahead of you. The restaurant is on your left. Entrées €5-6.5. plats €10-12.5. Lunch time menu €12.5, dinner menu €20. ☑ Open M-W 7:30-11pm, Th-F noon-1:30 and 7:30-11pm, Sa 7:30-11pm.

L'INCONTOURNABLE
TRADITIONAL $$
2 quai Louis XVIII   ☎05 56 44 59 59

The Garonne is beautiful, but on a summer day, the banks of the river can be scorching hot. Escape the summer heat and duck into the AC at this river-side restaurant and your best bet for a cheap meal on this street. The €13 and €17 menus come with a glass of that famous local wine to help you forget the heat.

i Quai Louis XVIII is the avenue that follows the Garonne River. The restaurant is between pl. de la Bourse and Esplanade des Quinconces. Menu €9-17 ☑ Open daily 7am-midnight.

NIGHTLIFE

🏮 LA CALLE OCHO
BAR
24 rue des Piliers de Tutelle   ☎05 56 48 08 68 www.calle-ocho.eu

Make your way past overzealous salsa dancers and tipsy head-bobbers to get your drink on at one of Calle Ocho's three bars, then shake your hips to the remixed Latin grooves in this shrine to all things Cuban. The place gets crowded after 11pm, so if you want some elbow space, get there beforehand.

i From pl. de la Comédie, walk along cours de l'Intendance. Rue des Piliers de Tutelle is the 2nd right turn. Beer €5.5. Tequila €6.5-7.5. Rums €6.5-12. ☑ Open M-Sa 5pm-2am.

EL BODEGON
BAR
14 pl. de la Victoire   ☎05 56 96 74 02

El Bodegon dominates nightlife in pl. de la Victoire, the most popular party quarter for Bordeaux's students. The DJ plays the latest top 40 hits, bartenders light booze on fire, and on the weekends, an exuberant crowd dances the night away, frequently on top of the bar. For those who'd rather drink than dance, a terrace offers a quieter spot.

i A straight shot down rue Ste-Catherine to pl. de la Victoire. Karaoke or theme nights on W. Happy hour buy 1 drink get 1 free. Free Wi-Fi. Bee €6.2-8.2. 1 liter of sangria €16. Cocktails €7. ☑ Open M-Sa 7am-2am, Su 1pm-2am. Kitchen open M-Sa 11am-3pm. Happy hour 4-9pm.

LE TROU DUCK
BAR, GLBT-FRIENDLY
33 rue des Piliers de Tutelle   ☎05 56 52 36 87

The zebra-striped bar here functions mostly as an excuse to gyrate to'90s hits and Rihanna. The dance floor of this intimate gay bar gets pretty crowded, and the disco lights may be a bit cheesy, but you might not mind when you find yourself sandwiched between the cute guys who flock here.

i From pl. de la Comédie, walk along cours de l'Intendance. Rue des Piliers de Tutelle is the 2nd right turn. The bar is at the very end of the street. Beer €5-6.50. Mixed drinks €6. ☑ Open M-W 6pm-2am, Th-Sa 5pm-2am, Su 6pm-2am.

bordeaux

ARTS AND CULTURE

GRAND THÉÂTRE OPERA
pl. de la Comédie ☎05 56 00 85 95 www.opera-bordeaux.com
This 18th-century neo-classical opera house features an impressive façade with 12 pillars topped by statues of the Nine Muses and rounded out by the regal poses of Juno, Venus, and Minerva. And just to rub the neo-classical bit in more, inside the theater, Apollo and the Muses look down from the breathtaking blue dome of the concert hall. If goddesses aren't good enough and you want to see a real-life diva, you can snag €8 tickets to dance, opera, and orchestral shows by checking at the ticket office 48hr. before the curtain, or by getting a three-show subscription (paradis des étudiants; €24).
i Tram B to Grand Théâtre. Reserve tours at the tourist office or by phone. Tickets €8-110. Students receive 50% off and €8 rush tickets available 48hrs before performance. Guided tours €3, under 12 €2. ☑ Performances Sept-Jul. Tours year-round. Ticket office open Sept-Jul Tu-Sa 1-6:30pm.Guided tours W, Sa at 2:30pm, 4pm, 5:30pm, call in advance to reserve.

ESSENTIALS

Practicalities

- **TOURIST OFFICES:** The main tourist office provides maps, brochures, and a guide with hotels, walking itineraries, and listings. There's also an entire desk dedicated to arranging visits to the vignobles (wineries). (12 cours du XXX Juillet ☎05 56 00 66 00 www.bordeaux-tourisme.com *i* Tram line B or C to Quinconces. ☑ Open May-Jun M-Sa 9am-7pm, Su 9:30am-6:30pm; Jul-Aug M-Sa 9am-7pm, Su 9:30am-6:30pm; Sept-Oct M-Sa 9am-6pm, Su 9:30am-6:30pm; Nov-Apr M-Sa 9am-6:30pm, Su 9:45am-4:30pm.)

- **CONSULATES:** US. (89 quai des Chartrons from outside France ☎05 56 48 63 85; from within France ☎05 56 48 63 85; http://bordeaux.usconsulate.gov ☑ Open M-F 9am-5pm, best to call in advance to set up appointment.) UK. (353 bd du Président Wilson ☎05 57 22 21 10 http://ukinfrance.fco.gov.uk ☑ Open M, W, F 9am-12:30pm, phone lines M-F 9am-12:30pm, 1:30-4:30pm, emergency service ☎05 57 22 21 10)

- **CURRENCY EXCHANGE:** You'll have to ring multiple doorbells and climb one flight of stairs to reach the security-heavy Bureau de Change Kanoo. (11 cours de l'Intendance ☎05 56 00 63 33 *i* €8 fixed commission on all cash exchanges. 3% commission on travelers' checks. ☑ Open M-F 9:30am-6pm, from Jun-Sept 9:30am-1:30pm)

- **YOUTH CENTER:** Centre Régional Information Jeunesse (CIJA) helps with employment, internships, long-term accommodations, and cultural information. They offer 15min. free internet access and SNCF train ticket purchase, and distribute LINDIC, a student guide to Bordeaux published in late Jul or early August. (125 cours d'Alsace Lorraine ☎05 56 56 00 56www. info-jeune.net *i* Tram to Hôtel de Ville. ☑ Open M 9:30am-6pm, Tu-W 9:30am-6pm, Th 9:30am-8pm, F 9:30am-5pm.)

- **INTERNET:** I.Phone. (24 rue du Palais Gallien ☎05 57 85 82 6 *i* €2 per hr., €10 for 10 hrs. ☑ Open M-F 10am-8pm, Sa-Su noon-8pm)

- **POST OFFICES:** The post office has a Western Union. (43 pl. Gambetta ☑ Open Jan-mid Jul M-F 9am-6pm, Sa 9am-4pm; mid-Jul-Aug M-F 9am-5pm, Sa 9am-1pm; Sept-Dec. M-F 9am-6pm, Sa 9am-4pm.)

Emergency

- **POLICE:** L'Hôtel de Police. (23 rue François de Sourdis ☎05 57 85 77 77 ☑ Open 24hr.)

- **LATE-NIGHT PHARMACIES:** Bordeaux has two 24hr. pharmacies. Pharmacie des Capucins near the Marché des Capucins. (30 pl. des Capucins ☎05 56 91 62 66 *i* Bus #11, 16,

45B, or 58 to Capucins. At the corner of the big intersection that leads to the market.) Near the Palais de Justice is Pharmacie d'Albret. (71 cours d'Albret ☎05 56 96 68 36 *i* Tram A to Palais de Justice. Turn right at the big intersection, it's down one block on your right.)

- **HOSPITALS/MEDICAL SERVICES:** Hôpital St-André. (1 rue Jean Burguet ☎05 56 79 56 79)

Getting There
BY PLANE
Bordeaux-Mérignac Airport is 11km. west of Bordeaux (BOD; ☎05 56 34 50 00 www.bordeaux.aeroport.fr). Public bus line #1 runs from the airport to Esplanade des Quinconces, near the tourist office. There are stops at Gare St-Jean, the main Tourist Office, and pl. Gambetta (to Gambetta 30min). The airport also runs the Jet'bus, which goes from the airport to Gare St-Jean and stops at Place de la Victoire, Cours du Maréchal Juin, Pellegrin, and Fontaine d'Arlac on the way to the airport. (☎05 56 34 50 72. *i* €7, €6 for under 26. ☺ Departs from airport Porte 11, 30-40mins., arrives every 45min., departures from the airport from 8:30am-10:45pm, Sa-Su additional departure at 7:45am.)

BY TRAIN
Gare St-Jean (rue Charles Domercq 36 35. Ticket office open M-Th 4:30am-midnight, F 4:30am-1:30am, Sa 4:30am-midnight, Su 4:30am-1:30am) receives trains from: Lyon €30-163 6-7hr., 1-2 direct trains per day); Marseille €20-127 6-7hr., 7 direct trains per day); Nice €40-170 9-12hr., 2 direct trains per day); Paris €30-120 3hr., 25 per day); Toulouse €18-35 2-3hr., 17 per day).

Getting Around
Bordeaux is entirely walkable—or at least entirely walkable once you get there (far-off youth hostels, we're looking at you). The extensive public transportation system can be used for a fast hostel-to-centre-ville commute, and to get to the airport and train station.

BY PUBLIC TRANSPORTATION
TBC runs a bus and tram system. (☎05 57 57 88 88www.infotbc.com, www.reseaut-bc.com *i* 1 ticket €1.40; 10 tickets €11.3, under 28 €6.30; 1-day pass €4.30; 7-day pass €11.30, under 28 €8.20; night pass valid 7pm-7am €2. ☺ Trams A, B, and C run M-W 5am-12:30am, Th-Sa 5am-1:15am, Su 5am-12:30am.) During the school year, the very helpful night bus #58 runs Thursday through Saturday nights, 1:30-5:30am. The ticket and information offices are at 9 pl. Gambetta (☺ Open M-F 7am-7pm, Sa 9am-6pm.), Esplanade des Quinconces (☺ Open M-F 7am-7:30pm, Sa 9am-6pm) and at the Gare St-Jean train station (☺ Open M-F 7am-7pm, Sa 9am-6pm).

BY BIKE
Bordeaux's popular bike-share program has bicycle stands everywhere from the centre-ville to the other side of the Garonne. (☎09 69 39 03 03 http://vcub.fr *i* 24hr. subscription €1, 7-day €5; 1st 30min. free, then €2 per hr.) However, the stands require access to a €200 deposit and a smart-chip enabled bank card, so Americans will probably be out of luck. Bikes can be rented from Pierre Qui Roule. (32 pl. Gambetta ☎05 57 85 80 87 www.pierrequiroule.fr *i* €15 per day, €28 per weekend, €59 per week. ☺ Open M 2-7pm, Tu-Sa 10am-7pm, in the summer 10am-1pm, 2-7pm.)

BY TAXI
Taxi Télé. (☎05 56 96 00 3 *i* €1.50 per km during the day, €2.50 per km after 7pm; €40-50 to the airport.)

bordeaux

marseille

We could call Marseille a true immigrant city with a vibrant local culture, but we prefer to think of it as the Tijuana of France. A Tower of Babel produced by the train-with-cut-brakes that is globalization, this (in)famous port town is the stomping ground of sailors, backpackers, mobs of immigrants, and (we suspect) unsavory characters involved in the import-export business. Expect color, chaos, and a lingering smell of trash and urine. Located in the center of Provence, Marseille is an ideal home base for visits to the *calanques* along the coasts or to the Provençal cities of Avignon, Arles, and Cassis. This may not be the prettiest town on the French Riviera, but it does host the closest train station that will take you to other Mediterranean coastal towns. Avoid certain neighborhoods, and schlep it to the sweet smell of lavender only an hour away.

ORIENTATION

Marseille is organized into four main areas, situated around the roughly rectangular **port** that cuts into the city's heart. The area on the south side of the port, extending east roughly to rue de Rome and north to la Canebière, is the **Vieux Port,** with the

get a room!

Stick to Belsunce or the city's outskirts for the cheapest hotels and hostels, but know that these are not areas to come stumbling home to late at night. Spend a little more at Vieux Port's quiet B&Bs and nicer, centrally located hotels. For more suggestions, visit **www.letsgo.com.**

VERTIGO CENTRE
42 rue des Petites Maries   ☎04 91 91 07 11 www.hotelvertigo.fr
HOSTEL $

Jimmy Stewart won't be here to complain to you in his Ameri-British accent or push you off the top of a church, but you will find plenty of other Anglophones at Vertigo. The hostel offers a large, homey lobby armed with a bar, self-service kitchen, and full living room with couches, chairs, a TV, and plenty of soccer fans. Rooms are big and can get hot under Marseille's seemingly never-setting sun, so always come with a fan.

i From the train station, walk down the Grand Staircase onto bd d'Athènes and take the 1st right. Turn left onto rue des Petites Maries; the hostel is on the left, close to the top of the hill. Bar and communal kitchen available. Other location in Vieux Port (38 rue Fort Notre Dame). 2- to 6-person dorms from €23.50; doubles €55-65. ☯ Reception 24hr.

AUBERGE DE JEUNESSE DE BONNEVEINE
Impasse du Docteur Bonfils   ☎04 91 17 63 30 www.fuaj.org/Marseille-Bonneveine
HOSTEL $

Like many other FUAJ youth hostels around the world, Auberge de Jeunesse de Bonneveine is big, bright, boisterous, and booming with international youth debauchery. A pool table and foosball table keep gamers happy alongside the bar and lounge area.

i Bus #44 to pl. Bonnefon. Turn toward the intersection and take the angled left onto av. Joseph Vidal, then turn left onto Impasse du Docteur Bonfils. Or from ⓂVieux Port, take bus #83 about 20min. to La Plage, transfer to bus #19 across the street, and take that to Les Gatons Plage. Turn around and take the 1st right onto rue des Gatons, then the 3rd left onto av. Joseph Vidal, and then turn right onto Impasse du Docteur Bonfils. Breakfast included. FUAJ Card required. Dinner menu €6.80. 2- and 5-day sea kayak package available at reception and online. 4- or 6-bed dorms €21.40. 3 nights max. in summer. ☯ Reception until 1am. Bar open 6pm-1am.

france

glimmering Notre Dame de la Garde on the hilltop behind. The ancient quarter on the north side of the port is **Le Panier,** where you'll find Marseille's oldest buildings, cutest corners, and most cramped 6ft. wide alleys. Just downhill from Le Panier, the quai du Port is lined with expensive hotels, boutiques, and upscale waterfront cafes. The area to the east of the port (near its shortest side) is **Belsunce,** home to a large part of Marseille's sizable immigrant population; this is where you'll find the Gare St-Charles SNCF station and the main thoroughfare of la Canebière. We recommend exploring—just not at night. Uphill farther east is **Notre-Dame du Mont,** a district with a gritty feel but great food and nightlife around cours Julien and the pl. Jean Jaurès.

Vieux Port and Le Panier

Vieux Port is one of the busiest parts of Marseille and boasts shopping, the biggest tourist attractions, and the city's oldest *boulangerie.* The best nightlife can be found right along the southern border of the port on **quai Rive Neuve,** with a slew of restaurants scattered throughout the blocks behind it. **Notre Dame de la Garde** is the cherry on top of Vieux Port's diverse sundae, rising on the hill to the south and capping off Vieux Port before the mountains and dividing it from the good beaches in the west.

When the Greeks landed in Marseille 2600 years ago, they landed in Le Panier; this neighborhood is far and away the oldest section of Marseille. The area tends to be a little more expensive, a little more cramped, and generally lacking the attractions of other parts of the city. The **quai du Port** running along the port's northern shore is where you'll find a number of nice restaurants, but the population thins out the farther away from the water you wander. Narrow winding streets work their way away from the port and up the hill toward the **Vieille Charité,** the neighborhood's best-known landmark. In general, the area is most accessible by tram.

Belsunce and Notre-Dame du Mont

Little North Africa teems with kebab stands and carpet stores, making it an ideal place to shop cheap and eat cheaper. Nestled in the northeast corner of the city, **Belsunce** fans out from the short end of the port; Ⓜ︎Colbert and the Porte d'Aix mark the western border that separates Belsunce from le Panier, and La Canebière cordons Belsunce off from the comfort of the port's shores in the south. As the sun sets, the storefront gates drop and the litter seems to wander about the streets as suspiciously as its inhabitants. Unless you're large, male, and have a knack for knife fights, take the long way to the port and skip Belsunce at night.

Follow rue Aubagne away from La Canebière across cours Lieutaud and you'll find yourself up in **Notre-Dame du Mont,** a rough-and-tumble but up-and-coming neighborhood filled with quirky but cool food and nightlife. The **cours Julien** is lined with a diverse array of restaurants and the **place Jean Jaurès** has some of the city's best bars—but, as always, exercise caution at night.

SIGHTS

Vieux Port and La Panier

▨ **NOTRE DAME DE LA GARDE**   CHURCH
Top of the hill   ☎04 91 13 40 80

This elegant basilica is the crown jewel of Marseille. Our Lady of the Guard has been watching over all of the city since 1214. The view from the hilltop is breathtaking (and just imagine what the 10,000kg golden Mary and baby Jesus can see from on top of this thing!). Services are still held in the crypt of the church, a tradition that's probably a holdover from the days when the Nazis were taking shots at the basilica (you can still see the bullet holes in the east wall), but the droves of tourists that flood this church on a daily basis prefer the immaculately conceived interior of the basilica. Mosaics make the walls and ceiling shine with pride over the silver mother and child above the altar. We don't know what's up with Marseille and its religious icons made of precious metals, but we like it.

i Take bus #60 from Vieux Port straight to the basilica. It's the giant church at the top of the giant hill that you can see from pretty much anywhere in Marseille. Mass in the basilica Su 8, 10am, noon, 5pm in summer; 8, 10am, noon, 4:30pm the winter. Mass in the crypt M-F 7:25, 9am, 5pm; Su 9 and 11am in summer. M-F 7:25, 9am, 4:30pm; Su 9 and 11am in winter. Free. ☑ Open daily 7am-7pm.

▨ CHÂTEAU D'IF   PRISON
1 quai de la Fraternité, Île d'If   ☎04 91 59 02 30 or 06 03 06 25 26

The legendary home of the Count of Monte Cristo and the Man in the Iron Mask, this island-fortress-turned-prison is famous for its notorious detainees. Alexander Dumas's criminal hero was only a fictional prisoner here, but the mysterious and still anonymous Man in the Iron Mask was the real deal under Louis XIV. Even an Asian rhino took up residence at the château when his trip to Portugal, where he was to be presented to the king, was interrupted by damage to the ship. The building itself is beautiful, and the view of the coast from the roof is unparalleled. Although the prison was built to make escapes nearly impossible (this place is an island, after all), don't worry if you miss the ferry you intended to take back—there will be another one, and there are worse places to be stranded.

i Ⓜ️Vieux Port. Guided tours in French free. Boat tickets (buy at the port €10.10, family €7.60, groups of 10 or more €9.60. Château €5.50; reduced €4; under 18, 18-25 year old EU citizens, non-European permanent residents of France, and handicapped free. ☑ Open May 15-Sep 16 daily 9:30am-6:30pm; Sep 17-Mar Tu-Sa 9am-5:30pm; Apr-May 14 daily 9am-5:30pm.

VIEILLE CHARITÉ   HISTORIC BUILDING, MUSEUM
2 rue de la Charité   ☎04 91 14 58 80 www.vieille-charite-marseille.org

In 1640 the powers that be in Marseille decided all beggars and poor people should be locked up. So the somewhat less powerful powers that be built the Vieille Charité to give the homeless a place to sleep. The place later evolved into an orphanage where wooden planks blocking the windows would allow the nuns to turn a blind eye to the local Mother or Father of the Year dropping their kid off in front of the church. Today, you can enjoy the Baroque Chapel in the center of the courtyard, the Musée des Arts Africains, Océaniens, et Amérindiens, the Musée d'Archéologie Méditerranée, Le Miroir cinema, or a temporary exhibit highlighting local history.

i Tram 2 to Sadi Carnot. Walk north on rue de la République and turn left onto the little alleyway labeled rue Lorette before the next intersection. Go up the stairs and continue straight; the museum is on the right. Permanent exhibits €3, students €1.50, French university students and children under 12 free. Temporary exhibits €4, student €2.50. ☑ Museums open Jun-Sept Tu-Su 11am-6pm; Oct-May Tu-Su 10am-5pm.

Belsunce and Notre-Dame du Mont

▨ MUSÉE DE LA MODE   MUSEUM
11 La Canebière   ☎04 96 17 06 00 www.m-mmm.fr

The ultimate window shopper's dream, this museum showcases the history of clothing from the 1940s to the present and boasts 6000 garments—Lady Gaga's meat dress is sadly omitted.

i Ⓜ️Vieux Port. Walk up the block; the museum is on the left €2, students free. ☑ Open Oct-May 10am-5pm, Jun-Sept 11am-6pm.

THE GREAT OUTDOORS

◪ SORMIOU CALANQUE

One of the easiest to hike and most breathtaking of the calanques, this trail leads down to a small cove where it's just too pretty to not swim, even if it means stripping down to your skivvies to enjoy it.

i Ⓜ*Rond-Point du Prado. Then take bus #22 to the end of the line.*

◪ SUGITON CALANQUE

The calanque to the east of Sormiou is equally pretty. Make your way along a windy trail for about 20min. until it becomes flat for another 30min. Head down to the water's edge, where cliff jumpers can be seen leaping from high ledges into the lagoon.

i *Bus #21 to the end.*

FOOD

Vieux Port and Le Panier

◪ AU FALAFEL
FALAFEL, SHAWARMA $$

5 rue Lulli   ☎04 91 54 08 55

Au the joy of falafel. This falafel, shawarma, kefta, and everything-Israeli eatery makes homemade to-die-for hummus and grills all of its food in the small open kitchen at the front of the store. This can make the place steam up inside, so although the stone walls and generic coffee shop art are charming, you'll probably prefer to enjoy the breeze from the patio.

i Ⓜ*Vieux Port. Walk south along the port onto cours Jean Ballard, then turn left onto rue Francis Davso. Rue Lulli is on the right. Pita sandwiches €6-8. Entrées €4-11. plats €12-22.* 🕐 *Open M-Th noon-midnight, F noon-4pm, Su noon-midnight.*

◪ FOUR DES NAVETTES
BOULANGERIE $

136 rue Sainte   ☎04 91 33 65 69 www.fourdesnavettes.com

Four des Navettes has been baking (you guessed it) navettes since 1781. The traditional lemony biscuits are meant to resemble the boats that first brought evangelists to France's shores, and if by boats they mean rather cylindrical driftwood, then yes, they've got it right. The Abbaye St-Victor blesses the navettes as they come out of the oven at 6am every February 2 on Candlemas.

i *Down the street from the Abbaye St-Victor. Dozen navette €9.* 🕐 *Open Sept-Jul M-Sa 7am-8pm, Su 9am-1pm and 3-7:30pm; Aug daily 9am-1pm and 3-7:30pm.*

LE SOUK
NORTH AFRICAN $$$

100 quai du Port   ☎04 91 91 29 29 www.restaurantlesouk.com

Holy Marrakesh, is this food somethin'. Le Souk specializes in couscous and tajines that you might consider sharing with your significant other unless you're feeling especially ravenous. The couscous here isn't just couscous—it's a royal spread of semolina, vegetables and broth, raisins, chickpeas, spicy sauce, and your choice of meat on handmade dishes from North Africa. The cramped interior will make your eating experience feel more authentic, but you may need the breeze from the port outside to cool your senses.

i Ⓜ*Vieux Port. Walk around the port to the right-hand side. Lunch men €13.50. Entrées €6.50-9. Couscous €14.50-20. Tajines €15-20.* 🕐 *Open Tu-Su noon-3pm and 7:30-11:30pm.*

Belsunce and Notre-Dame du Mont

◪ MARCHÉ CAPUCIN
MARKET $

pl. du Marché des Capucins

Fresh fruit and vegetables color this small but lush market in the plaza just outside the Noailles Métro stop. Prices here are so cheap you could probably feed a family of four on €10. The water draining from the seafood market at the foot of the plaza gives this market a distinct aroma if you approach from below. Smelly or not, the food is high-quality and worth a visit, especially if you're looking to stock up your hostel fridge or picnic basket for the beach.

i Ⓜ*Noailles. The market is right outside the Métro stop. Tomatoes €1.20 per kg. Potatoes €0.90 per kg. 🕐 Open M-Sa during the day.*

ARABESQUE
NORTH AFRICAN $$

20A rue d'Aix ☎04 91 91 96 75

Belsunce is filled with lots of good, cheap North African food, but Arabesque is particularly good and especially cheap. A bit more rustic and hodge-podge than other places on the port, Arabesque looks a little bit like an American highway rest stop cafeteria inside. The food, however, is much tastier and more authentic than Subway. You will find an almost entirely local population here that may give you sideways looks for showing up in this neck of the woods, but don't let that scare you away. Instead, look for the desserts that line the windows and regularly lure in unsuspecting lunchers.

i Ⓜ*Colbert. Turn left onto rue Puvis de Chavannes and follow it to rue d'Aix. Arabesque is on the left. Bakery items €1-3. Entrées €3. plats €6-11. 🕐 Open daily 7:30am-8pm. Lunch noon-3pm.*

O'PAKISTAN
PAKISTANI, INDIAN $$

11 rue des Trois Rois ☎04 91 48 87 10 or 04 91 48 02 55

Since 1990, O'Pakistan has kept customers overjoyed with over-the-top delicious food. Royal wooden chairs and a bar that glitters like the euro that will still be in your pocket after leaving this place, O'Pakistan takes you out of Marseille and across the sea for the evening. Most diners opt for the thali plate that comes with a sampling of eight different *entrées* and a side of Pakistani bread. The tray of small bowls is as colorful as it is flavorful and will keep your senses busy for a long time.

i Ⓜ*Notre Dame du Mont-Cours Julien. Take rue Pastoret or rue Bussy l'Indien and turn left onto rue des Trois Rois. Entrées €4.50-10. plats €8.50-13. 🕐 Open daily noon-2pm and 7pm-midnight.*

NIGHTLIFE
Vieux Port and Le Panier

BAR 13 COINS
BAR

45 rue Ste-Françoise ☎04 91 91 56 49

Bright, multi-colored tables and chairs match the energetic yet light-hearted energy of this chill bar. Friday nights bring in live bands on the patio where families and young couples alike enjoy jazz, pop, and rock concerts. The interior of the bar is barely big enough for the bar itself, so the crowd can always be found outside next to the bright murals of soccer players. Start your evening out in Marseille with a few drinks here, then move on to greener pastures when the sun begins to set.

i Ⓜ*Joliette. Walk south on av. Robert Schuman, turn left at the police station, then right, then left onto Ste-Françoise. Beer €3-4.50. Wine €3. Mixed drinks €6. 🕐 Open daily in summer 9am-midnight; in winter 9am-9pm.*

BARBEROUSSE
CLUB

7 rue Glandèves ☎04 91 33 78 13 www.barberousse.com/ville/marseille

The Marseille branch of this three-club chain is the original, and the pirate theme makes much more sense in this port city. A young crowd comes here for the nightly DJ, the house specialty rum, and flavored vodka shots.

i Ⓜ*Vieux Port. Turn right when you exit the Métro and walk about 2½ blocks; the club is on the left. DJ every night. Shots €2.50. Piña Colada €2.50. Havana Club mojito €9.50. 🕐 Open Tu-Th 9pm-2am, F-Sa 9pm-4am.*

france

Belsunce and Notre-Dame du Mont

◪ **PETIT NICE**   BAR

28 pl. Jean Jaurès

If you're in the mood for a night of sitting around, chatting with friends, and drinking to your heart's (responsible) desire, this is the place to do it. Drinks are unbeatably cheap and the bar has a cute nautical Nice theme going on, but all that's negligible when everyone is out on the enormous patio. This is the perfect place to get lost in conversation and blissfully forget about your budget for a while, since your bill won't add up too quickly.

i ⓂNotre-Dame du Mont-Cours Julien. Bee €2-3.50. Rum and mixed drinks €3-3.50. ⌚ Open Tu-Sa noon-2am.

ESSENTIALS
Practicalities

- **TOURIST OFFICE: Office de Tourisme et des Congrès.** Free maps and accommodations bookings. **Marseille City Pass** includes unlimited access to public transportation, access to 7 museums, city guided tours, ferry to Île d'If, tourist train to Notre-Dame de la Garde, and discounts for shopping, city music festivals, and other events. (4 La Canebière ☎04 91 13 89 00 www.marseille-tourisme.com *i* ⓂVieux Port. Walk away from the port entrance on La Canebière. City Pass 1-day €22; 2-day €29. ⌚ Open M-Sa 9am-7pm, Su 10am-5pm.) Tourist desk at **Gare St-Charles.** (☎04 91 50 59 18 ⌚ Open M-F 10am-12:30pm, 1-5pm.)

- **TOURS:** Tourist office offers walking tours of the city in French. (*i* 1 tour per week in English; ask for schedule. €7. ⌚ Daily at 2pm.) Almost always full of families and tourist groups, the **Petit Train** is a Disneyland-esque trolley that takes tourists around the major sites of the city. (☎04 91 25 24 69 *i* Departs on 3 different tracks. Call or book at tourist office. ⌚ Old Marseille departs every 30min. Apr-Nov 15 10am-12:30pm and 2-6pm.) Notre-Dame de la Garde runs every 20min. Apr-Nov 10am-12:20pm and 1:40pm-6:20pm; every 40min. Dec-Mar or on the hr. 10am-noon and 2-4pm. (*i* Old Marseille €6, children €3. Notre-Dame de la Garde €7, children €4. Frioul Island €4, children €2.)

- **CONSULATES: UK.** (24 av. du Prado ☎04 93 15 72 10 ⌚ Open M-F 9:30am-noon and 2-4:30pm by appointment only.) **US.** (12 pl. Varian Fry ☎04 91 54 92 00 ⌚ Open M-F 9am-noon and 3-5pm by appointment only.)

- **LOST PROPERTY:** 41 bd de Briançon. (☎ 04 91 14 68 97 ⌚ Open M-F 8:45am-noon and 12:45-4:30pm.) Also located at Gare St-Charles Platform A.

- **YOUTH CENTER: Centre Régional Information Jeunesse** (CRIJ) Provence. Information on long-term housing, short-term employment, vacation planning (once you get that job), and services for the disabled. (96 La Canebière ☎04 91 24 33 50 www.crij.com *i* ⓂNoailles. ⌚ Open M 10am-5pm, Tu 1-5pm, W-F 10am-5pm. Limited hours Jul and Aug.)

- **GLBT RESOURCES: Centre Gay et Lesbien Marseille Provence.** (1 rue Ferrari ☎04 91 42 07 48 beatrice.bouillaut.free.fr/bbclub/cgl13/present.html or www.gay-sejour.com *i* ⓂRéformé or ⓂNotre-Dame du Mont-Cours Julien. ⌚ Open M 4-8pm, W 4-8pm, F 4-8pm.)

- **INTERNET ACCESS:** Free internet at the CRIJ. Some internet cafes are scattered around Belsunce and the Vieux Port as well as around Gare St-Charles, especially on rue des Petits Maries.

- **POST OFFICE:** One in each arrondissement. **1er:** (1 pl. Hôtel des Postes ☎ 04 91 15 47 00 *i* Take La Canebière toward the sea and turn right onto rue Reine Elisabeth as it becomes pl. Hôtel des Postes. *i* Currency exchange available. ⌚ Open M-W 8am-6:45pm, Th 9am-6:45pm, F 8am-6:45pm, Sa 8am-12:15pm.)

- **POSTAL CODE:** 13001

Emergency

- **SOS VOYAGEURS:** Gare St-Charles. (☎04 91 62 12 80)

- **POLICE:** Dial ☎17 for emergencies. 2 rue du Antoine Becker (Non-emergency ☎04 91 39 80 00) and 66 La Canbière (Non-emergency ☎04 88 77 58 00 *i* Ⓜ️Noailles. Branch at train station next to Platform A).

- **PHARMACY:** There are pharmacies everywhere, but there is always 1 in each *arrondissement* that is open 24hr.; call for more information. (7 rue de la République ☎04 91 90 32 27 Ⓩ Open M-Su 8:30am-7pm.)

- **HOSPITAL: Hôpital Timone.** (264 rue St-Pierre ☎04 91 38 00 00 *i* Ⓜ️Timone.) **Vieux Porte Medical Center.** (48 rue de la République ☎04 91 14 68 97. Ⓩ Open daily 9am-8pm, Su and holidays 9am-1pm.)

- **AMBULANCE:** ☎15, **Doctors:** ☎3624, **Dentists:** ☎04 91 85 39 39

Getting There

BY PLANE

Aéroport Marseille-Provence (MRS; ☎04 42 14 14 14 www.marseille-airport.com) is a popular destination served by several major carriers. **AirFrance** offers flights from Paris. **Ryanair** also has service from London and various secondary airports throughout Europe. Shuttles (☎08 91 02 40 25 *i* €0.30 per min.) run every 15-20min. between the airport and Gare St-Charles (*i* €8, €8.50 for shuttle plus RTM ticket Ⓩ 25min.).

BY TRAIN

Gare St-Charles is the hub of the city and runs frequent trains within France, including from Lyon (€58 Ⓩ 1hr., 20 per day), Nice (€32 Ⓩ 2hr., 20 per day), and Paris (€105 Ⓩ 3hr., 15 per day). International trains usually arrive through Paris. For up-to-date and accurate fare information, visit www.sncf.com. For those under 25, a €15 TER pass, valid for one year, provides a 50% discount on regional travel in Provence-Alps-Côte d'Azur (PACA). Trust us, you don't want to take the slow TER trains from Marseille to Paris—it's a long haul.

BY BUS

Buses depart from rue Honnorat, behind the train station. (☎08 91 02 40 25 *i* Gare St-Charles. Ⓩ Ticket counters open M-F 6:15am-7:30pm, Sa 6:30am-6:30pm, Su 7:30am-12:30pm and 1:30-6pm.) Depending on location, you can buy tickets on board the bus (the closer the destination is, the more likely you will be able to do this), but we recommend buying tickets at the window. Buses travel from: Aix-en-Provence (€5.50 Ⓩ Every 10-15min. 6:30am-8:30pm, 2 per hr. 9-11:30pm); Nice (€28, students €19 Ⓩ 2hr., 1 per day); and Cannes (€25, students €19 Ⓩ 2-3hr. 4 per day).

BY FERRY

There are a few different options available to travelers who want to get to Marseille by ferry. **SNCM.** (61 bd des Dames ☎08 25 88 80 88 Ⓩ Office open M-F 9am-6pm.) **Corsica Ferries.** (7 rue Beauvau ☎08 25 09 50 95 www.corsicaferries.com *i* Departs from Toulon. To Corsica €32-65; Algeria €105-315; Sardinia €60-85. Ⓩ Open M-Sa 8am-8pm, Su 9am-7pm.) **MPCT.** (Marseille Provence Cruise Terminal www.marseille-cruise. com *i* From Gare St-Charles, take Métro line 2 to Joliette. From there take bus 35 to Gate 4 of the port entrance. From the port entrance, you may have to walk 2-3km to the departure quay.)

france

BY TAXI

Traveling to Marseille by taxi is expensive, but if you must, **Taxi radio Marseille** (☎04 91 02 20 20) and **Taxi Marseillais** (☎04 91 92 92 92) are available. There are 24hr. taxi stands surrounding the Gare St-Charles and Vieux Port. A trip to Vieux Port from Gare St-Charles will cost €20-30, while a trip to the airport will be €40-55.

BY CAR

There is a stand at the Gare St-Charles. **Avis.** (☎04 91 64 71 00 www.avis.fr *i* Must be 21 or older. Under 25 surcharge €25 per day. ☼ Open M 7am-10:30pm, Tu-W 7am-9pm, Th-F 7am-10:30pm, Sa 7am-7pm, Su 8am-8pm.)

Getting Around

RTM runs the Métro, tram, and bus systems; all three have the same fares and take the same tickets and passes. Don't try to cheat the system and ride the bus, tram, or even the Métro without a ticket—RTM security are everywhere, constantly checking for tickets and handing out fines day and night. One trip is €1.50, and you can also buy a Carte of 10 journeys (€12.80), an unlimited day pass (€5), an unlimited 3-day pass (€10.50), or an unlimited 7-day pass (€13). Métro stations are open M-Th 5am-11:30pm, F-Su 5am-12:30am, while the tram runs M-F 5am-12:30am. Bus lines that you might want to use depart from Gare St-Charles, Castellene, and Vieux Port. There are **Le Vélo bike stands** throughout the city, but they require a €150 deposit on your credit card unless you have a European bank card (in which case it's a screaming deal at €1 per hr., free for first 30min).

avignon

Though we may never understand why anyone would move their capital from Italy to France, Avignon still maintains the unique privilege of being the city that seven rebellious popes chose as their new home. For a brief 39 years during the 14th century, Avignon became Catholicism's hub, which naturally warranted a grand residence **(Palais des Papes)** and an influx of culture and politics. As time passed, however, and the Church moved back to Rome, the already famous and centuries-old Pont d'Avignon would gradually lead from somewhere to nowhere. Nevertheless, a trip to Avignon is still worth at least a solid day, if not for the sights, then to sample a seemingly disproportionate amount of good food sprinkled throughout barely more than 4 sq. km. If you come in July during the Festival d'Avignon, expect a certain level of organized chaos and an infinite measure of culture.

ORIENTATION

The town of Avignon is surrounded by a giant wall, so there are only so many ways you can get lost in it. **Rue de la République,** the main road from the train station, runs north-south and leads straight to the **Palais des Papes.** Just east of the rue de la République, before it hits **place de l'Horloge,** is a small web of pedestrian-only streets that contain mostly shopping spots. This area is roughly the center of the city, though **place Pie** and **Les Halles** (Avignon's covered market) are arguably its true heart. Radiating out from this center is **rue Thiers** running east and **rue Carnot,** which turns into **rue de la Carreterie,** running northeast. You can find lots of good cafes along and just off of rue de la Carreterie, but the farther you go, the more residential and quieter it gets. The Rhône River runs over the northern and western sides of the city, and the famous **Pont d'Avignon** spans the rushing currents roughly where the river bends. Across from the banks of Avignon is the southern tip of the Rhône's **Île de la Barthelasse,** where you can find a cheap campsite and Avignon's only hostel.

get a room!

For more recommendations, visit **www.letsgo.com**.

HOTEL MIGNON   HOTEL $$$
12 rue Joseph Vernet   ☎04 90 82 17 30 www.hotel-mignon.com
Hotel Mignon truly lives up to its name—this place is pretty darn cute
(you're confused about the steak part now, aren't you?). With delicate
wallpaper and velvety drapes adorning the windows and headboards, this
quiet little hotel has charm that's through the roof. Hopefully the person
you're sharing a bathroom with is as adorable as your accommodations.
   *i From the tourism office, turn left onto rue Joseph Vernet and follow it almost to the end.
   Single €56-65; doubles €71-86; triples and quads €89-119. ☑ Reception 24hr.*

SIGHTS

PALAIS DES PAPES   PALACE
Montée Jean XXIII   ☎04 90 27 50 00 www.palais-des-papes.com
In early 1309, Pope Clement V decided it was time for a change of scenery from
the Vatican, so he moved Catholicism's headquarters to Avignon whereupon this
grand Gothic palace was built and completed in less than 20 years. At the time,
Matteo Giovannetti was the next big thing in the ever-growing Italian art scene
and was recruited to paint frescoes all over the palace's interior, some of which
are still intact. The building would later suffer a series of attacks and sieges by
anti-papal armies and French revolutionaries and even spent time serving as a
prison, stables, and army barracks. Today, the palace is owned by the city and is
one of France's most visited monuments.
   *i Right next to the Avignon cathedral on the Place du Palais. Free audio guide with entrance
   €10.50, reduced €8.50. With Pont d'Avignon €13, reduced €10. ☑ Open daily Nov-Feb 9:30am-
   5:45pm; Mar 9am-6:30pm; Apr-Jun 9am-7pm; Jul 9am-8pm; Aug 9am-9pm; Sept-Oct 9am-7pm.
   Last entrance 1hr. before close.*

MUSÉE DU PETIT PALAIS   MUSEUM
pl. du Palais des Papes   ☎04 90 86 44 58 www.petit-palais.org
The Musée du Petit Palais is home to the Campana collection of Renaissance
Italian art, first bought by Napoleon III and later bestowed upon the Louvre,
which then gifted the collection and other paintings to the Petit Palais. Most
of the museum is a standard offering of sad paintings of the crucified and the
martyred. The museum is very large and a little bit redundant, so we suggest
focusing your time on the exhibits toward the back, which feature the works
of Giotto and other Italian artists, 14th-century attempts at perspective, and the
trials and tribulations of a burgeoning Renaissance. Also of note is The Calvary,
the gory 14th-century equivalent of the Passion of the Christ that depicts a gold,
sad, and bleeding Jesus that would make even Mel Gibson cringe.
   *i Behind Palais des Papes, at the end of the square on the left-hand side. Info brochures are
   scattered around the museum. Guided visits available upon request. Permanent and temporary
   exhibit €7, reduced €4. Temporary exhibit only €3. ☑ Open M 10am-1pm and 2-6pm, W-Su 10am-
   1pm and 2-6pm.*

france

FOOD

MAISON NANI
TRADITIONAL $$

rue de la République
☎04 90 82 60 90

Maison Nani will make you feel young again. Tintin cartoons, brightly colored chairs, and a mini-carousel in the window will take you back to the good ol' days. And we don't mean the first week of your vacation, you lucky dog, you—we mean back in the day when your biggest concern was finishing your spinach before wolfing down Mom's homemade cookies.

i *Corner of rue Théodore Aubanel and rue du Provôt. Just off of rue de la République. Menu with tart, salad, and coffee €9.80. plat du jour with dessert and coffee €14.20. plats €9-17. Salads €10-11.* ☒ *Open daily noon-3pm and 7-11pm.*

FRANÇOISE
TRADITIONAL $

6 rue du Général Léclerc
☎04 32 76 24 77 www.melido.fr

Françoise is a simple, cafeteria-style French eatery with prepared and fresh homemade foods at the ready. Every eat-in order is accompanied by a salad—and by salad, we mean a bowl of lettuce—with homemade dressing. Avignon's working class and cheap teenagers flood Françoise at lunchtime. We don't know if they're aiming for old-school or organic with the wooden cutlery, but it makes us feel like we're eating at Uncle Larry's Amish farm, and strangely enough, we like its simplicity.

i *From pl. Pie with your back to Les Halles, walk straight up rue du Général Léclerc. The restaurant is on the left. Free Wi-Fi. Credit card min. €10. Sandwiches €3-4. Salads €3-4.50. Apple crumble €4. Hot meal and two sides €9.* ☒ *Open M-Sa 8am-7pm.*

NIGHTLIFE

WALL STREET
BAR

pl. Pie
☎04 90 27 09 28

This bar has absolutely nothing in common with its namesake—the lack of suits, elitism, and palpable greed make this Wall Street a much more enjoyable place than the one in New York. This bar is where young, respectable folk come out for drinks and occasional dancing. Above ground, red and purple lighting gives the place a jazzy feel, but downstairs you'll find a different sort of scene; the rotating circular bar in the center of the room keeps things interesting with the company of DJs from in and out of Avignon on the weekends.

i *In pl. Pie behind the tower on the corner. DJ Sept-Jun Th-Sa. Student night on Th. DJ from outside Avignon on F. Basement closed Jul-Aug. Shooter €2.50. Beer €2.50 half pints, €4.50 pints; happy hour €2 and €3.50. Mixed drinks €6, happy hour €3. Bottles €55, happy hour €45.* ☒ *Open daily 8am-1am (3am in Jul).*

CUBANITO
BAR, CLUB

51 rue Carnot
☎04 90 86 98 04

Cubanito won't let you forget that hips don't lie. Always alive with salsa, merengue, cha-cha, or other generally hot Latin beats, Cubanito is la loca place to be. Watching those gifted with the ability to actually look sexy when they dance may be tortura, so get on your feet, ask for a lesson on the basic moves, and let your she-wolf out of its den.

i *Bee €3.30. Mixed drinks €6.* ☒ *Open Tu-Su 4pm-3am.*

ESSENTIALS

Practicalities

- **TOURIST OFFICE:** The tourist office offers maps, guided tours by appointment, Rhône River cruise tickets, and a free pass that discounts Avignon sights by 10-50% after the first full-price ticket. (41 cours Jean Jaurès ☎04 32 74 32 74 www.avignon-tourisme.com *i* Walk straight down the main drag from the train station. Tourist information is on your right after 200m. ☺ Open Apr-Oct M-Sa 9am-6pm, Su 10am-5pm; Nov-Mar M-F 9am-6pm, Sa 9am-5pm, Su 10am-noon. During July Festival open daily 9am-7pm.) There is also a tourist info desk inside Les Halles market. (pl. Pie ☺ Open F-Su 10am-1pm.) Tourist info desk inside TGV station open during peak season only.

- **TOURS: Petit Train** takes you to all the major sights in Avignon. (Leaves from Palais des Papes every 30min. ☎06 10 32 85 24 *i* €7, children €4. ☺ 40min. Open daily Mar 14-Jun 10am-7pm; Jul-Aug daily 10am-8pm; Oct daily 10am-7pm; Nov-Mar 15 W 2-6pm, Sa 2-6pm.)

- **POST OFFICE:** Cours Président Kennedy (☎04 90 27 54 10 ☺ Open M 8:30am-6pm, Tu 8:30am-8pm, W-F 8:30am-6pm, Sa 9am-4pm.) Next to Les Halles. (rue de la Petite Meuse ☺ Open M-F 9:30am-5pm, Sa 9:30am-noon.)

- **HOSPITAL: Hospital de la Durance.** (1750 chemin du Lavarin ☎08 26 88 98 11 www.crd84. fr) **Centre Hospitalier Avignon.** (305 rue Raoul Follereau ☎ 04 32 75 33 33 www.ch-avignon. fr)

- **YOUTH CENTER:** 102 rue de la Carreterie. (☎04 90 14 04 05 ☺ Open M-F 8:30am-noon and 1-5pm.)

- **GLBT RESOURCES: Le CIDcafe.** Loud and proud cafe with brochures for the popular GLBT clubs and bars, such as Le Cage and l'Esclave, and a schedule of GLBT theme nights in Avignon. (11 pl. l'Horloge ☎04 90 82 30 38 www.lecidcafe.com ☺ Open daily 6:30am-1am.)

- **LAUNDROMAT: La Blanchisseuse.** (248 rue de la Carreterie *i* €2.50 per 5.5kg, €3.50 per 7kg. ☺ Open daily 7am-8pm.) There is also a large laundromat at the Bagatelle Camping site (see Accommodations.)

- **INTERNET:** You can find free internet almost anywhere in Avignon; look out for the green sticker on the entrance to cafes, laundromats, and stores. **Françoise** has free Wi-Fi (see **Food**). **Taxi-phone.** (24 rue Carnot *i* €1 per 30min.)

Emergency

- **SAMU:** ☎15

- **POLICE:** Municipal Police. (13 ter quai St Lazare ☎04 90 85 13 13) National Police. (Caserne de Salles bd St-Roch ☎17 or ☎04 32 40 55 55)

- **PHARMACIES:** Pharmacies are located throughout the city. Like many cities in southern France, there is one pharmacy, on a rotating schedule, that is open 24hr. each week. To find a pharmacy on duty call ☎3237 or visit www.3237.fr.

- **FIRE:** ☎18.

Getting There

BY PLANE

Avignon Caumont Airport (AVN; ☎04 90 81 51 51 www.avignon.aeroport.fr) is 8km from the city center. Regular flights go to and from Birmingham, Exeter, London, and Southampton; connecting flights to Belfast, Dublin, Edinburgh, Glasgow, Guernsey, Jersey, and Newcastle are also available.

BY TRAIN

Avignon has three main train stations: the **TGV station, Avignon Centre,** and **Auto Train Avignon Sud.** Gare Avignon TGV is a 15min. bus ride from the city center. (pl. de l'Europe www.sncf.com or www.sncf.fr) Direct trains within France from: Paris (€70-80 ☺ 2½hr.); Roissy Charles de Gaulle airport (€80-100 ☺ 3hr.); Montpellier (€15 ☺ 1-2hr. depending on stops); Lyon (€25 ☺ 1½-2½hr. depending on stops); and Lille,

Nantes, Rouen, Metz, Marne la Vallée, Rennes, Toulouse, and Strasbourg. Trains also run from Brussels (€100-140 ⏱ 5hr.) and Geneva.

Avignon Centre (bd St-Roch www.sncf.com or www.sncf.fr) is the closest to the city center and has the most frequent trains to and from popular destinations, including express regional trains, inter-city trains, and Paris TGV. Eurostar has a train between Avignon and London every Saturday in July and Aug. (€130-180 ⏱ 7-8hr.)

Auto Train Avignon Sud. (Chemin de la Poulasse St-Chamand ☎04 90 27 81 70 ⏱ Trains between Avignon and Paris daily late Apr-Sept in winter 3 times per week on Tu, Th, Sa. Trains between Avignon and Berlin on Th. Trains between Avignon and Metz, Strasbourg, and Lille in summer only.)

BY BUS

The **Edgard bus** is based in Nîmes and serves smaller cities and attractions in Provence. The E51 line connects Avignon and Nîmes, and four other lines connect Avignon and less frequented destinations. (☎08 10 33 42 73 www.edgard-transport.fr)

Getting Around

Avignon is a small city with lots of narrow, winding, one-way, and pedestrian-only streets, so the best way to get around is on foot. **Vélopop** is a bike service with more than 200 bicycles that are available for rent 24/7 at 17 stations throughout the city. (☎08 10 45 64 56 www.velopop.fr). You can also rent bikes from **Provence Bike,** which is located outside of the city walls just southeast of Avignon Centre. (7 av. St-Ruf www.provence-bike.com ☎04 90 27 92 61 *i* 1st 30min. free; 1-day package €1 for access, then €1 per additional 30min.; 7-day package €5/1. Credit card only. ⏱ Open Apr-Oct daily 9am-6:30pm.) You can also call a taxi from **Taxi Avignon.** (☎04 90 82 20 20)

arles

Combine the mystique of ancient Rome with the culture of France and a touch of a troubled Dutch artist and you get the eccentric historical cocktail that is Arles. Every street in this town seems to end in a Roman ruin, a cafe that inspired a Van Gogh painting, or both. This historical legacy has transformed Arles into a hotspot for busloads of French tourists and retired Americans. Nonetheless, the city is worth enduring the brief clamor of chatty, camera-clicking tourist groups. Every corner of Arles manages to offer a new kind of Provençal charm, whether it be the friendly bustle of a plaza or the quiet solitude of a flower-boxed alleyway. Local tortured artists and musicians cultivate a small but active bar and concert scene, and the hype peaks around July during the local photography festival.

ORIENTATION

Getting into Arles is fairly easy from the **Gare SNCF,** which is located just north of the city center and east of the Rhône. If you're starting at the Gare SNCF (which you probably are), follow the signs to enter the city center through the northern gate. From there it's a straight shot down **rue Voltaire** to the **Amphithéâtre,** the city's most iconic sight and a good place to get your bearings. Just behind the Amphithéâtre is the **Théatre Antique.** Following rue de la Calade past the theater, you will arrive at a number of other sights as well as the Hôtel de Ville, the city hall. The pl. de la Forum is where you will find most of Arles's crowds and young locals enjoying music and drinks well into the night. **Boulevard des Lices** and **boulevard Georges Clemenceau** hug the southern border of the city and are home to the police, post office, and tourist office. The **Musée Départemental d'Arles Antique** is on the western tip of the city along the Rhône. Everything south of these boulevards is mostly residential.

For more recommendations, visit **www.letsgo.com**.

MAISON DU PÈLERIN
HOSTEL $

26 pl. Pomme   ☎04 90 96 11 89 for Le Calendal www.arles-pelerins.fr

Although just marginally pricier than the Auberge de Jeunesse, Maison du Pèlerin is a budget backpacker's dream; the location, in particular, pays for itself. Inside a charming, rustic old building, dorm rooms here are rather spacious and bright, if nothing else, and there is a large full-service kitchen with no shortage of coffee, Nesquick, and butter for your morningbaguette.

i Just behind Le Calendal, caddy-corner to the Théâtre Antique and the Amphithéâtre. Reception is at Le Calendal reception desk. Wi-Fi can be used in the lobby of Le Calendal. Breakfast and linens included. Dorms €25 per person per night. ☒ Reception 24hr.

AUBERGE DE JEUNESSE
HOSTEL $

20 av. Maréchal Foch   ☎04 90 96 18 25 www.fuaj.org

Although this Auberge de Jeunesse isn't in the city center, fortunately it's not much of a hike. With plain dorm rooms, a standard common area and bar, and lively young people speaking every language under the sun, this place is your best option for meeting other travelers in Arles, even if the staff claims that it isn't much ofa party hostel.

i Walk or take bus #3 to the tourist office from the train station (last bus 7:15pm). Behind the tourists office is bdÉmile Zola; walk straight and follow the road as it bends left over the train tracks. Look for Auberge de Jeunesse signs and turn left onto av. du Maréchal Foch.. Dorms €19 per person per night. ☒ Reception 7-10am and 5-11pm (midnight Jul-Aug). Bar closes at midnight. Lockout daily 10am-5pm.

SIGHTS

AMPHITHÉÂTRE D'ARLES
AMPHITHEATER

Rond-point des Arènes   ☎04 90 49 36 86 www.arenes-arles.com

Easily Arles's most visited, exciting, and beloved attraction, this ancient Roman amphitheater dates back to the first century CE. After the fall of the Roman empire, the amphitheater was transformed into a town with houses, chapels, and its own public square. Eventually its function changed again, and it became the stadium it is today. Les Arènes now hosts twice-annual bullfights that bring crowds from near and far. You can also see horse shows, art festivals, and reenactments of gladiator battles in the summer.

i From the train station, follow av. de Stalingrad to the end of rue Voltaire. Or follow signs in the city for the Amphithéâtre. Bullfights at Easter and 2nd weekend in September, sometimes more in the summer. €6.50, reduced €5. Entrance to Théâtre Antique included. ☒ Open daily May-Sept 9am-7pm; Oct 9am-6pm; Nov-Feb 10am-5pm; Mar-Apr 9am-6pm.

MUSÉE DÉPARTEMENTAL ARLES ANTIQUE
MUSEUM

Presqu'il-du-Cirque-Romain   ☎04 90 18 88 80 www.arles-antique.cg13.fr

This small, triangular museum houses some of Provence's most antique Roman ruins. Despite its geometric rigidity, the museum takes visitors through a chronological and thematic documentation of the glory that was the Roman Empire in Arles. Statues, sarcophagi, pottery, jewelry, and modern models of ancient wonders make for an impressive rendition of times long gone. The nearly complete mosaics and segments of aqueducts are particularly astounding, especially for you Latin geeks. Before you get to the museum, you will encounter the Hortus

Garden, modeled after the Roman Circus, where you can have a romp in the grass or come for mock-Olympic Games and other events during the summer.

i *Open M 10am-6pm, W-Su 10am-6pm. Hortus Garden open daily Apr-Sept 10am-7pm; Oct-Mar 10am-5:30pm.*

THÉÂTRE ANTIQUE
THEATER

rue de la Calade
☎04 90 93 05 23

Although it has been a UNESCO World Heritage Site since 1981, the Théâtre Antique's authentic antiquity seems a bit diminished by its present-day usage, which brings dancing, singing, and theater to the modern stage set-up in the center of the ruins. There is a fee to enter this theater, but most of it can be seen through the fence from the outside, so we suggest you only pay if you're dying to touch some old rocks. One ticket will get you entrance to the Théâtre Antique as well as the Amphithéâtre, so don't see one without seeing the other.

i *Located 1 block south of the Amphithéâtre on rue de la Calade. Entrance at the corner of rue de la Calade and rue du Cloître. €6.50, reduced €5. Entrance to Amphithéâtre included. Cash only. ☺ Open daily May-Sept 9am-7pm; Oct 9am-6pm; Nov-Feb 10am-5pm; Mar-Apr 9am-6pm.*

ABBAYE DE MONTMAJOUR
ABBEY

Route de Fontvieille
☎04 90 54 64 17   montmajour.monuments-nationaux.fr

Five kilometers from the center of Arles, this medieval abbey has been greeting visitors ever since the mid-19th century, when the Prosper Mérimée decided that it was about time to show the place off. And it was quite a lot to brag about. Over the centuries, the abbey amassed a fortune in donations and unofficial payments for religious ceremonies and blessings. A UNESCO World Heritage Site, the courtyard reveals the magnificent Pons de l'Orme tower, and the arched ceilings will keep you gazing up in awe (be careful not to walk into any of the columns).

i *From Gare SNCF or bd Georges Clémenceau, take bus #29. 10-15min., €3.80 1 way. Check bus schedule. €7.50, reduced €4.50, adult group €6, under 18 and EU citizens under 26 free. ☺ Open Jul-Sept daily 10am-6:30pm; Oct-Mar Tu-Su 10am-5pm; Apr-Jun daily 9:30am-6pm. Last entry 45min. before close. Guided tours available by reservation.*

FOOD

✦ FAD'OLI
SANDWICHES, SUSHI $

46 av. des Arènes
☎04 90 49 70 73 www.fadoli.com

Olive oil is the name of the game at this small, walk-up window sandwich shop near the busy pl. du Forum in the center of Arles. One of the owners is a former judge of olive oils, so whether it's for cooking, dipping, or dressing, these people know quality. They now stock and sell only three types of oil after converting their large storage area to indoor seating, but each oil is award-winning and mouth-watering. What's more, the sandwiches are crazy cheap and always delicious.

i *Near the pl. du Forum. Sandwiches €4-6. Salads €4.50-15. Sushi €7. ☺ Open daily noon-11pm.*

✦ DUNE
LEBANESE $$

8 rue Reattu
☎04 90 49 66 67

Dune has a simple menu of eight dishes and a handful of sides, but the flavors here are seriously complex. Plates of tabouli, feta, hummus, kebab meat, tzatziki, and more make for the kind of meal where you get a different taste with every bite. A sweet after-meal shot of thé à la menthe tops off a delicious meal.

i *Down the street from Musée Réattu, at the corner of rue Reattu and rue du 4 Septembre. Vegetarian plates available. plats €7.50-13. Sides €3. ☺ Open M-Sa noon-2pm or 3pm and 7pm-whenever the owner feels like closing.*

arles

LA COMÉDIE
ITALIAN $$

10 bd Georges Clemenceau ☎04 90 93 74 97

There is nothing funny about how good the pasta here is. While it doesn't take any extravagance to set these dishes apart, everything here is still really freakin' good. Perfect for a romantic Italian date or a family dinner, La Comédie serves the best pasta in town at very reasonable prices.

i Behind the bus stops. Pasta, salad, and other plat €9.50-18. ☑ Open M 7-11pm, Tu-Sa noon-2pm and 7-11pm.

SOLEILÏS
SORBET, ICE CREAM $

9 rue Docteur Fanton ☎04 90 93 30 76

The summer heat in Arles can be as rude as that girl who won't stop popping her bubble gum, and souvenir shops often tempt overheated tourists with slurpees on every corner. But the secret to cooling off is to get closer to the sun—Soleilïs has the best all-natural sorbet and ice cream in town. All 12 flavors are made with organic milk and eggs from local, grass-fed farms. Portions here are a bit skinny for the price but are still worth every lick.

i From the pl. du Forum, with your back to the hotel, go straight down rue des Thermes; the shop is on the corner. Free English book exchange. 1 scoop €1.50-2.70, 2 scoops €2.50-3.70, 3 scoops €3-4.20. ☑ Open Jul-Aug M 2-6:30pm, Tu-Su 2-6:30pm and 8:30-10:30pm. Oct-Apr daily 2-6:30pm.

NIGHTLIFE

WALLABEER
BAR

7 rue Molière ☎06 67 42 84 84

If you're walking down Arles's main boulevards after dark and you hear any noise that sounds like fun, it's probably coming from Wallabeer. Popular among young locals and tourists, Wallabeer throbs with a hot DJ and sweats with greasy dancers. The Australian theme is a bit forced in this decidedly French bar, but who doesn't love a little "Kangaroo Crossing" sign on the wall? Enter the street level bar and dance floor in the front or head back to the patio that looks over bd Georges Clémenceau.

i Behind the bus stops, above La Comédie. Entrance behind the main road on rue Molière. DJ F-Sa. Beer €5. ☑ Open daily 10am-2am.

L'APOSTROPHE
BAR, CAFE

7 pl. du Forum ☎04 90 96 34 17 www.lapostroph-arles.com

L'Apostrophe is where Arles's young, fun, and happy buzz through the night in the pl. du Forum. The crowd at this local favorite can often be found dancing to a DJ or a booming street band.

i Cocktail party Sa nights in the summer. DJs usually on weekends. Beer €5. Mixed drinks €8. ☑ Open daily 8am-2am or later.

ESSENTIALS

Practicalities

- **TOURIST OFFICES:** A tourism office branch is located inside **Gare SNCF;** ask for a map and other basic services there. The main tourism office is on **Esplanade de Charles de Gaulle.** (☎04 90 18 41 20 www.arlestourisme.com *i* From the train station, turn left and walk down av. Paulin Talabot; take the 1st left. From av. de Stalingrad, walk right and through the round-about and continue straight down rue Voltaire. Walk around the right side of the Amphithéâtre to the opposite side, pass the Théâtre Antique on your right, and continue straight through the garden to bd des Lices. Cross the street and turn right; the tourism office is just past the post office. ☑ Open M-Sa Jul-Aug 9am-6:45pm; Sept 9am-6:45pm; Oct-Mar 9am-4:45pm; Apr-Jun 9am-6:45pm. Open Su and holidays 10am-1pm year-round.)

france

- **LUGGAGE STORAGE: Hotel Acacias.** (2 rue de la Cavalerie ☎04 90 96 37 88 *i* Large bag €3 per day, small bags €2 per day. ☼ Open daily 7:30am-10pm.) **Hôtel Régence.** (5 rue Marius Jouveau ☎04 90 96 39 85 *i* €2 per bag per day. ☼ Open daily 7:30am-9:30pm.)
- **INTERNET ACCESS: Cyber City.** (31 rue Augustin Tardieu ☎04 90 18 87 40 and 38 bd Clememceau ☎04 90 96 19 70 €0.50 for 10min.) **Cafe Taxiphone.** (31 pl. Voltaire ☎04 90 18 87 40 €1.50 per hr. ☼ Open daily 9am-noon and 2:30-9pm.)
- **POST OFFICE:** 5 bd des Lices, next to tourist office. (☎04 90 18 41 15 *i* Currency exchange available. ☼ Open M-F 8:30am-6pm, Sa 8:30am-12:30pm.)
- **POSTAL CODE:** 13200.

Emergency

- **POLICE:** On the corner of bd des Lices and av. des Alyscamps, down the street from the main tourism office. (☎04 90 18 45 00), **Ambulance: SMUR.** (☎04 90 49 29 99), **Poison Control:** ☎04 91 74 66 6, **Hospital: Quartier Fourchon.** (☎04 90 49 29 29)

Getting There

Arles is usually a town that you stop at in the middle of your tour of the French Riviera, so the best way to get here is by train. **SNCF trains** run regularly between Montpellier and Marseille and between Marseille and Avignon, with Arles as a stop along those routes. Trains run to Arles from: Marseille (€10-15 ☼ 1hr.), Avignon (€8-10 ☼ 1hr.), and Nîmes (€8-10.50 ☼ 20-30min.). Tickets can be bought online at www. sncf.com or www.sncf.fr or at the train station at least 5min. before departure.

Getting Around

You can make your way around Arles by **train** or by **bus.** The **Petit Train** leaves from the main tourist office and Les Arènes every 40min. to tour the old city. (Office 17 bis av. de Hongrie ☎04 90 18 81 31 €7 for 30min. ☼ Open daily Apr-Oct 10am-7pm.) **Navia A** provides public buses that travel counterclockwise around the border of the *centre ville* between the Musée Départmental de l'Arles Antique and the Gare SNCF. (Free. ☼ Open M-Sa roughly 7am-7:30pm.)

nice

Nice has been on the backpacker must-see list since the youth of the world discovered its beaches and cheap wine. Combining a wealthy reputation with an affordable underbelly, Nice neatly condenses everything amazing about the Cote d'Azur into one sizzling Métropolis. While those of you who'd like to escape the tourists will groan when you see the busloads of cruise-shipping retirees and loudmouthed Anglophones in the *vieille ville*, you'll cheer when you see the rock-bottom happy hour prices at the local bars and grin as you interact with a well-established youth culture that goes out of its way to make travelers feel welcome. Daytime activities revolve around the rocky beaches and immense seaside promenade; extensive shopping opportunities and an unparalleled array of museums are available for those of you who can't just lie around all day. The city just about explodes at night, with live music in almost every bar and club and non-stop parties in the old town.

ORIENTATION

Nice is among the larger cities in southern France, though that's not saying much. The extreme ends of the city span 7km of coastline, but the heart of Nice is concentrated on the western side of the Port de Nice in **Vieux Nice**, the old town. This is where you will probably be spending most of your time, hitting a few sights and

get a room!

Nice is a popular destination on the French Riviera and charges accordingly; lucky for you, however, budget accommodations in Nice are very accessible. Nice is the only city that has an ⬛Auberge de Jeunesse that's actually in the city. Let the drinking games begin. For more, visit **www.letsgo.com**.

⬛ HOTEL VILLA LA TOUR   HOTEL $$$
4 rue de la Tour   ☎04 93 80 08 15 www.villa-la-tour.com

Rooms at the Villa la Tour look like they're waiting for a photo shoot for the latest issue of Pottery Barn's catalogue. Fortunately, this former 18th-century monastery feels less studio-stale and more country-home cozy. From simple art to birds and fruit painted on the walls, the decor is quaint and friendly. If your room isn't relaxing enough as it is, lounge on the patio out front or head to the small rooftop terrace with your book to get away from the street noise.

i *Tram: Cathédrale-Vieille Ville (dir.: Pont Michel). Walk in same direction as tram for 2-3 blocks and turn right onto rue de la Tour. Singles €66-137; doubles €70-115; triples from €120. 🕐 Reception 24hr.*

⬛ AUBERGE DE JEUNESSE   HOSTEL $
3 rue Spitalieri   ☎04 93 62 15 54 www.fuaj.org

Located right in the middle of the Masséna, just a few blocks from the tram, this international hub is frequented by travelers who are more interested in Nice's hardcore nightlife than the backpackers playing King's Cup at the Villa Saint Exupéry. Hang out in the common area and make some friends before hitting the town.

i *Tram: Jean Médecin. Walk around the Nice Etoile shopping mall. The hostel is directly behind mall. Dorms €26. 🕐 Lockout 11am-3pm.*

⬛ VILLA SAINT EXUPÉRY   HOSTEL $$
22 av. Gravier   ☎08 00 30 74 09 www.villahostels.com

Among Europe's "most famous hostels," Villa Saint Exupery has no shortage of things to do, even if it is farther from the centre ville than Saturn is from the sun. The Petit Prince-themed hostel makes even a 14-bed dorm feel cozy. The hostel also organizes an impressive set of day trips and adventurous activities that include canyoning, scuba diving, sailing, skiing, and Bikram yoga.

i *Tram: Comte de Falicon. Walk past the Casino supermarket on the left and take the right fork past the soccer stadium onto av. du Ray. Continue straight as the road turns into av. Gravier. Walk 2 blocks and take a sharp left; walk up the hill until the stairs marked with the villa's name. Or, take the angled left for a shorter but steeper climb to the villa, which is on the left. Female-only dorms available. High season 8- to 14-bed dorms €32-50; 4- to 7-bed dorms €37-60; singles €90; doubles €65-70; triples €50-65. Low season €16-40/18-45/35-60/28-55/25-50. 🕐 Reception 8am-midnight.*

choosing from a high concentration of restaurants and bars. A stretch of gardens and fountains surrounded by **place Masséna** in the southwest and the **Musée d'Art Moderne et d'Art Contemporain** and **place Garibaldi** in the northeast separate Vieux Nice from the Masséna neighborhood. Masséna is topped off by the SNCF train tracks in the north. A number of sights north of the **Gare Nice-Ville** shouldn't be missed, including the **Musée Matisse** and the **Musée National Marc Chagall**.

Vieux Nice

Vieux Nice is where the best of everything in Nice can be found: bars, restaurants, churches, markets, and tourist hordes. The area forms a rough triangle bounded by the coast in the south, the **Port de Nice** in the east, and **boulevard Jean Jaurès** and rue Cassini to the northwest, which intersect at **Place Garibaldi** on the northern tip. The tram line runs along bd Jean Jaurès. The winding streets can be difficult to navigate, so we suggest getting one of the big, fold-up maps from the tourism office to help you along the way. **Cours Saleya** is lined with restaurants and is also home to Nice's **Marché aux Fleurs** (flower market). The **Château Castle Hill** rises over the eastern side of the old town. Though the best bars are pretty evenly spread across the city, the northern part of town tends to be slightly deserted at night; if you are going to venture into the depths of Vieux Nice at night, use the buddy system.

Masséna

In general terms, Masséna covers the area north of Vieux Nice and south of the Gare SNCF and the rest of the train tracks. Even more generally, it includes everything north of the train tracks as well, most notably a handful of sights that include the Cimiez area, where you'll find the **Musée Matisse** and the **Monastère de Cimiez**. The tram runs straight through Masséna along **avenue Jean Médecin,** goes further north past **Église Ste-Jeanne d'Arc,** and continues north of where you will probably be exploring. Getting to Cimiez is easy via the frequent buses and well-distributed bus stops for the **Lignes d'Azur.** The area closest to the train station is probably among Nice's least charming (read: dirty) sections. However, hotels tend to be cheaper and quieter in this area due to their distance from the tourist crowds and the Vieux Nice nightlife.

Sea Front

The Sea Front is the easiest part of Nice to navigate. Step one: face the water. Step two: walk left or walk right. Boom, you have just oriented yourself along the only axis of this neighborhood. Dotted with the **Musée Masséna, Hotel Negresco,** and **Opéra** along the **Promenade des Anglais,** the Sea Front is the least budget-friendly place to be in Nice, but it's still nice for a short stroll. The **Musée des Beaux Arts** is essentially the western limit, while in the east, the **Jardin Albert 1er** separates this area from Vieux Nice where the Promenade des Anglais turns into **quai des Etats-Unis** along the shore.

SIGHTS

Vieux Nice

⚐ MUSÉE D'ART MODERNE ET D'ART COMTEMPORAIN   MUSEUM
Promenade des Arts   ☎04 97 13 42 01 www.mamac-nice.org

Nice's modern art museum presents minimalist galleries that generally focus on French new realists. The permanent exhibits start off a bit traditional (if you can call contemporary art traditional), with the crushed cars and halved coffee grinders that are to be expected. But march on, troops, because things get more interesting upstairs, where you'll discover a full-length gown with train made entirely of plastic bottles and bags. The Niki Saint-Phalle collection and the Yves Klein collection are accompanied by in-depth displays about their life and works, while the rooftop offers a nice panoramic view of the city.

i On the Promenade des Arts. Take tram (dir.: Pont Michel) to Garibaldi. Turn back in the opposite direction that you just came from on the tram and exit pl. Garibaldi to the west; the museum is straight ahead. Free. Guided tours W 4pm by reservation €3, students €1.50. ⚏ Open Tu-Su 10am-6pm.

▨ COLLINE DU CHÂTEAU

FORTRESS
☎04 93 85 62 33

We won't lie to you: getting to the top of the Castle Hill takes some stamina, but it is well worth the climb. The ruins of this hilltop fortress date back to the Celtic-Ligurians in the 11th century and, in addition to its role in military defense, Colline du Château served as a central icon of the region for hundreds of years. The operation was shut down by Louis XIV during the War of Spanish Succession and has since lost its functional purpose. Cemeteries were erected in the 18th century, and in the 1800s the whole place was modified into the tourist attraction that it is today. You may see archaeologists hard at work playing in the ruins; otherwise, admire the waterfall and what is arguably the best view of Nice and France's Mediterranean.

i Make your way to the big hill on the eastern end of the old town, then follow signs for "Site de l'Ancien Château." If you're going up, you're doing it right. Free. ☒ Open Jun-Aug daily 8am-8pm; Sept 8am-7pm; Oct-Mar 8am-6pm; Apr-May 8am-7pm. Info booth open Jul-Aug Tu-F 9:30am-12:30pm and 1:30-6pm.

CATHÉDRALE SAINTE-RÉPARATE

CATHEDRAL

pl. Rossetti   ☎04 93 92 79 10 http://cathedrale-nice.com

Dedicated to Ste. Réparate, the city's patron saint, this cathedral is the largest and most dramatic in Nice. Inspired by early Baroque architectural models from Rome, it is not an accident that the design is a miniature version of the larger and more famous St. Peter's in Rome. Chapelettes line the sides of the church and are covered with art dedicated to figures such as Santa Rosa of Lima, St. Joseph, and St. Sacrament. Fortunately, someone noticed that the interior of the church is rather dark and in need of a facelift; throughout 2013 and likely into 2014, some sections of the church will be covered up for restoration.

i Tram: Cathédrale-Vieille Ville. Walk straight into the old town down rue Centrale and continue right as it turns into rue Mascoinat. The cathedral is on the right. Or tram: Opéra-Vieille Ville. Walk straight down the steps into the old town and take an immediate left onto rue de la Préfecture. Walk past the Palais de Justice and turn left onto rue Ste-Réparate. The cathedral is on the left. Free. ☒ Open Tu-Sa 9am-noon and 2-6pm, Su 9am-1pm and 2-6pm. Office open M-F 9-11:30am.

MAISON D'ADAM ET EVE

HISTORIC SIGHT

rue de la Poissonnerie

The House of Adam and Eve is the Lonesome George of painted Niçois architecture (except it's not going to die). The side of the house has a carved bas-relief from 1584 that depicts Adam and Eve naked in the Garden of Eden, coming at each other with clubs. Apparently this WWE version of the Bible never made it into the King James translation.

i Turn left onto rue de la Poissonnerie from cours Saleya and look up; the painting is above a soaps and spices shop. Free.

Masséna

▨ MUSÉE MATISSE

MUSEUM

164 av. des Arènes   ☎04 93 81 08 08 www.musee-matisse-nice.org

The beautiful renovated Genoese villa that houses the Matisse Museum is mostly dedicated to his papiers gouachés découpés works, better known as his paper cut-outs. The more complex Danseuse Creole (Creole Dancer) and Nu Bleu IV (Blue Nude IV), however, might catch your attention for a bit longer. A recent donation from Matisse's collection of more than 400 cut-outs that never made it into his final pieces are a beautiful complement to the permanent exhibit. These coulda-been, woulda-been masterpieces have been arranged into a display designed by Matisse's son.

i Take bus #15, 17, 20, 22, or 25 to Arènes/Musée Matisse. Follow the signs through the garden to the museum, which is a red building. Tours in English by reservation. Free shuttle between Chagall and Matisse museums. Free. ☼ Open M 10am-6pm, W-Su 10am-6pm.

MUSÉE NATIONAL MARC CHAGALL   MUSEUM
av. Docteur Ménard ☎04 93 53 87 20 www.musees-nationaux-alpesmaritimes.fr/chagall
This museum's permanent collection highlights Chagall's 12 canvas paintings depicting his personal interpretation of the Hebrew Bible and more than 100 of the artist's prints. The adjacent rooms display his "creative" blending of the Bible and Russian Revolution (because when you say Lenin, we think crucifixion). Must-sees include a beautifully decorated piano and stained glass depicting the story of Creation as well as an outdoor mosaic that can be viewed through a window from inside the museum. Occasionally, the museum features temporary exhibits in conjunction with other museums, such as a 2012 exhibit that highlighted the profound effect exile had on the art of famous painters like Picasso, Léger, and Kandinsky as well as Chagall himself.

i Walk to the left along the train tracks of Gare SNCF and follow the signs. Or take bus #22 (dir.: Rimez) to Musée Chagall. €7.50, reduced €5.50, EU citizens under 26 and handicapped free. Temporary exhibits are €1-2 more. 1hr. guided tour €4.50, reduced €3.50. 1½hr. guided tour €6.50/5. 2hr. guided tour €8.50/6.50. 1st Su of the month free. Free audio guide. ☼ Open May-Oct M 10am-6pm, W-Su 10am-6pm; Nov-Apr M-10am-5pm, W-Su 10am-5pm. Last entry 30min. before close.

Sea Front

MUSÉE MASSÉNA   MUSEUM
65 rue de France and 35 Promenade des Anglais   ☎04 93 91 19 10
Though the building itself is modeled after an ancient Italian villa, the Musée Masséna (also known as the Palais Masséna or Villa Masséna) is a distinctly French landmark that chronicles Nice's history. A large collection of furniture, paintings, posters, and other objects document Nice's history in terms of politics, art, and culture. You may not believe that the late 19th-century photos of Nice and the old carnival pier are real, but you won't have a hard time grappling just how elaborate wardrobes of Masséna's ladies and gents once were.

i On the Promenade des Anglais, about 4 blocks past the tourist office. Next to Hotel Negresco. Free. ☼ Open M 10am-6pm, W-Su 10am-6pm.

MUSÉE DES BEAUX ARTS   MUSEUM
33 av. des Baumettes ☎04 92 15 28 28 www.musee-beaux-arts-nice.org
When Napoleon III came to Nice after the annexation of France in 1860 and found not a single fine arts museum, he was quick to remedy the situation. Well, maybe not that quick; by 1928, however, the museum was finally opened in the Villa Kochubey that now sits in the far west corner of Nice's sea front. The museum's permanent collections include works by Picasso and Rodin, along with Carle Van Loo's particularly breathtaking, full-wall mural of the Greek hero, Theseus, totally owning a bull. A rather macabre display of frightening Surrealist pieces by Gustac-Adolf Mossa will haunt you with its crazy clowns and bloody knives that make Chuckie look tame. Finish on a higher note with the father of the modern poster Jules Chéret's bright paintings on the top floor.

i Walk down rue de la Buffa and continue onto rue Dante. When you reach bd François Grosso, follow the signs. The museum is a peach and white villa at the top of a bunch of steps. Guided tours W and Th at 3pm €5, reduced €2.50. Free. ☼ Open M 10am-6pm, W-Su 10am-6pm.

nice

FOOD

With heavy Italian and Corsican influences, many Niçoise dishes include lots of olives and olive oil. Niçoise salad is made with lots of raw vegetables, hard-boiled egg, tuna or anchovies, olives, and olive oil. *Socca* is a chickpea-based pancake usually eaten with ground pepper, and *socca* joints are as common in Nice as *creperies* are in Paris. And of course you can't forget *ratatouille*, Nice's most famous culinary invention.

Vieux Nice

🍴 LA FERME SALEYA   NIÇOISE $$$
8 rue Jules Gilly   ☎06 71 84 07 32

Inside, surrounded by cool stone walls and wooden cross beams, this traditional maison Niçoise serves French cuisine that will make you forget you're in the city and think you've been dropped off somewhere in the countryside. Order a house dish for a most authentic experience.

i Tram: Opéra-Vieille Ville. Walk east all the way down rue de la Préfecture and turn right onto rue Jules Gilly. The restaurant is on the next corner on the left. Entrées €10-15. plats €18-24. Pastas €16-18. ☒ Open Tu-Sa noon-2pm and 6-10pm, Su 6-10pm.

RENÉ SOCCA   SOCCA $
2 rue Miralheti   ☎04 93 92 05 73

You may or may not have noticed little socca shacks sprinkled throughout the city by now, but René Socca is where you will find the most authentic and fin-ger-lickin' good socca in the city. The pancake-like fried snack comes stacked high on a plate for just €2.80. Signs on the block-long patio will remind you that your hands are the most appropriate utensils here, even if you skip the socca for other fried goodies.

i From pl. Garibaldi, walk south down bd Jean Jaurès and take the 1st left onto the small street where everyone is eating pancakes. Socca €2.80. ☒ Open Tu-Su noon-9pm.

Masséna

🍴 VOYAGEUR NISSART   TRADITIONAL $$$
19 rue d'Alsace Loraine   ☎04 93 82 19 60 www.voyageurnissart.com

A little countryside gem just a stone's throw from the train station, the Voyageur Nissart has been a Niçois favorite since 1908. The menu offerings change daily but usually include blette, the Swiss chard that is native to Nice. Tear yourself away from the old town to enjoy a real French evening of traditional Niçoise food, soft music, checkered tables, and a glass or two (or three or four) of fine wine.

i From the train station, walk straight ahead down the stairs to get to av. Durante and turn left onto rue d'Alsace Loraine. The restaurant is on the right. Menus €16.50, €19.50, and €25. Some items available à la carte. ☒ Open Tu-Su noon-2:30pm and 7-10:30pm.

🍴 L'ATELIER ST-ANTOINE   TRADITIONAL, CAFÉ $$
8 av. Durante   ☎06 72 63 96 00

The Atelier St-Antoine is your classic French cafe. Simple carpaccio or tartare de boeuf are nothing new but are still delicious, served up in portions big enough for a hungry traveler. L'Atelier St-Antoine doubles as an art gallery and features bright paintings of celebrities like Michael Jackson, Elvis, and Charlie Chaplan. The art perfectly complements the colorful patio furniture and gives this place a jazzy edge.

i From the train station, walk straight ahead down the stairs to get to av. Durante and walk 1½ blocks. The restaurant is on the left. plats €10-14. ☒ Open M-Sa 7am-7pm.

france

SPEAKEASY

7 rue Lamartine

VEGAN $$

☎04 93 85 59 50

Although the hand-written manifestos espousing the nutritional evils of an omnivorous diet may be a bit of a turn-off for those of us who can appreciate a good hunk o' meat, we can understand the enthusiasm when the food here tastes like ambrosia. Besides, it's hard to argue with Leonardo da Vinci and Lamartine, famous vegetarians to whom the restaurant pays homage. The owner and chef is a fantastic cook and offers a new short menu each day.

i Tram: Jean Médecin. Facing south (toward pl. Masséna), turn left onto bd Dubouchage and take the 2nd left onto rue Lamartine. The restaurant is on the left, around the corner from the Auberge de Jeunesse. plats €10. Entrée, plat, and dessert €14-16. ☒ Open M-Sa noon-2:30pm and 7-9pm.

NIGHTLIFE

The variety of nightlife in Nice is huge, but the density is uneven, so if you're going to wander away from the more populated areas around pl. du Palais, make sure you bring a map and a friend or two. It's definitely worth searching for Nice's hidden gems (there are a lot of them), but use your good judgment where the streets get narrower, darker, and quieter in the north and east of Vieux Nice.

Vieux Nice

BULLDOG PUB POMPEII

14, 16 rue de l'Abbaye

PUB

☎04 93 85 04 06

Don't be surprised to see a long line outside the door to the Bulldog. Even though it's by no means VIP, it's a Niçois favorite and fills up quickly. Live rock music keeps the beats high all night, every night. The floor in front of the stage is packed with people dancing and sweating to the music, while the upper level is a bit more relaxed for those who want to sit back and listen.

i Tram: Opéra-Vieille Ville. Walk down the steps and take an immediate left onto rue de la Préfecture, then turn left onto rue de l'Abbaye. Pub Pompeii is on the next block. Live music. Smoking lounge upstairs. Beer €6-7. Mixed drinks €8. 6 shots €18. ☒ Open daily 11pm-5am. Live music 10pm.

WAYNE'S BAR

15 rue de la Préfecture

PUB

☎04 93 13 46 99

Every tourist-heavy, backpacker city has to have at least one bar that boasts an almost entirely foreign clientele. So schwing schwing over to Wayne's for party time. It's totally awesome, man.

i Tram: Opéra-Vieille Ville. Walk straight down the steps and take an immediate left onto rue de la Préfecture. Wayne's is on rue de la Préfecture, just opposite the Palais de Justice. Live music every night, usually rock. Pints €6-7. ☒ Open daily 11am-2am. Kitchen open noon-11pm.

THE SNUG&CELLAR

corner of 22 rue Droite and 5 rue Rosetti

PUB

☎04 93 80 43 22 www.snugandcellar.com

Although the staff is all Irish or English, Anglophones and Francophones alike take refuge at the Snug for a lighter, chiller atmosphere than your typically crowdy (crowded and rowdy—it's a thing) Irish pub. The upstairs bar is bright, open, and welcoming to newcomers. You'll find more of a party downstairs, where live music and regular soccer and rugby games draw crowds to the cavernous space downstairs.

i From pl. Rosetti, turn your back to the church and look straight ahead. The pub is on the left. Open mic and live music in the cellar M 8pm. Curry night on Tu. Pub quiz W 8pm. Th live music in the cellar Th 9pm. Fish'n' chips on F. Roast on Su. Pints €5-6.50, happy hour €4-4.50. Mixed drinks €6.50-8.50, happy hour €4.50-6.50. ☒ Open daily noon-2am. Kitchen open noon-12:30am. Happy hour 8-10pm.

nice

LE SIX
CLUB, GLBT
6 rue Raoul Bosio ☎04 93 62 66 64

Le Six is the gayest thing to happen to Nice since Elton John vacationed at the Hotel Negresco. Nice's gay crowd comes here for the nightly DJ and endless dancing. Flashing colored lights add to the steel shine of the bar's interior, just in case the video of nude photo shoots wasn't flashy enough. If you're tired of dancing, climb the ladder to the second floor loft; just don't leave until after the most muscled man in France does his strip-tease from the shower positioned in the back of the bar. It's mesmerizing.

i Tram: Opéra-Vieille Ville. Walk straight down the stairs, down rue Raoul Bosio into the old town. Le Six is ahead on the left. DJs and shower boy every night. Mixed drinks €7-10. ☼ Open daily 10pm-4am.

3 DIABLES
BAR
2 cours Saleya ☎04 93 62 47 00 www.les3diables.com

Among the food-centric cafes and brasseries on cours Saleya, 3 Diables adds some spice with a nightly DJ playing Top 40 hits that keeps the student-heavy crowd on its feet. The inside is set up more like a pub with a wooden interior, but the aisles between chairs and tables, along with the tops of chairs and tables themselves, are taken over by dancing.

i Walk east down cours Saleya to the end of the street. The bar is on the right. Karaoke on W. Beer €7-9. Mixed drinks €9-11. ☼ Open daily 5pm-3am. Happy hour 5-9pm.

ARTS AND CULTURE

CINEMATHEQUE DE NICE
MASSÉNA
3 esplanade Kennedy ☎04 92 04 06 66 www.cinematheque-nice.com

This historic theater screens old black-and-white films, documentaries, and art-house staples. The prices here are an absolute steal, but don't expect box office hits or convenient show times. The schedule changes weekly and is available at the tourism office and local museums.

i Tram (dir.: Pont Michel) to Acropolis. Continue in the direction of the tram. The theater is 2 blocks ahead on the left inside the giant building. Membership (€1) required. Tickets €2, students €1.50. 10 shows for €18. ☼ Showings between 11am-8:15pm. Closed in the summer.

OPÉRA DE NICE
SEA FRONT
4-6 rue St-François de Paule ☎04 92 17 40 79 www.opera-nice.org

The Nice Opéra started out as the Maccarani Theater, when the King of Sardinia's old house was turned into a theater. The theater was purposely razed in 1826 to build a new Italian-style opera, then accidentally razed in 1881 when an explosion caused by a gas leak burned the theater down. Rebuilt a year later in an inspired style of Italian-French fusion by a pupil of Gustave Eiffel, the current building is now one of the prized gems of Nice. Today the Opéra hosts a number of operas, concerts, and ballets between September and June.

i Tram: Opéra-Vieille Ville. Walk straight into the old town, south toward the beach, and turn right onto rue St-François de Paule 1 block before the quai des États-Unis. Opera tickets €10-70. Concerts and ballets €8-40. Discounted student tickets as low as €5. ☼ Box office open M-Th 9am-5:45pm, F 9am-7:30pm, Sa 7am-4pm. Open 5min. before start of the show.

ESSENTIALS

Practicalities

- **TOURIST OFFICE:** The tourist information branch on av. Thiers does last-minute accommodations bookings with partner hotels and offers restaurant guides, city maps, and free tourist guides. (*i* Next to the train station. ☎08 92 70 74 07 www.nicetourisme.com ☼ Open mid-Jun to mid-Sept M-Sa 8am-8pm, Su 9am-7pm; mid-Sept to mid-Jun M-Sa 8am-7pm, Su

france

10am-5pm. Hours subject to change.) **Main Office.** (5 Promenade des Anglais ☎08 92 70 74 07 ☒ Open mid-Jun to mid-Sept M-Sa 8am-8pm, Su 9am-7pm; mid-Sept to mid-Jun M-Sa 9am-6pm.) **Airport location.** (Terminal 1 ☎08 92 70 74 07 *i* Limited services. ☒ Open daily Apr-Sept 9am-8pm; Oct-Mar 9am-6pm.)

- **CONSULATES: Canada.** (2 pl. Franklin ☎04 93 92 93 22 ☒ Open M-F 9am-noon.) **UK.** (22 av. Notre-Dame ☎04 93 62 94 95 ☒ By appointment only.) **US.** (7 av. Gustave V ☎04 93 88 89 55 ☒ By appointment only.)

- **YOUTH CENTER:** The **Centre Regional d'Information Jeunesse (CRIJ)** posts summer jobs for students and provides info on long-term housing, study, and recreation. (19 rue Gioffredo, near the Museum of Contemporary Art. ☎04 93 80 93 93 www.crijca.fr ☒ Open M-F 10am-6pm.)

- **LAUNDROMATS:** Laundromats are plentiful throughout the city of **Lavomatique.** (11 rue de Pont Vieux ☎04 93 85 88 14 *i* Wash €4 per 7kg. Dry €0.80 per 5min. ☒ Open daily 8am-10pm.) **Laverie des Peintres.** (39 rue de la Buffa Wash €4.50, dry from €0.50. *i* Ironing and dry cleaning available.)

- **POST OFFICE:** 23 av. Thiers (☎36 31 www.lapost.fr ☒ Open M-W 8am-7pm, Th 8am-5:45pm, F 8am-7pm, Sa 8:30am-12:30pm.) Additional branches throughout the city.

- **POSTAL CODE:** 06000

Emergency

- **POLICE:** 1 av. Maréchal Foch (☎04 92 17 22 22)

- **LATE-NIGHT PHARMACY: Pharmacie Masséna.** (7 rue Masséna ☎04 93 87 78 94 ☒ Open M-Sa 24hr.) **Pharmacie Riviera** (66 av. Jean Médecin ☎04 93 62 54 44 ☒ Open M-Sa 24hr., Su 7pm-midnight.) To find a pharmacy at any time call ☎32 37.

- **HOSPITAL:** 5 rue Pierre Dévoluy. (☎04 92 03 33 33)

Getting There

BY PLANE

Aeroport Nice-Cote d'Azur (NCE ☎08 20 42 33 33 www.nice.aeroport.fr) is France's second-busiest airport after the Paris airport and is serviced by most major national and international European airlines. Lignes d'Azur buses (☎08 10 06 10 06) regularly shuttle people to and from the city. Take the #98 bus from the airport to Riquier bus station in *centre ville*. (€1. ☒ 20min., every 20min. daily 6am-8:30pm.) Take the #99 from the airport to Gare SNCF. (€1. ☒ 15min.; every 30min., daily 8am-9pm.)

BY TRAIN

Gare SNCF Nice-Ville is the mostly centrally located and frequently used train station. (av. Thiers ☎36 35 www.sncf.com) Trains run to and from: Cannes (€4-6 ☒ 40min.; daily every 15-30min., 5:30am-10:30pm); Marseille (€31 ☒ 3hr.; daily every hr., 5:30am-9pm); Monaco (€3-4 ☒ 20min.; daily every 15-30min., 5:30am-11pm); Paris (€100-130 ☒ 5hr.; daily every 1-2hr. 6am-8pm). **Gare de Nice Chemins de Fer de Provence** is located at 4 bis rue Alfred Binet, behind Nice-Ville. (☎04 97 03 80 80 www.train-provence.com) Chemins de Fer de Provence runs to Digne-les-Bains (€20 ☒ 3½hr.; 10 per day M-F 6am-7:30pm, Sa-Su 8am-6:15pm) and Plan du Var (€2 ☒ 40min.; 8 per day, 6:30am-5:15pm).

BY BUS

Buses to regional, national, and international destinations operate through the **Gare Routière,** though it's less of a station and more of a glorified bus stop (5 bd Jean Jaurès ☎08 92 70 12 06). Regional buses go to Menton, Monaco, Cannes, and Grasse. All tickets cost €1.

nice

BY FERRY

Nice Côte d'Azur is the overhead that runs all ferries from the port (☎08 20 42 55 55 www.riviera-ports.com). The primary ferry companies in Nice are **Corsica Ferries** (quai d'Entrecasteaux ☎08 25 09 50 95 www.corsicaferries.com ☼ Open mid-Mar to mid-Nov M-Sa 9am-noon and 2-5:30pm; mid-Nov to mid-Mar M-F 9am-noon and 2-5:30pm) and **SNCM** (quai d'Entrecasteaux ☎32 60 www.sncm.fr ☼ Open daily Apr-Sept 8am-6pm; Oct-Mar 9am-12:30pm and 1:30-5:30pm). High-speed ferries leave from Port de Nice terminals 1 and 2, which are on opposite sides of the port. Reduced rates for those under 25 and over 60. Take bus #1 or 2 to the port.

Getting Around

BY BUS AND TRAM

Lignes d'Azur is the public transport company in Nice. The tram is the best way to get anywhere in Nice. A new tram line runs straight through the middle of the city between Las Planas in the north and pl. Masséna in the south, where it turns northeast along bd Jean Jaurès. The tram runs every day starting at 4:25am, with trams arriving every 4min. during the day. An extensive bus system will get you anywhere you need to go across the city. The office is across from the Gare SNCF (17 av. Thiers ☼ Open M-F 8am-7pm, Sa 8am-3pm) or at pl. Masséna (3 pl. Masséna ☼ Open M-F 7:45am-6:30pm, Sa 8:30am-6pm). The bus and the tram take the same ticket. Single-journey tickets can be bought onboard from the bus driver; otherwise, tickets and passes must be bought from machines at tram stops or at one of the offices. (1-way €1, 10 journeys €10, unlimited day pass €15). **Noctrambus** night service has less frequent trams and four buses that run 9pm-1:35am.

By Taxi

Central Taxi Riviera (☎04 93 13 78 78) runs throughout the city. To book a taxi in advance call ☎08 99 70 08 78. **Taxi Nicois Indépendant** picks up from behind Gare SNCF (☎04 93 88 25 82). Be sure to ask for the price before boarding and make sure the meter is turned on. Night fares 7pm-7am.

BY BIKE

Vélo Bleu (☎04 93 72 06 06 www.velobleu.org) is Nice's bike rental company and has 173 stations throughout the city. You must have a European credit card to make an account over the phone or online to be able to check out a bike. Call to register (☎04 30 00 30 01 Registration fee €1 per day, €5 per week, €10 per month. After this fee, the first 30min. is free, the second 30min. is €1, and every hr. after that is €2.

cannes

Cannes seems to always smell distinctly of sunblock, salt water, and affluence. But if you look past the fabulously dressed (or undressed, if you're at the beach), Cannes is an extremely dynamic and surprisingly affordable destination. With the world-famous Cannes Film Festival held in May, cinema is definitely the name of the game here, but it certainly does not limit the city's cultural offerings. The Palais des Festivals hosts numerous festivals that feature dance, music, and theater; the Malmaison boasts a contemporary heart for the modern soul, and a number of cinemas across the city play every kind of film around. Before you even get to your cultural indulgences, whether enjoying a show or following the paparazzi to see what they've found, you could spend meal upon meal sampling the fresh catch or homemade pizza at any one of the city's numerous restaurants and still have enough cash left over for the cinema. Regardless of where you go or what you do, you will find Cannes to be a place of both excitement and relaxation, all at the same time.

get a room!

For more recommendations, visit **www.letsgo.com**.

⬛ CAMPING PARC BELLEVUE
CAMPGROUND $

67 av. Maurice Chevalier ☎04 93 47 28 97 www.parcbellevue.com

Cannes's only camping option offers an impressive five hectares of cabins and tent space. With playgrounds and a large swimming pool, Bellevue attracts a lot of young families in the summertime. If you're lucky, you might catch Wii karaoke or dancing on the patio of the epicerie.

i Take bus #2 (direction Les Bastides) to Les Aubépines. Continue in the direction of the bus and turn right at the small traffic circle; the campground is just ahead on the right. Pool, playgrounds, and restaurant on site. €13 per tent, caravan, or camping car; €4 per person, €3 per child under 5 years; €4 per car; €4 electricity. High season cabins €285-730, low season €190-300. ☼ Reception 8am-8pm.

⬛ HOTEL ALNEA
HOTEL $$$

20 rue Jean de Riouffe ☎04 93 68 77 77 www.hotel-alnea.com

The less expensive of the two hotels owned by Noémi and Cedric Dewavrin, Hotel Alnea is a relaxing, beach-themed hotel in the center of Cannes. You may feel like you don't want to leave your cozy, sound-proofed and individually air-conditioned room, but paintings of beaches and sun will inspire you to go out, and Noémie will be happy to lend you mats and an umbrella for the beach.

i From the train station, turn right and walk until you hit the big intersection. Turn left onto rue Jean de Riouffe (go down the steps). The hotel is on the left on the corner. Singles €50-80; doubles and twins €95-120. ☼ Check-in 2pm. Check-out 11am. Reception 8am-8pm.

HOTEL MIMONT
HOTEL $$

39 rue Mimont ☎04 93 39 51 64 www.canneshotelmimont.com

Hotel Mimont is, without competition, the best budget hotel in Cannes. Just a couple minutes' walk from the train station, Mimont is happily a bit removed from the busier tourist areas south of the train station. While you probably won't find better prices elsewhere inCannes, this is a quiet, nondescript hotel; solo travelers, don't expect to meet traveling compadres during your stay here (that's what the nearby nightlife is for).

i From the train station, turn left and take the underpass next to the tourist office to rue Mimont. Take the angled right and walk 3 blocks. The hotel is just past the post office on the left. Free Wi-Fi. Breakfas €6.40. ☼ Reception closes 11pm.

cannes

ORIENTATION

Cannes is a very easy city to get around; it's a lot smaller than you imagined it was in that dream where you won the Palme d'Or and exchanged room keys with ⬛**Vincent Cassel**. The *centre ville* is roughly wrapped by the SNCF train tracks that curve over the top of the city with the sea as the lower boundary. The **Gare SNCF** runs smack dab through the middle of the city on rue Jean Jaurès. Between rue Jean Jaurès and **rue d'Antibes,** you will find mostly hotels and cafes. Keep heading down rue d'Antibes and the hotels will get bigger, the shopping more expensive, and everything just a little bit shinier. You can find some hot nightlife along **rue des Frères Pradignac;** pretend you're among the high rollers and you might just catch a glimpse of Brad Pitt. Going all the way down to the sea will take you to **boulevard de la Croisette** and **Plage de la Croisette,** where you will have to shell out at least €20 for a beach chair. Behind the Vieux Port and the **Hôtel de Ville** (next to the **Gare Routière**), the Cannes population swells during the day, particularly along the shopping road **rue Meynadier** and around the **Marché**

Forville. The **Musée Castre** and the **Église Notre-Dame d'Esperance** overlook the city from atop the hill just west of the Hôtel de Ville.

SIGHTS

MUSÉE DE LA CASTRE
MUSEM

pl. Castre ☎04 93 38 55 26

Formerly the private castle of the monks of Lérins, the Musée de la Castre is a quaint little museum with an eclectic permanent exhibit featuring an array of artifacts from across the world. Ancient art from the Americas and Oceania as well as a musical instruments exhibit will make you feel a bit more worldly. Throw in an Etruscan sarcophagus and some 19th-century Provençal paintings for good measure, and be sure to climb to the top of the watchtower at the exit for a spectacular panoramic view of Cannes.

i From the Hôtel de Ville, head down rue St-Antoine and take the stairs up to the left. Continue following the stairs until you're out of breath; the museum is just at the top of some more stairs behind the church. €6; 18-25 €3; under 18, students under 26, and handicapped free. ☼ Open daily Jul-Aug M-Tu 10am-7pm, W 10am-9pm, Th-Su 10am-7pm; Sept-Jun 10am-1pm and 2-6pm.

ÉGLISE NOTRE-DAME D'ESPÉRANCE
CHURCH

pl. Castre ☎08 99 54 07 71

The Église Notre-Dame d'Espérance was originally built as an overflow church when Cannes' population grew enough in the 1500s to warrant extra worship space. A beautiful carved oak door and imposing clock tower define the church from the outside. Unfortunately, the church is currently undergoing massive restorations on its interior and won't be finished until the end of 2013, so at the moment all you can really see inside the church is the altar. The ceiling and sides around the pews are covered by a tarp with a printed image of what you would see there if not for the tarp. At least they're keeping up for appearances.

i From the Hôtel de Ville, head down rue St-Antoine and take the stairs up to the left. Continue following the stairs; the church is at the top. Free. ☼ Open daily 9am-noon and 2-6pm.

FOOD

🞖 PHILCAT
SANDWICHES, SALADS $

Promenade de la Pantiéro

Philip and Cat own this small port-side kiosk that serves some of the biggest and cheapest sandwiches and salads you'll find anywhere. Fresh helpings of rice, tomatoes, cucumbers, corn, cheese, and just about anything else you could ask for are stacked high on giant salads, and hot sandwiches good enough to eat even on a hot day.

i On the promenade at the top of the Vieux Port. Sandwiches and salad €3.50-5. Drinks €2. ☼ Open daily 8am-7pm.

🞖 AKWABAMO EXOTICK
AFRICAN $$

36 rue Mimont ☎04 93 99 89 10

When you go to Akwabamo, it's like you're actually transported to Africa. Upbeat traditional African music accompanies vibrant patterns and assorted African drums, baskets, and small statues. The place is nothing fancy, but the food is so delicious, you will want to get up and dance to the music.

i Go behind the train station and turn right onto rue Mimont; the restaurant is just past the post office on the right. Credit card min €15. plats €8-16. ☼ Open M-Sa noon-2:30pm and 7-11pm.

france

NIGHTLIFE

Cannes has its fair share of flashy, high-end nightclubs, particularly along **rue des Frères Pradignac**. But take the time to wander around the small city at night, and you will also find a delightful offering of Irish pubs, laid-back lounges, and GLBT hotspots.

◪ THE STATION TAVERN   PUB

18 rue Jean Jaurès   ☎04 93 38 34 91

For budget travelers who are running out of money and struggling with a steep learning curve when it comes to French, the Station Tavern is a glorious respite of cheap drinks and Anglophones. Tons of international students (especially Americans) come to the tavern on a nightly basis for karaoke, beer, and merriment. The Tavern also has a basement lounge room complete with '70s and '80s music and plenty of flashing lights.

i From the train station, exit and look to your left; the tavern is right there on the corner. DJ on M and W. Theme nights on Th and Su. Karaoke in summer daily 8pm-2am, in winter Th-Sa 8pm-2am. Poo €2 per game. Darts free. Pints €4. 10 shots or 10 beers for €16. 5 vodkas for €20. Happy hour mixed drinks €5. ☼ Open daily 9am-3am.

◪ BROWN SUGAR   BAR, RESTAURANT

17 rue des Frères Pradignac   ☎04 93 39 70 10

Wedged among the more fashion-forward, cocktail-sipping types that frequent rue des Frères Pradignac, Brown Sugar is much more laid back and much more Dutch than its neighbors. Bicycles, guitars, hats, and sleds hang from the ceiling in this cozy bar, where a chill crowd imbibes homemade beer while watching over-dressed girls try to pick up guys across the way. Brown Sugar doesn't have a happy hour, but it does offer a free plate of tapas when you order a drink between 6 and 9pm. Now who wouldn't call that a happy three hours?

i From the train station, walk south (straight) toward the sea and turn left onto rue d'Antibes. Turn right onto rue Macé and take the 1st left onto rue des Frères Pradignac. Brown Sugar is a block and a half ahead on the left. Pints €6-7. Mixed drinks €10. ☼ Open daily 5:30pm-2:30am. Kitchen open daily 6-11:30pm.

LE SPARKLE AND L'APPART   CLUB, BAR, RESTAURANT

6/8 rue des Frères Pradignac   ☎04 93 39 71 21

The bar doesn't so much sparkle as it does flash, so if you're in the mood to groove, head over to L'Appart and find a spot on the dance floor amid a stylish crowd that knows where the party's at. The red ropes and imposing bouncer may seem intimidating, but there is (usually) no VIP list at Le Sparkle.

i From the train station walk south (straight) toward the sea and turn left onto rue d'Antibes. Turn right onto rue Macé and take the 1st left onto rue des Frères Pradignac. The club is on the right. No dress code, but you'll regret showing up in just your jeans and a clean shirt. Pints €8. Mixed drinks €10-12. ☼ Open daily 11:30pm-7am. Restaurant open daily 6pm-midnight.

LE 7   CABARET, CLUB

7 rue Rouguière   ☎04 93 39 10 36

Le 7 confirms the claim that great things come in small packages. Le 7 is the ultimate night-owl spot that doesn't start to see customers roll until 1am. The party really starts at 2am on the weekends and features popular cabaret shows; don't miss Coco, she's a real diva.

i Walk down rue Félix Fauvre toward the Hôtel de Ville with the sea on your left and turn right onto rue Rouguière. Cabaret Th-Su at 2am. DJ Th-Sa. Cover €13, includes 1 drink. Drinks €9-11. ☼ Open daily midnight-7:30am.

cannes

ARTS AND CULTURE

ESPACE MIRAMAR
CINEMA, EXHIBITION SPACE
35 rue Pasteur
☎04 93 43 86 26 www.cannes.com

A 400-seat cinema and 130 sq. m exhibition floor comprise the Espace Miramar, one of Cannes's cultural and artistic cornerstones. Dedicated to the visual arts, six exhibitions (mostly of photography) are scheduled here each year.

i Walk down bd de la Croisette with the sea to your right, past the Malmaison, and turn left onto rue Pasteur. Espace Miramar is on the right. ☒ Exhibitions open Tu-Su 2-6pm. Cinema open select evenings.

ARCADE THEATRE
CINEMA
77 rue Félix Fauvré
☎04 93 39 10 00 www.allocine.fr

If you're feeling extra homesick and need a quick escape from all the swallowed r's and o là là's, head to the Arcade for a Hollywood blockbuster. With only five screens, there is usually a fair mix of American movies, other English-language films, and new French flicks to be found here.

i One rue Félix Fauvré between rue Louis Blanc and rue Maréchal Joffre. All films in original language. €9.50, students and seniors €7. W special €6.50 for everyone. Sa and Su 10:30am show €4.50. ☒ Open daily, last showing usually 9:30 or 10pm.

ESSENTIALS

Practicalities

- **TOURIST OFFICE:** In the Palais des Festivals. Provides limited accommodations bookings, free maps of the city, and information about events. (1 bd de la Croisette ☎04 92 99 84 22 www. cannes.travel ☒ Open Mar-Jun 9am-7pm; Jul-Aug 9am-8pm; Sept-Oct 9am-7pm; Nov-Feb 10am-7pm). Also a branch next to the train station. (pl. de la Gare ☎04 92 59 35 11 ☒ Open M-Sa 9am-1pm and 2-6pm.)

- **CURRENCY EXCHANGE: Trevelex.** €80 min. cash advance. (8 rue d'Antibes ☎04 93 39 41 45 ☒ Open Jul-Aug M-Sa 9am-8pm, Su 10am-6pm; Sept-Jun M-F 9am-6pm, Sa 10am-6pm.)

- **YOUTH CENTER: Bureau Information Jeunesse.** Info on jobs and housing. (3 rue Georges Clemenceau ☎04 97 06 46 25 ☒ Open M-Th 8:30am-12:30pm and 1:30-6pm, F 8:30am-12:30pm and 1:30-5pm.)

- **INTERNET: Cyber Atlas.** (Corner of rue Jean Jaurès and rue Helene Vagliano ☎04 93 69 42 82 €3 per hr. ☒ Open daily 9am-11pm.)

- **POST OFFICE:** 22 rue de Bivouac Napoleon. (☎36 31 ☒ Open M-W 9:30am-6:30pm, Th 9:30am-12:30pm and 2-6:30pm, F 9:30am-6:30pm, Sa 9am-1pm.) Branch at 34 rue Mimont. (☎04 93 06 27 00 ☒ Open M-F 9am-noon and 1:30-6pm, Sa 9am-12:30pm.)

- **POSTAL CODE:** 06400.

Emergency

- **PHARMACY:** Pharmacies are easy to find in Cannes and are usually open during the day M-Sa. **Pharmacie des Allées.** (2 av. Felix Fauvre ☎04 93 39 00 18)

- **POLICE:** 1 av. de Grasse (☎04 93 06 22 22) and 2 quai St-Pierre. (☎08 00 11 71 18)

- **HOSPITAL: Hopital des Broussailles.** (13 av. des Broussailles ☎04 93 69 70 00)

Getting There

Trains leave from the **Gare SNCF** in the center of the city. (1 rue Jean Jaurès ☒ Open M-Th 5am-10:30pm, F-Su 5am-1am.) Trains run from: Antibes (€3 ☒ 10-15min.); Grasse (€3-4 ☒ 25-30min.); Marseille (€25 ☒ 2hr.); Monaco (€7-10 ☒ 1hr.); Nice (€5 ☒ 30min.); St-Raphaël (€5-7 ☒ 30min.); Paris (€70-120 ☒ 5hr.).

france

The regional bus company is the **Rapide Côte d'Azur** (pl. Cornut Goutille) and departs from the Gare Routière at the Hôtel de Ville and the Gare SNCF. The #200 bus leaves from the Hôtel de Ville and goes to Nice. (🕐 1-2hr.; M-F 6am-9:45pm every 10-20min., Sa 6am-9:45pm every 20-30min., Su 7:45am-9:40pm every 20-30min.) The #600 bus leaves from the Gare SNCF and goes to Grasse. (🕐 1hr.; M-Sa 6am-9pm; Su 7:30am-7:30pm, every 20-30min.). All journeys on the Rapide Côte d'Azur are €1 except the #210 Express, which leaves from the Hôtel de Ville and goes to the Nice Airport. (*i* €16.50, under 26 €13. Round-trip €26.50. 🕐 7am-7pm daily.)

Getting Around

If you're staying within the *centre ville*, walking is your best bet. The **Bus Azur** is Cannes's local bus system that departs from the Gare Routière and the Gare SNCF (☎08 25 82 55 99 www.busazur.com). The tourist office sells 10-trip, weekly, monthly, and student passes, along with other long-term passes on sale at the Gare Routière. Single-journey passes can be bought for €1 directly from the driver. The **é-lo** is a minibus that services a loop around the *centre ville*. (🕐 9am-7:20pm, every 10-12min.)

france essentials

MONEY

Tipping

By law in France, a service charge, called "service compris," is added to bills in bars and restaurants. Most people do, however, leave some change (up to €2) for sit-down services, and in nicer restaurants it is not uncommon to leave 5% of the bill. For other services, like taxis and hairdressers, a 10-15% tip is acceptable.

Taxes

The quoted price of goods in France includes value added tax (VAT). This tax on goods is generally levied at 19.6% in France, although some goods are subject to lower rates. Non-EU visitors who are taking these goods home unused may be refunded this tax for purchases totaling over €175 per store. When making purchases, request a VAT form and present it at a Tax Free Shopping Office, found at most airports, road borders, and ferry stations, or by mail. Refunds must be claimed within six months.

SAFETY AND HEALTH

Drugs and Alcohol

Although any mention of France often conjures images of black-clad smokers in berets, France no longer allows smoking in public as of 2008. The government has no official policy on berets. Possession of illegal drugs (including marijuana) in France can result in a substantial jail sentence or fine. Police may arbitrarily stop and search anyone on the street.

There is no drinking age in France, but restaurants will not serve anyone under the age of 16, and to purchase alcohol you must be at least 18 years old. Though there is no law prohibiting open containers, drinking on the street is considered uncouth. The legal blood-alcohol level for driving in France is 0.05%, which is less than it is in the US, UK, New Zealand, and Ireland, so exercise appropriate caution if operating a vehicle in France.

france essentials

KEEPING IN TOUCH
Cellular Phones
In France, mobile pay-as-you-go phones are the way to go. The two largest carriers are SFR and Orange, and they are so readily available that even supermarkets sell them. Cell-phone calls and texts can be paid for without signing a contract by using a Mobicarte prepaid card, available at Orange and SFR stores, as well as tabacs. You can often buy phones for €20-40, which includes various amounts of minutes and 100 texts. Calling the US from one of these phones is around €0.80 a minute, with texts coming in at around €0.50.

france 101

HISTORY
Eccentrics of Yore (Antiquity-500 CE)
French tourism began 50,000 years ago, when early humans wandered to the region in search of a mild climate. Not much happened until Celtic and Belgae tribes decided they too wanted to visit the area, gradually invading it all between 1500 and 500 BCE. This assortment of Druids and headhunters were collectively christened "Gauls" by the Romans, whose imperial superiority complex didn't jive well with Gaulish military culture. Centuries of conflict were ignited in 393 BCE, when a Gaulish band of miscreants led by Brennus invaded Rome. After laughing hysterically, the Roman army swiftly obliterated them, then conquered most of Gaul in 58 BCE under the leadership of one Julius Caesar. Druid necklaces of human heads were exchanged for aqueducts and amphitheaters as Gaul underwent a cultural makeover.

Frankly My Dear... (500-1300)
For the next five centuries or so, France was subjected to routine invasions and coups as a motley crew of monarchs attempted to control it. A whole bunch of kings worked to unite the country and succeeded in cementing Catholicism as France's religion of choice. By the eighth century, the Carolingian Dynasty had taken hold, reaching its pinnacle during the rule of Charlemagne. Like all good things though, this empire did not last. France went into one of its cycles where no one really controlled anything, although Hugh Capet successfully managed to unseat the Carolingians in 987. After several centuries of an extensive royal game of Risk, the Capetians expanded and consolidated their kingdom beyond their stronghold in Paris, but were never quite able to get a handle on their nobles. Capetian international influence reached its own peak when Saint Louis IX became king in 1226. Though he lost every crusade he participated in, Saint Louis received kudos points from Rome for trying and was awarded an additional gold star by the Papacy for channeling his inner Jesus and kicking the Jews out of France. So great was the Papacy's approval that, for the next 70 years, the Papacy resided in Avignon.

Plague, War, Death, and Other Happy Developments (1300-1610)
As if the Black Death wasn't cheerful enough, a succession crisis over the French crown catalyzed the Hundred Years' War between England and France, which lasted 16 years longer than its name suggests. At one stage it looked like the English might take over France, until a valiant and possibly schizophrenic teenager named Joan of Arc kicked Les Anglais out of Orléans. The French monarchy now expanded in both

size and power, discovering an uncanny and uncharacteristic ability to win wars. The French managed to sabotage everything, though, with the Wars of Religion, a conflict between Catholics and Protestants (known as Huguenots) that resulted in a series of seriously unpleasant genocidal massacres. Out of the chaos rose the gallant Henry IV, who guaranteed the Huguenots' religious freedom through the Edict of Nantes in 1598. Henry IV converted to Catholicism to appease the people, but had trouble appeasing the psychotic contingent of his new religion and was knifed by a deranged Jesuit in 1610. In the spirit of brotherly love, a Parisian mob executed his assassin by scalding and then quartering him.

You Say You Want a Revolution (1610-1799)

Unfortunately for the French aristocracy, this was not the end of unrest in France. Perhaps due to Louis XIV's obscenely luxurious lifestyle during his rule from 1643-1715, and also to the suggestion of his grandson's wife (a young Austrian by the name of Marie Antoinette) that those short on bread should just eat cake, the dregs of French society decided it was time to do something. Storming the Bastille prison seemed like a good idea, and that's just what they did on July 14, 1789. Three years later, the monarchy crumbled. These would be seen as the calm years of the revolution once Robespierre and his Committee of Public Safety decided in 1793 to ensure the safety of Louis XVI, Marie Antoinette, and around 3000 others by politely offing their heads.

Shorty Breaks It Down (1799-1914)

Fed up with Robespierre's unhealthy relationship with the guillotine and the ineffectiveness of those who followed him, Napoleon Bonaparte overthrew the revolutionary government in 1799. Rewriting the constitution and issuing his own standardized "Napoleonic Code," Napoleon had ambitions that were larger than he was. In 1804, he somehow managed to convince people that naming himself Emperor was totally consistent with the ideals of the revolution. Though his domain at one point stretched from Spain to Russia, the 1815 Battle of Waterloo put a damper on his plans. Defeated, Napoleon was exiled to the tropical island of Saint Helena, setting a precedent that the punishment for trying to take over the world is to be forced to chill out in paradise for the rest of your life.

The next hundred years witnessed steady growth in technology, infrastructure, and culture, as well as a healthy smattering of further revolutions. Napoleon's nephew even showed up and defied both democracy and the rules of counting by ruling for 18 years as Napoleon III.

Check Out These Guns (1914-present)

While the stalemate on the Western Front prevented the German forces from conquering France in WWI, the second time around they were not so lucky. Hitler's forces swept through the country in just a few weeks. The north of the country was occupied by the German army until 1944, while the southern half was ruled along Fascist lines from the town of Vichy.

In 1958, undaunted by the failure of the first four, France embarked on the Fifth Republic. This nearly fell in May 1968 when student demonstrations took over the streets of Paris and eventually escalated into a nationwide general strike. The crisis passed, however, and since then the French government has demonstrated an uncharacteristic stability.

france 101

We all know that being a tourist is fun (if you didn't agree, chances are you wouldn't be reading this book). And France, with its countless monuments and museums, its culture and cuisine, its world-renowned art and architecture, certainly provides ample opportunity to be a fanny-packing foreigner. However, if your trip to *l'hexagone* consists of nothing more than visiting museums and snapping artsy cover photos from your favorite Parisian bridge, you will miss out on countless opportunities to gain a deeper appreciation for the country and to feel like you've truly lived in France. Learning the language and history of the country will make your explorations all the more rewarding (in addition to making you feel like a pro when a less-enlightened tourist asks you for directions or if you speak English), while tackling many of the country's problems (such as poverty and an increasingly aging population) will allow you to forge meaningful connections with the community you're visiting. Finally, while finding a job may not be on the top of your to-do list, it's a way to experience a new culture (and having the money to pay for your flight home is never a bad thing)

STUDY

Tired of receiving an ominous glare every time you attempt to order a *café crème*, ask directions to the nearest *salle de bain*, or mutter a simple *bonjour madame* to the proprietor of your favorite Parisian boulangerie? Scared you'll receive even more ominous glares from your ever-judgmental French waiter because you don't know which wine should accompany your meal? Want to impress your friends with your substantial knowledge of the Louvre's holdings? Whether you're looking to *améliorer votre français* (improve your French) or become a certified wine snob, France, and Paris in particular, offers no shortage of educational opportunities for the foreign student.

- **FRANCE LANGUE:** France Langue offers French-language classes for every level of proficiency in five locations (two in Paris, as well as ones in Nice, Bordeaux, and Biarritz) as well as au pair and internship-based language programs. Host family, residence hall, hotel, or apartment lodgings are provided for students in need of accommodations. (Paris location: ☎33 01 45 00 40 15; Bordeaux location: ☎33 05 24 72 14 65)

- **INSTITUT DE FRANÇAIS:** Located in the village of Villefranche on the French Riviera, the Institut de Français offers intensive two- or four-week French language classes designed to acquire rapid proficiency. Unlike many other language programs, classes here run eight hours a day, five days a week, so a full commitment to the program is necessary. (. ☎33 493 01 88 44)

- **ALLIANCE FRANÇAISE MARSEILLE-PROVENCE:** The Alliance Française offers a more flexible, low-key array of classes in the south of France (ranging from four to 20 hours per week), more suitable for someone looking to study the language in addition to pursuing other activities. Classes are offered in both Marseille and Aix-en-Provence. (en.afmarseille.org ☎0033 04 96 10 24 60)

- **O CHATEAU WINE TASTING AND WINE BAR:** Described as "the most irreverent wine tastings in Paris" by *TIME Magazine*, O Chateau offers several different wine tasting classes sans snobbery. In addition to the classes at its 1er location, O Chateau offers private or group daytrips to several French wine regions. (☎011 33 1 44 739 780)

- **LE CORDON BLEU PARIS:** Arguably the most renowned culinary institute in the world, Le Cordon Bleu offers an array of "Gourmet & Short Courses" that last no longer than a day and cover specific aspects of French cuisine. (☎33 01 53 68 22 50)

- **LA CUISINE PARIS:** La Cuisine Paris offers English-language cooking classes spanning the French culinary tradition. Day classes range from traditional pastries to cheeses, while food tours offer a chance to explore the cuisines of individual neighborhoods. (☎33 01 40 51 78 18)

- **WICE:** One of the oldest Anglophone communities in Paris, WICE's mission is to provide cultural and educational enrichment to the international community of Paris. WICE offers a variety of courses through its many members, ranging from instructional classes in the visual arts to creative writing to cooking. (☎33 1 45 66 76 67)

- **PARIS LOISIRS CULTURELLES:** For a relatively low price €35 for three hours), Paris Loisirs Culturelles offers painting classes at its atelier in the 11ème for all levels of experience. Members may also take advantage of the free French-English conversation groups and monthly museum trips (☎33 09 83 68 70 26)

- **ÉCOLE DU LOUVRE:** Located in the Palais du Louvre, the École du Louvre is an institution of higher education run by the French Ministry of Culture, offering classes in art history, archeology, epigraphy, the history of civilizations, and museology. Many of the École's daytime courses (conducted in French) are open to auditing by the public. (☎01 55 35 18 00)

VOLUNTEER

Ever since the French decided that they did not, in fact, want to be slaves to a ruling 1%, they've had something of a love affair with protests and social activism. No wine break during work? Protest it. Too much American music on the radio? Protest it. Though the spirit of *La Révolution* is very much alive and well in modern France, we wouldn't suggest taking to the streets orbeheading any monarchs if you decide that you, too, would like to change the world. Volunteer opportunities abound throughout the country, providing opportunities to give back to the community without a complimentary overnight stay in a French prison.

- **ORANGE ROCKCORPS:** The concept behind Orange RockCorps is simple: find a project, give four hours of your time, and receive concert tickets for your efforts (artists such as Snoop Dog, David Guetta, and Sean Paul have participated in the past). In addition to the free concert

tickets, volunteering with Orange RockCorps is a great way to meet other young people in France. (☎0811 287 287).

- **WICE:** If you're already mastered the fine details of French culture, consider lending a helping hand to the poor Anglophones who haven't. In addition to offering classes, WICE accepts volunteers to help with everything from curriculum development to website maintenance. (☎33 1 45 66 76 67)

- **RESTOS DU COEUR:** Les Restaurants du Coeur is a French charity that distributes free meals to the homeless and other individuals living in poverty. With locations throughout the country, Restos du Coeur is an easily accessible way to give back to the community. (☎01 53 24 98 09)

- **SOS HELP:** SOS Help is an anonymous, English-language emotional support line serving the international community in France. Volunteers are trained by psychologists and may assist as either listeners (answering the phone and listening to callers) or supporters (helping with other tasks). A long-term commitment is required. (☎01 46 21 46 46)

- **CROIX ROUGE:** Being the behemoth NGO that it is, the Red Cross is constantly in need of volunteers to help with its day-to-day activities. If your talents or interests include organizing donation drives, performing office tasks, or assisting medical-response teams, this may be for you. (☎01 44 43 11 00)

- **SECOURS POPULAIRE FRANÇAIS:** SPF is a charity that aids poor families and children by providing things such as social support, food, or clothing. SPF is currently seeking volunteers for its "copain du Monde" program, similar to Big Brothers Big Sisters in America. (☎01 44 78 21 00)

- **FONDATION CLAUDE POMPIDOU:** The Fondation Claude Pompidou provides volunteer-based support to sick and elderly people in hospitals as well as to disabled children and their families at their homes. Some French language ability may be necessary. (☎01 40 13 75 00)

- **WWOOF:** In exchange for room, board, and enough granola-scented self-satisfaction to pay for your flight home, volunteering on an organic farm through WWOOF (World Wide Opportunities on Organic Farms) may provide the perfect opportunity to escape your studies and city.

WORK

So you're finally living the life of your dreams in France: people watching from a streetside cafe, making trips to sophisticated museums with unpronounceable names, and shopping along the Champs Élysées…that is, until you realize that your cup of *café au lait* isn't any cheaper than a Starbucks latte, museums aren't free, the sales tax is 20 percent, and you're still on a student budget. Long-term work may be difficult to acquire, as France is currently facing record high unemployment rates and many jobs require appropriate visas, but short-term and English-speaking positions are often available.

- **TEACHING ASSISTANT PROGRAM IN FRANCE:** The Cultural Services Department of the French Embassy and the French Ministry of Education send approximately 1500 US citizens and permanent residents to teach English in France each year. The program lasts seven months and €950 per month stipend is provided. French proficiency is required. (http://highereducation.frenchculture.org/teach-in-france ☎202 944 6000)

- **EVEIL BILINGUE:** Eveil Bilingue is an organization that specializes in early language acquisition for children in the Paris area. They are currently recruiting native English speakers for teaching and babysitting positions. (☎09 81 61 20 43)

- **FEDERATION UNIS DES AUBERGES DE JEUNESSE:** Through this organization, you may apply to work at hostels throughout the country, assisting with day-to-day tasks and management. Jobs are typically offered on a short-term basis. (☎0033-1 44 89 87 27)

- **ERASMUSU:** Erasmusu is a student network that lists job postings in cities around the globe. Postings are all from private families, individuals, or companies, and compensation varies. ()

- **AU PAIR:** Working as an au pair allows you to live and eat with a French family while receiving an allowance for personal expenses. In exchange, you help with domestic tasks and childcare, often serving as an older sibling for young children in the family. Many au pair placement services are available in France and abroad. Au Pair World (☎49 561 310 561 17) and Accuiel International Services (☎01 39 73 04 98) are both good options.

CUSTOMS AND ETIQUETTE

How to Win Friends

Everyone knows the stereotype of the unfriendly, pretentious Frenchman, but if you exhibit basic manners, most will simply label you as a foreigner and remain civil. It is important to greet everyone that you interact with as monsieur or madame. Meeting friends, it is common to kiss once on each cheek, but upon first introductions, a handshake is acceptable. Simply saying please (*s'il vous plaît*) and thank you (*merci*, optional *beaucoup*) will earn you respect. Along those lines, Parisians will appreciate any attempts at speaking French; bonjour, bonsoir, and pardon are your three favorite words starting now.

Table Manners for Dummies

Simply staying nourished in Paris may be the most difficult task of all. At a meal, don't think about eating before someone says, "Bon appétit!". Resist the temptation to fill wine glasses up to the top, no matter how delicious the wine. Although knives and forks are used to eat almost everything (even fruit) don't think about touching a knife to your salad leaves, since to all with some common sense it is inexcusably offensive. And while the French generally abhor finger food, do not cut a baguette on the table—tear it. You may (rightfully) insist that these customs are peculiar, prissy, or pompous, to which we can only bid thee good luck.

FOOD AND DRINK

Filet Mignon With a Side of Snails, S'il Vous Plaît

Whether you sit down at a bistro, bar, or sidewalk cafe, you won't run out of different dishes to enjoy. For breakfast, try a croissant, or a chocolate-filled pain au chocolat. Lunch typically consists of simple salads, sandwiches on baguettes, crepes, croques-monsieur (a fancy-pants version of a grilled ham and cheese), or heavier meat dishes. Dinner may include a few fishy options: bouillabaisse is a popular traditional soup made from many different types of fish, and escargots are available at elegant restaurants for those who dare to try cooked snails. Perhaps the best part of dinner is dessert—from éclairs to chocolate mousse to crème brûlée, you'll find you have much to gain, and some bigger clothes to buy.

Drink (Read: Wine)

Okay, the header is a slight exaggeration—the French appreciate a good espresso in the morning and the occasional coffee after dessert. But while in France, it may be worthwhile to do as the French do, by which we mean drink wine and lots of it. Just don't be intimidated by the inordinate selection; the wine menu might look more like a textbook. If worse comes to worst, ask the waiter for a cup of the house best.

GERMANY

Anything that ever made it big is bound to attract some stereotypes, and Germany is no exception. Beer, crazy deaf composers, robotic efficiency, sausage, Inglourious Basterds—just to name a few. Germany has some of the best collections of art in the world, incredible architecture, and a history that makes it clear no one bosses Germany around. Whether giving the ancient Romans a run for their money or giving birth to Protestantism, Germany has always been a rebel. Even behind its success as a developed country, it hasn't given that up.

The damage from World War II still lingers in city skyscapes, and the country is keenly embarrassed of its Nazi and communist pasts. Even though its concrete wall has been demolished, Berlin, the country's capital, still retains a marked difference between east and west after decades of strife, tempering the picturesque castles and churches of earlier golden ages.

Plenty of discounts, cheap eats, and a large student population make Germany an exciting place to visit and study. It's also incredibly accessible for Anglophone visitors, as many Germans have no qualms about slipping from their native tongue into English. The nightlife and culture of Berlin or Munich will grab you and never let you go, while thriving smaller university towns will charm you into wanting to stay another semester.

greatest hits

- **COLD WAR KIDS.** Admire the Berlin Wall murals painted by artists from around the world at the **East Side Gallery** (p. 248).
- **BUTTERFLY KISSES.** Emerge from **Cocoon Club** (p. 300) a drunken butterfly after spending the night wrapped in some German hottie's arms.
- **BEAMER, BENZ, OR BENTLEY.** Sport the classiest threads you own, and head to the **BMW Welt and Museum** (p. 307) to test drive a new whip.
- **DOWN IN ONE.** Pace yourself and avoid using the vomitorium at Munich's most famous beer hall, **Hofbräuhaus** (p. 312).

If we had to recommend one neighborhood to the student travelers of Berlin, it would probably be Kreuzberg. With the cheapest food (can we get a hell yeah döner kebabs?) and the coolest, grungiest clubs, it seems to be designed specifically for the young budget traveler. While in Munich, we suggest checking out what we're calling the University Area if you want young people and cheap digs. Finally, in Hamburg, the area around Schanzenviertel is quiet and a nice spot to find budget accommodations.

berlin

So you've decided to visit Berlin. Congratulations. Your pretentious friends went to Paris. Your haughty friends went to London. And your lost friends went to Belarus. But you decided on Berlin. You've probably heard that Berlin is the coolest city in the world, or that it has one of the best clubs in Europe, or that it sleeps when the sun comes up. Well, don't believe the hype. It's not the coolest city in the world; it's several of the coolest cities in the world. It doesn't have one of the best clubs in Europe; it has 10. And to top it off, Berlin never sleeps.

Berlin's rise began with some normal history, taken to epic heights. King Friedrich II and his identically named progeny ruled from canal-lined boulevards, built palaces like middle-fingers to all the haters, and developed Prussia into an Enlightened European powerhouse, with Berlin at the helm. But after centuries of captaining Europe, Berlin went crazy in the 20th. As the seat of Hitler's terror and with World War II drama in its streets, Berlin rebooted in the '50s, only to become a physical manifestation of Cold War divisions. The Berlin Wall rose in 1961, slicing the city and fueling the enmity of a radical student and punk population. Ten years after the Wall crumbled in 1989, the German government decided to relocate from Bonn to Berlin. And from there, Berlin became today's European champion of cool.

Sorry about your friends.

ORIENTATION

Charlottenburg

Should you tire of the immense bustle or forget that Berlin was an old European capital, venture into Charlottenburg. Originally a separate town founded around the grounds of Friedrich I's palace, it became an affluent cultural center during the Weimar years and the Berlin Wall era thanks to Anglo-American support. The neighborhood retains its original old-world opulence, from the upscale Beaux-Arts apartments to the shamelessly extravagant **Kurfürstendamm,** Berlin's premiere shopping strip. **Ku'damm,** as the locals call it, runs from east to west through southern Charlottenburg. Popular sights include the Spree River in the northwest and the absurdly splendiferous **Schloß Charlottenburg** to the north, both of which bolster Charlottenburg's old-Berlin appeal. Aside from the sights, the neighborhood's high rents keep out most young people and students, so the Charlottenburg crowd tends to be old and quiet and prefers the sidewalk seating of expensive Ku'Damm restaurants to crazy ragers in the area's few clubs.

germany

GERMANY

DENMARK
Baltic Sea

North Sea

Sylt
Westerland
North Frisian Islands
Amrum
Husum
St. Peter Ording
Tönning
Helgoland
East Frisian Islands
Norden
Jever
Emden
Cuxhaven
Bremerhaven

Flensburg
Schleswig
Kiel
Plön
Lübeck
Ratzeburg
Lauenburg

Fehmarn
Rügen
Binz
Stralsund
Greifswald
Usedom
Rostock
Wismar
Güstrow
Schwerin
Waren
Neubrandenburg
Müritzsee
Neustrelitz

SCHLESWIG HOLSTEIN

MECKLENBURG - VORPOMMERN
(MECKLENBURG-UPPER POMERANIA)

NETHER-LANDS

Oldenburg
Bremen
Hamburg
Lüneburg
LÜNEBURGER HEIDE

BRANDENBURG
POLAND

NIEDERSACHSEN
(LOWER SAXONY)

Osnabrück
Bielefeld
Münster
TEUTOBURG FOREST
Detmold
Bodenwerder

Celle
Hannover
(Hanover)
Hameln
(Hamelin)
Wolfenbüttel
Hildesheim
Goslar
Göttingen

Bräunschweig
(Brunswick)
Magdeburg
Wernigerode
Harz Mountains
Quedlinburg
Dessau

Berlin
Potsdam
Brandenburg
SPREEWALD
Frankfurt an der Oder
Lübben
Lübbenau
Cottbus

SACHSEN-ANHALT
(SAXONY-ANHALT)
Wittenberg

NORDRHEIN-WESTFALEN
(NORTH RHINE-WESTPHALIA)

Essen
Dortmund
Düsseldorf
Mönchengladbach
Aachen
Bonn
Köln
(Cologne)
Hamm
Münden
Kassel
Fritzlar
Marburg
HESSEN
(HESSE)

THÜRINGEN
(THÜRINGIA)
Eisenach
Gotha
Erfurt
Naumburg
Weimar
Jena
Gera
THÜRINGER WALD

Halle
Leipzig
SACHSEN
(SAXONY)
Chemnitz
Zwickau
Meißen
Dresden
Bautzen
Görlitz
Zittau

BELGIUM

Koblenz
Limburg
RHEINLAND PFALZ
(RHINELAND PALATINATE)
Eifel Massif
Cochem
Trier
Bingen
Mainz
Worms
Wiesbaden
Darmstadt
Aschaffenburg
Frankfurt
Lahn
Fulda
Taunus Range
Coburg
Bamberg
Bayreuth
CZECH REPUBLIC
Prague

LUX.
SAARLAND
Saarbrücken
Mannheim
Speyer
Heidelberg
Karlsruhe
Pforzheim
Baden-Baden
Würzburg
Main
BAYERN
(BAVARIA)
Erlangen
Nürnberg
(Nuremberg)
Rothenburg o.d. Tauber
Dinkelsbühl
Schwäbisch Hall
Heilbronn
Eichstätt
Schwäbisch Gmünd
Nördlingen
Ingolstadt
Regensburg
Straubing
BAYERISCHER WALD
Passau

FRANCE
Freudenstadt
Rottweil
BLACK FOREST
Stuttgart
Tübingen
Schwäbian Jura
Ulm
Augsburg
Landshut
Burghausen
Donau (Danube)
AUSTRIA
München
(Munich)
Wasserburg
Chiemsee
Prien
Salzburg
Bad Reichenhall
Berchtesgaden

Breisach
Freiburg
BADEN-WÜRTTEMBERG
Memmingen
Starnberger See
Garmisch-Partenkirchen
Oberammergau
Bavarian Alps
Bodensee
(Lake Constance)
Friedrichshafen
Konstanz
(Constance)
Bregenz
Füssen
Zugspitze

SWITZERLAND

0 50 kilometers
0 50 miles

berlin

Schöneberg and Wilmersdorf

South of Ku'damm, Schöneberg and Wilmersdorf are primarily quiet residential neighborhoods, remarkable for their world-class cafe culture, bistro tables, relaxed diners, and coffee shops spilling out onto virtually every cobblestone street. Also, nowhere else in Berlin, and perhaps in all of Germany, is the GLBT community quite as spectacularly ready to party as in the area immediately surrounding **Nollendorfplatz.** To the west lies one of Berlin's most convenient outdoor getaways: **Grunewald** rustles with city dwellers trading their daily commute for peaceful strolls with the family dog among the pines. But if you don't have the time for the 20min. bus or tram ride— or if a palm reader once predicted that you would be mauled by dogs in a German forest—then Schöneberg and Wilmersdorf offer a gracious handful of shady parks scattered among their apartment façades, where you can sit in the grass and kick back the cups of joe.

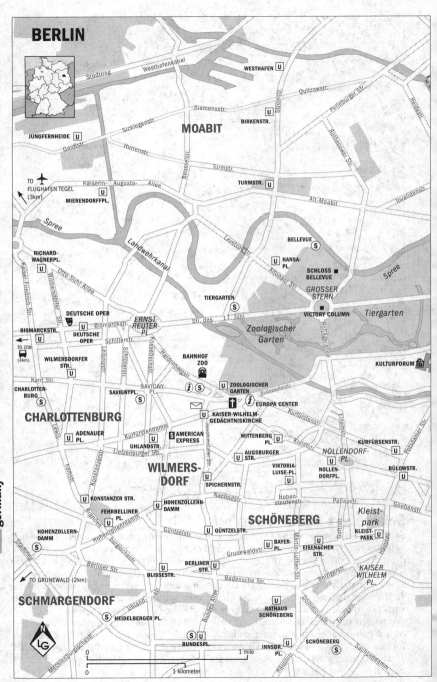

BERLIN

WESTHAFEN Ⓤ

Städtring
Westhafenkanal
Siemensstr.
Sickingenstr.
Quitzowstr.
Perleberger Str.

MOABIT

JUNGFERNHEIDE Ⓤ
BIRKENSTR. Ⓤ

Gaußstr.
Huttenstr.
Berlichingenstr.
Turmstr.
Sellerstr.

TO
FLUGHAFEN TEGEL
(3km)

Kaiserin- Augusta- Allee
TURMSTR. Ⓤ

MIERENDORFFPL. Ⓤ
Alt-Moabit
Invalidenstr.

Spree
Landwehrkanal
Levetzowstr.
Altonaer Str.
BELLEVUE Ⓢ

RICHARD-
WAGNERPL. Ⓤ
HANSA-
PL. Ⓤ
SCHLOSS ■
BELLEVUE

Kaiser-Friedrich-Str.
Otto-Suhr-Allee
Wilmersdorfer Str.
TIERGARTEN Ⓢ
GROSSER
STERN
Spree

DEUTSCHE OPER 🎭 Ⓤ
Bismarckstr.
ERNST-
REUTER-
PL.
Str. des 17. Juni
VICTORY COLUMN ■
Tiergarten

BISMARCKSTR. Ⓤ
DEUTSCHE
OPER
Schillerstr.
Zoologischer
Garten
Hofjägerallee

TO ZOB
(4km)
Leibnizstr.
Schlüterstr.
Hardenbergstr.
Bleibtreustr.
BAHNHOF
ZOO 🚉
KULTURFORUM 🏛

WILMERSDORFER
STR. Ⓤ
Kant Str.
SAVIGNYPL. Ⓢ
SAVIGNY-
PL.
ⓘ Ⓢ
ZOOLOGISCHER
GARTEN Ⓤ
Budapesterstr.

CHARLOTTEN-
BURG Ⓢ
✉ 🕍
Tauentzienstr.
ⓘ EUROPA CENTER
Kurfürstenstr.
Einemstr.

CHARLOTTENBURG
ADENAUER
PL. Ⓤ
Kurfürstendamm
$ AMERICAN
EXPRESS
KAISER-WILHELM-
GEDÄCHTNISKIRCHE
WITTENBERG
PL. Ⓤ
Kleiststr.
KÜRFÜRSTENSTR. Ⓤ
Potsdamer Str.

Leibnizstr.
Konstanzerstr.
UHLANDSTR. Ⓤ
Lietzenburger Str.
Joachimstaler Str.
AUGSBURGER
STR.
NOLLENDORF-
PL. Ⓤ
BÜLOWSTR. Ⓤ

WILMERS-
DORF
SPICHERNSTR. Ⓤ
VIKTORIA-
LUISE-PL.
NOLLEN-
DORFPL.

KONSTANZER STR. Ⓤ
HOHENZOLLERN-
DAMM Ⓤ
Nachodstr.
Hohen-
staufenstr.
Pallasstr.
Goebenstr.
Kleist-
park

FEHRBELLINER
PL. Ⓤ
Hohenzollerndamm
SCHÖNEBERG
Goltzstr.
KLEIST-
PARK Ⓤ

HOHENZOLLERN-
DAMM Ⓢ
Berliner Str.
Güntzelstr.
GÜNTZELSTR. Ⓤ
Grunewaldstr.
BAYER-
PL. Ⓤ
EISENACHER
STR.
Belzigerstr.
KAISER
WILHELM
PL.

TO GRUNEWALD (2km)
Brandenburgischestr.
Hohenzollernpl.
BERLINER
STR. Ⓤ
Badensche Str.
Martin-Luther-Str.
Dominicusstr.
Hauptstr.

SCHMARGENDORF
BLISSESTR. Ⓤ
Uhland
Bundes Allee
RATHAUS
SCHÖNEBERG

Mecklenburgischestr.
HEIDELBERGER PL. Ⓢ
BUNDESPL. Ⓢ Ⓤ
INNSBR.
PL. Ⓤ
SCHÖNEBERG Ⓢ
Sachsendamm

Städring

0   1 mile
0   1 kilometer

germany

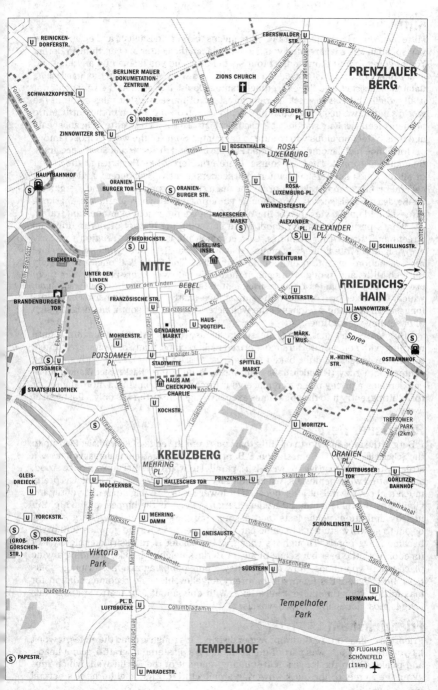

berlin

Mitte

Mitte lives up to its name. Literally, Mitte means "center" in English, and every second you spend in Mitte will remind you that it is, in fact, the center of everything in Berlin. You're going to find thousands of tourists in Mitte, and you'll also find anything and everything political, historical, and cultural. Southwest Mitte boasts the **Brandenburg Gate**, the **Reichstag**, and the exceedingly famous **Jewish Memorial**. At the very center of it all, you'll find **Museuminsel**, literally an island of museums that piles some of the world's most awe-inspiring sights practically on top of each other. In the north, Mitte borders **Prenzlauer Berg** starting at **Rosenthaler Platz**. This area has Mitte's cheapest eats and tons of techno clubs you're sure to encounter. Some of the world's most famous performance halls, including the **Berlin Philharmonic** and the **Deutscher Staatsoper**, grace this cultural capital. Then, of course, there's the forest-like **Tiergarten** at the center of Mitte, which shelters sunbathers, barbecuers, pensive wanderers, and probably several breeds of magical creatures. The main street cutting through the Tiergarten, **Straße des 17 Juni**, serves as a popular gathering place where carnivals, markets, protests, and public viewings of the World Cup take precedent over constant traffic.

What's perhaps most fun about Mitte is tracing the history of Berlin down its streets and through its buildings. One common phrase used in relation to nearly every sight in Mitte is "heavily damaged in World War II," and original buildings and reconstructions are often difficult to distinguish. The **Berlin Wall** once ran directly through Mitte, and, though the signs of the divide fade with every passing year, there are still many remnants of a more fragmented Berlin, like the DDR-built **Fernsehturm**, which, for better or worse, is Mitte's most incessantly visible landmark. One of the longest still-standing stretches of the Wall deteriorates in the south, an unsightly sign of unsettling recent times.

But Mitte isn't just about the sights; it also burns brightly from night until morning with some of Berlin's most prized techno clubs, many of which are named, for whatever reason, after baked goods (e.g., **Cookies**, p. 264). Plus, with shopping centers both ritzy (**Friedrichstraße**) and intimidatingly hip (**Hackescher Markt**), Mitte can serve as a pricey place to replace your threads with something more flannel or form-fitting; entry into the sometimes exclusive nightlife options is only a flashy strut away.

Prenzlauer Berg

P'Berg is the area just north of Mitte that runs from the edge of **Rosenthaler Platz** up to the **Schönhauser Allee** U-Bahn station. P'Berg's most famous street is **Bernauer Strasse**, a street which runs east(ish) to west(ish), parallel to where the Berlin Wall once stood, and is dotted with memorials. When the Wall came down, Prenzlauer Berg was pretty much a ghost town. But after decades of lower rents drawing students, youth, and vitality, by the millennium, Prenzlauer Berg had become the hippest of the hip. But hip, by definition, never lasts, and as time progressed, Prenzlauer Berg steadily began to gentrify: students became parents, hippies gave way to yuppies, and parks became playgrounds. Though it's changed, Prenzlauer Berg hasn't completely lost its cool: with the best bar scene of any of Berlin's neighborhoods, including a wine place where you choose how much to pay, a ping-pong bar, and more vintage sofas than *Mad Men*, P'Berg can still be pretty unbelievable. One recommendation for maximizing your time here: rent a bike. With only about four metro stations, this Berg is most accessible on two wheels.

Friedrichshain

Friedrichshain is one of Berlin's cheaper districts. It's rough around the edges, it won't let you forget that it was part of the DDR, and it's plastered in graffiti, metal-heads, and punks. From the longest still-standing remnant of the Berlin Wall, which runs along the Spree, to the stark, towering architecture of the neighborhood's central

germany

axis, **Frankfurter Allee**, the ghost of the former Soviet Union still haunts the 'Hain. Fortunately, this ghost only seems to scare the population out into the night, when any crumbling factory, any cobwebbed train station, and any complex of graffiti with enough grime is fair game for F'Hain's sublimely edgy nightlife. Friedrichshain is wonderfully inexpensive and unique. Travelers should keep a lookout, though, at night, because its often desolate infrastructure can hide shady characters.

Kreuzberg

If Mitte is Manhattan, Kreuzberg is Brooklyn. Graffiti adorns everything, and the younger population skulks around while chowing down on street food fit for a Last Supper. The parties start later, end later, and sometimes never stop. The neighborhood's alternative soul sticks around like an especially persistent squatter. Underground clubs in abandoned basements, burned-out apartment buildings, and oppressive warehouse complexes shake off their dust when the sun disappears and rage until well after it reappears. The area is also home to most of Berlin's enormous Turkish population (hence the nickname "Little Istanbul"). *Döner* kebabs, the salty scraps cut from those gigantic meaty beehives in every other storefront, go for €2-3 all across this district, and the **Turkish Market** along the southern bank of the **Landwehrkanal** is one of the most exciting, raucous, cheap, and authentic markets in Western Europe. If you want to learn about Berlin, head to Mitte. If you want to not remember what you learned, come to Kreuzberg.

SIGHTS

Charlottenburg

Charlottenburg shouldn't be at the top of your list of places to visit in Berlin. It's removed from the city center, meaning it's more residential and less crazy. That said, if you have more than a couple of days in the city, Charlottenburg does have a few scattered and exceedingly impressive sights. Be warned: Charlottenburg is huge.

KADEWE

Tauentzienstr. 21-24 ☎030 212 10 www.kadewe.de

This is it, folks. This place is one of the coolest things you'll see in Charlottenburg. Fifty thousand people pass through KaDeWe daily (and just think: you could be one of them!!!). KaDeWe is one of the world's largest department stores, and it stocks seven gargantuan floors of things you want but can't afford, from Longchamp bags to over 100 varieties of jam. The sheer size of this place is seriously impressive: KaDeWe's floors are equivalent in square footage to nine football fields. If you do decide to visit KaDeWe, you should keep a close eye on your wallet because you're going to want to buy something you can't afford. For anyone on a budget, this place is pretty much just a spectacle, but if KaDeWe is cool enough for David Bowie to sing about, it must be cool enough for you to visit.

i *U1, U2, or U3: Wittenbergpl. ✿ Open M-Th 10am-8pm, F 10am-9pm, Sa 9:30am-8pm.*

KÄTHE-KOLLWITZ-MUSEUM   MUSEUM

Fasanenstr. 24 ☎030 882 52 10 www.kaethe-kollwitz.de

Berlin is full of grand museums, but even so, the Käthe-Kollwitz-Museum sets itself apart. This place is extremely affecting from beginning to end. As a member of the Berlin *Sezession* (Secession) movement and one of Germany's most prominent 20th-century artists, Kollwitz protested World War I and became silent for the duration of World War II. This museum takes you through her life, from following her rise as an acclaimed artist to illustrating how the death of her own son in WWI impacted her work. All of her depictions of war, pregnancy, starvation, death, and the innocent reflect her riveting emotional authenticity.

berlin

Travelers with just a few nights in Berlin should consider shelling out for a room in Mitte to be near the city's major sights and nightlife. Charlottenburg is dotted with cheap pensions and hostels, while Schöneberg and Wilmersdorf can be pricey for a solo backpacker. Prenzlauer Berg's few hostels have great proximity to bars and cafes, and club-goers should consider a bed in Friedrichshain. If you're looking to meet fellow travelers, Kreuzberg's your best bet. These are some of our favorite spots; for more, visit **www.letsgo.com**.

■ HAPPY GO LUCKY HOTEL   HOSTEL $$
Stuttgarter Pl. 17   ☎030 327 09 072 www.happygoluckyhotel.com

The outside of this place is an appropriately bright orange; we promise you won't miss it. Happy Go Lucky's proximity to the U-Bahn make this place convenient for access to most of Berlin. The hostel caters to people of all types, but we'd recommend it especially for lone travelers who are looking to meet other cool cats.

i *S3, S5, S9, or S75: Charlottenburg, or U7: Wilmersdorfer Str. Free Wi-Fi. Breakfas €6. Dorms €19; singles €30-36; doubles €38-47; triples €40-55; quads €46-60. ② Reception 24hr.*

■ CIRCUS HOSTEL   HOSTEL $$
Weinbergsweg 1A   ☎030 200 03 939 www.circus-berlin.de

From the moment you step into the front door, you'll recognize the themed decorations. The rooms are big, with stylish minimalist furniture and huge windows. Circus Hostel is one of the friendliest places around for students, families, or old fogeys—they succeed at pleasing everyone.

i *U8: Rosenthaler Pl. It's visible as you exit the metro. Free Wi-Fi. The breakfast buffet €5) is probably the freshest and biggest you'll find in a Mitte hostel. Linens included. Lockers €10 deposit. Towels €1. 8- to 10-bed dorms €19; 4-bed dorms €23; singles €46; doubles €56. €2 service charge when paying with credit card. Bikes €12 per day. ② Reception 24hr.*

■ PFEFFERBETT   HOSTEL $
Christinenstr. 18-19   ☎030 939 35 858 www.pfefferbett.de

This charming hostel is housed in an old brew house. Though the rooms are simple, Pfefferbett has really high ceilings and pretty, exposed bricks that exude a homey vibe.

i *U2: Senefelderpl. Head to the south exit and look immediately to the right; there's a sign in a large doorway directing you to Pfefferbett. Go up the left flight of stairs, turn right, and walk to the back of the courtyard. Turn left; the hostel is just around the corner. Free Wi-Fi in common room. Breakfast €6.50. Linens €2.50. Laundry €5. Women-only dorms available. 8-bed dorms from €12; 6-bed from €15, with shower from €19; 4-bed from €20; singles with bath from €47; doubles with bath €64. ② Reception 24hr.*

■ SUNFLOWER HOSTEL   HOSTEL $
Helsingforser Str. 17   ☎030 440 44 250 www.sunflower-hostel.de

Sunflower isn't as pretty as its name suggests, but it packs one hell of a punch of characters (like Darth Vader and Sesame Street). The young staff and an indie-electro mix make this hostel just one Habermas book away from a college cafe.

i *U1, S3, S5, S7, S9 or S75: Warschauer Str. Walk north on Warschauer Str. and turn left onto Helsingforser Str.; it's on the right. Free Wi-Fi. Breakfas €3. Linens €3 deposit. Laundry €4.50. 7- to 8-bed dorms €10-15; 5- to 6-bed €13-17; singles €30-37; doubles €38-48; apartments €70-75. Bikes €12 per day. ② Reception 24hr.*

germany

Without so much as a hint of narcissism, her self-portraits are refreshing and moving, reflecting her maturation and suffering during the wars.

i U1: Uhlandstr €6, students €3. ☼ Open daily 11am-6pm.

SCHLOSS CHARLOTTENBURG
PALACE

Spandauer Damm 10-22 ☎030 320 92 75

Schloß Charlottenburg is a gigantic Baroque palace. And, if you care about history, you'll delight in knowing that it was commissioned by Friedrich I in the 1600s as a gift for his wife. Here's the bottom line: getting into this place will set you back €12 and, at the end of the day, you'll overdose on the fanciful furnishings of the über-rich. Think about forgoing the upholstery experience to go and visit the majestic, exquisitely manicured (and free!) Schloßgarten around the back of the palace. Like the fairy tales you dreamed up as a small child, these tremendous grounds are packed chock-a-block with small lakes, fountains, and those secretive, forested paths your inner child has coveted for so long. During the summer months, Schloßgarten is the ideal picnic spot.

i Bus #M45 from Bahnhof Zoo to Luisenpl./Schloß Charlottenburg, or U2: Sophie-Charlotte Pl. Altes Schloß €12, students €8; Neuer Flügel €6/5; Belvedere €3/2.50; Mausoleum free. A Tageskarte (day ticket; €15, students €11) covers them all. Audio tours (available in English) included with admission. ☼ Altes Schloß open Apr-Oct Tu-Su 10am-6pm; Nov-Mar Tu-Su 10am-5pm. Schloßgarten open sunrise to sunset.

SCHWULES MUSEUM (GAY MUSEUM)
MUSEUM

Lützowstr. 73 ☎030 695 99 050 www.schwulesmuseum.de

The Schwules Museum started out small, but having recently relocated, this place is rapidly expanding. Schwules remembers homosexual persecution and packs exhibits with everything GLBTQ. Most of Schwules exists only as temporary exhibitions, but these exhibits keep things fresh, and, like a box of chocolates, you never know what you're going to get. Penises are one a penny, but so are 19th-century canvases, issues of *Der Eigene* (the world's first gay newspaper), and mug shots of gay men prosecuted by the Nazis.

i English exhibit guide available. €6, students €4. ☼ Open M 2-6pm, W-F 2-6pm, Sa 2-7pm, Su 2-6pm.

MUSEUM BERGGRUEN
MUSEUM

Schloßstr. 1 ☎030 326 95 80

If you feel strongly about Picasso, you should visit this museum. They keep two whole floors devoted almost solely to his work, plus a couple of random African masks. You're sure to notice Picasso's *"Le matador et femme nue"* ("The matador and the nude woman"), with its colorful, captivating show of big-lipped figures with fleshy protrusions. On top of the expansive Picasso collection, this museum keeps a whole room of Matisse, showcasing every side of his artwork. You'll see Matisse's oh-so-famous nudes alongside black-and-white, exceedingly simple prints. As a final attempt to get you to visit this place, we'll also tell you that the museum houses a significant collection of Klee's work, including the exceptionally adorable and lively *"Rotes Mädchen mit gelbem Topfat"* ("Red girl with yellow hat").

i Bus #M45 from Bahnhof Zoo to Luisenpl./Schloß Charlottenburg or U2: Sophie-Charlotte Pl. €12, students €6, children free. Audio guide included. ☼ Open Tu-Su 10am-6pm.

OLYMPIASTADION
STADIUM

Olympischer Pl. 3 (Visitors Center) ☎030 250 02 322 www.olympiastadion-berlin.de

This massive stadium was originally built for the 1936 Olympics. Looking back, it seems pretty amazing that Germany was holding the Olympics in 1936. The stadium helps you reflect on the time. If you haven't heard of a guy named Jesse Owens, this whole place might as well be a tribute to him. Jessie Owens was an African-American track and field athlete who scored four gold medals during

berlin

the '36 Games, but Hitler refused to recognize his accomplishments. In (slightly) more recent years, the Brits used the main field as a headquarters immediately after World War II. If you come to this place at the wrong time (aka, right after a soccer match), you won't be able to get into the museum, but you'll get to observe hundreds of drunk German folk drinking beer by the liter and singing nationalist songs.

i *U2: Olympia-Stadion. S5 or S7: Pichelsburg €7, students €5. Families (2 adults and up to 3 children) €16. Guided tour €10, students €8, under 6 free. Audio guides €3. ☑ Open daily Mar 20-May 31 9am-7pm; Jun 1-Sept 15 9am-8pm; Sept 16-Oct 31 9am-7pm; Nov 1-Mar 19 9am-4pm. Last entry 30min. before close.*

KAISER-WILHELM-GEDÄCHTNISKIRCH (MEMORIAL CHURCH)   CHURCH
Breitscheidpl.   ☎030 218 50 23

Memorial Church was mostly destroyed in World War II, and to this day it serves as an ominous reminder of wartime destruction. The dramatic, battered church tower is currently being restored and won't be visible from the street for the foreseeable future. All that remains during the interim construction period is a tiny museum in the foyer of Memorial Church. Still, if you're nearby, this exhibition is totally worth checking out. Admission is free, and the exhibition includes some eye-opening, grievous images of wartime Berlin. Right next door is the overstated "New Church," complete with blue glass bling windows reaching far into the sky. Don't bother with the shiny new stuff and stick to contemplation in Memorial Church.

i *On the Kurfürstendamm in the center of Breitscheidpl. ☑ Church open daily 9am-7pm. Exhibit open M-Sa 10am-6pm, Su noon-5pm.*

Schöneberg and Wilmersdorf

Schöneberg sights are a mix of pastoral parks and whatever cultural bits and pieces ended up in this largely residential neighborhood. Travelers with limited time in Berlin should note that attractions here are few and far between and aren't easily and efficiently visited. If you want to see them all, map out your plan and attack these sights in groups.

🏛 GRUNEWALD AND THE JAGDSCHLOSS   PARK
Am Grunewaldsee 29 (Access fromPücklerstr.)   ☎030 813 35 97 www.spsg.de

This 3 sq. km park, with winding paths through wild underbrush, gridded pines, and a peaceful lake, is popular dog-walking turf and a great change from the rest of bustling Berlin. About a 1km walk into the woods is the **Jadgschloß**, a restored royal hunting lodge that houses a gallery of portaits and paintings by German artists like Anton Graff and Lucas Cranach the Elder. The lodge is a picture of understated elegance, surrounded by even more blooming botany. The one-room hunting lodge is worth skipping, unless you find pottery shards particularly enthralling. Instead, walk around the grounds or take a hike north in the forest to **Teufelsberg** ("Devil's Mountain"), the highest point in Berlin that was made from WWII rubble piled over a Nazi military school.

i *U3 or U7: Fehrbelliner Pl., or S45 or S46: Hohenzollerndamm, then bus #115 (dir. Neuruppiner Str. or Spanische Alle/Potsdamer): Pücklerstr. Turn left onto Pücklerstr., follow the signs, and continue straight into the forest to reach the lodge. Check the Jagdschloß visitor center for a map. Hunting lodge €4, students €3. Tours in German €1) offered on weekends. ☑ Open spring-fall Tu-Su 10am-6pm, last entry 5:30pm; winter Sa-Su 10am-4pm, last entry 3:30pm.*

BRÜCKE MUSEUM   MUSEUM
Bussardsteig 9   ☎030 831 20 29 www.brueckemuseum.de

The Brücke (The Bridge) houses a number of brightly-colored oil paintings which you'd think were put together by Monet. Think again. For us non-artistic folk, no-names line every wall of this museum. Their works are part of *Die*

Brücke movement, which showcases thick brushstrokes, super-bright yellows, and other energetic colors. This museum is tiny and extremely far from almost everything else, but for anyone who's heard of *Die Brücke* before, it'll be worth the trek. It's not often you get to experience your passion in a modern building nestled at the edge of a German wood.

i *U3 or U7: Fehberlliner Pl., then bus#115 (dir. Neuruppiner Str. to Spanische Allee/Potsdammer): Finkenstraße, then walk back up Clayallee about 50ft. and turn left onto the footpath leading into the woods. Look for signs. €5, students €3. Cash only. ☺ Open M 11am-5pm and W-Su 11am-5pm.*

ALTER SANKT-MATTHÄUS-KIRCHHOF — CEMETERY
On Großgörschen Str., right next to the lower Yorckstr. S-Bahn Station entrance

We're fairly sure Hansel and Gretel and the mean-nasty witch they killed are all buried in this cemetery. Well, maybe not, but both of the Grimm brothers are. This *Kirchhof* is an expansive and sloping retreat from the city around, and it's isolated from the bustle by tall trees and hushed gardens. Besides the infamous Brothers Grimm, this cemetery is the eternal resting place of Romantic composer Max Bruch. A grand, mid-19th-century chapel juts out from the shrubbery, as do a number of gigantic and increasingly impressive structures that old Berlin families built for their deceased. After you've spent an hour grave hunting, stop by the cafe and flower shop to ease yourself back into the hassles of the living.

i *U7, S2, S25: Yorckstr. ☺ Open in summer M-F 8am-8pm, Sa-Su 9am-8pm; winter M-F 8am-4pm, Sa-Su 9am-8pm. Hours vary by month. Cafe open M-Sa 9am-6pm.*

VIKTORIA-LUISE-PLATZ — PARK
Intersection of Motzstr. and Winterfeldstr.

Come young, come homeless! Like the best German *Plätze*, Viktoria-Luise-Platz just seems to bring everyone together during those blissfully sunny afternoons. There's probably a kid trying out his new skateboard tricks on one side and a young mother watching her child take its first steps on the other. This oasis of a park is named after Wilhelm II's daughter and, in keeping with its name, channels the extravagance of an older, pre-war, bourgeois Berlin, with a central geyser of a fountain and a Greco-Roman-looking row of columns standing guard at one side. Take advantage of the lack of an open container law and bring your booze collection and a blanket to sip lazily amid the perfectly green grass and flowers.

i *U4: Viktoria-Luise-Pl.*

RATHAUS SCHÖNEBERG — COURTHOUSE
John-F.-Kennedy-Pl. 1

The *Rathaus* (literally, "courthouse") here is pretty unremarkable, being the stark, early 19th-century building that it is (so many straight lines!). Still, JFK came here to establish that he was a jelly-filled doughnut during his Translation 101 case study-worthy speech in which he declared, "Ich bin ein Berliner." But this place isn't just a dull and historical courthouse. It also houses a flea market every Saturday and Sunday on the *Platz* out front bearing Jack's name. Even if you come here midweek, the huge park is an ideal spot to romp around, catch some sun, and nibble on whatever foodstuffs you happen to bring with you.

i *U4: Rathaus Schöneberg. ☺ Flea market open Sa-Su 10am-6pm.*

GAY MEMORIAL — MEMORIAL
Just outside the Nollendorf U-Bahn station

Don't blink! You might miss it. This slightly hidden memorial is shaped like a Crayola crayon, with six ultra-neon colors running down its sides. The small monument commemorates homosexuals killed during World War II. There's not a whole lot to see here—the memorial is tiny, and the markings are virtually nonexistent. Still, it's worth turning your head if you happen to pass by on the way to the Nollendorfplatz U-Bahn stop.

i *U1, U3, U4, or U9: Nollendorfpl.*

berlin

Mitte

You might not be looking for any advice, but we'll give it to you anyway: *do not*, we repeat, *do not* plan to do everything and see everything Mitte has to offer. This place is huge, and the sights vary from fountains to state buildings to art museums to museums about the Kennedys to museums about ancient Egypt. Prioritize! Plan ahead! And be selective! There's something here for everyone.

▨ MEMORIAL TO THE MURDERED JEWS OF EUROPE   MEMORIAL
Cora-Berliner-Str. 1   ☎030 263 94 311 www.stiftung-denkmal.de

Stark concrete blocks arranged in a grid pattern across an entire city block commemorate the Jews killed by the Nazis. Though the commotion of the busy streets and cheap apartment blocks surrounding the memorial may seem to discourage reflection, as you walk deeper into the gradually growing blocks, the city recedes in silence. Lose yourself on the uneven paths in the memorial, then head below ground for a moving, informative exhibit on the history of Judaism during World War II. Especially devastating is the "family" room, which presents pre-war Jewish family portraits and then investigates the individual fates of the family members. The last room continuously plays one of thousands of compiled mini-biographies of individuals killed in the Holocaust. To read the bios of every murdered Jew would take over six years.

i U2: Potsdamer Pl. From the metro, walk north on Ebertstr. Free. ☼ Open daily Apr-Sept 10am-8pm; Oct-Mar 10am-7pm.

▨ PERGAMON MUSEUM   MUSEUM
Am Kupfergraben 5   ☎030 209 05 577 www.smb.museum

We aren't kidding when we say that people come all the way to Berlin just to check this place out. Heck, Museum Island might as well be renamed Pergamon Island. So here's the gist: Pergamon was the capital of a Hellenistic kingdom, and the museum reconstructs its temple to nearly its full size, so you can walk up its steep steps. The awe-inspiring battle relief on the wall displays jagged-toothed snakes ripping off heroes' arms while titans tear lions' mouths apart. The Mesopotamian Ishtar Gate, reconstructed tile-by-tile from the original, rises 30m into the air, then stretches 100m down a hallway. You'll hardly believe it, so come see it.

i S5, S7, S9, or S75: Hackescher Markt. From the metro, head south on Burgstr., turn right onto Bodestr., and then right again onto Kupfergraben after crossing the bridge €10, students €5. A Tageskarte (€18, students €9) grants entry to all museums on Museum Island on the day of purchase. ☼ Open M-W 10am-6pm, Th 10am-10pm, F 10am-6pm.

▨ NEUE NATIONAL GALERIE   MUSEUM
Potsdamer Str. 50   ☎030 266 424 510 www.smb.museum

Not to be confused with the **Neues Museum** (p. 243), the Neue Nationalgalerie houses some of the most famous works by early German Modernists (think early 1900s). Featured artists include Franz Marc, Max Ernst, and Ernst Ludwig Kirchner. Sadly, key works were labeled "degenerate" by the Nazis in the 1930s and have since disappeared from the collection. Missing works haunt the gallery in the form of black-and-white photocopies. The permanent exhibition fills the basement, while the spacious, Louvre-like "Temple of Light and Glass" that greets you on the ground floor holds spectacular contemporary exhibits.

i U2: Potsdamer Pl. From the metro, head west on Potsdamer Str. and follow it as it curves south. €10, students €5; with Tageskarte €18/9. Admission includes audio tour. ☼ Open M-W 10am-6pm, Th 10am-10pm, F-Su 10am-6pm.

germany

☒ HOMOSEXUAL MEMORIAL
MEMORIAL

On Ebertstr.   www.stiftung-denkmal.de/en/homosexualmemorial

While Berlin's current acceptance of homosexuality is matched by few other places in the world, this wasn't the case until 1969. Before that, homosexuality was illegal in both East and West Germany under a law passed by the Nazis. As a result, homosexuals were not included in many WWII memorials. This memorial, which opened in 2008, consists of a giant block of gray stone, like a misplaced part of the Memorial to the Murdered Jews of Europe across the street, but with one big difference: if you gaze fixedly into a small window, you can watch a video of two men kissing in slow motion projected on a permanent loop. While containing a definite middle-finger-to-Hitler message, the looped video is also intensely humanizing and worth looking into (quite literally).

i U2: Potsdamer Pl. From the metro, walk north on Ebertstr. The memorial is on the left, in the garden. ☒ Open daily 24hr.

☒ TOPOGRAPHY OF TERROR
MUSEUM

Niederkirchner Str. 8   ☎030 254 50 950 www.topographie.de

The Topography of Terror takes you way back to 1930, and from then it takes you to explore the development of Nazi-/Gestapo-/Secret Service-induced terror. Seriously, prepare to be terrorized. The main exhibit consists of an extended series of maps, graphs, photographs, and an enormous amount of context—you could spend an entire afternoon reading through all the captions and explanations, which are fortunately provided in both German and English. That said, the images are so consistently powerful—and the exhibition so unbelievably exhaustive—that it is a must for any nuanced understanding of the development of Nazi terror. Outside, a newer exhibition of the development of Nazi influence in Berlin runs along the block-long remaining segment of the Berlin Wall.

i U6: Kochstr., or U2: Potsdamer Pl. From the metro, head east on Leipziegerstr. and take a right onto Wilhelmstr. Free. ☒ Open daily 10am-8pm.

FERNSEHENTURM
TOWER

Panoramastr. 1A   ☎030 242 33 33 www.tv-turm.de

At 368m the Fernsehehturm (literally "TV Tower") trumps all other sky pokers in the EU. It's shaped like a lame 1950s space probe on purpose: the East Berliners wanted their neighbors to the west to remember Sputnik every time they looked out their windows in the morning. For better or for worse, capitalism has since co-opted the DDR's (East Germany's) biggest erection, giving you the chance to rocket up into the tower's crowning Christmas ornament for a steep fee. Fortunately, in spite of the hordes of tourists that will inevitably get in your way, the view is incredible and especially worth checking out at the end of your stay, once you have a working vocabulary of Mitte's sights. Otherwise, it's just a big, beautiful mess of towers and roofs.

i U2, U5, or U8: Alexanderpl €12.50, ages 3-16 €8, under 3 free. Entrance requires you to pass through security, so be sure to leave any pocket knives at your hostel. ☒ Open daily Mar-Oct 9am-midnight; Nov-Feb 10am-midnight.

ROTES RATHAUS
CITY HALL

Rathausstr. 15   ☎030 90 260

Take heed at the name: this is about as close as you'll ever come to seeing a house for rats. Well, maybe not. This place is just full of tame politicians these days, though it used to serve as East Berlin's town hall. Today, it houses the Berlin Senate. Berlin, after all, is its own state, so each district has individual state senators who meet at the Rathaus every week. Inside, there are rolls of red carpet and a few small, loosely-related exhibits for intrepid tourists, like a series of aerial photographs of central Berlin from 1943 to 2004. Make sure to check the place out at night: its four brightly glowing clock faces make it look like a robot owl monster.

i *U2: Klosterstr., then head north. Or U2, U5, or U8: Alexanderpl.* 🕐 *Open daily 8am-6pm.*

MARIENKIRCHE   CHURCH
Karl-Liebknecht-Str. 8   ☎030 242 44 67 www.marienkirche-berlin.de

Given Berlin's past, it's pretty incredible to find a building this old in town. St. Marienkirche was built in 1270, and despite periodic renovations (including a major Baroque makeover in 1470), it's still standing. The main draw of this church is an ancient and terrifying mural. In the *Dance of Death,* a line of members of medieval high society (kings and knights) perform said dance alongside skeletons. More recently, the church's new murals consist of badly-drawn graffiti around the back of the main façade.

i *U2, U5, or U8: Alexanderpl. From the metro, walk southwest along Karl-Liebknecht-Str. Free.* 🕐 *Open daily 10am-6pm.*

BERLINER DOM   CHURCH
Am Lustgarten   ☎030 202 69 119 www.berlinerdom.de

You'll have to get over the cringe of paying to enter a church (damn) since this is one of Berlin's grandest buildings. *Dom* means "cathedral," but this 1905 church is Protestant (thus, not really a cathedral). Nonetheless, when it comes to grandeur, it crushes most of the cathedrals you've seen. A museum upstairs shows various failed incarnations of the church, and if you climb some back stairs that seem to get sketchier and sketchier as you proceed, you can actually get to a spectacular rooftop terrace lookout. Don't forget the basement, which contains an enchanting crypt that houses the ghosts of lightweights like the Hohenzollern kings.

i *U2, U5, or U8: Alexanderpl. From the metro, walk southwest on Karl-Liebknecht-Str. Admission €7, students €5, children under 18 free.* 🕐 *Open Apr-Sept M-Sa 9am-8pm, Su noon-8pm; Oct-Mar M-Sa 9am-7pm, Su noon-7pm.*

ST. HEDWIG'S CATHEDRAL   CATHEDRAL
Hinter der Katholischen Kirche 3   ☎030 203 48 10 www.hedwigs-kathedrale.de

Named after Harry Potter's owl (if only!), the biggest and oldest Catholic cathedral in the city is like no cathedral you've seen before; with a billowing dome and an angled overhang, it looks more like God's baseball cap than a church. Due to money troubles, it took about 140 years to build (1747-1887), only to be destroyed about 60 years later by British bombs and eventually reconstructed in the 1960s. As a result, it's got '60s written all over the interior, with long strings of glowing glass balls, perhaps representing a crystalline universe, and abstract stained glass. It's a beautiful and unique cathedral to see, both inside and out, and due to some acoustic miracle, it might be the quietest place you'll find to read this book.

i *U2: Hausvogteipl. From the metro, walk north along Oberwallstr. Look for the copper dome. Free.* 🕐 *Open M-F 10am-5pm, Su 1-5pm.*

REICHSTAG   PARLIAMENT
Pl. der Republik 1   ☎030 227 32 152 www.bundestag.de

The Reichstag serves as the German parliament building. In an attempt to hold politicians and citizens alike to a standard of "openness," the top of the grand building is a 1200-ton glass dome. From the dome, visitors can see parliamentary debates beneath them or look across the waterways and skyline of Berlin. The glass structure also channels sunlight into the government chambers via an aggressive spire of mirrored fragments that juts down toward the floor. A free, automated audio tour tracks your movement up and down the nearly 300m ramp. Stop off at the top for a swell view of the Berlin skyline and to marvel at the fact that this dome—and therefore the Reichstag—is roofless. Rain, snow, and sleet all fall into the building and land in a giant "cone" located on the dome's floor. Visitors can trek around the roof terrace while avoiding the solar panels that make the Reichstag the world's only zero-emission congress.

i Bus #100: Pl. der Republik. U55: Reichstag. To access the roof, you must reserve an appointment online at least 2 days beforehand. Free. ☼ Open daily 8am-10pm.

SOVIET MEMORIAL   MEMORIAL
Str. des 17 Juni

While most of Berlin's memorials were built in reflection, the Soviet Memorial was put together in 1945, during the action. As such, it tries to make you feel like the Battle of Berlin was just yesterday. The memorial is flanked by WWII tanks, anti-aircraft guns, and boyish, Lego-loving men to admire them. A famed, larger-than-life copper soldier is the image of the 2000 unnamed men buried in this complex. After taking several photos of a writing system you can't even sound out, make sure to check out the tiny outdoor exhibit behind the memorial to get some historical context that has been translated into English. Haunting photos of a desolate post-war Berlin and of Soviet battlefields covered with bodies make this memorial more than just an overbearing sign of Soviet militarism.

i Bus #100: Pl. der Republik. Head south through Tiergarten to Str. des 17 Juni and take a right. Free. ☼ Open daily 24hr.

NEUE WACHE   MEMORIAL
Unter den Linden 4   ☎030 250 025

Neue Wache (literally "New Watch") originally housed the royal palace guards. In 1969, after both devastating World Wars, an unnamed soldier and an unnamed concentration camp victim were laid to rest here. The memorial is nothing short of eerie, with a small amount of light propagating from the roof toward a mesmerizing sculpture by Käthe Kollwitz. The sculpture is aptly titled "Mother with her Dead Son." Aside from this grand adornment, the room is empty. There's little so affecting as the echo of a footstep within this room.

i U2: Hausvogteipl. From the metro, walk north along Oberwallstr. Free. ☼ Open daily 10am-6pm. The interior of the monument is still visible when the gate is closed.

BEBELPLATZ   SQUARE, MEMORIAL
Bebelpl.

In 1933, a crazed group of Nazi students raided the Humboldt library and burned over 20,000 volumes of "un-German" books written by Jews, communists, and homosexuals. A plaque displays Heinrich Heine's prophetic words: "Where they burn books, they will eventually burn people." Visitors can look down through a glass window into a library full of empty white shelves. It's a haunting sight to see, especially if you happen upon it accidentally. Unless you just want to see a reflection of the sky or your face, come at night, when the memorial is lit from the inside.

i U2: Hausvogteipl. From the metro, walk north along Oberwalstr. The window lies in front of the Humboldt University building labeled "Juristische Fakultät."

NEUES MUSEUM   MUSEUM
Bodestr. 1   ☎030 266 424 242 www.neues-museum.de

Oddly enough, the Neues Museum (literally "New Museum") houses the old. Tourists don't just visit this place because it's on Museum Island—its collection earned it a spot among the stars. As one of the best museums in Berlin, Neues keeps an incredibly vast collection of unbelievably well-preserved artifacts from the ancient world, with everything from jewelry to sculpture to the most intricate coffins you've ever seen. Mummies run rampant, sarcophagi multiply, and somewhere in it all, that famous bust of Nefertiti—yeah, that one—sits glowing in her own gallery. The building was heavily damaged in WWII, and this new New Museum incorporates the old collection into a spectacularly modern complex.

Wander into the central chamber on the second floor, and you might just feel like the slab of granite you're standing on is floating through some esoteric Egyptian incantation. To avoid the lines, reserve a ticket online.

i *U6: Friedrichstr., or S5, S7, S75, or S9: Hackescher Markt. From the S-Bahn, head south on Burgstr., then turn right onto Bodestr. The museum is on the right, but the ticket office is on the left before the river. Tickets correspond to a time; once they've been purchased, visitors must return at the time printed on their ticket. €10, students €5; with Tageskarte €18/9. ☉ Open M-W 10am-6pm, Th-Sa 10am-8pm, Su 10am-6pm.*

TACHELES
GALLERY
Oranienburger Str. 53   ☎030 282 61 85 www.tacheles.de

When was the last time you went to check out a bombed-out department store? That's what we thought. Well, here's your chance. Though you can no longer enter Tacheles, it remains an unforgettable experience, day or night. Once a street-art metropolis, all that remains for the public to admire is a graffiti-covered and bomb-damaged exterior. There's a courtyard around back that attempts to keep the spirit of Tacheles alive, but unfortunately, said spirit is drowning underneath capitalism. Almost every sculpture in the Tacheles courtyard is for sale, and not for cheap sale either. Tacheles is likely in the process of dying; there's even been talk in the town of ripping this place down, so go and look while you still can.

i *U6: Oranienburger Tor. From the metro, head east on Oranienburgerstr. Tacheles is on the right. Courtyard free. Building closed. ☉ Open daily 8am-late.*

THE KENNEDYS
MUSEUM
Pariser Pl. 4A   ☎030 206 53 570 www.thekennedys.de

The Kennedys is half museum, half art gallery. It houses an exhibit of photographs and rare memorabilia— JFK's suitcases, matches, and pens—and shows museum-goers the Kennedys' progression from Irish immigrants to America's political elite. Berlin seems to be extremely fond of the Kennedys, and not just for JFK's über-famous *"Ich bin ein Berliner"* comment—the city's relationship with the Kennedys started what the museum repeatedly refers to as the great German-American friendship. You may end up learning more about the Kennedys than you ever wanted to know, and the exhibition can often seem far too starry-eyed for its handsome protagonist, but the photographs are engaging, especially the ones you don't recognize. Anticipate seeing hundreds of pics of the Kennedys playing with their children, but don't expect to see any snaps of JFK wearing his reading glasses.

i *S1, S25, or U55: Brandenburger Tor. From the metro, walk west toward Brandenburg Gate, then turn right into the square immediately before the Gate. €5, students €2.50. ☉ Open daily 10am-6pm.*

HAMBURGER BAHNHOF MUSEUM
MUSEUM
Invalidenstr. 50-51   ☎030 397 83 439 www.hamburgerbahnhof.de

If you're expecting a museum devoted to trains, try not to be too disappointed. This massive museum stretches the entire length of an old station, but it showcases modern masterworks from the art world. Expect to see gigantic Andy Warhol prints (including a very colorful Chairman Mao) alongside several pioneering Minimalist works, with boldly (and often annoyingly) conceptual works. You may find yourself playing a Guitar Hero version of a one-note Lamont Young piece; then again, you may also find yourself lost and trembling in the back of a dark tunnel. Wherever it is, it will take a lot of walking to get back to the entrance—this museum stretches for leagues in every direction.

i *S5, S7, S9, or S75: Hauptbahnhof. From the metro, exit through the northern exit, then walk northeast on Invalidenstr. On the left, the museum is set back in a small court hidden by vegetation. €12, students €6. ☉ Open Tu-F 10am-6pm, Sa 11am-8pm, Su 11am-6pm.*

ALTE NATIONAL GALERIE

Bodestr. 1-3

GALLERY

☎030 209 05 577 www.smb.museum

This wide collection of mostly German *fin de siécle* and early 20th-century art does special justice to masters like Adolph Menzel, whose Realist canvases are all over the first floor, including a grotesque painting of his own feet. The exhibition is also very Romanticism-heavy, so you may get a little tired of the same idealized golden cliffs and imaginary castles after you've seen them several times over. Music fans will note the famous portrait of Richard Wagner. One of the museum's main strengths is its small assortment of French Impressionist works on the second floor, including absolute beauts by Monet, Manet, Munet (okay, maybe not Munet), and Renoir.

i S3, S5, or S75: Hackescher Markt. From the metro, head south on Burgstr. and turn right onto Bodestr. The museum is on the right. €10, students €5; with Tageskarte €18/9. ☒ Open M-W 10am-6pm, Th 10am-10pm, F-Su 10am-6pm.

ALTES MUSEUM

Am Lustgarten

MUSEUM

www.smb.museum

This *alt* ("old") museum looks like it's smiling widely, with its pillarly teeth next to the Berliner Dom. True to its name, the collection focuses on the old—it's filled with Roman and Etruscan antiquities, including a wide range of pottery, sculpture, jewelry, and other artifacts from the daily lives of the long dead. After seeing the Pergamon and the Neues Museum, you might feel a little relieved once a gilded bronze victory goddess waves goodbye atthe end of this permanent exhibition. But don't let this museum be overshadowed by its flashier neighbors; its rebuilt central hall, with imposing marble busts surrounding you at every angle, may induce euphoria.

i U2, U5, or U8: Alexanderpl. From the metro, head southwest on Karl-Liebknecht-Str. and turn right after the Berliner Dom €10, students €5; with Tageskarte €18/9. ☒ Open M-W 10am-6pm, Th 10am-10pm, F-Su 10am-6pm.

HOUSE OF WORLD CULTURES

John-Foster-Dulles-Allee 10

EXHIBIT HALL

☎030 397 87 175 www.hkw.de

The House of World Cultures is pretty much always doing something different, so we can't promise you anything about the exhibits you'll see here, but we can promise that you'll feel like you're entering an analog world. This place was first put together by Yanks who wanted to show off to the nearby East Berliners. These days, the House of World Cultures hosts festivals, movie screenings, lectures, and a bookstore with more instances of the word "revolution" than hundreds of high school history textbooks combined. A bizarre structure that's been affectionately dubbed "The Pregnant Clam," this place is only worth the walk when something's afoot inside, so check the website before plotting your route.

i U55: Bundestag. From the metro, head west on Paul Löbe Allee. Free. Event prices vary. ☒ Open daily 10am-7pm. Exhibitions open M 11am-7pm, W-Su 11am-7pm.

MUSEUM FOR FILM AND TELEVISION

Potsdamer Str. 2

MUSEUM

☎030 300 90 30 www.deutsche-kinemathek.de

Before Hollywood, Germany was the queen of cinema. This fun little exhibit commemorates those times, with a special emphasis on the work of Fritz Lang and Marlene Dietrich. Sometimes it feels like attending a party where you don't know anyone, but the production photos and set drawings of *The Cabinet of Dr. Caligari* and *Metropolis* are worth the admission price alone. Film buffs will be rewarded, and film gruffs will still find a few things to tickle them. One such tickler is perhaps the strangest cola ad you've ever seen, involving a girl, some straws, a nicotine patch, and a heavy dose of jarring camera cuts.

i U2: Potsdamer Pl. From the metro, head west on Potsdamer Str. €6, students €4.50. ☒ Open Tu-W 10am-6pm, Th 10am-8pm, F-Su 10am-6pm.

berlin

AKADEMIE DER KÜNSTE

Pariser Pl. 4

EXHIBIT HALL

☎030 200 570 www.adk.de

Exhibits change every two months in this glassy modern hall that serves as the headquarters for the Akademie der Künste, a society of famous German artists. Independent exhibitions tend toward the bold and progressive in media, ranging from photography to design to traditional painting to interactive video installations. One recent exhibition on female film directors featured a long table lined with constantly looping computer screens. Though the shiny exterior stands out from the buildings around it, incredibly, the walls of the exhibit hall are the original 17th-century pieces, and the modern hall has been built around it.

i Bus #100, #200, or S1, S2: Brandenburger Tor. From the metro, head west toward the Brandenburg Gate. The hall is on the left as you enter the square, before the Gate. €5, students €3-4. Free 1st Su of the month. ⧖ Open Tu-Su 11am-8pm.

BERTOLT BRECHT HAUS

Chausseestr. 125

MUSEUM

☎030 200 571 844 www.adk.de

Bertolt Brecht and his wife revolutionized theater through one of the most influential dramatic theories of the 20th century, and this tour lets you not only glimpse but downright stare at his personal life. Brecht's apartment, preserved by his wife, the actress Helene Weigel, is comprised of two studies, the bedroom where he croaked, and part of his library, all of which are filled with small, noteworthy artifacts. Come with an English-speaking crew so they'll do the tour in English; otherwise, you'll be stuck reading along and wondering if the Germans are mocking you whenever they laugh.

i U6: Oranienburger Tor. From the U-Bahn, head north on Chausseestr. The house is on the left. There's no real sign, so look for the address. Guided tours are obligatory. €4, students €2.50. ⧖ Tours every 30min. Tu 10-11:30am and 2-3:30pm; W 10-11:30am; Th 10-11:30am and 5-6:30pm; F 10, 10:30, and 11:30am; Sa 10-noon and 1-3:30pm; Su 11am, noon, and every hr. 1-6pm.

TIERGARTEN

Tiergarten

PARK

www.berlin.de/orte/sehenswuerdigkeiten/tiergarten

Stretching from the Brandenburg Gate in the east to the Bahnhof Zoo in the west, this enormous park at the heart of Berlin contains some of the city's most iconic monuments, including the **Victory Column** and the **Soviet Memorial** (p. 243). Str. des 17 Juni bisects the park from east to west and frequently hosts parades, celebrations, and markets. The park is perfectly manicured in parts and wild in others and also contains some beautiful paths, ponds, and gardens that can offer solace from the heat and hordes of hipsters.

i Bus #100, #200, or S1, S2: Brandenburger Tor. From the metro, head west on Unter den Linden.

BRANDENBERG GATE

Pariser Pl.

GATE

☎030 226 33 017

You've already seen its image obnoxiously covering the windows of every passing U-Bahn train, but upon approaching the real Brandenburg Gate for the first time, trumpets may still blare in your head. During the day, tourists swarm this famous 18th-century gate; however, the wise traveler will return at night to see it ablaze in gold. Friedrich Wilhelm II built the gate as a symbol of military victory, but Germans these days prefer to shy away from that designation. A system of gates (and, independently, a certain famous wall) once surrounded it, but today only this most famous gate remains.

i S1, S2, or S25: Brandenburger Tor.

Prenzlauer Berg

Prenzlauer Berg isn't the place for sightseeing. There are a couple of treasures, namely **Mauerpark** and random bits of the remaining Berlin Wall, but this part of the city is mostly about hip bars, boutiques, and cafes.

▨ MAUERPARK   PARK
Extends north of the intersection between Eberswalder Str. and Schwedter Str.

Mauerpark is the heart and soul of Prenzlauer Berg. It's a grungy, sprawling, all-in-one park: you'll find a flea market, a stadium, some unique graffiti (if your name is Alex, there's even a marriage proposal!), day-drinking, a huge playground, men walking their dogs, and Sunday afternoon karaoke. In summary, Mauerpark is a park designed to exemplify the very essence of Berlin—perhaps as a thesis, spoken through a loudspeaker. We don't recommend taking a nap here, but we do recommend spending some time appreciating everything it has to offer.

i U2: Eberswalder Str. From the metro, walk west on Eberswalder Str. Mauerpark extends far to the north after you pass the stadium. Free.

▨ BERLINER MAUER DOKUMENTATIONSZENTRUM   MUSEUM, MONUMENT
Bernauer Str. 111   ☎030 464 10 30 www.berliner-mauer-gedenkstaette.de

A remembrance complex, museum, chapel, and entire city block of a preserved portion of Berlin Wall (complete with watch tower) come together in this memorial to "victims of the Communist tyranny." The church is made of an inner oval of poured cement walls, lit from above by a large skylight and surrounded by a transparent skeleton of two-by-fours. The museum has assembled a comprehensive collection of all things Berlin Wall, including original recordings, telegrams, blueprints, film footage, and photos. Climb up a staircase to see the wall from above.

i U8: Bernauer Str. From the metro, walk north on Brunnen Str., then turn left onto Bernauer Str. The church and memorial are on the left before Ackerstr., and the Dokumentationszentrum and exhibition are on the right immediately after Ackestr. Free. ☐ Open Apr-Oct Tu-Su 9:30am-7pm; Nov-Mar 9:30am-6pm.

JÜDISCHER FRIEDHOF   CEMETERY
Schönhauser Allee

Prenzlauer Berg was one of the major centers of Jewish Berlin during the 19th and early 20th centuries. This ivy-covered Jewish cemetery contains the graves of composer Giacomo Meyerbeer and artist Max Liebermann and is studded by impressively high, dark tombs under towering trees. It's currently in a disappointing state of disrepair, with countless overturned tombstones and fallen trees, but it's still a beautiful grove worth wandering through. Nearby, **Synagogue Rykstrasse** (Rykestr. 53, right next to the Wasserturm) is one of Berlin's loveliest synagogues and one of the few spared on *Kristallnacht*. Since the synagogue still operates as a school, visitors aren't allowed to enter, but the red-brick, turn-of-the-century façade is impressive enough to warrant a visit.

i U2: Senefelderpl. From the metro, walk north on Schönhauser Allee. The gate to the cemetery is on the right, near the Lapidarium. Free. ☐ Open M-Th 8am-4pm, F 8am-1pm.

ZEISS-GROSS PLANETARIUM   PLANETARIUM
Prenzlauer Allee 80   ☎030 421 84 50 www.astw.de

In 1987, this spherical planetarium opened as the most modern facility of its kind in the DDR. Would you believe that they had technology as advanced as the radio? The technology paled in comparison to what was going on in the West at the time, but today it can still show you the stars, sometimes with accompanying Bach or commentary for children. There are no exhibits, only shows, so check the website or call ahead for times.

i S8, S41, S42, or tram M2: Prenzlauer Allee. From the metro, the planetarium is across the bridge, on the left €5, students €4. ☐ Shows Tu-Th 9am-noon and 1-5pm, F 9am-noon and 1-9:30pm, Sa 2:30-9pm, Su 1:30-5pm.

berlin

Friedrichshain

VOLKSPARK FRIEDRICHSHAIN
PARK

Volkspark Friedrichshain isn't the largest park in Berlin; it loses out to the **Tiergarten** in Mitte in terms of both size and class. But this brings us to the age old question: does size really matter? Volkspark compensates by attracting tons of people, from dog-walkers to kite-fliers to sunbathers. Monuments have popped up around the park as well, the most popular being the **Märchenbrunnen,** or the "Fairy Tale Fountain," a fountain that depicts 10 Grimm characters around a tremendous cascade of water. **Mount Klemont** gained its mass from the enormous pile of rubble swept beneath it in 1950 from two bomb-destroyed World War II bunkers; today, it occasionally serves as a platform for open-air concerts and movie screenings. With perhaps too much history for its own good, the park still draws thousands from their homes on nice days.

i *S8 or S10: Landsberger Allee or U5: Strausbg. Pl. From Strausbg. Pl., walk north on Lichtenberger Str. Bounded by Am Friedrichshain to the north, Danziger Str. to the east, Landsberger Allee to the south, and Friedenstr. Str. to the south.*

EAST SIDE GALLERY
MONUMENT

Along Mühlenstr.
www.eastsidegallery.com

The longest remaining portion of the Berlin Wall, this 1.3km stretch of cement slabs has been converted into the world's largest open-air art gallery. The Cold War graffiti is unfortunately long departed; instead, the current murals hail from an international group of artists who gathered in 1989 to celebrate the Wall's fall. One of the most famous contributions is by artist Dmitri Wrubel, who depicted a wet, wrinkly political kiss between Leonid Brezhnev and East German leader Erich Honecker. The stretch of street remains unsupervised and, on the Warschauer Str. side, open at all hours, but vandalism is surprisingly rare.

i *U1, U15, S3, S5, S6, S7, S9, or S75: Warschauer Str. or S5, S7, S9, or S75: Ostbahnhof. From the metro, walk back toward the river. Free.*

STASI MUSEUM
MUSEUM

Ruschestr. 103, Haus 1
☎030 553 68 54 www.stasimuseum.de

It's odd to imagine that this was once the most feared building in all of Germany: the Stasi Museum is housed in the gigantic headquarters of the East German secret police, the **Staatssicherheit,** or **Stasi.** During the Cold War, the Stasi kept dossiers on some six million of East Germany's own citizens, an amazing feat and a testament to the huge number of civilian informers in a country of only 16 million people. Since a 1991 law made the records public, the "Horror Files" have rocked Germany, exposing millions of informants and destroying careers, marriages, and friendships at every level of German society. The museum exhibition presents a wide array of original Stasi artifacts, among which is a mind-blowing collection of concealed microphones and cameras. All we want to know is how nobody noticed the bulky microphone concealed under a tie.

i *U5: Magdalenenstr €5, students €4. Exhibits in German; English info booklet €3. ⏰ Open M-F 10am-6pm, Sa-Su noon-6pm.*

Kreuzberg

None of Kreuzberg's sights are essential, especially compared to their glamorous cousins in Mitte, but if you're interested in something other than grunge, there are several museums, parks, and buildings you should consider stopping at. In addition to the sights we've listed, Kreuzberg also has several beautiful 19th-century churches that are worth a peek, including **Saint-Michael-Kirche** (Michaelkirchpl.), the **Heilig-Kreuz-Kirche** (Zossener Str. 65), and **Saint Thomas-Kirche** (Bethaniendamm 23-27).

germany

DEUTSCHES TECHNIKMUSEUM BERLIN   MUSEUM

Trebbiner Str. 9   ☎030 902 54 0 www.sdtb.de

With 30 full-size airplanes, 20 boats—including a full-size Viking relic—and a train from every decade since 1880, this museum could be a city in itself. Its permanent exhibitions cover everything from aerospace to road traffic to photo technology, but the special exhibitions also manage to be enticing. Most recently, Technikmuseum showed off 30 years in 30 photographs, a small but incredibly charming tour of the museum's technological prowess. But if photographs don't appeal, we find it hard to believe that World War II planes used for the Berlin Airlift, a U-boat, and a WWII rocket won't please.

i *U1 or U2: Gleisdreieck. From the metro, head east on Luckenwalder Str. and turn right onto Tempelhofer Ufer. Walk under the train tracks and turn right onto Trebbiner Str. The entrance is about¾ of the way down Trebbiner Str. Many exhibits in English. €6, students €3.50; after 3pm, admission is free for children and students under 18. ⚅ Open Tu-F 9am-5:30pm, Sa-Su 10am-6pm.*

SOVIET WAR MEMORIAL   MEMORIAL

Treptower Park

This memorial, a commemoration of Soviet soldiers who gave the ultimate sacrifice during the Battle of Berlin, is humongous. At 20,000 sq. m, it puts Mitte's **Soviet Memorial** to shame. Two jagged triangular slabs, each bearing the hammer and sickle, guard a tremendous rectangular square lined by exquisitely cut shrubs and surrounded by marble reliefs of Soviet soldiers helping the poor and the huddled. Quotes from Stalin in the original Russian and in German surround you at every step. But the most impressive piece stands at the end of the square: a tremendous, grassy mound bears a giant bronze statue of a Soviet soldier crushing a broken swastika and lugging a sword.

i *U1 or U15: Schlesisches Tor. From the metro, walk southeast on Schlesische Str. Cross both canals and continue until you reach a fork in the road, between Puschkinallee and Am Treptower Park. Take Puschkinallee and walk along the park until you reach a large, semicircular courtyard with an entrance gate. Turn into this courtyard; the memorial is on the left. Free. ⚅ Open 24hr.*

JEWISH MUSEUM   MUSEUM

Lindenstr. 9-14   ☎030 259 93 300 www.jmberlin.de

You'd know the Jewish Museum was important just from a single glance from outside the building: traffic blockades and security personnel swarm around the place, and you have to go through a security checkpoint to enter the museum. The building itself plays a significant role in the portrayal of its exhibitions: Daniel Libeskind designed the building to reflect the discomfort, pain, and the inherent voids in Jewish history, manifesting these characteristics as tremendous, triangular shafts, inaccessible rooms, and uneven floors. It's an amazing museum that actually succeeds at being experiential: it's disorienting, frightening, and historical.

i *U1 or U6: Hallesches Tor. From the station, head east on Gitschinerstr. and take a left at Lindenstr. €7, students €3.50, under 6 free. Audio tour €3. ⚅ Open M 10am-10pm, Tu-Su 10am-8pm. Last entry 1hr. before close.*

CHECKPOINT CHARLIE   HISTORIC SITE

Zimmerstr. and Friedrichstr.

Though we really don't like this place, we can't leave it out: Checkpoint Charlie is incredibly popular, absurd, and has hundreds of tourists and multiple Starbucks cafes (which practically don't exist in Berlin) on one street. Never, ever have we seen more of a tourist trap. Though Checkpoint Charlie was once important to Berlin as the entrance to the American sector of West Berlin, today it's nothing but a mock entrance point, with German men dressed as American soldiers. You guessed it—you can take your picture with them for two badly-spent euro. A set of placards along Kochstr. provides a somewhat interesting history on the

berlin

checkpoint and the various escapes it witnessed. Skip the museum: with admission at €12.50, you're better off buying a few beers.

i U6: Kochstraße. From the metro, walk north on Friedrichstr. Free. Museum €12.50, students €9.50. ☒ Open 24hr.

FOOD

Charlottenburg is not known for its budget-friendly fare, so head north to Moabit for cheap, authentic Turkish or Vietnamese food. Check out Schöneberg's relaxed cafe culture around the intersection of Maaßenstr. and Winterfeldstr. In Mitte, it's best to avoid overpriced restaurants and cafes near major sights. Prenzlauer Berg is another cafe capital: check out Kastanienallee or the streets around Helmholtzpl. for the highest concentration of caffeine. Some of Friedrichshain's narrow cobblestone streets are lined with cheap cafes, ice cream joints, and reasonably priced restaurants. The intersection of Simon-Dach-Str. and Grünbergerstr. is a good place to start. For the best international cuisine in a city known for cheap ethnic fare, head to Kreuzberg, where incredible restaurants line Oranienstraße, Bergmannstraße, and Schlesische Straße.

Charlottenburg

KASTANIE
BEER GARDEN

Schloßstr. 22 ☎030 321 50 34 www.kastanie-berlin.de

Ashoka Kastanie is a traditional beer garden hidden on the west side of Schloßstr. It serves up most of the classic German favorites, including *Warmer Leberkäse mit Laugengebäck* (meatloaf with pretzels, €3.50) and makes an especially delightful Spargelquiche (asparagus quiche, €6.50). Complete with weathered wooden tables spreading across the shaded grounds and packed bike-racks outside, Kastanie is quite the authentic neighborhood restaurant. Still, the colorful wooden masks hanging above the *Biergarten* suggest a quaint quirkiness. Kastanie is a perfect spot for brunch on a sunny afternoon. An added bonus: Kastanie is only a stone's throw from **Schloß Charlottenburg** (p. 237) and its surrounding museums.

i U2: Sophie-Charlotte Pl. Walk up Schloßstr. toward the Schloß. Kastanie is on the left-hand side of Schloßstr. Entrees €4-8. Beer €3. Cash only. ☒ Open daily 10am-2am.

ASHOKA
INDIAN $

Grolmanstr. 51 ☎030 310 15 806 http://www.myashoka.de

Charlottenburg is expensive, but Ashoka is not. It's totally possible to eat a full, delicious, warm meal in this restaurant for less than €6, especially if you keep to the vegetarian options. Every curry (€4-8) comes with rice or bread and a salad. Try the Mattar Panir (€4.60) for creamy peas and cheese curry to write home about. This restaurant is a hole-in-the-wall without that much seating, but the space available is comfortable and backpacker friendly. No promises, but if you're lucky, Ashoka might even serve you tap water!

i U2 or U9: Zoologischer Garten. From the metro, walk south on Joachimstaler Str. and turn right onto Kantstr. Turn right onto Savignypl., then right onto Grolmanstr. Ashoka is on the right. ☒ Open daily noon-midnight.

SCHWARZES CAFE
BAR, RESTAURANT $$$

Kantstr. 148 ☎030 313 80 38

Get this: Schwarzes Cafe is open 24/7, and it's not a *Dönerkebab* stall. In fact, it's everything but *Dönerkebab*. The hip cafe that it is, Schwarzes serves up every meal at every hour of the day, making it a perfect place to find a hummus platter (€6.20) at 4am. It's expensive, but you're probably going to stop caring after you've kicked back an absinthe. Literally meaning "black cafe," we'd guess that

germany

the (partially) black interior alongside the classic exposed bricks of this place was designed by a guy who wears a fedora. Just a guess.

i S3, S5, S7, S9, or S75: Savignypl. Weekly special €7-13 (served 11:30am-8pm). Breakfast €5-8.50. Drinks €3-7. Cash only. ☼ Open daily 24hr.

FAM DANG
Hutten Str. 5

VIETNAMESE $$
☎030 755 67 526

Located in a predominantly Vietnamese area, Fam Dang's bright rooms, outdoor patio, and ridiculously inexpensive daily menu make it a must. Drop by during the busy noon hour to watch the waitresses careen around with tremendous white bowls as they rapidly rail away in accented German at a middle-aged, professional crowd on its lunch break. The soup menu includes a wide variety of Vietnamese favorites, like glass noodle soup. Portions are gigantic, so be sure to come starving and thirsty.

i Bus M27: Turnstr./Beusselstr. Entrees €5. Cash only. ☼ Open M-F 11am-9pm, Sa noon-9pm.

ABBAS
Huttenstr. 71

MIDDLE EASTERN $
☎030 343 47 770

A candy store turned Middle Eastern joint, this sprawling shop sells dozens of varieties of baklava, nuts, and desserts on the cheap, from chocolate-covered lentils to pistachio-cashew pastries. Try the specialty baklava (€3); you'll be licking sweet, delicious honey off your fingers for hours. Abbas is an ideal place to swing by and pick up a box of some yummy nibbles for a later hour. Abbas is situated in a poorer area of Charlottenberg. Dress conservatively, lest you enjoy a potential scowl from the folks in charge.

i Bus M27: Turmstr./Beusselstr. Cash only. ☼ Open M-Th 10am-5pm, F-Su noon-8pm.

MENSA TU
Hardenbergerstr. 34

CAFETERIA $
☎030 939 39 7439

No, your IQ doesn't have to be in the 98th percentile to eat at Mensa TU. This Mensa is a cafeteria for TU Berlin, the city's premiere technical institute. It caters to students, so meals here are dirt cheap (€2-5). The Mensa is a vibrant TU social spot and is constantly buzzing with loud conversation. The best part? You get to load up your own plate with as much as you can fit on it. In keeping with its being a cafeteria, it's easy to fill up on the food but a little harder to enjoy it. Unless you're looking for a cup of joe, watch your euro and be careful to avoid the higher-priced cafe downstairs.

i U2: Ernst-Reuter-Pl. or bus #245: Steinpl. The cafeteria is a 10min. walk from Bahnhof Zoo. Meal €4-5, students €2-3. Cash only. ☼ Open M-F 11am-2:30pm.

LA PETIT FRANCE CROISSANTERIE
Nürnberger Str. 24A

CAFE $
☎017 817 11 3826

With enough room inside to fit all of about 10 people, this cafe is tiny. Really tiny. But they serve up some fresh and inexpensive French-style lunches, and these make for an especially easy impromptu picnic. Try the baguettes with a variety of toppings, including tomato, mozzarella, and basil ("grande" size €3.50). It might be hard to feel full after lunch at Le Petit France Croissanterie, so use this place for a break in your day rather than a full meal.

i U3 to Ausgburger Str. Baguettes from €2.50. Pasta and salad combo €4.50. Cash only. ☼ Open M-Sa 8am-6:30pm.

Schöneberg and Wilmersdorf

Schöneberg's relaxed cafe culture is best experienced around the intersection of **Maaßenstrasse** and **Winterfeldstrasse**. More popular cafes and inexpensive restaurants crowd the **Akazienstrasse,** which runs from the U-Bahn station at Eisenacherstr. to Hauptstr. All in all, come for the foamy coffee but stay for the eclectic foreign cuisine.

berlin

CAFÉ BILDERBUCH

CAFE $$

Akazienstr. 28 ☎030 787 06 057 www.cafe-bilderbruch.de

We're fairly sure that Café BilderBuch was decorated in the 19th century by a crazy woman who was convinced she was royalty. The antique cabinets, fringed lamps, deep-cushioned sofas, and adjoining library make this a unique place to visit. But none of that matters as much as the food and coffee. While this place is a little more expensive than the coffee shop, **Double Eye,** just down the street, Café BilderBuch provides a delightfully leisurely experience. This joint is especially well known for its delicious brunches and bowls of coffee (*ein Milchkaffee*, €2.60). The brunch menu is good enough to compel you to shove grandmothers out of the way to get in the door. Try the *"Der Froschkönig"* ("The Frog Prince") combo, which includes salmon, trout, caviar, and a glass of prosecco. The menu, printed on the cafe's own press, doubles as a weekly newspaper and includes the neighborhood's goings-on.

i U7: Eisenacher Str. Free Wi-Fi. Soup from €3.70. Salads from €6. Entrees €8. Coffee €1.50. Cash only. ⏰ Open M-Sa 9am-midnight, Su 10am-midnight. Kitchen closes daily 11pm.

BAHARAT FALAFEL

TURKISH $$

Winterfeldtstr. 37 ☎030 216 83 01

Don't confuse this Turkish restaurant for a *döner* stand. Baharat Falafel makes all of its falafel fresh and fried to order, nestling them in a fluffy pita with lots of tomatoes, lettuce, and mango or chili sauce. Wash down Baharat's slightly expensive plates (hummus, tabbouleh, and salad, €8) with fresh-squeezed *Gute-Laune Saft* (good-mood juice, €1-2), which tastes sublimely refreshing in a land where even water is a soft drink. Indoor seating (with a map of Iraq on the bright walls) or an outdoor bench under a striped awning are comfortable settings for your messy nom-nom-nomming.

i U1, U3, U4, or U9: Nollendorfpl. Sandwiches from €3.50. Entrees €7-9. Cash only. ⏰ Open M-Sa 11am-2am, Su noon-2am.

HIMALI

TIBETAN, NEPALESE $$$

Crellestr. 45 ☎030 787 16 175 www.himali-restaurant.de

Step into Himali and prepare to be greeted by the delightful aroma from the tandoori oven. This place keeps that thing fired up and spitting out piping hot Nepali and Tibetan classics all day long. You don't come here to eat and leave— you come here to eat, relax, nibble, and enjoy. Seriously, lunch can easily take an hour and a half here. Everything on the menu is spiced into submission, with the spices grown and ground in-house. This is an excellent stop for vegetarians, with many meat-free dishes available, but (sorry PETA) we prefer the carnivorous *Seekh Kebab* (tandoori-prepared lamb, €10.50).

i U7: Kleistpark. Walk up Langenscheidtstr. uphill and turn right onto Crellestr. Entrees €6.50-12. ⏰ Open daily noon-midnight.

DOUBLE EYE

CAFE $

Akazienstr. 22 ☎017 945 66 960 www.doubleeye.de

Don't come to Double Eye expecting to relax. If you want to relax, pay twice as much and head to **Cafe BilderBuch** just down the street. Double Eye means business. The cafe is tiny but constantly busy. Want to know how they manage it? They give you 10min. to down your perfect, delicious, foamy, delightful coffee—10min. tops. Okay, so maybe no one's timing you as you glug your latte, but there really isn't space here for you to lounge around. Come, buy coffee, drink coffee, read newspaper headlines, leave. It's that simple. One final warning: if you ask for anything syrupy or sugary in your coffee, DoubleEye baristas reserve the right to laugh in your face. Coffee purists rejoice.

i U7: Eisenacher Str. All drink €1-3. Milchkaffee (soup bowl-sized coffee with milk) €2.20. Cash only. ⏰ Open M-F 8:33am-7:29pm, Sa 9:01am-6:29pm. No, we are not kidding.

germany

CAFÉ EINSTEIN
VIENNESE CAFE $$$

Kurfurstenstr. 58   ☎030 261 50 96 www.cafeeinstein.com

You don't have to be a rocket scientist to enjoy Café Einstein. Nope, Berlin's premier Viennese coffee shop welcomes all. That is, it welcomes all who are well-dressed. And by "well-dressed," we don't mean that awesomely hideous Christmas sweater you wear year-round. The estate is grand, and it's almost intimidating to enter, especially if you're living the rugged backpacker life and haven't showered for days. You'll want time to slow down as you cherish a small cake or **Apfelstrudel**, which are some of the least expensive (but quite possibly the tastiest) ways to enjoy the cafe's dark, wood-paneled walls and detailed molding.

i *U1, U3, U4, or U9: Nollendorfpl. Entrees €15-22. Breakfast from €5.80. Su brunch bar €13.* ⏰ *Open daily 6am-1am.*

BERLIN BURRITO COMPANY
BURRITOS $

Pallasstr. 21   ☎030 236 24 990 www.berlin-burrito-company.de

All right, we see you. You're narrowing your eyes and muttering self-righteously to yourself, "Burritos have nothing to do with Berlin." It's okay, we forgive you. For those college kids who have spent an entire year eating a burrito for every meal, locating the nearest cheap burrito place could make or break their time exploring Berlin. Anyway, this place isn't your usual Chipotle. This place is cheap and delicious, with fillings like lime chicken and spicy tomato habañero sauce (yum). And with the clean and colorful walls, see-through barber shop chairs, and some dark electro-tunes you've never heard before, this little burrito place has a definite Berlin flavor.

i *U1, U2, U3, U4: Nollendorfpl. Walk down Maasenstr. toward the church and turn right on Pallasstr. Burritos from €4. Cash only.* ⏰ *Open M-Su 11:30am-11pm.*

BAR TOLUCCI
TUSCAN $$

Eisenacher Str. 86   ☎030 214 16 07 www.bar-tolucci.de

With stone oven pizzas and outdoor seating on wood-slated bistro tables that line a quiet street corner, this restaurant is casual eating and generous portions at their finest. The pizzas are cheap (€5.50-8.50) and eclectic (smoked salmon? *Bitte!*). Be sure to arrive after the oven starts firing at 5pm; non-pizza options can be a bit pricier.

i *U7: Eisenacher Str. Pizza €5.50-8.20. Entrees €7-12.* ⏰ *Open M-F 10am-midnight. Garden open noon-midnight. Pizza oven in use M-F 5pm-midnight.*

Mitte

🔲 MONSIEUR VUONG
VIETNAMESE $$

Alte Schönhauserstr. 46   ☎030 992 96 924 www.monsieurvuong.de

The moment you step in the door (which might take a moment, because this place is extremely popular), the Monsieur Vuong brand will be right up in your face. Everything from the neon pink and orange menus to the glossy picture of Monsieur Vuong on the wall to the packed, fine wooden benches screams "branded." Grin and bear it because the food here is delicious. The prices are a little high compared to most Vietnamese places, and the portions are not as fantastically large, but Monsieur Vuong rationalizes its stinginess with some of the tastiest and most beautifully presented Vietnamese food you'll find in the city.

i *U2: Rosa-Luxemburg-Pl. From the metro, take the alleyway from the park across Rosa-Luxemburg-Str., then turn left onto Alte Schönhauserstr. Entrees €6-10. Vietnamese "shakes" €3.40-5.80.* ⏰ *Open daily 10am-midnight.*

🔲 DOLORES BURRITOS
MEXICAN $

Rosa-Luxemburg-Str. 7   ☎030 280 99 597 www.dolores-online.de

If you're looking for the cheapest good food you can find in Mitte, head to Dolores. Think Baja Fresh, but better. The menu is super cheap, and the burritos

berlin

are massive, making it unsurprising that this place is crazy popular. You might have to wait in line, but these calorically badass burritos are totally worth it. You pick the style of your food and the meat you want; meat lovers should go for the carnitas and veggie-heads should opt for something seitan, and everyone should go for the smoky peanut salsa. You'll end up with a massive burrito, burrito bowl, or quesadilla (all €4.50, plus extras).

i U2, U5, U8, S5, S7, S9, or S75: Alexanderpl. From the metro, head north on Rosa-Luxemburg-Str. Burritos around €5; prices vary depending on your ingredients. Cash only. ☒ Open M-Sa 11:30am-10pm, Su 1-10pm.

BERLINER MARCUS BRÄU
GERMAN $$
1-3 Münzstr. ☎030 247 69 85 www.brau-dein-bier.de

This little microbrewery has only been serving up *Bier* since 1982. While the beer is smoother than air, we don't recommend eating a full meal here. With Dolores right around the corner, it's a crying shame to spend more than twice as much dough on your supper and end up with some all-too-standard German *Wienerschnitzel*. Tl;dr: skip the food, but stop in for a Pils.

i U2, U5, U8, S5, S7, S9, or S75: Alexanderpl. From the metro, head north on Karl-Liebknecht-Str., then turn left onto Münzstr. Entrees €7.50-11. Drinks €1-7. Beer from €2.60 per 0.3L, €7.40 per L. ☒ Open M-F noon-midnight, Sa-Su 4pm-midnight.

GOOD MORNING VIETNAM
VIETNAMESE $$
Alte Schonhauserstr. 60 ☎030 308 82 973 www.good-morning-vietnam.de

Good Morning Vietnam is only a block away from Monsieur Vuong, and while both restaurants serve up delicious Vietnamese food, they could hardly be more different. Good Morning Vietnam serves up massive portions, for one thing. Entrees are also about €2 cheaper than their MV counterparts and include crispy duck, mango chicken skewers, and tofu platters. And although the food here is a little less spiced and flavored, the larger portions will definitely please your belly.

i U2: Rosa-Luxemburg-Pl. From the metro, take the alleyway across Rosa-Luxemburg-Str. from the park. Entrees €7-7.50. ☒ Open daily noon-midnight.

TIPICA
MEXICAN $$$
Rosenstr. 19 ☎030 250 99 440 www.tipica.mx

Tipica manages to pull off upscale Tex-Mex food while still featuring a pick-your-poison taco menu. Large portions of meat, cilantro, onion, and lime come with four tortillas; you add the sides and salsas and roll your own creations. The meats get crazy (think veal tacos), but the portions stay large and the selection crowd-pleasing. Get any meat Alambre-style (fried with peppers, onions, and bacon) for no extra charge.

i S5, S7, S9, or S75: Hackescher Markt. From the station, head east and turn right at An der Spandauer Brucke, immediately after the Markt. Follow it 100m or so as it curves to the right. Tacos start a €8. Sides €2. Salsa €1.50. Entrees €11.50-14. ☒ Open M-Th 11am-11pm, F-Sa 11am-1am, Su 11am-11pm.

DADA FALAFEL
FALAFEL $
Linienstr. 132 ☎030 275 96 927 www.dadafalafel.de

Ever stood in line at a falafel place and thought, "This place could use more Duchamp"? Well, even if you haven't, this is the place for you. The high walls and ceiling of this tiny takeout place are covered in thick, multi-colored paint swirls, as if to reflect the smear of sauces that will soon cover your face. There's usually a fair amount of outdoor seating, though securing one of these prized tables may require minor feuds with other tourists. The crispy-on-the-outside, soft-on-the-inside falafel (€3.50) is appropriately packed with flavor, the plates (€5) are beautifully and smearfully arranged, and everything just seems to taste

germany

better with the classic jazz playing from the speakers. After feasting your belly, feast your eyes on Derdasdie, the Dada art exhibit next to the restaurant.

i *U6: Oranienburger Tor. Cash only.* ☼ *Open M 9am-2am, Tu-F 8:30am-midnight, Sa-Su 9am-2am.*

FASSBENDER&RAUSCH CHOCOLATIERS
CHOCOLATE $$$

Charlottenstr. 60 ☎030 204 58 443 www.fassbender-rausch.de

Prepare to experience the wacky world of Willy Wonka. Well, not quite. This sprawling chocolate shop showcases a huge, chocolate reconstruction of the *Titanic*, a bubbling, exploding chocolate volcano, and a chocolate reconstruction of a Boeing 767, among hundreds of other, smaller chocolate goodnesses available for purchase. Anticipate a crowd of people piling into Rausch the moment you enter; this chocolate is pretty much a German staple and is wildly popular and sold everywhere. Truffles (€5.95 for 100g) come in 100 flavors, and most of them are *lecker*, or delicious. We're especially fond of the booze-filled truffles, but then, who would ever doubt chocolate and cognac in one mouthful?

i *U2 or U6: Stadtmitte. Chocolate €0.50-300.* ☼ *Open M-Sa 10am-8pm, Su 11am-8pm. Cafe open daily from 11am.*

GLÜCKLICH AM PARK
CAFE $

Kastanienallee 54 ☎030 417 256 51

Feeling down? Glücklich am Park is sure to bring a smile to your face. Between the dozens of children licking ice cream cones in the sprawling outdoor seating area and the cheap and delicious waffles (and the birds stealing nibbles of those waffles), Glücklich am Park is a jovial and delicious place to kill sometime on a Sunday afternoon. True to its name, Glücklich am Park is right across from a park, where you can frolic to your heart's content. We recommend you take your frolicking with a caramel waffle (€2.40).

i *U8: Rosenthaler Pl. Walk north on Kastanienallee. Glücklich am Park is on the left. Waffles, ice cream, and crepes €2-4.* ☼ *Open daily 10am-11pm.*

CURRY 61
CURRYWURST $

Oranienburger Str. 6 ☎030 400 54 033 www.curry61.de

There's a horde of currywurst stands across this city, but not all currywurst is created equal. Curry 61 has recently become an upscale currywurst joint, with currywurst mit pommes costing €5.90. This particular currywurst stand has an avid following of both locals and tourists. The curry sauce here is on the sweeter side, but the sausage is still as good as could be. Try it without skin, or "Darm," and you'll be eating a piece of history—East Berlin sausage skin shortages led intrepid currywursters to serve their product without any wrapping. The economy may have perked up, but the taste was so compelling that some hawkers just continued to omit the skins.

i *S5, S7, S9, or S75: Hackescher Markt. From the metro, head west on Oranienburger Str. Currywurst from €3. Cash only.* ☼ *Open M-Sa 11am-midnight, Su 11am-8pm.*

Prenzlauer Berg

Prenzlauer Berg is smitten with its cafes: nearly every street hides a cafe (or six), so a cheap, tasty cup of joe or a small, inexpensive meal are never hard to come by. Check out **Kastanienallee, Kollwitzstrasse,** or the streets around **Helmholtzplatz** for the highest concentration of caffeine. If your place is kitchen equipped, stock up at any of the several **REWE** stores around P'Berg.

W—DER IMBISS
VEGETARIAN $$

Kastanienallee 49 ☎030 443 52 206 www.w-derimbiss.de

Der Imbiss has done its best to isolate the flavors common to Italy, India, and Mexico. The result is both weird and wildly popular with the fedora-donning and the plaid-wearing. Stop in for a "famous" naan pizza (our favorite is the Jewish Naan, with smoked salmon, capers, and caviar (€8). If pizza doesn't appeal, you might fancy a burrito (€7), a wrap (€6-10), or an Indian thali (€7). The link between 'em all? The bread. Der Imbiss has figured out that naan passes for pizza crust, burrito shells, and, well, naan.

i U8: Rosenthaler Pl. From the metro, walk north on Weinbergsweg until it becomes Kastanienallee. The restaurant is on the left. Cold or grilled wrap €6-10. Burritos €7. Cash only. ⏰ Open M-Th noon-10pm, F-Sa noon-midnight, Su noon-10pm.

LA FOCACCERIA ITALIAN $
Fehrbelliner Str. 24   ☎030 440 327 71

Are you tired of going into Italian restaurants and paying €10 for some heat-lamp-warmed lasagna? Goodness, have we found the place for you. La Focacceria serves incredibly good value pastas (lasagna, €4.20) and focaccia (€1.50 per slice, cheaper if you buy more), and everything is made fresh in front of you. If you order pasta, your dish will be delightfully warm and still bubbling when you pick it up. The only downside is that this place is both tiny and crazily popular, so you might have to take your food across the street to the local park to nom. We figure that's a small price to pay for such a good deal.

i U8: Rosenthaler Pl. From the metro, walk north and away from the TV Tower on Weinbergsweg. Turn left onto Fehrbelliner Str. La Focacceria is on the right. Pasta €4.20. Focaccia €1.50 per slice. ⏰ Open M-Sa 11am-11pm.

DAS FILM CAFÉ BURGERS, THEATER $$
Schliemannstr. 15   ☎030 810 19 050   www.dasfilmcafe.de

An old-but-good gimmick, Das Film Café pairs food and films. Although the cafe is open all day, it's usually pretty empty, unless there's a show starting. The burgers (from €6.90) are loved by all, but the brunch-and-a-movie deal has us singing in the rain. "Eat the Movie" film breakfasts (cheese, ham, fruit, prosecco, and movie ticket; €9.90) precede the Sunday 2pm showing, while a monthly film quiz is, according to one waitress, a quiz that's about film. Films are never dubbed and are usually in English.

i U2: Eberswalder Str. From the metro, head north on Pappelallee, turn right onto Raumerstr., left before the park on Lychenerstr., then right immediately so you're walking along the park. Take a left onto Schliemannstr. The cafe is on the right. Burgers from €7. Breakfast €4.90-8.50. Hummus plates €5.50. Cappuccino €2. Tickets €4.50, students €4. Film quiz €5. Cash only. ⏰ Open M-F 3pm-late, Sa-Su 11am-late.

BONANZA COFFEE HEROES CAFE $
Oderberger Str. 35   ☎017 156 307 95   www.bonanzacoffee.de

Bonanza might be the world's best coffee house. The beans are roasted in house, and when ordering your espresso drink, you get to pick between two daily grinds, one of which is usually the perfectly smooth Bonanza standard. Order a latte with the Bonanza roast (€2.90), and enjoy the splendiferous flavors Starbucks wishes you never discovered.

i U8: Bernauer Str. From the metro, walk west on Bernauer Str. Turn right onto Schwedter Str., but keep left and turn onto Oderberger Str. Bonanza is on the right. Coffe €2-4. ⏰ Open M-F 8:30am-7pm, Sa-Su 10am-7pm.

SUICIDE SUE CAFE $$
Dunckerstr. N2   ☎030 648 34 745   www.suicidesue.com

Based on the extended backstory of some *Kill-Bill*-like, samurai-sword-wielding woman who gave up slicing Yakuza brains to slice bread, Suicide Sue is a bright and beautiful place to enjoy some inexpensive internet, coffee, and lunch. Sizeable *Stullen* (sandwiches) comprise the main food options, but they're large enough, cheap enough, and varied enough that they transcend the thousands of other sandwiches that Prenzlauer Berg offers. When you're not surfing the web, check out the coffee table books on photography and film.

i *U2: Eberswalder Str. From the metro, walk east on Danziger Str., then take the 3rd left onto Dunckerstr. Suicide Sue is immediately on the right. Stullen €3-5. Breakfast €2.40-8.50. Cake €2-3 per slice. Cash only. ⏱ Open M-F 8am-6pm, Sa 9am-6pm, Su 10am-6pm.*

ANNA BLUME

CAFE $$

Kollwitzstr. 83   ☎030 440 48 749 www.cafe-anna-blume.de

Anna Blume could cater the world's best wedding—they sell flowers, delicious cakes, and some marvelous hor d'oeuvres. This cafe is expensive, but we wouldn't recommend it if we didn't think it was worth the cost. Skip the coffee and the expensive drinks unless you're coming for a deliciously fruity, milky smoothie (€4.10). Though the signature "tree-tiered" breakfast isn't cheap, the locals love it (€17.50 for two people or €24.50 for four). Stick to a plate of their cheap yet marvelous cold crepes (€4.30; we recommend the variety plate). Delicious, healthy, simple, and filling.

i *U2: Eberswalder Str. From the metro, head east on Danziger Str., then turn right onto Kollwitzstr. The cafe is on the right, at the southwest corner of Kollwitzstr. and Stredzkistr. Breakfast €4-8. Crepes €4-8.50. Coffee €2-3. ⏱ Open daily 8am-2am.*

LIEBLING

CAFE $

Raumer Str. 36A   ☎030 411 98 209

With a mostly organic menu, plenty of outdoor seating, and chill Berlin vibes, Liebling makes sure its patrons will be pleased. Try one of the daily soups (€5.20) or the New York cheesecake (that is, if that locals' favorite isn't already sold out). There's plenty of seating on the quiet street opposite the park, making Liebling a great choice for outdoor, mid-afternoon day drinking.

i *U2: Eberswalder Str. From the metro, walk east on Danziger Str., then turn left onto Dunckerstr. The cafe is at the northeast corner of Dunckerstr. and Raumerstr. Milchkaffee €2.50. Hot drinks €2-3. Aperitifs €2.50-4. Mixed drinks €2-3.50. Cash only. ⏱ Open M-F 9am-late, Sa-Su 10am-late.*

SOUPANOVA

SOUP $$

Stargarder Str. 24   www.myspace.com/soupanovaberlin

The creation of soups at Soupanova begins with your choice of broth (options include Thai coconut milk and miso). Then, choose the solid component, whether it be wontons, chicken, or tofu. Finally, pick a seat outdoors from perhaps the most eclectic collection of sidewalk furniture you'll find outside of a flea market; otherwise, enjoy the couches, dim lighting, and old wood floors indoors.

i *U2: Eberswalder Str. From the metro, head east on Danziger Str., then turn left onto Schliemannstr. Head north and walk through the park; continue walking north on Schliemannstr. Soupanova is on the right. Soup €5-6.50. Cash only. ⏱ Open M-Sa 6pm-late*

KREUZBURGER

BURGERS $

Pappelallee 19   ☎030 746 95 737 www.kreuzburger.de

Kreuzburger is not in Kreuzberg. Big whoop. The only thing we really care about here are the cheap-as-sin burgers, served all day and late into the night. Kreuzburger is plastered with kitschy old newspapers, but the burgers are as cheap as €3.90. For a cleaner conscience, consider asking for an organic patty, with a €0.70 upcharge. And though we don't want to support your drunk munchies too enthusiastically, there's no better place in P'Berg to prevent a hangover with some tasty fried foods. Bigger and greasier make the morning after easier!

i *U2: Eberswalder Str. From the metro, head northeast on Pappelallee and take the 1st right onto Raumerstr. Kreuzburger is on the corner of Raumerstr. and Pappelallee. Burgers €4-8. Fries €2. Cash only. ⏱ Open daily noon-3am.*

berlin

DESI INDIAN $

Dunckerstr. 2a ☎030 609 46 009

Though it lacks that Prenzlauer Berg cafe character that you've come to know and love, Desi offers a huge selection of tasty Indian dishes. If you visit Desi between noon and 4 pm, you can score a majorly cheap lunch. For just €4, you can pick any of the vegetarian dishes, and they come with all the fixings. Meat costs a little more, but we'll forgive you for giving into temptation—unless you order the super-pricey scallops. Come here for lunch, not dinner; you'll get more bang for your buck while the sun is still up.

i *U2: Eberswalder Str. From the metro, head east on Danziger Str., walk 3 blocks, and turn left onto Dunckerstr. The restaurant is on the right. Entrees normally €5.50-8. Cocktails €5-7. Cash only. ⏰ Open daily noon-late. Lunch noon-4pm.*

BABEL LEBANESE $

Kastanienalle 33 ☎030 440 31 318

With the exception of Che Guevara's portrait, which inexplicably adorns the back wall, Babel is a quintessential Middle Eastern eatery. Babel's menu is simple. Almost everything is a hummus plate, where you pick the meat. The prices aren't ridiculously cheap, but the hop in quality is worth the extra cost. The lamb, salad, and hummus plate (€8) is a particular favorite; the locals keep coming back for more, and while that means Babel is delicious, it also might mean you have to wait for your food. But at least you get to wait with a free cup of Middle Eastern tea.

i *U2: Eberswalder Str. From the metro, head southwest on Kastanienallee. The restaurant is past Oberberger Str. on the right. Falafel €3-6. Shawarma €3.50. Vegetable wrap €3.50. Cash only. ⏰ Open daily 11am-midnight.*

Friedrichshain

FRITTIERSALON GERMAN $$

Boxhagener Str. 104 ☎030 259 33 906

Frittiersalon serves up the usual cheap Berlin grub: currywurst and burgers. What sets this place apart is the vegan and vegetarian options. We aren't sure who would want to eat vegan currywurst (what's the point?), but if you do, Frittiersalon's the place. The name literally means "Frying Salon," and, though it might not be the most memorable lunch ever, all dishes are fried to order. They offer a whole host of homemade sauces and some lip-smackin' French fries, too.

i *U5: Frankfurter Tor. From the metro, walk south on Warschauer Str. and turn left onto Boxhagener Str.; the restaurant is along the 2nd block on the left. Bratwurst and currywurst vegan variations available €2.40. Burgers €3.90-7.80. Cash only. ⏰ Open daily 1pm-midnight.*

AUNT BENNY CAFE $

Oderstr. 7 ☎030 664 05 300

Aunt Benny's brings everyone together: Wi-Fi crazed "entrepreneurs," regular cafe-goers, andmoms and their babes meeting friends here before heading to the playground across the street. People sit around on stuffed coffee sacks and benches, sipping lattes (€2.50) and discussing Berlin's best coffee roasteries. Regulars are almost aggressive with their enthusiasm for the cafe's *bricher-muesli*—a kind of Swiss cereal containing nuts, fresh apples, and oats, soaked overnight, served with yogurt, and usually sold out by 4pm.

i *U5: Frankfurter Allee. From the metro, walk west on Frankfurter Allee, then turn left onto Jessnerstr. The restaurant is on the left, opposite the park. Bagel €2. Cake €3.10 per slice. Coffee from €1.60. Smoothies €4.20-4.80. Su brunch €8. Cash only. ⏰ Open Tu-F 9am-7pm, Sa-Su 10am-7pm.*

KUCHEN RAUSCH

CAFE $$$

Simon-Dach-Str. 1 ☎030 55 95 38 55 www.kuchenrausch.de

Next to our other listings in Friedrichshain, the thing that makes Kuchen Rausch stand out is its price. This place isn't cheap. That said, if you're looking for somewhere nice to enjoy a slow meal and some delicious coffee and cake, Kuchen Rausch beats out all the rest. The coffee (*Milchkaffee* €3) is served in huge, pretty mugs and tastes nothing less than heavenly, and the *Vegi Ofenbrot* (bread stacked with brie, pears, and pesto; €7.40) is superb. Kuchen Rausch's tables spill out onto the corner of Simon-Dich-Str., where the people watching is unrivaled.

i U5: Frankfurter Tor. From the metro, walk east on Frankfurter Allee. Turn right onto Simon-Dich-Str. Kuchen Rausch is on the right. Breakfast €2.90-12.20. Lunch €7.40-11.80. ☼ Open daily 9am-midnight.

VÖNER

VEGETARIAN $

Boxhagener Str. 56 ☎030 992 65 423 www.voener.de

The first things you'll notice after walking into Vöner: the place is spotless, the staff wear incredibly skinny, brightly colored jeans, and the food is delicious. Though we don't really understand the concept of vegetarian *döner*, Vöner keeps it yummy with organic French fries and organic smoothies to boot. Everything on the menu is vegetarian—in fact, most of it is vegan. Veggie *döners* (*vöners*), veggie burgers, and veggie currywurst all compare quite nicely to their more savage cousins.

i U5: Samariter Str. From the metro, head south on Colbestr., then turn left onto Boxhagener Str., and follow it down until you pass Wühlischstr. Vöners €3.40. Veggie burgers €3.40. French fries €2.80. Organic soft drinks and smoothies €1.80. ☼ Open daily noon-11pm.

CARAMELLO EIS

ICE CREAM $

Wühlischerstr. 31 ☎030 503 43 105 www.caramello-dopamino.de

Caramello Eis is a little more expensive than a bunch of the nearby ice cream parlors, but people claim that the 20 extra euro cents are worth it. All of Carmello's ice cream is handmade and organic, and some flavors are even vegan. Though the staff claim that the chocolate *Eis* with chili powder is the best flavor in all of Berlin, our researchers found the chocolate and cocoa nibs flavor quite superior.

i U5: Frankfurter Tor. Ice cream €1.20 per scoop. Coffee €1-2.60. Smoothies €2-3. Cash only. ☼ Open daily 11am-10pm.

FLIEGENDER TISCH

ITALIAN $$

Mainzer Str. 10 ☎030 297 76 489

Unfortunately, there's no magic: the tables at "Flying Table" do not in fact fly, let alone hover. Still, what are flying tables compared to candlelight and inexpensive Italian food? If you've spent enough time in Berlin, you're probably tired of seeing those "Knock, Knock, Gnocchi on Heaven's Door" billboards, but the *gnocchi spinat* (€5.80) here is absolutely worth trying. Flying Table's other staples include risotto (€5.60-6.60), pizza (€6.80), and hamburgers (with seafood, spinach, and garlic; €3.30). The restaurant is small, and Fliegender Tisch feels a lot nicer than its low prices would suggest.

i U5: Samariter Str. Pizza €5. Pasta €4.30-6.60. Cash only. ☼ Open daily 5pm-midnight.

HOPS AND BARLEY

MICROBREWERY $

Wühlischstr. 22/23 ☎030 293 67 534 www.hopsandbarley-berlin.de

This microbrewery has British men on tap; that is, they love, they tap, and they keep coming back for more. The cider, pilsner, and *weizenbier* here are all made in house, and they're all delicious. The place gets wonderfully packed for German football games, when the bar opens early (3pm) and stays open late enough

berlin

for the hangovers to kick in. The guys here also make their own bread daily, so you can drink your grain and eat it, too.

i *U5: Samariter Str. From the metro, walk west on Frankfurter Allee, then turn left onto Mainzer Str. Follow the same street as it turns into Gärtner Str., then turn left onto Wühlischstr. Beer €3.10 per 0.5L. Cash only.* ✪ *Open daily 5pm-late.*

CAFE CORTADO CAFE $
Simon-Dach-Str. 9

Flowers and board games on breezy patio tables and a cozy, sofa-stuffed back room draw a young crowd. With a taste for international coffee blends, Cafe Cortado serves Turkish and Portuguese coffee, alongside beer and cocktails, from a mosaic bar.

i *U5: Frankfurter Tor. From the metro, walk south on Warschauer Str., turn left onto Grünberger Str., and turn right onto Simon-Dach-Str. The cafe is in the long line of restaurants on the left. Coffee €1.70. Chai latte €2.80. Beer €3. Mixed drinks from €6. Ciabattas €3.80. Bagels €3.50. Brownies €2. Cash only.* ✪ *Open M-F 9am-9pm, Sa-Su 9am-midnight.*

Kreuzberg

◪ **MUSTAFA'S** MIDDLE EASTERN $
Mehringdamm 32 ☎ www.mustafas.de

Kreuzberg has dozens of street food vendors, but one in particular stands out as (slightly) better than all the rest: Mustafa's. Even on hot, summery days, the queue outside Mustafa's lines the street, with everyone dancing to some thumpin' Bollywood tunes. Despite its popularity, Mustafa's is still priced for the street, and it's open daily 24hr., too. Chicken *döner* (€2.90) seems to be the local omnivore's favorite, while vegetarians can opt for the vegetable kebabs (€2.50).

i *U6 or U7: Mehringdamm. From the metro, cross to the west side of Mehringdamm, then walk south past the big building that looks like a cartoon medieval castle. Mustafa's is in the little stand on the sidewalk, immediately past the castle. Entrees €2.50-5. Cash only.* ✪ *Open 24hr.*

◪ **SANTA MARIA MEXICAN DINER** MEXICAN $$
Oranienstr. 170 ☎030 922 10 027 www.lasmarias.de

We hear a lot of young American folks complaining about the lack of "real" Mexican food in Berlin. Though the owner is Australian, not Mexican, this complaint doesn't exist at Santa Maria. The food is served in huge portions, and we're especially fond of the chorizo quesadilla (€7.70). Easily the cla$$iest place to get drunk before the clubs in the area open, Santa Maria serves up happy hour margaritas (€4) and tequila shots (€1) from 8-10pm. The *choriqueso* (€6.50) is a pot of melted cheese and sausage—just think about that for a second.

i *U8: Moritzpl. From the metro, head southeast on Oranienstr. The restaurant is on the left after Oranienpl. Entrees €5-8. Cash only.* ✪ *Open daily noon-late. Happy hour daily 8-10pm.*

◪ **CAFÉ MORGENLAND** CAFE $$
Skalitzer Str. 35 ☎030 611 32 91 www.cafemorgenland.eu

Morgenland's cult-like local following adores the cafe's breakfasts. Order by country: Englisches (€7.50) for the bland, Italienisches (€7) for the meaty, Spanisches (€8.20) for the feast. The menu is wildly extensive, so if none of those options catch your fancy, you're sure to find something suited to please. A baguette? A salad? An omelette? Something with rice? A decadent dessert? Tables are prized at this vibrant cafe, so unless you want to risk a long wait or an empty stomach, call ahead to make a reservation.

i *U1: Görlitzer Bahnhof. From the metro, walk west on Skalitzer Str. The cafe is in the little square next to the intersection between Skalitzer Str. and Manteufel Str. Entrees €5-15. All-you-can-eat weekend brunch €9.50. Cash only.* ✪ *Open M-F 9am-1am, Sa-Su 10am-1am. Business lunch M-F noon-4pm. Brunch Sa-Su 10am-4pm.*

RISSANI
MIDDLE EASTERN $

Spreewaldpl. 4 ☎030 616 29 433

Döner isn't hard to find in Kreuzberg. But a Middle Eastern restaurant that doesn't even serve *döner*? Now that's something! Rissani serves some of the cheapest sandwiches in Berlin. Order the falafel sandwich or the chicken shawarma sandwich (€2) and prepare to cover your face in yogurt and crumbs.

i *U1: Görlitzer Bahnhof. From the station, head east down Skalitzer Str. and take a right onto Spreewaldpl. Entrees €2-5. Cash only. ② Open M-Th 11am-3am, F-Sa 11am-5am, Su 11am-3am.*

HENNE ALT-BERLINER WIRTSHAUS GASTSTÄTTEN
GERMAN $$

Leuschnerdamm 25 ☎030 614 77 30 www.henne-berlin.de

Henne thinks that if you get to make decisions, you're going to make bad ones. So you don't really have much of a choice: you're going to order the one entree they serve. It's chicken. Not just any chicken—this is a perfectly fried half-chicken and a piece of bread (€7.90). While you wait, Henne brings you a bowl of Southern-style, mayo-heavy potato salad for you to devour. Complete with antler decorations and its very own beer garden, Henne provides the quintessential German experience. Even JFK thought so.

i *U1 or U8: Kottbusser Tor. From the station, head northwest on Oranienstr. Take a right onto Oranienpl. and follow the park about halfway to St. Michael's Church. The restaurant is at the corner of Leuschnerdamm and Waldemarstr. Reservations required for outdoor seating; they're a good idea for indoor seating as well. Sausage €2.40-3.50. Beer €2.60-3.80. Wine €4. Cash only. ② Open Tu-Sa 6pm-late, Su 5pm-late. Kitchen closes Tu-Sa 11pm, Su 10pm.*

CURRY 36
CURRYWURST $

Mehringdamm 36 ☎030 251 73 68 www.curry36.de

We postulate that currywurst stands were so plentiful and so hard to name that they gave up and just decided to refer to them by number. Somehow, 36 stands above the rest. With its super-crispy chippies (red and white €1.60) and its curry-powder-ketchup-sausage mess (€1.50), Curry 36 is the best of the 'wurst.

i *U6 or U7: Mehringdamm. From the metro, head south on Mehringdamm. The fast-food stand is on the right just before Yorck/Gneisenaustr. Currywurst €1.50, organic costs an extra €0.30. French fries €1.40. Cash only. ② Open daily 9am-5am.*

NIGHTLIFE

If you're reading this section and thinking, "I'm not sure I want to go clubbing in Berlin," then stop it. Stop it right now. Take a hint from Lady Gaga, patron saint of Berlin, and just dance... you won't regret it. The true *Diskotheken* await in the barren cityscape of Friedrichshain and the notoriously nocturnal Kreuzberg. Mitte does not disappoint, either—its tremendous multi-room clubs filled with exquisitely dressed 20-somethings are generally worth their hefty covers. The major parties in Schöneberg are at the GLBT clubs in the northern part of the neighborhood. For tamer nightlife, try the jazz clubs in Charlottenburg or the bar scene in Prenzlauer Berg.

Charlottenburg

Don't go to Charlottenburg expecting a wild time. We're pretty sure you won't be able to get *that* crazy here, since Charlottenburg is known for its residential feel, quiet cafes, and the 30-somethings who are busier starting families than throwing crazy ragers. The neighborhood is great for a mellow evening or some live jazz, but the real parties are eastward. The **Ku'damm** is best avoided after sunset, unless you enjoy chatting up drunk businessmen.

A-TRANE
BAR, CLUB

Bleibtreustr. 1 ☎030 313 25 50 www.a-trane.de

If you don't like jazz, A-Trane is too expensive for you to stop by. But if you do like jazz, boy, this place is glorious. The patrons are older (the kind of people who've probably gone to this club once a month for the past 35 years), but that's the jazz crowd for you. Every once in a while, this place will attempt to cater to the young kids, pursuing popularity over prowess by offering up a disappointing and terrible Red Hot Chili Peppers jazz cover. Skip these fads and either sit in on a Saturday night jam session (anticipate sticking around until sometime on Sunday morning) or check their website for shows, most of which will not disappoint.

i S3, S5, S7, S9, or S75: Savignypl. Cover €10-25, students €8-13. No cover Saturday after 12:30am. Cash only. ☑ Open M-Th 9pm-1am, F-Sa 9pm-late, Su 9pm-1am.

QUASIMODO
CLUB

Kantstr. 12A ☎030 312 80 86 www.quasimodo.de

By day, Quasimodo serves up *Kaffee*, and by night, the club showcases live music in an eclectic variety of genres—including funk, soul, disco, folk, and jazz—nearly every night of the week. What sucks is that the crowd here tends to be on the older side, and sometimes they can give this club an office-party kind of feel (remember: you're still in Charlottenburg). A spacious basement room with a large bar and stage lets all those awkward coworkers dance right up close to the performers.

i U2, S5, S7, S9, or S75: Zoologischer Garten. On the corner of Fasanenstr. and Kantstr. Check the website for music schedule. Cover for concert €8-30, cheaper if reserved in advance. Free entry every Tu. Drinks €2.50-4.50. Cash only. ☑ Open daily 10pm-late.

ANDA LUCIA
BAR, RESTAURANT

Savignypl. 2 ☎030 540 271 www.andalucia-berlin.de

Perhaps you're looking for a mild introduction to Berlin's crazy nightlife. Anda Lucia is exactly that: a tame bar experience where you pay a good amount of money for some good, gentle fun. If you arrive after 11pm, everyone around you should be drunk enough to show off their salsa moves despite Anda Lucia's lack of a dance floor. This place mostly functions as a warm Latin bar, with a cocktail list about a mile long. We love the pricey mojitos (€8.20, ouch...), but we've heard travelers complain that this place includes a €2 up-charge or tip on every bill, so keep that in mind while your tab is adding up.

i S5, S7, or S75: Savignypl. Wine from €4 a glass. Tequila €3. Tapas €3.70-5. ☑ Kitchen open daily noon-2am.

Schöneberg and Wilmersdorf

Schöneberg is Berlin's unofficial gay district, so most of the nightlife here caters to the GLBT community. A couple of distinctive cocktail bars may be worth visiting in the interest of broadening your buzz, but the neighborhood's real parties happen at the GLBT clubs and bars in northern Schöneberg.

◾ HAFEN
BAR, GLBT

Motzstr. 19 ☎030 211 41 18 www.hafen-berlin.de

Hafen is easily one of the friendliest (and best!) bars in Schöneberg. It's a wonderful little place, ideal for the start of a night on the town. Inside, you'll find plenty of locals all along the spectrums of age and attractiveness. Everything about Hafen is inviting, from the dancing neon lights to the expansive bar. With a large supply of tables and a consistently high level of volume and energy pulsing from its clean, drum-machine-heavy tunage, Hafen is a great place to go with friends. The weekly pub quiz (M at 8pm; conducted in English the first M of every month) is wildly popular, and every Wednesday night features a new DJ. On April 30, Hafen hosts its largest party of the year in honor of the Queen of the Netherlands. Hafen can be frenetic and totally crazy with a hoppin' party, or it can be more mellow depending on the particular night.

i U1, U3, U4, or U9: Nollendorfpl. Cash only. ☑ Open daily 8pm-4am (or later).

SLUMBERLAND

BAR

Goltstr. 24 ☎030 216 53 49

While pretending Berlin is located in the Caribbean generally makes us frown, Slumberland manages to pull it off. With its sand-covered floor and posters of old Spanish films, this bar allows patrons to "get away" in this island escape in the middle of land-locked Berlin. Try an obligatory beach favorite, like a piña colada or a Sex on the Beach (both €6.50), or go tropical with a fruit-flavored African beer (DjuDju, €3.90). The *Fußball* table is an awesome addition, but consider yourself warned: the beach may be relaxing, but things here get competitive.

i *U1 , U3, U4, or U9: Nollendorfpl. Most drink €2-7. Ⓚ Open M-Th 5pm-2am, F 5pm-4am, Sa 11am-4pm, Su 5pm-2am.*

PRINZKNECHT

BAR

Fuggerstr. 33 ☎030 236 27 444 www.prinzknecht.de

While most of the bars in the neighborhood don't help you meet new people, Prinzknecht almost guarantees it. Take a smoke break out front and some friendly 20- or 30-somethings will strike up a conversation. Prinzknecht is an ecstatic, gay-friendly spot with a huge wooden bar and disco ball reflections striping the place. Loud beats and crowds fuel Prinzknecht's insanely high energy levels. Even with levels upon levels of bar stools and couches extending far back into its purple and green, neon-lit interior, the bar fills up way past capacity on event nights, and people begin to resemble waves on the street. A mostly male clientele spread between 20-somethings and 50-year-olds nods to the almost oppressively loud beats inside, while some patrons cool off on the long benches that stretch across the pavement outside.

i *U1 or U2: Wittenbergpl. 2-for-1 drinks W 7-9pm. Cash only. Free Wi-Fi. Ⓚ Open M-Th 3pm-2am, F-Sa 3pm-3am, and Su 3pm-2am.*

BEGINE

BAR

Potsdamer Str. 139 ☎030 215 14 14 www.begine.de

In a neighborhood dominated by male gay clubs, Begine is a welcome retreat for women. No, really: a sign outside says *"Nur für Frauen"* (literally, "only for women"), and they mean it. As Berlin's biggest lesbian community center, Begine has a popular, low-key cafe and bar with comfortable sofas from which to enjoy readings and live music at night. Dim yellow lighting and an acre of empty floor space make for a quiet bar that offers a short and unremarkable list of beers, coffee, and cocktails. The bar is far removed from the nightlife center over by Nollendorfpl., but maybe that's precisely the point. An older crowd proudly patronizes this respectable neighborhood rarity.

i *U2: Bülowstr. Ⓚ Open M-F 5pm-late, Sa 7pm-late, Su hours vary.*

TRAIN

BAR

Corner of Potsdamer Str. and Langenscheidtstr. ☎030 017 734 441 23

Train is, quite literally, located inside an old, rusty locomotive wagon. It's a total gimmick, and the bar has all of no class, but we love it anyway. It manages to pull off cheesy, with chandeliers and aluminum foil ceilings, while still attracting a rockin' crowd of 20-somethings. Most of the cocktails here are locomotive-themed, like the fruity Train Fever (rum, lime juice, lemon juice, maracuja syrup, mango juice (€6). Chug-a-chug enough of 'em, and you might wake up the next morning feeling like you were run over by a caboose. Choo-choo!

i *U7: Kleistpark. Cocktail €6, €5 M-Tu and Su nights. Cash only. Ⓚ Open daily 6pm-late.*

HEILE WELT

BAR, GLBT

Motzstr. 5 ☎030 219 17 507

Even with the addition of two enormous, quiet sitting rooms, this bar still attracts enough 20-somethings to fill the place wall to wall (to the point that patrons begin to pool in the street outside). Heile Welt keeps its cool with a

berlin

fur-covered wall, chandeliers, gold tassels, and a row of comfy armchairs. But without much of the glamour or volume of its competitors, this kitsch bar is better suited to conversation with friends and is less a place to meet new people. We're not saying it's impossible to meet guys in Heile Welt, but the environment is laid-back and more suited for a mellow evening.

i U1, U3, U4, or U9: Nollendorfpl. Beer €2.50 per liter. Cash only. ☺ Open daily 6pm-4am, sometimes later.

Mitte

Mitte's techno clubs often offer the height of Berlin's dance scene. Nowhere else will you find clubs so well attended by exquisitely dressed locals in their early 20s, and, despite high covers, these tremendous multi-room clubs rarely disappoint. Most of these places are pretty close to **Rosenthaler Platz**, but some club is always just around the corner in Mitte. Don't expect to get a full night's sleep; the parties generally don't heat up until 2am.

▧ COOKIES
CLUB

Friedrichstr. 158   ☎030 274 92 940 www.cookies-berlin.de

If you're picking this guide up in the middle of the night, you might have started to salivate at the thought of cookies. Alas, you'll find none here. But what you will find is everything hot, sweaty, and sexy. Cookies is housed in a former Stasi bunker on one of the most famous strips in Berlin. Three bars lubricate your dancing joints with a long list of trendy, expensive cocktails, including the Watermelonman (Smirnoff, watermelon liqueur, grenadine, lemon juice, orange juice (€7.50). Once intoxicated, you get to choose between an awesomely huge dance floor with heavy techno and a tiny room devoted to your hometown's hip hop. The party don't start 'til 1am, so save your tears if you show up alone at midnight. Also, invest in some plaid or a cardigan beforehand if you want to have a hope in hell of getting in.

i U6: Französische Str. From the metro, head north on Friedrichstr. along the left side of the street. The club is unmarked, so look for a group of darkly-dressed dudes around a door as you near Dorotheenstr. Cover €5-15. Cocktails €7.50 €10. Coat check €1. Unfortunately, no baked goods. ☺ Open Tu 10:30pm-6am, Th 10:30pm-6am.

KAFFEE BURGER
CLUB

Torstr. 58-60   ☎030 280 46 495 www.kaffeeburger.de

So it's a Wednesday night, and you're buzzed from the hostel bar but can't find anywhere to show off your moves: Kaffee Burger is the perfect place to stumble into. There's a small but worthwhile dance floor packed by 20-year-olds in band T-shirts and scarves right next to 40- and 50-year-olds showing off how crazy they can still be. With a quieter, smokier "Burger Bar" next door, complete with plenty of cushy furniture to lounge on and a cocktail called the "Drunken Rihanna" (€7), Kaffee Burger will transform your week night from a bleak night into a freak night. Weekly programs include poetry readings, film screenings, and drunken sloppiness.

i U6: Rosa-Luxemburg-Pl. From the metro, walk 1 block to the east on Torstr. Cover M-T €1, F-Sa €5, Su €1. Beer €2.50. Shots €3-4. Cocktails €6-7. Cash only. ☺ Open daily 9pm-late.

WEEK END
CLUB

Alexanderpl. 5   ☎030 246 31 676 www.week-end-berlin.de

Don't take the name too seriously. Week End is one of the coolest clubs in town any night of the week. There's live music several nights a week. And if that's not enough to draw you in, two words: rooftop bar. And not a second-story, lame-ass rooftop. Nope, this one is on the top of a mini-, East Berlin-esque skyscraper. Besides the rockin' rooftop bar, this place has two whole floors of the skyscraper, both devoted to delicious cocktails, bright lighting, and crazy dancing. This

germany

awesome club does have one downside, which shouldn't be unexpected: there's hardly anyone here but tourists, and most of them don't seem to know what techno even is. Unfortunately, with a sky-scraping cover and drink prices, you may not want to spend every weekend at Week End, but it's worth at least a visit.

i *U6: Alexander Pl. From the metro, head northeast to the "Sharp" building. Cover €10-20. Coat check €1.20. ⏰ Open Tu-Su midnight-late.*

CLÄRCHENS BALLHAUS
CLUB
Auguststr. 24   ☎030 282 92 95 www.ballhaus.de

By day, it's a self-described gypsy cafe. But by night, it's an ideal spot for anyone looking to try out those swing dancing skills. Clärchens aims to be kitschy and unique, and it totally accomplishes both. The dancing tends to get sloppier and sloppier as the night wears on and the BAC of its patrons climbs higher and higher. The ball house has a 1920s flair to it, exemplified by its weekly offerings of cha-cha, salsa, and swing dancing. Come early for a drink in the beautiful patio garden, or come late to watch the surprisingly talented steppers of all generations kick it old school in a tremendous hall surrounded by silver tassels.

i *U8: Oranienburger Str. From the metro, head north on Tucholsky Str. and turn right onto August-str. M-Th programs €8, students €6, after midnight free; F-Sa €3; Su programs €8, students €6, after midnight free. ⏰ Open daily 10am-late. Dance programs start sometime between 7 and 9pm, depending on the day of the week. Check the website for more details.*

8MM BAR
BAR
Schönhauser Allee 177B   ☎030 405 00 624 www.8mmbar.com

8mm is officially open "every day, kinda." And that says a lot: crowd levels vary depending on the particular night, but when it's bustling, it's bustling. 8mm is both a dark, smoky bar and a live music venue. It's also a great place to meet new people and to chat about how ironic you are. Art films are sometimes projected on the walls, and frequent guest performers and live DJs make this more than just a place to wear flannel and look disaffected, although there's still plenty of that to go around.

i *U2: Senefelderpl. From the metro, head south on Schönhauser Allee. Beer €2.50-6. Mixed drinks €4-7. Cash only. ⏰ Open M-F 8pm-late, Sa 9pm-late, Su 8pm-late.*

SCHOKOLADEN
CLUB
Ackerstr. 169   ☎030 282 65 27 www.schokoladen-mitte.de

Schokoladen specializes in being loud and cheap. It's a great, grungy, raucous, student-centric place to start your evening. Live music tends to make evenings here worthwhile, so be sure to wear some grungtastic fishnet stockings you bought at an outdoor market, come see some indie music, and let the evening take off from there. Unfortunately, Schokoladen does not appear to serve chocolate.

i *U8: Rosenthaler Pl. From the metro, walk west on Torstr. and turn right onto Ackenstr. Schoko-laden is on the left. Cover up to €10. Beer sometimes as cheap as €1.50, but prices vary. ⏰ Hours vary, but shows usually start around 8pm. Check the website for details.*

NEUE ODESSA BAR
BAR
Torstr. 89   ☎017 183 98 991

Enter because of the bright lights drawing you in and the black-and-white vintage parlor look (with cushy furniture), but stay for the whiskey. Neue Odessa Bar serves some of the best top-shelf drinks around. Though the bar is small and a constant crowd of the best-dressed hipsters in town will aim to keep you from your gin, once you summon your drink, you'll be sure to find space to sip and breathe at one of the many tables around the bar. A live DJ spinning electro-poppy American indie rock completes the scene.

i *U6: Rosa-Luxemburg-Pl. From the metro, walk 2 blocks east on Torstr. to the corner of Torstr. and Chorinerstr. Beer €3. Cocktails €6-8. Cash only. ⏰ Open daily 7pm-late.*

berlin

Prenzlauer Berg

Prenzlauer Berg has one of the highest birth rates in all of Germany, meaning that you aren't going to find many crazy clubs that rage until the sun comes up. There's less techno, more lounging, and far earlier quiet hours (starting around midnight) than other parts of Berlin. Prenzlauer Berg's nightlife is calm but still worth checking out. The bars are some of the most unforgettable in town, and, since they fill and empty a bit earlier, they're perfect before you head out to later, clubbier climes.

▧ THE WEINEREI: FORUM
BAR

Fehrbelliner Str. 57   ☎030 600 53 072   www.weinerei.com

With its dim lighting and kitschy, mismatched, super comfy furniture, Weinerei Forum dillies up some of the best and cheapest coffee and food in the neighborhood. Wait, it gets better. From 8pm to midnight, this place holds Berlin's most lively wine tasting: you pay €2 for a glass, you try any of their several wine varieties, and at the end of it all, you put as much money as you "think you owe" in a jar. Now, if you just read this as "€2 for unlimited wine!!!" you're not the kind of cool cat the forum is trying to attract. As you leave without putting any money or just a few euro cents in that jar, you'll get scowled at and possibly called out. Weinerei Forum wants you to be the judge of the value of your wine and food; while that's totally awesome and a great way to spend an evening, it doesn't mean it's a freebie.

i U2: Senefelderpl. From the metro, exit by the northern stairs, then head west on Schwedter Str. Turn left onto Kastanienalle, then veer right onto Veteranenstr., a block down the hill. The bar is on the corner of Veteranenstr. and Fehrbelliner Str. Cash only. ☒ Open M-Sa 10am-late, Su 11am-late. Wine flows 8pm-midnight every night, so let that guide you.

▧ DR. PONG
BAR, PING PONG

Eberswalder Str. 21   www.drpong.net

Dr. Pong is a bar uniquely devoted to ping pong. Aside from a ping pong table and a drinks station, there's nothing else in the room. Watch the pros play a game or make a fool of yourself; though the environment is exceedingly competitive, beginners are still welcome. Order an Andro Susskind (€6), a delicious drink which Dr. Pong describes as "Sticky as a long, slow, summertime fuck."

i U2: Eberswalder Str. From the metro, head east on Eberswalder Str. The bar is on the left. Cover €3.50; includes 1 beer. Must be 18 or older to enter. Beer €2.70. Cocktails €4.50-5.50. Cash only. ☒ Open M-Sa 8pm-late, Su 6pm-late.

SCOTCH AND SOFA
BAR

Kollwitzstr. 18   ☎030 440 42 371

Retro. Stylish. Classic. Scotch and Sofa defines what a bar should be, with comfortable spaces to lounge about. Come to Scotch and Sofa to sip your scotch or whiskey, talk about something intellectual, and osmose the coolness of the atmosphere. Take some advice, though: if you aren't already experienced in the whole classy-scotch-drinking game, pick the cheapest option on the mile-long menu. It all tastes good, and your wallet will thank you.

i U2: Senefelderpl. From the metro, exit by the northern stairs, then head southeast on Metzer Str. After passing the grocery store, turn left onto Kollwitzstr. The bar is on the right, half a block up Kollwitzstr. Scotch from €5. ☒ Open daily 6pm-very late. Happy hour daily 6-7pm; cocktail of the day €3.80.

WOHNZIMMER
BAR

Lettestr. 6   ☎030 445 54 58   www.wohnzimmer-bar.de

This bar is laid back, and when we say that, we mean grab a beer (€2.60) and lie on a chaise lounge or one of the many super comfy couches in the "living room."

Wohnzimmer is a smoking bar, so the patrons tend to be in their late 20s and exude philosophical vibes. Nostalgia abounds.

i *U2: Eberswalder Str. From the metro, head east on Danziger Str., turn left onto Lychener Str., then right onto Lettestr., just past the park. The bar is on the left, at the corner of Lettestr. and Schliemannstr. Beer €2.50-3. Cocktails €4-5. Cash only. ⌚ Open daily 9am-late.*

DUNCKER
CLUB

Dunckerstr. 64 ☎030 445 95 09 www.dunckerclub.de

Duncker used to be a stable, and it still kinda looks like one. In all of Prenzlauer Berg, this is the craziest club, and it might even rival Stasi-bunker clubs. The interior is decorated with chain mail and armor and pretty much anything else you associate with horses. Dunker is frequented by 20-somethings and serves as a venue for a host of live music events. Ring the bell for entry.

i *U2: Eberswalder Str. From the metro,head east on Danziger Str., then turn left on Dunckerstr. Walk north on Dunckerstr. until you reach the bridge over the train tracks. The club is on the left, in the darkened building immediately past the bridge. Goth music M. Eclectic DJs Tu-W. Live bands Th. "Independent dance music" F-Sa. Throwback DJs Su. "Dark Market" goth flea market Su 1pm. Cover varies, usually less than €5; no cover on Th. Beer €2.50. Long drinks €4.50. F-Sa all drinks max. €2. Cash only. ⌚ Open M-W 9pm-late, Th 10pm-late, F-Sa 11pm-late, Su 10pm-late.*

ZU MIR ODER ZU DIR
BAR

Lychener Str. 15 ☎017 624 412 940 www.zumiroderzudir.com

Zu Mir oder Zu Dir literally means, "My place or yours?" and it's a question you're quite likely to find yourself asking or answering in this bar. Entrance is only permitted for those over 21, which turns our smiles upside down. Still, this might be the easiest place to drop the "Zu Mir oder Zu Dir?" question in Prenzlauer Berg, so we'll let you decide how to run with that.

i *U2: Eberswalder Str. From the metro, head east on Danziger Str., then turn left onto Lychener Str. Zu Mir oder Zu Dir is in the line of bars to the left. Beer €2-3. Cocktails €4.50-5. Long drinks €5-8. Cash only. ⌚ Open daily 8pm-late.*

PRATER GARTEN
BEER GARDEN

Kastanienallee 7-9 ☎030 448 56 88 www.pratergarten.de

Prater Garten claims to be the oldest and prettiest beer garden in all of Berlin, and, though we generally try to keep away from superlative adjectives, we do think it's pretty swell. Like any good beer garden, Prater Garten serves up its own cheap brews (0.4L Prater Schwarzbier €3.50), a lot of sunshine, and a whole bunch of rowdy nights.

i *U2: Eberswalder Str. From the metro, head southwest on Kastanienallee. The beer garden is halfway down the 1st block on the right. Weisswurst €3. Beer €2.50-3.50. Cash only. ⌚ Open in good weather Apr-Sept daily noon-late (usually until midnight or 1am).*

Friedrichshain

Barren factory-scapes, heavily graffitied walls, and blinding floodlights may not be the most inviting obstacles to navigate in the dead of night, but such is the environment that hides some of Friedrichshain's—and Berlin's—biggest and most bangin' techno clubs. The old warehouses along **Revaler Strasse** hold the lion's share of sprawling dance floors, but you might want to branch out a little to avoid a double-digit cover.

ROSI'S
CLUB

Revaler Str. 29 www.rosis-berlin.de

The first impression tells all: amazing music, amazing beats, amazing people. There's never a dull moment at Rosi's between its combination of indoor and outdoor clubbing. Outside, you'll find a dire pit, ping-pong, a small dance floor, and a tiny grill. Inside, you'll find more graffiti than you thought could exist in a single room, Indiana Jones-themed pinball, dancing, more dancing, and more music. Rosi's is at the opposite end of Revaler Str. from the main club complex,

berlin

meaning that natural selection weeds out most of the tourist riff-raff on the dark walk over. By the way, we don't advise you to take that dark walk, either. Just grab a cab, and if you're already sloshed, just be sure you can say "Rosi's" as you get in the car. Parties start and end late, so this is a perfect place to end your night.

i U1, S3, S5, S7, S9, or S75: Warschauer Str. From the metro, walk north on Warschauer Str., turn right onto Revaler Str., and walk about 10min.; Rosi's is on the right. Cover €3-7. Cash only. ☾ Open Th-Sa 11pm-late.

ASTRO-BAR
BAR

Simon-Dach-Str. 40   www.myspace.com/astrobar

Astro-Bar is quirky. The interior features Transformers action figures displayed behind the bar, with green light all around. Light-years of lounge and table space line the walls, while the dim lighting from orb-shaped lamps may make you feel lost in space. With a new DJ every night, Astro-Bar provides a ton of tunage, from punk to power pop to Britfunk to every head-scratching subgenre under the sun. Astro-Bar is an extremely popular bar with the 20-something set; the kids just keep coming back for the booze, the tunes, and the feeling that they're floating in space.

i U5: Frankfurter Tor. From the metro, head south on Warschauer Str., turn right onto Grünberger Str., then turn right onto Simon-Dach-Str. Beer from €2.50. Mixed drinks from €5. Cash only. ☾ Open daily 6pm-late.

K-17
CLUB

Pettenkoferstr. 17   www.k17.de

K-17 could hardly be farther from everything else. Literally: it's in the middle of nowhere. But you know what? A walk is all it takes to prevent fannypacking tourists from lining up outside. This towering club has a spacious dance floor and bar on each of its four floors. Metal and all things loud and crunchy blast from the speakers of each floor, attracting a mostly black-clad crowd that will inevitably think you're preppy. Concerts are usually once per week, so keep an eye on the website for dates and prices.

i U5: Frankfurter Allee. Once you're on Pettenkoferstr., keep an eye out for signs; the club is off the road on the right. Cover €6. Beer €2.50. Vodka and coke €3.50. ☾ Open F-Sa 10pm-late.

ABGEDREHT
BAR

Karl-Marx-Allee 140   ☎030 293 81 911   www.abgedreht.net

Abgedreht doesn't have very much personality. It tries to attract a metal crowd, but they're all too busy frequenting more authentic F'Hain hoots, like **Jägerklause** (p. 269) just around the corner. Sheet music papers the walls, and leather couches clump around antique sewing tables, all of which are puzzling in a bar whose name means "high" in colloquial German. Though the crowd generally falls in the 30+ range and you likely won't remember Abgedreht after you leave Berlin, this is one of the more accessible points of entry into the neighborhood's metal scene.

i U5: Frankfurter Tor. From the metro, walk west on Karl-Marx-Allee until you pass the building with the huge, copper tower. Beer €3-4 per 0.5L. Traditional German foods like bratwurst and Wiener-schnitzel around €9. Cash only. ☾ Open daily 5pm-late. Happy hour 7-9pm (cocktails from €4).

SANITORIUM 23
BAR

Frankfurter Allee 23   ☎030 420 21 193   www.sanatorium23.de

Located on one of those wide boulevard DDR streets, Sanitorium is another place designed to ease you into the Friedrichshain scene. This bar plays light, almost clinical techno to guests that lounge on sleek, backless couches shaped like cubes. As much as we hate blatant marketing, we do love free booze, so check in at Sanitorium on Facebook for a free shot.

i U5: Frankfurter Tor. Beer €2.50-3.50. Cocktails €5.50-8. Cash only. ☾ Open M-Sa 6pm-late, Su 7pm-late.

FRITZ CLUB

CLUB

Prinzessinnenstr. 1   ☎030 698 12 80 www.fritzclub.com

Though Fritz Club's top 40 dance floor is packed and its techno floor is sparsely attended, the venue still has some charm. This place has a heavy tourist following, but the club also has three dance floors that allow you to choose between techno, American pop, and American rock. A huge outdoor rock garden that's more desert than oasis provides some space to lounge and let your sweat evaporate, while bars strewn liberally about the complex prevent you from going dry. Though it's a bit far, a relatively cheap cover and a constant stream of 20-year-olds ready to pump their fists make this one of the highlights off Mühlenstr.

i *S3, S5, or S75: Ostbahnhof. From the metro, walk south on Str. der Pariser Kommune, turn left onto Mühlenstr., and take the 1st left toward the big complex of warehouses. The club is on the right side of these warehouses. Beer €3-3.50. Cover €6. Cash only. ☼ Club open F-Su 11pm-late and select weekdays. Check the website for a calendar of events. Concerts start at 9pm.*

RED ROOSTER

BAR

Grünbergerstr. 23   ☎030 290 03 310 www.redroosterbar.de

Though the Red Rooster fills up with a crowd of international backpackers pretty much every evening, it retains an only-in-Berlin atmosphere. We aren't sure if the red and black aesthetic is meant to channel the DDR, but with an outdoor patio and a porch swing, the Rooster is hardly an oppressive environment. Inside, the bartenders serve cider and Czech beers on tap from behind an old wood countertop. For the particularly outgoing (or the desperate backpacker), "perform 4 stay" events invite you to sing for a free beer—or even a free bed! The drunken crowing that results is where we assume the name comes from.

i *U5: Frankfurter Tor. Walk south on Warschauer Str. and turn right onto Grünberger Str. Beer from €2.50-3. Cash only. ☼ Open M-Th 5pm-1am, F-Sa 5pm-3am, Su 5pm-1am.*

CASSIOPEIA

CLUB, BEER GARDEN, RESTAURANT, MUSIC VENUE

Revaler Str. 99   ☎030 473 85 949 www.cassiopeia-berlin.de

Cassiopeia is set in a *Kunsthaus*, a word that makes us starry-eyed just thinking about it. The place is covered in graffiti, and it stays cool around the clock: there's clubbing, beer drinking, swinging, painting, rock climbing, eating, and listening, all wrapped into one awesome location. Occasionally, the club hosts concerts, usually starting around 8pm; check out the list of bands you've never heard of on the website. Unfortunately, the cover that can move into the double digits during prime times, so the budget traveler may have to remain content with gazing at the Cassiopeia in the sky.

i *U1, S3, S5, S7, S9, or S75: Warschauer Str. Cover €5-16. Vodka €2.50. Beer €2.50-3. Cash only. ☼ Open W-Sa 11pm-late.*

JÄGERKLAUSE

BAR, BEER GARDEN

Grünbergerstr. 1   ☎017 622 286 892 www.jaegerklause-berlin.de

Jägerklause is surrounded by an ornate iron fence and a bunch of shrubbery that makes this little beer garden feel like its in another country. If you're not the lounge and drink and eat *wurst* type, Jägerklause is also a wild bar. The bar is frequented by pin-up stylers, leather-cladbikers, and the old T-shirt and ripped-jeans crowd, and you'll know it from the presence of antlers in Jägerklause's decorations. The pub has a dance floor and features live bands from Wednesday to Saturday. Check the website calendar for dates and deets.

i *U5: Frankfurter Tor. From the metro, walk south on Warschauer Str. Turn right onto Grünberger Str. Jägerklause is on the right. Beer €3.10. ☼ Beer garden open Tu-F 2-10pm, Sa-Su 11am-10pm. Pub open Tu-Su 11am-late.*

berlin

Kreuzberg

If you came to Berlin for nightlife and you've visited some places in other neighborhoods, you've probably been left wondering why on earth Berlin has the reputation it boasts. And the answer, dear friend, is Kreuzberg. Kreuzberg is world-renowned for its unbelievable techno scene. Converted warehouses, wild light displays, destructive speaker systems, and packed dance floors cluster around **Schlesisches Tor**, but some of the best spots are scattered more widely. Kreuzberg is one of Berlin's most notoriously nocturnal neighborhoods, so expect the parties to rage from about 2am to well past dawn.

CLUB TRESOR   CLUB

Köpenicker Str. 70   ☎030 629 08 750 www.tresorberlin.com

Guess what? Club Tresor is housed in a massive warehouse. "Gee, just like every other club in Berlin, right?" Wrong! With its motto of "Berlin must be new," Club Tresor is like no other. For one, there's a strobe light, but it manages to be cool rather than kitschy. The dance floor in the basement is so big that you can easily get away from that one guy who manages to be lame in the coolest club in Berlin. Upstairs, a brighter, redder, and more comfortable floor plays tight house tracks, which serve as a perfect warm-up or cool-down. Make the trek, stay all night, and have your nightmares later.

i U8: Heinrich Heinestr. Cover €8-15. Cash only. ☺ Usually open W 11:59pm-late, F-Sa 11:59pm-late, but check the website for a schedule.

CLUB DER VISIONAERE   CLUB, BAR

Am Flutgraben 1   ☎030 695 18 942 www.clubdervisionaere.com

CDV is pretty much the only Berlin club that is not, in fact, in a warehouse. Instead, it's going for that whole "underrated" feeling, because it's still not as well-known as Watergate (see below) despite incredibly high ratings. It's a boat, it's a club, it's a riverfront cabana. Unfortunately, it's packed, and packed with slightly awkward British tourists at that. A DJ spins inside a mini, indoor club, but the fun is definitely outside, where you can sip rum drinks, dip your feet in the river, or jump into the river while screeching some Britney Spears lyrics you remember from your childhood. So relaxing, so visionary, so Berlin.

i U1: Schlesisches Tor. From the metro, head southeast on Schlesischestr. Cross the 1st canal; when you reach the 2nd, the club is on the left next to the bridge. Cover €4-15. Beer €2.50-3.50. Long drinks €5.50. Cash only. ☺ Open M-F 2pm-late, Sa-Su noon-late.

ARENA CLUB   CLUB

Eichenstr. 4   ☎030 533 20 30 www.arena-club.de

Though Arena's pool might be cooler than its dance club, it must be said: Arena is pretty damn awesome. Unfortunately, the club (unlike the pool/sauna) is not floating in the Spree. It's just another old, converted factory. There's a ton of space for lounging and taking a break from dancing to the beats, with cushy, square booths that are perfect for snuggling. Arena keeps the juice flowing with two full bars and two full dance floors, both of which scream techno all night long.

i U1: Schlesisches Tor. From the metro, head south on Schlesischestr. across both canal bridges. The Arena complex is the large industrial set of buildings on the left after the 2nd bridge. Cover €5-10. Cash only. ☺ Party hours vary, but usually open F-Sa midnight-late.

WATERGATE   CLUB

Falckensteinstr. 49   ☎030 612 80 396 www.water-gate.de

Oh the exclusivity! It's so enticing! Even if we didn't put this place in the book, you'd probably end up going anyway. You'll get to enjoy waiting in a long, *long* line (min. wait 30min.), but if you manage to endure the queue and get past the bouncer (are you sure your shirt isn't too casual?), you'll get to post a Facebook status bragging about visiting "the World's most exclusive club." Okay, enough ripping on Watergate: groups should split up, especially sausage fests. Inside, you'll find a gorgeous, Spree-level view, a boat where you can cool off, and a dance floor that's so packed, so loud, and so long that you'll probably momentarily forget the world while you're there. The whole place is spectacular and enticing, but for authenticity's sake, we urge you to seek out some other Kreuzberg clubs, too. Watergate is like Nixon's presidency: ruined by nosy Americans.

i *U1: Schlesisches Tor. From the metro, head toward the bridge. It's the unmarked door at the top of the stairs, just before the river. There'll be a line (there always is). Cover €8-20. Mixed drinks €6.50. Cash only. ☼ Open W midnight-late, F-Sa midnight-late.*

RITTER BUTZKE
CLUB

Ritterstr. 24   www.ritterbutzke.de

If you're looking for a place that's "off the beaten track" (at least for tourists), this is it. One of Berlin's only clubs to feature a *Gästeliste*, or guest list, in addition to regular admission for n00bs and natives without friends in high places, Ritter Butzke's complex, nestled in the alleyways of an old factory building, is one of Kreuzberg's most well-known and best-kept secrets. The three dance floors vary from small and intimate to medium-sized and cramped to expansive and accommodating to even the most notorious toe-steppers. Pick your poison.

i *U1: Prinzenstr. From the metro, head northeast on Prinzenstr. for 2 blocks, then turn left onto Ritterstr. Halfway down the block, turn into the courtyard shaded by trees on the right. The entrance to the club is at the end of this courtyard. Cover around €10. Shots €2-2.50. Beer €2-3. Long drinks €5-6. Cash only. ☼ Hours vary, but generally open F midnight-late, Sa 10pm-late. Check the website for full calendar of events.*

LUZIA
BAR, CAFE

Oranienstr. 34   ☎030 817 99 958 www.luzia.tc

Kreuzberg is covered with clubs, but where are all the bars? Well, they're superfluous because Luzia is such a great bar that they'd all fall short in comparison. Luzia is huge and tremendously popular with the Kreuzberg locals, most of whom are UK transplants who think of themselves as German artists. Whatever, this is still a great bar. Gold-painted walls glow softly in the light of flickering candles. The huge, L-shaped design allows for long lines of vintage, threadbare lounge chairs, cafe tables, and a bar so long that it can easily serve the crowd that swarms here at peak hours.

i *U1 or U8: Kotbusser Tor. From the metro, head northeast up Aldabertstr. and turn left onto Oranienstr. The bar is on the right. The only sign is a large, black rectangle with a gold coat of arms in the middle. Beer €2.50-3.50. Long drinks €5-6. Absinthe €3-7. Cash only. ☼ Open daily noon-late.*

MAGNET CLUB
CLUB, MUSIC VENUE

Falckensteinstr. 48   ☎030 440 08 140 www.magnet-club.de

Magnet wishes it were in New Orleans: it's the sort of place that hosts ladies' cage wrestling competitions. Patrons include locals who come for the DJ and furious tourists who got rejected from Watergate next door. Indie bands play on a short, shallow stage that makes it seem as though they're part of the crowd, and DJs spin a much lighter mix than their Kreuzberg counterparts—think indie electropop. Magnet tries hard to one-up its peaceful indie followers, offering free Jager shots (while the stock lasts) a couple of nights a week.

i *U1: Schlesisches Tor. From the metro, head toward the bridge. An "M" hangs above the door. Cover €3-7. Shots €2-2.50. Beer €2.50-3. Long drinks €6-6.50. ☼ Usually open Tu-Su from 10pm. Check online for exact schedule.*

SO36
BAR, CLUB

Oranienstr. 190   ☎030 614 01 306 www.so36.de

SO36 was probably amazing in 1970. For one thing, seeing David Bowie on a dance floor might make your heart stop. But today, SO36 is less of a club and

berlin

more of a relic, a tribute to better music and better times. The various parties, live shows, and cultural presentations that fill this huge hall attract a mixed gay/ straight clientele whose common denominator is that they like to party hardy. Gayhane, a gay cabaret that performs the last Saturday of every month, has become a staple of the Berlin GLBT scene and can get pretty epic.

i U1 or U8: Kottbusser Tor. From the metro, walk north on Adalbertstr. and turn right onto Oranienstr. The club is on the right. Cover varies. Shots €2.20. Beer €2.80-3.50. Wine €3. Long drinks €5.50, with Red Bull €6. Cash only. ⏰ Hours vary, but usually open F-Sa 10pm-late.

ROSES   GLBT, BAR
Oranienstr. 187   ☎030 615 65 70
At first glance, it might look like a kink shop, but, rest assured, the fuzzy pink walls and the omnipresent cheetah print make this gay bar a sight for sore eyes. Gay men, some lesbian women, and a couple of straight groups (there to camp out in campy glory) join together for small talk over some clean electronic. The bar's small size makes mingling easy, and the endless assortment of wall trinkets (glowing mounted antlers, twinkling hearts, a psychedelic Virgin Mary) keep everyone giggling.

i U1 or U8: Kottbusser Tor. From the metro, head northwest on Oranienstr. past Mariannenstr. The bar is on the left. Beer €2.50. Cocktails €5, with Red Bull €6. Cash only. ⏰ Open daily 9pm-late.

ARTS AND CULTURE

As the old saying goes, "Where there be hipsters, there be Arts and Culture." Though the saying's origins are unclear, it certainly applies to Berlin. Whether it's opera, film, or Brecht in the original German that you're after, Berlin has got you covered. For a magical evening at the symphony, grab a standing-room-only ticket to see the Berliner Philharmoniker or grab a rush seat to see the Deutsche Oper perform Wagner's four-opera cycle, *The Ring of the Nibelung*. If rock, pop, indie, or hip hop are more your style, head to Kreuzberg to check out Festsaal Kreuzberg and Columbiahalle. Nearby, English Theater Berlin will satisfy any Anglophone's theater cravings, while the Deutsches Theater in Mitte hosts performances of the German classics as well as the English canon in translation. The truly hip should head straight to Lichtblick Kino or Kino Babylon to find radical documentaries, avant-garde films, and a sea of retro frames and flannel.

Music and Opera

BERLINER PHILHARMONIE   MITTE
Herbert-von-Karajan-Str. 1   ☎030 254 88 999 www.berlin-philharmonic.com
If you fancy yourself to be a fan of classical music, you'd better have heard of the **Berlin Philharmoniker.** Led by Sir Simon Rattle, the Philharmoniker is considered one of the world's finest, if not the finest, orchestras. Concerts take place in the Philharmonie, a decidedly huge and weird-looking concert hall near Potsdamer Platz. The bright yellow building was designed to be pitch perfect: every member of the audience gets an adequately full view and incredibly full sound. With most concerts selling out about a month in advance, it can be pretty tough to get a seat, so check the website for availability. For sold-out concerts, some tickets and standing room may be available 90min. before the concert begins, but only at the box office. Stand in line, get some cheap tickets if you're lucky, and enjoy some of the sweetest sounds known to mankind.

i S1, S2, S25, or U2: Potsdamer Pl. From the metro, head west on Potsdamer Str. Tickets for standing room from €7, for seats from €15. ⏰ Open from Jul-early Sept. Box office open M-F 3-6pm, Sa-Su 11am-2pm.

DEUTSCHE STAATSOPER

Unter den Linden 7   ☎030 203 54 555   www.staatsoper-berlin.de

The Deutsche Staatsoper is notorious for its splendor. Though its presence and patronage suffered during the years of separation, this opera house is rebuilding its reputation and its repertoire of Baroque opera and contemporary pieces. Unfortunately, its exterior is under extensive renovation, and the usual opera house is closed until mid-2014. Until its main building reopens, the Staatsoper presents performances in the sticks—Schiller Theater in Charlottenburg.

i *U6: Französische Str. Or bus #100, 157, or 348: Deutsche Staatsoper. Tickets €14-260. For certain seats, students can get a ½-price discount, but only within 4 weeks of the performance and only at the box office. Unsold tickets €13, 30min. before the show. ⚄ Open Aug through mid-Jul. Box office open daily noon-7pm and 1hr. before performances.*

DEUTSCHE OPER BERLIN

Bismarckstr. 35   ☎030 343 84 343   www.deutscheoperberlin.de

The Deutsche Oper Berlin's original home, the Deutsches Opernhaus, was built in 1911 but (surprise!) was decimated by Allied bombs. Today, performances take place in Berlin's newest opera house, which looks like a gigantic concrete box. If you have the chance, don't pass up a cheap ticket to see one of Berlin's most spectacular performances.

i *U2: Deutsche Oper. Tickets €16-122. 25% student discount when you buy at the box office. Unsold tickets €13, 30min. before the show. ⚄ Open Sept-Jun. Box office open M-Sa 11am until beginning of the performance or 11am-7pm on days without performances, Su 10am-2pm. Evening tickets available 1hr. before performances.*

FESTSAAL KREUZBERG

Skalitzerstr. 130   ☎030 611 01 313   www.festsaal-kreuzberg.de

Free jazz, indie rock, swing, electropop—you never know what to expect at this absurdly hip venue. A tremendous chasm of a main hall accommodates acts of all shapes and sizes, plus an overflowing crowd of fans packed together on the main floor and the mezzanine. A dusty courtyard out front features a bar and novelty acts like fire throwers. Poetry readings, film screenings, and art performances fill out the program with appropriately eclectic material, making this one of Berlin's most exciting venues.

i *U1 or U8: Kottbusser Tor. From the U-Bahn, head east on Skalitzerstr. The venue is on the left. Tickets €5-20. Shots €2. Long drinks €6. ⚄ Hours vary. Usually open F-Sa 9pm-late. Check website for details.*

COLUMBIAHALLE

Columbiadamm 13-21   ☎030 698 09 80   www.columbiahalle.de

Any venue that features Snoop Dogg, The Specials, and Bon Iver in a matter of a couple months has a special place in our hearts. With a wildly eclectic collection of superstars and indie notables from all over the world, Columbiahalle's calendar is bound to make you gasp and say, "I definitely wanna see that," at least twice. Once a gym for American service members in south Kreuzberg, Columbiahalle may look dated and innocuous, but its standing-room-only floor and mezzanine sure can rage.

i *U6: Platz der Luftbrücke. From the metro, head east on Columbiadamm. The venue is in the 1st block on the right. Tickets €20-60, depending on the act. ⚄ Hours and dates vary, but concerts tend to start at 8pm. Check the website for more details.*

Film

Finding English films in Berlin is almost as easy as finding the Fernsehturm. On any night, choose from over 150 different films, marked **O.F.** or **O.V.** for the original version (meaning not dubbed in German), **O.m.U** for original version with German subtitles, or **O.m.u.E.** for original film with English subtitles.

berlin

LICHTBLICK KINO

Kastanienallee 77   ☎030 440 58 179 www.lichtblick-kino.org

Lichtblick is a charming cinema. The 32-seat theater presents avant-garde films and radical documentaries, as well as a wildly eclectic range of movies. English films are intermixed with all sorts of other international fare, and all films are shown with the original sound and accompanied by German subtitles, so you won't need to perform any amazing feats of lip-reading for any of the many English films. With a bar in the main entrance and a couple guys reading philosophical novels by candlelight, this is the quintessential art house experience.

i U8: Eberswalder Str. From the metro, walk southwest on Kastanienallee, past Oderberger Str. The theater is near the end of the next block on the left. Tickets €5, students €4.50. ☉ 2-5 films shown every night, check the website for a calendar. Usually 5-10pm.

KINO BABYLON

Rosa-Luxemburg-Str. 30   ☎030 242 59 69 www.babylonberlin.de

Americans, Brits, and Berliners alike flock to this spunky, independent film house with a commitment to classic international cinema. Silent films, fiction readings, and constant themed retrospectives guarantee that you'll have a chance to see something new and interesting alongside the classics. Casanova, anyone? Occasional summer screenings happen outdoors on the beautiful Rosa-Luxemburg-Pl.—and epic screenings of *Rocky Horror Picture Show* go down regularly. Unfortunately, outside of the frequent American classics, English is a bit hard to come by, as most subtitles are in German.

i U2: Rosa-Luxemburg-Pl. From the metro, walk south on Rosa-Luxemburg-Str. Tickets €4-8. ☉ The schedule changes daily; check website for details. Box office open M-F from 5pm until the 1st film of the evening.

ARSENAL

In the Filmhaus at Potsdamer Pl.   ☎030 269 55 100 www.arsenal-berlin.de

Run by the founders of Berlinale and located just below the **Museum for Film and Television,** Arsenal showcases independent films and some classics. Discussions, talks, and frequent appearances by guest directors make the theater a popular meeting place for Berlin's filmmakers. With the majority of films in the original with English subtitles, non-Germans can watch easy.

i U2, S1, S2, or S25: Potsdamer Pl. From the metro, head west on Potsdamer Str. and go into the building labeled "Deutsche Kinemathek." Take the elevator down to the 2nd basement level. Tickets €6.50, students €5. ☉ 3-5 films shown each night. Films usually start 4-8pm. Check the website for a full calendar.

CENTRAL KINO

Rosenthaler Str. 39   ☎030 285 99 973 www.kino-central.de

A small theater right in the middle of Mitte, this place shows indie German fare, award-winning American films, and other international cinema, mostly in the original language with German subtitles. While the screens aren't huge, the location is prime. It's located near Hackesher Markt in a heavily graffitied courtyard; one theater is even outside.

i S3, S5, or S7: Hackescher Markt. From the metro, walk north on Rosenthaler Str., past the Hackesche Höfe, and the theater is in a courtyard next door. €6.50, students €6. ☉ Open daily before the 1st movie noon-3pm.

Theater

ENGLISH THEATER BERLIN

Fidicinstr. 40   ☎030 693 56 92 www.etberlin.de

Though all the shows here are presented in English, it's hard to find a theater that is more "Berlin." From 10min. skits to full-out festivals, the English Theater tries out every edge of the spectrum, and, boy, is this place ever edgy. We hear that most shows feature naked people and cabbages.

i *U6: Pl. der Luftbrücke. From the metro, head north on Mehringdamm for 2 blocks and turn right onto Fidicinstr. The theater is on the left, within the 1st block. €13, students €8.* ☒ *Box office opens 1hr. before show. Shows are at 8pm unless otherwise noted. Check the website for a calendar of performances.*

DEUTSCHES THEATER   MITTE
Schumann Str. 13a   ☎030 284 41 225 www.deutschestheater.de

Built in 1850, this world-famous theater was once controlled by legendary director Max Reinhardt and is still a cultural heavy hitter in Berlin. With even English dramas in translation (Shakespeare and Beckett are rockstars here), Anglophones shouldn't expect to understand any of the words. Fortunately, the productions are gorgeous enough that they're worth seeing in spite of the language barrier.

i *U6: Oranienburger Tor. From the U-Bahn, head south on Friederichstr., take a right onto Reinhartstr., then another right onto Albrechtstr €5-30.* ☒ *Box office open M-Sa 11am-6:30pm, Su 3-6:30pm. Shows are at 8pm unless otherwise noted.*

VOLKSBÜHNE   MITTE
Linienstr. 227   ☎030 24 06 55 www.volksbuehne-berlin.de

Originally established to house productions of Socialist Realism at prices accessible to the working class, this imposing "people's theater" looks like it came straight out of a utopian sci-fi thriller. While the enormous stage goes dark during the summer, alive with concerts, German and English theater, and touring performances and festivals from Sept-May. Productions range from Büchner to Brecht to an interactive contemporary work called "Revolution Now!"—you'll probably leave more convinced of capitalist injustice than ever before. Before and after the shows, crowds gather in the beautiful plaza to smoke and talk.

i *U2: Rosa-Luxemburg-Pl. From the metro, walk south down Rosa-Luxemburg-Str. Tickets €6-30. Students get a 50% discount on certain performances; check the website.* ☒ *Box office open daily noon-6pm and 1hr. before performances. Shows are at 8pm unless otherwise noted.*

SHOPPING
Books
Finding English books in Berlin is about as easy as finding someone who speaks English: they're everywhere, but they're not always very good. Secondhand is the best way to offset the extra cost of English books.

🛢 ST. GEORGE'S BOOKSTORE   PRENZLAUER BERG
Wörtherstr. 27   ☎030 817 98 333 www.saintgeorgesbookshop.com

You'd be hard-pressed to find a better English-language bookstore on the continent. St. George's owner makes frequent trips to the UK and US to buy the loads of titles that fill the towering shelves. The books are stacked from the floor to the ceiling, and picturesque ladders stretch upward. Over half of the books are used and extremely well-priced (paperbacks €4-8), with a number of books for just €1. Pay in euro, British pounds, or American dollars (oh my!).

i *U2: Senefelderpl. From the metro, head southeast on Metzerstr. and turn left onto Prenzlauer Allee. Follow Prenzlauer Allee 3 blocks, then turn left onto Wörtherstr. The bookstore is halfway down the block, on the right. Used hardcovers €10.* ☒ *Open M-F 11am-8pm, Sa 11am-7pm.*

ANOTHER COUNTRY   KREUZBERG
Riemannstr. 7   ☎030 694 01 160 www.anothercountry.de

Browsing this cluttered secondhand English bookstore feels a little like walking around some guy's house, but a wide and unpredictable collection rewards your searching, especially since all books are €2-5. Another Country doesn't just want to be that forgettable place where you can buy a cheap copy of *Twilight* (which is in stock; €5); it wants to be a local library and cultural center. A small percentage of the books are labeled "lending only," meaning they're priced a little higher (around €10), and you get back the entire price, minus €1.50, when you return them. Plus, live acoustic performances, readings, and trivia add further incentive to return again and again. Check out the wide selection of "Evil Books," which includes a copy of L. Ron Hubbard's *Dianetics*, a book entitled *The Quotable Richard Nixon*, and *Bradymania*.

i U7: Gneisenaustr. From the metro, walk south on Zossener Str. Turn right onto Riemannstr., and Another Country is on the left. ꙮ Open Tu-F 11am-8pm, Sa-Su noon-4pm.

Music

⬛ SPACE HALL
KREUZBERG

Zossenerstr. 33, 35   ☎030 694 76 64 www.spacehall.de

They don't make them like this anymore in the States—maybe they never did. With two addresses (one of just CDs, the other strictly vinyl), Space Hall makes it nearly impossible *not* to find what you're looking for. The vinyl store never misses a beat, with the longest interior of any Berlin record store (painted to resemble a forest, of course) and easily one of the widest selections to boot. They also have an inspiring collection of rubber duckies.

i U7: Gneisenaustr. From the metro, head south on Zossenerstr. The record store is on the left. CDs regular €10-20, discounted €3-10. LPs €10-30. ꙮ Open M-W 11am-8pm, Th-F 11am-10pm, Sa 11am-8pm.

⬛ HARD WAX
KREUZBERG

Paul-Lincke-Ufer 44a   ☎030 611 30 111 www.hardwax.com

Walk down a silent alleyway, through an eerily quiet courtyard, up three flights of dim, graffitied stairs, and suddenly, you're in one of Berlin's best record stores for electronic music. Bare brick and concrete walls make it feel aggressively nonchalant, while an entire back room dedicated to private listening stations for patrons proves that Hard Wax is dedicated to helping you get out of the House. Here, you'll find dubstep, IDM, ambient, and subgenres upon subgenres. Fortunately, nearly every CD and LP bears a short description in English courtesy of Hard Wax's experts, so you'll never feel like you're randomly flipping through a lot of crap. Though the selection is small compared to some of Berlin's other electro-record stores, the offerings seem hand-picked.

i U1 or U8: Kottbusser Tor. From the U-Bahn, head south on Kottbusserstr. Take a left just before the canal, then enter the courtyard on the left just after crossing Mariannenstr. Records €5-30; most €8-12. CDs €10-20. ꙮ Open M-Sa noon-8pm.

ESSENTIALS
Practicalities

- **TOURIST OFFICES:** Now privately owned, tourist offices merely give you some commercial flyer or refer you to a website instead of guaranteeing human contact. Visit **www.berlin.de** for reliable info on all aspects of city life. **Tourist Info Centers.** (Berlin Tourismus Marketing GmbH, Am Karlsbad 11 ☎030 25 00 25 www.visitberlin.de. *i* On the ground floor of the Hauptbahnhof, next to the northern entrance. English spoken. *Siegessäule, Blu,* and *Gay-Yellowpages* have GLBT event and club listings. Transit maps free; city maps €1-2. The monthly *Berlin Programm* lists museums, sights, restaurants, and hotels as well as opera, theater, and classical music performances, €1.75. *Tip* provides full listings of film, theater, concerts, and clubs in German, €2.70. *Ex-Berliner* has English-language movie and theater reviews, €2. ꙮ Open daily 8am-10pm.) **Alternate location.** (Brandenburger Tor S1, S2, S25, or bus #100:

Unter den Linden. *i* On your left as you face the pillars from the Unter den Linden side. ⌚ Open daily 10am-6pm.)

- **STUDENT TRAVEL OFFICES: STA** books flights and hotels and sells ISICs. (Dorotheenstr. 30 ☎030 201 65 063 *i* S3, S5, S7, S9, S75, or U6: Friedrichstr. From the metro, walk 1 block south on Friedrichstr., turn left onto Dorotheenstr., and follow as it veers left. STA is on the left. ⌚ Open M-F 10am-7pm, Sa 11am-3pm.) **Second location.** (Gleimstr. 28 ☎030 285 98 264 *i* S4, S8, S85, or U2: Schönhauser Allee. From the metro, walk south on Schönhauser Allee and turn right onto Gleimstr. ⌚ Open M-F 10am-7pm, Sa 11am-4pm.) **Third location.** (Hardenbergstr. 9 ☎030 310 00 40 *i* U2: Ernst-Reuter-Pl. From the metro, walk southeast on Hardenbergstr.Open M-F 10am-7pm, Sa 11am-3pm.) **Fourth location.** (Takustr. 47. ☎030 831 10 25 *i* U3: Dahlem-Dorf. From the metro, walk north on Brümmerstr., turn left onto Königin-Luise Str., then turn right onto Takustr. ⌚ Open M-F 10am-7pm, Sa 10am-2pm.)

- **TOURS: Terry Brewer's Best of Berlin** is legendary for its vast knowledge and engaging personalities, making the 6hr.+ walk well worth it. Tours leave daily from in front of the Bandy Brooks shop on Friedrichstr. (☎017 738 81 537 www.brewersberlintours.com *i* S1, S7, S9, S75, or U6: Friedrichstr €12. ⌚ Tours start at 10:30am.) **Insider Tour** offers a variety of fun, informative walking and bike tours that hit all the major sights. More importantly, the guides' enthusiasm for Berlin is contagious, and their accents span the English-speaking world. (☎030 692 3149 www.insidertour.com. ⌚ Tours last 4hr.)

- **CURRENCY EXCHANGE AND MONEY WIRES:** The best rates are usually found at exchange offices with **Wechselstube** signs outside, at most major train stations, and in large squares. For money wires through Western Union, use **ReiseBank.** (Ⓜ Hauptbahnhof ☎030 204 53 761 ⌚ Open M-Sa 8am-10pm.) **Second location.** (Ⓜ Bahnhof Zoo ☎030 881 71 17.) **Third location.** (Ⓜ Ostbahnhof 030 296 43 93.)

- **LUGGAGE STORAGE:** In the Ⓜ Hauptbahnhof, in "DB Gepack Center," 1st fl., east side €4 per day). Lockers also at Ⓜ Bahnhof Zoo, Ⓜ Ostbahnhof, and Ⓜ Alexanderpl.

- **INTERNET ACCESS:** Free internet with admission to the **Staatsbibliothek.** During its renovation, Staatsbibliothek requires €10 month-long pass to the library. (Potsdamer Str. 33 ☎030 26 60 ⌚ Open M-F 9am-9pm, Sa 9am-7pm.) **Netlounge.** (Auguststr. 89 ☎030 24 34 25 97 www.netlounge-berlin.de *i* Ⓜ Oranienburger Str. €2.50 per hr. ⌚ Open daily noon-midnight.) **Easy Internet** has several locations throughout Berlin. (Unter den Linden 24, Rosenstr. 16, Frankfurter Allee 32, Rykestr. 29, and Kurfürstendamm 18.) Many cafes throughout Berlin offer free Wi-Fi, including **Starbucks,** where the networks never require a password.

- **POST OFFICES: Bahnhof Zoo.** (Joachimstaler Str. 7 ☎030 887 08 611 *i* Down Joachimstaler Str. from Bahnhof Zoo on the corner of Joachimstaler Str. and Kantstr. ⌚ Open M-Sa 9am-8pm.) **Alexanderplatz.** (Rathausstr. 5, by the Dunkin Donuts. ⌚ Open M-F 9am-7pm, 9am-4pm.) **Tegel Airport.** (⌚ Open M-F 8am-6pm, Sa 8am-noon.) **Ostbahnhof.** (⌚ Open M-F 8am-8pm, Sa-Su 10am-6pm.) To find a post office near you, visit the search tool on their website, www.standorte.deutschepost.de/filialen_verkaufspunkte, which is confusing and in German but could help.

- **POSTAL CODE** 10706.

Emergency

- **POLICE:** Pl. der Luftbrücke 6. U6: Pl. der Luftbrücke.

- **EMERGENCY NUMBERS:** ☎110.

- **AMBULANCE AND FIRE:** ☎112.

- **NON-EMERGENCY ADVICE HOTLINE:** ☎030 466 44 664.

berlin

- **MEDICAL SERVICES:** The American and British embassies list English-speaking doctors. The **emergency doctor** (☎030 31 00 31 or ☎018 042 255 23 62) service helps travelers find English-speaking doctors. **Emergency dentist.** (☎030 890 04 333)

- **CRISIS LINES:** English spoken on most crisis lines. **American Hotline** (017 781 41 510) has crisis and referral services. **Poison Control.** (030 192 40) **Berliner Behindertenverband** has resources for the disabled. (Jägerstr. 63d ☎030 204 38 47 www.bbv-ev.de ☼ Open W noon-5pm and by appointment.) **Deutsche AIDS-Hilfe.** (Wilhelmstr. 138 ☎030 690 08 70 www.aidshilfe.de) **Drug Crisis Hotline.** (☎030 192 37 24hr.) **Frauenkrisentelefon.** Women's crisis line. (☎030 615 4243 www.frauenkrisentelefon.de ☼ Open M 10am-noon, Tu-W 7-9pm, Th 10am-noon, F 7-9pm, Sa-Su 5-7pm.) **Lesbenberatung** offers counseling for lesbians. (Kulmer Str. 20a ☎030 215 20 00 www.lesbenberatung-berlin.de) **Schwulenberatung** offers counseling for gay men. (Mommenstr. 45 ☎030 194 46 www.schwulenberatungberlin.de.) **Maneo** offers legal help for gay victims of violence. (☎030 216 33 36 www.maneo.de ☼ Open daily 5-7pm.) **LARA** offers counseling for victims of sexual assault. (Fuggerstr. 19 ☎030 216 88 88 www.lara-berlin.de ☼ Open M-F 9am-6pm.)

Getting There

By Plane

Capital Airport Berlin Brandenburg International (BBI) is currently under construction and will be opened at an unknown future date. Until then, **Tegel Airport** will continue to serve travelers. (☎018 050 00 186 www.berlin-airport.de *i* Take express bus #X9 or #109 from U7: Jakob-Kaiser Pl., bus #128 from U6: Kurt-Schumacher-Pl., or bus TXL from S42, S41: Beusselstr. Follow signs in the airport for ground transportation.)

By Train

International trains (☎972 226 150) pass through Berlin's **Hauptbahnhof** and run to: Amsterdam, NTH (€130. ☼ 7hr., 16 per day); Brussels, BEL (€140. ☼ 7hr., 16 per day); Budapest, HUN (€140. ☼ 13hr., 4 per day); Copenhagen, DNK (€135. ☼ 7hr., 7 per day.); Paris, FRA (€200. ☼ 9hr., 9 per day.); Prague, CZR (€80. ☼ 5hr., 12 per day); Vienna, AUT (€155. ☼ 10hr., 12 per day.)

By Bus

ZOB is the central bus station. (Masurenallee 4. ☎030 301 03 80 *i* U2: Theodor-Heuss-Pl. From the metro, head southwest on Masurenallee; the station is on the left. Alternatively, S4, S45, or S46: Messe Nord/ICC. From the metro, walk west on Neue Kantstr. The station is on the right. ☼ Open M-F 6am-9pm, Sa-Su and holidays 6am-8pm.)

Getting Around

By Public Transportation: The Bvg

The two pillars of Berlin's metro are the **U-Bahn** and **S-Bahn** trains, which cover the city in spidery and circular patterns, (somewhat) respectively. **Trams** and **buses** (both part of the U-Bahn system) scuttle around the remaining city corners. (BVG's 24hr. hotline ☎030 194 49 www.bvg.de.) Berlin is divided into three transit zones. **Zone A** consists of central Berlin, including Tempelhof Airport. The rest of Berlin lies in **Zone B. Zone C** covers the larger state of Brandenburg, including Potsdam. An **AB** ticket is the best deal, since you can later buy extension tickets for the outlying areas. A **one-way** ticket is good for 2hr. after validation. (Zones AB €2.30, BC €2.70, ABC €3, under 6 free.) Within the validation period, the ticket may be used on any S-Bahn, U-Bahn, bus, or tram.

Most train lines don't run Monday through Friday 1-4am. S-Bahn and U-Bahn lines do run Friday and Saturday nights, but less frequently. When trains stop running, 70 night buses take over, running every 20-30min. generally along major transit routes; pick up the free *Nachtliniennetz* **map** of bus routes at a **Fahrscheine und Mehr** office. The letter "N" precedes night bus numbers. Trams continue to run at night.

Buy tickets, including monthly passes, from machines or ticket windows in metro stations or from bus drivers. **Be warned:** machines don't give more than €10 change, and many machines don't take bills, though some accept credit cards. **Validate** your ticket by inserting it into the stamp machines before boarding. Failure to validate becomes a big deal when plainclothes policemen bust you and charge you €40 for freeloading. If you bring a bike on the U-Bahn or S-Bahn, you must buy it a child's ticket. Bikes are prohibited on buses and trams.

Single-ride tickets are a waste of money. A **day ticket** (AB €6.30, BC €6.60, ABC €6.80) is good from the time it's stamped until 3am the next day. The BVG also sells **7-day tickets** (AB €27.20, BC €28, ABC €33.50) and **month-long passes** (AB €74, BC €75, ABC €91). The popular tourist cards are another option. The **WelcomeCard** (sold at tourist offices) buys unlimited travel (AB 48hr. €17, ABC €19; 72hr. €23/26) and includes discounts at 130 sights. The **City TourCard** is good within zones AB (48hr. €16, 72hr. €22) and offers discounts at over 50 attractions.

By Taxi
Call 15min. in advance for a taxi. Women can request female drivers. Trips within the city cost up to €30. (☎030 261 026, toll-free ☎0800 263 00 00)

By Bike
Biking is one of the best ways to explore the city that never brakes. Unless your hostel is out in the boonies, few trips will be out of cycling distance, and given that U-Bahn tickets verge on €3 and that the average long-term bike rental costs €8 per day, pedaling your way can be a better deal and a simpler way to navigate. **Fat Tire Bike Rental** (Panorama Str. 1a ☎016 389 26 427)and **Prenzlberger Orange Bikes** (Kollwitzstr. 35 ☎030 240 47 991 www.berlinfahrradverleih.com) are both great options.

cologne

Cologne is the fourth largest city in Germany (after Berlin, Hamburg, and Munich), but it feels decidedly provincial. Perhaps it's the way that its famous cathedral owns all the other buildings in town, or maybe it's because the locals speak their own funky dialect, called Kölsch. Cologne became a major pilgrimage destination in the 12th century, after relics of the Three Wise Men were transferred to its cathedral. Many know "cologne," thanks to Eau de Cologne, an 18th-century perfume that was all the rage back in the day and now makes for the perfect passive-aggressive gift. The city center was almost completely razed by bombings during World War II and has since been meticulously reconstructed.

The city never regained the power it once had in the Middle Ages, but that doesn't mean that it lives in the past. Trade fairs and conventions regularly bring in throngs of businesspeople. The city is also home to many art museums, and the nightlife scene stays vibrant thanks to the presence of the University of Cologne (Universität zu Köln), one of Germany's largest universities. Known as the "Gay Capital of Germany," Cologne is also the site of an enormous Pride parade every summer. Don't be fooled: Kölsch beer may be served in the smallest glasses you'll find in Germany, but people here like to enjoy life in big gulps.

ORIENTATION
The Rhein runs north to south through the middle of the city. The historic center is located on the west bank, where a semi-circle of streets, made up of the Hansaring, Hohenzollernring, Hohenstaufenring, Sachsenring, and Ubierring, separates the

city's Altstadt (Old Town, inside the ring) from the Neustadt (New Town, outside the ring). On the other side of the river is Deutz, home to Cologne's trade fairs.

Altstadt-Nord

The northern part of the Old Town is home to the majestic **Dom,** which sits next door to the **Hauptbahnhof,** Cologne's transportation hub. Many of the city's museums and churches can be found here, rubbing elbows with Western shops and overpriced German brewhouses. **Hohe Straße** and **Schildergasse** are the main shopping streets, stretching from the cathedral all the way to ⓂNeumarkt. This district is also where you'll find Eau de Cologne stores, including the famous **4711-Haus.**

Altstadt-Sud

The southern part of the Old Town begins at roughly the Deutzer bridge. **The Chocolate Museum** and the **Rautenstrauch-Joest Museum** remain this neighborhood's greatest assets, but recent construction along the banks of the Rhein has transformed the once-defunct **Rheinauhaufen** (Rhein harbor) into a posh residential area. The three inverted, L-shaped apartment buildings, called the **Kranhaus** (Crane House), have brought the city some modern architectural street cred. Cologne's gay hubs (the Heumarkt area and Rudolfpl.) can be found on the border between the northern and southern sections of the Old Town.

Neustadt

Thanks to the presence of the University of Cologne (located in the southwest part of Neustadt), this district has some of Cologne's most student-friendly restaurants and bars. The area around **Zülpicher Platz** has great restaurants and stores on every corner, while the **Belgisches Viertel** to the northwest has a reputation for trendy stores and bars. **Hohenzollernring** and the surrounding side streets make up another lively area that boasts many cafes, movie theaters, and nightclubs.

SIGHTS

Altstadt-Nord

🏛 KÖLNER DOM (COLOGNE CATHEDRAL)   CATHEDRAL
Domkloster 3   ☎0221 17 94 05 55 www.koelner-dom.de

To ascend the Südturm (southern tower), exit the church through the main gate and turn left to head down the stairs. The climb up the tower's 533 steps will take at least 15min. and will leave you wobbly-legged, but it offers a panoramic view of the city. Though Cologne's skyline sans cathedral is pretty underwhelming, the climb is definitely worth it. Catch your breath about three-quarters of the way up at the Glockenstube, a chamber for the tower's nine bells. Four of the bells date from the Middle Ages, but the loudest one is the 20th-century upstart called Der Große Peter, which is the world's heaviest swinging bell at 24 tons.

i By the Hauptbahnhof. The Dom Forum (☎0221 92 58 47 20www.domforum.de), across the street, organizes guided tours in English. A 20min. film in English shown inside the Dom Forum provides an introduction to the cathedral. Cathedral free. Schatzkammer €5, students €2.50; tower €2.50/1; combined €6/3; Dom Forum tours €6 €4; film €2 €1,free with a tour. ✪ Church open daily May-Oct 6am-9pm; Nov-Apr 6am-7:30pm. Schatzkammer open daily 10am-6pm. Tower open daily May-Sept 9am-6pm; Oct 9am-5pm; Nov-Feb 9am-4pm; Mar-Apr 9am-5pm. Dom Forum open M-F 10am-6:30pm, Sa 10am-5pm, Su 1-5pm. Tours M-Sa 10:30am and 2:30pm, Su 2:30pm. Dom Forum film M-Sa 11:30am and 3:30pm, Su 3:30pm.

🏛 MUSEUM LUDWIG   MUSEUM
Heinrich-Böll-Pl.   ☎0221 22 12 61 65 www.museum-ludwig.de

If you thought Cologne was too focused on its past to collect modern art, you were wrong. The interesting exterior of this building is a work of art in itself that contrasts beautifully with the historical cathedral next door. Still, the metal curves are nothing compared to the astronomic collection of 20th-century art inside. With almost 800 works by Pablo Picasso, the museum has the third largest Picasso collection in the world, documenting all stages of the artist's career. The entire bottom floor is dedicated to the biggest names in Pop Art, such as Andy Warhol, Roy Lichtenstein, and Robert Rauschenberg. Expressionism and the Russian avant-garde art also dominate the permanent collection.

i Behind the Dom, close to the Römisch-Germanisches Museum. Audio tour €3. €10, students €7; 1st Th of the month ½-price after 5pm. ☑ Open Tu-Su 10am-6pm. Open until 10am 1st Th of the month.

KOLUMBA   MUSEUM
Kolumbastr. 4   ☎0221 933 19 30 www.kolumba.de
This contemporary art museum run by the Church—yes, you read that right—displays religious artwork from the Middle Ages to the present. The museum is an amazing combination of past and present. Not only is the contemporary museum built upon the ruins of a church, but it is probably one of the few places where you can see centuries-old crucifixes side-by-side with contemporary installations, photographs, and paintings, often dramatically emphasized by spotlights in dark rooms. The museum was constructed over the ruins of the Gothic cathedral of St. Kolumba, which you can see on the ground floor.

i U3, U4, U5, U16, U18: Appellhofpl. Walk through the Opern Passage and turn left onto Glockengasse; Kolumba is 1 block past 4711-Haus. Free guidebooks available in English €5, students €3, under 18 free. ☑ Open M noon-5pm, W-Su noon-5pm.

NAZI DOCUMENTATION CENTER (EL-DE HAUS)   MUSEUM
Appellhofpl. 23-25   ☎0221 22 12 63 32 www.nsdok.de
Cologne had its own share of Nazi history, and this museum documents that very powerfully. The former Gestapo headquarters and jail here were converted into a museum that educates visitors on the city's history under the Nazis. Make sure not to miss the basement, where you can see original prison cells, where pleas, poems, and even self-portraits were all scratched into the plaster walls by the (mostly political) prisoners. The exhibit documents a number of individual stories, ranging from successful escape attempts to torture and executions. Although the top floors only have German explanations, the large black-and-white photographs transcend language barriers.

i U3, U4, U5, U16, or U18: Appellhofpl., then follow the signs. English explanations in the basement jail but not in the exhibits upstairs €4.50, students €2. Audio tour available in English and 5 other languages €2. Cash only. ☑ Open Tu-F 10am-6pm, Sa-Su 11am-6pm.

TWELVE ROMANESQUE CHURCHES OF KÖLN   CHURCHES
Twelve churches containing the bones of saints were built in a semicircle around the Altstadt during the Middle Ages to protect Cologne. Though each is dwarfed by the Dom, the churches attest to the glory and immense wealth of what used to be the most important city north of the Alps. The most memorable of these is probably **Saint Ursula Church** (Ursulapl. 24), dedicated to the British princess St. Ursula, who was so fond of her celibacy that she delayed her marriage to take a religious trip around Europe, during which she and her virgin companions were killed by the Huns. The church's treasury contains hundreds of human skulls wrapped in fabric, and the walls are decorated with bones. Another interesting church is the **Groß Saint Martin** (An Groß St. Martin 9-11), which was re-opened in 1985 after near destruction in WWII. The excavated cellar dates to the first century CE and once served as a training ground for wrestlers. St. Gereon has a history that dates back to the fourth century as well as a beautiful dome with interesting stained glass windows. Entry to the churches is free, so if you don't feel like paying for museums, you can get your dose of sightseeing simply by

cologne

touring these. As not many people choose to do this, you won't be surrounded by tourist crowds.

i St. Ursula is northwest of the Hauptbahnhof. Groß St. Martin is close to the river, between the Deutzer and Hohenzollern bridges. Churches free. St. Ursula treasury €2. Groß St. Martin excavations €0.50. ☎ St. Ursula treasury open M 10am-1pm, W 10am-1pm, and F-Sa 10am-1pm and 2-5pm. Groß St. Martin open Tu-F 9am-7:30pm, Sa 9:30am-7:30pm, Su 10am-7pm.

Altstadt-Sud

▨ SCHOKOLADENMUSEUM (CHOCOLATE MUSEUM)   MUSEUM
Am Schokoladenmuseum 1a   ☎0221 931 88 80 www.schokoladenmuseum.de

Give in to the temptation: it's worth it. Cologne's Chocolate Museum is every child's dream and is equally interesting for adults. What we appreciate most about this amazing place is that even though it has all the fun of free samples (check out the chocolate fountain—for best results, show up several times wearing different wigs), there's still a lot to be learned here, too. Besides exploring the complex history that turned our favorite dessert from a spicy drink into sweet candy, you can also see cocoa plants in the mini greenhouse, pyramids of Kinder Egg toys, and even a purple Milka cow. You'll also learn how hollow chocolate bunnies are made, and you can watch the stony-faced, lab-coated Oompa-Loompas—er, museum employees—make and package chocolates behind glass walls.

i U1, U7, or U9: Heumarkt. Walk east to the river, turn right, and continue along the bank. When you reach the island, turn left onto the small footbridge. All explanations in English €8.50, students €6, family €24. Cash only. ☎ Open Tu-F 10am-6pm, Sa-Su 11am-7pm. Last entry 1hr. before close.

MUSEUM SCHNÜTGEN AND RAUTENSTRAUCH-JOEST MUSEUM   MUSEUM
Cäcilienstr. 29-33   ☎Rautenstrauch-Joest:0221 221 31 356 www.museenkoeln.de

These two establishments follow Cologne's trend of museums with incredible architecture. Although located in the same building, the two museums seem to be polar opposites. The Schnütgen showcases one of world's largest collections of European medieval art; one of the most interesting parts, though, is the contrast between the plain, modern walls of the museum and the gorgeous stained glass taken out of its ordinary setting. The Rautenstrauch-Joest welcomes visitors with a video of people greeting each other in different languages. This ethnological museum examines artifacts from Africa, Asia, Australia, and America through themes such as prejudice, funerals, clothing, and religion. Again, the presentation of these exhibits alone, with large curtains and state-of-the-art interactive screens, makes for a worthwhile visit.

i U1, U3, U4, U7, U9, U16, or U18: Neumarkt. Head east a tiny bit on Cäcilienstr. Schnütgen €6, students €3.50. Rautenstrauch-Joest €7/4. Combined €10/7. Cash only. ☎ Both open Tu-W 10am-6pm, Th 10am-8pm, F-Su 10am-6pm.

FOOD

Altstadt-Nord

▨ WEINHAUS VOGEL   GERMAN $$
Eigelstein Str. 74   ☎0221 139 91 34

Don't be fooled by the wine glasses in the window: Weinhaus Vogel is an authentic local restaurant where great beer is more important than fancy wine. If you're still not convinced, just take a look around at the enormous collection of beer posters. Daily local specialties go for €5-6, but we also recommend entrees from the main menu, like the delicious *wienerschnitzel*.

i From the Hauptbahnhof, head past the Rolex building, then turn right at the roundabout. Continue straight through the tunnel; the restaurant is on the right about 300m down the street. Meal €6-18. Daily specials €5-6. Kölsch €1.30. Cash only. ☎ Open M-Th 10am-midnight, F-Sa 10am-2am, Su 10am-midnight.

get a room!

Below are a couple of Let's Go's top recommendations for catching some Z's in Cologne; for more, visit **www.letsgo.com**.

STATION HOSTEL FOR BACKPACKERS   HOSTEL $$
Marzellenstr. 44-56   ☎0221 912 53 01 www.hostel-cologne.de
This five-floor backpacker haven has the best location of any hostel in town and a lively atmosphere to match. The "What's On" part of their website and the knowledgeable staff will direct you to all the cool places in Cologne. The bar and lobby are on the smaller side, but the upstairs seating area with a great kitchen makes up for this. The building is far from new, but the young guests' spirits make the stay here worth it.
i Exit the Hauptbahnhof with the Dom to the left and walk past the Rolex building. At the roundabout, turn right onto Marzellenstr. Free Wi-Fi in common areas and free computer use. Linens included. Lockers outside of the room. 6-bed dorm €17-23; singles from €32; doubles from €48. ☒ Reception 24hr.

MEININGER HOTEL COLOGNE CITY CENTER   HOSTEL $$
Engelbertstr. 33-35   ☎0221 99 76 09 65 www.meininger-hotels.com
Meininger is as young and interesting as its guests: the intriguing velvet wallpapers are almost as cool as the hostel's location near the great nightlife around Zülpicher Pl. The hostel does everything right: the guest kitchen, game room, lounge, and bar are great for relaxing and socializing, while the colorful rooms with private bathrooms are quiet and clean. The free maps of the city, cheap snacks, and affordable bike rentals are extra perks.
i U1, U7, U12, or U15: Rudolfpl. From the station, walk south on Habsburgstr., turn right onto Lindenstr., then left onto Engelbertstr. Free Wi-Fi. Breakfas €5.90. Linens and towels included. Computers €1 per 20min. or €2 per hr. Bike rental €12. Women-only dorms available. Dorms €24, but the price can go up to €35 on Sa-Su; singles from €39; doubles from €79. ☒ Reception 24hr.

FRÜH AM DOM   GERMAN $$$
Am Hof 18   ☎0221 261 32 11 www.frueh.de
The enormous, red Gothic letters that spell out the name of this restaurant are only an introduction to the establishment's grandeur. Früh am Dom has colossal rooms, tile stoves, large wooden cabinets, an outside seating area, and even its own stained glass panel of the Cathedral. Due to its proximity to the famous Dom and the large plates of traditional food, Früh am Dom is the kind of landmark where locals send their out-of-town guests to get the typical Cologne experience. However, as great as this may sound (and it is pretty great), the prices aren't exactly geared toward the starving student.
i Walk south from the plaza of the Dom, then turn left onto Am Hof. The restaurant is on the right. Soup €4-4.60. Entrees €7.50-22.50. Kölsch €1.80. ☒ Open daily 8am-midnight. Warm food served until 11:30pm.

Altstadt-Sud

TOSCANINI   ITALIAN $$
Jakobstr. 22   ☎0221 310 99 90
Swinging green leaves near the entrance mixed with red brick arches and large windows make Toscanini a sweet and casually romantic restaurant. It is a bit of a trek from the main tourist path, but it's worth the trip if you're looking for au-

thentic Italian food. The restaurant is best known for its pizza, served fresh from the stone oven: try the Rustica, a delicious combination of cheese, prosciutto, and arugula. It's also one of the few places where the wait staff doesn't bring you a little *Kölsch* glass right away—wine is the beverage of choice here.

i U3 or U4: Severinstr. Head south down Severinstr. and turn right onto Jakobstr. Toscanini is on the right. Pizza €5.30-9.50. Pasta €6.10-12.90. Beer €2.10. Wine €2.10 per 0.1L. ☉ Open M-Sa noon-3pm and 6-11pm, Su 6-11pm.

Neustadt

HABIBI FALAFEL
MIDDLE EASTERN $

Zülpicherstr. 28 ☎0221 271 71 41 www.habibi-koeln.de

The marvelous aura of this tiny restaurant makes even the delicious smells and handsome, well-dressed men on their lunch breaks seem unimportant. The small, mosaic-covered tables and hanging newspaper articles come together to create a place very popular with local students, especially on late nights after a few rounds of drinks. The cheap falafel (€1.90) and shawarma (€2.50) are in demand at all times of the day, and the takeout is extremely cheap. If you have time to stay for a while, we recommend the generous plates, which come with a cup of cinnamon tea.

i U9, U12, or U15: Zülpicher Pl. Head down Zülpicherstr.; the restaurant is on the right. Plates €6.70-7.70, takeout €1.90-4. Espresso €0.70. Cash only. ☉ Open M-Th 11am-1am, F-Sa 11am-3am, Su 11am-1am.

BEI OMA KLEINMANN
SCHNITZEL $$$

Zülpicherstr. 9 ☎0221 23 23 46 www.beiomakleinmann.de

Perhaps the best-known *schnitzel* restaurant in Cologne, Bei Oma Kleinmann offers more than a dozen varieties, from "Weiner Art" to "Chili Lili" and "Olaf Maria," all of which are equally enormous. This place, full of old radios and taxidermied mountain goats, knows that dinner is the most important meal of the day (for your soul, not your health). Thus, the restaurant is open only in the evenings, and it gets crowded fast. Though the founder, Oma Kleinmann, recently passed away at the age of 95, she is remembered with framed photographs on the walls.

i U9, U12, or U15: Zülpicher Pl. Head down Zülpicherstr.; the restaurant is on the left. Schnitzel €12.90-20.90. Kölsch €1.50-2.50. Cash only. ☉ Open Tu-Th 5pm-midnight, F-Sa 5pm-1am, Su 5pm-midnight. Kitchen open 5-11pm.

NIGHTLIFE

Altstadt-Nord

GLORIA
VENUE, GLBT

Apostelnstr. 11 ☎0221 66 06 30 www.gloria-theater.com

Gloria is a must-see landmark of Cologne's GLBT scene. Not just a cafe and not just a club, this former movie theater offers the best of all worlds and hosts all sorts of awesome events, from parties to films to stand-up comedy. Although the cafe is nice, the real deal is the multi-purpose theater in the back, with red velvet walls and clusters of disco balls. Call or visit the website for the schedule of events; in the past, big names such as Sufjan Stevens and Coldplay have performed here.

i U1, U3, U4, U7, U9, U16, or U18: Neumarkt. Walk west toward St. Aposteln church and follow Apostelnstr. as it curves right. Cover €8-15. Theater tickets €15-25. Beer €1.90. Long drinks €6.50. Cash only. ☉ Cafe open M-Sa noon-8pm. Club hours vary based on event schedule.

germany

Neustadt

DIE WOHNGEMEINSCHAFT
BAR

Richard-Wagner-Str. 39 ☎0221 39 75 77 18 www.die-wohngemeinschaft.net

Whoever had the idea for this bar was a genius: the interior design combines cute, hipster, and awesome in the best possible way. The bar consists of four rooms, each decorated in the style of a fictitious university roommate—Annabel's cutesy vintage bed is good for chit-chatting, and JoJo's minibus is really cool to sit in (though we've never seen a dorm that would fit a minibus). Play ping-pong in Mai Li's smoky room, or listen to eclectic DJ mixes in Easy's abode. The adorable details don't stop at the rooms: the large bar has vintage fridges and awesome chairs. Aside from the bar, DW also runs a hostel with rooms just as creative as the bar.

i U1, U7, U12, or U15: Rudolfpl., then walk south 1 block to Richard-Wagner-Str. and head west. The bar is on the left. Live DJs W-Sa. Beer €1.60- 2.60. Long drinks €5-6. Cash only. ☼ Open M-Th 3pm-2am, F-Sa 3pm-3am, Su 3pm-2am.

DAS DING
CLUB

Hohenstaufenring 30-32 ☎0221 24 63 48 www.dingzone.de

"The Thing" is a smokey student disco with a bunch of neon lights everywhere, and it's the best place to show off your dance moves to your new hostel friends. Das Ding is incredibly student (and budget traveler) friendly, with dirt-cheap specials every night of the week. Tuesdays, for example, offer €1 vodka energy shots in addition to free-beer-o'clock from 9-11pm. And it doesn't stop there: the club even has a birthday special that includes 10 free shots, a bottle of champagne, and party goods. Student IDs are not required, but the bouncer outside keeps the crowd young.

i U9, U12, or U15: Zülpicherpl. Just past the Rewe supermarket. Cover €3-5. Beer €1.20. Shots €1.50-3. Cash only. ☼ Open Tu-W 9pm-3am, Th 10pm-4am, F-Sa 10pm-5am.

ESSENTIALS

Practicalities

- **TOURIST OFFICES:** KölnTourismus. (Kardinal-Höffner-Pl. 1, across from the Dom. ☎0221 22 13 04 00 www.koelntourismus.de *i* Books accommodations for a €3 fee. Inquire about local bus tours, which cost about €15. English-language walking tour €9, students €8. DIY iGuide €8 per 4hr. ☼ Open M-F 9am-8pm,Sa-Su 10am-5pm. English-language walking tour Sa 11:30am.)

- **CURRENCY EXCHANGE:** Reisebank. (Inside the Hauptbahnhof. ☎0221 13 44 03 www.reisebank.de *i* Exchanges traveler's checks for a €6.50 commission. ☼ Open daily 7am-10pm.) Exchange. (Kardinal-Höffner-Pl. 1, inside the tourist office ☎0221 92 52 596 ☼ Open M-F 9am-6pm, Sa 9am-4pm.)

- **WOMEN'S RESOURCES:** Frauenberatungszentrum. (Friesenpl. 9 ☎0221 420 16 20 ☼ Open M 2-5pm, Tu 9am-noon, W 2-5pm, Th-F 9am-noon.)

- **GLBT RESOURCES:** SchwIPS Checkpoint. (Pipinstr. 7, just around the corner from Hotel Timp. ☎0221 92 57 68 11 www.checkpoint-koeln.de ☼ Open M-Th 5-9pm, F-Sa 2-7pm, Su 2-6pm.) LSVD Emergency Hotline. (☎0221 19 228)

- **INTERNET:** Many cafes offer free Wi-Fi, including Starbucks in the Hauptbahnhof. Gigabyte. (Across the street from the Hauptbahnhof. *i* €2 per hr. ☼ Open 24hr.) A cheaper option is the Film Cafe. (Eigelstein Str., 40 *i* €1 per hr.)

- **POST OFFICES:** Breite Str. 6-26, near Appellhofpl. (☼ Open M-F 9am-7pm, Sa 9am-2pm.)

- **POSTAL CODES:** Cologne postal codes start with 50 or 51. The code for the post office listed above is 50667.

Emergency

- **112. POLICE:** ☎110.

- **DOM APOTHEKE:** (Courtyard between the Dom and the Hauptbahnhof. ☎0221 20 05 05 00 www.dom-apotheke-koeln.de ⌚ Open M-F 8am-8pm, Sa 9am-8pm.)

Getting There

By Plane

Flights from **Köln-Bonn Flughafen** (☎02203 40 40 01 02 www.koeln-bonn-airport.de), located halfway between Cologne and Bonn, serve most major European cities, in addition to Turkey and North Africa. The airport is also a budget airline hub. The **S13** runs between the Cologne Hauptbahnhof and the airport. *i* €2.50. ⌚ 15min., every 20-30min.) A taxi from Cologne to the airport costs no more than €30.

By Train

The Cologne Hauptbahnhof is located right by the Dom in the Altstadt-Nord. Trains go to: **Berlin** (€109. ⌚ 5hr., 1-2 per hr.); **Bonn** (€6.80. ⌚ 30min., 2 per hr.); **Frankfurt** (€64. ⌚ 1½hr., every hr.); **Munich** (€129. ⌚ 5hr., every hr.); **Amsterdam** (€58. ⌚ 3hr., every 2hr.); **Basel** (€111. ⌚ 4hr., every hr.); **Brussels** (€46. ⌚ 2hr., 4 per day); **London** (€400. ⌚ 5hr., 2 per day); **Vienna** (€154. ⌚ 10hr., 5 per day.) Prices may be lower if booked at least three days in advance.

Getting Around

By Public Transportation

Cologne's buses, trams, and subways are served by the **KVB**, or Kölner Verkehrs-Betriebe (☎0221 26 313 www.kvb-koeln.de). A **Kurzstrecke** ticket (€1.70, ages 6-14 €1) is good for a ride of four stops or less. A ride to anywhere in the city is €2.50 (ages 6-14 €1.30), but you can save money by buying a carnet of four (€9/4.90). A day pass is €7.30 for individuals, and €10.70 for groups of up to five. Validate tickets at the validating machines before boarding or face a €40 fine.

By Ferry

Köln-Düsseldorfer leaves from the dock in the Altstadt, between the Deutzer and Hohenzollern bridges, and offers trips up and down Rhein. (☎0221 208 83 18 www.k-d.de *i* To the Mainz €55, round-trip €60; to Bonn €14/16. Up to 50% discounts for students with valid ID. 1hr. panoramic cruises up and down Rhein in the Cologne area €7.80. 2hr. afternoon cruises €12. ⌚ Panoramic cruises Apr-Oct daily 10:30am, noon, 2pm, and 6pm. Afternoon cruises 3:30pm.)

By Gondola

Kölner Seilbahn sells scenic gondola trips across the Rhine, from the Zoo to the Rheinpark. (Riehlerstr. 180 ☎0221 547 41 83 www.koelner-seilbahn.de *i* U18: Zoo/Flora. 1-way €4; round-trip €6. ⌚ Open Apr-Oct daily 10am-6pm).

By Bike

Cologne is a big city, and renting a bike can help you conquer the distances more easily. Pay attention to the direction of bike traffic, as bike lanes are often one-way. In general, keep to the right side of the street. **Radstation** offers bike rental near the Hauptbahnhof. (Breslauer Pl. ☎0221 139 71 90 *i* Exit the Hauptbahnhof through the rear exit, then turn right. €50 deposit. €5 per 3hr.; €10 per day, €40 per week. ⌚ Open M-F 5:30am-10:30pm, Sa 6:30am-8pm, Su 8am-8pm.)

germany

hamburg

As the waterway to the North Sea, some claim that Hamburg has 2579 bridges, but the official count is "more than 2300." Whichever way you count, Hamburg has more bridges than Venice, London, and Amsterdam combined. And that's really something; the city's water is breathtaking. But if water, water, and more water isn't your thing, Hamburg's also the perfect place to try donning high heels on cobblestone streets. Or just take a break and explore Hamburg's copper roofs, fantastic parks, awesome boating opportunities, chic shops, and old factories. Like any good quintessential German city, Hamburg has been burned, bombed, and bisected with nightlife trashier than garbage (again outdoing Venice, London, and Amsterdam combined). Still, the city has somehow managed to draw in corporations, lawyers, and a whole bunch of immigrants. Maybe it's the nightlife. Hamburg is a port, after all.

ORIENTATION

Hamburg's geography is notoriously complex, so consider pulling out a map to look over as you read through this. Hamburg lies on the northern bank of the **Elbe River.** The city's **Altstadt,** full of old façades and labyrinthine canals, lies north of the Elbe and south of the **Alster lakes. Binnenalster,** the smaller of the two Alster lakes, is located in the heart of the Altstadt, with the bustling **Jungfernstieg** on the south corner. The much larger **Außenalster,** popular for sailing in the summer and skating in the winter, is slightly farther north, separated from the Binnenalster by the **Kennedy- and Lombardbrücken**.

Five unique spires outline Hamburg's Altstadt. Anchoring the center of the Altstadt is the palatial **Rathaus,** the ornate town hall, and its exquisite doorstep and regular home to both political protests and farmers' markets, the **Rathausmarkt. Alsterfleet Canal** bisects the downtown, separating Altstadt on the eastern bank from the **Neustadt** on the west. The city's best museums, galleries, and theaters are within these two districts.

The **Hauptbahnhof** lies at the eastern edge of the city center, along **Steintorwall**. Starting from the **Kirchenallee** exit of the Hauptbahnhof, Hamburg's gay district, **St. Georg,** follows the **Lange Reihe** eastward. Outside the Hauptbahnhof's main exit on Steintorwall is the **Kunstmeile** (Art Mile), a row of museums extending southward from the Alster lakes to the banks of the Elbe. Perpendicular to Steintorwall, **Mönckebergstraße,** Hamburg's most famous shopping street, runs westward to the **Rathaus.** Just south of the Rathaus, **Saint Pauli** bears long waterside walkways and a beautiful copper-roofed port along the towering cranes of the Elbe's industrial district. Horizontally bisecting St. Pauli is the infamously icky **Reeperbahn** (disingenuously pronounced "RAPER-bawn"), which is packed with strip joints, erotic shops, and a tourist mecca of clubs on the pedestrian off-shoot **Große Freiheit.**

To the north of St. Pauli, the **Schanzenviertel** is a radically liberal community on the cusp of gentrification. Here, rows of graffiti-covered restaurants and a busy, late-night cafe and bar scene show little edge but attract fleets of bargain-hunting students. In late summer, the **Schanzenfest** illegal street market consistently breaks out into a fullfledged war of Molotov cocktails and tear gas between cops and civil discontents. On the westernmost side of Hamburg, **Altona** celebrates with a mini-Schanzenviertel nightlife and restaurant scene; the area was an independent city ruled by Denmark in the 17th century before Hamburg absorbed it. Altona's shop-lined pedestrian zone, the **Ottenser Hauptstrasse,** runs west from the Altona train station.

hamburg

SIGHTS

◪ PLANTEN UN BLOMEN
BOTANICAL GARDEN

Next to the Hamburg Messe ☎040 428 232 125 www.plantenunblomen.hamburg.de

This park is fantastic. It's huge, it's laden with lily pads and manicured gardens, and it has something for everyone. There's a real botanical garden, a greenhouse growing things which we thought could only grow south of the Equator, coffee and bananas among them. There's a Japanese garden. There's a charming little rose garden. There are a whole handful of cafes and ice cream stands. There are wading pools. There are fountains. For the Harry Potter enthusiast, a giant (though inanimate) chess set is the arena of competition for many a muggle. Daily performances by groups ranging from Irish step dancers to Hamburg's police choir fill the outdoor Musikpavillion Sundays at 3pm May-Sept. The nightly Wasserlichtkonzerte draws crowds to the lake with fountains and choreographed underwater lights.

i S11, S21, or S31: Dammtor. Or U1: Stephanspl. ☒ Open daily 7am-11pm. Hours of the other attractions (Japanese garden, botanical garden, golf course, etc.) vary.

◪ HAMBURGER KUNSTHALLE (HALL OF ART)
MUSEUM

Glockengießerwall ☎040 428 131 200 www.hamburger-kunsthalle.de

The Kunsthalle is the Louvre of Germany. The museum is stately, massive, and located on prime Hamburg turf. Staring at every piece of artwork for 10 seconds each would take a few days, and just running quickly through the place sucks up a good two hours. Either way, it's time well spent. With an incredible collection of canvases from every period in art history—from early medieval religious paintings through Modernism—arranged chronologically across its spacious, skylit halls, this museum is freakishly gorgeous. After you've gotten your fill of everything pas, enter the cafe and take the underground passage behind you to the *Galerie der Gegenwart* (Gallery of the Present) for an expertly curated series of contemporary art exhibits, which may include anything from photographs to the skins of stuffed animals.

i Turn right from the "Sitalerstr./City" exit of the Hauptbahnhof and cross the street. The Kunsthalle has the domed ceiling. €12, students €6, under 18 free. Audio tour €2. ☒ Open Tu-W 10am-6pm, Th 10am-9pm, F-Su 10am-6pm.

◪ RATHAUS
TOWN HALL

Rathausmarkt ☎040 428 312 470

With more rooms than Buckingham Palace, the 1897 Hamburger Rathaus is an ornately carved stone monument to Hamburg's long history as a wealthy port city. Today, we have the privilege of seeing the post-fire original: during the extensive Allied bombing of the Innenstadt, a bomb fell on the Rathausmarkt just out front, but, due to the quick thinking of some invisible, architecture-loving time traveler, it never exploded. Accessible only with a thorough 40min. tour, the lavish chambers of the Rathaus overflow with expansive murals, disorienting ornate molding, and wedding-cake chandeliers.

i U3: Rathaus. Tours don't run on days that the state government convenes. Even on open days, certain rooms may be closed due to meetings, so call ahead. Tours €3, under 14 €0.50. ☒ English tours M-Th every hr. 10:15am-3:15pm, F 10:15am-1:15pm, Sa 11:15am-5:15pm, Su 11:15am-4:15pm.

MUSEUM FÜR KUNST UND GEWERBE
MUSEUM

Steintorpl. ☎040 428 134 880 www.mkg-hamburg.de

This museum aims to confuse: the complex is a concoction of 19th-century and hyper-modern construction, and the exhibited art and design is similarly varied. Works hail from everywhere and anywhere: a hall of 17th- and 18th-century pianos borders a room of Middle Eastern carved tile; Art Deco pottery squares

germany

off against a gigantic collection of 18th-century porcelain arranged by region of origin; and a hallway of late 20th-century chairs challenges your backside to figure out how to sit in them. And this is just the permanent collection. Special exhibits range from 1980s and'90s Japanese fashion to Art Nouveau advertisements. Yes, it's a disorienting jumble, but it's a pleasing one.

i *S1, S2, S3, S11, S21, S31, U1, U2, or U3: Hauptbahnhof. Leave through the Hauptbahnhof's south exit; the museum is across the street. €10, students €7, under 18 free. Admission €5 on Th after 5pm.* ☼ *Open Tu-W 10am-6pm, Th 10am-9pm, F-Su 10am-6pm.*

Outside Central Hamburg

KZ-GEDENKSTÄTTE NEUENGAMME   CONCENTRATION CAMP
Jean-Dolidier-Weg 75   ☎040 428 131 500 www.kz-gedenkstaette-neuengamme.de

It's quite a trek from Hamburg, but it's one you should make: seeing the complex that once housed a concentration camp is nothing short of a chilling experience. Since the camp lies out in the rolling Hamburg countryside, a visit will take at least three hours, but this lesser known center of Nazi terror is a humbling experience worthy of the trip. Between 1938 and 1945, this camp held more than 100,000 forced laborers. Close to half the occupants died from overwork, disease, or execution. Walk around the camp buildings, from the cafeteria and dorms—now reduced to stark piles of rubble—to the work camps, and browse the thorough and moving collection of photographs and artifacts, which includes artwork by some of the prisoners.

i *S21: Bergedorf. Then take bus #227 or #327: KZ-Gedenkstätte, Ausstellung (about 35-45min.). Buses leave the train station and the camp M-Sa every 30min., Su every 2hr. Free.* ☼ *Museum and memorial open Apr-Sept M-F 9:30am-4pm, Sa-Su noon-7pm; Oct-Mar M-F 9:30am-4pm, Sa-Su noon-5pm. Paths open 24hr. Tours in German Su noon and 2:30pm.*

FOOD

⊠ RISTORANTE ROCCO   ITALIAN $$$
Hofweg 104   ☎040 22 31 88 www.ristorante-rocco.de

From the outside, with its spot next to a small canal and outdoor tables tiered to approach the water, Ristorante Rocco looks way too cla$$y for budget travelers. Even on weekdays, Rocco always hosts business peeps out on date night. Despite the pretentious atmosphere, though, the food is unpretentious and the prices unassuming. For the local all-time favorite, opt for the *lasagne* (€9), which is baked in its own little dish and covered in deliciously-crispified cheese. Or, if you rather, satisfy your taste for Hamburg's seafood with any of the dishes containing scampi or *Meeresfrüchten.*

i *U3: From the metro, walk north on Winterhuder Weg for 3 large blocks. Then keep left as Winterhuder Weg splits off of Herderstr. Turn right onto Hofweg, and the restaurant is on the right, right next to the canal. Pasta €8-10.50. Entrees €10.50-18.* ☼ *Open M-F noon-3pm and 6-11:30pm, Sa-Su 6-11:30pm.*

⊠ AZEITONA   MIDDLE EASTERN $
Beckstr. 17-19   ☎040 18 00 73 71

They say that Hamburg is famous for its €2.50 falafel, and we think Azeitona scored the reputation for the whole city. This cafe is tiny and all vegetarian, and the falafel is pretty darn good. For the perfect sandwich, add some of Azeitona's antipasti for €0.50. The restaurant is decorated like a little slice of the Middle East, and even the benches are carpeted.

i *U3: Feldstr. From the metro, walk north on Sternstr. After a short block, turn left onto Beckstr. Azeitona is on the right. Entrees €2.50-6. Caipirina €4.* ☼ *Open M-Th noon-11pm, F-Sa noon-late, Su noon-11pm.*

hamburg

get a room!

Accommodations in Hamburg can get freakishly expensive, especially in the summer months. But like the good, cheap food, the good, cheap hostels are located in the Schanzenviertel and out west in Altona. For more recommendations, visit **www.letsgo.com**.

◪ INSTANT SLEEP   HOSTEL $$

Max-Brauer-Allee 277   ☎040 431 82 310 www.instantsleep.com

Instant Sleep combines the feel of a summer camp and the set-up of an institution: the beds aren't bunked, but they feel like cots and are all quite close together. Instant Sleep keeps a fully stocked kitchen and an awesomely social common room. Expect to find foosball, hammocks, and a comfy loft with bean bags and a television. A young backpacking crowd gathers here to hang out or fans out onto the balcony for a smoke.

i *U3, S11, S21, or S31: Sternschanze. Free Wi-Fi. Linens included. Laundry available. 12-bed dorm €15; 6- to 8-bed dorms €17; 4- to 5-bed €21; singles €39; doubles €54; triples €72. Cash only. ☼ Reception open M-W 8am-11pm, Th-Sa 8am-2am, Su 8am-11pm. Balcony open until 10pm.*

SCHANZENSTERN ALTONA   HOSTEL $$

Kleiner Rainstr. 24-26   ☎040 399 19 191 www.schanzenstern.de/hotel/altona

Altona has a hotel atmosphere, with a silent courtyard, a residential street, and a lack of common space. Still, the rooms here are tremendous, the beds are comfy and rarely bunked, every room comes with its very own bathroom, and the wide view of Altona will make you swoon. With the Altstadt and the Schanzenviertel each about a 5-10min. train ride away, the location can feel a little remote. Good thing there's a bustling shopping and nightlife center nearby.

i *S1, S2, S3, S11 or S31: Altona. From the metro, exit at Ottenser Hauptstr. and head west along the pedestrian walkway. Turn right at Spritzenpl. and take the right fork in the road. Turn left onto Kleiner Rainstr.; the hostel is on the left, just before the bend in the road. Free Wi-Fi and internet terminals available. Breakfas €6.50. Linens included. Dorms €19; singles €44; doubles €59-69; triples €74; quads €84; apartments €79-100. Cash only. ☼ Reception 24hr. Common room open 7am-2am.*

◪ EISCAFÉ AM POELCHAUKAMP   ICE CREAM $

Poelchaukamp 3   ☎040 27 25 17

It's just an ice cream parlor, but it's an exceptionally good one. The owners are Italian, and the *eis* is authentic, too. Get a couple scoops—the rum flavors, rum truffle and *malaga* or rum raisin, are the best. Take it to explore the nearby residential neighborhood.

i *U3: Sierichstr. From the metro, walk south on Sierichstr. for about 10min. Then turn right onto Poelchaukamp, and the Eiscafe is on the left near the canal. Each scoop €1. ☼ Open daily 11am-10pm.*

LA SEPIA   SEAFOOD $$

Schulterblatt 36   ☎040 432 24 84

When in Hamburg, eat seafood. It's simply a must, and this Spanish and Portuguese restaurant serves some seriously generous portions at seriously affordable prices (at least in comparison to similar cafes). The low prices justify the interior, which is impersonal and loaded up with tanks of crustaceans. Avoid the expensive dinner entrees and catch the lunch special (noon-5pm) for around

germany

€5-7, or try the fish sampler (€6) to get the full cornucopia of Hamburg's *Meeresfrüchte* (fruit of the sea).

i *U3, S11, S21, or S31: Sternschanze. Entrees €7.50-22. Soups €4.50.* 🍴 *Open daily noon-3am.*

HATARI PFÄLZER CANTINA
GERMAN $$

Schanzenstr. 2 ☎040 43 20 88 66

You'll be glad to hear that the word "eclectic" sums this cafe up quite nicely: it's decorated with Chinese **dragons** and hunting trophies. Students flock here for hamburgers (€7.80-8.20) and Hamburger-watching on the busy street corner. Hatari also serves German specialties, including *schnitzel* (€11-12) and *Flammkuchen* (€7.30-8.30), or "French pizza," a Bavarian thin crust spread with thick cream and piled with toppings.

i *U3, S11, S21, or S31: Sternschanze. Entrees from €7. Cash only.* 🍴 *Open daily noon-late.*

HIN&VEG
VEGETARIAN $

Schulterblatt 16 ☎040 594 53 402

This veggie diner is fittingly dog-friendly. As you enter, you might hear one of the servers adoring a dog: *"Wasser für den Hund."* If you're intimidated by meaty German classics, this is your chance to fill up on veggie versions of Deutschland staples. Hin&Veg serves dishes like vegetarian currywurst (€3) and *döner* (€4), all with vegan sauces. Also, a delicious collection of veggie burgers makes for a light, refreshing way to gain the requisite Hamburg/hamburger bragging rights.

i *U3, S11, S21, or S31: Sternschanze. From the metro, head south on Schanzenstr. and take the 3rd left onto Schulterblatt. The restaurant is on the right. Burger €2-4. Pizza €5.90-7.50. Cash only.* 🍴 *Open M-Th 11:30am-10:30pm, F-Sa 11:30am-midnight, Su 12:30-10pm.*

NIGHTLIFE

◪ AUREL
BAR

Bahrenfelderstr. 157 ☎040 390 27 27

Aurel identifies itself as a *Kneipe*, which is basically a pub. Despite the prevalence of beer drinking, one of the main attractions at Aurel is their delicious mojito special (€6.50 before 9pm). An early crowd sticks around Aurel until bedtime. A small, beleaguered bar keeps tabs on the incessantly large crowd, which packs the small tables and inevitably spills out onto the sidewalk. Check out the stained glass on the back wall (don't worry—we don't get it either).

i *S1, S3, or S31: Altona. From the metro, exit onto Ottenser Hauptstr., walk east, then turn right onto Bahrenfelderstr. The bar is on the left at the corner of Bahrenfelderstr. and Nöltingstr. Beer €2.60-3.50. Mojitos €8 after 9pm. Mixed drinks €6-8. Cash only.* 🍴 *Open daily 10am-late.*

◪ SHAMROCK IRISH BAR
BAR

Feldstr. 40 ☎040 432 77 275 www.shamrockirishbar.com

Our researchers were mystified by the outdoor flower garden at this punk bar: how, oh how, could leather-clad, whiskey-drinking old boys frequent this dark, smoky Irish bar without treading on them? True to its Irish heritage, Shamrock often fills to capacity with Guinness-drinking English-speakers. Irish football banners hang from the ceiling, and some of the funniest bartenders this side of the Channel fill huge steins with Guinness, Kilkenny, and Irish Car Bombs. Come Thursday nights at 9pm for a hilarious pub quiz and watch Germans mutter to each other in broken English about topics ranging from Bolshevism to Batman to beer.

i *U3: Feldstr. From the metro, head east on Feldstr. The bar is on the left. Guinness and Kilkenny 0.3 €2.90, 0.4L €3.80.* 🍴 *Open Tu-Th 6pm-1am, F 5pm-late, Sa 1pm-late, Su 6pm-midnight.*

hamburg

ROSI'S BAR

BAR

Hamburger Berg 7 ☎040 31 55 82

In an area famous for debauchery, Rosi's sets the standard. Though this bar is located on a strip of seemingly identical bars, nowhere else comes close to Rosi's age-old(going on 60 years) notoriety, fame, or motley collection of DJs. Come for soul one night and return for goth-rock the next; no two evenings are alike. Rosi, the one-time wife of Tony Sheridan, became the bar's manager at the tender age of 18 and still runs it now with her son. Dark wood walls are dressed up with a single disco ball and layers of music posters, all of which contribute to Rosi's wild nights.

i *S1, S2, or S3: Reeperbahn. Go east on Reeperbahn, take a left onto Hamburger Berg, and walk about 75m. DJs most nights from 11pm. Beer €2.50-3. Cocktails €5. Cash only. ⏰ Open M-Th 9pm-4am, F-Sa 9pm-6am, Su 9pm-4am.*

CAFÉ GNOSA

CAFE, BAR, GLBT

Lange Reihe 93 ☎040 24 30 34 www.gnosa.de

Café Gnosa is a Hamburg institution. It's a great cafe and perfect for a visit during the day, but it's most famous for its fabulous GLBT nightlife. Full of bright lights and decorated with dark wood, Café Gnosa has been serving warm and cold drinks and famous cakes since World War II. Hamburg's first gay bar attracts an older crowd—gay and straight—who remember its early days, plus some younger faces eager to enjoy the exquisite cakes and talk with the refreshingly friendly staff. You can also pick up free GLBT publications like *hinnerk* and Hamburg's Gay Map here.

i *From the north entrance of the Hauptbahnhof, follow Ernst-Mecke-Str. as it becomes Lange Reihe. Beer €2.70-3.60. Cocktails €5.50-8. Champagne €8.70. Coffee €1.90. Cakes €2-5. Cash only. ⏰ Open daily 10am-1am.*

KYTI VOO

BAR, GLBT

Lange Reihe 82 ☎040 280 55 565 www.kytivoo.de

Red neon lights and loud electro suggest a small club, but Kyti Voo is really a large, chic gay bar with an insatiable hunger for heavy beats. The bar inside is massive and many-sided, so it's too bad no one uses it in the summer, when 20- to 40-somethings snatch up the extensive outdoor seating. By about 10:30pm, Kyti Voo's sidewalk is one of the most popular places in St. Georg. Sip coffee or cocktails or chow down on a steaming hot *Flammkuchen* (€6.90-8.90).

i *From the north entrance of the Hauptbahnhof, follow Ernst-Mecke-Str. as it becomes Lange Reihe. The bar is on the right, about halfway down the block. Espresso €1.60. Beer on tap 0.3L €2.80, 0.5L €3.60. Cocktails €5.50-8. Wine €3.40-6.50. Cash only. ⏰ Open M-F 9am-late, Sa-Su 10am-late.*

YOKO MONO

BAR

Marktstr. 41 ☎040 431 82 991 www.yokomono.de

Yoko Mono is situated on the edge of a trash-covered, motor-biker-frequented park. The crowd that gathers here is student heavy and generally under 25. Yoko Mono is pretty much the ideal place to chat to someone about how much you love Bon Iver. A pool table heats up the side room, while the small main bar is dark, cozy, and packed. With all the cool, attractive friends it encourages you to meet, this bar could've easily broken up the Beatles.

i *U3: Feldstr. From the metro, head north on Laeiszstr., then west on Marktstr. Wine €2.50-2.80. Beer €2.80-3.50. Cash only. ⏰ Open daily noon-2am or later.*

FABRIK

CLUB

Barnerstr. 36 ☎040 391 070 www.fabrik.de

Fabrik used to be a factory for machine parts. Complete with a rusted crane on the roof, Fabrik is perhaps the only appropriate place to do the robot. Actually, no one does the robot, even here, though you can engage in some Fabrik boogie

germany

woogie. For years, crowds have packed this two-level club to hear live DJs, big-name rock acts, and an eclectic mix of other bands, with styles ranging from Latin to punk.

i S1, S3, or S31: Altona. From the metro, exit at Ottenser Hauptstr., walk along the pedestrian walkway to the east, turn right onto Bahrenfelderstr., and walk north until you reach Barnerstr. The club is on the right. Check the website for a schedule of events. Live DJ most Sa nights at 10pm. The club hosts a "Gay Factory" night each month. Cover €7. Tickets €17-36. ☼ Hours vary, and most acts start at 9pm.

ESSENTIALS

Practicalities

- **TOURIST OFFICES:** Hamburg's main tourist offices supply free English-language maps and pamphlets. All sell the Hamburg Card (€8.90), which provides discounts for museums, tours, and particular stores and restaurants, plus unlimited access to public transportation. The Hauptbahnhof office books rooms for a €4 fee and offers free maps. (☎040 300 51 300. *i* In the Wandelhalle, the station's main shopping plaza, near the Kirchenallee exit. ☼ Open M-Sa 9am-7pm, Su 10am-6pm.) The Sankt Pauli Landungsbrücken office is often less crowded than the Hauptbahnhof office. (Between piers 4 and 5. ☎040 300 51 203. ☼ Open M-W 9am-6pm, Th-Sa 9am-pm.)

- **CURRENCY EXCHANGE:** ReiseBank arranges money transfers for Western Union and cashes traveler's checks. (☎040 32 34 83 *i* 2nd fl. of the Hauptbahnhof near the Kirchenallee exit. Also sells telephone cards. Other branches in the Altona and Dammtor train stations as well as in the Flughafen. 1.5% commission. €6.50 to cash 1-9 checks, €10 for 10 checks, and €25 for 25 checks. Exchanges currency for a fixed charge of €3-5. ☼ Open daily 7:30am-10pm.) Citibank cashes traveler's checks, including AmEx. (Rathausstr. 2 ☎040 302 96 202 *i* U3: Rathaus. ☼ Open M-F 9am-1pm and 2-6pm.)

- **GLBT RESOURCES:** St. Georg is the center of the gay community. Hein und Fiete, a self-described "switchboard," gives advice on doctors, disease prevention, and tips on the gay scene in Hamburg. (Pulverteich 21 ☎040 240 333. *i* Walk down Steindamm away from the Hauptbahnhof, turn right onto Pulverteich ,and look for a rainbow-striped flag on the left. ☼ Open M-F 4-9pm, Sa 4-7pm.) Magnus-Hirschfeld-Centrum offers film screenings, counseling sessions, and a gay-friendly cafe. (Borgweg 8 ☎040 278 77 800. *i* U3: Borgweg. ☼ Cafe open M-Th 5:30-11pm, F 5pm-late, Su 3-8pm.) Magnus-Hirschfeld-Centrum also offers gay and lesbian hotlines. (Gay hotline ☎040 279 00 69. Lesbian hotline ☎040 279 0049. ☼ Gay hotline open M-W 2-6pm and 7-9pm, Th 2-6pm; Lesbian hotline open W 5-7pm, Th 6-8pm.)

- **INTERNET ACCES:** Free Wi-Fi is available in Wildwechsel (Beim Grünen Jäger 25 ☼ Open daily 4pm-late), at the Altan Hotel (Beim Grünen Jäger 23 *i* You don't have to be a guest to use internet in the lobby/bar. ☼ Open 24hr.), and at Starbucks. (Neuer Jungfernstieg 5 ☼ Open M-F 7:30am-9pm, Sa-Su 8am-9pm.) Staats- und Universitätsbibliothek has computers on the 2nd floor, but internet access is limited to library cardholders. (Von Melle-Park 3 ☎040 428 38 22 33. *i* Library car €5 per month, €13 per 6 months. ☼ Open M-F 9am-9pm, Sa-Su 10am-9pm.)

- **POST OFFICE:** Hauptbahnhof. (At the Kirchenallee exit. ☼ Open M-F 8am-6pm, Sa 8:30am-12:30pm.)

- **POSTAL CODE:** 20095.

Emergency

- **EMERGENCY NUMBERS:** ☎112.

- **POLICE:** 110. (*i* From the Kirchenallee exit of the Hauptbahnhof, turn left and follow signs for "BGS/Bahnpolizei/Bundespolizei." Another branch is located on the Reeperbahn, at the corner of Davidstr. and Spielbudenpl., and in the courtyard of the Rathaus.)

- **PHARMACY:** Adler Apotheke.(Schulterblatt 106 ☎040 439 45 90 *i* Schedule of emergency hours for Hamburg pharmacies out front. ☼ Open M-F 8:30am-7pm, Sa-Su 9am-4pm.) Hauptbahnhof-Apotheke Wandelhalle. (☎040 325 27 383. *i* In the station's upper shopping gallery. ☼ Open M-W 7am-9pm, Th-F 7am-9:30pm, and Sa-Su 8am-9pm.)

Getting There

By Plane

Air France (☎018 058 30 830) and **Lufthansa** (☎018 058 05 805), among other airlines, serve Hamburg's **Fuhlsbüttel Airport** (HAM; ☎040 507 50). **Jasper Airport Express** buses run from the Kirchenallee exit of the Hauptbahnhof directly to the airport. (☎040 227 10 610. *i* €5, under 12 €2. 25min. ☼ Every 10-15min. 4:45am-7pm, every 20min. 7-9:20pm.) Alternatively, you can take U1, S1, or S11 to Ohlsdorf, then take an express bus to the airport. (*i* €2.60, ages 6-14 €0.90. ☼ Every 10min. 4:30am-11pm, every 30min. 11pm-1am.)

By Train

The **Hauptbahnhof,** Hamburg's central station, offers connections to: Berlin (€56; 2hr., about 1 per hr.); Frankfurt (€109; 4hr., 1 per hr.); Hannover (€40; 1½hr., 2 per hr.); Munich (€185; 6hr., about 1 per hr.); and Copenhagen (€80; 5hr., 6 per day). The efficient staff at the **DB Reisezentrum** sells tickets (☼ Open M-F 5:30am-10pm, Sa-Su 7am-10pm), which are also available at the ticket machines located throughout the Hauptbahnhof and online at. **Dammtor** station is near the university, to the west of Außenalster; **Harburgdorf** is to the southeast. Most trains to and from Schleswig-Holstein stop only at **Altona,** while most trains toward Lübeck stop only in the Hauptbahnhof. Stations are connected by frequent local trains and the S-Bahn.

By Bus

The **ZOB** terminal is across Steintorpl. from the Hauptbahnhof. (☎040 24 75 76 ☼ Open M-Tu 5am-10pm, W 5am-midnight, Th 5am-10pm, F 5am-midnight, Sa-Su 5am-10pm.)

Getting Around

By Public Transportation

HVV operates the efficient U-Bahn, S-Bahn, and bus network. Tickets are validated upon purchase according to the station or time you buy them. Short rides within downtown cost €1.30, and one-way rides farther out in the network cost €0.80; when in doubt, use the starting point/destination input tool on any ticket machine to figure out which of the one-way tickets will suffice. Two different day cards may cause confusion: the **9-Uhr Tageskarte** (9hr. day card €5.50) works for unlimited rides midnight-6am and 9am-6pm on the day of purchase. A **Ganztageskarte** (full-day pass; €6.80) works for unlimited rides at any point throughout the day of purchase until 6am the next morning. A **3-Tage-Karte** (3-day ticket; €16.50) is also available. Passes are available for longer time periods, though anything over a week requires a photo. Frequent riders can bring a photo or take one in the nearby ID booths for €5.

By Ferry

HADAG Seetouristik und Fährdienst AG runs ferries. (☎040 311 70 70 *i* Departs the docks at St. Pauli Landungsbrücken. 21 stops along the river. Price included in HVV train and bus passes; €2.60 for a new ticket. ☼ All 21 stops 75min., every 15min.) Take the HVV-affiliated ferries in lieu of the expensive tour boats for an equally impressive view of the river Elbe.

By Taxi

All Hamburg taxies charge the same rates. Normally, it's about €2.70 to start, then about €1.80 per km for the first 10km and €1.28 per km thereafter. Try **Autoruf** (☎040 441 011), **Das Taxi** (☎040 221 122), or **Taxi Hamburg**. (☎040 666 666)

By Bike

Hamburg is wonderfully bike-friendly, with wide bike lanes on most roads. Rent a bike at **Fahrradstation Dammtor/Rotherbaum** (Schlüterstr. 11 ☎040 414 68 27 *i* €4-8 per day ✪ Open M-F 9am-6:30pm) or **Hamburg City Cycles**. (Bernhard-Nocht-Str. ☎040 742 14 420 *i* Offers guided bike tours €12 per day, €23 per 2 days, €7 per day thereafter. ✪ Open Tu-F on request, Sa-Su 10am-6pm.)

frankfurt

When you think of Germany, do you imagine timber houses, cobblestones and castles, *Lederhosen*, or *Oktoberfest*? Forget all that: Frankfurt has none of it. Allied bombs destroyed Frankfurt's Old European style, and all that remains is *"Mainhatten."* Frankfurt is located on the Main River, and while you'd imagine the place to be charming, exciting, and romantic, it's none of that, either. Frankfurt is all about business: banks, skyscrapers, corporations, colorless suits, transportation (and layovers). So, is it worth seeing? Well, if you're traveling on a budget, perhaps not. But like the rest of us, you're probably going to end up in Frankfurt because of a layover, and the city does have some worthwhile sights and museums. After all, Frankfurt did serve as the site of the Holy Roman Empire's imperial elections from 1562 until the empire's dissolution in 1807. The **Altstadt,** Frankfurt's tiny old town, features some leftovers from its medieval glory days, including adorable reconstructions of those half-timbered houses you've set as your computer's background and an exquisite Gothic cathedral, which, by the glory of luck or a chance deity, survived the Allied bombing of 1944. The **Main River,** which splits Frankfurt in two, offers some gorgeous views that almost make you forget the steel phalluses scraping the sky around you. Considered the epicenter of German techno back in the '90s, Frankfurt also has some of Germany's most literally (and not-so-literally) burned-out but once awesome clubs.

ORIENTATION

The Main River runs east to west through Frankfurt, splitting it in two. Most of the city is located to the north.

North of the Main

The historic city center right along the Main is called the **Altstadt,** and includes the **Römerberg** (a medieval square) and the (in)spired **Dom Sankt Bartholomäus,** site of those famous Holy Roman Empire elections. Just to the north is the **Innenstadt,** the city's commercial district, with high-class shops and restaurants stretching along the Zeil between Ⓜ Hauptwache and Ⓜ Konstablerwache. Immediately west of that, around **Taunusanlage,** the city's financial district holds the highest concentration of skyscrapers. To the southwest lies the **Hauptbahnhof,** surrounded by cheap restaurants and the city's red light district. Just to the north, near Ⓜ Festhalle/Messe, the **Frankfurter Messe** is the third-largest trade fair hall in the world and is surrounded by more glass pyramids than 31st-century Egypt. In the northwest corner, **Bockenheim** is home to the students of Johann-Wolfgang Universität and Frankfurt's few wallet-friendly cafes. The city's most upscale and exclusive nightlife lies along **Hanauer Landstraße** on the east side of the city, amid auto dealers, factories, and highway cloverleaves.

South of the Main

Immediately south of the Main, a row of museums called the **Museumsufer** stretches along Schaumainkai, which runs alongside the river. The neighborhood to the south is known as **Sachsenhausen.** In the middle, around **Schweizer Platz,** you'll find a collection of age-old restaurants specializing in *grüne Soße* (literally "green sauce," made with borrage, sorrel, chives, and other herbs) and *Apfelwein* (apple wine), while to the northeast, near **Frankensteiner Platz,** a hopping, cobbled nightlife district fills its diverse bars with throngs of ruddy-faced young people.

SIGHTS

North of the Main

🖼 MUSEUM FÜR MODERNE KUNST   ART MUSEUM
Domstr. 10   ☎069 212 30 447 www.mmk-frankfurt.de

The Museum für Moderne Kunst is one of the best ways to spend a couple of hours in Frankfurt. Sure, the collection could be located anywhere, but this modern city does modern art pretty damn well. MfMK has a little something for everyone: plastic, yellow mini skyscrapers; paintings of bound and nude women; rooms full of messy "found art" sculptures; video installations, including one of an elephant doing all its elephant things as it's circled by a camera; and works by some of the great pop artists, including Warhol's iconic Campbell's soup cans. Check out James Turrell's *Twilight Arch,* but try not to step on a fellow patron when you enter the completely dark room.

i U4 or U5: Römer/Dom. From the metro, walk up Hasengasse to the curvy building 1 block north of the Dom. Explanations in English. €10, students €5. Last Sa of the month free. 🕐 Open Tu 10am-6pm, W 10am-8pm, Th-Su 10am-6pm.

DOM SANKT BARTHOLOMÄUS   CHURCH
Dompl. 14   ☎069 133 76 184 www.dom-frankfurt.de

This cathedral is practically the only sight in Frankfurt that isn't shiny and new. Amazingly, the 66m spire survived the Allied bombing of 1944. Back when the Holy Roman Empire was a thing (from 1562-1792), seven electors chose continental Europe's most influential emperors here, and the glorious coronation ceremonies that followed filled the Dom's Gothic halls with splendor. Unfortunately, the church had to be reconstructed after an 1867 fire, but the resulting Gothic tower is among Germany's most famous. The Dom Museum in the main entrance, and its continuation in the Haus am Dom holds architectural studies of the Dom, intricate gold chalices, and the ceremonial robes of imperial electors. Though limited, this splendid collection of religious memorabilia is worth the small fee.

i U4 or U5: Dom/Römer. Cathedral free. Dom Museum €3, students €2. Tours €3/2. Cash only. 🕐 Cathedral open M-Th 8am-8pm, F noon-8pm, Sa-Su 9am-8pm, except during services. Tours (in German) Tu-Su 3pm. Museum open Tu-F 10am-5pm, Sa-Su 11am-5pm. Haus am Dom open M-F 9am-5pm, Sa-Su 11am-5pm.

RÖMER   CITY HALL
Römerberg 25

Are you ready to dish out €15 for a scoop of ice cream? Römer's the place: this alleged "medieval masterpiece" is set against the most touristy square in all of Frankfurt. At the west end of the Römerberg, the blocky façade of the Römer has marked the site of Frankfurt's city hall since 1405. Named for the merchant family who inhabited it before the city council snatched it up, the Römer is distinct and marred only by the fact that today's version is a simplified post-war reconstruction. Since most of the building is still used by the municipal government, tourists can only access the Kaisersaal, which features an impressive se-

germany

get a room!

Frankfurt doesn't really do "deals." Hostels are hard to come by, and hotels are mostly full of bankers and businessmen. The West End/Bockenheim area has some more affordable options in a quieter setting, though nightlife is more accessible from Sachsenhausen and near the Hauptbahnhof. The two listed here are relatively cheap and are right near public transportation; for more, visit **www.letsgo.com**.

FIVE ELEMENTS HOSTEL   HOSTEL $$

Moselstr. 40   ☎069 240 05 885 www.5elementshostel.de

Five Elements is in the middle of Frankfurt's red light district, so we weren't expecting much when we visited. Thankfully, we were pleasantly surprised. Every night is special at Five Elements, which offers a free pasta night, free barbecue night, free movie night, and constantly updated list of free surprises. If this weren't enough, the rooms are superior, with tall metal bunks, plenty of floor space, and huge windows looking out on the skyscrapers. Reserve ahead of time, as Five Elements fills early in the summer.

i From the Hauptbahnhof, walk down Kaiserstr., turn left onto Moselstr., then walk across Taunusstr. The hostel is on the right. Free Wi-Fi. Breakfas €4. Linens €1.50. Laptops and bicycles available with deposit. 10% discount with Backpacker Network card. 5- to 7-bed dorms €18-24; singles €36-66; doubles from €50; quads from €72. ☑ Reception 24hr.

HAUS DER JUGEND   HOSTEL $$$

Deutschherrnufer 12   ☎069 610 01 50 www.jugendherberge-frankfurt.de

Haus der Jugend has one of the best locations of all the hostels in Frankfurt. It's located on the river and is only a 5min. walk from Frankfurt's best sights, including the Altstadt and the Museumsufer, and Sachsenhausen's nightlife. Unfortunately, Haus der Jugend does have a curfew in place, which limits the awesomeness of its closeness to Sachsenhausen. Despite gorgeous river views, like any hostel with over 400 beds, Haus der Jugend feels more like a hospital than a B&B. Still, anonymity is a small price to pay for good amenities and an unrivaled location.

i Bus #46: Frankensteiner Pl. From the bus stop, backtrack a tiny bit to the hostel. Alternatively, take tram 14 to Frankensteiner Pl. and walk west on Deutschherrnufer. The hostel is just before the Alte Brücke. Wi-Fi €5 per day. Breakfast and linens included. Laundry €2. 8- to 10-bed dorms €18; singles €37; doubles €53-63; quads €84-102. ☑ Reception 24hr. Curfew 2am.

ries of 19th-century portraits of every Holy Roman Emperor, from Charlemagne to Francis II. It's only worth the €2 admission if you want to play the lookalike game with some of the most influential leaders in human history.

i U4 or U5: Dom/Römer. Admission to Kaisersaal €2, students €0.50. Cash only. ☑ Kaisersaal open daily 10am-1pm and 2-5pm.

ARCHÄOLOGISCHER GARTEN   ARCHAEOLOGICAL SITE

Between the Dom and the Römerberg are the Schirn Kunsthalle and a plant-less "garden" of crumbled building foundations, some of which date back to a 2000-year-old Roman settlement. Three sets of ruins, from the first century BCE and the ninth and 15th centuries CE, were uncovered during excavations in 1953. Today, they rest undisturbed in a well-maintained garden, where you can wander around the ancient remains of Roman baths, military walls, an imperial palace, and middle-class resident houses. We suggest you pause to wonder whether

frankfurt

ancient residents of Frankfurt wore business suits, too. The only drawback to this place is that nothing's translated into English.

i *U4 or U5: Dom/Römer. From the metro, head toward the Dom.*

South of the Main

🏛 STÄDEL

ART MUSEUM

Schaumainkai 63　　　　　　　　　☎069 605 09 80 www.staedelmuseum.de

The Städel Museum, with its collection dating back to 1300, is probably the most successful and complete museum you're going to find in Germany. Masters like Botticelli, Rembrandt, and Dürer dominate one end of the timeline, while modern gods like Renoir, Kirchner, and Picasso command the other. The contents of this museum were hidden in a Bavarian castle during World War II, and everything survived the war except the main gallery, which was rebuilt in 1966. Excellent presentation, curatorial decisions, and organization will turn you into an art history beast after a single visit.

i *The Städel is at the south end of the Holbeinsteg. M-F €12, students €10, under 12 free; Sa-Su €14, students €12. 🕐 Open Tu 10am-6pm, W-Th 10am-9pm, F-Su 10am-6pm.*

🏛 MUSEUM FÜR ANGEWANDTE KUNST (MUSEUM FOR APPLIED ART)

MUSEUM

Schaumainkai 17　　　　　　　☎069 212 34 037 www.angewandtekunst-frankfurt.de

You might be wondering what "applied art" is. Not to worry—MfAK will set you straight. Art is everything. Art is the car your parents used to drive, the clothes you're wearing, the broken umbrella in the bin out front. This place offers a relatively comprehensive collection that immerses you in the everyday life of every continent and every time period (within reason). Check out the modern room, which contains a timeline of chairs—that's right, chairs—from 1859 to the present. The futuristic new villa, which connects to the original museum by a second-floor bridge, contains furnished rooms representing several different eras, including a Baroque music hall and a Jugendstil dining room.

i *On the eastern end of the Museumsufer, by the south end of the Eisernersteg footbridge €9, students €4.50. 🕐 Open Tu 10am-6pm, W 10am-8pm, and Th-Su 10am-6pm.*

LIEBIEGHAUS

MUSEUM

Schaumainkai 71　　　　　　　　　☎069 650 04 90 www.liebieghaus.de

A museum not solely devoted to art comes as a shock in Frankfurt, but Liebieghaus's collection of all things Egyptian, Classical, medieval, Renaissance, Baroque, and Rococo makes this museum stand out. After all, one era is just never enough. Some collections are more impressive than others: if you want to fill up on medieval wood sculptures of the Virgin Mary or Roman busts, you're set, but if you thirst for Egyptian sculpture, you'll stay thirsty. A climb up the tower leads to several rooms still furnished in the house's original style, which includes cozy wooden nooks and outstanding views of the Main. If the admission price is asking too much, consider just touring the museum's grounds: they're gorgeous, artistic, and free.

i *Adjacent to the Städel. €7, students €5, family ticket €12, under 12 free. Audio tours €4, students €3. 🕐 Open Tu 10am-6pm, W-Th 10am-9pm, F-Su 10am-6pm.*

FOOD

North of the Main

🏛 CAFÉ SÜDEN

CAFE, TAPAS $

Berger Str. 239　　　　　　　　　　　　　　　　　　☎069 956 333 00

Süden is an awesomely comfortable cafe in the middle of Bornheim. The cafe's colorful tables and umbrellas and joyous, slightly drunken banter spill out onto the quiet street. The ambiance could hardly be more pleasant, so we'll try not to

germany

scare you: tapas. At *Let's Go*, we don't often go for tapas unless we're in Spain. But Süden's tapas are honest-to-goodness cheap, they're filling, and they're delicious. Did we say awesome already? Try the *aubergine creme* (€3.50), a big bowl of hummus-like cream served with a comfortably large serving of bread. Süden's mint yogurt sauce is equally delectable: try it with grape leaves (€4) or chorizo (€4.50). If tapas aren't your thing, Süden also serves up good sandwiches, including tuna and egg for a mere €4.

i U4: Bornheim Mitte. From the metro, walk northeast on Berger Str., through the pedestrian-only square. After 3 blocks, Süden is on the left. Tapas €3.50-5. Sandwiches €4-5. Coffee €2-3. ☒ Open M-F 8:30am-midnight, Sa 10am-midnight.

KLEINMARKTHALLE
MARKET $
Hasengasse 5-7   ☎069 212 33 696   www.kleinmarkthalle.de

Kleinmarkthalle isn't just a restaurant. It's a collection of independent stalls, all competing for your attention under one roof. You get to assemble your own lunch: pick from bakeries, butchers, Middle Eastern specialty shops, and produce stands. Our motto, at least in Kleinmarkthalle, is "try before you buy," and most of the stalls are all-too-eager to indulge us. After you fill up on free samples of everything from peppered mango to cherries, buy some food for the road. Find enough (mostly raw) meat to feed a small nation, or seek a more civilized meal on the mezzanine, where you can watch the bartering below.

i U4 or U5: Römer/Dom. Head toward the Dom and continue north about ½ block past the Museum für Moderne Kunst. Cash only. ☒ Open M-F 8am-6pm, Sa 8am-4pm.

ZUR SONNE
GERMAN $$
Berger Str. 312   ☎069 45 93 96   www.zursonne-frankfurt.de

Zur Sonne is the idyllic, über-traditional beer garden you dreamed of finding in Germany: think sausages and dumplings. Despite Sonne's extremely German atmosphere, veggie food is both available here and thoroughly decent. Try the *Vegetarische Gemüsemaultaschen* (€7.40). You can stay here practically all night drinking house-made *Apfelwein* by the pitcher €3.30 per person) and wondering where the sun went. By the time you've eaten your second round of *Wildgoulash* (€13.20), it'll dawn on you.

i U4: Bronheim Mitte. From the metro, walk through the pedestrian-only square and continue northeast onto Berger Str. After 4 blocks, Zur Sonne is on the right. Apfelwein €1.40-7.60. Beer €2.90. Entrees €5.90-14.10. ☒ Open M-Sa 5pm-midnight, Su noon-11pm.

DAS LEBEN IST SCHÖN
ITALIAN $$
Hanauer Landstr. 128   ☎069 430 57 870   www.daslebenistschoen.de

Das Leben ist Schön means "Life is beautiful," and as much as we'd like to believe them, the location of this restaurant makes it a whole lot harder to believe. It's in the middle of nowhere, surrounded by car dealerships and outlet stores. Still, the restaurant showcases a sea of vintage photographs on the walls, and that's a beautiful sight. A bite of the piping hot pasta or freshly baked pizza only confirms the sentiment. Tremendously popular among 30-something locals (most of them sans business suit) thanks to its long communal tables and thick-crust pizza, Das Leben ist Schön rings loud and jolly despite the 30min. tram ride you'll have to take to get here.

i Tram 11: Schwedlerstr., then keep heading west½ block. Pasta €6.80-13. Pizzas €6-9. Salads €3-12. Apfelwein 0.2L €2.20, 0.5L €4. ☒ Open M-Sa 11:30am-11pm, Su noon-9pm. Pizza served until midnight F-Sa.

CAFÉ LAUMER
CAFE $$
Bockenheimer Landstr. 67   ☎069 72 79 12   www.cafe-laumer.de

Laumer has set up a display case in front of the cafe showcasing all the ways they can enhance your wedding, and that encapsulates the cafe's ambiance. Dine on the sunny, plant-filled front patio or in the backyard garden of this celebrated

frankfurt

cafe just a few blocks from the university. An older crowd of local businessmen on their lunch breaks enjoys the hearty *echt deutsch* special of the day (€6.40-9.80), while neighborhood *Stammgäste* (regulars) read the newspaper, drink coffee (€2.20), and eat generous slices of cake (€2.40-3.20).

i U6 or U7: Westend. Head east on Bockenheimer Landstr. The restaurant is on the right. Entrees €4.60-9.80. Breakfast €5-8. ☼ Open M-F 8am-7pm, Sa 8:30am-7pm, Su 9:30am-7pm.

South of the Main

▨ SCHIFFER CAFÉ

CAFE $$

Schifferstr. 36 ☎069 61 99 32 21 www.schiffercafe.de

At Schiffer, every new day comes with a new list of yummy daily specials and remarkably few suits attending business lunches. The lack of business folk lends the cafe a personality—we know, unbelievable, right? Schiffer is located directly opposite a small park, and the perimeter of the cafe is lined with little outdoor tables perfect for a coffee and some people watching. Location isn't everything, though. Schiffer also serves some absurdly good food without Frankfurt prices (scrambled eggs start at €3.40).

i U1, U2, U3, or U8: Schweizer Pl. From the metro, walk east on Gutzkowstr. Turn left onto Bodenstedtstr, then turn right onto Schifferstr. The cafe is on the left. Coffee €1.90-3.20. Breakfast €3.20-9.20. Sandwiches €2.40-5.50. ☼ Open M-F 8am-8pm, Sa 8am-7pm, Su 9am-7pm.

LA MAISON DU PAIN

FRENCH $$

Schweizer Str. 63 ☎069 78 07 46 46 www.lamaisondupain.de

When you think of France, do you think of the smell of freshly baked bread, of lavender bunches, of wooden furniture? Well, so does the rest of the world, and especially La Maison du Pain. Literally "the house of bread," this cafe has perfected the usual French stereotype, serving delicious croques (€6.40), quiches (€6.90), tarts (€4.30), and bowls of coffee (cafe au lait, €3.30). After a while, you might get sick of the French music and the whole schtick—seriously, they've even decorated the windows with decals of French landscapes—but fortunately, the motif does come with good food.

i U1, U2, U3, or U8: Schweizer Pl. From the metro, walk south on Schweizer Str. La Maison is on the left. Breakfast €4.80-9.80. Entrees €6-9. Macaroons €1.30. ☼ Open M-F 7:30am-8pm, Sa-Su 8am-8pm.

ADOLF WAGNER

GERMAN $$$

Schweizer Str. 71 ☎069 61 25 65 www.apfelwein-wagner.de

Saucy German dishes and some of the region's most renowned *Apfelwein* (0.3L €1.80) keep patrons jolly at this Sachsenhausen icon. Sit with regulars and try some of the *Grüne Soße* (green sauce) that you keep hearing about, preferably slathered atop the Frankfurter schnitzel (€12). The sauce is creamy and sour, and the wine fills your mouth with a lingering apple aftertaste. As you drink and digest, bask in either of the two sunny courtyards.

i U1, U2, or U3: Schweizer Pl., then head south on Schweizerstr. The restaurant is on the left. English menu available. Entrees €7-14. Sausages €4.50-7.50. ☼ Open daily 11am-midnight.

NIGHTLIFE

▨ COCOON CLUB

CLUB

Carl-Benz-Str. 21 ☎069 90 02 00 www.cocoon.net

Cocoon is in the middle of nowhere. It'll cost you €20 to get over here with a taxi (alternatively, you can take a tram), but despite the hassle and the cover, those looking for a legit night out won't want to miss it. The complex is gigantic and feels kind of like you're descending into the lair of some monstrous, postmodern spider, and the decor is so weird that it's impossible not to call this place cool. The main floor, which pumps house music at maximum volume with one of

germany

Europe's best sound systems, is enclosed by a gargantuan white-plastic lattice: the cocoon, where your spasms may metamorphose into dancing. Outside the inner sanctum, expensive cocktail bars greet you at every curve in the halls; two smaller (but still huge) dance floors bump to lighter house blends; and couples get cozy in comfy indentations punched into the cocoon's exterior. The bouncers are picky about wardrobe, but this is Frankfurt's premiere club.

i *U11 or U12: Dieselstr., then walk down Carl-Benz-Str. Cover €10. Cocktails €8-10. Open F-Sa 9pm-6am.*

⬛ PULSE AND PIPER RED LOUNGE

BAR, CLUB, GLBT

Bleichstr. 38a ☎069 138 86 802 www.pulse-frankfurt.de

Pulse and Piper features two dance floors, two lounges, a restaurant, and a beer garden. It's the ultimate all-in-one nightlife paradise. Despite its size, the club maintains some coziness as bartenders greet regulars on their way in. Piper, the smoking section, comprises a separate bar and loads of lounge space and is one of the largest of its kind in Frankfurt. Officially a gay club, Pulse attracts a clientele both gay and straight with its sublimely social spaces and hair-splitting house music that prompts patrons to dance far more wildly than the usual German two-step.

i *U1, U2, U3, or U8: Eschenheimer Tor. Head northwest on Bleichstr. Pulse and Piper Red Lounge is on the left. Martini Mondays all martini €5. Beer €2.50-3.80. Cocktails €8-10, happy hour €4-5. Restaurant entrees €6-22. Pulse open M-Th 11am-1am, F 11am-4am, Sa 10am-4am, Su 10am-1am. Piper Lounge (entry within Pulse) open daily 6pm and closes with Pulse. Happy hour M-W 7-9pm, Th 6pm-1am, F-Su 7-9pm. Kitchen open until 11pm.*

KING KAMEHAMEHA

CLUB

Hanauer Landstr. 192 ☎069 480 09 610 www.king-kamehameha.de

King Kamehameha, much like Cocoon, is in the middle of nowhere, but at least it's less in the middle of nowhere. This place lies in Frankfurt's southeast industrial district, where business folk shop for their new kitchen interiors and schmancy new Benz cars by day. Devastatingly loud house music from seasoned DJs threatens to shake this former brewery (with smokestack still standing) to the ground on Friday and Saturday nights, while Thursdays feature the renowned King Kamehameha Club Band, which ignites crowds with everything from '60s dance hits to top 40. Next to the packed main dance floor, a partially covered "garden" is the perfect place to take a break from the dancing, drinking, and steam.

i *Tram 11: Schwedlerstr. From the tram stop, head northeast on Hanauer Landstr. and turn into the alleyway next to Das Leben ist Schön. The club is set far back from the street, in the building with the brick smokestack. Cover €10. Shots €4. Beer €4-5. Cocktails €10. Cash only. Open Th 9pm-4am, F-Sa 10pm-5am. Open on select W; check the website for a calendar of events.*

ESSENTIALS

Practicalities

- **TOURIST OFFICES:** Hauptbahnhof. (☎069 212 38 800. *i* Near the main exit, next to the car rental. Brochures, tours, and map €0.50-1. Books rooms for a €3 fee; free if you call or email ahead. Open M-F 8am-9pm, Sa-Su 9am-6pm.) Alternate location at Römerberg 27. (Open M-F 9:30am-5:30pm, Sa-Su 10am-4pm.)

- **CURRENCY EXCHANGE:** ReiseBank in the Hauptbahnhof has slightly worse-than-average rates but, unlike most banks, stays open on Saturday. (☎069 24278591 *i* Go down the stairs inside the main entrance and walk down the hallway to the right. Open M-F 7am-6:30pm, Sa 10am-6pm.) Deutsche Bank. (*i* Across the street from the Hauptbahnhof. Open M-Th 9am-1pm and 2-5pm, F 9am-1pm and 2-4pm.) Germany's only remaining American Express branch exchanges currency, handles traveler's checks, and arranges hotel and rental car reservations. (Theodor-Heuss-Allee 112 ☎069 979 71 000 ☒ Open M-F 9:30am-6pm, Sa 10am-2pm.)

- **RESOURCES FOR WOMEN:** Frauennotruf is a hotline for female victims of sexual violence or abuse. (☎069 70 94 94 www.frauennotruf-frankfurt.de ☒ Open M 9am-1pm and 3-5pm, Tu 9am-1pm, W 9am-1pm and 6-8pm, Th-F 9am-1pm.)

- **GLBT RESOURCES:** The Switchboard is home to a popular bar/cafe, Café der AIDS-Hilfe Frankfurt, run by a local AIDS foundation. (Alte Gasse 36 ☎069 29 59 59 www.frankfurt-aidshilfe.de/ag36/switchboard. Cafe ☎069 28 35 35. *i* Take the U- or S-Bahn to Konstablerwache, walk west on Zeil briefly, and take the 1st left onto Großer Friedberger Str., which becomes Alte Gasse. Anonymous AIDS testing M 5-7:30pm, €15. ☒ Cafe open Sept-Jun Tu-Th 7pm-midnight, F-Sa 7pm-1am, Su 2-11pm; Jul-Aug M-Th 7pm-midnight, F-Sa 7pm-1am, Su 7-11pm.)

- **LAUNDROMATS:** Wash-World. (Moselstr. 17 ☎061 015 565 910 U4, U5, S1-S6, S8, or S9: Hauptbahnhof. *i* From the metro, walk northeast on Kaiserstr. and take the 1st right on Moselstr. The laundromat is on the right. Wash €3.50, dry €1 per 15min.) SB Waschsalon. (Wallstr. 8, near Haus der Jugend in Sachsenhausen. *i* Wash €3.50, dry €0.50 per 10min. ☒ Open daily 6am-11pm.)

- **INTERNET ACCESS:** Plenty of Internet-Telefon stores can be found on Kaiserstr., directly across from the Hauptbahnhof. Starbucks offers unlimited free Wi-Fi without a password, so you don't even need to buy an expensive drink. Visit Kaiserstr. 26 (☒ Open M-F 7am-8pm, Sa-Su 9am-7pm), Braubachstr. 36 (☒ Open M-F 7:30am-9:30pm, Sa 8:30am-9:30pm, Su 9am-9pm), or An der Hauptwache 7. (☒ Open M-Th 8am-9pm, F 8am-10pm, Sa 9am-10pm, Su 10am-8pm.) CyberRyder. (Töngesgasse 31 ☎069 91396 754 www.cyberyder.de *i* Internet €1.30 per 15min. Drinks €1.60-3. ☒ Open M-F 9:30am-10pm, Sa 10am-10pm, Su noon-9pm.)

- **POST OFFICE:** Inside the Hauptbahnhof, opposite track 22. (☒ Open M-F 7am-7pm, Sa 9am4pm.) Second location on Goethpl. (☒ Open M-F 9:30am-7pm, Sa 9am-2pm.)

- **POSTAL CODE:** 60313.

Emergency

- **EMERGENCY:** ☎110. Fire and Ambulance: ☎112.

- **POLICE:** Adickesallee 70. (☎069 755 00.) U1 or U2: Miquel Adickesallee. From the metro, head east on Adickesallee. The station is on the left.

- **PHARMACY:** Apotheke im Hauptbahnhof (Station's Einkaufspassage ☎069 23 30 47 *i* Take the escalators heading down toward the S- or U-Bahn trains, then turn left. ☒ Open M-F 6:30am-9pm, Sa 8am-9pm, Su 9am-8pm.) Adler Apotheke. (Neue Kräme 33 ☎069 283 525 *i* From the Römer, walk north along the square past Subway, cross Berliner Str., and continue north on Neue Kräme. The pharmacy is on the left at the end of the block. A sign in the window lists the schedule of after-hours emergency service. ☒ Open 8am-7pm, Sa 9am-4pm.)

Getting There

By Plane

The **Frankfurt Airport** (☎0180 537 24 636 www.frankfurt-airport.de) is the gateway to Germany for thousands of travelers from all over the world. From the airport, S-Bahn trains S8 and S9 travel to the Hauptbahnhof every 15min. (*i* Buy tickets from the green Fahrkarten machines before boarding. Tickets €3.90.) Most public transportation and trains to major cities depart from Airport Terminal 1. Take the free bus (every 15min.) or walk through the skyway to reach the terminal from the main airport. Taxis to the city center (€20) can be found outside every terminal.

By Train

The **Hauptbahnhof** is on the west side of the city, close to the Main. (☎0180 599 66 33 Visit www.bahn.de for reservations and information.) Trains leaving from Frankfurt go to: Berlin (€90-120 ⌚ 5hr., every hr.); Dresden (€82-87 ⌚ 5hr., every hr.); Heidelberg €19-26 ⌚ 1½hr., every hr.); Köln (€40-60 1-2hr., 2 per hr.); Munich (€91 ⌚ 3½hr., every hr.); Amsterdam (€70-130 ⌚ 4-7hr., every 2hr.); Basel (€75 ⌚ 3hr., every 2hr.); and Paris (€110-120 ⌚ 4-5hr., 6 per day).

By Rideshare

Mitfahrzentrale arranges rides to Berlin (€20); Köln (€11); Munich (€15); Amsterdam (€20); Vienna (€24); and other cities. (Stuttgarterstr. 13 ☎069 19440 www.mfz.de *i* Take a right on Baselerstr. at the side exit of the Hauptbahnhof on track 1 and walk 2 blocks toward the river. ⌚ Open M-F 9:30am-5:30pm, Sa 10am-2pm.)

Getting Around

By Public Transportation

Buy tickets from the green-blue **Fahrkarten machines** before boarding the metro; tickets are automatically validated upon purchase. Einzelfahrkarte (single-ride) tickets are valid for 1hr. after purchase. Check to see if your destination qualifies for a Kurzstrecke ("short-stretch" ticket) by looking through the stops at the top of the machine and then punching in the appropriate number before selecting your ticket. For rides within Frankfurt, use the code "50" (€2.40, children €1.40; short rides €1.50, children €1; day tickets €6, children €3.60, group of up to 5 adults €9.50). Failure to buy a ticket results in a €40 fine, and Frankfurt is notorious for checking, especially during rush hour.

By Taxi

Try **Taxi Frankfurt** (☎069 230 01 or ☎069 230 033), **Time Car GmbH** (☎069 20 304), or **SGS Taxi** (☎069 793 07 999).

By Boat

Several companies offer tours of the Main that depart the Mainkai on the river's northern bank near the Römerberg. Check out **KD.** (☎069 285 728 www.k-d.com *i* €7.50 per person, under 13 €5. ⌚ 1hr. Apr-Oct daily 10:30am, noon, 2pm, 3:30pm, 5pm, and 6:30pm.) **Primus-Linie** (☎069 133 83 70 www.primus-linie.de) cruises to a long list of towns along the Main, making for great day trips.

By Bike

Frankfurt has an excellent network of bike paths, and, with few cobblestones outside of the Altstadt, biking is a fun and easy way to find those harder-to-reach places. Just watch out for Mercedes-driving businessmen: they won't stop. Deutsche Bahn (DB) runs the citywide bike rental, **Call a Bike.** Look for the bright red bikes with the DB logo in racks throughout the city. Retrieve unlocking code by phone or online. (☎07000 522 55 22 www.callabike.de *i* €0.08 per min., €15 per day, or €45 per week.) **NextBike** is similar, but you must return bikes to specific locations throughout the city. (☎030 692 05 046 www.nextbike.de *i* Check the website for a map of locations. €1 per hr., €8 per day.)

munich

If you ask the average traveler about this Bavarian capital, you'll hear beer, beer, and more beer. The birthplace of Oktoberfest, Munich is the third largest city in Germany (pop. 1,380,00) and one of the country's most expensive. It's difficult to believe that this affluent, beer-soaked city is where the Nazi NSDAP Party had its first headquarters. Hitler's first attempt to seize power took place in Munich, and the Führerhimself spoke at some of the beer halls that you can still visit today. The first Nazi concentration camp, Dachau, is just 30min. away from the city. Today, Munich is trying to put much of this history behind it and has become a thriving center of European commerce, with world-class museums, parks, and architecture. Salzburg (only 1½hr. away by train) is a popular daytrip for many Munchkins—er, Müncheners—and the fairytale castle of Neuschwanstein is a major tourist attraction.

ORIENTATION

City Center

The city center is the hub of all tourist activity in Munich. Many of the city's historical sights and brand-name stores are packed into the few blocks between Marienpl. and Odeonspl. For the stereotypical Bavarian experience, struggle through the throngs of international camera-flashers for a night at the famous Hofbräuhaus and a stroll through the Residenzmuseum. There's a long pedestrian zone between Marienpl. and Karlspl., a square with fountains that is popularly known as "Stachus." South of Marienpl., bustling, yuppie Isarvorstadt is home to Munich's GLBT district. To the west, Theresienwiesen borders on the huge Oktoberfest field. Backpacker hostels cluster around the Hauptbahnhof, Munich's central train station, which is north of Theresienwiesen.

University Area

"University area" is the common nickname for the districts of Schwabing and Maxvorstadt, immediately north of the city center. Maxvorstadt is home to Kunstareal, the city's museum district, and Königspl., a former Nazi stronghold. Schwabing, to the north, is a student's dream district; Ludwig-Maximilian Universität intellectuals fill the area's cozy bars and restaurants. West of Schwabing, everything goes greener with the charming Englischer Garten, where you'll find Munich's beloved beer garden by the Chinesischer Turm (Chinese Pagoda).

Olympic Area

The 1972 Munich Olympics was Germany's chance to prove itself in the international spotlight after the racist disasters that had devastated the 1936 Berlin Olympics under the Nazis. But the Munich games were overshadowed by the killing of 11 Israeli athletes by Palestinian terrorists. Now known as the Munich Massacre, the attack was the subject of Steven Spielberg's 2005 film *Munich*. Today, you can visit the Olympiapark and marvel at the site of the Games. The imposing Olympiaturm (Olympic Tower) is the highest point in all of Munich, and the iconic Olympiastadion's (Olympic Stadium) curtains of acrylic glass drape over lime green seats. The enormous shopping mall, Olympia-Einkaufszentrum, is west of the park.

Au-Haidhausen

These two neighborhoods, located across the Isar river, housed laborers before WWII bombing nearly demolished Au (Haidhausen was left surprisingly intact). Today, these regions play a large role in Munich's cultural scene. The Gasteig cultural complex contains the Munich Philharmonic, a conservatory, the main branch of the public library, and an experimental theater. Giant clubs surround the Ostbahnhof station—talk about being on the right side of the tracks.

Neuhausen

Neuhausen remains one of Munich's hidden gems, relatively undiscovered by tourists. Take tram 17 toward Amalienburgstr. and you'll find some of Munich's prettiest landscapes, from the world's largest beer garden at Hirschgarten to the extravagant Schloss Nymphenburg. For a more urban feel, head to Rotkreuzpl. and meander down Nymphenburgstr. for the city's best cafes.

SIGHTS

City Center

MARIENPLATZ   SQUARE
Marienpl. 1

The pedestrian area around Marienpl. is the heart of Munich. Its name comes from the Mariensäule, a 17th-century monument to the Virgin Mary that sits at the center of the large square as a tribute to the city's miraculous survival of the Swedish invasion and the plague. The square is dominated by the impressively ornate Neo-Gothic Neues Rathaus, or new city hall, which was built in the early 20th century. Camera-toting tourists gawk at its central tower during the thrice-daily Glockenspiel mechanical chimes displays, which may be one of the most underwhelming tourist attractions you'll ever see and hear. At the eastern end of the square, the Altes Rathaus (Old Town Hall) houses a small and boring toy museum.

i *S1, S2, S3, S4, S5, S6, S7, S8, U3 or U6: Marienpl.* 🕐 *Glockenspiel displays in summer 11am, noon, and 5pm; in winter 11am and noon.*

ALTER PETER (SAINT PETER'S CHURCH)   CHURCH
Rindermarkt 1   ☎089 26 04 828

As the poster inside explains, Alter Peter was severely damaged during World War II. The Gothic-inspired church was then meticulously rebuilt, but most of the interior walls remain plain and white. However, you can still see an original cannonball lodged in the church wall (behind the church, take the steps leading up to Cafe Rischart and look around the top right corner of the window frame). Check out the freakish, gem-studded skeleton of St. Munditia, exhibited in a glass case that looks more like a diamond ad gone wrong than holy remains. The church's tower offers a bird's-eye view of Munich and is definitely worth climbing. However, the ascent to the (almost) heavens is challenging, as the staircase of 306 steps is too narrow for two-way traffic. Watch out for others and observe the decades of cool signatures and stickers on the walls.

i *S1, S2, S3, S4, S5, S6, S7, S8, U3 or U6: Marienpl. Church free. Tower €1.50, students and children €1. Cash only.* 🕐 *Tower open in summer M-F 9am-6:30pm, Sa-Su 10am-6:30pm.; in winter M-F 9am-5:30pm, Sa-Su 10am-5:30pm.*

RESIDENZ MUSEUM AND HOFGARTEN   MUSEUM
Residenzstr. 1   ☎089 26 06 71 www.residenz-muenchen.de

The 130-room Residenz palace, once home to Bavarian dukes and electors, is now a museum that takes the word "excess" to new dimensions, with mirrors, porcelain, and blinding gold leaves galore. Highlights include the ancestral gallery, hung with over 100 family portraits tracing the royal lineage, and the spectacular Renaissance antiquarium, replete with stunning frescoes. A separate ticket is needed for the Treasury, full of shiny expensive stuff.

i *U3, U4, U5, or U6: Odeonspl. Residenz and treasury each €7, students €5, under 18 free; combined Residenz and treasury ticket €11/9/free; Cuvilliés Theater €3.50/2.50/free; combination Residenz, treasury, and theater €13/10.50/free. Audio tours included.* 🕐 *Residenz and Treasury open Apr-Oct daily 9am-6pm; Oct-March 10am-5pm. Last entry 1hr. before close. Theater open Apr-Jul M-Sa 2-6pm, Su 9am-6pm; Aug-Sept daily 9am-6pm; Sept-Oct M-Sa 2-6pm, Su 9am-6pm; Oct-Mar M-Sa 2-5pm, Su 10am-5pm.*

munich

University Area

PINAKOTHEKEN   MUSEUMS
Barrerstr.   ☎089 23 80 52 16 www.pinakothek.de

Don't let the whole "five museums" thing scare you away from Pinakotheken:
think of all these museums as just one giant and super impressive art gallery.
The five buildings are part of the Kunstareal, a museum district in Maxvorstadt
that comprises the majority of Munich's art museums. Start with **Alte Pinakothek,**
the one with the collection that some would affectionately call "boring, old art"
(14th- to 17th-century art, including works of European masters such as da Vinci

get a room!

As a city of beer, Munich sees its fair share of young philanthropists looking to aid
the local industry. With that comes a proliferation of clean and reasonably priced
hostels smack in the city center. Here are a couple noteworthy places to rest your
head; for more, visit **www.letsgo.com**.

WOMBATS   HOSTEL $$$
Senefelderstr. 1   ☎089 59 98 91 80 www.wombats-hostels.com/munich

A party hostel par excellence, Wombats is always hopping. The free drink
voucher you receive at check-in gets you started with a small beer at
the"WomBar" downstairs, while quieter types can hang out in lovely ham-
mocks in the courtyard garden. All rooms have private bathrooms and
high-tech key card lockers, and the hostel's custom city map is a big plus.
   i S1, S2, S3, S4, S5, S6, S8, U1, U2, U4, or U5: Hauptbahnhof. Exit at Bayerst., cross the
   street, and continue to Senefelderstr. If you're facing the station, it's on the left. Free Wi-Fi
   in the lobby. Breakfas €3.80. Linens included. Computer use €0.50 per 20min. Dorms
   €22-29; doubles €38-40. ☺ Reception 24hr. Happy hour daily 6-8pm and midnight-1am.

EURO YOUTH HOTEL   HOSTEL $$
Senefelderstr. 5   ☎089 59 90 88 11 www.euro-youth-hotel.de

Euro Youth Hotel has one of the most luxurious reception and common
areas in the city. The 12-person dorms are surprisingly cheap, so make
sure to book in advance, as beds fill up very early. The lounge and its
wrap-around bar are the site of many entertaining nights, which range
from quizzes to'80s dances to karaoke.
   i S1, S2, S3, S4, S5, S6, S8, U1, U2, U4, or U5: Hauptbahnhof. Exit the station at Bay-
   erst., cross the street, and continue to Senefelderstr. Free Wi-Fi. Breakfas €4.50; included
   for private rooms. Linens included. 12-bed dorms €15-20; smaller dorms €19-28. Private
   rooms available. ☺ Reception 24hr. Happy hour M-Tu 6-9pm, W 6-10pm, Th-Su 6-9pm.

THE TENT   CAMPGROUND $
In den Kirschen 30   ☎089 141 43 00 www.the-tent.com

When Munich prepared to host the 1972 Olympics, the government
kicked out all the hippies camping out at the English Garden, who then
skipped out to the northeast corner of town to set up permanent camp
here. So the not-for-profit Tent was born. Two tents are filled with bunk
beds, while the third makes space for the bravest travels: those who sleep
on a thin, rainbow-colored mat on the floor. This is by far the cheapest
place to stay in Munich.
   i Tram 17: Botanischer Garten. Take a right onto Franz-Schrankstr. and a left at the end
   of the street. Free Wi-Fi. Lockers available. Floor spac €7.50 (including floor pad and
   blankets); beds €11. Camping €5.50 per person; €5.50 per tent. Bike rental €9 per day.
   Cash only. ☺ Reception 24hr. Open Jun-Oct.

germany

and Dürer). What's surprisingly cool is that the whole collection is arranged in one giant hallway of multiple rooms, so you can really experience how much art changed over the course of 300 years. The Pinakotheken can be a lot of art all at once, so consider visiting over several days or run (not literally) through the museums on Sundays, when admission is only €1.

i U2: Theresienstr. Walk east on Theresienstr. until you see the big museum complex. Museum Brandhorst, Alte, and Neue Pinakothek each €7, students €5; Pinakothek der Moderne €10/7; Sammlung Schack €4/3; 1-day pass to all 5 €12/9; 5-entry pass €29. All museums €1 on Su. ☒ Alte Pinakothek open Tu 10am-8pm, W-Su 10am-6m. Neue Pinakothek open M 10am-6pm, W 10am-8pm, Th-Su 10am-6pm. Pinakothek der Moderne open Tu-W 10am-6pm, Th 10am-8pm, F-Su 10am-6pm. Museum Brandhorst open Tu-W 10am-6pm, Th 10am-8pm, F-Su 10am-6pm. Sammlung Schack open daily 10am-6pm.

▨ ENGLISCHER GARTEN
PARK

Strolling through the open emerald fields and leafy paths of the enormous Englischer Garten may be one of the most relaxing things you can do on a summer day in the city. The park is one of the largest metropolitan public parks in the world, dwarfing both Central Park in New York and Hyde Park in London. The amazingly healthy residents of Munich do everything from walk their dogs, ride their bikes, and bathe in the sun here. Some choose to do this last activity in the nude, in areas designated FKK or *Frei Körper Kultur* ("Free Body Culture"). There are also several beer gardens here, but the most famous one surrounds a wooden Chinese pagoda. In the southern part of the garden, a former Nazi art exhibition space, Haus der Kunst (Prinzregentenst.1 089 21 12 71 13 www. hausderkunst.de), is now Munich's premier venue for contemporary art, with changing international and domestic exhibitions.

i U3: Universität, Giselastr., or Münchner Freiheit. Park free. Haus der Kunst €5-12. Student discounts available. ☒ Haus der Kunst open M-W 10am-8pm, Th 10am-10pm, F-Su 10am-8pm.

KÖNIGSPLATZ
SQUARE

The Königsplatz was comissioned by King Ludwig I to be Munich's tribute to Greek and Roman antiquity. During the Third Reich, the Nazis, who also admired ancient Rome, made the square their headquarters and used the large roads for rallies. The infamous book burning of 1933 took place here, and the famous Munich Accord was signed in Hitler's "Führerbau," just east of the square (strangely, the building is now home to a music and theater university). The square is not just for squares though; on sunny days, dozens of people spend their time just chilling on the stairs or sunbathing in the large grassy fields.

i U2: Königspl. Glyptothek and Antikensammlungen each €3.50, students €2.50; combined ticket €5.50/3.50. Every Su €1. ☒ Antikensammlungen open Tu 10am-5pm, W 10am-8pm, Th-Su 10am-5pm.Glyptothek open Tu-W 10am-5pm, Th 10am-8pm, F-Su 10am-5pm.

Olympic Area

▨ BMW WELT AND MUSEUM
MUSEUM

Am Olympiapark 1 ☎018 02 11 88 22 www.bmw-welt.com

Do you know what BMW stands for? Regardless of your answer, you must stop by the BMW Welt and Museum. (BMW stands for "Bayerische Motoren Werke," by the way.) The amazing, futuristic architecture of the entire BMW complex alone would make your visit worthwhile. However, you can also jump into all sorts of cars, play racing computer games, and watch shows of handsome Germans driving motorcycles up and down stairs while you're here. And this is only in the BMW Welt, which is the car company's showcase. The museum is almost as cool (although perhaps not as interactive), with state-of-the-art exhibits detailing the history, development, and design of Bavaria's second-favorite export. Frosted glass walls and touch-sensitive projections lead visitors past engines,

munich

chassis, and concept vehicles with exhibits in both English and German. Visitors can also make reservations to tour the adjacent production factory, with a tunnel that runs through the entire assembly line.

i U3: Olympiazentrum. BMW Welt is the large steel structure visible upon exiting the metro; the museum is located across the street. Factory and BMW Welt tours available only with a reservation. BMW Welt free. Museum €9, students €6, family €12. Special discounts with Olympiapark ticket or the City Tour Card. ⏰ BMW Welt open daily 7:30am-midnight. Museum open Tu-Su 10am-6pm; last entry 5:30pm. 2 factory tours in English daily 11:30am and either noon or 4pm.

OLYMPIAPARK   SPORTS COMPLEX
Olympiapark   ☎089 30 67 24 14 www.olympiapark.de
Built for the 1972 Olympic Games, the lush Olympiapark contrasts with the curved steel and transparent spires of the Olympic Stadium and the 290m Olympiaturm, Munich's tallest tower. The Olympic area (including the stadium) can be accessed for free, but you can buy a self-guided audio tour for in-depth information about the various structures. Otherwise, three English-language tours are available. The Adventure Tour gets you into many of the buildings and introduces you to Olympiapark's history; the Stadium Tour focuses just on the stadium; and the Roof Climb lets you unleash your inner Spider-Man and climb the stadium's roof with a rope and a hook. The building where Palestinian terrorists captured Israeli athletes during the Munich Massacre is in the northern half of the park (Connellystr. 31).

i U3: Olympiazentrum. Audio tours and tickets for tours can be purchased at the information desk in the southeast corner of the park (close to the ice rink). Audio tour €7, deposit €50. Adventure Tour €8, students €5.50. Unguided entrance to stadium €3. Stadium Tour €7.50, students €5. Roof climb €41, students €31. Tower and Rock Museum €5.50, under 16 €3.50. Admission includes discounts at Sea Life and the BMW Museum. ⏰ Tours offered daily Apr-Nov. Adventure Tour 2pm. Stadium Tour 11am. Roof Climb 2:30pm (weather permitting). Tower and Rock Museum open daily 9am-midnight. Audio tour available 9am-5pm, but can be returned any time before 11:30pm.

Au-Haidhausen

DEUTSCHES MUSEUM   MUSEUM
Museumsinsel 1   ☎089 217 91 www.deutsches-museum.de
An hour or so in the Deutsches Museum will teach you more than all your introductory science classes combined. This incredible museum presents you with the power of German engineering—prepare for everything from key mechanisms, musical instruments, and oil rigs to timekeeping microchips and the frontiers of nanotechnology. Reading all the explanations throughout the giant rooms, spread over eight floors, is impossible for us mere mortals, but anywhere you go, you're guaranteed to find something mindboggling. Before you think you've had enough knowledge for the day, be sure to check out the claustrophobic mining exhibit, which is appropriately situated in the basement.

i S1, S2, S3, S4, S5, S6, S7, S8: Isartor. On the island between the city center and the Au neighborhood. From the metro, head toward the river, cross onto the island, and turn right €8.50, students €3, children under 6 free. Cash only. ⏰ Open daily 9am-5pm.

Neuhausen

SCHLOSS NYMPHENBURG   PALACE
Schloss Nymphenburg   ☎089 17 90 80 www.schloss-nymphenburg.de
This palace was supposedly modeled after Versailles and built in 1675 for Bavarian royalty. The main building, the lavish, three-story Stone Hall, has all your typical, intricate frescoed ceilings and enormous dangling chandeliers, but the real charm of this property is the enormous, gorgeous garden. Few tourists venture beyond the space immediately behind the castle, so the area with four ornate pavilions (Amelienburg, Badenburg, Magdaleneklause, and Pagoden-

germany

burg) remains peaceful. Highlights of the property include the bedroom in which King Ludwig II was born and the Gallery of Beauties, featuring portraits of the 36 women whom King Ludwig I considered to be the most beautiful in Bavaria (our favorite is Helene Sedlmeyr). Summertime brings classical concerts to the park grounds; check kiosks for details.

i Tram 17: Schloss Nymphenburg. Palace €6, students €5. Porcelain and carriage museums €4.50, students €3.50; pavilions €4.50/3.50; combination ticket €11.50/9. Audio tour €3.50. Gardens free. Museum Mensch und Natur €3, students €2, Su €1. ☼ Complex open daily Apr-Oct 9am-6pm; Oct-Mar 10am-4pm. Badenburg, Pagodenburg, and Magdalenklause closed in winter. Museum Mensch und Natur open Tu-W 9am-5pm, Th 9am-8pm, F 9am-5pm, Sa-Su 10am-6pm.

Outside Munich

◙ NEUSCHWANSTEIN CASTLE   CASTLE
Schwangau, near Füssen   ☎083 62 93 08 30 www.neuschwanstein.de
Depending on who you ask, Neuschwanstein Castle is either a gorgeous, fairy-tale fortress or a 19th-century, Disney-esque castle that borders walks a fine line between cool and kitschy. We definitely don't deny the charms of the white Neuschwanstein, or "New Swan Rock," castle, which was commissioned by King Ludwig II and is perched precariously on a hilltop in the beautiful Bavarian Alps. The only way to get inside the castle, which is almost completely covered in paintings of scenes from Wagner's operas, is with a 30min. guided tour. No visit to this castle is complete without a walk across Marienbrücke, a slightly rickety wooden bridge across a waterfall that leads to a stunning side view of Neuschwanstein.

i Take the 2hr. DB train to Füssen (every hr.; €21 for Bayern ticket, €50 round trip normal ticket). Walk right across the street and take either the #73 or #78 bus to the last stop, Schwangau (10min.; free with Bayern ticket or €1.90 1-way). To get to the castle from the bus stop, you can either walk up the hill (40min.), take a bus (10min.; up €1.80, down €1, round trip €2.60), or take a horse-drawn carriage (15min.; up €6, down €3). Check the schedule of buses going back to Füssen—they leave every hr., synchronized with train departures. The main ticket office is approximately 100m uphill from the #78 bus stop. English tours are frequent, but earlier tours sell out quickly; it's a good idea to book in advance €1.80 surcharge). Guided tours of Neuschwanstein €12, students €8, under 18 free; Hohenschwangau €10.50/8/free; combined ticket €23, students €21. ☼ Castle open Apr-Sept daily 9am-6pm; Oct-Mar 10am-4pm. Ticket office open Apr-Sept daily 8am-5pm; Oct-Mar 9am-3pm.

DACHAU CONCENTRATION CAMP MEMORIAL SITE   MEMORIAL SITE
Alte Römerstr. 75, Dachau   ☎081 31 66 99 70 www.kz-gedenkstaette-dachau.de
The first thing prisoners saw as they entered Dachau was the inscription *"Arbeit Macht Frei"* ("Work will set you free") on the camp's iron gate. One of the most moving parts of the memorial site is actually part of the audio guide: survivors tell their life stories and the unimaginably inhumane life in the camp. The barracks, originally designed for 5000 prisoners, once held 30,000 at a time—two have been reconstructed for visitors, and gravel-filled outlines of the others stand as haunting reminders. It is impossible to prepare yourself for the camp's crematorium, which has been restored to its original appearance. The museum at the Dachau Memorial Site, in the former maintenance building, examines pre-1930s anti-Semitism, the rise of Nazism, the establishment of the concentration camps, and the lives of prisoners.

i S2 (dir.: Petershausen): Dachau (30min.; 4 stripes on the Streifenkarte, free with Munich XXL ticket). Then, take bus #726 (dir.: Saubachsiedlung): KZ-Gedenkstätte (1 stripe on the Streifenkarte; €1.20, or free with Munich XXL ticket). All displays have English translations. Museum and memorial grounds free. Audio tours €3.50, students €2.50. Tours €3 per person. ☼ Memorial grounds open daily. Museum and information office open Tu-Su 9am-5pm. Tours 2½hr. in English daily 11am and 1pm; in German noon. Documentary 22min. in German 11am and 3pm; in English 11:30am, 2pm, and 3:30pm.

FOOD

City Center

⚄ CAFE RISCHART

CAFE $

Marienpl. 18   ☎089 231 70 03 20 www.rischart.de

Budget travelers can always count on Cafe Rischart: it's cheap, fast, and simple. There are two cafes on Marienplatz that have touristy outside seating areas, but there are also multiple locations at subway stops and train stations where even locals stop by to grab something to go. The delicious sandwiches are made from mouthwatering bread, with plenty of tasty German or Italian fillings inside (€3-4). A scoop of gelato (€1.20) is also obligatory on sunny days.

i S1, S2, S3, S4, S5, S6, S7, S8, U3, or U6: Marienpl. Locations on the southeast corner of the square and behind Alter Peter. Coffee €1.80-3. Cash only. ☒ Open M-Sa 6:45am-9pm, Su 9am-9pm.

ZUM AUGUSTINER

GERMAN $$$

Neuhauserstr. 27   ☎089 23 18 32 57 www.augustiner-restaurant.com

Augustiner beer halls and beer gardens are an essential part of Munich, but that doesn't take away from the bustling milieu created by the happy voices of tourists and locals here. Get your hearty German standards here, but don't forget about the delicious Weissbier. If you're really hungry, go for the gravy-laden roasted pork with a giant potato dumpling and sauerkraut. Enjoy the subdued beer hall ambience in the main hall, in the picturesque courtyard, or at one of the busy street tables—but beware, those pretzels on the table cost €1.

i S1, S2, S3, S4, S5, S6, S7, S8, U4, or U5: Karlspl. Walk past the fountain and under the arches to Neuhauserstr.; restaurant is on the right. Multilingual menu. Entrees €5-19. ☒ Open daily 10am-midnight.

University Area

BAR TAPAS

TAPAS $$

Amalienstr. 97   ☎089 39 09 19 www.bar-tapas.com

Grab a pen and a slip of paper from the bar and write down your selections from the displays of tapas at this romantic Iberian outpost. We recommend the spicy chorizo and the tortilla pie with cheese, potatoes, and onions. At lunch time, Bar Tapas offers cheap bocadillos, tortillas, and tacos (€4.80-7.80). If you're in the neighborhood but don't feel like Spanish food, just walk around Amalienstr. and Türkenstr., which are packed with small restaurants and cafes.

i U3 or U6: Universität. Turn left onto Adalbertstr. Tapas €4.30. Cocktails €5 after 10:30pm. ☒ Open daily 11:30am-1am.

CAFE IGNAZ

VEGETARIAN $$

Georgenstr. 67   ☎089 271 60 93 www.ignaz-cafe.de

Cafe Ignaz is a vegetarian oasis in the land of pork and beef. It's also just an oasis in general, as all of the locals from the neighboring streets seem to be packed into the two small rooms and outdoor seating area. The narrow passage that connects these two areas has a counter filled with gorgeous cakes and sweet and salty pastries that you can purchase for takeaway. Otherwise, the vegetarian and vegan cafe serves gnocchi, risotto, crepes, and more, all perfect antidotes to Bavarian cuisine. Every meal comes with a free cake, which may be either sweet or made from vegetables.

i U2: Josephspl. Take Georgenstr. east for 3 blocks. English-language menu. Entrees €9.90. Breakfast buffet €7, includes hot drink. Lunch buffet €5.90. Brunch buffet €9.90. ☒ Open M 8am-11pm, W-Su 8am-11pm. Breakfast buffet M 8-11:30am, W-F 8-11:30am. Lunch buffet M noon-2:30pm, W-F noon-2:30pm. Brunch buffet Sa-Su 9am-2pm. Happy hour M-F 3-6pm.

germany

Au-Haidhausen

CAFÉ VOILÀ
CAFE $$$

Wörthstr. 5 ☎089 489 16 54 www.cafe-voila.de

Looking for a perfect place for a delicious Italian-Bavarian breakfast cafe? Before you shout *"Voilà!"* after happening upon this popular establishment, we recommend that you make a reservation, especially on the weekends. Café Voilà is lovely for sitting outside at any time of the day, but the enormous traditional interior with large mirrors is just as nice on rainy days. After breakfast, the cafe offers reasonably priced, three-course lunch menus, along with burgers, pasta, and salads. A selection of some 60 cocktails (€5 during happy hour) attracts customers in the evening.

i S1, S2, S3, S4, S5, S6, S7, S8, or U5: Ostbahnhof. Exit onto Wörthstr. and walk 1 block past the small park between the roads. Breakfast €4-11. Entrees €5.50-16. Beer €2.80-3.50. Cash only. ⊠ Open M-Th 8am-1am, F-Sa 8am-late, Su 8am-1am. Happy hour M-Tu 5pm-1am, W-Sa 5-8pm and 11pm-1am, Su 5pm-1am.

WIRTSHAUS IN DER AU
GERMAN $$$

Lillienstr. 51 ☎089 448 14 00 www.wirtshausinderau.de

Wirtshaus in der Au, on the "other side" of the Isar, is a beautiful, traditional Bavarian restaurant both in decor and in taste. Farther from the touristy crowds, the restaurant's enormous interior and impressively large outdoor area is perfect for large groups. And we're still not done admiring Wirtshaus' size: the establishment also claims to serve the largest dumplings in all of Munich, both in girth and variety. During Oktoberfest, they have a tent with 26 different varieties; during the rest of the year, there's usually five to pick from. Try the tomato olive dumpling filled with mozzarella, with a side of marinated eggplant.

i Tram 18: Deutsches Museum. Cross the bridge, head past Museum Lichtspiele, and turn right onto Lillienstr. English menu available. Entrees €7.80-17. Maß €6.90. ⊠ Open M-F 5pm-midnight, Sa-Su 10am-midnight.

Neuhausen

⌧ RUFFINI
CAFE $$

Orffstr. 22-24 ☎089 16 11 60 www.ruffini.de

The plain white walls, straight lines, large mirrors, and stacks of simple, clear glasses makes this enchanting cafe a nice break from the (also awesome) Bavarian over-decoration. This cooperative cafe, located on a quiet residential street, buzzes with locals chatting or reading the morning paper. Order a frothy cappuccino and a flaky croissant and take them to the sunny terrace upstairs. For lunch, there are many vegetarian options, and the meat dishes usually comes from eco-friendly sources. Ruffini is owned collectively by over two dozen people, ranging from designers to policemen who all put in hours working at the cafe. If you're in a hurry, you can also stop by the small bakery that sells beautiful cakes and fancy wines.

i Tram 12: Neuhausen. Turn perpendicular to tram route so that the park is to the left. The cafe is 2 blocks down Ruffinistr. Rooftop terrace is self-service. Small bakery attached; enter on Ruffinistr. Breakfast €5.80-8.50. Dinner €4-14. Cash only. ⊠ Cafe open Tu-Su 10am-midnight. Shop open Tu-F 8:30am-6pm, Sa 8:30am-5pm, Su 9am-5pm.

⌧ AUGUSTINERKELLER
GERMAN $$

Arnulfstr. 52 ☎089 59 43 93 www.augustinerkeller.de

This restaurant's authentic Bavarian dishes will surely not disappoint. Since Augustiner was first concocted in 1824, it has been widely viewed as the most prized of Bavarian brews, and this beer garden is among the best in town. Sit beneath the century-old chestnut trees and wait for the traditional bell-ringing ritual, which happens whenever a new wooden barrel is tapped. The beer garden

munich

is divided into two parts; the self-service counter is much cheaper and just as great for delicious food and beer.

i S1, S2, S3, S4, S6, S7, or S8: Hackerbrucke. Turn right onto Arnulfstr. Maß €7.80. Beer garden is cash only. ☒ Beer garden open daily 11:30am-midnight. Restaurant open daily 10am-1am.

Thalkirchen

ALTER WIRT   GERMAN $$
Fraunbergstr. 8   ☎089 74 21 99 77

Thalkirchen isn't really a culinary destination, but if you're in the area, Alter Wirt is your best bet. This dimly lit restaurant consistently prepares great Bavarian fare as well as cheap burgers and quesadillas. Large portions make this a local favorite—even the "small" meals are filling enough for an entire dinner, while the delicious potato wedges with sour cream are about the cheapest hot meal you'll find in town. If you want a break from Bavarian food, we recommend the burger and fries. The family-friendly beer garden is a great place to go on a sunny day.

i U3: Thalkirchen, then head down Fraunbergstr. Schnitzel Tu; for €5.10, get an enormous plate of schnitzel with fries and a drink. Entrees €6-13. Maß €5.60 ☒ Open daily 9am-midnight. Kitchen closes at 11pm.

NIGHTLIFE

City Center

▨ HOFBRÄUHAUS   BEER HALL
Platzl 9   ☎089 29 01 36 10 www.hofbraeuhaus.de

We could easily list this place under Sights—no trip to Munich is complete without a visit to its most famous beer hall. This is "das original" Hofbräuhaus beer hall that gave rise to dozens more around the world. Figures like Lenin, Hitler, and Mozart are mere footnotes in the long history of the place, which was royalty-only until King Ludwig I opened it to the public in 1828. Beer here comes in liters (€7.30); if you ask for anything less, they'll chortle and probably bring you a Maß anyway. By the end of the night you'll either be singing at the top of your lungs or singing a different tune at the famous vomitorium.

i S1, S2, S3, S4, S5, S6, S7, S8, U3, or U6: Marienpl. Take a left before the Altes Rathaus onto Burgstr. Then walk past the Alter Hof courtyard and take a right onto Pfisterstr. Arrive early to guarantee a spot, especially for large groups. Entrees €9.50-17. ☒ Open daily 10am-11:30pm. Shows at 7pm.

CAFE AM HOCHHAUS   BAR
Blumenstr. 29   ☎089 290 13 60 www.cafeamhochhaus.de

This tiny one-room bar proves that it's not size that matters—it's how you use it. The bottle-shaped disco ball and shiny bull skull are almost normal compared to the weird wallpaper that covers almost the entire area and depicts people swimming in what could be a reflecting pool of a palace. The nightly DJs spin anything but the mainstream and thus attract an assorted clientele that may include well-known German soccer players or models.

i U1, U2, U3, or U6: Sendlinger Tor. With the brick arches of Sendlinger Tor behind you, walk toward the tram stop and turn left onto Sonnenstr. Follow as it becomes Blumenstr. and curves multiple times before you reach the cafe on the right. Gay T-Dance on Su. Shot €6.50-7.50. Cocktails €8. ☒ Open M-Th 8pm-2am, F-Sa 8pm-late, Su 8pm-2am. The party usually gets started around 11pm.

germany

University Area

ALTER SIMPL
BAR

Türkenstr. 57   ☎089 272 30 83 www.eggerlokale.de

The gothic letters, wooden tables, hundreds of old posters, liters of beer, and great Bavarian food make Alter Simpl a genuinely awesome place to have a traditional meal or a beer at any time of the day. However, Alter Simpl stands out from its simpler cousins in a number of ways. Founded in 1903, the bar takes its name from an old satirical magazine called "Simplicissimus," with the magazine's iconic logo of a dog breaking the chains of censorship reworked into a dog breaking open a champagne bottle. There's even a statue of this red dog inside the establishment. Although the bar was once a second home to Munich's artists and intellectuals, it is now a lively hangout packed with students and a young crowd.

i *U3 or U6: Universität. Turn right onto Schellingstr. and then right onto Türkenstr. Beer €3.80. Snacks and entrees €5.60-15. Cash only.* ☒ *Open M-Th 11am-3am, F-Sa 11am-4am, Su 11am-3am. Kitchen open M-Th 11am-2am, F-Sa 11am-3am, Su 11am-2am.*

SCHELLING SALON
BAR

Schellingstr. 54   ☎089 272 07 88 www.schelling-salon.de

The clanking of beer glasses won't be the only collision you hear in Schelling Salon: the bar is filled out with red and green pool tables. This Munich institution once welcomed the likes of Lenin, Rilke, Brecht, and Hitler (legend has it that Hitler was banned from the restaurant due to unpaid bills), but nowadays, any tourist or local can enjoy the surprisingly cheap beer and big plates of Bavarian food among the old newspaper articles, photos, and posters. Unless you're the type of guy or gal who frequents establishments with pool tables, we recommend you check out this bar, as it will definitely be something you haven't seen before. Don't miss the giant chess board on the ceiling!

i *U3 or U6: Universität, then head away from the Siegestor and take a right onto Schellingstr. Beer 0.5L €2.90. Breakfast €3.20-5.40. Entrees €5-11.50. Pool €4.50 per hr. before 5pm, €9 per hr. after. Cash only.* ☒ *Open Oct-Jul M 10am-1am, Th-Su 10am-1am.*

Au-Haidhausen

▨ MUFFATWERK
CONCERT VENUE

Zellstr. 4   ☎089 45 87 50 10 www.muffatwerk.de

This converted power plant hosts all kinds of concerts, from hip hop to jazz, and has hosted such names as Santana and Smashing Pumpkins. On Fridays and Saturdays, crowds storm the massive performance hall to hear live DJs. The attached beer garden, bar, and cafe all provide a more relaxed venue during the afternoon or evening. On your way here, check out the beach with a view of the dam.

i *Tram 18: Deutsches Museum. Cross the bridge and turn left (follow the signs). Cover F-S €7-12. Concerts €15-35. Cash only.* ☒ *Shows generally start 8:30-9:30pm; the hall opens 1hr. earlier. Check website for events. Beer garden open M-F 5pm-midnight, Sa 2pm-midnight, Su noon-midnight.*

▨ KULTFABRIK AND OPTIMOLWERKE
CLUB

Friedenstr. 10   ☎089 450 69 20 www.optimolwerke.de

Kultfabrik and Optimolwerke are amusement parks, except these ones will take you on a different kind of wild ride (one that may result in a technicolor yawn). The two establishments, or rather collections of establishments, lie in adjacent lots, each containing enormous assortments of smaller bars and clubs. Hours, covers, and themes vary among the individual venues, which range from the fun-in-the-sun Bamboo Beach (Kultfabrik), complete with imported sand, to the darker Drei Turme (Optimolwerke), with its castle-like interior. Also within

munich

Kultfabrik is Kalinka, where you can fill up on vodka and party against a giant, seven-foot bust of Lenin. Kultfabrik prints a monthly magazine with the club schedules.

i S1, S2, S3, S4, S5, S6, S7, or S8: Ostbahnhof. Walk through the underground tunnels past all the tracks to the back of the station and follow the crowds. On F, a single cover of €5 gets you inside many of Kultfabrik's clubs. Covers vary; generally around €5. Cash only. ☺ Hours vary, but most parties start 10-11pm; check schedule online.

Neuhausen

🏛 BACKSTAGE

BAR, CLUB

Wilhelm-Hale-Str. 38 ☎089 126 61 00 www.backstage.eu

Backstage may be a converted gas station, but the abundance of trees and plants (lit up with vibrating green lights) makes this venue totally awesome, without the touch of scary-abandoned-factory feeling. The complex features live music from the indie underground scene. The local crowd varies depending on the act, but during the summer, you can always expect a crowded Biergarten with one of the best beer deals in town (Maß €4.80) and cheap shots (Th-Sa €1). The entire area includes three performance venues and multiple outdoor seating areas.

i Trams 16, 17: Steubenpl. Walk south on Wilhelm-Hale-Str. and take the 3rd left, before the bridge. Follow the road as it curves until you reach Backstage. Freakout Party on Sa. Check the website for more events. Concert €15-30. Sa cover €7.50; includes 2 drinks. Shots €2.50. ☺ Summer beer garden open M-Th 5pm-1am, F-Sa 5pm-5am, Su 5pm-1am.

LÖWENBRÄUKELLER

BEER HALL

Nymphenburgerstr. 2 ☎089 54 72 66 90 www.loewenbraeukeller.com

Marienplatz has Hofbräuhaus, Neuhausen has Löwenbräukeller, and we don't want to hear complaining about how similar beer gardens and halls can get. That's part of the magic. After all, you go for the beer, the company, and the waitresses in the Bavarian dresses. This beer garden may look like the other famous ones, but the entrance of Löwenbräukeller is easily identifiable thanks to its green tower and the characteristic Löwenbräu lion on the terrace.

i U1: Stiglmaierpl. English menu available. Maß €8.40. Entrees €5-14. ☺ Open daily 10am-midnight. Kitchen closes 11pm.

ESSENTIALS

Practicalities

- **TOURIST OFFICES:** English-speaking staff books rooms for free with a 10% deposit. München Ticket, a booking agency for concerts, theater, and other events, has locations at each tourist office. (Bahnhofspl. 2 ☎089 23 39 65 00 www.muenchen.de *i* Outside the train station. Map €0.40. ☺ Open M-Sa 9am-8pm, Su 10am-6pm.) 2nd location. (Marienpl. 2 ☎089 23 39 65 00 www.muenchen.de *i* Inside Neues Rathaus. ☺ Open M-F 10am-7pm, Sa 10am-5pm, Su 10am-2pm.)

- **CURRENCY EXCHANGE:** ReiseBank has decent rates, and Western Union will cash traveler's checks at a 1.5% commission. (Hauptbahnhof ☎089 55 10 80www.reisebank.de ☺ Open daily 7am-10pm.)

- **LUGGAGE STORAGE:** Lockers are in the main hall of the Hauptbahnhof. (☎089 13 08 50 36 *i* Max. 3 days €5 per day. ☺ Open M-F 7am-8pm, Sa-Su 8am-6pm.)

- **GLBT RESOURCES:** Bavarian queer publications include Leo, Blu (www.blu-magazin.de), and Rosa Muenchen (www.rosamuenchen.de). Gay & Lesbian Information Line. (Men ☎089 260 30 56; women ☎089 725 42 72 Open F 6-10pm.) LeTra is a resource for lesbians. (Angertorstr. 3 ☎089 725 42 72 www.letra.de ☺ Hotline M 2:30-5pm, Tu 10:30am-1pm, W 2:30-5pm.) Schwules Kommunikations und Kulturzentrum has resources, counselors, a small cafe, and a library for gay men. (Müllerstr. 43 ☎089 260 30 56 www.subonline.org ☒ Open M-Th 7-11pm, F 7pm-midnight, Sa 8pm-1am, Su 7-11pm.)

- **WOMEN'S RESOURCES:** Kofra offers job advice, books, and magazines and has a small cafe. (Baaderstr. 30 ☎089 201 04 50 www.kofra.de ☒ Open M-Th 4-10pm, F 2-6pm.) Frauen-treffpunkt Neuperlach offers services for women, including an international coffee house and English conversation nights. (Oskar-Maria-Graf-Ring 20 ☎089 670 64 63 www.frauentreff-punkt-neuperlach.de ☒ Open Tu 11am-noon, Th 11am-noon, and by appointment).

- **INTERNET:** San Francisco Coffee Company has locations throughout the city. (Tal 15 www.sfcc. de *i* Free Wi-Fi with any purchase. ☒ Open M-F 7:30am-9pm, Sa 8am-10pm, Su 9am-8pm.) Coffee Fellows Cafe has an internet cafe and printers on the 2nd floor. (Schuetzenstr. 14 *i* Wi-Fi or computer us €1.50 per 30min.; €2.50 per hr. Free Wi-Fi 1hr. with any €5 purchase. ☒ Open M-F 7am-11:30pm, Sa-Su 8am-11:30pm).

- **POST OFFICE:** Hauptbahnhof Post Office. (Bahnhofpl. 1; www.deutschepost.de *i* The yellow building opposite the train station. ☒ Open M-F 8am-8pm, Sa 9am-4pm.)

- **POSTAL CODES:** Munich postal codes begin with 80 or 81. The Hauptbahnhof postal code is 80335.

Emergency

- **EMERGENCY NUMBERS:** ☎112. Police: ☎110. Ambulance: ☎089 19 222.

- **CRISIS LINES:** Frauennotruf Muenchen operates a rape crisis hotline. (Saarstr. 5 ☎089 76 37 37 www.frauennotrufmuenchen.de ☒ Available M-F 10am-midnight, Sa-Su 6pm-midnight.) Munich AIDS Help. (☎089 54 33 30.)

- **PHARMACIES:** (Bahnhofpl. 2 ☎089 59 98 90 40 www.hauptbahnhofapo.de *i* Exit the train station and take a right. ☒ Open M-F 7am-8pm, Sa 8am-8pm.)

- **HOSPITALS/MEDICAL SERVICES:** Klinikum Schwabing (Kölner Pl. 1 ☎089 30 680 www. klinikum-muenchen.de) and Red Cross Hospital Neuhausen (Nymphenburgerstr. 163 ☎089 12 78 97 90 www.swmbrk.de) both provide 24hr. emergency medical services.

Getting There

By Plane

Munich's international airport, Flughafen München (Nordalee 25 ☎089 975 00 www. munich-airport.de) is a 45min. train ride from the city center. Take S1 or S8 to Flughafen. (€9.80 on a Streifenkarte. ☒ Every 10-20min. 4am-1:30am). A cab ride to the airport from the city center cost €60.

By Train

Munich's central train station, München Hauptbahnhof (Hauptbahnhof 1 ☎089 130 81 05 55 www.hauptbahnhof-muenchen.de *i* S1, S2, S3, S4, S6, S7, S8, U1, U2, U4, or U5: Hauptbahnhof), has arrivals and departures to a host of European cities. Connected cities include **Berlin** (€120 ☒ 6hr., 2 per hr.); **Dresden** (€100 ☒ 6hr., 2 per hr.); **Frankfurt** (€91 ☒ 3hr., 2 per hr.); **Hamburg** (€129 ☒ 6hr., every hr.); **Köln** (€129 ☒ 5hr., 2 per hr.); **Amsterdam,**NHE (€150 ☒ 6hr., every 2hr.); **Paris,** FRA (€150 ☒ 6hr., every 2hr.); **Prague,** CZR (€60 ☒ 6hr., 2 per day.); **Zurich,** CHE. (€70 ☒ 4hr., 3 per day.) These prices are the official ones if you purchase the day of departure; you can often get heavy discounts (30-40%) by buying a ticket between three months and three days in advance.

Getting Around

By Deutsche Bahn

The S-Bahn is under the operation of the Deutsche Bahn (DB) network, which means that Eurail, InterRail, and German rail passes are all valid. Before beginning your journey, validate your ticket by getting it stamped in the blue boxes. DB officers often check for validation, and those without properly validated tickets are charged a heft €40 fine. The S-Bahn generally runs between 3:30am and 1:30am.

By Public Transportation

The U-Bahn, trams, and buses are all part of the city's MVV network (☎089 41 42 43 44 www.mvv-muenchen.de) and require separate ticket purchases. Pick up maps at the tourist office or at the MVV Infopoint office in the Hauptbahnhof. Transportation schedules vary, but the U-Bahn opens around 4:30am and closes around 1am during the week (2am on weekends). Nachtlinien (night trams) run every 30min. and cover most of the city. Tickets come in multiple forms based on how far you're traveling and how long the pass is valid. The simplest form is the single Einzelfahrkarte (€2.50), which is good for 2hr. for a trip in one direction. All other trips depend on the distance, for which the Munich area is split into 16 different zones of concentric circles around the city center. For short trips (within the same zone), get a Kurzstrecke (€1.20). For multiple rides, buy a Streifenkarte (stripe ticket; €12), which usually comes with 10 stripes. The zones are further grouped into four different colors (white, yellow, green, and red), for which you can get one-day or three-day passes. For the most part, tourists will stay within the white zone, for which a one-day pass costs €5.40 and a three-day €13.30. Partner tickets can save you money if you're traveling in a group. There are several cards available:

- **ISARCARDS:** An IsarCard is a week- or month-long pass that can be even cheaper than the three-day pass. One-week passes cost €12.30-17.60, depending on whether you pick two, three, or four zones. IsarCards, however, are only valid during the week or the month proper (e.g., a weekly pass will only work from Su to Su, and 1-month passes work for specific months), so plan accordingly.

- **CITY TOUR CARDS:** This card gets you transportation, along with some tiny discounts to attractions in Munich. That said, these attractions are not always the most popular ones in town. The City Tour card probably isn't worth it if you're not getting the partner ticket.

- **BAYERN TICKET:** The Bayern Ticket gets you access to any public transportation within Bavaria for an entire day. (€21. ☼ Valid M-F 9am-3am, Sa-Su midnight-3am.) The ticket also covers neighboring cities, including Ulm and Salzburg, making it perfect for day trips. The greatest savings can be achieved by getting a group Bayern Ticket, which covers up to five people for just €29.

By Taxi

Taxi-München-Zentrale (☎089 216 10 or ☎089 19 410 www.taxizentrale-muenchen.de) is a large taxi stand just outside the Hauptbahnhof. Taxi stands are located all around the city. The pricing algorithm is complicated, but there is a flat fee of €3.30, and shorter distances generally cost €1.70 per km.

By Bike

Munich is extremely bike-friendly. There are paths on nearly every street, and many locals use bikes as their primary mode of transportation. Renting a bike can be a great way to see a lot of the city in just a few days. Remember to stay within the bike lanes and that many lanes are one-way.

germany

germany essentials

MONEY

Tipping

Service staff are paid by the hour, and a service charge is included in an item's unit price. Cheap customers typically just round up to the nearest whole euro, but it's customary and polite to tip 5-10% if you are satisfied with the service. If the service was poor, you don't have to tip at all. To tip, mention the total to your waiter while paying. If he states that the bill is €20, respond "€22," and he will include the tip. Do not leave the tip on the table; hand it directly to the server. It is standard to tip a taxi driver at least €1, housekeepers €1-2 a day, bellhops €1 per piece of luggage, and public toilet attendants around €0.50.

Taxes

Most goods in Germany are subject to a value added tax—or mehrwertsteuer (MwSt)—of 19%, which is included in the purchase price of goods (a reduced tax of 7% is applied to books and magazines, food, and agricultural products). Non-EU visitors who are taking these goods home unused may be refunded this tax for purchases totaling over €25 per store. When making purchases, request a MwSt form and present it at a Tax Free Shopping Office, found at most airports, road borders, and ferry stations, or by mail. Refunds must be claimed within six months. For more information, contact the German VAT refund hotline (☎0228 406 2880 www.bzst.de).

SAFETY AND HEALTH

Local Laws and Police

Certain regulations might seem harsh and unusual (practice some self-control city-slickers, jaywalking is €5 fine), but abide by all local laws while in Germany; your embassy will not necessarily get you off the hook.

Drugs and Alcohol

The drinking age in Germany is 16 for beer and wine and 18 for spirits. The maximum blood alcohol content level for drivers is 0.05%. Avoid public drunkenness; it can jeopardize your safety and earn the disdain of locals.

Needless to say, illegal drugs are best avoided. While possession of marijuana or hashish is illegal, possession of small quantities for personal consumption is decriminalized in Germany. Each region has interpreted "small quantities" differently (anywhere from 5 to 30 grams). Carrying drugs across an international border—drug trafficking—is a serious offense that could land you in prison.

Prescription Drugs

Common drugs such as aspirin (Kopfschmerztablette or Aspirin), acetaminophen or Tylenol (Paracetamol), ibuprofen or Advil, antihistamines (Antihistaminika), and penicillin (Penizillin) are available at German pharmacies. Some drugs—like pseudoephedrine (Sudafed) and diphenhydramine (Benadryl)—are not available in Germany, or are only available with a prescription, so plan accordingly.

germany 101

HISTORY

Germanation (Ancient Times to 900 CE)

The Roman Empire conquered the autonomous tribes that had occupied the area; Roman ruins can still be seen in Cologne and elsewhere. After the collapse of the empire in the fifth century CE (which was largely thanks to the invasions of "barbaric" Germans), the Germanic tribes separated again. In the eighth century, Charlemagne reunited (read: conquered) them into what is now known as the First Reich, or first empire. Along the way, he forcibly converted thousands of pagans to Christianity.

"Neither Holy, nor Roman, nor an Empire" (900-1517)

After Charlemagne's death, power was decentralized, and the historical oddity known as the Holy Roman Empire emerged. The empire remained a presence across Germany and surrounding regions until 1806, despite its lack of an explicit religious purpose or connection to Rome. It wasn't even a real empire, as it didn't govern the states it comprised. Instead, it can be seen as a kind of medieval European Union, in which all the states are independent but meet occasionally to pretend they like each other. The Golden Bull of 1356 finally gave a constitution-of-sorts to the empire, stating how the electors would convene to elect an emperor. Don't get excited and think this was an early form of democracy: there were only seven electors, and they were all princes. Over time, the Habsburgs of Austria monopolized the imperial throne and turned it into a de facto hereditary title.

In 1439, Johannes Gutenberg invented the world's first printing press. Rapid production of books led to increased literacy, putting information—and the power that comes with it—into the hands of laypeople (or at least the few percent of laypeople who were literate). 95 Theses, 30 Years of War (1517-1648) In 1517, Martin Luther posted his 95 Theses, which railed against the failings of the Catholic Church, on the door of a local church in Wittenberg. Luther's controversial beliefs sparked religious strife across Germany and Europe. His supporters protested so vehemently that they became known as Protestants, creating the division in Christianity that exists to this day. Religious conflict eventually escalated into the devastating 30 Years' War, which ravaged Germany from 1618 to 1648. As much as a third of the German population may have died in the conflict, and some regions lost 75% of their pre-war population through killings, diseases, and famines. Just about the only good outcome of the war was that it ended the age of religious conflicts that had dominated European politics since Luther's emergence. The Holy Roman Empire survived the war and continued in its stable and boring fashion for another 150 years.

End of Empire (1648-1815)

In the 18th and 19th centuries, the northeastern state of Prussia, governed from Berlin, became the most powerful force in Germany. Under a long sequence of kings named Frederick, the Prussian army grew as mighty as its helmets were pointy. But the combined strength of Prussia, Austria, and much of the rest of Europe was still no match for Napoleon Bonaparte when he advanced east across Europe. Napoleon put the Holy Roman Empire out of its misery following his decisive victory in the 1805 Battle of Austerlitz. He replaced the empire with the Confederation of the Rhine, which retained much of the federal structure of its predecessor. Once Napoleon was defeated a decade later, Austria reestablished its control over Germany with the German Confederation, which was yet another example of a weak body exercising minimal control over the many German states. The organization of Germany was greatly rationalized at this time. Before the Napoleonic Wars, there had been more than 300 states in Germany; after 1815, there were just 39.

No Austrians Allowed (1818-1871)

Prussia focused throughout this period on one-upping Austria, while German nationalists yearned to unite the country somehow. The revolutionary year of 1848 seemed promising, and nationalists convened in Frankfurt to attempt to unite the country. After months of slow discussions over what the new country should look like, they offered the German crown to Prussian King Frederick William. He refused, saying it was not theirs to give. Unification found a more willing, if devious and self-serving, champion in Prussian Prime Minister Otto von Bismarck. In 1866, Bismarck engineered a war with Austria that the Prussians won comfortably, ensuring their supremacy over Germany. In 1871, Bismarck stared down Napoleon III, and Prussia's defeat of France in the Franco-Prussian War left it strong enough to combine all the non-Austrian German states into the German Empire.

Round One (1871-1918)

Following unification, Bismarck, a notorious pragmatist, carefully maintained the balance of power in Europe. Germany also began collecting colonies, mainly in Africa. Under Wilhelm II, who became kaiser (king) in 1890, Bismarck's realpolitik was abandoned, as Germany focused on military expansion and rivalry with Great Britain. The tension caused by this exploded into World War One in 1914. Germany attempted to knock out France before invading Russia, but became bogged down in a two-frontal, attritional war. Though Russia was defeated in 1917, years of stalemate in the west and deprivation on the home front forced Germany to surrender in 1918. Bitterness at the defeat and the harsh Treaty of Versailles that followed it were major causes of the Second World War.

Round Two (1918-1945)

In 1923, a young former soldier named Adolf Hitler tried to start a revolution. He began in what is obviously the best place to seize power in Germany: a beer hall. He persevered after this failure, and his Nazi Party won the most votes of any party in the 1932 election (receiving 37% of votes). Hitler became Chancellor the following year. He set about dismantling the democratic constitution, rebuilding the army, and expanding German territory. In 1938, Austria was absorbed into Germany with almost no resistance from the Austrian citizens. Invading Poland didn't go so well, though, as it pushed Britain and France to declare war. For a thorough history of the war, consult published works (yes, we know you're just going to read Wikipedia). Safe to say, invading the Soviet Union turned out to be a terrible idea, and the combined force of the US, USSR, and UK (no one can beat all those Us) led to Germany's defeat. Hitler committed suicide on April 30, 1945, and Germany surrendered a few days later. Much of the country was leveled by the fighting, with aerial bombing destroying cities like Dresden and Hamburg, while the advancing Red Army laid waste to eastern Germany and Berlin. The later stages of the war revealed its most terrible element: the Holocaust. Hitler's anti-semitic policies were carried to their logical, hideous conclusion, as the Nazis sought to eradicate all the Jews of Europe. Two-thirds of Europe's Jews, some six million people, were killed.

Germany Divided (1945-1990)

After the war, Germany was divided into four occupied zones, one for each of the three victorious countries and one as charity for France. Berlin, which lay well inside the Soviet zone, was divided in the same way. In 1949, the French, American, and British zones (plus their sectors of Berlin) were united into West Germany, while the Soviet zone became East Germany. West Germany recovered quickly from the war

germany 101

Sometimes, a week of vacation isn't enough to get all you want out of Germany. Take a few months to study, work, or volunteer in the land of Goethe, and you will find out that not everyone wears Lederhosen (but that the pretzels are delicious everywhere). Germany's public education system has long attracted foreigners, and veryhigh quality education can be had here for a steal. If you intend to make a fortune becoming the next Michael Otto, however, be warned: Germany's job market is highly competitive, and opportunities are hard to come by for non-native speakers. But this shouldn't deter you from spending a few months in the country that gave the world Copernicus, Hegel, and Heidi Klum. Adopt the German work ethic, savor sauerkraut, and save up your money before blowing it all on your first Oktoberfest.

STUDY

Germany is one of the world's most popular study abroad destinations, and not just because of the blonde milkmaids. Most universities are public and considerably cheaper than their US counterparts. As the motor of the European Union, Germany also has extensive experience receiving international students. Its schools also offer a vast array of English courses. If the role of eternal tourist appeals to you, you can get an entire degree without stepping foot inside a German class!

- **INSTITUTE OF EUROPEAN STUDIES (IES):** If you have yet to master your German tenses, IES provides you with the opportunity to take part in an intensive German courses, in addition to an internship and a German-taught course at a partner university. Your host family will be delighted to feed you some *kartoffel* and correct your pesky grammar mistakes.

- **GERMAN ACADEMIC EXCHANGE SERVICE (DAAD):** Feeling like you won't be able to afford any German beer after seeing that study abroad bill? Think again. The German Academic Exchange Service can pay for your entire master's if you recently graduated from a US or Canadian university. You don't even have to speak German! (www.daad.org)

- **CULTURAL EXPERIENCES ABROAD (CEA):** If a whole semester of German seems a little too ambitious, start small with a summer school program in Berlin. The Cultural Experiences Abroad staff will serve as your German mom by organizing airport pickups, gourmet tours of Berlin and Eurotrips to provide decoration for your Facebook wall. (www.gowithcea.com)

- **ACADEMIC PROGRAMS INTERNATIONAL (API):** More interested in winter sauerkraut than summer landscapes? Every January, Academic Programs International offers an intensive language course in Berlin to fill up that awkward hole in your winter vacation (www.apistudyabroad.com)

- **EDUCATION FIRST (EF):** Education First accommodates both the lazy and the hardworking. Select either the intensive, general, or "interested" track to strike a balance between work and study as you enjoy the beautiful city of Munich. (www.ef.com)

- **FREIE UNIVERSITÄT:** Go big or go home. Besides having a stereotypical German name to impress your friends back home, this renowned university has one of the largest international student bodies in the world. Earn your entire bachelor's or master's in Germany, gradually easing into the German language thanks to the university's vast English offerings. (www.fu-berlin.de)

- **HEIDELBERG UNIVERSITY:** True German connoisseurs know there is more to Germany than Berlin and Munich. If you already have a strong background in German, head to the world-famous Heidelberg University for bucolic views of the German countryside. (www.uni-heidelberg.de)

- **UNIVERSITY OF BÖNN:** The University of Bönn knows how important you like to feel. Their international degree programs are specifically tailored to foreign students and offer a mix of English and German courses, as well as specialized international counseling. (www.uni-bonn.de)

- **GERMANY INTERNSHIP PROGRAM:** Pad your resume German-style and learn all about Germany's unique work culture with an internship placement. Fields of internships in Cologne cover everything from agriculture to fashion design. (www.international-internships.com)

- **FRENCH GERMAN ALLIANCE:** Apprenticeships have been a praised aspect of German education for decades, providing an opportunity for students to gain hands-on experience in fields such as cooking or artisanal work. The French-German alliance allows you to kill two European languages with one stone by completing an apprenticeship in both countries. (www.afasp.net)

VOLUNTEER

Why volunteer in Germany, you ask? Between its pristine recycling systems, its stellar international test scores, and its filling cuisine, this country seems to have itself together. But just to add to the orderliness, the volunteering ethic is deeply embedded in German culture. Volunteer programs often offer opportunities to travel and learn German for free in a vast number of service areas.

- **VOLUNTEER ECOLOGICAL YEAR:** Come learn about environmental protection from the pros of recycling. This volunteer program will have you work on a hands-on project to protect the environment, providing you with pocket money, board, and lodging in exchange for your hard work. No German necessary. (www.foej.de)

- **FRIENDS OF WALDORF:** This German institute runs an Incoming Program, which offers foreigners the opportunity to spend 12 months in Germany working on various community service projects. Participants get to choose from areas of service as well-defined as homes for the elderly to ones as obscure as curative education. Conversational German necessary.

- **INTERNATIONAL YOUTH AND CULTURE CENTRE:** Even though Germany might not be the first place you associate with free-spirited artists, the land of efficiency and order has something for

the creative mind. Help organize cultural events and run workshops with children for anywhere from six months to a year. (www.kiebitz.net)

- **SONNTAGS CLUB:** Volunteer for a year at the headquarters of the German LGBT association to work toward ending homophobia in Germany. The year-long volunteer programs include various trips across Europe as well as German language lessons for non-native speakers. (www.sonntags-club.de)

- **YOUTH HIKING IN SAXONY-ANHALT:** If you're always pushing your friends to go to the gym, well, now you can do it in Germany. Help the Germany Youth Hostel Association trick European youth into hiking by developing new trails and designing promotional material. Basic German required.

- **KANDERN RESIDENTIAL HOME:** Deep into the Black Forest, practice your German and help with geriatric care. Prepare snacks, clean rooms, and listen to the World War II stories of the residents over some well-deserved pretzels. Basic German required. (www.t-online.de)

- **FRAUENBERG KINDERGARTEN:** If you've always had a soft spot for toddlers, expose yourself to the German educational methods in the rural village of Frauenberg. As you change the diaper of one of your screaming students, remember: your job also includes free train tickets across Germany and professional language training. (www.jugendsozialwerk.de)

- **EUROPEAN COMMISSION YOUTH:** The European Commission coordinates a number of volunteer opportunities throughout Europe. If you feel like your burgeoning sense of European solidarity needs some tending, spend anywhere from a month to a year creating presentations about Europe and organizing trips for European youth. (http://ec.europa.eu/youth)

- **WORKAWAY:** This global website connecting volunteers to volunteer opportunities has been particularly successful in Germany. Work a few hours a day in an art research institute, on a German farm, or on a horse ranch in exchange for a bed for the night. Most hosts have at least an elementary command of English, but German requirements vary. (www.workaway.info)

WORK

Due to the high levels of education across Germany, securing a high-paying job without fluent spoken German will not be an easy task. Fear not, however: even if all you have to offer is your English tongue, there are plenty of opportunities to earn a few euro.

- **CERTIFICATE IN ENGLISH LANGUAGE TEACHING TO ADULTS (CELTA):** While you do not need a diploma to tutor English at a person's home, a English Language Teaching Certificate is necessary to hold a more formal position. This 4-week long course provides you with a certificate and a counseling network to secure a permanent teaching position. (www.suarez.de)

- **AU PAIR CARE:** Being an au pair is serious business in Germany. After finding a position through an accredited agency, you will be able to share bratwurst with your new family alongside your typical home dishes for a period of six to 12 months. (www.aupaircare.com)

- **AYUSA ENGLISH TUTORING PROGRAM:** If six months is a lot to commit, Au Pair Care offers you a compromise between work and fun as a home-stay tutor in a German family for one to three months. (www.aupaircare-germany.de)

- **LEO LINGO:** If you enjoy wielding complete authority over defenseless German children, being a camp counselor may just be the job for you. Leo Lingo organizes seven-week-long language sports camps in various places in Germany; counselors get room and board, as well as a modest salary. (www.leo-lingo.de)

- **YOYO CAMPS:** YoYo Camps are week-long summer day camps to teach English to German children in a cheery, Boy Scout atmosphere. Camp counselors get a lot of flexibility when designing their programs and are encouraged to let their creative juices flow. (www.yoyocamps. de)

- **BUNDESTAG INTERNSHIP:** This program of the German Academic Exchange Service offers you the opportunity to spend two months interning in the German Parliament. Learn about German politics and maybe even rub shoulders with Angela Merkel, all while getting paid by the German state. Excellent spoken German required.

and became a prosperous, democratic state. East Germany could not shake the Soviet influence, becoming a Communist, one-party state with an active secret police and restricted civil liberties. It wasn't hard for those in East Germany to see it slipping behind its neighbor, and many people sought to escape to the west. In an attempt to stop this mass migration, the East German government built the infamous Berlin Wall in 1961, dividing the capital city clean in two to block the path from east to west. The wall stood until 1989, when it was stunningly demolished following sudden backtracks by the Soviet and East German governments. A year later, Germany was reunited under Chancellor Helmut Kohl.

Germany Ascendant (1990-present)

Unification was not as simple as some had hoped, and the need to absorb the economically sluggish eastern half of the country slowed the west's previously relentless growth. Nevertheless, Germany today has retaken its place as the most powerful country in Europe. When Greece's economy fell apart in 2010, it was Germany that rode to the rescue. Some Germans are bitter at being expected to save weak, irresponsible governments from default, and Chancellor Angela Merkel has had to carefully balance the responsibilities of Germany's role in Europe with its domestic needs. Under her stewardship, though, today's Germany remains united, highly developed, and central to European politics.

CUSTOMS AND ETIQUETTE

Dining

Traditionally, German restaurants allow self-seating if no host is present. Water with your meal is on request and you must specify if you want tap water. Otherwise, the restaurant will rack up your bill by bringing you expensive bottled water. Note that restaurants may charge you for bread or rolls.

Meet and Greet

If you are invited to a German home, it is best to bring chocolates or flowers as a gift. Since many flowers carry particular stigmas, it is safest to bring yellow roses or tea roses. After all, you don't want to give funeral flowers to your kind host.

When entering a room, shake hands with everyone in the room individually, including children. Until you're told otherwise, address a person with her official title and surname. When entering a store, always greet with a "Guten Tag." Upon leaving the store, even if you did not buy anything, it is polite to say "auf Wiedersehen" (goodbye).

FOOD AND DRINK

What do Germans eat? In a word, meat. And more meat. And some more meat. Currywurst, slices of sausage served in a curry sauce, is an extremely common option in the city; in Berlin it's sold on street corners and in restaurants alike. Bratwurst, another common street food, resembles an American hotdog. Traditionally it is made from pork, but today, it's frequently made from a combination of meats. Kassler is a cured and smoked slice of pork. Simple but yummy. If meat isn't your thing, fret not—vegetarian options are becoming increasingly popular in major cities.

Germans prefer their coffee thin, dark, and bitter. If you're unable to wrap your American head around the idea of a black coffee, you can order a Milchkaffe (that's right—coffee with milk); just don't complain when the locals scoff. Berliners also take pride in their pastries, particularly the jelly-filled doughnut (one of JFK's favorites). Outside of Berlin, it's called a Berliner, but in the city, they're usually referred to as Pfannkuchen. And of course there's beer. Germans take their beer seriously. In fact, all beer is brewed in accordance with Reinheitsgebot or "beer purity law," which regulates the ingredients.

GREAT BRITAIN

What is the coolest country in the world? Everyone will have his or her own answer to this question—Hollywood wannabes will say America, sappy romantics will say France, and bold (possibly crazy) adventurers will say Nepal. But the answer just might be Britain. Name anything you love, and Britain has it. Music? The Beatles. The arts? The Edinburgh Festival. Learning? Oxford and Cambridge. History? On every street corner. Sports? "Football." Literature? Shakespeare. Celebrity gossip? The royal family.

Britain has everything a traveler could want, and it's one of the most accessible countries in the world. There's no language barrier, the waiters aren't judging you,and everything is crammed into a convenient island-sized package. But don't think Britain is resting on its laurels. This country continually invents and inspires, as musicians create new beats, modern-art museums deliver mind-blowing spectacles, and boy wizards save the world. In 2012, the Olympic Games even came to London for a record third time. Whether you spend your trip touring all of London's free museums or curled up in front of the BBC with a cuppa, you'll be experiencing British culture at its best. Forget about Nepal, get over France, and bid good day to the USA, because Britain is where it's at.

greatest hits

- **GOOD WILL PUNTING.** Need a break from all the colleges at Cambridge University? Rent a punt from **Scudamore's** (p. 386) and cruise down the River Cam.

- **GO ASK ALICE.** Visit **Christ Church College** (p. 375) in Oxford to see where Lewis Carroll first met the real Alice, before she headed off to Wonderland.

- **THE BIRTHPLACE OF WIZARDS.** Follow in JK Rowling's literary footsteps at the **Elephant House Café** in Edinburgh (p. 397), where Harry Potter was born

GREAT BRITAIN

N

0 — 100 kilometers
0 — 100 miles

SHETLAND ISLANDS
Lerwick

ORKNEY ISLANDS
Stromness
Kirkwall

Thurso

Lewis
OUTER HEBRIDES

Ullapool

Uig
The Uists
Skye
Inverness

Aberdeen

Fort William

Mull
INNER HEBRIDES

Oban
SCOTLAND
St. Andrews

Glasgow
Edinburgh

Arran

NORTHERN IRELAND
Belfast

Dumfries
Stranraer
Newcastle-upon-Tyne
Carlisle
Durham

Isle of Man
Douglas

ISLE OF MAN

IRELAND

York
Manchester
Leeds
Liverpool
Isle of Anglesey
Chester
Bangor
Sheffield
Llangollen
Lincoln
Nottingham

ENGLAND

Aberystwyth
Birmingham
King's Lynn
Norwich

Stratford-upon-Avon
Cambridge

WALES
Fishguard
Cheltenham
Pembroke
Swansea
Oxford
Cardiff
LONDON
Bristol
Bath
Canterbury
Salisbury
Dover

Portsmouth
Exeter
Brighton
Plymouth
Isle of Wight

Penzance

Channel Islands

FRANCE

great britain

Great Britain is the land of the student. Britain is home to renowned centers of learning like Oxford, Cambridge, LSE, and Hogwarts, helping it to attract students from around the world. Just about every city in Britain has a major university, and you can rest assured that British students love a good time. **London** alone has 135,000 students. For an intellectual crowd, **Oxford** and **Cambridge** are the obvious stops. Nonetheless, **Edinburgh,** the capital of Scotland, is Great Britain's capital for student life. The University of Edinburgh is home to over 24, 000 students who live, study, and drink just south of the Royal Mile. The forward-thinking city also has some of Britain's most talented artists. As a result, mobs of students from around the world head to Edinburgh every August for one of the world's largest arts festivals. If you thought London was all Britain had to offer, a few days with the students in Edinburgh will quickly change your mind.

london

London evades a one sentence summary besides the oft-trotted out maxim by Samuel Johnson: "When a man is tired of London, he is tired of life." That being said, a certain clump of neurons fires to the tune of "God Save the Queen" when the idea of "London" settles through the senses. If you haven't been before, your mind will of course fancy that it's all very much like *Sherlock Holmes*, *Harry Potter*, a Hugh Grant movie, or *Skins*. You wouldn't be wrong.

There is definitely the adventure of *Sherlock Holmes* in the city, a cold sort of mystery where people on the street have closed faces that need to be deduced. Seeing everything will be a fruitless chase, and you'll gape in awe at Holmes' eidetic, A-Z memory of the city after blankly not registering the Tube map in Heathrow Terminal 5 in a sort of sensory overload. For an aesthetic ideal, *Harry Potter* isn't a bad mental picture to hold. It's shocking to see Westminster Abbey and St. Paul's exceed the Ministry of Magic's grandeur and the crowded Bank area seem just like Gringotts. The rows of identical houses in the books can appear cartoonized and unbelievable in the movies, but in Notting Hill and Chelsea, that's exactly what lines block after block.

As for the Hugh Grant canon, the residents do hold an embarrassed charm, although with less eyelash-fluttering. And you're very likely to meet Americans and go aimlessly shopping. As for *Skins*, just head to Camden, Dalston, or Shoreditch. The grittier side to London exists all the same, with a clear divide between the posh, well-tailored skirt and heels crew and the black skinny jeaned ruffian type that haunts those neighborhoods.

Whether you're here for exhibitions of royal or imperial grandeur, an unparalleled theater scene, or a city that is becoming modern amidst its love of the past, London can only be approximated, for it contains multitudes.

ORIENTATION

To say that London is a sizeable city is to adopt the infamous British tendency for understatement. London is bloody massive. The central knot of museums, historical sights, shopping, and entertainment stretches along the Thames from the City of London (yes, a city within a city) through the West End to Westminster. The luxurious residential neighborhoods of Chelsea, Kensington, Notting Hill, and Marylebone lie to the north and west. Add in the university neighborhood of Bloomsbury and the

london

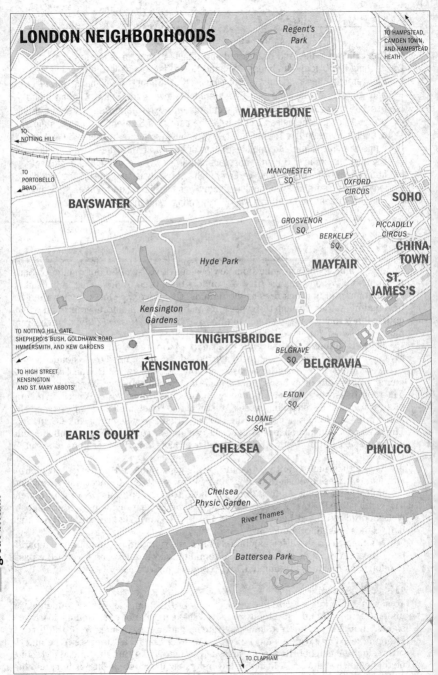

LONDON NEIGHBORHOODS

Regent's Park

TO HAMPSTEAD, CAMDEN TOWN, AND HAMPSTEAD HEATH

MARYLEBONE

TO NOTTING HILL

TO PORTOBELLO ROAD

MANCHESTER SQ.

OXFORD CIRCUS

SOHO

BAYSWATER

GROSVENOR SQ.

PICCADILLY CIRCUS

BERKELEY SQ.

CHINA-TOWN

Hyde Park

MAYFAIR

ST. JAMES'S

Kensington Gardens

TO NOTTING HILL GATE, SHEPHERD'S BUSH, GOLDHAWK ROAD, HMMERSMITH, AND KEW GARDENS

KNIGHTSBRIDGE

BELGRAVE SQ.

BELGRAVIA

KENSINGTON

TO HIGH STREET KENSINGTON AND ST. MARY ABBOTS'

EATON SQ.

SLOANE SQ.

EARL'S COURT

CHELSEA

PIMLICO

Chelsea Physic Garden

River Thames

Battersea Park

TO CLAPHAM

great britain

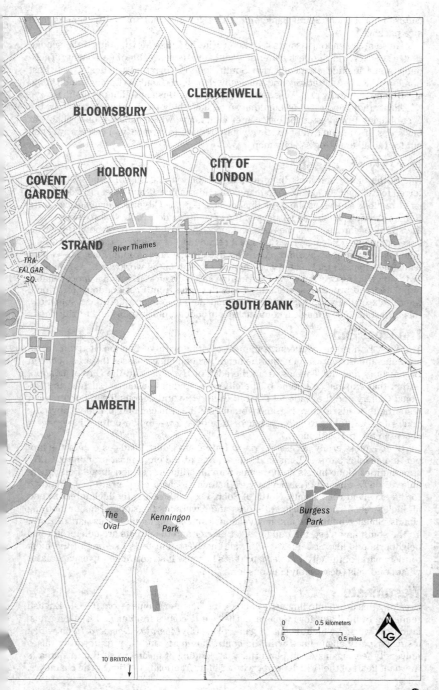

CLERKENWELL

BLOOMSBURY

COVENT
GARDEN

HOLBORN

CITY OF
LONDON

STRAND

River Thames

TRA-
FALGAR
SQ.

SOUTH BANK

LAMBETH

The
Oval

Kennington
Park

Burgess
Park

0   0.5 kilometers
0   0.5 miles

N
LG

TO BRIXTON

culturally prominent South Bank, and you've got the whole of central London in a nice package.

These areas encompass most of Zone 1 in the Tube. Moving out to the second ring, a traveler will find less material wealth and more wealth of personality. These outer areas include ethnically rich South London (Brixton),artistically rich East London (Hackney), literarily and musically rich North London (Camden and Hampstead), and culturally rich West London (Shepherd's Bush and Hammersmith).

Navigating the sprawl of London can be incredibly frustrating. Fortunately, the ever-obliging Britsplaster the city center with maps, which can be found reliably at bus stops. If you don't want to leave your direction to chance, you can always shell out for the all-knowing A-Z city map.

The City of London

One of the oldest and most historic parts of London, the City of London, often referred to as "the City," is home to many of London's finest (and most crowded) tourist attractions as well as the city's financial center. The City holds many of London's Roman artifacts, including vestiges of the ancient London Wall. Next to these relics, the spires of famous churches are juxtaposed with the towers of powerful insurance companies. Because the City's real estate market was locked down sometime a couple of centuries ago, no one really lives in the area around Fleet St.—which lends the City a 28 Days Later vibe anytime other than the workweek. As you head farther north, the City fades into Farringdon and Clerkenwell, which is more reliably populated and provides something of a buffer zone from East London. Here you'll find a mix of the yuppie-gentrified City and the hipster-gentrified East; somehow, this turns out to be a magical combination, producing quirky pubs and terrific food.

The West End

The West End is one of the largest, most exciting parts of London. Its twin hearts are Soho and Covent Garden, but the neighborhood encompasses the area between Bloomsbury and the Thames, from the edge of Hyde Park to the City of London. Within that expanse are some of the city's best public museums (such as the National Gallery and the National Portrait Gallery), world-famous theater, interesting restaurants, loads of shopping, and vibrant nightlife. You can find just about anything you're looking for here (except maybe a good curry—Indian culture is strangely absent in this part of London).

Soho—most easily accessible via ⊖Tottenham Court Road—is one of the hipper and seedier parts of London. Home to one of the city's most prominent GLBT communities, Soho bursts at the seams with nightlife for gay and straight clubgoers alike. By day, this area (particularly Chinatown, located off Gerrard St.) is known for its excellent restaurants. North of Soho, Oxford Street is the high street to end all high streets, with department stores and cavernous flagships of major clothing chains. Smaller boutiques and many salons can also be found in this part of town. To the south and west, the buildings get fancier and the streets are quieter in regal neighborhoods like St James's. All in all, the West End feels like one of the most touristy parts of the city, but perhaps that's because it so conveniently encapsulates what London is (deservedly) famous for.

Westminster

Breaking this down into linguistic chunks, the "minster" comes from the Old English rendering of the Latin for monastery. The "west" comes from an Old English translation of "whist," which meant "a game played by*Liberalus Democratius*in which a smaller party aligns itself with the controlling party and then traitorously raises university fees against their platform." Just kidding. It means west. But this area *is* the giant heart of the British power with all of its frantically beating aortic chambers:

Buckingham Palace, Westminster Palace and the Houses of Parliament, and Westminster Abbey. Other than wandering around this massive London Legoland, there's not much to do. The area around Victoria has your usual lottery of fastfood cafés, and Belgravia can be counted on for a quiet pint. Otherwise, the nearby West End is a much more exciting place to roam.

The South Bank

Back in the Puritan days, the South Bank was one giant den of sin. A trip across the river meant you and Satan would pal it up in the blasphemous theater district and maybe frequent a hooker or two while you were in the area. Now, it's a thoroughly un-gritty mecca of culture that hosts the biggest cinema in Britain, a half dozen theatres, the Tate Modern, and the fearsomely awesome Southbank Centre. Its purview extends—quite unsurprisingly—along the south bank of the Thames across from the City of London and Westminster. The main riverside path is called the Millennium Mile and stretches from the London Eye in the west eastward along the Thames, making for a beautiful walk, especially around sunset. No hookers though.

South Kensington and Chelsea

Welcome to the poshest part of London, where anything less than perfectly coiffed hair, a believable tan, and the flash of a Louboutin sole will earn you the curled-up lip of British disdain. Tired tourists—who flit in and out of the museums and buy only from the food section of Harrods—are easily distinguished from the fleet of glamazons who use cabs to travel mere blocks. So use the hostel iron for your best shirt and don't feel too bad when the staff of designer stores look at you you're wearing a Nazi costume—they're pretty much paid to hate on anyone who's not Madonna. This area—for our plebeian purposes—extends from Cromwell Rd. down to the Thames and is enclosed by Sloane St. and Redcliffe Gardens.

Hyde Park to Notting Hill

Hyde Park is, we promise, actually a park and not terrible movie with Bill Murray. It's roughly rectangular with a Tube stop at pretty much every corner—Marble Arch, the incredibly unhelpfully named Hyde Park Corner, High Street Kensington, and Queensway. North of the park are a set of neighborhoods that get progressively nicer as you move west. Paddington, Edgware Rd., and Queensway mix fairly fancy houses on their back streets with main roads that have plenty of cheap ethnic eateries, souvenir shops, and stores of questionable legality that can unlock your phone, cash your checks, and wire your money across the world. Notting Hill has the mansions you would imagine, but popping out of the Tube at Notting Hill Gate may be a bit of a shock if you're expecting instant British charm—it's pretty much dull commercial real estate. Head slightly north, though, and you'll find the villas you were expecting. In the middle of that, Portobello Road has a market, antique stores, vintage clothing, and the kind of minimalist, hip cafes and restaurants that seem to appear anywhere you can get a secondhand prom dress or a pair of cowboy boots.

Marylebone and Bloomsbury

It doesn't get much more British than Marylebone—from the fact that Sherlock Holmes lived here to its mystifying pronunciation (it's Mar-leh-bone). Lush Regent's Park is surrounded by gleaming mansions, Marylebone Lane is lined with pubs, and the side streets are pocketed with clusters of Indian and Middle Eastern restaurants. The neighborhood stretches from Regent's Park south to Oxford St., and from Edgware Rd. east until it bleeds into Bloomsbury. While Marylebone is fun to poke around in, the prominence of fancy residential areas and spiffy office buildings means that good values here are hard to find.

london

Bloomsbury, on the other hand, is famous for its bohemian heritage. The namesake Bloomsbury Group included luminaries like Virginia Woolf, John Maynard Keynes, and E.M. Forster. Today, you can feel the continuation of all that cleverness emanating from the British Library and University College London—though creeping gentrification means there are few affordable garrets left for the burgeoning artist-intellectuals of today. Bloomsbury, centered on Russell Square, stretches east to King's Cross Rd., and is bounded on the north and south by Euston Rd. and High Holborn, respectively. The western part is now very high-end, while the eastern and northern bits retain more of the old student vibe. You can find some cheap pubs and restaurants throughout the streets surrounding the university, and the area is packed with good hostels, especially around King's Cross.

North London
Even though the area encompassing North London is only 3-4 miles from the city center, it boasts its very own self-contained Künstlerroman narrative. As soon as a creatively-inclined British youth begins to feel those vengeful lashes of rebellion, it's off to Camden Town, where safety pins replace school badges and everyone drinks themselves dizzy. The hard rocker vibe the area staked its reputation on is now a mere kitschy shadow, but it hasn't yet been completely overrun with tourists searching fruitlessly for the "London Look" of the Stones. As the under-eye wrinkles of the insomniac university student become permanent, she might find herself in the northeast regions of Angel or Islington, which hosts both up-and-coming bankers and the outer regions of the Hackney hipster scene. This is more of an adult-friendly space (not necessarily in the sexual sense), as the Upper St. is a less juvenile shopping experience than Camden town (less skulls, more structure). So what happens when you've paid your dues/soldout? It's time to reward yourself with a several million pound house in Hampstead! While this beautiful, peaceful oasis of stately townhouses and kaleidoscopic gardens had been the residence of hundreds of not-yet-successful literati, it's now more of a "good job, ol' chap" prize for celebrities. Nevertheless, Hampstead's greatest resource—its marvelous heath—comes as freely as lines to Keats.

East London
Isn't it just so ironic that an area that was once a slum is now a completely choice place for artists trying to screw the man (and each other)? But really, the music scene is so authentic—nothing like those horrid megaclubs that are corporate fronts dishing out soma like candy. Did you know that they don't have Urban Outfitters here (except the one they do)? No, it's completely organic, local, microbrewed, ephemeral, a yawning Communist utopia with some of the absolutely best market steals. Fancy a free art gallery? And it's just absolutely brimming with diversity. Lots of immigrants here (even though it's relatively segregated to Brick Ln.–as you go north, it gets more homogenous). Why live anywhere else in a bougie, cloned London when you can thrive in a place that really understands that you're above that? Grab your Nietzsche, your tortoiseshells, your bleeding heart, and enjoy East London. If that's your sort of thing.

South London
South London has long been maligned as one of London's dodgier neighborhoods. While the area has enjoyed something of a renaissance in recent years, it's still not as safe as much of central London. Clapham is a good place to find pubs and restaurants full of young professionals. Clapham has also become a cultural hub as the home of the Battersea Arts Centre, renowned for its groundbreaking productions. Brixton is less quaint, but a bit more fun. Bible-thumpers preach the Apocalypse from convenience store pulpits, and purveyors of goods set up shop at the nearby

Afro-Caribbean market, despite the overpowering smell of fish. Brixton is the place to come if you've started missing fast food, though some truly excellent restaurants peek out from between the fried-chicken stands. At night, it's a popular place to hear underground DJs and live reggae shows. The local Underground stations across the south of the city play classical music, thought by many to be a tactic for keeping young people from accumulating in the Tube, Clockwork Orange-style.

West London

West London is one of the most shape-shifting parts of the city. Shepherd's Bush is a hub of ethnic life, evident in the varied restaurants lining Goldhawk Rd., culminating in the veritable World's Fair of Shepherd's Bush Market. Shepherd's Bush is also home to Westfield's, a 43-acre ode to consumerism that makes American strip malls look like rinky-dink cornerstores. Hammersmith, the neighborhood to the south of Shepherd's Bush, is quieter and more gentrified. It feels more like a seaside resort than London— once you get out of the thriving area surrounding the Tube station, that is. Farther south and west are Kew and Richmond, which have the luscious greenery of Kew Gardens and Hampton Court, two easily accessible places to escape the urban jungle.

SIGHTS

It's a known secret that while Americans coo over Kate Middleton's baby and tsk over the antics of Prince Harry, the Brits keep the royal family around as a tourist trap (and their palaces and residences are going to be the most expensive sights). It's definitely working: tourism accounts for about 8% of the UK's GDP. It's not that *everything* in London costs loads of money. In fact, many of the most famous historical and artistic sites—like The British Museum, National Gallery, National Portrait Gallery, Victoria&Albert, and Tate Modern—are free. Also, for St. Paul's Cathedral and Westminster Abbey, you can avoid the £16 ticket and visit during their Evensong services. However, the most overlooked set of free sights in the city is the lava game of parks and gardens that blanket London. We recommend Hampstead Heath whole-heartedly, as well as St. James's Park. Regent's and Hyde Park are more frequently traveled and provide a nice afternoon out, but the wilder heath types play up more of the Albion spirit that converts most non-Brits to Anglophilia. In terms of ticketed attractions, avoid the London Eye, the Tower of London, and Madame Tussaud's. Instead, if you're on budget, take the Tube out to Hampton Court or Kew Royal Gardens.

The City of London

▩ SAINT PAUL'S CATHEDRAL

CHURCH

St. Paul's Churchyard   ☎020 7246 8350 www.stpauls.co.uk

The upper levels of the cathedral are open to the hearty and hale. This means you'll be climbing enough stairs to practically ascend to heaven yourself. Two hundred and fifty-one steps up is the acoustically marvelous **Whispering Gallery**, where you can hear someone whisper to you from 32m opposite. For 119 steps more you can visit the outdoor Stone Gallery, then another climb will take you to the pinnacle Golden Gallery, which provides exquisite views of the city (although smokers and otherwise respiratorily-challenged visitors can zoom through the same views on the free video tour).

i ⊖*St. Paul's. Signs outside the station lead you to the cathedral. 1½hr. free guided tours are offered at 10am, 11am, 1pm, and 2pm. Briefer introductory tours run throughout the day. A hand-held multimedia tour is included in the price of admission. £16, concessions £14, children £7. £1.50 discount if you book online.* ⌂ *Open M-Sa 8:30am-4pm (last ticket sold). You can get in for free (though you'll have limited access) during church services. Matins M-Sa 7:30am. Eucharist M-Sa 8am and 12:30pm; Su 8am, 11am, and 6pm. Evensong M-Sa 5pm, Su 3:15pm. Free organ recitals Su 4:45-5:15pm. Service times subject to change; check the website or the signs outside the cathedral.*

london

THE TEMPLE
HISTORICAL SITE

Between Essex St. and Temple Ave.   ☎020 7427 4820

When Shakespeare gave the line "Let's kill all the lawyers" to an insurgent in *King Henry VI*, the Bard meant corrupt hooligans, not the upstanding barristers of The Temple, who premiered **Twelfth Night** for him here in 1602. We can sense your confusion: isn't this a church? Well, yes. The whole stunning complex of medieval, Elizabethan, and Victorian buildings was first established by the Knights Templar in 1185 as the English seat for the order (and catapulted into stardom by *The Da Vinci Code*). After the crusades proved a bit of a lost cause, The Temple stopped crusading for those who wore suits of armor and became the HQ for those who brought suits instead. Now, the site is devoted to two of London's Inns of Court, which are the location of legal offices and training grounds for baby lawyers. The gardens, medieval church, and Middle Temple Hall are occasionally open to the public. Middle Temple Hall is an excellent example of Elizabethan architecture, with its beautiful double hammer beam roof. The large gardens are perfectly manicured with lush shrubberies and provide a handy dell for a spot of quiet reflection. The church itself has gorgeous carved effigies and sinister organ music often sifting through the columns.

i ⊖Temple. Go to the Victoria Embankment, turn left, and turn left again onto Temple Ln. Book 1hr. tours in advance. You can book to stay for lunch if you're appropriately dressed. Church admission £4. Services Oct-Jul Su 11:15am. Organ recitals W 1:15-1:45pm. Tours Oct-Jul Tu-F 11am. ⌚ Middle Temple Hall open M-F 10am-noon and 3-4pm, except when in use. Hours for church vary, but are posted

MUSEUM OF LONDON
MUSEUM

150 London Wall   ☎020 7001 9844 www.museumoflondon.org.uk

The Museum of London is an incredibly thorough archeological and sociological survey of the city from its Celtic pre-history to its melting pot present. Some of the highlights include a gargantuan 19th-century map of the city, color-coded by class (including "criminal"), and the ruins of the original Roman wall that ran below the site of the present museum. Even if you're a modernist and don't enjoy the historical navel-gazing at which Brits excel, the end of the museum has a fascinating touchscreen projector that surveys problems the city will face in the future (like population growth, carbon emissions, and NHS solvency).

i ⊖St. Paul's. Go up St. Martins and Aldersgate. Free. ⌚ Open M-F 10am-6pm. 45min. tours at 11am, noon, 3pm, and 4pm.

COURTAULD GALLERY
MUSEUM

Somerset House, Strand   ☎020 7872 0220 www.courtauld.ac.uk

Back in the '50s, when red was the new black, a fondness for Marx was quite commonplace in the academic sphere. Thus, infamous**KGB** double agent Anthony Blunt (spy code name: "Tony." Seriously.) served as director of this gallery for nearly 30 years despite suspicions of defection. Housed as part of the palatial Somerset House, the collection includes medieval and Renaissance art from the likes of Botticelli and Rubens—but it's most renowned for its delightful Impressionist and Post-Impressionist collection, featuring paintings by Degas, Monet, Manet (including **A Bar at the Folies-Bergère**), Seurat, and van Gogh.

i ⊖Temple. Turn right onto Temple Pl., left onto Arundel St., then left onto Strand. £6; concessions £5, £3 on M. ⌚ Open daily 10am-6pm.

TOWER BRIDGE
BRIDGE

Tower Bridge   ☎020 7403 3761 www.towerbridge.org.uk

While the Golden Gate is the one that usually gets knocked down in apocalyptic films, Tower Bridge has its own history of action film moves, as when a bus driver not only minded the gap but sailed his passengers over it when the bridge began to rise without warning. Compared to London Bridge, Tower

great britain

To breathe the air of London, you're going to be shelling out more than you would in European capitals on the continent. Thus, for most travelers, it'll be a merry hostel life where, out of three categories (central location, markedly cheaper prices, and good amenities), you get to pick two. For the light sleeper or introvert, there are a few B&Bs and budget hotels whose rates start around $50 for a single, and if you're traveling in a group, these hotels offer doubles, triples, and quads that go for just a little bit more than hostel rates.

For more places to stay, visit **www.letsgo.com**.

✪ YHA ST PAUL'S   HOSTEL $
36 Carter Ln.   ☎0845 371 9012 www.yha.org.uk
Most hostels play a game called "pick two;" not so with this hostel. Rooms come with ensuite washbasins and large lockers for your ever-accumulating horde of souvenirs; the premise also has laundry, an on-site restaurant, and blackboards thoroughly covered with upcoming events.
i ⊖St. Paul's. Go right down New Change, turn at the cathedral onto Cannon St., then take a left onto Carter Ln. All dorms single-sex. 6- to 11-bed dorms £22-28; triples, quads, quints, and sextets all around £25 per person. ⌚ Reception 24hr.

✪ ST. CHRISTOPHER'S VILLAGE   HOSTEL $
165 Borough High St.   ☎020 7939 9710 www.st-christophers.co.uk
It takes a village to raise a party, and St. Christopher's is built for that purpose: in-house bar, restaurant, chill-out room, cinema room, condom machines on every floor, and a relatively unadvertised rooftop terrace. The dorms are set up with the beds pushed against the walls, leaving the floor open as glorious space. Given St. Chris's karaoke and dance-filled nights, light sleepers and those in town for a less socially-motivated experience should either procure a room on the third floor.
i ⊖London Bridge. Walk down Borough High St. with the bridge at your back. Free Wi-Fi. Breakfast included. 4- to 22-bed dorms £12-37; doubles around £80.

✪ ASTOR HYDE PARK   HOSTEL $
191 Queen's Gate   ☎020 7581 0103 www.astorhostels.co.uk
Location, location, location. However, that maxim of real estate implies that you'd be ecstatic in a trash heap as long as the post code is good, which would be uncharitable to this grandiose yet friendly hostel in the heart of the museum district. The flagship Astor hostel not only has sky-high ceilings and spacious dorms, but it also employs an energetic staff that organizes hostel-wide events like pub quizzes and beer olympics.
i ⊖High St. Kensington. Turn right onto Kensington High St., then right onto Queen's Gate. Ages 18-35 only. Dorms £22-33; doubles £80-100.

✪ PALMER'S LODGE SWISS COTTAGE   HOSTEL $
40 College Crescent   ☎020 7483 8470 www.palmerslodge.co.uk
The set-up is bunks of dark-stained wood, with trunks underneath for storage, and bathrooms that are the cleanest we've seen in the London hostel gamut; the common areas feature chandeliers, bay windows that span to ceiling to floor,and a bar with a beautiful outdoor terrace.
i ⊖Swiss Cottage. Take exit 2 from the station, turn left onto Eton Ave., then right onto College Crescent. Free Wi-Fi. Breakfast included. 18+. 4- to 28-bed dorms £18-37; doubles from £70.

london

Bridge definitely wins on the aesthetic front (unless we're counting children's nursery rhymes). The exhibition you can pay to get into is enjoyable and runs through anecdotes and the history of the bridge's construction. Still, this might not be for those afraid of heights. On the whole, it's less of a tourist trap than the Tower of London, though you can skip the ticket price and just enjoy its stunning architecture for free.

i ⊖*Tower Hill. Follow signs to Tower Bridge. £8, concessions £5.60, ages 5-15 £3.40, under 5 free. ☼ Open daily Apr-Sept 10am-6:30pm; Oct-Mar 9:30am-6pm. Last entry 1hr. before close.*

The West End

◪ THE NATIONAL GALLERY

MUSEUM

Trafalgar Sq.   ☎020 7747 2885 www.nationalgallery.org.uk

When they say "National Gallery," it's not just code for "country's coolest collection." Really, the "National" stands for a distillation of British aesthetics and the "Gallery" means really famous art. Accordingly, you have the stunning slate of van Goghs (including *Sunflowers*) and Rubens. And then you have what seems like every painting of the Thames in existence. There's a gorgeous collection of Monet and Manet, and then you have Turner's 1001 ways to draw a naval fleet (the painting that Ben Whishaw and Daniel Craig discuss in *Skyfall* is indeed housed here). That's not to say that highbrow art and British sensibility never mix, but rather that aestheticians and Anglophiles alike will enjoy the expansive hall. The best way to explore is to buy a map (£1) and pick and choose which rooms you want to peruse. For the undecided, we recommend the Dutch room and most of the **Sainsbury** wing, which includes some great examples of medieval art.

i ⊖*Charing Cross. Free. Special exhibits around £10. Audio tours £3.50, students £2.50. 1hr. guided tours daily at 11:30am and 2:30pm; meet at Sainsbury Wing info desk. 10min. talks on individual paintings Tu 4pm. ☼ Open M-Th 10am-6pm, F 10am-9pm, Sa-Su 10am-6pm.*

◪ NATIONAL PORTRAIT GALLERY

MUSEUM

St. Martin's Pl.   ☎020 7306 0055 www.npg.org.uk

Allow us to draw a comparison: the National Portrait Gallery is the Platonic ideal of Facebook. Everyone picks a flattering or interesting image (with the exception of Kate Middleton, whose portrait is merely creepy). You put it in one space that's easily accessible and free, there's no advertising, and you don't have to listen to said person's political opinions. It's just the faces of those you recognize, love, and love-to-hate. The NPG starts at sculptures of Tudor kings and works its way up to modern-day Last Supper parodies (news alert: Dame Judi Dench is immaculate not only in concept) and some definitely non-traditional representations of figures like Stephen Fry and Germaine Greer. Starting from the beginning of the collection, the early subjects are only royalty until the 1600s, when portraits of artistic figures such as Shakespeare and Milton are included as well. The larger political tableaus, such as Copley's *The Death of the Earl of Chatham*, are fascinating depictions of political bodies, but the most interesting is the 20th-century section—filled with images of Thatcher, McCartney, and Princess Diana—where familiarity intersects with a break from red-cheeked men in coiled wigs.

i ⊖*Charing Cross. Walk down Strand to Trafalgar Sq. and turn right. Free. Small special exhibits £6, large exhibits £12. Audio tours £3. ☼ Open M-W 10am-6pm, Th-F 10am-9pm, Sa-Su 10am-6pm. Open until 10pm on select nights; check website for details.*

TRAFALGAR SQUARE

HISTORICAL SITE

The Thames is a snottish brown, London puddles are murky pitch, and the Trafalgar fountain is as aquamarine as a cruise ship pool. Welcome to one of the world's most famous plazas, flanked by memorials to art, war, and God. From the designer of the Houses of Parliament, Charles Barry (this should be read in

great britain

a deep movie announcer voice), Trafalgar Square commemorates **Admiral Horatio Nelson.** A sandstone statue of the military hero atop his eponymous column looks out toward the Thames to protect the English from the French/Germans/Russians/Immigrants, depending on the political flavor of the times. The **National Gallery** stands to the north of the square, and the surrounding perimeter is lined with various embassies and consulates. The sprawling center area serves as a meeting point, demonstration area, and the home of an annual Christmas tree (donated by Norway in thanks for service given in World War II, and we think to say "sorry" for Quisling). Pinch-hitting for God is **St Martin-in-the-Fields,** whose spires peek out at the edge of the plaza.

i ⊖*Charing Cross.*

ST MARTIN-IN-THE-FIELDS

CHURCH

Trafalgar Sq.
☎020 7766 1100 www.smitf.org

Exhibiting the logic of "Look something pretty!", King Henry VIII significantly renovated the medieval version of this church to keep plague victims away from his palace. The strategy still works on tourists today, who visit for the Cafe in the Crypt and the concerts instead going to pray that things don't fall off. St Martin's is also the parish church of the royal family, but it's better known for its great musical tradition. Every Monday, Tuesday, and Friday at 1pm, the church holds a 45min."lunchtime concert," a classical recital from students at musical academies and colleges. In the evening, professional artists run the gamut of Mozart to modern works in the beautiful (for a Protestant church) space.

i ⊖*Charing Cross. It's on the east side of Trafalgar Sq. Jazz concerts W 8pm. Free. Lunchtime concerts £3.50 suggested donation. Reserved ticket for jazz £12, unreserved £9. ☼ Open M-Tu 8:30am-1pm and 2-6pm, W 8:30am-1:15pm and 2-5pm, Th 8:30am-1:15pm and 2-6pm, F 8:30am-1pm and 2-6pm, Sa 9:30am-6pm, Su 3:30-5pm. Open at other times for services and concerts.*

Westminster

▨ WESTMINSTER ABBEY

ABBEY, HISTORIC SITE

Off Parliament Sq.
☎020 7222 5152 www.westminster-abbey.org

No matter how maudlin the foundation, the church's day-to-day work is for the living, and it is still primarily a functioning house of worship. Nearly all important British church ceremonies take place here—including William and Kate's wedding—with the notable exception of Diana and Charles's marriage, which took place in **St. Paul's** (p. 333). *Let's Go* almost automatically recommends attending a free service for touristy, ticketed cathedrals, but even if you pay admission, we recommend coming back for Evensong regardless. Seeing the Abbey in action with the accompanying sound of the choir is an experience you won't soon forget.

i ⊖*Westminster. Walk away from the river. Parliament Sq. and the Abbey are on the left. The Abbey vergers offer 90min. tours. £18, students and seniors £15, ages 11-18 £8. Verger-led tours £3. ☼ Admission M-Tu 9:30am-4:30pm, W 9:30am-7pm, Th-F 9:30am-4:30pm, Sa 9:30am-2:30pm. Last entry 1hr. before close. Verger-led tours M-F 10am, 10:30am, 11am, 2pm, and 2:30pm; Sa 10am, 10:30am, and 11am. Services: M-F Matins 7:30am, Holy Communion 8am and 12:30pm, choral Evensong 5pm (spoken on W); Sa 8am morning prayer, 9am Holy Communion, 3pm choral Evensong (5pm Jun-Sept); Su 8am Holy Communion, 10am choral Matins, 11:15am sung Eucharist, 3pm choral Evensong, 5:45pm organ recital, 6:30pm evening prayer.*

▨ CHURCHILL MUSEUM AND CABINET WAR ROOMS

MUSEUM, HISTORICAL SITE

Clive Steps, King Charles St.
☎020 7930 6961 www.iwm.org.uk/cabinet

Winston Churchill is all things to all Britons: courageous prime minister, fearless leader, vivacious wit, amateur painter, not Neville Chamberlain. Really, he was a geopolitical Renaissance man. Britain doesn't produce that many multi-taskers, and so what did they do to preserve and protect their best? Stick him under-

london

ground in a bunker that oozes trapped anxiety from its windowless walls like a haunted house. Opened in 1939 a few days before the beginning of the long winter for Poland and France, the Cabinet War Rooms were used as a shelter for important government officers, and Churchill spent six years pacing around the map room, whose lights still burn brightly. Connected to the Cabinet War Rooms is the Churchill Museum. Visitors can step on sensors to hear excerpts from some of his most famous speeches and watch videos detailing the highs and lows of his career. Also on display are his alcoholic habits, which included drinks with every meal, and his signature "romper," better known as a onesie. The interactive, touchscreen "lifeline" is phenomenally detailed; be sure to touch his 90th birthday and August 6th, 1945, but be prepared to draw stares from the other museum patrons. The memorialization grows a bit absurd: there's a lock of his hair on display, the possession of which is generally a universal sign for "stalker."

i Θ*Westminster. Turn right onto Parliament St. and left onto King Charles St. £15.45, students and seniors £12.35 (without voluntary donation), under 16 free. ☒ Open daily 9:30am-6pm. Last entry 5pm.*

HOUSES OF PARLIAMENT
Westminster Palace

HISTORIC SITE
www.parliament.uk

There are a number of ways members of the public can visit the Houses of Parliament. Debates in both Houses are generally open to the public; visitors can queue for admission during sitting times, though entrance is not guaranteed. Nor is it guaranteed that anything interesting will be going on—we recommend checking the website to see what bills are on the table. Prime Minister's Questions is a rowdy back and forth stand-up comedy session between the PM and the Shadow Chancellor, though tickets may only be reserved by UK residents, and foreign visitors can only take the rare leftover spaces. Finally, tours of the Houses are given throughout the year, but foreign visitors can only attend on Saturdays and during the Summer Recess (Aug and Sept).

i Θ*Westminster. The public entrance is at Cromwell Green, on St. Margaret St., directly across from Westminster Abbey. Debates and committee sessions free. Tours £16.50, concessions £14, children £7. ☒ When Parliament is in session, House of Commons open M 2:30-10:30pm, Tu 11:30am-10:30pm, W 11:30am-7:30pm, Th 9:30am-6:30pm, sometimes F 9:30am-3pm; House of Lords open M-Tu 2:30-10pm, W 3-10pm, Th 11am-7:30pm, sometimes F 10am-close of business. Tours leave every 15min. Aug M 1:15-5:30pm, Tu-F 9:15am-4:30pm; Sept Tu-F 9:15am-4:30pm; Oct-Jul Sa 9:15am-4:30pm (for UK residents).*

BUCKINGHAM PALACE
The Mall

PALACE, MUSEUM, HISTORIC SITE
☎020 7766 7300 www.royalcollection.org.uk

The interior of the palace is, for the most part, closed to the public—we can't imagine the Queen would be pleased with plebes tramping into her private chambers. From late July to early October, though, the royals head to Balmoral, and the **State Rooms** are opened to the public. As befits their status, the rooms feature fine porcelain, furniture, paintings, and sculptures by famous artists like Rembrandt and Rubens. In addition to the permanent pieces, the rooms often exhibit treasures from the Royal Collection—jewels, Fabergé eggs, and Kate Middleton's wedding dress. The **Royal Mews,** open most of the year, functions as a museum, stable, riding school, and a working carriage house. The carriages are fantastic—especially the "Glass Coach," which carries royal brides to their weddings, and the four-ton Gold State Coach. Unfortunately, the magic pumpkin carriage used to escape from evil step-royals is only visible after midnight, but if you're in the Royal Mews when the clock strikes 12am, you have other problems (namely, how to scale the layers of barbed wire that surround the palace). Finally, the **Queen's Gallery** is dedicated to temporary exhibitions of jaw-droppingly

great britain

valuable items from the Royal Collection. Five rooms designed to look like the interior of the palace are filled with glorious artifacts that the Queen holds in trust for the nation. They feature everything from Dutch landscape paintings to photographs of Antarctic expeditions to Leonardo da Vinci's anatomical drawings.

i ⊖Victoria. *Turn right onto Buckingham Palace Rd. and follow it to Buckingham Gate. Audio tour provided for State Rooms. State Rooms £19, students and seniors £17.50, ages 5-16 £10.85, under 5 free; Royal Mews £8.50/7.75/5.30; Queen's Gallery £9.50/8.75/4.80; combined ticket to Royal Mews and Queen's Gallery £16.25/14.90/9.10; Royal Day Out ticket (access to all 3) £33.25/30.50/18.85.* ☼ *State Rooms open late Jul-Oct daily 9:30am-6:30pm. Last entry 4:15pm. Royal Mews open Apr-Oct daily 10am-5pm; Nov-Dec 22 daily 10am-4pm; Feb-Mar M-Sa 10am-4pm. Last entry 45min. before close. Queen's Gallery open daily 10am-5:30pm. Last entry 4:30pm.*

The South Bank

The Globe Theatre of Shakespeare's day was not the fun, middle-class night of historical edification it is now—rather a step up from the prostitution and animal fighting for which the South Bank was known. Now, the only cocks present are the skyline's phallic symbols, such as Tate Modern's obelisk tower and the Shard, a self-explanatory skyscraper that casts its blueish glaze over the entire bank. For those envious of the view, you can always buy a ticket for **The London Eye**, but at about £19 per ride, it's much more reasonable to just crane your neck on the plane flight down.

▧ TATE MODERN   MUSEUM, MODERN ART
53 Bankside   ☎020 7887 8008 www.tate.org.uk

The movement of modern art as the worship of novelty has no better standard than Jackson Pollock—boldly painting what no man had painted before (namely, paint). And in addition to hosting one of Pollock's most famous works, Tate Modern is itself a novelty made concrete. The building is a converted power station whose insides are the sort of striking minimalism one would expect out of *1984*. Yet within the gallery rooms are Rothko and Picasso, Mondrian and Delvaux in glorious relief to such stark surroundings. The permanent galleries entitled **Poetry and Dream, Transformed Visions, Structure and Clarity,** and **Energy and Process** range from sculptures that touch the high ceilings to paintings of chaos to neon lighting and mirror work. Art exists for interpretation, so bring your open mind and free associate for a bit—or just stare at the Rothkos until your mind becomes a calm atmosphere in kind.

i Open M-Th 10am-6pm, F-Sa 10am-10pm, Su 10am-6pm. Free guided tours of each permanent gallery 11am, noon, 2pm, and 3pm.

▧ IMPERIAL WAR MUSEUM   MUSEUM
Lambeth Rd.   ☎020 7416 5000 www.iwm.org.uk

Housed in what was once the infamous Bedlam insane asylum, the Imperial War Museum is mad for history. The exhibits start out with two massive naval guns standing sentinel over the imposing building's entrance. The first room is cluttered with enough war-making machinery to make any general salivate. Highlights include a Polaris A3 Missile, the first submarine-launched missile, a full-size German V2 Rocket, and the shell of a"Little Boy," the type of atomic bomb detonated above Hiroshima. Luckily, the bomb is non-functional, but it's still disconcerting when kids whack the casing. The third floor houses a haunting, expansive Holocaust exhibition, which traces the catastrophic injustice of WWII Nazi atrocities with cartographic precision, its miles of film exploring everything from the rhetoric of the Nazi party to the history of anti-Semitism. If this subject matter is too light for your fancy, take solace in the Crimes Against Humanity video exhibition one floor down. The first floor houses the exciting, if sensational, "Secret War" exhibit of WWII spy gadgetry, which provides a

london

brief history of MI5 and the Special Operations Executive. Art nuts will enjoy the museum's unique art collection, called "Breakthrough." The ground floor is devoted to the World Wars, with artifacts, models, videos, and the popular Blitz Experience and Trench Experience exhibits that recreate the feeling of hiding during an air raid and living in the trenches. Also down here is a section on post-1945 conflicts, sure to make you feel chipper about the state of the world.

i ⊖Lambeth North. Exit the station and walk down Kennington Rd., then turn left onto Lambeth Rd. The Blitz Experience daily schedules downstairs; it lasts around 10min. Free. Special exhibits £6, students £5. Multimedia guides £4.50. ⏰ Open daily 10am-6pm.

SHAKESPEARE'S GLOBE   THEATER, HISTORIC SITE
21 New Globe Walk   ☎020 7902 1500 www.shakespearesglobe.com
When film producer and director Sam Wanamaker took his own tour to Britain in the 1940s, he traipsed over to the South Bank to pay homage to the patron saint of theater, only to find a sullen plaque that said, "Shakespeare wuz here." Or something like that. What commenced was a decades-long fundraising and construction project to recreate the Globe of Elizabethan glory. A ticket to the exhibitions and tour (for information on productions, see **Arts and Culture**) includes a 45min. walkthrough of the theater, chock full of anecdotes about bear-baiting, current productions, and the list of fire hazards that threatened the original Globe's integrity (namely, firing cannons inside a building with a thatched roof and the blazing oratory of Puritans that resulted in the closure of the theater during the English Revolution). The exhibits are a bit drier but a good starting point if you want to brush up on film and TV adaptations or Shakespeare's lesser-known works.

i ⊖Southwark. Turn left onto Blackfriars Rd., right onto Southwark St., left onto Great Guildford, right onto Park St., then left onto Emerson St. The entrance faces the river, around the corner from the main entrance to the theater. Exhibition and Globe tour £13.50, students £11. ⏰ Exhibition open daily 9am-5:30pm. Tours M 9:30am-5pm, Tu-Sa 9:30am-12:30pm, Su 9:30am-11:30am.

South Kensington and Chelsea

🏛 **VICTORIA AND ALBERT MUSEUM**   MUSEUM
Cromwell Rd.   ☎020 7942 2000 www.vam.ac.uk
It is sadly political that female monarchs often tack on their husband's name (William and Mary as well) while the reverse never happens. Nevertheless, the V&A stands primarily as a fitting tribute to the 19th-century golden age of industrialization and art. Founded in 1851 at the Great Exhibition, the original museum focused more on manufacturing art than Dutch Old Masters—still seen today in such items as The Great Bed of Ware (that could sleep 12 people) and the exhibits on 19th-century dress straight out of Cranford and Jane Austen. Not that there's not your requisite dose of high-brow options, too. The Renaissance sculpture gallery has some beautiful examples of Samson strangling a Philistine and a Narcissus that looks like he's punching his own reflection, while St. George loosely holds what looks like Mushu in the back (British saints are so much more docile than those pagans, you know). Also worth your time is the giant room filled with the Raphael Cartoons (not TMNT)—prints of the tapestries in the Vatican that are as large as the School of Athens itself. The rotating ticketed exhibitions are drawn to please, the most recent crop including "David Bowie Is," a labyrinth of costumes and documents from Britain's favorite Starman.

i ⊖South Kensington. Turn right onto Thurloe Pl. and left onto Exhibition Rd. The museum is to the right across Cromwell Rd. Free. Special exhibitions generally £6-10. Free daily tours available; check screens at entrances for times. ⏰ Open M-Th 10am-5:45pm, F 10am-10pm, Sa-Su 10am-5:45pm.

SAATCHI ART GALLERY
ART GALLERY

Duke of York Sq.   ☎020 7811 3085 www.saatchigallery.co.uk

While Tate Modern certainly has the tourist monopoly on contemporary art in the city, the Saatchi embodies its spirit of edginess and wonder. Take the bottom floor gallery, for example, hosting Richard Wilson's *20:50*. When you walk in, it looks relatively simple: a room has been painted in darker colors until the halfway point of the wall, and the lighter top half looks like a mirror image. Until you peer over the railing and notice that you are mirrored as well. You can even walk out on a steel platform so that the black liquid void surrounds you at waist level. Another brilliant piece shown when we visited was Annie Kevan's series of portraits of cruel dictators as children—notably, little Hitler is the only one painted to have blue eyes. While the exhibits are best approached with an open mind, we recommend buying the exhibition guide on the way out if you're an art aficionado (you can always come back, as the gallery is free!).

i ⊖*Sloane Sq. Go straight out of the Tube and continue onto King's Rd. The square is on the left. Free as the wind. Exhibition guides £13.* ⏲ *Open daily 10am-6pm. Last entry 30min. before close.*

ST. MARY ABBOTS
CHURCH

High St. Kensington   ☎020 7937 5136 www.stmaryabbotschurch.org

Tucked away behind the usual slag of big-box fashion stores is a wooded grove with a pastoral flower shop outside. Behind the foliage and the flora, a church stands where churches have stood for over 1100 years, through which time Issac Newton, Beatrix Potter, and Princess Diana all worshiped here. When you enter, the silence swallows you; all the better to notice the scorch marks from Satan prowling around (just kidding, World War II).

i ⊖*High St. Kensington. Turn right onto Kensington High St. and left onto Kensington Church St. Free.* ⏲ *Open M-Tu 8:30am-6pm, W-F 7:10am-6pm, Sa 9:40am-6pm, Su 8am-7pm.*

ST. LUKE'S GARDENS
PARK

Sydney St.

If you're in London for a long stay, then this hideaway a mere block from King's Rd. is perfect for a *private* repose. Because it's primarily in use for residents (and their too-young-for-daycare toddlers), it won't do to bring out the alcohol, 20 of your friends, and the speakers. You'll simply have to make due with the circlets of fiery roses laced around the towering Gothic church that overlooks this Arcadia.

i ⊖*Sloane Sq. Go down King's Rd. away from the Tube. Turn right onto Sydney St.* ⏲ *Open daily 7:30am-dusk.*

BROMPTON ORATORY
CHURCH

Brompton Rd.   ☎020 7808 0900 www.bromptonoratory.com

"Look at that sumptuously *gorgeous* Puritan church," said no one ever. Luckily, the grand Brompton Oratory keeps holy the Roman Catholic tradition of beauty first, confession later. However, the marble-laden sanctuary also keeps up the pesky habit of the state being suspicious of Catholics: it was used as a drop point for KGB agents during the Cold War.

i ⊖*Knightsbridge. Turn left onto Brompton Rd. Free.* ⏲ *Open daily 6:30am-8pm. Services M-F 7, 8, 10am, 12:30, 6pm (in Latin); Sa 7, 8, 10am, 6pm; Su 8, 9, 10, 11am (Latin), 12:30, 4:30, 7pm.*

KENSINGTON PALACE
PALACE

Kensington Palace Gardens   ☎0844 482 7777 www.hrp.org.uk/kensingtonpalace

When William of "William and Mary" had one too many asthma attacks, he moved out to the 'burbs and into Kensington Palace. Since its establishment in the 17th century, it has played host to the likes of Georges I and II (after this, it became a home for minor royals like the pre-queen Victoria, Princess Diana and Charles, and, most recently, Will and Kate). A tour will take you through the state rooms done up as they were when the kings and queens were in residence.

london

Also be sure to see the web of lace and Swarovski crystals in the center of the palace that look like something straight out of *Tron*. When you're finished with tour, stop by The Orangery to sip tea and method act your way into believing you could live here, too.

i ⊖High St. Kensington. Turn right leaving the station and head down the road, then enter the park and make for the palace (it's kind of hard to miss). £15, concessions £11.40. ⏰ Open daily 10am-6pm.

NATURAL HISTORY MUSEUM

MUSEUM

Cromwell Rd.   ☎020 7942 5011 www.nhm.ac.uk

You might be thinking that once you've seen one Natural History Museum, you've seen them all. Rock collection, erect skeletons, stuffed animals, walk-in womb... wait, are we sure this museum is for children? Well, regardless, as the spawn of tired parents will jostle around you like 100 angry garden hoses, beeline for the back of the museum to see the unrepeatable Cadogan Gallery: a collection of British treasures including the most expensive book in the world (John James Audubon's "The Birds of America" at £7.3 million) and a moon rock so graciously given to Britain by a country that they used to own.

i ⊖South Kensington. Turn right onto Thurloe Pl. and left onto Exhibition Rd. The museum is to the left across Cromwell Rd. Book early for tours of Darwin's special collections. Free. Special exhibits around £8; discounts for students. ⏰ Open daily 10am-5:50pm. Last entry 5:30pm.

Hyde Park to Notting Hill

SPEAKERS' CORNER

HISTORICAL SITE, PERFORMANCE SPACE

Hyde Park, Park Ln.

In this alcove of free speech, London pays credence to its more democratic constitution: the Corner has been the stage for political, religious, and social debates for more than a century. In some ways, it's sort of like stand-up comedy, since you have to be quick on your feet to answer questions from the Corner regulars/hecklers (some of whom have frequented for decades). Famous speakers of yesteryear include Marx, Lenin, and George Orwell, but today you're as likely to find a fundamentalist Christian as a **Communist**. Anyone is welcome to speak, so young revolutionaries and Ciceros, prepare your oratory!

i ⊖Marble Arch. Go through the arch into the park. The area where most people speak is the paved section between the arch and the beginning of the main grassy area. Free. ⏰ Hours vary, but around 9am-10pm in the summer.

APSLEY HOUSE

HISTORICAL SITE, MUSEUM GALLERY

Hyde Park Corner   ☎020 7499 5676 www.english-heritage.org.uk

Named for Baron Apsley, the house later known as "No.1, London" was bought by the Duke of Wellington in 1817 (his heirs still occupy a modest suite on the top floor and provide their best impersonations of Bill Nighy in contributions to the audio tour). The house is a stunning architectural triumph dotted with spoils from the Napoleanic Wars—including a beautiful collection of sabres abandoned in Napoleon's war carriage when he was on the run from Wellington—and gifts from grateful European monarchs. One of the unforgettable treasures is an 11ft. naked Napoleon statue at the foot of the staircase that the scourge of Europe was ashamed of because it made him look "too athletic." Other marvels include an original statue of Cicero hiding among 20 other reproduction busts, the key to the city of Pamplona (granted after the Duke captured the city), the death masks of Wellington and Napoleon, and a stunning 6.7m-long Egyptian service set given by Napoleon to Josephine as a divorce present. Scholars maintain that the dessert service was meant as a mean joke about Josephine's weight—it's huge. If you're an English history buff, the careful curation will delight you; otherwise, the exhibit pays for itself in droll audio tour commentary.

i ⊖*Hyde Park Corner. Jun 18 is Wellington Day, so check for special events. £6.70, concession £6, children £4; joint ticket with Wellington Arch £8.60/7.70/5.20. Audio tour free.* ⏰ *Open Apr-Oct W-Su 11am-5pm. Last entry 30min. before close. Closed Nov 2013-Mar 2014 for refurbishment.*

THE WELLINGTON ARCH
Hyde Park Corner

HISTORICAL SITE

☎020 7930 2726

If you're creating an art film that includes a fast time lapse of cars shooting around traffic circles, then congratulations! This sight is perfect for you. Otherwise, visitors are treated to a history of the arch and an unspectacular view from the observation deck, which is more or less tree-level with Hyde Park. Due to the better angels of our nature, the original statue of the Duke of Wellington was replaced with a symbol of peace—the angel Quadriga—in 1883 (and no fighting ever happened again!). However, despite the anti-climactic view, the Arch is worth it if you buy the joint ticket with Apsley House.

i ⊖*Hyde Park Corner. Adult £4, concessions £3.60, children £2.40; joint ticket with Wellington Arch £8.60/7.70/5.20.* ⏰ *Open Apr-Sept W-Su 10am-5pm; Oct-Mar 10am-4pm. Last entry 30min. before close.*

Marylebone and Bloomsbury

THE BRITISH MUSEUM
Great Russell St.

MUSEUM

☎020 7323 8299 www.british-museum.org

Another treasure is the **King's Library** on the eastern side of the ground floor, which holds artifacts gathered from throughout the world by English explorers during the Enlightenment. Some of the central display cases bear descriptions, but much of the collection is jumbled together without explanation—a curatorial choice meant to recreate the feel of collections from the period. We think it works pretty well. Mixed in with the artifacts are shelves full of books from the House of Commons' library—get your dork on and try to find an 18th-century copy of your favorite Roman poet or Greek historian.

i ⊖*Tottenham Court Rd., Russell Sq., or Holborn. Tours by request. £5 suggested donation. Prices for events and special exhibitions vary, most £8-12. Excellent color maps with self-guided tours £2. Multimedia guide £5. Free daily tours in specific exhibition rooms 11am-3:45pm; check website for details. 20min. free spotlight tours F 5-7pm. Weekend tours £12, Sa-Su 11:30am and 2pm.* ⏰ *Museum open daily 10am-5:30pm. Select exhibitions M-Th 10am-5:30pm, F 10am-8:30pm, Sa-Su 10am-5:30pm.*

THE BRITISH LIBRARY
96 Euston Rd.

LIBRARY

☎020 7412 7676 www.bl.uk

The British Library is at once what a library would suggest—reading rooms, archives, member cards for UK residents, and, oh yes, a Gutenberg Bible thrown in just because. For tourists, the Treasures of the British Library is a compendium of scores, manuscripts, and illustrations that will register familiarity and awe. The literature section is comprised of words, words, words, not surprisingly focused on Shakespeare—although John Milton's common-place book, Oscar Wilde's *The Ballad of Reading Gaol*, and Jane Austen's reading desk are proffered non-Bard treasures. Even though Britain is not renowned for its musical tradition, the **Music** section makes due with circumstance and celebrates Vaughn Williams and Elgar; also included are several original Haydn scores, along with Beethoven's tuning fork and Mozart's marriage contract. However, the real highlights are related to God and Country, with one of 50 documented Gutenberg Bibles modestly hiding in the illuminated manuscripts section and the **Magna Carta** commanding its own exhibition room. Most of the treasures given space in the main room offer either something of visual beauty—as in the Armenian

london

Bible or several illuminated Qu'rans—or historical significance, including a loving shout-out to the 1945 creation of the welfare state (admittedly not as flashy as the 2012 Olympics Opening Ceremonies). In addition to the permanent collection, the library has two rotating exhibition spaces, one free and located in the atrium outside of the Treasures gallery and the other a ticketed affair behind the museum shop. If you are aiming to become a luminary of your own, the cafe connected to the main floor has a majestic view of the 65,000 volumes that King George III assembled as a royal library. That shall surely inspire you as you greedily gorge on pastries and coffee without restraint, knowing that you are fighting intellectual death.

i ⊖*Euston Sq. or King's Cross St. Pancras. From Euston Sq., turn left. From King's Cross, turn right. Free Wi-Fi with registration. To register for use of reading room, bring 2 forms of ID, 1 with a signature and 1 with a permanent UK address. Free. Tours free. Group tours (up to 15 people) £85. Tours M-F 9:30am-6pm, Sa 9:30am-5pm, Su 11am-5pm, call020 7412 7639 to book. Individual tours M-Sa 10:30am and 3pm, Su 11:30am, call019 3754 6546 to book. ☒ Open M 9:30am-6pm, Tu 9:30am-8pm, W-F 9:30am-6pm, Sa 9:30am-5pm, Su 11am-5pm. Reading rooms closed on Su.*

REGENT'S PARK
PARK

☎020 7486 7905 www.royalparks.org.uk

While the Prince Regent (George IV) was a laudanum addict who amassed today's equivalent of £50 million in debt, his legacy now lies in some of the most aesthetically pleasing spaces in London. At the Queen's pleasure, the British and a smattering of internationals take to the 300 acres of the royal park for sport (football, rugby, and tennis are popular choices) or rest. The children at heart can wander through **The London Zoo,** and those who feel the same emotion for a flower or butterfly as they do a cathedral or picture will delight in **Queen Mary's Garden,** which boasts such plant species as "Conspicuous" and hosts over 40,000 roses, best viewed in early June. In the rain, the **Open Air Theatre** is your best bet to avoid muddy treks (although bring a waterproof raincoat, as Open Air is self-evident). If one craves solitude, rainy days are ideal for creepily standing by the pond MI6-style; however, even on sunny days, the farther you travel from the southern gates, the more number of baskers drops dramatically.

i ⊖*Regent's Park. Deck chair £1.50 per hr., £4 per 3hr., £7 per day. Boats £7.50 per hr., £5.50 before noon. Zoo £23, concessions £21, children £17. ☒ Park open daily 5am-dusk. Zoo open daily 10am-5:30pm.*

THE WALLACE COLLECTION
GALLERY

Manchester Sq. ☎030 7563 9552 www.wallacecollection.org

If Netflix were to suggest a museum to you based on your love of 18th-century French period pieces, art with a strong naked female lead, and themes that deal with the transience of life, then the Wallace Collection would be front and center on your recommendation list. Housed in the palatial **Hertford House,** the collection is a multi-layered experience of silk wallpapered walls, whole furniture sets owned by Marie Antoinette, at least five clocks per room, symbolic busts of "Summer" and "Autumn," some requisite British paintings of hounds, and the exquisite *Francesa da Rimini* by Ary Scheffer that shows Dante and Virgil gazing upon the punishment of the lustful in Hell. The ground floor's four **Armoury Galleries** boast scads of richly decorated weapons and burnished suits of armor, while the **State Rooms** hold a collection of sumptuous Sèvres porcelain. On the upper floor, you'll find coral and cerulean rooms, dreamy paintings by artists like Rubens and some darker, sterner stuff by Rembrandt and van Ruisdael, as well as one of the collection's most celebrated pieces, Frans Hals's *The Laughing Cavalier* (who wasn't a cavalier at all).

i ⊖*Marble Arch. Turn left onto Oxford St., left onto Duke St., and right onto Manchester Sq. Gallery free; suggested donation £5. Audio tour £4. ☒ Open daily 10am-5pm.*

North London

◪ HAMPSTEAD HEATH
PARK
Hampstead   ☎020 7332 3030

These 1000 acres of unmanicured forest, fresh ponds, dusky grass, and silent dells are the most underrated attraction in London. Few tourists make it out here (probably because of the more centrally located park options like Regent's, Hyde, and St. James), and the only "look, Facebook friends, isn't this cool?" photo opportunity involves climbing to the top of Parliament Hill and gazing upon the dusky, futuristic London below. As you move farther north up toward the Kenwood estate, the paths become more hilly and less touched by human hands (save for the odd champagne cork on the ground). The east part of the Heath features a slew of gender-separated bathing ponds. However, the best way to experience the widening brume is to start at the entrance near Hampstead and take as many side paths into the dark forest as possible, working your way through silence dearly purchased.

i Bus #210 will drop you at the north of the Heath. Alternatively, get off at ⊖Hampstead, turn right onto Heath St., go up North End Way, turn left onto Inverforth Close, and left onto a path to arrive at the hill gardens. Bus #214 allows easy access to Parliament Hill. ⌖ Heath open 24hr. Hill Garden open daily 8:30am-1hr. before sunset.

KEATS HOUSE
HISTORICAL SITE
Keats Grove   ☎020 7332 3868 www.cityoflondon.gov.uk/keatshousehampstead

When the developers came round in 1920 and wanted to demolish this house to build flats, just imagine the lexicon of Keats quotes the council used to prevent its demise ("A thing of beauty is a joy forever," perhaps?). Now, fans of the tragic consumptive can appreciate the house and surrounding gardens where he wrote "Ode to a Nightingale." The house is comprised of historically preserved Regency-era rooms stocked with artifacts from his life (as well as those of his friend, Charles Brown, and fiancée, Fanny Brawne).

i ⊖Hampstead Heath. Turn left onto South End Rd. and follow it until it hits Keats Grove. £5, concessions £3, under 16 free. 45min. free guided tours; schedule varies. ⌖ Open Easter-Oct 31 Tu-Su 1-5pm; Nov-Easter F-Su 1-5pm.

KENWOOD HOUSE
GALLERY
Hampstead Ln.   ☎020 8348 1286 www.english-heritage.org.uk

Lord Iveagh, a barrister and Lord Chief Justice, lived here in the 18th century. Visitors to Kenwood House can now admire his fabulous art collection and see how the 18th-century elite lived. Iveagh's bequest fills the house with paintings that are essentially odes to the London of yore. The house is currently undergoing renovations and is scheduled to reopen in November 2013.

i Bus #210 stops on Hampstead Ln. at the Kenwood House stop. The park is across the road. Free. Booklets £4. ⌖ Open daily 11:30am-4pm. Last entry 3:50pm.

East London

◪ WHITECHAPEL GALLERY
ART
77-82 Whitechapel High St.   ☎020 7522 7888 www.whitechapelgallery.org

In 1901, the Whitechapel Gallery began as an exemplar of *noblesse oblige*. Over a century later, the resident hipster probably knows more about art (or seems to) than the elite ever could have imagined for their cute, East End charity cases. But even under the pall of its patronizing beginning, the space debuted Rothko, Pollock, and Kahlo to London audiences; it also served as the only British stop of Pablo Picasso's *Guernica*. Prepare yourself for challenging works of all media types as well as a few mid-career retrospectives.

i ⊖Aldgate East. Turn left onto Whitechapel High St. Free. Special exhibits and events normally under £10, £2 student discount. ⌖ Open Tu-Su 11am-6pm.

london

◪ GEFFRYE MUSEUM
136 Kingsland Rd.

MUSEUM

☎020 7739 9893 www.geffrye-museum.org.uk

Pemberley, Satis House, Brideshead, Downton Abbey—all accounts of these fictional houses are accompanied with obsessively lavish descriptions of their furnishings (re: indicators of yearly income) in a singularly British way. In the Geffrye Museum, you can see how domestic style evolved from 1630 to the present through a series of mock-up rooms. While it's a bit weird to imagine any British living room without a TV, the exhibits do a great job of putting you in the mindset to Bible read or play a good round of gin rummy.

i ⊖*Hoxton. Make a right onto Geffrye St., a left onto Pearson St., and a left onto Kingsland Rd. Free. Special exhibits around £5.* ⏰ *Open Tu-Sa 10am-5pm, Su noon-5pm.*

West London

◪ HAMPTON COURT PALACE
East Molesey, Surrey

PALACE

☎0844 482 7777 www.hrp.org.uk/hamptoncourtpalace

There's something slightly bizarre about being led through a historical audio tour by a more paranoid version of Francis Urquhart/Frank Underwood/Richard III (depending on your fourth wall experience). But then again, the whole of Hampton Court is an eclectic mix of architecture, curiosity, and historical appeal. The humongous palace was given by Henry VIII to Cardinal Wolsey and then abandoned until William and Mary gloriously restored it (well, actually, it's really just another episode of "Christopher Wren Strikes Again"). The tours will take you through the lives of all three monarchs and their chapels, kitchens, bedchambers, and apartments. Outside of the walls lie the magnificent grounds, replete with hedge maze (portkey not included) and several gorgeously landscaped gardens. Don't miss the ornate, gilded astronomical clock, which was used for a quick check on the current sun sign and the London Bridge water levels.

i *Trains run from Waterloo to Hampton Court (£5.50). The palace is just across the bridge from the train station. Alternatively,* ⊖*Richmond. Take the R68 toward Hampton Court. Audio and guided tours included with admission. £16, concessions £13.40, children under 16 £8; gardens only £5.72/4.84/free; maze only £4.40, children £2.75.* ⏰ *Open daily Jan-Mar 10am-4:30pm; Apr-Oct 10am-6pm; Oct-Dec 10am-4:30pm. Last entry 1hr. before close. Last entry to maze 45min. before close.*

ROYAL BOTANIC GARDENS, KEW
Richmond, Surrey

BOTANICAL GARDENS

☎020 8332 5000 www.kew.org

Combine a cultural legacy of landscaping and royal extravagance, and you get Kew Gardens—a sprawling Shangri-la only visited by the most thorough of tourists (even London locals don't get out to it very often). These botanical gardens host the largest collection of plants in the world, and visitors can eat up gorgeous assemblages of roses, orchids, and cacti (or be eaten up by the carnivorous plants). For those not so enamored with flora, peacocks strut the 121 hectares at their leisure; for architecture aficionados, the asiatic pagoda and Kenyan-style treetop walkways are funky contributions to an otherwise solidly British collection of cottages and houses on the grounds. The greenhouses are a nice escape if it starts raining on your journey, but the highlight is the sizable lake near the back of the gardens, spanned by the Sackler Crossing. Take some champagne, don't pluck the roses, and lounge on its banks in peace.

i ⊖*Kew Gardens. Exit the station and walk down Litchfield Rd. to the Gardens' Victoria Gate. £14.50, concessions £12.50, under 17 free.* ⏰ *Open M-F 9:30am-6:30pm, Sa-Su 9:30am-7:30pm. Last entry 30min. before close. Galleries close daily at 5:30pm. Free guided tours leave Victoria Plaza at 11am and 2pm.*

FOOD

British food doesn't have a great reputation. Yes, it is bad for you and no, it doesn't have complex flavors, but it is so intrinsically a part of British life that to forgo it would be a grave error for any visitor. Fish and chips, bangers and mash, tikka masala (a British invention), and warm ale are all different names for the same thing: comfort food. Neighborhoods like Brixton and Shoreditch serve up a span of ethnic cuisine, from Caribbean to Indian, while gourmet restaurants whip up inventive dishes. "Pub grub" still rules over everything. In case you hadn't noticed, Brits like to operate in certain set ways. There's a reason that old war propaganda line, "Keep Calm and Carry On," is plastered all over the place; there's a reason the Queen still rolls down the Mall every June; there's a reason the Brits always think England will win the Cup; there's a reason fair Albion still uses the pound; and for that same reason, you'll always be able to get a pie and a pint on any corner in London. Now eat your mushy peas—the cod's getting cold.

The City of London

CITY CÀPHÊ

17 Ironmonger Ln.

VIETNAMESE $

www.citycaphe.com

During their lunch break, businesspeople in pleated pants and skirts quietly turn onto Ironmonger Ln. for one of the only non-chain restaurants in the area. The goods? Bánh mì and perfectly cooked rice noodle dishes. As opposed to the Vietnamese food stalls you'll find in Brick Ln. or Camden, this small, modern joint reflects its yuppie clientele in presentation (even though the prices don't require a Centurion Card).

i ⊖ *Bank. Head down Poultry away from the stop, then turn right onto Ironmonger Ln. Bánh mì £4. Other dishes £4-6. 🕑 Open M-F 11:30am-3pm.*

J&A CAFE

4 Sutton Ln.

CAFE $

☎020 7490 2992 www.jandacafe.com

The two young sisters who run this rustic hideaway (Johanna and Aoife) offer some rarities in British cafe culture: relatively long opening hours, a diverse menu, and a venue larger than an airplane aisle. It's easy to miss because of its off-road alleyway locale, which is filled with picnic benches and patrons. However, once settled in, you can spend hours nursing a coffee or one of their lemonades (that have extracts like rhubarb, elderflower, and pear).

i ⊖ *Barbican. Turn left onto Goswell Rd., left onto Great Sutton St., and left onto Sutton Ln. Free Wi-Fi. Breakfast, sandwiches, and lunch dishes £4-8.50. 🕑 Open M-F 8am-6pm, Sa-Su 9am-5pm.*

COACH AND HORSES

26-28 Ray St.

PUB $$

☎020 7278 8990 www.thecoachandhorses.com

London pub food evokes the same attitude that something like Rubinoff does: "Oh God. Never again...but I'll probably end up with it anyway after five drinks." Coach and Horses does not deal in mushy peas and food so oily it's a hazard to nearby aquatic wildlife—instead, the grub here is a foodie's take on the standard pub line-up. Try the venison ragout or an 8oz. West Country steak or something simple like the delicious pea and ham soup.

i ⊖ *Farringdon. Walk north on Farringdon Rd. and turn left onto Ray St. Appetizers £4.75-7.25. Main courses £11-15. 🕑 Open M-F noon-11pm. Kitchen open noon-3pm and 5-10pm.*

THE CLERKENWELL KITCHEN

31 Clerkenwell Close

BRITISH, SEASONAL $$

☎020 7101 9959 www.theclerkenwellkitchen.co.uk

Despite the trope of bad British cuisine and worse execution, the locally sourced movement has gained traction. Clerkenwell Kitchen, an IKEA-modern cafe, is a good example of the free-range/organic trend done without too much snobbery. The menu items are inventive—such as the squid with watercress and chili—and the waiters are a jovial bunch that will actually talk to you, either about the menu or your book (the rarest of rarities in socially-repressed London).

i ⊖Farringdon. Turn right onto Cowcross St., right onto Farringdon Rd., right onto Pear Tree Ct., and right onto Clerkenwell Close. Walk straight as if still on Pear Tree Ct. If you see the church, you've gone too far. Main courses £7.80-12. ⏰ Open M-F 8am-5pm.

The West End

🖼 KULU KULU
SUSHI $$

76 Brewer St.   ☎020 7734 7316 www.kulukulu.co.uk

Kulu Kulu is an onomatopoetic play on "Kuru Kuru," the noise that conveyer belts apparently make. And that is what you'll get here: a steady stream of small sushi dishes whirling around the runway while discerning businesspeople pluck them for consumption. Different plates indicate different prices; when you're ready to pay, a waiter will come over and add up your plates. Granted, you're not going to getüber-modern low-lighting and black lacquered bars like you will at some uppity West End joints, but the prices here are more competitive than even what you'll find at Tesco's.

i ⊖Piccadilly Circus. Go down Glasshouse St., keep right onto Sherwood St., and turn left onto Brewer St. Dishes £2 (4-5 dishes make a good meal). Sushi combos from £6. ⏰ Open M-Sa noon-10pm.

🖼 MONMOUTH COFFEE COMPANY
CAFE $

27 Monmouth St.   ☎0872 148 1409 www.monmouthcoffee.co.uk

The English have a more estranged relationship with filter coffee than the States, no better evidenced by the fact that the only variety of black coffee offered in most brand-name shops is the Americano. However, Monmouth is one of the few places in the city where you can buy individually filtered coffee, and the resulting heaven can power you through an entire morning of Covent Garden tourism. There's limited seating available, but most customers take a coffee and croissant either to work or to wait outside one of the nearby theaters for rush tickets.

i ⊖Leicester Sq. Turn right and then left onto Upper St. Martin's Ln., which becomes Monmouth St. Coffee £2.50. Baked goods £1.50-2. ⏰ Open M-Sa 8am-6:30pm.

FORTNUM&MASON
TEA $$$$

181 Piccadilly   ☎020 7734 8040 www.fortnumandmason.com

Fortnum&Mason is basically the Malfoy family's ideal of what Hogsmeade should look like: specialty tea, truffles, champagne, picnic hampers filled with china, roulette sets, fancy cologne, and animal-topped canes. However, a more universal highlight is the tea service that includes scones, sandwiches, cakes, and options like Scotch Egg and Welsh Rarebit. Admittedly, this is all quite expensive, so a good option for those with a budget is The Parlour, for a less formal tea experience ($5.75 per pot), or the lowest floor, where you can grab a solitary cuppa ($1.80).

i ⊖Piccadilly Circus. Turn left down Piccadilly. Afternoon tea £40-50 per person. ⏰ Open M-Sa noon-9pm, Su noon-8pm.

Westminster

🖼 POILÂNE
BAKERY $

46 Elizabeth St.   ☎020 7808 4910 www.poilane.com

As you wander through the traveler's gauntlet of plastic-wrapped sandwiches, it's easy to forget what bread is like. Not "vessel for my jam" or "clamp for my ham and cheese." Actual, thick, chewy, crispy, soft, warm, salty bread. There's literally one option in the city for a heavenly manna experience: the only non-French branch of the famous Parisian bakery chain, Poilâne. Like the cobbling elves that help the shoemaker at night, many of the bakers live upstairs and cook through the night so the bread is fresh for the die-hard morning crowd. Interestingly enough, they bake the bread in the same model that was responsible for burning down half of London once upon a time.

i ⊖Victoria. Turn left onto Buckingham Palace Rd., then right onto Elizabeth St. Loaves generally from £4-10. Walnut bread £4.50. ☒ Open M-F 7:30am-7pm, Sa 7:30am-3pm.

▨ PIMLICO FRESH
CAFE, MEDITERRANEAN $

86 Wilton Rd. ☎020 7932 0030

Even though a dish like fish and chips has a simple composition *technically*, British food sometimes seems confusing and excessive. Why does this potato have so much stuff in it? Who eats baked beans for breakfast/ever? Is it normal that my plate has enough oil left over to be the next Deepwater Drilling scandal? Pimlico Fresh is a rare bird in that it freshens up British staples and ignores the "acquired taste" options, like oil, tuna, mayo, and cress. Instead, the options here are simple and delicious: porridge, toast, baked eggs, pies, and some lighter fare. They also serve Monmouth coffee, which you can enjoy at the communal picnic benches or at the window-facing countertop.

i ⊖Victoria. Wilton Rd. runs behind the station, toward Pimlico, away from Buckingham Palace. Takeout available. Main dishes £5-7.50. Coffee from £2. ☒ Open M-F 7:30am-7:30pm, Sa-Su 9am-6pm.

JENNY LO'S TEAHOUSE
ASIAN FUSION $$

14 Eccleston St. ☎020 7259 0399 www.jennylo.co.uk

As most tea-drinking Brits live a quiet, domestic life where the kettle is never that far away, there are surprisingly few tea-centric spots in the city. And when there are, it's usually for minor royalty who should be congratulated on not drinking something stronger at 2pm. However, this unassuming tea shop is the original deal (remember: imperialism), with an equally good menu of Thai and Vietnamese options as well. And the best part is that the tea doesn't come with stony British judgment.

i ⊖Victoria. Turn left onto Buckingham Palace Rd., then right onto Eccleston St. Takeout and delivery available. Tea £2-4. Main courses £8-10. Cash only. ☒ Open M-F noon-3pm and 6-10pm.

The South Bank

▨ PIEMINISTER
PIES $

Gabriel's Wharf, 56 Upper Ground ☎020 7928 5755 www.pieminister.co.uk

The South Bank is lined with refuge for the diaspora of tourists coming from Tate Modern, the London Eye, and London Bridge. Avoid anything saying "Fish and Chips" and head straight to the best pies in London (but actually—no demon barbers and psychotic mistresses running this happy joint). These fist-sized pies are a healthier take on the British staple, with options such as the Heidi (sweet potato and goat cheese) alongside comfort favorites like kidney and beef. Enjoy them outside during the summer or as takeaway in the winter, since there's no indoor seating.

i ⊖Waterloo. Walk toward the main roundabout and onto Waterloo Rd., then turn right onto Upper Ground. Pies £4.25; with gravy, mashed potatoes, and mushy peas £5.95. ☒ Open daily 10am-6pm.

TSURU
JAPANESE $

4 Canvey St. ☎020 7928 2228 www.tsuru-sushi.co.uk

Some of the packages looks suspiciously like dressed-up Tesco sushi, but as soon as you indulge, you can taste the handmade, succulent difference. The interior is not very large, but there are large seating areas outside on the closed street. If you're hungry before seeing a production at The Globe or the National

london

Theatre, just try one of the takeaway boxes that sometimes goes for half-price in the early evening.

i ⊖Southwark. Walk down Blackfriars Rd. toward the river, then turn right onto Southwark Rd. and left onto Canvey St. Sushi boxes £4-6. Katsu £6. ☑ Open M-F 11am-9pm, Sa noon-9pm.

South Kensington and Chelsea

▨ BUONA SERA JAM   ITALIAN $$
289A King's Rd.   ☎020 7352 8827

Chelsea is a neighborhood where the disheveled traveler will be looked down upon: if you're not in a suit or similar finery, you'll be marked as a tourist. Now, however, you can look down on them. Climb up a ladder to one of the second-story stacked booths of Buona Sera and enjoy your affordable risotto while you feel like you're a T-block in a giant Tetris game.

i ⊖Sloane Sq. Exit the Tube and head straight down Sloane Sq. Turn onto King's Rd., which slants gently off to the left. Alternatively, take bus #11, 19, 22, 211, or 319. Salads £5. Pasta and risotto £9. Meat and fish entrees £14. ☑ Open M-F noon-11pm, Sa-Su noon-10:30pm.

BUMPKIN   BRITISH $$$
109 Brompton Rd.   ☎020 7341 0802 www.bumpkinuk.com

Bumpkin has the same hearth and earth feel of a country pub, but that's about as "bumpkin" as it gets. Of course, they *are* referring to their patriotic menu of nosh only hailing from British farm, field, and shore (notable exceptions are most of the items on the wine menu and the coffee, but we think that's better for all involved). As the patronage views tennis matches and feasts on duck and pudding, we declare them successful and also recommend the eggs royale if you find yourself in a brunching mood.

i ⊖South Kensington. Exit down Old Brompton Rd. The restaurant is on the right. Appetizers £5.50-10. Main courses £11-22. ☑ Open daily 11am-11pm.

MY OLD DUTCH PANCAKE HOUSE   DUTCH $$
221 King's Rd.   ☎020 7376 5650 www.myolddutch.com

While IHOP attempts diplomatic overtures, this tucked away pancake diner is unapologetically Dutch. For example, the 12in. pancakes (roughly, crepes) are served on blue and white porcelain emblazoned with windmills. How quixotic then that the diner hosts "Monday Madness," where you can choose a sweet or savory option for only £5.

i ⊖Sloane Sq. Exit the Tube and go straight down Sloane Sq. The street slanting gently left is King's Rd. Pancakes £5-9. ☑ Open M-F 10am-9:30pm, Sa-Su 9am-9:45pm.

Hyde Park to Notting Hill

▨ OTTO   PIZZA $
6 Chepstow Rd.   ☎020 7792 4088 www.ottopizza.co.uk

Otto's confidence in its cornmeal pizza crust is exemplified by a map of continental America with arrows pointing to Alaska, Hawaii, and apparently the 51st state: Otto. Then again, with the sound of Mumford & Sons and the smell of delicious hope wafting through the dining area, this restaurant has enough popularity to level such a claim. Pick one of eight or so options (we recommend the No. 114) and enjoy the crispy crust and piled-on toppings. The commitment-phobic can order the Chef's Taster—which has six different slices—and even the seminal pizza hater can order a broccoli, black bean, and mushroom salad that makes a great side dish as well.

i ⊖Notting Hill Gate. Make a right down Pembridge Rd., which will turn into Pembridge Villas, and then a left onto Chepstow Rd. Takeaway available. Gluten-free and vegetarian options always available. Slices £3.85-4.95; half pizza £10; whole pizza (serves 2-3) £18. ☑ Open M-F noon-3pm and 5:30pm-11pm, Sa noon-11pm, Su noon-10pm.

great britain

DURBAR RESTAURANT
INDIAN $

24 Hereford Rd.   ☎020 7727 1947 www.durbartandoori.co.uk

It's hard to resist the warm smells from the kitchen of Durbar, where the same family has served up Indian specialties for the last 54 years. This was a popular Indian restaurant before Indian restaurants were popular, and—in a city now brimming with this kind of food—it still manages to be one of the best values. The menu ranges across India, with a collection of favorites and some unexpected dishes, such as the Brinjal Jalfrezi—an entire eggplant spiced with chilies.

i ⊖*Bayswater. Turn left onto Queensway, left onto Moscow Rd., and right onto Hereford toward Westbourne Grove. Starters £2-5. Main courses £6-9. Lunch special £4.50.* ⏰ *Open M-Th noon-2:30pm and 5:30-11:30pm, F 5:30-11:30pm, Sa-Su noon-2:30pm and 5:30-11:30pm.*

SNOWFLAKE GELATO
GELATO $

43 Westbourne Grove   ☎020 7221 9549 www.snowflakegelato.co.uk

A constant stream of customers slip in and out of this über-modern gelateria in the heart of Hyde Park. The signature flavor—Snowflake—is a feathery mix of white chocolate, coconut, and almond that transcends ice cream and lands somewhere between whipped, frozen nectar of the gods and really great gelato. Takeaway is a popular option, but the pure white leather booths and delicate lighting makes you feel like you're eating in the Snow Queen's palace (happily, the mirrors remain on the wall instead of as a shard in your eye).

i ⊖*Bayswater. Turn left out of the station onto Queensway, then turn left again onto Westbourne Grove. The gelateria is on the left. 1 scoop £3, 2 scoops £4, 3 scoops £5.* ⏰ *Open M-Th 10:30am-11:30pm, F-Sa 10:30am-12:30am, Su 10:30am-midnight.*

Marylebone and Bloomsbury

LA FROMAGERIE
CHEESE $

2-6 Moxon St.   ☎020 7935 0341 www.lafromagerie.co.uk

Cheese. Everywhere. In the cheese room. In the cafe. On your plate. In your stomach. Oh there *is* a reason heroin is nicknamed as such, and while *Let's Go* does not condone drug use, you can quit che—alright, we shall enable you. Sample one of the cheese plates (we recommend the British one) from the quaint, rustic cafe; then pick out some cheese from vault-like cheese room. Then buy some of La Fromagerie's special cheese crackers. Then, declare madness. For how can you claim sanity when you think there is no way your cheese can be better than last time, when, in fact, it is and will be with each bite, you fool!

i ⊖*Baker St. Turn left onto Marylebone Rd., right onto Marylebone High St., and right again onto Moxon St. Cheese prices vary wildly. Small cheese plate £8.75; large £13.50. Wine pairings by the glass £5-10.* ⏰ *Open M-F 8am-7:30pm, Sa 9am-7pm, Su 10am-6pm.*

SPEEDY'S CAFÉ
CAFE $

187 North Gower St.   ☎020 7383 3485 www.speedyscafe.co.uk

Because of the commercialization of Baker St. proper, North Gower St. has become the new home of Sir Arthur Conan Doyle's hero in the deerstalker (or shall we say ear hat?). Despite its newfound fame due to its prominence in BBC's *Sherlock*, Speedy's and its delicious sandwiches remain cheap ($3-5), and the decor very modestly acknowledges its role in the series with only a few pictures and drawingsof the cast. Moreover, the friendly staff couldn't possibly include someone that would lead on Mrs. Hudson while having wives in Doncaster and Islamabad. Enjoy your own seven percent solution (of coffee beans) and a sarnie after a visit to the British Library—a resource we're admittedly not sure could help with cataloging 243 different types of tobacco ash.

i ⊖*Euston Square. Take the Euston Rd. exit, turn right onto Euston Rd., then right onto North Gower St. Speedy's is on the left. Entrees £6-8.* ⏰ *Open M-F early-3:30pm, Sa early-1:30pm.*

london

NEWMAN ARMS
PIES $$
23 Rathbone St. ☎020 7636 1127 www.newmanarms.co.uk

Newman Arms recently faced the wrath of the Westminster City Council, which decreed that it must serve its pies "more slowly" as a strategy to reduce the number of after-work drinkers milling on the street outside. However, the fact that this is even a problem is just good testament to the charm of the three-centuries-old purveyor of pies. Head upstairs to the Pie Room to try such delicacies as lamb and rosemary or beef and Guinness. Afterward, do not make the mistake of thinking Spotted Dick has anything to do with your cutaneously-challenged ex-boyfriend (or his member). It's simply vegetable pie with currants. And delicious.

i ⊖*Goodge St. Turn left onto Tottenham Court Rd., left onto Tottenham St., left onto Charlotte St., and right onto Rathbone St. Enter through the corridor next to the entrance to the pub. Pies £10-12.50. Desserts £4.50. Pints from £3.50. ☼ Open M-F noon-3pm and 6-10pm.*

SHIBUYA
JAPANESE $$
2 Acton St. ☎020 7278 3447 www.shibuyalondon.co.uk

In the city proper, sushi this fresh would cost a sum thrice that of Shibuya's offerings. The restaurant's atmosphere is a modern zen haven filled with the lilting birdsong of light J-pop hits and natural fresh light (that streams through some heraldry stained glass). Enjoy one of the sake choices, and if sushi is too raw/too bougie for your taste, select a curry or rice dish. Admittedly, Shibuya does cater to yuppies that seemingly teleport through the less-coiffed St. Pancras area from business-formal Marylebone. However, Shibuya remains a wonderful place to clear your palate and your head and ultimately emerge unsullied by the suited, hunched patrons surrounding you.

i ⊖*King's Cross St. Pancras. Make a left leaving the station, stay on Euston as it turns into Pentonville Rd., then make a right onto King's Cross Rd. The restaurant is on the corner with Acton St. Sushi from £3.80. Sushi combos from £15. Entrees £9.50- £10. ☼ Lunch M-F noon-3pm. Dinner daily 6pm-10:30pm.*

North London

LA CRÊPERIE DE HAMPSTEAD
CREPERIE $
Around 77 Hampstead HighSt.

Hampstead natives swear that this creperie saves a trip across the Channel. Hampstead natives also hit the level of privilege where going across the Channel merely for some crepes isn't that strange. Regardless of its posh patrons, you can snag a delicious, filling crepe here in a cone for under £5 with little to no wait; then, take it to the Heath.

i ⊖*Hampstead. Turn left onto Hampstead High St. No seating. Most crepes from £3.90-4.50. ☼ Open M-Th 11:45am-11pm, F-Su 11:45am-11:30pm.*

LE MERCURY
FRENCH $$
140A Upper St. ☎020 7354 4088 www.lemercury.co.uk

Complete your English experience by expatriating your palate to France. In London, your Gaul options are usually limited to Michelin star restaurants and Pret a Manger. Le Mercury strikes a happy medium, with low prices (all dishes under £9) and ambitious items like *Poir pochee et bleu* (white wine poached pear, blue cheese and roast walnuts) and slow-roasted pork belly with celeriac confeit. Enjoy them in the yellow interior dotted by flickering candlelight.

i ⊖*Angel. Exit and turn right onto Upper St. Starters £4. Main courses £9. Desserts £3. ☼ Open M-Sa noon-1am, Su noon-11:30pm.*

great britain

MANGO ROOM

CARIBBEAN $$

10-12 Kentish Town Rd.   ☎020 7482 5065 www.mangoroom.co.uk

Stables Market is filled with black-clad teenagers arguing through mouthfuls of dried-out stall rice about who is faker (the girl with the avian-themed dress or the boy with the horn-rimmed glasses?). Ignore that "scene" and head to a truly authentic restaurant dominated by bright paintings, reggae, and delicious Caribbean dishes—like ackee and saltfish, jerk chicken, and curries.

i ⊖Camden High St. Turn left onto Camden High St., left onto Camden Rd., and left onto Kentish Town Rd. Lunch entrees £7.50-9. Dinner entrees £11-15. ☒ Open daily noon-11pm.

East London

◼ CAFE 1001

CAFE $

91 Brick Ln.   ☎020 7247 9679 www.cafe1001.co.uk

After you've picked up some avian-emblazoned apparel at Old Spitalfields Market, walk over to this alleyway coffee shop whose patrons converse enough to rival Scheherazade. The warehouse space is a solid option for an afternoon coffee, but is good for heartier grill fare like barbecue and burgers. At night, the salad bar transitions to a real bar, and the back room becomes a venue for up-and-coming bands and DJs. Bloc Party filmed their video for "The Prayer" here; in their apt, immortal words, "East London is a vampire."

i ⊖Aldgate East. Turn left onto Whitechapel Rd., left onto Osborn St., then continue onto Brick Ln. Free Wi-Fi. Live bands on Tu (rock) and W (folk and jazz). Swing dancing classes Th 11am-5pm. Club night F-Su 7pm-midnight. Cover £3-5 after midnight. Burger and chips £5. Coffee £1.20-2. ☒ Open daily 7am-midnight, often stays open all night F-Su.

MIEN TAY

VIETNAMESE $

122 Kingsland Rd.   ☎020 7729 3074 www.mientay.co.uk

What Brick Lane is to Bengali food, this stretch of Kingsland Rd. is to Vietnamese cuisine. Mien Tay sets itself above the rest the hackneyed options with low prices and high-quality, crispy spring rolls, fragrant *pho*, and tasty noodle dishes (try the lemongrass and curry noodles). The service is swift, and the dining room is bright and roomy. We recommend coming before or after a visit to the nearby Geffrye Museum.

i ⊖Hoxton. Make a left after leaving the station, then a right onto Cremer St., and a left onto Kingsland Rd. Starters £2-5. Main courses £5-9. ☒ Open M-Sa noon-11pm, Su noon-10pm.

South London

◼ FRANCO MANCA

PIZZERIA $

Unit 4, Market Row   ☎020 7738 3021 www.francomanca.co.uk

It's not the most inviting of scenarios, winding your way through the back alley corridors of a Brixton shopping complex to reach Franca Manca. Nevertheless, the boisterous flow of Italian and divine smells of pizza toppings other than "cheese" are worth the strange approach. The crust is a light sourdough concoction, the olive oil is organic, and the toppings include some bold choices like courgettes and aubergines (that's zucchini and eggplant, y'all) and yellow peppers. If we have not yet convinced you, the bottles of libation are quite liberally priced, all under £20.

i ⊖Brixton. Make a left leaving the Tube, a quick left onto Electric Ave., then a right onto Electric Ln., and a left onto Market Row. Pizza £4.50-7. ☒ Open M noon-5pm, Tu-Sa noon-11pm, Su noon-10:30pm.

◼ NEGRIL

CARIBBEAN $$

132 Brixton Hill   ☎020 8674 8798

Brixton is famous for its Afro-Caribbean food, and Negril is the place to sample some of its greatest hits. You can try regional specialties like callaloo (a leafy

london

green), saltfish fritters, and goat curry or go with something more familiar, like roasted chicken or barbeque ribs (as well as smoothies). They also have quite a few vegan options, in accordance with the traditional Rastafarian diet. The weekend brunch is very popular and allows patrons to spread out on Negril's picnic benches for hours.

i ⊖Brixton. *Make a left leaving the Tube and continue as the road becomes Brixton Hill. Delivery and takeaway available. No alcohol served, but you can BYOB for a £2.50 corkage charge per person. Entrees £7-12.* ⏰ *Open M-F 5-10pm, Sa-Su 10am-10pm.*

West London

▨ **SUFI** PERSIAN $$
70 Askew Rd. ☎020 8834 4888 www.sufirestaurant.com

Nestled in the streets connecting Goldhawk Rd. and Uxbridge Rd. is what many locals will swear to be the best Persian food in London. It's a small place with a nice but ultimately unmemorable façade and decor (excluding the dozens of award stickers hanging near the bottom of the window), but the delights within—namely a satisfying meal for £8—will blow away first impressions. Sample the saffron ice cream after your meal for only £3 more.

i ⊖Shepherd's Bush Market. *Make a right down Uxbridge Rd. when leaving the station, then walk about 15min. and make a left down Askew Rd. You can also take Bus #207 to the beginning of Askew Rd. Starters £2-4. Entrees £7-13.* ⏰ *Open daily noon-11pm.*

NIGHTLIFE

The City of London

▨ **FABRIC** CLUB
77A Charterhouse St. ☎020 7336 8898 www.fabriclondon.com

It feels like the space-time fabric is bending underneath you at London's most famous club. Oh wait, that's just the vibrating dance floor. The biggest contributor to this club's legitimacy is the soundtrack: they eschew not only top 40 but more mainstream DJs like Tiësto and Paul Oakenfeld as well. The space—a renovated warehouse full of deconstructed industrial decor—is equally serious (especially compared to the fun-loving dance crowd). Look out for hidden quirks and flourishes, like 3D floor maps in the stairwells and a copy of Rubens's *Samson and Delilah* presiding over the smokers' courtyard. This being said, if you're over 21, you'll probably feel a bit old, as the bulk of the clientele are teenagers drinking £10 rum and cokes to their newfound clubbing freedom.

i ⊖Farringdon. *Turn left onto Cowcross St. and continue until you hit Charterhouse St. Cover F-Sa £15-20, Su up to £10. Get discounts by buying tickets in advance. Beer £4.50.* ⏰ *Open F 10pm-6am, Sa 11pm-8am, Su 11pm-6am.*

▨ **THE JERUSALEM TAVERN** PUB
55 Britton St. ☎020 7490 4281 www.stpetersbrewery.co.uk

The Jerusalem Tavern is the kind of London pub where you might be convinced you're back in the 18th century (or turn of the BCE Jerusalem for all we know). The tavern is as bare as they come: it's just a narrow, wooden interior without any music playing. It's the only tavern in London to offer all of the St. Peter's ales. These specialized brews—including the trifecta of Golden Ale, Ruby Red Ale Honey Porter, and Cream Stout—are enough to renounce your prior beer preferences. Then again, if you don't want the walk back to seem like a Calvary trudge, we recommend multiple trips.

i ⊖Farringdon. *Turn left onto Cowcross St., left onto Turnmill St., right onto Benjamin St., and left onto Britton St. Pints from £3.* ⏰ *Open M-F 11am-11pm.*

THE SLAUGHTERED LAMB   PUB
34-35 Great Sutton St.   ☎020 7253 1516 www.theslaughteredlambpub.com
Don't be put off by this pub's macabre name (or the pentacle logo)—it's merely a
remnant of the district's old meat-packin' days. The Slaughtered Lamb feels a bit
like a gigantic old gentleman's club, with leather couches, comfy armchairs, and
framed pictures around a fireplace...and a hip hop soundtrack. Downstairs, the
music continues with frequent live shows and occasional comedy acts.
i ⊖Barbican. Turn left onto Goswell Rd. and left onto Great Sutton St. Pints around £4. ☼ Open
M-Th 11:30am-midnight, F-Sa 11:30am-1am, Su 12:30-10:30pm.

THE BETSEY TROTWOOD   PUB
56 Farringdon Rd.   ☎020 7253 4285 www.thebetsey.com
The namesake Betsey Trotwood was a colorful, man-hating character in Dickens's *David Copperfield*. The pub has retained the verve of Dame Maggie Smith
and done away with the sexism, so most patrons just quietly enjoy a pint of one
of many cask ales. The space opens out onto the street, and sunshine streams in
through the large windows, creating a comfortable lazy vibe in summer. Various
events,like bluegrass shows and poetry readings, are held downstairs.
i ⊖Farringdon. Turn right onto Cowcross St. and right onto Farringdon Rd. Pints from £3.50. ☼
Open M-F noon-11pm, Sa noon-11:30pm, Su noon-10:30pm.

The West End

▨ THE BORDERLINE   CLUB
Orange Yard, off Manette St.   ☎020 7734 5547 http://venues.meanfiddler.com/borderline/
Though Borderlineis essentially a bare basement with the same drunken dancing as you'll discover at any London club, the all-important variable is the playlist
of indie artists like Joy Division, The Smiths, The Kooks, and Vampire Weekend.
The crowd is quite devoted to the music, and you can't help but get into the spirit
of things when everyone is shouting lyrics to purposely obscure songs. The club
also hosts live music, for those who have the "Christopher Columbus saw it first"
approach to performers (or, as a true hipster would say, Leif Erikson).
i ⊖Tottenham Court Rd. Turn right onto Charing Cross Rd. and right onto Manette St. Punk on W.
Student night on Th. Indie rock and Brit pop on F-Sa. Cover W-Th £5, F-Sa £7. Frequent £2 drink
specials. ☼ Open W-Sa 11pm-4am.

▨ DIRTY MARTINI   BAR, CLUB
11-12 Russell St.   ☎0844 371 2550 www.dirtymartini.uk.com
Martinis: the ode to gin made by James Bond and countless other debonair sirs.
This club in the heart of Covent Garden does not relinquish this tradition, even
though the cool, tuxedoed, cigar-smoking associations have metamorphosed
into tightly dressed women and their suit jacket-less friends. Society has traded
in fussiness for accessibility, and that's great for the student traveler, as the expert mixology is a steal compared to other clubs charging the same for a lousy,
too-sweet mojito.
i ⊖Covent Garden. Head down James St. to the Covent Garden Piazza, turn left and go around it
until you come to the corner of Russell St. Happy hour M-Th until 10pm, F-Sa until 8pm, Su all day.
Cover £5 high-capacity weekend. Beer £4. Cocktails £8-9. ☼ Open M-W 5pm-1am, Th 5pm-3am,
F 4pm-3am, Sa noon-3am, Su 1-11pm.

▨ AIN'T NOTHIN' BUT...   BAR, LIVE MUSIC
20 Kingly St.   ☎020 7287 0514 www.aintnothinbut.co.uk
Has your wife left you? Has your dog died? Has your life been nothing but a
meaningless parade of drivel-filled observations? Well then, dear, the blues are
your anthem, and in an area filled with pop hits of the later '00s, this R&B stalwart provides a haven for both good times and bad. Most patrons lounge around

london

the bar, but the back room hosts live music, so you can really sink your teeth into the existential pain of your plight.

i ⊖*Oxford Circus. Head down Regent St., turn right onto Great Marlborough St., then right onto Kingly St. Cover £5 F-Sa after 8:30pm. Beer from £4.* ☼ *Open M-Th 5pm-1am, F 5pm-2:30am, Sa 3pm-2:30am, Su 3pm-midnight.*

HEAVEN
CLUB, GLBT

Under the Arches, Villiers St.   ☎020 7930 2020 www.heavennightclub-london.com

Loudly announcing that heaven is in a Tube Station is a one-way ticket to being committed. Nay, the paradise we refer to is one of London's largest gay clubs, replete with giant video screens, a warehouse for a dance floor, and enough campy men to staff a production of *La Cage Aux Folles*. Mondays have "Popcorn," a student-friendly event with good drink specials and a welcoming door policy; the music varies from hip hop to techno to classic dance tunes. Thursday through Saturday, the club is run by G-A-Y, London's biggest GLBT party organization. Friday night brings "Camp Attacks" (with amazingly cheesy disco music) and performances by famous pop stars.

i ⊖*Charing Cross. Turn right from the station and head down Villiers St. The club is under the archway about halfway down. Cover £5; usually free before midnight or if you sign up on the guest list.* ☼ *Open M 11pm-3am, Th 11pm-3am, F-Sa 11pm-5am.*

FREUD
BAR

198 Shaftesbury Ave.   ☎020 7240 9933

Freud said in *Interpretation of Dreams* that dreaming of staircases was indicative of sexual suppression. Well, climb on down into your mother's womb—er, a totally normal West End bar. The place is more Kafkaesque than Freudian, with no chaise lounges and a lot of concrete, but the drinks are clever (Slippery Nipple, anyone?), and the prices are right.

i ⊖*Piccadilly Circus. Turn right onto Shaftesbury Ave. Beer £3.50. Mixed drinks £5.50-7.50. Credit card min. £10.* ☼ *Open M-Th 11am-11pm, F-Sa 11am-1am, Su noon-10:30pm.*

VILLAGE
BAR, GLBT

81 Wardour St.   ☎020 7478 0530 www.village-soho.co.uk

Early in the evening, Village looks like just another after-work bar with a happily iridescent logo. Then the go-go dancers climb up onto their perches, and a veritable parade of attractive men—and their equally attractive flame dames—swarm in to enjoy the night (with associate flame dames as well). Throughout the week, you can expect drag queens, karaoke (Tuesdays and Wednesdays), and more.

i ⊖*Piccadilly Circus. Turn right onto Shaftesbury Ave. then left onto Wardour St. Cocktails £6-7.* ☼ *Open M-Sa 4pm-1am, Su 4-11:30pm.*

Westminster

CASK
BEER HEAVEN

6 Charlwood St.   ☎020 7630 7225 www.caskpubandkitchen.com

Maybe you're not a beer person, and maybe you're bitter about not knowing why everyone orders a "lager." Cask is a great introduction to this expansive world of acquired taste, and would you want your first great nicotine experience to be with a pack of Lucky Strikes behind a KFC or a Cuban cigar? The beer "menu" is actually a binder full of hundreds upon hundreds of bottled beers from around the world. A couple dozen more are on tap, and they rotate the selection so they can accommodate as many rare and novel brews as possible.

i ⊖*Pimlico. Turn right onto Tachwood St.; Cask is on the right, at the corner with Charlwood St. Free Wi-Fi (as if you needed an excuse to spend more time here). Pints start around £4, but vary wildly from there.* ☼ *Open M-Sa noon-11pm, Su noon-10:30pm.*

BRASS MONKEY

PUB

250 Vauxhall Bridge Rd.　　　　　　　☎020 7834 0553 www.brass-monkeybar.co.uk

Vauxhall Bridge Rd. can be a bit intimidatingly run-down as it prepares to shoot over the Thames. However, this charming, twinkly pub stands out as a solid option, especially if you're staying in the area. It's not a rowdy scene, and a good indicator of calm is that a decent proportion of patrons enjoy food with their drink.

i ◉*Victoria. Turn right onto Vauxhall Bridge Rd. Wine £5-6. Pints around £4. ☼ Open M-Sa 11am-11pm.*

The South Bank

◤ THE HIDE

BAR

39-45 Bermondsey St.　　　　　　　☎020 7403 6655 www.thehidebar.com

The isolated elements of The Hide would hint at pretention: fancy cocktails with snarky descriptions, red velvet curtains, obscure jazz, and suited men in various state of dishevelment. However, it's mostly a local crowd that's just as happy with a modern concrete bar and mood lighting as an old-fashioned wooden one with fringe lamps. The cocktails are quite good: try your liver at the Parliamentary Brandy (Jensen's Old Tom Gin, cubed sugar, Peychaud's bitters; £9), modeled after a moonshine recipe used during one of the temperance periods.

i ◉*London Bridge. Walk toward the bridge and turn right onto Tooley St., then right onto Bermondsey St. Most spirits £4. Beer from £4.80. Cocktails £9-10. ☼ Open Tu 5pm-midnight, W-Th 5pm-1am, F-Sa 5pm-2am, Su 5pm-10:30pm.*

SOUTHWARK TAVERN

PUB

22 Southwark St.　　　　　　　☎020 7403 0257 www.thesouthwarktavern.co.uk

You can try your hand at the certifiably hokey London Dungeon "experience," or you can drink in Southwark Tavern's basement—a series of converted prison cells that exceed their original charm (then again, it often seems as if half the South Bank is a prison and the other half a brothel). The ground floor is your standard warm welcome with some surprises: would you like some quail eggs, ox cheek, or edamame with that pint?

i ◉*London Bridge. Exit down Borough High St.; the pub is where Southwark St. splits off. Quiz night on Tu. Pints £4. ☼ Open M-W 11am-midnight, Th-F 11am-1am, Sa 10am-1am, Su noon-midnight.*

MINISTRY OF SOUND

CLUB

103 Gaunt St.　　　　　　　☎087 0060 0010 www.ministryofsound.com

In club years, this staple of the EDM scene is ancient and has hosted world-famous DJs like Tiësto, Armin van Buuren, Afrojack, and Deadmau5 for over 20 years. Now, the scene is a mix of techno die-hards and dilettantes in Jeffrey Campbell high heels and plaid shirts that use the trance interludes to take selfies. Your music options are the main dance floor with go-go dancers, smoke hoses, and light shows; the smaller boutique floor on the second floor; the VIP lounge; and the outside patio that streams in music from the main floor.

i ◉*Elephant and Castle. Exit toward the roundabout, walk down Borough High St., and turn left onto Gaunt St. Cover £13-20; £5 discount with student ID. ☼ Open F 10:30pm-6am, Sa 11pm-7am. Weekday hours vary; check the website.*

South Kensington and Chelsea

◤ THE DRAYTON ARMS

PUB

153 Old Brompton Rd.　　　　　　　☎020 7835 2301 www.thedraytonarmssw5.co.uk

The Drayton Arms is a aesthete's pub, with a sun-catching wall of windows that breaks the mold of the typically dark and cloistered London joint. It's really the perfect mix between its post code (chandeliers and leather booths) and a liberal spirit (in-house theater and a not exclusively yuppie crowd). The theater is a rarity as well, hosting five nights a week of comedy, film, and drama in the evenings.

i ⊖*Gloucester Rd. Turn right onto Gloucester Rd. and right onto Old Brompton Rd. Theater productions Tu-Sa. Quiz night M (£1 buy-in). Pints around £3.70. Wine £4-7. Cocktails £6-7.* ⏰ *Open M-Sa noon-11pm, Su noon-10:30pm.*

THE TROUBADOUR CLUB

LIVE MUSIC, BAR

263-267 Old Brompton Rd.   ☎020 7370 1434 www.troubadour.co.uk

A Troubadour is a sublime thing to call an artist: it means a poet who puts lyric to music. But instead of merely a pretty name, this bar has earned its title, playing host to Bob Dylan, Joni Mitchell, Paul Simon, and Jimi Hendrix. More recently, it was the site of Adele's first gig. The adjacent bar and cafe is intimate with coffee cups and wine glasses hanging from the ceiling and a strip adjacent to the bar packed with aspiring artists themselves.

i ⊖*Gloucester Rd. Turn right onto Gloucester Rd., then right onto Old Brompton Rd. Live music most nights. Poetry night every other M. Friday shows 21+. Happy hour Tu-Su 8-9pm. Cover usually £6-12. Cash only.* ⏰ *Cafe open daily 9am-midnight. Live music M-W 8pm-midnight, Th-Sa 8pm-2am, Su 8pm-midnight.*

AZTECA LATIN LOUNGE

LATIN BAR

329 King's Rd.   ☎020 7352 4087 www.aztecalatinlounge.com

Azteca is a perfect cocktail itself. Mix together sultry Latin music, giant party drinks that serve four, salsa lessons, and cheap, delicious food. Within this absurdly colorful environment, Chelsea's residents swap chatting on bar stools with a pint in hand for shooting tequila on comfy couches.

i ⊖*Sloane Sq. It's a 10-15min. walk from the station, so you can also take bus #11 or 22. Salsa lessons Tu 7:30-8:30pm. Beer from £3. Cocktails from £6. Party cocktail (serves 4) £25.* ⏰ *Open M-Th 5pm-midnight, F-Sa 5pm-3am, Su 5pm-midnight.*

THE BLACKBIRD

PUB

209 Earl's Court Rd.   ☎020 7835 1855

The Blackbird is your friendly neighborhood pub with all of the infrastructural necessities: long bar, lots of booths, cheap drinks, soft rock, and healthy local contingent. The food runs the gamut from roasts to British staples and is served up quick. Stop here for a calm night instead of rushing to one of the self-proclaimed "local English pubs" to the east.

i ⊖*Earl's Court. Just across the road from the station, slightly to the right. Pints from £3.50.* ⏰ *Open M-W 8:30am-11pm, Th-Sa 8:30am-11:30pm, Su 8:30am-10:30pm.*

Hyde Park to Notting Hill

NOTTING HILL ARTS CLUB

CLUB

21 Notting Hill Gate   ☎020 7460 4459 www.nottinghillartsclub.com

As you burst forth into the club's urban grotto, you would never suspect its well-to-do neighborhood would condone such gritty revelry. The concrete walls reverberate hard-hitting techno as 18- to 25-year-olds kick back absinthe and dance precariously on the stage. Art installations include words projected onto the lounge couches,resulting in patrons' smiling faces imprinted with words like "sweet sounds memory" in a new level of Instagram nostalgia. Of course, you can always just have a pint and a conversation, but with the level of visual performance around here, relaxation is achieved more through sensory overload.

i ⊖*Notting Hill Gate. Walking up from the subway, it is on the right side of the road between two segments of the A204 (look for the large triangular crosswalks). The door isn't well marked, but look for the smoking area and metal fences keeping the entrance line in place. 18+, be sure to bring proof of age. Check the website beforehand for specific opening times and events. Cover varies, generally £5-8. Beer £3. Cocktails from £8.* ⏰ *Open M-W 7pm-2am, Th 7:30pm-2am, F 7pm-2am, Sa 8pm-2am, Su 6pm-1am.*

great britain

PORTOBELLO STAR
BAR

171 Portobello Rd.   ☎020 7229 8016 www.portobellostarbar.co.uk

The Portobello Star has gentrified itself from a old-timey, Modest Mouse "Float On" aesthetic to a yuppie affair, but the cocktails remain fearsomely good. We recommend taking a friend and splitting the strongest drink on the menu—the W11 Zombie (four types of rum, Pernod absinthe, and an exotic medley of passion fruit, grenadine, and pineapple; £15). Enjoy it as the DJ (posted at the bar with a laptop) spins pepped-up R&B and rock; take your drink to the back lounge room if the trussed-up crowd near the front starts networking too enthusiastically.

i ☻*Notting Hill Gate. Take a right onto Pembridge Rd., then a left onto Portobello Rd.Cocktails £7.50-15.* ☼ *Open M-Th 11am-11:30pm, F-Sa 11am-12:30am, Su 11am-11:30pm.*

PORTOBELLO GOLD
PUB

95 Portobello Rd.   ☎020 7229 8528 www.portobellogold.com

Portobello Gold is an old-fashioned pub with live music and a patronage that sings along to rock hits (and includes Bill Clinton). The front is your traditional, wood-paneled bar with pub-dwellers ranging from 18 to 80; the back is a sort of greenhouse, with candles and plants shielding patrons from prying eyes (although ears can pick up all manner of accents in this multi-culti bar). If you can wrangle it, try to snag the one table upstairs that overlooks the bar: romance personified.

i ☻*Notting Hill Gate. Turn right onto Pembridge Rd., then left onto Portobello Rd. Live music Su 7pm. Pints from £3.50. Wine £4-6.* ☼ *Open M-Th 9am-midnight, F-Sa 9am-12:30am, Su 9am-11pm.*

SUN IN SPLENDOUR
PUB

7 Portobello Rd.   ☎020 7792 0914 www.suninsplendourpub.co.uk

As the summer solstice nears, the apex of this fun pub is its secret beer garden (which sadly closes up shop when the sun does at 9:30pm). Otherwise, take a drink in the main room bedecked with wood-latticed windows, giant mirrors, gold chandeliers, and faux-distressed Victorian wallpaper. The crowd tends towards a mixed bunch of well-worn regulars, youth, and professionals that seem to all enjoy the electronic rock soundtrack in kind.

i ☻*Notting Hill Gate. Take a right onto Pembridge Rd., then a left onto Portobello Rd. Free Wi-Fi. Pints £4-6. Wine £3-6. Spirits from £3.* ☼ *Open M-Th noon-11pm, F 10am-midnight, Sa 9am-midnight, Su 10am-10:30pm.*

Marylebone and Bloomsbury

THE SOCIAL
BAR, CLUB

5 Little Portland St.   ☎020 7636 4992 www.thesocial.com

During the evening hours, the pubs of Bloomsbury play host to clutches of students waving about their pints with well-meant frivolity. The Social is a welcome energy outlet: downstairs, hip hop and dance music blasts through the quiet oeuvre of the alley. Upstairs, the intimate bar plays Motown numbers (quirkily enough, pictures of birds à la The Audobon Society lined the walls when we visited). Weekly events include Bashment, a Jamaican dance set on Wednesdays, and Hip Hop Karaoke on Thursdays.

i ☻*Oxford Circus. Turn right onto Regent St. then turn right onto Little Portland St. Live acts on the ground fl. most nights. Student cards will get you discounts on most covered nights. Cover £5-7. Pints £4-5. Cocktails £8.50.* ☼ *Open M-Sa noon-midnight, Th-Sa noon-1am.*

PURL
BAR

50/54 Blandford St.   www.purl-london.co.uk

Designed to look like an Al Capone speakeasy—interesting if only for the fact that Britain has never prohibited alcohol—Purl caters to a posh modern crowd

london

that's probably never broken a nail much less someone's legs. Sipped by patrons in the darkened, intimate labyrinth of nooks and crannies, the drinks are less a cobbling of lighter fluid and rubbing alcohol and more a creation from an MIT lab. Liquid nitrogen, ice cream, grape jelly, and candied bacon make appearances in the cocktails and work together splendidly (try the Corpse Reviver #1, which mixes grape jelly and blue cheese foam).

i ⊖*Bond St. Turn eft onto Oxford St. and right onto James St., which eventually turns into Thayer St. Then turn right onto Blandford St. Reservations recommended for tables; book online through the website. Cocktails £9-12. ☒ Open M-Th 5-11:30pm, F-Sa 5pm-midnight.*

THE GOLDEN EAGLE   PUB
59 Marylebone Ln.   ☎020 7935 3228

There are plenty of spots in London where leaning against the bar, tossing or flipping your hair with that devilish charm, and playing it cool is encouraged. Or you can do something truly spectacular and sing along with the boozy crowd to bespectacled Tony "Fingers" Pearson on the piano every Tuesday, Thursday, and Friday; have fun with old-timey hits that weren't old-timey when the crowd was your age. Given the cheap pints and your resulting inebriation, you just might be the one belting out tunes the loudest.

i ⊖*Bond St. turn right onto Oxford St. and left onto Marylebone Ln. Music Tu 8:30pm, Th-F 8:30pm. Pints £3.50-4. Wine from £3. ☒ Open M-Th 11am-11pm, F-Sa 11am-midnight, Su noon-7pm.*

THE FITZROY TAVERN   PUB
16A Charlotte St.   ☎020 7580 3714

By our count, there are at least 30 "oldest" pubs in London and dozens more that had famous patrons—although Britain's density of well-known thinkers and their personal drinking levels means that claim is a little less impressive. But the Fitzroy has some genuine history to keep the old and comedy shows to bring in the new. Dylan Thomas and George Orwell met here after work at the BBC, and the walls of the pub are lined with some hilarious memorabilia from the war (including a poster saying "We're here for the duration, we hope" and another one with a white box in a field of black that served as directions for finding the pub in a blackout).

i ⊖*Goodge St. Turn left onto Tottenham Ct. Rd., left onto Tottenham St., and left onto Charlotte St. Comedy night W 8:30pm. Pints around £2.50-3. Burgers from £6. ☒ Open M-Sa 11am-11pm, Su noon-10:30pm.*

SCALA   CLUB
275 Pentonville Rd.   ☎020 7833 2022 www.scala-london.co.uk

Repurposed from a cinema, this simply cool, four-level club has seen acts from Coldplay to The Scissor Sisters to Lionel Richie. The place is popular with a younger crowd that makes its presence known on the dance floor, and the older patrons congregate more toward the bar. Both dance floors are usually packed on a club night, but leave the high heels at home, as some patrons can be a bit over exuberant.

i ⊖*King's Cross St. Pancras. Head left when leaving the station. Cover varies, usually £8-16. Club nights F-Sa 10pm-4am or later. ☒ Opening hours depend on the night; check website for details.*

THE ROCKET   PUB
120 Euston Rd.   ☎020 7388 5796 www.therocketeustonroad.co.uk

This pub has shifted its clientele from primarily youngsters to a more professional/student mix. Inside, wrought iron chandeliers support multicolored light bulbs, and patrons pass barbs at each other near the warmly lit bar. Outside is a bit harsher, as the pub's location on Euston Rd. means that traffic and pedestrians streaming from King's Cross might put a damper on your night out with friends.

i ⊖*Euston. Make a left down Euston Rd. Pints around £3. Wine £3-5.* ☒ *Open M-W 11:30am-midnight, Th-F 11:30am-2am, Sa-Su 10am-2am.*

North London

🔲 69 COLEBROOKE ROW
BAR

69 Colebrooke Row · ☎075 4052 8593 · www.69colebrookerow.com

69 Colebrooke Row's advertising of the venue as "The Bar with No Name" sounds like a bad secondary title, yet the effort put into their mixology makes the hokeyness a bit more acceptable. Of the cocktails, we liked the "Death in Venice" (Campari with grapefruit bitters topped with prosecco). Popular among Islington yuppies and cocktail connoisseurs, the bar's vibe is saved from pretension by the impromptu ditties played by patrons on the upright piano.

i ⊖*Angel. Turn right after leaving the station and stay to the right as you pass Islington Green. Then turn right onto Colebrooke Row. It's number 69. Cocktails £9.* ☒ *Open M-W 5pm-midnight, Th 5pm-1am, F-Sa 5pm-2am, Su 5pm-midnight.*

SLIM JIM'S LIQUOR STORE
BAR

112 Upper St. · ☎020 7354 4364 · www.slimjimsliquorstore.com

It sounds like a convenience store that never has any cars parked in front of it, but it's actually an American dive bar with enough bras hanging from the ceiling to clothe a feminist commune (you can add yours if you'd like). A nice selection of bourbons and beers make this a solid option even if you don't have any particular love of rockabilly style.

i ⊖*Angel. Turn right and continue up Upper St. Bourbon and scotch £3-10. Pints from £3.75.* ☒ *Open M-W 4pm-2am, Th 4pm-3am, F-Sa noon-3am, Su noon-2am.*

East London

🔲 THE BOOK CLUB
BAR, CLUB

100 Leonard St. · ☎020 7684 8618 · www.wearetbc.com

We don't even want to know what a Book Club in this part of town would look like. Ironically reading Dan Brown? Commentary on how every Nicholas Sparks novel boils down to pretty people finding each other in the rain? Thankfully, this cafe/bar/lecture hall/dance club/art installation is more about how to live like F. Scott Fitzgerald than how to read him. During the week, events range from speed dating ("Are you a fan of Soviet-era film? Me too! Let's have sex. Capitalism hates sex."), drawing classes ("The body is merely a canvas for our pain."), and beer pong ("Alcohol!"). Thursday through Saturday are usually reserved for dancing the depression away.

i ⊖*Shoreditch High St. Make a left after leaving the station, then a right onto Great Eastern St., and a left onto Leonard St. Cover varies from free to £12; on most weekends, it's £5 after 9pm.* ☒ *Open M-W 8am-midnight, Th-F 8am-2am, Sa 10am-2am, Su 10am-midnight.*

🔲 STRONGROOM BAR
BAR

120-124 Curtain Rd. · ☎020 7426 5103 · www.strongroombar.com

Did you know that in order to be a "cool" bar, you have to be in an alleyway? So goes the East London nightlife scene, young imbiber. The Strongroom makes understandably less use of its dark, sparse indoors than the umbrella tables in the space between brick buildings. The crowd is a bit older than the expected cadre of "Dalston Superstars" but has some concessions, like a great series of cocktail options and late hours during the weekend.

i ⊖*Shoreditch High St. Make a left after leaving the station, then a right onto Great Eastern St., and a right onto Curtain Rd. Pints around £4.* ☒ *Open M 9am-11pm, Tu-W 9am-midnight, Th 9am-1am, F 9am-2am, Sa noon-2am, Su noon-10pm.*

london

CALLOOH CALLAY   BAR
    65 Rivington St.   ☎020 7739 4781 www.calloohcallaybar.com

After your first time trying Callooh Callay's cocktails, we bet you'll jabber away
to your friends about how the drinks are made of high-quality booze, are sometimes served ingramophones, and are perfectly titled for a Shoreditch crowd
like "Respect Your Elders." The Upstairs Bar isn't Lewis Carroll-themed (e.g.
you don't have to go through the looking glass to go to the bathroom), but rather
changes every six weeks from themes like "Dutch Gin House" and "Havana
Nights." The crowd tends to be a bit more upper crust than other places in the
area, but the chummy bartenders create a comforting den.

i ⊖*Old St. Make a right down Great Eastern Rd., then a left onto Rivington St. Cocktails £9.
Upstairs bar closed on M and Su. Make a table reservation if you don't want to stand at the bar.* 🕐
Open M-W 6pm-midnight, Th-Su 6pm-1am.

South London

🏴 **HOOTANANNY**   BAR, CONCERT VENUE
    95 Effra Rd.   ☎020 7737 7273 www.hootanannybrixton.co.uk

Hootananny during the day is a bit like what we'd imagine the downtime bar for
circus workers would be. For example, there are the swaths of fabric draped big
top-style in the back alcove, the red velvet booths, the pool tables, and the celebratory tone that the bright red house brings to the drab surrounding area—it's
as if something magical could happen anytime. Well, it *is* magical, as Hootananny hosts musicians and DJs playing everything from death disco to Central Asian
folk melodies—you can almost feel the East End's envy of authenticity.

i ⊖*Brixton. Make a left as you exit the station and continue on Effra Rd. as it forks off. 21+. Most
shows are free; occasional £5 cover. Shows W-Su start at 8 or 9pm. Beer from £3.80.* 🕐 *Pub open
M-W 3pm-midnight, Th 3pm-2am, F 3pm-3am, Sa noon-3am, Su noon-midnight. Hours vary*

West London

🏴 **DOVE**   PUB
    19 Upper Mall   ☎020 8748 9474

The only thing recognizing the existence of this bar to a Ulysses of pub crawls
is an arrow pointing into an alleyway near the Thames. Through the stone walls
lies the best riverside pub for the cheapest prices you're going to find in the city.
Another bonus is the fact that only locals frequent the Dove, and pints and comforting pub grub litters the tables as the conversation continues into the night. In
the summer, sit out on the river patio and try to snag a set in the upper balcony.

i ⊖*Ravenscourt Park. Make a left down Ravenscourt Rd., cross King St. (you'll need to go under
the road in the subway) onto Rivercourt Rd., and make a left onto Upper Mall. Pints around £4.* 🕐
Open M-Sa 11am-11pm, Su noon-10:30pm.

ARTS AND CULTURE

For both cultural connoisseur and dilettante, London offers a truly terrifying spectrum of performance art. With Shakespeare's word-smithing running through all of
the English language, the **Globe Theatre** pays due homage to the dramatic poet. The
theater scene then spreads to include musicals and their revivals, off-beat British
comedies, experimental works, and some celebrity showcases (staffed by a cadre
of British actors whose stage presence eclipses the film roles for which they're
generally known). But, of course, it's not all sitting in a dark auditorium in regulation
cocktail attire, for Britain is also known for its incredible rock music tradition. British singers and bands almost always begin their journey to stardom in the London
circuit of cafes and small performance venues. It's this divide between centuries-old
and seconds-old art that approximates a city—with its reliance on the past and the
contrarian reaction against it fighting each other on the battlefield of art.

great britain

Theater

Ah, "theatre" (thee-ya-tah) in London. The city is renowned for its affordable performances—tickets for big musicals in the **West End** can be had for as little as £25, a pittance compared to the $100 tickets sold on Broadway. In the West End, London's main theater district, you'll find big musicals that stay in residence at a single theater for decades. Other theaters put on more cutting-edge works. Many pubs have live performance spaces where theater groups rehearse and perform for audiences that, after a few pints, tend to find the second act more confusing than the first. Some churches, like St. Paul's in Covent Garden, host shows during the summer. Only buy discounted tickets from booths with a circle and check mark symbol that says **STAR** on it; this stands for the Society of Tickets Agents and Retailers, and it vouches for the legitimacy of a discount booth.

ROYAL COURT THEATRE · SOUTH KENSINGTON AND CHELSEA
Sloane Sq.   ☎020 7565 5000 www.royalcourttheatre.com

The Royal Court has built its reputation as the antidote to all the orchestral swoons and celebrity cameos sweeping through the West End. The Royal Court's 1956 production of John Osborne's *Look Back in Anger* (not to be confused with the Oasis song) is credited with single-handedly launching modern British drama. Royal is primarily writers' theater, purveying high-minded works for audiences that will appreciate them.

i ⊖Sloane Sq. Tickets M £10, Tu-Sa £12-28. Student discounts available on day of performance. ⟨⟩ Box office open M-F 10am-6pm or until the doors open, Sa 10am-curtain (if there's a performance).

THE NATIONAL THEATRE · THE SOUTH BANK
Belvedere Rd.   ☎020 7452 3400 www.nationaltheatre.org.uk

Okay, it looks a bit like a Kafkaesque prison, especially when the brutalist structure displays Helvetica advertisements for £12 Travelex tickets that can be seen from the other side of the river. Prison structure aside, the National Theatre's multiple stages host new and classic British drama, including many premieres, revived lost classics from around the world, and a standard repertoire of Chekhov and Ibsen.

i ⊖Waterloo. Turn right onto York Rd. and left onto Waterloo Rd. Tickets £12-44. ⟨⟩ Box office open M-Sa 9:30am-8pm, Su noon-6pm.

THE OLD VIC · SOUTH LONDON
The Cut   ☎0844 871 7628 www.oldvictheatre.com

This famous, stately theater was built in 1818 and has hosted the likes of Ralph Richardson and Laurence Olivier. Though showcasing a huge range of styles, the Old Vic focuses on the classics, including star-studded Shakespeare productions. Kevin Spacey—when he's not playing men in mid-life crises—serves as artistic director (and has since 2003).

i ⊖Southwark. Turn right onto The Cut. Tickets £11-52. ⟨⟩ Box office open M-Sa 10am-7pm on show days, 10am-6pm on non-show days.

SHAKESPEARE'S GLOBE · THE SOUTH BANK
21 New Globe Walk   ☎020 7401 9919 www.shakespearesglobe.org

There are definitely two tribes that attend Globe Performances: groundlings and non-groundlings. Since the Globe is a near replica of the original theater, an open roof and standing area are available for said "groundlings." An experience of being so close to the actors that you can see the spit fly from their perfectly dictating mouths, this special opportunity can be yours for £5. The other seats are spread across three semi-circled tiers around the stage, which can become fairly uncomfortable if you don't shell out for a cushion as well. The Globe stages works not only by the Bard, but also two new plays per season. Understandably

london

for an open-air theater, the season runs from Apr-Oct, although the recently opened Sam Wanamaker Playhouse hosts performances year-round.

i ⊖*Southwark. Turn left onto Blackfriars Rd., right onto Southwark St., left onto Great Guildford St., right onto Park St., then left onto New Globe Walk. Standing £5; seats £15-35, under 18 £12-32. ☼ Box office open M-Sa 10am-8pm, Su 10am-7pm.*

Cinema

London is teeming with traditional cinemas, the most dominant of which are **Cineworld** (www.cineworld.co.uk) and **Odeon** (www.odeon.co.uk). But the best way to enjoy a film is in one of the hip repertory or luxury cinemas like **Everyman** or **Curzon**. *Time Out* publishes showtimes, as does www.viewlondon.co.uk.

▧ BFI SOUTHBANK AND IMAX

SOUTH BANK

Belvedere Rd.   ☎020 7928 3232 www.bfi.org.uk

There are two reasons the BFI is awesome. First, it has the BFI Southbank, which is a champagne-drinking, bougie madhouse hidden under Waterloo Bridge. It showcases everything from early premieres to challenging foreign works and runs themed "seasons" that focus on the work of a particular director, cinematographer, or actor. Also, their Mediatheque is free and allows you to privately view films from their archives. The second reason is that the largest screen in all of Britain—the BFI IMAX—is just down the street, meaning you can see your favorite art house film and then catch the latest rock-'em-sock-'em comic book adaptation in a sensory overload chamber of win.

i ⊖*Waterloo. Follow the signs to either BFI Southbank (along the river) or the IMAX theater (so large you can't miss it). Note: you must go underground to reach the IMAX theater. Several exits spin off from it like wheel spokes. £11, concessions £8.50, matinee £6. ☼ Open daily 11am-11pm. Mediatech open Tu-F noon-8pm, Sa-Su 12:30-8:30pm.*

Comedy

The English are famous for their dry, sophisticated, and sometimes ridiculous ("We are the knights who say 'Ni!'") sense of humor. This humor thrives in the stand-up and sketch comedy clubs throughout the city. Check *Time Out* for listings, and be warned that the city virtually empties of comedians come August, when it's Fringe Festival time in Edinburgh.

▧ COMEDY STORE

THE WEST END

1A Oxendon St.   ☎0844 871 7699 www.thecomedystore.co.uk

Hands-down the most famous comedy venue in London, the Comedy Store made a name for itself in the'80s as a home for up-and-coming comedians like Jennifer Saunders, Dawn French, and Mike Myers (who was one of the founding members). Nowadays, visiting comics perform Thursday through Saturday, and the resident sketch-comedy team takes the stage on Wednesdays and Sundays. Tuesdays have stand-up on recent topical events, while the last Monday of the month hosts would-be comedians who are either encouraged or heckled by the audience. Famous comedians like Eddie Izzard have been known to pop in from time to time for impromptu performances.

i ⊖*Piccadilly Circus. Turn left onto Coventry, then right onto Oxendon. Tickets £14-20. ☼ Box office open M-Th 6:30-9:30pm, F-Sa 6:30pm-1:15am, Su 6:30-9:30pm. Doors open daily 6:30pm. Shows usually 8 and 11pm.*

Pop and Rock

Clubs are expensive, and many pubs close at 11pm. Especially given the current economic climate, fewer young people are willing to shell out £10-15 to get into a club, especially since beers inside cost an additional £4-5 apiece. To find the heart of London's nightlife, you have to scratch beyond the pub-and-club surface and head into the darkened basements of bars and seismically loud music clubs. With a history

great britain

of homegrown musical talent—including **The Rolling Stones, Radiohead,** and **The Clash,** all of the bands from the infamous **"British Invasion,"** and many of the best '90s pop groups—London's fantastic music scene goes way back. Today, it has all of the big name acts you'd expect a major city to draw, in addition to an underground focus on indie rock and a surprisingly ample dose of folk and blues.

🎵 KOKO   NORTH LONDON
1A Camden High St.   ☎0870 432 5527 www.koko.uk.com

Koko's isn't a typical rock and roll venue. Originally a theater, then a cinema, then one of the BBC's first broadcasting locations, and then the famous Camden Palace Nightclub, Koko holds a 110-year history within its music-soaked red walls and gilded balconies. Bringing in mostly big-name indie acts, along with some pop and rock acts (they've had everyone from Madonna to Usher to Justice), Koko is one of the premier venues in London. It also hosts an indie night with DJs and dancing on Friday.

i ⊖*Mornington Crescent. Turn right onto Hampstead Rd. Koko is on the right. Tickets sold online. Concerts £10-30. Beer £3.50-4. Cash only for in-person purchases.* 🕐 *Box office open M-Th noon-4pm, F noon-5pm.*

🎵 BORDERLINE   THE WEST END
Orange Yard, off Manette St.   ☎020 7734 5547 http://venues.meanfiddler.com/borderline/

This simple venue (which is also a fantastic club) lacks the outlandish Art Deco trappings of other London concert halls, but it oozes the spirit of rock and roll from every beer-soaked wall and ear-blowing speaker. Big-name artists often play the Borderline when starting solo careers. Townes Van Zandt played his last show here; Eddie Vedder, Jeff Buckley, and Rilo Kiley have played here; and **Spinal Tap** performed here right after the movie came out. The amps go up to 11, the music's piping hot, and the location is prime.

i ⊖*Tottenham Court Rd. Turn right onto Charing Cross Rd., and right onto Manette St. Tickets £3-30.* 🕐 *Doors open daily 7pm. Tickets available at the Jazz Cafe box office M-Sa 10:30am-5:30pm.*

HMV APOLLO   WEST LONDON
15 Queen Caroline St.   ☎020 8563 3800 www.hmvapollo.com

Like many of the big, architecturally stunning venues in London, the Art Deco HMV Apollo used to be a cinema. It was originally called the Hammersmith Odeon and was the site of Bruce Springsteen's 1975 concert film. It's also hosted big acts like Oasis, R.E.M., Elton John, the Rolling Stones, and even the Beatles.

i ⊖*Hammersmith. Apollo is opposite the Broadway Shopping Centre. There are plenty of signs leading to it. Call08448 44 47 48 for tickets. Ticket prices vary; check online for more info.* 🕐 *Box office open on performance days 4pm-start of the show.*

O2 ACADEMY BRIXTON   SOUTH LONDON
211 Stockwell Rd.   ☎020 7771 3000 www.o2academybrixton.co.uk

Home to Europe's largest fixed stage, the O2 Academy Brixton's set list is rife with the big names of our generation—past acts include MGMT, Morrissey, Pavement, LCD Soundsystem, and Wiz Khalifa. They also occasionally host club nights. You can also check the lineups at the other O2 Academies in Shepherd's Bush and Islington.

i ⊖*Brixton. Turn right onto Brixton Rd. and left onto Stockwell Rd. Ticket prices vary, generally £20-35. Pints £4. Bar cash only.* 🕐 *Box office opens 2hr. before doors on gig nights.*

Classical Music

🎵 ROYAL OPERA HOUSE   THE WEST END
Bow St.   ☎020 7304 4000 www.roh.org.uk

Admittedly, the glorious glass façade of the Royal Opera House makes it look like a train station (albeit a nice one). However, the only tracks running out of this Opera House are world-class arias. Tickets go on sale about two months before performances, and it's a good idea to book early. Or you can wait for standby tickets, which are offered 4hr. before performances for half price and are only £15 for students. The ROH also sponsors free outdoor film screenings. For information on dance performances at the ROH, see **Dance**.

i ⊖*Covent Garden. Turn right onto Long Acre, then right onto Bow St. Tickets £4-150.* ☼ *Box office open M-Sa 10am-8pm.*

THE LONDON COLISEUM   THE WEST END
33 St. Martin's Ln.   ☎0871 472 0600 www.eno.org

Home to the **English National Opera,** the London Coliseum showcases new, cutting-edge ballet and opera. They also perform unique reworkings of classic opera productions, like a version of Donizetti's *L'Elisir' Amore* set in a 1950s diner.

i ⊖*Charing Cross. Walk toward Trafalger Sq. on Duncannon St., turn right at the square onto St. Martin's Pl., and St. Martin's Ln. splits off to the right. Sometimes students and other concessions can get discounted tickets 3hr. before the performance. Tickets £15-90.* ☼ *Box office open M-Sa 10am-8pm on performance days, 10am-6pm on non-performance days.*

Jazz

⊠ RONNIE SCOTT'S   WEST END
47 Frith St.   ☎020 7439 0747 www.ronniescotts.co.uk

Ronnie Scott's has been defining "hip" in Soho for the last 51 years. It was the first British club to host American jazz artists, and everyone from Chick Corea to Tom Waits (ok, not jazz, but who's complaining?) has played here. The venue is all flickering candlelight and dulcet reds and blues. Black-and-white photos of jazz giants line the walls, and a diverse crowd imbibes cocktail creations like Jazz Medicine (Jägermeister, sloe gin, Dubonnet, fresh blackberries, and angostura bitters). Really, it's medicine to recover from the snooty expressions of West End clubbers that make them look like they've just been ill.

i ⊖*Tottenham Court Rd. Turn onto Oxford St. with your back to Tottenham Court Rd., then turn left onto Soho St., right into the square, and right onto Frith St. Cover £10, more for big acts. Cocktails £8.50-9.* ☼ *Open M-Sa 6pm-3am, Su noon-4pm and 6:30pm-midnight. Box office open M-F 10am-6pm, Sa noon-5pm.*

SHOPPING

London is one vital quarter of the "Paris, New York, Tokyo, London" list that most major designers plaster on their store windows. Of course, most European capital high streets have some mix of Valentino, Burberry, and Hermes, so we'll skip to the singular: **Harrods** and **Harvey Nichols.** These megalithic department stores cater to the upper classes (the royal classes are more the custom-made type). It's not all for McQueen and the Queen, though—Soho is full of vintage clothing stores and independent record shops. The East End (when not tacitly ignoring its Urban Outfitters) is a reliable source of fun boutiques. As the eponymous movie showcases, Notting Hill has a gauntlet of secondhand shops. And for those who can't break in a city without scouring a bookstore, London has a litany of quirky independent retailers that round out the major chains like Waterstone's and Daunt.

Bookstores

⊠ JOHN SANDOE BOOKS   SOUTH KENSINGTON AND CHELSEA
10 Blacklands Terr.   ☎020 7589 9473 www.johnsandoe.com

Undaunted by his father's vocal disapproval, John Sandoe founded this independent bookstore in 1957, and the bohemian writerly crowd of Chelsea adored it. Today, besides the modish, pretty covers that are hand-selected by edition, the store retains old-fashioned charm antithetical to the somewhat sterile displays at Waterstone's. Books are piled up on the sides of the staircase, moving shelves

great britain

in the back leave more space for books, and the staff have read almost every title in stock.

i ⊖*Sloane Sq. Exit the Tube and go straight down Sloane Sq. Veer left onto King's Rd., and turn right at Blacklands Terr.* ⏰ *Open M-Tu 9:30am-5:30pm, W 9:30am-7:30pm, Th-Sa 9:30am-5:30pm, Su noon-6pm.*

▥ SKOOB
MARYLEBONE AND BLOOMSBURY
66 The Brunswick, off Marchmont St.   ☎020 7278 8760 www.skoob.com

Evol: a palindromic ode to this secondhand bookstore that lionizes the written word. Amid the Brunswick complex—a series of stores posher than the next—walk down Skoob's stairs and prepare to be confronted with an astoundingly complete collection (unlike some secondhand bookstores, where there are only 10 copies of *Wuthering Heights* because no one liked it). Whether travel, science fiction, crime fiction, literary criticism, poetry or mathematics beckons to your sensibilities, expect to walk out pounds lighter and heavier.

i ⊖*Russell Sq. Turn right and then left up Marmont St. Skoob is at the far end of Brunswick, on the right.* ⏰ *Open M-Sa 10:30am-8pm, Su 10:30am-6pm.*

Music

▥ MUSIC AND VIDEO EXCHANGE
HYDE PARK TO NOTTING HILL
42 Notting Hill Gate   ☎020 7221 2793 www.mgeshops.com

Music and Video Exchange will provide hours (if not days) of entertainment to any audiophile. The staff engage in constant *High Fidelity*-esque conversations and practically ooze musical knowledge, while customers browse through vinyl, CDs, and cassettes in the bargain area. Upstairs in the rarities section, you can find anything from a £12 original vinyl of the Rolling Stones's *Get Yer Ya-Ya's Out!* to the original German sleeve for the Beatles's *Let it Be*. Customers can trade their own stuff in exchange for cash or—in a move betraying MVE's cold-hearted understanding of a music-lover's brain—twice the cash amount in store vouchers.

i ⊖*Notting Hill Gate. Walk out of the south entrance of the Tube and go down Notting Hill Gate.* ⏰ *Open daily 10am-8pm.*

▥ SISTER RAY
THE WEST END
34-35 Berwick St.   ☎020 7734 3297 www.sisterray.co.uk

An old-school record shop of the best kind, Sister Ray's stellar staff is adept at creating musical matches made in heaven. Hip, cheap books about music line the check-out counter, and listening stations are located throughout the store. And when they're not selling £500 special edition LPs, the prices are quite cheap. The store also buys, so if you want to sell your classic punk records to fund the next leg of your vacation, this is the place for you.

i ⊖*Tottenham Court Rd. Turn left onto Oxford St., left onto Wardour St., and left onto Berwick St.* ⏰ *Open M-Sa 10am-8pm, Su noon-6pm.*

THE SCHOTT MUSIC SHOP
THE WEST END
48 Great Marlborough St.   ☎020 7292 6090 www.schottmusic.co.uk

Opened in 1857, Schott is the oldest sheet music shop in London. This quiet, spacious store sells everything from the Beatles to Bartók. The expert staff is the type that knows not only all of the pieces but also different recordings and can help recommend the best. Especially notable for music-starved travelers are the three **practice rooms** beneath the shop (each with a baby grand Steinway) available to rent by the hour.

i ⊖*Oxford Circus. Turn left onto Regent St. and left onto Great Marlborough St. 10% student discount on print music. Practice rooms £10 per hr. before noon, £12 per hr. noon-6pm, £15 per hr. after 6pm.* ⏰ *Open M-F 10am-6:30pm, Sa 10am-6pm.*

london

Markets

BOROUGH MARKET
Southwark St.

THE SOUTH BANK
www.boroughmarket.org.uk

Even though the advent of globalization has removed any excuse for horrible British food, it's still a stereotype that proves true. And if you come from a culture where fresh produce is taken for granted (basically any other culture), Borough Market is your gateway ticket to fresh French cheeses, English strawberries that wouldn't be caught dead in a Tesco's, and baked goods that were made for high tea. You can spend days (three per week to be precise) browsing the stalls, or you can pick the "I'm feeling lucky" option and take a break at one of the cafes and restaurants that share the space.

i ✪London Bridge. Exit the Tube and walk down Southwark St. away from the river. The market is on the right, starting where Southwark St. and Borough High St. split off. ⏰ Open Th 11am-5pm, F noon-6pm, Sa 8am-5pm.

Department Stores

HARRODS
87-135 Brompton Rd.

SOUTH KENSINGSTON AND CHELSEA
☎020 7730 1234 www.harrods.com

Pick your favorite trappings of capitalism. You can choose spectacle—the sight of thousands of tourists and the upper classes looking at the soles of Christian Louboutins and slipping on Helmut Lang. Or perhaps status symbols would suffice, for what will make you evolutionarily desirable more than casually buying a Patek Phillipe? As they say, you just hold onto it for the next generation. Let's be real, though: unless you're a mogul/celebrity/smuggler, it's going to be the awesome food section, with rooms devoted to chocolate, unpronounceable wine, tea, etc., that seems attainable (and you get to eat away the pain of poverty).

i ✪Knightsbride. Take the Harrods exit. ⏰ Open M-Sa 10am-8pm, Su 11:30am-6pm.

ESSENTIALS

Practicalities

For all the hostels, cafes, museums, and bars we list, we know some of the most important places you visit during your trip might actually be more mundane. Whether it's a tourist office, free Wi-Fi hotspot, or post office, these practicalities are vital to a successful trip, and you'll find all you need right here.

- **TOURIST OFFICES:** The main central tourist office in London is the Britain and London Visitor Centre (BLVC). (1 Regent St. www.visitbritain.com *i* ✪Piccadilly Circus. ⏰ Open Apr-Sept M 9:30am-6pm, Tu-F 9am-6:30pm, Sa-Su 10am-4pm; Oct-Mar M 9:30am-6:30pm, Tu-F 9am6pm, Sa-Su 10am-4pm.) Also useful is the London Information Centre. (Leicester Sq. ☎020 7292 2333 www.londoninformationcentre.com *i* ✪Leicester Sq. ⏰ Open daily 8am-midnight.)

- **TOURS:** Original London Walks offers walking tours with themes like "Jack the Ripper" and "Harry Potter." (☎020 7624 9255 www.walks.com *i* £9, students and over 65 £7.)

- **CURRENCY EXCHANGE:** Thomas Cook. (30 St James's St. ☎084 5308 9570 ⏰ Open M-Tu 10am-5:30pm, Th-F 10am-5:50pm.)

- **CREDIT CARD SERVICES:** American Express (www.amextravelresources.com) has locations at 78 Brompton Rd. (☎084 4406 0046 *i* ✪Knightsbridge. ⏰ Open M-Tu 9am-5:30pm, W 9:30am-5:30pm, Th-F 9am-5:30pm, Sa 9am-4pm) and 30-31 Haymarket. (☎084 4406 0044 *i* ✪Piccadilly Circus. ⏰ Open M-F 9am-5:30pm.)

- **GLBT RESOURCES:** The official GLBT Tourist office offers information on everything from saunas to theater discounts. (25 Frith St. www.gaytouristoffice.co.uk *i* ✪Leicester Sq.) Boyz

great britain

(www.boyz.co.uk) lists gay events in London as well as an online version of its magazine. Gingerbeer (www.gingerbeer.co.uk) is a guide for lesbian and bisexual women with events listings. *Time Out London's* magazine and website (www.timeout.com/london) also provide a good overview of the city's GLBT establishments and the city in general.

- **TICKET OFFICES:** Albermarle of London agency provides official tickets for all major West End theater productions. Book tickets via web, phone, or visiting the office. (5th fl., Medius House, 63-69 New Oxford St. ☎020 7379 1357 www.albemarle-london.com ☒ Open M-F 8am-8:30pm, Sa 8:30am-8pm, Su 10am-6pm.)

- **INTERNET:** Wi-Fi abounds in this technologically advanced city. Most cafes provide internet access. Chains like Starbucks (www.starbucks.co.uk) and McDonald's (www.mcdonalds.co.uk) almost always have free Wi-Fi. Other chains with Wi-Fi include the Coffee Republic (www.coffeerepublic.co.uk), Wetherspoon (www.jdwetherspoon.co.uk), Pret a Manger (www.pret.com), COSTA (www.costa.co.uk), and Caffé Nero (www.caffenero.co.uk). Public areas also have Wi-Fi. The area between Upper Street and Holloway Road, also known as The Technology Mile, is the longest stretch of free internet in the city.

- **POST OFFICES:** Trafalgar Square Post Office. (24-28 William IV St. ☎020 7484 9305 *i* ⊖Charing Cross. ☒ Open M 8:30am-6:30pm, Tu 9:15am-6:30pm, W-F 8:30am-6:30pm, Sa 9am-5:30pm.)

Emergency

- **EMERGENCY NUMBER:** ☎999.

- **POLICE:** City of London Police. (37 Wood St. ☎020 7601 2455 ☒ Open M-F 7:30am-7:30pm.) Metropolitan Police. (☎030 0123 1212)

- **RAPE CRISIS CENTER:** Solace. (136 Royal College St. ☎0808 802 5565 www.rapecrisis.org.uk)

- **HOSPITALS/MEDICAL SERVICES:** St. Thomas' Hospital. (Westminster Bridge Rd. ☎020 7188 7188) Royal Free Hospital. (Pond St. ☎020 7794 0500) Charing Cross Hospital. (Fulham Palace Rd. ☎020 3311 1234) University College Hospital. (235 Euston Rd. ☎0845 155 5000)

Getting There

By Plane

London's main airport is **Heathrow** (LHR ☎0844 335 1801 www.heathrowairport.com), commonly regarded as one of the world's busiest airports. The cheapest way to get from Heathrow to central London is on the Tube. The two Tube stations servicing Heathrow form a loop at the end of the Piccadilly line, which runs to central London. (☒ 1hr.; every 5min. M-Sa 5am-11:54pm, Su 5:46am-10:37pm.) **Heathrow Express** (☎084 5600 1515 www.heathrowexpress.com) runs between Heathrow and Paddington station four times per hour. The trip is significantly shorter (though comparably pricier) than many of the alternatives, clocking in at around 15-20min. (*i* £20 when purchased online, £25 from station. ☒ 1st train departs daily around 5:10am.) The **Heathrow Connect** also runs to Paddington but is cheaper and takes longer, since it makes five stops on the way to and from the airport. There are two trains per hour, and the trip takes about 25min.

The **National Express bus** (☎08717 818 178 www.nationalexpress.com) runs between Victoria Coach Station and Heathrow three times per hour. Though cheap and often simpler than convoluted Underground trips, the buses are subject to the travails of London traffic. Posing a similar traffic threat, **taxis** from the airport to Victoria cost around £60 and take around 45min. In short, they aren't worth it.

london

Getting to **Gatwick Airport** (LGW ☎0844 335 1802 www.gatwickairport.com) takes around 30min., making it less convenient than Heathrow but less hectic, too. The swift and affordable train services that connect Gatwick to the city make the trip a little easier. The **Gatwick Express** train runs non-stop service to Victoria station. You can buy tickets in terminals, at the station, or on the train itself. (☎0845 850 1530 www.gatwickexpress.com *i* 1-way £19.90; 2-way £34.90. Round-trip ticket valid for a month. ☼ First train at 3:30am, then 4:30am, then every 15min. from 5:00am-11:45pm., then last trains at midnight and 12:30am.)

National Express runs buses from the North and South terminals of Gatwick to London. The National Express bus (☎0871 781 8178 www.nationalexpress.com) takes approximately 1½hr., and buses depart for London Victoria hourly. Taxis take about 1hr. to reach central London. **easyBus** (☎084 4800 4411 www.easybus.co.uk) runs every 15min. from North and South terminals to Earls Court and West Brompton. (Tickets from £2. ☼ 65min., every 15min.)

By Train

Europeans are far ahead of Americans in terms of train travel, and London offers several ways to easily reach other European destinations. Multiple train companies pass through the city. The biggest are **Eurostar** (☎08432 186 186 www.eurostar.com), which travels to Paris and Brussels, and **National Rail** (☎08457 48 49 50 www.nationalrail. co.uk), which oversees lines running throughout the United Kingdom. Train travel in Britain is generally reliable but can be unreasonably expensive. Booking tickets weeks in advance can lead to large savings, but spur-of-the-moment train trips to northern cities could cost more than £100.

By Bus

Bus travel is another (frequently cheaper) option. **Eurolines** (☎08717 818 181 www. eurolines.co.uk ☼ Open 8am-8pm) is Europe's largest coach network, servicing 500 destinations throughout Europe. Many buses leave from **Victoria Coach Station**, at the mouth of Elizabeth St. just off Buckingham Palace Rd. Many coach companies, including National Express, Eurolines, and Megabus, operate from Victoria Coach. National Express is the only scheduled coach network in Britain and can be used for most intercity travel and for travel to and from various airports. It can also be used to reach Scotland and Wales.

Getting Around

Though there are daily interruptions to Tube service, the controlling network, Transport of London, does a good job of keeping travelers aware of these disruptions to service. Each station will have posters listing interruptions to service, and you can check service online at www.tfl.gov.uk or the 24hr. travel information service (☎0843 222 1234). The website also has a journey planner that can plot your route using any public transport service ("TFL" is a verb here). Memorize that website. Love that website. Though many people in the city stay out into the wee hours, the Tube doesn't have the same sort of stamina. When it closes around midnight, night owls have two choices: cabs or night buses.

Travel Passes

Travel passes are almost guaranteed to save you money. The passes are priced based on the number of zones they serve (the more zones, the more expensive), but Zone 1 encompasses central London, and you'll rarely need to get past Zone 2. If someone offers you a secondhand ticket, don't take it. There's no real way to verify whether it's valid—plus, it's illegal. Under 16s get free travel on buses. Passengers ages 11-15 enjoy reduced fares on the Tube with an Oyster Photocard. Students18 and older must study full-time (at least 15hr. per week over 14 weeks) in London to qualify for the Student Photocard, which enables users to save 30% on adult travel cards and bus passes. It's worth it if you're staying for an extended period of time (study abroad kids, we're looking at you).

Oyster cards enable you to pay in a variety of ways. Fares come in peak (M-F 6:30-9:30am and 4-7pm) and off-peak varieties and are, again, distinguished by zone. Oysters let you "pay as you go," meaning that you can store credit on an as-needed basis. Using an Oyster card will save you up to 50% off a single ticket. Remember to tap your card both on entering and leaving the station. You can use your card to add Travelcards, which allow unlimited travel on one day. This will only be cost-effective if you plan to use the Tube a lot. They cost £8.80 for anytime travel or £7.30 for off-peak travel. You can top up your Oyster at one of the infinite off-licences, marked by the Oyster logo, that are scattered throughout the city.

Season Tickets are weekly, monthly, and annual Travelcards that work on all public transport and can be purchased inside Tube stations. They yield unlimited (within zone) use for their duration. (*i* Weekly rates for Zones 1-2 £30.40, monthly £116.80.)

By Underground

Most stations have Tube maps on the walls and free pocket maps. The Tube map barely reflects an above-ground scale, though, and should not be used for even the roughest estimation of walking directions (seriously). Platforms are organized by line and will have the colors of the lines serviced and their names on the wall. The colors of the poles inside the trains correspond with the line, and trains will often have their end destination displayed on the front. This is an essential service when your line splits. Many platforms will have a digital panel indicating ETAs for the trains and sometimes type and final destination. When transferring within a station, just follow the clearly marked routes.

The Tube runs from Monday to Saturday from approximately 5:30am (though it depends on the station and line) until around midnight. If you're taking a train within 30min. of these times (before or after), you'll want to check the signs in the ticket hall for times of the first and last train. The Tube runs less frequently on Sunday, with many lines starting service after 6am. Around 6pm on weekdays, many of the trains running out of central London are packed with the after-work crowd. It's best to avoid these lines at this time of day.

You can buy tickets from ticket counters (though these often have lines at bigger stations) or at machines in the stations. You need to swipe your ticket at the beginning of the journey and then again to exit the Tube. Random on-train checks will ask you to present a valid ticket to avoid the £80 penalty fee (reduced to £40 if you pay in under 21 days).

The Overground is a new addition to the London public transportation scene. It services parts of the city past Zone 1, where Tube lines are sparse, and is particularly useful in East London. Fares and rules are the same as the Tube; you can just think of it as another line, except with a better view.

By Bus

While slower than the Tube for long journeys (thanks to traffic and more frequent stops), buses are useful for traveling short distances covered by a few stops (and several transfers) on the Tube.

Bus stops frequently post lists of buses servicing the stop as well as route maps and maps of the area indicating nearby stops. These maps are also very helpful for finding your way around a neighborhood. Buses display route numbers.

Every route and stop is different, but buses generally run every 5-15min. beginning around 5:30am and ending around midnight. After day bus routes have closed, night buses take over. These typically operate similar routes to their daytime equivalents, and their numbers are usually prefixed with an N (N13, for instance). Some buses run 24hr. services. If you're staying out past the Tube's closing time, you should plan your night bus route or bring cab fare. (Single rides £2.40, Oyster card £1.40.)

london

oxford

Oxford has prestige written all over it. This city is home to the oldest university in the English-speaking world, and over the course of nearly 1,000 years, it has educated some of the most influential players in Western civilization. Students around the globe aspire to join the ranks of Adam Smith, Oscar Wilde, Stephen Hawking, and Bill Clinton—not to mention 26 British prime ministers and 12 saints.

But if you can't join them, you might as well visit them. The city has plenty to entertain travelers of all persuasions: stunning college courtyards, centuries-old pubs, leafy river paths, occasionally rowdy clubs, and shops aplenty. During term time, rub shoulders with Oxford's thousands of students; in the summer, the colleges empty, and the city fills with photo-hungry tourists and eager summer-school imports. Either way, you can expect to be in the comradely company of students and budget travelers—don't panic if one or two of them actually refer to you as "comrade."

Unlike Cambridge, though, Oxford does not hold its time-resistant bubble for long. Once you get outside of the center's ancient streets and medieval architecture, the city comes (surprisingly) close to a modern metropolis. Don't limit yourself to the sights you've seen on postcards—the town rewards those willing to take the short trek to the outlying neighborhoods or venture down its tiny, twisting side streets.

ORIENTATION

Carfax, at the crossroads of Oxford's main shopping district, is the pulsing heart of the city. **High Street, St. Aldate's, Cornmarket Street,** and **Queen Street** all converge by the Town Hall to create a tourist-mobbed area—beware of the stampede of gaping cameras and more-than-over-eager parents who will callously trample you as potential competition. Most of the university's best-known colleges are located along High St. and the parallel roads to the north and south, with **Christ Church** around the corner on St. Aldate's. The bus station is in the eastern corner of Carfax, following the direction of **Queen Street,** while the train station is a bit farther in the same direction, across the river.

If you walk north up **Saint Giles** (Cornmarket St. becomes Magdalen St., which then turns into St. Giles), then make a left onto **Little Clarendon Street,** you'll reach **Jericho.** Home to the Oxford Canal, the Oxford University Press, and vibrant nightlife, this is Oxford's up-and-coming bohemian neighborhood. The main Jericho drag, **Walton Street,** runs off of Little Clarendon.

On the other side of the city center, down the hill and across Magdalen Bridge, is the **Cowley Road** neighborhood, centered around the eponymous street and home to numerous ethnic eateries and local pubs, which offer a nice change of pace from blue-blooded, tourist-jammed Oxford.

SIGHTS

Most people come to admire Oxford's dozen or so aesthetically pleasing colleges, and we advise you to look at the university's free info booklet, which details all of the colleges' opening hours and admission fees. You can find it on the university's website (www.ox.ac.uk) under "Visiting the University." However, due to conferences, graduations, and general eccentricity, the hours open to tourists might change without further notice, like your favorite bureaucratic Kafka novel. If you're traveling by yourself, you shouldn't have a problem getting admitted, but as a tour group size increases, you might have to book a Blue Badge tour through the Tourist Information Centre (TIC). One of the best ways to get into the colleges for free—especially during term-time—is to attend a church service in the college chapels. Show up 15min. before a service starts and tell the people at the gate that you'd like to attend; they'll usually let you in for free.

get a room!

Compared to Cambridge, Oxford has a surprisingly good selection of budget accommodations. Establishments are clustered around the train station and on **Iffley Road;** the former are closer to town and the city's nightlife, but the latter are in a quieter and more sedate area near the shops and cafes on Cowley Rd. You can also visit **www.letsgo.com** for more Let's Go recommendations.

🏨 CENTRAL BACKPACKERS   HOSTEL $
13 Park End St.   ☎01865 242 288 www.centralbackpackers.co.uk

True to its name, this hostel is not only central but also filled with friendly backpackers excited to experience the latter part of Oxford's "think and drink" culture. The rooftop garden is a lovely anomaly in the hostel scene, and the rooms are clean and not cramped. The clubs on the street level don't stop believing until 3am. However, you can usually find a group to tag along with and partake in the libations yourself.

i From the train station, follow Botley Rd. east toward the town centre; 12-bed dorms £20; 8-bed £21; 6-bed women-only £22; 4-bed £24. ☑ Reception open 8am-11pm.

Attractions

🏛 ASHMOLEAN MUSEUM   MUSEUM
Beaumont St.   ☎01865 278 000 www.ashmolean.org

The Ashmolean befits its dual honors of being the oldest university museum in the world and the most smorgasbordy collection in the UK (that's just our own award). While the British Museum is great for a survey of colonialism, the Ashmolean tries to work within a world narrative by organizing their collection into equal parts "Eastern," "Western," and "West meets East." As befits a university museum, the exhibits are highly educational; well-organized displays teach you about everything from the consolidation of northern European tribes to the decipherment of ancient Aegean scripts. As you feast on knowledge in this ivory tower, you can also feast on food, as the Ashmolean has Oxford's only rooftop restaurant.

i From Carfax (at the west end of High St.), head up Cornmarket St., then turn left onto Beaumont St. Free lunchtime gallery talks for 1st 12 who express interest Tu-F 1:15-2pm; pick up tokens at the information desk. Special exhibits £5-6. ☑ Open Tu-Su 10am-6pm.

📚 BODLEIAN LIBRARY   LIBRARY
Broad St.   ☎01865 277 178 www.bodleian.ox.ac.uk

The Bodleian is one of the greatest libraries in the world, holding millions of volumes, including the normal trifecta of rare manuscripts (Shakespeare's First Folio, the Gutenberg Bible, and the Magna Carta). However, there are also some neat deep cuts, like the oldest copy of The Song of Roland, the earliest surviving work of French Literature, and the Huntington MS 17, which is not a type of rifle but rather the oldest printing of the gospels in the West Nile dialect of Bohairic. The complex of 17th-century buildings surrounding the courtyard are impressive enough to justify the visit, but if you want to experience some inevitable Harry Potter déjà vu, you can take a tour. All tours go to the Divinity School, the oldest teaching room in the university; longer ones take you to the gorgeously ancient Reading Room and by the rotund Radcliffe Camera (a vital part of every TV serial that takes place in the city).

i Entrances on Broad St., Catte St., and Radcliffe St.; take Catte St. off High St. Entrance to the courtyard free. Entrance to Divinity Hall £1. 30min. tour of Library and Divinity Hall £5, 1hr. tour £7, extended tour £13. Audio tour £2.50. ☑ Open M-F 9am-5pm, Sa 9am-4:30pm, Su 11am-5pm.

oxford

THE PITT RIVERS MUSEUM

MUSEUM

Park Rd.　　　　　　　　　　　　　　　☎01865 270 927　www.prm.ox.ac.uk

There's no such thing as referencing colonialism too many times, so we're going to breach it once more. While not every one of the thousands of artifacts in Oxford's archaeological and anthropological museum was acquired by colonial shopping at a 1000% discount, at least they're not exploiting the items that were (admission is free). From macabre shrunken heads to provocative fertility statues, razor-like samurai swords to practical Maori spears, real Inuit furs to golden feathered cloaks, every shelf in every glass case teems with fresh wonders of the creativity and ingenuity of the human species. In classic Victorian style, every case is arranged not by culture, as is now the norm, but by theme, which brings the wonderfully stark comparisons to the dim, somber light around you. Giving you just enough information to whet your appetite for travel, understanding, and worldly experience, this is a must for any globetrotter.

i *From High St., take Catte St., which becomes Parks Rd. Walk through the Museum of Natural History on the right. Tours W 2:30 and 3:15pm. Audio tour £2. Free.* ☑ *Open M noon-4:30pm, Tu-Su 10am-4:30pm.*

MODERN ART OXFORD

GALLERY

30 Pembroke St.　　　　　　　　　　☎1865 722 733　www.modernartoxford.org.uk

Oxford's entire appeal is founded on the fact that it is not modern *at all*. It's such a creature of the past that you can barely go for a meal, drink, or piss without finding out that Tolkien ate, drank, and pissed there, too. That's why this is your antidote to leaving the town covered in a thin film of historical dust. The museum rotates exhibits that are equal parts bizarre and incomprehensible: documentary films on things you didn't even know you were interested in, strange series of short film collages, sculptures without plaques. Unlike the other Oxford museums, which justify their exhibits by over-explaining, the Modern Art museum justifies itself by not, and thus allows the visitor's mind to wander creatively.

i *From Carfax, walk down Queen St. Turn left onto St. Ebbe's St. Turn left onto Pembroke St. The gallery is on the left. Check online for current exhibits and night events. Bar open on event nights. Free.* ☑ *Open Tu-W 10am-5pm, Th-Sa 10am-7pm, Su noon-5pm.*

CARFAX TOWER

TOWER

Junction of St. Aldate's, Cornmarket, High, and Queen St.　　　　　☎01865 792 633

This was the site of the former City Church of Oxford (St. Martin's Church). However, in 1896, university leaders decided that the bulk of the church needed to be demolished in order to make room for more traffic in the downtown area. Given the stagnant mass of tourist crowds that now mill around it below, that was probably a bad move. Despite its name sounding like an auto insurance price quote company, it actually comes from the French *carrefour*, or "crossroads," which makes sense, as the tower marks the official center of Oxford. To prevent the Tower of Babel II (and thus more linguistic majors), no building in the city center may be taller; this means that from the top, you get an extraordinary view over the university's spires.

i *£2.20, under 16 £1.10.* ☑ *Open daily Apr-Sept 10am-5:30pm; Oct 10am-4:30pm; Nov-Mar 10am-3:30pm.*

OXFORD CASTLE

CASTLE

44-46 Oxford Castle　　　　　　☎01865 260 666　www.oxfordcastleunlocked.co.uk

Sometimes disappearing down a dark passageway while following an underpaid, faux-torch-bearing actor is exactly what the doctor ordered. Oxford Castle will remind you that this hasn't always been the safe student haven it is today. A shot of medieval intrigue and a sudden understanding of the immense past behind every street corner can finely tune your appreciation for Oxford (even if it is done in costume and outrageously overacted bits). Life was tough, no question.

great britain

People were thrown into dungeons, hanged, murdered, tortured, and even brought back from the dead—all slightly more fun than clubbing in Cambridge.

i Directly behind the Castle St. bus stop. Tours approximately every 20min. £9.25, students £7.25. ☼ Open daily 10am-5pm; last tour 4:20pm.

Colleges

☒ CHRIST CHURCH   COLLEGE
St. Aldate's   ☎01865 276 492 www.chch.ox.ac.uk/college

Oxford's most famous college has the university's grandest quad and some of its most distinguished alumni. During the English Civil War, "The House" was home to Charles I and the royal family, who retreated to the Royalist-friendly university during Cromwell's advance (and, when the city came under threat, escaped dressed as servants). Speaking of "Off with their heads," the college is also notable as the place where Lewis Carroll first met Alice—the young daughter of the college dean. More recently, exploits in fantasy include the *Harry Potter* films, as some of the scenes were shot in the dining hall and central quad. For the Dark Ages version of magic, come here for Evensong to take a gander at the college for free and to experience the wonderful choir. Later on in the evening, listen for Great Tom, the seven-ton bell that has been rung 101 times (the original number of students/dalmatians) every evening since 1682 at 9:05pm to mark the original undergraduate curfew. And they say we live in an over-personalized age now. Today, it merely ushers in the beginning of an all-nighter sponsored by Red Bull, the internet, and shame.

i Down St. Aldate's from Carfax (at the west end of High St.). Depending on season £7-8.50, concessions £5.50-7. ☼ Open M-Sa 10am-4:30pm, Su 2-4:30pm. Evensong daily 6pm.

MAGDALEN COLLEGE   COLLEGE
High St.   ☎01865 276 000 www.magd.ox.ac.uk

Magdalen is spelled differently from its Cambridge counterpart, but pronounced in the same manner (MAUD-lin). With its winding riverbanks, flower-filled quads, and 100-acre grounds, Magdalen is possibly Oxford's most attractive college. The contrast between the medieval quad and the 18th-century New Building (where C.S. Lewis lived) also makes for some impressive architectural observations. Magdalen boys have traditionally been quite a catch—the college has housed seven Nobel Prize winners, Dudley Moore, and Oscar Wilde—so put your wooing cap on. The college also has a pleasant deer park, where equally attractive deer have grazed aimlessly for centuries.

i At the east end of High St., by the river. £5, concessions £4. ☼ Open Jul-Sept daily noon-7pm; Oct-Jun 1-6pm or dusk.

BALLIOL COLLEGE   COLLEGE
Broad St.   ☎01865 277 777 www.balliol.ox.ac.uk

Along with Merton and University, Balliol, founded in the 1260s, has a legitimate claim to being the oldest college in Oxford. Renowned for its PPE subject (Politics, Philosophy, and Economics), Adam Smith, Aldous Huxley, Christopher Hitchens, three British prime ministers, and six members of the Obama administration were produced from Balliol's mismatched spires. Its grounds feel impressively medieval, complete with crenellated parapets surrounding the first court (for a less intimidating view, go through the hedges on the right-hand side, past the first court, for a picturesque garden).

i From Carfax (at the west end of High St.), take Cornmarket St., then turn right onto Broad St. £2, students £1. ☼ Open daily 10am-5pm or dusk.

oxford

MERTON COLLEGE
COLLEGE

Merton St.   ☎01865 276 310   www.merton.ox.ac.uk

Though Balliol and University were endowed before it, Merton has the earliest formal college statutes (1274), which helps to legitimize its boast of being the oldest college. Its traditions and high-achieving student body also give it a nerdy reputation. For example, the annual Time Ceremony has students dance around the Fellows Quad in full regalia, drinking port in celebration of the end of British Summer Time. JRR Tolkien was the Merton Professor of English here and spent his time casually inventing the Elvish language and writing a well-received minor trilogy on the side. The college's 14th-century Mob Quad is Oxford's oldest and one of its least impressive, while the nearby St. Alban's Quad is home to some of the university's best gargoyles.

i *From High St., turn down Magpie Ln., then take a left onto Merton St. £3. ☒ Open M-F 2-5pm, Sa-Su 10am-5pm.*

ALL SOULS COLLEGE
COLLEGE

Corner of High St. and Catte St.   ☎01865 279 379   www.all-souls.ox.ac.uk

Despite its misleadingly inclusive name, this is the most exclusive school of the Oxford lot, and its entrance exam is considered to be the world's hardest (although the Kobayashi Maru is the universe's). Only a few dozen rise to the annual challenge; one past prompt was"Does the moral character of an orgy change when the participants wear Nazi uniforms?" Answer: if Prince Harry is there, no. Finalists are then invited to a dinner, where the dons confirm that they are "well-born, well-bred, and only moderately learned." Ultimately, anywhere from zero to two graduate fellowships are offered each year (and include the great state architect T.E. Lawrence and great architect Christopher Wren). A walk around the college itself is one of quiet beauty and stony regality.

i *Entrance to the right of Catte St. from High St. Free. ☒ Open Sept-Jul M-F 2-4pm.*

FOOD

Here's one major perk of visiting a student town: **kebab trucks.** These student favorites line High St., Queen St., and Broad St. (we recommend Hassan's on Broad St.), and stay open until 3am during the week and 4 or 4:30am on weekends.

▨ THE VAULTS AND GARDEN
CAFE $$

St. Mary's Church, Radcliffe Sq.   ☎01865 279 112   www.vaultsandgarden.com

In the summer, this garden is hands-down the best place for lunch in the entire city. Based out of the University Church of St. Mary the Virgin, the large garden offers picturesque views of the Bodleian Library, Radcliffe Camera, and nearby colleges. You can even stretch out and soak up the sun on picnic blankets while enjoying the Brideshead life (although the emphasis is less on champagne and strawberries than on scones and tea). Notwithstanding, the eponymous vaults are a worthy consolation prize if rain reigns. The organic, locally sourced menu changes daily, with fresh salads, sandwiches, and soups, as well as coffee, yogurt, and pastries.

i *Turn up St. Mary's Passage off Queen St. or High St. 10% student discount. Lunch entrees £7-10. Tea items £2.20 each. ☒ Open daily 8:30am-6:30pm.*

GEORGINA'S
CAFE $

Avenue 3, The Covered Market   ☎01865 249 527

Hiding above the furor of the Covered Market sits this fantastically unpretentious coffee shop. The old movie posters papering the ceiling and the cluttered seating arrangements ensure that you can lounge here comfortably while tackling a large-portioned meal. If you need a solid breakfast after a regrettable late-night kebab run, their custom omelettes (£4.75) are a solid victory in the eternal struggle against hangover.

i From Carfax, walk down High St. Turn right and enter the Covered Market. Go onto Avenue 3 and look for a staircase about halfway down. Tends to be full or nearly full from noon-1pm. Bagels, ciabatta, and panini £3.20-3.95. ☒ Open M-Sa 8:30am-5pm.

THE EAGLE AND CHILD   PUB $
49 St. Giles'   ☎01865 302 925
This pub was a favorite watering hole of JRR Tolkien, C.S. Lewis, and the group of writers who dubbed themselves the "Inklings." However, while visiting a bar that a serial alcoholic like George Orwell or Charles Bukowski frequented is a legitimate chance to channel their energy, it's harder to link the author of "Mere Christianity" with a drinking establishment. This brick and wood pub is now more of a tourist destination than a charming bar, although the booths at the front can shield you from cameras and hushed awe.

i From Carfax (at the west end of High St.), follow Cornmarket St., which becomes St. Giles'. Sandwiches £5.75-9.75. Burgers £8-11.50. ☒ Open M-Th 11am-11pm, F-Sa 11am-midnight, Su noon-10:30pm.

ATOMIC BURGER   BURGERS $$
96 Cowley Rd.   ☎01865 790 855 www.atomicburger.co.uk
This funky, outer space-themed restaurant offers a pop culture laden litany of delicious burgers, sides, shakes, and drinks. You can blow out your brain's capacity *Hitchhiker's Guide*-style with Zaphod's Flaming Gargleblaster Margherita (tequila, triple sec, and absinthe; £7.50) or *Pulp Fiction*-style with a Big Kahuna burger. The inside of the restaurant looks like the bedroom of a child yearning to be an astronaut (or that of an adult with arrested development), but the joint is so earnestly not self-conscious that it makes you forget the heavy use of Comic Sans.

i Follow High St. past Magdalen College and across Magdalen Bridge and head down Cowley Rd. All burgers come with a free side. 10% discount on takeout. Gluten-free options, vegetarian options. Burger with 1 side £6.75-9.25. ☒ Open M-F noon-10:30pm, Sa-Su 10am-10:30pm.

FREUD   CAFE, BAR $
119 Walton St.   ☎01865 311 171 www.freud.eu
We're pretty sure there's nothing in *Interpretation of Dreams* that explains what drinking and dancing in a cathedral means. Regardless of the inexplicable premise, Freud inhabits the vaulted interior of a 19th-century Greek Revival church, stained glass and all—if it wasn't for the cafe tables on the portico outside, you'd never guess that this place serves food. The cafe progresses into a cocktail bar at night, with a DJ on the weekends. That may explain the disco ball, but it doesn't make the presence of a cocktail menu above a church pew any more comprehensible.

i From the train station, follow Botley Rd. toward the town center, bear left onto Hythe Bridge St., then left onto Worcester St., which becomes Walton St. Freud is on the right, next to Radcliffe Infirmary. Sandwiches and pizza £5.50-8. Appetizers and snacks £1.75-4.50. Cocktails £6-7. ☒ Open M 5pm-midnight, Tu 5pm-1am, W 10:30am-1am, Th-Sa 10:30am-2am, Su 10:30am-midnight. Kitchen open daily until 10pm.

NIGHTLIFE

If the London clubbing scene is a nice Talisker, Oxford is a fair glass of Pinot Blanco, and Cambridge is a paper bag that once had Rubinoff and now has piss in it. Point being, nightlife here doesn't incur the excitement of London, but it could be much, much worse. The main clubbing area in Oxford is near the train station, on **Park End** and **Hythe Bridge Streets**. Both of these split off from **Botley Road** (the train station's home). The center of town has little in the way of dancing, but its many excellent pubs are perfect for a more laid-back evening.

▨ PURPLE TURTLE UNION BAR
BAR, CLUB

Fewin Ct.   ☎01865 247 007 www.purpleturtlebar.com

Prepare yourself for claustrophobic tunnel vision as you consume enough flaming absinthe shots to become the green fairy incarnate. This underground bar is directly under the Oxford Union Debating Society, and true to form, you're probably going to host the largest internal debate of your life when trying to decide which one of the 40 shooter options (based on the personalities of the different colleges) is really you. We're going to put on our Sorting Hat and recommend the Slytherin shooter (green absinthe, apple sours) regardless. The dance floor can get a bit insanely cramped, but the DJs spin with a deft hand.

i From Carfax, walk down Cornmarket St. Turn left onto Frewin Ct. Beer from £2. Shooters £2.50. Shots from £1.50. ⏰ Open M-Sa 8pm-3am, Su 8pm-2am.

▨ THE BEAR INN
PUB

6 Alfred St.   ☎018 6572 1783 www.bearoxford.co.uk

The Bear may be the oldest pub in Oxford—the current building was built in the 18th century, but previous incarnations go all the way back to 1242 (and since bears in Oxford went extinct in the 10th century, who knows?). Anyway, the pub does show its age with low ceilings and rickety stairs that make it slightly perilous for the tall and/or clumsy patron. But don't let this put you off; the Bear is a great, unfussy place to enjoy a pint. The ties in the display cases have been given in exchange for half pints and hail from clubs and colleges around the world.

i Off High St., just behind Christ Church. Pub quiz Tu 8:30pm. Live music W 9pm. Pints £3.50. ⏰ Open M-Th 11am-11pm, F-Sa 11am-midnight, Su 11:30am-10:30pm.

THE KING'S ARMS
PUB

40 Holywell St.   ☎018 6524 2369 www.kingsarmsoxford.co.uk

The King's Arms embraced only men from 1607-1973, and as befits an old-guard vestige of the patriarchy, there are enough leather-bound booths and pervasive whiffs of mahogany to sufficiently prove its masculinity. However, the various traditional rooms don't ooze the fabricated pubbiness of the chains, and it's no surprise that professors sometimes hold office hours here. Brass tacks, it's on students' list of reliable pubs to hit when a Royal Baby is born, when Andy Murray wins Wimbledon, or when anything that will make day-drinking more excusable occurs.

i Across the street from the Bodleian Library. On the corner between Holywell St. and Park St. Beer from £3.40. ⏰ Open daily 10:30am-midnight. Kitchen open until 9:30pm.

JERICHO TAVERN
PUB, LIVE MUSIC

56 Walton St.   ☎018 6531 1775 www.thejerichooxford.co.uk

Radiohead debuted here back in 1984; since then, Jericho Tavern has been sold and bought, remodeled and rebranded, but has always remained an indie favorite and a good spot to find live music in Oxford. The heated outdoor beer garden is also a plus, especially if you get a Fruli Strawberry Beer (or, you know, something less girly) to enjoy out there. There's live acoustic at 8pm on Sundays, and board games are available for further entertainment.

i From Carfax, walk north on Cornmarket St., which becomes Magdalen St. Turn left onto Beaumont St., then right onto Walton St. The tavern is near the Phoenix Picturehouse. Pints around £3.50. ⏰ Open M-F noon-midnight, Sa 11am-midnight, Su noon-midnight. Kitchen closes at 10pm.

THE CELLAR
LIVE MUSIC

Frewin Ct.   ☎018 6525 0181 www.cellaroxford.co.uk

"Underground" music is one of those phrases that is immediately coded as"-furtive," "obscure," and "authentic." But the Cellar brings it back to its roots by being very obviously underground, with tunnels echoing the newest, boldest rock groups and alternative DJs. Going through phases of greatness and less-than-greatness over the last few years, the Cellar is on the upswing again, clinging to its independent identity and subterranean culture. In other words, it has not sold out like the Bridge (which joins artists to corporations, obviously).

i *From the Town Center, walk down Cornmarket St. Turn left onto Frewin Ct. Check events online. Cover £5-12. ♨ Open M-Sa 10pm-3am, Su 10pm-2am.*

ARTS AND CULTURE

OXFORD PLAYHOUSE   THEATER
11-12 Beaumont St.   ☎01865 305 305 www.oxfordplayhouse.com

Known to locals as "The Playhouse," this independent theater hosts student and amateur dramas, contemporary dance and music, comedy, lectures, and poetry. Whether it's Philip Pullman and Neil Gaiman chatting or a production staged completely in the dark, whatever event is on will not be your average sit-and-pretend-to-appreciate-theater experience. In the summer, the theater puts on Shakespeare performances in the quad in front of the Bodleian Library (and also hosts Globe Theatre touring companies, meaning a trip to London is not necessary).

i *Down Beaumont St. from the Ashmolean Musem. Ticket prices vary. Advance concessions £2 off. Student standbys available day of show for £9.50. ♨ Box office open M-Sa 10am-6pm or until 30min. after curtain, Su from 2hr. before curtain to 30min. after (performance days only). Cafe open 10am-11pm (closes at 5:30pm on non-performance nights).*

ESSENTIALS
Practicalities

- **TOURIST OFFICES:** The Tourist Information Centre (TIC) provides the free "What's On In Oxford" guide, sells discounted tickets to local attractions, and books rooms with a 10% deposit. (15-16 Broad St. *i* From Carfax, take Cornmarket St., then turn right onto Broad St. ☎01865 252 200 www.visitoxford.org ♨ Open M-Sa 9:30am-5pm, Su 10am-4pm. Closes 30min. earlier in winter.)

- **STUDENT TRAVEL OFFICES:** STA Travel. (Threeways House, 36 George St. *i* From Carfax, take Cornmarket St. Turn left onto George St. The office is on the right. ☎0871 702 9839 www.statravel.co.uk ♨ Open M 10am-6pm, Tu-Th 9am-7pm, F 10am-7pm, Sa 10am-6pm, Su 11am-5pm.)

- **TOURS** :The official Oxford University Walking Tour leaves from the TIC and provides access to some colleges otherwise closed to visitors. The 2hr. tours are capped at 19 people and are booked on a first-come, first-served basis. You can get tickets up to 48hr. in advance at the TIC, by phone,or online. (☎01852 726 871, ☎01865 252 200 to book tickets www.visitoxford.org *i* £8, children £4.50. ♨ Tours daily in summer 11am and 1pm (additionally 10:45am and 2pm on Sa). Themed tours, like the C.S. Lewis, Harry Potter and J.R.R. Tolkien Tours run on a varied schedule; check with the TIC. (*i* £15, concessions £10.)

- **CURRENCY EXCHANGE:** Banks line Cornmarket St. Marks and Spencer has a bureau de change with no commission. (13-18 Queen St. *i* From Carfax, walk down Cornmarket St. M&S is on the right. ☎01865 248 075 ♨ Open M-W 8:30am-6:30pm, Th 8:30am-7:30pm, F 8:30am-6:30pm, Sa 8:30am-6:30pm, Su 11am-4:30pm.) There is also a bureau de change with no commission attached to (but not affiliated with) the TIC.

- **INTERNET:** Free at Oxford Central Library; however, there is often a wait during prime hours. Some stations are open to pre-booking if you know exactly when you'd like to use it. (Westgate *i* From Carfax, walk down Queen St. The library is ahead. ♨ Open M-Th 9am-7pm, F-Sa 9am-5:30pm.) Offered for free at most cafes in the area.

oxford

- **POST OFFICE:** 102-104 St. Aldate's. (☎01865 513 25 postoffice.co.uk *i* From Carfax, take St. Aldate's. Bureau de change inside. ☑ Open M-Sa 9am-5:30pm.

Emergency

- **EMERGENCY SERVICES:** In any emergency, dial ☎999.

- **POLICE:** On the corner of St. Aldates and Speedwell St. (St. Aldates ☎08458 505 505 ☑ Open 24hr.)

- **HOSPITALS/MEDICAL SERVICES:** John Radcliffe Hospital. (Headley Way ☎01852 741 166 *i* Bus #13 or 14.)

Getting There

Botley Road Station (Botley Rd., down Park End St. ☎01865 484 950 ☑ Ticket office open M-F 5:45am-8pm, Sa 7:30am-8pm, Su 7:15am-8pm) receives trains from: **Birmingham** (₤34 ☑ 1hr., every 30min.); **Glasgow** (₤116 ☑ 5-6hr., every hr.); **London Paddington** (₤23.40 ☑ 1hr., 2-4 per hr.); and **Manchester** (₤62.80 ☑ 3hr., 2 per hr.).

By Bus

Gloucester Green Station is the city's main bus station. The Oxford Bus Company (☎01865 785 400 www.oxfordbus.co.uk) runs the **Oxford Express** (*i* Free Wi-Fi. ₤14, students ₤11 ☑ 1½hr., every 15-30min.) and the **X70 Airline** runs from Heathrow Airport. (*i* Free Wi-Fi. ₤23. ☑ 1½hr., every 30min.) It also runs the **X80 service** from Gatwick Airport. (*i* Free Wi-Fi. ₤28 ☑ 2½hr., every hr.) It's best to book tickets in advance on the Oxford Bus website. The **X5 bus** connects Oxford with Cambridge. (*i* Free Wi-Fi. ₤12.50 ☑ 3¼hr., every 30min.)

Getting Around

By Bus

Oxford Bus Company (☎01865 785 400 www.oxfordbus.co.uk) provides service throughout the city. Fares vary depending on distance traveled. (*i* Day Pass ₤4, weekly pass ₤14.) Weekly passes can be purchased at the Oxford Bus Company Travel Shop. (*i* 3rd fl. of Debenham's department store, on the corner of George St. and Magdalen St.☑ Open M-W 9:30am-6pm, Th 9:30am-8pm, F 9:30am-6pm, Sa 9am-6pm, Su noon-4pm.) **Stagecoach** (☎01865 772 250 www.stagecoachbus.com) also runs buses in the city and to some surrounding villages. One-way tickets within the city usually cost ₤1.80. Buy a pass for a week of riding within Oxford for ₤16. Be careful when buying Day Passes because they don't apply to both companies. For real-time information on buses in Oxford, use www.oxontime.com, which will also text you the schedule.

By Taxi

Call **Radio Taxi**(☎01865 242 424) or **ABC** (☎01865 770 077) for taxis. There are taxi ranks at Oxford Station, Saint Giles, Gloucester Green, and in the evening at Carfax. Taxis may be hailed in the street.

By Bike

You can rent some wheels at **Cyclo Analysts.** (150 Cowley Rd. ☎01865 424 444 www.oxfordcycles.com *i* Includes lock. ₤10, 2 days ₤18, 3 days ₤24, every additional day ₤3. ☑ Open M-Sa 9am-6pm, Su 10am-4pm.)

great britain

cambridge

Eight centuries of history, 31 colleges, and the energy of a living university town, all in one easily accessible package. It was here that James Watson and Francis Crick (with the oft-forgotten Rosalind Franklin's help) discovered the double helix, Sir Isaac Newton deduced gravity, Lord Byron and John Milton wrote their famous poetry, and 🖼Winnie-the-Pooh was born. The city is dominated by its eponymous university; the school's medieval buildings line the winding streets, and every pub, club, and cafe seems to exist to serve students. If you're looking for the definitive Cambridge experience, try the "P and P" formula: Punting and Pimm's—in American, boating and boozing. This is best done in the summer, when the banks of the Cam turn green and flowers bloom in the college gardens, but to get a sense of the real Cambridge, you'll have to come during term-time, when the town fills with its 18,000 students.

ORIENTATION

With just two avenues—and helpful maps galore—Cambridge is relatively easy to navigate. The main shopping street starts at **Magdalene Bridge,** north of the River Cam, and appears alternatively as Bridge St., Sidney St., St. Andrew's St., Regent St., and Hills Rd. The other principal thoroughfare begins at **Saint John's Street** (just off Bridge St.), and becomes Trinity St., King's Parade, and Trumpington St. To get into town from the Drummer St. bus station, take **Emmanuel Road,** which leads to St. Andrew's St. and a bank-heavy block with loads of ATMs. To get to the center of town from the train station, follow **Station Road,** turn right onto Hills Rd., then follow it straight until it becomes St. Andrew's St. in the town center. The River Cam runs along the northern and western edges of the city center.

SIGHTS

Cambridge is quite different from Oxford—its "peer institution"—in that the colleges are more homely, with a few grandiose exceptions like King's and Trinity. We've listed our favorites below, but all the city-center colleges are beautiful (the "new," 20th-century colleges can be skipped), but if you're only in town for a few days,you can take a punt and see six or seven of them from behind in one go. The town itself—which is a sight in its own right—has the close-to-the-ground feel of an agricultural market (quite a contrast from Oxford's warren of gothic castles). As for the museums, most showcase what Cambridge is famous for: excellence in the sciences, from the poles of botany to engineering.

🖼 KING'S COLLEGE
King's Parade

COLLEGE

☎01223 331 100 www.kings.cam.ac.uk

Founded by Henry VI in 1441, King's College was the feeder school for Eton until it relaxed its admission policy in 1873 and reluctantly began to accept students from vastly inferior schools like Harrow. These days, King's draws more students from state schools than any other Cambridge college, and it has gained a reputation as the most socially liberal of the institutions. Still, you wouldn't guess that from the massive buildings and the rolling grounds that scream privilege. Catch a look from the other side of the river to see the college in all its glory, then come visit the Gothic King's College Chapel, where spidering arches and stunning stained glass will wow even the most church-weary tourist. King's alumni include John Maynard Keynes, E.M. Forster, and Salman Rushdie.

i *King's Parade is the western of the city center's 2 main avenues, the northern continuation of Trumpington St. £7.50, concessions and ages 12-18 £5, under 12 free.* 🕓 *Open during term time M-F 9:45am-3:30pm, Sa 9:30am-3:15pm; outside of term time M 9:45am-4:30pm, Tu-Su 9:30am-5pm. During term time, Evensong in chapel M-Sa 5:30pm; Su Eucharist 10:30am, Evensong 3:30pm.*

TRINITY COLLEGE
COLLEGE

Trinity Ln. ☎01223 338 400 www.trin.cam.ac.uk

Welcome to the largest and richest college in Cambridge. Glib descriptions attribute its founding to Henry VIII, but it was really Catherine Parr who persuaded the ornery king to create a new college instead of destroying the whole Oxbridge system monastery-style. Now, Trinity is famous for its illustrious alumni, which include literati Dryden, Byron, Tennyson, and Nabokov; atom-splitter Ernest Rutherford; philosopher Ludwig Wittgenstein; and Indian statesman Jawaharlal Nehru. The epically beautiful Great Court is the world's largest enclosed courtyard—and also the track for young runners who attempt to beat the 12 strikes of the clock in under 43 seconds as shown in Chariots of Fire (even though it was filmed at Eton). The supposed great-great grandchild of the apple tree that inspired Issac Newton's theory of gravity stands near the gate; in the north cloister of nearby Neville's Court, Newton calculated the speed of sound by stamping his foot and timing the echo. In less practical exercises, Lord Byron used to bathe nude in the college's fountain and kept a pet bear because college rules forbade cats and dogs. The Wren Library houses alumnus A.A. Milne's handwritten copies of Winnie-the-Pooh and Newton's personal copy of his Principia. Trinity also has punts, available for rent by the river near Garret Hostel Ln.

i *Turn left off Trinity St. onto Trinity Ln. £3, children £1.50. Punts £14 per hr. with £40 deposit.* ☉ *Courtyard open daily 10am-4:30pm. Wren Library open M-F noon-2pm. Hall open 3-5pm. Punts available spring-summer M-F 11am-5:30pm, Sa-Su 10am-5:30pm.*

THE FITZWILLIAM MUSEUM
MUSEUM

Trumpington St. ☎01223 332 900 www.fitzmuseum.cam.ac.uk

This grandiose revivalist museum has the variety of the British Museum without the crushing realization that all of the exhibits came about directly via colonialism (then again, an argument can be made for structural violence in the case of the absurdly wealthy British collector who started the museum). Loosely centered around "art and antiquities," the collection hosts a fearsome selection of Italian and French painters; Greek and Middle Eastern pottery; Egyptian sarcophagi; and illustrated medieval manuscripts. On the more modern side of things, there are some excellently preserved works by Thomas Hardy and Virginia Woolf as well.

i *Free. Audio tours £3, students £2. Guided tours £4.* ☉ *Open Tu-Sa 10am-5pm, Su noon-5pm. Guided tours depart from the courtyard entrance Sa at 2:30pm.*

ST. JOHN'S COLLEGE
COLLEGE

St. John's St. ☎01223 338 600 www.joh.cam.ac.uk

The motto of St. John's—*"souvent me souvient"*—is a triple pun, and none of them have to do with souvenirs. One meaning is "Often I remember," which is appropriate given that the college celebrated its quincentennial in 2011. William Wilberforce, William Wordsworth, Sir Cecil Beaton, and Douglas Adams are only a few of the students that have studied here through its history. A second meaning of the slogan is "Think of me often"—not difficult when considering the gorgeous chapel, Bridge of Sighs, or the 93ft.-long Fellows' Room where some of the D-Day planning happened. St. John's is also associated with its choir, which has been singing Evensong for over 300 years. The final pun is "I often pass beneath it," which could possibly be interpreted now as snooty Trinity College rivals passing by while humming "We'd Rather Be at Oxford than St. John's" (sung to the tune of "She'll Be Coming 'Round the Mountain").

i *Head north on Sidney St., which becomes Bridge St. Take a left onto St. John's St. £5, ages 12-17 £3.50, under 12 free.* ☉ *Open daily Mar-Oct 10am-5:30pm; Nov-Feb 10am-3:30pm.*

great britain

MAGDALENE COLLEGE
COLLEGE

Magdalene St.   ☎01223 332 100 www.magd.cam.ac.uk

Magdalene College (pronounced MAUD-lin) was not only purposely built on the other side of the river in order to protect its Benedictine monks from the town's licentious crowd, but it was also the last Oxbridge college to admit women in 1988 (students protested vigorously by wearing black armbands). This is all a bit strange given the college's namesake, Mary Magdalene, and the fact that they host the most lavish May Ball every year (it's also the only college that insists on a white tie dress code). Academically, it's famous for the Pepys Library, which holds some of the diaries of C.S. Lewis, who, though an Oxford man, occasionally lived in Magdalene. The long riverfront area behind the main courtyards is technically closed to visitors, but some travelers report that if you look like a student—and act like you know what you're doing—it's possible to stroll unbothered along the willow-lined path.

i Walk south down Huntington Rd. as it changes into Castle St., then into Magdalene St. Free. 🅾 Open daily until 6pm. Library open daily Apr 20-Aug 31 11:30am-12:30pm and 2:30-3:30pm; Oct 6-Dec 5 2:30-3:30pm; Jan 12-Mar 13 2:30-3:30pm.

WHIPPLE MUSEUM OF THE HISTORY OF SCIENCE
MUSEUM

Free School Ln.   ☎01223 330 906 www.hps.cam.ac.uk/whipple

The trope of "Oxford for humanities, Cambridge for sciences" goes a long way to explain the focus of this museum. Robert Whipple donated a collection of 1000 scientific devices to the university, and many of these are on display here. Newer additions include the Gömböc (a mathematically precise object that rolls to the same resting position no matter where you place it) and Fred, a 19th-century anatomical model whose parts have been mercilessly scattered across the mu-

---

get a room!

Budget lodging options in Cambridge are notoriously bad, as people who come to visit or live here either fall into the categories of "student with pre-arranged dorm room" or "parent with some dough to burn." There are few affordable rooms near the town center, and overpriced, occasionally sketchy bed and breakfasts fill the area to the north and south of town. In particular, B&Bs cluster on **Arbury Road** and **Chesterton Road** to the north; several can be found close to the station on **Tenison Road.** Bus #1 goes between Tenison Rd. and the town center, while bus #2 serves Chesterton Rd. When the university is not in session, many of the colleges offer their rooms (generally called "digs") at competitive prices (usually £30-70 for a single); check www.cambridgerooms. co.uk for more information. For more recommendations, visit **www.letsgo.com.**

LYNWOOD HOUSE
B&B $$$$

217 Chesterton Rd.   ☎01223 500 776 www.lynwood-house.co.uk

This recently renovated B&B traded in predictable floral motifs that commonly grace Victorian hotels for a bolder, modern theme. The rooms are nice, large, and well designed, with rich, tasteful color combinations and great furnishings. Though Lynwood House is a bit to the north of the city center, there's a convenient cluster of pubs and stores nearby.

i From the town center, take either Victoria Ave. or Bridge St., then turn right onto Chesterton Rd. Free Wi-Fi and ethernet. Breakfast included. Ensuite bathrooms. Often 2-night min. stay. Check website for details. Singles £65-85; doubles £85-120.

cambridge

seum. Several intriguing planetariums, some microscopes and telescopes, and a wealth of pocket calculators round out the quirkily fascinating collection.

i Turn left off St. Andrew's St. onto Downing St. Follow it until it becomes Pembroke and turn right onto Free School Ln.Free. 🕒 Open M-F 12:30-4:30pm.

CHRIST'S COLLEGE COLLEGE

St. Andrews St.   ☎01223 334 900   www.christs.cam.ac.uk

"Tempered to the Oaten Flute / Rough Satyrs danced and fauns with cloven heel" would be an epic testimonial on the "Is Christ's College Right For You?" admissions page. And indeed, that was how John Milton—called by his friends "The Lady of Christ's"—described the college in *Lycidas*. A portrait and bust in the Great Hall pay homage to Milton and another of Christ's famous alums: Charles Darwin, who didn't lionize the college nearly as much. Sacha Baron Cohen also graduated from Christ's, so we all look forward to the day when a picture of Borat will adorn the wall.

i Continue north on Hills Rd. until it turns into Regent St., then into St. Andrew's St. Free. 🕒 Open daily 9:30am-noon.

JESUS COLLEGE COLLEGE

Jesus Ln.   ☎01223 339 339   www.jesus.cam.ac.uk

Yes, it's hard to keep all of the colleges straight when the names are only variations on a New Testament theme. A good memory aide is to think of Jesus being tempted to stay hours in this college's 25 acres of lovely gardens and courts. Keep an eye out for some strange art installations that include the annual Sculpture in the Close (when we visited, it was 10 mannequins re-enacting a crime scene). Attracting an eclectic set, the college's alumni include Thomas Cranmer, Samuel Taylor Coleridge, and Nick Hornby.

i Go north on Sidney St. and turn right onto Jesus Ln. Free. 🕒 Open daily 8am-dusk.

FOOD

For a "college town," Cambridge has more upscale dining options than off-licenses and supermarkets. However, there are a number of cheap cafes that can set you up with a meal for less than £5. The summer months see students camping out on one of the "Pieces" with wine and sandwiches or strolling the streets with wine and ice cream cones.

THE EAGLE PUB $$

8 Bene't St.   ☎01223 505 020

Even though Cambridge students might roll their eyes at this pub's high tourist profile, it remains genuine enough to still draw crowds of locals. Why the fame? It's a veritable monument to life and death. On February 28, 1953, Francis Crick and James Watson burst into the Eagle to announce their discovery of the "secret to life"—the double helix. And toward the back, look for the messages and squad numbers that RAF men scorched into the ceiling on the evenings before piloting missions during World War II. For your hopefully less dramatic purposes, the bar adds to its storied charm with affordable alcohol and classics of the pub food genre—sausage and mash, a slab of a burger and chips, or a steaming steak and ale pie.

i Heading south on King's Parade, turn left onto Bene't St. Entrees £8-14. Pints around £3.50. Credit card min. £5. 🕒 Open M-Sa 10am-11pm, Su 11am-10:30pm.

STICKYBEAKS CAFE $

42 Hobson St.   ☎01223 359 397   www.stickybeakscafe.co.uk

There's something beautiful about a cafe that provides all of the white, blinding modern vibe of a gallery while serving you gourmet food as well. The menu items here are a bit fancier than your average ham and cheese toast (think more continental, like bruschetta and olives), but you can nab some heartier breakfast staples for cheap prices if you're not satisfied with the usual hostel corn flakes and toast.

i Hobson St. splits off to the right of Sidney St., next to Christ's College. Breakfast dishes £1.50-3. Lunch dishes £4.50-7. ☼ Open M-F 8am-5:30pm, Sa 9am-5:30pm, Su 10am-5pm.

DOJO'S NOODLE BAR
ASIAN $

1-2 Millers Yard ☎01223 363 471

The closest a dignified Cambridge student is going to come to a real dojo is in a Pokémon game, but the only things getting beaten to death in this establishment are noodle puns (place settings are bordered with "Noodfucius," little words of wisdom). Every imaginable Asian noodle dish is served here: Japanese, Chinese, Thai, and Malaysian are all fair game. The quick service, large portions, and low prices make this a popular and worthy student haunt.

i Turn onto Mill Ln. off Trumpington St., then left onto Millers Yard. Entrees from £7-9. ☼ Open M-F noon-2:30pm and 5:30-11pm, Sa-Su noon-11pm.

INDIGO COFFEE HOUSE
CAFE $

8 St. Edward's Passage ☎01223 295 688

A student favorite, the Indigo Coffee House has two tiny floors of British charm tucked off an equally cute alley. Plentiful sandwich options (available on sliced bread, baguette, or bagel) extend from the standard ham and cheese to chorizo and tomato. They also serve up a host of cakes, croissants, and salads. Note the sign that threatens to levy a £1 fine for incorrect usage of the word "literally."

i Head toward Trinity on King's Parade and turn right onto St. Edward's Passage. It's 1 street to the right of St. Mary's Church when you're facing it. Sandwiches £3-5. Coffee from £1.50. Cash only. ☼ Open M-F 10am-6pm, Sa 9am-6pm, Su 10am-5pm.

NIGHTLIFE

Nightlife in Cambridge is split between pubs that close at 11pm and clubs that don't get going until midnight. Clubs are generally reserved for extremely drunken student nights out, which, depending on what you're looking for, can either make for a great time or a total nightmare. The pubs tend to be of an extremely high quality—full of good beer (almost universally £3.50-4) and even better conversation. Keep in mind that, during term-time, colleges run their own bars, some of which are open to the public.

THE MAYPOLE
PUB

20A Portugal Pl. ☎01223 352 999 www.maypolefreehouse.co.uk

This lively pub is known affectionately as "The Staypole" thanks to it being one of the few bars in Cambridge with a late-night license. It takes advantage of its status as a "free house" (meaning that it's independent from any brewery and can serve whatever beers it wants) by stocking a selection of a dozen rotating beers on draft and many more in bottles. It's a tremendously popular spot, where students drink pints and pitchers of cocktails late into the night.

i When walking toward the river on Sidney St., turn right onto Portugal Pl. Pints from £3.50; pitchers £12-14. ☼ Open M-Th 11:30am-midnight, F-Sa 11:30am-1am, Su noon-11:30pm.

THE ELM TREE
PUB

16A Orchard St. ☎01223 502 632 www.theelmtreecambridge.co.uk

The pub may look very English, but its specialty is Belgian beer. Over 50 brews are represented here, and as you step inside, you'll be offered an incredibly helpful menu. The two rooms hold dusty bottles and tables filled with locals, while pictures of drinking customers cover the walls. Outside, the smoking crowd spills out as the only acknowledgment there's a pub in the quiet area. Occasionally, the space hosts live music.

i Walking south on Parker St., make a left onto Clarendon St. The pub is on the corner with Orchard St. Beer from £3.50. Cash only. ☼ Open daily 11am-11pm.

cambridge

HIDDEN ROOMS

BAR

7A Jesus Ln.   ☎01223 514 777   www.hiddenthing.com

The curtained booths and leather upholstery of this cocktail bar recall the days when Churchill and de Gaulle would meet in this underground lounge. Even if state-making isn't on the evening's agenda, you'll feel sufficiently sophisticated as you sip on one of the dozens of classic and unclassic cocktails twirled and poured behind the glamorous bar. When the ol' peripheral vision inevitably starts to go, make a beeline to the club room, which offers a darker, louder section with quickly changing tracks and dazzling light shows.

i With the ADC Theater on your right, head to the end of Park St. Turn right onto Jesus Ln. It's on the right. 2-for-1 cocktails M-W.Cocktails £6.80-9.20. ☼ Open M-Sa 3pm-12:30am, Su 3-10:30pm.

ARTS AND CULTURE

▨ ADC THEATRE

THEATER, COMEDY, DANCE

Park St.   ☎01223 300 085   www.adctheatre.com

"It was grown-up and polished, yet at the same time bashful and friendly; it was sophisticated and intelligent but never pretentious or pleased with itself; it had authority, finish, and quality without any hint of self-regard, vanity, or slickness," wrote Stephen Fry of the first Cambridge Footlights show he saw. The"Arts Dramatic Club" is the student-run theater that hosts the Footlights, which launched the comedic careers of Hugh Laurie, Fry, and half of Monty Python. Many other famous actors who attended Cambridge—including Ian McKellen, Emma Thompson, and Rachel Weisz—performed here as well. During term-time, there are usually two performances per day, while out of term there are still shows most days. There are occasional dance shows in addition to the usual theater and comedy.

i Head away from town center and take a left off Jesus Ln. to get to Park St. Tickets £5-10, concessions sometimes available. ☼ Box office open Tu 12:30-7pm, W-Th 3-7pm, F 12:30-7pm, Sa 3-7pm.

▨ SCUDAMORE'S

PUNTING

Quayside   ☎01223 359 750   www.scudamores.com

For North Americans, punting is solely related to kicking a football across half a stadium. For Cantabrigians (excluding the Boston variety), it is glamorously sticking a pole in mud and vaulting your way along the river Cam. Unless you're an old hand or an idiot, it's best to avoid the self-hire option and get a tour guide to regale you with over-the-top accounts of alumni and their youthful exploits. Scudamore's is the gold standard, with a small kiosk on the river and a fleet of attractive men roaming around the banks aggressively advertising the punting experience.

i Underneath Magdalene Bridge. Take a right off Bridge St. Another location is at the end of Mill St. Self-hire £22 per hr., students £16; plus £90 deposit taken in the form of an imprint of your credit or debit card. Guided tours £16, concessions £14.50, under 12 £8. Discounts if you buy tickets online. Private and specialty tours can be pre-booked. ☼ Open daily 9am-dusk.

CAMBRIDGE CORN EXCHANGE

LIVE MUSIC

Wheeler St.   ☎01223 357 851   www.cornex.co.uk

Probably the largest music venue in Cambridge, the Corn Exchange has hosted most of the big-name musical acts that come through Cambridge, from the Beatles and Pink Floyd to The Smiths and Oasis. It also presents musicals, dance performances, and opera. The 19th-century building was established as a space for merchants to trade grain; nowadays, it serves as an exam room for the university when it's not being used for concerts (sadly, they don't play "School's Out" when you finish).

i Heading south on King's Parade, turn left onto Bene't St. and go straight until it becomes Wheeler St. Prices vary. Occasional student discounts. ☼ Open M-Sa 10am-6pm.

ESSENTIALS
Practicalities

- **TOURIST OFFICES:** The Tourist Information Centre at Peas Hill has National Express tickets, discounted punting tickets, and sightseeing bus tickets and also offers accommodations bookings and an access guide to the city for disabled visitors. (☎0871 226 8006 www.visitcambridge.org ⏰ Open M-Sa 10am-5pm, Su 11am-3pm.)

- **STUDENT TRAVEL OFFICES:** STA Travel (38 Sidney St. ☎0871 702 9809 www.statravel.co.uk ⏰ Open M-Th 10am-7pm, F-Sa 10am-6pm, Su 11am-5pm.)

- **TOURS:** Several walking tours leave from the Tourist Information Centre. The Guided Tour features King's College and Queens' College. (*i* £17.50, concessions £15.50, children £8. ⏰ Tours leave daily at 1 and 2pm.)

- **INTERNET:** Jaffa Net Cafe. (22 Mill Rd. ☎01223 308 380 *i* £1 per hr. ⏰ Open daily noon-midnight.)

- **POST OFFICES:** Bureau de Change. (9-11 St. Andrew's St. ⏰ Open M 9am-5:30pm, Tu 9:30am-5:30pm, W-Sa 9am-5:30pm.)

Emergency

- **POLICE:** on Parkside. (☎0345 456 4564 ⏰Open daily 8am-10pm.)

- **HOSPITALS/MEDICAL SERVICES:** Addenbrookes Hospital. (Hills Rd., by the intersection of Hills Rd. and Long Rd. ☎01223 245 151)

Getting There

By Train

The only significant starting point for trains to Cambridge is London. Trains arrive at **Station Road.** (*i* 20min. walk southeast from the town center. ⏰ Ticket office open M-Sa 5:10am-11pm, Su 7am-10:55pm.) You can catch trains at London King's Cross (£22. ⏰ 50min., 2 per hr.) and **London Liverpool St.** (£15.30. *i* 1¼hr., 2 per hr.)

By Bus

The bus station, mostly for short-distance buses, is on **Drummer Street.** (⏰ Ticket office open M-Sa 9am-5:30pm.) Airport shuttles and buses to more distant destinations run from **Parkside.** Buses arrive from: London Victoria (*i* Transfer at Stansted. £12.70. ⏰ 3hr., every hr.); Gatwick (£34. ⏰ 4hr., every 2hr.); Heathrow (£28.60. ⏰ 3hr., every hr.); Stansted (£10.50. ⏰ 50min., every 2hr.); Oxford. (*i* Take the X5 bus. £12.50. ⏰ 3¼hr., every 30min.)

Getting Around

By Bus

CitiBus runs from stops throughout town, including some on **Saint Andrew's Street, Emmanuel Street,** and at the train station. The most useful routes are C1 (from the station) and C2 (goes out along Chesterton Rd.). Single rides cost £2.20. **Dayrider Tickets** (unlimited travel for 1 day; £3.90) can be purchased on the bus; for longer stays, you can buy a **Megarider** ticket (unlimited travel for weeks; £13 per week).

By Taxi

For a taxi, call **Cabco.** (☎01223 312 444 ⏰ Open 24hr.)

By Bike

You'll see students on bikes everywhere in Cambridge. To fit in, go to **City Cycle Hire.** (61 Newnham Rd. ☎01223 365 629 www.citycyclehire.com *i* £7 for 4hr., £10 for 8hr., £12 for 24hr., £17 for 2-3 days, £25 for 4-7 days, £35 for 2 weeks, £80 for up

cambridge

to 3 months. ☺ Open Easter-Oct M-F 9am-5:30pm, Sa 9am-5pm; Nov-Easter M-F 9am-5:30pm.)

stonehenge

As the Stonehenge audio tour will explain, Stonehenge is not only an enigma, but a mystery (jury's out on whether either one is wrapped in the other). But the question remains: what is it all for? Is it a calendar? A status symbol? A sacrificial altar? Proof of extra-terrestrials? We're sad to inform you that merely visiting will not leave you with one definitive answer. However, whatever its purpose or maker, the stone circle really does inspire a sense of wonder—and that's enough of a reason for 21st-century tourists to visit.

🗿 **STONEHENGE**   MONUMENT

Amesbury   ☎019 8062 2833 www.english-heritage.org.uk

A trip to Stonehenge paired with a stop in Salisbury—the nearest major city—is a full-day event that basically repeats the message of Ken Follett's *The Pillars of the Earth*: building stuff is hard. Stonehenge itself is a tricky customer. While only 30 years ago, the place was an out-of-the-way tourist spot that only very thorough travelers would attempt to visit, there are now bus tours that drop thousands of visitors next to the highway that Stonehenge overlooks. For casual appreciation of pagan architecture, an hour is all you need; the audio tour will walk you through the materials, construction, layout, and purpose of the pi-shaped masonry. Surprisingly, even though you'll share your magical experience with hundreds of people, the design of the walkway is expertly shaped so that you can get as many mystical selfies as your heart deigns without someone in a red windbreaker wandering into the shot. If you have more time and money saved up, traveling here via Salisbury instead of via the A303 is a nice way to get a more rounded survey of British history (and pre-history).

i By train: take the National Rail from Waterloo to Salisbury (around £40). Once in Salisbury, the Stonehenge Bus leaves from the train station for the site every 30min. from about 9:30am-6pm in summer and 10am-2pm in winter (£12). By bus: tours leave the city (£30 with price of admission). Adult £8, concessions £7.20. By barge, with 50-ton rocks: leave that to the pagans. ☺ Open daily Jan-Mar 15 9:30am-4pm; March 15-May 9:30am-6pm; Jun-Aug 9am-7pm; Sept-Oct 15 9:30am-6pm; Oct 15-Dec 9:30am-4pm.

edinburgh

Edinburgh is a city that moves. Visitors are constantly streaming through Scotland's capital, and the population of the city swells by roughly one million during the month of August. Festival season, or Fest, as it's known to locals, is a time of both great joy and chagrin, as free entertainment reigns supreme but walking down the street to the supermarket takes nearly half an hour. Even when Edinburgh isn't party central, its residents aren't afraid to sing its praises. The city is full of locals with an intense pride in their city, and you might have to coax information out of them over a pint and a blether (Scottish-speak for drink and a chat), at which point they will reveal a certain attitude toward the rest of the British Isles. A majestic city, it's one of those places where you watch the sun go down over the castle from the top of a hill and wonder just how you managed to wander into such a spectacular place. However you did it, keep going: Edinburgh was made for it. Downhill is always easier.

great britain

ORIENTATION

Edinburgh's most famous neighborhoods, **Old Town** and **New Town,** are easily divisible, as they are separated by a large gully that houses **Waverley Station** and **Princes Street Gardens.** This ravine is bisected by three bridges: **Waverley Bridge, North Bridge,** and **The Mound.** Stockbridge is to the north of New Town (walk as if you were heading to Leith and the sea) and **Haymarket** and **Dalry** are in the area west of New Town. **The Meadows, Tollcross,** and the **West End** are all over the hill from Old Town, off toward the south end of town.

Old Town

The Old Town is heralded by the imposing castle that holds court atop the rocky crags of an extinct volcano, dividing Old Town from New Town. Its winding, cobbled streets are surrounded by four- and five-story Georgian buildings that house everything from storytelling centers to party-driven hostels. Going down the **Royal Mile** you can expect to see all manner of characters, from camera-clutching tourists to sharp-eyed street performers and blasting bagpipers to slouching alley cats. Old Town is where it's at. It's where you'll take the most pictures, it's where you'll drink, sleep, shop, and eat. You'll be hard-pressed to even find another neighborhood some days—there's just too much to do. However, everyone else knows this, too, so make sure to only hit up Old Town when you're feeling particularly ready for a tourist onslaught.

New Town

New Town isn't actually that new. It was considered new when it was designed by James Craig in the 1760s, which certainly qualifies it as elderly by this point. One advantage of having a designer, however, is easy navigation. Following a simple, grid-like pattern, the neighborhood is bordered by **Queen Street** to the north, with grand old residences housing everything from the Royal Society of Physicians to the Society of Single Malt Scotch. **Princes Street** to the south, meanwhile, holds the line between Old and New with a healthy shopping thoroughfare, along with its share of sights. **George Street,** running through the middle, is the heart of the neighborhood, with traffic to match (read: generally unfriendly to pedestrians). The various intersecting thoroughfares have branches of their own, usually smaller streets with houses or shops. **Rose Street,** infamous for its tourist trade, remains irresistible for its high quantity and quality of pubs running the complete length. The challenge: crawl from one end to the other.

Stockbridge

Put on your best polo, because we're heading to the Edinburgh Country Club—Stockbridge. Full of the top tier of the upper crust of society, it's a bit like its own village, with its own restaurants, drinking, and way of life. Forgot your monocle? No worries, just find one among the posh leftovers sold in the copious Stockbridge charity shops. As we always say, if you can't beat 'em, join 'em; if you can't join 'em, wear their cast-offs. When you're not scrounging through the thrift stores, you can meander through the streets, pop into a cafe, stop off at a trim restaurant, or just wander on down to the **Water of Leith.**

Haymarket and Dalry

Haymarket and Dalry are not that pretty, at least compared to the rest of Edinburgh. This may be why they are home to some of the city's cheaper housing. There are a bunch of slightly battered, cheaper hotels for those looking to avoid the more inner-city hosteling experience, though you do end up getting what you pay for (in terms of both location and facilities). A few good food stops can be found, and those

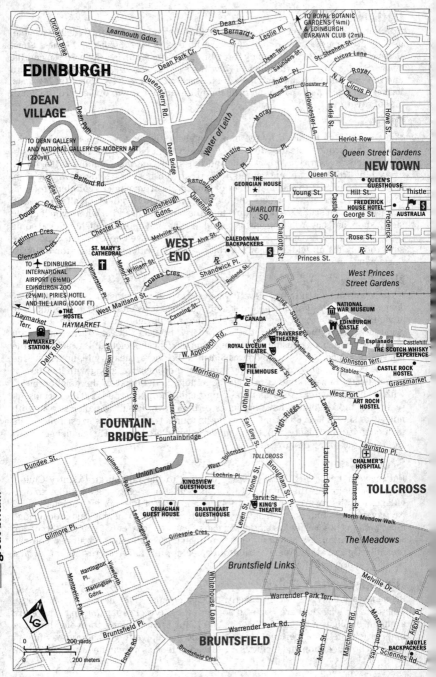

EDINBURGH

DEAN VILLAGE

Learmouth Gdns.

Orchard Brae

Dean St.
St. Bernard's Cr.
Dean St.
Leslie Pl.

Dean Park Cr.

TO ROYAL BOTANIC
GARDENS (¼mi)
& EDINBURGH
CARAVAN CLUB (2mi)

Dean Terr.
Saunders St.
St. Stephen St.
Circus Lane

India Pl.
Glouster Pl.
Doune Terr.
Gloucester Ln.

Royal
N.W. Circus Pl.
Circus

India St.
Howe St.

Heriot Row

Queensferry Rd.

Water of Leith

Dean Path

Dean Bridge

TO DEAN GALLERY
AND NATIONAL GALLERY OF MODERN ART
(220yd)

Belford Rd.

Ainslie Pl.
Stuart St.
Randolph Cres.
Queensferry St.

Moray Pl.

Queen Street Gardens

NEW TOWN

THE GEORGIAN HOUSE ★
Queen St.

● QUEEN'S GUESTHOUSE
Hill St.
Thistle St.

Douglas Gdns.
Douglas Cres.
Eglinton Cres.
Glencairn Cres.

Chester St.
Drumsheugh Gdns.
Melville St.

ST. MARY'S CATHEDRAL ✝

WEST END

Alva St.
Young St.

CHARLOTTE SQ.

S. Charlotte St.
Castle St.

FREDERICK HOUSE HOTEL ●
George St.
Frederick St.

AUSTRALIA $

Rose St.
℞

TO ✈ EDINBURGH
INTERNATIONAL
AIRPORT (6½MI),
EDINBURGH ZOO
(2¼MI), PIRIES HOTEL
AND THE LAIRG (500F FT)

William St.
Manor Pl.
Palmerston Pl.
Coates Cres.

CALEDONIAN BACKPACKERS $

℞
Shandwick Pl.
Rutland St.

Princes St.

West Princes Street Gardens

West Maitland St.
Canning St.

Haymarket Terr.
● THE HOSTEL
HAYMARKET

HAYMARKET STATION

Dalry Rd.

Morrison Link

CANADA

W. Approach Rd.
Gardner's Cres.
Grove St.

ROYAL LYCEUM THEATRE

Cambridge St.
TRAVERSE THEATRE
Cornwall St.
Grindlay St.

NATIONAL WAR MUSEUM

EDINBURGH CASTLE
Esplanade
Castlehill

King's Stables Terr.

THE SCOTCH WHISKY EXPERIENCE

Morrison St.
THE FILMHOUSE
Lothian Rd.
Bread St.
Lady Lawson St.
King's Stables Rd.
Johnston Terr.

CASTLE ROCK HOSTEL

Grassmarket

FOUNTAIN-BRIDGE

Earl Grey St.
High Riggs
West Port
ART ROCH HOSTEL

Fountainbridge

Dundee St.

Gilmore Park
Union Canal

West Tollcross
TOLLCROSS
Home St.
Brougham St.

Lauriston Pl.
CHALMER'S HOSPITAL

Lauriston Gdns.

TOLLCROSS

KINGSVIEW GUESTHOUSE
Lochrin Pl.

Tarvit St.
Brougham St. Pl.
Chalmers St.

CRUACHAN GUEST HOUSE
Leamington Terr.
BRAVEHEART GUESTHOUSE
Leven St.
KING'S THEATRE

North Meadow Walk

Gillespie Cres.

The Meadows

Gilmore Pl.

Bruntsfield Links

Hartington Pl.
Viewforth
Hartington Gdns.
Montpelier Park

Whitehouse Loan

Melville Dr.

Warrender Park Terr.

Bruntsfield Pl.
Warrender Park Rd.

BRUNTSFIELD

Bruntsfield Cres.
Spottiswoode St.
Arden St.
Marchmont Rd.
Marchmont Cres.
Argyle Pl.
ARGYLE BACKPACKERS
Sciennes Rd.

0   200 yards
0   200 meters

great britain

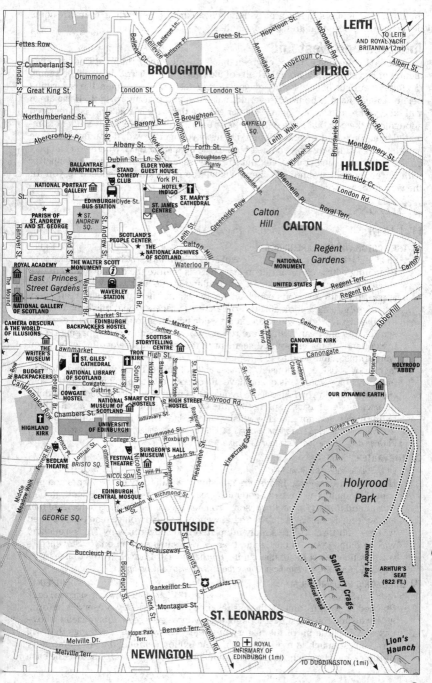

looking for a night out in this area will find cheap drinks. Be warned, there are some old-guard pubs here that aren't the friendliest.

Tollcross and West End

Dominated by the vast expanse of green that is the meadows, the West End is conveniently only a short walk from the hubs of **Old Town** and **New Town.** But you'll be seeing far fewer tourists out this way, except during festival time, when the swarming begins. **Lothian Road** is home to several great pubs, and continuing up to **Home Street** will take you to the local cinema, **The Cameo.** The **University of Edinburgh** is integrated enough into the city that none of the pubs or bars in the area are solely student-dominated, but you'll find several full of a distinctly younger crowd. If you fancy it, take a putter and a chipping iron and head out to the **Bruntsfield Links,** where you can play on the public chipping course. Get out to Tollcross and West End—you'll feel better with fewer tourists around, and the locals will be more kindly disposed to you for the very same reason.

SIGHTS

Old Town

☒ THE SCOTCH WHISKY EXPERIENCE

TOUR

354 Castlehill   ☎0131 220 0441 www.scotchwhiskyexperience.co.uk

Beginning with a carnival ride in giant barrels (before the drinking, mercifully), you'll be explained the process of distilling single-malt whisky by a ghostly apparition with a serious penchant for the elixir. Then after a short, and very impatiently rushed, look at the barrel-making process, you'll finally be ushered into the tasting room, where an expert guide will offer you smells on a very retro scratch-and-sniff card, which are representative of each whisky-making region in Scotland. At the end of that segment of the tour, you'll select the whisky you want to taste and head to the display room, where the Diageo Claive Vidiz Collection of whiskies is housed…almost 3500 of them. There you'll learn how to properly enjoy your whisky and have the opportunity to purchase a bottle from the store, should you find one that you really enjoy. If you are already something of a whisky enthusiast, splurge for the ☒**Gold tour.** Sure, it's pricey, but where better to get a comprehensive whisky knowledge? Good luck walking home!

i Silver tour (basic): £12.50, concessions £10. Gold tour (advanced): £22, concessions £19.50. ☒ Open daily 10am-6pm. Last tour daily 5pm.

☒ THE WRITERS' MUSEUM

MUSEUM

Lady Stair's Close, The Royal Mile   ☎0131 529 4901

Housed in the majestic Ladystairs mansion is a sanctuary of the works and personal belongings of three of Scotland's greatest authors: Sir Walter Scott, Robert Burns, and Robert Louis Stevenson. From mannequined displays to locks of hair and writing desks, it's great for a quiet wander whether you've read the collected works of all three or are simply interested in discovering why Treasure Island was so damn good. In particular, there is one small section on RL Stevenson's travels and even some of his opining on the theory of travel. Words to live by.

i Free. ☒ Open M-Sa 10am-5pm. During the festival, also Su noon-5pm.

☒ SURGEON'S HALL MUSEUM

MUSEUM

Nicholson St.   ☎0131 527 1649 www.museum.rcsed.ac.uk

Stacked high with some of the nastiest body parts perfectly preserved in formaldehyde and the wickedest-looking tools you've ever seen, this museum showcases every little bit of the history of surgery as well as a few things that will turn your stomach. A morbidly fascinating exhibit detailing the gruesome story of Burke and Hare, who murdered innocent citizens in order to receive the cash for supplying early doctors with bodies, actually displays a pocketbook made from Burke's own human skin. Before we had photography, we had painting, and there are several technically beautiful oils of festering wounds. What can we say? It's great. Just don't come on a full stomach.

i £5, concession £3. ☺ *Open Apr-Jul daily noon-4pm; Aug M-F 10am-4pm and Sa-Su noon-4pm; Sept-Oct daily noon-4pm; Nov-Mar M-F noon-4pm.*

THE NATIONAL MUSEUM OF SCOTLAND
MUSEUM

Chambers St. ☎0131 247 4422 www.nms.ac.uk

Housed in an enormous, modern castle complete with winding staircases and massive open spaces, this museum features nine floors to check out. The exhibits here are as wide-ranging as you would expect, from "The Kingdom of the Scots," featuring powder horns and ancient Pictish stonework, to "Scotland: A Changing Nation," illustrating Scotland in ways you'd never expect—inventors, innovators and even Ewan MacGregors. If that doesn't make it clear enough, this is a testament to Scottish national pride on the deepest level. You aren't in Britain here: you are in Scotland. As a final stop, hit up the rooftop terrace for some awesome castle photo-ops. But beware: you'll be fair game for the Camera Obscura tours up there. They're watching.

i Free. ☺ *Open daily 10am-5pm.*

get a room!

Possibly more so than any other city in the UK, Edinburgh's accommodation options are defined by its neighborhoods. See our full list of recommendations at **www.letsgo.com**.

▨ CASTLE ROCK HOSTEL
HOSTEL $$

15 Johnston Terr. ☎0131 225 9666 www.castlerockedinburgh.com

Not only a spot fit for a castle, it occupies a smaller side street, which makes for next to no tourist traffic. Castle Rock offers solid wooden bunks, a colorful, youthful lounge area, and—it's rumored—the option to work off your next night's stay. Though, of course, this all depends on whether or not there's work to be done, so don't take that accommodation money to the pub just yet.

i *Dorms £13-15.* ☺ *Reception 24hr.*

▨ ART ROCH HOSTEL
HOSTEL $

2 W. Port ☎0131 228 9981

You feel the vibrant wayfarer spirit in every corner of this hosteler's hostel with worn black walls, and an even more worn reception. Dorms are cool and airy, featuring sturdy wooden bunks (instead of squeaking metal). The lounge-and-kitchen area is the size of a small aircraft hangar and fits the requisite cooking appliances, TV, chairs and couches, and even a hammock, all with plenty of room to spare.

i *High-season dorms £11; low-season dorms £9. Singles £20.* ☺ *Reception 24hr.*

▨ CALEDONIAN BACKPACKERS
HOSTEL $

3 Queensferry St. ☎0131 226 2939 www.caledonianbackpackers.com

By far the best budget option in New Town, this 250-bed monster will remind you how good hostel living can be—comfortable and crazy all at the same time. With free Wi-Fi, an available kitchen, and a fully stocked bar, it's not cheap fun, it's cheap and fun.

i *Dorms £13-20.* ☺ *Reception 24hr.*

edinburgh

CAMERA OBSCURA AND THE WORLD OF ILLUSIONS

MUSEUM, MINDBENDING

Castlehill ☎0131 226 3709 www.camera-obscura.co.uk

Just across the street from the Scotch Whisky Experience is this slightly more kid-friendly option. The actual camera obscura, a combination of reflecting lenses and mirrors, presents a live-action, birds-eye view of the city. However, if it's overcast, your picture will be dimmer (read: you're in Scotland—your picture will be slightly dim), and if you're not on the bottom level of seating, chances are high that some little kid's noggin is going to be eagerly "obscuring" yours. The rest of the exhibition is a series of floors full of holograms, illusions, and distortions. All very well, but you will probably be fighting the hordes of yelling school kids to get your own hands on things. Infuriatingly, you have to get through a mirror maze in order to exit. Good luck getting out.

i £9.25, students and seniors £7.25, ages 5-15 £6.25. ⏰ Open Apr-Jun 9:30am-7pm, Jul-Aug 9:30am-9pm, Sept-Oct daily 9:30am-7pm, Nov-Mar daily 10am-6pm.

EDINBURGH CASTLE

CASTLE

Castlehill ☎0131 225 9846 www.edinburghcastle.gov.uk

Hauntingly gothic at night, radiantly regal at high noon, and glowingly warm at dusk, Edinburgh Castle has a lot to offer. From the top, there are the brilliant photo-ops you'll want when you get home. Of course, don't be surprised to later find after jockeying for frame space that you have a very nice photo of a charming couple up from Glasgow for the weekend. The Honours of the Kingdom (or the Scottish Royal Jewels) exhibit funnels you along a winding display of murals and mannequins before finally reaching the jewels. If the place is busy, it can take up to 40min., so be warned. Stop by at the top of the hour to see the acclaimed changing of the guard, though wear pads to avoid bruises in the scrum afterward.

i £16, concessions £13, children £9.20. ⏰ Open daily in summer 9:30am-6pm, winter 9:30am-5pm; last entry 1hr. before close.

THE NATIONAL WAR MUSEUM (NWM)

MUSEUM

Hospital Sq., Castlehill ☎0131 247 0413 www.nms.ac.uk

The National War Museum explores facets of life as a soldier, from the role of Scots in war to how injured soldiers are, sometimes literally, rebuilt. There is also the required smorgasbord of death, whether your tastes favor old decorative swords or old decorative admiral's pistols. The exhibit follows the evolution of the Scottish soldier and his weaponry all the way to present day. Tales of ancient Scotland, or maybe the Castlehill tourists, may put you in a warlike mood, and here you have a release.

i Free (with entrance to the Castle). ⏰ Open daily in summer 9:45am-5:45pm; in winter 9:45am-4:45pm.

ST. GILES' CATHEDRAL

CATHEDRAL

High St. ☎0131 225 9442 www.stgilescathedral.org.uk

Sitting in a grand position on the Royal Mile, the stonework on the outside is finer than lace, and the inside is just as beautiful. With glowing stained glass that casts enormous rainbows onto the walls in the late morning and an ornate wooden organ near the center of the building, St. Giles' is so photo-worthy that you'll find yourself looking like the ultimate tourist trying to get a shot of everything. However, you won't be the only one, and the constant flow of tourist traffic means that St. Giles' is hard-pressed for the calm atmosphere associated with cathedrals. Still, get someone to take your picture in front of a jewel-like window and you'll have your very own technicolor coat.

i Free. ⏰ Open May-Sept M-F 9am-7pm, Sa 9am-5pm, Su 1-5pm and services; Oct-Apr M-Sa 9am-5pm, Su 1-5pm and services.

great britain

New Town

◪ NATIONAL GALLERY OF SCOTLAND

MUSEUM

The Mound, just across Princes St.   ☎0131 624 6200 www.nationalgalleries.org

The idea of a National Gallery is to ensure that the general population has a chance to appreciate great art. Including some landmark pieces by Raphael and El Greco, you don't want to rush your way through this extensive collection. The National Gallery of Scotland brings some of the best for everyone. Even the octagonal rooms in which the artwork is hung seem designed to make you take your time.

i Free. Special exhibits £5-10. ⓩ Open M-W 10am-5pm, Th 10am-7pm, F-Su 10am-5pm.

ST. MARY'S CATHEDRAL

CATHEDRAL

York Pl.

More reminiscent of an Italian or Catholic cathedral, the garishly bright colors of the kings with angel wings and altogether obnoxious wall paintings rather detract from the genuine beauty of brilliantly creative stained glass and some of the biggest organ pipes you could never need. If you need a moment of quiet reflection in a big open space, though, you could do much worse.

i Free. ⓩ Open daily 8am-7pm.

THE NATIONAL ARCHIVES OF SCOTLAND

MUSEUM

2 Princes St.   ☎0131 535 1314 www.nas.gov.uk

A small collection of dusty old documents inhabits the much larger National Archives. Luckily, feather quills and old ink blotters are way cooler than you would think; the"Open Secret" exhibit demonstrates how governments through the ages have sought to conceal information from the public. Might sound dull, but when it comes to 15th-century governments—the gloves come off. Or, if you are in a more fantastical mood, look for the facsimile reproductions of government documents ascertaining the existence of the Loch Ness monster on the display boards.

i Free. ⓩ Open M-F 9am-4:30pm.

Stockbridge

THE ROYAL BOTANIC GARDENS

BOTANIC GARDENS

20A Inverleith Row   ☎0131 552 7171 www.rbge.org.uk

A center for plant research and conservation, this place is nuts (seeds, and spores, too) for plants. The entrance and visitors' center is beautifully impressive, with a glass façade and white, spinning windmill in front. Entrance to the gardens themselves is free, but to get into the Glasshouses for the real, misty green experience, you'll have to pay.

i Open daily Mar-Sept 10am-6pm; Oct 10am-5pm; Nov-Jan 10am-4pm; Feb 10am-5pm.

WATER OF LEITH

NATURE WALK

Meandering down a riverbank is always a bubbling joy. A place to clasp the hand of a date or silently meditate, the Water of Leith provides a good opportunity to forget city life and just listen to the soothing sounds of the water. Flowing through New Town and Stockbridge, this stream will never be too far away, which for you nature-lovers might be a comforting truth. Low-hanging trees and tumbling bushes hang over the path, providing some shade for when you want to rest your eyes. Careful if that running stream gets too intense, though. Not to scare you off, but flash floods are not entirely unheard of.

i From the Dean St./Deanhaugh St. intersection, walk down St. Bernard's Row. There are entrances to the footpath on the right.

STOCKBRIDGE MARKET

At the junction of St. Stephen Pl. and St. Stephen St.

Before you go grab your all-hemp recycled grocery bag and head off to get your fix of farmers' market veggies, it's worth knowing that the Stockbridge Market no longer exists—it's been replaced by houses. However, the old archway, with its engraved lettering and protruding lamp, is still there, making for quite a picturesque scene. Grab the camera, snap a few quick shots and stroll down through the garden, sheltered by trees. Or just head off to the art gallery next to the entrance.

i From Deanhaugh St. Bridge, walk up Kerr St. Turn left onto St. Stephen St., then left onto St. Stephen Pl. The archway is ahead.

ALPHA ART

GALLERY

52 Hamilton Pl. ☎0131 226 3066 www.alpha-art.co.uk

Before entering this art gallery, like most art galleries, remind yourself that you really can't afford anything inside. Then step through the cool doors and resist temptation. With a collection of original and limited-edition prints from artists that are local, UK-based, and international, Alpha Art's collection has a huge range. Great oils, silk-screens, and sculptures abound.

i Browsing free. Artwork expensive. ⏰ Open Tu-F 10am-6pm, Sa 10am-5pm, Su noon-5pm.

SCOTLANDART.COM

GALLERY

1 St. Stephen Pl. ☎0131 225 6257 www.scotlandart.com

With over 1000 original pieces between their Glasgow and Edinburgh branches, as well an extensive online selection (they've got computers right there in the gallery if you want to check it out), the guys at www.scotlandart.com are there to make sure you find what you're looking for. For those of us on a traveler's budget, however, we will just browse around.

i Browsing free. Artwork expensive. ⏰ Open Tu-F 10:30am-5:30pm, Sa 10am-5:30pm, Su noon-5pm.

Tollcross and West End

⬛ EDINBURGH CENTRAL MOSQUE

MOSQUE

50 Potterrow ☎0131 667 1777 www.edmosquelibrary.com

Combining elements of Islamic and Scottish baronial design, this towering castle of a building dominates the skyline of the area. A change from the sometimes monotonous monopoly of Scottish Presbyterianism, you can find some peace and quiet in the famously complete library and maybe even explore beyond your own beliefs.

i Across the street from the University visiting center. ⏰ Library open M-Sa 11:30am-6pm. Prayers F 12:50-1:50pm.

⬛ THE MEADOWS

PARK

5 Millerfield Pl. ☎0131 444 1969

Located on the southwestern end of town, the Meadows are a beautiful, welcome respite from the honking cars and blabbing people inside the city. With wide-open, grass-covered fields intersected by paths covered by the shade of trees, it's no wonder that during the festival the Meadows become a hotspot for people to gather and throw frisbees, barbecue, and generally just have a great time. There are 16 tennis courts and a playground on one end, while the public Bruntsfield Links chipping field, great for messing about with ballsand sticks if you're into that, is at the other.

i Walk from the intersection of Home St. and Brougham St. down Home St. The Meadows is on the left. Call ahead to reserve a tennis court during summer months. ⏰ Courts open Apr-Jun M-F 4-9pm, Sa-Su 10am-6pm; Jul-Aug M-F 9am-9pm, Sa-Su 10am-7:30pm; Sept M-F 4-9pm, Sa-Su 10am-6pm.

great britain

FOOD

Edinburgh, like any heavily touristed city, has just about any kind of cuisine you might be hankering for. So if you haven't quite gotten up the gumption to try haggis yet, try some fantastic veggie creations over at David Bann's or a huge plate of beef curry over at the Mosque Kitchen. You can do a wine and cheese night at the hostel if you stock up at IJ Mellis in Stockbridge. In short, the possibilities are endless.

Old Town

▧ OINK

HOG ROAST $

34 Victoria St.   ☎0131 220 0089 www.oinkhogroast.co.uk

For those of you who think that"This little piggy went to market" ends happily, you probably want to avoid this restaurant, although if you do, you will find the words "I've made a huge mistake" escaping from your lips. It doesn't get any more real than a roast pig (complete with head and trotters) on display in the window, from which every customer is served until a fresh one is needed. If that doesn't sound appetizing (understandable), imagine instead the hot pulled pork being piled into the soft white roll, then topped with homemade apple sauce, pepper, and a healthy dose of crunchy crackling on the top for good measure. There is no better food to munch on while you walk the medieval Royal Mile. Prices range from "The Piglet" (£2.60), for little stomachs, to "The Oink" (£3.60), the classic, and "The Grunter" (£4.60), named for the noises made by their owners.

i Sandwiches £2.60- £4.60. ⓩ Open M-Th 10am-8pm, F-Su 10am-10pm.

▧ MAXIE'S BISTRO

BISTRO $$$

5B Johnston Terr.   ☎0131 226 7770

To get to Maxie's, you'll have to descend two sets of stairs flanked by paintings of old cigarette ads to the basement of the building. The interior decor, a cross between traditional pub and student hang-out, is nice enough. While it's acceptable to sit inside there, if you're smart you'll immediately walk out onto the terrace, below which plunges the edge of the hill, offering a dramatic setting for your meal. Overlooking the city 50ft. above the ground, it's the perfect place to sit back and have a pint and a classic set of haggis, neeps, and tatties.

i Starters £3.50-7. Entrees £8-17. ⓩ Open daily 11am-11pm.

THE ELEPHANT HOUSE CAFÉ

CAFE, BAR $$

21 George IV Bridge   ☎0131 220 5355 www.elephanthouse.biz

▧Harry Potter and company were born here on scribbled napkins, a fact proclaimed loudly on several walls. The cafe serves both coffee and booze, making you wonder which one JK Rowling was drinking when she had her inspiration. If you are of a more macabre lilt, Ian Rankin is also a regular, featuring the cafe in several of his books and writing here often. Choose yours. They also have a selection of pastries and pies, though, infuriatingly, no internet—a great detriment to all writers less inclined to the napkin option.

i Coffee £1.50-2.75. Beer £3. ⓩ Open M-Th 8am-10pm, F 8am-11pm, Sa 9am-11pm, Su 9am-10pm.

CAFÉ TRUVA

CAFE $$

251-253 Canongate St.   ☎0131 556 9524 www.cafetruva.com

Cafes on the Royal Mile are plentiful, but there may not be any that can rival Café Truva in terms of great outdoor seating. With small tables set out underneath the stone arches of the entryway, the cafe boasts a view that overlooks the Royal Mile along a row of picturesque houses. The food is Turkish and Mediterranean, but they also have a great selection of truffles and chocolates.

i Coffee £1.50-2.10. Toasted sandwiches £5.50. ⓩ Open daily 8:30am–7pm.

edinburgh

THE LITTLE INN
SANDWICHES $
1 Johnston Terr.
☎0775 661 4407

One of the smallest places on the Royal Mile (the only seating is a little bench outside the shop), The Little Inn is probably so small because it doesn't need anything grand to attract the line that stretches out the tiny door and down the street. Forget trying to sit down, try getting in first. Grab a soup and a baguette for just £2. Even the milkshakes (tasty!) are only £2.50.

i Breakfast rolls £1.40-2.80. ☒ Open daily 7am-3pm. Open late during festival.

New Town

WOLFITS
DELI $
200 Rose St.
☎0131 225 5096   http://wolfits.co.uk

We have no idea why this restaurant is called "Wolfits." What we do know is that this small establishment sells good food cheap. You can certainly see the popularity as the local office workers queue down the street for food, and the aroma seals the deal. Soups and buttered baguettes go for under £3. There's not really an atmosphere beyond the tense excitement for cheap, delicious food, but you can watch music videos on the television while you wolf it down—oh, now we get the name.

i Sandwiches from £2. ☒ Open M-F 7:30am-4pm, Sa-Su 8am-4pm.

MUSSEL INN
SEAFOOD $$$
61-65 Rose St.
☎0131 225 5979   www.mussel-inn.com

The white and blue front to this seafood specialist almost takes you back to some salt-blown waterfront where mussels are brought in straight through the front door. Sadly, this is not the case; but with regards to the freshness at Mussel Inn, it might as well be true. Serving mussels brought in from the West Lochs of Scotland and the Shetland Isles, the Inn dishes out food that is the most savory the waters of Scotland has to offer. As if the natural taste weren't enough, they serve mussel pots with Moroccan, shallot, and bleu cheese flavors as well. It's a crowded place, so book ahead.

i 1kg. pot of mussels £10.10-12.20. 0.5kg pot of mussels £5.10-6.20. ☒ Open M-Th noon-3pm and 5:30-10pm, F-Su noon-10pm, Su 12:30-10pm.

NINE CELLARS THALI RESTAURANT
INDIAN $$$
1-3 York Pl.
☎0131 557 9899   http://9cellars.co.uk

A multiple award-winning Indian restaurant is a rare find. To find one that you don't feel the need to be rolled from afterward is rarer still. Nine Cellars is enjoyably both. While slightly limited in terms of options, there is no limit to the signature Indian flavors that never disappoint. Try the spiced lamb, but ask for some date chutney to eat it with. It's a combination you do not want to miss.

i Fixed 3-course lunch £7.50. Dinner entrees £15-20. ☒ Open M-Sa noon-2:30pm, 5:30-11:30pm, Su 5:30-11:30pm.

THE CONAN DOYLE
PUB $$
71-73 York Pl.
☎0131 557 9539

In the neighborhood where Sir Arthur Conan Doyle himself used to live, there's memorabilia—Sherlock Holmes and otherwise—galore in this pub. Unfortunately, as with so many historically interesting pubs, the specter of the "Nicholson pub" has swooped in and made another kill. The memorabilia, rather than accentuating the experience, is a pathetic reminder of what should be in the place of this conglomerated nightmare. True, the standardization means a decent meal at a decent price, with some drink to boot. But where is the soul, Watson?

i Breakfast from £5. Burgers from £8. ☒ Open M-Th 9am-11:45pm, F-Sa 9am-1am, Su 12:30pm-midnight.

great britain

Stockbridge

BELLS DINER
DINER $$$

7 St. Stephen St.   ☎0131 225 4673

At Let's Go, we are not picky about burgers. For us, as long as it's hot, has a bun, and isn't from a franchise with a drive-thru, we're pretty happy. However, there are occasions in one's life when one is exposed to a truly great burger, resonating with perfection. Bells Diner is one of those experiences. The burgers cost a bit more than you'd usually pay ($8-10) but are well worth the expenditure. While alone they might be a splurge, the full plate includes chips (fries) and a mouth-watering selection of six different dipping sauces.

i Burgers £8.95-11. ☼ Open M-F 6-10pm, Sa noon-10pm, Su 6-10pm.

HENRI
DELI $$

48 Raeburn Pl.   ☎0131 332 8844 www.henrisofedinburgh.co.uk

Half cafe with sit-down coffees and an outdoor terrace and half specialty food and wine paradise, Henri has mastered what a modern, trendy deli should be. The attractive, warm interior is matched with brushed-steel accents and a sophisticated lunch menu. And yet, its merchandise has a surprising, all-important affordability. Get a freshly-baked loaf of bread (from $1) and then supplement it with any number of cheeses, salamis, or quiches.

i Sandwiches £3-5. ☼ Open M-W 9am-8pm, Th 9am-9pm, Sa 9am-7pm, Su 9:30am-6:30pm.

PATISSERIE MADELEINE
CAFE $$

27B Raeburn Pl.   ☎0131 332 8455

An intensely modern cafe, the quiet coolness is perfect for sitting down to a flat white (like a latte, but sweeter) and book, along with enjoying the most futuristic bathrooms you've ever seen (seriously, it's like NASA designed the loo). Madeleine earns a thumbpick, though, for the best ▧macaroons this side of Paris. These light wafery cookied sandwiches are sweet but tart, in flavors like vanilla, chocolate, raspberry, and mango ($0.80 each). You can't stop eating them. Seriously, we tried. You can't (mumble crunch yum!) stop...

i Cakes and coffees £1.50-5. ☼ Open W-Sa 9am-6pm, Su 11am-5pm.

CAFÉ PLUM
CAFE $

96 Raeburn Pl.   ☎0795 781 1703

Plum is a tiny, purple and white cafe down on Raeburn with one hell of a coffee and tea selection, along with some tasty (and cheap) toasted sandwiches. If your budget is tight and you just need something to tide yourself over, grab a hot, sweet mug of tea and a ham-cheese toastie—easy, quick, and satisfying.

i Toasted sandwiches £2.50. Coffee £1.50-2.50. Full breakfast £7. ☼ Open M-W 8am-5pm, Th-F 8am-6pm, Sa 9am-5pm, Su 10:30am-5pm.

Haymarket and Dalry

GOOD SEED BISTRO
BISTRO $$$

100-102 Dalry Rd.   ☎0131 337 3803 www.goodseedbistro.com

While the menu might be a little limited, don't be afraid to try something that might test your palate in this surprisingly gourmet spot in decidedly lower-end Dalry. The relaxed interior belies the depths of flavor they can prepare. Try the cocoa tagliatelle, with smoked salmon, shallots, cherry tomatoes and a dash of vodka ($9.95). Admittedly, it is a little pricey, but you get what you pay for in both quality and quantity. So, foodies, when the fast food on the road becomes just too much, this is where to find a haven.

i Entrees £7.95-12.95. ☼ Open M-Th noon-10pm, F-Sa noon-11pm, Su noon-4pm.

edinburgh

SCOOBY'S

SANDWICHES $$

95 Morisson St.

☎0131 221 1877

A do-it-yourself sandwich shop with a bantering attitude, expect to be waiting in line outside this tiny sandwich place—the secret is out. Scooby's does a mean spicy tuna mayo or spicy meatball soup. Or if none of the stuff on the board strikes your fancy, just take a look at the ingredients and go nuts.

i Soup and sandwiches from £2.50. ☼ Open M-F 6:30am-4pm.

PG'S SANDWICH BAR

SANDWICHES $

127 Morrison St.

☎0131 228 8763

PG's is on a lower key and playing field compared to Scooby's, but it is still a great option for a cheap sandwich and a relaxing lunch. Maybe it is seriously lacking in cool decor, but the prices and savory smells are sure to satisfy.

i Sausage and haggis rolls £1. Sandwiches £3.50. ☼ Open M-F 7am-2pm.

XIANGBALA HOTPOT

CHINESE $$$

63 Dalry Rd.

☎0131 313 4408

A slightly different take on restaurant culture, the Xiangbala Hotpot is £15 per person all-you-can-eat for 2hr. With a silver boiling pot in the middle of the smooth black hotplates on your table, meats, seafood, and veggies are all thrown into the boiling broths and then scooped out to be slurped up through smacking lips.

i Entrees £15. ☼ Open daily 3-10pm.

MORISSON BAKERY

BAKERY $

147 Morisson St.

☎0131 229 6470

You'll know you're getting close to Morisson Bakery by the smell. There's no doubt that the wafting scent of fresh pies tempts all of Edinburgh between 2-3am. With fresh cakes and donuts as well as meat pies, it's an excellent stop at any time of the day or night (considering they're open for most of both). Though, probably due to the strange hours, do not expect service with a smile.

i All pastries under £1. Pies £1-2. ☼ Open daily 1am-5pm (not a typo).

Tollcross and West End

▨ THE MOSQUE KITCHEN

CURRY $

31 Nicholson Sq.

☎0131 667 4035 www.mosquekitchen.com

Like all the best takeout curry places, these guys don't mess around—why waste time on atmosphere? But once you see your gigantic plate of savory rice and spicy curry, you could care less what the room looks like. For a light snack, grab a seekh kebab (£1) to munch on while you walk.

i Seekh Kebab £1. Chicken curry plate £4, vegetable £3.50, meat £4.50. ☼ Open daily 11:30am-11pm, closed F 12:50-1:50pm for prayers.

▨ VICTOR HUGO CONTINENTAL DELICATESSEN

DELI $$

26-27 Melville Terr.

☎0131 667 1827 www.victorhugodeli.com

A true combination of deli and cafe, Victor Hugo's has little booths along the walls perfect for snuggling up with a coffee. The inside is a great place to wonder when the driving rain is going to stop. Or if the weather has a slightly more benevolent attitude, you can sit outside and enjoy the rare sun—from underneath the awnings of course. With locals who've been coming back since 1940 as well as students who come for the belly-filling mac 'n' cheese, it's everybody's favorite. Try the award-winning Ramsay of Carluke bacon roll (£3).

i Sandwiches £4-6. Teas £1.60. ☼ Open M-F 8am-8pm, Sa 9am-6pm, Su 10am-5pm.

PETER'S YARD

CAFE $$$

27 Simpson Ln.

☎0131 229 5876 www.petersyard.com

Peter's Yard, a Swedish-style cafe housed right in the heart of the University of Edinburgh, serves hot cinnamon buns as well as kladdkaka (a Swedish chocolate cake). Beware, though, the cafe is housed in a clear glass box, so those sitting outside on the balcony may 🍴spy on those sitting inside and vice versa. Recently, they undertook a project to create the perfect pizza, a sourdough creation they call the "No-compromise pizza." They have come damn near close, with unbelievably powerful ingredients: salami, ham, or anchovies (£10).

i Kladdkaka £2.70. Coffee £1.75-3. ☼ Open M 7am-6pm, Tu-F 7am-10pm, Sa 9am-10pm, Su 9am-6pm.

MADE IN FRANCE
CAFE, FRENCH $$
5 Lochrin Pl.   ☎0131 221 1184

Made in France is your own little slice of a Parisian cafe in the heart of Edinburgh. Of course, if you are really looking for a Parisian cafe, you should have gone to Paris. But we budget travelers are dreamers, so dream on. With French posters and framed Monet prints, it's a nice place to enjoy the tiny quiches and tarts. You can also pick up some wine or preserves from their shelves and take them home. La vie...c'est très belle.

i Baguettes from £2.60. ☼ Open M-F 9:30am-4:45pm, Sa-Su 10am-4pm.

MUMS
BRITISH $$
4A Forrest Road   ☎0131 260 9806 www.mumsgreatcomfortfood.com

This one's a belly-buster of comfort food. Seriously. The fare here includes your typical British staples—sausages and mash, cooked to perfection, as well as an assortment of gravies, and great towers of haggis and mashed potato. The plates are huge—come by at dinnertime and you won't need breakfast the next morning.

i 2 sausages and mash £7, haggis £7.25. ☼ Open M-Sa 9am-10pm, Su 10am-10pm. During festival open until 11pm.

NIGHTLIFE

Edinburgh, despite being the "prettier little sister" to Glasgow, has nowhere near the same club scene. This town, full of pubs and bars, however, buzzes happily on the weekends, while intensely skyrocketing during the festivals in August. Each specific neighborhood has its own take on the classic pub, from the tourist-heavy areas along the Royal Mile, to the strange collection of odd and local watering holes on Rose Street in New Town, to the posh, hip new bars in Stockbridge.

Drinking in Scotland, and in Edinburgh especially, isn't about "going on the piss" (though that is a part of it), but about finding the right place for yourself, your group, your night, and your state of mind—no matter how much that last one may be altered throughout the night.

Old Town

▨ BANNERMAN'S
BAR, MUSIC VENUE
212 Cowgate   ☎0131 556 3254 www.bannermanslive.co.uk

With a subterranean, half-barrel auditorium for the live acts, the soundproofing in Bannerman's is so good that if you want to sit in the bar and have a friendly chat, you can, even while a rock show goes on next door. A wide selection of beers and cask ales is available, but if you want to try the house special, go for the Jäger U-boat. What is a Jäger U-boat, you ask? Just place your fingers in your ears, grab a small bottle of Jäger with your teeth, tilt your head back and—Whoosh! hear the bubbles of the deeps as you descend...into a drunken stupor. Don't worry, you'll be fine.

i Jäger U-boat £2. Shot shelf £1. Pints £3.40-3.65. ☼ Open Sept-Jul M-Sa noon-1am, Su 12:30pm-1am; Aug open daily noon-3am.

edinburgh

BLACK BULL
PUB

12 Grassmarket St.   ☎0131 225 6636

The floors, the walls, and the ceiling look like the inside of an oak tree. A really big oak tree. The Black Bull is enormous, with ample room for you and a party to find seats in one of the warmly lit booths or on a plush leather sofa. Serving real cask ales, you couldn't ask for a better place to while away a night cuddled in a corner with a pint or two, laughing over a trivia game. The live music tends to be a warbling folk singer strumming on a guitar. This isn't a place for wild parties, more for the quieter joys of company.

i *Spirits £2-2.60. Pints £2.60-3.45.* ☑ *Open M-F 11am-1am, Sa-Su 10am-1am.*

WHITE HART INN
PUB

34 Grassmarket St.   ☎0131 226 2806

The Grassmarket's most ancient pub (est. 1516), the White Hart Inn retains its wizened feel, with faded photographs on the walls, beer steins hanging from the ceilings, and one watchful bust of William Burke by the door. Famous ex-patrons of the pub include Scotland's favorite poet, Robert Burns. Grab a pint and see if your poetic stylings are loosed.

i *Pints £2.85-4. Spirits £3-12.50.* ☑ *Open M-Th 11am-midnight, F-Sa 11am-1am, Su 12:30pm-midnight.*

THE BANSHEE LABYRINTH
CLUB

29-35 Niddry St.   ☎0131 558 8209   www.thebansheelabyrinth.com

Built into the side of a hill and just above Edinburgh's famous "haunted vaults" (the Auld Reekie tours actually end here), the Banshee Labyrinth is a maze of stairs and tunnels, low-ceilinged, cave-like rooms and Addams-Family-inspired bars. They are also apparently haunted, though any ghostly noises are more than drowned out by the raucous partying on every level. There are three bars, seven rooms, a pool hall, a cinema, plus, for the more athletic clubbers, a pole-dancing area. Note the sign that absolves the bar from any injuries you may sustain from your "sexy dancing."

i *Spirits with mixer £2.50. Pints £2.70-3.40.* ☑ *Open M-Th 2pm-3am, F-Su 12:30pm-3am.*

CABARET VOLTAIRE
CLUB

36-38 Blair St.   ☎0131 220 6176   www.thecabaretvoltaire.com

One of Edinburgh's most popular nightlife spots, Cabaret Voltaire has a line that begins to lead out the door as soon as the club opens up around 11:30pm. And if you think that's an early rush, the queue only grows longer throughout the night. Located just above the "haunted vaults" used by the Ghost tours,the actual club has that low-ceilinged, brick, underground feel. Plenty of red neon keeps things a little naughty without crossing the bridge into being strip-club worthy.

i *Cover up to £7.* ☑ *Open daily noon-3am.*

SIN
CLUB

207 Cowgate   ☎0131 220 6176   www.club-sin.com

A regular fixture in Cowgate's nightlife options, Sin lives up to its name, getting scandalously crazy during the week, on the weekends, pretty much whenever. With enough fog and twirling lights to make your head spin, the massive downstairs dance floor where trance and house music crashes like waves onto the writhing crowd entertains partiers late into the night. You can head up to the more relaxed, and less squirming, mezzanine level if you—ahem—have had just one sip too many and need to find your friends again.

i *Cover W-Th free; F free before midnight, £4 after midnight; Sa £5. Bottles £2.25. Pints £2.50.* ☑ *Open W-Su 10pm-3am. During festival open daily 1pm-5am.*

great britain

WHISTLE BINKIES
4-6 S. Bridge

BAR, LIVE MUSIC

☎0131 557 5114 www.whistlebinkies.com

A popular place to see smaller live acts, Whistle Binkies has a sort of "pre-ripped jeans" feel—there are lots of old barrels and comfortable ratty stools, but the holes in the wall with brick underneath are definitely stylized. Framed photos of famous musicians are carefully hung and illuminated, but the veneer of class slips later in the night, when the real night-dwellers come out.

i Pints £3.50-3.60. Spirits £1.60-3.50. ⏲ Open M-Th 5pm-3am, F-Su 1pm-3am.

GREYFRIARS BOBBY'S BAR
30-34 Candlemaker Row

PUB

☎0131 225 8328 www.nicholsonspubs.co.uk

Greyfriars Bobby's Bar is named after one of Edinburgh's local legends—Greyfriars Bobby, a terrier so faithful that he slept at his owner's grave for 14 years until his own death. The citizens buried him next to his beloved owner and the loyal pooch entered the annals of local legend. There's a statue of Bobby outside this pub, making for a popular photo spot for tourists of all nationalities. The pub itself is a pretty standard alehouse, having succumbed to the tide of the Nicholson concept pubs, but if you want to contemplate Bobby's loyalty from across the street, you can sit outside and have a beer.

i Ales £2.80-3. Spirits £3. ⏲ Open M-Th 11am-11pm, F-Sa 11am-midnight, Su 12:30-11pm.

New Town

DIRTY DICK'S
159 Rose St.

PUB

☎0131 260 9920 dirtydicksedinburgh@gmail.com

I spy, among the bric-a-brac housed in Dirty Dick's: a sea of upside-down golf clubs on the ceiling, a full upside down pint of beer, a picture of ◙Alfred Hitchcock, somewhat creepy teddy bears, and an accordion. Cozy up to a glass of scotch and some proper Scottish food—their famous haggis, of course—and enjoy the eclectic jumble of things around you. Edinburgh, the way it should be.

i Pints £3.30. Spirits £2.60. ⏲ Open M-Sa 11am-late, Su noon-late.

BLACK ROSE TAVERN
49 Rose St.

BAR

☎0131 220 0414 www.blackrosetavern.com

If you've ever grown a beard to impress the guys in your heavy-metal band or ever bought a guitar with more sharp ends than your Swiss Army knife, you'll enjoy the Black Rose. With rock karaoke on Wednesdays and a major skeleton obsession, the Black Rose is great for rockers of all types. Don't be put off by all the ripped black clothing…or the male makeup—you can make some good friends in this kind of environment. Jägermeister is the self-proclaimed house wine—all those pretentious bars can go boil their heads in their Chardonnay.

i Pints £2.80-3.65. Spirits from £1.20. ⏲ Open M-Sa 11am-1am, Su 12:30pm-1am.

EL BARRIO
47 Hanover St.

BAR, CLUB

☎0131 220 6818 www.elbarrio.co.uk

New Town's only club is rowdy enough on its own to blast out the quota of loud music. Open until 3am every day, this basement of brightly colored walls and Latin music becomes packed with stumbling, sweaty, messy people on the weekends, as the photos clearly rejected from Facebook that adorn the walls will attest. The trick is to laugh at the most intoxicated people you see on the walls and then to make sure you don't join their ranks.

i Mixed drinks £3- £5. ⏲ Open M-Th 8pm-3am, F-Sa 6pm-3am (or later), Su 8pm-3am.

QUEEN'S ARMS
49 Frederick St.

PUB

☎0131 225 1045

Cunningly hidden beneath street level, the Queen's Arms takes the idea of a pub and inserts a level of class and sophistication needed to make it a trendy watering hole. It's still got that traditional feel, with a padded bar, bookshelf full of classics, and wiry chandeliers. But it has that new-pub smell, making it feel more like a cocktailbar than anything else. No matter, take it all in over one of their hand-pulled ales, and let the night come down around you.

i *Pints £3-3.50. Spirits £2.75 and up.* ☑ *Open M-Sa 11am-1am, Su 12:30pm-1am.*

Stockbridge

This slightly older, more residential quarter of Edinburgh, is not the place for a wild night out. In fact, most bars are restaurants, and very nice restaurants at that, so if some fine food and cocktails are on the menu, take to the village of Stockbridge.

THE ANTIQUARY BAR   PUB
68-72 St. Stephen St.   ☎0131 225 2858 www.theantiquarybar.co.uk

Its entrance may be hidden at the bottom of a small stairwell in Stockbridge, but this bar lets its people and atmosphere do the talking. It's tough to find a truly local pub, but get immersed in this one and, by haggis, you'll feel like a Scotsman before you leave. A great local crowd with a jovial attitude hangs out here, and if you come by on Tuesday night around 8pm, you can get in on one hell of a poker game.

i *Spirits £2.10-3.50. Pints £3-3.55.* ☑ *Open M noon-11pm, Tu-W noon-midnight, Th-Sa noon-1am, Su noon-12:30am.*

HAMILTON'S   RESTAURANT, BAR
16-18 Hamilton Pl.   ☎0131 225 8513 www.hamiltonsedinburgh.co.uk

With lots of posh leather couches and very"in" pop-art prints on the back wall, it's no surprise to see that everyone in Hamilton's is well-dressed, mild-mannered, and sipping on glasses of wine. If you do like they do, you will order one of Hamilton's delectable plates, like the deliriously rich marinated chicken breast with charred asparagus, spiced Bombay potatoes, and toasted coconut (£11). Should you like to live so well, though, you'd be wise, though it's certainly not necessary, to spiff yourself up a bit. Look at you, you need to wash behind those ears!

i *Pints £3.30-4.50. Spirits £3.10. Entrees £9-19.* ☑ *Open daily 9am-1am. In Aug open daily 9am-3am.*

HECTOR'S   BAR
47-49 Deanhaugh St.   ☎0131 343 1735 www.hectorsstockbridge.co.uk

The huge windows and enormous letters spelling out the name on the front of this hip, trendy bar in the heart of Stockbridge bring what might easily be a pretentious bistro-bar into the light. In fact, Hector's burns the candles all night long, until the wax falls onto the tables. It has an elegant but laid-back feel, thanks to wraparound couches complete with funky pillows and a dark purple interior that enhance the aura. A heavily local patronage keeps things from getting too fancy-schmancy. Hector's stocks a wide selection of wines, ales, and beers as well as an organic cider.

i *Pints £3-3.50. Organic cider £3.10.* ☑ *Open M-W noon-midnight, Th-F noon-1am, Sa 11am-1am, Su 11am-midnight.*

THE STOCKBRIDGE TAP   PUB
2-6 Raeburn Pl.   ☎0131 343 3000

A great local place right next to Hector's, the Stockbridge Tap is for those who want serious beverage variety. From vast numbers of ales to enormous quantities of single malts, you will find anything your palate could want here. While the outside might scream gastropub, don't be deterred. The interior is surprisingly spacious and has the comfortably familiar air of a pub of the non-gastro variety. If you've got the time and the liver for it, try to drink a full range.

i *Spirits £2.40. Pints £3-3.30.* ☑ *Open M-Th noon-midnight, F-Sa noon-1am, Su 12:30pm-midnight.*

ST. VINCENT BAR

BAR

11 St. Vincent St.

☎0131 225 7447

From the outside, the St. Vincent Bar looks like a normal pub, catering to locals and not toerag tourists. However, it's a Let's Go favorite in terms of pub quirks: St. Vincent's allows you to purchase two pints of your favorite ale "to go." That's right. Tell 'em you feel like drinking at home and they'll give you a lovely carton of beer. Now that's brilliant.

i Pints £3-4. ☼ Open M-Sa 11am-1am, Su 12:30pm-1am. During festival open until 3am.

Haymarket and Dalry

CARTER'S

BAR

185 Morrison St.

☎0131 228 9149

Unlike the chain-owned concept pubs of Haymarket and Dalry, Carter's has an artsy and original elegance, accentuated by the candle wax dripping down the stairs and the mismatched couches and chairs in the loft. Even better, that artsiness is offset by a cheery and welcoming bar on entry, immediately dispelling any fears of being excluded for reasons of non-regularity. They set up small shows in the downstairs space (mostly on Th), so as long as you're not looking for a really flailing club, this could be for you. As the sign painted on the wall says, "Are you gonna piss about all day?—Or are you coming in?" Do the latter.

i Spirits £2.50-3.30. Pints £2.80-3.40. ☼ Open M-Sa noon-1am, Su 12:30pm-1am.

Tollcross and West End

HENRICKS

BAR

1A Barclay Pl.

☎0131 229 2442 www.henricksbar.com

A classy yuppie bar, identifiable by a decor that could have been pulled out of an interior design catalogue, this is a good spot for a pre-theater drink. Thistle wallpaper and little black lamps above the bar illuminate the little black dresses that show up on the weekends. No live music or trivia over here though, guys. This place is fancy.

i Pints £3.15-4.50. Mixed drinks 2-for-1 M-Th £5.50. ☼ Open M-Sa 11:30am-11pm, Su 11am-11pm.

CUCKOO'S NEST

BAR

69 Home St.

☎0131 228 1078

A smaller student bar with a tiki feel, the booths here are lined with a row of bamboo pieces and the mirrors on the walls are framed by what looks to be bird's nest gatherings. Unless you're really going nuts here though, it looks like the only thing making the name pertinent is the empty bird cage at the back of the bar. There's trivia on Mondays, musical bingo on Thursdays, and an open mic night the second Wednesday of every month.

i Pints £2.50-3.50. Mixed drinks from £3.50. ☼ Open daily noon-midnight or 1am.

THE EARL OF MARCHMONT

PUB

22 Marchmont Crescent

☎0131 662 1877

A talker's bar, don't be intimidated by the older folks: they won't bite—maybe stare at you for a bit, but that'll be all. Despite the distinct "regulars" vibe, the Earl fills up with students around 9pm during most of the year, but they are there for the jazz, classical, and Celtic music that plays above the buzz of conversation for much of the night. The wide windows and comfortable booths make it a perfect place to sip and watch the night fall around you.

i Pub food £8. Pints £3. Addlestone's (hard cider) £3.60. ☼ Open M-Sa 11am-1am, Su 11am-midnight.

edinburgh

BENNETS BAR

PUB

8 Leven St. ☎0131 229 5143

A perfectly quaint older pub, Bennets Bar is separated from the busy street by a pair of double doors with flowered stained glass. A great local haunt right next to the King's Theatre (currently under renovation), Bennets has seen actors act out pantomimes over pints (in lieu of a beer-laden rehearsal) or nip in for a quick one during intermission for some Dutch courage.

i Spirits £2-2.50. Pints £2.80-3.60. ☒ Open M-Sa 11am-1am, Su 5-11pm.

THE BLUE BLAZER

PUB

2 Spittal St. ☎0131 229 5030

A completely local place, the Blue Blazer refuses to let rules cramp their sense of humor. As the sign above the door says, "We at the Blue Blazer take our drinking very seriously. Anyone who appears to be having fun will be asked to leave." We're pretty sure they're kidding.

i Pints £3.10-3.60. ☒ Open M-Sa 11am-1am, Su 12:30pm-1am. In Aug open until 3am.

ARTS AND CULTURE

Edinburgh becomes the world capital for arts and culture every August during the Edinburgh Fringe Festival. The Fringe publishes its own program of activities, available in hard copy from the Fringe office and online. A world-famous orgy of performing arts, the Fringe Festival encompasses shows in theater, dance, comedy, opera, and more. The festival began in 1947 when eight rebellious theater groups not invited to perform at the International Festival decided that "the show must go on." The organization was formalized, and thus the world's largest arts festival was born. (180 High St. ☎0131 226 0026 www.edfringe.com.) For all listings and local events during the rest of the year, check out The List (www.list.co.uk £2.25) available at newsstands.

Music

■ THE JAZZ BAR

OLD TOWN

1A Chambers St. ☎0131 220 4298 www.thejazzbar.co.uk

This is the perfect venue to hear blues, hip hop, funk, and all that jazz. The Jazz Bar hosts not one, but three shows most nights: "Tea Time" (Tu-Sa 6-8:30pm) is acoustic, "The Early Gig" (daily 8:30-11:30pm) is jazzy and "Late N' Live" (daily 11:30pm-3am) is funky and electric.

i Cover after Tea Time £1-5. No cover during Tea Time. ☒ Open M-F 5pm-3am, Sa 2:30pm-3am, Su 5pm-3am. Open until 5am during Fringe Festival in Aug.

HMV PICTURE HOUSE

WEST END

31 Lothian Rd. ☎0131 221 2280 www.meanfiddler.com

With an old-school glamor about the place, you can sense that HMV Picture House used to be an old theater—that image soon fades into the evening. A beautiful place to watch things get messy, the HMV Picture House sees the likes of Bat for Lashes and Santigold, plus other big names, on the reg. On Thursday nights they do the intense "Octopussy Club night," with a bouncy castle, Jacuzzi, and plenty of chart-topping music. HMV Picture House is popular with students because of its £1 drinks. Every Saturday is "Propaganda night," launching plenty of great indie bands at hordes of Jäger-clutching students.

i Prices vary. ☒ Box office M-Sa noon-4pm.

THE BONGO CLUB

CANONGATE

37 Holyrood Rd. ☎0131 558 8844 www.thebongoclub.co.uk

Half club, half live music venue, half arts space…wait, how many halves is that? Bongo does it all, throwing raging parties on the weekends in their jungle-esque main room, with a stage for bands and live DJ set-ups. Perhaps most famously,

great britain

this is the host of the "Confusion is Sex" party which "offers people the opportunity to be something they aren't." Yeah, things get pretty crazy. Head upstairs during the day to check out the rotating art exhibits in the cafe.

i Prices vary. Cover entrance F-Sa £3-12 depending on the act. ⏰ Cafe open daily 1-7pm. Club open daily 11pm-3am.

Dance

GHILLIE DHU   WEST END
2-4 Rutland Pl.   ☎0131 222 9930 www.ghillie-dhu.co.uk
A heavily-touristed bar in what used to be a stone church building, the room upstairs, with an organ, high columned ceilings and three brilliant chandeliers, is still a popular choice for weddings. More importantly, however, the space is used for ▧traditional Scottish jigs. Head on over if you feel like getting down to some serious bagpipes.

i Pints £3-3.60. Spirits £2.75. Whiskies £2.75-17.50. ⏰ Open daily noon-3am.

Film

▧ THE CAMEO   WEST END
38 Home St.   ☎0871 902 5723 www.picturehouses.co.uk
There was a time when movie theaters were great. They had character and a good bar on the ground floor for after the magic-making on the upper floors. The screens were silver and the seats were plush. Now, in the age of Netflix and pirated movies, we have forgotten those days when movies were something to do, rather than consume. Well, the Cameo reminds us of the glory days. From the great bar downstairs to the independent and interesting movies shown, there is no better way to go to the movies.

i £7.30, matinee £6.30, student concession £4.80-5.80. ⏰ Open M-Th 11am-midnight, F-Sa 11am-1am, Su 11am-midnight.

Theater

▧ THE BEDLAM THEATER   OLD TOWN
11B Bristo Pl.   ☎0131 225 9893 www.bedlamtheatre.co.uk
The oldest student-run theater in Great Britain, the Bedlam (named after a nearby mental institution) is full of fun and crazy performances, several by the Edinburgh University Theatre Company (EUTC). The "Improverts," the University Improv group, who play every Friday at 10:30pm and every night at 12:30am during the festival, shouldn't be missed.

i Tickets £7.50-9, students usually receive a £1 discount. ⏰ Closed Jun-Jul. Aug-May, just knock and someone will be there to greet you.

EDINBURGH PLAYHOUSE   NEW TOWN
18-22 Greenside Pl.   ☎0844 847 1660 www.edinburghplayhouse.org.uk
Originally built as a cinema, which it remained for 40 years, the Edinburgh Playhouse underwent a massive renovation in 1993. It now revels in its status as one of the most popular theaters in the city. This is the place where the big acts of the Fringe come to wrangle laughs, roars, and howls from the crowd.

i Ticket prices vary. ⏰ Box office open M-Sa noon-6pm, show nights noon-8pm.

ESSENTIALS
Practicalities

- **TOURIST OFFICE: Visit Scotland Information Centre** is the largest tourist information center in Scotland. (3 Princes St. ☎0131 473 3868 www.visitscotland.com *i* Across from Waverley Station. *i* Credit cards accepted. ⏰ Open Jul-Aug M-Sa 9am-7pm, Su 10am-7pm; Sept-Jun

M-Sa 9am-5pm, Su 10am-5pm.) The friendly representatives from this Edinburgh branch will help you book accommodations, city tours, and coach and bus tours. The office also houses a souvenir shop and internet center.

- **POST OFFICE: Newington Branch.** (41 S. Clerk St. ☎0131 667 1154 *i* Walk from Edinburgh Station down Nicholson St. The post office is on the left at the intersection with Melville Dr. ☺ Open M-Sa 8:45am-5:30pm, Su 8:45am-1pm.) **Forrest Road Post Office.** (32 Forrest Rd. *i* Walk from the National Museum of Scotland, away from the Castle. The post office is on the left. ☎0131 225 3957 ☺ Open M-F 9am-5:30pm, Sa 9am-12:30pm.) **St. Mary's Street Post Office.** (46 St. Mary's St. ☎0131 556 6351 *i* Walk down the Royal Mile toward the Palace. Turn right onto The Pleasance. The post office is on the left. ☺ Open M-F 9am-5:30pm, Sa 9am-12:30pm.) **Frederick St. Post Office.** (40 Frederick St. *i* Walk from St. Andrew Sq. down George St. Turn left onto Frederick St. The post office is on the right. ☎0845 774 0740 ☺ Open M 9am-5:30pm, Tu 9:30am-5:30pm, W-F 9am-5:30pm, Sa 9am-12:30pm.)

- **INTERNET CAFE: E-Corner Internet.** (54 Blackfriars St. ☎0131 558 7858 www.e-corner. co.uk *i* Walk down the Royal Mile toward the Palace. Turn right onto Blackfriars St. The cafe is on the right. Internet £0.50 per 10min., £1.80 per hr. Printing £0.29 per page. International calls £0.10 per min. to landlines. ☺ Open M-F 9am-10pm, Sa-Su 10am-9pm.)

- **PHARMACY: Boots Pharmacy.** (32 W. Maitland St. Walk from Haymarket up W. Maitland St. The pharmacy is on the left. ☎0131 225 7436 *i* Credit cards accepted. ☺ Open M-F 8am-6pm, Sa 9am-6pm.) **Royal Mile Pharmacy.** (67 High St. ☎0131 556 1971 www.royalmilepharmacy.co.uk *i* Adjacent to the John Knox House on the Royal Mile. Credit cards accepted. ☺ Open M-F 9am-6pm, Sa 9am-5pm.)

- **ATM: Barclays** has 24hr. ATM out front. (72 George St. ☎0131 470 6000 www.barclays. co.uk. *i* At the intersection of George St. and Frederick St. ☺ Open M-F 9am-5pm, Sa 10am-2pm.)

Getting There

BY PLANE
Edinburgh's airport is **Edinburgh Turnhouse Airport** (EDI; ☎0870 040 0007 www.edinburghairport.com). The simplest way to get from the airport to central Edinburgh is on the AirLink bus. (£3.50. ☺ Every 5min.)

BY TRAIN
Waverley Train Station (☎0845 748 4950 www.networkrail.co.uk *i* Between Princes St., Market St. and Waverley Bridge ☺ Open M-Sa 4am-12:45am, Su 6am-12:45am) has trains to: Aberdeen (£35 ☺ 2½hr.; M-Sa every hr., Su 8 per day); Glasgow (£11.20 ☺ 1hr., 4 per hr.); Inverness (£32 ☺ 3½hr., every 2hr.); London King's Cross (£114 ☺ 4¾hr., every hr.); Stirling (£6.10 ☺ 50min., 2 per hr.). **Haymarket Train Station** is smaller, but has service to destinations throughout Scotland. (www.scotrail.co.uk Haymarket Terr. ☺ Open M-Sa 5am-12:30am, Su 7:45am-12:45am. Ticket office open 7:45am-9:30pm.)

Getting Around

Getting around in Edinburgh is always easiest on ⚡foot, so unless you've just completed your trip through the Himalayas, you shouldn't find yourself too sore at the end of the day. However, for those who really dislike hoofin' it, **Lothian Buses** have routes zigzagging all over the city. (☎0131 555 6363 www.lothianbuses.com *i* £1.40. Day pass £3.50. City singles—detachable day passes—20 for £28. All-night ticket for night buses £3.) Most bus stops have an electronic screen alerting you which lines are in service and their estimated time of arrival at the stop. Major Lothian bus lines include #24, 29, and 42, running from Stockbridge through the city center all the way to Newington St. on the South End. The #24 heads off toward M into St. and Arthur's

Seat, the #42 bends west to end at Portobello by Dynamic Earth, and the #29 ends at the Royal Infirmary. The #12, 26, and 31 all come in from the northwest and the Haymarket/Dalry area, the #12 bending off to the northeast after passing through city center, the #26 heading south toward Newington and Minto St. and the #31 pulling the same route but diverging to head southwest into Liberton and Gracemount. For a taxi, call **Central Taxis,** or book online. (☎0131 229 2468 www.taxis-edinburgh.co.uk)

great britain essentials

VISAS

Britain is not a signatory of the Schengen Agreement, which means it is not a member of the freedom of movement zone that covers most of continental Europe. Fortunately, its visa policies are fairly simple (for casual travelers, at least). EU citizens do not need a visa to visit Britain. Citizens of Australia, Canada, New Zealand, the US, and many other non-EU countries do not need a visa for stays of up to six months. Those staying longer than six months may apply for a longer-term visa; consult an embassy or consulate for more information. Because Britain is not a part of the Schengen zone, time spent here does not count toward the 90-day limit on travel within that area. Entering to study or work will require a visa. Check www.ukvisas. gov.uk for more information.

MONEY

Tipping and Bargaining

Tips in restaurants are sometimes included in the bill (it will appear as a "service charge"). If gratuity is not included, you should tip your server about 10%. Taxi drivers should receive a 10% tip, and bellhops and chambermaids usually expect £1-3 per night. To the great relief of many budget travelers, tipping is not expected at pubs and bars in Britain (unless you are trying to get jiggy with the bartender). Bargaining is practically unheard of in the upscale shops that overrun London. Don't try it (unless you happen to be at a street market or feel particularly belligerent).

Taxes

The UK has a 20% value added tax (VAT), a sales tax applied to everything but food, books, medicine, and children's clothing. The tax is included in the amount indicated on the price tag. The prices stated in Let's Go include VAT unless otherwise mentioned. Upon exiting Britain, non-EU citizens can reclaim VAT (minus an administrative fee) through the Retail Export Scheme, although the process is time-consuming, annoying, and may not be worth it, except for large purchases. You can obtain refunds only for goods you take out of the country (not for accommodations or noms). Participating shops display a "Tax-Free Shopping" sign and may have a minimum purchase of £50-100 before they offer refunds. To claim a refund, fill out the form you are given in the shop and present it with the goods and receipts at customs upon departure (look for the Tax-Free Refund desk at the airport). At peak times, this process can take up to an hour. You must leave the country within three months of your purchase in order to claim a refund, and you must apply before leaving the UK.

SAFETY AND HEALTH

Police

Police are a common presence in Britain and there are many police stations scattered throughout the city. There are two types of police officers in Britain: regular officers with full police powers, and police community support officers (PCSO), who have limited police power and focus on community maintenance and safety. The national emergency number is ☎999.

Drugs and Alcohol

The Brits love to drink, so the presence of alcohol is unavoidable. In trying to keep up with the locals, remember that the Imperial pint is 20oz., as opposed to the 16oz. US pint. The legal age at which you can buy alcohol in the UK is 18 (16 for buying beer and wine with food at a restaurant).

Despite what you may have seen on Skins, use and possession of hard drugs is illegal throughout the United Kingdom. Do not test this—Britain has been cracking down on drug use amongst young people in particular over the past few years. Smoking is banned in enclosed public spaces in Britain, including pubs and restaurants.

Terrorism

The bombings of July 7, 2005 in the London Underground revealed the vulnerability of large European cities to terrorist attacks and resulted in the enforcement of stringent safety measures at airports and major tourist sights throughout British cities. Though eight years have passed, security checks are still as thorough as ever. Allow extra time for airport security and do not pack sharp objects in your carry-on luggage—they will be confiscated. Unattended luggage is always considered suspicious and is also liable for confiscation. Check your home country's foreign affairs office for travel information and advisories, and be sure to follow the local news while in the UK.

MEASUREMENTS

Britain uses a thoroughly confusing and illogical mix of standard and metric measurement units. Road distances are always measured in miles, and many Brits will be clueless if you give them distances in kilometers. For weights, don't be surprised to see grams and ounces used side-by-side. There's also a measurement called a "stone," equal to 14lb., that is regularly used for giving body weights. Paradoxically, meters and centimeters are the most common way to give body heights. How the British ever accomplished anything in this world when they can't settle on a consistent system of measurements, we'll never know.

great britain 101

HISTORY

No One Expects the Vikings (Ancient Times to 1066)

Brits proudly declare that they haven't been successfully invaded since 1066, but that conveniently overlooks the fact that they were invaded a host of times before then. In prehistoric times, the islands were occupied by the Celts, who built Stonehenge and wore lots of blue face paint. Julius Caesar failed in an invasion attempt in 55 BCE, but the Romans took over for good in 43 CE. When the Roman Empire crumbled a few centuries later, the Saxons and Angles invaded from what is now Germany, bringing the language that would evolve into the English we know and abuse. According to myth, King Arthur and his knights can be credited with holding off the invading Germans for the duration of his reign. Merlin could not be reached for comment. The Vikings took a liking to raiding the Anglo-Saxons, pillaging the coast from bases in Scotland. In 886, King Alfred the Great negotiated peace with the Vikings, ushering in Anglo-Saxon supremacy and a mostly united England.

Parlez-vous français? Yeah, We Don't Either (1066-1485)

The Normans were a different kind of invader, bringing a feudal social organization to England following their victory at the Battle of Hastings in 1066. The Norman leader, William the Conqueror, made London his capital. Occasional rebellions against the feudal system gave us mostly fictional legends like Robin Hood and mostly ignored constitutional documents like the Magna Carta. During the 13th century, Edward I expanded his kingdom into Wales. The dominant issue of the age, though, was war with France. The English kings felt they had the right to the French throne; the French kings understandably disagreed. It took 116 years of fighting for this to be resolved. It looked for most of this Hundred Years' War like England would win, but somehow they managed to lose all their gains in the last few years of the war. The English love nothing more than a good war, so a civil war known as the War of the Roses followed quickly behind. This was ended in 1485 when no one would give Richard III a horse for his kingdom, and his defeat enabled Henry Tudor (Henry VII) to establish peace under the Tudor dynasty.

Break Up, Make Up, Shake Up (1485-1707)

Henry VII's main achievement was ending a giant war. Henry VIII's main achievement was being terrible at marriage. Obviously it makes sense that the latter is more famous. Henry made his way through six wives, changing the country's religion in the process just so he could get a divorce. The Church of England Henry created was a cross between Catholicism and Protestantism that predictably made no one happy. Catholic opposition to it led Spain to attempt, and fail, to invade England with the Spanish Armada of 1588. Guy Fawkes and a few Catholic friends tried to blow up Parliament and the king in the 1605 Gunpowder Plot, but their plan was foiled just a day before it would have succeeded. Hardcore Protestants were a little less troublesome, as they just set sail for the Americas to establish the first colonies there. Persistent religious troubles back home, combined with a disagreement between Charles I and Parliament over who should control the country, led to the English Civil War (1642-1651). This ended with Parliament victorious, and they took the unprecedented step of cutting off the king's head. No one was really sure what to do now, and the Parliamentary ruler, Oliver Cromwell, basically just ruled as a king-in-all-but-name until 1658. Once he died, things really fell apart, and the only solution was to go back to the monarchy. Charles I's son became Charles II. When this Charles's Catholic (!!!) brother James II became king in 1685, people were understandably a little worried, but they quickly got rid of him by persuading William of Orange to come over from the Netherlands to become William III. This Glorious Revolution involved almost no bloodshed, and ended in a stable (but unwritten) agreement that the monarchy existed mainly for ceremony while Parliament held the real power.

In the middle of all this, Elizabeth I, one of history's greatest prudes, decided to marry herself to the state rather than a man. Since states are notoriously impotent, she died childless. The only available heir was King James VI of Scotland. He became James I of England, setting the stage for the unification of England and Scotland into Great Britain, which was formalized in 1707.

If you're ready to hop the pond and not hop back, to perfect your British accent, or to pull a Beatles in reverse and take London by storm with your electro-funk country band (you know they're ready for it), then this is the section for you. We've got you non-tourist visitors covered for places to study, volunteer, and work (they'll warm to your music eventually, but you need some ca$h money in the meantime).

STUDY

- **UNIVERSITY COLLEGE LONDON (UCL):** Known as "London's global university," UCL has top marks in both student satisfaction and quality of teaching. Together with King's College, UCL formed the foundation of the University of London system back in 1836. (www.ucl.ac.uk)

- **KING'S COLLEGE LONDON:** You'll be steeped in history both royal and pop at this college, which is the third oldest university in England and an inspiration for Dan Brown's imagination. (www.kcl. ac.uk)

- **LONDON SCHOOL OF HYGIENE AND TROPICAL MEDICINE (LSHTM):** The most intriguingly named school in the University of London system, LSHTM is also a top postgraduate school in the fields of public health and tropical medicine. (www.lshtm.ac. uk)
- **TRINITY LABAN CONSERVATOIRE OF MUSIC AND DANCE:** As the label "Conservatoire" would suggest, this is a place to develop highly specialized artistic skills. However, the school also offers some classes that are open to the public. (www. trinitylaban.ac.uk)

VOLUNTEER

- **MUSEUM OF LONDON:** What could be cooler than spending your free time learning to work with artifacts and archiving historical objects? (www. museumoflondon.org.uk/Get- involved/ Volunteers)
- **THE CONSERVATION VOLUNTEERS:** If you've got a green thumb and have already checked with the doctor that it's not gangrene, put your unusual pigmentation to good use greening urban spaces and "reclaiming green spaces." (http://www.tcv.org. uk)
- **ZOOLOGICAL SOCIETY OF LONDON:** Think less Eliza Thornberry and more Lyra Belacqua when she's in Oxford; volunteer positions do not generally involve contact with animals. (http://www.zsl.org/ membership/volunteering)
- **LONDON HEALTH SCIENCES CENTER:** If you have a lot of joy and a big heart, there's no better way to share it than with people whose health is not as strong. (http://www.lhsc.on.ca/About_Us/Volunteer_Services)
- **NATURAL HISTORY MUSEUM:** What better way to get in touch with London's natural history roots than to volunteer at the Natural History Museum. (www.nhm.ac.uk/ support-us/volunteer)
- **ENGLISH HERITAGE:** If you're looking to connect with London's history and roots beyond what's Natural, check out this organization. (www. english-heritage.org.uk/caring/get-involved/ volunteering)
- **DOGS TRUST:** That's right, there's a charity that lets you hang out with dogs (walk them, play with them, cuddle with them) in your free time. (www.dogstrust.org. uk/giving/supportyourcentre/ volunteer)

WORK

- **RECRUITMENT AGENCIES:** One of the best ways to locate where the jobs are in London is to visit a recruitment agency specific to your field. (www. agencycentral.co.uk)
- **GOVERNMENT-RUN JOB CENTERS:** Another avenue to tracking down jobs in your area of interest and expertise, though if you want to snag that job, best start referring to these as government-run job 'centres.' (https://www.gov.uk/ jobsearch)
- **NEWSPAPER POSTINGS:** You can never go wrong with some good, old-fashioned scouring of the classifieds. Try The Guardian jobs, for instance. (http://jobs. theguardian.com/jobs/uk/england/greater-london)
- **PEEK-A-BOO CHILDCARE:** Au pair gigs are like free homestays, but with way more responsibility. They are a great way to learn about London culture while also making lifelong bonds with a family. Check out Peek-a-Boo Childcare for a reputable and established au pair agency based in London. (www. peekaboochildcare. com/for-au- pairs.aspx)
- **GREATER LONDON TUTORS:** Knowing English is not exactly a marketable skill in London, so teaching English is not a great way to make money here, but tutoring other subjects is a viable option. (www. greaterlondontutors.com)

BEYOND TOURISM

www.letsgo.com

Rule, Britannia (1707-1914)

With religious questions mostly settled (answer: 42), the 18th century saw Britain begin to build the largest empire the world has ever seen. By the end of the Seven Years' War (1756-63), Britain controlled Canada, 13 unruly colonies in America, and much of the Caribbean. Meanwhile, the East India Company, a technically independent company, took control over a large part of India. The loss of the American colonies was seen as a fairly insignificant development, as the empire elsewhere continued to flourish. Napoleon felt he could challenge British supremacy, but he was sent packing at the Battles of Trafalgar and Waterloo. During the reign of Queen Victoria, imperial expansion went into overdrive, as Britain took power throughout India, Australia, and much of Africa. Back home, the Industrial Revolution gave Britain the economic strength to control all of this territory, while also driving a population boom in cities like Liverpool and Glasgow. The country was also intellectually formidable, with thinkers like Sir Isaac Newton and Adam Smith revolutionizing scientific and philosophical thought.

Low Expectations (1914-1945)

Many people would later look back to the pre-WWI era as one of greatness and prosperity for Britain. This totally misses the fact that the working classes lived in appalling poverty and that the empire rested on exploitation of native peoples. Of course, things got worse before they got better. Colonial rivalry and embarrassing diplomatic failures led to World War One breaking out across Europe. The war lasted for four years, led to the death of nearly a million British men, and achieved virtually nothing. Twenty years later, Britain again found itself at war with Germany in World War Two. This war brought the fighting into Britain itself, with Hitler's bombers attacking London and other cities. Nearly half a million Brits lost their lives in the war.

The Myth of Decline (1945-2011)

Despite victory in the war, Britain was devastated by years of fighting. Its decimated economy and military could no longer sustain the empire, and most colonies declared independence in the next 20 years. The left-wing Labour government that held power after the war focused on internal issues, establishing free universal healthcare and taxation levels that would make the Tea Party cry. Despite the decline in Britain's international power, the standard of living rose dramatically. The cultural boom of the 1960s saw Britain produce the best music and the shortest skirts the world has ever seen. Things went downhill in the strike-ridden 1970s, but a boom returned under the leadership of Margaret Thatcher's Conservative Party in the late 1980s. The Labour government of Tony Blair focused on improving public services like healthcare and education, but rising debt levels and the economic crisis have led the new Conservative government of David Cameron to cut back government spending. Alienation exploded in the riots of last August, where bitter youths looted shops in London and other cities. Despite these recent troubles, modern Britain is one of the richest and most stable countries in Europe.

great britain

HUNGARY

Throughout Hungary, the vestiges of Ottoman and communist rules can be found on the same block. Castles stand staunchly and thermal baths pool beside concrete Soviet monuments, overlooking the graves of 20th-century writers and medieval poets. Döner kebabs, bockwurst, and cheeses are peddled side by side, while Budapest locals frequent Turkish bathhouses.

But Hungary's real draw may be the freewheeling youth and a relentless drive toward the modern. Streets are packed with hip hangouts and their patrons exude a vehemently chill attitude, making this city one of the best student urban destinations in Europe. And even though the locals might be too cool for school, they do appreciate a tenacity to learn about their culture. So make the effort and immerse yourself in all that is Hungary, with endless plates of goulash, sleepless nights at ruin pubs, and countless cups of coffee with some newfound friends.

greatest hits

- **RUBBER DUCKIE, YOU'RE THE ONE.** Get squeaky clean at **Széchenyi-Gyógyfürdő**, one of Budapest's many public bath complexes (p. 424).

- **INSTAFAN.** Hipsters will appreciate the chill vibe and kooky décor at **Szimpla Kert** (p. 434), Budapest's original ruin pub.

- **ICE, ICE, BABY.** In the winter, an area of historic **Hősök tere** (Heroes' Square, p. 424) functions as a skating rink.

- **FRESH TO DEATH.** Learn proper hummus-and-pita-eating techniques at **Hummus Bár** (p. 429).

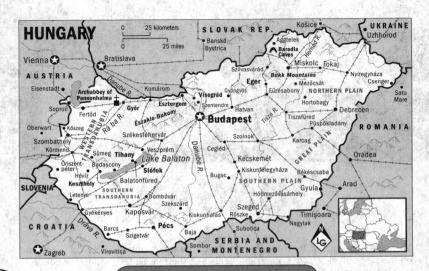

student life

You won't have to spurge on club attire if you're planning to backpack through Budapest. Ruin pubs—the trendiest new nightlife destinations—observe a come-as-you-are attitude. Twenty-somethings lounge in mismatched chairs while enjoying film screenings, concerts, or cold brews. Bring your new buzzed buddies for some mid-party munchies at **Cafe Alibi**—a little coffee shop in the center of student-city. Nurse your hangover in the parks around Józsefváros—an up-and-coming district popular with young locals—and pick up a hipster hottie at the Budapest film school while you're in the neighborhood. Take your new beau on an impromptu date to **Grand Market Hall** for some cheap eats, and stroll off the calories along the Danube in the Belváros. Now that's cut-rate courting.

budapest

Perhaps the single most underrated city in Europe, Budapest is a town for lovers and dreamers. It's a place where the grocery store clerk will chat you up even if he can't understand a word you're saying, a land where ruins become late-night bastions for beer-swilling hipsters, where people flock to museums until three in the morning, and where every building has its own character, name, and color. Nowhere else can you play chess with half-naked old men in the warm waters of a Turkish bath. You might be hard-pressed to find a picture comparable to one taken at sunset from Fisherman's Bastion on the top of the Gothic Parliament, whose dangerously honed spires melt under the fairy tale-blue hue of the sky. A walk on Margaret Island makes you feel as if you've stumbled upon a rainforest oasis, while a stroll down Andrássy út, with its tree-lined walkway of purple and yellow flowers, leads you to one of the most towering monuments in Europe: the Millennial Monument, around which people once stood with candles in their hands to form a giant, blazing peace sign. In the years since Hungary entered the European Union and money began to flow into the once severely impoverished nation, Budapest has become a city under constant repair and reconstruction; the result is a city of juxtaposition. Modern, newly erected buildings stand alongside ancient, 18th-century structures whose crumbling façades become endearing rather than appalling. Perhaps what makes the city most remarkable is that rather than concealing the scars and scabs left by its bloody history, Budapest bears them to the world like the proud warrior that it is.

ORIENTATION

Belváros, District V

Belváros holds the best and worst of what Budapest has to offer. Wide streets packed with tourist traps like **Váci utca** merge and intertwine with back alleys filled with crowded pubs and dimly lit restaurants to which locals possessively slink. Every city has its Belváros, where "INSERT CITY NAME HERE" is emblazoned on bags blowing from metal hooks on street carts; unlike every other city, though, Budapest's tourist trap district is just as popular with locals as it is with visitors. From **Erzsébet tér,** the northern city park filled with Tony Hawk wannabes and teens in ripped black everything, to the southern terminus of **Grand Market Hall** (a testament to capitalism if there ever was one), to the western shimmering border of the Danube, Belváros is a laid-back district of over-priced real estate with a heart to fill it. After a night of partying in Erzsébetváros or antiquing in Lipótváros, Belváros quietly stands with wide boulevards and hushed coffeehouses, welcoming those whose aim is the aesthetic.

Lipótváros, District V and XIII

Lipótváros includes parts of District V and XIII, beginning after Arany János utca, adjacent to Belváros, and continuing along the river past Margit Island. This neighborhood boasts the majestic **Parliament Building,** with its Gothic spires overlooking the island, as well as the hand of God (or at least St. Stephen's mummified one) in **St. Stephen's Basilica** near the south. Between these two competing landmarks lies the ironically-named **Liberty Square,** nestled between the locked-and-guarded American embassy and Budapest's Wall Street. Lipótváros also extends into Budapest's former factory district. While not much attracts the average tourist past Margit Bridge, the more adventurous will find a few hidden treasures nestled between the towering residential complexes.

Erzsébetváros, District VII

After hearing that the largest synagogue in the world lies in New York City, you'd probably think that the second-largest place of worship for the Jewish people would be in Israel. Nope. It's in the center of Pest, in domed and towered splendor, heralding the western entrance to the city's Jewish district: Erzsébetváros. Just south of the bourgeoisie's domain, Terézváros, this district is carpeted in kosher delis, Torah education centers, and two of the city's most famous theaters: Madrach and Magyar Szinhaz. However, the district's rich, Semitic cultural tradition isn't what brings most young travelers to its newly renovated streets. No, the big draw is the thread of ruin pubs stitched between **Andrassy utca** and **Rakoczi utca,** including **Szimpla Kert,** rated by ☒**Lonely Planet** users as the third best bar in the world.

Terézváros, District VI

Perhaps the busiest district in Budapest, Terézváros is home to an international train station, corporate offices, giant supermarkets, import stores, and the most globally diverse selection of dining opportunities you'll find in the city. The district's main draw is **Andrássy út,** which runs north to south from **Heroes' Square** to the **State Opera House.** The area near Andrássy út intersecting **Hajós utca** boasts some of the city's coolest new ruin pubs, while **Liszt Ferenc tér,** a few blocks from the **Oktogon** (a surprisingly descriptive cognate), offers outstanding budget eateries, from Hungarian

budapest

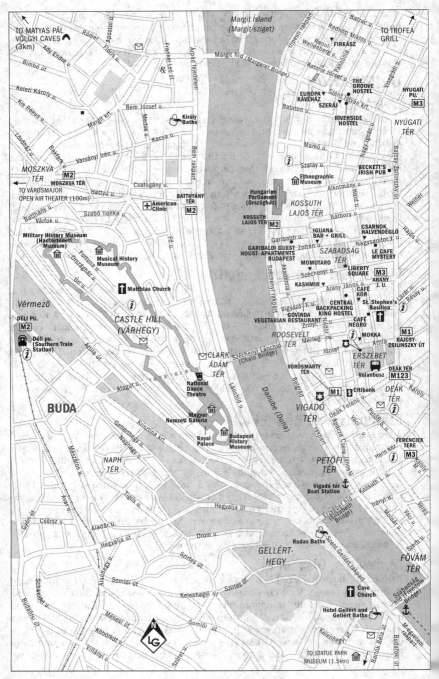

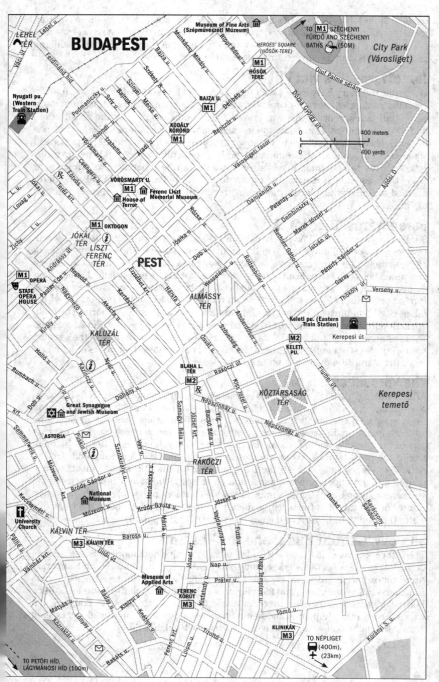

BUDAPEST

LEHEL TÉR

Nyugati pu. (Western Train Station)

Museum of Fine Arts (Szépművészeti Múzeum)

HEROES' SQUARE (HŐSÖK-TERE)

TO M1 SZÉCHENYI FÜRDŐ AND SZÉCHENYI BATHS (50M)

City Park (Városliget)

M1 HŐSÖK TERE

BAJZA U. M1

KODÁLY KÖRÖND M1

0   400 meters
0   400 yards

VÖRÖSMARTY U. M1

Ferenc Liszt Memorial Museum

House of Terror

OKTOGON M1

JÓKAI TÉR

LISZT FERENC TÉR

PEST

ALMÁSSY TÉR

OPERA M1

STATE OPERA HOUSE

Keleti pu. (Eastern Train Station)

M2 KELETI PU.

Kerepesi út

Verseny u.

KALUZÁL TÉR

BLAHA L. TÉR M2

KÖZTÁRSASÁG TÉR

Kerepesi temető

Great Synagogue and Jewish Museum

ASTORIA

RÁKÓCZI TÉR

National Museum

University Church

KÁLVIN TÉR

M3 KÁLVIN TÉR

Museum of Applied Arts

FERENC KÖRÚT M3

KLINIKÁK M3

TO NÉPLIGET (400m), (23km)

TO PETŐFI HÍD, LÁGYMÁNYOSI HÍD (100m)

budapest

canteen-style joints to fancier sit-down places. As in most cases, a busier environment means more commotion, and while there's no reason to fret on an average day, heed the area around the train station and the Oktogon for pickpockets, peddlers, and obnoxious drunks—even during daylight hours.

Józsefváros, District VIII

Bordering the fancy Belváros district to the west and just south of Erzsébetváros, the Józsefváros district has never been known for its glam or historical edification. Rather, up until a few years ago, it was known for its homeless population, prostitution, and dicey sex shops. Ever since the installation of public cameras, Józsefváros has metamorphosed into a district that now has some of the city's friendliest parks and squares, a fantastic artist community, the Budapest film school, and the gorgeous National Museum building. Take a stroll down the northern boundary of **Rakoczi út** or enjoy the west side of **Muzeum korut** for a dose of new charm. You will also be hard-pressed to find a young local who doesn't recommend this area for its underground nightlife.

Ferencváros, District IX

Similar to Józsefváros, Ferencváros is an up-and-coming district with newly renovated Baroque buildings and winding cobblestone streets. The past few years of city rehabilitation projects have left the inner half-circle of the district (the area contained between **Ferenc körút** and the Danube) looking freshly polished, albeit a bit empty. As the renovated areas became prettier, they also became more expensive, forcing previous dwellers to move to communities outside of the boulevard, where dilapidated buildings and streets with homeless people are still the norm. The main attraction for tourists in this part of town is **Ráday utca,** a small pedestrian street lined with restaurants and bars. While it can be an enjoyable place to dine in the evening hours, strict district codes that force establishments to close their doors at midnight leave the nightlife seekers at a bit of a loss.

The Városliget *City Park*

After walking through Budapest's seemingly endless matrix of Neo-Baroque, Neo-Classical, and Art Nouveau architecture, the Városliget will quench your thirst for greenery. Located in the northeastern corner of the urban sprawl, you can bathe yourself in history in **Heroes' Square** (located at the entrance of the park) or in art at one of the two national museums flanking the plaza; you can also literally bathe in one of the most famous spa complexes in Europe, smack dab in the middle of the park. If you're awash with cash, there are plenty of high-falutin' restaurants that have poured attention upon popes, queens, and pop stars; if the money flow has dried up, you can still stop by Kertem, a somewhat hidden outdoor pub in the southern corner. But if you are thirsting for serenity, merely let the sun swish through the trees like water through your fingers, and enjoy the scenery of the park for free.

Varhegy, Central Buda, and the Vizivaros

These three adjacent districts are Buda's most attractive neighborhoods and include **Castle Hill,** the famous **Chain Bridge,** and some of the city's most authentic Hungarian restaurants. It's easy to spend a whole day perusing the cobblestone streets of Castle Hill, marveling at the views, and learning about Hungarian art at the National Gallery. For the adventurous traveler, we recommend taking a bus from **Margit Bridge,** which winds through the Buda hills and behind the castle, for some unofficial sightseeing among the palatial abodes of the wealthy **Rózsadomb** neighborhood.

Gellért Hegy *Gellért Hill*

As you cross Erzsébet Híd from Pest into Buda, you'll appreciate just how hard Gellért Hegy would be to besiege. Composed of dramatically jutting volcanic rock and carpeted in dense forest, the hill is Budapest's one-stop-totally-free-shop for snapping city-wide shots. Climb up spidery paths from Hotel Gellért on the south side (and stop at the cave churches on the way up), or approach from the north for a more gradual sloping climb past a waterfall and statue to the hill's namesake, St. Gellért. Once you reach the top, the **Citadella** and **Liberty Monument** will greet you in stark military splendor, flanked by the Greek gods Marathon and Hercules. You'll wish you had those gods' strength after the arduous climb.

Margit-Sziget *Margaret Island*

Named after a girl sent to a convent, Margaret Island is both beatified and beautiful. With a thick, woodsy scent enveloped by the quiet swish of the Danube, this 2km long island is the locals' version of the Városliget and is conveniently located smack-dab between Buda and Pest. In the morning, you can join the quiet padding of runners' feet on the springy 5km trail that loops around the island or soak in the palatial Palatinus baths on the western side. In the afternoon, stop by the ruins and the Musical Fountain to the north, then repose in a grassy field while watching Hungarian youth play any number of games.

SIGHTS

It's a cliché reserved for advertisements to state that "X has something for everyone." But Budapest actually does.

Belváros

UNIVERSITY CHURCH

CHURCH

Papnövelde utca 7

University Square is accented by the glowing orange Baroque architecture of University Church, built in 1725. Pauline monks spent 17 years constructing and then perfecting every nook and cranny of the church while hiding valuable goblets and costumes in the cupboards lining the interior. This somewhat-secret chapel is located between rows of tall buildings and several streets up from the main downtown tourist area, but its darkish Roman Catholic symbolism is worth a visit. Contemplate life in one of the pews, but don't take it too easy—the backs have a jutting piece of wood on the top to keep you at attention.

i M3: Ferenciek tere. Head east on Kecskeméti utca and turn right on Papnövelde utca. Just your undying love for the Virgin Mary. ⚐ Services M-F 7am and 6pm; Su 8, 9, 11am, 12:30, 5, 7:30pm.

Lipótváros

ORSZÁGHAZ (PARLIAMENT)

GOVERNMENT BUILDING

Plaza Kossuth   ☎01 441 4000 www.parlament.hu

"The motherland does not have a house," lamented Hungarian poet Mihály Vörösmarty in 1846. Built in response to the growing sense of Hungarian nationalism during the period, this palatial Gothic revival building looks more like a set from The Lord of the Rings than a seat of government. Interestingly enough, during Communist times, a red star was placed on top of the building to make it slightly higher than the top of St. Stephen's Basilica, but the star was removed after the change to democracy. Take a guided tour to gaze admiringly upon a symbol of another dead political regime: the original Holy Crown of Hungary.

i M2: Kossuth tér. Head toward the river. Tours start at Gate XII and last about 50min. Entrance and tour 2850Ft, students 1410Ft. Free with EU passport. Ask a guard for permission to buy a ticket at Gate X. ⚐ English-language tours daily 10am, noon, 2pm; buy tickets early, especially in summer. Ticket office opens at 8am.

get a room!

For more accommodations recommendations, visit **www.letsgo.com**.

For more accommodations recommendations, visit **www.letsgo.com**.

ALL CENTRAL HOSTEL
HOSTEL $$

Bécsi utca 2 ☎01 328 0955 www.allcentral.hu

All Central Hostel is a real estate agent's dream: location, location, location defines this no-frills hostel with airy dorms, pristine bathrooms, and unbeatable prices. A kind-of-creepy elevator whisks weary pack-toting travelers up to one of the four floors for a night of repose in sleek bunks that might leave you feeling like you're sleeping in an infirmary. Just a couple blocks away from the Parliament building, the Danube River, the basilica, and Váci utca, this place is a steal.

i M1, M2, or M3: Deák Ferenc tér. Head down Bárczy István utca toward the river and turn right onto Bécsi utca. Lockers available. Dorms 3000-5000Ft; doubles 14,000Ft. 🕐 Reception 24hr. Check-out 10am.

10 BEDS
HOSTEL $$

Erzsébet körút 15 ☎3620 933 59 65

With an open layout and plenty of international guests, this happy and friendly hostel is so appealing that long-term guests sometimes become quasi-staff members and welcome you to the city with a pub crawl or trip to a bath. Eat breakfast at the minimalist bar or simply relax in a hostel that feels like it could be the house of a friend back home.

i M2: Blaha Lujza tér. Head north on Erzsébet körút 1½ blocks; the hostel is on the right. Free Wi-Fi. Linens, laundry, and lockers included. Dorms from 3000Ft. 🕐 Reception 24hr.

HOME-MADE HOSTEL
HOSTEL $$

Teréz körút 22 ☎302 21 03 www.homemadehostel.com

If you plan on hopping between restaurants, clubs, and cultural sights, the Oktogon will be your geographical center; this hostel, located only one block away from the eight-sided center of mayhem, goes against all of those surroundings by providing an earth-toned asylum. The proof? No bunks, large rooms, a decor of nicely-aged suitcases and bookshelves, and cooking lessons to teach you how to create homemade food. The calming experience begins as soon as you walk off the streets into the gorgeous, classical-style courtyard within.

i M1: Oktogon. Take Teréz körút east from Oktogon; the hostel is on the left. Free Wi-Fi. Towels and linens included. Laundry 2000Ft. Dorms from 3300Ft; doubles from 12,000Ft. 🕐 Reception 24hr.

MAXIM HOSTEL
HOSTEL $$

Ráday utca 34 ☎2360 404 02 22 www.maximhostel.com

Located on the main street of Ferencváros, this hostel is a great option for those who want to stay in a quieter part of the city. Amazing wooden beds will help you rest easy underneath crazy wall murals of dancing French ladies, and a spacious bathtub will wash the city grime off your skin and provide you with some respite from the energy of the street. Occasional free Hungarian meals cooked by staff members cap off an unbeatable deal—although since the hostel is on Ráday utca, you'll have more options than you know what to do with.

i M3: Ferenc körút. Head west on Üllői út and turn left onto Kinizsi utca. The hostel is on the corner of Kinizsi utca and Ráday utca. Free Wi-Fi. Breakfast, linens, and towels included. Dorms from 3000Ft; doubles from 9000Ft. 🕐 Reception 24hr.

hungary

SAINT STEPHEN'S BASILICA (SZENT ISTVÁN BAZILIKA)   CHURCH
Hercegprímás utca 7   ☎06 1 311 0839   http://bazilika.biz
Completed in 1905 after 50 years of construction, this towering monument and its majestic cupola smile on Budapest's Wall Street. The red-green marble and gilded interior attracts both local worshippers and gaping tourists who come to see the Panorama Tower—the highest 360-degree view of the city. After you take in the glorious view, go down to the church and notice that the statue of Jesus at the front altar looks more like St. Stephen than the Nazarene. Not surprisingly, the basilica's most prized treasure is the eponymous saint's mummified right hand, and Roman Catholicism's long history of relic-worship hasn't changed much: a 200Ft donation will illuminate the relic for two minutes.

i *M1, M2, or M3: Deák Ferenc tér. Follow the signs. Entry to tower 500Ft, students 400Ft. 200Ft church donation.* ⊕ *Church open daily 7am-7pm. Chapel open May-Oct M-Sa 9am-5pm, Su 1-5pm; Nov-Apr M-Sa 10am-4pm. Mass M-Sa 8am and 6pm, Su 8, 9, 10am, noon, 6, 7:30pm. Tower open daily Apr-Oct M-Sa 10am-6pm.*

Erzsébetváros

🏛 GOZSDU UDVAR   WALKWAY
Between Király utca 13 and Dob utca 16
If it wasn't for the continual, meandering stream of people emanating from a normal-looking apartment complex, you'd walk right past this 200m-long secret passageway of bars, cafes, and shops. Mere capitalism, however, isn't the only thing to be savored under the breezy archways—live music and comedy shows create an equally cool ambience during the summer.

i *M1: Oktogon. Head east on Erzsébet körút and turn right onto Király utca. Summer months bring open-air concerts and events. Check www.culture.hu for more information and event listings.*

SYNAGOGUE AND JEWISH MUSEUM   MUSEUM, SYNAGOGUE
Corner of Dohány utca and Wesselényi utca   ☎36 70 533 5696   www.greatsynagogue.hu
The largest synagogue in Europe and the second-largest in the world, Pest's Great Synagogue (Zsinagóga) was built in 1859 and heavily damaged during WWII when the Nazis used it as a radio base during the Siege of Budapest. Today it stands as the gloriously desert-rose colored, onion-domed place of worship guarding the city's Jewish district. The post-war reconstruction isn't the only beautiful thing about the synagogue—an enormous metal weeping willow called the Tree of Life stands in the courtyard as a stunning Holocaust memorial. Next door, the Jewish Museum (Zsidó Múzeum), built at the birthplace of Zionist Theodor Herzel, displays Budapest's most prominent Jewish artifacts.

i *M2: Astoria. Covered shoulders required. Men must cover their heads inside; yarmulkes available at the entrance. Admission to museum included with entrance to the synagogue. 2500Ft, students 1100Ft. Tour prices vary.* ⊕ *Open Mar-Oct M-Th 10am-5:30pm, F 10am-3:30pm, Su 10am-5:30pm; Nov-Feb M-Th 10am-3:30pm, F 10am-1:30pm, Su 10am-3:30pm. Services F 6pm. Admission starts at 10:30am. Tours M-Th 10:30am-3:30pm every 30min.; F and Su 10:30, 11:30am, 12:30pm.*

Terézváros

🏛 ANDRÁSSY ÚT   BOULEVARD
Budapest's Champs-Élysées, Andrássy út extends from Erzsébet tér northeast to Heroes' Square (Hősök tér) and the Városliget. Once the headquarters for the Nazi and Communist regimes, this street now stands as tribute to the arts, with the Hungarian State Opera House and statues waxing rhapsodic to national hero, Franz Liszt. While the M1 line runs directly under the boulevard, it would be a shame to skip the 30min. walk above ground, which takes you past rows of UNESCO-preserved buildings as well as a litany of excellent dining options and even fancier fashion establishments.

i *M1: Hősök tér through Bajcsy-Zsilinszky. Free.*

⬛ EIFFEL TÉR

GRASSY KNOLL

No assassinations have yet occurred around this brand-spanking new nook next to the train station, although you might still see a few budding tourists/Zapruders snapping shots of the fountains and beautiful, velvety greenery. Recently transformed from a parking lot to a grassy knoll for reading and lounging, the area is enhanced by its location between the dramatic architecture of the Nyugati rail station and an equally dramatic, modern office building that rents ground floor spaces out to cafes and bars. A terrace also hosts nightlife activities.

i M3: Nyugati. Free.

⬛ NYUGATI PÁLYAUDVAR

RAILWAY STATION

Teréz körút 55

This railway station is smaller than its eastern cousin, though it has the advantage of being in a neighborhood you'll actually want to visit. The building was designed and built by the Eiffel Co., though it turned out notably less phallic than the company's Parisian masterpiece. If you're itching to explore the rest of the country and region, this station is the hub for several intra-Hungary train routes as well as a few toward Austria, but if you're planning on staying put, the station itself is a beautiful, Baroque construction connected to the most lavish McDonald's you'll ever see.

i M3: Nyugati. Free.

The Városliget

⬛ HŐSÖK TERE (HEROES' SQUARE)

MONUMENT

Spanning the space of a stadium, Heroes' Square is a flat construction of white stone that can get super hot on a summer's day. However, surrounding this bizarre field marauding tourist groups are some of Budapest's greatest landmarks. The Millennium Monument commemorates both the supernatural and the human: the pillar in its center is topped by the Archangel Gabriel, while the base is surrounded by the seven chieftains said to be the leaders of the Magyar tribes that settled the Carpathian Basin. On the left side of the square stands the Museum of Fine Arts, and on the right stands the Palace of Art (quite flattering that art is considered so heroic, no?).

i M1: Hősök tere. You can't miss it! Free.

⬛ SZÉCHENYI-GYÓGYFÜRDŐ (SZÉCHENYI BATHS)

BATH, MONUMENT

Állatkerti körút 11 ☎363 32 10 www.szechenyibath.com

Tourists and locals flock to this sprawling bath complex in droves in order to relax in the swimming pool, take the cure (the water contains a cocktail of minerals that would make a Long Island Iced Tea jealous), or shock their systems by jumping in and out of thermal baths. With chess matches between grizzled elders and young up-and-comers scattered amid the bath's startlingly gorgeous neo-Baroque visage, Széchenyi is the perfect place to rest your body and your eyes alike.

i M1: Széchenyi Fürdő. Bring your own bathing suit and towel. Daily tickets from 3400Ft. Massages from 3000Ft. ⏰ Open daily 6am-10pm.

Varhegy, Central Buda, and Vizivaros

⬛ ROYAL PALACE

MUSEUM

Szent György tér 2

After being occupied by the Ottomans, crusaded by the Christians, and rented by the Revolutionaries, you'd think that the royal residence would have been allowed a reprieve after rehabilitation in the late 19th century. But after the Nazis came (and went), you can imagine what the Communists thought of the Royal Palace's lavishness. Despite its trying past, today the palace serves as the holder of all things Hungarian as the site of the National Gallery, the National History Museum (which includes a rather moving collection of artists' portraits of the palace), and even a public library. However, for those not interested in the castle's more dusty legacies, the flowering courtyards, fountains, and positively panoramic views of Pest provide ample value for no cost at all.

i M1, M2, or M3: Deák Ferenc tér. Take Bus #16 across the Danube. Or, from Moszkva tér; walk up to the hill on Várfok utca. "Becsi kapu" marks the castle entrance. Free.

FISHERMAN'S BASTION (HALÁSZBÁSTYA)   MONUMENT
Szentháromság tér

It is said that a man called Jesus Christ of Nazareth once provided fish for 5000 people; since then, the outcropping of a castle wall called Fisherman's Bastion has provided photos for a lot more than 5000 tourists. While bastions were originally built to give castle defenders more visibility to shoot at the advancing hordes, this one has about as much defensive capability as the Magic Kingdom's Cinderella Castle—and looks just like it, too. But you're not here to preserve your empire—just your money—so make the climb at sunset or nightfall to gaze down upon the river without paying the daytime fee. Then again, you might just see some falconry if you pass by under the scourge of the sun.

i In front of Matthias Church; walk toward the river. Daytime 300Ft, nighttime free.

MATTHIAS CHURCH (MÁTYÁS TEMPLOM)   CHURCH
Szentháromság tér 2   www.matyas-templom.hu

Electric blue, neon orange, and earthy brown wouldn't intuitively make for the most aesthetic color palette, but the diamond-shaped tiles on the roof of continuously-photographed Matthias Church exceed expectations. After a brief stint as a mosque during the 16th and 17th centuries (during which the interior was gutted and white-washed), the church suffered further during its reconstruction at the hands of an ambitious nobody. We say nobody because history rarely rewards failure, and it wasn't until the 19th century that Frigyes Schulek procured some ancient plans and rebuilt the church in Neo-Gothic style in the flash of a tourist's camera (23 years, more specifically, but that's pretty remarkable for a church). Teeter up the spiral staircase to visit The Museum of Ecclesiastical Art if you think relic precedes angelic; if you believe all that glitters is not gold, go outside and take a photograph (the park directly south of the church is slightly elevated and an excellent spot to snap a shot).

i Bus 16, 16a, and 116: Szentháromság tér. Church and museum 1000Ft, students 700Ft. Open M-F 9am-5pm, Sa 9am-1pm, Su 1-5pm. High mass M-Sa 7, 8:30am, 6pm, Su 7, 8:30, 10am, noon, 6pm.

SZÉCHENYI CHAIN BRIDGE (SZÉCHENYI LÁNCHÍD)   BRIDGE

After waking up in Budapest, don't take Erzsébet or Margit híd and let Budapest's first bridge over the Danube be the sight that got away. You've probably already seen the city's famous bridge, as Katy Perry used Széchenyi as a triumphant runway for her music video for "Firework," but it wasn't that long ago that a less inspirational kind of explosion destroyed the bridge when the Axis powers retreated after WWII. Rebuilt soon after, it now connects the heart of Belváros to the belly of Buda. On the Buda side, stop by the Zero Kilometer Stone from whence all Hungarian highways are measured.

i Bridge spans between Clark Ádám tér, on the Buda side, and Roosevelt tér, on the Pest side. Free.

MAGYAR NEMZETI GALÉRIA (HUNGARIAN NATIONAL GALLERY)   MUSEUM
Buda Palace, wings A, B, C, and D   ☎356 00 49   www.mng.hu

The halls of Buda Castle now house the world's largest collection of Hungarian fine art. Spread across three floors and divided by historical period, the permanent collection traces the development of Hungarian painting and sculpture

budapest

from the Gothic period to the second half of the 20th century. The collections of painters like Gyárfás Jenő and Károly Lotz are some of the museum's best, but for those who crave a more modern take, look for pieces by Impressionist Béla Czóbel in the 20th-century galleries, including his 1922 work, In the Atelier.

i Hike up or take the tram to Buda Castle. The museum is housed in the giant building that you can't possibly miss. 1200Ft. Hapsburg crypt 600Ft. Audio guides 800Ft. ⏰ Open Tu-Su 9am-5pm. Last entry 4:30pm.

Gellért Hegy

🏛 LIBERTY MONUMENT (SZABADSÁG SZOBOR)
Gellért Hill
MONUMENT

Budapest has a complicated history with the term "liberty," as the city intimately knows that "liberators" can easily morph into freshly-molded tyrants. Its most famous tribute to freedom, however, guards the city with the intimidating advantage of a palm frond (okay, and a frightfully defensible fortress—the Citadella). Overlooking Buda and Pest, this green Lady Liberty will take your breath away, mostly because of the insanely steep ascent required to gaze upon her visage. Then again, you're free to take the bus, but that's going to cost you 320Ft. (Also, there's no such thing as a free lunch: the food options on top of the hill are devotees of the free market, you know.)

i The monument is at the top of the hill, near the Citadella. Only wheelchair-accessible if you take bus #27 from Moricz Zsigmond. Free.

HOTEL GELLÉRT AND GELLÉRT BATHS
Szent Gellért tér 1
BATH
☎466 61 66 www.spasbudapest.com

At the foot of Gellért Hill lies one of the mementos that the Turkish occupation left behind: thermal baths. This isn't just your standard Jean-Paul Marat bathtub—Hotel Gellért's Art Nouveau halls contain baths at varying degrees of steaming, baths separated by gender, a swimming pool, several Sahara-level saunas, and even a wave pool and sun terrace outside. While the hotel itself is probably beyond most students' budgets, the bath's richly tiled and statued interior is the perfect after party following a sweaty climb up the hill.

i Tram 49: Szent Gellért tér. Towel rental available, but bring your own bathing suit. Check www.danubiushotels.com for hotel details. Admission with locker 4200Ft. ⏰ Open M-F 6am-7pm, Sa 6am-10pm, Su 6am-8pm. Last entry 1hr. before close.

Outer Buda

🏛 MEMENTO PARK (SZOBORPARK)
On the corner of Balatoniút and Szabadkai utca
MONUMENT

While in the rest of the former Soviet republics people were happily dismantling and demolishing the symbols of their hated regimes, the monument-loving people of Budapest decided it might be worthwhile to keep theirs around, even if they didn't want them anywhere near the city itself. Forty of these statues now reside a 25min. bus ride away in Memento Park as a testament to a bygone political and artistic period. At the gates to the park, you can see an authentic replica of the infamous Stalin statue that was torn down so thoroughly during the 1956 revolution that only the dictator's boots were left behind; the remains of the statue became a symbol of the revolution. An indoor exhibit shows unnerving clips from old secret police training videos. If you pay attention, you may even learn a thing or two about how to hide secret messages in crushed soda cans.

i Express bus #7: Etele tér. Take the yellow Volán bus from terminal #7 bound for Diosd-Érd and get off at Memento Park. You'll need to buy a separate ticket from the Volánbusz ticket office. There is also a white direct bus from Deák Ferenc tér (M1, M2, or M3) daily Jan-Jun 11am, Jul-Aug 11am and 3pm, Sept-Dec 11am. The bus costs 4500Ft, students 3500Ft; includes price of admission and return ticket. 1500Ft, students 1000Ft. ⏰ Open daily 10am-dusk.

Margit-Sziget

RUINS
RUINS

Margit Sziget

Though it may be hard to imagine now, there was once a time when this island was used for something besides outdoor drinking and sunbathing (in fact, its medieval name was Island of the Rabbits). More seriously, however, Margaret Island was the place to be cloistered in Budapest. King Béla IV built the convent in the 13th century and sent his daughter, Margaret, there as a thank you gift to God for helping him beat the Mongols. Motivation aside, her seclusion at least guaranteed her a kind of immortality when the island was renamed after her death (something Béla never achieved). Today, you can still see the ruins of the Franciscan priory as well as the Dominican convent, and Princess Margaret is buried at the site of the old nave. To the north of the ruins, you can take a look around St. Michael, a charming little chapel that holds the oldest bell in all of Hungary. If poetry is your thing, try a verse or two near the nearby Promenade of Hungarian Artists, a collection of busts of famous Hungarian artists, writers, and poets.

i Take the main road from the Margit Bridge entrance; pass the Franciscan priory 1st, on the left, between the Hajós Alfréd swimming pool and the Palatinus Baths. The convent is farther along, on your right near the water tower. Free.

PALATINUS STRANDFÜRDŐ (PALATINUS BATHS)
BATH

Margit Sziget ☎340 45 05 www.spasbudapest.com

When these baths opened in 1921, the city's residents were all at once madly, clumsily, shamelessly, and agonizingly in love. You don't have to be an artist or a madman to appreciate the sprawling complex with enormous fountains, waterslides, and jets across three large pools, all fed by the thermal springs underground. If quiet and simple soaking is what your mind and body needs, go in the early afternoon on a week day. If raucous splashing and the cry of youth are what you crave, go on the weekend in this kingdom by the sea (well, river).

i From the Árpád Bridge entrance, take Soó Rezső sétány south; the baths are on the right. Admission with lockers M-F 9am-4pm 2400Ft, 4-7pm 1700Ft; Sa-Su 2800Ft. ☒ Open daily May-Aug 9am-7pm.

Óbuda

▓ PÁL-VÖLGYI AND MÁTYÁS CAVES
CAVES

☎325 95 05 http://szemlohegyi.hu

Budapest is famous for its thermal baths, but few people realize that the heated water that eats up entire afternoons has also spent hundreds of thousands of years eating through the limestone hills beneath the city. One result: the second longest of Hungary's cave systems, the Pál-völgyi and Mátyás Caves, which offer the unskilled numerous spelunking opportunities. The walking tours (no climbing involved) are informative and interesting without asking you to do anything more stressful than make your way up a short ladder. Those looking for something a little more challenging should consider taking one of the 2½-3hr. tours that will have you crawling through the Sandwich of Death.

i Bus #86: Kolosy tér. Backtrack up the street and take the 1st right to reach the bus station. From there, catch bus #65 to get to the caves (Pál-völgyi). Bring warm clothing. English tours available; call ahead for times. 1000Ft, students 800Ft. ☒ Open Tu-Sa 10am-4pm. Tours every hr. English tours M, W, F afternoons.

budapest

FOOD

Budapest isn't exactly a movable feast—it's a very sedentary one, really. With heavy meat dishes (emphasis on the meat) and national specialties that include goulash (a meat and vegetable soup) and goose liver (exactly what it sounds like), you won't be hunting for satiation. When the Turks invaded, they brought their love of coffee to the country, and thus the Kávéház of Budapest is almost as popular as the Sörház celebrating that other hydrating fluid, beer. Besides cheap draughts, the national spirit of Hungary is pálinka, liquor distilled from fruit (technically making it a brandy). Drink up!

Belváros

■ CENTRAL KÁVÉHÁZ
CAFE $$$

Károlyi Mihály utca 9   ☎266 2110 www.centralkavehaz.hu

Don't let the marble tables, chandeliers, and a professionally decked-out staff fool you—while this coffee/bar/restaurant/sweetshop might appear to be out of Beauty and the Beast, you are more likely to find a modern-day Belle hitting her Kindle rather than the ball. Admittedly, the prices wouldn't satisfy Gaston on a particularly violent day; however, the cafe is as old as time (well, all right, 1887). In addition to a variety of entrees, confectionaries and alcohol will lift whatever curse lies upon your soul, and the chill staff will convince you to, yes, be their guest.

i M3: Ferenciek tere. Take Károly Mihály utca east. Nosh 1500-2900Ft. Entrees 2500-4500Ft. Mixed drinks 1400-2300Ft. ◘ Open daily 8am-11pm.

■ CAFE ALIBI
CAFE $$

Egyetem tér 4   ☎01 317 4209 cafealibi.hu

An old-fashioned cash register and your grandmother's fine china will greet you at this little coffee shop in the center of student-city. While the prices are up there, you're unlikely to find a more tasteful, less touristy cafe in this neighborhood. Most importantly, view this place as a way to test if your alibi is good enough to blend in with the locals (stares are a bad thing, traveler).

i M3: Kálvin tér. Take Kecskeméti utca west and turn left onto Egyetem tér. Salads 900-1600Ft. Coffee from 320Ft. ◘ Open daily 8am-11pm.

Lipótváros

■ SZERÁJ
TURKISH, FAST FOOD $

Szent István körút 13

This joint mixes Turkish fast food with a deft Hungarian touch. If waiters and tips are becoming tedious, stop by this "self-serve" (it means that someone else serves you from behind a buffet line—in Hungary, the self is obviously chastised) restaurant on the ever-bustling Szent István körút. If even limited human contact with the servers has your teeth grinding, take a seat in one of two upstairs balconies while you enjoy fried food whose moral quotient still seems higher than McDonalds. Try a simple falafel sandwich stuffed with red cabbage (650Ft).

i M3: Nyugati. Head down Szent István körút toward the river; the restaurant is on the left. Entrees from 400Ft. Desserts from 300Ft. ◘ Daily 9am-4am.

TRÓFEA GRILL ÉTTEREM
GOURMET, BUFFET $$$

Visegrádi utca 50A   ☎01 270 0366 www.trofeagrill.net

Gourmet meals and all-you-can-eat buffets don't usually hold hands on the playground, but somehow this place pulls it off. Large chandeliers entwined with reindeer antlers overlook the large wooden dining area while soft American tunes play in the background (unless it's your birthday, in which case the Hungarian version of "Happy Birthday" will start blasting as waiters deliver a sparkler-topped chocolate cake to your table). With an over 100-dish menu, unlimited drinks, and occasional comedy and folk performances, your dining experience and stomach will be full.

i M3: Nyugati. Take Szent István körút toward the river and turn right onto Visegrádi utca. Free Wi-Fi. Buffet M-F lunch 3500Ft, dinner 5000Ft; Sa-Su all day 5500Ft. ☑ Open M-F noon-midnight, Sa 11:30am-midnight, Su 11:30am-10:00pm.

Erzsébetváros

▧ CASTRO BISZTRÓ   BISTRO $
1075 Madách tér 3   ☎215 01 84 www.castrobistro.hu

With an experimental electronic soundtrack humming in the background, this is an easy cafe in which to stew alone or with others. An eclectic decor boasts Buena Vista Social Club posters as well as a vague Cuban theme (Castro as in Fidel?). A handsome bar serves a sizzling Illy roast and a selection of beer and wine that you can enjoy on old-timey tablecloths lit by the heavenly window light. Outside, the terrace almost rivals the coolness of the melody within.

i M1, M2, or M3: Deák Ferenc tér. Head north on Király utca, turn right onto Rumbach Sebestyén utca, and right onto Madách tér. Espresso 290Ft. Entrees from 900Ft. 30min. free Wi-Fi included. ☑ Open M-Th 10am-midnight, F 10am-1am, Sa noon-1am, Su 2pm-midnight.

▧ HUMMUS BÁR   ISRAELI $
Kertész utca 39   ☎321 74 77

This isn't a bar where you mix your hummus with Manichevitz (although we'd be interested to see that combination). Inside the comic-covered walls of Hummus Bár, you can choose to observe the Sabbath inside in a den-like backroom and savor something like the mushroom hummus plate (1000Ft) speckled with olives and accompanied by a pair of piping hot pita.

i M1: Oktogon. Head east onto Erzsébet körút, turn right onto Király utca, and left onto Kertész utca. Falafel from 800Ft. Entrees 400-1800Ft. ☑ Open daily noon-11pm.

KÖLEVES   RESTOBAR $$
Kazinczy utca 35   ☎322 10 11 www.koleves.com

With wooden floors and chairs, the tree theme ends with a Köleves specialty: stone soup. Jewish-influenced cuisine and a continually rotating list of live music events will have you saying mazel tov in no time. Outside, a large umbrella-filled bar with a playground theme evokes strange subliminal messages; the children painted on the wall have tan, super skinny legs and white stockings that look like cigarettes.

i M1, M2, or M3: Deák Ference tér. Head north on Király utca and turn right onto Kazinczy utca. Nightly entertainment. Soup from 650Ft. Entrees 2450-3400Ft. ☑ Open daily noon-midnight.

Terézváros

FŐZELÉK FALO   HUNGARIAN $
Nagymező utca 18

This place treats Fözelék, a Hungarian every-man dish containing vegetables and meat cooked into a thick soup, as the equivalent of the cupcake phenomenon in the States. Every possible derivation of this stew is presented in a fast, get-in-get-out manner but remains so comforting that you won't mind the rush. Try the squash if you feel like Thanksgiving or the wiener schnitzel for a more international take.

i M1: Oktogon. Head south from the metro on Andrássy út and turn right onto Nagymező utca. Fözelék 430Ft. Entrees 430-690Ft. ☑ Open M-F 9am-10pm, Sa 10am-9pm, Su 11am-6pm.

KAJA.HU   HUNGARIAN $$
Nagymező utca 41   ☎374 04 68 www.kaja.hu

Promoted as a "cybergastro," this place certainly does look like the inside of some futuristic spaceship. Kaja.Hu relies on an absurdly modern black, white, and silver decor and an equally untraditional view on health (try the Fitness Canteen section of the menu for grilled chicken in every possible permutation). Have a drink at the bar before disembarking to go to the distinctly anti-modern ruin pub scene.

i M1: Oktogon. *Head south from the metro on Andrássy út and turn right onto Nagymező utca. Delivery available. Soups from 590Ft. Salads from 690Ft. Entrees from 990Ft.* ☒ *Open M-Th 11am-10pm, F-Sa 11am-midnight, Su 11am-10pm.*

Józsefváros

▦ SIRIUS KLUB   TEA HOUSE $
Bródy Sándor utca 13   ☎266 17 08 www.sirius-se.hu/teahaz

Given how difficult this place is to find, you might as well think the address was 12 Grimmauld Place rather than 13 Bródy Sándor (oh come on, we're being Sirius). However, if you look very carefully, you'll see a tiny silver plaque and a fuzzy glow through the window; you've reached one of Budapest's best teahouses, where a giant selection of teas is served through a small window connected to the main seating area. Tibetan prayer flags and floor cushions invite you to kick off your walking shoes and mellow out, and cookies provide sweet relief from the grim old city air.

i M3: Kálvin tér. *Head north on Múzeum körút and turn right onto Bródy Sándor utca. Tea from 690Ft. Cookies 300Ft.* ☒ *Open daily noon-10pm.*

▦ DARSHAN UDVAR   INTERNATIONAL $$$
Krúdy Gyula utca 7   ☎266 55 41 www.darshan.hu

With enough variation to keep 11 different Dr. Whos happy, Darshan Udvar is definitely bigger on the inside. With an outdoor eating patio, an inner courtyard, a separate indoor eating area, and a rooftop garden, dining here should be a tenet of your trek through Józsefváros. In good weather, the rooftop garden provides the most solace for those far away from their homeland, with mosaic-covered walls, thatched roofs, and woven tablecloths. Order the Olaszos csibe (chicken, smoked slod, mushroom, potato, and mozzarella; 1850Ft) and exterminate your delicious meal before you can blink.

i M3: Ferenc körút. *Head north on József körút and turn left onto Krúdy Gyula utca. Soups from 790Ft. Noodles 1290-1690Ft. Entrees 1790-2990Ft. Desserts 650-790Ft.* ☒ *Open daily 11am-midnight.*

BÉCSISZELET   HUNGARIAN $$
Üllői út 16/a   ☎267 49 37 www.becsiszelet.hu

Usually, when something is described as "spreading across a city," it is some type of fevered pathogen. Thankfully, Bécsiszelet has broken this pandemic mold with a total of six restaurants in Budapest stemming from its original down to earth location on Üllői út. With a common denominator of maximal portions for minimal prices, choose the wiener schnitzel (2490Ft) and fall in love with your subsequent food baby.

i M3: Kálvin tér; head east. *Coffee from 270Ft. Beer from 290Ft. Soup 290-490Ft. Entrees 1190-2490Ft.* ☒ *Open M-Sa 11:30am-11pm, Su 11:30am-10pm.*

Ferencváros

▦ SHIRÁZ PERZA ÉTTEREM   PERSIAN $$$
Mátyás utca 22   ☎218 08 81 www.shirazetterem.hu

On all of the signs that herald Radáy utca as the street to eat, there should be a small parenthetical saying the best place is an ornate Persian eatery on the intersecting Mátyás utca. Sit on soft, jewel-toned cushions inside and listen to the chirping of two canaries in a golden cage, or do your best caterpillar from Alice and Wonderland with a water pipe outside (perhaps your voice will even

hungary

become as deep as Alan Rickman's). With a selection of kebabs that will skewer your previous culinary experiences, Shiráz will make you wish magic carpets existed just so you could return anytime you want.

i M3: Ferenc körút. From the station, head toward the river on Üllői út, then turn left onto Köztelek utca, which runs right into Ráday utca. The restaurant is on the corner of Ráday utca and Mátyás utca. Khoresh 1750Ft. Kebab plates 2400Ft. Shisha 1490Ft. ☉ Open daily noon-midnight.

The Városliget

KERTEM
Olof Palme sétány 3   CAFE $$
☎3630 225 13 99   www.kertemfesztival.hu
Its name simply means "my garden," but this outdoor pub and grill serves as so much more. With absurdly cheap alcohol for the Városliget and a soundtrack of old-timey '40s ballads, you'll have a difficult time wanting to move on to the sights outside of Kertem's wooden-fenced walls. If you're into delayed-gratification, head here toward the end of your day and take in a live music performance and draft beer.

i M1: Hősök tere. As you're entering the park, turn right and walk for about 5min. Kertem is on the left. Check online for concert and program listings. Coffee from 280Ft. Burgers around 1000Ft. ☉ Open Jun-Sept daily 11am-4am. Kitchen open noon-1am.

CAFE KARA
Andrássy út 130   CAFE $$
☎269 41 35   www.cafekara.hu
This Turkish cafe not only boasts a positively epic view of Heroes' Square but also has the sweetest scent around due to the prodigious number of customers puffing on colorful, mango- or banana-loaded hookahs (1700Ft). While many of the eateries inside the park will smoke you out with their ring of successively intimidating prices, you can munch on some gooey turkey and cheese sandwiches here for only 1150Ft.

i M1: Hősök tere. At the corner of Andrássy út and Heroes' Sq. Turkish coffee 360Ft. Salads 900-1500Ft. Sandwiches 1150-1500Ft. ☉ Open daily 10am-10pm. Belly dancing F-Sa 8pm.

ROBINSON RESTAURANT
Városligeti tó   HUNGARIAN $$$
☎663 68 71
If you take a dip in the Városliget's artificial pond, you might just wash up on Robinson Restaurant, whose terrace stands on a patio above the sun-glinted water. Housed in a building out of a Frank Lloyd Wright sketchbook, this sit-down restaurant has served gourmet food to the likes of David Bowie and Robert Redford. While the menu can be a labyrinth of Gatsby-appropriate prices, try the risotto with tenderloin strips and forest mushrooms (3100Ft) for a filling lunch or dinner.

i M1: Hősök tere. Walk through Heroes' Sq., and then turn left; the restaurant is in the park across from the zoo. Soups 900-1600Ft. Entrees 2600-6300Ft. ☉ Open daily noon-5pm, 6pm-midnight.

Varhegy, Central Buda, and the Vizivaros

⊠ NÁNCSI NÉNI VENDÉGLŐJE
Ördögárok utca 80   HUNGARIAN $$$
☎398 71 27   www.nancsineni.hu
This place is so far away from the city center that you might be tempted to cross it off of your list of possibilities and move along. We forbid you. With truly delectable meat dishes and a clever menu, Nánsci Néni distinguishes itself with an absurd attention to detail and some of the friendliest service this side of Buda.

i M2: Széll Kálmán tér. Take tram 61 to Hűvösvölgy út. Then, at the station, take bus 57 toward Hűvösvölgy út (yes, again) and get off at Széchenyi utca after 3 stops. Turn left onto Nagyret utca; the restaurant is at the corner of Ordogarok utca. Soups from 850Ft. Entrees 1750-2850Ft. ☉ Open daily noon-11pm.

budapest

◼ DAUBNER CUKRÁSZDA
CAFE $$

Szépvölgyi út 50   ☎335 22 53 www.daubnercukraszda.hu

While locals rave about the cakes and ice cream, this place is all too easy for tourists to miss due its location on a road less traveled; the prices, however, make it worth stumbling out of your way. It is a sweet place to get something small to go and eat in the privacy of your hostel bed; then again, you can always get an eight-slice masterpiece of a cake to share with the rest of your dorm. While the cases are stocked with enough sugar to make a bottle of grape-flavored cough syrup go down, make sure to wait your turn, as a long line of fellow sugar addicts will be clamoring for a taste as well.

i *Tram 17: Kolosy tér. Walk a few blocks up Szépvölgyi út; the cafe is on the left. Sweets from 150Ft. 8-slice cake from 1600Ft. Ice cream from 190Ft. ☼ Open daily 9am-7pm.*

ARANYSZARVAS BISZTRÓ
HUNGARIAN $$$$

Szarvas tér 1   ☎375 64 51 www.aranyszarvas.hu

If Slytherin House had a restaurant in Buda, this would be it. With fancy table settings, an overwhelming emphasis on game meat, and a motto that translates to "we don't make any compromises," we only wish that it anagrammed to "I am Lord Classymort." If you're running low on cunning (Salazar would be ashamed), then pick something simple like cold tomato soup with tomato granita (1150Ft). If you're ambitious to the max, pick the leg of deer, hunter-style (3450Ft).

i *Trams 18 or 19: Döbrentei tér. Take Döbrentei tér away from the river, turn right onto Attila út, and then veer left; the restaurant is on the corner. Reservations recommended. Appetizers 1150-2450Ft. Entrees 2890-3490Ft. Desserts 990-1400Ft. ☼ Open daily noon-11pm.*

Margit-Sziget

◼ HOLDUDVAR
HUNGARIAN, MEDITERRANEAN $$

Margit Sziget   ☎236 01 55 www.holdudvar.net

In the middle of an island devoted to confectionary stands, this restaurant, with its soft orange lanterns and cream-colored decor, will be your best chance of getting a traditional sit-down meal for not much cash. Try the roasted duck leg with steamed cabbage and onion-flavored mashed potatoes (2250Ft) for a traditional Hungarian meal after a long day of island-exploring.

i *From the Margit Bridge entrance, take the main road; the garden is on the right, across from the Hajós Alfréd swimming pool. Film screenings in the open-air cinema Su 9pm. Soup 990Ft. Entrees 1300-4200Ft. ☼ Open daily in summer 11am-5am.*

Óbuda

◼ EMIL CUKRÁSZDA
CAFE $

Bécsi út 314   ☎240 75 35 www.emilcukraszda.hu

Yes, it's far out. However, think of this as a reward for successfully navigating Óbuda. With enough sugar to insulinate yourself against vegetables for life, the hundreds of cakes, pastries, and gelato will also cure you of any disappointment you might have had with Óbuda as a whole. A limited seating area (i.e., a bench next to the entrance) means this place is an in-and-out sort of ordeal, but the courageous traveler will not be disappointed once he's taken his first bite of triple chocolate cake with raspberry filling and buttercream accents.

i *Bus #260: ATI. Keep walking a bit in the direction of the bus and cross the road. Sweets from 250Ft. Coffee from 210Ft. ☼ Open Tu-Su 10:30am-6:30pm.*

NIGHTLIFE

Nightlife in Budapest centers around three types of establishments. Firstly, there is the ruin pub. Get well acquainted with this style of graffitied and artfully-falling-apart bar, as it is what your hostelmates and friends will be gunning for. The most famous of these is Szimpla Kert, a gargantuan courtyard serviced by more bars than you'll find in a jail cell. The second type of establishments are concentrated on the Buda side of the Danube from Liberty Bridge to Petófi Bridge, a three-hit group of guaranteed good times: Zöld Pardon, A38 and Rudas Romkert. Dress up and put on those boots that were made for walking. The third type is quieter and more reserved for locals who crave a calmer sort of evening, and Budapest provides these quiet, tucked-away bars in full.

Belváros

▨ AKVÁRIUM

CLUB

Erzsébet tér ☎01 860 3368

Formerly the"Gödör Klub," Akvárium, situated in the former foundation of what was supposed to be the new National Concert Halls, possesses conspicuously bare concrete walls and might seem unfinished. But patrons don't seem to mind, and on weekends you can hardly move in this crowded concert arena, where rock, jazz, world, techno, and folk deafen the swarming teens and other party-goers. If you arrive early enough, you might snag a table on the long staircase or a seat on one of the benches along the retaining walls. During the day, you can watch the liveliness of youth in the nearby Erzsébet tér.

i M1, M2, or M3: Deák Tér. Beer from 350Ft. Shots 200-1000Ft. ⌖ Open M-W 6pm-2am, Th-Sa 6pm-5am, Su 4pm-2am.

▨ CAPELLA CAFE

CLUB, GLBT

Belgrád rakpart 23 ☎70 597 7755 www.capellacafe.hu

It's not a cafe for a barbershop quartet (although perhaps that will be a theme night sometime). Budapest's first gay discotheque draws a crowd of all orientations to its three levels, even during the week. Themed dance rooms, a variety of music, and occasional drag nights promise an evening unlike any other in a largely heteronormative city, and those who want a more quiet night will find a laid-back bar upstairs with a balcony surrounding the dance floors.

i Trams 2 and 2a: Március 15 tér. Follow the river toward the castle. Cover W-Sa usually 1000Ft. Beer and wine 600Ft. Shots from 800Ft. ⌖ Open daily M-Sa 10pm-5am.

KATAPULT

PUB

Dohány utca 1 ☎01 266 7226

Local 20-somethings squeeze into this tiny but lively pub that functions as a cafe by day. Red walls and trippy lamps oversee a range of evenings, from political debates to head-banging and grinding; the space leaves it up to the clientele to decide its vibe for the night. Try to eat beforehand, as the kitchen closes in the afternoon.

i M2: Astoria. Walk west up Károly körút from the metro and backtrack to the right onto Dohány utca. Beer from 500Ft. ⌖ Open daily 8am-2am.

Lipótváros

LE CAFE M

BAR, GLBT

Nagysándor József utca 3 ☎01 312 1436 www.lecafem.com

Also known as the "Mystery Bar," Le Cafe M is a stylish, small gay bar in the heart of District V. Catering to a low-key crowd, it draws a mix of locals and tourists with subdued conversation and tasteful drinking. Brick walls, leather booths, and atmospheric lighting set a similar mood. While anyone can have a good time here, the bar is frequented mostly by gay men.

i M3: Arany János. Take Bajcsy-Zsilinszky út north and turn left on Nagysándor József utca. Beer from 450Ft. Shots from 300Ft. Mixed drinks from 990Ft. ⌖ Open M-F 4pm-4am, Sa-Su 6pm-4am.

budapest

Erzsébetváros

SZIMPLA KERT
RUIN PUB

Kazinczy utca   ☎352 41 98 www.szimpla.hu

A hodge-podge of furniture ranging from colorful lighting, a movie screen, and a concert stage to your grandmother's Victorian loveseat and the old beach lounger you threw in the garage make for a chilled out night of hipster glory at Budapest's original ruin pub. Smoke in the courtyard, take a hookah to share with friends, or buy a cheaper-than-thou beer from one of the many bars to take upstairs to the mezzanine. Films such as Die Hard are screened with Hungarian subtitles almost every night and nicely compliment the dream-like atmosphere.

i M2: Astoria. Head east on Rákóczi út and turn left onto Kazinczy utca. Check the website for event listings. Beer from 350Ft. Shots from 600Ft. Mixed drinks 1500-2500Ft. ☼ Open daily noon-3am.

SZÓDA
BAR

Wesselényi utca 18   ☎3670 389 64 63

This lounge-like locale stands in stark contrast to the area's sometimes overly enthusiastic ruin pub scene. Bathed in satanic red light, with a ceiling covered in life-sized manga comics, Szóda caters to patrons whose moods range from subdued to slightly amused. For a more lively scene, head downstairs to have your heartbeat elevated by a weekly rotation of DJs.

i M2: Astoria. Head east on Rákóczi út and turn left onto Kazinczy utca; the bar is near the corner of Kazinczy utca and Wesselényi utca. Check online for event listings. Beer from 300Ft. Shots 350-650Ft. ☼ Open M-Th noon-3am, F noon-5am, Sa 2pm-5am.

Terézváros

PIAF
LOUNGE

Nagymező utca 25   ☎312 38 23

Head to the address, talk in hushed tones to the seemingly all-knowing waitress, and then relax on red velvet couches that make you feel like you've stumbled upon a sexless brothel. Yeah, we're serious. This joint gets poppin' after 3am, and even that's a little early to show up. Haunted by both young and old, Budapest's oldest nightclub will guarantee you an experience unlike any other and help you recover after a night of ruin pub romps with its refreshingly old style. Bounce around downstairs to an eclectic mix of dance music, or lounge upstairs while listening to the sonatas and adept flourishes of live piano playing.

i M1: Oktogon. Head south on Andrássy út and turn right onto Nagymező utca. 1000Ft cover. Wine from 450Ft. Beer from 650Ft. ☼ Open daily midnight-6am.

MOST
RUIN PUB

Zichy Jenő utca 17   ostjelen.hu

A new take on the ruin pub, Most offers a slew of options for backpackers, party hoppers, and resigned adults with its array of styles that range from classic grunge furniture inside to sleeker decor on the terrace. Climb the steps up to the balcony for a romantic drink (cheap enough that you can get a second), or chill indoors on the first floor and get your hipster on amid the wall-length bookcase and wine bottles-made-candelabras. Then again, you might never want to leave the unassuming garden where you entered—a plot of land transformed into a quiet oasis of happy conversation and, again, cheap drinking. Did we mention it's cheap?

i M1: Opera. Head east on Andrássy út, turn left onto Nagymező utca, and left onto Zichy Jenő utca. Wine 240Ft. Beer 300Ft. ☼ Open daily M 10am-2am, T 10am-3am, W 10am-4am, Th-Sa 10am-5am, Su 10am-2am.

SZILVUPLÉ RUIN PUB
Ó utca 33 ☎3620 992 51 15 szilvuple.hu

In refreshing contrast to typical ruin pub decor (which seems to thrive on finding furniture on the street), Szilvuplé has matching tables and chairs. With a modern bar illuminated by recessed, train station-like skylights, Szilvuplé's walls are hidden under quirky murals (an effective assurance that the building won't collapse in a matter of minutes). Go upstairs to witness some intrepid salsa dancing (M-W at 9pm), or just console yourself with the particularly cheap house wine.

i M1: Oktogon. Head south on Andrássy út, turn right onto Nagymező utca, and right onto Ó utca. Check online for event listings. Wine from 200Ft. Beer from 290Ft. ☼ Open M-W 6pm-2am, Th-Sa 6pm-4am.

Ferencváros

RUMBA CAFÉ BAR
Lónyay utca 27 ☎3670 503 69 69 www.rumbacafe.hu

After hopping from club to club with the same menus of Soproni, pálinka, and a variety of straight shots you just can't swallow anymore, Rumba will come as a fresh island breeze. With the largest assortment of tropical-themed drinks in Budapest, you can contently sip your "Sex in the Rumba" (white rum, brown rum, apricot brandy, pineapple juice, orange juice, and lime, 1350Ft) or take the "Revenge of the Grandmother," a series of six shots whose ingredients are remain a secret (2250Ft). Enjoy it all within the comfy atmosphere of '70s decor and soft lighting.

i M3: Ferenc körút. Head west on Üllői, turn left onto Kinizsi utca, and then turn right onto Lonyay utca. Shots from 850Ft. ☼ Open W-Sa 6pm-1am.

Varhegy, Central Buda, and the Vizivaros

▨ ZÖLD PARDON ENTERTAINMENT COMPLEX
Goldmann György tér ☎279 18 80 www.zp.hu

You know a club is cool when the state shuts it down—that's exactly what happened with "Green" Pardon in November 2011, when the District XI municipality had enough with its loud shenanigans and shut it down, which then prompted Hungarian politicians to stop debating the Euro-crisis and focus on this club's fate instead. It has since reopened in technicolor splendor about a kilometer south of its original location. With a gamut of raucous fun, Zöld Pardon boasts live music events almost every night, about 100m of bars, and a group of young, enthusiastic party-goers that have made this place famous.

i Trams 4 or 6: Petőfi híd. Walk away from the city (follow the stream of people) for about 10min. The club is on the right. Check website and Facebook for event listings. Cover 400Ft. Beer from 350Ft. Mixed drinks from 1000Ft. ☼ Open Apr-Oct daily 11am-5am.

RUDAS ROMKERT RUIN PUB
9 Döbrentei Square ☎30 351 52 17 www.rudasromkert.hu

A relatively new open-air ruin pub located at the foot of Gellért Hill, Rudas Romkert caters to an upscale clientele and feels more like a club than a chill hangout spot. Later on in the evening, the large outdoor dance floor plays host to dance remixes of pop songs as the purple paper lanterns swing overhead and pretentiousness is dampened. The posse of bouncers at the door, however, might make Birkenstock-wearing backpackers think twice about entering.

i Bus 7: Rudas gyógyfürdő. Beer from 450Ft. Mixed drinks from 900Ft. ☼ Open daily 5pm-late.

budapest

Margit-Sziget

◙ HOLDUDVAR
OUTDOOR BAR

Margit Sziget · ☎236 01 55 · www.holdudvar.net

Hold on tight. Nestled in the woods of Margaret Island is the sweet smell of gourmet cooking, roasted meat, and the clink of cool glasses condensing in air that smells of pine and petrichor. The projector that screens films flickers with each passing frame, whirring quietly among the chatter of patrons splashed against the stars. At five, as the morning becomes lighter with the promise of another try, the guests part ways only to see each other again another night.

i From the Margit Bridge entrance, take the main road; the garden is on the right, across from the Hajós Alfréd swimming pool. Film screenings on the open-air cinema Su 9pm. Beer from 300Ft. Shots 790-1400Ft. ☼ Open in summer daily 11am-5am.

ARTS AND CULTURE

One word: ballet. It's the highest of art forms, and Hungary offers the best of the best (with no knowledge of Hungarian required!). Admittedly, Budapest has more culture to offer than merely ballet; it has an opera as well, with seats alternately filled by tourists and Hungarian hob-nobbers. The two main theater houses in the Jewish district often perform world-renowned plays, and if you're lucky, you might even get a chance to visit the Liszt Ferenc Music Academy, which houses the next generation of rhapsodic composers.

◙ THE LISZT ACADEMY OF MUSIC
OPERA

Liszt Ferenc tér 8 · ☎342 01 79 · www.zeneakademia.hu

It seems like you can't walk five feet in Budapest without seeing some bookshop, statue, coffeehouse, or street paying tribute to Franz Liszt. But for this academy, which now serves as the center of edification for the next generation of geniuses, the moniker is all too appropriate: the school was in fact founded by the city's famed, rhapsodic prodigy. While it might be difficult to procure a seat for a summer concert here (students are off traveling in July and August), stop by the building nonetheless for a nice dose of Art Nouveau architecture.

i M1: Oktogon. Head east on Teréz körút and turn right onto Király utca; the academy is on the right 1 block down. Check the website or call for concert listings. Schedules vary; there are rarely concerts during the summer. Prices vary depending on performance. ☼ Box office open daily 2-8pm.

◙ MADÁCH SZÍNHÁZ
THEATER

Erzsébet körút 29 · ☎478 20 41 · www.madachszinhaz.hu

A local favorite, Madách Színház is one of the few theaters in the city that suits all tastes. Not only can you create memories by taking in a performance of Cats, Anna Karenina, or Phantom of the Opera, but you can also get your fill of culture in all its many shades.

i Tram 4 or 6: Wesselényi utca; theater is located across the street. Check online for listings and prices. Prices vary from approximately 1000-4900ft. ☼ Box office open daily 10am-12:30pm and 1-6:30pm.

MAGYARÁLLAMI OPERAHÁZ (STATE OPERA HOUSE)
OPERA

Andrássy út 22 · ☎353 01 70 · www.opera.hu

Housed in a magnificent, neo-Renaissance building that took nine years to construct, the Hungarian State Opera hosts some of the continent's finest operas, ballets, and classical performances. While some seats sell out a year in advance, rush tickets are sometimes available at a fraction of the normal price 1hr. before the performance.

i M1: Opera. Call for show schedules or check the poster at the gate. Tickets 400-9000Ft. ☼ Box office open M-Sa 11am-7pm, Su 4-7pm. Closes at 5pm on non-performance days. 1hr. tours daily in 6 languages at 3 and 4pm.

SHOPPING
Music

◪ FERENC LISZT MUSIC SHOP
Andrássy út 45

TERÉZVÁROS

☎322 40 91

Named after Hungary's most famous composer, this tiny store carries classical music as well a great selection of major operas. Perchance you happen to fall in love with one of the tunes you heard at the Opera House just down the street, Ferenc Liszt Music Shop will likely possess the score.

i M1: Oktogon. Walk south toward the Opera. 🕒 Open M-F 10am-6pm, Sa 10am-1pm.

◪ WAVE MUSIC
Révay köz 1

TERÉZVÁROS

☎269 07 54 www.wave.hu

With some titles that you could easily find at Urban Outfitters mixed with a more eclectic mix of jazz and alternative punk, Wave Music will satisfy your need to solidify your music collection with its abundance of CDs and LPs.

i M1: Bajcsy-Zsilinszkyút. Head north on Bajcsy-Zsilinszky út and turn right onto Révay köz. 🕒 Open M-Sa 10am-8pm.

Specialty

◪ LEHEL PIAC
Lehel tér

DISTRICT XIII

A better option than the tourist trap that is the National Market Hall, Lehel Piac is the best open-air market to buy fruits and veggies for pennies or less. All local growers and the lack of a middle man make it a sweet option if you want to do your own cooking.

🕒 Open M-F 6am-6pm, Sa 6am-2pm, Su 6am-1pm.

ESSENTIALS
Practicalities

- **TOURIST OFFICES: Tourinform** arranges tours and accommodations. (Sütő utca 2. ☎429 97 51 www.budapestinfo.hu 🕒 Open daily 8am-8pm.) If you're only going to be in Budapest for a short period, consider a **Budapest Card** (Budapest Kártya), which provides discounts, unlimited public transportation, admission to most museums, and can be ordered online. (www.budapest-card.com *i* 1-day card 3900Ft, 3-day 7900Ft. 🕒 Open M-F 9am-6:30pm, Sa 9am-2:30pm.)

- **DOMESTIC OPERATOR:** ☎190, INFORMATION: ☎199

- **GLBT RESOURCES: GayGuide.net Budapest** posts an online guide and runs a hotline with info and a reservation service for GLBT-friendly lodgings. (☎06 30 932 33 34 www.budapest.gayguide.net 🕒 Hotline open daily Apr-Oct 4-8pm.) **Na Végre!** publishes an up-to-date guide to gay nightlife, available at any gay bar (www.navegre.hu).

- **POST OFFICE: Városház utca 18** (☎318 4811 *i* Poste Restante, Postán Mar, is in office around the right side of the building. 🕒 Open M-F 8am-8pm, Sa 8am-2pm.) Alternative branches at Nyugati station, Teréz körút; 105/107 Keleti Station, Baross tér 11/c; and elsewhere. (🕒 Open M-F 7am-8pm, Sa 8am-2pm.)

- **POSTAL CODE:** Depends on the district. Postal codes are 1XX2, where XX is the district number.

Emergency

- **TOURIST POLICE:** Sütő utca 2, inside the Tourinform office. (☎438 80 80 M1, M2, or M3: Deák tér. *i* Beware of imposters demanding to see your passport. 🕒 Open 24hr.)

- **HUNGARIAN POLICE:** ☎107, POLICE HEADQUARTERS: ☎343 00 34, AMBULANCE: ☎104, FIRE AND EMERGENCY: ☎105

- **PHARMACIES: Frankel Leó út 22.** (☎314 36 95. *i* Look for green signs labeled Patika or Gyógyszertár. ☼ Open M-F 7:30am-9pm, Sa 7:30am-2pm. Minimal after-hours service fees apply.)

- **MEDICAL SERVICES: Falck (SOS) KFT.** (Kapy út 49/b ☎224 90 90. *i* The US embassy maintains a list of English-speaking doctors.)

Getting There

BY PLANE

Ferihegy Airport (BUD; ☎235 38 88). From the airport to the city center, take Bus #93 (270Ft ☼ 20min.; every 15min., 4:55am-11:20pm), then #3 to Kőbánya-Kispest (15min. to Deák tér, in downtown Budapest). **Airport Minibus** (☎296 85 55) goes to hostels (2990Ft).

BY TRAIN

The major train stations, **Keleti Pályaudvar, Nyugati Pályaudvar,** and **Déli Pályaudvar,** are also metro stops (☎3640 49 49 49). Most international trains arrive at **Keleti Station,** but some from Prague go to **Nyugati Station.** For schedules, check www.mav.hu. Prices change often and sometimes depend on time of day and time of year. Trains arrive from: Berlin (15,800Ft ☼ 12-13hr., 4 per day); Bucharest (23,600Ft ☼ 14hr., 5 per day); Prague (16,300Ft ☼ 7-8hr., 5 per day); Vienna (3600Ft ☼ 3hr., 17 per day); Warsaw (18,500Ft ☼ 11hr., 2 per day). The daily **Orient Express** stops on its way from Paris to Istanbul. Trains run to most major destinations in Hungary. Purchase tickets at an **International Ticket Office** (☼ Keleti Station open daily 8am-7pm; Nyugati Station open M-Sa 9am-9pm; info desk 24hr.). Or try **MÁV Hungarian Railways.** V, Andrássy út 35 ☎461 55 00 *i* Branches at all stations. ☼ Open Apr-Sept M-F 9am-6pm; Oct-Mar M-F 9am-5pm.) The **HÉV Commuter Railway Station** is at Batthyány tér, opposite Parliament. Trains head to Szentendre. (460Ft. ☼ 45min.; every 15min., 5am-9pm.) Purchase tickets at the station for transport beyond the city limits.

BY BUS

Buses to international and some domestic destinations leave from the **Népliget Station.** (Üllői út 131 ☎329 14 50 M3: Népliget. ☼ Cashier open daily 6am-8pm.) Check www.volanbusz.hu for schedules.

Getting Around

BY TRAIN

The **HÉV Commuter Rail Station** is across the river from Parliament, one metro stop (M2) past the Danube in Buda at Batthyány tér. On the list of stops, those within the city limits are displayed in a different color. For these stops, a regular metro ticket will suffice. Purchase tickets at the counter to travel beyond the city limits. Békásmegye is the final stop within the city limits.

BY BUDAPEST PUBLIC TRANSIT

The **subways** and **trams** run every few minutes. **Buses** are generally on time and some run 24hr.; schedules are posted at stops. **Budapest Public Transport** (BKV ☎36 80 40 66 86 www.bkv.hu) has information in Hungarian and English on its website. Single-fare tickets for public transport (320Ft 1-way on 1 line) are sold at metro stations, Trafik shops, and sidewalk vendors at tram stops. Punch tickets in the orange boxes at the gate of the metro or on buses and trams; punch a new ticket when you change lines, or face a fine of 6000Ft from the undercover ticket inspectors. (*i* Day pass 1550Ft, 3-day 3850Ft, 1-week 4600Ft, 2-week 6200Ft, 1-month 9400Ft.)

The metro has three lines: **M1 (yellow), M2 (red),** and **M3 (blue).** M1 runs west to east from downtown Pest, past City Park along Andrássy út. M2 runs west to east and connects **Deli Train Station** in Buda with **Keleti Train Station** in Pest along Rákóczi út. M3 runs north to south through Pest and provides a transfer bus (200E) to the airport from the southern terminus (Kőbánya-Kispest). A fourth metro line that will connect southern Buda to northeastern Pest is currently under construction and is expected to open in spring 2014. The metro runs 4:30am-11:30pm.

Bus stops and tram stops are easily identifiable (most notably because trams have to travel on rails). The major tram lines are **4/6,** which runs from Széll Kalmán tér north to Margaret Island and back south to Pest before crossing at Petöfi Bridge to return to Buda again, and **2,** which runs along the Danube from its northern terminus at Jászai Mari tér (on the Pest side near Margaret Island) to Közvágóhíd, just south of the National Market Hall. Unfortunately, while bus tickets can be purchased for 400Ft from the driver, tram tickets must be purchased in advance. Most buses and trams stop running at 11pm. After you've missed the last tram, transportation is available in the form of **night (É) buses,** which run from midnight-5am along major routes: #7É and 78É follow the 2 route; #6É follows the 4/6 tram line; #14É and 50É follow the 3 route.

hungary essentials

MONEY
Although part of the European Union, Hungary's official currency is the forint (Ft).

Tipping and Taxes
Tipping is customary in all situations where the customers and service workers—waiters, taxi drivers, and hotel porters—come face to face. Depending upon how satisfied you are with the service, plan to tip 10-15%. Goods, products, and services in Hungary are subject to a value added tax (VAT) of 27% (a reduced tax of 18% is applied to basic consumer goods). Non-EU visitors who are taking these goods home unused may be refunded this tax for purchases totaling over 48,000Ft per store. When making purchases, request a VAT form and present it at a Tax Free Shopping Office, found at most airports, road borders, and ferry stations, or by mail. Refunds must be claimed within six months.

SAFETY AND HEALTH
Local Laws and Police
You should not hesitate to contact the police in Budapest if you are the victim of a crime. Be sure to carry a valid passport, as police have the right to ask for identification. Police can sometimes be unhelpful if you are the victim of a currency exchange scam; in this instance, it may be better to seek advice from your country's embassy or consulate.

Drugs and Alcohol
Avoid public drunkenness as it will jeopardize your safety. In Hungary, drinking is permitted at age 18. Marijuana is entirely illegal throughout the country. Carrying drugs across an international border—considered to be drug trafficking—is a serious offense that could land you in prison.

Smoking is incredibly popular in Budapest. If you are sensitive to cigarette smoke, ask for a non-smoking room in a hotel or hostel, or to be seated in the non-smoking area of restaurants.

Located between Western and Eastern Europe, Hungary is a country of a millennium of riveting history and a beautiful, unique language. Most opp ortunities are centered in Budapest, but many programs offer trips to other charming cities, and other Central European countries. Studying, volunteering, or working in Hungary will leave room for countless crazy nights of dancing to folk, underground, and techno music and drinking pálinka.

STUDY

Most educational opportunities are located at well-respected universities in Budapest and most include full-year, semester, and summer programs.

- **BUDAPEST SEMESTER IN MATHEMATICS:** The Budapest Semester in Mathematics is said to be the most prestigious undergraduate study abroad program in mathematics. For 14 weeks, students take classes influenced by the Hungarian tradition of mathematical thinking. (☎1-507-786-3114 www.budapestsemesters.com)

- **LEXIA: BUDAPEST AREA STUDIES AND CULTURE:** Immerse yourself in Hungarian history, art, politics, and society through culture seminars. Visit less touristy locations such as Transylvania and Lake Balaton while working on a research project such as "Magyar Minorities outside Hungary". (☎1-617-945-2621 www.lexiaintl.org)

- **CIEE BUDAPEST: CENTRAL EUROPEAN STUDIES:** Students take a variety of courses while exploring Budapest, other cities of Hungary, and Transylvania. Qualified students can take advantage of internships at local newspapers, NGOs, and even Hungarian ministries. (☎1-800-407-8839 www.ciee.org)

- **NRCSA: BUDAPEST, HUNGARY:** You will live in the homes of native Hungarian speakers while learning the language with private or semi-private tutors. Choose from standard, intensive, and super intensive programs. (☎1-888-678-6211 www.nrcsa.com)

- **AFS: GAP YEAR IN HUNGARY:** High school or gap year students live with host families while attending Hungarian public schools. (☎1-800-237-4636 www.afsusa.org)

VOLUNTEER

There are several volunteer projects aimed at helping the lowest socioeconomic classes and areas affected by natural disasters. Budapest is also always open to volunteers.

- **AIESEC:** AIESEC, a youth-run organization, offers several projects to those who wish to help Hungary grow through work with NGOs. Past and current projects include interning in kindergartens, career planning for high school students, and more. (☎46-0-185-01-597 www.aiesec-uppsala.se)

- **WORKAWAY INFO:** Find hostels, summer camps, and families looking for international and English-speaking volunteers on this database. (www.workaway.info)

- **WWOOF:** WWOOF Hungary has dozens of organic farms on the beautiful great plains as well as just outside of Budapest. The website offers free memberships to everyone. (www.wwoof.hu)

- **HABITAT FOR HUMANITY:** Help vulnerable groups and low-income families affected by the economic crisis or focus on natural disaster protocols through Habitat for Humanity's projects in Hungary. (☎36 1-374-0606 www.habitat.hu)

- **VOLUNTEERS FOR PEACE:** The Volunteers for Peace website lists affordable and rewarding opportunities. For example, volunteers can help organize English learning sessions for underprivileged rural children. (☎1-802-540-3060 www.vfp.org)

WORK

- **CENTRAL EUROPEAN TEACHING PROGRAM (CETA):** CETA recruits native English teachers to work in one of about 100 Hungarian public schools. Contracts are 10 months long and include accommodation. (☎1-503-287-4977 www.cetp.info)

- **TEFL INSTITUTE:** Become a certified TEFL teacher after this four-week intensive course. Tuition includes job placement assistance. (☎1-773-880-5141 www.teflinstitute.com)

- **LANGUAGE CORPS:** Language Corps offers a four-week TESOL Certification program in Budapest. Many participants find teaching jobs after completing training. (☎1-877-216-3267 www.languagecorps.com)

- **BUDAPEST JOBS:** Budapest Jobs is an English-language database that has freelance, full-time, part-time, and student job listings in Budapest. (www.budapestjobs.net)

hungary 101

HISTORY

The nomadic Magyar tribe, led by warlord Arpad, conquered the Slavs and took over the region now known as Hungary in 896 CE. A decentralized clan system prevailed until the end of the 10th century, when Arpad's less exotically named descendant, Stephen, instituted tribal aristocracy and Christianity. He also, incidentally, named himself the first King of Hungary. For more than 200 years Stephen's kin ruled over a relatively prosperous Hungary, and slowly developed the cities of Buda and Pest. In 1541, the city met its new family when the Ottomans moved in, leading to the construction of some fine Turkish baths and the enmity of the Habsburg empire, which had conquered Western Hungary but had failed repeatedly in their efforts to claim the capital. In 1686, the Habsburgs finally got their way, destroying most of Buda in the process and eventually kicking out the Ottomans entirely in 1718. However, repeated uprisings of the native Magyars and disgruntled bourgeoisie occurred over the next 150 years, culminating in the 1848 revolution, which was put down within a year.

In 1867, the "Year of Reconciliation," Austria and Hungary teamed up and Buda and Pest were merged into one capital of this dual monarchy. In 1873, Buda combined with Pest and Óbuda to officially rebrand as Budapest. Budapest flourished as a political and cultural center of Europe until 1914, when the Austro-Hungarian empire collapsed and WWI commenced. By 1918, Hungary was flying solo as an independent republic. Hungary further suffered in WWII, during which 38,000 civilians were killed in the 1944-45 Battle of Budapest and 20-40% of the Budapest area's 250,000 Jews were murdered.In 1949 Budapest became part of the Soviet Union. Peaceful resistance to Communism in the '50s was put down violently, and Hungarians were forced to succumb to the regime, which worked to downplay Hungarian national identity. From the '60s to the '80s, much of Budapest's war-damaged infrastructure was repaired, and the city was dubbed the "happiest barrack" of the Eastern bloc countries. This title didn't stop citizens from rejoicing when the Iron Curtain fell in 1989 and Hungary became an independent state. In 2004, Hungary joined the European Union.

FOOD AND DRINK

Hungarians don't take food lightly. Accordingly, traditional Hungarian fare is as heavy as it comes, usually starring meat, potatoes and paprika (the Hungarian kind, which is hot). No city does savory stews and meaty pancakes better than here. Nowhere else can you dig into the ooey-gooey deliciousness of hortobágy palacsinta (fried pancakes with veal chunks, sour cream, and paprika) or főzelék (a hearty vegetable stew, often flavored with bacon or sausage). Another meatier stew is goulash, Hungary's ubiquitous meat, potatoes, and paprika stew. For those who don't want any veggies adulterating their meat, kolbász (Hungarian sausage) or fatányéros (barbecue dish of mixed meat, like mutton, beef, veal, and pork) are great options. Pescetarians can enjoy halászlé is a traditional soup made of river fish and spiced with a good dose of paprika.

Hungary has become an active wine producer in recent years (especially since the fall of the Soviet Union), a point of pride among modern Budapestians—so much so that a national wine festival is celebrated in the city each September. To impress the locals or expand your palate, try ordering a Budai Zöld, Furmint, Juhfark,Hárslevelu, Kadarka, Kéknyelu, or Királyleányka (and if you successfully get one, make sure to toast your pronunciation skills). Budapest also boasts numerous czardas (old-fashioned taverns), pinces (beer/wine cellars) and sorozos (pubs) that serve as good a selection of local and international beers as anywhere on the continent. Be careful to order what you want by name—order just sor (beer), and restaurants will often automatically bring you their expensive imported beer, instead of a cheaper brand.

IRELAND

If you haven't yet heard that Ireland is the land of shamrocks, shillelaghs, and 40 shades of green, you should probably purchase a television, a copy of Darby O'Gill and the Little People, or a guide to Western culture since 1855. Surprisingly prominent in the international imagination for an island of six million people, Ireland is a place that the rest of the world feels it understands very well, and the Irish themselves find much more complex. Their native country was originally chopped up into several dozen regional kingships, and today it's still split between two different countries, two different religions, and 11 different Wikipedia disambiguations. (Eight-seven percent of native Irish find that last division to be the most contentious.)

OK, we made that last statistic up. It's still no wonder, though, that Ireland and "Irishness" can be difficult to categorize. Its two capitals—Belfast in the North, and Dublin in the Republic—are at once the least and most "Irish" cities on the island. Belfast, home to the island's largest Orangemen parade and some its strongest pro-British sympathies, is Ireland's second-largest city and the one-time centerpiece of the iconic, tragic Troubles. Dublin, capital of the Republic and site of the Easter Rising, is increasingly urban and international, making it feel more like modern London than magical Glocca Morra. However, these cities' entanglement with issues of national identity, history, and globalization is a lot more Irish than that Claddagh ring your friend paid €50 for. Like pouring a perfect stout, dancing with Michael Flatley, or spelling a one-syllable word in Gaelic, visiting Ireland should be a wonderfully complicated experience—otherwise you're not doing it right.

greatest hits

- **REJOYCE.** At the **James Joyce Centre** (p. 454), pay homage to one of the fathers of literary Modernism.
- **CLUBLIN.** Head to **Gogarty's** (p. 457) in Dublin to rage all night.
- **PRIDE OF BELFAST.** Immerse yourself in the history of the *Titanic* in Belfast's **Titanic Quarter** (p. 464). As they proudly say, "It was fine when it left us."

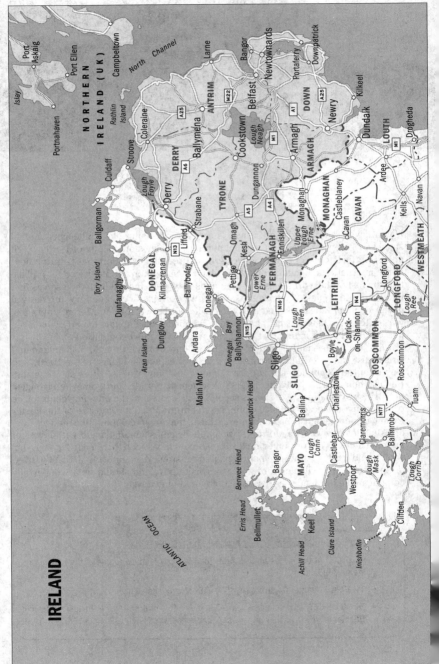

IRELAND

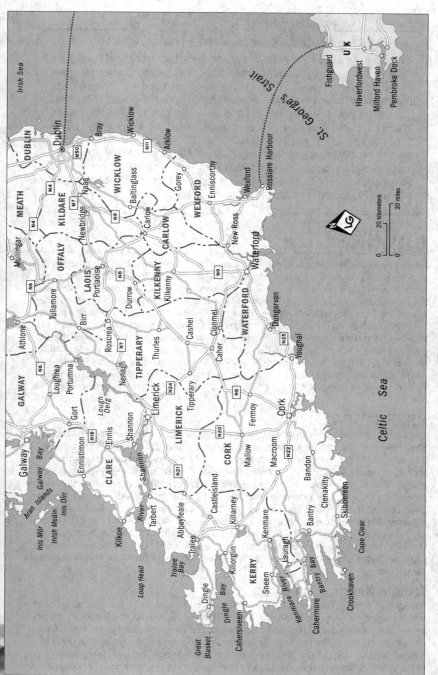

As the dominant cities in Ireland, **Dublin** and **Belfast** attract most of the island's students. Fun is among these cities' main attractions, but jthe fact that the young people here party hard doesn't mean they don't work hard, too. Trinity College, Dublin, Ireland's foremost university, is among Europe's top centers of learning. You'll find it just off Grafton St., and it is an integral part of Dublin life, hosting Ireland's national library and putting on public events like June's Trinity College Dublin Shakespeare Festival, which features over 50 outdoor performances across the city. The 17,000-student University College Dublin, meanwhile, is about 4km south of the city center. In Belfast, there's an entire University District around Queen's University Belfast. The campus is beautiful enough to justify a tourist visit, and, with 25,000 students around, you might not leave.

dublin

Grab a pint of ▓Guinness, sit down, and listen up. If you're reading this, chances are you've recently arrived in Dublin, capital of the Republic of Ireland. Now that you're here, however, what's to be done? You can't very well sit around drinking Guinness the whole time you're here. Oh wait—of course you can! Fortunately, Dublin has something for every type of traveler. You can get wasted in Temple Bar with a motley crew of tourists, visit museums of everything from natural history to modern art, tour both the Guinness Storehouse and the Jameson Distillery, while away the day poking your head into luxury clothing stores on Grafton St., see live music, and hit the impressive club scene around Camden, Wexford, and Harcourt Streets—we could go on and on. See as much of it as you can, and don't constrain yourself to specific areas because you're sure that things just couldn't get any better. They can and will.

ORIENTATION

Dublin is more of a sprawling metropolis than a concentrated urban center. The **Liffey River** cuts the city in two, making navigation easy even for the direction illiterate. The south side is tightly condensed, home to Dublin's most famous neighborhoods, including **Temple Bar** and **Grafton Street.** Just west of these areas lies the historic and scenic neighborhood known as **Georgian Dublin.** Expect a different scene on the north side of the river, where prices are cheaper and the neighborhoods less touristy, for good reason: they certainly lack the charm that is so abundant on the south side. The **O'Connell Street** neighborhood is the economic center on this side of the river, and serves as a great place for cheap shopping and local pubs. The farther north you go, the less we advise going out at night. The area north of O'Connell Street has some great finds during the day, but is of little interest after dark for those without a taste for heroin.

Temple Bar and the Quays

Navigating Temple Bar pretty much consists of stumbling from one pub to the next while singing, or—more likely—shouting Irish drinking songs. On a weekend, chances are you'll be so drunk that just making it to the end of the block will seem like a challenge. However, in the clear light of day, when you feel like walking around in a soberer state of mind, take the main east-west drag, **Temple Bar,** and diverge onto any of the multiple lanes that run north-south from there. Heading north will take you up toward the **River Liffey** and **the Quays,** while heading south will take you toward **Dame St., Trinity College,** and neighboring **Grafton Street.**

The Quays (pronounced "keys") are even easier to maneuver. You'll walk either on the north side (**Ormond Quay** and **Bachelors Walk**) or the south side (**Aston** and **Wellington Quay**) of the Liffey. Keep an eye out for the little restaurants lining the Quays; some of the best are easy to miss.

Grafton Street

Ah, **Grafton Street,** pedestrian highway of purchasing pleasure. Taking off from the intersection of **Suffolk** and **Nassau Streets,** Grafton Street climbs on a slight incline up from **Trinity College** to **St. Stephen's Green.** Small pedestrian walkways branch off from either side of the street, leading to more shops and—more importantly—several excellent pubs.

Shopping on Grafton Street is not for the faint of heart...or those strapped for cash. Several top-tier brands have outlets here, but the south side is hardly a penny-pincher's paradise. Cheaper shopping can be found elsewhere if you're looking to salvage your Guinness fund. Even if you're not buying, though Grafton Street is a place you don't want to miss. Window shopping here is made more enjoyable by the presence of a hodgepodge collection of street performers who busk from dawn until dusk; the best acts come out on weekends.

O'Connell Street

O'Connell Street, the main drag of its namesake neighborhood, runs north-south away from the Liffey. Most hostels are concentrated on **Gardiner Street,** which runs parallel to O'Connell St. and can be found a few blocks to the east. **Henry Street** intersects O'Connell St. about halfway up; follow it west, away from O'Connell, for great shopping. Most of the neighborhood's sights and restaurants (sometimes one and the same) are in the area west of O'Connell St.; others can be found around **Parnell Square,** north of **Parnell Street.**

Georgian Dublin

When you've had enough of Temple Bar's late-night shenanigans and Grafton Street has lost its charm (read: when your credit card maxes out), head west. Much like Temple Bar, **Georgian Dublin** is compact and raring to go; every corner offers a variety of things to see. This neighborhood is home to some of the city's most famous attractions: **Dublin Castle** and **St. Patrick's Cathedral** are located just south of **Lord Edward St.** Stretched out to the west, Georgian Dublin also includes some of Dublin's best (in our humble, alcohol-loving opinion) attractions: **The Guinness Factory** and **Jameson Distillery.**

North of O'Connell Street

Something you should know about the area north of O'Connell Street: it's dodgy. As in, not a place you want to take Fluffy for a walk after dark. Located far past the Parnell Monument, this neighborhood has a few hostels and restaurants, but not enough to keep someone happy for more than a day or two. What you will find is an area with smaller and more local shops, and a much lower percentage of tourists on the sidewalk.

SIGHTS

Dublin is not a huge city. For the rushed traveler, the city's hotspot sights can be hit in less than a day, and the dedicated might find that a 3hr. walking tour is enough. Those who can, however, should dig a little deeper. Dublin is a city rich with history, and its sights won't let you forget it. From the city's early roots and its Viking period to the War of Independence, Dublin—like rock 'n' roll—never forgets.

dublin

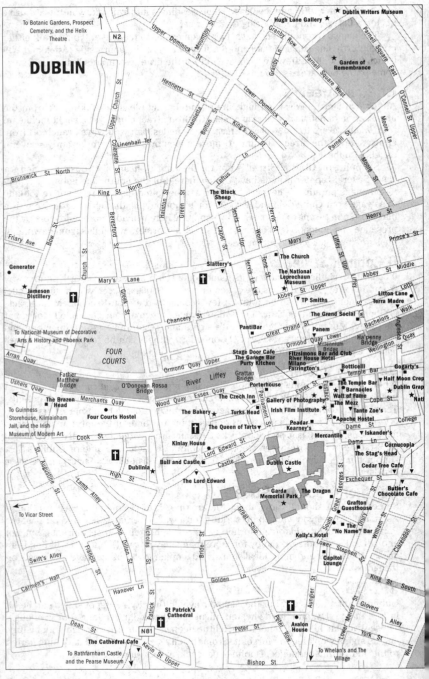

★ Dublin Writers Museum

Hugh Lane Gallery ★

To Botanic Gardens, Prospect
Cemetery, and the Helix
Theatre

★ Garden of
Remembrance

DUBLIN

Brunswick St North

King St North

Friary Ave

Linenhall Ter

Henry St

Prince's St

● Generator

The Black
Sheep ▼

★ Jameson
Distillery

✝

Slattery's ▼

✝

The Church ■

Mary's Lane

Mary St

Abbey St Middle

Chancery St

The National
Leprechaun
Museum

Lotts

Abbey St Upper

TP Smiths ■

Litton Lane
Terra Madre

To National Museum of Decorative
Arts & History and Phoenix Park

FOUR
COURTS

PantiBar ■

Great Strand St

The Grand Social ■

Panem ■

Bachelors Walk

Ha'penny
Bridge

Ormond Quay Lower

Wellington Quay

Arran Quay

Stage Door Cafe
The Garage Bar
Purty Kitchen

Fitzsimons Bar and Club
River House Hotel
Milano

Boticelli ■

Gogarty's ★

Ormond Quay Upper

Farrington's ■

Temple Bar

Half Moon Crep

To Guinness
Storehouse, Kilmainham
Jail, and the Irish
Museum of Modern Art

Father
Matthew
Bridge

Grattan
Bridge

Porterhouse ■

The Temple Bar ■
Barnacles ■

Dublin Grap

O'Donovan Rossa
Bridge

River Liffey

Wall of Fame ★

★ Nati

Ushers Quay

Wood Quay Essex Quay

The Czech Inn ■

Gallery of Photography ★

The Mezz ■
Tante Zoe's

Cape St

● The Brazen
Head

Merchants Quay

The Bakery ●

Turks Head ■

Irish Film Institute ★

Apache Hostel ■

College

Four Courts Hostel ●

✝

The Queen of Tarts ▼

Peadar ■
Kearney's

Dame St

Iskander's ■

To Vicar Street

Kinlay House ●

Mercantile ■

Dame Ln

Cornucopia

✝

Bull and Castle ▼

Lord Edward St

The Stag's Head ■

Dublinia ★

Castle St

Cedar Tree Cafe

● Dublin Castle ★

Butler's
Chocolate Cafe

The Lord Edward ▼

Garda
Memorial Park

The Dragon ■

Grafton
Guesthouse ■

Swift's Alley

The
"No Name" Bar ■

Carmen's Hall

Kelly's Hotel ●

✝

Capitol
Lounge ■

St Patrick's
Cathedral ✝

● Avalon
House

To Whelan's and The
Village

The Cathedral Cafe ▼

To Rathfarnham Castle
and the Pearse Museum

Bishop St

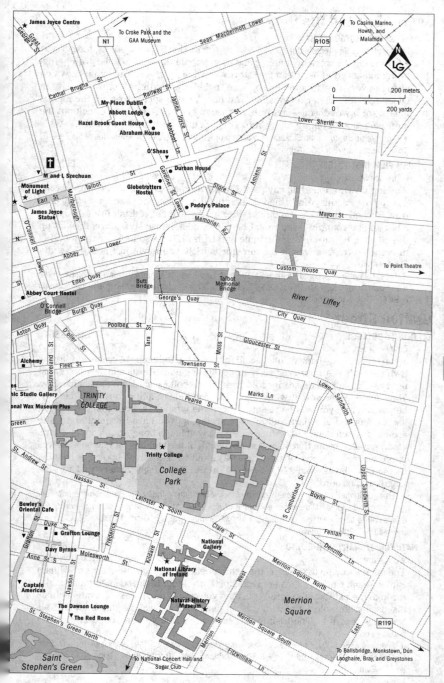

- James Joyce Centre
- To Croke Park and the GAA Museum
- N1
- To Casino Marino, Howth, and Malahide
- R105
- N LG
- 0 — 200 meters
- 0 — 200 yards
- Great George's St
- Cathal Brugha St
- Sean Macdermott Lower
- Railway St
- James Joyce Ln
- Marlbot St
- Foley St
- Lower Sheriff St
- My Place Dublin
- Abbott Lodge
- Hazel Brook Guest House
- Abraham House
- O'Sheas
- Durban House
- M and L Szechuan
- Monument of Light
- Talbot St
- Gardiner St Lower
- Earl St
- James Joyce Statue
- Globetrotters Hostel
- Store St
- Amiens St
- Mayor St
- O'Connell St Lower
- Marlborough St
- Abbey St Lower
- Paddy's Palace
- Memorial Rd
- Custom House Quay
- To Point Theatre
- Abbey Court Hostel
- Eden Quay
- Butt Bridge
- Talbot Memorial Bridge
- George's Quay
- River Liffey
- O'Connell Bridge
- Burgh Quay
- City Quay
- Aston Quay
- Poolbeg St
- Tara St
- Moss St
- Gloucester St
- Alchemy
- D'Olier St
- Fleet St
- Westmoreland St
- Townsend St
- Marks Ln
- Lower Sandwith St
- ...ic Studio Gallery
- ...nal Wax Museum Plus
- Green
- TRINITY COLLEGE
- Pearse St
- Upper Sandwith St
- St. Andrew St
- Trinity College
- College Park
- Nassau St
- Leinster St South
- S Cumberland St
- Boyne St
- Bewley's Oriental Cafe
- Duke St
- Grafton Lounge
- Davy Byrnes
- Frederick St
- Molesworth St
- Clare St
- National Gallery
- Kildare St
- National Library of Ireland
- Merrion Square North
- Fenian St
- Denzille Ln
- Captain Americas
- Anne St S
- Dawson St
- Natural History Museum
- Merrion St West
- Merrion Square
- R119
- Grafton St
- The Dawson Lounge
- The Red Rose
- St. Stephen's Green North
- Merrion Square South
- Merrion St
- Merrion Square East
- Saint Stephen's Green
- To National Concert Hall and Sugar Club
- Fitzwilliam Ln
- To Ballsbridge, Monkstown, Dún Laoghaire, Bray, and Greystones

dublin

Temple Bar And The Quays

GALLERY OF PHOTOGRAPHY
GALLERY

Meeting House Sq., Temple Bar   ☎1 671 4654 www.galleryofphotography.ie

Showcasing the work of students and professionals alike, the Gallery of Photography makes good use of its two stories of winding space. The exhibits, which change every two months or so, have included everything from "Creativity in Older Age" to "Under a Grey Sky." An hour or two spent perusing the photos makes for a wonderful—and free, free is always good—activity. Check out the large selection of photography books or pick up a postcard in the lobby.

i *From Dame St., turn onto Eustace St. walk½ block, and turn left into Meeting House Sq. Free.* ☒ *Open Tu-Sa 11am-6pm, Su 1-6pm.*

IRISH FILM INSTITUTE
CINEMA

6 Eustace St.   ☎1 679 5744 www.irishfilm.ie

Walking down a long hallway paved in movie reels and plastered with classic movie posters, this refurbished Quaker building is a movie junkie's dream come true. Skylights let the natural light filter in as you enjoy a drink from the bar or a bite to eat from the restaurant. Check out the in-house DVD store, then hit up the cinema; be sure to see the indie and Irish flicks. Also look for the monthly director's retrospectives; if the director is Irish, you might just get to attend a Q&A session.

i *From Dame St., turn onto Eustace St. The Irish Film Institute is halfway down the block on the left. Movie ticket €7.50 until 6pm, €8.90 after 6pm.* ☒ *Film institute open M-F 10am-6pm; cinema open M-F 10am-9:30pm.*

Grafton Street

⬛ TRINITY COLLEGE
UNIVERSITY

College Green   ☎1 896 1000 www.tcd.ie

Jump on a tour of Trinity College and follow in the footsteps of greats like Joyce, Swift, and oh, yes, your ever-sassy student tour guide. Ghosts and deadly student feuds await you, as do stories told with all the college sarcasm money can buy. Your guide leaves you at what seems like too long of a line to the Old Library; be patient, and you will be rewarded with the famous Book of Kells. The book itself is housed in a dark and crowded room, so you have to squint and jostle around to get a good look. More easily enjoyed is the Long Room, a wonderful, wood-paneled room that stretches the length of the building and houses shelves upon shelves of some of the university's oldest and rarest books. A rotating themed exhibit is available for perusal in the glass display cases that run the length of the room.

i *From O'Connell Bridge, follow Westmoreland St. for 5min.; Trinity College is on the left. Tour plus admission to the Old Library and Book of Kells €10, tour without admission to library €5, admission to library without tour €9.* ☒ *Tours M-Sa roughly every 30min. 10:15am-12:45pm and every 45min. 2:15-3:40pm.*

NATIONAL LIBRARY OF IRELAND
LIBRARY

2-3 Kildare St.   ☎1 603 0200 www.nli.ie

The main show, so to speak, is the exhibit detailing the life and works of William Butler Yeats, whose poems are read aloud in a lilting Irish accent as you wander through the exhibit. It's more Yeats than you ever thought possible; intellectuals discussing him, old journals of his on display, and—wait, is that a lock of his hair? Yes. Yes, it is. The Irish love their Yeats, and if you do, too, then this is a must-see.

i *Follow Nassau St. along Trinity College; turn right onto Kildare St. The library is on the left. Free.* ☒ *Open M-W 9:30am-7:30pm, Th-F 9:30am-4:45pm, Sa 9:30am-4:30pm. Guided tours W 1pm and Sa 3pm.*

get a room!

Hostels on the north side will cost less, but you'll have to sacrifice proximity to Temple Bar/Grafton Street. For more recommendations, visit **www.letsgo.com**.

🖼 BARNACLES TEMPLE BAR HOUSE   HOSTEL $
19 Temple Ln. S.   ☎1 671 6277 www.barnacles.ie

The lime-green exterior of Barnacles makes it hard to miss, and you'll be glad for that. This gem of a hostel probably has the best location in Dublin, right in the heart of Temple Bar. Grab a drink and head to the common room, where you'll have five new friends before you know it. For those bored of Dublin, try their "Coast to Coast Special": a night in Dublin, a bus to Galway and a day there, a night at the Barnacles Hostel in Galway, and a return bus to Dublin €50).

i Take Dame St. from Trinity College. Turn right onto Temple Ln. S. Breakfast included. Free Wi-Fi. Laundr €8 per bag. Towel and lock rental €1.50, plus €5 returnable deposit. Dorms €10-33; private rooms €30-44. ☑ Reception 24hr.

🖼 GLOBETROTTERS HOSTEL   HOSTEL $$
47-48 Lower Gardiner St.   ☎1 873 5893 www.globetrottersdublin.com

There's a reason Hostelworld frequently ranks Globetrotters among its best accommodations. An incredible variety of large and eclectically decorated common spaces will make it hard to leave the hostel. In fact, if you're staying in single or double rooms, dial "0" on your phone to order a drink from the bar and have it delivered to your room.

i From O'Connell Bridge, turn onto Eden Quay, then left onto Beresford Pl. When you hit Lower Gardiner St., turn left and walk 1 block. The hostel is on the left. Free Wi-Fi. Linens included. Kitchen available. Free secure bicycle parking. Free luggage storage. Safety deposit boxes available for small fee. Private rooms ensuite and include breakfast. Dorms M-F €18; singles €60-70; doubles €80-90. ☑ Reception 24hr.

🖼 FOUR COURTS HOSTEL   HOSTEL $$
15-17 Merchants Quay   ☎1 672 5839 www.fourcourtshostel.com

This might just be the best hostel in Dublin; at the very least, it's among the most fun-loving. The staff are determined to keep things lighthearted, evidenced by the tip jar that reads, "St. f Drink fund: We need beer!" Tons of services (DVD, Wii, and guitar rental, to name a few) are all available with the presentation of ID. The dorms themselves are comfortable, with lofty ceilings that reduce stuffiness but amplify snores.

i From Grattan Bridge, head down Essex Quay as it turns into Wood Quay and then Merchants Quay. Hostel is on the left. Breakfast included. 24hr. cancellation policy. Free Wi-Fi. 8- and 10-bed dorm €16-27, 6-bed €18-32, 4-bed €19-34. Family rooms €20-36 per person. Singles €45-55, with bathroom €50-60. ☑ Reception 24hr. Check-out 10:30am.

🖼 KINLAY HOSTEL   HOSTEL $$
2-12 Lord Edward St.   ☎1 679 6644 www.kinlaydublin.ie

Kinlay escapes the noise of Temple Bar but certainly not the fun. St. dard rooms are nothing to call home about, but there is free dinner. That's right—Monday through Thursday, go crazy on the included meal, which fills you up while you get to know that cute fellow traveler you've been eyeing.

i From Trinity College, take Dame St. and continue as it turns into Lord Edward St. Breakfast included. Free Wi-Fi. Kitchen available. 12-, 16-, and 20-bed dorm €15; 4-, 5-, 6-, and 8-bed dorms €16; private doubles €50. ☑ Reception 24hr.

dublin

NATIONAL GALLERY OF IRELAND

MUSEUM

Merrion Sq. W. ☎1 661 5133 www.nationalgallery.ie

While you're on the museum kick, head to the National Gallery, home of the Irish Masterpieces Collection. Get an eyeful of Ireland's other Yeats (Jack B.) and his dark, slightly abstract works, or head to the ever-so-Irish Dubliners display. Don't like art? (Or just don't appreciate the less-than-renowned work of Irish painters?) It's still worth the trip. The cafe has all-organic, all-delicious selections. Get some work done with the free Wi-Fi while simultaneously stuffing your face with some ham and white cheddar quiche €8.95).

i From Trinity College, take Nassau St. Continue as it turns into Leinster St. S. and then Clare St. Take a right onto Merrion Sq. W. Free. ✪ Open M-W 9:30am-5:30pm, Th 9:30am-8:30pm, F-Sa 9:30am-5:30pm, Su noon-5:30pm, public holidays 10am-5:30pm.

O'Connell Street

JAMES JOYCE STATUE

STATUE

Grab a photo with one of Ireland's biggest names ever. Jauntily leaning into everyone who puts their arm around him, the Joyce statue provides a photo-op for an oh-so-Irish souvenir from Dublin.

i From O'Connell Bridge, take O'Connell St. Lower; statue will be at the intersection with Earl St.

Georgian Dublin

DUBLIN CASTLE

CASTLE, GOVERNMENT BUILDING

Off Dame St. ☎1 645 8813 www.dublincastle.ie

The original Dublin Castle, built by the English in the 13th century, burned down in an accidental fire (ouch). The castle was rebuilt in the 18th century and was the headquarters of British rule in Ireland until the Irish Revolution in 1920. Today, it's a series of government buildings, which doesn't sound nearly as cool as a burned-out castle. The tour will take you through several impressive state rooms, including the blue-carpeted ballroom where the President of Ireland's inauguration takes place. The tour ends in the bowels of one of the castle's original towers. You can see the darkly colored waters that once formed a pool in the castle gardens, giving the city its name—Dubh (black) and Linn (pool).

i Walk over the O'Connell Bridge past Temple Bar and turn right onto Dame St. Follow Dame St. for 10min.; Dublin Castle is on the left. €5.50, students and seniors €4.50, under 12 €2. ✪ Open M-F 10am-4:45pm, Sa-Su and public holidays 2-4:45pm.

JAMESON DISTILLERY

MUSEUM

7 Bow St. ☎1 807 2355 www.jamesonwhiskey.com

Hurray! A tour that rewards you with free drinks! Volunteer at the beginning of the tour for an opportunity to become an official whiskey taster, certificate and all. Not up to the task? Don't worry, everyone gets a taste of the famous Irish whiskey at the end of the hour-long tour. Spend some time in the cask room; the evaporating whiskey gives the air a sweet vanilla scent. Because even angels drink Jameson. Especially angels.

i From the O'Connell Bridge, take Bachelors Walk and continue as it becomes Ormond Quay, Inns Quay, and finally Arran Quay. Turn right onto Church St., then turn left onto May Ln. €12.50, students €10.50. ✪ Open M-Sa 9am-6pm. Tours every 15min.

ST. PATRICK'S CATHEDRAL

CATHEDRAL

Patrick St. ☎1 453 9472 www.stpatrickscathedral.ie

It should come as no surprise that a church named for St. Patrick is one of Dublin's must-see sights. The sky-high archways house exhibits of Ireland's holy history and the legends that go with it. Come pay tribute to Ireland's favorite saint or just to the amazing architects of year 1191 CE. Be sure to leave some

ireland

time to lounge in the gardens out front—the views of the cathedral's exterior are quite a backdrop for a lazy afternoon.

i Follow Dame St. until it turns into Lord Edward St., then Christ Church Pl. Turn left onto Nicholas St., which turns into Patrick St. The Cathedral is on the left €5.50, students and seniors €4.50. ② Open M-F 9am-5pm, Sa 9am-6pm, Su 12:30-2:30pm and 4:30-6pm.

West Of Temple Bar

GUINNESS STATEHOUSE
BREWERY

St. James's Gate ☎1 408 4800 www.guinness-storehouse.com

This isn't a tour. It's an ambush (albeit a welcome one) of everything Guinness. The old brewery has been transformed into an overload of information that requires every one of your senses to take it in. At the Guinness Statehouse, you can examine old Guinness ads, learn how to drink a pint properly (free samples!), and even enjoy a free mug of Guinness at the Gravity Bar, a circular glass bar that overlooks all of Dublin. Tl;dr: great tour, great views, free beer. Sound good? You betcha.

i Follow Dame St. as it turns into High St., then Cornmarket, and then Thomas St. Turn left onto Crane St. Tour brochures available in multiple languages €15, students and seniors €11, students under 18 €9, children 6-12 €5. ② Open daily Jul-Aug 9:30am-7pm; Sept-Jun 9:30am-5pm.

KILMAINHAM GAOL
MUSEUM, JAIL

Inchicore Rd. ☎1 453 5984 www.heritageireland.ie/en/dublin/kilmainhamgaol

This former prison holds the secrets to nearly every street name, monument, and government building in Dublin. The 45min. required tour digs into the gritty details of Ireland's fight for independence. Why here? First built by the British, most of the major Irish leaders were at one point jailed or put to death here. Take our word for it:, history becomes a little too real when you stand in the same place as firing-squad victims.

i From Christ Church Cathedral, take Thomas St.; continue as it turns into James's St. Stick to the right of the fork to continue onto Bow Ln., and continue as it turns into Kilmainham Ln. Take a right onto S. Circular Rd., then the 1st left onto Inchicore Rd. Guided tour mandatory. €6, students and children €2, families €14. ② Open daily Apr-Sept 9:30am-6pm; Oct-Mar M-Sa 9:30am-5:30pm, Su 10am-6pm.

PHOENIX PARK
PARK

Parkgate St. www.phoenixpark.ie

It's a bit of a hike from the city center, but this park is bursting with a full day's worth of activities. Come with a picnic lunch; any spot in the 1752-acre grounds makes for a good place to sit and relax a while. The visitor's center is itself a sight: it's located in the Ashtown Castle, which dates back to the 15th century. You also probably noticed the Wellington Testimonial, the tallest obelisk in Europe (62m). A tribute to the Duke of Wellington, the bronze plaques at the base are cast from cannons. The Magazine Fort is closed to the public, but a climb to the hilltop where it's located gives good views of the city. The giant white cross commemorates the Pope's visit in 1979, a day that any Irish citizen over 40 still remembers. Phoenix Park is also home to many recreational facilities, including camogie fields, football fields, polo grounds, and a model airplane arena, to name a few.

i Take bus #37, 38, 39, or 70. Concerts held in summer; check website for details. Free. ② Open 24hr., but Let's Go does not recommend visiting after dark.

North Of O'Connell Street

For the Hugh Lane Gallery and the Garden of Remembrance, head behind the Parnell Monument to the northern end of Parnell Square. Leaving the Hugh Lane Gallery, turn left to get to the Writers Museum; the James Joyce Centre is just a few blocks down in the same direction.

JAMES JOYCE CENTRE

MUSEUM

35 N. Great George's St. ☎1 878 8547 www.jamesjoyce.ie

You can find those that claim to understand Ulysses, but we know better. The James Joyce Centre is part museum, part headquarters for Joyce fanatics in Dublin and, mecca for Joyce fanatics from around the globe. And trust us, there are plenty. Pieces to note include a copy of Joyce's deathmask, a table at which part of Ulysses was written, and the door to 7 Eccles St., the fictional residence of Leopold Bloom.

i From the O'Connell Bridge, walk up O'Connell St. to the Parnell Statue; turn right onto Parnell St. and then left onto N. Great Georges St. Group discounts available. €5, students and seniors €4. ☒ Open Tu-Sa 10am-5pm, Su noon-5pm.

DUBLIN WRITERS MUSEUM

MUSEUM

18 Parnell Sq. ☎1 872 2077 www.writersmuseum.com

James Joyce may have his own digs just up the road, but Ireland's other literary greats are surely not forgotten. The Dublin Writers Museum showcases old manuscripts, first editions, and tons of memorabilia and journals galore. You don't need to like Irish literature to enjoy a visit here: the building itself, former home of John Jameson, is worth the trip. Stained-glass windows and marble archways? Looks like whiskey's not a bad business in Ireland.

i From the O'Connell Bridge, head up O'Connell St. Continue onto Parnell St., then turn left onto Parnell Sq. N.; the museum is on the right. €7.50, students and seniors €6.30, children €4.70, families €18.70. ☒ Open M-Sa 10am-5pm, Su 11am-5pm. Last entry 45min. before close.

FOOD

Temple Bar And The Quays

⬛ PANEM

CAFE $

21 Lower Ormond Quay ☎1 872 8510

Run by a Sicilian man and his Irish wife, Panem has got your coffee and pastry fix covered. It's a tight squeeze into the tiny cafe, where you will be surrounded by Irish regulars and curious travelers all eyeing up the quiche and hot ham sandwiches on display. With imported Italian coffee (€2.50-3) and mind-meltingly delicious Sicilian almond biscuits (just €1 each), don't be surprised if Panem becomes your morning, afternoon, and evening ritual.

i Cross the Millennium Bridge from Temple Bar. Sweets fro €0.90. Sandwiches as much as €6.50. Cash only. ☒ Open M-Sa 9am-5:30pm.

⬛ HALF MOON CREPES

CAFE $

5 Crown Alley ☎1 649 3748 www.halfmoon.ie

Hand made crepes—check. Nutella—check. An option for bacon on anything—check! If you're looking for a deal, Half Moon offers giant, (we're talking 2ft. in diameter) crepes from €3.50. Go for a meal (we recommend the Traditional Irish) or stop by for something sweet (ice cream and Nutella, anyone?). Open early, with a good coffee selection, this cafe has got your day covered from start to finish.

i From Dame St., turn onto Anglesea St., then left onto Cope St., and finally right onto Crown Alley. Free Wi-Fi. Crepes start a €3.50. Wine €3.50. ☒ Open M-Th 10am-8:30pm, F-Sa 10am-12:30am, Su 10am-8:30pm.

⬛ TERRA MADRE

ITALIAN $$

13A Bachelors Walk ☎1 873 5300

Escape the clamor of the Quays and dip into Terra Madre's basement restaurant. Mismatched chairs give a casual, eclectic vibe, but it's not the chairs you're there for. It's the oh-so-mouth-watering pasta and panini that make this place hard to beat. Try the Gricia, made with pig's cheek, if you're feeling adventurous.

i From the O'Connell Bridge, turn left onto Bachelors Walk. Stop by early in the day to make a reservation. Entrees €6.50-13. ☼ Open M-Sa 12:20-3pm and 5-10pm.

GALLAGHER'S BOXTY HOUSE
TRADITIONAL $$$
20-21 Temple Bar
☎1 677 2762 www.boxtyhouse.ie

Nearly all of the pubs in the Temple Bar area serve some kind of Irish food, but Gallagher's takes it a step further than the rest. An interior most reminiscent of a 19th-century Irish household gives off a welcoming, comforting vibe—it's as though you're eating in a home in the Irish countryside. Try some Boxty (a potato dish offered in ten different variations), and be sure to pair it with a Beamish stout if you want to fit in with the rest of the diners.

i On Temple Bar, just off Anglesea St. Appetizer €4-11. Entrees €19-23. ☼ Open daily 11am-11pm.

TANTE ZOE'S
CREOLE $$$
1 Crow St.
☎1 679 4407

The food is all Creole, all the time (jambalayas and gumbos are the plats du jour, toujours), but the ambience is divided—sit upstairs for the feel of a French bistro or head downstairs for a close-quartered jazz club. Come on Saturday nights with hopes to hear the singing waitress.

i From Dame St., make a right onto Crow St. (1 block over from the Central Bank plaza). Entree €7-30. ☼ Open Tu-Th noon-10pm, F-Sa noon-11pm, Su noon-10pm.

Grafton Street

▨ CORNUCOPIA
VEGAN, VEGETARIAN $$$
19-20 Wicklow St.
☎1 677 7583 www.cornucopia.ie

Prepare to get your health on. Cornucopia serves meals that are vegan, gluten-free, wheat-free, yeast-free, dairy-free, egg-free and low-fat. While meals here don't quite compare to the food coma-inducing splendor of a double bacon cheeseburger, it is worth waiting in line with the well-to-do granola babies for a surprisingly sweet wheat grass shot €3.50). Come Thursday through Saturday nights to enjoy some organic wine €5.35 per glass, €21.50 per bottle) and live harp and guitar music.

i From Trinity College, head down Grafton St., then take a right onto Wicklow St. Upcoming bands post flyers for upcoming shows in the entrance. ☼ Open M-Tu 8:30am-9pm, W-Sa 8:30am-10:15pm, Su noon-9pm.

▨ THE BLEEDING HORSE TAVERN
TRADITIONAL $$
24 Upper Camden St.
☎1 475 2705

Established in 1649, this bar boasts the exposed brick, wooden tables, and leather that make it feel like it hasn't changed a bit since its founding; the four flatscreens and riled up Irish rugby fans, however, will quickly remind you that this is the 21st century. Stick by the bar if you're keeping an eye on the game, or hole up in one of the many nooks with a pint of Guinness €3.80) and some bangers and mash €10) for a quieter night.

i From Trinity College, take Dame St. Turn left onto S. Great Georges St. and follow it as it turns into Aungier, Wexford, and then Camden. The bar is on the left. DJ Th-Sa. Entree €8-13. Pints €3.80. ☼ Open M-W 10am-11:30pm, Th-Sa 10-2:30am, Su 10am-11pm.

BEWLEY'S ORIENTAL CAFÉ
CAFE $$
78-79 Grafton St.
☎1 672 7720 www.bewleys.com

A Grafton Street institution, Bewley's is something to see in and of itself. Beautiful stained glass windows by Dublin's own Harry Clark line the downstairs walls, making the place look more like a cathedral than a cafe. If you're looking for a "cafe's cafe," then head upstairs, where you can sit out on a tiny balcony overlooking the street. Enjoy some delicious coffee made from beans roasted inhouse, as you ponder the extensive dessert menu.

i *From Trinity College, go down Grafton St. The cafe is on the right about 2 blocks down. Coffee €2-4.50. Lunch €6-16. ☼ Open M-W 8am-10pm, Th-Sa 8am-11pm, Su 9am-10pm.*

O'Connell Street

⚥ THE BLACK SHEEP
61 Capel St.

CAFE $$

☎1 878 2157

The wooden tables and bookshelves will make you feel as though you've walked into an Irish country home, and your first bite of the lamb stew will make you sure of it. Offering simple food, Black Sheep delivers in the tastiest ways possible. Make sure to grab a drink from their selection of over 110 craft beers.

i *From O'Connell Bridge, take Bachelors Walk and follow it until the end of Lower Ormond Quay. Take a right onto Capel St. Entrees €4.50-20. ☼ M-Th 10:30am-11:30pm, F-Sa 10:30am-12:30am, Su noon-11pm.*

⚥ TP SMITHS
9-10 Jervis St.

PUB $$

☎1 878 2067   www.thesmithgroup.ie

If you're ever in the mood for a Thai/Mexican/Middle Eastern/Irish place, this place has got you covered. After catching a glimpse of the classic Irish pub exterior (read: Guinness signs and Jameson casks), the menu at TP Smiths may come as a surprise. Paninis, wraps, couscous, burritos, curry—looks like someone couldn't make up their mind on a genre. Sit downstairs near the giant landscape mosaic or head up the winding copper staircase to the balcony seats above.

i *From O'Connell Bridge, take O'Connell St. Turn left onto Middle Abbey St., continue onto Upper Abbey St., then take a right onto Jervis St. Entrees €5-13. Pitchers €12.30. ☼ M-Th 10:30am-11:30pm, F-Sa 10:30am-1:30am, Su 12:30-11:30pm.*

SLATTERY'S
129 Capel St.

CARVERY $$$

☎1 874 6844   www.slatterysbar.com

Once the smell of roasting meat hits you, there's no turning back from this carvery popular with both tourists and locals. Although there's not a large selection at the bar, the essentials are available. This place isn't trendy, so don't expect its drinks to be. The meat, however, will leave you smiling.

i *From O'Connell Bridge, take Bachelors Walk and follow it to the end of Lower Ormond Quay. Take a right onto Capel St. Free Wi-Fi. Lunch €4-12. Dinner €7-15. ☼ Kitchen open M-Sa 8am-9:30pm, Su 10:30am-9:30pm.*

North Of O'Connell Street

⚥ LA VITA
77A Dorset St. Upper

CAFE $

☎1 860 2541

If you're looking for something other than pub grub, La Vita offers a nice change. Mostly vegetarian options make it a good lunch place for the non-meat eaters, and the fresh fruit smoothies €4.50) appeal to all types. We suggest the Salad of Hearts €5), partly because of the gruesome name, but mostly because those artichoke hearts are pretty darn good.

i *From O'Connell Bridge, take O'Connell St. toward the spire. Turn left onto Parnell St. and follow as it becomes Cavendish Row. Continue onto Parnell Sq. E. then Frederick St. N. Turn right onto Dorset St. Upper. The cafe is on the left. Meals €4 €9. Free Wi-Fi. ☼ Open M-F 8am-5pm Sa 11am-4:30pm.*

NIGHTLIFE

Temple Bar And The Quays

◪ MERCANTILE
PUB

28 Dame St.   ☎1 670 7100 www.mercantilehotel.ie

A favorite among hostelgoers, Mercantile is the start to the ever-so-famous hostel pub crawl. Expect a pretty rowdy, foreign crowd around 9pm and a bit of debauchery after that. No live music, but this bar doesn't need it to keep the 20-something crowd coming back.

i *From Trinity College, head down Dame St.; the pub is on the left. Free Wi-Fi. Pint €5. ◷ Open daily 10:30am-midnight.*

GOGARTY'S
BAR, LIVE MUSIC

58 Fleet St.   ☎1 671 1822 www.gogartys.ie

Okay, you'll be hard-pressed to find a local here, and it's basically a tourist trap, but it's a pretty cool tourist trap: three floors, two bars, a beer garden, and a very posh à la carte restaurant on the top. Live music starts as early as 1:30pm, moves upstairs at 8pm, and continues all night long. Grab a few extra euro and those dancing shoes; you won't want to leave this bar.

i *From Dame St., turn onto Anglesea St. Turn right onto Fleet St. It is the big yellow building. Bar foo €5-15, prices increase upstairs. ◷ Open M-Sa 10:30am-2:30am, Su noon-1am.*

THE TEMPLE BAR
BAR

47-48 Temple Bar St.   ☎1 672 5287 www.thetemplebarpub.com

With possibly the best beer garden in the area, The Temple Bar is a pun-merited hotspot on a sunny day. Expect to pay the TB standard €5 for a pint and slightly more for a mixed drink. Music starts with traditional Irish tunes at 2pm and changes to U2 at night. You'd be hard pressed to find a local here, but you'll also be hard-pressed to care.

i *From Dame St., turn onto Temple Ln. S. and continue to the intersection with Temple Bar St. No cover. Guinness €5, lager €5.50. ◷ Open M-W 10:30am-12:30am, Th 10:30am-2am, F-Sa 10:30am-2:30am, Su noon-1am.*

PEADAR KEARNEY'S
PUB, LIVE MUSIC

64 Dame St.   ☎1 707 9701 www.peadarkearneys.com

Named for the composer of the Irish National Anthem who was raised upstairs, it's only fitting that this pub has great live music seven nights a week. Come in early and score a cheap drink (€3.50) or wait until the band starts up at 9pm. Brian Brody is a one-man musical powerhouse on Saturday nights, playing traditional Irish tunes intermixed with several classic American requests. He's also quite the cutie. Don't miss it.

i *From Trinity College, head down Dame St. The pub is on the right. Cash only. When daily specials end, drinks start around €5. ◷ Open daily noon-1am. Happy hour M-F noon-7pm, Sa-Su noon-5pm.*

ALCHEMY
CLUB

13 Fleet St.   ☎866 629 575 www.alchemyclub.ie

While the two flights of stairs to get down to this club may be unfortunate for drunks and those in heels (especially if you're both), the NYC-inspired interior is worth the perilous venture down. Top-40 hits blare all night long, while upturned liquor bottles behind the bar get constant use. Students should come late on Wednesdays for discounted drinks or late on Sundays for free admission. Things don't heat up until after 1am.

i *From Trinity College, head up Westmoreland St. towards the Liffey. Turn left onto Fleet St. Cover F-Sa €9. Guinness and lager €5. ◷ Open W-Su 10:30pm-3am.*

FITZSIMONS BAR AND CLUB
BAR, CLUB

21-22 Wellington Quay   ☎1 677 9315 www.fitzsimonshotel.com

Located in the heart of Temple Bar, Fitzsimons has five different floors, including a nightclub, a cocktail bar, and an open-air rooftop terrace. Hugely popular on the weekends, this emporium of nightlife entertainment is open until 2:30am daily. Be forewarned, there's no A/C in the club downstairs, so it can turn into a sweatbox; but it's a fun sweatbox, nonetheless. The multiplicity of tourists in this bar do make it a prime place to get scammed, though, so keep a sharp eye.

i From Dame St. turn onto Eustace St. It's on the corner of Eustace and E. Essex St. Fitzsimons also has a hotel and restaurant. Stout €4.85, lager €5.35. ☼ Open daily noon-2:30am.

Grafton Street

🔲 WHELAN'S
BAR, MUSIC VENUE

25 Wexford St. ☎1 478 0766 www.whelanslive.com

The place for Dublin's alternative music, Whelan's boasts a large interior with several bars, an excellent balcony area, and two stages. The main stage hosts the biggest names in up-and-coming music (ever heard of John Mayer? Franz Ferdinand?), while the smaller upstairs stage handles local and acoustic acts. Featured in the blockbuster hit PS I Love You, don't be surprised if you find love here yourself—either with the overly talkative old man at the bar or the brooding German smoking in the beer garden. Whelan's is a must for music lovers and curious travelers alike.

i From Dame St. turn onto S. Great Georges St. and continue as it turns into Aungier and then Wexford. Whelan's is on the right. €5-10 cover for the club after 10:30pm on weekends. Guinness €4.40. Lagers €4.90. ☼ Open M-F 2:30pm-2:30am, Sa 5pm-2:30am, Su 5pm-1:30am.

🔲 THE DRAGON
BAR, CLUB, GLBT

64-65 S. Great Georges St. ☎1 478 1590 thedragon@capitalbars.com

A heady combination of Paris chic, Vegas neon, and Addams macabre, The Dragon is a popular gay bar whose younger crowd gets hopping around midnight. Check out the wildly believable drag shows on Monday, Thursday, or Saturday, and throw your sexual orientation out the window.

i From Dame St. turn onto S. Great Georges St. The club is a few blocks down, on the right. Mezzanine and 2nd dance floor upstairs. Pint €3-6. ☼ Open M 8pm-3am, W-Sa 8pm-3am.

THE DAWSON LOUNGE
PUB

25 Dawson St. ☎1 671 0311

Protect yourself from nuclear fallout by climbing down the stairs into "the smallest pub on earth" (or in Dublin, at least). A bit of a novelty, it's a fun place to stop during the afternoons when you can benefit from its dimly lit, cool ambience. Let it get crowded, however, and you'll come to the uncomfortable realization that it's really just a walk-in closet with a Guinness tap. For stout lovers, it's worth the trip. Claustrophobics might want to stay above ground.

i From Trinity College, head down Grafton St. then around the bend onto Nassau St. Turn right onto Dawson St. and head to the end. The pub is on the right. Tiny packages of peanuts available for purchase. ☼ Open M-Th 12:30-11:30pm, F-Sa 12:30pm-12:30am, Su 3-11pm.

THE STAG'S HEAD
PUB

1 Dame Ct.   ☎1 679 3687 www.louisfitzgerald.com/stagshead

Established in 1895, the Stag's Head is the everyman pub of Dublin. Everybody drinks here—businessmen drink next to soccer hooligans, next to punk rockers. When we say next to, we truly mean elbow to elbow; this place gets packed weekend nights. Oh yeah, and there's a giant stag head inside.

i From Dame St. turn onto Trinity St. then a quick right onto Dame Ln. Continue to the intersection with Dame Ct. Guinness €4.55, lager €4.90. ☼ Open M-Sa 10:30am-1am, Su 10:30am-midnight.

ireland

DAVY BYRNES
PUB

21 Duke St.   ☎1 677 5217 www.davybyrnes.com

Getting a famous mention in James Joyce's Ulysses, this literary pub fills up on Bloomsday with patrons looking for Gorgonzola sandwiches and glasses of "burgundy" (the same meal consumed by the novel's main character). If impossible-to-read novels aren't your thing, it's still worth making a stop. Mingle with happily inebriated locals and young travelers in one of Ireland's most famous landmarks.

i From Trinity College, head down Grafton St. then turn left onto Duke St. Entree €6-20. Extensive wine selection at €5-7.50 per glass. ② Open M-Th 11am-11:30pm, F-Sa 11am-12:30am, Su 11am-11pm.

O'Connell Street

🔲 PANTIBAR
BAR, CLUB, GLBT

7-8 Capel St.   ☎1 874 0710 www.pantibar.com

Probably the friendliest nightclub in town, PantiBar is a GLBT playground. Bright neon lights give a good view of the tight T-shirt wearing men serving €5 cocktails all night, but the drinks are hardly the best part. Thursday night is craft night, affectionately referred to as "Let's make a do-do." Come early for a chance to meet Panti and play with her ever-so-adorable terrier. Yes, the club is dog-friendly. How often do you find that?

i From Parliament St. and Temple Bar, take the Grattan Bridge over the Liffey to Capel St. The bar is on the right. Pint €4. Cocktails €5. Drinks ½ price on Su. ② Open M-F 5-11:30pm, Sa 5pm-2:30am, Su 5-11:30pm.

THE CHURCH
CLUB

3A Jervis St.   ☎1 828 0102 www.thechurch.ie

Also a restaurant and a Dublin landmark, this bar is not the place for cash-strapped travelers. For those with a little extra to spend, worship in the Irish way in this bar and Dublin landmark. This church-turned-bar is nearly sinful. Head through the late-night restaurant and down to the basement to find the high-class tourists and well-to-do Irish businessmen sipping on specialty cocktails.

i From O'Connell Bridge, turn left onto Bachelors Walk. Continue along the river and turn right onto Jervis St. Pints and cocktails €5. ② Open M-Th 4pm-midnight, F-Sa 4pm-2am.

Georgian Dublin

🔲 PORTERHOUSE BREWING COMPANY
BAR

16 Parliament St.   ☎1 679 8847 www.porterhousebrewco.com

Beer bottles line the four different floors, back-lit by an orange glow. There is nothing a beer drinker could desire that isn't in this bar. Brewing ten different types of beers, the Porterhouse still manages to diversify its drink menu by serving craft beers from all over the world. Grab a beer from any one of the four levels; there is a bar on each one.

i From Trinity College, head down Dame St. Turn right onto Parliament St. Free Wi-Fi. Meal €7-13. Pints €3.50-7. ② Open M-Th 10:30am-11:30pm, F-Sa 10:30am-12:30am, Su noon-11pm.

🔲 FARRINGTON'S
BAR

29 E. Essex St.   ☎1 671 5135 www.thesmithgroup.ie

On the border of Temple Bar and the Georgian District, this bar embodies the best of both. It's got the "we're Irish and we know it" feel of Temple Bar, minus the masses of tourists. Come early to order the whiskey tasting platter (€10) or later for the Irish music.

i From Trinity College, take Dame St. Turn right onto Eustace St. The bar is at the corner of Eustace and Essex St. Free Wi-Fi. Pint €5. Cocktails €6. ② Open M-Th 10:30am-11:30pm, F-Sa 10:30am-2:30am, Su 12:30-11:30pm

dublin

PURTY KITCHEN   CLUB
    34-35 E. Essex St.   ☎1 677 0945 www.purtykitchen.com

Girls, get out the high heels and short skirts. Boys, get ready to buy some drinks. Top-40 hits pumping, walls that look like disco balls, and three levels of dance floors? This is your standard, hoppin' nightclub. Though it doesn't have much to make it stand out, the Purty Kitchen does a great job at good, ol' fashioned clubbin'.

   i From Trinity College, take Dame St. Turn right onto Sycamore St. then left onto E. Essex St. €3.50 pints on Th. Pints €5. Cocktails €6. ⚇ Open Tu-Sa 10pm-3am, Su 10pm-1am.

THE CZECH INN   CLUB
    Essex Gate   ☎1 671 1535 www.czech-inn.org

A large central hallway leads to the dance floor at the back, past all the almost see-through windows to the tiny rooms that line the place. Posters of grinding models smile down on you as you get crazy to Top-40 hits under the laser lights. This is the sort of place you don't tell your mother about.

   i From Trinity College, take Dame St. Turn right onto Parliament St. then a left onto Essex St. Don't come before 1am; it will be dead. Pints €5. Cocktails €6-8. ⚇ Open M-Sa noon-3am.

ARTS AND CULTURE

Theater

▨ **THE GAIETY THEATRE**   GRAFTON ST.
    S. King St.   ☎1 677 1717 www.gaietytheatre.ie

A beautiful old house theater with three levels of red velvet seating showcases Irish drama at its finest. Student discounts are offered up to 15%, but another good money-saving tip (regular prices run anywhere fro €25-55) is to go for the "restricted view" seats. Rumor has it that the large drop in price is coupled with a minimal loss in stage visibility. Check the website for a complete show schedule. Riverdance comes for two months every summer.

   i From Trinity College, take Grafton St. to the end and turn right onto S. King St. No exchanges or refunds. Doors close promptly when the show begins. Concessions available. Ticket €19-55. ⚇ Box office open M-Sa 10am-7pm.

ABBEY THEATRE   O'CONNELL ST.
    26-27 Lower Abbey St.   ☎1 878 7222 www.abbeytheatre.ie

First opened in 1904 through the efforts of a certain Mr. William Butler Yeats, the Abbey Theatre has burned down, moved away, moved back, and rebuilt on its original location. Apparently the physical space is doing its best to mimic the creative atmosphere, which has promotes an ever-changing landscape of new Irish writers. Some say it falls short; we think that it's still Ireland's National Theater, so it's worth a visit.

   i From O'Connell St. turn onto Lower Abbey St. Tickets €18-40. ⚇ Box office open M-Sa 10:30am-7pm.

BEWLEY'S CAFÉ THEATRE   GRAFTON ST.
    78-79 Grafton St.   ☎86 878 4001 www.bewleyscafetheatre.com

Soak up some of the best of Irish culture at Bewley's Café Theater. Famous for being one of James Joyce's writing spots, this Dublin landmark is a good place for lunchtime entertainment as well as jazz or cabaret in the evenings. Don't expect too many locals here—they already have enough of that good ol' Irish culture.

   i From Trinity College, take Grafton St. Look for the theater on the right. Ticket €10. ⚇ Doors open at 12:50pm for lunchtime performances and 8pm for evening performances.

ireland

Rock And Roll

🏛 GYPSY ROSE ROCK AND BLUES CLUB TEMPLE BAR AND THE QUAYS
5 Aston Quay www.gypsyroseclub.com

A skull, cross, and rose painted on the windows out front invite every Deadhead and Springsteen lover alike. Old rock posters cover the ceiling of the small bar entrance, but don't be fooled: this club has three different venues inside. Start upstairs for live music at the acoustic bar or take the stairs covered in drug-fueled wall murals to the downstairs lounge. Hang a sharp right to check out the club venue, perfect for rocking out to some Guns N' Roses (yeah, they play here).

i *From O'Connell Bridge, walk down Aston Quay on the Temple Bar side of the Liffey. Before 11pm all drinks €4. After 11pm all drinks €5.* ☼ *Open M 5pm-1am, Tu 5-9:30pm, W 5pm-1am, Th-Sa 5pm-3am, Su 6pm-1am.*

THE ACADEMY O'CONNELL ST.
57 Middle Abbey St. ☎1 877 9999 www.theacademydublin.com

It's new, it's hot, and it has all the...well, medium names anyone in Dublin could want to see. Sticking to the rock genre, The Academy varies from punk to indie, so make sure you know what's playing before you go. With two stages and a whole lot of buzz, this is one of the top rock venues in Dublin.

i *From O'Connell Bridge, take O'Connell St. then turn left onto Middle Abbey St. Outdoor smoking patio and full bar. Tickets €5-25.* ☼ *Open daily 10am-5:30pm.*

FIBBERS ROCK BAR O'CONNELL ST.
80 Parnell St. ☎87 914 1249 www.fibbermagees.ie

Get your party shirt on, and we mean the all-black Korn party shirt—we found the best metal venue in Dublin. The music is loud and it is angry (although the people are really quite pleasant). Check the website to hit up a live show, or just stop by for some pool and like-minded people.

i *From O'Connell Bridge, take O'Connell St. and turn right onto Parnell St. Outdoor smoking patio. Pints start at €3.50.* ☼ *Open daily noon-3am.*

ESSENTIALS
Practicalities

- **TOURIST OFFICES: College Green Tourism Office,** Dublin's only independent tourist agency, will help you get a jump on any tour you have in mind. From booking tickets for the Guinness Storehouse to reserving your stay for the night, they do it all. (37 College Green ☎1 410 0700 info@daytours.ie ☼ Open daily 8:30am-10pm.) However, it's worth stating that they are a booking service, and while they can answer most of your questions, if you're looking for information, take the short walk over to **Dublin Tourism** on Suffolk St. Located in a converted church with beautiful arched ceilings and stained glass windows, this may be the only tourist office that's a sight in itself. The staff are knowledgeable and friendly. Head to the general information desk with general questions or head over to one of the many tour companies that have desks in the office. (The former St. Andrew's Church, Suffolk St. ☎1 605 7700 www.visitdublin.com From College Green, walk up Suffolk St. Dublin Tourism is on the right. ☼ Open daily 8:30am-9pm.) To get to the **O'Connell St. branch** from the river, walk up O'Connell St. An off-shoot of the Dublin Tourism head offices in the converted St. Andrew's cathedral, this office offers many of the same services (e.g., tour bookings, room reservations, and general tourist information), just in a slightly more boring building. (14 O'Connell St. ☎1 874 6064 www.visitdublin.com ☼ Open M-Sa 9am-5pm.) The **Northern Ireland Tourist Board** is the place to go for information on Belfast and Northern Ireland, they're also a booking service and will make any reservations you require, free of charge. (Inside Dublin Tourism, Suffolk St. ☎1 605 7732 www.discovernorthernireland.com ☼ Open Sept-June M-Sa 9am-5:30pm, Su 10:30am-3pm; July-Aug M-Sa 9am-7pm.)

dublin

- **LUGGAGE STORAGE: Global Internet Café.** As a nice internet cafe (and they actually do serve coffee), possibly the best thing about this place is their luggage storage rates. A lot of hassle averted for a little money. (8 Lower O'Connell St. Head over the bridge and onto O'Connell St.; the cafe is on the right. ☎878 0295 www.globalcafe.ie *i* Wi-Fi: 20min. €1.85, students €1.70; 40min. €2.25/2; 1hr. €2.95/2.65. Luggage storage: 1st day €4.50, each additional day €2.15. ☼ Open M-F 8am-10pm, Sa 9am-9pm, Su 10am-9pm.)
- **CURRENCY EXCHANGE: €6,000 LIMIT. (1 WESTMORELAND ST. ☎670 6724 ☼ OPEN M-TH 9AM-6PM, F-SA 9AM-8PM, SU 10AM-6PM.)**
- **ATMS:** A 24hr. ATM can be found at the bottom of Grafton St., across Nassau St. from the Molly Malone statue. There are also two 24hr. ATMs at the **Ulster Bank** on Dame St. across from the Wax Museum Plus. ATMs are also located in every **SPAR.**
- **GENERAL POST OFFICE:** From the O'Connell St. bridge, it is a few blocks away from the river along O'Connell St. on the left. Look for a new museum detailing the role of the post office in Irish society over the years. (O'Connell St. ☎1 705 7000 www.anpost.ie *i* Cash only. ☼ Open M-Sa 8:30am-6pm.)

Emergency

- **EMERGENCY NUMBER:** ☎999 or 112. Ask for the service (ambulance, fire, or police) you require.
- **POLICE:** There are several **Garda** (police) stations located around Dublin. To get to the Harcourt station, follow Harcourt St. away from the city center and away from St. Stephen's Green (Harcourt Sq. ☎01 666 666 www.garda.ie ☼ Open 24hr.). On the north side, follow the Quays from O'Connell Bridge, taking Bachelors Walk as it becomes Lower Ormond Quay then Upper Ormond Quay. Take a right onto Chancery Pl. then a right onto Chancery St. (Chancery St. ☎1 666 8200 www.garda.ie ☼ Open 24hr.)
- **PHARMACIES: Hickey's Pharmacy** is up Grafton St. on the left. (21 Grafton St. ☎1 679 0467 ☼ Open M-Th 8:30am-8:30pm, F 8:30am-8pm, Sa-Su 10:30am-6pm.) Another Hickey's Pharmacy is located on O'Connell St., right after the bridge (55 Lower O'Connell St. ☎1 873 0427 www.hickeyspharmacy.ie ☼ Open M-F 7:30am-10pm, Sa 8am-10pm, Su 10am-10pm). **Temple Bar Pharmacy.** (21 Essex St. ☎1 670 9751 www.templebarpharmacy. ie ☼ Open M-W 9:30am-7pm, Th-Sa 9:30am-8pm, Su 1pm-5pm.)
- **SEXUAL ASSAULT: Dublin Rape Crisis Center** provides a 24hr. hotline, free counseling, advocacy, and legal advice for victims of recent rape or sexual abuse. (70 Lower Leeson St. 24hr. toll-free national hotline ☎1 800 77 8888; office number ☎1 661 4911 www.drcc.ie Free. ☼ Open M-F 8am-7pm, Sa 9am-4pm.)

Getting There

BY PLANE

Flights go through **Dublin International Airport** (DIA; www.dublinairport.com).

Getting Around

BY BUS

Dublin Bus runs using a system of stages. The price of your bus fare in Dublin depends on how far you're traveling: 1-3 stages €1.40, 4-7 €1.90, 8-13 €2.15 and over 13 stages is €2.65. The "Rambler Pass" is advertised for tourists, but though it lets you travel on any bus for a set amount of time, it is priced pretty steeply, so only buy it if you're sure to be moving around quite a bit (1-day pass €7, 3-day €14, 5-day €23). Bus times vary, but can usually be caught every 8-20min. 6am-8pm and every 30min. 8pm-midnight. (☎1 873 4222 www.dublinbus.ie.)

BY TRAIN

Luas, Dublin's light rail tram system, traverses the city, making its way to several of Dublin's suburbs. One-way tickets are €2-3, depending on the distance traveled and time, while round-trip tickets are €3-6. The fares are divided into zones, much like the bus system. Maps at each station let you know which zone you need to get to. For longer stays, a 7-day (€13-30) or 30-day (€50-89) bargain pass is available. Use it to get from one end of the city to the other or to hit up Dublin's suburbs quickly and for cheap. (☎800 300 604 www.luas.ie ☒ Operates M-F 7am-7pm and Sa 10am-2pm.) Dublin Area Rapid Transit (DART) runs along Dublin's coast southward from Malahide and Howth to Greystones. One-way tickets are €2-5, depending on the destination, and round-trip tickets are €4-10. Student discount tickets and special offers for tourists are often available. (☎1 703 3504 www.irishrail.ie)

BY TAXI

Taxis in Dublin are, much like everything else, expensive. Expect to pay anywhere from €7-10 to get from one destination to another, and more if you're heading across town. Obey the general rules of foreign taxi travel—ask ahead to find the shortest route to your destination, and then make sure the cabbie follows it. **Blue Cabs** is the most popular taxi company in Dublin. They offer wheelchair-accessible cabs. Call ahead of time to book. It's an extra €2 to order a cab ahead by phone and an extra €1 for each passenger. (☎1 802 2222 www.bluecabs.ie.) There are taxi stands (or "ranks") all over the city, as well.

BY BIKE

Dublin is a bikable city. It's not common for bike shops to do rentals; get ready to bargain if you're going that route.

belfast

Think of Belfast as Dublin's badass older brother who plays in a band: he's cool, gritty, and gets tons of groupies. The city has an air left over from a history of recent war and strife, so don't be surprised if there is some enmity between members of the population on cultural lines. The city's people are some of the friendliest, though, and you only need to sit in one of the traditional pubs for a short while before you find someone who not only remembers "the Troubles" (as the conflict is called), but can also recall a time when a police frisking was requisite before entering the city center. But far from having resentment or a "hush-hush" attitude, the people of Belfast engage with their history; black cab tours of West Belfast, the area of hottest conflict, have become a popular tourist attraction. With all the history behind it, Belfast is reinventing itself as a tourist paradise, with a wonderful balance of sights, restaurants, and nightlife to make it a completely perfect starting point for an adventure through the island.

ORIENTATION

What's with all the Donegalls? Okay, get this: **Donegall Square** surrounds the city hall, **Donegall Road** runs from the west, crossing through town at **Shaftesbury Square** and becoming **Donegall Pass;** and finally, there's **Donegall Street,** which runs right through the heart of the **Cathedral Quarter.** Lesson to be learned? If someone gives you directions via a "Donegall" anything, make sure you get a second opinion. Belfast is a narrow city, running mostly north-south, with the previously conflicted **Falls** and **Shankill Roads** in West Belfast usually best visited hurriedly. The **University Quarter,** comprising **Queen's University,** lies south of the city center along **University Road** (follow Bedford St. and Dublin Rd. from city hall) and houses most of the student life and nearly all of

belfast

the budget accommodations in Belfast. What was called the "Golden Mile" in past years—the triangle formed by Dublin Rd., Great Victoria St., and Bruce St. —is now pretty much dead. A few fast-food joints and the odd pub can be found there, but the new hotspot for nightlife is the **Cathedral Quarter,** the area above city hall near the **River Lagan.** The developing **Titanic Quarter** lies to the east and, while still not exactly a hotspot, is up and coming, with a new be-all and end-all **Titanic Exhibition** as its crown jewel.

The University Quarter

The University Quarter centers on **Queen's University** but extends into the residential neighborhoods to the west and south. The **Students' Union, The Botanic Inn,** and **Eglantine Inn** are all popular student bars, and there are several hostels and B&Bs on **Eglantine Avenue** and **Fitzwilliam Street. Lisburn Road** provides the other, far-side north-south channel, and also has several good restaurants and cafes. If you ever get disoriented, ask for either Lisburn Rd. or University Rd. and you'll be able to get yourself back toward the city center.

The Titanic Quarter

Over the river to the east of the city center, the Titanic Quarter was once home to Belfast's massive shipbuilding industry. Indeed, it is still home to the historic **Harland & Wolff** shipyard, whose enormous cranes are still visible from almost any point in the area. Today, the Titanic Quarter is being subjected to a thorough redevelopment project, which includes the glowingly enormous **Titanic Exhibition** perched on the banks of the river. Most spots in this area can be seen from the **Titanic Trail** stretching from the Bridge End bridge along the river. While this is a small quarter at the moment, keep an eye on the website **www.titanic-quarter.com** for new events and openings.

Cathedral Quarter

Boasting the hottest nightclubs and independent restaurants, the Cathedral Quarter is the place for a night out. Here is where you'll find the newest pubs, the hippest crowds, and the sweetest cocktails. **High Street** provides a neat "bottom" to the neighborhood, which extends up to the **University of Ulster** and east over to **North Street.** The smaller streets have a lot to offer as well: Waring St., for instance, has some good bars and luxury hotels. It's all held together by the ubiquitous backbone known as **Donegall Street**

City Center

Not one to mess around with misnomers, the City Center is indeed in the center of the city. Mostly focused around **Belfast City Hall** in **Donegall Square,** the **Cathedral Quarter** is to the north, while following **Dublin Road** all the way to the south will eventually lead to the **Queen's Quarter.** Most of the chain shopping areas and more upscale restaurants can be found between Donegall Sq. and **Castle Place,** while nightlife and accommodations are found from the square to **Donegall Pass.** If you don't get confused by the number of Donegalls around here, buy a Guinness, then see how you feel.

SIGHTS

The University Quarter

🖾 **ULSTER MUSEUM**   MUSEUM
Botanic Gardens   ☎28 9042 8428
This museum can't decide whether it is a natural history museum, a human history museum, an art museum, or a local history museum. In fact, joyously, it is all four. Gaping Tyrannosaurus jaws will make you wonder why they seemed to have better dentists in the Jurassic era, while mummified remains might

get a room!

For more *Let's Go* recommendations, visit **www.letsgo.com.**

▨ VAGABONDS
9 University Rd.   ☎28 9543 8772 www.vagabondsbelfast.com

HOSTEL $$

More focused on the glamorous and stylish elements of travel, rather than the rough-and-ready quality most backpackers adopt, Vagabonds conjures quite the modern and chic image. Clean dorms, comfy common spaces, and a friendly staff (mostly travelers just passing through themselves) are what you will find here. Most walls are covered with some celebration of traveling for travel's sake, from globally sourced photos to quotes from greats like Paul Theroux. This is a break from the horror stories of the road. You might even want to stay home for a night and just relax. That's okay, though—Monday movie night means free popcorn.

i From Shaftesbury Sq., walk down Bradbury Pl. Bear left onto University Rd. The hostel is on the right. Breakfast included. Free Wi-Fi. Bike hire available. Laundry available. Dorms £13-16; doubles £40. ☒ Reception 24hr. Check-in after 1pm. Check-out 11am.

▨ THE LINEN HOUSE HOSTEL
18 Kent St.   ☎28 9058 6400

HOSTEL $

This hostel is undoubtedly the best value you will find in the Cathedral Quarter, and probably in Belfast as a whole. If you can put up with sleeping in a dorm with 20 other people, as well as the noise emanating from the late-night party crowd (it is in the heart of the Belfast nightlife, after all), you'll get more than your money's worth. With a reasonably comfortable, if not feathery-soft bunk, a kitchen whose major attraction is plenty of countertop surface area, and a simple, nondescript dining room, you will not be living in the lap of luxury. Fortunately, the price is definitely right.

i Large mixed dorm £6.60; large female-only dorm £7.50; 8- to 10-bed £8; 6-bed £9. Singles £20; doubles £15; quads £11. ☒ Reception 24hr. Check-in from 2pm. Check-out 10:30am.

belfast

tempt you as a burial option. Prehistoric Irish river fish floating menacingly in formaldehyde will make you wonder why a minnow like Jaws was such a big deal, and sketches by Leonardo Da Vinci will put to rest any traditional artistic leanings you might have. In short, the sprawlingly extensive collection caters to any kind of whimsical desire you might find simmering within.

i Free. ☒ Open Jul-Aug daily 10am-5pm; Sept-Jun Tu-Su 10am-5pm.

QUEEN'S UNIVERSITY
University Rd.   ☎28 9097 5252

UNIVERSITY

Sprawling lawns and classic brick buildings could definitely make you wonder if you made the right university choice (i.e., the choice not to go here). While Queen's does have plenty of modern buildings, the older, central sections have to be walked through to be properly admired. We recommend calling ahead and getting a guided tour. Yes, you will be one of those touristy people intruding on a campus, but it is definitely worth the distasteful stares. If you don't want to bother with that, you can simply pick up the "Walkabout Queen's" pamphlet, which will take you through a similar route as that of the guided tours, without the obligation to tip the brochure when you're done—unless, of course, you thought the brochure was cute; then you could maybe ask it to dinner.

i Free. ☒ Visitors' center open M-F 9:30am-4:30pm.

Cathedral Quarter

◾ GOLDEN THREAD GALLERY   GALLERY
84-94 Great Patrick St.   ☎28 9033 0920

Without question one of the most challenging and refreshing galleries of modern art, this out-of-the-way find is particularly impressive in a city where modern art is something of a rarity. While two continuously shifting exhibits occupy the main spaces, the real gem is the community art project space. It doesn't get much fresher than works finished one day, only to be on the wall the next. If there is a place to feel the glow of creativity, it is here.

i *Free entry.* ◙ *Open Tu-F 10:30am-5:30pm, Sa 10:30am-4pm.*

NORTHERN IRELAND WAR MEMORIAL EXHIBITION   MUSEUM
21 Talbot St.   ☎28 9032 0392

Often, war museums become far too big, overwhelmed by the need to cover the entire breadth and depth of the realities of wartime experiences and tragedies. Usually, trying to do that ends up obscuring the real message. In this case, the intimate and real experiences of Ulster County and the rest of Northern Ireland shine through in such a way that you can truly feel the history, not simply read about it. This museum is a great monument to those men and women who were touched by the First and Second World Wars and how they overcame the dangers of the past.

i *Free.* ◙ *Open M-F 10:30am-4:30pm.*

SINCLAIR SEAMEN'S CHURCH   CHURCH
Corporation Sq.   ☎28 9071 5997

Bedecked in seafaring memorabilia, from the lifeboat-shaped collection boxes to the ship's shining wheel and compass, it might be a little distracting were you to come here for a service. But for a secular visit, you can enjoy the strong seafaring tradition in Belfast. Dating back to 1857, this particular church probably hosted some of the men who worked aboard the RMS Titanic, the fantastically ill-fated "Pride of Belfast."

i *Donations welcome.* ◙ *Open W 2-4:30pm.*

ST. ANNE'S CATHEDRAL   CATHEDRAL
Donegall St.

Mixing Gothic architecture with modern art installations can sometimes work in particularly interesting or arresting ways. Unfortunately, in St. Anne's Cathedral, it did not quite work out. The cavernous interior of the gaudy cathedral, with the requisite number of glowing candles and small side chapels, is broken up by the "Spire of Hope," a towering space needle jutting through the center of the ceiling and extending up into the sky above. Apparently they were trying to get the attention of someone overhead, but unfortunately all they got were some very confused birds and one perplexed aircraft.

i *Donations welcome.* ◙ *Open M-F 10am-4pm.*

The Titanic Quarter

◾ TITANIC BELFAST   MUSEUM
Queen's Rd.   ☎28 9076 6399

This museum is a source of pride of Belfast, but hopefully this one won't sink. Vaunted as the most complete Titanic experience in the world, the shimmering sides and pointed prows (as they are best described) of this miracle of architecture dominate the Titanic Quarter. Once inside, though, the tourist machine will mobilize. After your (expensive) ticket has been purchased, take the escalator to the upper level, but beware, this is not an exhibit in which you are free to roam. It is an "experience" in the way that cattle herding is an "experience" for the cattle. Your cycle through the process includes a ride through a replica of the shipbuilding yards, a look out over the sea from a replica bow of the Titanic itself (above water), a glance at a holographic, quarrelsome first-class passenger, and then a full-blown movie dive to the wreckage. You might be struck by the amount of time spent on the engineering breakthroughs and building process compared to the more famous wreck, but as they say in Belfast "It was fine when it left us," and that is their focus. Less romantic than the movie (which you will undoubtedly want to watch afterward), but still everything you ever wanted to know about the unsinkable ship.

i £13.50, students £9.50. ☒ Open Apr-Sept M-Sa 9am-7pm and Su 10am-5pm; Oct-Mar daily 10am-5pm. Last admission 1hr. 40min. before closing.

THE TITANIC DOCK AND PUMP HOUSE   HISTORIC BUILDING
Northern Ireland Science Park, Queen's Rd.   ☎28 9073 7813

Unlike the"Experience" located next door, this is a piece of real Titanic history. The only one, in fact, unless you happen to have the thousands of dollars necessary for a dive to the wreck itself. It is the sheer scale of the ship that really hits you here. It becomes apparent that this wasn't big in the old-fashioned sense, something which wouldn't actually seem so impressive today. No, this was a behemoth of steel and engineering. At the time, the Pump House launched the single largest ship ever to float in its day. When it was first released, it was the largest object ever moved by human beings. That's big. Wander through by yourself and enjoy the echoes of footsteps, or get the guided tour for plenty of tidbits and factoids you would have missed in the more grandiose "Experience."

i £4.50, students £3.60. With guided tour £4.50, students £5.40. ☒ Open M-Th 10am-5pm, F 9:30am-5pm, Sa-Su 10am-6pm.

HARLAND & WOLFF   SHIPYARD
Queens Rd.   ☎28 9024 6609

Don't go wandering too far through here, as it remains a very active shipyard. Unless you happen to have a penchant for welding, probably best to give most of this a wide berth. But you can't be anywhere in Belfast without seeing the towering outfitting cranes Samson and Goliath. Indeed, there is a fair portion of new stained glass in the city which features their yellow bulk in some corner. So wander in and get those definitive holiday snaps, while deepening your understanding of Belfast through the once single greatest employer of Belfastians in times gone by. And, yes, it is also a Titanic sight. It is its birthplace, in fact. For the best experience, get one of the Laganside River Tours, which will take you around the whole place by water.

i From the Bridge End bridge, turn left. Walk along the riverside footpath until its end. Continue onto Queens Rd. The shipyard is on the right.

City Center

❈ BELFAST CITY HALL   CITY HALL
Donegall Sq.   ☎28 9032 0202

Very pretty on the outside, but if you want to get at the fascinating stuff on the inside, we recommend the pro tour. Admire giant silver scepters and gawk at funny old clothing, even those still being used by a councilman. Maybe sit on the seats of all the bigwig politicos using that unusual garb or take time to touch furniture that missed the Titanic's maiden voyage and wonder about their fellows at the bottom of the sea.

i Free. ☒ Exhibition open M-F 9am-4:30pm, Sa 10am-3:30pm. Tours M-F 11am, 2, and 3pm; Sa 2 and 3pm.

▨ THE LINEN HALL LIBRARY
17 Donegall Sq.

LIBRARY

☎28 9032 1707

Among the creaky bookshelves and deeply engraved reading desks, you can plunge yourself into the collected written history of Belfast and Northern Ireland. You could spend hours diving for buried factoids among dusty shelves, while all the time spying on the frolicking in Donegall Sq. below. But it is vacation time, so you probably aren't researching. In that case, come for the erudite atmosphere, strong coffee, and free Wi-Fi.

i Donations welcome. ☼ Open M-F 9:30am-5:30pm, Sa 9:30am-4pm.

ST. GEORGE'S MARKET
12 E. Bridge St.

MARKET

☎28 9043 5704

First opened in 1890, some things about St. George's Market haven't changed—you'll still get a strong smell of raw fish and meat as you walk in the entrance, and catcalls from one vendor to another are still the norm. You'll now also find everything from handmade jewelry to pungent spices to questionable antiques. Check it out on Saturday mornings and listen to the live music that goes on right in the middle of everything.

i Prices vary. Haggle. ☼ Open F 6am-2pm, Sa 9am-3pm, Su 10am-4pm.

GRAND OPERA HOUSE
2 Great Victoria St.

OPERA

☎28 9024 1919

There are few opera houses you'd expect to see adorned with elephants and Hindu gods, least of all in Belfast. But indeed, inspired by England's former Indian territories, the architect of the Grand Opera House incorporated his experiences of the then-empire into this building's interior design. If you can't get in to see a show (which can be done on the cheap if you call in for standby tickets), at least try and get in to see the theater space. An elephant would never forget it.

i Prices vary, but expect to pay £8-30. ☼ Box office open M-F 9:30am-5:30pm, Sa noon-5pm.

FOOD

Trying to pin down exactly what Irish cuisine is might take quite some time. Let's just say that it focuses on local ingredients fed in the pub-grub form. And there are Irish pubs aplenty, never fear. Should you decide to venture away from the safe confines of a memorabilia-bedecked bar, however, there are some savory options awaiting you.

A particular favorite around these parts is the all-day **Ulster Fry,** which includes a fried "farl" of soda bread, fried potato "farls," bacon, eggs, and sausage—all locally sourced, of course. Mix it all up and dive into the fried goodness.

The University Quarter

▨ BOOKFINDER'S CAFE
47 University Rd.

CAFE $

☎28 9032 8269

Long before the commercial chains started throwing coffee shops into their upper stories, this dusty bookshop was welcoming scholars from the nearby university into its tiny cafe. Let yourself be ushered through the once-loved, worn secondhand books piled high around you, before finding yourself in a small grotto among them all. There is nowhere better to sip on a latte reading your newest favorite.

i Coffee £2. Soup £4. ☼ Open M-Sa 10am-5.30pm.

THE MAD HATTER
2 Eglantine Ave.

BRITISH $$

☎28 9068 3461

Join the rest of the local residents in their Sunday best for a solid fry up on a weekend morning. Ideal for soaking up the mistakes from last night, bite into the crisp fried bread and smother those sausages and bacon in plenty of ketchup.

For the real experience, mix everything on your plate into one great big fried mess. Grab a paper from the rack by the door and settle in to munch contentedly, and then stay for a while longer while you try to move.

i *Ulster Fry £4.45. Entrees £4-7.50.* ⏰ *Open M-Sa 8am-6pm, Su 8:30am-5pm.*

Cathedral Quarter

☒ MADE IN BELFAST   IRISH $$$
23 Talbot St.   ☎28 9024 4107
From the eclectic decor around you to the breakdown of the menu into"smalls" and "bigs," you know you have stumbled into a backpacker's paradise of a restaurant. With overstuffed pillows and wall hangings, the vibe is right—and we haven't even gotten to the food. Try the Irish dexter beef, Belfast black stout, and oyster pie (£12) for a succulent, drool-worthy, and deliciously Irish meal.

i *Entrees £9.50-22.* ⏰ *Open M-W noon-10pm, Th-Sa noon-11pm, Su noon-9pm.*

☒ THE DARK HORSE   CAFE $$$
30 Hill St.   ☎28 9023 7807
Outfitted in dark wood paneling, darker leather booths, and painted mirrors behind the bar, this little sister to the nearby Duke of York is reminiscent of an old-school gentlemen's club—think pipes rather than strippers. Putting some of the style back into coffeehouses, this place is perfect for a more refined sandwich at lunchtime or a proper sit-down meal in the evening before you join the fray in Commercial Ct.

i *Entrees £6.50-16.75. Free Wi-Fi. Take-out available.* ⏰ *Open M-Th 9am-6pm, F-Sa 9am-1am.*

WHITES TAVERN   PUB $$
2-4 Winecellar Entry   ☎28 9024 3080
Tucked away in a side entry, this small public house is undoubtedly best described as a tavern. Whites Tavern has a warm heart and is full of the smell of freshly pumped Guinness and the chuckling of regulars on their well-worn wooden benches. The food is hot and pubby, just what you need on those rainy Belfast days. Sure, on weekends it swells full to bursting and even spills out onto the cobblestones, but the glowing golden light bathing the street keeps the party bright and merry.

i *Pints from £2. Entrees £4-12.* ⏰ *Open M-Th noon-11pm, F-Sa noon-1am, Su noon-11pm.*

BLINKERS   BRITISH $$
1 Bridge St.   ☎28 9024 3330
This is a greasy spoon that serves up British home-style favorites. Blinkers is best known for their full, all-day Ulster Fry (£8), which pulls in plenty of children with eyes six or seven times the size of their stomachs. For a starving backpacker though, there isn't a much better breakfast than a huge plate piled high with fried, greasy wonderfulness. You certainly won't leave hungry.

i *Entrees £7-19.* ⏰ *Open M-Sa 9am-7pm.*

City Center

☒ ARCHANA   INDIAN $$
53 Dublin Rd.   ☎28 9032 3713
With enormous plates of creamy, fragrant curries and rice, this is the Indian spot in Belfast. If an endorsement is needed, the Indian national cricket team themselves ate here when they were visiting Belfast on their world tour (apparently there is no higher endorsement as far as Indian food goes). The small size of the restaurant means that seats fill up quickly, even the rickety tables on the upper level, so arriving on the earlier side will ensure that you can enjoy your classic tikka masala with almonds and cashews (£10) like a cricketer.

i *Entrees £10-12.* ⏰ *Open daily noon-2pm and 5-11pm.*

belfast

THE ALLOTMENT

BISTRO $$$$

48 Upper Queen St.

☎28 9023 3949

Quality ingredients is certainly the name of the game, and the fresh fare here comes from nearby allotments and personal plantations. And they transform those local ingredients into stunning dishes of gastronomic excellence. The atmosphere remains relaxed, with light wood tables and chalkboards belying the exquisite menu, which is admittedly limited but changes frequently. While it might seem expensive at first, you are encouraged to BYOB and, with no corkage fee, you will have all the fun you want over great food with plenty of the bottle for good measure.

i *Entrees £10-17.* ☒ *Open M-W 7:30am-6pm, Th-F 7:30am-4pm and 6-10:30pm, Sa 9am-4pm and 6-11pm, Su 9am-3pm.*

BRIGHTS RESTAURANT

BREAKFAST, CAFE $$

23 High St.

☎28 9024 5688

You know those mythical breakfast places with platters of scorchingly fried food just waiting to be slathered in ketchup and devoured by hordes of towering rugby players? Those myths are the shadowy reality of Brights. Serving all sorts of other foods throughout the day, the real find here is the "Brights Ulster Fry," a truly magnificent concoction of eggs, bacon, fried bread, black pudding, sausages, tomato, and mushrooms (to appease the herbivores). And at only £4 before noon, there is no better value across the land.

i *Entrees £6.25-10. Full Ulster Fry £4 before noon.* ☒ *Open M-W 9am-5:30pm, Th-F 9am-8pm, Sa 9am-5pm.*

POPPO GOBLIN

SANDWICHES $

23 Alfred St.

☎28 90246 894

A tiny sandwich shop tucked into a back street of central Belfast, the locals head here for a taste of the gourmet at less-than-gourmet prices. True, the size of the place limits the amount of real atmosphere you can pack in here, but thankfully the flavors of the food pack in enough to speak for themselves. Try the sesame chicken in spicy peanut sauce on pita (£3.25) for the biggest bang—both for your buck and your palate.

i *Sandwiches £3.25-5.* ☒ *Open M-Sa 9am-3pm.*

NIGHTLIFE

The University Quarter

▦ THE BELFAST EMPIRE

VENUE

42 Botanic Ave.

☎28 9024 9276

Boasting two stage and bar areas, the Empire is not somewhere you go for a quick pint. With live performances advertised around the city that span from local tribute bands to classic artists, the small club's rock 'n' roll spirit is not dead. The dark wood interior is emphasized by the powerful spotlights trained on the stage. You can almost imagine you are at a petite rock concert all for you. Without even walking in, the large, stone front of the building is impressive, with plenty of gently curving balustrades and oak doors. For the most part, tickets are available on the night of, but book online to be safe.

i *Tickets £6-12. Beer from £3.* ☒ *M-Sa 11:30am-1am.*

▦ LAVERY'S

PUB, CLUB

12-18 Bradbury Pl.

☎28 9087 1106

Everybody has heard of it and mostly everyone has been, provided they aren't living in a ditch somewhere. With three floors, Lavery's is huge. The first floor is a traditional pub bar, with a great outdoor beer garden; the second floor is a black, compact music venue and bar, with all the finesse twirling bartenders can bring; and finally, a club with spinning green strobes and a serious dance floor sits up top. Each level feels spacious…that is, until the weekends, when the crowd spills out the door. Happy hours M-Th means all drinks are $2.85. During the week, the third floor, "The Ballroom," is a fantastic pool hall, where it is not a heinous crime to be less than world-ranked.

i *Pints £3.20. Top 2 floors £5 cover. ⏰ Open M-Sa 11:30am-1am, Su 12:30pm-midnight.*

▧ THE ELMS
BAR, VENUE

36 University Rd.
☎28 9050 9840

The music is the all-important component here, mostly sticking to the classics of rock and alternative. If you are a fan of anything from Jimi Hendrix to The Black Keys, you will feel right at home in here. With all the hard rock feel, but none of the potentially upsetting grunge, true diehards might feel a bit out of place. But forget the funky-patterned wood bar…and the classy cocktails…and the perfectly arranged posters on the walls, just let the beat of those classic tracks take over as you swig something strong and sharp.

i *Beer from £3.20. Cocktails £5. Food £5-7. ⏰ Open M-W 4pm-1am, Th-Sa 7pm-1am, Su 7pm-midnight.*

CUCKOO
BAR

149 Lisburn Rd.
☎28 9066 7776

Wickedly cheerful and wildly colorful, Cuckoo makes no apologies for itself. Indeed, it proclaims its motto very clearly over the front entrance:"Still making sense." Inside, there is a brilliantly inspired mixture of graffiti art combined with more traditional dark wood, wicker, and leather fittings. Check out the layers of artistry covering the floor from the comfort of a leather armchair. You can't beat this place on its eclecticism,its passion, or its style. And, with a theme for every night of the week, you will rarely go astray here.

i *Pints from £3. Cocktails £4.50. ⏰ Open M-Sa noon-1am, Su noon-midnight.*

THE BOTANIC INN
BAR, CLUB

23-27 Malone Rd.
☎28 9058 9740

Like a Swiss army knife of nightlife,"the Bot" has a little bit of everything. It gets packed on the weekends and during sporting events thanks to its reputation as Belfast's sports bar. Check out signed rugby jerseys, boxing gloves, and a shiny, shiny trophy case. On Saturday, the downstairs suddenly becomes a buzzing local watering hole, before those same customers head upstairs to the tightly packed dance floor in the club. Show up on Sunday for the carvery menu ($6) and wash it down with some local Belfast Ale. Framed photos of burly men in short-shorts abound. Don't catch the eye of the Toucan, though: there could be trouble.

i *Pints £3.10-3.60. ⏰ Open M-Sa 11:30am-1am, Su noon-midnight.*

QUEEN'S UNIVERSITY STUDENTS' UNION
BAR, CLUB

75 University Rd.
☎28 9097 3106

Impossible to get any more studenty than the student union, this one will make you wonder how Queen's students get any work done at all. With not one, but three bars, this complex can keep you entertained all night long, where new friends are not hard to come by. The Speakeasy Bar upstairs is generally the quietest of the three, but when the evening gets going, the space gets so packed that those comfy-looking chairs are a dream from long ago. Downstairs, meanwhile, there is the more lounging Bar Sub, with plenty of comfy couches and TVs, should you decide that you would rather not talk to your friends. Finally, there is Bunatee Bar, where most of the student-run organizations hold their"evening get-togethers"—over pints, of course.

i *Pints £3-3.50. ⏰ Open M-Sa 8:30am-late, Su noon-midnight.*

belfast

THE EGLANTINE INN
BAR

32-40 Malone Rd.   ☎28 9038 1994

Across the street from "the Bot" is "the Eg," a heavily student-patronized bar with chic red lighting and black leather couches. Sit near the wide windows facing the Bot and enjoy the cool darkness, a stark contrast to the other's cheery, loud merriment.

i *Most pints £3. ☼ Open M-Sa 11:30am-late, Su noon-late.*

Cathedral Quarter

☒ OLLIE'S
CLUB

35-39 Waring St.   ☎28 9023 4888

Below the undeniably opulent Merchant Hotel lies a basement that most hotels can only dream of. Low, exposed brick covers the ceilings and glowing, seductive art hangs out in the corners, while cheerful chattering can only just be heard over the bass reverberating through the tunnel walls. Here, you'll see all kinds, from students to some older folks who have definitely still got it. If all the dry ice, drums, and bass gets to be too much, take a break in the enclosed Heineken Lounge, where you can enjoy a chilled bottle of the stuff, surrounded by mounted, green-glowing bottles in the night air.

i *M cover £3, all drinks £2.50; Th-F cover £5; Sa cover £10. ☼ Open M 10pm-late, Th 9pm-late, F 10pm-late, Sa 9pm-late.*

☒ THE DUKE OF YORK
PUB

11 Commercial Ct.   ☎28 9024 1062

You would be forgiven for thinking that the cramped entry of Commercial Court has exploded into a rowdy street party on a Saturday night. The outdoor cobblestones are flooded with light and slick with spilled drinks. A traditional pub downstairs, the Duke of York often sees its hubbub spill out into the street, whose cramped quarters would rival those of any club. If you can get there, though, the tiny upstairs club is complete with walls covered in framed Guinness ads and old portraits alike, along with spinning tinted disco lights.

i *Beer from £3. ☼ Open M 11:30am-11pm, Tu-F 11:30am-1am, Sa 11:30am-2am, Su 2-8pm.*

21 SOCIAL
RESTAURANT, BAR, CLUB

1 Hill St.   ☎28 9024 1415

One of the most chic places on the block, 21 Social has three floors: the restaurant downstairs, the main bar upstairs and the VIP bar on the top floor—"Cigarette Girl," which you probably won't see unless you've got a big wad of cash in your pocket. This place will satisfy any time of day or night, so head here in the day to try the risotto with forest mushrooms and cashel bleu cheese topped with truffle foam ($9), or else go at night to join the heaving mass of the rest of Belfast.

i *Upstairs club cover £10-20. Entrees £9-17. ☼ Open M-Tu noon-11pm, W noon-midnight, Th-Sa noon-1am, Su 1-9pm.*

THE SPANIARD
BAR

3 Skipper St.   ☎28 9023 2448

Even if you can get in over the steep 25+ age requirement, you might have a difficult time squeezing into this miniature rum house, where there are so many people you'll worry the floor might collapse. If you manage to make your way upstairs, don't be disturbed by the omnipresent pictures of Jesus—no one quite knows why they're there, but they work oddly well as decor. Try the "Extraordinary," with Havana Cuba rum, squeezed lime, and ginger beer ($5.25).

i *Pints £3.30. ☼ Open M-Sa noon-1am, Su noon-midnight.*

THE NORTHERN WHIG   BAR
2-10 Bridge St.   ☎28 9050 9888
Dominating the top of Donegall St., this large bar is housed inside an old bank
building, which lends it a sprawling amount of floorspace, along with a high,
echoing ceiling. During the day, these extravagances might seem somewhat
presumptuous, but by the time night comes around, every inch of extra space is a
blessing. Plenty of plush, scattered seating, nimble bartenders, and a diligent DJ
discharging all sorts of favorites from the charts lends the place an atmosphere
just shy of a club. If you're looking for a place to start your night, you just found it.
i Cocktails £5.25-5.75. ☺ Open M-Tu noon-11pm, W-Sa noon-1am, Su 1-11pm.

KREMLIN   CLUB, GLBT
96 Donegall St.   ☎28 9031 6061
The self-described hottest gay experience in Europe, the Kremlin lives up to
its boasts. Separated into three distinct areas, everyone will find somewhere to
embrace the night regardless of their political leanings. First, there is"Tsar," the
relaxed cocktail area that is most suitable for some conversation and a sweet
drink before moving to the more lively areas. Next you might come to the "Long
Bar," the louder alternative to the cocktail lounge—you can expect plenty of
laughing and disco spinning over two levels while music blares. Finally, once
courage is at its highest, ramp it up to the "Red Square," a two-level clubbing
arena usually outfitted with a backdrop reflecting that night's theme. By the time
you get to the arena, you will be a true member of the Party.
i Free entry until midnight, £10 after. ☺ Open Tu, Th-Su 10pm-2am.

City Center

⚐ MCCRACKEN'S   PUB
4 Joy's Entry   ☎28 9032 6711
A newer, trendier version of the traditional Irish pub, McCracken's has substi-
tuted funky, green seats for boring bar stools and installed some portraits of
famous Irish writers à la Andy Warhol. The crowd is trendier as well and tends to
offer more for the well-dressed, young professionals than the older Irish regulars
or crazy high school kids.
*i Pints £3.15-3.25. ☺ Open M-W 11:30am-9pm, Th-F 11:30am-11pm, Sa 11:30am-3am, Su
6:30-8:30pm.*

⚐ VOODOO   BAR, LIVE MUSIC
9-11 Fountain St.   ☎28 9027 8290
One of the best live music bars in the City Center, you can expect to be downing
pints in good style at Voodoo. The downstairs bar is stylish, with red wood detailing and a full selection of whiskeys and beers. Delve farther into the venue,
though, and you will quickly come across some long-haired punk rockers and
beams of blue or green light exploding in a wild crowd.
i Prices vary depending on performance. Beer from £3.50. ☺ Open M-Sa noon-2am.

THE STIFF KITTEN   CLUB
1 Bankmore Sq.   ☎28 9023 8700
On a Saturday the Stiff Kitten rivals Berlin or Amsterdam in terms of pulse-pound-
ing tracks and streaming lights. When you get tired of dancing, head over to the
Blue Bar, where you can sit down; if you really want to take a break from the
sound, head next door to the SK bar, where all-age groups mingle in a much
more relaxed environment.
*i From the Europa Hotel, turn right and walk down Great Victoria St. Turn left onto Bruce St. Turn
right onto Dublin Rd. Turn right onto Bankmore Sq. The club is on the right. Come on Th and F for
£1.50 and £2 drinks respectively. ☺ Open M noon-1am, Tu noon-2am, W noon-1am, Th-F noon-
2:30am, Sa noon-3am.*

ESSENTIALS

Practicalities

- **TOURIST OFFICES: Belfast Welcome Centre** is one of the only tourism offices (and by far the biggest) in Belfast and is also the only place to go for **luggage storage.** (*i* £3 for up to 4 hr., £4.50 for over 4hr.) Aside from taking in your bags and bothering to be open every day except Christmas, the BWC provides all the tourism info you could ever want, assistance booking tours, a gift shop, **currency exchange,** and an **internet cafe.** They must be listening to a lot of Vanilla Ice over there, because their mantra seems to be, "You got a problem? Yo, I'll solve it." (47 Donegall Pl. ☎28 9024 6609 www.gotobelfast.com *i* From Belfast City hall, walk up Donegall Sq. The center is on the left. Touch-screen information kiosk available. Two 24hr. ATMs located outside Belfast Welcome Centre. ☒ Open Oct-May M-Sa 9am-5:30pm, Su 11am-4pm; Jun-Sept M-Sa 9am-7pm, Su 11am-4pm.)

- **BANKS: Bank of Ireland.** (28 University Rd. *i* Two 24hr. ATMs. ☒ Open M-Tu 9:30am-4:30pm, W 10am-4:30pm, Th-F 9:30am-4:30pm.) **First Trust Bank.** (*i* Across the street from the front of city hall. 2 24hr. ATMs. ☒ Open M-Tu 9:30am-4:30pm, W 10am-4:30pm, Th-F 9:30am-4:30pm.) **Belfast Post Office** has currency exchange. (12-16 Bridge St. ☎28 9032 0337 postoffice.co.uk ☒ Open M-Sa 9am-5:30pm.)

- **INTERNET ACCESS: Revelations** gives a discount to students and hostelers, if your hostel doesn't have internet already. (27 Shaftesbury Sq. ☎28 9032 0337 www.revelations.co.uk *i* £1.10 per 15min. ☒ Open M-F 8am-10pm, Sa 10am-6pm, Su 11am-7pm.)

- **POST OFFICES: Belfast Post Office** can tend to all of your postal service needs. (12-16 Bridge St. ☎28 9032 0337 postoffice.co.uk ☒ Open M-Sa 9am-5:30pm.) You can also head to the **Bedford Street** branch. (16-22 Bedford St. ☎28 9032 2293 ☒ Open M-F 9am-5:30pm.)

Emergency

- **POLICE:** (60 Victoria St. ☎845 600 8000 for switchboard, ☎999 for emergencies; www.psni.co.uk ☒ 24hr. assistance.)

- **PHARMACY:** At **Boots,** wade through an enormous makeup section and head upstairs to get to the pharmacy. (☎28 9024 2332 www.boots.com *i* From Belfast City Hall, walk up Donegall Sq. The pharmacy is on the left. 35-47 Donegall St. ☒ Open M-F 8am-9pm, Sa 8am-7pm, Su 1-6pm.)

- **HOSPITALS: Belfast City Hospital.** (Lisburn Rd. ☎28 9032 9241 for switchboard, ☎999 for emergencies; www.belfasttrust.hscni.net ☒ Open 24hr.)

Getting There

BY PLANE

Belfast International Airport (BFS; ☎28 9448 4848 www.belfastairport.com *i* Passengers who require additional mobility assistance should call ☎28 9448 4957) has flights all over Europe, the US, and beyond, and hosts the following airlines: **Aer Lingus** (☎871 7185 000 www.aerlingus.com), with flights from Barcelona, Faro, Lanzarote (Arrecife), London Heathrow, Málaga, Munich, Rome, Tenerife; **Continental** (www.continental.com/uk), with flights from New York; **easyJet** (☎905 821 0905 www.easyjet.com), with flights from Alicante, Amsterdam, Barcelona, Bristol, Edinburgh, Faro, Geneva, Glasgow, Ibiza, Krakow, Liverpool, London Gatwick, London Stansted, Málaga, Newcastle, Nice, Palma de Mallorca, Paris Charles de Gaulle; **Jet2.com** (☎871 226 1 737 www.jet2.com), with flights from Blackpool, Chambery, Dubrovnik, Ibiza, Jersey, Leeds Bradford, Mahon, Murcia, Newquay, Palma de Mallorca, Pisa, Toulouse, Tenerife; **Manx2.com** (☎871 200 0440 www.manx2.com), with flights from the Isle of Man, Galway, Cork; **Thomas Cook** (☎871 895 0055 www.thomascook.

com), with flights from Alicante, Antalya, Bodrum, Corfu, Cancún, Dalaman, Faro, Fuerteventura, Heraklion, Ibiza, Lanzarote, Larnaca, Las Palmas, Mahón, Monastir, Palma, Puerto Plata, Reus, Rhodes, Sanford Orlando, Sharm el Sheikh, Tenerife, Toulouse, Veronal; **Thompson Airways** (☎871 895 0055 www.thomson.co.uk), with flights from Bodrum, Bourgas, Dalaman, Grenoble, Lanzarote, Lapland, Las Palmas, Málaga, Naples, Palma de Mallorca, Reus, Tenerife. **Belfast City Airport** (BHD; ☎28 9093 9093 belfastcityairport.com) hosts **flybe.com** which runs from destinations within the UK, including London, Edinburgh, Manchester, and Glasgow.

BY TRAIN

Belfast Central Train St. ion takes trains from all over Northern Ireland and down to the Republic as well. Major origins include Dublin (2hr.), Londonderry (2¼hr.), and Neary (50min.). Check the website for times and prices, as both are subject to frequent change. (Central Station, E. Bridge St. ☎28 9066 6630 www.translink.co.uk ⏰ Open M-Sa 6:20am-8:10pm, Su 10am-7:30pm.)

Getting Around

While a walking city for the most part, transportation cards and tickets are available at the **pink kiosks** in Donegall Sq. W. (⏰ Open M-F 8am-6pm, Sa 9am-5:20pm) and around the city.

BY BUS

Belfast has two bus services. Most local bus routes connect through **Laganside Bus St. ion, Queens Square.** Metro bus service (☎28 9066 6630 www.translink.co.uk) operates from Donegall Sq. Twelve main routes cover Belfast. **Ulsterbus** "blue buses" cover the suburbs. (*i* Day passes £3.50. Travel within the city center £1, £2.50 beyond, under 16 £1.50). **Nightlink** buses travel from Donegall Sq. West to towns outside Belfast (*i* £3.50 ⏰ Sa 1 and 2am).

BY TAXI

Metered taxis run through the city 24hr. Look for the following companies: **Value Cabs** (☎28 9080 9080), **City Cab** (☎28 9024 2000), and **Fon a Cab** (☎28 9033 3333).

BY BICYCLE

For bike rental, head to **McConvey Cycles.** (183 Ormeau Rd. ☎28 9033 0322 www.mcconvey.com *i* Helmets and locks supplied. £20 per day; £80 per week. £50 deposit. ⏰ Open M-W 9am-6pm, Th 9am-8pm, F-Sa 9am-6pm.)

ireland essentials

VISAS

Citizens of almost all major developed countries (including Australia, Canada, New Zealand, the UK, and the US) do not need visas to enter the Republic of Ireland. Citizens of these countries can stay for up to 90 days without a visa, but after this period will have to apply for a longer-term visa. Note that the Republic of Ireland is not a signatory of the Schengen Agreement, which means it is not a part of the free movement zone that covers most of the EU. The advantage of this is that non-EU citizens can visit Ireland without eating into the 90-day limit on travel within the Schengen area. Some travelers have been known to use Ireland as a convenient location for "stopping the Schengen clock" and extending their Eurotrip. The only real disadvantage of Ireland's non-Schengen status is that you will be subject to border controls on entry, so don't forget your passport.

Those hoping to study or work in Ireland will have to obtain special visas to do so; consult your nearest Irish embassy or consulate for information on applying. You will generally need a letter of acceptance from a university or company in order to apply. You can find more information on all visa questions at the website of the Irish Department of Foreign Affairs and Trade (www.dfa.ie).

Since Northern Ireland is in the United Kingdom, its visa rules are the same as for Britain. For information on these policies, see the Great Britain chapter.

MONEY

Tipping and Bargaining

Some restaurants in Ireland figure a service charge into the bill; some even calculate it into the cost of the dishes themselves. The menu often indicates whether or not service is included. If gratuity is not included, consider leaving 10-15%, depending upon the quality of the service. Tipping is not necessary for most other services, such as taxis and concierge assistance, especially in rural areas. In most cases, people are usually happy if you simply round up the bill to the nearest euro. But if a driver is particularly courteous and helpful, consider tipping 5-10%. Hairdressers, at least for women, are typically tipped 10% of the bill. Never tip in pubs—it's considered condescending. In general, do not tip bartenders, though some bartenders at hip urban bars may expect a tip; watch and learn from other customers.

Taxes

The Republic of Ireland has a 23% value added tax (VAT), although some goods are subject to a lower rate of 13%. Northern Ireland edges its southern neighbor with the UK VAT rate of 20%. The prices stated in *Let's Go* include VAT unless otherwise noted. Given the Irish government's serious cashflow problems, don't be surprised if the rates increase even more.

SAFETY AND HEALTH

Although Ireland has a long history of serious sectarian violence and terrorism, the situation has improved considerably in the last 15 years. It is still probably best to avoid incendiary discussions with strong opinions on the Northern Ireland question or by stating your undying love for Oliver Cromwell (this will not go down well). Always be aware of your surroundings and don't assume that the Troubles are completely over: there are still many fringe groups who are prepared to commit acts of terrorism.

Drugs and Alcohol

The Republic of Ireland and Northern Ireland both regulate the possession of recreational drugs, with penalties ranging from a warning to lengthy prison sentences. Possession of marijuana results in a fine, though repeated offenses can result in prosecution. Harder substances are treated with severity. If you carry prescription drugs with you, have a copy of the prescription and a note from a doctor readily accessible at country borders. The drinking age, 18 in both the Republic of Ireland and Northern Ireland, is more strictly enforced in urban areas. While there is no national legislation prohibiting drinking in public, local authorities may pass by-laws enforcing such a policy. Drinking is banned in many public places in Northern Ireland. Contact the local authority for more information.

Ireland

ireland 101

HISTORY
Saint Patrick, Vikings, and Normans (400-1495 CE)
By 400 CE, seven independent kingdoms had evolved among the Celtic tribes in Ireland. These kingdoms often allied their armies to raid neighboring Roman Britain and the continent. On one of these raids, a 16 year-old lad was captured, returned to Ireland, and sold into slavery. Rather than whiling away his spare time hunting wild animals and girls (or whatever normal 16 year-old lads did back then), this boy spent his years of enslavement studying religion. Once he escaped at age 22, he began a lifelong quest of converting the Irish to Christianity. This lad was none other than Ireland's patron saint, Saint Patrick.

Accompanying the spread of Christianity was an expansion in the study of Latin learning and Christian theology. Irish missionaries traveled to Continental Europe to spread their beliefs, and scholars from other countries came to Irish monasteries. This period of Insular Art produced such treasures as the Book of Kells (an illuminated Gospel book in Latin), the Ardagh Chalice (a large, two-handled silver cup), and many of the carved stone crosses that adorn the island. In the ninth and 10th centuries, the Golden Age of Irish scholasticism was interrupted by Viking invasions, as scholarly work often is. Eventually these Vikings built settlements on the island, many of which grew into important cities, including Dublin, Limerick, Cork, and Wexford.

The invasions, however, did not end there. In 1169, an invasion of Norman mercenaries marked the beginning of more than seven centuries of Norman and English rule in Ireland. From the end of the 12th century to around 1400, many Normans from England moved to Ireland, settling in the eastern areas, particularly around Dublin. Even though some Normans assimilated, strife persisted between native Irish and the colonists. The Kilkenny Act passed in 1367 kept the two populations separate.

Tumultuous English Rule (1495-1801)
Over the next few centuries, the English increased their control over Ireland and decided to settle down for a nice, long occupation. In 1495, Henry VII extended English law to Ireland and assumed supremacy over the existing Irish government. Over the next couple of decades, however, the effective rulers of Ireland and many of their allies openly rebelled against the crown. By 1536, Henry VIII resolved once and for all to bring Ireland under English governmental control so that Ireland could not become a base for future rebellions and attacks against England. He upgraded Ireland from a lordship to a full kingdom, and Henry VIII was proclaimed King of Ireland at a meeting of the Irish parliament in 1541. As made clear by the women (and the food) in his life, Henry VIII was not easily satisfied. Next, he wanted to extend the control of the English Kingdom of Ireland over all of its claimed territory. This process took nearly a century and was marked by internal conflicts between independent Irish and Old English lords.

From the mid-16th into the early 17th century, the English government played favorites, confiscating land from Irish Catholic landowners and giving it to Protestant settlers from England and Scotland through a series of policies known as Plantations. Alongside land reforms, the 17th century was also marked by extreme violence, with Ireland suffering 11 years of warfare. It began with the Rebellion of 1641, when the Irish Catholics rebelled against the domination of English and Protestant settlers. The Catholics briefly ruled the country until Oliver Cromwell reconquered Ireland on behalf of the English. By the end of the conflict, up to a third of Ireland's pre-war population was dead or in exile. Following the bloodshed, Ireland became the main arena for battle during the Glorious Revolution of 1688, during which the Irish Catholics fought to reverse the Penal Laws and land confiscation policy. Irish antagonism towards the English was further aggravated by the economic situation in Ireland in the 18th century, when two frigid winters led to a famine between 1740 and 1741. Without the all-powerful potato or any aid from English rulers, about a million people died of starvation or disease.

Autonomy (Finally?) (1801-1922)

Following the famine, Catholic Ireland gradually increased in prosperity. The Catholics slowly gained parliamentary power, and in 1801, the British and Irish parliaments enacted the Acts of Union. This merger created a new political entity called the United Kingdom of Great Britain and Ireland.

With the Irish fixated on their goal of full national sovereignty (and the sovereign potato) another potato blight, along with the political and economic factors of the time, led to the second of Ireland's "Great Famines." Again, this famine led to mass starvation and emigration. As Ireland slowly recovered from its second Great Famine, there were additional efforts to gain home rule (a demand for self-government within the United Kingdom of Great Britain and Ireland) and better living conditions.

The Home Rule Act was passed in 1914, which would have given Ireland some autonomy, but it was suspended for the duration of World War I. The period from 1916 to 1921 was marked by political upheaval and turmoil. From 1919 to 1921, the Irish Republican Army (IRA) waged a guerilla war (the Irish War of Independence). Amidst the fighting, the Fourth Government of Ireland Act of 1920 implemented Home Rule while separating the island into "Northern Ireland" and "Southern Ireland." The terms of the war-ending truce abolished the Irish Republic (Southern Ireland) and created the Irish Free St. e. The free state renamed itself Ireland in 1937 and declared itself a republic in 1949.

Autonomy (Finally!) (1922-1948)

The decision to sever the Union divided the Republican movement into anti-Treaty (those who wanted to fight on until an Irish Republic was achieved) and pro-Treaty (those who accepted the Free St. e as a first step towards full independence) supporters. Between 1922 and 1923, the opposing sides fought the bloody Irish Civil War, but ultimately, the treaty stood.

From 1922 to 1937, the Irish Free St. e existed against the backdrop of the Great Depression and the growth of dictatorships in mainland Europe. In contrast with many contemporary European states, Ireland remained a democracy. At the same time, the Roman Catholic Church exerted powerful influence over Irish society, forbidding divorce, pornography, contraception, and abortion, as well as encouraging the censoring and banning of many forms of media. Ireland remained neutral during WWII, and though this saved the state from many of the horrors of the war, tens of thousands of Irishmen volunteered to serve with the British forces.

In 1937, a new Constitution of Ireland was drawn up, re-establishing the state as Ireland. A republic in all but name, it remained formally within the British Commonwealth. This lasted only 11 years before the ties with the Commonwealth were completely severed and the Republic of Ireland was born (finally!) in 1948.

The Republic Today (1948-present)

During the 1960s, under Taoiseach (Prime Minister of Ireland) Sean Lemass's government, Ireland underwent a series of economic reforms, including the provision of free secondary education in 1968. Global economic troubles in the 1970s, augmented by a set of misjudged economic policies caused the Irish economy to stagnate. Along with economic troubles, there was also social and political unrest. There were sectarian conflicts in Northern Ireland between the Nationalists, Catholics who wanted Northern Ireland to unite with the Irish Republic, and the Unionists, Protestants who were loyal to Great Britain. This revived the Provisional Irish Republican Army (PIRA), whose violent attempts were aimed at the creation of a new Irish Republic. The civil unrest marked a period called The Troubles and did not officially end until 1998.

The 1980s and 1990s were marked by prosperous economic and social growth, driven by solid economic policies and investment from the European Community. Economic growth accelerated alongside social liberalization. Irish society adopted liberal social policies, such as the legalization of divorce and the decriminalization of homosexuality. The recent global financial crisis has hit Ireland hard, however; the economic boom is over.

CUSTOMS AND ETIQUETTE

Meet and Greet

The basic greeting is a nice firm handshake and a hello (or salutation appropriate for the time of the day). It is expected that you will maintain eye contact with the person you are talking to, and even if you do not know your partner in conversation very well, the Irish are a bunch of chummy blokes (and dames), so don't be surprised when the conversation takes a friendly turn.

Things That Will Piss the Irish Off

There are several topics that you should definitely not address. Please don't talk about homosexuality or abortion, as a majority of the Irish are very religious and conservative when it comes to social values. Never refer to the Republic of Ireland as part of the United Kingdom. Don't mention "The Troubles" (see History). And never refer to someone or call someone a "mick" (a derogatory term for an Irishman) or "Briton," as this is considered a major insult.

FOOD AND DRINK

Food

Along with the potato, food staples that have played a constant role in the Irish diet are grains (especially oats), dairy products, and soups. The Irish have been accomplished cheese makers for centuries. And Irish soups are thick, hearty, and filling, made with potatoes (duh), seafood, and various meats. Representative Irish dishes are Irish stew, bacon and cabbage, boxty, coddle, and colcannon. Traditional Irish stew is made from lamb or mutton, as well as potatoes, carrots, onions, and parsley. Bacon and cabbage, as the name implies, consists of unsliced back bacon boiled with cabbage and potatoes. Sometimes other vegetables, such as turnips, onions, and carrots, are also added. Boxty is a traditional Irish potato pancake, similar to a latke. There are many different recipes, but they all contain finely grated, raw potatoes and all are served fried. Coddle consists of layers of roughly sliced pork sausages and rashers (thinly sliced, fatty bacon) with sliced potatoes and onions. Finally, colcannon is yet another potato-based dish that consists mainly of mashed potatoes with kale or cabbage.

Drinks

Let's be honest here—Ireland is not famous for its food. In 1759, Arthur Guinness began brewing his popular London "porter." He, his family, and the entire drinking world hasn't looked back since. Guinness is known around the world for its impenetrable blackness. Although it is no longer given away free in Dublin hospitals to new mothers as a lukewarm restorative (true story), it is available on tap everywhere.

ireland 101

STUDY

- **DUBLIN ENGINEERING PROGRAM:** If your idea of fun is long nights at the lab and getting cozy with technology, spend your fall semester taking three technical and engineering courses at Dublin City University and one elective on Irish art or literature. (www.bu.edu/abroad/programs/dublin-engineering-program/, www.dcu.ie)

- **NATIONAL UNIVERSITY OF IRELAND, GALWAY:** Immerse yourself in the Irish higher education system with a potpourri of course selections from the internationally renowned faculties of Arts, Law, Business, Engineering, Medicine, and Science—NUIG is ranked in the top 3% of schools on a global scale. The school is best known for its Marine Science, Irish Literature, Women's St. ies, Classical Civilizations, and Information Technology departments. (☎353 91 524411 www.nuigalway.ie/international-students/)

- **DUBLIN CITY UNIVERSITY INTERNSHIP PROGRAM:** At DCU, your Irish history- and culture-focused coursework is paired with a full-time, four days per week professional work experience in the Dublin area. (☎617-353-9888, www.bu.edu/abroad/programs/dublin-internship-program, www.dcu.ie)

- **UNIVERSITY COLLEGE CORK:** Choose from among 40 degree courses across the college of Arts, Celtic St. ies and Social Sciences, the College of Business and Law, the College of Science, Engineering and Food Science, and the College of Medicine and Health. (☎353 (0)21 490 3000, www.ucc.ie/en/international)

- **TRINITY COLLEGE DUBLIN:** As an international student, you'll have access to over 400. Trinity College Dublin has a reputation for approachable lecturers and small group work in undergraduate tutorials and seminars. (☎353 1 896 3150 www.tcd.ie/international)

VOLUNTEER

The **National Volunteer Development Agency** (www.volunteer.ie) is an excellent database.

- **BALLYTOBIN CAMPHILL COMMUNITIES:** Ballytobin is a therapeutic community for 75 children and adults with multiple disabilities. Some volunteers work on the farm and in the garden, providing the community with fresh organic vegetables, milk, and meat, while others care and support disabled children or adults, assisting in the classroom or in craft workshops. All community members live together in an extended family home and partake in cooking, cleaning, and other chores. (☎01-2694406 www.camphill.ie/ballytobin)

- **DUBLIN CONSERVATION VOLUNTEERS:** Do you love woodland management, laying hedges, maintaining grasslands, creating paths, erecting fences, and cleaning up public parks? Try your green thumb and plant a tree every Saturday for four hours in different locations around the Dublin area. Volunteers are welcome for one-time or multiple-week commitments. (☎087 1214 641 www.conservationvolunteers.ie)

- **ST. S SCHOOL COMPLETION PROGRAMME:** Connect with your inner science nerd by helping to tutor vulnerable young populations in Junior Cert level science on Wednesday afternoons. Some teaching experience is required. (☎061-609 603 www.stepsscp.com)

- **LGBT HELPLINE:** In 2012, the lesbian, gay, bisexual, and transgender helpline received 10,000 calls but could only manage less than a quarter of them due to a lack of volunteers available to answer the phone. Volunteers take an initial six-week training course and are expected to contribute four hours a week. Listening and empathy skills are key. (☎1890 929 539 www.lgbt.ie)

WORK

Search engines like jobs.goabroad.com, www.overseasjobs.com, jobsinireland.org, and www.pickingjobs.com/ireland are a good place to start.

- **ESL OPPORTUNITIES:** ESL Opportunities is partnered with the Irish College of English and Swan Training Institute, so you'll have some hands-on teaching experience before your first day on the job. (☎353 1 8453744 www.eslopportunities.com)

- **THE ACCREDITATION AND CO-ORDINATION OF ENGLISH LANGUAGE SERVICES (ACELS):** ACELS compiles a list of recognized English Language Training (ELT) schools and organizations. Once you are TEFL certified, ACELS can put you in touch with member schools for that oh-so-dreamy ESL teaching job. (☎01 9058185 www.acels.ie)

- **MARKETING ENGLISH IN IRELAND (MEI):** MEI is an association of 55 English language schools, including large, medium, and small schools that serve almost 200,000 students from around the world each year. If you're already TEFL certified, MEI can help place you in an institution. MEI also offers TEFL courses that are accredited by the Department of Education. (☎353 1 6180910/11 www.mei.ie)

- **SPORTS DATA AG:** Check out this job with Sports Data AG, a worldwide information supplier for sports related data based in Switzerland. The freelance job in Ireland involves attending local sports events to gather stats for real time publishing. (☎41 71 517 72 00 www.sportsdata.ag)

BEYOND TOURISM

www.letsgo.com

In addition to stout, Irish whisky is also immensely popular, and it comes in many forms, including single malt, single grain, and blended whisky. Other famous Irish drinks include cider, mead, cream liquor, and Irish coffee.

ITALY

For the home of the papacy, Italy certainly knows how to do sensual pleasures right: stylish Vespas, intoxicating vino, vibrant piazze, and crackling pizzas covered in garden-fresh produce will light up your eyes, ears, nose, and taste buds as you make your way across the Mediterranean's favorite boot. In a country where la dolce far niente ("the sweetness of doing nothing") is a national pastime, you will nonetheless find yourself with a wealth of opportunities to pursue la dolce vita. And as a student traveler, you are uniquely situated to experience Italia in all its ridiculousness and sublimity. Striking out on your own, likely on a budget, you will open yourself up to what someone who stays in the swankiest hotels and eats at all the five-star restaurants will miss: making connections with the people and the way of life in Italy's many storied cities and towns. Wander your way along the canals in Venice and marvel at the famed mosaics of Ravenna. Try to dodge the sharp glances of the fashionistas in Milan and discover the moving stories of the flood-ravaged Ligurian Coast as you make your way along the Cinque Terre. Eat pizza in Naples, climb the Duomo inFlorence, and explore ruins in Sicily. With its Renaissance art, Roman grandeur, and religious relics, Italy presents curious and intrepid travelers with an experience that is at once cultural, historical, and truly divine.

greatest hits

- **ANCIENT ANTIQUES.** The relics of ancient Rome pop up all over the place. **Rome** (p. 486) is obviously the place to start, but even cities like **Verona** (p. 566) and **Milan** (p. 525) share this fascinating history.

- **WHERE REBIRTH WAS BORN.** Thanks to the Renaissance, there's more art in Italy than even a Medici can handle. Get the best possible primer at the king of Italian museums: Florence's **Uffizi** (p. 589).

- **MONDO MANGIA.** You've been eating Italian food all your life, so you might as well sample the real deal, right? For where pizza was invented, head to **Naples** (p. 624). For the birthplace of lasagna, try **Bologna** (p. 570).

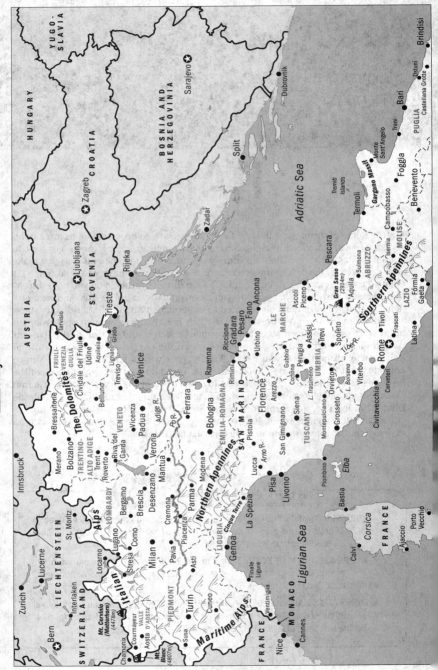

italy

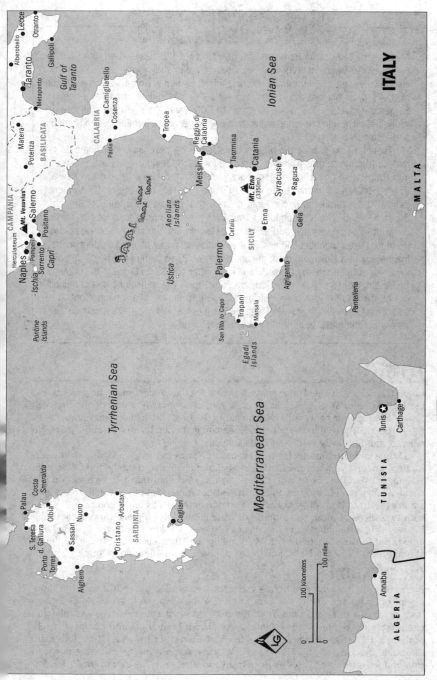

ITALY

Ionian Sea

MALTA

Lecce
Otranto
Alberobello
Gallipoli
Taranto
Gulf of Taranto
Metaponto
Camigliatello
Cosenza
CALABRIA
Matera
BASILICATA
Potenza
Tropea
Paola
Reggio di Calabria
Taormina
Messina
Catania
CAMPANIA
Herculaneum
Mt. Vesuvius
Naples
Salerno
Positano
Pompeii
Sorrento
Ischia
Capri
Mt. Etna
(3350m)
SICILY
Enna
Syracuse
Ragusa
Cefalù
Palermo
Gela
Agrigento
Ustica
Aeolian Islands
Pontine Islands
San Vito lo Capo
Trapani
Marsala
Egadi Islands
Pantelleria

Tyrrhenian Sea

Mediterranean Sea

Palau
Costa Smeralda
S. Teresa
Porto d. Gallura
Torres
Olbia
Nuoro
Arbatax
SARDINIA
Sassari
Oristano
Alghero
Cagliari

N
LG

0   100 kilometers
0   100 miles

Tunis
Carthage
TUNISIA
Annaba
ALGERIA

Italy may be famous for its antiquities (monuments, Renaissance art, the Roman Forum, Pope Benedict XVI), but this doesn't mean that young people haven't claimed the past as their own. Nowhere is this truer than in **Rome,** which has many of Italy's most ancient attractions and yet also an incredible amount of vitality. Sapienza University has no fewer than 147,000 students, so there's plenty of young people around to round out a great nightlife scene in Termini, Centro Storico, and Testaccio.

Though Rome may be the biggest beast, there are dozens of cities lining up to rival its youthful culture. **Milan** is renowned for uptight fashion and business dealings, but it also has a looser and more youth-oriented scene around the Navigli district. **Bologna** is home to the Western World's oldest university, and, with more than 100,000 students packed into a city with a population a tenth of Rome's, the students are pretty much taking over. **Pisa** may be famous for a leaning tower, but with three universities and an awful lot more bars, the student scene stands up much better than its buildings. Even in cities with a less obvious student scene, like **Venice** and **Florence,** there are still plenty of 20-somethings to be sought out if you make the effort—try Dorsoduro in the former and Santa Croce in the latter to find them. Wherever you are in Italy, don't just think that museums and churches are all there is for you to see. Hit up an aperitivo bar or take a pitcher out to a piazza and drink like the locals. That's just as much a part of today's Italian culture as any amphitheater or crumbling chapel roof.

rome

Rome. The city that ruled an empire. A center for the Renaissance, the papacy, and the birthplace of Western civilization. A gorgeous, sprawling metropolis that will *veni vidi vici* your heart with its art, history, Vespas, and gelato. Crazy amounts of gelato. So bid farewell to the wine-dark sea and gather up those household gods. No need to wait for oracles—the Eternal City calls.

People come to this city for many reasons. For fresh mozzarella and tomato pizza, breathtaking views of the Sistine Chapel, the chance to romp by the Colosseum at 3am, or all of the above, all on the same day (#wheninrome). It's where you can wander down streets too tiny to be mapped, eat more pasta than you'll ever admit, admire the art of Bernini by day and the art of twerkology by night, and dodge Vespas with two slices of pizza and a bottle of wine in hand. It's a place that's easy to fall in love with, although it's not an easy city to conquer (the Carthaginians tried and failed).But fortune favors the brave, so sail up the Tiber. Let's leave those elephants at home, *semper ubi sub ubi*, and fasten up those togas—let's go to Rome.

ORIENTATION

Rome is easily navigable on foot—every time you think you're lost, another monument pops up and you're back on track. The best way to think of Rome is as a body: a few major arteries (some with significant blockage problems) will take you from region to region, while countless capillaries branch off into compact neighborhoods. P. Venezia is not really the heart of Rome, but it's where the city's main thoroughfares convene. V. Cavour and V. Nazionale are the legs leading down to Rome's foot—Termini, the city's main transportation hub. The arm of the V. dei Fori

italy

Imperiali takes you back in time, passing the Roman Forum and the Colosseum. The other arm, the V. del Corso, heads into the very commercial present, as it's filled with shops and the crowds that go with them. This then becomes the V. Flaminia, which navigates around the Villa Borghese. Rome's "neck" is the Centro Storico, a mass of winding streets where navigation by map is much more difficult than navigation by monument. The C. Vittorio Emanuele II is a useful throughway which leads across the Tiber River into Rome's slightly less crazy head, home to Trastevere and not-technically-part-of-Rome-but-we're-still-including-it-for-obvious-reasons Vatican City.

Ancient City

With one of the highest cameras-to-square-inches-of-sidewalk ratios in Rome, the Ancient City doesn't exactly feel "ancient" anymore. The **Via dei Fori Imperiali** is the main thoroughfare for ruin-seekers, passing the **Colosseum** and **Roman Forum** before reaching **Piazza Venezia,** where the road ends with the classical pastiche that is the Vittorio Emanuele II Monument. Around the P. Venezia, even more Roman ruins await at **Via del Teatro di Marcello,** although these are less famous (but only moderately less impressive). **Via Cavour** leads from the Roman Forum to the pleasant Monti area and Esquiline Hill, full of narrow, picturesque streets that aren't clogged with tourist traps.

Centro Storico

To the traveler who has paid one too many euro after waiting in one too many 4hr. lines, the Centro Storico offers a reprieve: nearly all the churches, monuments, and *piazze* you'll find here are free. With most of the main attractions clustered on either side of **Corso Vittorio Emanuele II,** this tangled web of streets is manageable in size, though not the easiest to navigate. Expect to get lost as *vie* suddenly split into numerous *vicoli,* so use C. Vittorio Emanuele II as a departure point and the vibrant urban living rooms of **Campo dei Fiori** and **Piazza Navona** as your major landmarks.

Piazza di Spagna

Nestled between the Tiber and the grounds of the Villa Borghese, the area around the P. di Spagna is Rome's answer to Fifth Avenue, the Champs-Élysées, and the West End. From the **Piazza del Popolo,** the neighborhood branches off into three main roads: the quieter **Via della Ripetta,** the overbearing **Via del Corso,** and the **Via del Babuino.** The last of these leads to the **Spanish Steps.** For the fashion-obsessed, **Via dei Condotti** is home to the shops of some of the most exclusive Italian designers. Sightseers on a budget will not be disappointed, either, as many landmarks (like the **Trevi Fountain**) are free to the public. To avoid the capitalist onslaught, take a stroll on the elevated **Viale di Trinita dei Monti,** which offers the best view of P. di Spagna and its artistic marvels.

Jewish Ghetto

Just across from Trastevere is the small area known as the Jewish Ghetto, the first of its kind in Western Europe. Bordering the **Lungotevere dei Cenci** is the impressive **Great Synagogue,** the spiritual and physical center of the area. It's a small, residential neighborhood that is renowned for delicious kosher food, especially **carciofi alla giudia** (insanely delicious fried artichokes) which are found mainly in the restaurants of the **Via del Portico d'Ottavia.** Friday evenings and Saturdays are not, of course, the time to visit, as residents will be at home observing the Sabbath.

Vatican City

The people-to-square-foot ratio is significantly cockeyed in this part of the city: the madhouse of tourists in the Vatican contrasts sharply with the empty boulevards in the surrounding region of **Prati.** If the plastic souvenirs, bright flags, and English menus aren't enough to indicate which neighborhood you're in, the brick wall that physically separates Vatican City from Prati should give you a clue. On the Prati

rome

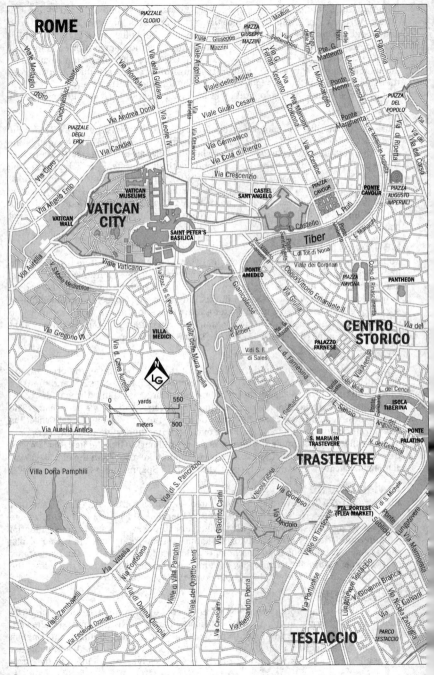

ROME

PIAZZALE
CLODIO

PIAZZA
GIUSEPPE
MAZZINI

PIAZZA
DEL
POPOLO

VATICAN
MUSEUMS

VATICAN
WALL

VATICAN CITY

SAINT PETER'S
BASILICA

CASTEL
SANT'ANGELO

PIAZZA
CAVOUR

PONTE
CAVOUR

PIAZZA
AUGUSTO
IMPERIALE

Castello

Tiber

PIAZZALE
DEGLI
EROI

VILLA
MEDICI

PIAZZA
NAVONA

PANTHEON

**CENTRO
STORICO**

PALAZZO
FARNESE

ISOLA
TIBERINA

PONTE
PALATINO

S. MARIA IN
TRASTEVERE

TRASTEVERE

PTA. PORTESE
(FLEA MARKET)

Villa Doria Pamphili

TESTACCIO

PARCO
TESTACCIO

N
LG

0   yards   550
0   meters   500

italy

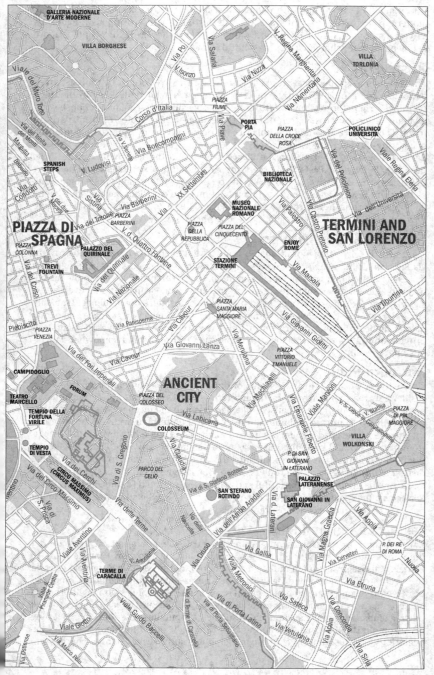

GALLERIA NAZIONALE
D'ARTE MODERNE

VILLA BORGHESE

VILLA
TORLONIA

Viale del Muro Torto

Via Po

V. Isonzo

Via Salaria

Via Nizza

V. Regina Margherita

Via Nomentana

PIAZZA
FIUME

Corso d'Italia

Via del Policlinico

POLICLINICO
UNIVERSITA

Viale Regina Elena

Via del Tritone
dei Monti
Margutta

PORTA
PIA

PIAZZA
DELLA CROCE
ROSA

SPANISH
STEPS

V. Ludovisi

Via V. Veneto

Via Boncompagni

BIBLIOTECA
NAZIONALE

Via Condotti

Via Sistina

Via Barberini

XX Settembre

Via del Policlinico

Via Castro Pretorio

Via dell'Università

PIAZZA DI
SPAGNA

Via del Tritone

PIAZZA
BARBERINI

MUSEO
NAZIONALE
ROMANO

Via Palestro

TERMINI AND
SAN LORENZO

PIAZZA
COLONNA

PALAZZO DEL
QUIRINALE

V. d. Quattro Fontane

PIAZZA
DELLA
REPUBBLICA

PIAZZA DEL
CINQUECENTO

ENJOY
ROME

TREVI
FOUNTAIN

Via del Quirinale

STAZIONE
TERMINI

Via Marsala

Via del Corso

Via Nazionale

PIAZZA
SANTA MARIA
MAGGIORE

Via Tiburtina

Plebiscito

Via Panisperna

Via Cavour

Via Giovanni Giolitti

PIAZZA
VENEZIA

Via dei Fori Imperiali

Via Giovanni Lanza

Via Merulana

PIAZZA
VITTORIO
EMANUELE

CAMPIDOGLIO

Via Cavour

Via Machiavelli

Viale Manzoni

V. S. Croce V. Statilia

PIAZZA
DI PTA.
MAGGIORE

TEATRO
MARCELLO

FORUM

PIAZZA
DEL
COLOSSEO

ANCIENT
CITY

Via Emanuele Filiberto

VILLA
WOLKONSKI

TEMPIO DELLA
FORTUNA
VIRILE

Via Labicana

COLOSSEUM

P. DI SAN
GIOVANNI
IN LATERANO

Via Appia

TEMPIO
DI VESTA

Via dei Cerchi

Via di S. Gregorio

Via Claudia

PALAZZO
LATERANENSE

Via Magna Grecia

CIRCO MASSIMO
(CIRCUS MAXIMUS)

PARCO DEL
CELIO

SAN GIOVANNI IN
LATERANO

Via del Circo Massimo

Via d. Laterani

P. DEI RE
DI ROMA

S. Prisca

Via delle Terme

Via di S. Stefano Rotondo

SAN STEFANO
ROTONDO

Via dell'Amba Aradam

Via Druso

Via Gallia

Via Cerveteri

Nuova

Viale Aventino

Via di
Piramide Cestia

Via di
Antoniana

Viale Metronio

Via Satrico

Via Etruria

Via Adalia

Via Concordia

TERME DI
CARACALLA

Viale Giotto

Viale Guido Baccelli

Viale di Terme di Caracalla

Via di Porta Latina

Via di Porta San Sebastiano

Via di Porta Latina

Via Vetulonia

Via Sira

Via Ostiense

Via Marco Polo

side, you'll find surprisingly affordable hotels and casual *trattorias* scattered among modern, pastel residential buildings. For all this talk about crowds in Vatican City, as you make your way back toward the pope's digs, the throng of people is more manageable than what you'll find in Central Rome.

Trastevere

Trastevere is to Rome what Brooklyn is to New York: overlooked by tourists, loved by locals, and removed from the metropolitan center while still being in the thick of things. There aren't any metro stops nearby, but you can play choose-your-own-adventure by crossing one of the three main bridges into different parts of town. The **Ponte Fabricio** and the **Isola Tiberina** open into the quieter, right side of the neighborhood where there are plenty of restaurants and laid-back bars. The **Ponte Garibaldi** leads into **Piazza Giuseppe Gioachino Belli** and the less-than-beautiful **Viale Trastevere.** Finally, the **Ponte Sisto** brings you right into the **Piazza Trilussa** and the heart of Trastevere's extensive nightlife. While you probably won't end up sleeping here, as there are few budget-friendly accommodations, the excellent bar and club scene and unpretentious, homegrown restaurants make this a good bet for evenings, while daytime strolls provide plenty of picturesque photo-ops.

Termini and San Lorenzo

Termini is the city's transportation hub—and it's got the blocks of hostels to prove it. **Via Giovanni Giolitti,** which runs alongside Termini, and the streets surrounding **Piazza Indipendenza** are lined with budget accommodations. With prime access to the metro, major bus lines, great nightlife (read: international student mania), and even a few sights of its own, no other part of Rome matches Termini's convenience. Our only advice: try to arrive by daylight. With a backpack or an unwieldy suitcase and a long plane ride behind you, trekking through the maze of people and advertisements can provide not only a disheartening first impression of Rome but a somewhat dangerous one as well.

Northern Rome

Unlike the city center, Northern Rome offers visitors more contemporary sights and residential areas. Villas from the 17th and 18th centuries are scattered throughout the area, most notably in the expansive **Villa Borghese** and the more modest **Villa Torlonia.** Practically every *piazza* and museum features a sculptural or architectural work of the great Gian Lorenzo Bernini. If you're hoping to find something even more recent, Rome's modern and contemporary art museums are nearby. The **Piazza del Popolo,** originally an important entry point into the city, is now at the top of a shopping district and right next to the grounds of the Villa Borghese. To the east, the **Porta Pia** marks the beginning of the beautiful and primarily residential (or ambassadorial) **Via Nomentana.** Inexpensive food can be hard to come by, so take advantage of the many open spaces for picnics and leisurely strolls.

Testaccio and Ostiense

Located south of the Colosseum, Testaccio and Ostiense are left off most tourist itineraries and are literally off Rome's central map. ⓜB toward **Piramide** leads to **Piazzale Ostiense,** from which radiate a number of large streets: **Via Marmorata** crosses the river into Trastevere, and **Via Ostiense** is the area's main thoroughfare. Composed of newer, residential housing and paved streets, these uncongested neighborhoods let you put away the guidebook for an afternoon, but be sure to save energy for the pulsing clubs. They may have long lines and be far from the center of Rome, but they offer some of the best nightlife in the city. You might not come here with high expectations, but the culinary, cultural, and clubbing surprises are sure to charm you.

Southern Rome

Just because it's off the tourist map doesn't mean Southern Rome isn't worth at least a day of exploring. This stretch of the city is home to residential streets, enough churches to convert you to Catholicism, and yes, more ruins. The churches are along the **Via Labicana** and near the **Piazza di San Giovanni in Laterano,**so keep an eye out for towers, nuns, and priests to orient yourself. The **Appian Way** has enough sights to demand its own day-long visit and is marked at every bend in the road by ruined aqueducts, entrances to catacombs, and fragments of statues. Less touristed than central Rome, this area is a great place to view some amazing Christian monuments without waiting in Vatican-sized lines.

SIGHTS

Ancient City

COLOSSEUM   ANCIENT ROME
V. di San Gregorio, V. Cello Vibenna, and V. Nicolai Salvi   ☎06 39 96 77 00 www.pierreci.it

It's the Colosseum. We don't need to tell you to see it. In fact, you've probably already seen it everywhere from movies to postcards to that one time you were riding the night bus and saw it through a drunken haze and tried to convince the bus driver to stop. But as the largest amphitheater in the world and an architectural marvel, the Colosseum was originally used for public spectacles showcasing mock battles, Greek dramas, and, of course, gladiatorial combat. After you take hundreds of pictures with the gladiators outside, do as the Romans did and follow the swarming crowds inside. You'll get a great view of the tourists on the other side of the complex, along with a spectacular look at the arches, arena, and passageways through which gladiators, emperors, and other ferocious beasts once passed. Afterward, head out to the sides to look at the Arch of Constantine and Roman Forum down below and to wave at your adoring fans before you head into the rotating museum exhibitions and gift shop. Tickets to the Colosseum are joint with the Palatine Hill and Roman Forum.

i Ⓜ*B: Colosseo or Termini, then bus #75. Tickets are purchased for entrance to the Colosseum, Palatine Hill, and Roman Forum; they allow 1 entrance per sight over the course of 2 days €12, EU students ages 18-24 €7.50, EU citizens under 18 or over 65 free. Guided tour €5. Audio tour €5.50. Cash only. Buy a ticket at the Roman Forum to avoid lines* 🕐 *Open daily 8:30am-1hr. before sunset.*

ARCH OF CONSTANTINE   ANCIENT ROME, MONUMENT
V. San Gregorio, south of the Colosseum near the Palatine Hill entrance

It's an arch! And it commemorates Constantine! Bet you didn't see that coming. But it's also drop-dead gorgeous and will turn heads nonetheless. As big as Constantine's ego and elaborately decorated with photoshopped versions of what the emperor looked like, this triumphal arch was built in honor of the Stan's victory over Maxentius at the Battle of the Milvian Bridge. What makes this striking for the art historian in you, though, is the extensive reuse of old material and reliefs taken from other monuments. Copyright is *so* this century.

i Ⓜ*B: Colosseo or Termini, then bus #75. Walk down V. San Gregorio from the Colosseum. Free.*

ROMAN FORUM   ANCIENT ROME
The heart of Ancient Rome. The center of all public life. A place once alive with markets, celebrations, religious ceremonies, and Ciceronian orations. Even if you're a Vestal Virgin, you should be getting a historical boner. Though not quite the social and political center that it once was, the Roman Forum now opens up its rather rocky paths to visitors who can stumble around through the broken-down ruins and call out "O tempora! O mores!" because sometimes after five years of Latin, that's really all you remember. Start your trek into this dusty plot of land, and you'll soon come across the **Arch of Titus.** Check out the relief on the

rome

interior of rowdy Romans carrying off a menorah from the Temple of Jerusalem. Farther ahead is the round **Tempio di Romolo,** with its Christian artwork right next to the imposingly beautiful columns of the **Tempio di Antonino and Faustina.** One of the prettiest and more intact sites at the Roman Forum is the **House of the Vestal Virgins,** which has been left untouched by even time. Further along is the **Curia,** the austere meeting place for the Roman Senate, right next to the elaborately decorated **Arch of Septimus Severus,** marking the foot of the Capitoline Hill. Look up and you'll see the enormous columns that are the only remains of what was once the enormous **Temple of Saturn.**

i Ⓜ*B: Colosseo or Termini, then bus #75. Enter at V. San Gregorio (near the Arch of Constantine), V. dei Fori Imperiali (halfway between Trajan's column and the Colosseum), or directly opposite the Colosseum. The entrance to the Forum is joint with the Palatine Hill. Tickets are purchased for entrance to the Colosseum, Palatine Hill, and Roman Forum; they allow 1 entrance per sight over the course of 2 days. €12, EU students ages 18-2 €7.50, EU citizens under 18 or over 65 free. Audio tour €5, combined with Palatine Hill €7; available in English. Cash only.* ⏰ *Open daily 8:30am-1hr. before sunset.*

PALATINE HILL
ANCIENT ROME

You should always arrive fashionably late to Flavian's Palace for dinner. A couple thousand years late? Still counts. The Palatine Hill (from which we derive the word "palace") is a lovely glimpse into the lifestyles of the rich and famous in Rome, if you take the time difference into consideration. From the Palatine Hill, you can also look out over the **Circus Maximus,** once home to chariot races and now a large field with mosquitoes and concerts in the summer. By the ruins of the palaces is the **Palatine Museum,** housing some household artifacts, and farther up are the **Faranese Gardens,** filled with beautiful roses and nurseries for exotic plants. From such great heights, you'll also get a lovely panorama of the Roman Forum, Colosseum, and Capitoline Hill, and you'll understand luxurious living at its finest. Afterward, walk down past the **Nymphaeumm of the Rain,** a cave with running water (because the natural world is the only palace you need).

i Ⓜ*B: Colosseo or Termini, then bus #75. Enter at V. San Gregorio (near the Arch of Constantine), V. dei Fori Imperiali (halfway between Trajan's column and the Colosseum), or directly opposite the Colosseum. Tickets are purchased for entrance to the Colosseum, Palatine Hill, and Roman Forum; they allow 1 entrance per sight over the course of 2 days. €12, EU students ages 18-24 €7.50, EU citizens under 18 or over 65 free. Audio tour €5, combined with the Forum €7; available in English. Cash only.* ⏰ *Open daily 8:30am-1hr. before sunset. Palatine Museum open daily 8am-4pm; 30 people per floor, 20min. at a time.*

CAPITOLINE HILL
PIAZZA, MUSEUM

One of the seven hills of Rome, the Capitoline (*Campidoglio* in Italian) is your go-to hill when you want to be greeted by gorgeous naked men. But like all the other gorgeous men you've met, they'll be cold as marble to your advances. Nevertheless, this hill is full of Renaissance palaces surrounding the beautiful **Piazza di Campidoglio,** designed by Michelangelo himself. From the outside, the famous equestrian statue of Marcus Aurelius steals the show, but take a look inside the **Capitoline Museums** for the oldest and perhaps most impressive public collections of ancient art in the world. Everything from the *Dying Gaul* to the famous *Capitoline Wolf* are housed in this beautiful museum, with its elaborately frescoed walls and modern touches like mini informational movies and interactive exhibits. Afterwards, step outside for a beautiful vista over the Roman Forum, Colosseum, and Fori Imperiali (if you time it well, you can catch them at sunset) while you photobomb all the wedding photos being taken here.

i *From V. dei Fori Imperiali, veer left toward the Vittorio Emanuele II Monument. Turn onto V. Teatro Marcello and head uphill. Capitoline Museum €12, EU students ages 18-25 €10, EU citizens under 18 or over 65 free; combined ticket with Centrale Montemartini €14, EU students 18-25 €12. Audio tour €5; available in English.* ⏰ *Capitoline Museums open Tu-Su 9am-8pm. Last entry 7pm.*

get a room!

In terms of convenience, residential feel, and cost, Trastevere, Testaccio and Ostiense, and San Giovanni (south of Termini) are ideal places to find your home away from home. Termini is best for last-minute and conveniently located accommodations, especially for travelers arriving by train. Below are some of the best beds in Rome, and more are available on **www.letsgo.com**.

M&J PLACE HOSTEL
HOSTEL $$

V. Solferino 9   ☎06 44 62 802 www.mejplacehostel.com

Colorful walls, lively social spaces, and cheap prices? We had you at colorful walls. If you can score a bed in this hostel, take it. Along with the daily organized outings to museums or flea markets and the bar next door, you too can live out all those dreams of being in Rome while surrounded by fellow young travelers.

i ⓜTermini. Walk down V. Marsala away from the station and turn right onto V. Solferino. Wi-F €2 per hr., €5 per 4hr. Breakfast included in some packages, otherwise €3. Lockers included. Free luggage storage until 9pm. Female-only dorms available. High-season dorms €25-38; low-season dorms €12-20; singles €75; doubles €80-100; triples €135; quads €160. Cash only. ☒ Reception 24hr.

ALESSANDRO PALACE
HOSTEL $$

V. Vicenza 42   ☎06 44 61 958 www.hostelsalessandro.com

You know what frescoes and a mini Augustus statue at reception mean? Hardcore partying. At night, the frequent free pizza parties, happy hour specials, and rowdy late-night drinkers will make sure that this isn't one of those hostels you only come back to when you're ready to hit the hay.

i ⓜTermini. Walk up V. Marsala and turn right onto V. Vicenza. Free Wi-Fi up to 1hr. €1 per hr. thereafter. Breakfast included. Free luggage storage before 3pm. Reserve 1 week in advance in high season. Free pizza daily Apr-Jul 8:30pm. Dorms €19-45; doubles €60-130, with bath €70-130; triples €78-147/85-147. ☒ Reception 24hr.

LA CONTRORA HOSTEL
HOSTEL $$

V. Umbria 7   ☎06 98 93 73 66

La Controra is the IKEA of hostels. Most of the clean, catalogue-looking dorms have three or four weary travelers. With only 14 beds overall, you'll be no stranger to your fellow hostel dwellers, whether you're cooking together or sitting in that look-how-much-fun-rooms-are pose that every Pottery Barn model knows how to rock.

i ⓜA: Barberini. Walk down V. di Santa Nicola da Tolentino and then take a left onto V. Umbria. The hostel is on the right; buzz for entry. Free Wi-Fi. Breakfast included. Kitchen. A/C. Key deposit €10. Lockers available, but bring your own lock. During high season, make reservations about 1 week in advance. Dorms €30-40. ☒ Reception open 8am-midnight.

COLORS
HOTEL, HOSTEL $

V. Boezio 31   ☎06 68 74 030 www.colorshotel.com

Fresh, new, clean, and yes, colorful. The free Wi-Fi and air conditioning will make you never want to leave, even though you're blocks away from St. Peter's Square. The staff is very helpful and friendly, and the kind (but less rowdy) travelers who stay here only make this place even brighter.

i ⓜA: Ottaviano. Walk down V. Ottaviano and turn left onto V. Cola di Rienzo, then right onto V. Terenzio. Colors is at the intersection with V. Boezio. Breakfast included in hotel €7 in dorm. Dorms €20-30; singles €40-70, with bath €50-80; doubles €52-100; triples €70-100. Cash preferred. ☒ Reception 24hr.

rome

FORI IMPERIALI
V. dei Fori Imperiali

☎06 67 97 702

Rome is one of those places where even walking down a street counts as a site. And as you walk down V. dei Fori Imperiali, you'll see why. With the Colosseum at one end and the Vittorio Emanuele II Monument at the other, a casual stroll down this road will give you a chance to see the Imperial Fora. Once four bustling business districts, this site is now packed with broken down columns and walls. The most famous fora is the **Fora of Trajan** with the even more famous **Trajan Column**. A beautiful, continuous frieze decorates this column, which commemorates Trajan's victories in the Dacian Wars on a 98ft.-long shaft. Definitely not compensating for anything. But if you think your imaginary girlfriend's face is beautiful when lit by the setting sun, wait until you see the Fori Imperiali. As everything turns golden-orange in the late evening, get some overpriced gelato from the street vendors and soak in some of the beauty while you walk (maybe it will transfer).

i From the Colosseum, walk down V. dei Fori Imperiali. Free. ⏱ Exhibition and info center open daily 9:30am-6:30pm

THE VELABRUM

ANCIENT ROME

The Velabrum knows all about getting low. Located in an ex-swamp that was the spot where Romulus and Remus's basket was saved, this low-lying area was extremely sacred to the ancient Romans. So they naturally built a giant sewer (the Cloaca Maxima) through it. But now, this de-swamped region is home to the ruins of temples, arches, and random piles of stones that let your imagination run wild. The main sight is the **Chiesa di Santa Maria in Cosmedin,** which holds the oh-so-famous **Bocca della Verità.** According to legend or, you know, *Roman Holiday,* anyone who places their hand in the stone mouth will have it bitten off if they are a liar. So go ahead and test it out if you're feeling brave. Or just man up and tell us where you really were last night.

i From the Circo Massimo, walk down V. dei Cerchi until you reach P. di Sant'Anastasia. The Velabrum and its sights are in the flat region at the base of the hill. Suggested donation for picture €0.50. ⏱ Church open daily 9:30am-5:50pm.

CHIESA DI SAN PIETRO INVINCOLI
P. di San Pietro in Vincoli, 4A

CHURCH

☎06 48 82 865

Skeletons and chains? Hardcore. St. Peter is famous for being a rock(star) in Christianity, and this church is a testament to that. The sculptures of skeletons are about as bare-boned as the walls, but if this wordplay isn't convincing enough, check out this church to see Michelangelo's famous statue of Moses—complete with horns (since someone somewhere botched up a Latin translation of the Bible—clearly he was not AP Vergil material). Along with attracting Michelangelo groupies, this church also houses the very chains that bound St. Peter himself in Jerusalem.

i From V. Cavour, turn onto V. di San Francisco di Paola and walk up the stairs to the piazza in front of the church. Modest dress required. Free. ⏱ Open daily 8am-12:30pm and 3-6pm.

Centro Storico

🏛 PANTHEON
P. della Rotunda

ANCIENT ROME

☎06 68 30 02 30

One does not simply go to Rome and not see the Pantheon. One of the most beautiful and well-preserved buildings from Ancient Rome, this temple was originally built during the reign of Augustus as a temple for all the gods (and we mean *all* the gods) but has since been converted to a Catholic church (one god, all the gods—close enough). An architectural marvel in its own right, this temple is the largest unsupported structure of its kind, much like your ego. Snap some pictures and remain in silence (a priest will shush you) while you walk around this circular building and pass by the tombs of royalty and the crowds of tourists who've all come in because, well, maybe they need to know the time.

i From P. Navona, follow the signs for the Pantheon toward V. della Dogana Vecchia. Free. Audio tou €5, students €3.50. ☉ Open M-Sa 8:30am-7:30pm, Su 9am-6pm.

PIAZZA NAVONA
PIAZZA

Surrounded by V. di Santa Maria dell'Anima and C. del Rinascimento

Originally a stadium built by Domitian in 86 CE, the only gladiatorial action Piazza Navona sees now are skirmishes between knock-off bag vendors and Roman authorities. But when you're done buying watches from that man in the coat, take a look at how beautiful the *piazza* actually is. With its large open expanse and Bernini's magnificent **Fontana dei Quattro Fiumi** depicting four enormous river gods in the center, you'll have no shortage of photo opportunities for your Facebook album. A favorite of tourists and street performers alike, you can stumble upon anything from an old guy breaking down to dubstep to a series of men painted as sculptures who only move when you throw money at them (which sounds like us on a lazy weekend). Though the cafes and restaurants in this area are more expensive, savor the moment and buy a beer to drink while sitting (and photobombing) in Rome's most famous *piazza*.

i Entrances at Palazzo Braschi, V.Agonale, V. di Sant'Agnese di Agone, and Corsia Agonale.

CHIESA DI SAN LUIGI DEI FRANCESI
CHURCH

P. San Luigi dei Francesi 5 ☎06 68 82 71

You might walk right by this church a few times, since it's rather unimpressive from the outside. But like your mother said: you can't change that face, so it's your inner beauty that counts. Thus, Chiesa di San Luigi dei Francesi hides a beautiful butterfly within (that butterfly beingthe spirit of Christ). With marble walls, gold decor, and three of Caravaggio's most famous pieces—**The Calling of Saint Matthew, Saint Matthew and the Angel,** and **The Crucifixion**— inside, this church sheds its Catholic exterior and goes all out with pride inside. But no one said enlightenment was free. Even Caravaggio's halos come at a cost, so deposit (aka, wait for someone else to deposit) €1 to see the paintings lit up by their heavenly electric glow. And always remember that this place is still a church first, so watch the dress code and expect some rather counterproductive shouts of "Silenzio!" from the mike when everyone's prayers get too rowdy.

i From P. Navona, exit onto Corsia Agonale, turn left onto C. del Rinascimento and right onto V. Santa Giovanna d'Arco. Free. ☉ Open M-W 10am-12:30pm and 4-7pm, Th 10am-12:30pm, F-Su 10am-12:30pm and 4-7pm.

VITTORIO EMANUELE II MONUMENT
MONUMENT, MUSEUM

P. Venezia , museum 06 67 93 526 ☎06 67 80 664 www.risorgimento.it

Nicknamed the "Wedding Cake" (no, not because you can eat it), the Vittorio Emanuele II Monument, with its layers of columny goodness, is an inescapable sight from most heights in Rome. It's built on the ground left when Mussolini razed many medieval and Renaissance neighborhoods (including Michelangelo's house), and the surrounding *piazza* now stands as an enormous rotary for cars, scooters, and buses that have all decided to kill you today. What takes (or is) the cake, though, is the enormous monument to Italian unification and national pride centered around the equestrian statue of Vittorio Emanuele II, whose mustache is—trivia time—over 1m long (definitely not compensating for anything). Get some great shots of the building from Piazza Venezia or even from a couple blocks away. If you manage to climb up all the steps of this monument, you'll be rewarded with another lovely view, including Trajan's Column and a chance to enter the dimly lit **Museo Nazionale Emigrazione Italiana** and the **Museo del Risorgimento** (where you'll finally be able to see exhibits such as "Garibaldi Calzoni's jeans in which he landed at Marsala"). But if you're not such a revolution nerd, just stay outside and take a moment to enjoy being so high. Physically, that is.

i *In P. Venezia. Free. ✪ Monument open M-Th 9:30am-6:30pm, F-Su 9:30am-7:30pm. Museum open daily 9:30am-6:30pm.*

Piazza di Spagna

FONTANA DI TREVI   FOUNTAIN
Beyond P. dell'Accademia di San Luca

The only time to really see Trevi Fountain is at 4am, when the moonlight hits the water just right and you can fawn over its majesty while ignoring the guy reading a newspaper next to you. Because yes, it's always crowded. Full of tourists, shop vendors, or policemen making sure you don't pull a *La Dolce Vita* and hop in, Trevi is one of those iconic Roman places you have to see. Nicola Salvi's beautiful fountain cut from rock and stone depicts an enormous Neptune surrounded by the goddesses of abundance and good health, as well as two brawny horsemen chilling out just because. Do as the Roman tourists do and save up on those one euro cent coins to toss in here: one ensures a prompt return to Rome, two will bring you love in the Eternal City, and three will bring about your wedding.

i Ⓜ*A: Barberini. Proceed down V. del Tritone and turn left onto V. Stamperia.*

PIAZZA DI SPAGNA AND THE SPANISH STEPS   MONUMENT, PIAZZA
People from all over the world come to shout an *hola* to the Spanish Steps. Take that, escalators. Built in 1723 to connect P. di Spagna to the heavens via 135 steps that lead up to the **Trinità dei Monti** church, these steps have been a favorite of internationals for hundreds of years, with the Italians (who designed it), the British (who occupied it), the French (who financed it), and the Spanish (who had an embassy here and gave it a name—solid effort) all pitching in. Nowadays, these steps are mainly used for, well, going up and down and for the crowds of tourists who come to eat gelato during the day and the rowdy young folk who come to drink here at night. The best view is from the church itself, where you'll get a vista over the stairs, tourists, gelato, and the *piazza*, with Bernini the Elder's **Fontana della Barcaccia,** or the Fountain of the Ugly Boat, in clear view.

i Ⓜ*A: Spagna.*

MUSEO DELL'ARA PACIS   MUSEUM
At intersection of Lungotevere in Augusta and P. Porto di Ripetta   www.arapacis.it

It's a museum housing one piece. But it's one gorgeous and important piece, so you should go see it. The Ara Pacis, an altar to the goddess Pax, was built to commemorate Augustus's military conquests throughout Spain and Gaul (and peace, too). Visitors are allowed to walk in to get a true sense of its size and view the beautiful sculptural friezes depicting the Senate and a goddess who no one really recognizes anymore. Some models (not the sexy kind) and informational panels surround the Ara Pacis, but the next big attraction is the building itself. A sleek white and wood-paneled example of modern architecture, this building has seen its fair share of controversy considering the very classical artwork it keeps. But sometimes the past simply must coexist with the present.

i Ⓜ*A: Spagna. Take V. del Carrozze toward V. del Corso and proceed into P. Augusto Imperiale €6.50, EU students 18-25 €4.50, EU citizens under 18 and over 65 free. Audio tour in English €3.50. ✪ Open Tu-Su 9am-7pm. Last entry 6pm.*

Jewish Ghetto

🔳 THE GREAT SYNAGOGUE   SYNAGOGUE
Corner of Lungotevere dei Cenci and V. del Tempio

You can't not like a building with a rainbow ceiling. And as the oldest and largest in Rome, this synagogue, much like your Frosted Flakes, is grrrreat. Built in

1904 after all the others were demolished, the Great Synagogue might be a baby compared to other Roman buildings, but it exists in one of the oldest continuous Jewish communities in the world (around since 161 BCE). Enormous and beautifully decorated with starry skies, palm trees, and furnishings from the older *Cinque Scole* (Five Synagogues) of the ghetto period, this synagogue is a breathtaking place to visit, whether you're coming in for one of the three daily prayer services or taking advantage of the guided tour.

i *At the corner of Lungotevere dei Cenciand V. del Tempio. Open for services or with a tour from the Museo Ebraico. Free.*

MUSEO EBRAICO
MUSEUM

Corner of V. del Portico d'Ottavia and V.Catalana ☎06 68 40 06 61 www.museoebraico.roma.it
Our two-sentence Jewish Ghetto introduction not good enough for you? Well if you want to know more, head to the Museo Ebraico, which will drop some learning on your ass. After walking around the entire building to find the entrance, take a look inside and get a general overview of Jewish culture and traditions, along with specific information on the ghetto you are about to adventure time into. With everything from tapestries and coins to crowns and a reconstruction of a Jewish kitchen during Shabbat, this small museum fits in a lot.

i *From Ponte Garibaldi, turn right onto Lungotevere de Cenci and take a left onto V. del Portico d'Ottavia to reach the museum entrance €10, over 65 €7.50, EU students €4, under 10 and the disabled free. Free guided tours of the Great Synagogue and the Spanish Synagogue available in English 15min. past every hr. ☼ Open Jun 16-Sept 15 M-Th 10am-6:15pm, F 10am-3:15pm, Su 10am-6:15pm; Sept 16-Jun 15 M-Th 10am-4:15pm, F 9am-1:15pm, Su 10am-4:15pm.*

Vatican City

▓ PIAZZA DI SAN PIETRO
PIAZZA

At the end of V. della Concializione ☎06 69 88 16 62 www.vaticanstate.va
Rome has a way of making you feel like a little girl (or boy or person of unspecified gender) in a big city. So walking into St. Peter's Square is like getting a big, marble columned hug. Which is exactly what you need. Designed by Bernini, the long colonnaded arms and welcoming oval interior of this *piazza* are meant to be as welcoming as the arms of the Catholic Church, which is a lot of metaphors to take in. But the effect is stunning. Even when it's filled with tourists snapping photos or waiting in long lines to the Basilica, the square lined with statues of saints and angels itself is a beautiful sight and is always happy to see you. Which kind of melts your stone cold heart.

i *Bus #23, 34, 40, 271, or 982 to P. Pia or bus #62 down V. della Conciliazione. Pilgrim Tourist Office, to the left of the basilica, has a multilingual staff, a gift shop, free bathrooms, a first-aid station, brochures, maps, currency exchange, and Vatican post boxes inside or nearby. Free. ☼ Piazza open 24hr. Tourist Office open M-Sa 8:30am-6:15pm.*

▓ WW
CHURCH

At the end of V. della Concializione ☎06 69 88 16 62 www.vaticanstate.va
With one of the most iconic domes in the world, Saint Peter's Basilica is more than a building to be admired from the outside. Much like you, this basilica is rich—on the inside. After going through the airport-like security (hey, you're in a different country after all), head inside and prepare to feel the power of Christ. And of enormous buildings. With cavernous ceilings, windows that barely light up the interior on cloudy days, and statues of saints that you literally have to look up to, everything in this church is massive. As soon as you walk in, turn to your right, and you'll see the famous **Pietà** by Michelangelo, a beautiful and heartbreaking rendition of Mary and Jesus. Below is the twisted and ornately decorated *baldacchino* (canopy), with its whimsical sculpted bumblebees, marking the pope's altar. To the right of the *baldacchino* is the statue of St. Peter

rome

himself with its lucky foot. Every June 29, this statue is dressed up in papal regalia from the Treasury for his feast day. Though most people come to this basilica
as tourists, consider coming here for mass as well in front of Bernini's **Cathedra
Petri**, an area closed off to tourists. It's a once in a lifetime opportunity, and you'll
be praying in the most famous church in the world. Make those prayers count…
You asked for a date with a Swiss Guard, didn't you?

i Free guided tours in English leave from the Pilgrim Tourist Information Center. No shorts, mini
skirts, or tank tops. Free. ☉ Basilica open daily Apr-Sept 7am-7pm; Oct-Mar 7am-6:30pm. Tours
Tu 9:45am, Th-F 9:45am. Mass M-F 8:30, 10, 11am, noon, and 5pm; Su and holidays 9, 10:30,
11:30am, 12:15, 1, 4, and 5:45pm. Vespers daily 5pm.

SAINT PETER'S GRAVE (PRE-CONSTANTINIAN NECROPOLIS) TOMB
Office left of the basilica, tombs below Scavi Office ☎06 69 88 53 18 www.vaticanstate.va

Not everyone from Christianity is resurrectable. Hence the large necropolis here
in Vatican City, most famously housing the bones of St. Peter himself. Though
paying a visit down to the first pope's tomb requires some 90 days preordination,
you'll be rewarded for your patience with a claustrophobic walk through the
tombs and some explanations of the sight's historical and religious significance.
In 1939, the discovery of ancient ruins and a number of bones in the area was
convincing enough for the once-infallible pope to claim that St. Peter's remains
did in fact exist under the original altar. Successive popes have also affirmed
the presence of the holy remains, but many still believe that the bones were
removed during the Saracen pillaging of Rome in 849 CE.

i In the piazza. Instead of entering the Basilica, veer left and look for Swiss Guards dressed in
stripes who will grant you access to the courtyard. The Scavi Office is on the courtyard's right side.
The necropolis can only be seen on a guided tour organized by the Scavi Office. Reservations must
be made at least 1 day ahead but should be made as early as possible (as early as 90 days in
advance). Pick up a reservation form at the office and hand deliver it, or email scavi@fsp.va with
name, number of attendees, tour language, desired dates, and address and telephone number of
where you are staying. Fully covered attire required. No backpacks or bulky items. €12. ☉ Scavi
Office open M-Sa 9am-5pm. Tours last 1½hr.

▧ VATICAN MUSEUMS MUSEUM
Vle. Vaticano 97 ☎06 69 88 38 60 www.museivaticani.va

And now, you patient and cultured world traveler, it's time for the main event.
Let's go to the **Sistine Chapel**. It's not difficult to find: just follow the mass of
tourists leading you into what is the most monumental and beautiful part of
the Vatican Museums. Gorgeous, awe-inspiring, life-changing. No photography
or talking is allowed, so you get to admire the enormous **Last Judgment** covering
the entire altar wall and the iconic **Creation of Adam,** one of nine panels depicting
scenes from Genesis. There are some lovely tidbits to be discovered while you're
here. For example, Michelangelo had originally wanted full frontal nudity for
the entire piece, but when Cardinal Carafa wouldn't let him go the full monty,
the artist covered everyone up (including Carafa himself, whose Speedo-zone is
being chomped on by a giant snake). Spend as long as you can staring up at this
masterpiece before you get crowd surfed out.

i Ⓜ A: Ottaviano. Head down V. Ottaviano, turn right onto V. dei Bastioni di Michelangelo, and
follow the wall until you see the end of the line for the museums. The entrance is on Vle. Vaticano
€16, ages 6-18 and EU citizens 18-26 €8, under 6 free. Free last Su of each month and on World
Tourism Day (September 27). Special viewings €4. Entrance with guided tour €32, ages 6-18 and
EU citizens 18-26 €24. Audio tours with map €7. ☉ Open M-Sa 9am-6pm. Open last Su of each
month 9am-2pm. Last entry 2hr. before close. Open Apr-Jul F 7-11pm for special viewing only; online reservation required. Check the website for hours as there may be additional closings.

MUSEO NAZIONALE DI CASTEL SANT'ANGELO

CASTLE, MUSEUM

Lungotevere Castello 50   ☎06 68 19 111 www.castelsantangelo.com

A round brick structure spiting all the marble around it, this mausoleum for Hadrian and his family turned palace, castle, prison, and (finally) museum, stands on the banks of the Tiber, inspiring childish wonder in all with its dried up moats and electric torches. Once a fortress as impenetrable as your Catholic girlfriend, Castel Sant'Angelo now offers visitors a chance to walk up a winding ramp to the beautiful statue of the archangel Michael, then up a few more steps to take in a panorama of Rome from the terrace. No catapults here, only gorgeous views of St. Peter's Dome and the statue-lined Ponte Sant'Angelo. And a full bar. So after you finish pre-gaming, check out the papal chambers, with their beautifully mosaic'd walls and collection of ancient statues, pottery, and busts below. Or, you know, just keep drinking. Forget the king: God save the Spritz.

i Bus #23, 34, 40, 271, or 982 to P. Pia. The castle is at the end of V. della Conciliazione and at the intersection with Ponte Sant'Angelo €8.50, EU citizens ages 18-25 €6, EU citizens under 18 and over 65 free. Audio tour €4. ☼ Open Tu-Su 9am-7pm. Last entry 6:30pm.

Trastevere

Really, the main sight in Trastevere is, well, Trastevere. Down every *vicolo*, in every *piazza*, by every fountain, there's a photo waiting to happen. No one will blame you if you fill numerous Facebook albums with the kind of rustic charm you thought only existed in movies.

▧ SANTA MARIA IN TRASTEVERE

CHURCH

P. Santa Maria in Trastevere   ☎06 58 14 802

Santa Maria in Trastevere is a sight for weary eyes lost in the winding streets of Rome. Just when you start giving up faith, the wide *piazza* opens up before you with a large fountain and the unmistakable figure of the Virgin Mary greeting you from the first church built exclusively for her in Rome. After parting the crowds of tourists and school groups Red Sea-style, make your way inside the church and admire the shimmering golden apse mosaic made in the Byzantine style (aka, before Christ had quite reached the third dimension) and realize that enlightened sheep are your new favorite art subjects. And when you're done buying your own Pope Francis bookmark from the gift shop, take a moment to bask in the sunlight, perhaps with some gelato, on the steps of the fountain outside.

i From Vle. Trastevere, turn right onto V. San Francesco a Ripa and walk 5min. Free. ☼ Open M-F 9am-5:30pm.

ISOLA TIBERINA

OPEN SPACE

Before Aeneas entered Italy, the Tiber did not know the feeling of ships. But now it can know the feeling of your toes! Isola Tiberina is a beautiful island in the middle of the river. Home to both the **Fatebenefratelli Hospital** and the **Basilica San Bartolomeo,** this is your one-stop shop for physical and spiritual healing. According to legend, the island is made of the silt-covered remains of Tarquin, an Etruscan ruler who caused the end of the monarchy after raping the beautiful Lucretia. But out ofthe ashes rises this peaceful island. After crossing the Ponto Fabrico (aka, the Ponte dei Quattro Capi, with its four stone heads of the architects who restored the bridge), the cobblestone plaza, cafes, and pharmacy won't make you feel too far away from the city. But take the steps down to ground level, and you'll get a beautiful (and often private) view of the mighty Tiber itself. Walk along the white stone paths lined with trees, take countless selfies, crash some romantic picnics, and see fishermen pull in their catch. Rome is a beautiful city, but if you need to get away and found a new empire or two, do as the Romans did and settle down by the Tiber.

i From V. del Teatro Marcello, walk toward the water and onto Lungomare dei Pierleoni. Turn right to reach Ponte Fabricio. Free.

GIANICOLO HILL
PANORAMIC VIEW

It's not one of the famous Seven Hills of Rome (sorry, you have to be on the other side of the Tiber for that), but Gianicolo Hill is still a worthwhile place to hike up. The winding V. Garibaldi will give you a workout, but just remember that there's a gorgeous view of Rome when you reach the top. And gelato. (We all go through great lengths for gelato.) For teasers on your way up, you'll get a chance to see the **San Pietro in Montorio** church and the **Fonte Acqua Paola** among the forested hill before you head into the **Piazzale Giuseppe Garibaldi**. The latter will present you with a beautiful vista of the city that will leave you breathless (and that's not just from the rather steep climb). Head around the back of Garibaldi's horse, and you'll catch a glimpse of St. Peter's dome, along with graffitied declarations of love (just like the true love between you and your gelato).

i From P. San Egidio, turn left onto Vicolo del Cedro, climb the stairs, and take a left onto V. Garibaldi. Free.

Termini and San Lorenzo

BASILICA DI SANTA MARIA MAGGIORE
CHURCH

In P. dell'Esquilino
☎06 69 88 68 17

Located just minutes away from Termini Station, Basilica di Santa Maria Maggiore is an enormous basilica dedicated to everyone's favorite virgin (no, not you). Legend has it that this basilica was built after Mary sent a miraculous snowfall in the middle of summer. So, obviously, a basilica had to be built in that spot. Despite the questionable history, it is a sight to see, with its elaborate gold ceiling, giant statues of saints, and beautiful frescoes covering every inch of the walls. There is a small museum attached with artifacts and artwork relating to the church's history, but you can also spend your time sitting on the red plastic chairs pretending to be pews and enjoy the glory of Gold. And God, too.

i ⓂTermini. Turn right onto V. Giolitti and walk down V. Cavour. Modest dress required. Basilica free. Museu €4, EU students and over 65 €2; Loggia €5/3. Audio tour (available in English) €4. ⓩ Basilica open daily 7am-7pm. Museum open daily 9am-6pm.

CHIESA DI SANTA MARIA DEGLI ANGELI
CHURCH

P. della Repubblica
☎06 48 80 812 www.santamariadegliangeliroma.it

Don't let the rough-hewn exterior ruin your expectations. Built in the ruins of the Baths of Diocletian, this *chiesa* designed by Michelangelo focuses more on inner beauty and Christ (or something artsy and historical like that) rather than a pretty façade. With high vaulted ceilings, faux-marble walls, and a meridian line running from the east transept to the altar that acts as a sundial, you gotta give Michelangelo some credit despite the less-than-impressive exterior. Make sure to check out the modern art at this church, such as a wiry angel figure and paintings with white swirls that are hidden saints. And after you've decided you just aren't going to have a religious epiphany, head out to the sacristy to view the baths that are as broken down as your dreams of proper backpacker hygiene.

i ⓂTermini. Walk into the P. dei Cinquecento and veer left toward V. Viminale. Sundial viewing schedule posted in church. Reserve sundial demonstrations 2 days in advance Jun 15-Sept 15. Call06 48 70 749 for more information. Free. ⓩ Open M-F 7am-6:30pm, Sa-Su 7am-7:30pm.

BATHS OF DIOCLETIAN
MUSEUM

V. Enrico de Nicola 79
☎06 39 96 77 00 www.archeoroma.beniculturali.it

Most misleading site name ever. There are no more baths here—just ruins. And some fountains. You brought your towel all the way here for nothing. But don't worry. You can still see some naked Romans, but they'll all be in statue form in the snazzy new museum that is built on the site. While you won't find anything postcard worthy here, there are some lovely pottery fragments, proto-historic altars (aka slabs of rock), and a lovely walk around Michelangelo's Cloister, so you can bathe in knowledge or beauty or something ethereal like that.

i Ⓜ*Termini. Walk into P. dei Cinquecento; enter on V. Volturno. Part of the Museo Nazionale Romano group, which also includes the Palazzo Massimo across the street, the Palazzo Altemps near the P. Navona, and the Crypta Balbi near the Largo Argentina. Buy 1 ticket for entrance to all 4 sights over 3 days €7, EU students €3.50, EU citizens under 18 and over 65 free. ☑ Open Tu-Su 9am-7:45pm. Last entry 6:45pm.*

Northern Rome

Northern Rome is not only home to embassies (boring) but also boasts a ton of museums, parks, and historic *piazze* (exciting!). Set away from the ancient ruins, this area of the city is home to more recent monuments, at least in Roman terms: 17th-century villas, Bernini's sculptural masterpieces, and modern and contemporary art all reside here.

▧ GALLERIA BORGHESE
MUSEUM

Ple. del Museo Borghese 5   ☎06 84 16 542 www.galleriaborghese.it

If you thought the walk in the Villa Borghese was breathtaking, wait until you get to the Galleria Borghese. Gorgeous, sumptuous, and extremely popular (be sure to book tickets in advance), this is not a place to miss in Rome. With every inch of this museum covered in paintings and frescoes by everyone in the index of your art history textbook, the Borghese is home to the works of Caravaggio, Titian, Rubens, and Raphael. But the showstopper here really is Bernini. Maybe you were a Play-Doh sculpture prodigy, but take a look at Bernini and see the limits of what man can do to marble. The **Rape of Proserpina** is a beautiful example of Bernini turning marble into flesh, as Pluto's fingers leave indents on Proserpina's body. Note, too, how poor Proserpina's toes delicately curl up. **Apollo and Daphne** will also require a good 10min. to walk around as you see the latter change from soft flesh to hard tree bark, all done in marble as the tips of Daphne's fingers and toes dynamically transform into leaves and roots. These two sculptures often attract large crowds, and since everyone enters the museum at once, start your visit at the top floor and work your way down to finish with these masterpieces.

i Enter on V. Pinciana, near V. Isonzo. Proceed up Vle. dell'Uccelleria for about 5min. Reservations are required and tend to fill up quickly; call06 32 810 or visit www.ticketeria.it €13, EU citizens ages 18-25 €8.50, EU citizens under 18 and over 65 €2. Tours €5. ☑ Open Tu-Su 9am-7pm. Last entry 6:30pm.*

▧ VILLA BORGHESE
GARDENS

Bordered by Vle. Trinita dei Monti and V. Porta Pinciana   ☎06 32 16 564

A gorgeous, sprawling garden that defies the bustling city around it by offering shady walks, grassy hills, and benches to sit on and ponder life. Surrounded by busts of Romans (such Tacitus) and non-Romans (everybody loves Gogol) alike, the trails are a perfect getaway for you and your lover (or even you and your friend-zoned buddies). Bring along a picnic basket and lie out on the grass. Wander your way over to the carousels, where children ride on fake horses, or stumble upon the large tract of land where real horse shows happen. And when you've had your fill of greenery, head on over to the Galleria Borghese for artistic beauty to match the natural aesthetics of the park. Although this is the perfect place to bring along a date (peddlers will try to sell you roses), even if you're all alone, there's always Tacitus to get down and dirty (if you're into talking about the *Annales*).

i Ⓜ*A: Spagna or Flaminio. There are multiple entrances to the park: Porta Pinciana, Ple. Flaminio, Vle. Belle Arti, V. Mercadante, and V. Pinciana. Gardens free. Bike renta €4 per hr., €15 per day. Visit www.ascolbike.com for more information. ☑ Gardens open daily Apr-Aug 7am-9pm; Sept 7am-8pm; Oct-Dec 7am-6pm; Jan-Feb 7am-6pm; Mar 7am-8pm.*

■ CAPUCHIN CRYPT
V. Veneto 27

CHURCH

☎06 48 71 185 www.cappucciniviaveneto.it

Walk into the Capuchin Crypt, and it will seem like a modern museum, complete with sleek wooden panels and life-sized TV screens with monks telling you to listen to that inner voice of Jesus. But walk down to the crypt, and you'll be met with all sorts of legends about its creation, the most romantic perhaps being that the idea came from a sinner seeking refuge from his own tortured soul (or from a man mocking death because he was so assured of resurrection). And then you'll enter the crypt itself. Made entirely out of human bones—from pelvises lining the wall to vertebrae in the lamps—the crypt is the perfect setting for a horror movie, especially given the skeletons still dressed in their monk's robes bowing to crosses. Perhaps you'll even hear the voice of Jesus (or maybe that's just the monks talking again). Either way, the words before you enter, "What you are now, we were; what we are now, you will be" will haunt you even after you ascend back into the sunlight.

i Ⓜ A: Barberini. Follow V.Veneto uphill; the church is on the right. To enter, take the stairs on the right. There is a strict dress code, so avoid low-cut or sleeveless shirts and short skirts or shorts; at the very least, bring something to cover up €1 min. donation. ⛄ Open M-W 9am-noon and 3-6pm, F-Su 9am-noon and 3-6pm.

GALLERIA NAZIONALE D'ARTE MODERNA
Vle. delle Belle Arti 131

MUSEUM

☎06 32 29 81 www.gnam.arti.beniculturali.it

Housed inside a very Neoclassical building, this museum might leave you with doubts as to how modern it actually is, but once you walk inside and onto the cracked mirror floor, you'll know where you are. Opening with some of Duchamp's most famous ready mades, this museum follows the path of naturalism all the way to pop art and postmodernism. You'll get everything from van Goghs, Klimts, and Mondrians to long, dark halls with buzzing electric exhibits. This is definitely a place to hit if you're a modern art enthusiast or even if you just want to see Duchamp and his (in)famous *Fountain*, a testimony to the truly immortal and universal power of bathroom humor.

i From Vle. del Giardino in the Villa Borghese, veer right and exit the park onto Vle. delle Belle Arti. The museum is on the right €12, EU students ages 18-25 €9.50, under 18 and over 65 free. ⛄ Open Tu-Su 8:30am-7:30pm. Left half of the building (19th-century Italian paintings) open Tu-Su 12:30-7:30pm. Last entry 6:45pm.

Testaccio And Ostiense

■ BASILICA DI SAN PAOLO FUORI LE MURA
Ple. San Paolo 1

CHURCH

☎06 69 88 08 00 www.basilicasanpaolo.org

In an enormous *piazza* where all the little *bambini* have water fights (ideally Catholics vs. heretics: water guns of instant baptism) stands the Basilica di San Paolo Fuori le Mura. As long as its name, this ancient basilica was built over St. Paul's tomb, which rests below the altar. Since then it has expanded significantly, perhaps just in case—St. Paul's gotta be down there somewhere. Inside, you'll see the wonders of heaven (or at least an intricately decorated ceiling), statues of enormous saints, 200 mosaic'd popes, and a hilarious pastor who makes everyone laugh while you sheepishly grin and await the Good Shepherd. Any day now...

i Ⓜ B: Basilica San Paolo, or bus #23 to Ostiense/LGT San Paolo stop. Modest dress required. 1hr. guided visits available; reserve online. Basilica free. Cloiste €4. ⛄ Basilica open daily 7am-6:30pm. Cloister open daily 8am-6:15pm.

CENTRALE MONTEMARTINI

V. Ostiense 106   ☎06 06 06 08 www.centralemontemartini.org

MUSEUM

Screw logic. Sometimes you just want to make a museum with gorgeous marble Aphrodite sculptures in front of hulking gray steam boilers. That's what Centrale Montemartini was thinking. Built inside Rome's first public electricity plant, this museum winds you through man's achievements in history, starting with frescoes from Republican Rome and culminating with Apollos backdropped by pipes and diesel engines. Art for the new age, man. Don't miss the hidden gems of ancient art, such as an enormous mosaic of hunting scenes and fragments of a colossal Fortuna found in the Area Sacra Argentina. It's almost as powerful and thought-provoking as your steampunk prom pictures.

i Ⓜ️B: Ostiense. The museum is a 10min. walk down V. Ostiense €5.50, EU citizens ages 18-25 €4.50; combined ticket with Musei Capitolini €11/8.50 (valid for 1 week). Cash only. ☒ Open Tu-Su 9am-7pm. Last entry 6:30pm.

Southern Rome

THE APPIAN WAY

V. Appia Antica   ☎06 51 35 316 www.parcoappiaantica.it

ROME

Get your wagons out; the Appian Way is calling. A historically famous and important road, the Appian Way stretches 16km from Porta San Sebastiano to Frattocchie (which is far, for all you metric-illiterates) and gives you the opportunity to follow the footsteps of celebrities like Virgil, St. Peter, and Spartacus (...and the bodies of his followers). As soon as you arrive, you'll realize that walking the Appian Way is equivalent to playing in traffic, as it still is a functioning thoroughfare for motor vehicles. So head out on a Sunday, when the road is closed and there's less traffic. If you choose to bike it, just know that parts of the Appian Way are not well paved and the cobblestones only get a gold star for effort. The main attraction for the first part of the road will be the 3rd-century **catacombs**, filled with dead people. And some frescoes. But continue on your way, and you'll encounter more dead people in tomb ruins and also some beautiful vistas of uncultivated land, parrots, wildflowers rustling in the wind, and some funky cacti. Perfect place for a new profile picture. For a shorter but rockier trip, take V. della Caffarella (to the left of V. Appia Antica) to see some Roman ruins and the remains of your sneakers.

i Ⓜ️A: San Giovanni. Head through Porta San Giovanni into the piazza. Take bus #218; to reach the info office, push the button to request a stop after you turn left onto V. Appia Antica. The bus continues up V. Ardeatina and drops you off near the Santa Domitilla and San Calisto Catacombs. Alternatively, take Ⓜ️B: Circo Massimo or Ⓜ️B: Piramide. Take bus #118, which runs along V. Appia Antica to the San Sebastiano Catacombs. If you want to walk, head down V. delle Terme di Caracalla from the Circo Massimo. At Ple. Numa Pompilio, veer right onto V. di Porta San Sebastiano through the city wall and onto V. Appia Antica. Info office at V. Appia Antica 60 offers bike rental, free maps, brochures, a bus ticket machine, and suggestions for activities along the way. For info on Archeobus tours leaving from Termini, call 800 281 281 or visit www.trambusopen.com. Road and park free. Bike rental €3 per hr., €15 per day. Archeobus with audio tour €10. ☒ Info office open May-Jul M-Sa 9:30am-1:30pm and 2-5:30pm, Su 9:30am-6:30pm; Aug M-Sa 9:30am-1:30pm and 2-5:30pm, Su 9:30am-5:30pm; Sept-Apr M-Sa 9:30am-1:30pm and 2-4:30pm, Su 9:30am-4:30pm. Archeobus tours daily every 30min. 9:30am-4pm.

FOOD

Trattoria, caffè, osteria, ristorante, pizzeria, gelateria—these are all Italian words for one thing: food. For meals on the go, cafes and *pizzerias* are the best option, offering panini and thin crust pizza in numerous varieties. Sit-down meals are a social and time-consuming affair in Rome, so don't expect to see many solo diners. You'll also have to acclimate to late dinners: most places don't open until 7:30pm or later, and they don't get busy until well after 9pm. Expect added fees for table service and bread, and, while water spews freely out of the myriad fountains in Rome, restaurants refuse to give out free tap water. Tipping isn't usually expected, but this also means that servers are considerably less attentive than you might be used to; you'll need to be aggressive if you want another glass of wine or the check.

Ancient City

It's a shame that eating is necessary. Well, not really, but since everyone has to do it—and nearly everyone in Rome comes to the Ancient City to do it—restaurants here are often overcrowded and overpriced. For the best deals, avoid the options closest to the sights and meander down quieter streets.

LA CUCCUMA

RISTORANTE, PIZZERIA $

V. Merulana 221   ☎06 77 20 13 61

You don't need to impress the cute waiter. You need chicken wrapped in bacon. Here at La Cuccuma, the generously portioned, €9 *prix fixe* meal (*primi, secondi, contorni*, and bread) is a steal and comes with delicious options like ham and cheese lasagna, fried chicken, and a large variety of vegetables (since you're part-time health conscious). A favorite not just among tourists but locals, too, this spacious restaurant, with its rustic sunflower and cat decor, also serves up slices of thin crust pizza for those less ambitious. But don't be one of them, 'cuz remember: bacon.

i Ⓜ A: Vittorio Emanuele. Walk down V. dello Statuto and turn right onto V. Merulana. Primi €4-5. Secondi €5-6. Pizza €8-16 per kg. Pizze tonde (after 7pm) €4-8.50. ☼ Open daily 10am-11pm.

PIZZERIA DA MILVIO

PIZZERIA $

V. dei Serpenti 7   ☎06 48 93 01 45

A deceptively small *pizzeria* from the front, this place backs it up into a large, open seating area with neon orange chairs, pictures of the chef with celebrities you don't recognize, and *so much food*. We're talking about pastas for *primi*, fried chicken and baked fish for *secondi*, and about half a counter filled with dessert. Everything from the cherry pies to the tiramisu will have you shaking your head at your silly self for thinking this was just another *pizzeria*. Though it can get rather crowded during lunchtime, wait for the other customers to clear out and then prepare yourself to feast.

i Ⓜ A: Cavour. From V. Cavour, turn onto V. dei Serpenti and walk 2min. Pizza €0.80-1.40 per etto. Primi €5. Secondi €6. Cash only. ☼ Open daily 7am-midnight.

LA TAVERNA DA TONINO E LUCIA

RISTORANTE $$

V. Madonna dei Monti 79   ☎06 47 45 325

Modernity is overrated in Rome. Check out this old-fashioned little restaurant off the busy V. Cavour. At La Taverna da Tonino e Lucia, you can cozy up next to your neighboring table (since space is limited) but also enjoy the coziness that comes with vintage lanterns, rustic furniture, and traditional Roman food. Try the recommended veal rolls with tomato sauce or any of the affordable entrees. You'll feel right at home, if your home also has cork-lined walls.

i Ⓜ B: Cavour. Walk down V. Cavour toward the Fori Imperiali, turn right onto V. dei Serpenti, and turn left onto V. Madonna dei Monti. Primi €8. Secondi €9-14. Cash only. ☼ Open M-Sa 12:30-2:30pm and 7-10:30pm.

LA CARBONARA

OSTERIA $$

V. Panisperna 214   ☎06 48 25 176 www.lacarbonara.it

Serving Rome for 106 years ensures that you rack up an impressive wine cork collection. And at La Carbonara, a massive wine list also goes along with a deliciously famous selection of pasta and classic dishes like *carciofi alla giudia* (fried artichoke) and *cacio e pepe* (cheese and peppers). Yes, the *spaghetti alla carbonara* is good, as the restaurant's name suggests. Don't believe our reviews?

Check out the walls of this restaurant, which are covered with scribbled love notes to the food. Because, as you might have discovered in Rome, sometimes only really good pasta can rekindle that passion in your heart.

i From Basilica di Santa Maria Maggiore, walk down V. di Santa Maria Maggiore, which becomes V. Panisperna. Primi €6-9. Secondi €9-15. ⏰ Open M-Sa 12:30-2:30pm and 7-11pm.

Centro Storico

Catering to hungry tourists, food in the Centro Storico tends to be overpriced. Your best bet for a quick meal is to head to a *panificio* (bakery), *pasticceria* (confectionery), or *pizzeria* and eat your grub in a nearby *piazza*. For a sit-down meal, wander down narrow, out-of-the way streets rather than central ones.

▨ DAR FILETTARO A SANTA BARBARA
FISH $

Largo dei Librari 88 ☎06 68 64 018

Sure, Rome's famous for its pizza and pasta and gelato. But Dar Filettaro a Santa Barbara could make it famous for cod as well. A local and tourist favorite, this restaurant is always busy, and there's nothing fishy about that. After being handed a one-sided menu featuring the restaurant's famous fried cod for only €5, almost everyone orders this one delicious meal. Getting a plate with just one cod on it might not seem that impressive by your Big Mac standards, but once you taste it in all its fried and seasoned glory, you'll realize why people keep coming here. The inside of the restaurant a bit small and cramped, with tables lining every possible wall, so if the weather's nice, opt to sit and listen to a mandolin player or kids playing soccer in the small *piazza* outside.

i From Campo dei Fiori, walk down V. dei Giubbonari and turn left onto the tiny Largo dei Librari. Salads, antipasti, and fried fis €5. Desserts €0.50-3.50. Beer €2.50-4.50. Cash only. ⏰ Open M-Sa 5:30-11:30pm.

GELATERIA DEL TEATRO
GELATERIA $

V. di San Simone 70 ☎06 45 47 880 www.gelateriadelteatro.it

It's gelato. Do we need to tell you more? How about this: there's no such thing as bad gelato, but if there had to be the best gelato, it might just be here. Always crowded with locals and tourists alike, Gelateria del Teatro will force you to pull a ticket number and wait your turn oh-so-patiently while you stare at mouthwatering flavors like Sicilian pistachio and cheese and almond and fig. And while you're here, take a look at the window outside and you'll see cooks making your gelato from fresh ingredients right before your very eyes. In that moment, all your problems will fade, and you'll realize the world is a beautiful place.

i From P. Navona, turn left onto V. dei Coronari and look for the tiny V. di San Simone on the left. Free tours offered for groups; call to reserve a spot. Cones and cup €2-10. Credit card min. €20. ⏰ Open daily in high season 11am-1am; in low season 11am-midnight.

FORNO MARCO ROSCIOLI
BAKERY $$

V. dei Chiavari 34 ☎06 68 64 045 www.salumeriaroscioli.com

Everyone needs a box of pasta shaped like Roman monuments in their pantry. And what better place to get it than at Forno Marco Roscioli? At this bakery, deli, and grocery store, you can also grab some flaky rolls with almonds and raisins or some thin crust pizza while you're here. And if you're feeling especially hungry, try the hot tomato gnocchi. While the food is great, don't expect to find somewhere to sit. There's always a crowd in here (no, that's not just your personal paparazzi), so grab your food to go and eat it while you wander the small streets of this neighborhood.

i From Campo dei Fiori, walk down V. dei Giubbonari and turn left onto V. dei Chiavari. Primi €5-7. Pizza €9.50-18 per kg. ⏰ Open M-Sa 7am-8pm.

rome

PIZZERIA DA BAFFETTO PIZZERIA $$
V. del Governo Vecchio 114 ☎06 68 61 617 www.pizzeriabaffetto.it

Pizzeria de Baffetto is as crowded with patrons as its walls are with pictures of famous people who've stopped by over the years. So it's pretty crowded. Thanks to what is arguably the best pizza in Rome, lines start forming fast, so get here early. And while there are no Soup Nazis, service can be brusque; be prepared to order fast and don't worry too much about what you pick—everything here is delicious.

i From P. Navona, exit onto P. Pasquina and continue as it becomes V. del Governo Vecchio. Pizza €5-9. Cash only. ⌚ Open M 6:30pm-12:30am, W-F 6:30pm-12:30am, Sa-Su 12:30-3:30pm and 6:30pm-12:30am

CUL DE SAC RISTORANTE $$
P. Pasquino 73 ☎06 68 80 10 94 www.enotecaculdesac.com

Given the four walls covered with bottles of wine, Jesus must have been especially fond of this restaurant. Cul de Sac definitely caters to the alcoholic in you and makes sure that even after you've tried all 1500 types of wine, you can still read the menu in your native tongue, whether it's English or Russian. Although this place is popular among the tourists, don't dismiss it just yet, since this just means you can get anything from the international *baba ghanoush* to the more local pig's head sausage—all while taking your Eucharist very seriously.

i From P. Navona, walk onto P. Pasquino. Primi €7.30-9. Secondi €6.60-10. Desserts €4.30. ⌚ Open daily noon-4pm and 6pm-12:30am.

Piazza di Spagna

▧ FRASCHETTERIA BRUNETTI RISTORANTE $$
V. Angelo Brunetti 25B ☎06 32 14 103 www.fraschetteriabrunetti.it

"Baked" and "pasta" are two of your favorite words. So when you hear of the baked pasta at Fraschetteria Brunetti, it's okay to fall in love. Specializing in various types of lasagna, ranging from your classic cheese and bacon to a fancy date-level salmon and broccoli to gorgonzola and walnuts, this cozy restaurant will make sure you get your fill of fresh, unique pasta at some of the most affordable prices in the area. Also, their mascot is a pig eating a carrot. It's adorable. You can't not go in.

i ⓜA: Flaminio-Piazza del Popolo. From P. del Popolo, exit onto V. di Ripetta and turn right onto V. Angelo Brunetti. Panini €3.50. Primi €10. Prix-fixe lunch of entree, coffee, and drink €9. Cocktails €4. ⌚ Open M-Sa 11am-2am, but may close earlier or later depending on the crowd.

CAMBI PIZZERIA, BAKERY $
V. del Leoncino 30 ☎06 68 78 081

There are a lot of Spanish Steps; you probably need some sugar to make it up all of them. Correction: you probably need *a lot* of sugar. Here at Cambi, you can stock up on delicious, chocolatey cookies, cream-filled pastries, and those fruit tarts that you eat every day for your vitamin intake. If you can make it past the siren song of the pastries, go west, young man, to consider your pizza, panini and *tramezzini* options, all of which could be yours for a very reasonable price. And to avoid V. del Corso's designer-priced water, stop by here for a bottle of dihydrogen monoxide for only €1.

i From Ara Pacis/Mausoleo di Augusto, walk down V. Tomacelli and turn right onto V. Leoncino. No seating. Cookie €0.80, €33 per kg. Panini €3.50. Pizza €8-15 per kg. Crostatine €11 per kg. Cash only. ⌚ Open M-Sa 8am-8pm.

GIOLITTI GELATERIA $
Via degli Uffici del Vicario 40 ☎06 69 91 243 www.giolitti.it

Have you had enough gelato? Your teachers were wrong, and there are such things as stupid questions. You always need more gelato. So after wandering through designer shops, wander your way over to this *gelateria*. Caught between V. del Corso and the Pantheon, this spot boasts an enormous green sign, crowds of tourists, and occasional visits from celebrities like Obama and Justin Timberlake. Which is probably why the waiters always have their suit and tie out. After serving customers for over 100 years though, Giolitti can show you a few things about gelato. An enormous selection of flavors and fancy wooden and marble counters give you a taste of luxury without the high price. Try the pistachio and limoncello.

i From V. del Corso, turn left onto V. del Parlamento and left onto V. di Campo Marzio. At the end of the road, turn left onto V. degli Uffici del Vicario. Gelat €2.50-5. ☒ Open daily 7am-1:30am

NATURIST CLUB
V. della Vite 14, 4th fl.

RISTORANTE, VEGETARIAN $$$
☎06 67 92 509

Much to your chagrin, the macrobiotic diet does not mean supersized portions of everything. But that doesn't mean you shouldn't try the menu at this macrobiotic restaurant. Focusing on organic, grain-based food, this restaurant cooks up delicious, atypical meals like ravioli stuffed with creamy tofu and pesto (€8) or seitan escalope with grilled vegetables (€9). Depending on the dishes of the day, offerings include fresh fish, grain-based pasta, and even homemade ice cream.

i Directly off V. del Corso around P. di San Lorenzo in Lucina; turn right onto V. della Vite from V. del Corso and look for #14. Buzz and walk to 4th fl. Primi €8-9. Secondi €9-11. Lunch combo €8-10. Fixed vegetarian dinner €16. Dinner combo €20-25. Organic wine €12-16 per bottle. ☒ Open M-F 12:30-3pm and 7:30-10:30pm, Sa 7:30-10:30pm.

Jewish Ghetto

Most restaurants in this neighborhood are on **Via del Portico d'Ottavia,** and while some of the prices might force you into a real ghetto, they're a great alternative to classic Italian fare. Most restaurants are kosher and close early on Friday and Saturday.

▨ ANTICO FORNO DEL GHETTO
P. Costaguti 31

BAKERY, GROCERY $
☎06 68 80 30 12

A grocery store and a restaurant? Your love affair with food is going to get intense. Tell your significant other that you're going to be working late because Antico Forno del Ghetto will have you swooning. With large selections of fresh bread, smoked meat, mounds of olives, and yes, even pastries, you'll never want to leave. Pick up some fresh pizza, some fruits and vegetables to take home, and as many cannoli as you can fit in your embrace—and all of it at a price that will make you truly believe that love is sweet and kind.

i From Ponte Garibaldi, walk down V.Arenula, turn right onto V. di Santa Maria del Pianto, and continue into P. Costaguti. Only pizza and bread guaranteed kosher. Pizza and focacci €1.20-2 per slice, €7.70-9.70 per kg. Cash only. ☒ Open M-F 8am-2:30pm and 5-8pm, Sa-Su 8am-1pm.

LA TAVERNA DEL GHETTO
V. del Portico d'Ottavia 8

KOSHER $$$
☎06 68 80 97 71 www.latavernadelghetto.com

La Taverna del Ghetto might appear to be another one of the small, intimate Middle Eastern cafes that line the Jewish Ghetto. But this cafe has junk in the trunk when you check it out from behind. An enormous dining area and party space for all your kosher-loving friends, you'll get served—anything from fish to *fiori di zucca* (zucchini flowers) to your stomach's fill of fried artichoke. And just when you think you've had enough, La Taverna will bring out some ricotta pies and finish you off.

i From Teatro Marcello, walk down V. del Piscaro and veer right as it becomes V. del Portico d'Ottavia. Primi €12-14. Secondi €16-25. ☒ Open M-Th noon-11pm, F noon-4pm, Sa 9-11pm, Su noon-11pm.

KOSHER BISTROT CAFFÈ
CAFE, KOSHER $$$

V. Santa Maria del Pianto 68/69

☎06 68 64 398

Sleek glass counters, modern white bar stools, and a full display of delicious (and kosher!) meals—welcome to the ghetto. Here, Kosher Bistrot Caffè's flaky breads and pasta selections are what bring all the boys to the yard. Sprawl out on the spacious patio seating outside or choose the glassy and classy tables inside as you holla at some curry chicken with zucchini or a massive plate of *salumi*. Damn, it feels good to be a gangsta.

i From Ponte Garibaldi, walk up V. Arenula and turn right onto V. Santa Maria del Pianto. Primi €9-11. Secondi €8-9. Beer and wine €6-7. Cocktails €7-8. ☼ Open M-Th 9am-9pm, F 9am-sundown, Su 9am-9pm. Aperitivo 5-9pm.

Vatican City

The longest lines in Rome eventually become hungry crowds. The selection of neighborhood *trattorias* and small stores that lines the quiet streets outside the Vatican won't disappoint, but the bright English menus and beckoning waiters closer to the museums will.

◼ CACIO E PEPE
RISTORANTE $$

V. Giuseppe Avezzana 11

☎06 32 17 268 www.cacioepeperistorante.com

One does not name their restaurant after a single dish unless that dish is pretty damn good. Though it's a bit far from Vatican City (making it okay for us to swear, right?), Cacio e Pepe is worth the walk. Plenty of checkered tables and the friendly staff will welcome you in like the arms of St. Peter's Square. And you'll be converting to Pastafarianism while spaghetti is flying into your mouth if you order the main dish, *cacio e pepe* (fresh egg pasta topped with oil, grated cheese, and black pepper). So for some of the most delicious pasta in Rome (at quite affordable prices), come here.

i Ⓜ️A: Lepanto. From the metro, walk up V. Lepanto (away from the Vatican), turn right onto Vle. delle Millizie, then left onto V. Giuseppe Avezzana. Primi €8. Secondi €8-10. Cash only. ☼ Open M-F 12:30-3pm and 7:30-11:30pm, Sa 12:30-3pm.

◼ OLD BRIDGE GELATERIA
GELATERIA $

Vle. dei Bastioni di Michelangelo 5

☎06 38 72 30 26

This *gelateria* is as crowded as the Vatican Museums at noon, but the reward is just as sweet. Service is fast, prices are cheap, and portions are St. Peter's Basilica-sized (read: big). And we know guys and guides have lied to you about size before, but the €2 medium with three flavors that barely fit into your cup, all topped with copious amounts of whipped cream, will convert you into a believer. Flavors range from classic strawberry to mango to pistachio with ricotta. Delicious. God bless the Vatican.

i Off P. Risorgimento and across the street from the line to the Vatican Museums. Gelat €1.50-5. Frappes €2-3. Cash only. ☼ Open M-Sa 8am-2am, Su 3pm-2am.

FA BIO
CAFE, ORGANIC $

V. Germanico 43

☎06 64 52 58 10

Healthy is the new sexy. And even if this cafe's name refers to said healthy organic produce, all those freshly made sandwiches and fruit smoothies may be just what you need to attract a dreamy Italian. Or just a dreamy Italian sandwich with prosciutto, mozzarella, arugula, mustard, and olive oil. We consider that a delectable date. Try a drink for your health that's not red wine, like one of the fresh fruit smoothies, and then go against everything you stand for and order a salad.

i Ⓜ️A: Ottaviano. Walk down V. Ottaviano and turn left onto V. Germanico. Panini €4. Salads €4.50. Cookies €0.50-1. Fruit juices and smoothies €3.50. Cash only. ☼ Open in summer M-Sa 9am-8pm; in winter M-Sa 9am-5pm.

BROWN&CO.

V. Tacito 20

BAKERY $

☎06 32 35 133

Fresh fruit tarts, cream-filled croissants, warm cookies dipped in chocolate. Dare we say…heavenly? At this bakery, with its sleek wooden and glass counters, comfy white cushioned bar stools, and delicious selections of pastries, you should indulge a little. There are worse sins than gluttony. Try the creamy lemon tart topped with a fresh blueberry, or just get an entire tray full of your heart's desire of fruity and chocolate-covered goodness. It'll be the best €5-6 you'll ever spend, and they even wrap it up all fancy (even though you're probably just going to eat it all on a park bench a couple blocks down).

i Ⓜ️A: Lepanto. Walk down V. Ezio and continue straight as it becomes V. Tacito. Also sells basic groceries. No seating. Pizza €7-13 per kg. Cookies €9.50 per kg. Fruit and cream tarts €1.50 each. Cash only. ☼ Open M-Sa 8am-2:30pm and 4:30-8pm.

Trastevere

There are plenty of dining options in Trastevere, whether you want a luxurious sit-down meal, a bite on the go, or something in between. While the *piazze* are full of great choices, explore smaller side streets for some of the harder-to-find gems.

◪ LE FATE

Vle. Trastevere 130/134

RISTORANTE $$

☎06 58 00 971 www.lefaterestaurant.it

Once upon a time, there was a restaurant that gave students bruschetta, pasta, dessert, and a glass of wine all for €10. Fairy tale? Nope. Forget free will: go to Le Fate. Witchcraft, you may cry, but with a student ID, you'll be let into this fantastical world with cheap, delicious food and an atmosphere that can only be described as, well, magical. With fairies gracing the lamps, bramble and flashing lights on the ceiling, and even a hidden trap door we spotted a staff member slip down, live out that childhood dream to be in a fairy tale and run with woodland sprites. Have a bit more money to spend? The candlelit Le Fate is also a lovely and affordable place to take your date on a romantic evening without selling your soul to an evil sorceress. With its decent selection of wine, fresh homemade pasta, and ethereal ambient lighting, any visit to Le Fate will end with a happily ever after.

i About 15min. down Vle. Trastevere from P. G. Belli. Free Wi-Fi. Inquire about cooking classes and apartment rentals for students. Primi €9-12. Secondi €10-18. Cash only. ☼ Open daily 6-11pm.

◪ LA RENELLA

V. del Moro 15/16

PIZZERIA, BAKERY $

☎06 58 17 265

Walk into La Renella at any hour and you'll probably find a line of people waiting to buy food. While it may take you some hazy conversions to figure out the metric system as you stare at the menu, you'll soon come to know that the pizza is pretty cheap—and delicious. Watching everyone else get their slices before you will be a test of patience and endurance. Surrounded by kilograms, Italian speakers, and flyers for local events and sales, you'll also get a taste of a true Italian neighborhood eatery. And when you pass by the cookies and pies, you'll probably want to get a taste of their cherry pie as well.

i From P. Trilussa, walk down V. della Renella. Back entrance on V. del Politeama. Pizza €6-17 per kg. Sweet tortes and crostate €11-18 per kg. Biscotti €11-20 per kg. ☼ Open daily 7am-2am.

PIZZERIA DA SIMONE

V. Giacinto Carini 50

PIZZERIA, DELI $

☎06 58 14 980

Need some extra calories before you approach the summit of Gianicolo Hill? Stop by Pizzeria da Simone. Don't let the long line scare you away. Though Simone's is usually crowded, the staff works fast and will get you some delicious, hot pizza in no time. With anything from shrimp on your pizza to a wide selection of fresh pasta, you'll get it here and get it cheap. Due to the flocks of people who

rome

rush to this *pizzeria*, there's not much space to sit, so take your pizza with you and eat it sitting at the top of Gianicolo Hill. Or, if the temptation is too great, eat it on your way up.

i From the Porta San Pancrazio on Gianicolo Hill, walk downhill on V. Garibaldi, then take a left and follow V. Giancinto Carini for about 7min. Pizza €1.50-4 per slice, €7-17 per kg. Vegetables €12-17 per kg. Pasta €13-17 per kg. Cash only. ☒ Open M-Sa 7am-8:30pm.

CASETTA DI TRASTEVERE
RISTORANTE $$

P. de Renzi 31/32 ☎06 58 00 158

Clotheslines, checkered tablecloths, and plastic lawn chairs outside might remind you of home. While it's not the same as your mom cooking free meals for you, the food at Casetta di Trastevere is still pretty damn cheap (we'll put money in the swear jar later, Ma). With plenty of outdoor seating overlooking the trees and vines crawling up Trastevere's alleyways and the feeling of an old brick home inside, this place is a perfect spot to rest your tired feet. While it does attract quite a few tourists, you can't blame them, since the prices are good and so is the pizza. And if Italy has given you more than your fair share of pizza, order some bruschetta or pasta, also decently priced. So pull up your lawn chair, join the crowds, and feel at home with the dozens of strangers surrounding you.

i From P. Santa Maria in Trastevere, walk down V. di Piede until you hit V. della Pelliccia. P. de Renzi is just beyond. Pizza €3-6. Primi €5-8. Secondi €5-12. Desserts €3-5. Cash only. ☒ Open daily noon-11:30pm.

Termini and San Lorenzo

Termini and San Lorenzo are dominated by restaurants representing both extremes of the price range: cheap eats and overpriced tourist menus. Avoid restaurants near the station and head to the side streets for better options. Hostel dwellers with kitchen access should befriend the huge **SMA** grocery store on P. dell'Esquilino. (Open M-Sa 8am-9pm, Su 8:30am-8:30pm.)

▨ ANTICA PIZZERIA DE ROMA
PIZZERIA $

V. XX Settembre 41 ☎06 48 74 624

Pizza and video games are what made you a social butterfly in high school. Live out those glory days again at Antica Pizzeria de Roma, where you can order a slice of some of the cheapest pizza in the neighborhood and try out the arcade games in the corner. There's some seating against the wall facing a mirror, too, so you get to have a hot date to go along with your bargain price but still delicious pizza.

i From P. della Repubblica, walk down V. Vittorio Emanuele Orlando and turn right onto V. XX Settembre. Individual pizza €2.20-5.50, €0.70-2 per etto. Cash only. ☒ Open M-Sa 9:30am-9:30pm.

PASTICCERIA STRABBIONI ROMA
CAFE, BAKERY $

V. Servio Tullio 2 ☎06 48 72 027 www.strabbioni.it

If you thought your outfit today was vintage, wait until you see Pasticceria Strabbioni Roma. Opened in 1888, this cafe still rocks the hand-painted flowers on the ceiling and old-fashioned lamps like it's nobody's business. But what really makes this place stand out is its food. Order one of their sandwiches, or perhaps a freshly baked pastry will do. The *budino di riso*, a small rice pudding cake, is a specialty of theirs. And since drinking is a specialty of yours, order one of their cocktails. At €3.50-4 a drink, you can't afford not to.

i From Porta Pia, walk down V. XX Settembre and turn right onto V. Servio Tullio. There is also a sit-down restaurant down the street at V. Servio Tullio 8/10. Panini €3-5. Pastries €0.80-3. Cash only. ☒ Open M-Sa 7am-8pm.

FASSINO

CAFE, GELATERIA $

☎06 85 49 117

You've got class. But you've also got needs. Gelato needs. That's why you should step inside Fassino and understand what true luxury feels like. Not only will this cafe satisfy all your "covered in cocoa powder and in a fancy cup" gelato cravings, but they'll also take your beloved treat and reinvent it in all sorts of beautiful ways. Try the *brivido caldo* (gelato with a warm cookie in the center and topped with whipped cream) in the winter or the *cioccarancio* (dark chocolate and orange) in the summer. If you've come for lunch, the set menu (a crepe, drink, dessert, and coffee; €8.50) will make all your dreams come true, especially if you frequently dream about lunch.

i From the end of V. XX Settembre, turn left onto V. Piave and walk until you hit P. Fiume. Turn right onto V. Bergamo. Gelat €2-5. Brivido Caldo €3 (winter only). Cocktails €4.50-5. Cash only. ☼ Open M-F 8am-midnight, Sa-Su 4:30pm-1am.

RISTORANTE DA GIOVANNI

V. Antonio Salandra 1A

RISTORANTE $$

☎06 48 59 50

With a giant sign hanging out over the street corner, Ristorante Da Giovanni makes sure that underground doesn't mean hidden. Follow the lanterns down the stairs and past some old typewriters into this family-owned restaurant, where your hip vintage outfit will perfectly complement the old posters and handwritten menu. The restaurant can thank you later. But first try some of their homemade classic dishes, like the fettuccine, roast veal, or *cacio e pepe*, and admire the recipes that have been in use for over 50 years.

i From P. della Repubblica, walk up V. Vittorio Emanuele Orlando, turn right onto V. XX Settembre, then left onto V. Antonio Salandra. Primi €6-7. Secondi €5-14. ☼ Open M-Sa noon-3pm and 7-10:30pm.

Northern Rome

Because Northern Rome is primarily residential, dining out tends to be pricey. Your best bet is to pack a picnic and eat it in one of the lovely gardens.

STAROCIA LUNCH BAR

V. Sicilia 121

CAFE $

☎06 48 84 986

Starocia Lunch Bar is a great place to make up for all those calories you lost walking in the Villa Borghese. And you might as well make up for future calories you were going to lose anyway. With enormous portions of panini or pasta and anything from cocktails to coffee, Starocia's will be sure to leave you with enough calories to last at least until happy hour at 6pm. And with its modern, black-and-white decor and sleek bar stools, this cafe turned bar at night will take you away from the classically themed villas and galleries you've been visiting and help you fit in with that young, hip crowd that comes in after lunchtime for drinks.

i Walking south on V. Po (away from the Villa Borghese) and turn right onto V. Sicilia. Tramezzini and panini €1.60-3.50. Pasta and secondi €4-7. Coffee €1-2. Cocktails €5-6. Happy hour buffet €4, with wine €6. Cash only. ☼ Open M-Sa 5:15am-9:30pm. Happy hour M-Sa 6pm.

TREE BAR

V. Flaminia 226

CAFE $$

☎06 32 65 27 54

Your wanderings on the concrete desert of V. Flaminia seem endless. The sun beats down, your water supply is running out, and the trams have scared away your camel. Then a little green oasis filled with your dreams of delicious pasta and countless wine options rises up through the haze: you've reached Tree Bar. With wooden panels and glass, this tree house, inspired by Japanese architecture, is a sight for weary travelers. Jazzy music blasts out as crowds gather on the patio to eat dinner or grab a drink as children play soccer in the nearby plaza. Sheltered by trees and park benches, this is a perfect place to stop for a drink or some fettuccine while reminiscing about that tree house you never actually had.

i Ⓜ️B: Flaminio. Walk about 25min. up V. Flaminia or take tram #2 to Belle Arti. Primi and secondi €4-15. Beer €3-5. Wine €5-7. 🕓 Open M 6pm-2am, Tu-Su 10:30am-2am.

IL MARGUTTA RISTORARTE
V. Margutta 118

VEGETARIAN $$

☎06 32 65 05 77 www.ilmargutta.it

Being vegetarian (or vegan!) is so in right now. Il Margutta RistorArte completely agrees. Unleash your artsy side by dining in what is practically a modern art museum filled with comfy black couches and white tablecloths to accommodate all your non-meat needs. Anything from detox teas to delicious pastas is available at this enormous restaurant, which takes up almost an entire block. Its colorful paintings, fancy decor, and tempting dishes will make anyone consider being vegetarian—even if it's just for one meal. .

i Ⓜ️A: Flaminio. From Ple. Flaminia, walk into P. del Popolo and veer left onto V. del Babuino. Walk 5min. and turn left onto the small alley street, V. Margutta. Primi €10-12. Secondi €10-15. 🕓 Open daily 12:30-3:30pm and 7-11:30pm.

Testaccio and Ostiense

Testaccio is known among Roman residents as one of the city's best spots for high-quality, reasonably priced food. Its location farther from the sights means fewer tourists have caught on. Whether you want an upscale restaurant or a cheap trattoria, you'll have no trouble finding it here.

🔖 IL NOVECENTO
V. dei Conciatori 10

RISTORANTE $$$

☎06 57 25 04 45 www.9cento.com

Homemade? Bitch, please. Il Novecento will change your perception of homemade family food. Step inside the dark wood paneled restaurant, past the dressers and bookshelves, and you'll find yourself right at home. If your home is full of delicious Italian food being made right before your very eyes, that is. With cooks rolling out pizza dough and cutting up pasta, your delicate art of making PB&Js may pale in comparison. But it's okay. Your family might not be a line of cooks, but you do specialize in eating pizza and roasted meats—a perfect match of skill sets here.

i Ⓜ️B: Piramide. Walk down V. Ostiense and turn right onto V. dei Conciatori. Pizza €5-9. Primi €9-10. Secondi €12-18. 🕓 Open M-F 12:30-2:30pm and 7:30-11pm, Sa-Su 7:30-11pm.

🔖 FARINANDO
V. Lucca della Robbia 30

PIZZERIA, BAKERY $

☎06 57 50 674

You can twerk those calories away at night. Right now, you need some cookies, and Fairinando can help with that. With everything from pastries dripping in chocolate to coconut macaroons to cookies filled with fruity jams whose names that one Italian lesson you saw on YouTube didn't cover. If you're craving something more like pizza, well, have the pizza. Loaded with toppings and fired in a huge wood-burning oven, the pies here make it easy to indulge yourself here. Remember, you still live in a world dictated by #yolo.

i Ⓜ️B: Piramide. Walk up V. Marmorata. Turn left onto V. Galvani and right onto V. Lucca della Robbia. Calzone €3. Pizza tonda €4-6, €7-16 per kg. Pastries €16-22 per kg. 🕓 Open M-F 8am-2:10pm and 4:30-8:30pm, Sa 5-9pm.

LA MAISON DE L'ENTRECÔTE
P. Gazometro 1

RISTORANTE, ENOTECA $$$

☎06 57 43 091 www.lamaisondelentrecote.it

So it's not what you expected when your date said he'd take you to Paris for dinner. But it's good enough. With a bohemian Paris theme, Le Maison's stained glass lamps, French music, and vintage mirrors will carry you away to a time and place you secretly don't know anything about. But you do know about eating, and the classic French dishes, such as cheesy onion soup, paired with Italian gnocchi will have you falling in love with the food (if not with your date). Guys are great, but trust us—transnational desserts like the *crema* gelato topped with Grand Marnier are better.

i Ⓜ*B: Ostiense. Walk down V. Marmorata away from Piramide for 5min. and turn right onto P. Gazometro. Salad €5-7. Primi €8-10. Meats €7-15. Beer €4. Cocktails €6. Wine by the bottle €12-16. Cash only.* Ⓐ *Open Tu-Th 1-3pm and 8pm-midnight, F-Sa 8pm-midnight.*

OSTERIA DEGLI AMICI
V. Nicola Zabaglia 25

RISTORANTE $$$

☎06 57 81 466 www.osteriadegliamici.info

It's okay. You don't really need *amici*. All you need is some of Osteria degli Amici's hot saffron risotto sprinkled with smoked Scamorza cheese and drizzled in balsamic vinegar. Served in an old-fashioned restaurant, with those wooden chairs, black and white photos, and arched doors that make everything look old-fashioned, this restaurant can be your new best friend with its delicious pasta, large wine selection, and chocolate soufflés for dessert. Friendship is sweet.

i Ⓜ*B: Piramide. Walk up V. Marmorata, turn right onto V. Luigi Vanvitelli, and turn left onto V. Nicola Zabaglia. Primi €7-9. Secondi €12-18.* Ⓐ *Open W-Su 12:30-3pm and 7:30pm-midnight.*

Southern Rome

▨ LI RIONI
V. dei Santi Quattro 24

PIZZERIA $$

☎06 70 45 06 05

So you're something of a pizza connoisseur. We get it. We won't just send you to cheap *pizzerias* that you'll probably drunkenly stumble into later anyway. So head over to Li Rione. Open only for dinner (or, you know, a really, really late brunch), this place, much like you, specializes in pizza. With dishes like the *prato fiorito* pizza (made with fresh mozzarella, mushrooms, peas, sausage, egg, and olives) served out on the patio or inside the large interior with 19th-century photographs, you can admire black-and-white pictures of the Colosseum while using your refined tastes to judge the pizza you're devouring.

i Ⓜ*B: Colosseo. Take V. Nicola Salvi to V. Labicana. Turn right at P. San Clemente and walk to V. dei Santi Quattro. Pizza €4.80-8.* Ⓐ *Open M 7:30pm-midnight, W-Su 7pm-midnight.*

OSTERIA IL BOCCONCINO
V. Ostilia 23

RISTORANTE $$$

☎06 77 07 91 75 www.ilbocconcino.com

An entrance lined with awards and amphorae. What's not to love? Serving up classics using seasonal ingredients, Osteria Il Bocconcino will have you feeling nostalgic for those old Roman times you never actually knew. Rustic wooden chairs, vines lining the doorway, and classic dishes like *rigatoni alla carbonara*, *polpette con sedano e cannella* (meatballs with celeriac and cinnamon) will have you feeling like an emperor. The amphorae outside might be for show, but after eating here, you'll realize that the awards are not.

i Ⓜ*B: Colosseo. Follow P. del Colosseo around to V. di San Giovanni in Laterano and turn right onto V. Ostilia. Primi €8-12. Secondi €11-14.* Ⓐ *Open M-Tu 12:30-3:30pm and 7:30-11:30pm, Th-Su 12:30-3:30pm and 7:30-11:30pm.*

L'ARCHEOLOGIA
V. Appia Antica 139

RISTORANTE $$$$

☎06 78 80 494 www.larcheologia.it

You're on the Appian Way and your wagon hasn't fallen into a ditch yet. Time to celebrate. Unfortunately, unlike your pickup lines, nothing is cheap here. But at L'Archeologia, located at an ancient post station for horses, you can exchange your physical and intellectual hunger for some dinner served with a side of history. Located next to a mausoleum and above an ancient wine cellar (jeepers!), enjoy the ancient sites while dining on anything from fresh prawn to

rome

sirloin steak, which is indeed expensive, but it's served in what special style? The Appian Way! (Cue pity laughter.)

i Take bus #118 to the San Sebastiano stop. L'Archeologia is on the corner of V. Appia Antica and Vicolo della Basilica. Primi €13-16. Secondi €15-28. ☑ Open M 12:30-3pm and 8-11pm, W-Su 12:30-3pm and 8-11pm.

NIGHTLIFE

Don't spend all your money and energy at the museums—Rome's nightlife is varied and vast, giving you a whole separate itinerary to attack after the guards go home and the cats come out to prowl the ruins. Enoteche (wine bars, often with *apertivi*), which cater to those seeking high-quality drinks and low-key conversation, are especially prevalent in the Ancient City and Centro Storico. Irish pubs and American-style bars populate Trastevere, busy *corsi*, and the areas surrounding Termini. Upscale lounges are common around Piazza di Spagna, while anyone looking to rage should head to the discos in Testaccio. If the weather is warm, it's easy to avoid cover fees and pricey cocktails by simply heading to the many busy *piazze*.

Ancient City

The Ancient Romans might have been known for bacchanalian orgies, but these days the wine bars that crowd the streets of Ancient City are Bacchus's only heirs. These upscale places rarely reach orgasmic levels, but Irish pubs provide rowdier options.

SCHOLAR'S LOUNGE   IRISH PUB
V. del Plebiscito 101B   ☎06 69 20 22 08 www.scholarsloungerome.com

You're an intellectual. So when you need to get schwasted, you do the smart thing and go to Scholar's Lounge. Irish flags, a wooden interior, and nine enormous TVs make this the famous and rowdy bar in the area. Always packed and open late, Scholar's is the place to head when all the other bars close at 2am and you still need to get your Thirsty Sunday going (just in time for karaoke!). Join all the studious students here, admire the impressive whiskey list, and drink up. You have brain cells to spare.

i From P. Venezia, follow V. del Plebiscito to the intersection with V. del Corso. Karaoke Tu and Su. Live music Th-F. Student shot €1. Pints €4-6. Cocktails €8-10; during the day €5; student cocktails €5. ☑ Open daily 11am-3:30am. Happy hour until 8pm.

▨ LIBRERIA CAFFÈ BOHEMIEN   CAFE
V. degli Zingari 36   ☎33 97 22 46 22

And sometimes you are actually an intellectual. So when you need to discuss the intricacies of that Dickens novel you never finished, head to Libreria Caffè Bohemien. With dim lighting, chandeliers, a piano, and rows of bookshelves, this lounge is the perfect place to whip out your MacBook or to curl up on one of the Victorian couches with a glass of wine in hand. Enjoy the ambiance, the indie rock playing, and that hipster pride that comes with spending an elegant evening indoors while your peers make questionable life decisions in Campo di Fiori.

i Ⓜ B: Cavour. From V. Cavour, turn right onto P. degli Zingari and left onto V. degli Zingari. Beer €3-5. Cocktails €5-6. Appetizers €6-10. Aperitivo buffet €8; with drink purchase €3. ☑ Open M 6pm-2am, W-Su 6pm-2am. Aperitivo buffet 7-9pm.

CAVOUR 313   ENOTECA
V. Cavour 313   ☎06 67 54 96 www.cavour313.it

Colosseum put you in a classy mood? Hit up Cavour 313. With over 100 varieties of wine and delicious meat plates ranging from hot salami to fish in olive oil, this place was made to cater to your classy needs. Act knowledgeable about wine and order the gorgonzola cheese with honey and the sweet Marsala wine (they complement each other!) or go for one of the savory meat plates with smoked hams, sun-dried tomatoes, and olives. The wooden booths offer more privacy than regular bars, so you can engage in whatever conversation classy people have (we're guessing Trajan Column penis jokes).

i Halfway up V. Cavour coming from V. dei Fori Imperiali. Wine €3.50-8. Meat plates €8-10. Mixed cheese plates €8-12. ☼ Open M-Sa 12:30-3:30pm and 7pm-midnight.

FINNEGAN PUB
BAR

V. Leonina 66 ☎06 47 47 026 www.finneganpub.com

A rowdy Irish pub complete with a pool table, flat screen TVs, and drafts starting a €3—welcome home, expats. With a ceiling lined with international currency bills that are just out of your reach and walls with sports jerseys, people come here for two things: alcohol and sports. If you want less rowdy fun, come earlier in the evening to sip a Corona on the patio outside. But later at night, get ready for a drunken crowd who down their beers and spirits, but no cocktails—real Irishmen always drink it straight.

i Ⓜ B: Cavour. Walk up V. Leonina. Live music F. Wine €3-5.50. Drafts €3-6. Spirits €4-6.50. Cash only. ☼ Open M-Th 1pm-12:30am, F-Su noon-1am.

Centro Storico

The Centro Storico may be old, but it packs in a young crowd at night. One of the best places to find bars and clubs, this area remains busy into the early hours of the morning. If you don't feel like hunkering down somewhere inside, spend the evening in the **Campo dei Fiori.**

MOOD
CLUB

C. Vittorio Emanuele II 205 ☎06 68 80 86 19

You can't spend every night with that ass on a barstool. Sometimes you just gotta twerk. So when you're in the mood to shake it like a polaroid picture, head on over to Mood. Accompanied by flashing lights, comfy lounges, cheap drinks, and incredible DJs, you'll be able to dance the night away listening to anything from Eiffel 64 and Daft Punk to Nicki Minaj and Usher. The club gets pretty packed after 1am, so there'll be no shortage of witnesses as you school everyone in the true art of breaking it down at one of the hottest clubs in the area.

i From Campo dei Fiori, take P. della Cancelleria to C. Vittorio Emanuele II and turn left; Mood is on the right. Shots for women €2. Beer €5. Cocktails €7. 2 drinks for €10 or open bar €15 until 1am. ☼ Open Tu-Su 11pm-4am.

SALOTTO 42
BAR

P. di Pietra 42 ☎06 67 85 804 www.salotto42.it

Black and white floral decor, artsy magazines, and a Buddha head next to some bottles of vodka: welcome to Salotto 42. A swanky but still hip and enlightened bar near Hadrian's Temple, this is where an older crowd comes to help their butts find nirvana on the most comfortable bar stools ever. Drinks are served with flowers in them (free snack!), and you can sip them while talking about all those important things in life, like karma, religion, and that topical reality show everyone loves.

i From the Pantheon, turn right onto V. di Pastini and veer left toward the Tempio Adriano. Beer €6. Cocktails €10. Free buffet with drink purchase during aperitivo. ☼ Open M-Sa 10am-2am, Su 10am-midnight. Aperitivo daily 7:30-9pm.

DRUNKEN SHIP
BAR, CLUB

Campo dei Fiori 20/21 ☎06 68 30 05 35 www.drunkenship.com

College parties? Please, you majored and minored in Partying 101. So come hell or high water, you're ready to steer the Drunken Ship. Made for all you nostalgic college-kids-at-heart, this bar caters to a rowdy, predominantly American crowd ready to watch the Yankees on TV or play some beer pong on the tables. With great deals every night (like 2-for-1 Tuesdays), grab a drink, sit on the Heineken

rome

bar stools, and listen to drunk American girls try to explain "Ms. New Booty" to the Italians who occasionally stop by.

i In Campo dei Fiori. Student discounts nightly.½-price drinks for women M-Th until 11pm. Buy 1 drink get 1 free Tu until 11pm. Shots €3-6. Long drinks €6. Cocktails €7. Happy hour pint of wine with free buffet €4. ☺ Open M-Th 3pm-2am, F-Sa 10am-2am, Su 3pm-2am. Happy hour M-F 4-8pm.

ABBEY THEATRE
IRISH PUB

V. del Governo Vecchio 51/53   ☎06 68 61 341 www.abbey-rome.com

Sure, you've seen a lot of saints in Italy, but don't forget to pay St. Patrick a visit while you're here. Complete with W. B. Yeats painted on the wall, Abbey Theatre Irish pub will have you wondering if you've gotten your flags mixed up and are actually on the Emerald Isle. With a wooden interior, bar food, and multiple rooms where you can listen to live music, Abbey Theatre is a perfect place to catch the latest sports game or just sit and talk to your friends over a glass of "mixed beer" (try the hard cider and grenadine, €5.50). This enormous pub will have you embracing that Celtic blood you're pretty sure you have in you.

i From P. Navona, exit onto P. Pasquina and continue as it becomes V. del Governo Vecchio. Check the website for weekly specials. Shot €4-5. Beer €4-6.50. Cocktails €7-8. ☺ Open daily noon-2am. Happy hour daily 3-8pm.

ARISTOCAMPO
BAR

Campo dei Fiori 30

For all those nights when you just can't make it two more steps into Campo dei Fiore, stop right at Aristocampo's doorstep. Don't feel too lazy—you'll be in good company here, as this bar and restaurant attracts large crowds of Italian and international students to its huge patio outside. Drink some cocktails, order a freshly made panini, and listen to the loud music blasting from the bar. It's a good place to sit down and enjoy the company of all those friends you have (popular, much?), but if you'd rather scream and shout and let it all out, head further into Campo dei Fiore and join the rowdy rascals in their drunken revelry.

i In Campo dei Fiori. Beer €5-6. Cocktails €7. Panini €5. Salads €8. Aperitivo drink and buffet €7. ☺ Open daily noon-2am. Aperitivo daily 6-8:30pm.

Piazza di Spagna

There's a reason the Spanish Steps are so popular at night, and it's not because they're pretty. Young travelers seeking nightlife in this neighborhood are wise to lounge on the steps rather than pay €15 for drinks and music at the nearby lounges. The few options here will all do damage to your bank account, so unless you've just hit it big in Monaco, try another neighborhood for nighttime entertainment.

HIGHLANDER PUB
IRISH PUB

Vicolo di San Biagio 9   ☎06 68 80 53 68 www.highlanderome.com

With a kilt-wearing, bagpipe-playing mascot, Highlander lets you know this isn't one of Rome's Irish pubs. Welcome to Scotland. Popular with the international students in the area, this pub, with its dark wooden bar and large flat screen TVs, keeps a schedule of NHL, NBA, and all those other acronymed sports posted so you and your friends can always catch the big game. And with plenty of beers on tap, ranging from Guinness to the Italian Poretti, you'll have no problem getting rowdy and a little tipsy here.

i Ⓜ A: Spagna. From the Spanish Steps, walk down V. dei Condotti, which becomes V. Fontanella di Borghese. When it becomes Largo Fontanella di Borghese, turn left onto V. della Lupa. Highlander is on the corner with Vicolo di San Biagio. Offers free tours of Rome daily at 5pm. Ladies' Night on Tu. College Night on Th. Draft beer €4-6. Cocktails €6-7. Wine €5-8. Cash only. ☺ Open M-Th 5pm-2am, F-Sa 12:30pm-2am, Su 5pm-2am.

ANTICA ENOTECA DI VIA DELLA CROCE ENOTECA
V. della Croce 76B ☎06 67 90 896

You can't work hard and play hard every day. Save those rowdier nights for tomorrow. Take a vacation from your weekend and head to this charming, rustic enoteca. With high ceilings, twisted iron bookshelves, wooden tables and bar, and plenty of wine bottles, this enormous space is usually full in the evenings with people sipping wine and quietly discussing their love for wine and quiet discussions.

i Ⓜ️A: Spagna. From the Spanish Steps, walk down V. della Croce. Beer €5. Cocktails €8. Wine €4-10 per glass. Antipasti platters €14-16. Primi €9-10. Secondi €12-24. Pizza €9-12. 🕐 Open daily 11am-1am.

Trastevere

Trastevere is home to some of the best nightlife in the city. American college kids, people inexplicably walking dogs at midnight, Italian teens, and connected-at-the-mouth couples intermingle in the streets with no apparent destinations. With so many great places to choose from, why make a plan? The **Piazza Trilussa,** right over the Ponte Sisto, is a great starting point.

D.J. BAR BAR, CLUB
Vicolo del Cinque 60 ☎338 85 98 578

You always wanted to get closer to those Roman boys. Well, here at the tiny D.J. Bar, you can! Though it barely takes up a street corner, you'll always know where to find this bar thanks to the enormous crowd of people outside. This is only a fraction of the throng inside, though, so you'll have to fight your way through to order a drink as the DJs blast "Teach Me How to Dougie" from their platform above (NB: most people here might not speak English, but they all know how to Dougie). The drinks are good, the music is loud, and although there isn't much space to dance, you'll get to see people drink entire bowls of alcohol and scream all the words to Flo Rida's "Low," and sometimes after a long week, that's all you need.

i From P. Santa Maria in Trastevere, veer into P. San Egidio and turn right onto Vicolo del Cinque. Shot €3. Beer €5. Cocktails €7-8. Cash only. 🕐 Open daily 5pm-2am. Happy hour F-Sa 7-10pm.

BACCANALE BAR
V. della Lungaretta 81 ☎06 45 44 82 68

No maenads raving or Bacchic revelry here—at Baccanale, blaring Bon Jovi and cheap beer will suffice. As a fairly low-key bar, this is the place for older couples coming in for dinner or groups of students looking for a cheap drink. By no means seeking to impress the Council of the Gods, the small but well-stocked Baccanale offers outdoor seating, fast service, and rows of foreign money hanging from the ceiling, paying homage to its international student population. Whether you're alighting from Olympus for a sandwich or a quick drink, Baccanale will not disappoint.

i From Vle. Trastevere, turn right onto V. della Lungaretta. Beer €3-5. Cocktails €5-7. 🕐 Open Tu-Su 11am-2am.

CAFÉ FRIENDS BAR, CLUB
P. Trilussa 34 ☎06 58 16 111 www.cafefriends.it

By day, Café Friends serves out a full breakfast and lunch in its brightly lit, tropical-colored dining area. But by night, its swanky and sleek bar at the front becomes the main attraction, especially for the international student crowd. With special drinks like the Zombie (rum, Jamaicano, cherry brandy, orange juice, and lime; €8) and a large lounge area and patio, you'll find large groups of

rome

friends (like the cafe's name! we get it!) lounging about while the music blasts on until the early morning.

i From Ponte Sisto, head into P. Trilussa. Free Wi-Fi. Beer €4-5.50. Cocktails €8. Aperitivo drinks €6-8. 15% discount for international students with ID. ☒ Open daily 7am-2am. Aperitivo daily 7-9pm.

GOOD
BAR, CAFE

V. di Santa Dorotea 8/9   ☎06 97 27 79 79

Bookshelves lined with bottles of wine and Jack—somehow Good has turned even this college staple from your dorm into a classy affair. With swanky music playing, candlelit tables, and elaborately colorful chandeliers, Good is the romantically warm and friendly bar that is popular with the post-graduate crowd. While the bartenders might still rock the plaid shirt over a Captain America tank top, most of the clientele for the week is older couples coming in for a drink, some food, and a chance to hear live jazz. Right on.

i From P. San G. de Matha, take V. di Santa Dorotea as it veers left. Free Wi-Fi. Beer €5-8. Cocktails €9. Happy hour drinks €8. ☒ Open M-Sa 8am-2am, Su 8:30am-2am. Happy hour daily 6:30-9:30pm.

Termini and San Lorenzo

Termini and San Lorenzo have two very different nightlife scenes. Dozens of bars near Termini's hostels cater primarily to international travelers with drink specials and loud dance music. San Lorenzo, on the other hand, is near the university and thus popular with artsy, 20-something Italians. Late-night bookstores, laid-back bars, and pulsing clubs litter the otherwise quiet neighborhood, so the best tactic is to follow the people until you find a place that looks interesting.

AI TRE SCALINI
CAFE, ENOTECA

V. Panisperna 251   ☎06 48 90 74 95 www.aitrescalini.org

Nothing says wild Friday night like wicker chairs and fake grapes hanging on the walls. Don't expect any ragers from this older crowd, but if you want the best place to sit around and talk about how much you love wine, hit up Ai Tre Scalini. A small enoteca, you'll fine only wine glasses (no shots here) in the hands of this crowd as they spill out the vine-covered doorway onto the street. Very popular among locals, it's a lovely little bar with frescoed walls and warm lighting to spend a relaxing Thursday night in before you continue your love affair with vodka later this weekend.

i From the intersection of V. XXIV Maggio and V. Nazionale (near Trajan's column), walk up V. Panisperna. Free Wi-Fi. 10% discount at lunch. Beer €3-5. Wine €4.50-6 per glass; €12-70 per bottle. Sfizi (bite-sized appetizers) €2.50-3. Primi €6-13. ☒ Open M-F noon-1am, Sa-Su 6pm-1am.

SOLEACLUB
BAR

V. dei Latini 51   ☎328 92 52 925

The mismatched cushions and orange curtains might make the sassy gay friend in you cry out murder, but hey €1 shots. Guess you can put up with it. With great drink specials advertised on the chalkboard outside and an artsy university crowd inside, live out those drunken hipster dreams you have while rocking out to Bowie. Though it might be a bit removed from Termini, that just makes it less mainstream(ergo, so hipster).

i Tram #3 or 19. Or Ⓜ Termini. Follow traffic down V. Marsala and turn left onto V. dei Ramni. Turn right onto V. dei Luceri, then right onto V. dei Sabelli; Solea Club is on the corner of V. dei Sabelli and V. dei Latini. Beer €3-5. Wine €4.50. Cocktails and shots €5.50. Cash only. ☒ Open daily 9pm-3am.

7SETTE CL.   BAR, CLUB

V. degli Aurunci 35   ☎06 97 61 24 28 www.7cl.it

It might be a long walk from your hostel in Termini, but with its extra long *aper-itivo* (6-10pm; buffet free with drink purchase), 7sette cl. will wait. After kicking back a few drinks, this dimly-lit bar with purple walls transforms into one of the better discos in the area, with live music and DJs spinning house. A large lounge area with sleek bar stools and couches also welcomes you in to sit and ponder the important questions in life. Like how exactly one would pronounce the name of this bar.

i Tram #3 or 19. Or Ⓜ*Termini. Follow traffic down V. Marsala and turn left onto V. dei Ramni. Turn right onto V. dei Luceri and then left onto V. dei Sabelli. Continue into the piazza and, with the church behind you, turn right onto V. degli Aurunci. Art and cinema night on M. Theme night on Tu. Live music on W and Th. DJ on F and Sa. Salsa and swing on Su. Beer €3-5. Wine €4-5. Cocktails and shots €5-7. Cash only. ☒ Open M-Th 3pm-2am, F-Sa 3pm-4am, Su 3pm-2am.*

YELLOW BAR   CAFE, BAR

V. Palestro 40   ☎06 49 38 26 82 www.the-yellow.com

Nothing cures American homesickness like a **Chuck Norris Roundhouse Kick to the Face Crazy Shot** (don't ask what's in it, just drink up). Catering to the young international crowd (hey, that's you!), this bar is always filled with a younger generation sitting out on the patio or at the sleek wooden bar on leather seats that get comfier as you get tipsier. With a giant Corona bottle by the entrance, music blasting, and a beer pong room (only for the hostel-dwellers) located downstairs, this famous hostel bar will cure any longings for America, especially with its full American breakfast that you can try to stomach the morning after.

i Ⓜ*Termini. From V. Marsala, near track 1, walk down V. Marghera and turn left onto V. Palestro. Pub quiz on €5. Open bar on F €15. Cocktails €8. Pitchers €15. Happy hour spirits €2.50; wine €1.50. ☒ Open daily 7:30am-2am. Kitchen open 7:30am-noon. Happy hour 3-9pm.*

Northern Rome

Near the cluster of hostels around Termini, **Via Nomentana** is a great option for those who want to venture a bit farther from their hostel. Good bars and *discoteche* are always popping up. Bars are the best year-round option.

NEW AGE CAFÉ   BAR, CAFE

V. Nizza 23

In an area without many bars, New Age Café stands out with its neon lights, top 40 hits, and the line of Vespas parked outside. Catering to mostly an older crowd that comes in for beer or coffee, this bar serves everything from alcohol to pastries to even Gatorade (in case you've just run up the not-so-well-lit street). With an interior balcony, outdoor seating, and bar stools lined up by the window, this bar takes in a decent number of people before getting too crowded, but watch out for nights with football (read: soccer) games. It's not blood sport, but it still makes Romans rowdy.

i From P. Fiume, walk down V. Nizza. Shot €3. Draft beer €5-6. Cocktails €7. Lunch panini and primi €4-6. Cash only. ☒ Open daily 7am-2am. Aperitivo daily 6:30-9:30pm.*

BÒEME   CLUB

V. Velletri 14   ☎06 84 12 212 www.boeme.it

Go down the rabbit hole at Bòeme, and you'll enter a world with dizzying black-and-white walls, elaborately Baroque chairs, and yes, a dance club that lets you party *all* night. Take an extended tea break before hitting this club, since doors don't even open until 11pm. Despite the late start, you'll get your money's worth with top 40 hits on blast until 5am. The crowd is a little grungy, so be prepared to see a lot of camouflage pants and hoodies. And most importantly, know that this wonderland is in a dark area with mostly deserted concrete buildings, so be sure to bring friends along to avoid sketchy encounters with the Cheshire Cat on your way home.

i *From P. Fiume, walk up V. Nizza and turn left onto V. Velletri. Cover €15-20, includes 1st drink. Drinks €10. ☒ Open F-Sa 11pm-5am.*

Testaccio and Ostiense

Locals who've sought out the best clubs head to Testaccio and Ostiense for big nights out. The strip of clubs, restaurants, and lounges surrounding **Via di Monte Testaccio** begs to be explored. The streets closer to the train station tend to have smaller, low-key establishments that stay open late and are a good option if you don't feel like heavy-duty clubbing.

▧ AKAB   CLUB
V. di Monte Testaccio 69   ☎06 57 25 05 85 www.akabcave.com

You're not in Rome as a tourist. You're here to werk it. So when wine bars and chitchat have got you down, hit up one of Rome's hottest nightclubs. An enormous dance space with flashing lights and occasional confetti thrown in your face, Akab is the go-to disco in this area. The cover charge might be high, but you'll be surrounded by large speakers, energetic DJs, and huge crowds who understand how to shut up and dance. And sometimes that's all you really want.

i Ⓜ*B: Piramide. Walk up V. Marmorata toward the river, turn left onto V. Galvani, and veer left onto V. di Monte Testaccio. Electronic music on Tu. House on Th. Rock on F. Commercial and house on Sa. Cover €10-20; includes 1 drink. Cocktails and beer €10. ☒ Open Tu 11:30pm-4:30am, Th-Sa 11:30pm-4:30am.*

▧ COYOTE   BAR, CLUB
V. di Monte Testaccio 48B   ☎340 24 45 874 www.coyotebar.it

And everyone laughed when you brought cowboy boots to Rome. Little did they know that Italians have a thing for the Wild West, and here at Coyote, they're all about the faux-mud brick patio decked-out in Christmas lights and US license plates along the walls. Amurica! With a beautiful location on a rooftop overlooking Testaccio and DJs spinning house and Latin music well into the night, this club is a favorite for locals who stay here until they can live out that real American cowboy dream to drunkenly stumble off into a sunrise.

i Ⓜ*B: Piramide. Walk up V. Marmorata toward the river, turn left onto V. Galvani, and veer left onto V. di Monte Testaccio. Cover F-Sa after midnight €10. Beer and wine €5. Cocktails €8. ☒ Open daily 9pm-5am.*

TOP FIVE   RISTORANTE, BAR
V. di Monte Testaccio 48   ☎06 57 45 453 www.topfivebar.it

Nothing says American bar like *A Clockwork Orange* posters, Spock paintings, and English graffiti on the bar counter. So while you're here, fill up on American nostalgia and some panini and drinks. There's plenty of seating and service is fast, so you can always satisfy your late-night pizza cravings and early morning breakfast calls at this bar before venturing out into club-lined streets of Testaccio again. Because you didn't choose this clubbing life; it chose you.

i Ⓜ*B: Piramide. Walk up V. Marmorata toward the river, turn left onto V. Galvani, and veer left onto V. di Monte Testaccio. Beer €4-6. Cocktails €8. Happy hour shots and beer €4; cocktails €6. Food €2-8. ☒ Open Tu-Su 8pm-5am. Happy hour 8:30-11pm.*

ARTS AND CULTURE

"Arts and culture," you ask, "isn't that Rome itself?" Well, yes—Renaissance paintings, archaeological ruins, and Catholic churches do count. But aside from these antiquated lures, Rome offers entertainment that makes it much more than a city of yore. Soccer games might not quite compared to man-fights-lion spectacles, but with hundreds of screaming Italians around, it comes close.

ALEXANDERPLATZ JAZZ CLUB

V. Ostia 9 and Villa Celimontana   ☎06 39 74 21 71 www.alexanderplatz.it

One of Rome's most popular jazz clubs and Italy's oldest, the Alexanderplatz Jazz Club operates in a hideout-like basement in the winter months for all your underground jazzy needs. Host to many famous musicians, enjoy the daily jazz as you decipher the multilingual scrawled notes that artists such as Stefano Bollani and Joshua Redman have left behind on the walls. In June, the jazz moves outside to the beautiful Villa Celimontana in the Ancient City.

i Ⓜ️A: Ottaviano. Exit on V. Barletta and turn right onto Vle. delle Milizie, then turn left onto V. Tolemaide. Turn right onto V. Ostia. For summer concerts at Villa Celi, Ⓜ️B: Colosseo. Follow V. Nicola Salvi and veer right onto Vle. del Parco del Celio. Then veer left onto V. Claudia, which becomes V. Navicella. Membership €15 per month, €45 per year. ⌚ Open daily 8pm-2am. Shows M-Th 9:45pm, F-Sa 10:30pm, Su 9:45pm. Happy hour 7-8:30pm.

TEATRO NAZIONALE

V. del Viminale 51or 06 48 17 003   ☎06 48 161 www.operaroma.it

Forget Neoclassical architecture—Teatro Nazionale's more modern building is lacking chandeliers and frescoes but still has state-of-the-art acoustics and is one of Rome's beloved opera houses. With the ubiquitous ads for its operas plastering the metro and the streets, curiosity alone might drive you here, while the affordable prices will make you stay and soak in that culture you came to Rome to discover. From June 30 to early fall, additional performances are held outdoors at the beautiful **Baths of Caracalla** *(Terme di Caracalla)*.

i Ⓜ️A: Repubblica. Walk down V. Nazionale, then turn left onto V. Firenze and left again onto V. del Viminale. Tickets can also be purchased online at www.amitsrl.it. Oper €33. Ballet €23. Outdoor performances at the Baths of Caracalla €25-135. Students and over 65 receive 25% discount; 10% discount for Baths of Caracalla shows. Check website for last-minute tickets with 25% discount. ⌚ Box office open Tu-Sa 9am-5pm, Su 9am-1:30pm, and from 1hr. before performance to 15min. after its start. Box office for Baths of Caracalla open Tu-Sa 10am-4pm, Su 9am-1:30pm.

ACCADEMIA NAZIONALE DI SANTA CECILIA

Vle. Pietro de Coubertin 30, for tickets06 89 29 82   ☎06 80 82 058 www.santacecilia.it

Founded as a conservatory in 1585, the Accademia is now both a training ground for musicians and a professional symphony orchestra. Concerts are held in three metallic and massive futuristic halls rising in the Parco della Musica near Flaminio. With (very) past conductors having included **Debussy, Strauss, Stravinsky,** and **Toscanini**, crowds still gather here to eat at the restaurant, shop at the music store, and catch concerts that occur between one to four times a week.

i Ⓜ️A: Flaminio, then tram #2 to P. Euclide. Or take the special line "M" from Termini (every 15min. starting at 5pm) to Auditorium. Last bus after last performance. Box office at Vle. Pietro de Coubertin 34. Tickets €18-50. Under 30 receive 25% discount when purchasing from the box office. ⌚ Box office open daily 11am-8pm and 1hr. before concerts.

SHOPPING

🔖 LIBRERIA DEL VIAGGIATORE

V. del Pellegrino 78   ☎06 68 80 10 48 www.libreriadelviaggiatore.com

If Aeneas had stopped by Libreria del Viaggiatore, it might have taken him less than 10 years to wander into Rome. A narrow old bookstore covered in posters of Marco Polo and with globes atop almost every bookshelf, this place is a traveler's delight. Spend 10min. wandering the seas of its dusty shelves and uncover travel guides and maps of practically anywhere your wanderlust might want to take you. If you don't seek different shores, just know that most of the non-travel books here are in Italian.

i From Campo dei Fiori, walk up V. Pellegrino. Cash only. ⌚ Open M 4-8pm, Tu-Sa 10am-2pm and 4-8pm.

PORTA PORTESE   TRASTEVERE
From P. Porta Portese to P. Ippolito Nievo   www.portaportesemarket.it

You don't need $20 in your pocket €1 will do. With vendors selling everything from cheap clothing, furniture, antiques, and jewelry, if you need something for less than €5, you'll probably find it here. The enormous piles of €1 and even €0.50 clothing are worth taking a dive into. If you're lucky, you'll score something fashionable. Grab onto it quickly before someone else in the Vatican Museum-sized crowds whisks it away and leaves you with all the XXL shirts that you haven't eaten enough pizza to fit into.

i Take bus #40 to Largo Argentina and tram #8. Cash only. 🕐 Open Su 7am-2:30pm.

MERCATO DI VIA SANNIO   SOUTHERN ROME
V. Sannio

Ain't nobody got time for laundry, so when you're in desperate need for some cheap clothes, head on over to V. Sannio. Specializing in all sorts of used and vintage clothing, this market will force you to jostle your way through the crowds to get what you want. But the prices will bring out that bargain hunting warrior in you, so go off and fight the good fight.

i Ⓜ A: San Giovanni. Cash only. 🕐 Open M-Sa 9am-1:30pm.

ESSENTIALS

- **TOURIST OFFICES: Comune di Roma** is Rome's official source for tourist information. Green **PIT Info booths,** located at most major sights, have English-speaking staff and sell bus and metro maps and the **Roma Pass.** (V. Giovanni Giolitti 34 in Termini, P. Sidney Sonnino in Trastevere, and V. dei Fori Imperiali ☎06 06 08 www.turismoroma.it, www.060608.it 🕐 Most locations open daily 9:30am-7pm; Termini location open daily 8am-8:30pm.) **Enjoy Rome** provides tour bookings, information on bike and scooter rental, and city maps. (V. Marghera 8A; 2nd office in P. San Pietro ☎06 44 51 843 www.enjoyrome.com *i* Ⓜ Termini. Walk down V. Marghera. 🕐 Both locations open M-F 8:30am-6pm, Sa 8:30am-2pm.)

- **LUGGAGE STORAGE: Termini Luggage Deposit.** (☎06 47 44 777 www.grandistazioni.it *i* Below Track 24 in the Ala Termini wing. *i* Storage for bags up to 20kg. Max. 5 days. 1st 5hr. €4, €0.60 per hr. for 6th-12th hr., €0.20 per hr. thereafter. After 1st day, €5 per day. Cash only. 🕐 Open daily 6am-11:50pm.)

- **GLBT RESOURCES:** The Comune di Roma publishes a free guide to gay life in Rome, *AZ Gay.* Pick one up at any PIT Info booth. **ARCI-GAY** offers medical, legal, and psychological counseling as well as free courses and general advice. (V. Zabaglia 14 ☎06 64 50 11 02, helpline 800 71 37 13 www.arcigayroma.it *i* Ⓜ B: Piramide. Walk up V. Marmorata and turn right onto V. Alessandro Volta; it's at the intersection with V. Zabaglia. *i* ARCI-GAY cards allow access to all events and services run by the program throughout Italy. 3-month card €8; 1 year €15. 🕐 Open M-Sa 4-8pm. Helpline operates M 4-8pm, W-Th 4-8pm, Sa 4-8pm.)

- **POST OFFICES: Poste Italiane** are located throughout the city. (☎800 160 000 www.poste. it) The main office is located at **Piazza San Silvestro 19.** (☎06 67 98 495 🕐 Open M-F 8:30am-6:30pm, Sa 8:30am-1pm.)

Emergency

- **POLICE: Police Headquarters.** (V. di San Vitale 15 ☎06 46 86 *i* Ⓜ A: Repubblica.) **Carabinieri** have offices at V. Mentana 6 (☎06 44 74 19 00 *i* Near Termini.) and at P. Venezia. (☎06 67 58 28 00) **City Police.** (P. del Collegio Romano 3 ☎06 69 01 21)

- **CRISIS LINES: Telefono Rosa** provides legal, psychological, and medical counseling for women. (Vle. Giuseppe Mazzini 73 ☎06 37 51 82 82 www.telefonorosa.it 🕐 Operates 24hr.) **Samaritans** provides psychological counseling in many languages; call for in-person guidance. (☎800 86 00 22; www.samaritansonlus.org 🕐 Operates daily 1-10pm.)

- **LATE-NIGHT PHARMACIES:** The following pharmacies are open 24hr.: **Farmacia della Stazione.** (P. dei Cinquecento 49/51 ☎06 48 80 019) **Farmacia Internazionale.** (P. Barberini 49 ☎06 48 25 456 *i* ⓂA: Barberini.) **Farmacia Doricchi.** (V. XX Settembre 47 ☎06 48 73 880) **Brienza.** (P. del Risorgimento 44 ☎06 39 73 81 86)

- **HOSPITALS/MEDICAL SERVICES: Policlinico Umberto I.** (Vle. del Policlinico 155 ☎06 49 97 95 14 or 06 49 97 95 15 www.policlinicoumberto1.it *i* ⓂB: Policlinico or bus #649 to Policlinico. Emergency treatment free. Non-emergencies €25-50. ◳ Open 24hr.) **International Medical Center** is a private hospital and clinic. (V. Firenze 47 ☎06 48 82 371 www. imc84.com *i* ⓂA: Repubblica. *i* Call ahead for appointments. ◳ Open M-F 9am-8pm.) **Rome-American Hospital.** (V. Emilio Longoni 69 ☎06 22 551 for emergencies, ☎06 22 55 290 for appointments www.rah.it *i* Well to the east of the city; consider taking a cab. To get a little closer, take bus #409 from Tiburtina to Ple. Prenestina or tram #14 from Termini. English-speaking. Private emergency and laboratory services, including HIV testing. ◳ Open M-F 8am-8pm, Sa 8am-2pm. 24hr. emergency care.)

Getting There

BY PLANE

DA VINCI INTERNATIONAL AIRPORT (FIUMICINO; FCO)

30km southwest of the city   ☎06 65 951

Commonly known as Fiumicino, Da Vinci International Airport oversees most international flights. To get from the airport, which is located right on the Mediterranean coast, to central Rome, take the **Leonardo Express** train to Termini Station. After leaving the airport's customs, follow signs to the Stazione Trenitalia/Railway Station, where you can buy a train ticket at an automated machine or from the ticket office. (€14. ◳ 32min., every 30min. 6:47am-11:37pm.) The **Sabina-Fiumicino Line (FR1)** will take you to Trastevere Station and other Roman suburbs. (www.trenitalia.i *i* €8. ◳ 20-45min., every 15min. 5:57am-11:27pm.) Don't buy a ticket from individuals who approach you, as they may be scammers. If you arrive after 8:30pm, you'll have to use an automated machine. Before boarding the train, make sure to validate the ticket in a yellow box on the platform; failure to do so may result in a fine of €50-100. To get to or from Fiumicino before 6:30am or after 11:30pm, the easiest option is to catch a **taxi.** (€40 flat rate for central Rome, including baggage and up to four passengers.)

ROME CIAMPINO AIRPORT (CIA)

15km southeast of the city   ☎06 65 951

Ciampino is a rapidly growing airport that serves budget airlines like Ryanair and EasyJet. There are no trains connecting the airport to the city center, but there are some buses. The **SIT Bus Shuttle** (☎06 59 23 507 www.sitbusshuttle.it ◳ 40min., every 30-60min. 7:15am-11:30pm) and **Terravision Shuttle** (☎06 97 61 06 32 www.terravision.eu ◳ 40min., every 20-60min. 8:15am-12:15am) run from the airport to V. Marsala, outside Termini Station. For easy and cheap access to the metro, the **COTRAL bus** runs to ⓂA: Anagnina. (€1.20. ◳ 30min., every 40min. 6:30am-11:10pm.)

BY TRAIN

Trenitalia (www.trenitalia.com) trains run through Termini Station, central Rome's main transport hub. International and overnight trains also run to Termini. City buses #C2, H, M, 36, 38, 40, 64, 86, 90, 92, 105, 170, 175, 217, 310, 714, and 910 stop outside in the P. del Cinquecento, so you definitely aren't short on options for the next leg of your journey. The station is open 4:30am-1:30am; if you arrive in Rome outside of this time frame, you will likely arrive in Stazione Tiburtina or Stazione Ostiense, both of which connect to Termini by the night bus #175. Trains run from: **Bologna** (€26-59 ◳ 2-5hr., 42 per day 6:15am-12:47am); **Florence** (€18-45 ◳ 1½-4hr., 52 per day 5:58am-10:36pm); **Naples** (€11-45 🕐 1-3hr., 50 per day 4:52am-9:50pm); **Venice** (€46-76 🕐 4-7hr., 17 per day 6:45am-10:36pm); **Milan** (€46-89 🕐 3-8½ hr., 33 per day 6am-12:47am).

Getting Around

BY BUS

The best way to get around the city other than walking is by bus. Dozens of routes cover the entire city center as well as the outskirts. Bus stops are marked by yellow poles and display a route map for all lines that pass through the stop.

BY METRO

Rome's metro system consists of two lines: Line A, which runs from Battistini to Anagnina (hitting P. di Spagna), and Line B, which runs from Laurentina to Rebibbida (hitting the Colosseum, Ostiense, and southern Rome). The lines intersect at **Termini Station.** While the metro is fast, it doesn't reach many regions and is best for getting across long distances. Stations are marked by poles with a red square and white M. Tickets are validated at turnstiles upon entering the station. The metro usually operates 5:30am-11:30pm (1:30am on Saturdays). A third metro line, Line C, is currently under construction.

BY TRAM

Trams make many stops but are still an efficient means of getting around. A few useful lines include **#3** (Trastevere, Piramide, Aventine, P. San Giovanni, Villa Borghese, P. Thorwaldsen), **#8** (Trastevere to Largo Argentina), and **#19** (Ottaviano, Villa Borghese, San Lorenzo, Prenestina, P. dei Gerani).

BY BIKE

ATAC runs **Bikesharing.** Purchase a card at any ATAC ticket office. (☎06 57 03 *i* Ⓜ A: Anagnina, Spagna, Lepanto, Ottaviano, Cornelia, or Battistini, or Ⓜ B: Termini, Laurentina, EUR Fermi, or Ponte Mammolo. Bikes can be parked at 19 stations around the city. Cards are rechargeable. Initial charge €5, €0.50 per 30min. thereafter. 🕐 Open M-Sa 7am-8pm, Su 8am-8pm. Bikes available for max. 24hr. at a time.) Plenty of other companies also rent bikes, including **Bici and Baci** and **Eco Move Rent** (see below).

BY SCOOTER

Rome is truly a city of scooters. Depending on the vehicle, prices range from €19-95 per day. A helmet (required by law) and insurance are usually included. **Bici and Baci** rents bikes and scooters. (V. del Viminale 5 ☎06 48 28 443 www.bicibaci.com 🕐 Open daily 8am-7pm.) **Treno e Scooter Rent** also rents scooters with a lock and chain included. (Stazione Roma Termini ☎06 48 90 58 23 www.trenoescooter.com. 🕐 Open daily 9am-2pm and 4-7pm.) **Eco Move Rent** rents scooters, Vespas, and bikes, with a lock included. (V. Varese 48/50 ☎06 44 70 45 18 www.ecomoverent.com 🕐 Open daily 8:30am-7:30pm.)

BY TAXI

Given the scope of Rome's bus system, taxis should only be reserved for desperate or time-sensitive affairs. Legally, you may not hail a cab on the street—either call **RadioTaxi** (☎06 35 70 www.3570.it) or head to a cab stand (near most major sights). Ride only in yellow or white cars and look for a meter or settle on a price before the ride. Fares start a €2.33 for rides between 7am-10pm and €4.91 for 10pm-7am and are then calculated per kilometer. Sunday and holiday daytime fares start at €3.36. **Rate 1** is charged for rides within the center (€0.78 per km). **Rate 2** is applied to rides outside the center (€1.29 per km). Though it's hard to tell what rate is being applied, write down the license number if the cost seems especially high. Tips are not expected.

milan

Milan is a major city, a sea of asphalt punctuated by breathtaking strips of green, where the bustle of daily life sometimes overshadows *la dolce far niente*. That's not to say Milan doesn't know culture; in fact, it earns its cultural Megatron status from the P. del Duomo alone, which is built on the four great pillars of the Milanese lifestyle: the church, art, commerce, and rich Renaissance people. This is a city where all the women wear heels, where even the least fashion-conscious can pick out the knock-off, where art is free and plentiful, and where it's normal to save up for one nice meal instead of several crappy ones. With opera notes trilling from the famous La Scala and Renaissance artwork, including Leonardo's breathtaking *Last Supper*, hiding around every corner, Milan has a rich well of culture from which to draw. It's evident in everything from the delicate Lombardian culinary specialties to the even more delicate (and expensive) clothing in the windows of the Fashion District. It is a cultural energy that pulses to the beats of the elite *discoteche*, vibrates in the crowds cheering on the AC and Inter Milan soccer teams, and glows in the city's edgy and vibrant contemporary art scene.

ORIENTATION

Piazza del Duomo

Sitting in the heart of Milan's downtown *centro*, the Duomo is the geographical and spiritual center of the city as well as its tourist hub. Beneath the plaza, ⓜ**Fermata Duomo** is one of the underground's busiest stations and connects the 1 (red) and 3 (yellow) lines. Northeast of the *piazza*, international banks and luxury hotels draw a more suited-up crowd. To the northwest, along **Via Dante**, is **Castello Sforzesco,** the city's other main tourist attraction. Affordable accommodations can be found along **Via Manzini. Via Torino** heads southwest, linking up with **Corso di Porta Ticinese** in an area that contains many more authentic restaurants, cool students, and hoppin' bars. Except for these main thoroughfares, this area's street "grid" is more like a deformed spider web, with few streets extending in a straight line for more than a few blocks, making a map critical for any successful exploration of this neighborhood.

Fashion District

Perhaps not coincidentally, Milan's most elegant area, once called the **Quadrilatero d'Oro,** is located right in the middle of everything. **Via Montenapoleone,** a street of brand-name shops with elaborate window displays and equally extravagant price tags, connects **Corso Vittorio Emanuele II** and **Piazza San Babila** (ⓜ1: San Babila) in the south to **Via Manzoni** (ⓜ3: Montenapoleone), home of Armani, in the north. V. della Spiga leads to **Piazza Cavour** and the famous gate that traditionally marked the entrance to the land of wealth within this upscale part of the city.

Giardini Pubblici

One of the city's most ethnically diverse and 🏳️‍🌈**GLBT-friendly** neighborhoods, Giardini Pubblici offers the peace of the gardens themselves, great museums lining the greenery, and dining and nightlife where the tourist population is far outnumbered by locals. Hotels that range from the fancy to the seedy can be found near the station and along the main roads of **Corso Buenos Aires** and **Viale Tunisia.** V. Torriani leads from the heart of the neighborhood toward the train terminal. The gardens are bordered by **Corso Venezia** to the east, **Via Palestro** to the south, **Via Manin** to the west, and **Bastioni di Porta Venezia** to the north. Along the streets parallel to the edge of Giardini Pubblici, including V. Castaldi, take your pick of the dozens of quaint (and snooty) cafes and bars that seem to fill every intersection. The area's primary metro station, ⓜPorta Venezia, is located on C. Buenos Aires at P. S. F. Romano.

Castello Sforzesco

Castello Sforzesco's environs are just far enough from the Duomo to feel like real, occupied neighborhoods, but they are close enough that most major attractions are within walking distance. At the center of it all is the castle, which, like the Duomo, can sometimes feel like a maze of museums and bracelet sellers. To escape the bustle, head north into the park, whose green expanse provides respite from the summer crowds during the day and is home to a number of clubs that heat up at night. You are absolutely not allowed to leave this part of Milan without seeing Leonardo da Vinci's **Last Supper.**

Navigli

The Navigli area is a triangle bounded by two waterways, the Naviglio Grande to the northwest and the Naviglio Pavese to the east, though the area's many bars and restaurants spread a few blocks beyond. The canals meet at the **Piazza XXIV Maggio,** which is marked by a traffic circle and a stone monument. ⓂPorta Genova, the nearest metro stop, is located a few blocks west of the *piazza* on V. Vigevano. The picturesque **Ripa di Porta Ticinese** runs along Naviglio Grande, while **Via Ascanio Sforza,** Navigli's main nightlife drag, sits on the east side of Naviglio Pavese. Most nightlife hotspots are on V. Ascanio Sforza, north of where the street is crossed by the tree-lined V. Liguria/V. Tibaldi, although some restaurants and hotels can be found on the southern end.

SIGHTS

Welcome to Milan, the city so full of Leonardo da Vinci that everyone and their mother refers to him by his first name—"Hey, wanna see some Leonardo?"—like he's a friend down the street. But the Milanese are buds with the big guy for a reason: from the 🖼**Last Supper,** which you must see, to the collections at the **Pinacoteca di Ambrosiana** to the more cutting edge exhibitions at the **Palazzo Reale,** Milan's more cultured than kefir. Besides a mother lode of art, Milan's got some awesome castles—okay, just one, **Castello Sforzesco,** but it's huge—and one of the largest churches in the world, the iconic **Duomo.** The **Fashion District** itself is like one huge museum—at least for all the commoners who won't be taking any of the super beautiful, super expensive pieces home any time soon. From the gilded halls of Renaissance *palazzi* to a contemporary palace to the **San Siro** sports stadium, Milano has some of the most spectacular sights in Italy—and arguably the country's most sophisticated population.

Piazza del Duomo

After touring the Duomo, head to some of the less-crowded attractions nearby. For the complete Milanese trinity—art, fashion, and Catholicism—you don't even have to leave the *piazza*.

🖼 **DUOMO**   CHURCH

P. del Duomo   ☎02 72 02 33 75 www.duomomilano.it

The second-largest cathedral in the world, the Duomo's sheer size is enough to take your breath away, though your gasp will echo all the way up the ginormous marble columns to the ornate ceilings, bouncing off more stained glass than all the first graders in the world have ever painted in art class. Famous people were pretty into this place, too: Giacomo de Medici's tomb, inspired by the work of Michelangelo, is inside. The rooftop, accessible by elevator or stairs, offers one of Milan's best vistas. The nearby Museo del Duomo houses paintings, tapestries, and artifacts dating back to the cathedral's construction and is probably one of the only warehouses in Milan where the luxury goods are not for sale.

i Ⓜ1: Duomo. Modest dress code strictly enforced. Free. Treasury €2. Roof access via elevator €12, children 6-12 and adults 65 and over €6; stairs €7, children and seniors €3.50. 🕐 Open daily 7am-6:45pm. Roof open daily 9am-9:30pm.

Milan's accommodations run the gamut. A few youth hostels can be found scattered around the city, and some are very conveniently located in quiet residential areas just a short metro ride from the *centro*. A number of quality one-star hotels surround the **Giardini Pubblici,** with a deliciously gritty vibe that evokes old-school European dives of yore, and lie to the southeast of Porta Venezia as well as along **Via Giorgio Washington.** International chains are clustered closer to the city center, where budget accommodations can be hard to come by. For more recommendations, visit **www.letsgo.com.**

HOTEL EVA AND HOTEL ARNO   HOTEL $$
V. Lazzaretto 17, 4th fl.   ☎02 67 06 093 www.hotelarno.com

In a strange twist on the Milanese budget hospitality scene, the brothers who run these sibling hotels are genuinely hospitable. And not in an"I want to rip you off" kind of way. Located in separate wings of a floor in an apartment building and sharing a reception, the rooms here are totally no-frills but are also clean, bright, spacious, and well-maintained.

i Ⓜ1: Porta Venezia. Walk up C. Buenos Aires and turn left onto V. Castati, then turn right onto V. Lazzaretto after about 5min. Ring the bell. Free Wi-Fi. Breakfast included. Free luggage storage. Singles €30-45; doubles €50-95; triples €65-130.

OSTELLO LA CORDATA   HOSTEL $$
V. Marco Burigozzo 11   ☎02 58 30 35 98 www.ostellolacordata.com

Home to a lively, international backpacking crowd headed for the disco lights of the Navigli district, Ostello La Cordata has a party-hostel reputation. With sociable common spaces, large dormitory rooms, and a killer location right by Navigli's most hoppin' club, this reputation is well deserved.

i Ⓜ2: Porta Genova. Take V. Casalle, cross the canal and turn left onto Alzaia Naviglio Grande. At the road's end, turn right onto Vle. Gorizia. Cross P. XXIV Maggio, turn left onto V. Samubo, and continue just past the 1st intersection. The hotel entrance is on the right on V. Giovanni Aurspa. Free Wi-Fi. Linens and towels included. Kitchen and lockers available. Dorms €21-25; singles €50-70; doubles €70-100; triples €90-120; quads €112-140. ⏰ Reception open 7:30am-12:30pm and 2:30pm-12:30am. Lockout 11am-2pm.

PINACOTECA AMBROSIANA   MUSEUM
P. Pio XI 2   ☎02 80 69 21 www.ambrosiana.it

The Pinacoteca Ambrosiana has more manifestations of the Madonna and her bambino than you previously thought possible: bambino with spikes coming out of his head (yes, that's supposed to be a halo); bambino making a peace sign as three fat, cavorting cherubs rock out on mandolins beside him; bambino breast-feeding; bambino all-grown-up. As exciting as the little guy is, don't you dare miss Rafael's truly enormous sketch of the School of Athens; seeing the work in its creation phase is like knowing Madonna before she was famous (no, not the Virgin—just like one). When you're too intimidated to continue staring at things of such large scale, check out Brueghel's tender, tiny Tapolino con Fiore ("Mouse with Flower") to bring things back to still-life size. Finish your trip with an awe-inspiring walk around the library, where Leonardo da Vinci's sketches will be on rotating display from now until the World Expo in 2015.

i Ⓜ1: Duomo. Follow V. Spadari off V. Torino, and turn left onto V. Cantu. €8, under 18 and over 65 €5. ⏰ Open Tu-Su 10am-6pm. Last entry 30min. before close.

milan

PALAZZO REALE
PALACE, ART MUSEUM

P. del Duomo 12 ☎02 88 451 www.comune.milano.it/palazzoreale

Formerly the palace of Milanese royalty, the Palazzo Reale is now an art museum featuring myriad rotating and often free exhibits. It's also perhaps the only place in the world you can see the ceiling friezes, opulent mirrors, and faded tapestries of a palace in the same room as a preserved bird carcass (it's art, we promise).

i Ⓜ1/3: Duomo. To right when facing the Duomo. Most galleries free; some exhibits require ticket purchases or pre-booking, which will generally be no more than €10 and will offer a student discount. ☒ Open M 2:30-7:30pm, Tu-Su 9:30am-7:30pm; last entry 1hr. before close.

MUSEO POLDI PEZZOLI
MUSEUM

V. Manzoni 12 ☎02 78 08 72 www.museopoldipezzoli.it

Gian Giacomo Poldi Pezzoli probably got made fun of as a child for the absurd, rhyming alliteration of his name and decided to stick it to all of them by acquiring lots of cool stuff. By "stuff," we mean a seemingly endless collection of precious and historical lace, gold, armor, and paintings, including Botticelli's Madonna and Pollaiuolo's Portait of a Young Woman. Works by some Flemish and Northern European painters are on display as well, including that picture of Luther that was probably in your European history textbook (send pics—no flash allowed—to your teacher for bonus points).

i Ⓜ1/3: Duomo. Follow V. Manzoni past La Scala. Audio tour included with admission. €9, students and seniors €6, under 10 free. ☒ Open M and W-Su 10am-6pm.

NOVECENTO
ART MUSEUM

Galleria Vittorio Emanuele 11/12 ☎02 88 44 40 72 www.museodelnovecento.org

The recently completed Novecento museum provides a well-organized look at 20th-century art. With a room or two dedicated—in chronological order—to each specific movement, you can move from Futurism to the future, one groovy escalator at a time.

i Ⓜ1/3: Duomo. On the right side of the piazza when facing the Duomo. €5, students and over 65 €3, under 25 free. ☒ Open M 2:30-7:30pm, Tu-W 9:30am-7:30pm, Th 9:30am-10:30pm, Fr 9:30am-7:30pm, Sa 9:30am-10:30pm, Su 9:30am-7:30pm.

GALLERIA VITTORIO EMANUELE II
ARCHITECTURE

P. del Duomo

Right next to one of the world's most impressive monuments to religion on P. Duomo is one of its most impressive monuments to shopping. A stroll through the structure, finished in 1877, reminds you of the culture and commerce that have shaped this industrial and art-crazy city. Big-name brands glare down from glinting shop windows inside, while tourists spend more euro than you'll ever have at one time on everything from purses to a few grams of caviar. The combination of art and money proves that in Italy, Prada and Puccini are never too far apart.

i Ⓜ1/3: Duomo. To the left when facing the Duomo. Free (entry, at least).

Fashion District

While the most significant monuments of the Fashion District are the stores themselves, the side streets hold some unique, less frequented museums to explore.

MUSEO BAGATTI VALSECCHI
MUSEUM

V. Santo Spirito 10/Gesu 5 ☎02 76 00 61 32 www.bagattivalsecchi.house.museum

Brothers Fausto and Giuseppe Bagatti Valsecchi apparently had a little too much time on their hands, and they spent it playing dress-up in this gorgeous *palazzo* filled with Renaissance artwork and artifacts as well as some pieces that are just meant to look authentic. One thing the brothers couldn't disguise, however, are genuine paintings by Renaissance artist Giovanni Bellini and the seriously threatening arms gallery, which is full of breastplates, helmets, swords, and spears worn in battle all over Europe during the Renaissance. The museum also displays a gorgeous collection of 20th-century Murano glass sculptures acquired after the brothers' deaths.

i Ⓜ3: Montenapoleone. Walk down V. Montenapoleone and turn left onto V. Gesu; the museum is through a courtyard on the left. €8; students, children, and over 65, and on W €4. Ⓧ Open Tu-Sa 1-5:45pm.

Giardini Pubblici

🏛 GIARDINI PUBBLICI   GARDENS
C. Venezia at Bastioni di Porta Vinezia   ☎02 88 46 32 89 93
Just like anything else you can think of, Italians do parks better than you do. The English might have inspired the design for these public gardens, but the Italians mastered the art of chilling in them. If you don't believe us, go take a stroll. From bambinos to little old signoras, a walk in the park in the afternoon or evening is practically a daily ritual for the locals. And who could resist the tree-lined paths, sunny fields, bubbling stream, and children's paleontology exhibit that constitute this park-going experience? Come in the afternoon, have a coffee at one of the various available cafes, bring your dog, bring your kid, bring your life partner (or one night stand), and learn la dolce far niente from the best of them.

i Ⓜ1: Porta Venezia or Palestro. It's the big green thing you can't possibly miss. Free. Ⓧ Open Jan-Feb 6:30am-8pm; Mar-Apr 6:30am-9pm; May 6:30am-10pm; Jun-Sept 6:30am-11:30pm; Oct 6:30am-9pm; Nov-Dec 6:30am-8pm

GALLERIA D'ARTE MODERNA   MUSEUM
V. Palestro 16   ☎02 88 44 59 47 www.gam-milano.com
Milan apparently has so much Renaissance art that the extra Jesus panels need to be hung in the stairwell of the Modern Art Museum. These comprise just part of the eclectic collection ranging from pieces by notables Paul Gauguin and Vincent Van Gogh to a seemingly random exhibit of Turkish rugs. Just go with it, though: for the grand total of free, East Asian ceramics interspersed with Italian Impressionism (which exists, all you Francophiles) are sure to make an enriching, if slightly quirky, trip to the museum.

i Ⓜ1: Palestro. Walk north on C. Venezia and take the 1st left onto V. Palestro. The museum is on the left. Free. Ⓧ Open Tu-Su 9am-1pm and 2-5:30pm.

Castello Sforzesco

Castello Sforzesco is kind of like the nesting dolls of Milanese tourism: you enter one sight only to find that it contains 25 others. With some of the most spectacular churches and museums in Milan, Castello Sforzesco is a great place to wander for an afternoon or three.

🏛 CHIESA DI SANTA MARIA DELLE GRAZIE AND CENACOLO VINCIANO   CHURCH, MUSEUM
P. Santa Maria delle Grazie 2   ☎02 89 42 11 46 www.cenacolovinciano.net
This sight consists of the Chiesa, which is a scrumptious example of Lombardian Gothic architecture, towering domes, gorgeous painted ceilings, and the Last Supper, which is an almost indescribably awesome and iconic piece of art. The former is totally worth a trip, offers free admission, and is easily accessed; the latter is not free, is difficult to access, but is also totally worth it. Go book your tickets now.

i Ⓜ1: Conciliazione or Ⓜ3: Cardona. From P. Conciliazione, take V. Boccaccio and turn right onto V. Ruffini; continue for 2 blocks. Many tickets for the Last Supper are bought up by tour companies months in advance, so be sure to reserve early online. By early, we mean the moment after you decide to go to Milan. Church free. Refectory €6.50, EU residents 18-25 €3.25, EU residents under 18 or over 65 free. Reservation fee €1.50. Ⓧ Church open M-Sa 7am-noon and 3-7pm, Su 7:30am-12:15pm and 3:30-9pm. Refectory open M-Sa 8am-6:30pm. Groups are let in at 15min. intervals to see the Last Supper.

milan

CASTELLO SFORZESCO

P. Castello

CASTLE, MUSEUM

☎02 88 46 37 00 www.milanocastello.it

This castle was constructed in 1368 to protect the city, and we're pretty sure the original planners' defensive design was meant to create so many awesome museums inside that invading enemies would be distracted by all the ancient coins, Leonardo da Vinci frescoes, and musical instruments. While the grounds themselves are free, a cheap fee gains you admission to more museums than you could actually visit in a day. Our main man Leonardo's studio could once be found within the castle that now pays tribute to him and many other artists in the Museum of Ancient Art, where his frescoes cover the ceiling. Also worth a look are the Museum of Musical Instruments and the Museum of Decorative Art.

i Ⓜ1: Cairoli. Grounds free. All-museum pass €3, students and seniors €1.50, under 25 free. Free admission M-Th 4:30-5pm, F 2-5pm, Sa-Su 4:30-5pm. ☉ Castle grounds open Apr-Oct daily 7am-7pm; Nov-Mar 7am-6pm. Museums open Tu-Su 9am-5:30pm.

PINACOTECA DI BRERA

V. Brera 28

MUSEUM

☎02 72 26 32 64 229 www.brera.beniculturali.it

Pinacoteca di Brera is known to induce the following questions in curious visitors: What is the meaning of art? Why do we so value Renaissance paintings? Why is the Christ child always so weird-looking? Providing a fascinating behind-the-scenes glimpse at the restoration process, the Pinacoteca was founded for art students' private studies, and its current collection reflects this focus. With highlights such as Raphael's Marriage of the Virgin, Caravaggio's Supper at Emmaus, and Francesco Hayez's hot 'n' heavy hit, Il Bacio (you'll know it when you see it), the museum also has an intriguing collection of 20th-century works that juxtapose ancient Etruscan stonework with Renaissance Christwork.

i Ⓜ2: Lanza or Ⓜ3: Montenapoleone. Walk down V. Pontaccio and turn right onto V. Brera. Or from La Scala, walk up V. Verdi until it becomes V. Brera. Visitors with disabilities enter V. Fiori Oscuri 2. €6, EU citizens from 18-25 €3, EU citizens under 18 or over 65 free. ☉ Open Tu-Su 8:30am-7:15pm. Last entry 45min. before close.

MUSEO NAZIONALE DELLA SCIENZA E DELLA TECNOLOGIA "DA VINCI"

21 V. San Vittore

MUSEUM

☎02 48 55 51 www.museoscienza.org

The perfect place to take kids or anyone who likes pulleys, knobs, buttons, videos, and generally shiny things, the Technology Museum offers a dizzying array of exhibits. Perennial favorites include reproductions of Leonardo's machines, with enough levers and gizmos to keep any easily distracted person busy for hours, and an extensive exhibit on the history of video and radio.

i Ⓜ2: Sant'Ambrogio. Walk against traffic on V. Giosuè Carducci and turn left onto V. San Vittore. €10, under 18 and students with ID €7, seniors €4. Submarine tours additional €8 with reservation, €10 without. ☉ Open Tu-F 10am-6pm, Sa-Su 10am-7:30pm. Leonardo's inventions section open Sa 2-6pm, Su 10am-1pm and 2-6pm.

Navigli

We recommend this student-friendly neighborhood more for bar-hopping than museum-hopping. Still, there are enough monuments, churches, and paintings of crucified Jesus to go around. Bring your camera and maybe find your lost dignity after those body shots last night—Navigli's sights aren't just that hottie at the bar next to you.

BASILICA DI SAN LORENZO MAGGIORE AND LORENZO COLUMNS

C. di Porta Ticinese 39

CHURCH

☎02 89 40 41 29 www.sanlorenzomaggiore.com

Only in Italy do people say things like, "Let's get mad wasted and go chill at one of the most valuable Roman relics in the city!" Maybe they don't actually say that (or they say it in Italian and we're not quick enough to pick it up), but the Lorenzo Columns—colonne colloquially—and the surrounding *piazza* are sweet examples of living history. During the day, the columns are a resting spot for the tired tourists and laconic hipsters that call this neighborhood either "Where's the Duomo?" or "home." Daytime is also the best (and most legal) time to pop into the church, whose soaring columns and round floor plan make it a model of Lombardian architecture and worth a visit.

i Ⓜ1: San Ambrogio. Follow V. de Amicis to Corso di Porta Ticinese; turn left and walk through the arches. The church and columns are ahead on the right. Free. ☼ Open daily 7:30am-12:30pm and 2:30-6:45pm.

TICINESE CITY GATE   RUINS
P. XXIV Maggio

This city gate, one of the last standing from Milan's original wall from the 1100s, might have been restored in the 1860s, but its milieu seems to come from a century later. During the day, the gate stands in the middle of the *piazza* looking badass as trams, cars, and fruit sellers bustle by, while at night and on weekends the place hosts a cool countercultural scene. Impromptu concerts fill the Friday night air, bars sprout from the back of parked VW buses, and communist rallies bring out the carabinieri. Not exactly the kind of fortifications the medievals had in mind, we're sure, but a cool testament to the evolving use of public spaces over time.

i Ⓜ2: Porta Genova. Free.

ST. EUSTORGIO BASILICA AND MUSEUM   CHURCH
P. Sant'Eustorgio 3   ☎02 89 40 26 71 www.santeustorgio.it

We especially recommend St. Eustorigio for guilty Catholics who want to see some dark, intense martyrdom scenes in the museum before popping over for a stroll through the church to pray off the angst. While the basilica has all the requisite Lombardian fanciness, including killer domes and striking columns, the museum is a bit confusing (much of the information is only in Italian) and doesn't hold more than some paintings and crosses by lesser-known Italian artists. It does, however, have a sweet crypt under the church where you can view Roman funerary epitaphs and pretend to be Indiana Jones, so that's a win.

i Ⓜ2: Porta Genova. Follow V. Vigevano to V. Gorzia. Take C. di Porta Ticinese from the piazza. The church is on the right. €6, students and over 60 €3, under 14 €1. ☼ Museum open Tu-Su 10am-6pm.

FOOD

There's much to be had from Milan's culinary scene, from slices of pizza enjoyed while sitting on the sidewalk to fine dining in the city's venerable sit-down, button-up establishments. Starting the night off right is easy with the happy hour *aperitivo* buffets offered by many bars, especially near the Navigli—all-you-can-eat spreads of bread, pasta, meats, and cheeses come included with the purchase of one drink. Sadly overlooked most everywhere except inside the city's ring road, Milanese cuisine, with its risotto and *cottoletta alla milanese* (breaded veal cutlet), is still served up in a number of quaint *trattorie*. Often hard to find in Italy, ethnic cuisines from Argentina to Eritrea and beyond take center stage in some neighborhoods, particularly around the **Giardini Pubblici.**

Piazza del Duomo

When it's time to sit down and eat after your day of sightseeing, identify the touristy spots on P. del Duomo...then steer clear of them. A better bet is to venture down a few side streets, where there are a number of great inexpensive options, including high-quality pizza and take-out places and small, out-of-the-way restaurants where the chic business crowd ventures for homey, cheap lunch.

PRINCI   BAKERY, PIZZERIA $
V. Speronari 6   ☎02 87 47 97 www.princi.it

Princi is like the Prada of bread, minus the unattainably expensive bit. Selling
square, crisp-bottomed pizza and focaccia, crusty wood-fired bread, and prepared salads, pasta, and vegetable dishes by the kilogram, Princi has everything
you need to take home a light, high-quality dinner.

i Ⓜ1/3: Duomo. Take V. Torino and make 1st left. Pizza and focaccia €16 per kg. ☼ Open Su-F
7am-8pm, Sa 8am-8pm.

PIZZA AND FRIENDS   PIZZERIA $$
V. Baracchini 9   ☎02 87 23 81 33 www.pizzaandfriends.com

If you believe the names of its dishes, this place should cost a fortune. Luckily,
it doesn't. The "St. Tropez" (tomato, mozzarella, tuna, leek, and basil; €9) isn't
nearly as expensive as the vacation destination it's named after, and the "Rocke-
feller" (mozzarella di bufala, truffles, egg yolk, arugula, and parmesan; €12)
doesn't require the bank account of America's famous oil tycoon. The greatest
part? These pizza pies still taste like a million bucks.

i Ⓜ3: Missori. From P. Missori, follow V. M. Gonzaga. At P. Diaz, turn right onto V. Baracchi-
ni. Pizzas €8-13. Sandwiches €5-12. ☼ Open M-F 11:30am-3:30pm, Sa 11:30am-3:30pm and
6:30pm-11:30pm.

Fashion District

Restaurant options can be limited within the central shopping zone of the Fashion
District, and much of what's here is overpriced fare aimed at tourists or fashionistas.
But if you can figure out where the workers eat, you're golden. For real budget meal
options, follow the business suits at lunch time to unbelievably inexpensive buffet
options.

RITA SELF SERVICE   BUFFET $
Largo Guido Donegani 2   ☎02 29 00 04 76 www.cir-food.it

Nearby but slightly outside the high-fashion hub, this buffet-style eatery is like a
pimped-out dining hall for laid-back business people, except instead of chicken
patties and chopped salad, you get gnocchi with squid.

i Ⓜ3: Turati. After exiting the station, walk to intersection and look for a red awning. Order pizza
at register. Affiliated snack bar also has sandwich lunch specials. Primi and secondi €3-6. Pizzas
€5-7. ☼ Open M-F noon-2pm.

BIANCO LATTE   CAFE, GELATERIA $$
V. Turati 30   ☎02 62 08 61 77 www.biancolattemilano.it

Bianco Latte is almost too hip to handle. We say almost, though, because with
gelato of this quality, we can't be anything but charmed by the clean white
storefront and colorful attached toy store. The clientele's spotless white blouses
and understated style matches the aesthetic of this crisply designed shop, where
colorful heaps of cool, creamy gelato decorate the dairy counter in an array of
nutty, chocolatey, and fruity flavors.

i Gelato €2.50-4. ☼ Open M 7:30am-7:30pm, Tu-F 7:30am-midnight, Sa-Su 8am-midnight. Dinner served Tu-Su.

Giardini Pubblici

From Argintinean to Japanese, Giardini Pubblici's selection of international and
Italian fare proves there's nothing quite like the remix—especially when the mix is
of the gastronomical variety.

PANDENUS
BAKERY $$

V. Tadino 15 ☎02 29 52 80 16 www.pandenus.it

Pandenus combines the best of Milanese chic with budget prices for super-cheap, super-quality bread, baked goods, and lunch specials. The loaves here are crusty and divine and will make you feel like you've never had bread before.

i Ⓜ1: Porta Venezia. Take C. Buenos Aires north and turn left onto V. Casati. The bakery is on corner of V. Casati and V. Tadino. Lunch €8-10. Bread and pastries €0.80-2. Coffee €0.80 (yes, we're excited about this, too). Happy hour drink and buffet €8. Brunch €18. Free Wi-Fi. ☒ Open M-Sa 7:30am-10:30pm, Su 9am-10:30am. Brunch Sa-Su noon-3pm. Happy hour daily.

L'OSTERIA DEL TRENO
RISTORANTE $

V. San Gregorio 46/48 ☎02 67 00 479 www.osteriadeltreno.it

L'Osteria del Treno is Slow Food certified, meaning the Italian, "we love awesome food that's prepared lovingly from responsible and quality ingredients" organization has given it a thumbs up. If you come during the lunchtime rush or at the end of the day, when the self-service morphs into a sit-down restaurant that often hosts large functions, you'll know why this place is so popular.

i Ⓜ2/3: Centrale F.S. Lunch primi €4.70; secondi €6.70. Dinner entrees €9-13. ☒ Open M-F 12:30-2:30pm and 8-10:30pm, Sa-Su 8-10:30pm

Castello Sforzesco

As is the case with the Duomo, restaurants within sight of Castello Sforzesco are designed to catch tourists who don't know where else to eat. Try **Corso Magenta** and some parts of the Brera district instead. If all else fails, there are always kebab stands.

SHOCKOLAT
GELATERIA $

V. Boccaccio 9 ☎02 48 00 16 35 www.shockolat.it

Chili-pepper chocolate, hazelnut chocolate, dark chocolate, orange chocolate, milk chocolate, and rum chocolate. Yes, indeed, there are six flavors of chocolate gelato at this cafe. Insanely beautiful chocolate tarts luxuriate in a case near the gelato.

i Ⓜ1/2: Cardona F. N. Exit the circle onto V. Boccaccio and continue for approximately 3min. Free Wi-Fi. Gelato €2.50-3.50. ☒ Open M-F 7:30am-1am, Sa 8am-1am, Su 10am-1am.

JAMAICA BAR
CAFE $$

32 V. Brera ☎02 87 67 23 www.jamaicabar.it

If Jamaica Bar were to have a 100th birthday party celebrating its thus far illustrious life (yes, it is indeed 100 years old), one of its most notorious party guests would be Benito Mussolini. Since the days of the dictator, this establishment has also played host to less fascist intellectuals whose black-and-white photos line the walls. They come for the pizza and panini and stay for the intellectual ambience.

i Ⓜ1: Lanza. Take V. Tivoli as it becomes V. Pantaccio. Turn right onto V. Brera. Panini €5.50-6.50. Entrees €7-14.50. Pizza €7-9. Ghosts of famous dictators free. ☒ Open daily 9am-2am.

Navigli

Navigli has one of the highest concentrations of cheap, high quality food in all of Milan—after all, it's not healthy to drink on an empty stomach. Besides the consistently awesome and budget-friendly *aperitivo* buffets, a full array of sandwich shops, pizza and kebab joints, and sit-down spots are available to nourish both the sophisticated and the sloppy.

BIG PIZZA: DA NOI 2
PIZZERIA $$

V. Giosue Borsi 1 ☎02 83 95 677 www.danoi2.it

In the American dream of Italy there exists a Mecca of carbohydrates near a canal, where the pizza is endless, the pasta flows in a river of starchy goodness, and corny Italian pop music plays under a darkening sky. That paradise is not

milan

Big Pizza, but that paradise is also pretty unrealistic, so this place is as close as you're going to get. With a seemingly endless pizza and pasta menu that nevertheless manages to remain authentic, Big Pizza is the carb high of all carb highs. You're welcome, America.

i Ⓜ2: Porta Genova. Take V. Casale to Alzaio Naviglio Grande. Has a smoker's room M-F. Pizza €7.50-11. Pasta €5-15. Ⓩ Open M-Sa noon-2:30pm and 7pm-midnight, Su 7pm-midnight.

▨ **IL FORNO DEI NAVIGLI**   BAKERY $
Alzaia Pavese 2   ☎02 83 23 372

Glowing marmalade shines from tender tartlets through Il Forno's windows as if they were stained glass. Yes, these pastries are awesome: apple fritters and dumplings stacked fat and crispy, luscious chocolate pistachio rolls, and shiny, beautiful cakes. The bakery is open late, too, so you can take your drunk munchies to a whole new level.

i Ⓜ2: Porta Genova. At intersection of V. Valenza and Alzaia Naviglio Grande. Pastries €20 per kg. Ⓩ Open daily 7am-midnight.

NIGHTLIFE

In terms of sheer variety, very few places on earth rival Milan when it comes to nightlife and there are plenty of locals eager to rave about their city's vibrant after-hours scene. **Corso Como** is home to the city's most exclusive and expensive clubs, where mere mortals can mingle with models and football stars provided their attire passes the judgment of the big man with the earpiece and clipboard. Dozens of small bars with big (and inexpensive) *aperitivo* buffets line the canals of the **Navigli** area, drawing students and young people to the neighborhood in droves. Beyond these hubs, the nightlife spokes stretch to all edges of the city, throughout which both local bars and international clubs are scattered.

Piazza del Duomo

Nightlife on P. del Duomo is pretty much the same as the daylife: a lot of tourists gawking at the pile of intricate stonework that is the Duomo and the Galleria Vittorio Emanuele.

▨ **CUORE**   BAR
V. Gian Giacomo Mora 3   ☎02 58 11 83 11 www.cuoremilano.it

If you've been wondering where the awesome has been hiding in Milan, it's here. Come here to find a crowd that has all the best of Milanese taste and a funky, artistic flare. With a DJ spinning trance music into late in the night, Cuore's vibe strikes just the right note between alternative and tasteful. As you drift between groups of young people clustered around intimate tables, chatting, then dancing to the music coming from the graffiti-covered DJ booth, you will feel like you've found the heart of Milan's hipster scene.

i Ⓜ1/3: Duomo. Follow V. Torino to C. di Porta Ticinese, and turn right onto V. Gian Giacomo. Mora before the columns. Drinks €2-8. Ⓩ Open daily 6pm-2am.

TASCA   ENOTECA
C. di Porta Ticinese 14   ☎02 83 76 915 www.iltasca.it

Tasca's clientele of generally young, generally attractive people sit sipping wine, gather in murmuring groups on the street, and leave lipstick on their glasses. While the Spanish theme is suggested only by the menu and a few pictures of dances and bullfighters on the wall, it's the "we're cool" theme that really shows through with the crowd here.

i Ⓜ2: Sant'Ambrogio. Follow V. Amicis and turn left onto C. di Porta Ticinese. White wine €5-6, red €5-9. Tapas €5-10. Ⓩ Open M-F 12:30pm-1:30am, Sa 7:30pm-1:30am.

Giardini Pubblici

Free from the tourists of the Duomo and the (overt) snobbery of the Fashion District, Giardini Pubblici is the place to go for chic nightlife that is never too intimidating. Additionally, an uber-inviting **GLBT** scene and more ethnically diverse hangouts than other neighborhoods in Milan make the Giardini Pubblici a hip place to be for just about anyone.

L'ELEPHANT   BAR

V. Melzo 22   ☎02 29 51 87 68 www.lelephant.it

One of Milan's oldest hangouts for the GLBT community, L'Elephant is a place for people of all genders and sexual orientations to chill under endearingly ugly fake palm trees and on awesomely cringe-worthy pleather chairs. While men dominate the scene, smaller groups of women also join in on the fun.

i Ⓜ1: Porta Venezia. Follow V. Melzo from P. Romana. Mixed drinks €5-8. Happy hour €6. Ⓣ Open daily 6:30pm-3am. DJ daily from 7:30pm.

MONO   BAR

V. Lecco 6   ☎33 94 81 02 64 www.myspace.com/monomilano

Having an official website on MySpace might make you see Mono as a bit immature, but if you actually check out the page—and their space—in question, you'll find far more zombie-themed parties and hipster haircuts than bikini shots and fish-lip faces. Mono is the place to be for the young, the artistic, and, apparently, the occasionally undead.

i Ⓜ1: Porta Venezia. Exit onto Vle. Vittorio Veneto. Take the 2nd right onto V. Lecco. Bar is 1 block ahead on right. DJ on Th-Sa. Drinks €7-9. Ⓣ Open Tu-Sa 6:30pm-2am.

Navigli

LE TROTTOIR   CLUB

P. XXIV Maggio 1   ☎02 83 78 166 www.letrottoir.it

Navigli is the place to be for student nightlife in Milan, and Le Trottoir is the place to be in Navigli. Welcome to the epicenter of the groovy student clubbing universe. With both live music and a DJ every night of the week, dance floors both downstairs and upstairs, and a crowd ranging from self-conscious hipsters to short-skirted clubbers, Le Trottoir is the place to talk about the Middle Eastern-themed pop at lunch, then get your groove on in the early evening.

i Ⓜ2: Porta Genova. Take V. Casale and turn left onto Alzaia Naviglio Grande. Continue straight onto Vle. Gorizia to P. XXIV Maggio. Located in the piazza, an island in a sea of roads. Concert schedule online. DJ and live music nightly. Cover M-Th free, F-Sa €10, Su free (includes 1 drink). 1st drink, aperitivo, and buffet €8. Ⓣ Open daily 11am-2am (although those in the know say it rarely closes until 3am).

SCIMMIE   BAR, RISTORANTE

V. Ascanio Sforza 49   ☎02 89 40 28 74 www.scimmie.it

Half old-school saloon, half alt-rock club, Scimmie's dimly lit bar space is also a performance venue for some of the hottest acts in the Milanese alt scene and beyond. With small, intimate tables, dangling glass chandeliers, and old-school posters of dudes who have performed here, Scimmie's crowd consists of music aficionados in their early 30s—until the night ages and the crowd grows younger as students drop in for some music.

i Ⓜ2: Porta Genova. From the metro stop, head south on V. Casale, cross the canal, and continue straight. At P. Arcole, continue on V. Giovanni Segantini and turn left onto V. Giosuè Borsi and cross the canal. Scimmie is on the right. Concert schedule online. 1st drink €10. Mixed drinks €4-9. Primi €8-12; secondi €18-22. Ⓣ Open daily 7:30pm-late ("If the crowd's really into it, we'll go as late as 6am," the bartender says). Live music begins 11pm.

milan

ARTS AND CULTURE

⚫ TEATRO ALLA SCALA
P. della Scala

THEATER

☎02 88 791 www.teatroallascala.org

No opera can be complete without having been performed at La Scala, the world's preeminent venue. Even after the enormous crystal chandelier dims, the beauty of the place remains palpable, as the opera house's stunning acoustics and the audience's unparalleled enthusiasm make seeing a show at La Scala a treat for patrons as far removed from the stage as the highest balcony.

i Ⓜ1 or 3: Duomo. Pass through the Galleria to P. della Scala. Dress code: jacket and tie for men, appropriate attire for women. The theater also occasionally hosts symphony concerts, typically in Dec and Mar. Ticket prices vary widely depending on performance. Students can get €10 preview ticketsfor select performances, so check the website for upcoming performances. ☑ Box office open daily noon-6pm inⓂ1: Duomo and at theater 2hr. before performances. Opera season is Sept-Jul.

SHOPPING

⚫ D MAGAZINE OUTLET
V. Montenapoleone 26

FASHION DISTRICT

☎02 76 00 60 27

We're not saying that the clothes here are cheap; in fact, Montenapoleone might be one of the only streets in the world where a €90 shirt is a bargain. But if you want quality without breaking the bank, there is no better place to be.

i Ⓜ3: Montenapoleone. Men's and women's apparel from €30; most pieces €50-120. ☑ Open daily 10am-7:30pm.

ARMANI
V. Manzoni 31

FASHION DISTRICT

☎02 72 31 86 00 www.armani.com

After gazing into the dark, tinted windows and walking past the black-clad guard into this lacquered and mirrored temple to fashion, one might begin to wonder: where are all the clothes? Each shelf bears only a few items, all looking as if they were pinned into perfect position by the designer himself. It's all right, though: there are few customers who could afford to buy more than one article of clothing here anyway.

i Ⓜ3: Montenapoleone. Clothing starting at €180. No big deal. ☑ Open M-Sa 10am-9pm, Su 10:30am-7:30pm

PRADA
V. Montenapoleone 6-8

FASHION DISTRICT

☎02 777 17 71 www.prada.com

The first thing you see when you walk inside Prada's flagship store? Purses and handbags neatly arranged on different blocks. And what can you put in handbags? Jackets and dresses and shoes and sunglasses and perfumes and anything else that Prada makes. How convenient.

i Ⓜ1: San Babila. Walk up V. Montenapoleone. Handbags €200-2000+. ☑ Open M-Sa 10am-7:30pm, Su 11am-7pm.

GUCCI
V. Montenapoleone 5-7

FASHION DISTRICT

☎02 77 12 71 www.gucci.com

Let's do the weight-to-euro ratio test for Gucci. Blouse price: €800. Mass: approx. 25g. That's €32 a gram—it's like fashion cocaine, only legal and probably even more expensive. Other specialties include a €4000 jacket that might just be made of zebra and also might just cost more than your semester in Europe.

i Ⓜ1: San Babila. Men's apparel from €120. Women's from €200. ☑ Open M-F 10am-7pm, Sa 10am-7:30pm, Su 10am-1pm and 2-7pm.

ESSENTIALS
Practicalities

- **TOURIST OFFICES: Informazioni Accoglienza Turistica** is Milan's central tourist office. It publishes *Hello Milano*, which offers information in English on events and nightlife, and the monthly *Milanomese*, which has a comprehensive list of events and exhibitions in Italian and English. Tour operators keep desks here as well, and the office has helpful English-speaking representatives. (P. Castello 1 ☎02 77 40 43 43 www.visitamilano.it *i* Directly on the left when facing the Castello. ☒ Open M-F 9am-6pm, Sa 9am-1:30pm and 2-6pm, Su and holidays 9am-1:30pm and 2-5pm.) **Stazione Central Branch.** (☎02 77 40 43 18 *i* Directly across from the tracks.)

- **TOURS: Autostradale** (☎02 72 00 13 04 www.autostradale.it) has a sales desk in the tourist office and operates hop-on, hop-off sightseeing city tours that circle the *centro.* Taped commentary available in English. 3hr. tours (€60) depart P. Duomo at 9:30am and include admission to Leonardo da Vinci's *The Last Supper.* Walking tours (€20-30) including the Duomo, Galleria Vittorio Emanuele II, and La Scala or Castello Sforzesco depart daily at 10am.

- **CONSULATES: Australia.** (V. Borgogna 2, 3rd fl. ☎02 77 67 41 www.italy.embassy.gov.au/ rome/home.html *i* Ⓜ1: San Babila. Appointments recommended. ☒ Open M-Th 8:30am-1pm and 1:30-5pm, F 8:30am-1pm.) **Canada.** (V. Vittor Pisani 19 ☎02 67 581 www.canada. it *i* Ⓜ2 or 3: Centrale F.S. ☒ Open M-F 9am-noon.) **New Zealand.** (V. Terraggio 17 ☎02 72 17 00 01 www.nzembassy.com/italy *i* Ⓜ1 or 2: Cardona F.N. ☒ Open M-Sa 8:30am-12:30pm and 1:30-5pm.) **UK.** (V. S. Paolo 7 ☎02 72 30 01 www.britain.it *i* Ⓜ1 or 3: Duomo. ☒ Open Nov-Mar M-F 8am-noon and 1-4pm; Apr-Oct M-F 7-11am and noon-3pm.) **US.** (V. Principe Amedeo 2/10 ☎02 29 03 51 www.milan.usconsulate.gov *i* Ⓜ3: Turati. ☒ Open M-F 8:30am-noon.)

- **CURRENCY EXCHANGE:** Banks and ATMs are abundant. (☒ Most banks are open M-F 8:30am-1:30pm and 3-4pm.) **Western Union** located in Stazione Centrale. (☒ Open daily 9am-7:45pm.) **American Express.** (V. Larga 4 ☎02 72 10 41 *i* Near the Duomo. ☒ Open M-F 9am-5:30pm.)

- **LUGGAGE STORAGE: Stazione Centrale.** (1st 5hr. €5. Each additional hr. up to 12hr. €0.70 per hr. Additional hr. after 12hr. €0.30 per hr. ☒ Open daily 6am-11:50pm.)

- **GLBT RESOURCES: ARCI-GAY Centro D'Iniziativa Gay.** (V. Bezzeca 3 ☎02 54 12 22 25 www. arcigaymilano.org ☒ Open M-F 3-8pm.)

- **DISABLED SERVICES: AIAS Milano Onlus.** (V. Paolo Mantegazza 10 ☎02 33 02 021 www. aiasmilano.it)

- **POST OFFICES:** (P. Cordusio 4 ☎02 72 48 21 26 *i* Near P. Duomo. Currency exchange and ATM. ☒ Open M-F 8am-7pm, Sa 8:30am-noon.)

- **POSTAL CODE:** 20100

Emergency

- **POLICE:** P. Cesare Beccaria, near the Duomo (☎02 772 71)

- **LATE-NIGHT PHARMACIES:** These can be found in **Stazione Centrale** (☎02 669 0735) and **Stazione Porta Garibaldi** (☎02 63 47 03 62). Most other pharmacies post after-hours rotations.

- **HOSPITALS/MEDICAL SERVICES: Ospedale Fatebenefratelli** (C. Porta Nuova 23 ☎02 63 631) and **Ospedale Maggiore di Milano.** (V. Francesco Sforza 35 ☎02 550 31 *i* 5min. from the Duomo on the inner ring road.) **Ospedale Niguarda Ca'Grande** is in the north of the city. (P. Ospedale Maggiore 3 ☎02 644 41)

milan

Getting There

BY PLANE

MALPENSA AIRPORT (MXP)

48km northwest of the city   ☎02 23 23 23 www.sea-aeroportimilano.it

Shuttles run to the right side of Stazione Centrale. (☎02 58 58 31 85 www.malpensashuttle.it *i* €10, round-trip €16. ⏱ 50min., every 20min. daily to airport 5am-9:30pm; to Stazione Centrale 6:20am-12:15am.) The airport also offers service between Malpensa and Linate airports. The Malpensa Express train departs Cardona Station (Stazione Nord). (*i* €10, round-trip €16. ⏱ 40min., every 30min. daily to airport 5:50am-8:20pm; to Stazione Nord 6:45am-9:45pm.)

LINATE AIRPORT (LIN)

7km east of the city   ☎02 23 23 23 www.sea-aeroportimilano.it

Serves domestic, European, and some intercontinental flights. Starfly buses (☎02 58 58 72 37 www.starfly.net) run to Stazione Centrale. (*i* €5. ⏱ 20min., every 30min. daily to airport 5am-10pm; to Stazione Centrale 6:15am-10:45pm.) City bus #73 runs to the downtown San Babila metro station (€1.50).

ORIO AL SERIO AIRPORT (BGY)

Bergamo, 58km northeast of the city   ☎035 32 63 23 www.sacbo.it

With 🗲 **budget airlines,** there's always a compromise that has to be made. And that compromise is location. So, although Bergamo might be a completely different city, it does provide a cheap option for arriving in Milan. Airlines that fly here include Ryanair and WizzAir. Inconvenience is greatly reduced by the shuttle bus that runs to Stazione Centrale. (*i* €7.90. ⏱ 1hr., every 30min. daily to airport 4am-11:30pm; to Milan 4:30am-1am.) General information, including a link to the transport workers' strike calendar (super convenient in Italy), can be found at the above number and website.

BY TRAIN

Milan's main train station (Italy's second busiest) is **Stazione Centrale.** (☎89 20 21 *i* Northeast of the city center in P. Duca d'Aosta.) It serves most **Trenitalia** trains, including high-speed **Frecciarossa (Eurostar)** lines. The ticket office on the ground floor is open daily 5:50am-10:20pm. The Trenitalia information booth located in the ticket office is open daily 7am-9pm. Trains run to Florence (*i* Eurostar €52, regional trains €27.50 ⏱ Eurostar 2hr., every hr. 5:45am-8:15pm. Regional train 3hr., every 3hr. 6:50am-8:15pm), Rome (*i* Eurostar €89, regional trains €46 ⏱ Eurostar 3½hr., departs more than once per hr. 5:45am-9pm. Regional train 6½hr., every 3hr. 6:50am-11:30pm), Turin (*i* €9.55 ⏱ 2hr., every hr. 5:15am-12:15am), Venice (*i* €30 ⏱ 2hr., every hr. 6:35am-9pm), and numerous local destinations.

Milan has several other, smaller stations on its periphery, accessible at the edges of the metro lines. The most significant of these is **Cardona-Stazione Nord** (☎199 15 11 52), hub for **Ferrovie Nord,** northern Italy's regional train company. **Malpensa Express** also departs from Cardona Station (see **By Plane**). **Stazione Porta Garibaldi** is a primary commuter station serving local destinations. Milan's oldest train station, **Porta Genova,** is slowly being phased out of the network, so you probably won't need to worry about it except as a metro stop for the phenomenal Cimitero Monumentale.

BY BUS

Airport buses depart from the southeast side of Stazione Centrale, with signs for times and prices posted outside. Tickets are available onboard. Most intercity buses arrive at the town's periphery. **Autostradale** arrives at Ⓜ1: Lampugnano and Stazione Porta Garibaldi. Other companies arrive at P. Castello near Stazione Nord (Ⓜ1: Cairoli). Bus service is available from virtually any town in the region, including Turin and basically anywhere you could (and couldn't) care about in Lombardy, in addition to some places beyond.

Getting Around

BY PUBLIC TRANSPORTATION

Milan's extensive and efficient transit network is the pride of the city. The **metropolitana Milanese** underground system runs from 6am-midnight and is the quickest and most useful branch of public transit, covering most areas in the city proper. Ⓜ**Line 1** (red) stretches from the suburbs of Sesto, northeast of the city (Sesto 1 Maggio F.S.), to the exposition centers of Rho-Fiera in the northwest and Bisceglie in the southwest. Ⓜ**Line 2** (green) links Milan's three primary train stations—Cardona F.N., Garibaldi F.S., and Centrale F.S.—while spanning from Cologno Nord and Gessate in the east to Abbiategrasso in the west. It crosses Ⓜ1 at Cardona and Loreto. Ⓜ**Line 3** (yellow) runs south from the up-and-coming neighborhoods near Maciachini to San Donato, crossing Ⓜ2 at Stazione Centrale and Ⓜ1 at the Duomo.

The subway's reach is not all-encompassing, so beyond its range is a system of **trams** and **buses** that connects metro stations to the less accessible parts of the city. Trams #29/30 circle the city's outer ring road, while bus #94 circles the inner road. Tickets (€1.50) are good for the metro, trams, and buses for 1hr. after validation; €4.50 buys a 24hr. pass and €13.50 gets 10 urban trips. Evening tickets (€1.80) are valid after 8pm until close on the day validated. For late-night travel, ATM operates a **Radiobus** service (☎02 48 03 48 03), which will pick up passengers holding valid ATM tickets anywhere in the city for a €2 surcharge (€1.50 if purchased in advance from the locations above), from 8pm-2am.

BY CAB

White taxis are omnipresent in the city, and cab stands in major *piazze* usually have cabs day and night. You can hail one on the street, but it's more common to pick them up at cab stands. Otherwise, call one of the major companies: **Autoradio Taxi** (☎02 85 85), **Taxi Blu** (☎02 40 40), or **RadioTaxi** (☎02 69 69).

BY BIKE

The new **bikeMi** (☎800 80 81 81 www.bikemi.it) program has installed dozens of pick-up and drop-off locations where locals and visitors can check out bikes and leave them at their destination. These are sprinkled throughout the city and its outskirts. (*i* Daily subscriptions €2.50, weekly €6, plus fees of €0.50 per 30min. after 1st 30min. up to 2hr. After 2hr., fines of €2 per hr. apply.)

venice

There will come a moment in Venice when you are standing on a bridge sandwiched in the middle of a mob of travelers, pinned between the shoving elbows of two sweaty tourists and fearing that you are about to meet your end. You will wonder why you even came to this city, where at any given time the tourists outnumber the locals, and you will rue the day you committed yourself to overpriced gelato, rapacious restaurant owners, and an endless parade of fake Gucci bags. Was it the fleeting visions of Tadzio or the myth of gorgeous gondoliers, the allure of a future Atlantis or the desire for cheap glass earrings at a tourist stall? All of the above, friends—all of the above. For underneath and even within this chaos, Venice is well-visited for a reason: it's magical. Not Harry Potter magical (though we have our suspicions), but bastion of art and culture, gorgeous ocean views, and killer food magical. In fact, Venice's concentration of fanny packs is surpassed only by its concentration of some of the best sights, tastes, and vibes in Europe. With a bit of time spent exploring

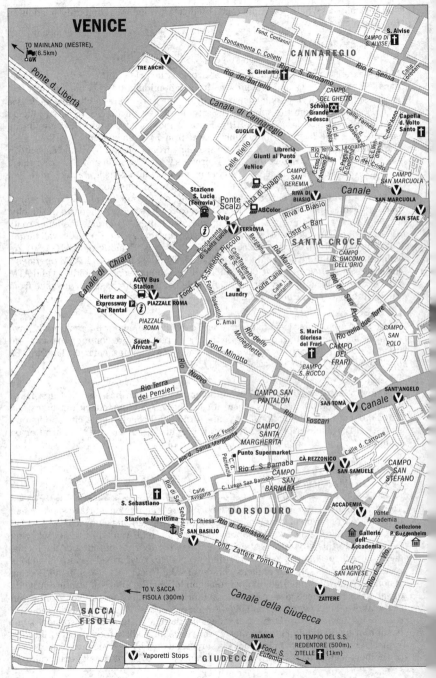

VENICE

TO MAINLAND (MESTRE), (6.5km)
UK

Ponte d. Libertà

TRE ARCHI

Fond. Contanni

Fondamenta C. Colletti

CANNAREGIO

S. Alvise
CAMPO DI S. ALVISE

S. Girolamo
Rio d. S. Girolamo

Rio dei Battello

Calle Loredana

Rio d. Sensa

Calle

Canale di Cannaregio

GUGLIE

CAMPO DEL GHETTO

Schola Grande Tedesca

Calle Farnese

C. d. Rabbia

Capella d. Volto Santo

Calle d.-all'Aseo

Calle Riello

Libreria Giunti al Punto

VeNice

Rio Terra S. Leonardo

C. Chiesa

C.d. Colonna

C. Pistor

C. del Cristo

C.Pegola

CAMPO SAN MARCUOLA

SAN MARCUOLA

Stazione
S. Lucia
(Ferrovia)

Ponte
Scalzi

Vela

Lista di Spagna

ABColor

CAMPO SAN GEREMIA

RIVA DI BIASIO

Riva d. Biasio

Canale

SAN STAE

FERROVIA

Fondamenta di Santa Lucia

C. S. Simeon Piccolo

Calle Traghetto

C. S. Lucia

C. Bergama

Lista d. Bari

SANTA CROCE

Canale di Chiara

ACTV Bus Station

Hertz and Expressway Car Rental

PIAZZALE ROMA

PIAZZALE ROMA

C. Bagomoro

Corte Canal

C. Contarina

Rio Marin

Rio d. San Polo

CAMPO S. GIACOMO DELL'ORIO

Laundry

C. Amai

Rio delle Muneghette

Fond. Minotto

S. Maria Gloriosa dei Frari

CAMPO DEI FRARI

Rio della due Torre

CAMPO SAN POLO

Rio Nuovo

Rio Terra dei Pensieri

CAMPO SAN PANTALON

CAMPO S. ROCCO

SAN TOMÀ

Rio Foscari

Canale

SANT'ANGELO

italy

South African

Fond. Foscani

CAMPO SANTA MARGHERITA

Rio d. Santa Margherita

Punto Supermarket

Rio d. S. Barnaba

Calle Pazienza

CAMPO SAN BARNABA

C. Lunga San Barnaba

CÀ REZZONICO

SAN SAMUELE

Calle d. Cartozze

CAMPO SAN STEFANO

Calle Avogaria

S. Sebastiano

Rio di San Sebastiano

Stazione Marittima

SAN BASILIO

C. Chiesa

Rio d. Ognissanti

DORSODURO

ACCADEMIA

Ponte Accademia

Gallerie dell' Accademia

Collezione P. Guggenheim

CAMPO SAN AGNESE

Rio d. S. Vio

Fond. Zattere Ponto Lungo

TO V. SACCA
FISOLA (300m)

Canale della Giudecca

ZATTERE

SACCA
FISOLA

PALANCA
Fond. S. Eufemia

TO TEMPIO DEL S.S. REDENTORE (500m), ZITELLE (1km)

GIUDECCA

V Vaporetti Stops

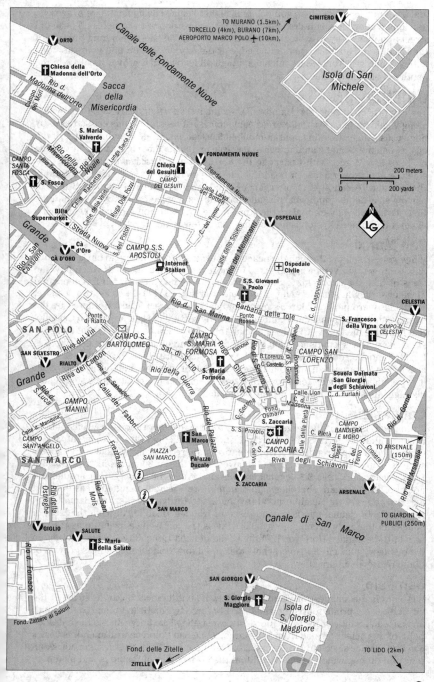

venice

and a willingness to get lost, you will realize that Venice has its fair share of secrets: unmapped alleyways, sun-drenched campos filled with locals at lunch, and peaceful streets populated by dreadlocked art students. Both in the glimmering interior of the Basilica di San Marco and at the edge of the city where you find yourself alone with sky and sea, Venice has an enchantment all its own that proves its place in the pantheon of Italian cities.

ORIENTATION

Venice's historical center is composed of six main *sestieri*, or districts. Often divided along vague boundaries, these areas each consist of several islands crisscrossed by numerous canals. Bustling, tourist-mobbed **San Marco** is the geographic center of the city. Cross the Grand Canal to get to **San Polo** and **Santa Croce. Cannaregio** lies to the north of San Marco, with **Castello** to the northeast and **Dorsoduro** to the south. Outside the city proper, a set of beautiful islands—including Lido, Giudecca, Murano, Burano, and Torcello—each offer unique windows into Venice's rich past. A maze of narrow streets, ubiquitous canals, and footbridges, Venice can be overwhelming at first. It's best to wander, soak in the atmosphere, and take comfort in knowing that a *vaporetto* (water bus) stop is never more than a few minutes away.

San Marco

When you're walking through the peaceful backstreets of Cannaregio or Castello, it's easy to forget that Venice is populated by more tourists than locals. If you follow the signs or take the *vaporetto* to San Marco, that fact hits you with full force: palatial museums, ritzy hotels, designer shops, and tourist throngs fill this central sestiere, particularly around San Marco's main landmark, **Piazza San Marco.** Bordered by the Grand Canal, the Canale della Giudecca, and the sestieri of Cannaregio and Castello, San Marco is the heart of Venice—and all the tourists know it. While having to stop short every few seconds lest you step into the frame of another traveler's photo is hugely annoying, don't let your fear of becoming a fixture of family albums scare you away from the area. San Marco may be chock-full of tourists (and tourist traps), but it is popular and pricey for a reason: it boasts some of the most impressive sights, distinguished museums, and upscale dining in all of Europe.

Cannaregio

Cannaregio is one of the largest and least touristy neighborhoods in Venice. Major avenues like Rio Terrà San Leonardo, Lista di Spagna, and Strada Nova cut across Cannaregio's smaller side streets; the entire sestiere is easily walkable and accessible by *vaporetto*, and San Marco is never more than a 30min. walk away. **Campo San Geremia** and **Campo S.S. Apostoli** are vibrant centers of activity built around the neighborhood's main churches. Most hotels are located along the eastern and western edges of the neighborhood (by the Rialto Bridge and Stazione Santa Lucia, respectively). Cannaregio is a good place to wander. Head north from the Lista di Spagna in the early evening and you'll witness the real Venice swim up as the sun sets into the canals. Here you'll find a scene of such tranquility—boats bobbing in the distance, gulls circling overhead—that you'll forget about the endless crowds of Cannaregio's main drags.

San Polo

San Polo is the smallest of Venice's six *sestieri*, but its location in the heart of the city makes it a prime tourist destination. Bordered by the Grand Canal to the south and east and Santa Croce to the north and west, the **Rialto Bridge** marks the entrance point of this neighborhood from San Marco, while San Polo's central anchor is **Campo San Polo,** Venice's second largest *piazza*. Many tourists favor this sestiere for shopping and dining, which means you'll find the normal mix of fabulous and mediocre restaurants (be wary, as always, of tourist menus and over-trafficked spots) despite a surprisingly limited selection of hotels. It's easy to get lost in San Polo, where finding your way around takes more of an intuitive, follow-the-crowd tilt. Stick to the wider streets, which usually lead to Rialto or Santa Croce—though, admittedly, navigation is a different beast in Venice than in most parts of the world. Nevertheless, if you have the patience and the stamina for exploration, the sights and smells of San Polo make getting lost in this neighborhood worthwhile.

Santa Croce

Though a small neighborhood, Santa Croce is incredibly diverse and easily accessible from western Cannaregio, San Polo, and Dorsoduro. While Santa Croce is defined in the northwest by **Piazzale Roma,** the main stop for most buses and taxis coming into Venice, the neighborhood's westernmost parts and the area bordering the Grand Canal fall prey to the same generic restaurants and hotels as most of the tourist hubs in Venice. Authentic Venetian food and affordable lodgings, however, remain surprisingly close by. In the western areas of Santa Croce, cheap, genuine neighborhood snack bars mix with tourist restaurants; in the north, lazy residential streets intersperse busy tourist thoroughfares. With a little digging, Santa Croce yields a peaceful vision of daily Venetian life.

Dorsoduro

Dorsoduro is the cool young aunt at the *sestiere* family reunion. As Santa Croce and San Polo sit on the porch in rocking chairs, San Marco and Castello compare family photographs, and Cannaregio bangs around the kitchen making lasagna, Dorsoduro's wearing a Gucci belly-top and doing yoga in the front yard. If you've ever wondered where Venice's under-40 crowd is hiding, you've come to the right place: **Ca' Foscari University** and the **Academy of Fine Arts** make this neighborhood the unsurpassable leader in number of deadlocks per capita. Bordered to the north by Santa Croce, Dorsoduro stretches east as a kind of peninsula, with the island of Giudecca to the south and San Marco to the north. With the perfect combination of bars, quality restaurants, awesome museums, youthful personality, and cheap kebabs, Dorsoduro is the anti-San Marco and the one place in Venice where fedora beats fanny pack.

Castello

Castello gets a lot of spillover traffic from San Marco, but as you head farther north and east, its charming local character begins to shine through. Residents proudly proclaim that eastern Castello represents the true, vanishing Venice, but most visitors are more interested in the western end, where crowded thoroughfares like **Salizada San Lio** and **Salizada San Provolo** offer excellent restaurants and easy access to the city center. If lost, navigate using landmarks like **Santa Maria Formosa,** a prominent church at the center of a big square of the same name, as well as **Rio dei Greci** and **Rio di San Lorenzo,** a canal that cuts through the heart of the neighborhood.

SIGHTS

An incredible number of churches, museums, palaces, and historic sights line Venice's canals—you could easily spend a month in the city and not see everything. With so many sights to see and so many admission fees to pay, your bank balance might start to sink as fast as Venice itself. The **Venice Card,** valid for one week from purchase, is available at any tourist office and provides free admission to the Civic Museums of Venice and 16 churches and reduced admission to temporary exhibits, art festivals, and other museums.

A "good deal" in Venice usually isn't a low-priced hotel—it's a hotel where the high price is matched by high quality. Some of the best bargains can be found in Cannaregio and Castello, while student apartments are available in Dorsoduro for those looking to stay longer. Unless you have money to burn, though, give up that vision of a room with a view of the Grand Canal. Here are a couple great deals we found; other budget finds—and a few splurges—can be found at **www.letsgo.com**.

ALBERGO CASA BOCCASSINI   HOTEL $$
Calle Volto 5295   ☎041 52 29 892 www.hotelboccassini.com
This isn't one of the palatial hotels along the Grand Canal, but it still has a doorbell made of silver and a marble staircase. Casa Boccassini is the hidden gem of Cannaregio, offering opulent lodging at reasonable prices. The shared-bathroom singles are a real steal.
i Breakfast included. Singles €30-60; doubles €50-90, with bath €70-140.

BACKPACKER'S HOUSE VENICE   HOSTEL $
Campo Santa Margherita 2967A ☎041 31 90 444 www.backpackershousevenice.com
This hostel is smack dab in the bustling nightlife center of Dorsoduro, but is still quiet and tucked away. There's not much to it besides dorm beds and doubles, but when the bars are done with you, you won't be in a state to appreciate anything else anyway. Plus, you'd be hard-pressed to find a bed this cheap anywhere else in Dorsoduro.
i Reception is in the restaurant bar in the northeast corner of Campo Santa Margherita. The hostel is across the campo and a few doors up the street. Free Wi-Fi. Ask for keys to a small kitchen. Dorms €23; doubles €46.

FORESTERIA VALDESE   HOSTEL, HOTEL $$
Palazzo Cavagnis 5170   ☎041 52 86 797 www.foresteriavenezia.it
One of few places in Venice offering dorms, Foresteria is run by a Protestant church and is an oasis of value in a sea o €90-per-person, one-star hotels. The shared dorm rooms and common spaces make it a good place for meeting fellow travelers, something that's difficult to do elsewhere in Venice.
i Breakfast included. Dorm €23-29; doubles €78-96; triples €90-111; quads €114-144.

OSTELLO DI VENEZIA (HI)   HOSTEL $
Fondamenta Zitelle 86   ☎041 52 38 211 www.hostelvenice.com
With 260 beds, a bar, restaurant, spacious common room, and state-of-the-art facilities, Ostello di Venezia sets the standard for hostels in Venice. Dorms are single-sex, though groups can book co-ed rooms in advance. The hostel is on Giudecca, but it doesn't feel detached from the city center at all, as it's less than a 5min. *vaporetto* ride to San Marco.
i Those without YHA membership must pay either €3 daily surcharge or leave a deposit. Breakfast included. Lockers included. Wi-Fi €3 per 20hr. 16-bed dorms €22. ☼ Quiet hours after 10pm.

HOTEL STELLA ALPINA   HOTEL $$$$
Calle Priuli detta dei Cavalletti 99D   ☎041 52 45 274 www.hotel-stellaalpina.com
Stella Alpina isn't cheap, but you'll get more for your money here than at many accommodations in Venice. The rooms are modern, with wide windows, amazingly comfortable beds, and lots of floor space.
i Breakfast included. Doubles €50-180; triples €70-200; quads €95-215.

italy

San Marco

◪ PALAZZO DUCALE
MUSEUM

P. San Marco 1   ☎041 27 15 911 www.museicivicivaneziani.it

Of the famous works, Sansovino's statues in the courtyard and Veronese's Rape of Europa are particularly renowned. Tintoretto's Il Paradiso, the longest canvas painting in the world, presides over the Great Council Room with a powerful, ominous presence. Also not to be missed is the grandiose Golden Stairway. Once you've had enough art and opulence, follow the signs to the prisons, a dark, extensive labyrinth in the lower eastern side of the palace. On your way out of the dungeons, peer out onto Venice from the Bridge of Sighs, named after prisoners who caught their last glimpses of freedom through the very same grates where visitors today pause to snap photos.

i *Ticket also valid for the Museo Correr, Museo Archeologico, and Sale Monumentali della Biblioteca Nazionale Marciana. Apr-Oct €14; students ages 15-25, ages 6-14, and over 65 €8. Nov-Mar €12/7. With Venice Card free.* ◷ *Open daily Apr-Oct 8:30am-7pm; Nov-Mar 9am-6pm. Last entry 1hr. before close.*

◪ BASILICA DI SAN MARCO
CHURCH

P. San Marco   ☎041 27 08 311 www.basilicasanmarco.it

See that impossibly long line trailing through P. San Marco from early morning to mid-afternoon? Everyone's in line for the basilica. This must-see is both ravishing and free, and, since visitors seldom spend more than 15min. inside, the line moves faster than you'd think. Once you make it inside, you'll be struck by the church's soaring domes, marble inlay, and golden mosaics, seamlessly incorporating Byzantine, Roman, and Northern European styles in typical Venetian fashion. Founded in the ninth century by two Venetian merchants who stole St. Mark's remains from Alexandria and smuggled them past Arab officials by hiding them in a case of pork, the original wooden church was destroyed by fire two centuries later. The current incarnation of the basilica dates to the 17th century. Those seeking to further explore the basilica's history will have to pay extra for its three affiliated sights: the Pala d'Oro, an altar depicting the life of St. Mark; the treasury, which houses precious religious objects; and St. Mark's Museum, a great primer in Venetian history that contextualizes the church.

i *Modest dress required—no bare shoulders or revealing skirts or shorts. Basilica free. Pala d'Oro €2. Treasury €3. St. Mark's Museum €4.* ◷ *Basilica open Easter-Nov M-Sa 9:45am-5pm, Su 2-5pm; Dec-Easter M-Sa 9:45am-5pm, Su 2-4pm. Pala d'Oro and treasury open Easter-Nov M-Sa 9:45am-5pm, Su 2-5pm; Dec-Easter M-Sa 9:45am-4pm, Su 2-4pm. Museum open daily 9:45am-4:45pm.*

◪ PALAZZO GRASSI
MUSEUM

Campo San Samuele 3231   ☎041 52 31 680 www.palazzograssi.it

A highbrow museum of modern art that's not afraid to laugh at itself, Palazzo Grassi is stimulating and refreshingly ridiculous. Affiliated with the Punta della Dogana museum in Dorsoduro, it features works by contemporary artists from around the world. The collection is so extensive and diverse that something is bound to interest, challenge, or amuse you, even if modern art usually leaves you mystified. The tickets aren't cheap, but you won't regret it once you're laughing at the gargantuan, patchwork-quilted stuffed toy invading the central atrium and coiling up the stairway.

i *€15; ages 12-18, students under 25, and seniors over 65 €10; under 11 free.* ◷ *Open M 10am-7pm, W-Su 10am-7pm. Last entry 6pm.*

PIAZZA SAN MARCO
PIAZZA

P. San Marco, the most important square in Venice, is a study in contrasts. Chaotic despite being at the heart of Venice's serene lagoon, this dignified seat of

Venetian government is now overrun by tour groups flocking to its many sights. Loaded travelers lounge with €12 cappuccinos at ritzy tea houses, while those on a budget buy stale bread from shrewd locals to feed the resident pigeons. Swing by early in the morning or in the evening to see the rare sight of P. San Marco sans tourists. In recent years, the *piazza* has been known to flood at high tide—when you're ready to soak up San Marco's old-world glamour, make sure to leave those new Ferragamo pumps at home.

CAMPANILE
TOWER

P. San Marco ☎041 27 08 31 www.basilicasanmarco.it

This tall brick bell tower is undeniably the dominant fixture of the Venetian skyline, so much so that, in 1997, a group of Venetian separatists stormed it to proclaim their message from its heights. The original tower, completed in 1514, collapsed in 1902; the reconstruction was completed a decade later. Today, visitors can take the elevator to the top to enjoy fantastic views over the city. The view may be excellent, but, considering the €8 admission fee, those on a tight budget might be better off just admiring the Campanile from the ground.

i €8. 🕐 Open daily Jul-Sept 9am-9pm; Oct 9am-7pm; Nov-Easter 9:30am-3:45pm; Easter-Jun 9am-7pm.

Cannaregio

🏛 CA' D'ORO
MUSEUM

Strada Nova 3932 ☎041 52 00 345 www.cadoro.org

This centuries-old private palace—a stunning example of Venetian architecture in itself—now houses one of the most impressive art collections in the city. The galleries contain humongous wall paintings, sculptures, and tapestries, and contemporary works are exhibited alongside Renaissance relics. Don't sweat the high ticket price; this is one of the best ways to spend €8 in Venice.

i €8, EU citizens 18-25 €6, EU citizens ages under 18 and over 65 free. 🕐 Open M 8:15am-2pm, Tu-Su 8:15am-7:15pm. Last entry 30min. before close.

🏛 THE JEWISH GHETTO
NEIGHBORHOOD

Campo di Ghetto Nuovo ☎041 71 50 12 www.moked.it/jewishvenice

The Jewish Ghetto provides a poignant window into the soul of old Venice. It consists of a small neighborhood around a large square with a towering obelisk at its center. Much of the ghetto's original architecture, including several synagogues, has been preserved through the years. You can see this area's history by just strolling around, though you can swing by the small Hebraic Museum for more context.

CHIESA SANTA MARIA IN NAZARETH O DEGLI SCALZI
CHURCH

Fondamenta dei Scalzi 54

Next to the hustle and bustle of the train station, Chiesa Santa Maria is a Baroque glory. Duck in for a few minutes if you want to inject some serious art into your life or if you're in need of a nice sanctuary from Venice's heat and crowds. Multi-colored marble forms the great swirls and statues of this impressive building. Take a second to reflect on the feat of engineering this building represents: all the people mining, cutting, constructing, and carving the marble into statues, altars, and altarpieces; people high on scaffolds painstakingly painting the angels on the ceiling. A few minutes in this marvel and you'll realize that is it truly a haven in the midst of the hoi polloi of Venice.

i Be conscious of appropriate attire; bare shoulders or legs are frowned upon. Open M-Sa 7:45am-11:30am and 4pm-7pm; Su 7am-11:45am and 4pm-6:45pm. Mass is celebrated several times a day during visiting hours, so be conscious of this possibility; mass times are posted on the door.

SAN POLO

Though a small neighborhood, San Polo has several sights that are well worth visiting. In addition to the Rialto Bridge and the area immediately surrounding it, several nearby churches and museums count among Venice's most rewarding destinations.

◪ RIALTO BRIDGE
BRIDGE

Over the Grand Canal

As the oldest bridge across the Grand Canal, Rialto draws a hefty tourist freight, and, despite the invariable disdain of local Venetians, the 1561 stone structure is worth a look. Not only does it boast a vantage to admire the Grand Canal's innumerable palazzi and gondole, but, when your camera battery dies, its three lanes are also lined with shops that stock every glass penguin and designer scarf you never knew you needed. Those seeking the perfect picture of the bridge should head south on the San Marco side and cross two smaller waterfront bridges to capture the full span of the bridge.

◪ BASILICA DEI FRARI
CHURCH

Campo dei Frari 3072 ☎041 52 22 637 www.basilicadeifrari.it

You may be skeptical about this church when you encounter its industrial-looking brick facade. As we all know, though, it's what's inside that counts, and the Frari is much more gifted when it comes to inner beauty. From Bellini to the remains of Titian, famous artists fill the spaces between carved arch ceiling beams and the orange-and-white checkered floor. A host of giant funerary monuments, including a marble pyramid and a sculpted skinless man bearing a banner, could each be a worthy sight in themselves, but you'll also find frescoes, rooms on church history, and gold pillaged by crusaders in the Holy Land. The best time to see the Frari is close to opening or closing, when the fewest tour groups are clunking through the halls.

i Open M-Sa 9am-6pm, Su 1-6pm. Last entry 5:30pm.

Santa Croce

Though not renowned for its sights, Santa Croce has a few that you could happily get lost in for an afternoon.

MUSEO DI STORIA NATURALE
MUSEUM

Santa Croce 1730 ☎041 27 50 206 www.msn.ve.it

It may seem odd to visit a natural history museum in Venice, but this extensive collection is truly exceptional. From human ancestor bones to taxidermy to comparisons of species' methods of motion, each extensive display seems to have been cooked up by some experimental interior designer. Fossils hewn into simulated archaeological sites (rather than glass cases with mood-setting soundtracks) make the museum feel like an interactive experience rather than a collection of inaccessible artifacts. If only we could convince them to open their doors a bit later—the ambient lighting and ample space would make for a fantastic nightclub.

i V: San Stae. Continue down Salizada San Stae and take the 1st right that leads to a bridge. Cross 2 bridges, take the 2nd right, and continue until you reach the museum. This museum is difficult to find, but if you follow the signs to Fontego dei Turchi, you'll get there. €8; students ages 15-25, ages 6-14, and over 65 €5.50; under 6 and holders of the Civic Museums pass free. ◫ Open Tu-F 9am-5pm, Sa-Su 10am-6pm. Last entry 1hr. before close.

CA' PESARO
MUSEUM

Santa Croce 2076 ☎041 72 11 27 www.museicivicivenezian.it

One of Venice's many fantastic modern-art museums, Ca' Pesaro exhibits a unique combination of East Asian artwork, late 19th- and early 20th-century paintings and sculptures by the likes of Miró and Klimt, and temporary exhibits that include things like feathered metronomes and warehouse canvases. The permanent collection is carefully presented to trace the development of Modernism, while the East Asian displays full of ornamental weaponry and Indonesian puppets have all the organization of your grandmother's attic. Remember to look up at the *palazzo*'s beautiful ceiling paintings.

i *€6.50; ages 6-14, over 65, students ages 15-25, and holders of the Rolling Venice Card €4; under 6 and holders of the Civic Museums pass free. ⏰ Open Tu-Su Apr-Oct 10am-6pm; Nov-Mar 10am-5pm. Last entry 1hr. before close.*

Dorsoduro

Dorsoduro is home to some truly remarkable modern art. But if colorful blobs or everyday objects with names like "Transcendence" never made sense to you, don't worry—there are also many examples of more classical works.

🔲 THE PEGGY GUGGENHEIM COLLECTION
MUSEUM

Dorsoduro 704   ☎041 24 05 411 www.guggenheim.org

Peggy Guggenheim was a sophisticated traveler. While most of us go from country to country collecting ticket stubs and mosquito bites, Peggy picked up every big artist of the 20th century. Her personal collection may be relatively small compared to some of Venice's other galleries, but everyone is here. You won't find a better place to finally straighten out that Pollock was the one who liked to throw paint, Picasso's people had funny noses, and Dalí liked clocks. The collection is a worthy visit for both art aficionados and those who just like pretty colors. Not to mention it's housed in a beautiful *palazzo* with a sculpture garden and frequent contemporary exhibits.

i *From Santa Maria della Salute, follow the signs west toward the Guggenheim Museum for approximately 4min €14, seniors €11, students €8, members and kids under 10 free. Free presentations at 11am, noon, 4pm, and 5pm. ⏰ Open M 10am-6pm, W-Su 10am-6pm. Last entry 5:45pm.*

🔲 SANTA MARIA DELLA SALUTE
CHURCH

Campo della Salute   ☎041 52 25 558

Got the plague? Of course you don't. Legend has it you've got Santa Maria della Salute to thank for that. Built between 1631 and 1687, the church was intended to pay homage to the Virgin Mary, who many Venetians believed was capable of protecting them from the ravages of the plague. And (depending on who you ask) it worked—1629 marked the last great outbreak of the plague in Venice, though the epidemic of obnoxious tourists had only just begun. Don't just content yourself with staring at the iconic dome from San Marco—hop on the *traghetto* and come on over. Paintings by Tintoretto and Titian highlight the interior of the church, whose gorgeous, sweeping arches and fabulous gold altarpieces are sure to keep you in good spirits and good health.

⏰ *Open daily 9am-noon and 3-5:30pm.*

PUNTA DELLA DOGANA
MUSEUM

Fondamenta della Dogana alla Salute 2   ☎041 52 31 680 www.palazzograssi.it

Terrifying, intriguing, and laughable, Punta della Dogana will make you dive off the deep end of your previous definition of art. Displays like a giant cube made of taxidermied animals or a sculpture of a man with a penis coming out of his eye will leave you anything but indifferent. The price is admittedly a bit steep, but the oddities along the waterfront windows of this huge palace are unforgettable. If also you plan to check out the Palazzo Grassi in San Marco, the joint ticket is a good deal.

i *€15, students and ages 12-18 €10; with Palazzo Grassi in San Marco €20/10. Audio tour €6/4. ⏰ Open M 10am-7pm, W-Su 10am-7pm. Last entry 6pm.*

GALLERIE ACCADEMIA   MUSEUM
Campo della Carità   ☎041 52 00 345 www.gallerieaccademia.org

It's time for I Spy: Accademia Edition. How many scenes of martyrdom can you spot? How many paintings are supposed to trick you into thinking they're architectural details? How many huge, precariously mounted masterpieces look like they're about to fall on your head? How many paintings feature people peeling off other people's thigh skin? (Answers: Too many; can't tell the difference; too scared to stand under them; only one, thank goodness.) If you can find all this, plus the buxom bar maids, stately virgins, and fat babies, you have made a thorough tour of the Accademia. Venice's prime museum for pre-19th century art, it's the place to be if you've got a hankering for huge paintings of Renaissance dudes adoring Jesus. Bonus points if you can spot the painting of ginger Jesus.

i €11, EU citizens 18-25 €9, for EU citizens under 18 and over 65 free. ⏰ Open M 8:15am-2pm, Tu-Su 8:15am-7:15pm.

Lido

Once the world's most popular beach resort, Lido has been largely forgotten by tourists. As a result, visitors can bike along Lido's long coastline, stroll on tree-lined streets, and sunbathe on sandy beaches without having to push past massive crowds. Lido feels the least stereotypically Venetian of the city's islands—its main promenade, Gran Viale, feels more like a California beach town-boulevard than an Italian street.

Giudecca

Giudecca—separated from Dorsoduro by the wide Giudecca Canal—is the most accessible of the lagoon islands. The *vaporetto* #2 makes several stops on the island, at Zitelle, Redentore, and Palanco. Giudecca was the epicenter of Venice's early 20th-century industrial boom. It fell into disrepair after WWII, but the island is now on the upswing with the development of high-end accommodations. The island's industrial past is still on display: the Molino Stucky Hilton, its most prominent landmark (and one of Venice's premier hotels), is located in a former granary and mill.

Murano

Known as "The Glass Island," Murano has been the center of Venice's glass industry since the 13th century, when concerns about fires in the city center led politicians to ban glass production there. Though the large brick buildings, open kilns, and occasional abandoned workshops give the island a gritty industrial feel, Murano also features tree-lined streets, unique churches, and the Museo del Vetro, which houses beautiful exhibits of the island's signature industry. Travel times to Murano vary; expect it to take 20-40min. by boat from the city center. *Vaporetto* lines #41, 42, and LN are generally the best options for getting here.

▨ MUSEO DEL VETRO   MUSEUM
Fondamenta Marco Giustinian 8   ☎041 73 95 86 www.museicivicivveneziani.it

For anyone interested enough in artisan glass to visit Murano in the first place—or anyone who likes pretty things in crazy shapes and vibrant colors—this museum is a must-see. The Museo del Vetro traces the development of Murano's glass industry from its earliest stages to the present day. Don't miss the centerpieces made by famed glassmaker Giuseppe Briati (popular among Venetian royalty and nobility in the 18th century) on the second floor.

i €8, students ages 15-25 €5.50, with Civic Museums Pass free. ⏰ Open daily Apr-Oct 10am-6pm; Nov-Mar 10am-5pm. Last entry 30min. before close.

Burano

Burano is a small island known for its handmade lace, fishing industry, lush parks, and brightly painted buildings. According to legend, the apparently directionally challenged fishermen of Burano painted their houses ostentatious colors so they could readily identify them when returning to the island. Though you can shop for Burano-style lace in Venice proper (see Venetian Artisan Goods), a wide selection of shops as well as a museum dedicated to the craft can be found on the island itself. Burano is also home to the beautiful Church of San Martino, with its infamous leaning campanile, just down the street from P. Galuppi.

FOOD

Food in Venice is serious business. With millions of tourists to feed every year and just as many restaurateurs looking to overcharge innocent travelers, dining can be a perilous and disheartening endeavor. Along the main drags like the Lista di Spagna and anywhere in San Marco, touristy, overpriced establishments with mediocre food are like an army of clones just waiting to attack. With some slyness and stealth, however, you can succeed in finding affordable, delicious food in Venice. Though it's true that restaurant food here costs sometimes twice as much as it might in a neighboring Italian city, the presence of snack bars, sandwich shops, and *pizzerias* offers a lot of cheap fare for the moneyless, while reasonably priced neighborhood restaurants and worth-it splurges are there for you to stumble upon, too.

San Marco

FUORI MENU
Calle del Spezier 2769

BAKERY, SANDWICHES $
☎041 24 10 176

Fuori Menu serves pizza, focaccia, and light sandwiches for wicked cheap. There's a cute yogurt and smoothie bar in the back, but the pastries are the real draw—don't leave Venice without trying their cannoli (€3.50).

i Pastries €1-4. Sandwiches €1.50-6. Pizza and focaccia €2.50-4. ☼ Open daily 8am-9pm.

BISTROT DE VENISE
Calle dei Fabbri 4685

RISTORANTE $$$$
☎041 52 36 651 www.bistrotdevenise.com

If there's one city in Europe where you're going to splurge, it's probably Venice. To treat yourself to some of Venice's best fine dining, come to Bistrot de Venise, where you'll be waited on hand and foot as you feast on dishes like homemade tagliolini with lagoon scallops and saffron-scented celery root (€19). Though you could spend more here than on a week's stay in some hostels, you can be smart and get a perfectly nice entree for €14.

i Entrees €14-38. 5-course tasting menu €80. ☼ Open M-Th noon-3pm and 7pm-midnight, F-Sa noon-3pm and 7pm-1am, Su noon-3pm.

RISTORANTE NOEMI
Calle dei Fabbri 912

RISTORANTE $$$$
☎041 52 25 238 www.ristorantenoemi.com

Situated in the upscale Hotel Noemi, Ristorante Noemi's antique-looking striped wall paper, mosaic floors, and subtly sophisticated Venetian fare make it a good option for students looking to indulge in a bit of Venice's old-school culinary grandeur. Mostly catered toward tourists with good taste and moderately fat wallets, the un-fussy northern Italian fare, including meat options absent from seafood-heavy restaurants (Scalopini milines €17) provides a solid dining experience for those looking for some tame glamor and a filling, classic meal.

i Antipasti €11-17; primi €12-16; secondi €9-25. ☼ Open daily 11:30am-midnight.

TRATTORIA PIZZERIA AI FABBRI
Calle dei Fabbri 4717

TRATTORIA, PIZZERIA $$
☎041 52 08 085

For a good meal at a good price, head to Ai Fabbri, one of few restaurants in Venice where culinary creativity doesn't come with a fat price tag. The *trattoria* offers a wide selection of pizzas and local specialties like liver alla veneziana with onions (€16). Simple brick walls and a TV make this place feel like a bar, but the back dining room offers a more serene setting.

i *Pizza €7.50-14. Entrees €9-17.* 🕓 *Open daily 11:30am-10:30pm.*

ACQUA PAZZA
SEAFOOD $$$$

Campo San Angelo 3808 ☎041 27 70 688 www.veniceacquapazza.it

Billing itself as an Amalfian restaurant and Neapolitan *pizzeria* in Venice, Acqua Pazza offers some serious sophistication with a menu brimming with fresh seafood. Meaning "crazy water" in Italian, Acqua Pazza certainly goes crazy with the aquatic theme: marble floors, a blue mosaic fountain, bright turquoise vests for the waiters, and an oar on the wall might overdo the under the sea idea, but the seafood is prepared perfectly. With a dress code for dinner and a clientele of mostly middle-aged, well-to-do tourists, Acqua Pazza is the place for some seriously fine dining—if you've got the dough for this catch, that is.

i *Men are required to wear long pants to dinner. Primi and secondi €25-80. Pizza €12-20.* 🕓 *Open daily noon-3pm and 8pm-midnight.*

RISTORANTE AL COLOMBO
RISTORANTE $$$$

Corte del Teatro 4619 ☎041 52 22 627 www.alcolombo.com

Go €150 for caviar? How about €49 for lobster? If you do, head to Ristorante Al Colombo for a seriously upscale feast. It's the kind of menu where, when you see that fish costs €12, assume it's by the 100g…with an 800g minimum. Not the kind of place your typical student traveler could afford to eat at more than once per trip, Al Colombo typifies a kind of Old World Venetian splendor for the padded pocketbooks of the middle-aged. Its officious service, scenic courtyard location, and, above all, ridiculously high-quality food provide a good backdrop for any marriage proposal—or a really dramatic breakup. Just don't drop the ring in the caviar.

i *Entree €19-80.* 🕓 *Open daily 11am-midnight.*

RISTORANTE ANIMA BELLA
RISTORANTE $$

Calle Fiubera 956 ☎041 52 27 486

This tiny restaurant offers a simple menu of spaghetti, ravioli, and lasagna. Those weary of Venice's seafood specialties will be pleased with Anima Bella's more meat- and vegetable-based menu.

i *Entrees €8-16.* 🕓 *Open daily 11am-3pm and 6-10pm.*

Cannaregio

🏴 GAM GAM
KOSHER $$

Canale di Cannaregio 1122 ☎041 71 52 84 www.jewishvenice.org/food/gamgam

Gam Gam will change your life in several ways. Life change #1: Italian Kosher food exists. Life change #2: Italian Kosher food is delicious. Life change #3: Italian Jewish waiters are sexy. If you were privy to this knowledge before going to Gam Gam, you are a privileged individual. If not, head to Gam Gam as soon as humanly possible for a cultural and culinary experience to rival any in Venice, with prices to match.

i *Entrees €5-15.* 🕓 *Open M-Th noon-10:30pm, F noon-5:30pm, Su noon-10:30pm.*

🏴 CASA BONITA DI GIOVANNI VACCARI
RISTORANTE, SEAFOOD $$

Fondamento San Giobbe 492 ☎041 52 46 164

In a city teeming with allegedly authentic tourist-friendly ristoranti, Casa Bonita manages to exist in a tourist-frequented area while staying genuinely Venetian. Reflecting Venice's culinary forte, the menu specializes in seafood pastas featuring cuttlefish, monkfish, and prawns. If you're fed up with seafood, try the tagliatelle in beef ragu (€14), a hearty take on Bolognese.

i *Appetizers €9-15. Entrees €10-20.* 🕓 *Open daily noon-2:30pm and 6:30pm-1am.*

venice

OSTERIA PARADISO PERDUTO   RISTORANTE $$$
Fondamenta Misericordia 2540   ☎041 72 05 81

Osteria Paradiso Perduto has a rare feature for Venice: an eclectic, colorful, genuinely cool feel. Your dad probably wouldn't come here, unless you have an awesome, jazz-playing dad, in which case you both should go and mangiare. Trays of seafood in various stages of preparation and a bowl of overflowing octopus tentacles might meet you at the front bar along with the boisterous chef. If you've ever wanted to hear what Italian Dixie sounds like, head to Paradiso Perduto the first Sunday of every month to hear the Venezia Cool and Dixie Swing Jazz band groove.

i Cash only. Entrees €9-20. ⏰ Open M 6pm-midnight, Th 6pm-midnight, F-Su noon-midnight.

OSTERIA BOCCADORO VENEZIA   RISTORANTE $$$$
Campo Widmann 5405A   ☎041 52 11 021 www.boccadorovenezia.it

Osteria Boccadoro serves up haute-cuisine reinterpretations of the region's traditional food. The dishes are pricey, but premium ingredients and elegant preparation justify the splurge. Come for exquisite specialties with long names, like the *gnocchi bianchi e neri con filetti di go e zucchine* (€20)—just be sure to practice your Italian pronunciation if you want to sound like a versed connoisseur.

i Appetizers €9-20. Entrees €13-26. ⏰ Open daily 11:45am-2:30pm and 7:30-10:30pm.

TRATTORIA STORICA   RISTORANTE $$$
Ponte dei Gesuiti 4858   ☎041 52 85 266 www.trattoriastorica.it

This upscale family-operated restaurant is a great place to savor a slow-paced meal in a quiet quarter of Cannaregio. The service is exceptional and the portions are generous. Trattoria Storica also offers two prix-fixe menus.

i Appetizers €9-13. Entrees €9-30. ⏰ Open daily 11am-4pm and 7pm-midnight.

San Polo

Along the Grand Canal, San Polo suffers from the same generic tourist cuisine that you'll find near all of Venice's sightseeing destinations, but if you manage to get away from the main drag around the Rialto, you'll be rewarded with the unique specialties and terrific ambience of Venice's best small restaurants.

FRARY'S   GREEK, MIDDLE EASTERN $$
San Polo 2559   ☎04 17 20 050

While the camel painted on the wall might strike the worldly as a little corny for a Middle Eastern restaurant, the red walls and groovy Greek jams of this small eatery make it a welcome and surprisingly affordable break from the lackluster tourist fare dotting San Polo. With a chill vibe, central location, and, perhaps best of all, a Tstudent discount, the spicy Greek-inspired pasta dishes (€9-12), ullah (basmati rice, spicy chicken, and cardamom; €6.50), and falafel (€6) are sure to shake it up.

i 20% student discount or free beer on weekdays. Entrees €9.50-15. ⏰ Open M 11:30am-3pm and 6-10:30pm, W-Su 11:30am-3pm and 6-10:30pm.

ANTICA OSTERIA GIORGIONE   RISTORANTE $$
San Polo 1022/B   ☎04 12 41 21 24

Though perhaps a bit upscale for most budget travelers, Antica Osteria Giorgione is the place to go for a splurge-worthy, phenomenal meal in San Polo. The historic restaurant, which has been in operation for over 120 years but is fully updated with a state of the art kitchen, combines traditional and modern influences to devise menu items you won't find in many other places, including incredible swordfish steaks and a delicious artichoke salad.

i Lunch €10-24. Dinner €16-24. ⏰ Open daily noon-3pm and 7:30-10pm.

ANTICO FORNO

PIZZERIA $$

Ruga Rialto 970/973 ☎041 52 04 110

Antico Forno is the perfect pizza pit-stop, with top-quality ingredients, adventurous vegetarian toppings, and substantial deep-dish slices. The convenient location and promise of fast, delicious pizza may have you eating here every time you pass.

i Slices €2-3.50. Cash only. 🕐 Open daily 11am-10pm.

BIRRARIA LA CORTE

RISTORANTE $$

Campo San Polo 2168 ☎041 27 50 570 www.birrarialacorte.it

Birraria La Corte, a great casual lunch or dinner spot in quiet Campo San Polo, boasts an adventurous menu without abandoning the Italian staples. They've perfected unconventional entrees like buffalo steak and chicken curry, both of which go great with the imported beers on tap.

i Entrees €6.50-19. 🕐 Open daily noon-2:30pm and 7-10:30pm.

OSTERIA NARANZARIA

RISTORANTE $$

Naranzaria 130 ☎041 72 41 035 www.naranzaria.it

Tucked just off Rialto, trendy Osteria Naranzaria has outdoor seating along the canal and a menu as diverse as its clientele. Without abandoning its Venetian roots, the restaurant adds unusual items like fresh sushi. Naranzaria is a great place for a light lunch by the bridge or some food and drinks before a night out.

i Cover €2. Entrees €11-14. Sushi €16. 🕐 Open Tu-Su noon-2am.

CIOCCOLATERIA VIZIOVIRTÙ

CIOCCOLATERIA $

Calle Balbi 2898A ☎041 27 50 149 www.viziovirtu.com

Venice's premier chocolatier, Cioccolateria VizioVirtù crafts a selection of creative, delicious, and (predictably) expensive chocolates every day. While they do an excellent job with pralines, truffles, and baked goods, their mastery of the fine art of confectionery is best displayed in their unconventional chocolates, including ones spiced up with red pepper. VizioVirtù also sells replica Venetian masks that make great I-really-did-think-of-you-in-Venice gifts.

i Various chocolate creations €1-2.50. Brownies €3.50. Mousse €4.90. 🕐 Open daily 10am-7:30pm.

Santa Croce

▧ RISTORANTE RIBOT

RISTORANTE $$

Fondamenta Minotto 158 ☎041 52 42 486

Ristorante Ribot pays tribute to the best of traditional Venice—regional cuisine, excellent Italian wines, and a beautiful patio garden—but keeps it fresh with an innovative kitchen and live music three to four times per week. Strategic ordering can make the exceptional food affordable. Lunchtime reservations are generally unnecessary, but you may want to save yourself a seat for dinner.

i Entrees €8-14. Prix-fixe menu from €13. Service 12%. 🕐 Open M-Sa noon-2:30pm and 7-10:30pm.

BACARETO DA LELE

SNACK BAR $

Campo dei Tolentini ☎04 15 24 68 52

Bacareto da Lele is a very crowded, very awesome, very hole-in-the-wall place for locals in the know and students on a budget to chill with the old-time owners who come through the door with groceries and assemble sandwiches of prosciutto, homemade salami, and various other fixings. The old wooden sign out front looks like the prices on it haven't changed since the snack bar's founding in 1968—which is a good thing for the crowds that gather outside and eat next to barrels in the sun. Bacareto da Lele is the place for the young, the broke, and the discerning to find lunch or a snack. Order one, two, or five sandwiches—no shame—grab a glass of wine, and relax.

i Sandwiches €1.80-2.20. Glasses of wine €0.60-1. No, we're not kidding. ☒ Open M-F 6am-8pm, Sa 6am-2pm.

ANTICA BESSETA
RISTORANTE $$$$

Salizada de Ca' Zusto 1395 ☎04 17 21 687 www.anticabesseta.it

A small restaurant serving fresh Venetian cuisine whose quality ingredients and careful preparation warrant the price, Antica Besseta is the place to go for a worth-it splurge in Santa Croce. Thankfully deviating from the overdone staples that characterize the woefully repetitive tourist restaurants on these islands, Antica Besseta varies its menu with seasonal ingredients while keeping it Venetian with dishes like taglioni con fiori di zucchini e gambi (taglioni pasta with zucchini flowers and shrimp).

i Entrees €10-28; fixed price €30 for meat and €35 for fish. ☒ Open M noon-3pm and 7-11pm, W 7-11pm, Th-Su noon-3pm and 7-11pm.

FRITTO&FRUTTA
SNACK BAR, SMOOTHIES $

Fondamenta dei Tolentini 220 ☎04 15 24 68 52 www.frittoefrutta.com

This is a cool little place catering to both travelers (you) and native Venetians (the gorgeous Italian men that enter after you). Accordingly, the pairing of fried food and smoothies here covers all the basics: a little fruit, a little sizzle, a little sweet—and a little student discount. The cold smoothies are perfect for a hot day, and, let's face it, may be the only time you've had fruit on your whole trip (no, we don't count sangria). The crispy fried fish, chicken strips, olives, artichokes, and, well, just about anything the chef thought to throw in the deep fryer are the perfect midday snack, light lunch, or Tdrunk food. Yes, you'd have to be drunk pretty early to get there before closing time, but this is Venice, where the bars go to bed at the same time as your grandma.

i 20% student discount on all sizes greater than small. €3.50-11 per cone of fried things. Smoothies €3. ☒ Open M-Sa 11am-9:30pm.

PANIFICO BAROZZI
BAKERY, GROCERY STORE $

Salizada San Pantalon 86A ☎041 71 02 33

One of the trickiest things about Venetian pastries is that every window display looks equally delicious. Panifico Barozzi's pastries are rare in tasting as scrumptious as they look. With an impressive number of delicacies to sample and the added bonus of a small grocery store stocked with inexpensive snacks, this is a one-stop shopping experience you shouldn't miss.

i Pastries €1-2. Cash only. ☒ Open daily 6am-7:30pm.

AGLI AMICI
SNACK BAR, RISTORANTE $

Santa Croce 189 ☎041 52 41 309

With impressive omelets and a great selection of cheeses, Agli Amici is a welcome anomaly in Venice, where breakfast usually consists of little more than coffee and a pastry. The seafood options are a bit expensive, but the good-value burgers and entrecôte are ideal for a quick but hearty lunch stop.

i Entrees €6-20. Service charge 10%. ☒ Open daily 8am-7:30pm.

Dorsoduro

Most of the nice restaurants in Dorsoduro tend toward the expensive side, but the neighborhood also offers some of the best cafes and *pizzerias* in the city, which makes the area appealing to travelers on a budget. Follow the students to the best and cheapest places for a greasy kebab or an even greasier slice—as always, Campo San Margherita is where it's at—or content yourself with some killer gelato and a bottle of wine (yes, this constitutes a meal).

SUZIE CAFE
CAFE $

Dorsoduro 1527   ☎041 52 27 502   www.suziecafevenice.com

Suzie distinguishes herself from other cafes with fresh daily pasta dishes and a vibrant personality. The cafe is decked out in classic rock memorabilia, highlighted by a sweet guitar that boasts half a dozen signatures on its body. You could spend weeks in Venice without finding a better place to enjoy a €8 meal.

i *Cover charge €2.50. Sandwiches and light meals €4-11. Primi of the day €7; secondi of the day €8. ☼ Open M-Th 7am-8pm, F 7am-1am.*

RISTORANTE LINEADOMBRA
RISTORANTE $$$$

Ponte dell'Umiltà 19   ☎041 24 11 881   www.ristorantelineadombra.com

Lineadombra is the place to go for a high-quality meal in Dorsoduro. The patio seating, located on a deck above the water, will make you feel like someone in a travel magazine, while the food comes straight from Gourmet. Dishes provide thankfully fresh spins on Italian classics—no reheated lasagna here—while diners sit on square red chairs inside the minimalist restaurant space. Try the shellfish and goat milk ricotta on eggplant cream (€24) or the black rice with vegetable ragu and shrimp (€23) for a healthier, fresher take on local seafood specialties.

i *Entrees €21-35. ☼ Open W-M noon-3pm and 7-10pm.*

RISTORANTE AI GONDOLIERI
RISTORANTE $$$$

San Vio 366   ☎041 52 86 396   www.aigondolieri.com

Ristorante Ai Gondolieri may have catered several events for the nearby Guggenheim Museum, but you don't have to be an eccentric billionaire or an art collector to enjoy Ai Gondolier's quality take on classic Italian. Dishes like baked canneloni with asparagus and veal ragu (€20) or cream of asparagus soup with quail egg croutons (€20) are kickin' it old school without the pitfalls of food stereotypes, while the expensive wine list will convince the more vino-oriented to break the bank. The dark wood bar and white table cloths in the dining room capture the same spirit of upscale elegance. Despite its catering history, however, the food at Ai Gondolieri is less Guggenheim and more Accademia; not a modern art piece trying to get all radical on us, but rather a Renaissance fresco doing the classics very right.

i *Entrees €20-33. ☼ Open M noon-3pm and 7-10:30pm, W-Su noon-3pm and 7-10:30pm.*

RISTORANTE MESSNER
RISTORANTE $$$

Fondamenta di Cà Bala 217   ☎041 29 60 695   www.hotelmessner.it

A great restaurant that you might unknowingly walk right past, Ristorante Messner serves solid and reasonably priced Venetian food in some of Dorsoduro's nicest garden seating. For those sick of seafood, Messner's grilled meats provide a welcome change of pace. Messner also offers something rarer still: a kid's menu.

i *Entrees €10-18. ☼ Open daily noon-3:30pm and 5:30-11pm.*

IL DOGE
GELATERIA $

Campo San Margherita 3058   ☎041 52 34 607

Most gelaterie in Venice look better than they taste, but Il Doge doesn't disappoint. Their fresh ingredients make for a better taste and texture. Even though the quality is high, the prices are among the lowest in Venice. Il Doge's inventive monthly specials, such as strawberry cheesecake, have helped at least one Let's Go researcher fatten up.

i *1 scoop €1.20, 2 scoops €2, 3 scoops €2.80. ☼ Open daily noon-11pm.*

venice

Castello

Since Castello is so close to P. San Marco, it gets a lot of tourist traffic, and restaurants with well-priced cuisine tend to be few and far between. There are quite a few good restaurants in Castello, but with some exceptions, they're typically a bit pricier than comparable establishments in other neighborhoods.

CIP CIAP
PIZZERIA $

Calle del Mondo Novo 5799/A   ☎04 15 23 66 21

Moses has come down from the mountain with a covenant from the pizza gods: Cip Ciap. Let's Go's top pick for pizza in Venice, Cip Ciap is a small, bright, and modern hole-in-the-wall that makes killer pies for wicked cheap. Cooked up in huge square pans, sliced, and sold by the weight, the restaurant's crispy-bottomed, cheesy-topped pies play with drool-inducing ingredients to make seriously delicious slices that will have you swearing off all that rubbery, lukewarm stuff you once believed was pizza.

i Pizza €1.50-1.70 per 100g. Calzones €3 per 100g. Joy free. ☼ Open M 9am-9pm, W-Su 9am-9pm.

TAVERNA SAN LIO
RISTORANTE $$$

Salizada San Lio 5547   ☎041 27 70 669   www.tavernasanlio.com

One of Venice's best restaurants, Taverna San Lio serves up elegant dishes that combine regional specialties with some international flair. Try the sea bass cannelloni in lobster sauce (€14), duck breast with red wine and plums (€22), or buffalo ricotta ravioli (€12). The Menu di Giorno (3 courses for €19) is an absolute steal for cuisine of this caliber.

i Pasta €10-15. Entrees €21-26. 3-course prix-fixe €19. ☼ Open M noon-11pm, W-Su noon-11pm.

LA MELA VERDE: GELATERIA ARTIGIANALE
GELATERIA $

Fondamenta de l'Osmarin 4977   ☎349 19 57 924

Murano does artisan glass. Burano does artisan lace. For Venice's best artisan gelato, head to La Mela Verde. Standing apart from the countless substandard gelaterie in this city, La Mela has fresh ingredients and flavors like the dark and decadent cioccolato fondente and the giotto, an irresistible concoction of white chocolate, almonds, and coconut.

i 1 scoop €1.50; 2 scoops €2.30; additional flavors €1 each; €13 per kg. Cash only. ☼ Open daily 11am-10pm.

RISTORANTE AL COVO
Ristorante $$$$

Campiello della Pescaria 3968   ☎04 15 22 38 12   www.ristorantealcovo.com

Ristorante al Covo's unintimidating, fresh, and homey dining room, coupled with lovely outdoor seating, belies its extremely high-quality food. Though pricey for most budget travelers, menu items prepared with fresh, seasonal ingredients, which often depend on the day's catch, are a far cry from the overdone tourist fare available in other parts of Castello. Shell out a few extra bucks to try the baked rack of lamb with lentils (€29) or Adriatic sole on celery root with baby artichokes (€31) for a taste of top-quality culinary refinement.

i Entrees €21-34. ☼ Open M-Tu 12:45-3:30pm and 7:30pm-midnight, F-Su 12:45-3:30pm and 7:30pm-midnight.

RISTORANTE LA NUOVA GROTTA
RISTORANTE $$$

Calle delle Rasse 358   ☎04 17 24 10 18

Tourists whose attention is captured by the catch displayed on ice outside of this restaurant can head into the kitschy, mirrored, and knick-knack-filled dining room for reasonably priced seafood entrees.

i Entrees €14-23. Tourist menu €17. ☼ Open M-Tu 11am-11pm, Th-Su 11am-11pm.

RISTORANTE ALLA CONCHIGLIA
Fondamenta San Lorenzo

RISTORANTE $$$
☎04 15 28 90 95

With great canal views and reasonable prices, Ristorante Alla Conchiglia attracts tourists with its powder blue seats, chandeliers, and decorative Venetian masks. Enjoy lunch or dinner on the terrace; if you're a seafood aficionado, the Venetian-style flounder is the restaurant's specialty and is reputed to be excellent.
i *Entrees €9-25. 🕐 Open daily noon-11pm.*

NIGHTLIFE

While you can hardly take a step without running into historic palazzi, excellent seafood, and lovely hotels in Venice, if you head out in search of a random bar, you'll likely end up heading home an hour later with nothing more than a kebab to show for it. Stick to the major hotspots listed here, and you'll have more success. Additionally, be prepared for a much more laid-back bar experience than in most major Italian cities. Venice's nightlife is kind of like its signature Spritz: it's light, it's fun, but nobody's getting schwasted.

San Marco

BACARO LOUNGE BAR
San Marco 1345

BAR
☎041 29 60 687

A minimalist bar just steps away from P. San Marco, Bacaro Lounge is one of the few establishments in San Marco that caters to the young and fashionable post-dinner crowd. With a sleek lounge setup conducive to mingling, an extensive list of wines and cocktails, and an understated playlist, Bacaro Lounge is the hottest place to be after dark in San Marco.
i *Drinks €3.50-13. 🕐 Open daily until 2am.*

RISTORANTE GRAN CAFFÈ QUADRI
P. San Marco 121

CAFE, BAR
☎041 52 22 105 www.quadrivenice.com

Caffè Quadri tends more toward refinement than debauchery. Sipping one of their excellent drinks (the wine list is unbeatable, and the coffee is reputedly some of Venice's best) to a string-quartet soundtrack is an elegant, ritzy experience. It'll almost make you think you're the class of person who can afford the jewelry from the shops lining the *piazza*—luckily they're all closed at this hour, so you won't do anything reckless.
i *Drinks €8.50-17. Desserts €3-7. 🕐 Open daily 9am-midnight.*

GRAND CANAL RESTAURANT AND BAR
Calle Vallaresso 1332

HOTEL BAR
☎041 52 00 211 www.hotelmonaco.it

The bar of the fancy Hotel Monaco has managed to steer clear of elitist snobbery, cultivating a clientele that stretches beyond the hotel's guest list. Kick back and enjoy exceptional wine and waterfront views without feeling out of place. After all, you're paying €15 for a cocktail—you've more than earned that comfortable canal side seat.
i *Wine and champagne €7.50-15. Mixed drinks €14-18. Snacks €14-23. 🕐 Open daily 10:30am-midnight.*

Cannaregio

Cannaregio's not the kind of place you go to if you want to get schwasty-faced and post embarrassing pictures on Facebook, Katy Perry-style. When one of the busiest places after midnight is a smoothie bar, you know you've got a nightlife deficit. Instead, Cannaregio's lovely and largely residential side streets are full of both locals and tourists whiling away the evening, sharing bottles of wine and light bar fare in the drowsy light of the setting sun. For any sort of nightlife, a good bet would be to try out the Irish Pub on game day: a wild night in Cannaregio will include a few beers, a game of calcio (soccer) on TV, and maybe a kebab to top things off. To be fair, though, there are few things more entertaining in this world than observing middle-aged Italian guys watching soccer. Cin cin, dear friend, cin cin.

CASINO' MUNICIPALE DI VENEZIA: CA' VENDRAMIN CALERGI
CASINO

Cannaregio 2040 ☎041 52 97 111 www.casinovenezia.it

One of the first things you might notice after getting off the plane at Aeroporto Marco Polo is that Venice takes its gambling seriously—even the baggage carousels have a roulette-wheel theme, sponsored by this (in)famous casino. Serious gamblers head straight to Lido, home to the main branch of this historic casino, so the Cannaregio location is mainly full of tipsy old couples and tourists silly enough to waste money playing the slots.

i *Men must wear suit jackets. Entry €5; guests at some hotels get in free. After that, it's up to you.* ☒ *Open M-Th 3pm-2:30am, F-Sa 3pm-3am, Su 3pm-2:30am.*

THE IRISH PUB VENEZIA
BAR

Cannaregio 3847 ☎041 52 81 439 www.theirishpubvenezia.com

A buzzing crowd of boisterous locals and rowdy tourists make the Irish Pub Venezia one of the best nightspots in Cannaregio. The drinks are strong and the space is cramped, but the loud music and proximity to a late-night kebab restaurant keep this place hopping long into the evening, even on weekdays.

i *Drinks €3-6. Snacks €6-12.* ☒ *Open daily noon-1:30am.*

San Polo

In terms of nightlife, San Polo is second only to Dorsoduro. The area around the Rialto Bridge, in particular, is home to some of Venice's best bars, popular with both Venetian locals and tourists.

JAZZ CLUB 900
JAZZ CLUB

San Polo 900 ☎041 52 26 565 www.jazz900.com

Just down Ruga Rialto from the bars near the Rialto Bridge, Jazz Club 900 is a *pizzeria* by day and a self-acclaimed live-music venue by night. With several shows per week and reasonably priced beer, the club can be a chill hangout or a lively music bar, depending on who's around.

i *From the Rialto Bridge, continue straight, turn left onto Ruga Rialto, where the market overhang ends. Continue for 2min. and turn right just after #789. Jazz Club 900 is ahead on the left. Drinks €2.50-5. Pizza €6-11.* ☒ *Open Tu-Su 11:30am-4pm and 7pm-2am.Concerts Oct-Apr 9pm.*

MURO VENEZIA
BAR

Campo Bella Vienna, Rialto 222 ☎04 12 41 22 29 www.murovenezia.com

A cool bar featuring actual young people sipping actual drinks under actual neon lights, Muro Venezia's silent movie grooves and lime green drink prices are perhaps as crazy as it gets in San Polo. Never fear, though: the crowd, which spreads onto the Campo, is a mix of travelers and locals chatting over drinks, and they all look like they have interesting things to say.

i *From Rialto Bridge in San Polo, make an immediate right, then take the 1st left, and go straight as if toward Rialto Market; the bar is straight ahead through Campo Bella Vienna. Drinks €2.50-7.* ☒ *Open daily 9am-1am.*

BAR AI 10 SAVI
BAR

Rialto 55 ☎04 15 23 80 05 www.ai10savi.com

A popular hangout for local guys and groups of tourists alike, Bar Ai 10 Savi lacks the pretense of some other Rialto bars and sticks to the basics: Pstrong drinks at great prices. The bar is crowded enough that patrons spill out onto the street in chatting groups to enjoy a cold one and the Campo di San Giacometto.

i *Drinks €2.50-5.50.* ☒ *Open M-Tu 8am-2am, Th-Su 8am-2am.*

ANCÒRA VENEZIA
BAR

Rialto 120   ☎041 52 07 066   www.ancoravenezia.it

Ancòra Venezia's subtle Asian and modernist aesthetics, plus the fact that most patrons are sipping wine, give it an upscale feel. If the bar is too crowded, you can always take your drink outside to Campo di San Giacometto.

i *Drinks €3-6.50. ☎ Open M-Sa 10am-2am.*

Santa Croce

In a city not known for its nightlife, Santa Croce is about the last place you'd want to go for an evening out. Unlike some other neighborhoods with at least a few bars and restaurants that stay open late, Santa Croce offers only a couple of places that keep the home fires burning after midnight.

BAR AL CARCAN
BAR

Salizada San Pantalon 133   ☎041 71 32 36

While most of Santa Croce shuts down around 11pm, Bar Al Carcan entertains an odd assortment of tourists looking for a quick nightcap and locals sipping drinks on the patio. The bar offers reasonably cheap drinks and good music.

i *Drinks €3-6. ☎ Open most days in summer until 1am.*

Dorsoduro

Enjoying nightlife in Dorsoduro is as simple as nursing a bottle of wine in Campo San Margherita. This might not sound as thrilling as, say, whipped cream and gummy bear body shots with a German hand model, but in reality Dorsoduro's energetic student scene gives it far and away the best nightlife of any neighborhood in Venice.

☑ VENICE JAZZ CLUB
JAZZ CLUB

Ponte dei Pugni/Fondamenta del Squero 3102   ☎041 52 32 056   www.venicejazzclub.com

The Venice Jazz Club is a great place to begin a night out in Dorsoduro. To get your cover's worth, grab an early dinner and spend the evening in the baby blue interior. While most bars are still in restaurant mode, this club is already serving drinks to the tune of the best jazz in Venice. It tends to attract an international crowd of 20-somethings and empties out once concerts end.

i *From Campo San Margherita, walk toward Campo San Barnaba, turn right before the bridge, and the club is ahead on the right. Cover €20; includes 1 drink. Drinks €5-10. Appetizers €5-15. ☎ Open daily from 7pm. Concerts 9-11pm.*

☑ MADIGAN'S PUB
IRISH PUB

Campo San Margherita 3053A

Unlike most bars in the area, at Madigan's Pub the bartenders are happy to chat. University names scrawled out in highlighter attest to the variety of international visitors that flock here for beer pong or flip cup, or to knock back some custom shots like the flaming "Sex in Italy."

i *Shots €3. Drinks €4-8. ☎ Open daily until 1:30am.*

CLUB PICCOLO MONDO
CLUB

Accademia Dorsoduro 1056A   ☎041 52 00 371   www.piccolomondo.biz

The closest thing to clubbing you'll find in Venice, Club Piccolo Mondo is nothing if not unique. The bar adorned with Venetian masks feels more like the bartender's kitchen than the hip counterpart to the leather lounge seats, while patrons dance in front of a screen playing music videos. This little club draws all kinds, from drunk students to middle-aged locals to big names like Mick Jagger and Naomi Campbell, and fills to the brim as bars close around 1am. If you've already had a few and are looking to dance until dawn, Piccolo Mondo is the place.

i *Cover €10. Drinks €9-12. ☎ Open daily 11pm-4am.*

venice

CAFFE ROSSO   BAR

Campo San Margherita 2963   ☎041 52 87 998

Caffe Rosso probably has the highest concentration of dreadlocks of any location in Venice. Students with yoga T-shirts and round glasses flock here to sip drinks, talk, and chill out amid posters for experimental theater and reggae festivals.

i *Drinks €1-6.50.* ☑ *Open M-Sa 7am-midnight.*

IMPRONTA CAFE   BAR, RESTAURANT

Crosera San Pantalon 3815   ☎041 27 50 386

Impronta is the antidote to all the corny, overdone antique-y Venetian establishments you'll find in other neighborhoods. Decked out with stainless steel, dark wood, modern seating, and a chalkboard sporting recipes for mixed drinks, this bar is filled with young Italians chatting over a drink or three. The menu, boasting quality dishes for cheap—try the gnocchi with salmon (€10)—makes Impronta a great place for dinner, while the stacks of wine bottles and cocktails remind you it's groovin' into the night as well.

i *Drinks €1-5. Entrees €8-16.* ☑ *Open M-Sa 7am-2am.*

MARGARET DUCHAMP   BAR

Campo San Margherita 3019   ☎041 52 86 255

In the summertime, the diverse visitors leave Duchamp's hot interior to sip quality cocktails outside on the campo. You can also get a sandwich to complement your tipsy.

i *Drinks €3.50-9.* ☑ *Open daily 9am-2am.*

ORANGE BAR   BAR

Campo Santa Margherita 3054A   ☎041 52 34 740 www.orangebar.it

While aged locals sprawl over the whole campo for a pleasant evening out and children hold toy car races, this bar is the place with the highest concentration of young adults. The colorful decor (guess what color!) adds energy to the buzzed atmosphere, and the green patio in the backyard is best for groups.

i *At the northwest end of the Campo San Margherita. Shots €3. Drinks €4-8.* ☑ *Open daily until 1:30am.*

Castello

A great place to sit outside at a cafe and relax well into the night, Castello isn't particularly notable for its nightclub scene. However, its selection of bars and cafes still draws large crowds during the summer.

TAVERNA L'OLANDESE VOLANTE   BAR

Salizada San Lio 5658   ☎041 52 89 349

With a prime location in one of Castello's best squares, a great selection of beers on tap, and a reggae playlist that blasts late into the night, L'Olandese Volante is one of Castello's most popular bars. The clientele includes tourists, students, and middle-aged locals, making this is a great place to get a feel for the diverse Castello crowd.

i *Beer €4. Mixed drinks €6-10.* ☑ *Open Jun-Aug M-F 9am-10pm, Sa-Su 9am-2am; Sept-May daily 9am-10pm.*

BAR VERDE   SNACK BAR

Calle de le Rasse 4525   ☎041 52 37 094

This standard Venetian bar boasts tasty drinks and even tastier late-night snacks, along with two TVs that usually broadcast sports. It's frequented mainly by tourists from nearby hotels, so the person sitting next to you may be a budget traveler sipping cheap beer or an elderly couple downing coffee in an attempt to stay awake.

i *Drinks €3-6. Snacks €1-12.* ☑ *Open daily 6am-1am.*

EL REFOLO
BAR

V. Garibaldi 1580 ☎04 15 24 00 16 www.elrefolo.it

Young tourists and Italians alike chill with drinks on the small tables in front of the simple, wood and brick bar. Hang out with the cool, genuinely fun bartenders who, according to some travelers, might just give you free shots as you sit with friends (or strangers who become friends under the influence of the tasty, cheap cocktails).

i Drinks €2.50-3. ☼ Open Tu-Su 11:30am-1am.

CAFFÈ INTERNAZIONALE
CAFE, BAR

Riva degli Schiavoni 4183 ☎041 52 36 047

Right on the waterfront, Caffè Internazionale is a great place to refuel before catching the *vaporetto* home after a long day of sightseeing. Enjoy the views with one of their cheap drinks or grab a quick bite to eat—just try not to get too jealous watching the luxurious yachts and party boats drifting past.

i Drinks €2-5. Snacks €5-10. ☼ Open Jun-Aug M-F 9am-midnight, Sa-Su 9am-1:30am; Sept-May daily 9am-midnight.

BACARO RISORTO
BAR

Campo San Provolo 4700

Perhaps the only place open this late in Castello (or at least Campo San Provolo), Bacaro Risorto is a great end (or beginning) of the night. The crowd of mostly Italians spills from the open bar onto the surrounding Campo, chatting over inexpensive drinks and super tasty (and super cheap) TItalian bar snacks while bantering with the pleasantly sassy bartenders.

☼ Open daily 7am-2am.

ARTS AND CULTURE

At the height of its power, the Venetian Republic was a center of artistic and cultural innovation. The profound legacy of the Renaissance is still evident in the architecture, music, painting, and theater that so many tourists flock here to enjoy. But Venice has also begun to incorporate modern influences into its creative scene, which means you'll find everything from classical orchestras to avant-garde performance art.

Orchestral Music

Venetian venues showcase elegant, inspiring classical music, performed by some of Italy's best choirs and orchestras.

▨ INTERPRETI VENEZIANI, CHIESA DI SAN VIDAL
SAN MARCO

Campo San Vidal 2862B ☎041 27 70 561 www.interpretiveneziani.com

Held in the striking San Vidal Church in San Marco, Interpreti Veneziani's concert series is regarded as the best orchestral music in the city. The high-caliber performances cater to serious aficionados—the kind of people who are willing to shell out for the experience.

i Tickets usually around €40.

CHIESA DI SANTA MARIA FORMOSA'S COLLEGIUM DUCALE
CASTELLO

Campo Santa Maria Formosa ☎04 19 88 155 www.collegiumducale.com

Collegium Ducale is a vocal group that produces some of the most highly regarded opera and Baroque music performances in the city, at a pretty decent price. With performances at both the Palazzo delle Prigioni and Santa Maria Formosa, it is the latter venue, with its excellent acoustics and sense of intimacy, that many opera aficionados rave about. The incredible chorus of voices ringing through the tiny church evokes Venice's historical splendor and reminds visitors of its artistic legacy today.

i Tickets €25, students and over 65 €20. Tickets available online. ☼ Concerts typically begin at 9pm.

Theater

🎭 TEATRO LA FENICE
SAN MARCO

Campo San Fantin 1965 ☎041 78 65 11 www.teatrolafenice.it

Venice's most versatile and prestigious venue, Teatro La Fenice is the place to go if you've spent your entire time in Venice eating gelato instead of seafood just so you'll have enough money to see one show. The classical concerts, opera, and ballet are often extraordinary, though the remarkable building—which earned its name, "the Phoenix," after rising from the ashes of three separate fires—is almost worth the price of admission on its own.

i *Concerts €10-60. Ballet €10-100. Opera €10-180.* 🕐 *Performances evenings and weekend afternoons.*

TEATRO GOLDONI
SAN MARCO

Calle dei Fabbri 4650 ☎041 24 02 014 www.teatrostabileveneto.it

Old-school opera is pretty darn scandalous, but when you want something a little edgier than Candide—at least stylistically—head over to Teatro Goldoni. Goldoni's shows tend to be contemporary and even provocative (latest offering: God and Stephen Hawking), and its performances prove that, in Venice, the art of theater is not merely antique but alive and innovating. Just don't look forward toany tours of this allegedly gorgeous building: Goldoni's performance schedule seems rather elusive, often with only a few performances scattered throughout May and June.

i *Prices vary according to seating and shows but can be as little a €5 for students; contact box office and consult web for up-to-date info and booking.*

Festivals

Venice is home to two of the premier arts festivals in Europe, the Venice Biennale and the Venice Film Festival. Although the city is a popular tourist destination year-round, the visitor numbers spike during these two events as art and film aficionados flock to the city.

LA BIENNALE DI VENEZIA
CASTELLO

Ca' Giustinian, San Marco 1364/A ☎041 52 18 711 www.labiennale.org

From June to November during odd-numbered years, Venice swallows art steroids. The Venice Biennale is one of the world's most celebrated festivals of contemporary artwork. Organized around numerous national pavilions that display contemporary artwork from their countries of origin, the festival allows visitors go from stall to stall interacting with the artwork of each country, while special events such as galas and performances also occur. While the Biennale is held only once every two years, it has become such a popular event that it has given rise to other festivals, including the International Architecture Exhibition and International Festival of Contemporary Music, among other workshops and events sponsored by the Biennale cultural organization. Because Biennale is held in odd-numbered years, the other festivals are typically held during even-numbered ones.

🕐 *Jun-Nov during odd-numbered years.*

MOSTRA INTERNAZIONALE D'ARTE CINEMATOGRAFICA
LIDO

Ca' Giustinian, San Marco 1364/A ☎041 52 18 711 www.labiennale.org

Venice is home to the world's oldest film festival, which was first held in 1932 and continues to draw thousands of artists, actors, directors, and film critics to the city each fall for screenings and celebrations of Italian and international cinema. The festival, held on the island Lido, has endured political turmoil (Mussolini Cups were once awarded as the festival's top prize) and its home island's gradual decline as a popular tourist destination. Nevertheless, the event itself hasn't waned in popularity. If you're just looking for a casual and quick visit to Venice, it's best to avoid the film festival; if you're looking for a chaotic but exciting cultural experience, get online now and book accommodations as far ahead as possible.

i Contact information above is for La Biennale di Venezia offices, which operate the administration of the Venice Film Festival. ☼ Early Sept.

SHOPPING

Venetian Artisan Goods

Of the top three artisan goods made in Venice—glass, masks, and lace—only the masks are typically produced in the city itself. Glass is produced in the northern lagoon island of Murano, while lace is generally produced in Burano. Though the islands offer numerous stores and the most extensive selection of glass and lace, there's no need to make a trip to the northern lagoon just to go shopping.

CA' MACANA
DORSODURO

Dorsoduro 1169   ☎041 27 76 142 www.camacana.com

Venice is overrun with mask shops, but Ca' Macana is one of the few places that focuses exclusively on Carnival masks. For those who care, this shop was the proud mask provider for Stanley Kubrick's Eyes Wide Shut. Not only can you browse the selection of strange and beautiful masks, you can watch the masters in action at Ca' Macana's workshops.

i Masks €15-60. ☼ Open daily 10am-7pm.

MA.RE
SAN MARCO

Calle Larga XXII Marzo 2088   ☎041 52 31 191 www.mareglass.com

With a location just off of P. San Marco, MA.RE stands out from the rows of similar shops all claiming to sell top-notch Murano glass. The products here range from wine glasses to unique ornamental pieces, like large ice-cube-esque blocks housing colorful octopedes, turtles, and jellyfish.

i Wine stopper €25. Chandeliers €15,000. ☼ Open Jun-Aug 9am-11pm; Sept-May 9am-7pm.

MURANO
SAN MARCO

370-368 Calle Larga San Marco   ☎041 63 17 79 www.duezeta.net

Murano (the store, not the island) is an island of authenticity in the midst of San Marco tourist mayhem. While a lot of the glass sellers around San Marco greet tourists with a smile and a 50% markup, the manager of Due Zeta is much more likely to introduce himself with a sneer and offers of steep discounts. That doesn't mean everything's cheap, though: in Murano, you pay a price for authentic artwork. The expansive store□which fills its three storefronts with its incredible selection of glass pieces□offers everything from €1 rings to elaborate sculptures for €1250 or more. The price of the Murano glass and 24-karat gold-rimmed tea set is not posted to avoid inducing a heart attack in frugal shoppers.

i Price ranges wildly, from €1 rings to €2000 sculptures. ☼ Open daily 9:30am-11:30pm. We suspect Murano offers some of the best nightlife in San Marco (this is a joke).

P. SCARPA
SAN POLO

Campo Frari 3007   ☎041 52 38 681

If, as Let's Go suspects, gruffness and authenticity have an inverse relationship, P. Scarpa is pretty darn authentic. A small, cramped lace shop offering a selection of both more quotidian (€2.50 doilies) and exquisitely rare (a €490, eighty-year-old lace collar) lace products, most of which are handmade, P. Scarpa's authoritative collection is matched only by the owner's pride in it.

i Prices vary widely. ☼ Open daily 9am-1pm and 2-6pm.

venice

Markets

Though Venice has relatively few open spaces and streets, it's the setting for a number of outdoor markets selling fresh fruit, vegetables, and seafood. Prices are typically posted, so you don't have to worry about getting overcharged. Make sure your produce isn't blemished or bruised, though, since some vendors try to pass the damaged wares off on tourists who are less likely to complain.

▦ RIALTO MARKET   SAN POLO

Don't miss Rialto market, one of the biggest street markets on the Mediterranean. If you come to the fish market around 7am, you'll find chefs and restaurateurs getting in on the cream of the crop. If scaled things make your skin crawl or you're allergic to waking up early, check out the miscellaneous stalls where you can bargain for anything from Murano glass to miniature crossbows.

i *Prices are variable but cheap. Cash only.* ✆ *Open M-Sa 8am-noon. Fish available Tu-Sa 7am-10am.*

ESSENTIALS
Practicalities

- **TOURIST OFFICES:** Head to the APT Tourist Office for maps, tours, the Venice Card, and theater and concert tickets. (P. Roma ☎041 24 11 499 www.turismovenezia.it ✆ Open daily 9am-2:30pm.) Additional offices near P. San Marco (San Marco 71) and on Lido (Gran Viale 6A).

- **LUGGAGE STORAGE:** Stazione Santa Lucia. (☎041 78 55 31 www.grandistazioni.it *i* 1st 5hr. €5, then €0.70 per hr. up to 12hr., €0.30 per hr. thereafter. ✆ Open daily 6am-midnight.)

- **DISABILITY SERVICES:** Citta per tutti provides information to physically disabled travelers. (San Marco 4136 ☎041 27 48 144 www.comune.venezia.it *i* V: Rialto. On Riva del Carbon, 2-3min. southwest of Rialto Bridge. ✆ Open Th 9am-1pm.)

- **INTERNET:** Look for internet cafes near the train station on Rio Tera Lista Spagna.

- **POSTAL OFFICES:** Poste Venezia Centrale. (San Marco 5554 ☎041 24 04 149 www.poste. it *i* V: Rialto. Off Campo San Bartolomeo, in front of the Rialto Bridge. ✆ Open M-F 8:25am-7:10pm, Sa 8:25am-12:35pm.)

Emergency

- **POLICE:** Polizia di Stato. (Santa Croce 500 ☎041 27 15 511 www.questure.poliziadistato.it *i* Near Ple. Roma.) Carabinieri. (Campo San Zaccaria, Castello 4693A ☎041 27 411 *i* V: San Zaccaria. Walk straight and follow the signs.) Other locations on Burano (V. San Martino 16), Lido (Riviera San Nicolò 33), and Murano (Fondamenta Riva Longa 1).

- **LATE NIGHT PHARMACIES:** Visit www.farmacistivenezia.it/turni2.php and click on "Asl 12 Venezia e isole" for a late-night pharmacy schedule.

- **HOSPITAL:** Ospedale Civile. (Campo Giovanni e Paolo Santissimi, Castello 6777 ☎041 52 94 111 www.ulss12.ve.it *i* V: Fondamenta Nuove. Walk east and turn right after the 1st bridge. The hospital has limited hours and is likely to direct you elsewhere for further treatment.)

Getting There

BY PLANE

Though **Aeroporto Marco Polo** (VCE ☎041 26 09 260 www.veniceairport.it) is billed as Venice's airport, once you arrive, the journey to the city's historic center has only just begun. A water taxi to reach the centro costs about €100, but there are several more economical ways to make it to Venice from the airport. **Alilaguna boats**(☎041 24 01 701 www.alilaguna.it) offer transport directly from VCE to the city center at €10 per passenger, but the service isn't necessarily expedient. The ultimate budget solution is to take one of the bus lines to Ple. Roma, near the Calatrava Bridge and just minutes away from Stazione Santa Lucia. The buses, which offer convenient transportation throughout the region, are operated by **ACTV** (☎041 24 24 www.hellovenezia.it) and cost as little as €1.30. This is comparable to the **ATVO Shuttle bus,** which also stops at Ple. Roma and costs €10 one-way. Buy any transportation ticket before leaving the airport—tickets are most easily purchased at the windows there.

BY TRAIN

Most travelers who are already in Italy will reach Venice by train. Several train lines run through **Stazione Santa Lucia** (☎041 26 09 260 www.veneziasantalucia.it) on the western side of the city. Trains arrive daily from Bologna (€11-30 ◩ 2hr., 30 per day), Florence (€11-43 ◩ 2-3hr., 20 per day), Milan (€18-42 ◩ 2½-3½hr, 15 per day), and Rome (€46-76 ◩ 3½-6hr., 15 per day). They often arrive in Venezia Mestre, which is one stop away from Santa Lucia Station. Tickets between the stations cost €1.10.

Getting Around

Although Venice has many great things to offer, convenient transportation isn't one of them. Within the city's six *sestieri*, there are absolutely no cars, buses, or trains. While poets and musicians have waxed nostalgic about the beauty of Venice's romantic, tangled streets, those same winding walkways are likely to provoke less lyrical outbursts from foreigners. Additionally, streets are often nameless or change names unexpectedly, and street numbers organized by neighborhood give only a general indication of where particular addresses are located. Your best bet is to memorize a few major landmarks, know the *vaporetto* stop closest to your hotel, know at least one campo, and keep the cardinal directions in mind.

BY BOAT

Before you spend a lot of money on an expensive *vaporetto* ticket, consider whether a *traghetto* might get you to your destination more quickly. *Traghetto*s (€2) are essentially gondolas without the kitsch, maneuvered by gondoliers-in-training who ferry people back and forth across the Grand Canal. Signs toward *traghetti* stops are clearly indicated, and odds are there will be one nearby. *Traghetti* hours vary and are limited during the winter. The *vaporetti* offer more extensive service throughout the city and operate 24hr. per day but are also more expensive. A single *vaporetto* ride costs €7 within a 60min. window, and you can buy a longer-term pass for unlimited service. (12hr. pass €18, 24hr. €20, 36hr. €25, 48hr. €30, 72hr. €35, 7 days €50.)

BY GONDOLA

Gondolas were once the primary method of transportation in Venice. Venetian aristocrats competed to have the most ostentatiously painted vessel, but the one-up-manship became so insufferable that the government eventually decreed that all gondolas must be painted black. Today, gondolas are not just a way to get from point A to point B but can also take you on a scenic loop back to point A again. These boats really are a beautiful way to see the city, and you'll appreciate the skill it takes to maneuver such a long vessel through the narrow canals, but they're wicked expensive. The going price is around €80 for about 10min. and gets more expensive as you approach St. Mark's Sq. You can try to bargain, but make sure you've agreed on the price before you set out, as gondoliers are a tight-knit group couched in tradition—probably not the people you want to piss off.

venice

verona

Think of Shakespeare's Juliet when you think of Verona, and you won't be wrong in your expectations. Now it is carefully tended and dressed up, just like a young lady from an important family: with extensive beauty tools and strict limitations. The whole city center exhibits signs here and there what people are not allowed to go to keep the city the perfect romantic location for travelers from all over the world. The city's impressively preserved historic buildings and significant medieval architecture have earned it distinction as an UNESCO World Heritage Site. But if our girl sounds too love-struck and delicate to you, it means you haven't yet been to its heart: a battered, brutal Roman amphitheater right in the middle of all the refined beauty. Even though the arena now only hosts musical events (mostly operas), everyone can still have a feeling that the crudeness is still there deep inside. Don't mess with Verona!

ORIENTATION

There is an incredible number of well-preserved historic sights and buildings in Verona, and though it's a sprawling city, it's still fairly manageable. Biking and walking are the best modes of transit, since much of Verona is difficult to navigate by car. Though traversing the city on foot may seem daunting, pretty much everything of interest is within a 15-20min. walk from the Arena that sits above the central Piazza Bra. The Adige River meanders through the city, yet most sites of interest can be found within the central peninsula. Verona University and its trail of kebab joints are on the east side of the Adige. Across the Ponte Navi from this area, V. Leoni leads northwest to the historic center of Piazza delle Erbe and then on toward Piazza Duomo. Walk west along the river to find the Castelvecchio.

get a room!

Sleeping in Verona on a budget can be challenging, but it's not impossible. Beware of opera nights, when hotels hike up prices for the influx of wealthy aficionados. These two are probably the best way to please your wallet; if you want to spend a bit more, check out the options on **www.letsgo.com**.

SLEEP EASY HOSTEL   B&B $$
  V. Venti Settembre 80   ☎392 915 5000 www.hostelverona.org

If there was a portrait of the word "irregular," it would be a picture of this hostel. Those who value an artistic combo of marble table set in the back yard and absence of a kitchen and the beauty of very bright-colored walls and Wi-Fi that works best (or only) on the stairs would not be disappointed. After all, rooms have balconies and private bathrooms, what other luxuries people might need?

i Cross Ponte Navi and follow v. XX Settembre for 10min. Hostel is on your right. Free Wi-Fi. Dorms €18-25, female dorms €20-28.
Lockers and ensuite bathrooms. Reception 1-8pm.

HOTEL SIENA   HOTEL $$$
  V. Marconi 41   ☎045 80 03 074

Hotel Siena is comfortable if not hugely exciting. The cramped singles facing the street are much less of a deal than the spacious doubles with mini-balconies that overlook the internal courtyard.

i From P. Bra, exit west onto V. Roma and turn left onto V. Daniele Manin, which becomes V. Marconi. Hotel Siena is on the left. Breakfast included. A/C. Single €86; doubles €142; triples €158; city tax included.

SIGHTS

Verona is full of Roman and Romanesque buildings that are among the most beautiful, historic, and architecturally significant in northern Italy. Most are concentrated
around the historic *centro* and are within comfortable walking distance of one another, but it still makes sense to plan a sightseeing route if you'll only be in the city for a
day or two. You shouldn't have to worry about budgeting your funds among Verona's
sights, though. If you invest in a 🗹**Verona Card,** you'll get free access to 12 sights, plus
four more at a reduced charge (2-day pass €15, 5-day €20; just church admissions €6,
students €5). The card is available at most major sights and local *tabbaccherie.* We
could be preachy and tell you that the many Romeo and Juliet attractions tend to be
overcrowded and of relatively little historic significance, but we wouldn't want to
rain on anyone's tragic love parade

🗹 ARENA DI VERONA
P. Bra
ANCIENT ROME
☎045 80 05 151 www.arena.it

As it often happens with romantic and pretty girls, beautiful Verona has a rough
heart with cruel and dark history. Battered, cave-like arena is located just on the
crossroad of the crossroads: the main *piazza.* It tries to become more elegant
by hosting opera concerts almost daily. But even strong preference of classics
can't conquer the brutal memories of gladiator fights (however, judging by the
tunnel condition those guys were real monsters). Such inner battle resolves in a
compromise and leaves ambiance of a soccer game.

*i From the train station, M-Sa bus #11, 12, 13, or 72; Su bus #90, 92, 93, 96, or 97 €6, students
and over 60 €4.50, kids 8-13 €1, with Museo Maffeiano €7 €5 with reductions). Opera tickets
€10-219. ⓩ Open M 1:30-7:30pm, Tu-Su 8:30am-7:30pm. Ticket office closes at 4:30pm. Most
performances at 9pm-9:15pm.*

MUSEO DI CASTELVECCHIO
C. Castelvecchio 2
CASTLE, MUSEUM
☎045 80 62 611 www.comune.verona.it/Castelvecchio/cvsito

If biblical themes are getting a bit old, this 14th-century fortress's collection of
paintings will be refreshing—many of the saints and Marys are actually up to
something instead of just standing there staring at you. Your museum admission
also lets you roam the castle ramparts overlooking the river.

*i From the train station, M-Sa bus #21, 22, 23, 24, or 41; Su bus #91, 93, 94, or 95. By foot, take
V. Roma from the west of P. Bra €6, students €4.50, ages 8-14 €1, with Verona Card and under 8
free. ⓩ Open M 1:30-7:30pm, Tu-Su 8:30am-7:30pm.Ticket sale closes at 6:45pm.*

TORRE DEI LAMBERTI
V. dalla Costa 1
TOWER
☎045 92 73 027

Like *The House That Jack Built,* this tower gathered quite a crowd over years
where everyone wanted to play a part in finishing it. It got higher and higher
every time when someone from the city decided it's time to throw in some more
stones. Now visitors can enjoy the magnificent cheat you'd wish every old tower
in Italy would have: an elevator that will steal 243 steps. If you've had your share
of towers, still consider climbing this one. Verona is beautiful up close (a rare
case!), imagine how gorgeous it is from afar!

*i Bus #72 or 73; right off P. Erbe €6, students and seniors €4.50, kids 8-14 €1. ⓩ Open daily
8:30am-8:10pm.*

COMPLESSO DEL DUOMO
P. Duomo 35
CHURCH
☎045 59 28 13 www.chieseverona.it

You don't need to be an architect to find Verona's Duomo fascinating. Since its
consecration in the fourth century CE, repeated natural disasters and subsequent rebuildings have added layers of architectural complexity. Even if you
aren't going to pay to see the red marble columns, vaulted ceilings, and Titian
paintings, the front facade of brick and marble stripes is still worth a look. Those

verona

who come inside close to the closure, have a chance to relax on a cool bench among strolling nuns and classical music in the air.

i Bus #72. From the eastern edge of P. Bra, take V. Leoncino until you reach V. Leoni. Follow this road past P. delle Erbe to the bridge and head right until you reach P. Duomo €2.50, with Verona Card free; combined ticket for 4 churches €6 €5 for students and people over 65). ☼ Open Su-Fr 10am-5:30pm, Sa 10am-3:30pm.

CASA DI GIULIETTA
PALAZZO, MUSEUM

V. Cappello 23 ☎045 80 34 303 www.comune.verona.it

Casa di Giulietta features a tunnel of love-graffiti, a worn statue of Juliette, a love-themed gift shop, a gate with locks, a balcony, and a billion of tourists jammed in between them. All the happiness above is free, but those willing to part with €6 can step into an empty house turned museum (empty with both tourists and exhibitions). There guests can walk on the balcony to be flashed by the crowd below and write a letter to Juliette while there is no Romeo in sight.

i Bus #72 or 73. From P. Bra, take V. Mazzini from the northeast and turn left onto V. Cappello €6, students €4.50. Combined ticket with Juliet's "tomb" €7, students €5. Cash only. ☼ Open M 1:30-7:30pm, Tu-Su 8:30am-7:30pm. Last entry 6:45pm.

FOOD

🏴 OSTERIA SGARZARIE
RISTORANTE $$$$

Corte Sgarzarie 14/A ☎045 80 00 312

Located in a beautiful courtyard just off P. delle Erbe, Osteria Sgarzarle serves phenomenal Veronese food. Try the lettuce salad with pears and maple syrup (€11), followed by the egg noodles with hare in amarone wine sauce (€10), for the perfect mix of earthy and fresh. It's a place for a date with long-term plans. In any other company hope that the delicious dishes would help you tune out all and every surrounding middle-aged couple.

i From P. Bra, head northwest on V. Fratta, turn right onto C. Cavour, and continue straight for about 5min.; the restaurant is ahead on the left. Entree €8-23. Cover €2.50. Wine €3-7. ☼ Open daily noon-4pm, 6:30pm-midnight.

🏴 TIGELLA BELLA
RISTORANTE $

V. Sottoriva 24 ☎045 80 13 098 www.tigellabella.it

The thing to order here is their *menu fisso* (€10.80), if you ever wondered how ham, warm bread, and nutella would taste together. Or another type of ham with mushrooms. Or yet another ham variety with white chocolate. (correct answer: actually, good, all of them.) Either way, such fun begs for a good company: someone has to mix that salsa with coconut crisps... Apart from this, the restaurant has some pretty cheap vegetarian options (€3-4.90).

i From the southeast corner of P. Bra, exit onto V. Pallone. Take the last left before the bridge onto V. Marcello. When the street ends, turn left and immediately right. Fixed menu with tigelle, fried gnocchi, ham, and 12 sauce €10.80. Entrees €3-9) ☼ Open Tu-Fr 7:30pm-0:30am, Sa-Su 12:30-2:30pm, 7pm-1am.

TRATTORIA AL SOLITO POSTO
RISTORANTE $$$

V. Santa Maria in Chiavica 5 ☎045 80 14 220

Nestled down a small alleyway, Trattoria al Solito Posto keeps it simple with top-quality Veronese cuisine prepared with fresh, local ingredients. Popular with locals, who are known to use it to host family parties, Trattoria al Solito Posto cooks up a mean polenta, while their risotto provides an excellent take on a regional favorite.

i From P. delle Erbe, turn right onto Corto Porsa Pasarito Chiesa S. Anastasia, then right onto V. San Pietro Martire for 2min., and right onto V. Santa Maria in Chiavica. Entree €10-36. ☼ Open Su-Mo, We-Th noon-3pm and 7-11pm, Fr-Sa noon-3pm and 7pm-midnight.

CANGRANDE OSTERIA AND ENOTECA   RISTORANTE $$$
V. Dietro Listone 19/D   ☎045 59 50 22 www.enotecacangrande.it

Cangrande is a place where perfectionism and tasteful self-irony walk hand-to-hand. Guests can choose to sit in the patio on a summer night to catch an opera playing in the Arena or walk pass the melted candle pile of human height inside. Seating options include a room with 800 wine bottles. Nowhere else a regional traditional dish of pumpkin tortelli with almonds and cinnamon (€9) tastes incredibly gourmet.

i *From the southwest corner of P. Bra, exit west onto V. Roma and take the 1st right onto V. Listone; the restaurant is shortly ahead on the left. Entree €8-24. Pizza €6-10. ☒ Open M-Sa 10am-1pm and 5pm-1am.*

NIGHTLIFE

Romeo and Juliet met at a party, so clearly Verona isn't completely dark after dinner. P. delle Erbe features some of the most sophisticated establishments, sporting a mix of locals and some tourists (though mostly Italians), while the area south of the Arena contains more hidden local gems.

LOCANDA DELLA 2NDA BALENA   CAFE, ENOTECA
Vicolo Balena 2   ☎045 493 63 82

Welcome to the cool kids' table. The place to see and be seen for the young, well-educated, and casually sophisticated Veronan crowd. Don't expect to find an international company here: the whole idea that they can be visited by tourists leaves owners very surprised. Instead, you could have fun, order wine, and test your "being like a true European" skills in this very brushed-up and artistic version of an Irish pub.

i *Exit P. delle Erbe onto V. Pallicciai. Turn left onto V. Spade then the 1st right onto Vicolo Balena. The bar is shortly ahead on right. Drinks €2.50-8.50. Free Wi-Fi. ☒ Open daily 11am-11pm. Aperitivo 8-10pm. Kitchen open 10am-10pm.*

OSTERIA A LA CAREGA   BAR
V. Cadrega 8   ☎045 80 69 248

This simple little *osteria* is not much more than a few wooden picnic tables, but the highly affordable drinks mean its usually crawling with students. Carega sometimes displays artwork and plays mainly jazz, electro, or rock and roll.

i *From P. delle Erbe, go north on V. Rosa until you reach V. Cadrega. Wine from €1.20. Beer from €2.30. Grappa €3.50. Free Wi-Fi. ☒ Open daily 10am-2am.*

ESSENTIALS
Practicalities

- **TOURIST OFFICES:** Central Tourist Office. (V. degli Alpini 9 ☎045 80 68 680 *i* Bus #13, 51, 61, 62 70, 71, or 73. Walk south from Arena di Verona into P. Bra. The tourist office is on the left behind the bike racks. ☒ Open M-Sa 9am-7pm, Su 10am-4pm.) Another location is at the airport (☎045 86 19 163).

- **INTERNET:** The city of Verona provides free Wi-Fi hotspots in P. Bra, P. delle Erbe, V. Mazzini, and Civic Library. Register for use at the Biblioteca Civica. (V. Capello 43 ☒ Open M 2pm-7pm, Tu-F 9am-7pm, Sa 9am-2pm.)

- **POSTAL OFFICES:** Poste Italiane. (V. Carlo Cattaneo 23 *i* From P. Bra, take V. Fratta and turn left onto V. Carlo Cattaneo. ☒ Open Mo-Fr 8:30am-2pm, Sa 8:30am-1pm.)

- **POSTAL CODE:** 37100

Emergency

- **POLICE:** Polizia di Stato. (Lungadige Antonio Galtarossa 11 ☎045 80 90 411 *i* From P. Bra, continue as it becomes V. Pallone. Cross over the river and turn right onto Lungadige Antonio Galtarossa.) Carabinieri. (V. Salvo D'Acquisto 6 ☎045 80 561 *i* Bus #72. From city center, continue along Corso Porta Nuova and turn right onto V. Antonio Locatelli.)

- **HOSPITAL:** Ospedale Civile Maggiore. (Ple. Aristide Stefani 1 ☎045 81 21 111 www.ospedaleuniverona.it *i* Bus #41, 62, 70, or 71 to P. Stefani 1.)

Getting There

Aeroporto Valerio Catullo Villafranca (VRN; ☎045 80 95 666 www.aeroportoverona.it) is Venice's small international airport. A shuttle from the airport to the train station runs every 15min. (€6). Verona Porta Nuova station (☎199 89 20 21 www.grandistazioni.it, www.ferroviedellostato.it) is where most travelers arrive. Trains arrive from Padua (€17 45-90min., 1-2 per hr.), Milan (€11 75min.-2hr., 1-2 per hr.), Venice €6.15 €21 1-2hr., 2-4 per hr.), and Rome (€45-85 3hr., approximately every hr.).

Getting Around

Verona is a walkable city, but buses are available. City bus (☎045 80 57 811 www.atv.verona.it) tickets can be purchased from tobacco shops and onboard. A stamped ticket (€1.10 in tobacco shops; €1.50 on board) is valid for 1hr. Most buses run from Verona Porta Nuova, where you can catch the regional bus (☎045 80 57 811 www.atv.verona.it) to Lago di Garda. Radiotaxi also has 24hr. taxi service. (☎045 53 26 66 www.radiotaxiverona.it)

bologna

Bologna: *la grassa, la dotta, la rossa*. The fat, the learned, and the red—this city sounds like an obese Commie professor. This proud local refrain summarizes what makes Bologna a great place. First, *la grassa*. Bologna is famous for its food, and rightfully so—a single meal here could make the whole trip worthwhile. Stuffed pastas like tortellini are local specialties, and lasagna alla Bolognese has become a household name far from Emilia-Romagna's dark, fertile soil. The town's other primary exports are caps and gowns—*la dotta*. Bologna is home to the Western Hemisphere's oldest university, whose 100,000 students swamp the city while classes are in session and leave it empty come summertime. With youthful exuberance (and livers), these students bring with them hopping nightlife and plenty of inexpensive booze. The university is also responsible for scores of free museums and sights that lack the tourist hordes of other Italian cities. What Bologna hasn't been so successful at is spreading the works of the national Communist Party, *la rossa*, which is headquartered in the city and has the sympathies of a number of its citizens.

ORIENTATION

Bologna is a pedestrian's town. Almost everything happens inside the *centro* walls, and a walk straight across takes less than 40min. Most travelers arrive at **Stazione Centrale**, in the north of the city. (Don't ask for directions to "the station," as you may end up at the regional station to the east.) Just left of the Stazione Centrale exit, **Via dell'Indipendenza** begins its run south to the *centro*, which culminates at **Piazza del Nettuno**. The larger **Piazza Maggiore**, Bologna's medieval center, connects to P. del Nettuno. From here, streets branch off and lead to the city's many museums. V. Francesco Rizzoli runs east from P. del Nettuno to the Two Towers of Bologna and to **Via Zamboni,** the hub of the city's university and a major student gathering spot. V. Ugo Bassi runs west from the *piazze* to **Via del Pratello** and its many bars. V. dell'Archiginnasio heads south alongside the basilica to Bologna's classiest quarter, where entrances to designer shops gleam beneath elaborate portico ceilings.

SIGHTS

Bologna's academic heritage is visible in its dozens of free museums. The **University Museums,** of which there are too many to count on one hand (or two hands and two feet, for that matter), cover every imaginable discipline and are clustered at the far end of V. Zamboni. The **Civic Museums,** full of surprisingly well-conserved art, are more spread out, as are the handful of tiny but engaging contemporary art galleries. **Piazza Maggiore** and **Piazza del Nettuno** feature Romanesque architecture, countless monuments, and, in the latter, a surprisingly sexual stone-and-bronze fountain of **Neptune and Attendants.** In P. di Porta Ravegnana, you'll discover that Pisa doesn't hold the monopoly on leaning with a visit to the **Two Towers:** one is still accessible to the public with a mere 1.3m overhang, while the other isn't doing so hot at 3m, which explains why it never did reach its neighbor's height. There are also some remarkable churches in Bologna with a completely different feel from the marble facades you find elsewhere in Italy.

▨ BASILICA MADONNA DI SAN LUCA
CHURCH, PANORAMIC VIEW

V. San Luca 36 ☎051 61 42 339

There's nothing holy about the climb to reach this secluded hilltop basilica. But if you complete it, you'll be able to say you survived the world's longest portico—the covered path has 666 arches. You'll also feel far less guilty about all your Bolognese feasts after you cover these 3.5km. Other rewards include the panorama of Emilia-Romagna's rolling countryside and the 1723 basilica, which contains purple-toned marble, elaborate frescoes around the central altar, and a prized icon of the Virgin Mary that is crowned and ensconced in gold. Legend has it that she was painted by St. Lukethe apostle himself.

i Head to Porta Saragozza in the southwest, or take bus #20 to Villa Spada. Follow the archways upward for a 40min. hike to the church (you can also take the tourist bus). Free. ⧖ Open daily 6am-12:30pm and 2:30-5:30pm.

bologna

get a room!

For a place with so many students, Bologna is woefully lacking in hostels—there's just one, and it's 4km from the *centro.* Thus, finding cheap accommodations in Bologna proper is all about finding which hotels are in their low season. Some operate by days of the week, others charge more when school's not in session, and still others increase prices in winter when hotels fill with business travelers. Several affordable places are clustered near **Via Guglielmo Marconi** and **Via Ugo Bassi.** For other ideas, visit **www.letsgo.com**.

HOTEL PANORAMA
HOTEL $$

V. Giovanni Livraghi 1, 4th fl. ☎051 22 18 02 www.hotelpanoramabologna.it

Indeed, the views from the windows of this hotel are quite picturesque. But when red-tiled roof after red-tiled roof starts to get boring, turn around to the walls: with the number of Italian-Spanish Impressionist reproductions you'll see, you'll think you're staying in an art gallery. While the beds are like those in any other hotel, there are some nice personal touches in the room (nothing says homey better than a small round table with a slightly worn tablecloth).

i Just off V. Ugo Bassi. Free Wi-Fi. Single €40; doubles €55, with bath €70; triples €75, with bath €90.

PINACOTECA NAZIONALE

V. delle Belle Arti 56

MUSEUM

☎051 42 09 411

The Pinacoteca has high ceilings to accommodate all its enormous gold-framed paintings of martyrs and angels, which date from ancient Rome through to the 18th century. While the themes don't stray from your standard religious scenes, the images are still remarkable for their surprisingly vivid colors—you'll worry that some of the extremely detailed, gory depictions might drip blood on your T-shirt. Artists include a few big names: Titian, El Greco, Vasari, and Raphael, notable here for his oddly calm *St. Cecilia in Rapture*.

i From the Two Towers, take V. Zamboni. Turn left at the opera house and right onto V. delle Belle Arti €4, students and teachers €2. ☼ Open Tu-W 9am-1:30pm, Th 9am-7pm, F-Su 2-7pm.

PALAZZO COMUNALE

P. Maggiore 6

MUSEUM

This *palazzo* has gored knights in its courtyard and free contemporary art exhibits. On the next floor, you'll find Bolognese art in the **Collezioni Comunali d'Arte,** which spans the 13th through 20th centuries. Gruesome depictions are in no short supply, and, beyond the dim frescoes, many unique pieces make the visit memorable. Next door, the **Museo Morandi** is less accessible to the casual art appreciator. If the painting you're looking at provokes instant and pervasive boredom, you're probably looking at a Morandi; here you'll find more monotone beige still lifes of vases than you can comfortably pretend to appreciate.

i On the west side of P. Maggiore. Lazy ones should take an elevator; the slippery staircase is not worth your time €5, over 65 and students €3, under 18 free. Palazzo Comunale free 1st Sa of each month 3-6:30pm. Museo Morandi free on W. ☼ Collezioni Comunali d'Arte open Tu-F 9am-6:30pm, Sa-Su 10am-6:30pm. Musei Morandi open Tu-F 11am-6pm, Sa-Su 11am-8pm.

BIBLIOTECA ARCHIGINNASIO

P. Galvani 1

PALAZZO

☎051 27 68 11 www.archiginnasio.it

This *palazzo* was home to Bologna's famous university from 1563 until 1805, and it has the coat of arms of more than 5000 instructors and students graffitied on its walls and ceilings to prove it. Today, the building houses the 800,000-volume **Biblioteca dell'Archginnasio,** arguably Italy's most important public library. You can also visit the *palazzo*'s famous **Anatomy Theater,** where instructors held dissections for medical student audiences and where actors now entertain without the use of corpses.

i From P. Maggiore, walk down V. Archiginnasio alongside the basilica. Free. ☼ Open M-F 9am-7pm, Sa 9am-2pm.

FOOD

This internationally acclaimed food capital is the place to take time for proper sit-down meals—it's a big part of the local culture. If you want to prepare your own food, there are several top-notch delis as well as a fresh produce market, the **Mercato delle Erbe,** accessible from the northwestern portion of V. Ugo Bassi. You should also know that dinner is on the later side in Bologna—if you show up at 7:30pm, the only other people in the restaurant will mostly likely be the waiter and the chef.

☒ OSTERIA DELL'ORSA

V. Mentana 1F

OSTERIA $

☎051 23 15 76

Welcome back to school! Long wooden tables with long wooden benches will take you back to your cafeteria days, but maybe it's just an attempt to cater to the main clientele—students from the neighboring university district. Regardless of the style of seating, students would flock here no matter what, lured by pasta specials and a wide selection of big panini.

i From P. del Nettuno, take V. dell' Indipendenza, turn right onto V. Marsala, then left onto V. Mentana. Panini grande €5. Crostini €1.50-8. Crescentini and piadini €4-5. Entrees €4-22. ⏰ Open daily noon-1am.

SPACCA NAPOLI
V. San Vitale 45A

PIZZERIA $

☎051 26 17 43

When the pizza arrives, first-time diners at Spacca Napoli frequently burst out laughing. It's not because the chef has carefully spelled out jokes with the toppings, but because a single pizza here could smother the sun. The menu has a wide variety of options, from the standard Margherita (€4) to such culinary adventures as Nutella and Grand Marnier (€6).

i Head down V. San Vitale from the Two Towers. Pizza €2.50-7.50. Primi and secondi €6-12. ⏰ Open M-F noon-2:30pm and 7-11:30pm, Sa-Su 7-11:30pm.

OLIVO
P. Aldrovandi 21b

RISTORANTE BAR $

☎051 087 88 72

P. Aldrovandi is an excellent stop for the hungry and the poor, with its cheap and varied open-air market (no fruit or vegetable costs more than €2 per kg) and a necklace of kebab cafes around it. But because everyone has to be (relatively) fancy every once in a while, this *piazza* also has Olivo, a cute and cozy restaurant with white wooden tables and a vast wine selection to make life even nicer.

i At the north end of P. Aldrovandi. Free Wi-Fi. Cover €1.50. Entrees €10-23. Wine from €4. ⏰ Open M-Sa noon-2am.Closed Aug 10-20.

LA ORTE GALUZZI
Corte Galuzzi 7

TRATTORIA $$

☎051 22 64 81

This *trattoria* is a hidden pasta Narnia. Tucked in a quiet courtyard away from the main streets, the place allows its guests to order from a menu that looks more like a medieval book of fairy tales. With a dozen varieties of tortellini varieties, from cream filling (€10) to pumpkin (€9), it's going to be a magical night.

i Just off V. Luigi Carlo Farini from Palazzo Archiginnasio. Cover €3. Primi €9-10. Secondi €12-40. Does not accept Diner's and American Express. ⏰ Open Tu-Su 12:30-2:30pm and 7:30pm-1am.

EATALY AMBASCIATORI
V. degli Orefici 19

RISTORANTE $$

☎051 09 52 820 www.eataly.it

Eataly Ambasciatori is what happens when you put a library cafe on steroids. This amusing venture combines a restaurant with a big bookstore and a wine shop with an information center for cultural events around the city. While it might be lacking your typical restaurant atmosphere, an unusual lunch experience is guaranteed by the waiters who walk out of bookshelves to deliver your pasta.

i Take V. Francesco Rizzoli away from P. del Nettuno and turn right onto V. degli Orefici. Panini €3.50-4.50. Primi €9-12. Secondi €9-15.50. ⏰ Restaurant open M-Sa 8am-midnight, Su 10am-midnight. Bookstore open daily 9am-midnight.

NIGHTLIFE

One hundred thousand students require a lot of booze. Bologna provides generously with a vast selection of bars, pubs, and nightclubs. **Via Zamboni** is student central, while across town **Via del Pratello** attracts a slightly older and more subdued crowd. **Piazza San Francesco** also fills with groups of students. In summer, nightclubs close and the partying moves to a number of outdoor discos, particularly in **Parco Magherita**.

🏙 PIAZZA SANTO STEFANO
P. Santo Stefano

BAR

Cynics beware. This small *piazza* takes everything picturesque and lovely in the world and glues it all together with a healthy dollop of starry-eyed romanticism.

People sit on the steps of a church under blooming tree branches or sip a drink at one of the slightly tilted tables in the cafe among the cheerful local crowd.

i From the Two Towers, follow Strada Maggiore for few blocks and turn right onto Corte Isolani.

CASSERO

CLUB, GLBT

V. Don Giovanni Minzoni 18 ☎051 09 57 200 www.cassero.it

Peer over an old wall to discover Cassero's beautiful colored lights, live music, and carousing students and locals. Inside, the thumping beat of the dance floor gets the crowd moving. As Bologna's premier gay and lesbian club, Cassero does the community proud.

i Take V. Guglielmo Marconi to P. dei Martiri and turn left onto V. Don Giovanni Minzoni. Beer €3.50. Mixed drinks €6-7. Cash only. ☼ Open in summer daily 7pm-6am; in fall, winter, and spring 9pm-6am.

CLURICAUNE

IRISH PUB

V. Zamboni 18B ☎051 26 34 19

Everybody lies. This is not a pub, even though the sign, the name, and our book tells you otherwise. It's a goddamn Irish *village*. Guests can fetch their *birra spina* (€5) and get lost in a multitude of endless rooms and cozy corners. Space, however, is a must in a place that is located right by the university district, and this place manages to fill up its copious wall space with embellishments like retro bikes with enormous front wheels.

i Take V. Zamboni from the Two Towers. Pin €5. Bottled beer €4.50. Mixed drinks €5.50-7. Cold punch €3.50. Happy hour drinks €2.50-5. Super happy hour drinks €2-4. ☼ Open daily noon-3am. Happy hour until 8:30pm. Super happy hour W 7:30-10:30pm.

ALTO TASSO

ENOTECA

P. San Francesco 6D ☎051 23 80 03 www.altotasso.com

In P. San Francesco, Alto Tasso serves affordable drinks to thirsty students and travelers. The bright walls of this casual enoteca display rotating exhibits of local artists' work., although the younger crowd of students, break-dancers, and artists prefer to take to the *piazza* outside the steps of San Francesco church.

i Take V. Ugo Bassi and make a slight left onto V. Pratello, then the 1st left onto V. San Francesco. Wine €3-5. Beer €3-5. Mixed drinks €5. ☼ Open M-Th 4:30pm-2:30am, F-Sa 4:30pm-3am, Su 4:30pm-2:30am.

ESSENTIALS

Practicalities

- **TOURIST OFFICES: IAT** provides information and is the starting point for walking and bus tours. (P. Maggiore 1E ☎051 23 96 60 *i* In Palazzo di Podesta. ☼ Open daily 9am-7pm.) Other locations at **Stazione Centrale** (☎051 24 65 41 ☼ Open M-Sa 8:30am-7:30pm) and **Aeroporto Guglielmo Marconi** (☎051 64 72 113 ☼ Open M-Sa 8am-8pm, Su 9am-3pm). **Bologna Incoming,** inside the main tourist office, books hotels, but not hostels. (☎800 85 60 65; www.bolognaincoming.it ☼ Open daily 9am-7pm.)

- **LUGGAGE STORAGE: Stazione Centrale.** (☎051 25 83 033 ☼ Open daily 6am-10pm.)

- **INTERNET: Sportello Iperbole** provides 3hr. free Wi-Fi and 2hr. free internet on public computers. (P. Maggiore 6 ☎051 20 31 84 *i* In Palazzo Comunale. *i* Reserve ahead for Wi-Fi. ☼ Open M-F 8:30am-7pm, Sa 8:30am-2pm and 3-7pm.)

- **POST OFFICES: Poste Italiane.** (P. Minghetti 1 ☎051 20 88 70)

- **POSTAL CODES:** 40100.

Emergency

- **POLICE: Polizia di Stato.** (V. degli Agresti 3 ☎051 23 76 32)

- **LATE-NIGHT PHARMACIES: Farmacia Comunali.** (P. Maggiore 6 ☎051 26 63 10 *i* In Palazzo comunale. ☒ Open 24hr.)

- **HOSPITALS/MEDICAL SERVICES: Policlinico Sant'Orsala Malpighi.** (V. Pietro Albertoni 15 ☎051 63 61 111 www.aosp.bo.it *i* Follow V. San Vitale to V. Giuseppe Massareti and turn right.)

Getting There

For those arriving by plane, **Aeroporto Guglielmo Marconi** (BLQ; V. Triumvirato 84 ☎051 64 79 615 www.bologna-airport.it) is northwest of the city center. ATC operates the **Aerobus** (☎051 29 02 90), which runs from the airport to Stazione Centrale's track D, with several stops in the *centro* along V. Ugo Bassi. (€6. ☒ Every 15min. 6am-12:15am.) To arrive by train, Stazione Centrale services: **Florence** (€30. ☒ 1½hr., 2 per hr. 7am-11:30pm); **Milan** (€23. ☒ 2-3hr., 2 per hr. 5:15am-11pm); **Rome** (€26. ☒ 2½-4hr., 2 per hr. 6:15am-10:36pm); **Venice** (€9.30. ☒ 2hr., every 30-60min. 5:57am-11:30pm).

Getting Around

ATC operates a comprehensive bus system throughout the city (☎051 29 02 90 *i* 60min €1.20; 24hr. €4), though most people walk in the *centro*. Find taxis in most *piazze* or call ☎051 37 27 27.

cinque terre

Just a few generations ago, little old ladies from Riomaggiore or Monterosso wore the same black dress their whole lives, the roads (not to mention cars) had not paved their way through the Cinque Terre, and fragrant wine hills glowed in the light of the setting sun, admired only by seagulls and the locals working the vineyards.

How times have changed. Though we'd be lying if we told you the Cinque Terre is the same virgin paradise it used to be—it's grown up a bit since then—it is still host to the stunning natural scenery and picturesque villages, pinned between mountain and *mare*, that make it so unforgettable to locals and tourists alike. These villages—"five lands" is the literal translation of *"Cinque Terre"*—include, from north to south, **Monterosso al Mare, Vernazza, Corniglia, Manarola,** and **Riomaggiore.**

ORIENTATION

A popular hiking path in a national park connects the five villages, each of which has its own unique character. Part of the pleasure of exploring the area on foot comes from getting to know the five coastal towns' distinct personalities. **Monterosso,** blessed with a welcoming expanse of sand, is the modern beach town, while **Vernazza** is the quieter but more sophisticated sister by the sea. Hilltop **Corniglia** is tiny and relatively withdrawn from the tourist circuit but offers the most stunning vistas and rocky descents. **Manarola** feels perhaps most removed from the tourist clamor but sports an excellent hostel and swim spot, while **Riomaggiore,** a crowded resort village, is a portal to the Cinque Terre from the south.

SIGHTS

Monterosso

🏖 **IL GIGANTE**   MONUMENT, BEACH

V. Mollina, near V. Fegina

He's the best-looking lifeguard on the beach. Too bad he's so hard to get into bed. Then again, that's because he's a stone giant carved from a cliff, watching over one of Monterosso's free beaches. Beyond the giant's gaze, you'll be able to view more of the town's public shores. The uncontrolled stretches tend to be mixed in with roped-off private areas for hotel guests and paying customers—look for the *ingresso libero* signs by the stairs or beach access to be sure that no cabana boys will come chasing you down with a bill.

i Turn right out of the train station onto Lungomare Fegina. Free.

Vernazza

VERNAZZA PORT
P. Marconi

BEACH

Once upon a time, this miniscule inlet was home to much of the wine shipping on the Italian Riviera. Now it sees a lot of toddlers in swim diapers taking their first dip with mom and dad. This strip of sand, located right in the heart of Vernazza, has no services or lifeguards, but its small size and protected water mean it remains very family-friendly. More athletic folks opt to scramble over the rocks at the far end of the dock and dive into the water at the end. (Note: don't be dumb and dive into shallow places).

i At the end of P. Marconi. Free. ☺ Open daily sunrise-sunset. Some travelers say they have disregarded this rule only to be told off by old fishermen.

Manarola

▨ ROCKY BEACH
At the end of V. Birolli

BEACH

The rock face leading down from town doesn't dissuade swimmers from nearby homes or from two continents away, and with good reason: this is one of the best places to swim in the Cinque Terre. While a little more adventurous than Vernazza's gentle wading beach but less daring than Corniglia's dramatic cliff, Manarola's cove is just right. As boats bob in and out of the harbor and sunbathers stretch in the midday heat, the more adventurous types jump 15ft. into the blue abyss from a central outcropping. And it's not just crazy teenagers who are plummeting off the ledge like lemmings; dads do belly flops into the salty water, too. Ironically, the quieter area to sunbathe is closer to the *piazza*, where a small concrete pier next to the rocks allows for a flatter bronzing plane and easy access to the water.

i Turn left from the tunnel and head down to the water on V. Birolli. Free.

Riomaggiore

▨ ARTWORK OF SILVIO BENEDETTO
In P. Rio Finale, the tunnel, and all over town

PUBLIC ART

www.silviobenedetto.it

Buenos Aires native Silvio Benedetto has a crush on the Cinque Terre, and apparently the V. dell'Amore wasn't enough. Oh, no—he wasn't satisfied with just scribbling his crush's name; instead, he emblazoned it across Riomaggiore with his monumental works of art. He started in the train tunnel (apparently no one told him it wasn't the tunnel of love) with abstract mosaic interpretations of sun, sea, and land. On a wall visible from the station, Benedetto's Storia di Uomini e de Pietre (History of Man and Stone) immortalizes the region's hardworking farmers in dramatic poses and eye-catching colors. Exploring the rest of town, visitors will unexpectedly happen upon Benedetto's influence in many places, which lends a little bit of whimsy to this less secluded sea town.

i Mural outside train station, mosaic in tunnel, and tile installation outside the tunnel's end. Above town, the municipal building on V. T. Signori also has a mural. Free.

get a room!

Most hotels can be found in the larger towns at either end of the Cinque Terre, Monterosso and Riomaggiore. Across the five villages you'll find *af-fittacamere*, apartments let out by locals on a short term basis. For more recommendations, visit **www.letsgo.com**.

HOTEL AGAVI (MONTEROSSO) · HOTEL $$$

Lungomare Fegina 30 · ☎0187 81 71 71 · www.paginegialle.it/hotelagavi

Hotel Agavi's rooms are simple, and its Monterosso location is perfect. While blue-checkered comforters keep the bright rooms feeling cheerful, great ocean views and the proximity to the water really steal the show.

i Turn left out of the train station. Sea breeze included. Single €60-80; doubles €80-120; triples €145.

HOTEL GIANNI FRANZI (VERNAZZA) · HOTEL $$$

P. Marconi 5 · ☎0187 82 10 03 · www.giannifranzi.it

Hotel Gianni Franzi's small, sunny rooms are located up their own steep set of steps. Inside, labyrinthine hallways and spiral steps give way to breathtaking ocean vistas and gorgeous terraces. You and your svelte calves should hightail it to Gianni Franzi; what you lose in calories climbing the steps you get to make up later in focaccia.

i Walk down V. Roma/V. Visconti and look left. Reception is in the restaurant. Single €45, with bath €70; doubles €80-120 depending on bathroom/sea view situation. ☼ Check-in before 4pm. On W call upon arrival.

OSTELLO CORNIGLIA · HOSTEL $$

V. alla Stazione 3 · ☎0187 81 25 59 · www.ostellocorniglia.com

Think about it: if they're brave enough to take on those stairs with their hefty packs, the mountain-trekking, backpacking crew that stays in this youth hostel must be interesting—or at least super fit.

i In the yellow building to the right before the centro storico. Wi-F €0.50 per 30min., €9 per day. Breakfast €3-5. Washing machine in hostel. Single-sex 8-person dorms €22-24; doubles €50-60. ☼ Reception 7am-1pm and 3pm-1:30am; lockout 1-3pm.

OSTELLO CINQUE TERRE (MANAROLA) · HOSTEL $$

V. Riccobaldi 21 · ☎0187 92 02 15 · www.hostel5terre.com

The second of only two hostels in all of the Cinque Terre, Ostello Cinque Terre provides a rare respite from middle-aged tourists holding hands in the heat. Visitors head up to simple single-sex dorms with bunk beds that include ocean views just as breathtaking as those of any four-star hotel.

i From the train station tunnel, turn right and walk 300m uphill to the church; the hostel is to the left. Wi-Fi free downstairs. 6-bed dorm €20-23; doubles €55-65; quads €88-100; 6-person rooms €126-144. ☼ Reception 7am-1pm and 4pm-1am. Lockout 10am-4pm.

RIOMAGGIORE RESERVATIONS · AFFITTACAMERE $$

V. Colombo 181 · ☎0187 76 05 75 · www.riomaggiorereservations.com

From student dorms to vast apartments, this room rental company seems to have it all. Each room includes an ensuite bath (or shared bath in the dorms), but beyond that, little is shared by the huge variety of properties. The dorms will probably be the best bet for budget travelers; housed in an apartment, they're clean, fairly spacious, and have kitchen access.

i After the tunnel, turn left up V. Colombo. It's ahead on the left. Wi-Fi in the office. Dorm €20-25; doubles and apartments €60-120. ☼ Office open daily 9am-1pm and 2-5pm.

cinque terre

HIKING

The trails connecting the five villages were once used to carry grapes and wine from the vineyards that fill the hilltops. Today they offer the chance for spectacularly beautiful and not especially difficult hikes.

Monterosso to Vernazza

The hike from Monterosso to Vernazza (90min.) is the most challenging of the four town-linking hikes, but without question, the pain is worth the gain: breathtaking vistas of the towns and spectacular panoramas of the sea crown the uphill journey. At higher elevations, the climb gives way to a relatively flat track notable for its wildflowers, butterflies, and gorgeous views over terraced vineyards back to Monterosso.

Vernazza to Corniglia

The trail from Vernazza to Corniglia (75min.), while still difficult due to a significant number of steps throughout, is more open than that from Monterosso to Vernazza. It begins along a wide path with continuous views of the ocean over a brush-covered hill. With less shade comes more cacti (in Italy—who knew?). The hike's most impressive point is near **Marker 15**, over 200m up, where the trail overlooks Corniglia—itself a city on a hill—with Manarola's orange and pink hues standing out against the many azure inlets in the distance.

Corniglia to Manarola

Talk about an inauspicious start to this trail (40min.). Even after climbing down 382 steps from Corniglia (a good reason to do the trail in this direction), the scenery scarcely improves, as the entry to this portion of the path runs past the train station, through a bunker-like concrete gully, and past a number of abandoned warehouses. Compared to the first two sections of trail, from Monterosso to Vernazza and Vernazza to Corniglia, the scenery here is only decent. The trail is much flatter and paved with gravel in many places, making it easier for hikers of all abilities.

Manarola to Riomaggiore

All's fair in love and walking, as demonstrated by the final stretch of the Cinque Terre's famous "Trail #2" (the blue line on the tourist-office map). Known as **Via dell'Amore,** or the "Lover's Trail," this 20min. walk can be completed by anyone, and with elevators at both ends, it is nearly wheelchair accessible except for a few steps in the middle. (Disabled visitors should call the park in advance at ☎0187 76 00 91 for lift information.) Smooth and paved, this hike provides more than just a mild introduction to the sea views further along. Indeed, its uniqueness comes from the so-called "Tunnel of Love," which has been thoroughly graffitied with sappy hearts and Cupid's arrows by countless paramours over the years, some of whom have even painted elaborate murals.

FOOD

Monterosso

▩ CANTINA DIE SCIACCHETRÀ   WINE SHOP $$
V. Roma 7

The only thing more magical than the sciacchetrà itself is the salesman at this spread-stuffed hole in the wall, where local products practically fall off the shelves. Or wait—it's just the row of free samples on the table. Play your cards right (or, you know, just ask) and you might be able to taste a free, shot-sized glass of the sciacchetrà; its sweet, syrupy taste will enlighten you as to what all the fuss is about. Buy a slightly cheaper bottle of wine and some tapenade

(€5.50) and make a meal of it—or just continue standing at the counter looking cute and asking for free alcohol.

i On the left before the 1st underpass over V. Roma. Cinque Terre wine €5-20. Sciacchetrà €27. Spreads €5.50-6.50. ✪ Open daily 9am-11pm.

RISTORANTE L'ALTAMAREA   SEAFOOD $$$
V. Roma 54   ☎0187 81 71 70

Fresh fish and even fresher homemade pasta are the hallmarks of this well-loved restaurant's traditional Ligurian menu. The fish ravioli with tomato cream (€11.90) will have the culinarily inclined among you swooning; follow it with the Ligurian rabbit with pine nuts and olives (€12.90) for a true feast. While the decor in this simple-seeming restaurant is nondescript, the food will leave a far more lasting impression.

i On the right after the 1st underpass on V. Roma. Primi €10-12; secondi €12-20. ✪ Open M-Tu noon-2:45pm and 6-10:30pm, Th-Su noon-2:45pm and 6-10:30pm.

PIZZERIA LA SMORFIA   PIZZERIA $
V. Vittorio Emanuele 730187 81 83 95

Okay, let's just get this out there: La Smorfia totally sounds like La Smurf. While there are no little blue friends to be found here, there's still plenty of pizza. In fact, there are as many as 90 different varieties. And with prices starting at €4.50, picking your pie may be the toughest decision you'll encounter in all of Liguria.

i Take the 1st left from the piazza after the tunnel onto V. Vittorio Emanuele. The pizzeria is up on the left. Small pizza €4.50-7, large €9-14. Calzones €8. ✪ Open daily 11:30am-3pm and 6-11pm.

Vernazza

🏷 BLUE MARLIN BAR   CAFE $$
V. Roma 43   ☎0187 82 11 49

Spanish guitar music + bacon = heaven? So maybe we have a simplistic definition of what to expect in the afterlife, but we're positively tickled by the English breakfast option and chill vibe at this casual cafe. The music isn't live, but the young locals are vivacious enough to make up for it.

i Down the hill from the train station, on the right. Pastries €1. Bruschetta €3-4. Pizza €5-7. Espresso drinks €1-2. ✪ Open daily 7am-6:30pm. Hot breakfast served 8:40-11:30am.

🏷 BATTI BATTI FRIGGITORIA   FRIGGITORIA $
V. Visconti 21   ☎334 92 423

Oh, wait—we found the only thing more exciting than bacon: fried stuff. This counts as a cultural experience, as you're less likely to find deep-fried Twinkies (though who knows what the influx of more Midwestern tourists will bring) and more likely to discover crisp, golden Ligurian food, such as anchovies, calamari, codfish, and bread with Nutella. Yes, deep-fried bread with Nutella—who said we're not at the county fair?

i From the train station, head toward the water; the friggitoria is on the right. Fried deliciousness €2.50-5 per cone. ✪ Open daily 10:30am-9:30pm.

Corniglia

🏷 CANTINA DI MANANAN   RISTORANTE $$$
V. Fieschi 117   ☎0187 82 11 66

Cantina di Mananan feels like an old-fashioned, local joint from the start; little do you suspect, however, that you are about to have the dinner of your life (or at least your trip). The interior proudly displays wine bottles, religious shrines, and old pictures of Corniglia, including one of a very naked man squatting over a wine barrel. Classy move, Cantina di Mananan. You'll forget promptly about the nudity, however, when you dig into the food. For the full experience, get ready to hunker down, count your euro to make sure you'll be able to pay at the end, and order away. If you're not happier and more full than you've ever been after this meal, you clearly just don't have a soul.

i From the centro storico, turn right onto V. Fieschi; the restaurant is on the left. Primi €10-12; secondi €12-18. ☼ Open M 12:30-3pm and 7:30-10pm, W-Su 12:30-3pm and 7:30-10pm.

TERRA ROSSA ENOTECA   ENOTECA $$
V. Fieschi 58   ☎0187 81 20 92

Tucked into a corner overlooking the valley, the delicate wooden tables and fresh flowers of this romantic spot are a mirage in the Mediterranean desert for weary hikers—or lovers—looking for a spot to rest. Candles glow in jars as sun-kissed couples sip Corniglia's Polenza, a dry white wine (€4-5), and dine on anchovies in olive oil (€11). For early risers, come for a piece of sweet focaccia with raisins (€1.50) and espresso as the morning sun trembles over the valley before heading down to Corniglia's exhilarating marina for a morning swim.

i Overlooking the valley; to the right from the centro storico when facing the valley. Appetizers up to €12. Wine €4-5. 3- or 5-wine tasting menu €10/15. Aperitivo features a glass of wine and 1 appetizer €8. ☼ Open M-Th 9am-9pm, F-Su 9am-11pm.

Manarola

TRATTORIA DAL BILLY   RISTORANTE $$$
V. Rollandi 122   ☎0187 92 06 28 www.trattoriabilly.com

There's a reason you can't just wander into Trattoria dal Billy on a weekend night and expect a table. Actually, there are several reasons, and they're all on the menu. Eating at Trattoria dal Billy is like realizing you've never eaten here. The octopus and potato salad (€10) will feel like the first octopus, potato, and drizzle of olive oil you have ever tasted. Especially if you've never actually eaten octopus before. You owe it to your taste buds, belly, and soul to book a table here.

i Turn right from the tunnel, then follow the road uphill 300m to the church piazza. Turn right up the steps at the far side of the piazza and follow the small street to the trattoria. Entrees €10-22. ☼ Open M-W noon-2:30pm and 6:30-10pm, F-Su noon-2:30pm and 6:30-10pm. Reservations strongly recommended.

LA CAMBUSA   PIZZERIA $
V. Birolli 110   ☎0187 92 10 29

The display case is always full. Maybe that's because there are so many choices that no customer can bear to pick just one dish. Beneath the hand-painted sign of this hole-in-the-wall establishment (there's no place to sit down, so be ready to grab and go), every bread product and delicacy known to humanity awaits, from doughy pizza slices (€2) to focaccia piled high with pesto, vegetables, and salami.

i Turn left from the tunnel and cross the piazza. The pizzeria is on the right. Focaccia €2. Pizza €2 per slice. ☼ Open daily 9am-8:30pm.

Riomaggiore

TE LA DO IO LA MERENDA   PIZZERIA, TAKEOUT $
V. Colombo 161   ☎0187 92 01 48

"Ligurian tasty here!" shouts a sign hanging in this restaurant. While grammar fiends might have something to say about that, we say it's poetry. One look at the explosion of focaccia behind the counter—not to mention the pizza and rice pie—will have you, too, convinced that tasty is a verb. Try the pasotti (ravioli) with walnut sauce (€7) for a meal on the go or simply stand gaping at the explosion of signs lining the walls of this place. Tasty, indeed.

i At the bend in V. Colombo, on the right. Medium pizza €5-7, slices €2-3. Ligurian dishes to go €5-8. ☼ Open daily 9:30am-9:30pm.

DAU CILA
V. San Giacomo 65

SEAFOOD $$$
☎0187 76 00 32

Located down the seemingly secret steps to the marina, Dau Cila's location is almost as beautiful as its food. Featuring tasty takes on the region's popular bruschetta, including a bacon rosemary version (€9), and creative dishes such as fried calamari with tomato petals and thyme (€15), Dau Cila is a great place to splurge on a truly top-quality meal in Riomaggiore.

i From the tunnel, take the steps down toward"Marina." Once outside, Dau Cila is on the left. Entrees €12-30. ⏰ Open daily noon-11pm. Bar open from 3-6pm when kitchen is closed.

NIGHTLIFE

Monterosso

📛 FAST BAR
V. Roma 13

BAR

It's rock all the time at this bar, whose rough, stone walls are augmented only by paraphernalia of American rock sensations—naked Red Hot Chili Peppers, anyone? Sporting perhaps the only Rocky Horror Picture Show poster in the Cinque Terre, Fast Bar equals fast times—or at least a great place to grab a drink with fellow tourists and alcohol-starved Italian dudes. Before the flood wiped away the old storefront, there was a wall of American dollar bills that stood as testament to late-night memories. Now, the tradition continues, as a new sheet of American (and some Canadian—don't cry for us, Canada) currency has notes left by travelers—thus proving that tradition is one thing that can't be dampened.

i After exiting the tunnel, pass under the railroad bridge and head left onto V. Roma. It's on the left. Sandwiches €3. Beer €4-4.50. Mixed drinks €5-6. ⏰ Open daily 10am-2am. Aperitivo 6-9pm.

CA DI SCIENSA
P. Garibaldi 17

BAR
☎0187 81 82 33

Sporting actual Cinque-Terrean youths chilling at aperitivo and swaying to reggae music among the old pictures of their fishermen forefathers, Ca di Sciensa is the place to be for relaxed night that doesn't involve watching a middle-aged couple giddily hold hands for the first time in years.

i From the tunnel, walk along the opposite side of the railroad bridge to P. Garibaldi. Beer €2-4. Mixed drinks €5. Sandwiches €5. ⏰ Open daily 10:30am-2am. Aperitivo 5:30-9pm.

Manarola

📛 LA CANTINA DELLO ZIO BRAMANTE
V. Birolli 110

BAR
☎0187 76 20 61

A dark-haired man plays Spanish guitar, flip-flop dangling off of bare foot, as tourists and locals linger into the night munching on bruschetta or apricot cake (€5) and sipping regional wines. Welcome to La Cantina dello Zio Bramante, started by Zio Bramante himself and family-owned for years. The owner and friends jam on the guitar (or didgeridoo) nightly at the front of the room, and patrons join in on the bongos, tambourines, and the tables. Music starts at 9:30pm, and the crowd—locals young and old and tourists who become regulars over the course of their vacations—arrives soon after as the songs start to sweep over the harbor.

i Turn left from the tunnel and cross the piazza; La Cantina is on the right. Wine €2.50-4.50. Mixed drinks €5-6. Sciacchetrà €5-9. ⏰ Open Jun-Aug daily 9:30am-1am; Sept-May M-Tu 9:30am-1am, Th-Su 9:30am-1am.

Riomaggiore

BAR CENTRALE
V. Colombo 144

☎0187 92 39 20

The primary gathering point for Riomaggiore's visiting international crowd isn't much to see on its own (except for caffeine junkies itching to gaze upon its high-tech espresso machine). When people start flowing in and the backpacker crowd begins to swap travel tales, however, it becomes easy to see why visitors return night after night.

i *Up V. Colombo on the left. Beer €3.50-5. Mixed drinks €6. ☼ Open daily 7am-1am.*

A PIE DE MA, BAR AND VINI
V. dell'Amore

BAR
☎0187 92 10 37

So your lover left you alone on V. dell'Amore to run off into the arms of a dashing Cinque Terrean. We've all been there. You now have two options: 1) Dramatically swan dive off the cliff into the sea, or 2) Go get a drink. Conveniently, A Pie de Ma is right at the end of the path and caters to lovers and lonely hearts alike. With a beautiful deck overlooking the water and a menu that stretches beyond just Italy, A Pie de vMa offers incredible views and seafood specialties to restore your broken spirit.

i *From the train station, take the steps up to V. dell'Amore. Turn right at the sign just before the ticket booth. Live music usually F-Sa at 9 or 9:30pm. Free Wi-Fi. Wine €2-6. Beer €3-4.50. Mixed drinks €5-6. Prix-fixe menu €46. ☼ Open W-Su 7:30am-1am.*

ESSENTIALS

Practicalities

- **TOURIST OFFICE: Cinque Terre National Park Office** provides information on trails and sells **Cinque Terre Cards**, which are necessary for hiking. (P. Garibaldi 20 ☎0187 81 70 59 www.parconazionale5terre.it *i* Also in the train station. ☼ Open daily 8am-8pm.) **Pro Loco** offers information on hiking and accommodations as well as **currency exchange.** (V. Fegina 38 ☎0187 81 75 06 www.prolocomonterosso.it *i* In front of the train station. ☼ Open daily 9am-7pm.)

- **INTERNET ACCESS:** As with most services, Monterosso is your best bet. **The Net** has computers and Wi-Fi. (V. Vittorio Emanuele 55 ☎0187 81 72 88 www.monterossonet.com €1 1st 10min., €0.10 per min. thereafter; €5 per hr.; €15 per day. ☼ Open daily 9:30am-9pm.)

- **POST OFFICE:** All five towns have their own post office, in Monterosso at V. Roma 73. (☼ Open M-F 8am-1:30pm, Sa 8am-12:30pm) and in Riomaggiore at V. Pecunia 7. (*i* Up the stairs from V. Colombo and to the left. ☼ Open M-F 8am-1pm, Sa 8am-noon.)

Emergency

- **POLICE: Carabinieri** in Monterosso (☎0187 81 75 24). There are also municipal police offices in all towns except Manarola.

- **LATE-NIGHT PHARMACIES:** The pharmacies at V. Fegina 44 in Monterosso, V. Roma 2 in Vernazza, and V. Colombo 182 in Riomaggiore post after-hours rotations outside.

- **MEDICAL SERVICES:** There is a doctor's office in the municipal building in Monterosso (P. Garibaldi). In a serious emergency, call an ambulance (☎118).

Getting There

All the town lies on the Genoa-La Spezia **train** line. A few trains arrive from Turin (€18 ☼ 4hr.; 5:20am, 1:20, 5:20pm), Milan, and Florence, but most arrivals from these cities transfer in Genoa or La Spezia. All trains from Genoa (€7. ☼ 90min.; about every hr., 5am-10:20pm) stop in Monterosso and Riomaggiore, but many skip the towns in between. Local trains run between Levanto and La Spezia, with stops at each of the five villages. (€2. ⏱ 2-19min.; every 30min. or less, 4:51am-11:39pm.) Train schedules to the towns are available at tourist offices. Note that for some of the villages (particularly Corniglia) the train station can be as much as a 15min. steep walk from the town itself.

Navigazione Golfo dei Poeti ferries connect the five towns. (☎0187 81 84 40 or 0187 73 29 87 www.navigazionegolfodeipoeti.it)

Getting Around

Walking is the best way to get around the towns of the Cinque Terre. **National Park Buses** (a.k.a. green vans) run through town regularly and connect to points in the hills (*i* €2, free with Cinque Terre Card).

florence

The Medici. Botticelli. Dante. What do these names, familiar to anyone who has studied history, art, or literature, have in common? All of them were natives of Florence, and their presence endures in the city today. As the birthplace of the Italian Renaissance and an epicenter for high culture, Florence has become one of the artistic treasure troves of the world. You can barely walk along the streets and *piazze* without running into famous works (or their replicas), and the myriad museums are rivaled in number by dozens of churches that house priceless artwork and frescoes all their own. But this city is so much more than that: you can sip regional Chianti at the many cafes and bars, enjoy traditional Tuscan cuisine in *trattorias* and *ristoranti*, and view spectacular live performances of everything from music to theater. This is a city of purely Florentine sights, tastes, and customs, and if you allow yourself to embrace that culture, you'll no doubt leave feeling like a true *fiorentino*.

ORIENTATION

The Duomo

Florence's distinctive Duomo is perhaps the most helpful feature for wandering tourists—it's easy enough to find your way back here, so learn the route from the Duomo to your hostel and you'll never be lost. If you imagine a *piazza*-compass, the **Baptistery** points west and the Duomo points east. The tall tower just south of the Duomo is the **Campanile.** While the streets south of P. del Duomo run straight, the northern ones veer eastward. This huge, bustling *piazza* is full of tourists during the day, but the incredibly diverse crowd makes it a surprisingly cool place to people watch.

Piazza della Signoria

Near the **Uffizi Gallery** and the Arno River, this *piazza* is perhaps the best part of the city to wander. Cheap food and accommodations are tucked away among the many ritzier options, but the eastern portion of this neighborhood (near the abominable **Casa di Dante**) is your best bet. Take **Via Calimari** toward the **Mercato Nuovo** to observe daily chalk art creations that are wiped clean by the noisy, street-cleaning trucks. Outside the Uffizi, you'll often find human statues and other street performers, while **Piazza della Repubblica** is the place to go for live music.

Santa Maria Novella

The Santa Maria Novella **train station** will likely be your first introduction to Florence, and the decision to venture east or south will color your earliest impressions of the city. To the east of the station, you'll find the cheap accommodations and casual

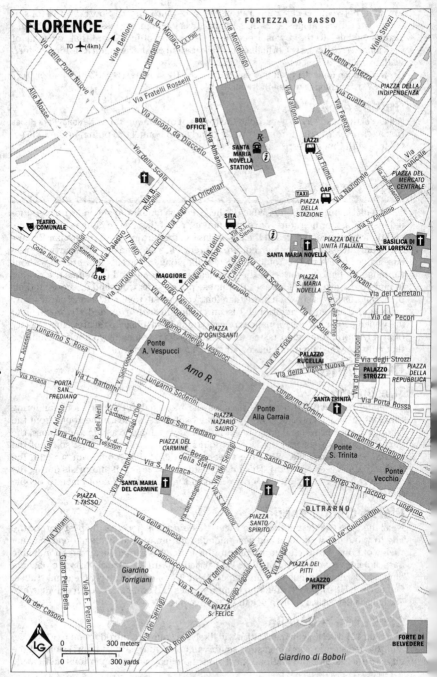

FLORENCE

TO ✈ (4km)

FORTEZZA DA BASSO

Via G. Monaco
V.I.Pari
Via Belfiore
Viale Belfiore
Via delle Porte Nuove
Via Cittadella
P. le Montelungo
P.le Montelungo
Via della Fortezza
Viale Strozzi
Alle Mosse
Via Fratelli Rosselli
PIAZZA DELLA
INDIPENDENZA
Via Valfonda
Via Guelfa
Via della Scala
Via Jacopo da Diacceto
Via Almanni
BOX OFFICE
SANTA MARIA NOVELLA STATION
R
LAZZI
Via Faenza
Via Fiume
Via Panicale
PIAZZA DEL MERCATO CENTRALE
Via degli Orti Oricellari
Via B. Rucellai
TAXI
CAP
Via Nazionale
Via S. Antonino
SITA
PIAZZA DELLA STAZIONE
Via S.C. da Siena
Via S.Antonino
TEATRO COMUNALE
Corso Italia
Via Garibaldi
Il Prato
Via Palazzo
Via S. Lucia
Via della Scala
Via dell' Albero
Via de' Canacci
SANTA MARIA NOVELLA
PIAZZA DELL' UNITÀ ITALIANA
BASILICA DI SAN LORENZO
Via de' Panzani
US
MAGGIORE
Via Curtatone
V. Finiguerra
Via de' Palazzuolo
PIAZZA S. MARIA NOVELLA
Via de' Cerretani
Via Montebello
Borgo Ognissanti
PIAZZA D'OGNISSANTI
Via del Sole
Via del Moro
Via de' Belle Donne
Via de' Pecori
Ponte A. Vespucci
Lungarno Amerigo Vespucci
Via dei Fossi
PALAZZO RUCELLAI
Via degli Strozzi
PIAZZA DELLA REPUBBLICA
Lungarno S. Rosa
Arno R.
Via della Vigna Nuova
PALAZZO STROZZI
Via d. Ancisella
Via Pisane
Via L. Bartolini
Via Sant'Onofrio
PORTA SAN FREDIANO
Lungarno Soderini
Lungarno Corsini
SANTA TRINITÀ
Via Porta Rossa
Via de' Tornabuoni
Ponte Alla Carraia
Ponte S. Trinita
Lungarno Acciaiuoli
Viale L. Ariosto
Via dell'Orto
P. dei Nerli
V. d. Cardatori
V. d. Tessitori
Borgo San Frediano
PIAZZA NAZARIO SAURO
Via di Santo Spirito
Ponte Vecchio
Borgo San Jacopo
Lungarno
P. d. Piede d'Oro
PIAZZA DEL CARMINE
Borgo della Stella
Via S. Monaca
SANTA MARIA DEL CARMINE
Via S. Agostino
OLTRARNO
Via de' Guicciardini
PIAZZA T. TASSO
Via del Leone
Via della Chiesa
PIAZZA SANTO SPIRITO
Via Mazzetta
Via Maggio
PIAZZA DEI PITTI
Via Villani
Via del Campuccio
Via delle Caldaie
Borgo Tegolaio
PALAZZO PITTI
Giano Pelta Bella
Viale F. Petrarca
Giardino Torrigiani
Via S. Maria
Via del Serragli
PIAZZA S. FELICE
Via del Casone
Via Romana
FORTE DI BELVEDERE
N
LG
0   300 meters
0   300 yards
Giardino di Boboli

italy

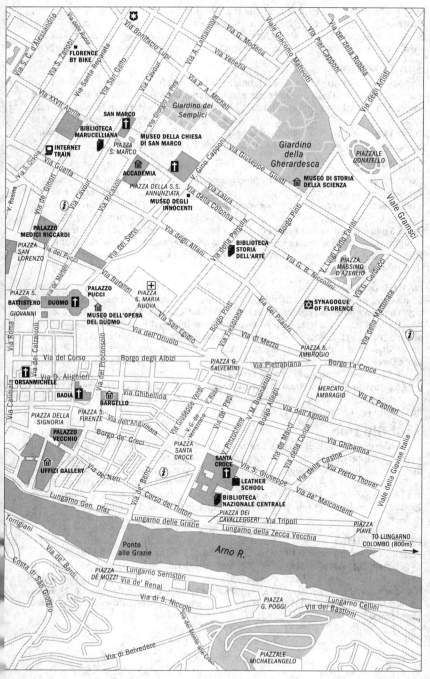

florence

food joints that you'd expect near the train station of any major city. To the south, clustered around the church that gives the station its name, you'll find art galleries, modern museums, and a calm stretch of the Arno. Don't bother venturing north or west, as you'll be leaving Florence's historic center before you've even set foot in it.

San Lorenzo

Just east of the train station lies a land of markets and 99-cent stores. Come for the cheap accommodations on **Via Faenza** and **Via Nazionale,**and stay for the food around San Lorenzo's vibrant outdoor market on **Via dell'Aviento** and the adjoining **Mercato Centrale.** If you're only here for a little while, these will be the most memorable sights in San Lorenzo, which is light on museums. Nightlife is more of the relaxed bar variety and a bit removed from the more happening Florentine clubs.

San Marco

By "San Marco," we mean pretty much everything between **Piazza San Marco** and the northern edge of the old city. The primary draw of this area is the density of museums and bus stops, not to mention the (real!) statue of David in the **Accademia** (which, unfortunately, also comes with a block-long line of tourists). To the east, **Piazza Santissima Annunziata** has its own concentration of sights worth exploring. Late at night, stick to the southern edge of the area or travel with a friend—north of P. San Marco is one of the quietest parts of the old city and can be unsafe after the buses stop running.

Santa Croce

Santa Croce is Florence's student and nightlife center and a great place to go exploring. The neighborhood spans the area east of the Duomo down to the river and is laced with cheap restaurants. As you wander, note the neighborhood's walls—though plaques marking the water line of the 1966 Arno flood can be found all over Florence, the profusion of watermarks here show that Santa Croce was hit the hardest. **Piazza Santa Croce** is concentrated with clothing and leather shops, and the antique market under **Piazza dei Ciompi's** old arches is worth checking out even if you don't plan on lugging anything home. **Piazza di Sant'Ambrogio** is the epitome of Florence's casual, *piazza*-based nightlife scene. If there were cheap accommodations in Santa Croce, this would be the best budget base in the city.

West Oltrarno

This is the cool, artsy half of the Oltrarno, the area on the south side of the Arno. With a concentration of pharmacies, supermarkets, and dogs, it feels more authentic and lived in than the other side of the river but still has a high density of hostels, museums, and study-abroad students. The main tourist draw is the **Palazzo Pitti** complex, but let the young and trendy vibe lead you a few extra steps to eat in **Piazza Santo Spirito** and explore the jewelry boutiques, art galleries, and studios nestled in the residential streets.

East Oltrarno

The most common reason to trek to East Oltrarno is for the unbeatable view from the **Piazzale Michelangelo.** This generally quiet residential area is laced with some of Florence's most active nightlife, which makes crossing the river worth your while. We've set the Oltrarnos' dividing line at **Ponte Vecchio,** but you'll find a large residential stretch between the bridge and the lively evening entertainment around **Ponte San Niccolo.**

italy

The best way to get your money's worth in Florence is to travel in a small group, so if you're still hesitant to invite that slightly annoying friend with the buckteeth on this trip, remember that he could save you a fair deal of cash. Unfortunately, solo travelers with a fear of hostel showers are out of luck—singles in otherwise affordable hostels often cost almost as much as doubles. Let's Go tracked down several reputable options; you can find more at **www.letsgo.com**.

ACADEMY HOSTEL   HOSTEL $$
V. Ricasoli 9   ☎055 23 98 665 www.academyhostel.eu

The art of hosteling here is polished to perfection. Young backpackers get a bed, free Wi-Fi at reception, privacy screens, lockers, private baths, a luxurious free breakfast, and a free snack of pasta and wine that could substitute for a light dinner. Everything is aimed to bring people together, though loud partying is not allowed.

i Less than a block north of the Duomo, on the left. Free Wi-Fi in reception. Breakfast included. Complimentary pasta and wine snack at 6:30pm. Dorm €30-38; singles €38. ☼ Reception 24hr. Lockout 11am-2pm.

FLORENCE YOUTH HOSTEL   HOSTEL $$
V. della Condotta 4   ☎055 21 44 84 www.florence-youth-hostel.com

Roll out of bed and into the Uffizi—you can't get much more central than this. You may love the location during the day, but you might be less of a fan at night when drunken student noise rises from the street. Here's what to do: down complimentary tea and coffee and take advantage of the staff's uncommon willingness to give you advice about the city.

i Coming from V. dei Calzaioli, the building is on the left. Florence Youth Hostel is on the top floor. *i* Wi-Fi, local calls and some international calls, maps, tea, and coffee included. No elevator. Breakfast M-Sa. Dorms €28; twins with bath €45; doubles €90; triples €105. Hot breakfast €2.50. ☼ Reception 24hr.

OSTELLO ARCHI ROSSI   HOSTEL $
V. Faenza 94r   ☎055 29 08 04 www.hostelarchirossi.com

Choose your room wisely—the lower the floor the better—to avoid the overcrowded bathrooms on the upper floors. Stroll through the garden or past the graffitied walls, gripping a free cappuccino and snacking on giant portions of pasta. This is definitely one of the best values in Florence, particularly for solo travelers on a budget.

i From the train station, take V. Nazionale and turn left onto V. Faenza. Free Wi-Fi available. Breakfast included. Lockers and computers available. Dorm €30; singles €45.

HOSTEL PLUS   HOSTEL $
V. Santa Caterina d'Alessandria 15   ☎055 46 28 934 www.plushostels.com

This chain hostel is better than chain smoking, chain mail, and maybe even daisy chains. TWhen the place is crowded, be sure to bring your own lock, as the constant flux of people makes it easy for non-guests to walk in. Special offers include a pasta and wine dinner and all-you-can-eat breakfast combo €10).

i Follow V. Nazionale until it changes names. Hostel Plus is the big gray thing on the left soon after P. dell'Indipendenza. Free Wi-Fi. Dorm €20-24. Doubles (can-be-made-singles) €60. Discount 10% when booked on their website. ☼ Reception 24hr. Walk-ins, come after noon to check availability.

florence

SIGHTS

This section can be summed up in a single word: Renaissance. Part of being in Florence is reaching the day when you've officially seen more of Jesus's face than your own mother's. You may be surprised by just how few Renaissance artists strayed from the biblical theme, but they'll still manage to wow you again and again. Because the art collection is so vast, attempting to see too much too quickly will leave you with nothing but a devalued mush of crucifixes and semi-attractive women. It's best to choose a few select spots and take your time. When you've had enough Medici and Michelangelo for one day, there are a handful of unusual spots that aren't rooted in the 16th century. You can also check out www.firenzeturismo.it for information regarding current exhibitions, festivals, and other events in Florence.

The Duomo

The Duomo-related sights (the church and its complex) are pretty much the main event in this neighborhood. You can enter the Duomo for free, but the rest of the complex requires a combined ticket (€10) to see the Baptistery, the Dome, the Campanile, the Museo and Santa Reparata. The ticket expires within 24hr. after 1st entrance and after 6 days if unused.

DUOMO
P. del Duomo   ☎055 23 02 885 www.operaduomo.firenze.it

CHURCH

Construction of Florence's Duomo began before anyone had come up with a solution to actually build and support the signature red dome that now pokes its head above the city. A man named **Filippo Brunelleschi** claimed he could build the largest and tallest dome ever made, and would do so without scaffolding. Though most called him a lunatic, he won the dome's commission in a contest without ever revealing how he actually planned to build it. Somehow, he came through in one of the greatest triumphs of Renaissance architecture. Unfortunately, all the Duomo's artwork has been moved to the Museo Opera complex (see below), and to get a real view of the Duomo fresco you'll need to pay for the separate climbing entrance. If the interior space and shallowness make you long for smaller spaces, you can take the stairs in the middle of the church's floor down to the low-ceiling basement and pay €3 to see the archaeological remnants of the Duomo's previous site.

i Come on, you can't miss it. Audio tour available in English. Free. Archeological site €3. Audio tour €5, students and under 18 €3.50, groups €2.50. Keep an eye open for free tours of the Duomo (inside). ☑ Open M-F 10am-4:30pm, Sa 10am-4:45pm. Holidays 1:30-4:45pm.

CAMPANILE AND DOME
P. del Duomo   ☎055 23 02 885 www.operaduomo.firenze.it

CHURCH

If slippery, narrow, and winding staircases sound romantic or you want to feel what's it's like to be a stone worm, try going up the Duomo for the sake of magnificent panoramas. The Campanile's 414 steps are steep, not too crowded, and lead to a view of the Duomo's exterior. The Duomo's 463 are more strenuous, though wider, and have a separate exit path, but their best feature is that they lead right past the bright Judgment Day fresco inside the dome. However, if a prospect of climbing nearly 1000 steps in a day sounds too harsh, *Let's Go* advises to opt for the Campanile: the climb is easier, and you can take cool pictures of the Dome (which you cannot do while being on top of it).

i Enter the dome from the north side of the round part of the Duomo. Enter the Campanile at the base of the big tower. Not for the out-of-shape. ☑ Dome open M-F 8:30am-6:20pm, Sa 8:30am-5pm. Campanile open daily 8:30am-7:30pm, last entrance 6:50pm.

Piazza della Signoria

Piazza della Signoria is one of the most beautiful parts of Florence. Home to the city's most famous museum, the **Uffizi Gallery**, the area also holds innumerable noteworthy outdoor spaces, from the **Ponte Vecchio** to the **Loggia**.

UFFIZI GALLERY
MUSEUM

Ple. degli Uffizi 6 ☎055 23 88 651 www.firenzemusei.it

Welcome to the Uffizi. The first thing you should know about this museum is that Michelangelo's David is not here—he's on the other side of town, in the **Accademia** (p. 592). Also, the Mona Lisa is in France, and de Nile ain't just a river in Egypt.

You're going to wait in line for what seems like an eternity. Consider passing the time by drawing terribly unflattering portraits of the people around you and trying to sell them for a euro. Alternatively, attempt to recreate Venus's hairstyle, guess the nationality of the others waiting in line, or convince everyone that you are the reincarnation of Botticelli and should be getting in for free.

Start the Uffizi from the top. Don't crumple up your ticket at the bottom of your bag because, after climbing two flights of the Uffizi's grand staircase, you'll be asked to flash your *biglietto* once more. At this point, you're standing in an enormous hallway lined with statues and frescoed within an inch of its life. To deal with all those numerous carved pieces of people, try finding the ones that look most like people you know (bonus points if the statue is naked).

Room 2 begins the long parade of Jesuses that you'll be visiting today. **Rooms 3-4** are particularly gilded. In Martini's Annunciation, Gabriel literally spits some Latin at Mary, who responds with the mother of all icy stares.

Room 8 is all about Fra Filippino Lippi and something that seems to be his ultimate life advice: when in doubt, pray. Greeting a baby, chatting with friends, finding love — there's no excuse why your hands shouldn't be folded.

Our second big-name artist is in **Room 9**. On your left, the seven virtues—which woman is which?—are lined up like dating show contestants, all painted by Pollaiolo. Well, all except for *Fortitude*, on the left. She is one of the earliest documented works by his student, a fellow by the name of Botticelli.

Rooms 10-14 are the main event. Where there be crowds and benches, there be the postcard works. Not that we need to tell you this, but Botticelli's **The Birth of Venus** is on the left—that's right, behind all those people. Push your way to the front to enjoy all the little details that don't come across in the coffee mug and mousepad reproductions, like the gold trim on the trees, the detail of the fabrics, the luminous, sleepy expression, and the weave Venus stole off Rapunzel.

Room 15 is another example of the student surpassing the teacher. Examine the painting by Andrea del Verrochio across the room on the right. Several of the painting's figures—it is still contested which ones specifically—were painted by his student, Leonardo da Vinci. Maybe you've heard of him? The two paintings to the left are fully Leonardo's.

Odds are, you're going to start speeding up at this point, so to keep pace, you might want to take a break at the **cafeteria**—go out into the main hallway and follow the signs. This is your typical overpriced museum cafe (coffee €1.80 without table service), give or take a balcony view of the Palazzo Vecchio. Take some snacks with you or buy an espresso at the bar (stand outside to avoid the pricey table service) and refresh your brain.

In **Room 35** is a *Massacre of the Innocents* by Daniele Ricciarelli. Despite the pile of dead babies in this painting, *Let's Go* does not condone the making of dead baby jokes. Downstairs in **Room 63**, the Hulk finally got a love story, even though a Romeo and Juliet one. **Room 64**'s gnome portrait represents Renaissance's version of 3D.

florence

If you have time and energy left at this point, the last few rooms are refreshingly different 18th-century stuff. If you don't, no one has to know. Congratulations on finishing the Uffizi; now you can go act like a Botticelli expert, even if the only thing you remember is Venus's terrible haircut.

i *It's the long narrow part of P. della Signoria. Enter (or stand in line) on the left; reserve tickets on the right. To avoid the lines without paying for a reservation, arrive late in the day, when your time in the museum will be limited by closing (but chances are, you won't have energy for all the rooms anyway). Expect to wait 2-3hr. to enter. €11, EU citizens 18-25 €5.50, EU citizens under 18 and over 65 and the disabled free. €4 reservation fee. Audio tour €5.50. ☒ Open Tu-Su 8:15am-6:35pm.*

THE BARGELLO   MUSEUM
V. del Proconsolo 4   ☎055 23 88 606 www.firenzemusei.it

Though you'd never know it from the inside, the Bargello was once the first public building in Florence: a brutal prison. The statues here seem to know this—most are mid-kill, mid-struggle, or mid-sprint. Bas-reliefs on the walls of the now-peaceful courtyard (where the executions took place) must be covering something—they are placed like the pictures that cover chipped paint in your dorm room. The mysterious halls have more than just dark history; there is now a rich collection of sculptures by some famous names, more baby Jesuses, and other curious little things exhibited that get weird once you take a closer look. Wait, what are you talking about—the monk statue standing on babies' heads is completely normal.

i *Behind the Palazzo Vecchio €7, EU citizens ages 18-25 €3.50, EU citizens under 18 and over 65 free. Cash only. ☒ Open daily 8:15am-4:50pm. Last entry 4:20pm. Closed 2nd and 4th M and 1st, 3rd, and 5th Su each month.*

PIAZZA DELLA SIGNORIA   PIAZZA

P. della Signoria is the place to go if you want to see sculptures without the museum prices. The **Loggia**, a portico full of statues that's as legit as any room in the Uffizi, is free. It features Cellini's **Perseus with the Head of Medusa**, Giambologna's **The Rape of the Sabine Women,** and other sculptures on exciting topics. Spoiler alert: the *David* in front of the **Palazzo Vecchio** is fake—the real deal is in the **Accademia.** The reproduction here stands just as proud as the original did when he was installed in this exact location to celebrate Florence's dominance over Tuscany. To the left of fake *David* is a giant fountain that Michelangelo despised so much he called it a waste of perfectly good marble. This bustling daytime *piazza* swirls with tour groups, art students sketching, and street musicians but gets calmer and more empty in the evenings, as you can't walk through it and stand in line for the Uffizi anymore.

i *This is the main piazza north of the Uffizi.*

PONTE VECCHIO   BRIDGE

This bridge has been called the "old" bridge for, oh, 400 years or so, ever since the Florentines built a second bridge over the Arno and had to find a way to distinguish this one from their new *ponte.* But its way to cope with aging is to revel in romance and gold. Gold shops line up on its curvy backside, providing couples on the promenade something to talk about. And if they happen to forget about their surroundings, oh well—the bridge is prettier from afar anyway.

i *From the Uffizi, walk to the river. It's the one with the shops on it.*

PIAZZA DELLA REPUBBLICA   PIAZZA

If bunk beds and complementary bed bugs (not that *Let's Go* would recommend such a place), long lines, and endless trains have killed your romantic mood, head straight over to this place to make your epic European adventure seem just like a movie again. Street musicians will provide a nice musical background. A carousel (with frescoes, just like anywhere else in Italy) is ready to sweep your date—or you—off your feet for just €1.50. The trick is to get a gelato somewhere else before walking over to this place, so you won't have to treat your date to a dinner in a pricey garden cafe.

i From P. della Signoria, walk north up V. del Calzaioli, and turn left onto V. Speziali.

PALAZZO VECCHIO

MUSEUM

P. della Signoria   ☎055 27 68 465 www.palazzovecchio-museoragazzi.it

So when was the last time you exercised? Remember those beautiful panoramas of Florence with the **Duomo** rising above all else? If you crawl two staircases and 233 steps to the very top of the tower, you can also make some pictures of your own. But if a pretty view from a high place is just too mainstream, there's a still a museum below—a potluck dinner of ceiling paintings, a fleur-de-lis room that might as well have belonged to Louis XIV, and a room walled with yellowing maps of the world. One of the highlights is the Room of the 500s, which features worryingly aggressive/erotic statues for a room that used to hold a political council. Finally, castle mystery lovers can call ahead and book a Secret Passages tour.

i The huge building in P. della Signoria. Activities and tours with costumed actors available; call for times. Museum €6.50, ages 18-25 and over 65 €4.50. Tower €6.50. Museum and tower €10. Tours €2. ☼ Museum open Oct-Mar M-W 9am-7pm, Th 9am-2pm, F-Su 9am-7pm; Apr-Sept M-W 9am-midnight, Th 9am-2pm, F-Su 9am-midnight. Tower open Oct-Mar M-W 10am-5pm, Th 10am-5pm, F-Su 10am-5pm; Apr-Sept M-W 9am-9pm, Th 9am-2pm, F-Su 9am-9pm.

Santa Maria Novella

▨ MUSEO DI FERRAGAMO

MUSEUM

P. Santa Trinita 5r   ☎055 33 60 456 www.museoferragamo.it

The shoes that you can see here (and in theory buy, if you can possibly afford them) are right at the entrance. For a more worthwhile experience, head deeper into the basement to the actual museum. Ferragamo was like the Leonardo da Vinci of shoes: he brought anatomy, chemistry, and engineering into the creation of footwear. The shoe molds of famous people might make you feel like Bigfoot, and Ferragamo's elegant designs may make your own shoes feel clunky and out of place. It's okay if it's a little over your head—you're on vacation now, so just enjoy the fact that you're in a museum about footwear.

i Enter at P. Santa Trinita on the side of the building that faces away from the river €6, under 10 and over 65 free. Ticket proceeds fund scholarships for young shoe designers. 1st and 2nd rooms are permanent; the rest of the exhibits change annually. ☼ Open daily 10am-7:30pm.

PALAZZO STROZZI

MUSEUM, PALAZZO

P. degli Strozzi   ☎055 27 76 461 www.palazzostrozzi.org

While this may seem like yet another old palace, no more impressive than any of the others, it isn't the seen-one-seen-'em-all Renaissance decor that makes Palazzo Strozzi worth visiting. The **Center for Contemporary Culture Strozzina,** which produces recent and contemporary art exhibits in the palace's halls, is the main draw here.Exhibitions on different themes come regularly and often with a sweet interactive bonus: touch everything you've longed to touch on small replicas of famous statues. The programming changes regularly, so check the website or stop by if you want to shake a little 21st-century dust into Florence's 15th-century aesthetic.

i West of P. della Repubblica. ☼ Prices and hours vary; check website for details.

BASILICA DI SANTA MARIA NOVELLA

CHURCH

P. Santa Maria Novella   ☎055 21 59 18 www.chiesasantamarianovella.it

If you're only going to bother with one of the non-Duomo churches, consider making it this one. Between the checkered floor and plethora of 3D figures, this church could be a giant's chessboard, and in the morning or early evening, sunlight streaming through the stained glass may remind you of last night's disco.

florence

Upon entering the church, you'll see a fresco of God doing the *Titanic* pose with Jesus on the cross. Do you notice anything strange about this picture? If God is standing on that back platform, how could he be leaning far enough forward to be touching Jesus in the front? Rather than believe that Masaccio could have made such a salient perspective error, some art historians argue that this is symbolic of God's capacity to be everywhere at once. Venture farther to walk in the courtyard and an additional museum, but mind your dress and manner—it's a working church.

i Just south of the train station; you can't miss it. Enter through the P. Santa Maria Novella entrance. €5; over 65 €3.50; visitors with disabilities, children under 5, and priests free. ✪ Open M-Th 9am-5:30pm, F 11am-5:30pm, Sa 9am-5pm, Su and religious holidays 1-5pm.

San Lorenzo

MEDICI CHAPELS
MUSEUM

P. Madonna degli Aldobrandini 6   ☎055 23 88 602   www.firenzemusei.it

The Medici Chapels would be the perfect setting for a Christopher Nolan movie. The dark **Cappella Principe** hovers over the sky and guards six mighty-looking tombs of Medici rulers. The **New Sacristy** is smaller and generally white, with an unfinished tomb (we'll forgive its designer, a fellow named Michelangelo, who left for the excitement of Rome). Curious visitors should peek behind the altar to find his pencil sketches on the walls, left over from the unfinished frescoes.

i It's the roundish building to the right of Basilica di San Lorenzo. Likely visit length 30min. tops €9, EU citizens ages 18-25 €4.50, EU citizens under 18 and over 65 free. ✪ Open daily 8:15am-4:50pm. Last entry 4:20pm. Closed 1st, 3rd, and 5th M and 2nd and 4th Su each month.

BASILICA DI SAN LORENZO
CHURCH

P. San Lorenzo   ☎055 26 45 184   www.sanlorenzo.firenze.it

The oldest church in Florence was born in 393 and became a grown-up in 1461. Now, it seems, it's ready to retire. Still, it's hard to have too much holiness, even when people come to have lunch on the stairs and bargain over leather items under the walls. Inside, the church emits an almost homey and welcoming vibe and features dramatic paintings (never has the Crucifixion looked so epic). The adjusted **Biblioteca Medicea Laurenziana** has a wide collection of manuscripts for additional €3.

i In P. San Lorenzo, just a little north of the Duomo €5, under 11 free. ✪ Open M-Sa 10am-5pm, Su 1:30-5pm.

PALAZZO MEDICI RICCARDI
MUSEUM

V. Cavour 1   ☎055 27 60 340   www.palazzo-medici.it

This *palazzo* argues once again that there was and is nothing more important for Italian rulers than art. Rooms and courtyards on the ground floor host modern sculpture installations, while the halls upstairs exhibit their own walls and ceilings, all splattered with some pretty cool pictures here and there.

i From San Lorenzo you can see the back of the huge brown palace. Enter from the reverse side on V. Cavour €7, ages 6-12 €4, people with disabilities and their assistants free. ✪ Open daily 9am-6pm. Ticket office closes at 5:30pm.

San Marco

▨ GALLERIA DELL'ACCADEMIA
MUSEUM

V. Ricasoli 60   ☎055 23 88 612   www.uffizi.com/accademia-gallery-florence.asp

Leonardo da Vinci once said that Michelangelo's figures resemble "a sack full of walnuts," but in a classic size comparison, whose masterpiece comes up a tad short? At an easy 17ft., it's no wonder the *David* can't find any robes in his size. Do you see those veins on his hand? The guy's a beast. Four unfinished statues by Michelangelo share *David*'s hall, trapped in the remaining block of marble like

Han Solo encased in carbonite. You may understand on an intellectual level that the master's statues are carved from a single piece of marble, but seeing these unfinished works (which go by The Slaves) drives it home. One man. A bunch of chisels. One big rock. If you've saved room for dessert after staring amorously at the *David*, head to the right of the entrance for a musical instrument gallery. In the next room on the left, you may notice the adored gnomish son about to pick his nose, or, we don't know, the enormous model of *The Rape of the Sabine Women*. Past the *David* gallery, on the left, is a 19th-century workshop overflowing with sculpted heads and busts. Upstairs, you'll see Jesus's face more times than you've seen your own mother's. But, at the very least, you will be one of a few who make it there. Right before the exit to the street, glance to the right to see the large photo of people frozen and staring at David.

It's worth noting that visiting the Accademia generally won't take more than an hour. Bear that in mind when weighing the choice between paying extra for a reservation or waiting in a line that lasts far longer than the time you'll spend in the actual museum.

i *Line for entrance on V. Ricasoli, off of P. San Marco. Make reservations at the Museo Archeologico, the Museo di San Marco, or the Museo del'Oficio. The non-reservation line is shortest at the beginning of the day. Try to avoid the midday cruise ship excursion groups. €11, EU citizens ages 18-25 €5.50, art students and EU citizens under 18 or over 65 free. Reservations €4 extra.* ⏰ *Open Tu-Su 8:15am-6:50pm. Last entry 6:20pm.*

MUSEO DI SAN MARCO
P. San Marco 3

MUSEUM

☎055 23 88 608 www.firenzemusei.it

Florence is hardly lacking in religious artwork, but Museo di San Marco packs in more than most. The themes may become repetitive, but the artistic importance of the works is impressive. The entrance courtyard features barely-there frescoes and some portraits that prove people had bad picture days before Facebook, too.

Upstairs you'll find monk cells, each with a personal fresco—from a Jesus that never minds bleeding to tranquil saints. Imagine living here for 40 years, copying manuscripts. Now compare the size of these rooms to your dorm room and be grateful that you only have to live in a closet for four years. Then look at Fra Angelico's famous fresco, **The Annunciation**, and imagine what it would be like if an angel arrived to announce that you were about to experience an unplanned pregnancy. The gallery on the right goes into the grinding details of copying manuscripts and has books on display, in case you wanted an even more in-depth lesson on how much it would stink to be a monk back then.

i *Located on the north side of the piazza. Approximate visit time: 30min. €4, EU citizens ages 16-25 €2. Closed 2nd and 4th M and 1st, 3rd, and 5th Su of each month. Last entry 30min. before close.* ⏰ *Open M-F 8:15am-1:50pm, Sa 8:15am-4:50pm, Su 8:15am-7pm.*

Santa Croce
Santa Croce is a little out of the way of the main attractions, but its scattered sights are some of Florence's most memorable.

SYNAGOGUE OF FLORENCE
V. Luigi Carlo Farini 4

SYNAGOGUE, MUSEUM

☎055 24 52 52

This beautiful building definitely doesn't fade into the surrounding Florentine architecture. Its conspicuousness was a bold choice: when it was built, the Jewish population still lived in a walled ghetto in the city center, and most synagogues were designed to blend in to avoid drawing attention to the community. Constructed in 1868, it's young by Florentine standards but has still managed to have quite a life. The Nazis used it as their headquarters during the occupation of the city, and when they evacuated, they rigged the temple to explode. Somehow, all but one of the bombs failed to detonate, which is why the building is still standing today. The beauty of its exterior is matched by the abstract and colorful geometric patterns of the interior, making it so different from other places of worship in the city that you'll wish you didn't have to leave your camera behind the metal detector at the entrance.

i From the Basilica di Santa Croce, walk 7 blocks north on V. dei Pepi. Turn right onto V. dei Pilastri and left onto V. Luigi Carlo Farini. Yarmulkes required and provided. Check bags and cameras at lockers before entering €6.50, ages 6-14 and students 15-24 €5, under 6 and disabled free. Cash only. ☼ Open M-F 10:30am-3pm, Su 10:30am-5:30pm.

BASILICA DI SANTA CROCE
CHURCH

P. Santa Croce 16   ☎055 24 66 105   www.santacroce.firenze.it

This enormous basilica has more celebrities than the Academy Awards. They happen to have been dead for hundreds of years, but no matter. Machiavelli lies in a chilling and understated tomb, Rossini under a subtle decoration of treble clefs and violin bridges, and Galileo with a globe and etching of the solar system. Michelangelo's tomb explodes with color and features a painting of the statue he'd intended for his final resting place. Dante's tomb is just gray, but it holds some inordinately large statues. You'll even find Marconi, inventor of the radio, here. The complex also includes exhibits, cloisters, and gardens, which are full of dead people of the less famous variety.

i Take Borgo dei Greci east from P. della Signoria €5, ages 11-17 €3, under 11 and disabled free. Combined ticket with Casa Michelangelo €8. Audio tour €5. ☼ Open M-F 9:30am-3:30pm, Sa-Su 1-5:30pm.

West Oltrarno

The major sights of West Oltrarno are all condensed into the enormous Palazzo Pitti. It's not hard to find the complex: just cross Ponte Vecchio and walk until you reach the very obvious *palazzo*. The Palazzo Pitti museums are grouped into two ticket combos. **Ticket One** gets you into Galleria Palatina, Galleria d'Arte Moderna, and Apartamenti Reali. **TicketTwo** is for the Boboli Gardens, Bardini Gardens, Museo degli Argenti, Galleria del Costume, and Museo della Porcellana. Overall, if you're choosing one ticket combo over the other, we recommend **Ticket Two.**

▨ BOBOLI GARDENS
GARDENS

www.uffizi.firenze.it/boboli

The Boboli Gardens feel like a cross between Central Park and Versailles. Imagine you're a 17th-century Medici strolling through your gardens—but don't imagine your way into a corset, ladies, because the gardens are raked at a surprising incline. They're easily large enough for you to hide from the inundating heat or finally get a tan while enjoying the green, green grass. Head uphill from the palace for the porcelain museum and a stunning view of the valley, where the city's packed red buildings give way to sprawling monasteries and trees. Farther from the main routes, statues stand mossy and cracked, but it's more fun to explore a place that seems slightly forgotten. As with any gardens, this one is most fragrant and lovely right after the rain.

i Ticket 2.

GALLERIA PALATINA
MUSEUM

www.uffizi.florence.it/palatina

Gold and statues and paintings of gold and statues cover every possible inch of this ridiculously ornate gallery. The permanent collection is housed in rooms named not for displays but for the ceiling art of figures like Saturn and Apollo. The quirkiest object in the collection sits alone in a small chamber between the Education of Jupiter and Ulysses rooms—it belonged to Napoleon and proves that great conquerors come in small bathtubs.

i Ticket 1.

GALLERIA DEL COSTUME

MUSEUM
www.uffizi.firenze.it/musei/costume

We assure you: this isn't just more Medici clutter. You can relax now. Instead, the fashions displayed here stretch all the way into the modern day. Try guessing which dress belongs to which time period, and you might be surprised at how difficult it is to guess correctly. If you do happen to be hankering for some an overly indulgent dose of the Medici, the one permanent display features the actual burial clothes of several dead Medici—these pieces were torn from their rotting corpses and preserved for your viewing pleasure. You're welcome.

i Ticket 2.

MUSEO DEGLI ARGENTI

MUSEUM
www.uffizi.firenze.it/argenti

This museum is a pirate's dream. The treasure map is simply a sign that says, "To the Treasure." Visiting Museo degli Argenti is like wandering through a painted jewelry box. There are no pure chunks of gold here, but lavish rings, minute ivories, precious jewels, dazzling crowns, and Chinese porcelain are booty enough.

i Ticket 2.

APARTAMENTI REALI

MUSEUM

The back end of the Galleria Palatina features a few preserved rooms of the palace that managed to evade the museum invasion of sculptures, china stalls, and extra paintings. You can practically see lords nonchalantly strolling ahead of you through the marble columns and chandeliers as they chatter about some fresco or another. By the end, you'll definitely wish these apartments were listed in the Accommodations section of this book.

i Ticket 1.

GALLERIA D'ARTE MODERNA

MUSEUM

☎055 23 88 616 www.uffizi.firenze.it/musei/artemoderna

Only in Florence could people define "modern art" as stuff that predates the French Revolution. This gallery begins in the 1780s, when art was no longer just for dukes, but for nobles, too. Talk about progress! The focus then moves toward 19th-century Naturalism as the motifs shift to motion, countrysides, and social scenes. It's a good palate cleanser to keep you alert as you make your way through these gilded rooms full of gods and angels—we promise you won't see any Madonna and Child renditions here.

i Ticket 1.

MUSEO DELLE PORCELLANA

MUSEUM
www.uffizi.firenze.it/musei/porcellane

It would seem weird to climb to the very top of the Boboli Gardens to check out a china exhibition, but you'll do it anyway for the sake of cool alleys and panoramic views. Plus, it turns out that whoever spent centuries amassing this collection of dishware really knew what he or she was doing. Even if you tune out all the floral plate motifs, there are some amazingly intricate painted scenes, including one that depicts lords and ladies milling in the garden in outlandishly fancy getups.

i At the highest point of the Boboli Gardens. Just keep walking up. Ticket 2.

East Oltrarno

You haven't seen Florence until you've seen it from the **Piazzale Michelangelo.** You'll find an extensive network of designated jogging routes and a number of small, lesser-known churches and sights amid the area's greenery. Some less typical gems, like the Bardini museum, await the determined explorer in East Oltrarno's residential area.

florence

"I climbed all the way to the top of the Ple. Michelangelo, and all I see is a parking lot, some tourist stalls, and an oxidized *David* reproduction," you may say in lament. But then you'll turn around. Suddenly, as Florence unfold all around you in stunning clarity, you won't care how many cars are behind you sharing the same view. If you stick around for the nighttime city lights, you may even begin to understand why the alien-colored *David* likes hanging out here so much.

i *From pretty much any bridge, bear east along the river until you reach P. Guiseppe Poggi, where the base of the steps is located. If you're not wearing walking shoes, take bus #12 or 13. Free.*

FOOD

Florence's cuisine is typical Tuscan fare: endless combinations of meat, olive oil, truffles, and (of course) pasta. Rustic *trattorias* are ubiquitous, and the good news is that you can't really go wrong with any of them. The only thing to note is the sneaky cover charge for table service, often tucked under a pushpin or typed in tiny font at the bottom of the menu. Get your cappuccino or latte macchiato fix before noon—coffee after noon in Italy is such a faux pas that some waiters may even refuse to serve it. Finally, as Florence claims to be the birthplace of gelato, it's totally acceptable to eat some every day that you're here, even if you're staying for the next five years.

The Duomo

The places in **Piazza del Duomo** offer some great deals, making it a good spot for a bigger meal. If you want quick food, though, skip the square's overpriced snack bars and venture a few blocks farther.

■ **VESTRI CIOCCOLATO D'AUTORE**   GELATERIA $
Borgo degli Albizi 11r   ☎055 23 40 374 www.vestri.it

If there was a contest of collecting adjectives, this place would hoard all the sweetest, nicest, and cutest words available. Guys, bring your dates here. Girls and gelato connoisseurs, simply come. Nowhere else in Florence can you get artisanal gelato in flavors such asdark chocolate and Earl Grey or white chocolate with wild strawberries. It's luxury for dirt cheap, pals.

i *From the Duomo, take V. Proconsolo south from the Duomo and turn left onto Borgo degli Albizi. Gelato from €1.80. Cash only.* ☼ *Open daily 10:30am-8pm.*

CAFFÈ DUOMO   RISTORANTE $$
P. del Duomo 29/30r   ☎055 21 13 48

This is a *trattoria* that finally interpreted international cuisine the right way! That is to say that they'll put chicken on your salad and turkey in any panini option if you're longing for dishes that will remind you of American fast-ish food. For the most homesick, there's even a sandwich box option with French fries and a salad (€5). All of the above does not cancel the fact that it's located right by the Duomo and serves nice Italian food, too.

i *On the north side of P. del Duomo. Bruschetta, salad, spaghetti/lasagna, and wine €10. Takeout panini €3.* ☼ *Open daily noon-11pm.*

LITTLE DAVID   RISTORANTE $
V. dei Martelli 14r   ☎055 23 02 695

Little David's crowds are smaller than the big *David*'s, making it a great spot to drop by to refuel and connect to the free Wi-Fi. Be sure to ask about the student special (pizza or pasta and a soft drinks (€7), as it's listed separately from the main menu.

i *Just north of the Duomo, on the right. Pizza €5.50-12. 0.5L wine €4.90.* ☼ *Open daily noon-1am.*

Piazza Della Signoria

Considering that this area teems with tourists of the well-heeled variety, there is still a surprising number of diverse, budget-friendly eateries. Good rule of thumb: the farther north or east of the Uffizi you go, the better off you are. This is also the place to find the city's best panini.

▧ I DUE FRATELLINI
V. dei Cimatori 38r

SANDWICHES $
☎055 239 60 96 www.iduefratellini.com

This open stall with an overhang and no seating dates to 1875, yet it still manages to draw crowds thanks to local wines, the tantalizing smell of panini, and the crowd psychology of seeing everyone else outside. We recommend panini #1 or #15 if the sight of endless cheap wine (from €1) still leaves you hungry.

i Come to the junction of V. dei Cimatoriand and V. dei Calzauoli; the stall is on the left. Sandwiches €2.50. ☒ Open daily 9am-7pm.

▧ DA VINATTIERI
V. Santa Margherita 4r

SANDWICHES $
☎055 29 47 03

With piles of bacon and salami in front of you at the stall or hanging from the ceiling and with lumps of fresh goat cheese laid out before you, the sandwich possibilities here seem endless. Indeed, they are. Add nutella in your panini? Why not! There is a huge jar at the counter for those who love food experiments. Otherwise, it's cheap, tasty, varied, and custom made on request.

i Across the alley from Casa di Dante, so just follow the signs for that attraction. Follow V. del Corso and take a right just before Lush. Panini €3.50. Tripe €5. ☒ Open daily 10am-8pm.

▧ FESTIVAL DEL GELATO
V. del Corso 75r

GELATERIA $
☎055 29 43 86

Whether the owners expect customers to dance with happiness as soon as they try this gelato remains a mystery. But in case you want to, the place comes prepared with glowing neon lights and thrusting party music. As if that's not enough, there's even a multi-colored dance floor on the ceiling—although the gelato here will have you jumping for joy even without the help of the decor.

i V. del Corso is east, off of P. della Repubblica. Look for the neon—you can't miss it. Gelato from €1.80. ☒ Open Tu-Su 10am-12:30pm.

O'VESUVIO
V. dei Cimatori 21r

PIZZERIA $
☎055 28 54 87 www.ovezuviofirenze.com

If you go to the gym, tan, do laundry daily, have an "I heart Vinnie" tattoo on your neck, and are still living in 2010, you might need a therapist. But you also won't want to miss the *pizzeria* where your favorite fist bumpers worked during the Florence season. For those who couldn't care less about *Jersey Shore*, it's actually really great pizza.

i 1 block west of the Baia on V. dei Cimatori; the restaurant is on the left. Pizza €5. T-shirt €10. ☒ Open daily 11am-10:30pm.

Santa Maria Novella

*Pizzeria*s, cafes, and kebab shops abound near the train station and church. This is a good neighborhood to find a cheap bite to eat, but look elsewhere for a sit-down meal.

BISTROT PANGIE'S
V. del Parione 43/45R

CAFE $
☎055 29 54 39

With so many curious things filling its interior, Bistrot Pangie's makes you feel as if you're eating in a gift shop. But looking at all the clutter might as well occupy your mind, since you won't have to worry about the budget when you get your panini and a glass of wine for €3 during happy hour. The staff remains carefree by serving food on paper plates and never getting stuck with the dishes.

i Right off P. Goldoni. Free Wi-Fi. Spaghetti alla carbonar €6.50. ☒ Open daily 11am-10pm. Happy hour daily 4-7:30pm.

RISTORANTE LA SPADA
V. della Spada 62r

TRADITIONAL $$

☎055 21 87 57 www.laspadaitalia.com

Roasting spits ooze an enticing scent at this to-go or sit-down locale for those who have worked hard and need some refueling. Meanwhile, slabs of meat and heaps of asparagus call your name from under a glass case. And there's always free taxi service for those who find that they can't walk after attacking the *Bistecca alla Florentina* (€30 per kg).

i *Near the corner of V. della Spada and V. del Moro. Mention the "free website after-dinner treat." Primi €7.50-11. Roast meat from the spit €8.50-13.50. Grill menu €8.50-43. ☒ Open daily noon-3pm and 6-11pm.*

50 ROSSO
V. Panzani 50r

CAFE $

☎055 28 35 85

It's on that main street near the train station, and you know that those areas are always filled with overpriced, low-quality places ready to catch the hungry traveler at his most vulnerable. But any poor kitties dying from hunger are lucky fishes if they duck in here for a quick bite. This tiny cafe's eclectic fare includes panini (€3), pizza (€3), and €1 espresso.

i *V. Panzani starts in the northeast corner of P. Santa Maria Novella, near the train station. Cappuccino €1.20. Cash only. ☒ Open daily 6:30am-midnight.*

San Lorenzo

The **Mercato Centrale** contains a feast of lunch options, but venturing outside to nearby restaurants is no step down. For dinner, **Via Nazionale** is lined with standard-fare pasta and pizza that isn't the cheapest in the area, but it gets the job done.

▧ NERBONE
P. del Mercato Centrale

RISTORANTE $

☎055 21 99 49

Nerbone is the love child of a garage and a picnic. It has stood in a corner of the Mercato Centrale for over 100 years. Crowd around the counter to order whatever happens to be on offer, take your tray, and squeeze in with some locals to remind yourself how fantastic your Italian isn't. A sign warns that tables are only for eating, so forget those autopsies you were planning on doing over lunch.

i *Enter Mercato Centrale from V. dell'Arte and go all the way to the right. Primi and secondi €4-9. House wine €3.50. Cash only. ☒ Open M-Sa 7am-2pm.*

▧ IL PIRATA
V. de' Ginori 56r

RISTORANTE $

☎055 21 86 25

Buy homemade food (pasta, meats, or vegetables) priced by the kilogram from a glass case opposite a line of stools and a counter. Refuel your immune system with a plate of vegetables (€5.50) or fill up with a big plate of pasta and side of vegetables (€6.50), but be careful when attempting to pour the self-serve olive oil. If business is slow, the owner may try to guess your nationality.

i *From P. San Lorenzo, walk north up V. de' Ginori for a few min. Takeout available. Primi €4-4.50. Meal combos €5.50-7.50. ☒ Open M-Sa 11am-9pm.*

▧ GELATERIA ALPINA
V. Filippo Strozzi 12r

GELATERIA $

☎055 49 66 77

No, you don't have to walk all the way to Alps to get gelato here, even though that's what Romans had to do when they wanted this treat. Still, those who want to try this award-winning ice cream will have to turn off the beaten and exhausted tourist path. While people behind the counter try to guess what is it that you want here, remember to check out the cakes and pastry. There are many delicious gelato places around Firenze, but only few, if any, offer the same selection of very cheap, savory, and fancy varieties.

i *One block north from P. Indipidienza. Gelato from €1.80. Pastries from €0.80. ☒ Open M-F6:45am-10pm, Su 8:13am-10pm.*

I'BRINCELLO   TUSCAN $
V. Nazionale 110r   ☎055 28 26 45
The battle between convenience and quality is over at last. May we present:
takeaway homemade pasta! And for a reasonable price! The sit-down option is less
exciting and more orange.
i *Just down V. Nazionale from the train station on the right. Primi €8-18. Secondi €9-20. Chianti
from €4. Cover €1.50.* ⏰ *Open daily noon-3pm and 7-11pm.*

San Marco

There are lots of self-evidently cheap places near the Accademia if you want to grab
something to snack on in the Botanic Gardens. Venture a few blocks farther for more
pleasant sit-down options.

▨ IL VEGETARIANO   VEGETARIAN $$
V. delle Ruote 30   ☎055 47 50 30
The farther you step through the door and into this rabbit hole, the curiouser
and curiouser this place gets. The calm and proper front room transforms into a
bustling wonderland, and you'll feel like Alice upon discovering the mad variety
of vegetables available for custom salads (cakes are also available for your tea
party). Once you go through the maze of placing an order, you can keep up with
the uncommon nonsense and sit yourself in the peaceful bamboo courtyard. Or
not so peaceful, if the neighboring yards happen to be kicking up a racket that
day. At the very least, the food is too good to shelve this gem.
i *From V. Nazionale, look for a subtle wooden sign on the left. Gluten-free and vegan options. Primi
€6-7. Secondi €8. Desserts €4.* ⏰ *Open Tu-Su 12:30-3pm and 7:30pm-midnight.*

GRAN CAFFÈ SAN MARCO   CAFE $
P. San Marco 11r   ☎055 21 58 33 www.grancaffesanmarco.it
Don't mind the rest of the world. Florence stands on three whales: pizza, gelato,
and pastries. This place is an aggregator that combines them all for hungry tour-
ists who can't decide what to eat first. Enter from the side street, and it's a cafe-
teria. Walk farther down to another side street entrance, and it's cafeteria meets
pastry place meets garden cafe. Avoid the table service and get self-service food
cheap on the cheap. Pizza toppings range from French fries to a classic tomatoes
and basil. For an endless selection of gelato flavors (from €2), peek to the left of
the *piazza* entrance and make your own transformation into a whale complete.
i *Located at the south end of the piazza. Primi €4-4.80. Secondi €4.50-6.50.* ⏰ *Open daily
8am-10pm.*

RISTORANTE TRATTORIA ZÀZÀ   RISTORANTE $$
P. del Mercato Centrale, 26/r   ☎055 21 54 11 www.trattoriazaza.it
If you have just scored the deal of the century by getting your hands on those
leather-whatevers (or even if you didn't but are still around Mercado Centrale),
you can visit Zàzà for a meal. This place is slightly classier than other eateries in
the area, but the quality makes up for the euro spent, especially if you are still in
that shopaholic mood. While waiting for your special dish and house wine, you
might marvel at the painted walls that parody Renaissance frescoes.
i *Northeastern corner of P. del Mercado Centrale. Primi from €7. House wine from €5. Table service €2.50.* ⏰ *Open daily 11am-11pm.*

Santa Croce

If you're craving something a little different, look no further than Santa Croce, where
cheap and late-night food options abound. There are even a few upscale establishments huddled around the Basilica di Santa Croce. We almost don't want to spoil the
fun you'll have discovering this quirky and diverse area on your own—in fact, we're
tempted to just give you a world map and send you on a scavenger hunt to check off

florence

each country's cuisine. Then again, it never hurts to have some options handy; here are a few spots to get you started.

🏵 THE OIL SHOPPE
SANDWICHES $

V. Sant'Egidio 22r   ☎055 20 01 092 www.oilshoppe.blogspot.com

The Oil Snoppe has a minor issue of consistency. Signs and chalkboard keep slipping from "panini" to "sub" and vice versa. But while this place makes up its mind, nothing can stop customers from munching on...whatever you call it. There is self-service, so please return the basket after having a delicious #24.

i From P. del Duomo, take V. dell'Oriuolo, turn right onto V. Folco Portiani then right onto V. Sant'Edigio. Sandwiches €3-4. Fries and drinks €2. Cash only. ☑ Open M-F 10am-7pm.

🏵 GELATERIA DEI NERI
GELATERIA $

V. dei Neri 20/22r   ☎055 21 00 34

Being a *Let's Go* researcher requires seating at a different *gelateria* each time in the quest of Florence's very best. So why can't we stop eating at this one? It might have something to do with the mousse-like *semifreddo*—try the tiramisu—or the insanely spicy Mexican chocolate, which we found too intense to finish.

i From Ponte Grazie, head north on V. dei Benci and turn left onto V. dei Neri. Gelato from €1.50. Cash only. ☑ Open daily 9am-midnight.

🏵 BRAC
SANTA CROCE

V. dei Vagellai 18r   ☎055 09 44 877 www.libreriabrac.net/brac

This chameleon of a place is the perfect daytime escape. You can spend a whole afternoon with a book or laptop while sampling delicious pie in the glass-walled courtyard. In the evening, the back room full of books, glass tables, and artsy placemats becomes one of the few quality vegetarian dinner spots in Florence. The front room is also a fully operational bar.

i From Ponte alle Grazie, walk 2 blocks down V. dei Berci and turn left onto V. dei Vagellai. It's a small, discreet door on the right just before the piazza. Free Wi-Fi; ask at bar for the code. Past €6-8. Dinner combo €12. Desserts €6. Beer from €3.50. Cover €1.50. ☑ Open M-Sa noon-midnight, Su 6pm-midnight.

🏵 LA GHIOTTA
CAFE $

V. Pietrapiana 7r   ☎055 24 12 37

Take a number at this student-friendly rotisserie—the line is out the door during lunchtime. Patrons don't seem to mind waiting to pick their meals from platters behind the counter. Order one of the 20 varieties of pizza and cram into the seats in the back. It's even cheaper if you take it to go: you can get half a rotisserie chicken or a giant slab of eggplant *parmigiana* for just a few euro.

i From Borgo Allegri, take a right onto V. Pietrapiana. Primi €5-9. Secondi €5-35. Pizza €5-7. Wine from €3.50 ☑ Open Tu-Su noon-2:30pm and 7-10pm.

RUTH'S
KOSHER, VEGETARIAN $$

V. Luigi Carlo Farini 2A   ☎055 24 80 888 www.kosheruth.com

This welcoming restaurant by the synagogue caters to Florence's Jewish community as well as local students. From the visitor drawings in the entryway to the bearded photos on walls, Ruth's has its own unique ambience.

i To the right of the synagogue.Primi €7-9. Secondi €10-24. ☑ Open daily noon-3pm, 7-10pm. Closed on Jewish holidays.

West Oltrarno

🏵 DANTE
RISTORANTE $$

P. Nazario Sauro 12r   ☎055 21 92 19 www.trattoriadante.net

Waiters and waitresses here do not read Dante's poetry or re-enact scenes from *Divine Comedy*, but even if visitors hoped for a meal for their soul, they will still get a meal for their body. Under the watchful eyes of Dante and his beloved

Beatrice, who adorn the walls of this establishment, make the most of the cheap menu by indulging in some of the least expensive fish and pizza in Florence.

i *A block south of Ponte alla Carraia, on the right. Fish €5-6. Pizza €6-9. Pasta €8-10. ① Open daily noon-1am; restaurant sometimes closes when it's not lunch of dinner time.*

LA SORBETTIERA
GELATERIA $

P. T. Tasso 11r
☎055 51 20 336

It's a mystery how this place has managed to be in business since 1934 and still be free of tourist crowds. We won't say it's completely crowd-free, though, since locals line up here to buy homemade ice cream by the kilogram (€18). Don't be shy: order as much gelato or as many frappes and semifreddos as you want (*Let's Go* recommends the lemon and sage flavor). Take your treat to the shade of the park and enjoy while watching Italian teenagers having the soccer match of their lives.

i *Across the street from the eastern side of park. Gelato from €1.20. ① Open M-Sa 12:30-11:30pm, Su and holidays 11am-1pm and 3-11:30pm.*

GUSTAPANINO
SANDWICHES $

V. dei Michelozzi 13r
☎333 92 02 673

A little brother of family-run restaurants Gusta Pizza and Gusta Osteria, Gustapanino tried hard to outdo its elder brothers. Whether or not it succeeded, it managed to score sweet outdoor seating right at P. Santa Trinita, where guests can chew on panini made with one of three bread options, all with a chiming fountain providing music in the background. If the sound of lapping water enchants you more than a sight of a candy bar excites a child, order to go and sit right on the water's edge.

i *In P. Santo Spirito; facing away from the Santo Spirito church, it's the 2nd building on the left. Focacce and piadine €3-4. ① Open Tu-Su 11:30am-3pm and 7-11pm.*

GUSTA PIZZA
PIZZERIA $

V. Maggio 46r
☎055 28 50 68

Run by the same family as Gustapanino (see above), Gusta Pizza serves Neapolitan-style, thin-crust pizza. Eat on location for some great personal service—some travelers say that if they really like you, they may even shape your pizza into a heart. Order to go if you want something warm and cheesy to eat by the river or if the inside of the restaurant fills up with students and other people who had the same idea as you.

i *On the corner of V. dei Michelozzi and V. Maggio. Facing the Santo Spirito church, turn right. Look for it on the next corner, on the right. Pizza €4.50-8. ① Open Tu-Su 11:30am-3pm and 7-11pm.*

East Oltrarno

In **Piazza di Santa Felicita,** there are a couple serviceable options for pit stops, including **Bibo, Ristorante Celestino,** and **Snack Le Delizie.** The eastern part of East Oltrarno is home to dinner gems frequented by locals, which means a lot less English on the menus.

L'HOSTERIA DEL BRICCO
RISTORANTE $$

V. San Niccolò 8r
☎055 23 45 037 www.osteriadelbricco.it

Behind an unobtrusive entrance, this gorgeous space with brick arches, flowers, and stained glass over the door is well worth the cover. A suit of armor stands casually on the side as L'Hosteria's most steadfast patron. The smell will kick start your appetite, and the meat or pasta from the handwritten menu will indulge all your senses.

i *Cross Ponte alla Grazie and turn left onto Lungarno Serristori. After 3 blocks, turn right onto V. Lupo, then left onto V. San Niccolò. Cover €2.50. Primi €7. Secondi €12-15. ① Open daily for lunch at noon and dinner from 7:30pm-late.*

florence

NIGHTLIFE

Florence specializes in laid-back nightlife rather than the dance-until-dawn variety. We know this may be hard for under-21s recently unleashed in Europe and looking to booze-cruise, but if you come here with the go-hard-or-go-home mentality, you may end up sorely disappointed. Instead, drink wine and mingle by the river, fall in love with the concept of *aperitivo*, and chill in *piazze* that are full of students. Still, from the hilariously huge selection of Irish pubs to a number of chic venues that turn more club-like as the night goes on, you should be able to find an ambience that suits your intensity level. During major sporting events and festivals, the streets fill with people and spill with wine. If you're really serious about clubbing, you should think about taking a taxi to larger venues outside the city proper.

The Duomo

This isn't exactly a traditional nightlife area. You'll find a couple of bars right by the Duomo, but you'll be better off venturing into other neighborhoods. When the weather is beautiful and the town is particularly crowded, people hang out on the Duomo steps all night.

SHOT CAFE   BAR
V. dei Pucci 5   ☎055 28 20 93

Like a bold and deviant teenager, Shot Cafe turns everything upside down. Vinyls serve as decor for the ceiling, and guitar balloons float throughout the bar. While American pop music from different decades fills the air, the young crowd mingles about. The best part is that this place won't slam you with a tough exchange rate—here, the dollar and the euro are one in the same, so party on, you economically recessed Americans.

i A block north of the Duomo. Free Wi-Fi. Beer €3.50; pitchers €10. 10 shots for €19. More expensive in winter. ☼ Open daily 6:30pm-2am.

ASTOR CAFE   BAR
P. del Duomo 20r   ☎055 23 99 318 www.astorcafe.com

Astor is like your favorite pair of jeans that works for both morning errands and a night at the club. In the morning, it's one of the few places where you can get a proper English breakfast. At night, blasting music adds to the wall projectors that flash arsty clips across the bar. Whether you start with breakfast and come later to party or start with the party and stay out till breakfast, Astor has you covered.

i On the northeast side of the piazza. Beer €5. Cocktails €7. 1L of whatever's on tap €10. ☼ Open daily 9am-1am.

Piazza Della Signoria

At night, this area lights up with bars and fills with wandering groups of students. For a range of options in a short stretch, try **Via dei Benci**, between P. Santa Croce and the river; Moyo is modern and trendy, the Red Gartello's karaoke entrance looks like the tunnel of love, and pubby Kikuya offers sandwiches and Dragoon Strong Ale. **Piazza della Signoria, Piazza Della Repubblica,** and **Ponte Vecchio** are other excellent places to hang out with a beer—get one to go from one of the local bars for some DIY nightlife.

MOYO   BAR
V. dei Benci 23r   ☎055 24 79 738 www.moyo.it

A sophisticated young crowd lounges in Moyo's modern black chairs. Candles and colorful disco lights that shine through a chandelier give this place a surreal, smoky atmosphere with an undulating beat.

i Just off P. Davanzati. Drinks €5-8. Buffet free. ☼ Open M-Th 8am-2am, F-Sa 8am-3am, Su 8am-2am. Lunch noon-5pm. Sushi aperitivo W 7-10:30pm. Every W Royal Party DJ set 10:30pm-late; drinks €5 with Erasmus card. Every Th free Tappafissa with D&B and electronic DJs; drinks €7.

AMADEUS

V. dei Pescioni 3

PUB

☎055 28 17 09

Amadeus attracts a healthy young crowd that is not too male-heavy for a pub. The genre changes nightly between happy music, house, R&B, reggae, and hip hop.

i Just off P. Davanzati. Beer €6. 3 drinks for €10. ☼ Open daily 7pm-2:30am.

THE OLD STOVE

V. Pellicceria 2r

IRISH PUB

☎055 29 52 32

Hey look, it's another Irish pub! Which, of course, actually means American, because Irish people know better than to go to Florence to drink. But the inside lighting is merciful, so just close your eyes, drink you beer, and think of Ireland. The soccer match board indicates the Old Stove's rowdy fan days.

i Walk to the side of P. della Repubblica that doesn't have the carousel and look down the street to the left. Pints €6, happy hour €4. Mixed drinks €7. ☼ Open M-Th noon-2am, F-Sa noon-3am, Su noon-2am. Happy hour M-Th 5-8pm.

TWICE

V. Giuseppe Verdi 57r

CLUB

☎055 24 76 356

Mostly sweaty guys, half-hearted dancing, and colored lights, Twice is the sort of place for clubbing when you don't feel like making a big production out of it. This cover-free club is a favorite among drunk students, people with no other club ideas, and Italian men on the prowl. The weird mix of music should have you giggling every time some forgotten hit from eighth grade plays. There's also a booth where people get hot and heavy and a fairly arbitrary VIP area in plain view—if you get waved in, just take the free drinks and roll with it.

i From the Duomo, head east on V. Oriuolo, then right onto V. Giuseppe Verdi. Beer €5. Mixed drinks €9. ☼ Open daily 9pm-4am.

Santa Maria Novella

In the evening, the streets of Santa Maria Novella are alive with youth. There are some stellar nightlife options, but in this area, it's best to choose a destination and stick to it rather than bar hop due to cover fees, distance, difference of style, or some combination of those. If you're trekking out to Central Park, be smart, pull a group together, and set aside funds for a cab home.

SPACE ELECTRONIC DISCOTEQUE

V. Palazzuolo 37

CLUB

☎055 29 30 82 www.spaceelectronic.net

Do you wish you could go clubbing at Epcot? Then join the happy young crowd around the aquarium bar in this conveniently located, space-age dance hall. Everyone joins in with whoever's blowing up the small karaoke stage. Meanwhile, the DJ upstairs rains techno down on you like a robot space god. If the bouncer waves you in, don't be fooled into thinking you got a free entrance—you'll pay the steep cover (€16) when you leave. Special events like guest bands and foam parties are extensively advertised on posters. The club's location means it's one of the few in the area that won't require you to take a cab home. And it'd be easy to find a company to share one, since the crowd is dominantly foreign and touring.

i From the river, take V. Melegnano to V. Palazzuolo, and turn right. Cover €16 with a drink included, students €10. Shots €3. Mixed drinks €6.50. ☼ Open daily 10pm-4am (or less, depending on a day of the week and business).

THE JOSHUA TREE PUB

V. della Scala 37r

PUB

☎01 23 45 67 89 www.thejoshuatreepub.com

Florence must be madly in love with its tourists because even the smallest places make sure that Americans have somewhere to go when they are inevitably homesick. Smaller than similar places in town, the Joshua Tree feels cozier and

florence

less deserted in the early evening hours. Launch your evening itinerary here or chill with the international regulars that often cluster on weeknights.

i *On corner of V. Benedetta. Pints €5.* ⏰ *Open daily 4pm-2am. Happy hour 4-9:30pm.*

PUBLIC HOUSE 27
BAR

V. Palazzuolo 27r   ☎339 30 22 330 www.publichouse27.com

This alternative music bar emits a sanguine glow and a cloud of smokers from early on in the evening. What it holds in, however, is an endless amount of rock bands, new and old, staring down the newcomers. If you aren't put off by the scary face stuck on the door, brave the red interior for €3 pint.

i *On the corner of V. della Porcellana. Pint €3.* ⏰ *Open M-Sa 5pm-2am, Su 2:30pm-2am.*

San Lorenzo

MOSTODOLCE
BAR

V. Nazionale 114r   ☎055 23 02 928 www.mostodolce.it

"In wine there is wisdom, in beer there is strength, in water there is bacteria." This is how the Mostodolce menu greets its patrons—in English, by the way, thanks to the influx of American tourists in the summer months. Come to watch a sporting event with big crowds, or just to drink artisanal beers brewed in Prato, and ponder the random duck above the bar. Warning: pondering increases with alcohol consumption.

i *On the corner of V. Guelfa. House beer €3.50. Chianti €3.50. Panini €4. Hamburgers €5.* ⏰ *Open daily 11am-2am. No table service 3:30-7:30pm.*

DUBLIN PUB
BAR

V. Faenza 27r   ☎055 27 41 571 www.dublinpub.it

If men in their 20s and 30s are your calling, they're calling you from Dublin Pub. This little bar is great for some international mingling, but is not so popular with women or those under 20 (though, if you're one of those, you can still have a good time). Also, the bar has **purse hooks**—score! Stick it out, because by the end of the night, an old man could be teaching you how to curse in Italian.

i *The far end of V. Faenza. Beer from €4. Cider €4.40. Pizza €5.* ⏰ *Open daily 5pm-2am.*

KITSCH THE PUB
BAR

V. San Gallo 22r   ☎328 90 39 289 www.kitsch-pub.com

What do you expect from a place called "kitsch" if not red velvet and stained glass? During the low season, try to nab some of the alfresco seating and mix with locals to avoid the TV that blares Gwen Stefani.

i *Off V. Cavour. Shot €2. Beer from €4. Cocktails from €6.* ⏰ *Open daily 5pm-3am.*

THE FISH PUB
BAR

P. del Mercato Centrale 44r   ☎055 26 82 90 www.thefishpub.com

While the ads for a "free crazy party" here every weekend night may seem slightly fishy, you might as well print the flyer on the website for discounts and a free shot. While you're at it, capitalize on the free champagne glass for students on Thursdays and free champagne on Mondays for women. Once you've looted the area, grab a handy plastic cup from the exit and take your drink to go. As for the bar itself, downstairs is loud and lit up blue, while upstairs features a quieter lounge area, a license plate collection, and a distorted portrait of the queen of England.

i *Right out of Mercato Centrale. Rock music on Tu. Bring your own iPod on W. Latin music on Su. 5 shots for €5. Discount for students after 9pm.* ⏰ *Open daily 4pm-4am. Happy hour 4-9pm.*

San Marco

There is no nightlife in San Marco. Why drink and party when you have an early morning line to stand in for the Accademia? An abundance of religious paintings might be doing something to the area. However, there are still a few places you should visit if you are up for a quieter night and don't mind meeting the locals.

THE CLUB HOUSE
BAR

V. de' Ginori 6r ☎055 21 14 27 www.theclubhouse.it

A curious place and a funky pill for terribly nostalgic Americans, this bar serves alcohol from dresser drawers under a theater-style chandelier while Nickelback and other American pop hits from a few years ago buzz in the air. Customers are often up to improvisation with their cocktails. In the midst of a number of quirky items (like colorful melted wax sculptures and random pieces of American football equipment),two flat screen TVs translate sports events.

i Off V. dei Pucci. Free Wi-Fi. Bomb €3.50. Beer €5.50. Long drinks €6. Cocktails €7. ☼ Open daily 3pm-3am.

FINNEGAN IRISH PUB
IRISH PUB

V. San Gallo 123r ☎055 49 07 94 www.finneganpub.com

Another **Irish pub!** This one has outdoor seating, pub booths, dedicated screenings of soccer and rugby, and rugby paraphernalia on the walls. You know the drill: a good place for casually watching the game (whatever the game may be) and hanging with the regulars. Finnegan displays its international flair with an eclectic collection of currencies stuck behind the bar and a skull to remind you what happens when money and alcohol get along all too well.

i North of P. San Marco. Shots from €3. ☼ Open M-F 4pm-midnight, Sa-Su 1am-1am.

BAR DEI CAVALIERI
BAR

V. San Gallo 33r ☎389 51 30 554

Do you ever really need anything else but coffee, sandwiches, and beer? This snack bar has these three life essentials, and it's enough to keep people dropping by for a quick drink or a longer stay at the outside tables until later hours. If you are staying in the area and love beer, ask for a stamp card (10 beers will get you one for free).

i 1 block northwest from P. San Marco. ☼ Open daily 7am-1am.

Santa Croce

Santa Croce is the soul of Florence's nightlife. If the street you're on seems oddly quiet, just keep walking—the lively spots show up in unexpected pockets. Try **Via dei Benci** for a rich selection. On nice evenings, join the swarm of young people lounging and drinking in **Piazza Sant'Ambrogio** and **Piazza Lorenzo Ghiberti**.

🎖 LAS PALMAS
PIAZZA

Largo Annigoni ☎347 27 60 033 www.laspalmasfirenze.it

What seems like a perfectly ordinary *piazza* by day tranforms into a rowdy, beach-themed block party when evening rolls around.We're talking palm trees, seafood, and straw screens right in the middle of Florence's cobblestone streets. Performers grace the enormous stage with theater, dance, music, or some combination of the three, setting the mood for a whole *piazza* of merriment. Groups of students, families, and older folks cram into the scores of tables and pile up on the generous *aperitivo* buffet, and children compete at foosball and table tennis. If you think the place is rowdy on a regular night, wait until you come when that they're projecting sporting events on the big screen.

i Off of P. Ghiberti, in front of the La Nazione building. Check website for performance and screening schedule. Live music Tu-Su. Movie screenings M. Beer and wine €4. Cocktails €5. Aperitivo €5. ☼ Open daily 6pm-1:30am.

⊠ RED GARTER   BAR
V. dei Benci 33/35r   ☎055 248 09 09

A place that claims to be the oldest American pub in Italy (since 1962) cannot be too local, but who cares if they borrowed all the right things from the US? During the day, this place is a steakhouse. When darkness falls, internationals blast the bar down with karaoke, live music, and beer pong on Tuesday nights.
i *From Ponte alle Grazie, follow V. dei Benci north. Events every night. Beer from €4. Cocktails €7.50. ⏰ Open M-Sa 3:30pm-2am, Su 11am-2am. Kitchen closes 1am.*

⊠ CAFFÈ SANT'AMBROGIO   BAR
P. Sant'Ambrogio 7r   ☎055 24 77 277

Location is a life-saver for this bar, which tries hard to be fancy with its minimalistic (read: boring) interior. Young crowds flood this bar no matter what due to its location, and the drinks are always affordable.
i *The piazza is at the end of V. Pietrapiana. Wine €4-7. Cocktails €6-7. ⏰ Open M-Sa 8:30am-2am. Aperitivo 6-9pm.*

OIBÒ   BAR, LOUNGE
V. dei Benchi 53r   ☎055 26 38 611 www.oibo.net

Florence's casual, chic crowd comes here to sip drinks on the large outdoor patio and dance under the disco ball. As the night goes on, the DJ tends to break out the Italian hits, and you might witness a bar full of elegant locals belting along. This is a great spot for *aperitivo* on your way to the Teatro Verdi.
i *On the corner across from the Basilica di Santa Croce. DJ "After Beach Party" on Su. Beer €6. Cocktails €7.50-10. ⏰ Open Apr-Nov daily 8am-2am. Aperitivo 6:30-9:30pm.*

NAIMA   CAFE, BAR
V. dell'Anguillara 54   ☎055 26 54 098 www.naimafirenze.it

The subtle violet-and-stone bar area of Naima is a great place to start the night, while the lounge has couches and candlelight for an intimate feel. Here you'll find lighthearted internationals and Euro-hipsters taking advantage of the affordable drinks.
i *From southeast of the Duomo, follow V. del Proconsolo south and turn right onto V. dell'Anguillara. Shot €3. Beer €5. Cocktails €7. ⏰ Open daily 3pm-2am.*

West Oltrarno

West Oltrarno has a good concentration of students, making it a lively and diverse evening locale, especially around the P. Santo Spirito. If you want to go dancing, you'll have to go somewhere else.

⊠ VOLUME   BAR, MUSEUM
P. Santo Spirito 5r   ☎055 23 81 460

There's a museum in Florence that's worth spending a night drinking at. And we don't mean taking bravery shots while running away from a dinosaur. What we do mean is that this little museum of wooden sculptures and a library cafe magically turns into a popular bar at night. *Let's Go* does not guarantee that the whole museum won't come to life after midnight (depending on how many drinks you've had).
i *To the right of the Santo Spirito church, sandwiched between 2 larger establishments. Cocktails €5. Crepes €4-7. ⏰ Open daily 9am-2am. Aperitivo 6-10pm.*

⊠ LA DOLCE VITA   WINE BAR
P. del Carmine 6r   ☎055 28 45 95 www.dolcevitaflorence.com

Trendy young adults with margarita glasses populate this happening, artsy bar. The bold interior hosts monthly photo shows as well as live Brazilian, jazz, or contemporary music every Wednesday and Thursday night. For travelers on a budget, break out that one nice outfit you brought, nab a spritz, and feast on the *aperitivo* buffet.

i *In P. del Carmine, by the Carmine church. Free Wi-Fi. Live music W-Th 7:30-9:30pm. Sprits €7.*
🕐 *Open M-Sa 11am-3am, Su 6pm-2am. Aperitivo buffet 7:30-9:30pm. Kitchen open noon-3pm.*

POP CAFE
BAR

P. Santo Spirito 18 ☎055 21 38 52 www.popcafe.it

Dim blue neon lightning, hipster-artsy pictures, and a quiet beat make Pop Cafe the least rowdy bar on the *piazza*. Pop is the ideal for those who do not have to be bouncing off the walls to be in a good mood or for those who long for a conversation that does not require shouting at the top of your lungs.

i *To the left of the Santo Spirito church. Beer, shots, and prosecco €4. Cocktails €6.* 🕐 *Open daily 11:30am-2am.*

ONE EYED JACK
BAR

P. Nazario Sauro 2 ☎055 62 88 040 www.thejackpub.com

You shouldn't have any trouble finding this Australian-run bar—a big painting of Jack in an eye patch spans the front shutter. It tries to look very wild for the international crowd, with blasting music and Marilyn Monroe gansta-style posters in the bathrooms. Live bands and international DJs come by many weekends; other nights, you can hit up the jukebox. This is a great spot for a pint and a bite.

i *Across the street from Gelateria La Carraia and Dante. Free Wi-Fi. Pints €3.50-6. Cocktails €6.*
🕐 *Open daily 11am-2am. Kitchen open 11am-1am.*

East Oltrarno

Far east of any part of Florence you're likely to visit, East Oltrarno is where the locals go to party. Since they're real people with real jobs, things tend to be most happening here on weekends. Investigate **Piazza Giuseppe Poggi** (at the base of the hill leading up to Ple. Michelangelo), **Via San Niccolò,** and **Via dei Renai** to get your game on.

📖 JAMES JOYCE PUB
BAR

Lungarno Benvenuto Cellini 1 ☎055 65 80 856

This enormous, comfortable bar (the oldest in Florence) is always filled with students for a reason. With foosball, literary kitsch on the walls, and a fun-loving local vibe, you hardly need quality beer to have a good time (though it helps, no doubt). Catch some air on a stroll by the river midway through your night. You don't even have to step back inside to order another round of drinks—a window in the bar opens onto the patio.

i *On the western side of the traffic circle after the Ponte San Niccolò. Wine from €4.50. Bottled beer €5.* 🕐 *Open daily until 3am. Aperitivo 7:30-10pm.*

ZOE
BAR

V. dei Renai 13 ☎055 24 31 11 www.zoebar.it

The colorful outdoor seating and zebra decorations give this place an upbeat feel as it floods with 20- and 30-somethings indulging in Zoe's renowned *aperitivo*. Take advantage of the extensive cocktail menu, grab an international newspaper, and relax.

i *Across the river from V. dei Benci. Cross Ponte alle Grazie, walk 1 block, and turn left onto V. dei Renai. Wine €7.* 🕐 *Open M-W 8pm-2am, F-Su 8pm-2am.*

ARTS AND CULTURE

Theater

Don't be scared off because you assume performances will be in Italian; going to the theater can be one of the best evening experiences in Florence, and the fact that shows are often free is the icing on an already awesome cake. In the summer, the

Bargello (p. 590) sometimes hosts site-specific productions in its courtyard, while temporary stages in the **Piazza della Signoria** host music and dance acts. If you're here a bit longer, there are some worthy venues just outside town, like the **Teatro Puccini,** the **Teatro Sotteraneo,** and the **Saschall.**

TEATRO DELLA PERGOLA
SAN MARCO

V. della Pergola 18   ☎055 22 641 www.teatrodellapergola.com

This opera house has been around since 1656, and it's understandable that anyone would want to retire at such a respectable age. However, this tough and elegant theater is still working, even though operas only pay a visit here during the *Maggio Musicale Fiorentino* festival. The rest of the time, you can enjoy a selection of about 250 drama productions each year from the comfort of plush red seats and gilded galleries. Old people don't have time to bother with foreign languages, so it's an impressive excuse to brush up on your Italian or choose a Shakespearian play you know too well to need a translation.

i At the intersection of V. della Colonna and V. Nuova dei Caccini. Prices vary by performance, usually €15-30. ☑ Box office open M-Sa 9:30am-6:30pm.

Rock and Jazz

The rock and jazz venues in Florence attract lively crowds and tend to cost no more than the price of a drink—and any drink tastes sweeter when sipped to the sound of a sweet serenade. Big-name artists have been known to show up anywhere from the **Teatro Verdi** to small cafes, so keep your eyes peeled for posters.

LA CITÉ LIBRERIA CAFE
WEST OLTRARNO

Borgo San Frediano 21   ☎055 21 03 87 www.lacitelibreria.info

When you look at a library cafe, it almost never is just a library cafe. For this, one books are merely a masquerade for the real thing: art and music. There's an event almost every day, with everything from jazz to swing to blues to Balkan recitals making appearances. And when music isn't playing, there's a high chance that you'll find a book presentation, an exhibition, or a play instead.

i From Ponte alla Carraia, walk west on Borgo San Frediano. The library cafe spans 3 windows on the right. Beer €3. ☑ Open M-W 3pm-1am, Th-Sa 3pm-2am, Su 3pm-1am. Almost daily events 6:30-10pm.

SEI DIVINO
SANTA MARIA NOVELLA

Borgo Ognissanti 42r   ☎055 21 77 91

Live music and elegant suits fill this *aperitivo* destination every Tuesday, Saturday, or Sunday. On all the other days, you can still count on a strict diet of music to go with your cocktails and wine. For some reason, the tourist crowds haven't discovered this gem yet, so, for your sake, please don't tell them.

i Go northwest on Borgo Ognissanti from Ponte alla Carraia. It's on the right. Live music on Tu, Sa, Su. Cocktails from €7. ☑ Open daily 7pm-2am.

SHOPPING

Open-Air Markets

Open-air markets are some of the most authentic experiences Florence has to offer. Try the enormous food and clothing market in **Parco delle Cascine** (P. Vittorio Veneto, Off Vle.Fratelli Rosselli on the western edge of the city. Open Tu 7am-1pm), the flower market in **Piazza della Repubblica** (Open Th 10am-7pm), or the antique market at **Giardini Fortezza Firenze.** (Follow V. Faenza north as it becomes V. Dionisi. Open Sept-June every 3rd Su of the month.)

MERCATO CENTRALE

P. del Mercato Centrale

This technically isn't an outdoor market, but it's chaotic enough to feel like one. At Mercato Centrale, you can find just about anything within the realm of food, from cheeses to spices to singing butchers. To stand out, stalls tack up random items (like a pair of striped purple and white balloon shorts) to their roofs or counters. You can also find unusually shaped pasta casually mixed in with the standard shapes: tortellini, spaghetti, penises, ravioli, striped farfale... Wait—striped farfale? If all this food ogling is making you hungry, some stalls in the center sell pizza and sandwiches by weight.

i It's the huge green-and-red building in the middle of all those sidewalk vendors. 🕐 Open spring-fall M-Sa 7am-2pm; winter Sa 7am-2pm.

SAN LORENZO

V. dell'Ariento

San Lorenzo's market spans the entire length of V.dell'Ariento. Vendors actively try to sell you hats, scarves, journals, or souvenirs as you pass, regardless of your apparent interest level. If you've got an eye for quality, this is the place to buy some of that famous Florentine leather. Vendors are used to ignorant tourists paying full price, so don't expect to shave more than a few euro off the price except through some hard-line bargaining. Since so many stalls have similar wares, you can always move on to the next one to get better prices.

i Walking away from the station on V. Nazionale, V. dell'Ariento is on the right just across from the fountain.

Artisan Goods

FARMACEUTICA DI SANTA MARIA NOVELLA

V. della Scala 16 ☎055 21 62 76 www.smnovella.com

This *farmaceutica* drowns you with the weight of its age (or it could be tantalizing smells of their brewed potions). The Santa Maria Novella monks have been bottling medicines in this museum-worthy space since the 13th century, but the "modern" pharmacy is straight from the Victorian age. Elixirs, perfumes, juleps, salts, spirits, waters, and protective oils are all available, displayed on shelving and sold in packaging that's been updated very little over the course of the past century. Browse the colored bottles of essence of myrrh under a chandelier and fancy yourself a Victorian aristocrat for an afternoon.

i At the corner of V. della Porcellana. Coming from P. Santa Maria Novella, turn right onto V. della Scala. Candle €10-50. 500ml liqueurs €50. Sun care from €20. 🕐 Open daily 10:30am-7:30pm. In Aug, closes Sa at 1pm.

ALICE ATELIER: THE MASKS OF PROF.AGOSTINO DESSÌ

V. Faenza 72r ☎055 28 73 70 www.alicemasks.com

Masks aren't just quick and easy Halloween costumes—at Professor Agostino's Dessì's studio, they are a true art form. Here, you can find the perfect two-faced mask to express your split personality. Handmade masks of things you never imagined, from bionic metal-faced creatures to puzzle people, are as good as a museum visit. Highly involved in Florence's art scene, Dessì has been making masks for world exhibitions since the '70s and brought his daughter, Alice, into the family business in 1997. The shop offers mask-making courses and will happily direct you to nearby exhibitions.

i From P. della Stazione, take V. Nazionale and turn left onto V. Faenza. Application form for mask-making courses can be found on the website. Masks from €50. 5-session course €500.

florence

ESSENTIALS

Practicalities

- **TOURIST OFFICES: Uffici Informazione Turistica** has its primary office at **Via Manzoni 16.** (☎055 23 3200pen M-F 9am-1pm.) Other locations include **Piazza Stazione 4** (☎055 21 22 45 Open M-Sa 8:30am-7pm, Su 8:30am-2pm), **Via Cavour 1r** (☎055 29 08 32 ② Open M-Sa 8:30am-6:30pm, Su 8:30am-1pm), and **Borgo Santa Croce 29r.** (☎055 23 40 444 ② Open Mar-Oct M-Sa 9am-7pm, Su 9am-2pm; Nov-Feb M-Sa 9am-5pm, Su 9am-2pm).

- **CURRENCY EXCHANGE: Best and Fast Change** has offices at V. dei Cerretani 47r (☎055 23 99 855) and Borgo Santa Lorenzo 16r. (☎055 28 43 91)

- **ATMS: BNL** (V. dei Cerretani 6) accepts Visa. **Banca Toscana** (V. dell'Ariento 18) accepts Mastercard.

- **LUGGAGE STORAGE:** At **Stazione di Santa Maria Novella.** (*i* By platform 16. 1st 4hr €4, 5th-12th hr. €0.60 per hr., €0.20 per hr. thereafter. Cash only. ② Open daily 6am-11:50pm.)

- **LAUNDROMATS: Onda Blue.** (V. degli Alfani 24 and V. Guelfa 221r ② Open daily 8am-10pm.)

- **INTERNET: Internet Train** can be found all over the city. For a central location, try **Via dei Benci 36r.** (☎055 26 38 555 www.internettrain.it *i* From P. Santa Croce, turn left onto V. dei Benci. Wi-Fi €2.50-3 per hr. Internet €3-4.50 per hr. ② Open daily 10am-10:30pm.) Many restaurants and library cafes offer free Wi-Fi. Try **BRAC.** (V. dei Vagellai 18r ☎055 09 44 877 ② Open daily 10am-11pm.)

- **POST OFFICES: Via Pellicceria 3.** (☎055 27 36 481 *i* South of P. della Repubblica. ② Open M-F 8:15am-7pm, Sa 8:15am-12:30pm.) Other locations include V. de Barbadori 37r (☎055 28 81 75), V. Pietrapiana 53 (☎055 42 21 850), V. de Barbadori 37r (☎055 28 81 75), and V. Camillo Cavour 71a (☎055 47 19 10).

- **POSTAL CODE:** 50100.

Emergency

- **EMERGENCY NUMBER:** 118.

- **POLICE: Polizia Municipale.** (24hr. non-emergency helpline ☎055 32 83 333) Help is also available for tourists at the mobile police units parked at V. dei Calzaioli near P. della Signoria and at Borgo Santa Jacopo in the Oltrarno, near Ponte Vecchio. The emergency **Carabinieri** number is 112.

- **LATE-NIGHT PHARMACIES: Farmacia Comunale.** (Stazione Santa Maria Novella055 21 67 61 ② Open 24hr. Ring the bell 1-4am.) **Farmacia Molteni.** (V. Calzaioli 7r ☎055 28 94 90 *i* Just north of P. della Signoria.) **Farmacia all'insegna del Moro.** (P. San Giovanni 20r ☎055 21 13 43 *i* A little east of the Duomo.)

- **HOSPITALS/MEDICAL SERVICES: Arcispedale Santa Maria Nuova** is northeast of the Duomo and has a 24hr. emergency room. (P. Santa Maria Nuova 1 ☎055 69 381) **International Medical Service.** (P. dell'Unita Italiana, 7 ☎055 287383, ☎349 7319461 ② Open M-F 2-4pm.) **Associazione Volontari Ospedalieri** provides free medical translation. (☎055 42 50 126 www.avofirenze.it ② Open M 4-6pm, Tu 10am-noon, W 4-6pm, Th 10am-noon, F 4-6pm.) **Tourist's Doctor.** (Instituto Prosperius, V. F.lli Rosselli 62 Firenze ☎338 89 41 809 ②24hr. medical assistance).

Getting There

How you arrive in Florence will be dictated by where you come from. Florence may have named its Amerigo Vespucci airport after the guy who in turn gave the Americas their name, but that doesn't mean the city has any flights from the US. Those flying across the Atlantic will have to transfer at another European airport. If flying from within Europe, it will probably be cheaper for you to fly into the budget-airline hub that is **Pisa Airport**. Buses run regularly from Pisa Airport to Florence; they take just over an hour and cost abou €10. If coming from within Italy, you will most likely catch a train, which will bring you into Santa Maria Novella station. If traveling locally, buses may be useful.

By Plane

Aeroporto Amerigo Vespucci is Florence's main airport. (V. del Termine 11055 30 615 main line, ☎055 30 61 700 for 24hr. automated service; www.aeroporto.firenze.it *i* For lost baggage, call ☎055 30 61 302.) From the airport, the city can be reached via the **VolainBus shuttle.** You can pick up the shuttle on the departures side. (*i* Exit the airport to the right and pass the taxi stand. Drop-off is at Santa Maria Novella station. €5. ☼ 25min., every 30min., 6am-11:30pm.) A cab from the airport to the city center costs about €20.

By Train

Santa Maria Novella train station dominates the northwest of the city. (www.grandis-tazioni.it ☼ Open daily 6am-midnight.) You can purchase tickets from the fast ticket kiosks or tellers. There are daily trains from: Bologna (€25-36 ☼ 40min., 2 per hr., 7am-11:26pm), Milan (€53 ☼ 1¾hr., 1 per hr., 7am-9pm), Rome (€45 ☼ 1½hr., 2 per hr., 8:30am-11:33pm), Siena €6.30 ☼ 1½hr., 6 per hr., 5am-9:18pm), and Venice (€43 ☼ 2hr., 2 per hr., 7:30am-7:30pm). For precise schedules and prices, check www.trenitalia.com.

By Bus

Three major intercity bus companies run out of Florence's bus station. From Santa Maria Novella train station, turn left onto on V. Alamanni—the station is on the left by a long driveway. **SITA** (V. Santa Caterina da Siena 17 ☎800 37 37 60 www.sitabus.it) runs buses to and from Siena, San Gimignano, and other Tuscan destinations. **LAZZI** (P. Stazione 4/6r ☎055 21 51 55 www.lazzi.it *i* For timetable info call ☎055 35 10 61) buses depart from P. Adua, just east of the train station. Routes connect to Lucca, Pisa, and many other regional towns. **CAP-COPIT** (Largo Fratelli Alinari 10 ☎055 21 46 37 www.capautolinee.it) runs to regional towns. Timetables for all three companies change regularly, so call ahead or check online for schedules.

Getting Around

The main thing that you should know is that Florence is a small city. Most visitors simply walk everywhere without any need for public transportation. This is ideal for the budget traveler, as you won't rack up metro and bus fares like you do in many other European cities. And if you're going to venture outside the compact city center, Florence has you covered.

By Bus

As the city's only form of public transportation, Florence's tiny orange buses are surprisingly clean, reliable, and organized. Operated by **ATAF** and **LI-NEA,** the extensive bus network includes several night-owl buses that take over regular routes in the late evenings. The schedule for every passing line is posted on the pole of each well-marked bus stop, complete with the direction the bus is going and a list of every stop in order. Most buses originate at P. Stazione or P. San Marco. Buses #12 and #13 run to the Ple. Michelangelo; bus #7 runs to Fiesole. You're unlikely to need the buses unless you're leaving the city center. You can buy tickets from most newsstands, ticket vending machines, or the ATAF kiosk in P. Stazione. (☎800 42 45 00 *i* 90min. ticket €1.20, €2 if purchased on board; for groups, there is *carta argile* for €10 that is equivalent to 10 tickets and can be used several times at once.) Stamp your ticket when you board the bus; you then have the length of time denoted by the ticket to re-use it. Be careful—if you forget to time-stamp your ticket when you board the bus (and can't successfully play the "confused foreigner" card), it's a min. €50 fine.

By Taxi

To call a cab, call **Radio Taxi.** (☎055 4390, ☎055 4499, ☎055 4242, or ☎055 4798). Tell the operator your location and when you want the cab, and the nearest available car will be sent to you. Each cab has a rate card in full view, and the meter displays the running fare, which is based on the distance traveled and any supplements charged. If you're going far or are nervous, it never hurts to ask for an estimate before boarding. There are surcharges for Sundays, holidays, luggage, and late nights. Unless you have a lot of baggage, you probably won't want to take a taxi during the day, when traffic will make the meter tick up mercilessly. At lunchtime, a 5min. ride from the Duomo to the Oltrarno will cost €10. Nevertheless, cabs are a manageable late-night option if you're outside the city, and especially if you're in a group. Designated cab stands can be found at P. Stazione, Fortezza da Basso, and P. della Repubblica. Cabs can also often be found at Santa Maria Novella.

By Bike

Most locals either ride a Vespa or cycle, and if you want to be one of them, there are many rentals around the city. However, keep in mind that while cycling is a great way to check out a longer stretch of the Arno's banks or to cover a lot of territory in one day, locals usually ride the quiet, deserted streets. If you're planning to bike to the sights, those routes are jam-packed with tourists; be ready to walk your bike most of the time. **Mille E Una Bici** (☎055 65 05 295 www.comune.firenze.it) rents bikes that can be picked up and returned at any of its four locations: P. Stazione, P. di Santa Croce, P. Ghiberti, and Stazione F.S. Campo Di Marte. **Florence By Bike** (V. San Zanobi 91r and 120/122r ☎055 48 89 92 www.florencebybike.it ☒ Open Apr-Oct daily 9am-7:30pm; Nov-Mar M-Sa 9am-1pm and 3:30-7:30pm) is another good resource. Staff will help renters plan routes, whether it's an afternoon or a multi-day trip outside of town.

pisa

This is what Pisa has to offer: one tower, leaning; one budget airline hub; and three universities. That may not sound like much, but the tower is actually really cool, the airport is remarkably easy to get to, and you can thank the universities for the city's many student-friendly bars. If Florentine nightlife left you doubting the Tuscan party scene, come to Pisa, where the cheap sangria will have you leaning at a 4.99° angle, too. Pisa's wide streets make it feel more like a city than other Tuscan towns. If you've forgotten how to live with the heat after so many shady alleyways, a 20min. bus ride will take you to Pisa's shoreline, where the plethora of swimmers belie the fact that you're not actually allowed to swim.

ORIENTATION

Whether you arrive in Pisa by train or plane, you will enter the *centro* from the **train station.** The city knows why people visit, so street signs bearing the image of a leaning tower and an arrow are everywhere. When you leave the station, you'll be in the southern end of the city. Take shop-lined **Corso Italia** straight ahead to reach the river, which is central to city life. **Via Santa Maria** will take you straight from the river to **Piazza dei Miracoli.**

Those staying overnight in Pisa are likely in transit—therefore, you may want to weigh access to the train station and airport over proximity to the tower. The one below is one of our favorite budget beds in the city; you can find more on **www.letsgo.com**.

WALKING STREET HOSTEL   HOSTEL $
Corso Italia 58   ☎393 06 48 737 www.walkingstreethostel.com
This hostel does not wait an extra second to remind you how international its crowd is. You're welcome to stand under a Chinese lantern or a Singaporean flag and feel completely at home. With a long list of amenities that includes everything from lockers to a DVD and game room, Walking Street Hostel is the best value you can get in Pisa.

i On Corso Italia, halfway from the train station to the river. Free Wi-Fi. Complimentary coffee and tea. Linens included. Wheelchair accessible. Dorm €19 (Jul €25); doubles €65-75. Cash only. 🕐 Reception open until 3am.

SIGHTS

Walled in and covered with trim green grass, Pisa's **Piazza dei Miracoli** is an island unto itself. True, the eager tourist crowds and relentless sun are free to barrage the square; even so, the clean-lined monuments maintain a sense of quiet grace—well, apart from that tall one in the back who can't seem to stop falling over. Entrance to the *piazza* itself is free, and possibly the best part of Pisa is hanging out in the shadow of the tower, watching tourists direct one another on how to take the perfect Leaning Tower photo. Meanwhile, if you're intent on scouring for sights beyond the square, Pisa offers the usual selection of grand old Italian churches, and everyday Pisa is at its prettiest along the Arno. The **Opera della Primaziale Pisana** sells tickets for all the monuments in the *piazza*. (☎050 83 50 11 www.opapisa.it Tower €18. Duomo free, but you need to pick up your ticket at the ticket office. Joint admission for non-leaning monuments: 1 monument €5, 2 monuments €7, 3 monuments €8, all 5 €9. Disabled visitors and 1 guest free. All monuments open daily June-Sept 8am-11pm; Oct 9am-7pm; Nov-Feb 10am-5pm; Mar 9am-6pm; Apr-May 8am-8pm. Last entry 30min. before close. Ticket office closes at 7:30pm).

LEANING TOWER   TOWER
We are jaded travelers here, but we admit: the hype for the Leaning Tower is not simply exaggerated by art historians. This thing is ridiculous, even more ridiculous than the tourists' creative poses with it, and that means something. You probably haven't noticed, but the tower's construction involved a few minor hiccups, leaving it only fully reconstructed and climbable in 2010, after 800 years of work. Climbing the tower is much like any other slanted, narrow, slippery tower climb in Tuscany, except more slanted, narrow, and slippery. Oh, and it's expensive, too. Maybe that's why even 17-year-olds need Mom or Dad with them if they want to scale this bad boy. Nevertheless, shell out the euro and climb for the sake of the only acceptable pictures with a tilted horizon.

i Make reservations in the Museo del Duomo or online. Visitors under 18 must be accompanied by an adult. Tickets are for a specific time; be prompt. The climb is 300+ narrow, twisty, and very slippery stairs; consider your health and tendency to experience vertigo before attempting. Guided visits last 30min.

DUOMO   CHURCH
For once, a church in great condition! Maybe it's cheating that it was heavily refurbished after a 1595 fire, but oh well. Pisa's Duomo skipped the sparse decor

pisa

trend and went for huge, vivid Renaissance-style paintings, an enormous mosaic of Jesus, and an intensely gold-flowered ceiling. Be sure to check out Adam, Eve, and an androgynous human-faced serpent in the left alcove.

i Pick up a free ticket at the ticket office. ☑ *Open daily Apr-Sept 10am-8pm; Oct 10am-7pm; Nov-Feb 10am-1pm and 2pm-5pm; Mar 10am-6pm.*

GIARDINO SCOTTO
PARK

Lungarno Leonardo Fibonacci   ☎050 23 044

For a change of scene and a breath of fresh air, Giardino Scotto is the place to be. Its main draws are the ruins and walkable portions of the Roman walls (now covered in love notes), but local students flock here on sunny weekends for the desk-like benches. There's also a permanent outdoor movie theater where films are screened every night of the summer. The playground will take you back to your childhood, provided you grew up in space and had a spinning gazebo. You likely won't be able to kick the happy children off the little in-ground trampoline; it's probably more socially acceptable to hang around on the swings.

i The park is at the bend in the river, east of the centro. Free. ☑ *Open daily Jul-Aug 8am-8:30pm; Sept 9am-8pm; Oct 9am-6pm; Nov-Jan 9:30am-4:30pm; Feb-Mar 9am-6pm; Apr 9am-7pm; May-Jun 9am-8pm.*

FOOD

This port city brims with seafood to spice up your carb-only diet. Unlike in Florence, you can get a Pisa pizza with actual toppings in the €5-6 range—you'll find about half a dozen similar but viable *pizzerias* along **Via Santa Maria**, just south of the monuments. Meanwhile, a number of Pisa's restaurants double as bars that offer cheap and delicious *aperitivo*. People tend to dine earlier here than in Florence, so don't roll up at 1pm and expect a closing restaurant to cook you *tagliatelle*.

ARGINI E MARGINI
SEAFOOD $

Lungarno Galilei   ☎329 88 81 972 www.arginiemargini.com

For a quick fix of beach-style escapism, look no further than this sandy bank of the Arno's southern shore. Argini e Margini's floating dock comes to life in the summer with fresh seafood and live jazz. They also serve *aperitivo* and cocktails along the pier under orange umbrellas and palm trees. Sounds pricey, right? Hardly—you won't need to shell out anything extravagant for fresh fish.

i Look over the wall at the edge of the river down near Ponte della Fortezza. Cover €1. Seafood priced by the kg. Fresh misto €4.50-5. Wine from €4. Cocktails €5. ☑ *Open in high season M-Th 6-11pm, F-Sa 6pm-midnight, Su 6-11pm.*

LA BOTTEGA DEL GELATO
GELATERIA $

P. Giuseppe Garibaldi 11   ☎050 57 54 67 www.labottegadelgelato.it

Even Florentines wouldn't turn up their noses at these generous servings of super smooth gelato. A word of warning, though: for a walk along the sunny and windy river, opt for a cup of gelato instead of a cone if you don't want to end up with more melty gelato in your hair than in your mouth.

i North of Ponte di Mezzo on P. Giuseppe Garibaldi. Gelato from €1.50. Ice cream sandwich €0.50. ☑ *Open daily high season 11am-1am.*

DOLCE PISA
CAFE $

V. Santa Maria 83   ☎050 56 31 81

Pastas, salads, and smoothies galore! Most things on the menu cost €6, so for once we cheapskates actually have options. Also, there's no cover charge at the tea salon tables, so no need to chomp pastries while awkwardly hovering by the bar.

i From the monuments, it's a 5min. walk down V. Santa Maria; it's on the right, on the corner with V. Luca Ghini. Pastries €1. Most entrees €6. Cappuccino €1.20. ☑ *Open M-Tu 7:30am-11pm, Th-Su 7:30am-11pm.*

NIGHTLIFE

You really don't need our help with this one. Pisa is jam-packed with bars and pubs, most of which are quite cheap. Basically, if you are paying more than €3 for a bottle of beer, then you'd better really like the atmosphere. Florentine *piazza*-based nightlife is less popular here, mainly becausethe *piazze* aren't as pretty and the pubs are more plentiful. The main gathering spot, **Piazza delle Vettogaglie,** is a near-hidden square lined with small pubs, picnic tables, and cheap late-night food. For slightly more upscale options, try **Borgo Stretto.** Like restaurants, bars tend to close a bit earlier in Pisa (around 1am). If you can make it here in June, Pisa takes to the streets for a line-up of large-scale nighttime festivals. The most happening spots change frequently, so your best bet is to explore. Here are a few scenic options on the water to get you started.

ZENIT CAFE   BAR
V. della Republica 8a, Marina di Pisa   ☎339 413 37 87

Zenit Cafe isn't actually too much of a nighttime haunt but is still deserves to be at the top of our list. A ways from Pisa, this is a great break from all the tourist shacks your likely to find closer to the sights. Here, you can enjoy the company of the patrons who hang here before you venture outside to explore the surrounding geography. With the sea and beach just opposite the door, Zenit is hard to pass up (the unique rocky beach requires some balancing skills to reach the water but also makes for some fun climbing).

i *From under the west archway in P. Vittorio Emanuele II, follow as it veers left to find the buses. Tickets (you want Corsi 2) ar €4 round-trip and can be bought inside on the right. Get off at Marina di Pisa; walk toward the shore and continue left. The cafe is one of the 1st ones in the buildings along the street. Beer €4-6. Cocktails €6. Aperitivo buffet €6.* ☼ *Open M-Tu 8am-midnight, Th-Su 8am-midnight. Last bus to Pisa leaves around 10:30pm.*

LA BERLINA   BAR
P. Cairoli 10   ☎340 880 68 81

The cheapest bar we have ever seen in Italy is named after a 15th-century wall that was located on this *piazza* to chain criminals to it for public display and condemnation. While nothing of this kind happens here anymore, P. Cairoli is still the place to come. Grab a drink to go (it's cheaper that way, and the interior isn't too exciting anyway) and enjoy one of the numerous competitions that are held here on warm June weekends.

i *Northwest side of P. Cairoli. Drinks (rum and pear) from €1.50. Artisanal beer €6. Discount on birthdays and Let's Go users.* ☼ *Open daily 10am-2am.*

BAZEEL   BAR
Lungarno Pacinotti 1   ☎340 28 81 113 www.bazeel.it

This upbeat corner bar on a major *piazza* dominates the scene around the Ponte di Mezzo, the most central of the *centro* bridges. The frozen cocktails make this a refreshing destination after a hot day. When it's cold, hang out on the catwalk above the cavernous indoor seating.

i *Just over the north side of Ponte di Mezzo. Beer €3-4.50. Frozen cocktails €6.50.* ☼ *Open daily 2pm-2am.*

ESSENTIALS
Practicalities

- **TOURIST OFFICES:** The office on **Piazza Vittorio Emanuele II** provides maps, an events calendar, and other assistance. (P. Vittorio Emanuele II 13 ☎050 42 291 www.pisaunicaterra. it ☼ Open daily 9:30am-4:30pm.) **Airport office.** (☎050 50 25 18 www.pisaunicaterra.it ☼ Open daily 9:30am-9:30pm.)

- **ATMS: Deutsche Bank** is on the corner of V. Giosuè Carducci and V. San Lorenzo. (Between P. Cavalieri and P. Martiri della Libertà. ☼ Open 24hr.)
- **LUGGAGE STORAGE:** In the **train station.** (At the left end of Binario 1 *i* €4 per 24hr., €2 for additional item. ☼ Open daily 6am-9pm.)
- **LAUNDROMATS: Lavenderia** provides washers, dryers, and detergent. (V. Carmine 20 ☼ Open daily 7am-11pm.)
- **INTERNET: Cyberia-Tribe** (V. San Martino 39, ☎050 500480), **Il Navigatore** (V. Palestro 10, ☎050 0980582). Visitto register for city Wi-Fi.
- **POST OFFICES:** (P. Vittorio Emanuele II 7/9 ☎050 51 95 14 *i* On the right of the *piazza.* ☼ Open M-F 8:15am-7pm, Sa 8:15am-1:30pm.)
- **POSTAL CODES:** 56100

Emergency

- **POLICE: Polizia Municipale.** (V. Cesare Battisti 71/72 ☎050 91 08 11), **Carabinieri** (V. Guido da Pisa, ☎050 97181).
- **LATE-NIGHT PHARMACIES: Lungarno Medicec 51.** (☎050 54 40 02 *i* On the north shore of the river, to the east. ☼ Open 24hr.)
- **HOSPITALS/MEDICAL SERVICES: Hospital Cisanello.** (V. Paradisa 2, ☎050 99 23 00, ☎050 99 21 11). **Santa Chiara.** (V. Bonanno Pisano ☎050 99 21 11 *i* Near P. del Duomo.)

Getting There

BY PLANE

Galileo Galilei Airport (☎050 84 93 00 www.pisa-airport.com) is practically within walking distance of the city, but the train shuttle (€1.50 on the bus) takes only 5min. The shuttle arrives at Arrivals. The airport is a major budget airline hub for all of Tuscany, including Florence. Some intercontinental flights serve Galileo Galilei, and you can fly directly to Pisa from most European cities.

BY TRAIN

Pisa Centrale will be your main port of entry from other Italian destinations. (P. della Stazione ☎050 91 75 91 *i* South of P. Vittorio Emanuele II. ☼ Ticket office open 6am-9pm, but there is always a long line; check out the 24hr. self-service machines.) Trains run to and from Florence (€7.80 ☼ 1-1¼hr.; 6 trains daily to Florence 4:15am-10:30pm, from Florence 7am-10:25pm), Rome (€23-51 depending on speed, but there's not much difference. ☼ 4hr., approximately every hr. 5:45am-7:56pm), and Lucca (€3.30. ☼ 27min.; approximately every hr. 6am-8pm). If leaving from San Rossore, Pisa's secondary station is in the northwest area of town; buy tickets at *tabaccherie.*

BY BUS

Aucostradaze Ryanair (€7.50) and **Terravision** (€6. ☎44 68 94 239 www.terravision.eu/florence_pisa.html) run buses between Pisa's airport and Florence, while **Lazzi** (☎058 35 84 876 www.lazzi.it) and **CPT** (☎050 50 55 11 www.cpt.pisa) run buses that leave from and arrive in P. Sant'Antonio. (☼ Ticket office open daily 7am-8:15pm.) Buses leave from Florence's Santa Maria Novella bus station. (*i* From the train station, take a left onto V. Alamanni; the station is on the left by a long driveway. (€6.10. ☼ 1¼hr., 1 per hr.) Buses to Lucca leave from Pisa Airport and run to and from P. Giuseppe Verdi in Lucca. (€4.40min., 1 per hr.) You can also easily take a bus to Marina di Pisa. (*i* From under the west side of the archway in P. Vittorio Emanuele II, follow as it veers left to find the buses. €2. ☼ 25min., every 20min.)

italy

Getting Around

ON FOOT

There's little need for anything but your feet while you're in Pisa. From the train station to P. dei Miracoli—the longest diameter of the city and also the route you're most likely to take—is about a 20-25min. walk, depending on the route.

BY BUS

LAM ROSSA runs a loop between the airport, train station, tower, and several other points in Pisa every 20min. (€1.10). Most buses stop at P. Sant'Antonio, just west of P. Vittorio Emanuele II. You can purchase bus tickets at *tabaccherie* or at ticket machines at Pisa Centrale and Galileo Galilei airport.

BY TAXI

RadioTaxi (☎050 54 16 00). There are taxi stands at the airport, Pisa Centrale, and P. del Duomo.

BY BIKE

Pisa is somewhat less bike-friendly than other Tuscan cities, with lanes that tend to disappear right when you actually need them. Rentals are available at **Eco Voyager.** (V. Uguccione della Faggiola 41 ☎050 56 18 39 www.ecovoyager.i *i* €4 per hr., €12 per day, €50 per week. ⏰ Open daily 9am-noon.)

lucca

Ask a native of Lucca to compare Florence to his beloved hometown, and he is likely to mutter dismissively about canine excrement. The fiercely proud Lucchesi have every reason to be protective of their little fortified Brigadoon, as it is everything Florence is not: musical, uncrowded, green, and slow-paced. You can throw away your map here and get lost—the walls will keep you safe as you wander labyrinthine alleys, distinctive *piazze*, and bicycling Lucchesi balancing cappuccinos. Those amazingly intact 16th-century walls that hug the city not only provide a gorgeous 4km stroll but also keep out most cars and two-days-per-country Round-the-Worlders. As the birthplace of Puccini, Lucca is an extremely musical city, with at least one concert every day of the year—your first stop might be at one of the ubiquitous poster kiosks to find out which university choir is touring through town that day. *Let's Go* recommends staying at least a night or two in Lucca—you don't want to miss the walls at sunset. And while these walls are undoubtfully the best thing the town has, it's still worth it venturing out and to the north: walk out Porta S. Maria and follow V. Borgo Gianotti for some modern shopping and, a few blocks later, a nice river stroll.

ORIENTATION

When you look at a map, you'll see a big, square-shaped area inside the ellipse of Lucca's walls. This square marks the original Roman city boundaries; inside it, streets form a surprisingly reliable grid. If they suddenly begin to spiral in on themselves, you are probably nearing the **Piazza Anfiteatro** in the north. Coming from the station, you will most likely enter from the south, passing Lucca's **Duomo.** A little west from here is **Piazza Napoleone,** the heart of community life. The other major gateway to the town is **Piazzale Verdi**—if you're here, it means you're in the westernmost part of the city. **Via Fillungo,** lined with posh shops and department stores, runs roughly north-south until it starts veering east into that wacky Anfiteatro zone. East of the canal on **Via del Fosso,** you'll find the city's "new" section, a 16th-century extension. The walls, of course, are always all around you.

get a room!

There's just one hostel in town, but it's big enough to accommodate everyone. Otherwise, you can find a cozy room in one of Lucca's 54 (and counting) bed and breakfasts for what you'd spend on a hostel in Florence. However, if you come in July, every bed in town will likely be stocked with music lovers: Lucca's **Summer Festival** attracts surprisingly big names for such a tiny town. The lone hostel, as well as a particularly worth-it B&B, are listed below; more accommodations can be found on **www.letsgo.com**.

▩ LA GEMMA DI ELENA   B&B $$
V. della Zecca 33   ☎0583 49 66 65 www.lagemmadielena.it

Most bed and breakfasts feel like they were decorated by your kooky aunt. This one feels like it was decorated by that awesome guy from college who lived in Tibet and now writes an antiquing blog. It's spacious yet cluttered in an utterly lived-in way, with colorful sarongs on the wall and a wind chime hanging from the chandelier. Each room has a distinct character and name—"Zelda," for example, has a crystal ball. Since Italian breakfast generally consists of one croissant, the B&B's buffet of bread, Nutella, jam, pastries, lunch meat, and cheese is a great incentive to get out of bed.

i Off V. del Fosso. Free Wi-Fi. Guests receive a key to the front door. Breakfast available 8:30-10am. Parking available. Pets welcome. Single €35; doubles €65-90. ⏰ Reception open until the last guest arrives.

OSTELLO SAN FREDIANO (HI)   HOSTEL $
V. della Cavallerizza 12   ☎0583 46 99 57 www.ostellolucca.it

Once upon a time, as you'll often find in Italy, this place was a monastery of the San Frediano church. It's unknown whether that saint was an avid traveler, but bless him anyway because not-so-touristy Lucca now has an enormous HI hostel. By enormous, we mean it looks ready to host five or six school groups to fill the vast courtyard and lavish common rooms.

i Just past V. San Frediano. It's the only hostel in town, so you can safely follow the Ostello signs. Free Wi-Fi in the lobby. Lockers included. Dorms €20, with bath €22 (mixed and gender-separated); doubles €65; triples €80; quads €105; quints €115. ⏰ Lockout 10am-2pm.

SIGHTS

The main sight in Lucca is the town itself. While you wander, there are several places of interest to explore. The **Basilica di San Frediano**, with its splendid Byzantine Jesus mosaic, displays the desiccated corpse of St. Zita in a glass case (kind of like a gruesome Snow White). The elliptical **Piazza Anfiteatro** was once the site of a Roman amphitheater. The **Torre dell'Ore** has been rented to clock-runners since 1390 and allows you to climb past the clock's inner workings, while the **Torre Guinigi** has tiny trees on top. We suggest you enjoy the towers from the ground, though, as don't provide Tuscany's most spectacular views. (*i* 1 tower €3, students and over 65 €2; 2 towers €5/4. Torre dell'Ore open daily June-Sept 9:30am-7:30pm; Oct-May 9:30am-6:30pm. Torre Guinigi open daily May-Sept 9am-midnight; Oct-Feb 9am-5pm; Mar-Apr 9am-7:30pm.)

▩ THE WALLS   WALLS
Some cities have a park. This park has a city. Lucca's walls were built as fortification in the second half of the 16th century. Despite all their ramparts, sally ports, and cavaliers, though, they never had to face an enemy worse than the flood of 1812. Today, the 4.2km of walls are mossy and tree-covered, and the

italy

old army quarters now serve as public facilities, cafeterias, and study centers. At any time of the day or evening, the town's residents can be found jogging or hanging out on the beautiful fortifications. Metaphorically, the walls continue to be a defense—they guard this Tuscan Atlantis from the outside world, protecting the tiny city's rhythm from being disrupted by the frantic tick-tock of modernity. "Once it was a place for military protection," says the city's official guide to the walls, "and now it protects memories."

i *Walk away from the town center and you're certain to hit them. For more info, visit the Opera delle Mura at Castello Porta San Donato Nuova (0583 58 23 20 www.operadellemura.it) or just pick up the guide to the walls from the tourist office.*

▨ PIAZZA NAPOLEONE   PIAZZA

Lucca is a small town with a huge heart. And while we do not diminish the town's charm and the friendliness of its citizens, Piazza Napoleone might just be the most appealing part of the city. Lucca's heart, P. Napoleone, is green, L-shaped, and has a lit-up carousel. It's tranquil on most days but blows up every time there's need for celebration, including the **Summer Festival** (p. 622) in July.

i *Just above the southern center walls. Free.*

DUOMO DI SAN MARTINO   CHURCH

P. di San Martino   ☎0583 49 05 30 www.museocattedralelucca.it

The Duomo di San Martino is a palace in a matchbox: you'll never know from the simple rectangular façade where all that glorious space on the inside comes from. Inside, a long-bearded Christ is crucified in a huge golden cage. You can also visit the **Tomb of Illyria** and the oldest surviving marble carving by Renaissance artist Jacopo della Quercia. Next door in P. Antelminelli, the **Museo della Cattedrale** displays graduals and other sparkly things from the Middle Ages to the 15th century.

i *From P. Napoleone, take V. Duomo. Duomo free. Baptistery €3, groups and children €2. Combined ticket to the baptistery, Tomb of Ilyria, and museum €7; groups and kids €5; family ticket (2 adults, 2 children) €20. ☒ Open M-F 9:30am-5:45pm, Sa 9:30am-6:30pm, Su 9:30-10:45am and noon-6pm. No tourist visits to the cathedral during Mass.*

PUCCINI OPERA   MUSEUM

V. Santa Giustina 16   ☎0583 95 58 24 www.pucciniopera.it

Though the information panels are rather dry, this free museum will help you understand why Puccini is important to Lucca and to opera in general. Peruse vintage poster art, costume design sketches, and souvenir schlock from the original runs of masterpieces like *Turandot, La Bohème, Madame Butterfy,* and *Tosca;* hear numbers from Gallone's cinematic interpretations of the operas; and read (but don't understand, unless you speak Italian) letters to and from the maestro himself. To extend the Puccini pilgrimage, grab one of the red postcards that bears his signature bowler hat and mustache for directions to his childhood home, which is not open to the public. The postcards also indicate the birthplace of legendary cellist Boccherini, in vain hope that someone cares.

i *Off P. San Salvatore. Free. ☒ Open M 10am-7pm, W-Su 10am-7pm.*

LU.C.C.A.   MUSEUM

V. della Fratta 36   ☎0583 57 17 12 www.luccamuseum.com

The full name of Lu.C.C.A is Lucca Center of Contemporary Art, proving that Lucca is as good at acronyms as it is at everything else. Those who like white-on-white designs and signs that say things like "this is the narrative plot of a peripheral network that harks back to the omnivorous particles of a tentacular research" will adore this museum. For everyone else, it's still a fascinating stage

lucca

for the latest avant-garde and experimental modern art, particularly in the realms of material and technique.

i At the intersection of V. Santa Gemma Galgani, V. della Zecca, and V. dei Fossi. Prices vary, but exhibits run from free to €10, sometimes with student discounts. ☑ Open Tu-Su 10am-7pm. Last entry 6pm.

PALAZZO PFANNER   MUSEUM

V. degli Asili 33   ☎0583 95 40 29   www.palazzopfanner.it

Those *nouveau-riches* of the 19th century certainly knew how to display wealth. At Palazzo Pfanner, before you even enter the museum itself, the statues lined up in the garden will lead you to an even more impressive fountain. What's inside is even more interesting, and the items collected here offer a more curious selection than you might expect. Prepare for a quirky mix of beer-brewing tools, vaginal irrigators, lemon trees, and Jesus sculptures. The visit is quick, but it's certainly unique.

i Near the San Frediano gate in the walls. Palazzo €4.50; students, ages 12-16, and over 65 €4. Garden €4.50/4. Combined ticket €6/5. Under 12 free. ☑ Open daily Apr-Oct 10am-6pm.

FOOD

Many of Lucca's loveliest dining spots are tucked into alleyways and hidden courtyards, but just follow lines of candles or paper lanterns, and they're easy to find. During the day, fresh produce, meat, and fish are available in **Piazza del Carmine** (open M-Sa 8am-1:30pm). Lucchese specialties tend to be pasta, such as the meat-filled *tortelli alla Lucchese.* You should also be aware that if you're coming from Florence, the gelato in Lucca is nothing to get excited about, so take a break from your regular treat and gorge on Nutella crepes, baked goods, and fruit-filled yogurt instead. However, locals sometimes add a jolt to their gelato with alcohol sundaes/granites, so look out for those specials.

SAN COLOMBANO   RISTORANTE, CAFETERIA $$

Baluardo di San Colombano   ☎0583 46 46 41   www.caffetteriasancolombano.it

Like all other establishments that scored a spot in an exceptionally unique and picturesque place, San Colombano is very proud of itself, for better and for worse. This pride results in fancy dishes and lots of seating spaces both outside and inside in a curving glass hall. But don't expect to savor your gnocchi with crab and mint (€12) while overlooking the views from the walls: "outside" means a small courtyard tucked inside the middle of the restaurant. Still, huge salads and experimental pizza combos "for those who want to dare" are worth a dinner here—try the pizza with tomatoes, two cheeses, and pears.

i Atop the wall, in the southeast at San Colombano. Cover €2. Pizza €5.50-9. Primi €8-14. ☑ Open Tu-F 8am-1am, Sa 8am-2am.

PIZZERIA BELLA MARIANA   PIZZERIA $

V. della Cavallerizza 29   ☎0583 49 55 65

Pizzeria Bella Mariana has the best pizza around, hands-down. You're expected to order at the desk and clean up after yourself, but this just means a lower price for the freshly fired pizza. Try the eggplant Pizza Siciliana. This is a great place to pick up some to-go pizza that you can eat while watching the sunset from the city walls.

i Across from the Ostello San Frediano. Pizza €5-8. ☑ Open M 12:30-2:30pm and 6:30-11:30pm, W-F 12:30-2:30pm and 6:30-11:30pm.

ANTICO SIGILLO   RISTORANTE $$

V. degli Angeli 13   ☎0583 91 042   www.anticosigillo.it

If magical forces brewed an essence of Lucca, after the vapor cooled down, they'd find Antico Sigillo. This place is located on a quiet street off the main touristic route and emits peaceful moods with it's light-colored and relaxing design. Moreover, it only serves local dishes, with gourmet specialties like *tortelli alla Lucchesi* with meat "inside and outside of pasta."

i *Off V. Fillungo. Free Wi-Fi. Cover €1.50. Primi €7.50-10. Chef's specials €8-15. Dessert €5.50.* ☒ *Open daily noon-10:30pm.*

FORNO ALIMENTARI G.GIURLANI
V. Fillungo 239
GROCERY STORE $
☎0583 49 62 33

When food places start to prey on your budget, head straight to this grocery store that is stuffed to the ceiling with everything from ham to local pastries to milk products to pre-cooked soups and dishes. Tip: even though there's no sign of pressed sandwiches, ask for a panini, and one will be made in front of your eyes just for €2. *Let's Go* recommends taking your food through the nearby walls and onto Baluardo S. Martino to enjoy it at a wooden picnic table. No *ristorante* in Lucca can offer such a view.

i *Just off P. S. Maria. Pastries from €0.40. Fruit from €1.50 per portion. Panini €2.* ☒ *Open daily 7am-2pm and 4-8pm.*

NIGHTLIFE

Nice bars and *enoteche* dot the old city, but **Piazza San Michele, Piazza San Frediano,** and the intersection of **Via Vittorio Veneto** and **Corso Garibaldi** are your best bet. Lucca is not the place to get your pre-game on and dance'til dawn, but it's a welcoming town for laid-back drinking and mingling. If there's a reason for celebration, you'll find the whole town out and about in **Piazza Napoleone.**

🔲 LELEMENTO
V. Carrara 16
ENOTECA, BISTROT
☎0583 49 32 04

While we at *Let's Go* debate the difference between minimalism and simply "not bothering to decorate," the black-and-white walls here are pleasing enough. And really, the important thing about Lelemento is that it keeps its doors open for *aperitivo* and the socializing that continues late into the night. To people watch and meet some locals, come between 7:30 and 8:30pm, when this place is at its busiest. Later hours will feature less of a crowd, but the alcohol will be relatively cheap regardless of the hour.

i *Across from Baluardo Santa Maria. Bottled beer €4. Cocktails €5. Live music on Fridays.* ☒ *Open M-F 7pm-1am, Sa 7pm-2am, Su 7pm-1am.*

BETTY BLUE CAFE
V. del Gonfalone 16/18
BAR
☎0583 49 21 66 www.betty-blue.eu

Although this place offers access to computers and Wi-Fi, this covert internet cafe is also a nice nightlife spot. If the weather is nice, guests of this bar mingle outside, while rainy evening see everyone lounging around inside on red plastic chairs. Up-to-date pop radio hits attract a younger crowd, but the prices keep the true youths away.

i *Between V. della Zecca and Porte dei Borghi, just behind the fountain. Draw beer €6. Cocktails €7-8. Internet €1.50 per 15min., €3.50 per hr. Free Wi-Fi.* ☒ *Open M-Tu and Th-F 5pm-1am, Sa 5pm-2am, Su 5pm-1am.*

GELATERIA GELATIAMO
Corso Garibaldi 42
GELATERIA
☎0583 46 95 13

Why can't a *gelateria* be a nightlife location? Think of it: a) sundaes with vodka and whiskey; b) corner pit-stop location that draws crowds after dark; c) gelato in Lucca is just like bar food that tastes even better when you've got the right chemicals in your system. Forget the cheap potato chips and venture over to Gelateria Gelatiamo the next time you're feeling a case of the drunchies.

i *At the intersection of V. Vittorio Veneto and Corso Garibaldi. Yogurt and gelato cones from €1.60. Sundaes €3-4.* ☒ *Open daily 10:30am-1am.*

ARTS AND CULTURE

Lucca is an extremely musical town. The **Puccini Festival** ensures at least one performance every day of the year, and summer time sees an explosion of concerts and musical events. Additionally, the town is a popular destination for university choirs and orchestras on tour, so stop by the box office at **Teatro Verdi**, visit www.comune.lucca. it, or take a look at one of the many poster kiosks to see what's happening during your visit. If you're here on a Friday night in the summer, you should also stop by the **Orto Botanico** (V. del Giardino Botanica 14) for free candlelit musical performances.

PUCCINI E LA SUA LUCCA OPERA
Chiesa di San Giovanni ☎0583 32 70 41 www.puccinielasualucca.com
We hope hometown hero **Giacomo Puccini** loves fame and glory (and occasional yawning)—here in Lucca, he's celebrated every single night of the year with recitals of his arias and art songs. Sometimes they spice it up with some Mozart and Verdi. Either way, this is the only permanent festival in the world, ensuring that every visiting tourist has a chance to be converted into a Puccini obsessive.
i Off V. Duomo. Coming from P. Napoleone, it's the church on the left before the Duomo. Concerts €20, students under 23 €16. 15% discount if you buy before 6pm at the official ticket point. Galas and staged opera performances €15-40. Advance sales online or at authorized festival sales points. ☒ All performances are at 7pm. Tickets sold at Chiesa di San Giovanni daily 10am-6pm.

SINGING OF THE TREES CLASSICAL MUSIC
Giardino Botanico ☎0583 58 31 50 www.comune.lucca.it
If you're lucky enough to be in Lucca on a Friday night in June, July, or August, you should be here for *Il canto degli alberi*. The city's botanical garden hosts chamber music concerts on Friday nights at 9:30pm during the summer. It's a great way to share in Lucca's passion for music without overly saturating yourself in too much Puccini. Better still, the whole garden is open and illuminated with candles along the pathways.
i In the botanical garden in the southeast corner of the city €3; disabled, under 14, and over 65 free. ☒ Performances in summer F 9:30pm.

SUMMER FESTIVAL FESTIVAL
P. Anfiteatro ☎0584 46 477 www.summer-festival.com
It's a true wonder how Lucca remains a quiet little town, unspoiled by tourist trash, despite hosting this summer festival. In July, P. Napoleone and P. Amphiteatro become mass concert stages for the latest names in music. This festival recruits a number of big names: previous line-ups have included The Killers, 30 Seconds To Mars, and Amy Winehouse. Some of the concerts are free, so check out who's playing while you're in town.
i Gates and seating vary by concert, but all are based out of P. Anfiteatro. Prices vary, but generally €30-100, with a couple free concerts each year. ☒ Concerts every few days in Jul.

ESSENTIALS
Practicalities

- **TOURIST OFFICES: Centro Accoglienza Turistica,** the main branch of Lucca's primary tourist office, schedules guided tours and provides audio tours, information about events, and internet access, including Wi-Fi (when it's working). (Ple. Verdi ☎0583 58 31 50 www.luccaitinera. it *i* Look for the "i" sign on the left. ☒ Open daily 9am-7pm.) **Ufficio Regionale** has accommodations booking assistance. (P. Santa Maria 35 ☎0583 46 99 64Look for the"i" sign on the right. ☒ Open late Jun-late Dec.)

- **CURRENCY EXCHANGE:** There is no currency exchange in town, and local bank branches provide this service to clients only.

- **ATMS: UniCredit Banca.** (*i* Corner of Viale Agostino Marti and V. San Paolino. 50m from the bank, off Ple. Verdi. ☼ Open 24hr.) **Deutschebank.** (*i* Corner of V. Fillungo and V. Mordini. ☼Open 24hr.)

- **LAUNDROMATS: Lavanderia Niagara.** (V. Michele Rosi 26 ☎349 16 45 084 *i* Off P. San Michele. ☼ Open daily 7am-11pm.)

- **INTERNET: Tourist offices** all provide computers with internet. The office at Ple. Verdi has Wi-Fi. **Betty Blue** internet cafe has both computers and Wi-Fi and keeps the longest hours. (V. del Gonfalone 16/18 ☎0583 49 21 66 www.bettybluelucca.it *i* Between V. della Zecca and Porte dei Borghi €1.50 per 15min., €3.50 per hr. Wi-Fi free. ☼ Open M-Tu 5pm-1am, Th-F 5pm-1am, Sa 5pm-2am, Su 5pm-1am.) Wi-Fi is also available at the **train station** in Ple. Ricasoli.

Emergency

- **POLICE: Polizia Municipale.** (Ple. San Donato 12 ☎0583 44 27 27 *i* At the westernmost point inside the walls.) **Carabinieri.** (Cortile degli Svizzeri 4 ☎0583 46 78 21 *i* In the southwest area of the *centro*.)

- **LATE-NIGHT PHARMACIES: Farmacia Comunale.** (P. Curatone 7 *i* Outside the city walls, opposite Baluardo San Colombano. ☼ Open 24hr.)

- **HOSPITALS/MEDICAL SERVICES: Campodi Marte.** (V. dell'Ospedale ☎0583 95 57 91 *i* Outside the city walls, northeast of the city. ☼ Open 24hr.)

Getting There

BY TRAIN

To get to Lucca from Florence, the train is your most reliable option. Take the Viareggio train—Lucca is the third to last stop before Viareggio. You can order your ticket (€7) from the self-service kiosk or the window. Validate your ticket before boarding by stamping it in the small green machine by your train. You will arrive in Ple. Ricasoli, just south of the city walls. (☼ Station open M-F 4:30am-12:30am, Sa-Su 5:30am-12:30am. Ticket office open daily 7am-7pm.) Direct trains run back to Florence (€7. ☼ 80min., 2 per hr. 5:05am-10:31pm.) and Pisa. (€3. ☼ 30min., 2 per hr. 7am-9:42pm.)

BY BUS

Take the **Vaibus** (☎0583 58 78 97 www.vaibus.it) from the Florence bus terminal. (*i* From the left side of the train station, take the 1st left and walk up the block. The terminal is on the left.) You'll arrive in Ple. Verdi. (€6. ☼ 1½hr., 1-2 per hr.)

Getting Around

BY TAXI

RadioTaxi (☎0583 02 53 53). Taxi stands (marked with codes identifying the pick-up point) can be found at the train station, P. Napoleone, P. Santa Maria, and Ple. Verdi.

BY BUS

Lucca offers both suburban buses and seven town buses around the city, all run by the company **CLAP** (☎0583 54 11 www.clapspa.it). You can catch pretty much any bus at Ple. Verdi, just inside the west side of the city walls. Buses stop running around 8pm. Ticket prices depend on your destination but start as low a €1.

BY BIKE

You'll find the same rates and hours at each of the major rental places around town. (*i* Street bike €3 per hr., €15 per day; mountain bikes €4/20; tandem bikes €5.50 per hr. ☼ Open daily 9am-7:30pm.) Here are some places to rent bikes: **Poll Antonio Biciclette** (P. Santa Maria 42 ☎0583 49 37 87), **Promo Tourist** (Porta San Pietro ☎348 38 00 126), and the **tourist office** in Ple. Verdi.

naples

Naples takes all of your preconceptions, pumps them full of steroids, and then makes you fall in love. Roman footsteps echo in the streets, and local conversations float from balcony to balcony; meanwhile, ancient amphitheater columns poke out from modern plaster, underground markets bustle with activity beneath dramatic *piazze*, and medieval churches soar to astonishing heights in inconceivably tight quarters. Even the grit and grime of Naples's alleyways become beautiful and endearing. Naples has no Colosseum, but it wasn't for nothing that UNESCO recently deemed the city's historic center a World Heritage Site. This port city was once the most important point of entry to western Italy and remains one to this day. Traces of its prior inhabitants grace both the streets and castles that breathe in the coastal air. Naples's fast pace may make it difficult to appreciate it all, but spare a few extra moments of your whirlwind time, slow down, and give this city the look that it deserves.

ORIENTATION

Centro Storico and Stazione Centrale

Naples's transit hub, Stazione Centrale, opens onto the vast, asphalt-and-exhaust-fumes expanse of **Piazza Garibaldi,** full of vendors and traffic that stops for no one. Hotels surround the *piazza* and line the nearby streets, but none of them are sarcastic enough to advertise "a room with a view." Head west during waking hours to find the Centro Storico. Also known as **Spaccanapoli,** this is Naples's oldest neighborhood, filled with tiny alleys, beautiful architecture, and a multitude of churches and chapels. This is what the tried and true locals call home. The **Duomo,** on the eponymously named via, is the religious center of the city. From the Duomo, you'll want to head back downhill toward the water and turn right onto V. San Biagio dei Librai. This street cuts straight through the **Piazza Gesu Nuovo** and, after passing five or six of the must-sees in Naples, eventually intersects with **Via Toledo,** one of the nicest walks in town.

Western Naples

The neighborhoods get nicer as you move farther away from the train station. **Piazza del Plebiscito,** home to the Palazzo Reale and a stunning church, is the unmistakable focal point of this part of town, and it's enormous. If you head up and out of its northern corner, you'll see the skylight-roofed shopping palace, Galleria Umberto I, straight ahead. The street to the left is V. Toledo; follow it for a few minutes to reach the **Spanish Quarter,** a cluster of streets with no specific boundaries that are always energetic, cramped, and loud. From P. del Plebiscito, a walk along the water will lead to to **Chiaia,** a fashionable, slightly more residential, and beautiful district of Naples. From Chiaia, most everything uphill comprises another classy, quiet neighborhood called **Vomero.** Best reached by any of the funiculars that sloth their way up the hill, Vomero is the place to head for some nice parks (Parco Virgiliano is a bit of a hike but very nice), better views, and a couple great museums.

SIGHTS

The Greeks, Romans, and Spanish have each left a unique mark on this remarkable metropolis. Along the water and nestled in the hills, ancient ruins, medieval castles and equally formidable churches like the **Chiesa di Gesu Nuovo** testify to the city's long history, while the winding streets make wandering easier and more enjoyable than following a strict itinerary.

naples

Naples will court you with a neon junkyard of hotel lights before you take five steps out of the Stazione Centrale. Hotels in these parts sacrifice general pleasantry for relative cheapness, but you should be careful when returning home at night. Below are some options Let's Go is fond of; you can find more at **www.letsgo.com**.

HOSTEL OF THE SUN   HOSTEL $
V. Guglielmo Melisurgo 15, 7th fl.   ☎081 42 06 393 www.hostelnapoli.com

Pop art on the walls and Peroni bottles in the fridge. Welcome home. This is a famously fun hostel, and the amusing staff, young crowd, and happy hour every night will make sure you always know where the party is. When you're not spending your time at the colorful bar or kicking ass on the Wii, carve out some time to explore the area with one of the organized daytrips, which range from checking out Capri to kayaking in the Bay of Naples to oh-so-classy wine tastings.

i From P. Garibaldi, take Tram #1 to the last stop. Alternatively, take the R2 bus from Corso Umberto I near the train station to the 2nd stop on V. Depretis. Free Wi-Fi. A/C. Breakfast and lockers included. 3- to 7-bed dorm €16-20; doubles €50-60, with bath €60-70; triples with bath €80-90. 10% Let's Go discount. ⚅ Reception 24hr.

HOTEL AND HOSTEL BELLA CAPRI   HOTEL, HOSTEL $
V. Guglielmo Melisurgo 4   ☎081 55 29 494 www.bellacapri.it

If the blue neon sign doesn't lure you in, the pictures of Capri lining the walls and summer beach house feel certainly will. Don't expect too much of a party hostel here, although nights are still lively, and you can always spend your evenings at bars in the *centro*. You only need to be up about 10min. before your ferry leaves anyway.

i From P. Garibaldi, take Tram #1 to the last stop. Alternatively, take the R2 bus from Corso Umberto I near the train station to the 2nd stop on V. Depretis. Free Wi-Fi. A/C. Dorm €15-21; singles €40-50, with bath €50-70; doubles €50-60/60-80; triples €70-80/80-100; quads €80-90/90-110. 10% Let's Go discount.

HOSTEL MANCINI   HOSTEL, PENSIONE $
V. Pasquale Stanislao Mancini 33 ☎081 55 36 731 www.hostelpensionemancini.com

It's right by the central station, and the hospitality of this family-run hostel will still make you feel more than welcome. Colorful, spacious rooms; flags on the walls; IKEA dream housekitchens; comfy common rooms: leave the ghetto surrounding the station behind and come here for luxury. Hostel Mancini's owner and his wife are kind and very helpful and create a small, tight-knit community.

i Directly across the piazza from the station. Free Wi-Fi. Breakfast included. A/C. Dorm €16-20; singles €30-45, with bath €40-50; doubles €40-50/50-70; triples €54-72/60-80; quads €64-80/70-90. 10% Let's Go discount. Cash only.

Centro Storico and Stazione Centrale

NAPOLI SOTTERRANEA (UNDERGROUND NAPLES)   ANCIENT ROME
P. San Gaetano 68   ☎081 29 69 44 www.napolisotterranea.org

Sunlight is too mainstream. Head underground. At Napoli Sotterranea, you'll be given a chance to take a tour along a labyrinth of Greek aqueducts, World War II bomb shelters, and secret nun/monk rendezvous areas, all of which are now empty (or so the nuns claim). If claustrophobia isn't one of your psychological issues (let's be honest, you just want to be held), take the narrow, candlelit tunnel walk to two beautiful blue grottoes left from the old aqueducts. It's the most cold, dark, and wet fun you'll ever have.

i Take V. dei Tribunali; the entrance is to the left of San Paolo Maggiore church.1½hr. tours depart every 2hr. €9.30, students €8. Cash only. ☒ Open M-F noon-4pm, Sa-Su 10am-6pm.

MUSEO ARCHEOLOGICO NAZIONALE   MUSEUM, ANCIENT ROME
P. Museo Nazionale 19   ☎081 29 28 23 http://museoarcheologiconazionale.
campaniabeniculturali.it

The saying is that more of Pompeii is here than in Pompeii. And after walking in, that's not hard to believe. This museum boasts a gorgeous and enormous collection of ancient sculptures, paintings, pottery, and mosaics. Start out in the Farnese Gallery, home to sculptures of emperors, Venuses, and the famous Farnese Weary Hercules. Next, either head up to see one of the most famous and vast collections of Roman wall paintings in the world, including the so-called "Sappho," or go straight to see every mosaic that has ever appeared in your Latin textbooks, from the beloved "Cave Canem" to the enormous Alexander Mosaic. And no trip to this museum is complete without a peek into the Secret Cabinet, which has more ass-grabbing, doggy-styling action than you've ever seen. This area is full of giant stone members and straight-up pornographic paintings, so spend some time here appreciating the art and history alongside some elderly patrons.

i Ⓜ1: Museo €6.50, EU citizens ages 18-24 €3.25, under 18 and over 65 free. Audio tour in English €5. Cash only. ☒ Open M 9am-7:30pm, W-Su 9am-7:30pm.

PIO MONTE DELLA MISERICORDIA   MUSEUM
V. dei Tribunali 253   ☎081 44 69 44 www.piomontedellamisericordia.it

So you skimmed the part of the Bible that covered the Seven Works of Mercy. It's a good book, but you're a busy person. Don't worry. Caravaggio's masterpiece by the same name shows all seven works and will have you reveling in the beauty of art and God and all things merciful. It's a powerful, complex piece that the prayin' and slayin' Caravaggio made in Naplesafter fleeing Rome for murder. Everyone needs hobbies during exile. While his piece stands as the highlight of this bright and beautiful round church, take a look at the Renaissance and Baroque picture gallery across the street, too. You can never have too much culture for the price of one ticket.

i On V. dei Tribunali, before V. Duomo when coming from the station. Church free. Galleries €5, students €4. Audio tour included with museum admission. Cash only. ☒ Open M-Tu 9am-2:30pm, Th-Su 9am-2:30pm.

CAPPELLA SANSEVERO   MUSEUM
V. Francesco de Sanctis 19   ☎081 55 18 470 www.museosansevero.it

Tucked away in a little alley are the hidden treasures of Cappella Sansevero. Built in 1590 by the sick Duke of Torremaggiore as a convenient chapel in his garden (lifestyles of the rich and famous), this small chapel was filled up with beautiful sculptures and a breathtaking ceiling fresco. The main attraction, however, is the famous *Veiled Christ* by Antonio Corradini. A masterful work that turned a single block of marble into a clinging veil over detailed, tortured flesh, this sculpture is as powerful as it is beautiful. Also be sure to also check out the sacristy down below, which has metallic bodies with exposed arteries so you know exactly where your heart lies on lackluster wordplay.

i From V. Tribunali, take a left onto V. Nilo and the 2nd right onto V. de Sanctis Francesco €7, ages 10-25 €5, under 10 free. ☒ M 10am-5:40pm, W-Sa 10am-5:40pm, Su and holidays 10am-1:10pm.

Western Naples

The sights in Western Naples prove that this city has been around for a while. Remnants of its time as an important seat of royal power blend with pretty and commercial streets to create an excellent area for exploring.

🏛 MUSEO DI PALAZZO REALE   MUSEUM
P. del Plebiscito 1   ☎081 40 05 47

When thug life in Naples is getting too gritty for you, break out the posh accent and play royalty for a day at Palazzo Reale. A beautiful and luxurious palace with magnificent rooms and halls, huge red arches, and paintings lining the walls, this place was once the seat to Bourbon kings and Spanish viceroys who had a taste for all things fabulous. Wander past the old tapestries, elaborate chandeliers, and velvet-draped throne of former kings. The palace also houses the 1.5 million volume Biblioteca Nazionale, with the carbonized scrolls from Villa dei Papiri in Herculaneum (in case you wanted to do some light reading on your vacation).

i In P. del Plebiscito €4, students €2. When there are special exhibitions, prices rise to €10/7. Cash only. ☒ Open M-Tu 9am-8pm, Th-Su 9am-8pm.

BASILICA DI SAN FRANCESCO DI PAOLA   CHURCH
P. del Plebiscito 10   ☎081 76 45 133

The Basilica di San Francesco di Paola is an impressive "What up?" to the Palazzo Reale across the way. As the faux-Pantheon of Naples, the soaring interior—54m high and 34m in diameter— of this church is filled with statues of saints gesticulating to the pews in the center. After you've been kicked out by the constant stream of weddings that occur here, head outside and sit on the steps to get a lovely view of a hopefully non-erupting Vesuvius across the bay.

i The domed building in P. del Plebiscito. Modest dress required. Free. ☒ Open daily 8:30am-noon and 4-7pm.

MUSEO NAZIONALE DI CAPODIMONTE   MUSEUM
V. Miano 2   ☎081 74 99 111 http://museodicapodimonte.campaniabeniculturali.it

This museum is located in yet another beautiful palace, and the gardens outside have been transformed into playgrounds sheltered by palm trees for all the *bambini*. But step inside the museum and get a look at the famous Farnese collection, which contains works by celebrity crushes like Masaccio, Simone Martini, and Caravaggio. The building itself, filled with ballrooms and chandeliers, is as much of a sight as its works.

i Ⓜ Piazza Cavour, then bus C63 or R4 €7.50, 2-5pm €6.50, EU students ages 18-25 €3.80. Cash only. ☒ Open M-Tu 8:30am-7:30pm, Th-Su 8:30am-7:30pm. Last entry 6:30pm.

CASTEL SANT'ELMO   CASTLE, MUSEUM
V. Tito Angelini 20   ☎081 22 94 401

Climb up to this castle that looms above most vistas in Naples, and you'll finally get a chance to have everyone look up to you. Dreams do come true. And you'll also get a gorgeous panorama over Naples, the bay, and Vesuvius as you walk around the ramparts, so that's pretty cool, too. After you've gotten enough fresh air to last you the climb back down, stop by the Napoli Novecento Museum, also housed in this castle, where you can join everyone in pretending to understand all the profound modern art kept inside.

i In Vomero. From the funicular at P. Fuga, turn right up the steps and follow the signs along V. Morghen to the castle €5, EU students ages 18-25 €2.50. Cash only. ☒ Open M 8:30am-7:30pm, W-Su 8:30am-7:30pm. Last entry 6:30pm. Museum entry every hr. 9am-6pm.

FOOD

When in Rome, do as the Ròmans do. When in Naples, eat pizza. If you ever doubted that Neapolitans invented this crusty, celebrated pie, the city's *pizzerias* will take that doubt, beat it into a ball, spin it on their collective finger, cover it with sauce and mozzarella, and serve it to you alla margherita. Centro Storico is full of excellent choices, especially along **Via Tribunali.**

Centro Storico and Stazione Centrale

◪ VOGLIA DI GRAFFA
BAKERY **$**

V. Tribunali 363 ☎081 29 56 23

You cannot tell a lie. Gelato is great. But sometimes you need something more deep-fried and chocolate-filled. And by sometimes, we mean always. So stop by the tiny Voglia di Graffa to order up a *graffa* or some bonbons and realize that a donut by any other name is just as sweet. All orders are freshly made on the sleek red counters, letting you spend the longest five minutes of your life watching dough be rolled out, deep fried, shaken up in sugar, and filled with chocolate and cream. Then, you can finally take a bite into it and know that if heaven were made, it would taste like your *graffa*. Take it as a sign that a benevolent God exists. And then order seconds.

i Between V. Arti and V. San Paolo on V. dei Tribunali. Graffa €1-1.50. Bonbons €1.50-2. ◪ Open M-Sa 4pm-midnight, Su 5:30pm-midnight.

PIZZERIA DI MATTEO
PIZZERIA **$**

V. dei Tribunali 94 ☎081 45 52 62 www.pizzeriadimatteo.it

Whether you're being chased by the Mafia or the paparazzi, sometimes you just need pizza fast and on the go. So turn to the tiny Pizzeria di Matteo for a quick slice of some folded-up pizza from the takeaway counter. It will cost you a vast fortune of €1. But just because the pizza here is cheaper than water doesn't mean it's not delicious. This *pizzeria* even managed to lure in Bill Clinton with its cheesy charms. And Bill Clinton doesn't fool around.

i On V. dei Tribunali, near V. Duomo. No table service. Pizza €2.50-6. Takeaway slices €1. Aranci-na €0.50-1. ◪ Open M-Sa 9am-midnight.

FANTASIA GELATI
GELATERIA **$**

V. Toledo 381 ☎081 55 11 212 www.fantasiagelati.it

Bright lights, huge men in tiny pink hats, and a delicious selection of gelato. That's what we fantasize about, too. Here at Fantasia Gelati, wait out the large crowds for a chance to realize all your dreams. The standards like pistachio and strawberry are always awaiting your call, and you can try the kiwi when you need to feel exotic.

i ⓜ1: Dante. On V. Toledo, south of P. Dante. Other locations at P. Vitelli 22, V. Gilea 80, Largo Lala 30, and V. Fragnito 39. Cones €2-5, gluten-free €2. ◪ Open in summer daily 7am-1am; in fall, winter, and spring Tu-Su 7am-11pm.

◪ L'ANTICA PIZZA DA MICHELE
PIZZERIA **$**

V. Cesare Sersale 1/3 ☎081 55 39 204 www.damichele.net

This is one of the most famous *pizzerias* in Naples, and tourists start flocking here early in the morning to sit inside and stare at the one picture of Julia Roberts behind which delicious pizza is made. Hot. Prepare for long waits, brusque service, and only two options (marinara and Margherita), so if the fame alone isn't cutting it for you, come here for the incredibly cheap prices, large portions, and, well, pizza. You can decide if it's the best in the world, and even if it's not, pizza is always good.

i Walk down Corso Umberto I and turn right onto V. Cesare Sersale. Pizza €4-5. Cash only. ◪ Open M-Sa 10am-11pm.

naples

Western Naples

▨ HOSTERIA TOLEDO
RISTORANTE $$

Vicolo Giardinetto 78A   ☎081 42 12 57   www.hosteriatoledo.it

It's just like home! Except with more delicious food. With warm lighting, rustic checkered tables, and dark wooden furniture, this Hosteria certainly gets points for being as homey as you are homely. Serving up classic Neapolitan dishes ranging from rigatoni to pasta with octopus to some well-done steak, this place has long been a favorite of locals and not-so-locals alike. So come over and eat up, but be sure to save some room for *baba* later—it's everyone's favorite phallic pastry.

  i Take Vicolo Giardinetto off V. Toledo. Primi €6.50-8. Secondi €7-14. ☼ Open M 1-4pm and 7pm-midnight, Tu 1-4pm, Th-Su 1-4pm and 7pm-midnight.

▨ TRATTORIA NENNELLA
RISTORANTE $$

Vicolo Lungo Teatro Nuovo 104   ☎081 41 43 38

You know it's probably a famous restaurant when they sell their own postcards outside. The large open patio, checkered tables, and rustic wooden charm attract everyone from construction workers to bankers to elite *Let's Go* readers hungry for the cheap and delicious prix-fixe lunch. Eat up some homemade Neapolitan food, ranging from pasta to steak, and enjoy the small neighborhood ambience of the Spanish Quarter. There's sometimes confetti on the ground. Don't ask questions.

  i Off of V. Toledo; walk up Vicolo Teatro Nuovo and look for the signs near Vicolo Lungo Teatro Nuovo. Prix-fixe men €10. Cash only. ☼ Open Sept-Jul M-Sa noon-3pm and 7-10:30pm.

FRIGGITORIA VOMERO
BAKERY $

V. Domenico Cimarosa 44   ☎081 57 83 130

When you need some warm *graffa* in your tummy (but extra money in your pockets), head on over to Friggitoria Vomero. About as spartan as it gets, this small bakery is basically just a flour-dusted kitchen with some counters thrown in for good measure. Everything from the fried goodness that is the *arancini* to the cream-filled *cornetti* is delicious and so cheap that you really should just order everything. You'll burn those calories by walking up some mountain in Naples later anyway.

  i In Vomero. Head away from the funicular at P. Fuga and look across the square. Fried food €0.20-2. Panini €2.50. Cash only. ☼ Open M-Sa 9:30am-2:30pm and 5:30-8:30pm.

PIZZERIA GORIZIA
PIZZERIA $$

V. Bernini 29-31   ☎081 57 82 248   www.gorizia1916.com

Forget eating your folded-up pizza on the street. Since 1916, Pizzeria Gorizia has been serving up pizza *and* class with mosaicked pizza ovens, real glasses (your parents raised you better than plastic cups), and old-fashioned chandeliers like the ones back in your mansion. But leave the family jewels at home—the class here comes at no extra charge. The pizza is both delicious and inexpensive, and look out for daily deals that include pizza/pasta and a drink for €9.

  i In Vomero. From the funicular at P. Fuga, take V. Domenico Cimarosa to the left and turn right onto V. Bernini. Cover €1. Pizza €5-8. Primi €6-13. Secondi €8-15. ☼ Open Tu-Su 12:30-4pm and 6:30pm-midnight.

NIGHTLIFE

Centro Storico and Stazione Centrale are sketchy enough in the daytime. After dark, there are a few cafes that may be okay once you're inside, but we recommend looking farther west for safer nightlife options. The *centro* offers a smattering of bars and clubs throughout the area, and students tend to congregate (sometimes literally just to congregate) at the *piazza* on V. Enrico de Marinis, just off V. Mezzocannone, and near many of Naples's popular hostels.

NEA ART GALLERY

ART GALLERY, LOUNGE

V. Santa Maria di Constantinopoli 53   ☎081 45 13 58 www.spazionea.it

Everyone loves modern art in Naples. Just take a look at any building's walls. But if you'd rather look at the walls inside a building, with drink and carrot cake in hand, stop by Nea. Here you can join all the cool cats who like to wander this art gallery, which showcases both local artists as well as heartthrobs like Jackson Pollack. You can then meander your way over to the bar and lounge area to admire the art of cocktails while sitting on Victorian couches and discussing how much you love your MacBook. The relaxed space attracts an artsy crowd, and they stay up and are artsy until way past your bedtime. But stop by and be rebellious. For art.

i Ⓜ1: Dante. Walk through Porta Alba and turn left onto V. Santa Maria di Constantinopoli. Check online for upcoming exhibits and performances. Entry free. 🕐 Open daily 9am-1am.

ST. JAMES' IRISH PUB

IRISH PUB

P. Bellini 72   ☎081 56 67 288 www.stjamespub.it

For those days when you need tequila and hot chocolate at 4pm, head to St. James' Irish Pub. Though not much of an Irish pub apart from the wooden decor and, well, the large selection of alcohol (read: beer), it's as Irish as it needs to be. And when you need those famous Irish bruschetta and olive dishes, they're on the menu, too. But save your rowdiness for Ireland (or Rome)—this quiet bar with plenty of *piazza* seating is more of a quiet place to chat and end the day rather than to stay up and meet it.

i Ⓜ1: Dante. Walk through Porta Alba and turn left onto V. Santa Maria di Constantinopoli; the piazza is immediately on the right. Beer €4-5.50. Mixed drinks €7-8. Cash only. 🕐 Open daily 10am-2am.

Western Naples

If you follow the road from P. del Plebiscito down to the coast and around to Chiaia, you'll find a few good spots, but the other nightlife center is in the cluster of streets surrounding **Via Alabardieri** and **Via Bisignano**.

🕮 GOODFELLAS

BAR

V. Raffaele Morghen 34   ☎340 92 25 475 www.goodfellasclub.com

Naples is full of pizza and beer, but if the bald eagle on your passport still isn't satisfied, head over to Goodfellas. A classic American bar with good cover bands playing, Chicago Bulls jerseys, and alcohol will make you feel like you're at home in a room full of Italians. Because nothing brings out that national pride in you quite like sitting in a dark wooden bar, watching some good old American music videos, and downing beers like your college years taught you. God bless the USA.

i In Vomero. Up the stairs from the funicular in P. Fuga and to the left. 0.5L wine €3.50. Beer €5. Mixed drinks €7. 🕐 Open Tu-Su 8pm-2am.

🕮 S'MOVE

BAR

Vico dei Sospiri 10   ☎081 76 45 813 www.smove-lab.net

It's like a disco. Except without the dancing. So pretty much, it's just a dimly lit bar with loud house music playing. Good enough. It's still the closest you'll get to a disco in this area, so head over to S'Move to twerk your way through various rooms with sleek black couches and silver barstools while all the cool locals sip on cocktails and talk about how mesmerizing they find your dance. Because, really, what else could they be talking about?

i In Chiaia. From P. dei Martiri, take V. Alabardieri, then take the 2nd left. Beer €5. Mixed drinks €7-8. 🕐 Open daily 7pm-4am. Aperitivo 7-9pm.

naples

LES BELLES CHOSES PUB

V. Cesario Console 15/16   ☎081 24 51 166

Dim lighting, jazzy beats, Union Jacks, and copious amounts of alcohol. *Perfecto.*Just steps away from P. del Plebiscito, this pub's dark wooden interior and flat screen TVs get little attention in the summertime, as everyone crowds outside on the patio for a gorgeous view of the Bay of Naples instead. So order up that pub food and down a couple drinks, because you haven't really been to Naples until you've seen the breathtaking Vesuvius through beer goggles. Now that's *amore.*

i Just south of P. del Plebiscito. Beer €3-6. Mixed drinks €6.50. Panini and snacks €5-7. ② Open daily 6pm-2am.

ESSENTIALS
Practicalities

- **TOURIST OFFICES:** The **Ente Provinciale per il Turismo (EPT)** (P. dei Martiri 58 ☎081 41 07 211 www.eptnapoli.info ② Open M-F 9am-2pm) books rooms and provides free maps and the indispensible ◾**Qui Napoli,** which includes hotel and restaurant listings. Qui Napoli is also available online at www.inaples.it/ita/quinapoli.htm. **Azienda Autonoma di Soggiorno Cura e Turismo di Napoli.** (P. del Plebiscito 1 ☎081 25 25 711 www.inaples.it) **Infopoint Azienda Autonoma di Soggiorno Cura e Turismo di Napoli** has locations at P. del Gesù 7 (☎081 55 12 701) and V. San Carlo 9 (☎081 40 23 94).

- **LUGGAGE STORAGE: Stazione Centrale,** near Platform 5. (☎081 56 72 181 *i* €5 for up to 5hr.; €0.70 per hr. 6-12hr., €0.30 per hr. thereafter. ② Open daily 7am-11pm.)

- **INTERNET:** Internet points are clustered around V. Mezzocannone and P. Bellini. **Lemme Lemme by Internet Bar** offers free Wi-Fi. (P. Bellini 74 ☎081 29 52 37 *i* Computers €0.05 per min. ② Open M-Sa 9am-3am, Su 5pm-3am.)

- **POST OFFICES:** The main post office is located at V. Monteoliveto 53. (☎081 55 20 870 ② Open M-F 8am-6:30pm, Sa 8am-12:30pm.)

Emergency

- **POLICE: Polizia Municipale.** (☎081 75 13 177) **Polizia di Stato** can be found at V. Medina or P. Garibaldi 22, directly across the *piazza* from the station.

- **HOSPITALS/MEDICAL SERVICES: Incurabili** is more helpful than its name might suggest. (P. Cavour ☎081 25 49 422 *i* P. Cavour or Museo. The emergency room is directly up V. Maria Longo.)

Getting There
BY PLANE

Aeroporto Capodichino (NAP) is located in the northeast section of the city and offers access to the areas surrounding the Bay of Naples. (Vle. Fulco Ruffo di Calabria ☎081 84 88 87 73 or ☎081 75 15 471www.gesac.it ② Open daily 5:30am-11:30pm.) The red-and-white **Alibus shuttle** runs from the airport arrivals terminal to P. Garibaldi and to the seaport near P. Municio. (€3. ② 15-20min.)

BY TRAIN

Naples's main railway station is **Stazione Centrale,** located in P. Garibaldi. (② Open daily 6am-11pm.) Trains run directly from: **Bologna** (€50-76. ② 3½hr.-6½hr., every hr. 6:10am-9:50pm); **Florence** (€49-68. ② 3-5½hr., every 30min. 5:50am-9:50pm); **Herculaneum** (€2.10. ② 15-20min., every 15min.); **Milan** (€60-110. ② 4½-5hr., every hr. 6:00am-5:15pm); **Pompeii** (€2.80. ② 20-40min., every 30min.); **Rome** (€22-45. ② 1-3hr., every 30min.); **Sorrento** via Circumvesuviana train (€4. ② 1½hr., every 30min. 6am-11pm).

italy

Getting Around

All regional buses and trains are included in the **UnicoCampania** system (www.unico-campania.it). The **UnicoNapoliticket** is valid for all modes of transportation in Naples. (☎081 55 13 10 www.unicocampania.it) Tickets can be bought at newsstands and *tabaccherie*. (€1.20, full day €3.60, weekend €3, weekly €15.) Public bus lines criss-cross the city; most accommodations and tourist offices provide bus maps. Most buses run from 6:30am to just before midnight. Trams, like the public bus lines, run across the city. With typical Naples logic, the tram system currently comprises three routes: lines 1, 2, and 4. A number of companies operate the city's white taxis (☎081 88 88; ☎081 57 07 070; ☎081 55 60 202; ☎081 55 15 151). Only take official, licensed taxis with meters and always ask about prices upfront.

pompeii

If Rome isn't Roman enough for you, take a daytrip to Pompeii, the city buried in time. Sailing around the Bay of Naples, you'll see Mt. Vesuvius lurking formidably over nearly all vistas. On August 24, 79 CE, the volcano erupted, blanketing Pompeii in a cloud of ash. Though tragic for the residents of this ancient metropolis, the eruption created a gold mine for archaeologists and a historical playground for tourists. Streets covered in stone blocks, fading frescoes, chipped mosaics, and a labyrinth of small rooms may get repetitive after a few hours but nonetheless inspire thoughts about how different life was nearly two millennia ago.

ORIENTATION

The ruins cover 66 hectares of land, although only 45 are accessible to the public. The area around the Circumvesuviana, the Porta Marina entrance, and Piazza Esedra is full of expensive restaurants and souvenir shops. A 20-25min. walk down V. Plinio and then V. Roma leads to the modern city's centro. From here, the Trenitalia train station is down V. Sacra in P. XXVIII Marzo. Inside the ruins, the most important sights are located on the western side, closer to the Porta Marina entrance. These sights include the Forum and the House of the Faun. A little to the east is the old city's brothel, and at the far eastern corner, you'll find Pompeii's amphitheater. Working your way back from there toward the entrance, you'll pass the Great Theater on the southern edge of the ruins.

SIGHTS

One ticket gives you the run of an entire ancient city. But touring the ruins is no simple undertaking—Pompeii was a true metropolis, complete with basilicas, bars, and brothels, and that kind of scope can be intimidating. Plenty of tour guides will try to coerce you into joining their group, which will cost €10-20. Rather than shelling out to become one of the crowd, opt for an informative audio tour (€6.50, 2 for €10). While both options will teach you a lot, one of the most fun ways to experience Pompeii is to navigate its maze-like streets solo—even with a map, you're likely to get lost. Of course, the pleasure of going at it alone can be mitigated when the city is packed, and at times, it's hard to walk down one of Pompeii's cobbled streets without running into another visitor. Come in the early summer or the fall for a slightly less crowded experience. If you plan on seeing more sites, a combined ticket allows entry to Herculaneum, Oplontis, Stabia, Boscoreale, and Pompeii over the course of 3 days. (*i* €11, EU citizens ages 18-24 €5.50, EU citizens under 18 and over 65 free; combined ticket €20/10/free. Cash only. ☑ Open daily Apr-Oct 8:30am-7:30pm; Nov-Mar 8:30am-5pm. Last entry 1½hr. before close.)

Near the Forum

As soon as you enter through Porta Marina, you can get down to business at the main market district in Pompeii, complete with the Basilica, Temple of Venere, and Forum. Stand in the middle of the Forum and look left, and you'll get a beautiful view of Mt. Vesuvius looming above the city. Next, wander into the Granai del Foro, which has plaster body casts, including the famous one of the dog. But if these are all too mortal for your divine tastes, walk into the Tempio di Apollo, which has copies of the statues of Apollo and Artemis that once dominated the area (the OG versions are at the Naples's Museo Archeologico Nazionale). If you're feeling dirty (because the showers in your hostel are always full), check out the well-preserved baths in the Terme del Foro. It can count as your proper hygiene care for the week.

Near the House of the Faun

To see more luxuries than you're getting at your one-star hostel, invite yourself over to the Casa del Fauno, an enormous and impressive ancient Roman home. With a bronze faun statue explaining the name and various mosaics, the lack of the famous Alexander Mosaic may be heartbreaking, but it's still a spacious, luxurious old home. For more tastes of wealth, go to the House of the Small Fountain, which has a fountain (no plot twist there). But also take a look at the frescoes, mosaics, and small sculptures while you're here. To see things on a larger scale, go to the House of the Vettii, where you'll find the famous frescoes of a well-endowed Priapus, who holds his place as the elephant in the otherwise gorgeous red room.

Near the Brothel

If ruins and an ancient city haven't left you all hot and bothered, you're probably just hard to please. But go to the ancient brothel, the Lupanare, and try to not be a little turned on (by history, of course). The explicit frescoes on the wall displaying various sex positions were either used to get the clientele excited or to give them a list of services provided. Various stone beds (which were covered with mattresses) occupy the surrounding rooms that were once sprinkled with graffiti about the ladies (and their various) there. Nearby, the Stabian Baths have a body cast and more mosaics for those who prefer non-pornographic images.

Near the Great Theater

To make your visit to Pompeii even more dramatic, head to the Great Theater, where rowdy Romans once gathered to watch bawdy plays and summer rock and roll concerts. Or something like that. Nearby, the Small Theater was built for the hipsters in the city to gather and listen to poetry readings in an acoustically impressive structure. The Botanical Garden next door offers some natural wonders of the area (because nature isn't all explosions and volcanoes).

Near the Amphitheater

To see what Pompeii residents did for fun when they weren't dying, check out the massive amphitheater where they gathered to watch others die. Holding 20,000 spectators during gladiator battles, it's almost large enough to accommodate all the tourists getting in your personal space. The Great Palaestra nearby is a lovely place for respite where you can sit under some trees and feel one with nature before you head to the Garden of the Fugitives to dampen your mood with some more plaster casts of the less-than-fortunate Pompeii-ers. But if you're set on ending things on a happier note, walk through the House of Octavius Quartio and House of Venus before you leave, where horticulture will give you some symbolic understanding of man's control over nature. And maybe convince you to take up gardening. (Your mom will be so proud.)

ESSENTIALS

Practicalities

- **TOURIST OFFICES:** Offices at P. Porta Marina Inferiore 12 (☎081 53 63 293) and at V. Sacra 1 (☎081 85 07 255) offer free maps of Pompeii, tickets for sightseeing buses around Campania, and pamphlets about area museums. (www.pompeiturismo.it ✆ Open daily 8:30am-6:30pm.)

- **LUGGAGE STORAGE:** Bag check at the archaeological site is free and mandatory for large bags.

Emergency

- **POLICE:** Carabinieri in Pompei Centro at V. Lepanto 61. (☎081 85 06 163)

Getting There

The best way to get to Pompeii's archaeological site is to take a train to Naples's Stazione Centrale from Termini Station. (€11-45. ✆ 1-3hr., 50 per day 4:52am-9:50pm.) Once in Naples, go to the lower level to catch the Circumvesuviana train (€2.90. ✆ 20-30min., every 15min.) toward Sorrento. Get off at Pompei Scavi. From the train, the ruins' main entrance, Porta Marina, is to the right. If you proceed down V. Villa dei Misteri, you can head through the less crowded entrance at P. Esedra (although audio tours are not available here). Alternatively, you can take a Trenitalia train from Naples. (€2.90. ✆ 20-40min., every 30min.) The train drops you off in modern Pompeii's centro. From the station, walk up V. Sacra until you reach P. Bartolo Longo. Turn left down V. Colle San Bartolomeo. It's a 20-25min. walk to the archaeological site's main entrance; it's better to enter at the less crowded P. Anfiteatro, a short way down V. Plinio.

palermo

Palermo will take your idea of "sensibly organized cultural destinations" and send it on a flight to Ancient Christendom, then to the Muslim lands of Arabia, then to wherever the Normans were from, then back to good old Italia. Mosaic tiles shine with a luster that hasn't been lost in nearly 1000 years, ancient churches bear Arabic inscriptions alongside biblical passages, and a 15min. walk in any direction from the **Quattro Canti Fountain** will put you in neighborhoods that serve up Chinese, Indian, and Middle Eastern cuisine (and some darn good Sicilian pizza, too). Perhaps not everything in Palermo is out in the open, though; the underground "economy" (we'll call it that) still dictates some of the city's shadier business transactions, but fortunately it's stuff you won't find unless you go looking for it. Enormous urban renovations have started to clean up the parts of town that until now were falling apart and have done a great job of preserving the city's most priceless sites, but the heart and soul of this dynamic, crazy, lovable place are still as unshakable as the Godfather's stare.

ORIENTATION

Palermo's train station will spit you out onto one of the city's two main north-south drags, **Via Roma** and **Via Maqueda**. Shoppers head for the former; sightseers head for the latter. V. Maqueda cuts right through the distinctive **Quattro Canti Fountain,** a four-piece architectural oddity that surrounds the V. Maqueda-V. Emanuele intersection. Some of the city's most brilliant sites, including the **Cattedrale di Palermo** and **Cappella Palatina,** are actually west of this crossroads, away from the water and the nicest parts of town. Head east of the fountain and you'll find cement-block sunbathers who don't seem to care that there isn't a beach in the city proper. North of the fountain, along V. Maqueda, you'll pass by the unmistakable **Teatro Massimo**, Italy's largest opera house, and its little brother, Teatro Politeama.

SIGHTS

CATTEDRALE DI MONREALE (DUOMO OF MONREALE)
CHURCH

P. Guglielmo il Buono ☎091 64 04 413

The 6340sq. m of glistening gold tiles that are enshrined in this 12th-century Byzantine"arts and crafts project" are actually rumored to have convinced several Franciscan friars to rescind their vows of poverty, but this place is just too damn beautiful for anyone to even half-consider taking a tile home as a souvenir. Plus, there's a 65ft.-high mosaic of Christ watching your every move. After concluding your staring contest with the Son of God—he will win—look to the left. There the mosaics begin a clockwise-moving depiction of scenes from the Old Testament. Outside and behind the church is a cloister about which many writers have waxed poetic; the manicured garden is bounded by more than 200 columns embossed with Arabic gold plating.

i *8km west of Palermo. Take bus #389 from Palermo's P. Indipendenza to Monreale's P. Vittorio Emanuele. Don't take a cab unless you want to try to argue down from a €30 asking price. Modest dress required. Don't waste money on the garden unless you are dying for some close-ups with columns and grass. You can see it from the terrace for a third of the price. Cathedral free. Terrace and northern transept €2 each. Garden and cloister €6.* ⏰ *Cathedral open daily 8:30am-12:45pm and 2:30-5pm. Terrace and northern transept open daily 9am-12:30pm and 2:30-5pm. Garden and cloister open 9am-5pm.*

CAPPELLA PALATINA
CHAPEL, MOSAICS

Inside the Complesso Monumentale Palazzo Reale ☎091 70 56 001 www.federicosecondo.org

Consecrated by King Ruggero II as a testament to just how much gold and luxury a certain caste of enterprising Normans could cram into a little house of God, this chapel exemplifies glorious craftsmanship rather than humble tributes. Check out the soft-faced, mosaic Jesus behind the altar. Then spend a while tracking the"Good Book" on the aisle to the right of the altar.

i *Head west on V. Vittorio Emanuele. Proceed past the Porta Nuova as the road becomes C. Calatafimi. Turn left onto P. Indipendenza (or cut through the little park diagonally) and hang left along the palace until you see a huge gate. The ticket office is just inside the gate €8.50, EU citizens 18-25 €6.50.* ⏰ *Open M-Sa 8:15am-5:40pm, last entrance 5pm; Su and holidays 8:15am-1pm, last ticket 12:15pm. Cappella Palatina is closed to visitors on some Su 9:45am-11:15am for religious ceremonies.*

CAPUCHIN CATACOMBS
CATACOMBS

P. Cappuccini 1 ☎091 21 21 17

It's eerie enough seeing one dead person, but the Capuchin Catacombs beg you to contemplate a somewhat larger figure. The bone-chilling passageways of this underground mega-tomb preserve 8000 men, women, and children, many dressed in (what was) their Sunday best. "Preserved" is a generous term; these corpses, some of which have been interred here for 400 years, hang by wire in notches along the walls or lie in repose in various crannies, all at the whim of gravity and somewhere between nightmarish mummification and total oblivion. In a corridor of her own, perhaps the Catacomb's most famous resident is also one of its youngest and best-preserved: 2-year-old Rosalia Lombardo lies in tragic peace, a golden ribbon in her equally golden hair, in a private glass case that you can walk right up to.

i *Bus #327. By foot (20-25min. from city center), head west on V. Vittorio Emanuele. Past the Porta Nuova, bear right onto V. Cappuccini. Turn right onto V. Ippolito Pindemonte. The catacombs are straight ahead. No photos €3.* ⏰ *Open daily 9am-1pm and 3-6pm.*

Palermo isn't quite homey enough to showcase a wealth of B&Bs, but you can still find plenty of character at a number of other accommodations around town, including a pair of killer hostels. Palermo is a big city, but travelers wll be pleased to find that almost all its lodgings tend to be located within a 10min. walk from the major sights. Staying near the train station is generally cheaper, and if you're only in town for a bit, those cheaper digs may be pretty attractive. The two hostels we mentioned are listed below; other options can be found at **www.letsgo.com**.

A CASA DI AMICI   HOSTEL $
V. Volturno 6   ☎091 58 48 84 www.acasadiamici.com

A Casa di Amici's logo is a tacky clip-art cartoon of some guy sleeping with a croissant- and coffee-filled dream bubble floating above his head. African-themed art gives this hostel a vaguely tribal feel, but you can be sure that the only wilderness you'll need to brave is Palermo itself. With sunflowers, mosaic floor tiles, and large rooms that come to life with shiny medallions and artwork hanging from the doors, this hostel has all the comforts of an eccentric savannah retreat.

i *Facing the front of the Teatro Massimo, walk down its right side on P. Giuseppe Verdi. Stay left at the fork and continue onto V. Volturno. A Casa di Amici is on the left. Free Wi-Fi. Breakfast included. Bikes available for rent. Laundry available. Dorm €17-23; singles €30-45; doubles €50-72; triples €60-96; quads €80-104. Some rooms with bath. ⏰ Reception 24hr.*

YOUR HOSTEL   HOSTEL $
V. Gagini 61   ☎091 32 04 36 www.yourhostel.it

Gleefully bright and recently refurbished rooms sparkle with modern character, warm common rooms dot each floor, and a rooftop terrace offers a prime opportunity for stargazing or schmoozing with new friends. The personal warmth that resonates here and makes for an excellent, albeit not too wild, cheery-cheap option.

i *Head north on V. Roma, then turn right onto V. Valverde. Take the 1st right onto V. Gagini. Your Hostel is on the right. Free Wi-Fi. Breakfast included. Laundr €5. Lockers available. A/C. Dorms €20; private rooms €25, contingent on availability.*

palermo

CATTEDRALE DI PALERMO   CHURCH
On V. Vittorio Emanuele   ☎091 33 43 73

The unmistakably hodge-podge exterior of this behemoth boasts Norman turrets, Arabic columns, Gothic archways, and a towering 18th-century dome. The site was originally occupied by an ancient Christian church, but when the Muslims came along, they took Allah the land and plunked a mosque right on top of the house of Jesus. After the Norman reconquests of the 1100s, the son of God started trending on Twitter again, and the folks decided they should treat him to a big cathedral. Rather than building it anywhere else on the entire freaking island, they took the easy route and built right on top of the mosque. Again. While the interior is somewhat less interesting than the exterior, be sure to check out the Tesoro (treasury) and its priceless Sicilian ivory works as well as La Meridiana, a bronze line in the floor that runs perfectly North-South and is flanked by cartoonish depictions of the signs of the Zodiac.

i *From the center of town, head west on V. Vittorio Emanuele; the cathedral is on the right. Modest dress required. Cathedral free. Crypt and treasury €2.50. ⏰ Cathedral open M-Sa 7am-7pm, Su 8am-1pm and 4-7pm. Crypt and treasury open M-Sa 9:30am-1pm and 2:30-5:30pm.*

CHIESA DELLA MARTORANA

CHURCH

P. Bellini 2

☎091 61 61 692

Often compared to the Cappella Palatina on account of its lavish interior design and unique blend of Islamic, Byzantine, and Norman art and architecture, the Chiesa della Martorana is another classic, way-too-nice-to-be-a-freebie freebie. You can direct your thanks to Jesus—he's up on the dome in glimmering mosaics surrounded by a whole fleet of angels. If you can suppress the "that's pretty, I want to touch that" impulse for just a moment or two, consider the fact that this church has some pretty remarkable history to go along with the visuals. It was herethat Sicily, in 1282, crowned its newest king, Peter of Aragon, with a headpiece that was probably almost as nice as the room in which the ceremony took place.

i *From the Quattro Canti Fountain, head south on V. Maqueda. Just past the Palazzo Pretorio, the church is on the left at a diagonal. Free. ⚐ Open M-Sa 8:30am-1pm and 3:30-5:30pm, Su 8:30am-1pm.*

CHIESA DEL GESU

CHURCH

P. Casa Profesa 21

☎091 58 18 80

If this church wasn't technically Baroque, it would surely fall under the category of Absurdism. There's plenty to see, but you'll have no idea what to look at. Everything in this nave is covered with some form of art, be it the many-colored marbles or Filippo Randazzo's Disney-like rainbow frescoes on the ceiling. Make sure to check out the second chapel on the right, featuring Pietro Novelli's depictions of St. Philip and St. Paul the Hermit.

i *From the Quattro Canti Fountain, head south on V. Maqueda and turn right onto V. del Ponticello; Chiesa del Gesu is straight ahead after a 2-3min. walk. Free. ⚐ Open daily 7am-noon and 5-6:30pm.*

TEATRO MASSIMO

THEATER

P. Verdi

☎800 65 58 58 or 091 60 90 831 www.teatromassimo.it

From the gallery of this 1350 seat temple to all things glorious and vibrato, you'll be able to see the massive 72m tall stage and the five levels of velvety red luxury boxes that circle the auditorium. Then you get to plop your rump down in the Royal Box, which offers the best view in the house and was home to Al Pacino's Mafia-tastic tush in The Godfather Part III. Having second thoughts about not catching a show? Get ready to shell out €110 a pop for each of the 27 chairs in this box—it's all or nothing. You might need to ask Berlusconi for a loan. After exiting, you'll head to the most interesting room on the tour: The Room of Echoes. Designed to privatize the conversations had within, only in the precise center of this circle can a speaker hear his or her own voice sans echo. At 30min., this tour is as effective and efficient as a real life Mafia job.

i *From the Quattro Canti Fountain, walk north on V. Maqueda; the theater is on the left. Buy tickets for performances and guided tours at the box office inside. Walk through the main gate and follow the signs to the left of the main staircase; the ticket office is inside the foyer. Guided tour €8. ⚐ Besides performances, only open with guided tours. Tours in English run every hour, usually on the 40min. mark, 9:30am-5pm. Tours last approximately 30min.*

GALLERIA D'ARTE MODERNA PALERMO

MUSEUM

V. Sant'Anna 21

☎091 84 31 605 www.galleriadartemodernapalermo.it

Modern art galleries aren't usually the place you go for a "release." Galleria d'Arte Moderna Palermo, however, is a bit unlike the rest. It makes a point of answering for the rest of Palermo's art scene with simple, accessible, and Palermo-centric contemporary beauty. You'll enter into a veritable viewing chamber to experience Mario Rutelli's early 20th-century, palpably violent bronze sculpture Gli iracondi, which depicts a man taking a wrathful vampire-chomp out of another man's calf. Head upstairs for portraits and landscapes; Francesco Lojacono's renderings of the Sicilian countryside are much more relaxing than the mess you get outside in Palermo, and the city's homeboys are pretty well represented, too.

i From the Quattro Canti Fountain, head east on V. Vittorio Emanuele. Turn right onto V. Roma, then left onto V. Sant'Anna. The museum is on the left. €7, ages 19-25 or over 59 €5, under 18 free. ☪ Open Tu-Su 9:30am-6:30pm. Ticket office open until 5:30pm.

QUATTRO CANTI FOUNTAIN

FOUNTAIN

Intersection of V. Vittorio Emanuele and V. Maqueda

At the intersection of V. Vittorio Emanule and V. Maqueda lies one of Palermo's most distinctive architectural features. The Quattro Canti (Four Quarters), however, is a four-part fountain that spices things up by surrounding this intersection from the outside. Four Baroque façades, each four stories tall, criss-cross the diagonals cut by the two roads, and the fountains and their enormous baths sit just above street level. The statues that adorn each of the four building faces represent the four seasons, the four Spanish kings of Sicily, and the four patron ladies of the city. This intersection also happens to be the rendezvous point for all of the horse-drawn taxi things in the city, and all the "solid waste" creates a rather distinctive odor that permeates area. So if you want to see the fountains and don't know how to read a map, follow your nose.

i In 4 parts on the corners of the intersection. Don't drink the water. Free. ☪ Open 24hr.

FOOD

🔖 ANTICA FOCACCERIA SAN FRANCESCO

STREET FOOD $

V. Alessandro Paternostro 58 ☎091 32 02 64 www.afsf.it

If the fact that this place has been serving up the same style of focaccia sandwiches—stuffed with everything from prosciutto to roasted eggplant—since 1834 doesn't convince you that they've been doing something right, maybe the hordes of locals, from overly but justifiably eager schoolchildren to slick-haired old men, will do the trick. If you have any room left after your main meal, make sure to get your hands on a ricotta-oozing cannolo. This place has known how to make those artery-clogging addictions the right way for a long time, too.

i Head east on V. Vittorio Emanuele toward the water. Turn right onto V. Alessandro Paternostro and continue 2-3min.; Antica Focacceria San Francesco is on the right, across the piazza from the Chiesa di San Francesco d'Assisi. Focaccia sandwiches €4-8. Pastas €3-6. Pastries and treats €1-4. ☪ Open daily 10am-midnight; slows down during siesta hours.

🔖 RISTORANTE PIZZERIA PEPPINO

RISTORANTE $$

P. Castelnuovo 49 ☎091 32 41 95

All this red-checkered tablecloth, extra nice version of your summer camp's mess hall is missing is some banjo music and a couple of counselors telling you about that time they "took on the mighty Colorado." The food here is gourmet compared to the meat-surprise stuff you can find at camp, but the real reason to come here is that it's still about as cheap as trail mix. The only pizza pie that breaches the €6 mark is the Pizza S. Daniele, which at just €8 is still probably a steal considering the generous amount of paper-thin aged prosciutto draped across the mozzarella and tomato sauce.

i With your back to the Teatro Politeama, Ristorante Pizzeria is in the back right corner of the same piazza, on the right side wall. Starters and primi €6-9; secondi €9-14. Pizza €5.50-6. ☪ Open daily noon-3pm and 7-11pm.

DI MARTINO DRINKS AND BRUNCH

CAFE $

V. Mazzini 52/58 ☎091 61 18 820

We're a little surprised this place isn't just called Di Martino Sandwiches and More Sandwiches. This ultra-popular brunch spot has almost 50 varieties of this culinary not-so-specialty, but something about the sheer breadth of the menu and the fact that half of the city seems to show up here between 11am and 2pm makes the simple man's treat feel one-of-a-kind. One thing you might not have expected to be "sandwiched," though, is a slab of locally caught swordfish. It's not quite as gourmet as a cut you'd get at a nice seafood place near the water, but when you can get that and a cup of coffee for under €10, it'll taste pretty rich.

i With your back to the Teatro Politeama, turn right onto V. della Libertà. Turn right onto V. Mazzini; Di Martino is on the right. Sandwiches €4-7. Coffee and drinks €2-5. ☼ Open daily 8am-1am.

CASA DEL BRODO
RISTORANTE $$$

C. Vittorio Emanuele 175 ☎091 32 16 55 www.casadelbrodo.it

At Casa del Brodo, the food does the talking. After getting a taste of the pork chops, swordfish, or, for the more adventurous, beef tongue or pig shin, you'll understand the under-investment in the not-so-elaborate decor—all the effort seems to have been pumped into the food. The upside of the down-to-earth atmosphere is that you won't need to dress up to get some of best and most authentic grub in town.

i Open M 12:30-3pm and 7:30-11pm, W-Su 12:30-3pm and 7:30-11pm.

NIGHTLIFE

⬛ BASQUIAT
BAR

V. Sant'Oliva 22 ☎091 60 90 090 www.basquiatcafe.altervista.org

Basquiat is a trendy, earthy, awesomely young cafe/bar on a quiet corner in Palermo. As the night wears on, make your way to the small lounge that is splatter-painted on one wall and features as much low-rise seating as you can cram into a space the size of a college dorm. Then and only then, once you've amassed some Sicilian street cred, should you attempt to snag one of the five or six chairs on the infinitesimally small patio in the back.

i With your back to the Teatro Politeama, head straight and slightly left along the left side of the piazza. Stay left at the fork onto V. Sant'Oliva; Basquiat is on the left. Mixed drinks €5. Tea €2-3. Coffee mixed drinks €2.50-3. ☼ Open daily 5pm-2am.

WHISKY AND DRINK
BAR

V. Carducci 38 ☎320 14 11 405

A crowd too large for the size of this establishment fine-tunes its air guitar skills along to a nightly playlist of rock'n' roll and cheap drinks. The lack of couches is kind of a bummer, but who cares about comfort when you're having fun?

i With your back to the Teatro Politeama, turn right onto V. XX Setembre, then left onto V. Carducci; it's on the left. Beer €2-3. Mixed drinks €4-5. ☼ Open M 7pm-2am, W-Su 7pm-2am.

VOLO
BAR, LOUNGE

V. della Libertà 12 ☎091 61 21 284

The shady, cosmopolitan patio and wide open lounge at Volo draw a casual but lively crowd on the weekends, and some who come early for the food wind up staying late for the drinks. With a location right on a main pedestrian thoroughfare, this place encourages drop-ins but discourages total debauchery; hardcore ragers may want to head elsewhere. Maybe you can challenge convention and go totally off the walls. It wouldn't be typical for Volo, but you know—YOLO.

i With your back to the Teatro Politeama, turn right onto V. della Libertà and walk 1-2min.; it's on the left. Beer €2-5. Mixed drinks €4-5. ☼ Open M-F 12:30pm-1:30am, Sa-Su 6:30pm-3am.

ROCKET BAR
BAR

P. San Francesco di Paola 42

Vintage indie-rock concert posters surround the interior of this rockin' place, and cheap figurines of Elvis and Blondie stand guard over the bar—we're not sure how they fit into the whole musical vibe, but that whole "cheap" thing is right in line with the rest of Rocket Bar's style. A young crowd descends upon this place on weekends to gorge on ridiculously cheap panini and wash it all down with €4 mixed drinks and some €2 beers. Feeling a little fancier? You can get a gourmet beer for €6, but just a heads up: it's coming out of a vending machine.

i Facing the front of the Teatro Massimo, walk to the right. At the fork, stay right on V. Aragona. Continue past the intersection with V. Stabile into P. San Francesco di Paola. Rocket Bar is on the right. Shot €2. Beer €2-6. Mixed drinks €4. Panini €2.50-3.50. ☼ Open M-Sa 8pm-3am.

ARTS AND CULTURE

SICILIAN PUPPET SHOWS
V. Collegio di Maria al Borgo 17
☎091 81 46 971 www.mancusopupi.it

PUPPETS

This puppeteering company takes their craft seriously. Come here to see as-pro-fessional-as-it's-gonna-get miniature epics of serious drama—stories of medieval royal strife, knights in shining armor, and Palermo's patroness, Santa Rosalia.

i The puppet shows take place in the Teatro Carlo Magno. From the P. Sturzo, head northeast along V. Scina. Turn right onto V. Collegio di Maria al Borgo. The theater is on the left after a 2-3min. walk. Approximately 5 shows per year, but they only run for a few days each €7, reduced €5. ☼ Shows usually 6pm.

TEATRO POLITEAMA
P. Politeama
☎091 60 72 532 www.orchestrasinfonicasiciliana.it

THEATER

Often overshadowed by the Teatro Massimo, the Teatro Politeama may actually house the most accessible aspect of Palermo's arts and culture scene. While the big dog down the road hosts the operas and the tourists, this slightly smaller but equally beautiful theater is the home turf of the Sicilian Symphony Orchestra, whose season runs the entire year.

i Head north on V. Maqueda until you reach P. Politeama; the theater is on the right. Orchestral season runs year-round. Some prices are as low a €10, some as high as €300. ☼ Check online or at the tourist office for program information.

ESSENTIALS

Practicalities

- **TOURIST OFFICES:** There are tons of tourist kiosks that dot the roads near the major sights in Palermo, but the main office is at P. Castelnuovo 34. (☎091 60 58 351 www.palermotourism. com *i* With your back to the Teatro Politeama, walk straight ahead. Also official branches at the airport and the train station. ☼ Open M-F 8:30am-2pm and 2:30-6pm.)

- **POST OFFICES:** The main office is an enormous, white, columned megastructure. (V. Roma 322 ☎091 75 39 392 www.poste.it *i* 5-10min. walk north of V. Vittorio Emanuele. There is a smaller office at the train station. ☼ Open M-F 8-6:30pm, Su 8am-1pm.)

Emergency

- **HOSPITAL:** The main hospital is the **Azienda Ospedaliera Universitaria Palermo.** (V. del Vespro 129). (Non-Emergency ☎091 65 51 111 www.policlinico.pa.it *i* Take C. Tukory west, then turn left onto V. Colomba, which cuts straight through the main grounds of the hospital until it hits V. del Vespro, where the main entrance is.)

- **POLICE STATION:** Main office V. Dogali 29. (Non-Emergency ☎091 69 54 111 *i* Head north and turn left onto V. Notarbartolo, just on top of the Giardino Inglese. Continue as it becomes V. Leonardo da Vinci, then turn left onto V. Rafaello Politi and cross V. Evangelisti Giovanni di Blasi onto V. Agordat. Then turn right onto V. Dogali.)

Getting There

The **Aeroporto di Palermo-Punta Rarsi,** also known as Falcone-Borsellino Airport, services mostly domestic flights but a few international ones, too. Located about 45min. northwest of Palermo's city center along the coast, the airport is connected to the Punta Rasi train station via a free shuttle; from the station, trains (€5.80) run every hour to Palermo's Stazione Centrale. Bus routes (€4-6) also run straight from the airport to Palermo's P. Castelnuovo and Stazione Centrale.

Trains are not only the best way to get around within Sicily but are also an easy way to get from mainland Italy to the island itself. Trains traveling to Sicily are loaded onto a gigantic barge and floated across the water to the Messina Centrale station. It's pretty cool. There's also a snack bar on the boat, and you can hang out on deck for the 45min. cruise. Trains run directly from: Messina (€11.80 ⏲ 3½hr., 1 per hr. 5am-8pm); Syracuse (€15 ⏲ 4hr., 1 per day); Salerno (€29 ⏲ 8½hr., 3 per day); Naples (€39 ⏲ 9-10hr., 3 per day); Rome (€50-60 ⏲ 10-12hr., 5 per day).

Ferries run to Palermo from Salerno on a fairly irregular schedule. **Grimaldi Group** runs boats a few times per week. (☎091 58 74 04 www.grimaldi-ferries.com *i* Sept-June €40; Jul-Aug €80. Check schedules online or call the ticket office to book.)

Getting Around

Though you can easily walk the entire city, a pretty good bus system will make the job a little easier on your feet. City buses run under the **AMAT** acronym. The main AMAT terminal is in the *piazza* just outside the train station, and routes run up and down all the major arteries of the city. Tickets cost €1.10 and are valid for 90min. You can purchase tickets at tobacco shops, ticket offices, tourist offices, or on the bus itself, although you'll get a frown from the driver if you go with the latter option. Taxis are a good option for getting back from outskirts of the city later at night. **Autoradio Taxi** (☎091 51 33 11) is a good choice. Be aware that if you ask a taxi to deliver you outside the Palermo city proper, rates will skyrocket. You'd be better off taking a bus to the outskirts, then getting a cab if your destination is a little off the beaten path.

italy essentials

MONEY

To use a debit or credit card to withdraw money from an ATM (*Bancomat* in Italian), you must have a four-digit Personal Identification Number (PIN). If your PIN is longer than four digits, ask your bank whether you can use the first four or if they'll issue you a new one. If you intend to hit up ATMs in Europe with a credit card, call your credit card company before your departure to request a PIN.

The use of ATM cards is widespread in Italy. The two major international money networks are MasterCard/Maestro/Cirrus and Visa/PLUS. Most ATMs charge a transaction fee, but some Italian banks waive the withdrawal surcharge.

In Italy, a 5% tip is customary, particularly in restaurants (10% if you especially liked the service). Italian waiters won't cry if you don't leave a tip; just be ready to ignore the pangs of your conscience later on. Taxi drivers expect tips as well, but luckily for oenophiles, it is unusual to tip in bars. Bargaining is appropriate in markets and other informal settings, though in regular shops it is inappropriate. Hotels will often offer lower prices to people looking for a room that night, so you will often be able to find a bed cheaper than what is officially quoted.

SAFETY AND HEALTH

Local Laws and Police

In Italy, you will mainly encounter two types of boys in blue: the *polizia* (☎113) and the *carabinieri* (☎112). The *polizia* are a civil force under the command of the Ministry of the Interior, whereas the *carabinieri* fall under the auspices of the Ministry of Defense and are considered a military force. Both, however, generally serve the same purpose, to maintain security and order in the country. In the case of attack or robbery, both will respond to inquiries or desperate pleas for help.

Drugs and Alcohol

The legal drinking age in Italy is (drumroll please) 16. Remember to drink responsibly and to **never drink and drive.** Doing so is illegal and can result in a prison sentence, not to mention early death. The legal blood alcohol content (BAC) for driving in Italy is under 0.05%, significantly lower than the US limit of 0.08%.

Travelers with Disabilities

Travelers in wheelchairs should be aware that getting around in Italy will sometimes be extremely difficult. This country predates the wheelchair—sometimes it seems even the wheel—by several centuries and thus poses unique challenges to disabled travelers. **Accessible Italy** (☎378 941 111 www.accessibleitaly.com) offers advice to tourists of limited mobility heading to Italy, with tips on subjects ranging from finding accessible accommodations to wheelchair rental.

italy 101

HISTORY

We Built This City (Beginning of Time-500 BCE)

The first evidence of human life in what is now Italy dates back around 50,000 years, but not a whole lot happened until the much-mythologized founding of Rome. The story goes that **Romulus** and **Remus,** two sons of the god Mars, were taken from their mother and raised by an oddly compassionate **she-wolf.** The brothers eventually wished to found a city of their own, and after much fighting and confusion, Romulus killed his brother and named his city Rome, after himself.

To the Republic (500-0 BCE)

Kings maintained the supreme power in Rome until 500 BCE, when the king's son raped Lucretia and sparked the overthrow of the monarchy. In its place, the revolutionaries founded the **Roman Republic,** which was cloaked as the foundation of democracy, but was kind of just an excuse for rich white men to vote in strangely comfortable white sheets that they dubbed "togas." When Gaul (a.k.a. France) thought they could grab some Roman territory for themselves in 58 BCE, the task of fighting them off fell to **Julius Caesar.** He drove out the Gauls and ruled Rome for four glorious years before that fiasco that brought us the phrase "stabbed in the back." Brutus and Cassius, two of Caesar's murderers, didn't quite get the power they thought they would. Instead, Caesar's adopted son, Octavian, defeated them and ruled what was now the **Roman Empire** under the title **Augustus** for the next five decades.

Age of Empire (0-476 CE)

The Roman Empire peaked around 117 CE. It regulated trade; collected taxes; created highways, aqueducts, and sewers; and killed Christians by the dozen. That last part ceased when Emperor Constantine converted the empire to **Christianity** in 313 CE. While Constantine was busy baptizing everyone he met, the Bishop of Rome was fitted with a shiny new title: **Pope.** Faced by ever-increasing hubris, a series of borderline-incompetent emperors, and some unfriendly German barbarians, the Roman Empire met its demise in 476 CE.

Turn out the Lights (476-1375)

Italy's division into rival city-states caused cultural and mental divisions that are obvious even today. Speaking of division, these **Dark Ages** were full of religious contention, mainly because someone was always annoyed by the pope and felt the need to let everyone know. The most dramatic instance of this prompted one of history's great unpronounceable developments: the **Great Schism.** This saw a rival pope set up shop in Avignon, France from 1378 to 1417. As if that weren't enough, the **Bubonic Plague** swept through Europe, killing a third of the total population.

All in the Famiglia (1375-1540)

The **Italian Renaissance** was in many ways brought to us by the powerful families who came to dominate the peninsula around this time. The most famous of these families, the **Medici** of Florence, set the standard for Renaissance rule, shifting their focus from banking and stabbing people to patronizing the arts. Some people weren't so happy with the spirit of humanitarianism and artistic freedom that flourished at this time. A wet blanket of a friar named **Girolamo Savonarola** encouraged his followers to burn thousands of "blasphemous" books, works of art, musical instruments, and other tools of sin in what became known as **The Bonfire of the Vanities.** Meanwhile, the feuding Italian princes left the country open to more petty wars, and Spanish armies took control of all the Italian cities except Venice by 1540.

Divided and Conquered (1540-1815)

After the highpoint that was the Renaissance, everything was kind of downhill for the next few centuries. When the last Spanish Hapsburg, Charles II, died in 1700, Italy was so weak that a game of geopolitical tug-of-war ensued, with Austria, France, and Spain all vying for possession of the decentralized peninsula. This back and forth ended when a Frenchman named **Napoleon Bonaparte** settled things by taking Italy for himself. In 1804, he united the northern city-states into the **Kingdom of Italy,** which had its capital in Milan. After he met his waterloo, however, the Congress of Vienna re-divided everything and gave much of it, including Milan and Venice, to Austria.

Make Way for Italians (1815-present)

A half-hearted but surprisingly effective nationalist movement followed the perceived injustice of the Vienna agreement. This **Risorgimento** sought to revive a spirit of Italian oneness, even though that had never really existed before. Cunning politicians in the northern state of Piedmont used these ideas as an excuse to unite (read: take over) northern Italy in 1860. The Piedmontese had no intention of dealing with what they considered the barbarian south of the peninsula, but populist hero Giuseppe Garibaldi forced their hand. Garibaldi conquered the land from Sicily to Naples with a grand force of 1000 men, and then offered this area to the Piedmontese king for free. He could hardly refuse this offer, so somehow Italy ended up a united country.

The history of Italy since unification has seen sporadic outbreaks of nationalism and persistent attempts to stabilize the country. Italy showed up late to the non-party that was **WWI,** fighting Austria for control of land in the Alps. Post-war disillusionment aided the rise of **Benito Mussolini,** a gifted orator who promised stability and a new Roman empire. Unfortunately, this involved establishing the world's first fascist regime. Italy fought alongside Nazi Germany in **WWII,** before realizing that this was a losing cause and, with typical pragmatism, switching sides halfway through.

The current constitution, instituted in 1948, allows for a democratic republic, with a president, a prime minister, a bicameral parliament, and an independent judiciary. Though the government has changed nearly 60 times since, one element remains consistent: powerful, bold leaders. Self-made tycoon **Silvio Berlusconi** is the latest in the lineup, having been elected as prime minister in 1994... and 2001... and 2008, with plenty of corruption scandals as well as two resignations in between.

essentials

CUSTOMS AND ETIQUETTE

A friendly (sometimes too friendly) bunch, Italians have their own ways of doing things. If you want to fit in, you might need a small course in Italian etiquette. Chances are, with four million visitors each year, they'll still know you're a tourist, but at least they'll think you're a polite one.

Italians place a lot of emphasis on first impressions, so don't get yourself into a *mi scusi* situation. When meeting someone for the first time, a handshake is the way to go—**air kissing** (left side first!) generally comes with more familiarity. The Italian people are known to stand pretty close, so get ready to readjust your personal space boundaries. When it comes to clothing, Italians find having *bella figura* (good image) very important and tend to value quality over quantity. Short skirts and shorts are slightly more risqué in Italy than America—revealing tops are a little less so.

ART AND ARCHITECTURE

Really Really Old Art

One of the many things the Romans did for us was leave behind an enormous artistic legacy. They did a good job of borrowing from the Ancient Greeks, with architectural motifs like columns, domes, and precise geometry being all the rage. The Roman taste for flair made its way into household art: sumptuous **frescoes** of mythical stories covered wealthy Romans' walls, while **mosaics** decorated the floor.

Middle-Aged Art

The Middle Ages started out pretty unoriginally, as far as architecture goes: the "in" style, **Romanesque,** mimicked the Romans' rounded arches, heavy columns, and windowless churches. Of course, when the hot new **Gothic** movement brought airy vaulted ceilings and giant stained-glass windows from France, the dark and heavy Romanesque style moved to the not list. Despite architecture's new, less gloomy beauty, sculptors and painters continued to specialize in dead or dying Christians.

Ninja Turtles Assemble

All that began to change during the Renaissance. **Botticelli's** *The Birth of Venus*, depicting the goddess rising from a seashell, marked the beginning of a new age for art. *David*, one of the most gawked-at **nude statues** of all time, did the same for sculpture, thanks to artist **Michelangelo.** Michelangelo also painted the ceiling of the Sistine Chapel, arguably one of the greatest works of all time, then declared to Pope Julius II, "I am not a painter!" Painter, sculptor, or Queen of England, the guy was an artistic genius. The other three ninja turtles' namesakes, **Raphael, Donatello,** and **Leonardo** (da Vinci) also left their marks on the Italian art scene. Raphael was a prolific painter, Donatello specialized in relief sculpture, and Leonardo... well, the man merits a whole paragraph to himself.

Genius, artist, inventor, sculptor, and author—Leonardo was, in short, the ultimate Renaissance Man. Some of his ingenious sketches have proven themselves to be perfectly viable plans for flying machines, testifying to their creator's visionary imagination. The Italians weren't always great at hanging onto his work, though, which is why you'll find his most famous painting in the **France** chapter.

Lets Talk About Our Feelings

By the end of the Renaissance, artists had nearly perfected the representation of a scene: the perspective, shadow, and human figures they painted were all completely realistic. Once this got boring, the natural next step forward was to depict how the artist really felt. This new approach to painting characterized a style now referred to as **Mannerism**. The most famous painter of this style, **Tintoretto**, gained a reputation for his temper, earning himself the nickname *Il Furioso*.

If you stopped reading after the "eat" part of Eat, Pray, Love and are planning to stay in Italy for a while, then you're in the right place.

STUDY

- **UNIVERSITY OF BOLOGNA:** University of Bologna is considered the oldest university in continuous operation, and it lives up to its motto: "Nourishing mother of studies." (www.unibo.it/it)

- **SAPIENZA UNIVERSITY:** With its main campus close to the heart of Rome, Sapienza is a city within a city, so you'll have no trouble finding anything you need. (http://en.uniroma1.it)

- **UNIVERSITY OF PISA:** Dating back to 1343, the University of Pisa is yet another world-class university where you'll be in good company, surrounded by figures both modern and historic, from Galileo and some Medici to Rubbia and Bombieri. (www.unipi.it/index.php/english)

- **LAZZARETTO NUOVO:** Join a summer field school to learn about archaeological techniques, metallurgy, plaster and painting techniques, and more. (www.lazzarettonuovo.com)

- **SYRACUSE UNIVERSITY FLORENCE:** Syracuse University offers a myriad of programs both at its own independent Center in Florence and through Italian universities in Florence; programs include language, culinary, architectural, and studio art options. (http://suabroad.syr.edu/destinations/florence)

- **ST. MARY'S COLLEGE IN ROME:** The semester-long Rome Program is best suited to sophomores with some Italian language skills, though others may apply. Participants in the program get a broad range of instruction in everything from Italian art history to international business, philosophy to Italian literature. Some of this instruction happens on site in museums. (www.saintmarys.edu/departments/modern-languages/study-abroad-programs/rome-italy)

- **WILLIAM & MARY SUMMER PROGRAM:** The College of William & Mary offers two summer programs in Italy, one in Florence and one in Sicily. (http://www.wm.edu)

- **SARAH LAWRENCE COLLEGE:** Sarah Lawrence's two Italy programs (one in Florence, one in Catania) are distinct from other study abroad programs because of their "emphasis on small discussion seminars and individual conferences." (www.slc.edu/international-exchange)

VOLUNTEER

- **LEGAMBIENTE:** Work in Lombardy on land conservation and sustainable living with this Italian environmental organization. (http://lombardia.legambiente.it)

- **MAGENTA FLORENCE:** Magenta is a "creative space for English-language interns in Florence" that offers exciting internships for those interested in photography and editing. Internships are open-ended and can involve conducting interviews, attending press conferences, and producing the magazine Vista. (www.magentaflorence.com/magenta/internship)

- **THE AMERICAN WOMEN'S ASSOCIATION OF ROME:** This organization's members volunteer with a wide range of programs throughout the community. Check out the website for inspiration; this is a good place to explore potential volunteer opportunities. (www.awar.org/volunteer.php)

- **MEYER HOSPITAL:** This pediatric hospital in Florence has eight outside volunteer associations you can choose from to help enrich the lives of children and their families. (www.meyer.it)

- **DYNAMO CAMP:** Dyanmo Camp is a place for children with serious/chronic illnesses to experience a fun, supportive camp community in the Italian countryside. (www.dynamocamp.org/en)

- **ASSOCIAZIONE TUMORI TOSCANA:** This association offers free home care to cancer patients in and around Tuscany. (http://associazionetumoritoscana.it)

- **PROGETTO ARCOBALENO:** If you are near Florence and want to help immigrants, the impoverished, and victims of trafficking, check out this organization. (www.progettoarcobaleno.it)

- **WWOOF:** An organization that connects you with organic farms where you can work in exchange for room and board. (www.wwoof.net)

- **LA FAULA:** Help out in the vegetable garden or with the grape harvest and get room and board free. Volunteers must stay at least six weeks. (www.faula.com/voluntee.php)

WORK

As a member of the EU, Italy requires a fair amount of paperwork and red tape for foreigners to be able to work legally.

- **TORRI SUPERIORE ECOVILLAGE:** Tori Superiore is a fully functioning ecovillage and cultural center. In the summer months, you can do a full work exchange, pitching a tent for free in exchange for helping out in the guesthouse and around the village. (www.torri-superiore.org)

- **BRITISH INSTITUTES:** You need to know Italian well to work here as an English teacher. (www.britishinstitutes.it/index.php/sections/lavora-con-noi)

BEYOND TOURISM

No More Order

From this time forward, art began to move and develop in a less uniform fashion. The **Baroque** style combined Renaissance grandeur with the emotional affect of Mannerism to create powerful but naturalistic works, best exemplified by Naples's **Caravaggio**. **Rococo** came a little later and focused on light motifs like seashells and clouds, leading to some ridiculously elaborate decorative art, particularly in Venice. The 19th century saw two of everyone's favorite -isms: **Impressionism** and **Neoclassicism.** The latter was particularly inspired by the interest in Ancient Rome that followed the excavations of Pompeii and Herculaneum.

The most notable 20th-century Italian movement was **Futurism**, which admired speed, violence, and the industrial city. Not surprisingly, many Futurists were supporters of Fascism. Recent Italian art has veered away from particular -isms, but, despite the country's reputation for masterworks of the past, many galleries like Venice's **Punta della Dogana** and Rome's **Galleria Nazionale d'Arte Moderna** focus on works that continue this thriving artistic legacy into the present day.

FOOD AND DRINK

The Three Squares

The first meal of the day in Italy generally isn't anything too elaborate: *la colazione* may consist simply of coffee and a *cornetto* (croissant). Lunch *(il pranzo)* can go either way: in rural regions you may find it to be a hugely elaborate affair that precedes a nap and separates the two halves of the workday. However, most Italians will just grab a simple panino (sandwich) or salad. The last meal of the day, *la cena*, is generally the most important, and starts at approximately 8pm. It can continue through most of evening, as it may contain any or all of the following courses: an *antipasto* (appetizer), a *primo* (starchy first course like pasta or risotto), a *secondo* (meat or fish), a *contorno* (vegetable side dish), a *dolce* (dessert), a *caffè* (coffee), and often an after-dinner liqueur.

Potent Potables

NON-ALCOHOLIC SHOTS

Italian-style coffee, or **espresso,** is famous, though the blend of coffee beans used is often from Brazil. The beans are roasted medium to medium-dark in the north, getting progressively darker as you move toward the south. *Caffè macchiato* is topped with a bit of steamed milk or foam; cappuccino is mixed with steamed, frothy milk; and *caffè latte* is equal parts espresso and steamed milk. Other varieties include the frowned-upon *caffè americano*, watered down and served in a large cup, and *caffè coretto*, a kicked-up version that includes a bit of strong liqueur.

PUTTING A CORK IN IT

Leading the world in both wine exports and national wine consumption, Italy is a country that values a good *vino*. Every year, over one million vineyards cultivate grapes for *rosso* (red wine) and *bianco* (white wine). The difference? Red wine includes the skins of the grapes in the fermenting process, while white wine does not. Try such regional beauties as Barolo, a classy (read: expensive) staple of Piedmont made from red grapes that are fermented for over 20 years, or Frascati, a cold, clean Roman white.

THE NETHERLANDS

There are few places in the world that can pull off the Netherlands's unique combination of reefer-clouded progressiveness and folksy, earnest charm. This part of Europe somehow manages to appeal both to tulip-loving grandmas and ganga-crazy, Red-Light-ready students. So, like everyother college student, come to Amsterdam to gawk at the coffeeshops and prostitutes, but don't leave thinking that's all there is to this quirky country. Take some time to cultivate an appreciation for the Dutch masters. Obviously, most Dutch people aren't pot-heads—they'll tell you that if marijuana was legalized in the states, 700,000 fewer people would need to be incarcerated annually. Consider what it would be like to live in a place where hookers are unionized and public works like windmills, canals, and bike lanes define the national character, and get ready to go Dutch!

greatest hits

- **LET'S (VAN) GOGH:** The area around Museumplein in Amsterdam features not one, but two of Europe's greatest art museums. Savor the Dutch Golden Age at the **Rijksmuseum** (p. 661) or *Sunflowers* at the **Van Gogh Museum** (p. 661).

- **DAM GOOD BARS: Leidseplein** is a nightlife haven, with laidback and musical bars littering the streets (p. 670).

- **IT'S ELECTRIC!: Electric Ladyland**, the world's "First Museum of Fluorescent Art," will take you on an unforgettably weird trip into the world of glowing rocks and "participatory art" (p. 661).

It's hard to think of many countries that are as friendly to students as the Netherlands is. Student scenes and discounts are easy to find, while the wealth of things to do means young people never need constrain themselves to any one place or activity. The Dutch make their cultural institutions extremely accessible to those under 26, offering them a 50% discount on the **Museumjaarkaart,** which gives unlimited access to most of the country's museums. Many places actively court student customers. If you're hungry, try 'Skek in Amsterdam, where you'll receive a 33% discount by showing a student ID. This might be the first place in the world where people try to borrow IDs from people who are actually under 21.

amsterdam

Tell someone you're going to Amsterdam, and you'll be met with a chuckle and a knowing smile. Yes, everyone will think you're going for the hookers and weed, but there's much more to Amsterdam. The Netherlands's permissive attitudes are the product of a long history of liberalism and tolerance that dates back far before the advent of drug tourism and prostitutes' unions. A refuge for Protestants and Jews in the 16th and 17th centuries, Amsterdam earned tremendous wealth as the center of a trading empire that stretched from the New York (sorry: New Amsterdam) to Indonesia. The city's wealth served as an incubator for the artistic achievements of the Dutch Golden Age and the economic and political birth of modern Europe. Today, Amsterdam is a diverse and progressive city as famous for its art museums and quaint canal-side cafes as for its coffeeshops and prostitution.

ORIENTATION

The first step to getting a handle on Amsterdam's geography is to understand its canals. The Singel wraps around the heart of the Centrum, which is made up from east to west of the Oude Zijd, Red Light District, and Nieuwe Zijd. Barely 1km in diameter, the Centrum's skinny streets overflow with bars, brothels, clubs, and tourists—many of whom won't leave this area during their whole stay in Amsterdam.

The next set of canals, running in concentric circles, are Herengracht, Keizergracht, and Prinsengracht (hint: "gracht" means "canal," so if you're looking for a "gracht" street and you don't see water, you're lost). These enclose a somewhat classier area filled with locals, tasty restaurants, and plenty of museums (some very worthwhile, others completely ridiculous). Rembrandtplein and Leidseplein, the twin hearts of Amsterdam party scene, are also nestled here.

To the east of the canal ring are Jodenbuurt and Plantage, the city's old Jewish quarter. Moving southwest, you get to De Pijp, an artsy neighborhood filled with immigrants and hipsters, then Museumplein and Vondelpark, home to the city's largest park and most important museums. Working back north to the west of the center, you'll find Oud-West and Westerpark, two largely residential neighborhoods that are experiencing a boom in popularity and culture. In between Westerpark and the canal ring is the reliably chic Jordaan. Finally, to the north, in between Jordaan and Centraal Station, lies Scheepvaartbuurt, the city's old shipping quarter.

THE NETHERLANDS

0   25 miles
0   25 kilometers

North Sea

TO
NEWCASTLE, ENGLAND

TO
HARWICH, ENGLAND
AND HULL, ENGLAND

Schiermonnikoog
Terschelling   Ameland
Vlieland   Wadden Islands
Texel   Waddenzee

Den Helder

Hoorn
Alkmaar
Zaanse Schans
IJmuiden   Edam
Haarlem
Zandvoort aan Zee   Amsterdam
Noordwijk aan Zee   Lisse   Aalsmeer
Scheveningen
The Hague   Leiden   Utrecht
Hoek van Holland   Delft   Amersfoort
Gouda   Rijn R.
Rotterdam   Waal R.   Nijmegen
Maas R.
Breda

Antwerp

Brussels

BELGIUM

Leeuwarden
Harlingen   Groningen
Heerenveen
Assen

Hoogeveen
Meppel
Vecht R.
Zwolle

IJsselmeer
IJssel R.

Apeldoorn
DE HOGE VELUWE
NATIONAL PARK
Arnhem

Maas R.
Rhine R.

Eindhoven

Roermond
Cologne

Maastricht

GERMANY

amsterdam

Oude Zijd

Many will delight in telling you that the Oude Zijd ("Old Side") is in fact newer than
the Nieuwe Zijd ("New Side"). That doesn't really say much about the character of
the neighborhood, which is sandwiched between the wild Red Light District and
the more relaxed, local Jodenbuurt and feels like a balance between the two. A
small, Chinatownesque area stretches along the northern part of **Zeedijk,** which spills
into **Nieuwmarkt,** a lovely square dominated by a medieval ex-fortress. The bars and
cafes lining Nieuwmarkt's perimeter are popular places for tourists and locals to
rub elbows over a beer. Farther south is **Kloveniersburgwal,** a canal lined with genteel
17th-century buildings (many now occupied by the University of Amsterdam). Fancier hotels and cafes start to replace the tourist traps and faux-British pubs where
the canal hits the Amstel.

Red Light District

Once defined by the sailors who frequented Amsterdam's port, the Red Light District
dates back to the 13th century, when business-savvy ladies began to capitalize on
the crowds of sex-starved seamen. Today, the only sailors you'll find are the fake
ones in the porn and costume shops, but the sex industry still flourishes here. The
neighborhood is remarkably well regulated and policed, but this is definitely no Dis-
neyland (though the number of families sightseeing here might surprise you). The
Oudezijds Achterburgwal, with its live sex shows and porn palaces, is the Red Light's

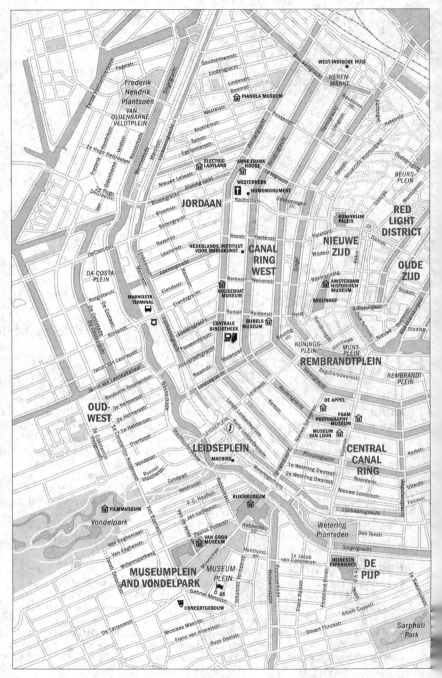

the netherlands

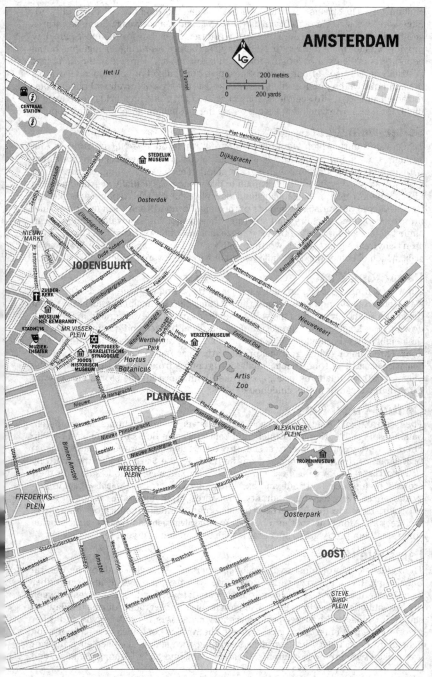

amsterdam

major artery. The streets perpendicular to this main thoroughfare are lined with girl-filled windows stretching to **Oudezijds Voorburgwal** and **Warmoesstraat**. Some sex stores and theaters have set up camp on these western streets, but for the most part they provide bars for male tourists to get liquored up before venturing through one of the neon-lit doors. Those not looking for prostitution can still carouse in the Red Light District's endless sea of bars and coffeeshops. You'll also find an immense army of the infamous Dutch public urinals here, as well as the type of traveler who feels comfortable using them. To see the hedonism at its peak, come on a Friday or Saturday night; for a less overwhelming visit, try strolling through on a weekday afternoon.

Scheepvaartbuurt

Scheepvaartbuurt, which would create quite a round on *Wheel of Fortune*, is Amsterdam's old shipping quarter. It was traditionally a working-class neighborhood with a lot of immigrants and once had a reputation as one of the rougher parts of the city. Nowadays, despite looking difficult to pronounce (it's actually not that bad…it's like "shape-fart-burt"), Scheepvaartbuurt is a pleasant area full of young people and largely devoid of tourists. Remnants of the neighborhood's salty, sea dog past—like bronze propellers, anchors, and steering wheels—dot the sidewalks, and you can almost detect a faint whiff of the sea breeze that once blew ships to this shore. There aren't any real sights, but it's worth a visit for the local shops that line **Haarlemmerplein**, which becomes **Haarlemmerdijk** as you move east toward residential Westerpark.

Canal Ring West

The Canal Ring West lies around—spoiler alert—a ring of three canals: the **Herengracht, Keizersgracht,** and **Prinsengracht** (helpful hint: they go in alphabetical order from the center of the city toward the west). It extends from Brouwersgracht in the north down to the Leidseplein. Chock-full of grand canal houses and quaint houseboats, the neighborhood provides a nice escape from the more crowded Nieuwe Zijd next door. Three major sights draw visitors here: the **Anne Frank House, Westerkerk,** and the **Homomonument.** The Nine **Streets,** small lanes running from the Prinsengracht to the Singel, south of Raadhuisstraat, are packed with more unique stores and vibrant cafes than we can fit in this guidebook.

Central Canal Ring

The Central Canal Ring tends to get overshadowed by its neighbors: Museumplein outshines its sights, Rembrandtplein and Leidseplein outdo its nightlife, and De Pijp offers a more exciting culinary scene. However, this neighborhood—the area from **Leidsestraat** to the **Amstel**, bordered on the north by the **Singel** and on the south by **Weteringschans**—enjoys the best parts of its surroundings without suffering their crowds, high prices, and soul- and cash-sucking tourist traps. **Utrechtsestraat** in particular offers lively cafes, restaurants, and stores, all frequented by a mix of locals and tourists, while the **Golden Bend** boasts some of Amsterdam's most impressive architecture. Along the southern border, **Weteringplantsoen** and **Frederiksplein** provide some small but pretty green spaces at which to stop and rest your feet.

Leidseplein

The Leidseplein, an almost exclusively commercial rectangle south of the Central Canal Ring, has a polarizing effect on those who pass through it, inspiring either devotion or disapproval. It's a busy, touristy part of town that lies in the area between the Nassaukade, Spiegelgracht, Prinsengracht, and Leidsegracht. During the day, the square is packed with street performers and promoters for pub crawls and other assorted evening entertainments. At night, the revelry continues in a bath of neon light and cheap beer. The few streets running through the Leidseplein's interior are packed with ethnic restaurants, theaters, bars, and clubs. Among the sushi and salsa, there are also a number of very Dutch establishments to be found. Numerous transport connections, including the elusive night bus, make this neighborhood a convenient and fun part of town. There are no sights to speak of, though look out for the enigmatic inscription, *"Homo sapiens non urinat in ventum"* ("A wise man does not piss into the wind") on the pillars above **Max Euweplein Square.** While many Dutch will frown in pity if you spend much of your trip here, the best part about Leidseplein is that some of those frown-bearers will secretly be living it up here all weekend, too.

Rembrandtplein

For our purposes, the Rembrandtplein neighborhood comprises the square itself, the area stretching from Herengracht to the Amstel, and the part of Reguliersdwarstraat between Vijzelstraat and the Bloemenmarkt. Once upon a time (the late 17th century), the area now known as Rembrandtplein was home to Amsterdam's butter market *(Botermarkt).* The construction of a few hotels in the 20th century brought tourists, and with the tourists came booze (and Euro-trance). With a few noteworthy exceptions, food and accommodations in Rembrandtplein often cost more than they're worth. The real reason to come here is the nightlife. Rembrandtplein's bars and clubs are as popular and numerous as those in the Leidseplein but tend to be larger and more exclusive, with more locals and GLBT establishments. Europe's largest LCD TV screen, located above Amsterdam's biggest club, **Escape,** lights up the square at night. From the middle of the square, **Rembrandt van Rijn** looks benevolently down at the madness. When you get tired of bar-hopping, take a rest in nearby **Thorbeckeplein,** a grassy stretch of trees named for Johan Rudolph Thorbecke (1798-1872), known colloquially as the first prime minister of the Netherlands. Thorbeckeplein is also the name of a song written by the popular Dutch singer Robert Long about a bittersweet gay love affair.

Nieuwe Zijd

Older than the Oude Zijd (but home to a church that's younger than the Oude Kerk, thus explaining the neighborhoods' confusing name swap), the Nieuwe Zijd offers a mix of history, culture, and a whole lot of tourists. **Damrak,** its eastern edge, stretches from **Centraal Station** to **Dam Square** and then turns into **Rokin.** These are some of the busiest streets in the city, full of souvenir shops and shawarma stands; they're best tackled on foot, as this is the one part of Amsterdam where bikes don't rule the road. As you head west to **Spuistraat,** the streets become less crowded and more hip. **Kalverstraat,** one of the city's prime shopping streets for centuries, is now home to department stores and international chains. The Nieuwe Zijd is tourist central, full of huge hostels and coffeeshops, and you're much more likely to run into drug-ready backpackers and elderly tourists taking pictures than any locals.

Jordaan

Once a staunchly working-class neighborhood, the Jordaan has been transformed into one of Amsterdam's prettiest and most fashionable areas. It provides a nice escape from the overwhelming hordes of tourists in the Red Light District to the east and has more energy than the residential Westerpark to the (surprise!) west. Streets are narrow, canals are leafy, and gabled houses are clumped together in colorful rows. You won't find any of Amsterdam's most famous sights here (well, except for Electric **Ladyland**), but the Jordaan's restaurants and cafes are not to be missed. Establishments in the northern part of the neighborhood are more often filled with locals, while tourists tend to wander over from Westermarkt into the area near **Rozengracht.**

amsterdam

Westerpark and Oud-West

Westerpark is a residential neighborhood northeast of the main city center; its eponymous park is a serene stretch of green that makes for a pleasant break from the urban jungle. It has a loyal and vocal community—just don't expect to hear any English—and is becoming increasingly popular among young people and artists, bringing ever-exciting cultural projects and nightlife to its streets. South of Westerpark lies the Oud-West, still dominated by locals but with a few large streets (**Kinkerstraat** and **Overtoom** in particular) that keep the area busy with their small ethnic cafes and cheap chain stores. The northern part of Oud-West is a little grungy, but the area farther south—north of Vondelpark, close to the Leidseplein—is probably the most tourist-friendly part of the neighborhood.

Museumplein and Vondelpark

Museumplein and Vondelpark lie just south of the main canal ring, close to the city center yet somewhat removed from its hectic disposition. Vondelpark is a gorgeous green space with some fine hostels not far from the excitement of Leidseplein and the ethnic eateries of the Oud-West. Museumplein, meanwhile, feels distinctly different from the rest of the city, attracting older and more affluent tourists than the backpacker-swarmed areas to the north. **P. C. Hooftstraat** is lined with designer stores like Prada and Tiffany, and the number of fancy French brasseries reflects the cash thrown around here. But just because you're young and on a budget doesn't mean you should shy away from these areas. Museumplein is a large, grassy field lined with some of the best museums in the world, and no visit to Amsterdam is complete without a trip to the **Van Gogh Museum** and **Rijksmuseum.** Most of the tourist-friendly action is sandwiched between Stadhouderskade to the north and Van Baerlestraat (which contains the Museumplein tram stop) to the south. Come here to get some space, culture, and class—three things that feel far away when you're downing Heinekens with the masses in a hostel bar on Warmoesstraat.

De Pijp

De Pijp ("duh pipe") may lack history and sights, but it more than makes up for that with modern culture. A mix of immigrants, students, and artists creates a haven of excellent ethnic restaurants, fun cafes, and relatively inexpensive housing. **Albert Cuypstraat** hosts the city's largest open-air market, along with a cluster of cafes, clothing stores, and cheap eats. Intersecting Albert Cuypstraat to the west is **Ferdinand Bolstraat,** which is home to a high concentration of restaurants and leads to the avoidable **Heineken Experience.** Still a little bit rough around the edges, De Pijp has all the charm of the Jordaan in a much younger and more urban setting.

Jodenbuurt and Plantage

A high concentration of sights and museums is the real draw here, but don't overlook the few excellent restaurants and small bars. The open space in these neighborhoods is a great antidote to the over-crowded city center. Jodenbuurt, centered around **Waterlooplein,** was historically the home of Amsterdam's Jewish population. Plantage, home to wide streets and numerous parks, stretches around Jodenbuurt to the east. Most commercial establishments can be found on the streets near the **Artis Zoo** or near the **Rembrandt House.**

SIGHTS

Between the pretty old churches, quaint canals, and nightly showcases of revelry and debauchery, Amsterdam is a sight in and of itself. You can see and learn a lot about the city, even with zero euro. If you're planning on visiting a number of museums, save some euro by investing in the Museumjaarkaart (www.museumjaarkaart.nl). For €40 (or €20 if you're under 26), you get free entrance to most museums in

Amsterdam and the Netherlands for a whole year. With the Museumjaarkaart, there's nothing to stop you from popping into one of the many small and weird museums and then popping right back out if it's not up to snuff. You cannot get the card at the tourist office (it's a great deal rarely advertised to tourists), but it's sold at some of the bigger participating museums.

Oude Zijd

While the best museums in Amsterdam are found elsewhere, the Oude Zijd is home to some worthwhile architecture and history. Make some erudite observations while passing these landmarks on your way to the Red Light District.

▓ NIEUWMARKT
SQUARE

Dominated by the largest still-standing medieval building in Amsterdam, Nieuwmarkt is a calm square lined with cafes and bars, making it one of the best places in the city for relaxed people watching. Originally a fortress gate, De Waag, the 15th-century castle-like structure in Nieuwmarkt's center, has housed a number of establishments over the years, including a weighing house, a gallery for surgical dissections, and, currently, a swanky restaurant. Some days the market is filled with freshly baked bread, local cheeses, flowers, clothes, and infinite knickknacks.

i *Nieuwmarkt. Or from Centraal Station walk 10min. down Zeedijk.*

Red Light District

Many tourists treat the Red Light District as a sight in and of itself, wandering through the crowded streets while pretending not to look at the prostitutes in the windows. But there are plenty of other worthwhile opportunities for travelers to learn about the parts of Dutch history and culture that don't involve sex, drugs, and drunk frat boys.

▓ OUDE KERK
CHURCH

Oudekerksplein 23   ☎020 625 82 84 www.oudekerk.nl

Since its construction in 1306, Oude Kerk, the oldest church in Amsterdam, has endured everything from the Protestant Reformation to the growth of the Red Light District, which today encroaches naughtily on this church's holy ground. (Case in point: the bronze relief of a hand caressing a breast set into the cobblestones outside.) Oude Kerk didn't escape all this history unscathed; during the Reformation of 1578, the church lost much of its artwork and religious figures. However, it remains a strikingly beautiful structure, with massive vaulted ceilings and gorgeous stained glass that betray the building's Catholic roots. You can occasionally hear concerts played on the grandiose **Vater-Muller organ,** which dates back to 1724, but Oude Kerk is now used mainly for art and photography exhibitions, including the display of the prestigious **World Press Photo** prizewinners. Whether you come for the art, music, or the sanctuary, tread lightly—you're walking on 35 generations of Amsterdam's dead.

i *From Centraal Station, walk down Damrak, turn left onto Oudebrugsteeg, then right onto Warmoesstraat; the next left leads to the church. Check the website for a calendar of performances* €7.50; students, seniors, and under 13 €5.50; with Museumjaarkaart free. ☒ Open M-Sa 10am-5:30pm, Su 1-5:30pm.

▓ ONS' LIEVE HEER OP SOLDER
MUSEUM

Oudezijds Voorburgwal 40   ☎020 624 66 04 www.opsolder.nl

The Ons' Lieve Heer op Solder ("Our Lord in the Attic") museum commemorates a beautiful Catholic church that was built…in an attic. When Catholicism was officially banned in the Netherlands, the Catholics were forced to practice in secret, and so this church was constructed. The Catholic's secret lair includes three houses whose connected offices make up the church and feature art and furniture from the period. The best part of the church comes when you can see three different periods of Dutch Catholic history at once. Through one window, you'll see Oude Kerk, built before the Protestant Reformation; beneath your feet, The Ons' Lieve Heer op Solder, highlighting the more muted Catholicism of the post-Reformation era; and then out the another window, Sint-Nicolaasbasiliek, which was built after freedom of religion was instated. The church is neat to walk through, but the real appeal is the understanding you'll gain of broader trends in Dutch history and culture.

i From Centraal Station, turn left onto Prins Hendrikkade, then right onto Nieuwebrugsteeg. Continue straight as Nieuwebrugsteeg becomes Oudezijds Voorburgwal €8, students €6, under 5 and with Museumjaarkaart free. ☼ Open M-Sa 10am-5pm, Su 1-5pm.

Nieuwe Zijd

The Nieuwe Zijd (despite its name) is one of the oldest parts of the city. Go back in time at the Amsterdam Historical Museum, then get a rude awakening into the present at some of the area's gimmicky attractions, such as Madame Tussaud's and the Sex Museum.

NIEUWE KERK
CHURCH, MUSEUM

Dam Sq. ☎020 638 69 09 www.nieuwekerk.nl

Built in 1408 when the Oude Kerk became too small for the city's growing population, the Nieuwe Kerk is a commanding Gothic building that holds its own amid the architectural extravaganza of Dam Sq. Inside, the church is all vaulted ceilings and massive windows. Don't miss the intricate organ case designed by Jacob van Campen, architect of the Koninklijk Palace. Today, the Nieuwe Kerk is the site of royal inaugurations (the most recent one being King Willem-Alexander's in 2013) and some royal weddings (like the new king's in 2002). Most of the year, however, the space serves as a museum. If the exhibitions do not interest you, come by for an organ concert held every Sunday.

i Any tram to Dam Sq. Nieuwe Kerk is on the northeastern edge of the square €15, with Museumjaarkaart free. Organ concerts €8.50; recitals free with cost of admission. ☼ Open daily 10am-5pm. Recitals Th 12:30pm. Concerts Su 8pm.

AMSTERDAM SEX MUSEUM
MUSEUM

Damrak 18 ☎020 622 83 76 www.sexmuseumamsterdam.nl

Unless you were previously unaware that people have been having sex since the dawn of mankind, there's not much new information about sex or sexuality at this museum. (The brief "Sex Through the Ages" presentation is hilariously simplistic, though the elegant British narration is priceless.) But let's face it: who needs information when you've got smut? Tons of pornographic photographs, paintings, and life-sized dolls fill the museum, along with models of various sexual icons.

i From Centraal Station, walk straight down Damrak. 16+ €4. ☼ Open daily 9:30am-11:30pm.

Canal Ring West

The Canal Ring West is home to a few must-see sights (the Anne Frank House and nearby Westerkerk should be near the top of your list), along with some wackier ones, like the **Nationaal Brilmuseum** and the **National Spectacles Museum** (Gasthuismolensteeg www.brilmuseumamsterdam.nl).

🖾 ANNE FRANK HOUSE
MUSEUM

Prinsengracht 267 ☎020 556 71 00 www.annefrank.nl

The Anne Frank House is by far the most popular sight in the entire city, with lines that start at least 30min. before opening and seem to grow throughout the day. The museum itself becomes a train of tourists watching videos, reading quotes, and looking at photographs of how the house looked when the Frank family was hiding there, as it now remains barren and unfurnished at the request of Anne's father, Otto. The museum itself is very well done in terms of emotional

Room rates fluctuate according by season and day of the week. Owners with unoccupied beds have been known to slash prices at less busy times. The following are only a few of our favorites; make sure to check out the rest of our recommendations online at **www.letsgo.com.**

▨ THE GREENHOUSE EFFECT HOTEL   HOTEL $$$
Warmoesstraat 55   ☎020 624 49 74 www.greenhouse-effect.nl

Somehow, this hotel has made the theme of extreme climate change and the future destruction of a livable earth into a good thing. How? Through affordable prices and uniquely themed rooms.

i From Centraal Station, walk south on Damrak, turn right onto Brugsteeg, then left onto Warmoesstraat. Single €65-85; doubles €95-130; triples €130.

▨ AIVENGO YOUTH HOSTEL   HOSTEL $
Spuistraat 6   ☎020 421 36 70 www.aivengoyouthhostel.com

Aivengo is different from most of the other hostels in a couple of ways, but the primary difference is the lack of social space. The hostel lobby does offer computers but has no real space for getting to know your fellow backpackers. The upside of this is the hostel has a reliably calm environment to retreat to after a night out.

i From Centraal Station, walk down Martelarsgraacht and keep straight onto Hekelveld, which becomes Spuistraat. Summer dorm €18-35. Private rooms €45-55 per person.

▨ FREDERIC RENT-A-BIKE   HOTEL $$
Brouwersgracht 78   ☎020 624 55 09 www.frederic.nl

It may sound cliche to say that this place feels like someone is opening up their home to you, but it's actually true here. There are three homey and uniquely decorated rooms sitting behind the bike rental shop.

i From Centraal Station, turn right, cross the Singel, and walk 2 blocks down Brouwers-gracht. Small rooms have shared bath. Single €50-60; doubles €65-105; Mondrian room €90-100; houseboats €120-175, with 15% reservation fee.

▨ HOTEL CLEMENS   HOTEL $$
Raadhuisstraat 39   ☎020 624 60 89 www.clemenshotel.com

Newly renovated, this hotel is an elegant option for those who can't afford the truly luxurious but prefer to avoid the hostel dorm. The rooms have a comfortable modern design that comes through in the breakfast room and hallways.

i Tram #13, 14, or 17 to Westermarkt. Walk across the bridge; the hotel is on the right. Free Wi-Fi. Breakfast included. Single €55-100; doubles €80-140; triples €125-160.

▨ STAYOKAY AMSTERDAM VONDELPARK   HOSTEL $
Zandpad 5   ☎020 589 89 55 www.stayokay.nl/vondelpark

This Ritz Carlton of hostels is humungous. You'll discover superb facilities and all kinds of entertainment. Right outside your door is the wonderful Vondelpark. Each room has its own bathroom.

i Tram #1, 2, 5, 7, or 10 to Leidseplein. Walk across the canal toward the Marriott, take a left, then make a right onto Zandpad after 1 block. Free Wi-Fi. Breakfast included. Single-sex dorms available. 2- to 20-bed dorm €26-48; private rooms €71-269.

amsterdam

power and will certainly give perspective on a horrible period of history. The end of the route includes information and interactive displays on contemporary issues in human rights and discrimination, reflecting the museum's mission as a center for activism and education as well as remembrance.

i *Tram #13, 14, or 17 to Westermarkt. Walk away from Keizersgracht down Westermarkt, then turn right onto Prinsengradcht €9, ages 10-17 €4.50, under 10 and with Museumjaarkaart free. ☼ Open daily Mar 15-Oct 31 M-F 9am-9pm, Sa 9am-10pm, Su 9am-9pm; Jul-Aug daily 9am-10pm; Nov 1-Mar 14 M-F 9am-7pm, Sa 9am-9pm, Su 9am-7pm.*

◙ WESTERKERK   CHURCH

Prinsengracht 281   ☎020 624 77 66 www.westerkerk.nl

This church was completed in 1631, a gift to the city from Maximilian of Austria (whose crown can be seen on the tower) as thanks for the city's support of the Austro-Burgundian princes. The church's brick-and-stone exterior is a fine example of Dutch late-Renaissance architecture. Inside, its plain white walls and clear glass windows are typical of the clean, Calvinist aesthetic. A 30min. guided tour to the top is a must (€4). The patient staff will pause to accommodate your huffing and puffing until you finish the climb and step out to behold the best view in Amsterdam. Only six people can go up at a time, so it's best to reserve your spot early.

i *Tram #13, 14, or 17 to Westermarkt. Walk away from Keizersgracht and turn right onto Prinsengradcht. Free. Tower tour €4. ☼ Open M-F 10am-5pm, Sa 11am-3pm. Tower tours every 30min.*

◙ HOMOMONUMENT   MONUMENT

Westermarkt   www.homomonument.nl

The Homomonument is the culmination of a movement to erect a memorial honoring homosexual victims of Nazi persecution, but it's also meant to stand for all people who have been oppressed for their sexuality. Designed by Karin Daan and officially opened in 1987, the monument consists of three pink granite triangles (in remembrance of the symbol the Nazis forced homosexuals to wear), connected by thin lines of pink granite to form a larger triangle. The Homomonument was designed to merge seamlessly with the daily life of the city, so it can be hard to discern amid picnicking tourists and whizzing bikes. *i* Tram #13, 14, or 17 to Westermarkt. The Homomonument is between Westerkerk and the Keizersgracht. Free.

Central Canal Ring

The grand buildings in the Central Canal Ring, architectural landmarks themselves, house a few historical museums as well as art galleries that lean toward the avant-garde. Kitsch aficionados can come here for some of the quirkier museums in the city, such as the **Museum of Bags and Purses** (Herengracht 573020 524 64 52 www.tassenmuseum.nl).

◙ FOAM   MUSEUM

Keizersgracht 609   ☎020 551 65 00 www.foam.org

In a city stuck in the past, this is one of the best places to find quality modern art in the medium of photography. This four level museum proves it has depth beyond by showcasing works from renowned photographers as well as young up and comers. During *Let's Go's* last visit, the museum was running four exhibitions, all showcasing different cultures and environments, including a village in Papa New Guinea and the streets of London. There are free tours available on Thursday nights, after which you will be able to at least fake a discussion about the effect of the framing of a photo or the transcendence of the medium as a whole.

i *Tram #4, 16, 24, or 25 to Keizersgracht. FOAM is about 50m east of the stop €8, students and seniors €5.50, under 12 and with Museumjaarkaart free. ☼ Open M-W 10am-6pm, Th-F 10am-9pm, Sa-Su 10am-6pm. Cafe open daily 11am-5pm.*

Jordaan

⬛ ELECTRIC LADYLAND   MUSEUM

Tweede Leliedwarsstraat 5   ☎020 420 37 76 www.electric-lady-land.com
As Hendrix himself sang, "It's time we take a ride." On this unforgettable ride,
let Nick Padalino, the passionate and eccentric owner/artist/remnant of the late
'60s, lead the way through his creation, the"First Museum of Fluorescent Art."
Nick seems to always be on duty and will happily spend hours explaining the
history, science, and culture of fluorescence to each and every visitor who walks
through the door. The most intriguing part of the museum is the fluorescent,
cave-like sculpture that Padalino terms "participatory art." Don a pair of foam
slippers and poke around the glowing grottoes and stalactites, flick the lights
on and off to see different fluorescent and phosphorescent stones, and look for
the tiny Hindu sculptures. When a tour is in progress, you may have to ring the
doorbell for a few minutes, but trust us—it's worth any wait.
  i *Tram #13, 14, or 17 to Westermarkt. Cross Prinsengracht and walk 1 block down Rozengracht,*
then make a right and walk a few blocks. The museum is just before you reach Egelantiersgracht
€5. ☼ Open Tu-Sa 1-6pm.

Museumplein and Vondelpark

The Museumplein is filled with museums—surprise! Plus, the beautiful **Concertgebouw,** at the southern end of Museumplein, is worth checking out even when there
isn't music playing (see **Arts and Culture,** p. 673).

⬛ VAN GOGH MUSEUM   MUSEUM

Paulus Potterstraat 7   ☎020 570 52 00 www.vangoghmuseum.nl
Van Gogh only painted for about a decade, but he left behind a remarkable
legacy of paintings and drawings, as well as his left ear. The highlight of the
museum is its impressive collection of Van Gogh's own work—the largest in
the world—ranging from dark, gloomy pieces like the *Skull of a Skeleton with
Burning Cigarette* to the delicateness of *Sunflowers.* We think this may be the
best museum in Amsterdam—unfortunately, so do a lot of other people. The
lines can get pretty painful; to avoid them, reserve tickets on the museum's
website or arrive when the throngs thin around 10:30am or 4pm.
  i *Tram #2, 3, 5, or 12 to Van Baerlestraat. Walk 1 block up Paulus Potterstraat €15, under 18*
and with Museumjaarkaart free. Multimedia tour €5. ☼ Open M-Th 9am-6pm, F 9am-10pm, Sa-Su
9am-6pm. Last entry 30min. before close.

⬛ RIJKSMUSEUM   MUSEUM

Jan Luijkenstraat 1   ☎020 674 70 00 www.rijksmuseum.nl
The heart of the museum is the second-floor gallery of art from the Dutch Gold-
en Age. They pull out the big guns in a room full of beautiful works by **Rembrandt**
and his pupils, evocative landscapes by Jacob van Ruisdael, and four luminous
paintings by **Vermeer,** including *The Milkmaid.* The big finish is the room devoted
to the **Night Watch,** one of Rembrandt's most famous paintings. Two audio tours
are available to guide you through the museum: one is more traditional and led
by the museum director, while the other is narrated by the Dutch artist, actor,
and director Jeroen Krabbé, who gives a more personal view of the artists and
paintings.
  i *Tram #2 or 5 to Hobbemastraat. Alternatively, tram #7 or 10 to Spiegelgracht. The museum is*
directly across the canal. Lines are shorter after 4pm €15, under 20 and with Museumjaarkaart
free. Audio tour €2.50 each. ☼ Open daily 9am-5pm.

⬛ VONDELPARK   PARK

The park is named after Joost van den Vondel, a 17th-century poet and playwright
often referred to as the Dutch Shakespeare. To those less knowledgeable about
Dutch literature, Vondel sounds phonetically like "fondle." People inhabit nearly

amsterdam

ever inch of the inviting grass, spread out alongside rolling streams and dotted with leafy trees, that makes up this 120-acre park. Its inhabitants include skaters, senior citizens, stoners, soccer players, and sidewalk acrobats. Locals bring out the barbecue and drink in the comfort of Vondel's green landscape. Our word association hits home with the knowledge that in 2008, the Dutch police decided that it's legal to have sex in Vondelpark—so long as it's not near a playground and condoms are thrown away. Thus, feel free to fondle when in Vondel. If you are looking for some more morally righteous entertainment, Vondelpark is also home to excellent cafes and an open-air theater (www.openluchttheater.nl), which offers free music and performances in the summer.

i Tram #2, 3, 5, or 12 to Van Baerlestraat. Walk down Van Baerlestraat to the bridge over the park and take the stairs down.

Jodenbuurt and Plantage

Some lesser-known but still worthwhile museums fill Jodenbuurt, historically the city's Jewish Quarter and now home to several sights focusing on Jewish culture and identity. Spacious Plantage, meanwhile, is home to the Botanical Gardens and Artis Zoo.

VERZETSMUSEUM (DUTCH RESISTANCE MUSEUM) MUSEUM

Plantage Kerklaan 61 ☎020 620 25 35 www.verzetsmuseum.org

This museum chronicles the five years the Netherlands spent under Nazi occupation during World War II. The permanent exhibit centers on the question that people faced in this period: "What do we do?" In the early days of the occupation, many struggled to decide whether to adapt to their relatively unchanged life under Nazi rule or to resist. As time went on, the persecution of Jews, gypsies, and homosexuals intensified, and as repression grew, so did the resistance. The museum masterfully presents individuals' stories with interactive exhibits and an extensive collection of artifacts and video footage. The museum pays tribute to the ordinary Dutch citizens who risked (and often lost) their lives to publish illegal newspapers, hide Jews, or pass information to Allied troops. A smaller portion of the exhibit details the effects of the war on Dutch colonies in East Asia. Verzetsmuseum is well worth your time and money, even if you're not a history buff.

i Tram #9 or 14 to Plantage Kerklaan. Across from Artis Zoo €7.50, ages 7-15 €4, under 7 and with Museumjaarkaart free. ☐ Open M 11am-5pm, Tu-F 10am-5pm, Sa-Su 11am-5pm.

FOOD

For some reason, when we think"Northern Europe," we don't think "awesome food." It's telling that in the vast world of Amsterdam restaurants, not too many of them actually serve Dutch cuisine. (Here's a quick run-down of what that looks like: pancakes, cheese, herring, and various meat-and-potatoes combinations.) Luckily, Amsterdam's large immigrant populations have brought Indonesian, Surinamese, Ethiopian, Algerian, Thai, and Chinese food to the banks of the canals. Finally, Amsterdam has this thing with sandwiches—they're everywhere, and they tend to be really, really good.

De Pijp, Jordaan, and the Nine Streets in Canal Ring West boast the highest concentration of quality eats, and De Pijp is the cheapest of the three. If you really want to conserve your cash, the supermarket chain Albert Heijn is a gift from the budget gods (find the nearest location at www.ah.nl). Keeping mind that most supermarkets close around 8pm. If you need groceries late at night (we can only guess why), try De Avondmarkt near Westerpark.

the netherlands

Oude Zijd

'SKEK

CAFE $$

Zeedijk 4-8 ☎020 427 05 51 www.skek.nl

'Skek is a self-described home for all those that work there and any guests that drop in. The place is completely run by students, and their young energy brings the place to life. 'Skek prepares hearty organic cuisine, with rotating options like a Japanese hamburger with wasabi mayonnaise, grilled vegetable lasagna, and braised eggplant. The interior is on a mission to be hip but tries not to seem like it. Thanks to whimsical fantasy board games painted on the tables, student art on the walls, and occasional live music, this eatery is the place to be from morning to night.

i *From Centraal Station, follow Prins Hendrikkade to Zeedijk. Lunch dishes around €5-7. Dinner entrees around €13. ☼ Open M 4pm-1am, Tu-Th noon-1am, F-Sa noon-3am, Su noon-1am.*

LATEI

CAFE $

Zeedijk 143 ☎020 625 74 85 www.latei.net

Walking into this colorful and eccentric restaurant, you're bombarded with random knickknacks and an assortment of mismatched furniture pieces that give Latei a playful atmosphere. When you discover that everything is for sale, the child inside you will emerge, and suddenly the wooden toy truck on the next table might be all you desire. But you better save your money for the simple and tasty food: sandwiches are made with artisan bread, the cafe makes its own olive oil, and "Home Cooked Food" is on the menu for dinner Thursday through Saturday nights. If you can't hold back from taking a piece of the place with you, we suggest the pins or key chains, as you're not going to find the likes of them anywhere else in Amsterdam.

i ⓂNieuwmarkt. Zeedijk is along the northwestern corner of the square. Sandwiches €3-5. Desserts €3-4. ☼ Open M-W 8am-6pm, Th-F 8am-10pm, Sa 9am-10pm, Su 11am-6pm.*

Nieuwe Zijd

CAFE SCHUIM

CAFE $

Spuistraat 189 ☎020 638 93 57

This artsy cafe takes the streets around it and perfectly blends their unique, graffitied charm with the kind of appeal found in a community club house (think big, padded leather seats grouped in circles that are perfect for large groups of friends). The place's picnic tables outside fill with a variety of hipsters, young professionals, and everything in between for dinner.

i *Tram #1, 2, 5, or 14 to Dam/Paleisstraat. Walk down Paleisstraat toward Singel and make a left onto Spuistraat. Sandwiches €4-7. Pasta €9.50-13. Beer from €2.20. ☼ Open M-Th noon-1am, F-Sa noon-3am, Su 1pm-1am.*

LA PLACE

CAFETERIA $

Kalverstraat 203 ☎020 622 01 71 www.laplace.nl

For a hungry traveler, walking into La Place will feel like stumbling off the street into heaven. Once inside, the air tastes sweeter (thanks to the aromas wafting from the endless bakery treats), the grass looks greener (that's just the fresh veggies at the salad bar), and the soundtrack is just right. Every culinary desire you have will be satisfied here. It's also affordable, so even if you are able to resist all of the temptations that come with the major shopping in the area, this is your chance to embrace rampant commercialism and indulge. The only problem you will have is trying not to slobber all over yourself in line.

i *Tram #4, 9, 14, 16, 24, or 25 to Muntplein. Note the giant V and D store and enter through the Kalverstraat door. The entrance to the cafeteria is on the left. Sandwiches €3-5. Pizzas €7. Entrees typically €3-8. ☼ Open M 11am-8pm, Tu-W 10am-8pm, Th 10am-9pm, F-Sa 10am-8pm, Su noon-8pm.*

amsterdam

Scheepvaartbuurt

HARLEM: DRINKS AND SOUL FOOD   AMERICAN $$

Haarlemmerstraat 77   ☎020 330 14 98

No, they didn't leave out a vowel: this place is the Dutch outpost of good ol' American soul food (or at least as close to it as you'll get in the Netherlands). Fill up on a variety of club sandwiches, soups, and salads at lunch or sup on dishes like fried chicken at dinner. As the night wears on, patrons stick around to imbibe and listen to the grooving soul and funk on the stereo (sorry, no sudden shaking will be taking place here), making Harlem one of Scheepvaartbuurt's livelier places come nightfall.

i From Centraal Station, turn right, cross the Singel, and walk down Haarlemmerstraat a few blocks. Harlem is on the corner with Herenmarkt. Sandwiches €5-8. Entrees €12-18. ☼ Open M-Th 10am-1am, F-Sa 10am-3am, Su 10am-1am. Kitchen closes 10pm.

Canal Ring West

'T KUYLTJE   SANDWICHES $

Gasthuismolensteeg 9   ☎020 620 10 45   www.kuyltje.nl

If you think you are unable to stomach another sandwich, this wonderful little deli will teach you better, for the delicious and large selection of sandwiches offered here come at a great price and with a nice helping of spicy mustard. The little shop offers nearly any meat you could desire and a couple Dutch cheeses that will remind you why you were so excited to come here to begin with. Ask the butcher for a recommendation or take ours and enjoy a traditional Dutch ham and cheese.

i Tram #1, 2, 5, 13, 14, or 17 to Dam/Radhuisstraat. Continue down Radhuisstraat and make a left at the Singel. Sandwiches €2.90-4.60. ☼ Open M-F 7am-4pm, Sa 10am-5pm.

TASCA BELLOTA   SPANISH $$

Herenstraat 22   ☎020 420 29 46   www.tascabellota.com

Due to a shared love of snacks, Spanish restaurants are popular in Amsterdam but few match the quality and value of this tapas and wine bar. Luckily, the Spanish enjoy lots of different kinds of snacks, and this menu features delicious dishes like spicy lamb meatballs, peppers stuffed with lentils and Manchego cheese, and dates with bacon. Strongly recommended by locals, Tasca Bellota also hosts live music some nights.

i Tram #1, 2, 5, 13, or 17 to Nieuwezijds Kolk. Cross Spuistraat and the Singel and continue on Herenstraat. Dishes for 1 or 2 fro €4.95-17.95. ☼ Open Tu-Th 6-10pm, F-Sa 5-11pm, Su 5-10pm.

DE KAASKAMER   CHEESE $$

Runstraat 7   ☎020 623 34 83   www.kaaskamer.nl

In this unique world that they call Amsterdam, cheese is a prized commodity that is sold in shops right next to jewelry stores and Gucci handbag shops. But to find the true diamonds in the cheese world, you must search in the rough and shop where the locals shop at De Kaaskamer. The store is overflowing with cheese and carries more than just Gouda. When you realize that making your own sandwiches is cheaper than paying someone to do it for you, come here and chow down on some cheese.

i Tram #13, 14, or 17 to Westermarkt. Walk down Prinsengracht, and Runstraat is on the left. Most cheese €2-5 per 100g, €7-9 per 500g. Cash only. ☼ Open M noon-6pm, Tu-F 9am-6pm, Sa 9am-5pm, Su noon-5pm.

the netherlands

Central Canal Ring

ZUIVERE KOFFIE
CAFE $

Utrechtsestraat 39 ☎020 624 99 99

Walking into this shop feels like walking back into the days when your mother made you a nice breakfast before school. There are also plenty of goodies (like croissants and tarts) to take with you, all of which are on display to delight you as you sit and plan your day. Before you hop back on your bike, make sure to grab a cookie from the cookie jar (yes, there is actually a cookie jar).

i *Tram #4, 16, 24, or 25 to Keizersgracht. Walk east on Keizersgracht and make a left onto Utrechtsestraat. Sandwiches €2.50-6.50. Apple pie €3.50. Drinks €2.25-4. ☼ Open M-F 8am-5pm, Sa 9:30am-5pm.*

GOLDEN TEMPLE
VEGETARIAN $$

Utrechtsestraat 126 ☎020 626 85 60 www.restaurantgoldentemple.com

This temple is built upon all the kitschy pillars that will delight anyone looking to feel like a hippie for an evening. The place is completely vegetarian, with vegan options available for almost every meal. To top it off, everyone on the second level sits on the floor. If you're lucky, you might be able to snag the love nest in the front of the restaurant, which is a raised bed fit with a variety of pillows and a table in the middle (remember to take off your shoes before entering).

i *Tram #4, 7, 10, or 25 to Frederickplein. Walk diagonally through the square and continue up Utrechtsestraat. Free Wi-Fi. Entree €8.75-17. ☼ Open daily 5-11pm. Kitchen closes at 9:30pm.*

Rembrandtplein

VAN DOBBEN
SANDWICHES $

Korte Reguliersdwarsstraat 5-9 ☎020 624 42 00 www.eetsalonvandobben.nl

An old-school deli and cafeteria that is everything most restaurants in Rembrandtplein are not: cheap, fast, and simple. The white ceramic tiling and chrome accents are a good match for the food's simplicity. Choose from a long list of sandwiches containing all kinds of different meats, many of which are on display at the counter. Take note from the true Dutch people seated around you and cover your roll and meat in gravy or another sauce. There is a limited selection of soups, salads, and omelets available as well. We're not sure how this place stays in business, seeing as everywhere else nearby seems to charge five times as much, so keep this deli in mind when looking for a satisfying meal for under €10 in the neighborhood.

i *Tram #9 or 14 to Rembrandtplein. The easiest way to find the small street is to get onto Reguliersdwarsstraat heading away from Rembrandtplein, then look for where the street veers off to the right. Free Wi-Fi. Sandwiches €2.50-5. ☼ Open M-W 10am-9pm, Th 10am-1am, F-Sa 10am-2am, Su 11:30am-8pm.*

RISTORANTE PIZZERIA FIRENZE
ITALIAN $

Halvemaansteeg 9-11 ☎020 627 33 60 www.pizzeria-firenze.nl

This pizzeria has a multitude of murals of Italian scenery on the walls to make you feel like you're actually in Florence. The pizza is not the best in the city, but the deals certainly are, as you can get a huge pie for only €5-7. We wonder if a certain Godfather has a hand in the business. With dozens of choices of both pizza and pasta, along with some meat and fish dishes, Pizzeria Firenze is definitely one of the best values for a meal around Rembrandtplein.

i *Tram #9 or 14 to Rembrandtplein. Halvemaansteeg is the street to the left of the line of buildings with the giant TV screen. Pizza and past €5-11. House wine €2.50 per glass. ☼ Open daily 1-11pm.*

Westerpark and Oud-West

Some of the best quality food can be found in these residential neighborhoods, where you're likely to be the only foreigner at the table.

⬛ DISH GLOBAL KITCHEN
Overtoom 255

SANDWICH $

☎06 414 65 881 www.dishglobalkitchen.nl

The size of the menu here is as big as the purported range of gastronomical offerings at this "global kitchen." This place dishes up Dutch-style sandwiches with twists from all over the map. You're still going to get the quality bread and cheese that you came to Holland to enjoy, but you'll get them paired with delicious hummus, Sandokan spicy chicken, or even meatloaf. Dish is cozy and very residential, so pull up a chair next to some locals and try to be worldly.

i *Tram #1 to J. P. Heijestraat. Sandwiche €5-6. Dessert €1.50-3.50.* ☺ *Open M-F 10am-4pm, Sa-Su 11am-4pm.*

⬛ BELLA STORIA
Bentinckstraat 28

ITALIAN $$

☎020 488 05 99 www.bellastoria.info

For people who miss their Italian nonna's home cooking (or missed out on having an Italian nonna entirely), this is the place to be. It's truly a family affair, run by a mother and her sons, all of whom chatter in Italian as they roll out dough. The best part is that you won't have to roll out too much of your own dough to enjoy a large portion of food. Since the restaurant sits in the middle of a residential area, expect to have the place to yourself in the middle of the day and to be surrounded by locals at dinner time. Make sure you finish off your meal with the most bizarre-sounding desserts ever (for example, *wittechocoladelimoncellomous me aardbeien*—a product only a combination of Dutch and Italian could possibly create).

i *Tram #10 to Van Limburg Stirumplein. Facing Limburg Stirumstraat, Bentinckstraat is on the right. Pizza and past €9-17.* ☺ *Open M-Sa 10am-9pm*

Museumplein and Vondelpark

⬛ BAKKERIJ SIMON MEIJSSEN
Van Baerlestraat 23

BAKERY $

☎020 662 8309 www.simonmeijssen.nl

It will be hard to miss this bakery, as it is almost literally overflowing with bread. Making your way inside will result in a yeasty bombardment of the senses. Sweet scents permeate the air, full loaves of artisan breads catch your eye, and all the while your heart is flooded with desire for the sandwiches stuffed with delicious meats and cheeses. Escaping this bakery with anything less than a sackful of treats for now and later would be a sin against the gods of good grain. Appease your stomach and the *pain*-theon by paying tribute in this holy haven of leavened wheat products, and don't worry—tidings here are cheap and worth every tithe.

i *Tram #2, 3, 5, or 12 to Van Baerlestraat. On the right when facing Vondelpark. Sandwiche €4. Treats €1-2.* ☺ *Open M-F 7:30am-6pm, Sa 8am-6pm.*

De Pijp

⬛ CAFE DE PIJP
Ferdinand Bolstraat 17-19

MEDITERRANEAN $$

☎020 670 41 61 www.goodfoodgroup.nl

This cafe serves up good food from all over the map, including curries, ravioli, and burgers. Then, after dinner, it takes on a new life as *the* place to hang, with local 20-somethings that swarm and linger over drinks on the patio or inside at the expansive bar. On certain nights, DJs will even come in and turn the place into a club of sorts.

i *Tram #16 or 24 to Stadhouderskade. Walk 2 blocks down Ferdinand Bolstraat. Cafe De Pijp is on the left. Entree €11-16.50.* ☺ *Open M-Th 4pm-1am, F 4pm-3am, Sa 3pm-3am, Su 3pm-1am.*

⬛ HET IJSPALEIS
Eerste Sweelinckstraat 20

ICE CREAM $

☎061 204 16 17

This gleaming white"Ice Palace" earns the coveted ranking of "totally dope," because there is no other way to describe it. The ice cream is absolutely delicious, from the standbys of chocolate and vanilla to the Dutch specialty, *stroopwafel flovor*. Every flavor is sweet, creamy, and heaped into a scrumptious cone.

i Tram #16 or 24 to Albert Cuypmarkt. Walk through the market and turn right. Scoops fro €1.10. 🕐 Open daily 11am-8pm.

⬛ BAZAR
Albert Cuypstraat 182

MIDDLE EASTERN $$

☎020 6732196 www.bazaramsterdam.com

Working your way through the bazaar that is the Albert Cuypmarkt, you will discover a bizarre restaurant named Bazar. Unlike this listing, the restaurant is far from redundant and stands out among the plethora of theme restaurants in Amsterdam as a great place to stop and enjoy a meal. The restaurant lives in a building that used to be a church and fills this huge space well with a variety of colorful decorations including a ceiling full of colorful lights that would put even the Griswold's to shame. The inexpensive and tasty Middle Eastern food here varies as much as the decor, from falafel to creative dinner specials like saffron veggie kebab.

i Tram #16 or 24 to Albert Cuypstraat. Walk through the market about 3 blocks. Sandwiches and lunch entree €6-11. Dinner entrees €9.50-15. 🕐 Open M-Th 11am-midnight, F-Sa 11am-1am, Su 11am-midnight.

Jodenbuurt and Plantage

⬛ EETKUNST ASMARA
Jonas Daniel Meijerplein 8

ERITREAN $$

☎020 627 10 02

Jodenbuurt started out as a neighborhood of immigrants, and this East African restaurant is a testament to the area's continuing diversity. The moment you walk into the place, you will be hit by a perfume of wonderful spices that seems to pervade the entire restaurant. If this doesn't stir up your hunger, then a quick look at the enormous platters of food around you will. The menu consists of varieties of delicately spiced meat and vegetables, all served with delicious *injera*, a traditional spongy, slightly tangy bread. This is one of the best values around and much more memorable than Amsterdam's unending parade of sandwiches.

i Tram #9 or 14 or Ⓜ Waterlooplein. Walk down Waterlooplein and turn right onto Wesperstraat. Jonas Daniel Mieijerplein is on the right, 1 street after the Jewish Historical Museum. Entrees €9.50-11.50. Beer €1.50. 🕐 Open daily 6-11pm.

NIGHTLIFE

Experiencing Amsterdam's nightlife is an essential part of visiting the city. Sure, you can go to the Rijksmuseum and see a dozen Rembrandts, but there's nothing like stumbling out of a bar at 5am and seeing the great man staring down at you from his pedestal in the middle of Rembrandtplein. That square and its debaucherous cousin, Leidseplein, have all the glitzy clubs, rowdy tourist bars, and live DJs you could ever hope for. For a mellower night out, bruin cafes are cafe-pub combinations populated by old Dutch men or hipster students, depending on which neighborhood you're in. The closer you get to the Red Light District, the fewer locals you'll find, and the more British bros on bachelor party trips you'll be forced to interact with. GLBT venues are a very visible and prominent part of Amsterdam's nightlife, and it's worth bearing in mind that in this city famous for tolerance, virtually every bar and club is GLBT-friendly.

NL20 is a free publication that lists the week's happenings—it's only in Dutch, but it's pretty easy to decipher the names of clubs and DJs. You can find it outside most stores, supermarkets, and tobacco shops. The English-language *Time Out Amsterdam* provides monthly calendars of nightlife, live music, and other events. It can be purchased at newsstands and bookstores.

Oude Zijd

Though the Oude Zijd is a little tamer at night than certain nearby neighborhoods, its close proximity to the Red Light District ensures consistent energy and some reveling tourists, especially along **Zeedijk.** If you're looking for a place to grab a drink, both Zeedijk and **Nieuwmarkt** are lined with pubs and cafe-bars. Follow the rainbow flags to find a smattering of GLBT bars in the northern part of Zeedijk, near Centraal Station.

◪ CAFE DE ENGELBEWAARDER   BAR

Kloveniersburgwal 59   ☎020 625 37 72 www.cafe-de-engelbewaarder.nl

The "Guardian Angel" Cafe seems to be looking out for you with regard to the quality of beer you are ingesting, and it takes its (exclusively) Belgian beer selection pretty seriously—and so should you. Located on the first floor of a canal house, with a comfortable and casual seating area by the water, it's the perfect place to converse with artsy young locals. Despite the hipness, welcoming bartenders will gladly help you find the perfect drink. The walls inside are covered with advertisements for local goings-on that will bring you up to speed on things to do throughout the city.

i ⓂNieuwmarkt. Walk south on Kloveniersburgwal for 5min. Live jazz Su 4:30pm. Occasional art showings; check website for details. Beer fro €3. ☿ Open M-Th 11am-1am, F-Sa 11am-3am, Su 11am-1am.

◪ HET ELFDE GEBOD   BAR

Zeedijk 5   ☎020 622 35 77 www.hetelfdegebod.com

Apparently the "11th commandment" ("*Het Elfde Gebod*") in some people's eyes is to drink only Belgian beer—that's all that's served here. For a country that produces so much beer, the Netherlands can be surprisingly unpatriotic in their brew selections. The place has seven beers on tap and over 50 in bottles (many of which come served in their own special glasses). Don't worry if you're overwhelmed by the choices; the knowledgeable bartenders are happy to provide recommendations. However, just as some of the commandments are a little dated nowadays, so are those that follow them, including the patrons of this bar. The weekends seem to attract an older and calmer crowd, but if you're looking for a relaxing and quality drink, this is the place.

i At the beginning of Zeedijk, near Centraal Station. Beer fro €3. Wine and spirits from €4. ☿ Open M 5pm-1am, W-Su 3pm-1am.

Red Light District

Ah, the Red Light District at night. Most of the neon glow bathes **Oudezijds Achterburgwal** and the nearby alleyways. Farther over on **Warmoesstraat,** you can still get a tinge of the lascivious luminescence but will find fewer sex-related establishments. Especially on weekends, the whole area is filled with slow-moving crowds of predominantly male tourists (although you might spot a surprising number of old women as well). When people get bored of window shopping, they wander the countless hotel bars on Warmoesstraat and Oudezijds Voorburgwal, which can be fun places to mingle with fellow backpackers. Despite police frequently strolling through, the area can turn into a meeting place for dealers and junkies late on weekends.

◪ WYNAND FOCKINK   BAR

Pijlsteeg 31   ☎020 639 26 95 www.wynand-fockink.nl

Many people avoid small alleyways in the Red Light District for fear of up-close-and-personal contact with a red-lit window, but this one holds a unique draw—a more than 300-year-old distillery and tasting room that makes the best *jenever* in the city. Perfect for day drinking, Wynand Fockink has no music and no flat screen TVs, and you can't use your phone while inside. But wait, that's not all—there aren't even any chairs, just rows of bottles on creaking shelves behind the small bar. An impressive mixologist is ready to splash together dozens of liquors, with flavorings like cinnamon, bergamot, and strawberry. Be adventurous and follow "Hansel in the Cellar" or drink from a "Naked Belly Button."

i From Dam Sq., walk down Dam to Oudezijds Voorburgwal, make the 1st left, and turn left onto Pijlsteeg. Spirits fro €2.85. ⏰ Open daily 3-9pm. Tours in English Sa 12:30pm.

Nieuwe Zijd

The Nieuwe Zijd has some decent nightlife, but it's not very concentrated. **Spuistraat** is the place to go for artsier cafes and bars, while **Dam Square** and **Rokin** are lined with larger, rowdier pubs. The small streets in the southern part of the neighborhood are home to good beer bars and a couple of energetic clubs. However, with fewer people around, it can feel a little less safe at night than the jam-packed Leidseplein and Red Light District.

🖾 PRIK
BAR, CLUB, GLBT

Spuistraat 109 ☎020 320 00 02 www.prikamsterdam.nl

Voted both best bar and best gay bar in Amsterdam on multiple occasions, Prik seems to attract its mostly male crowd like moths to a flame (or, in this case, to the glowing pink aura that lights up the entire street). Its atmosphere is about as light and fun as its name ("bubble" in Dutch). Come for cocktail specials all day Thursday and on Sunday evenings, or stop in to hear DJs spin pop, house, and disco classics on the weekends.

i Tram #1, 2, 5, or 14 to Dam/Paleisstraat. Walk down Paleisstraat and turn right onto Spuistraat. Beer fro €2. Cocktails from €6. ⏰ Open M-Th 4pm-1am, F-Sa 4pm-3am, Su 4pm-1am. Kitchen open until 11pm.

🖾 BELGIQUE
BAR

Gravenstraat 2 ☎020 625 19 74 www.cafe-belgique.nl

This small bar puts a more colorful and young spin on the classic, old-world Belgian bar. If you can muscle your way through to the bar, as it tends to be packed in here even on weekdays, you'll be rewarded with a choice of eight draft beers and dozens more Belgian and Dutch brews in bottles. "But I'm in the Netherlands," you say. "Should I really be at a bar called 'Belgium'?" Yes—they're basically the same, except Belgian beer is stronger and tastier, so just be quiet and enjoy.

i From Dam Sq., walk down Zoutsteeg. The bar is behind the Nieuwe Kerk, in between Nieuwendijk and Nieuwezijds Voorburgwal. Beer fro €2.50. ⏰ Open daily 2pm-1am.

🖾 DANSEN BIJ JANSEN
CLUB

Handboogstraat 11-13 ☎020 620 17 79 www.dansenbijjansen.nl

A student club with a rhyming name and a cheesy mix of top 40, R&B, and disco might seem like a recipe for disaster. Luckily, with beers for €1 euro on Thursdays, this rhyme is as awesome as Dr. Seuss's. It is seldom you will find true Amsterdammers here, but there are plenty of students and backpackers ready to embrace the lack of grace that these DJs have and get down to some super fre$h Robin Thicke.

i Tram #1, 2, or 5 to Koningsplein. Cross the canal, walk up Heiligeweg, and turn left onto Handboogstraat. Must have a student ID or be accompanied by someone who does. Cover M- €2, Th-Sa €5. Beer from €2. ⏰ Open M-Th 11pm-4am, F-Sa 11pm-5am.

BITTERZOET
BAR, CLUB

Spuistraat 2   ☎020 421 23 18   www.bitterzoet.nl

Bitterzoet just might be the most intimidating club in the city. Why? Because it's so damn cool, and you really want it to like you. The place fills with hipsteresque locals and seems to sell out nearly every event it puts on. Oftentimes, this means a high cover charge, but once inside, you'll discover one of the best parties in the city. The music varies widely from dance to bouncy house to smooth reggae to classic hip hop to live acts.

i *From Centraal Station, walk down Martelaarsgracht, which becomes Hekelweg and then Spuistraat. Cove €5-8. Beer from €2. ☼ Open M-Th 8pm-3am, F-Sa 8pm-4am, Su 8pm-3am.*

Scheepvaartbuurt

Nightlife in Scheepvaartbuurt isn't exactly happening. After dark, those who do stick around tend to congregate in the coffeeshops on **Haarlemmerstraat.** However, there are a few pleasant places to stop for a quiet drink.

DULAC
BAR

Haarlemmerstraat 118   ☎020 624 42 65   www.restaurantdulac.nl

The exterior may blend into the background of Haarlemmerstraat, but follow the young Dutch kids into this bar to find a good time. You'll know you're in the right place if you find crazy sculptures and many miscellaneous pieces of art inside. When the weather is nice, the party can be found in the nice garden terrace in the back, which is reminiscent of a New York high-rise in the way it combines chic and artsy with little effort.

i *From Centraal Station, turn right, cross the Singel, and walk down Haarlemmerstraat. Beer fro €2.50. Entrees €10-18. ☼ Open M-Th 3pm-1am, F 3pm-3am, Sa noon-3am, Su noon-1am.*

Canal Ring West

The Canal Ring West doesn't go wild after sunset, but the pubs along the water are great places to grab a beer, befriend some locals, and relax.

DE PRINS
BAR

Prinsengracht 124   ☎020 624 93 82   www.deprins.nl

"The Prince" may be a calm bar, but it seems like it wants you to recognize the teachings of Machiavelli. Inside, you'll find a charming wooden bar and lovely dinner area fit with candles, along with portraits of Al Pacino and Queen Beatrix. The lovely, old-world charm will teach you to love the place, while Pacino and Beatrix give it the power that reminds you to fear it. It may be better to be feared than loved for an actual ruling prince, but for this cafe, you need to overcome your fear of looking like a tourist and join the locals canalside to experience the true beauty of Amsterdam through a moonlit view Westerkerk.

i *Tram #13, 14, or 17 to Westermarkt. 2 blocks up Prinsengracht, on the far side. Beer fro €2.30. ☼ Open M-Th 10am-1am, F-Sa 10am-2am, Su 10am-1am. Kitchen closes at 10pm.*

Leidseplein

"Leidseplein" roughly translates to "more diverse nightlife per sq. ft. than anywhere else in the city." Some native Amsterdammers scoff at this area, considering it a sea of drunken British and American tourists. But the bars that cater to these liquored-up crowds are primarily confined to the Korte and Lange Leidsedwarsstraats. Many establishments are just as full of locals as they are of tourists.

the netherlands

WEBER

Marnixstraat 397

BAR

☎020 622 99 10

This place is poppin' and somehow achieves the impossible task of making the ever overdone theme of sex pretty damn classy and chic. Maybe it's the Magritte-style paintings, or possibly the taxidermied bison.

i Tram #1, 2, 5, 6, 7, or 10 to Leidseplein. Walk south of the main square and turn right onto Marnixstraat. Beer fro €2.50. Spirits from €4. ☼ Open M-Th 8pm-3am, F-Sa 8pm-4am, Su 8pm-3am.

PARADISO

Weteringschans 6-8

CLUB, CONCERT VENUE

☎020 626 45 21 www.paradiso.nl

You can have a very good Friday in this former church. Paradiso began in 1968 as the "Cosmic Relaxation Center Paradiso," and its laid-back vibe (at least as laid-back as you can get in one of the city's most popular clubs) keeps this place true to its roots. The club generally attracts less well-known artists than nearby Melkweg, though it has played host to big names like Wu-Tang Clan and Lady Gaga. Check out the live music every day and club nights five nights per week—including *Noodlanding!* ("Emergency landing!"), a party with "alternative dance hits" on Thursdays.

i Tram #1, 2, 5, 6, 7, or 10 to Leidseplein. Turn left onto Weteringschans. Cover for club night €5-20. Concert tickets €5-20, plus €3 monthly membership fee. ☼ Hours vary by event; check website for details.

Rembrandtplein

STUDIO 80

Rembrandtplein 17

CLUB

www.studio-80.nl

Studio 80 dominates the tricky balance between trashy and classy, between slutty and too-good-to-conform hipsterness. The place is decked out in the cheapest decor you've ever encountered, making it feel like a high school dance. Still, it's a pretty fun high school dance, and if at some point you fear that it's kind of pathetic that you're enjoying this place, another sick beat is thrown down, and you can't help but embrace it and have a good time.

i Tram #9 or 14 to Rembrandtplein. The entrance is next to Escape (see below), under the large balcony. Cover depends on the night, usually €6-10. Beer €2.50. ☼ Open W-Th 11pm-3:30am, F-Sa 11pm-5am.

VIVE LA VIE

Amstelstraat 7

BAR, GLBT

☎020 624 01 14 www.vivelavie.net

This long-established lesbian bar draws a diverse crowd of mostly young women and a few of their male friends. The atmosphere is refreshingly unpretentious and focused on dancing and having a good time. The excellent drink selections includes the Clit on Fire shot (€4). Music ranges from indie rock and bluesy country in the early evening to more dance and hip hop as the night progresses. If you need to cool off after too many of those shots, they have a large open patio separated from the craziness of the square.

i Tram #9 or 14 to Rembrandtplein. Beer fro €2.20. Spirits from €3. ☼ Open M-Th 4pm-3am, F-Sa 4pm-4am, Su 4pm-3am.

Jordaan

Nightlife in the Jordaan is much more relaxed than what you'll find in Leidseplein or Nieuwe Zijd, but that doesn't mean it's not popular or busy. Establishments tend more toward cafe-bars or local pubs than clubs, though some excellent music can be found in the neighborhood's southern stretches. If you're looking to seriously mingle with the locals, try one of the lively-on-the-weekends places along **Lijnbaansgracht** and **Noordermarkt**.

FESTINA LENTE
BAR

Looiersgracht 40B   ☎020 638 14 12 www.cafefestinalente.nl

Looking something like a bar stuck in the middle of an elegant vintage living room, this spot is enduringly popular with young and cultured Amsterdammers who want to "make haste, slowly." Bookshelves line the walls, and games of chess and checkers are readily available if you can find a spot to play. Poetry contests and live concerts are held often (check the website for details). The menu features *lentini*, small Mediterranean dishes, and an astonishing selection of bruschetta (on homemade bread!). For a more quiet and cultured evening out, this is the place to be.

i Tram #7, 10, or 17 to Elandsgracht. Go straight on Elandsgracht and turn right onto Hazenstraat; the bar is 2 blocks down on the corner. Beer fro €2. Wine from €3.30. ◻ Open M noon-1am, Tu-Th 10:30am-1am, F-Sa 10:30am-3am, Su noon-1am.

SAAREIN
BRUIN CAFE

Elandsstraat 119   ☎020 623 49 01 www.saarein.info

Putting a spin on the classic bruin cafe, Saarein offers a straightforward bar experience with a GLBT focus. The pink tones throughout make it more of a roze (pink) cafe, where you are sure find some fun, whether it be through Tuesday pool competitions or biweekly underground disco parties. Saarein is especially popular with the lesbian crowd, but no matter what your gender or orientation, you're sure to have fun.

i Tram #7, 10, or 17 to Elandsgracht. Turn left onto Hazenstraat and walk 2 blocks. Free Wi-Fi. Computer available. Beer fro €2. ◻ Open Tu-Th 4pm-1am, F 4pm-2am, Sa noon-2am, Su 2pm-1am.

Westerpark and Oud-West

OT301
CLUB

Overtoom 301   www.ot301.nl

Home to everything even remotely entertaining—a temporary handicrafts store, a cinema, live music, yoga and acrobatic classes, a vegan restaurant, and excellent DJ parties on most weekend nights—OT301 provides an escape from the typical tourist to-do list. The building was occupied by squatting artists in the late '90s, and OT301 eventually became a destination for Amsterdam's most hipster residents (after all, they were doing everything before it was cool). OT301's parties feature music ranging from electro house to soul and funk, and the place attracts a diverse and laid-back crowd.

i Tram #1 to J. Pieter Heijestraat. Check the website for upcoming events or just wander in and peruse the decorated handbills. Cove €3-5 most nights. ◻ Hours vary depending on programming; check website for details.

De Pijp

CHOCOLATE BAR
BAR

1e Van Der Helststraat 62A   ☎020 675 76 72 www.chocolate-bar.nl

Don't get too excited—this place doesn't serve some sort of magical, alcoholic candy bars, but it makes up for it by being just as rich and elegant as fine dark chocolate. A cocktail lounge with a long, glossy bar and seating area peppered with small, chic tables make the place classy, while the outdoor cabanas fitted with flaming lamps allow you to relax. On weekends, DJs spin laid-back dance tunes inside (after all, chocolate is meant to be savored slowly).

i Tram #16 or 24 to Albert Cuypstraat. Walk 1 block down Albert Cuypstraat and turn right. Beer fro €2. Cocktails €7. ◻ Open M-Th 9am-1am, F-Sa 9am-3am, Su 9am-1am.

Jodenbuurt and Plantage

🖾 DE SLUYSWACHT   BAR
Jodenbreestraat 1   ☎020 625 76 11 www.sluyswacht.nl
This tiny, tilting 17th-century building is the place that you come to Europe to discover, and although you were expecting to find this kind of bar on a lonesome seacoast instead of a bustling street, its contrast to the surroundings only make it a better place to hang out. The outdoor patio sits right above the canal, with giant umbrellas ready in case it starts to rain. When it gets really inclement, the plain wooden interior is invitingly snug, and you will have no choice but to make friends with the young locals that frequent the place. This bar is perfect for day-drinking and people-watching, with a good selection of draft and bottled beers.
i *Tram #9 or 14 or🅼Waterlooplein. Walk north from the stop and turn left onto Jodenbreestraat. Beer €2.20-4.60. 🕗 Open M-Th 12:30pm-1am, F-Sa 12:30pm-3am, Su 12:30-7pm.*

ARTS AND CULTURE

Classical Music and Opera
Classical music is a strong presence in Amsterdam thanks to the various high-caliber orchestras and innovative chamber ensembles that call this city home. Churches (especially the **Oude Kerk**) regularly hold organ and choral concerts and are particularly nice in the summer, when a lot of the concert halls close. Use this guide to begin your exploration of Amsterdam's arts scene, but, as with nightlife, keep an eye out for posters advertising upcoming events.

🖾 CONCERTGEBOUW   MUSEUMPLEIN
Concertgebouwplein 10   ☎020 573 05 73 www.concertgebouw.nl
Home to the highly renowned **Royal Concertgebouw Orchestra**, this performance space boasts some of the best acoustics in the world. They manage to fit in 900 concerts each year. Primarily classical, with some jazz and world music thrown in, there is even some that would appeal to those that who are not particularly into music and just want to sit inside the beautiful Neoclassical building and listen to the scores from their favorite movies, including **Star Wars** and **Harry Potter.**
i *Tram #3, 5, 12, 16, or 24 to Museumplein. Guided tours available. Varies by concert, but generally €20-100.*

Live Music
It's not hard to find great live music in Amsterdam. Many local artists tend toward electronic, techno, and house music, but you'll find home-grown bands and international indie, punk, pop,and hip-hop acts as well. Small jazz and blues joints can be found throughout the city. Leidseplein and the Oud-West boast particularly high concentrations of quality venues, ranging from large all-purpose clubs and concert halls to cozy bars and repurposed squats. In the summer,festivals explode in Amsterdam and the surrounding cities, often centered around electronic or reggae. Check the websites of major venues, look for posters around the city, and consult *NL20* or *Time Out Amsterdam* for the most up-to-date listings.

🖾 DE NIEUWE ANITA   WESTERPARK AND OUD-WEST
Frederick Hendrikstraat 111   ☎064 150 35 12 www.denieuweanita.nl
De Nieuwe Anita's popularity exploded recently when people realized that the cushy room at the front wasn't just some person's private living room. It's actually a great bar filled with creative and intellectual types. There is also a small, garage-like music room in the back where the true fun is found. American and Dutch underground and indie bands draw gangs of young local hipsters, while more diverse crowds show up for cheap movie screenings and readings. Check

amsterdam

the website for the what's going on—you are sure to find some cheap and quality entertainment here and a good introduction to Dutch subculture.

i Tram #3 to Hugo de Grootplein. Or take tram #10, 13, 14, or 17 to Rozengracht. Head north on Marnixstraat, make the 1st left before the Bloemgracht stop, cross the canal, and make another left at the traffic circle. Usually €5-10. ⏰ Hours vary; check website for details.

🏛 ALTO   LEIDSEPLEIN
Korte Leidsedwarsstraat 115   ☎020 626 32 49 www.jazz-cafe-alto.nl

Look for the giant alto saxophone adorning the door and slip inside the small, dark, and intimate interior to find a jazz club that wears its history and relevance on its walls, which are covered with photos and posters from past concerts. This is definitely the place to go on a night when you just want to sit back and enjoy the smooth grooves of some talented local artists. With a loyal following and nightly performances by renowned artists, this place fills up quickly, so show up early to get a good seat.

i Tram #1, 2, 5, 6, 7, or 10 to Leidseplein. Korte Leidsedwarsstraat is in the corner of the square. ⏰ Open M-Th 9pm-3am, F-Sa 9pm-4am, Su 9pm-3am. Music starts daily at 10pm.

Theater and Comedy

Traditional theater and musicals don't have the same presence in Amsterdam as they do in many other cities. The comedy scene is perhaps more varied and vibrant. For entertainment you can picnic to, don't miss the **Open Air Theater** in Vondelpark in July.

🏛 BOOM CHICAGO   JORDAAN
Rozengracht 117   ☎0900 266 6244 www.boomchicago.nl

Boom Chicago is the place for extremely popular improv comedy with plenty of audience participation. Boasting famous alumni, including Seth Meyers, Jason Sudeikis, Jordan Peele, and others, this is clearly the breeding ground for young, up-and-coming comedians. The current cast confirms this with reliably funny games and sketches that poke fun at the Dutch, which you'll probably appreciate after spending a while in Amsterdam.

i Tram #10 to Rozengracht or Tram #13, 14, 17 to Marnixstraat. 2min. walk down Rozengracht toward Centrum. ⏰ Most shows begin 8 or 9pm; check website for information.

Film

It's easy to catch a wide variety of old, new, and totally out-there films in Amsterdam. Most English-language movies are screened with Dutch subtitles. Look out for film festivals in the summer, like EYE institute's **North by Northwest.**

🏛 EYE INSTITUTE   THE IJ
IJ Promenade 1   ☎020 5891400 www.eyefilm.nl

The EYE moved in 2012 to this newly constructed building, which fittingly seems like something out of a movie as it pierces the sky with its futuristic design. This is one of the most impressive exhibition spaces in the entire city. Exhibitions here offer in-depth looks into specific film genres, motifs, actors and directors. The basement holds a free exhibition as well, which is just as engaging and even offers a chance to test your film knowledge with a movie quiz. The place has something to offer everyone, from the Netflix binging movie buff to the casual moviegoer.

i From Amsterdam Central Station, there is a 24hr. complimentary ferry to the other side of the IJ (Buiksloterweg, duration 3min.). Get on the middle pontoons, and when you step off the ferry in North, the EYE is on the left. Movie screening €10. Exhibition €12.50, free with Museumkaart. Basement free. €0.50 discount on tickets when you buy them online. ⏰ Exhibition open M-Th 11am-6pm, F 11am-9pm, Sa-Su 11am-6pm. Basement open daily 11am-6pm. Restaurant open Tu-Th 10am-1am, F-Sa 10am-2am. Check website for movie times.

PATHE TUSCHINSKI

REMBRANDTPLEIN

Reguliersbreestraat 26-28   ☎020 626 26 33 www.tuschinski.nl

One of Europe's first experiments with Art Deco design, this 1921 theater maintains its original luxury but now boasts better technology. The extravagant building and over-the-top interior will make you feel like you are at the premiere of a movie in the Golden Age of cinema. The snacks and drinks aren't so overpriced here, so grab a snack or some beer and enjoy a movie from the comfort of some of the biggest, cushiest seats you'll ever sit in. Catch artsier fare at the **Tuschinski Arthouse** next door.

i Tram #9 or 14 to Rembrandtplein. Walk down Reguliersbreestraat, and the cinema is on the right. Ticket €7.80-12.50. ☒ Open daily from 11:30am. Check website for showtimes.

Coffeeshops

Once upon a time, Amsterdam allowed tourists from far and wide to flock to its canals for cheap, legal drugs at its famous "coffeeshops." But those days have come and gone, and, as of late 2011, Dutch officials are planning to limit the use of legal marijuana to Dutch citizens. New regulations aside, coffeeshops and the relative permissibility of soft drugs in the Netherlands provide a fascinating window into Dutch culture and society. The listings that follow represent but a small introduction to the vast world of Amsterdam coffeeshops. If you happen to be Dutch, or if the government suddenly backtracks, you'll be able to get into them. We encourage you to do some research if you're interested in learning more about coffeeshops. Finally, though we may list a number of coffeeshops, *Let's Go* does not recommend drug use in any form.

PARADOX

JORDAAN

1e Bloemdwarsstraat 2   ☎623 56 39 www.paradoxcoffeeshop.com

Come to this local gem for the product and stay for the chill atmosphere. The walls and furniture are covered in oddball art (one table is adorned with a painting of a bare-breasted, two-headed mermaid), while bongs, vaporizers, and bowls are on hand. Select from over a dozen types of weed and an unusually broad selection of joints and spliffs. There are no gimmicky names for the different strains, and the helpful menu describes the effects of each variety, making it easy to get exactly what you want. There is also a nice selection of snacks, from warm toasties to smooth, sweet milkshakes.

i Tram #13, 14, or 17 to Westermarkt. Cross Prinsengracht and continue on Rozengracht, then turn left onto 1e Bloemdwarsstraat. Joint €3-5. Weed €5.50-11 per 1g. Hash €7-15 per 1g. Space cakes €6. ☒ Open daily 10am-8pm.

AMNESIA

CANAL RING WEST

Herengracht 133   ☎020 427 78 74

Amnesia is a well-regarded coffeeshop and with good reason—the place carries a sense of class just like a nice bar would. They have a variety of high-quality products, highlighted by nine Cannabis Cup winners. You can enjoy these with one of their vaporizers, which is both healthier for you and prevents the place from filing up with smoke. Either the place lives up to its name and forgot what "coffeeshop" means in this town or just wants to provide patrons with even more perks, but regardless, there's also a large coffee bar here for those who prefer the stimulating effects of caffeine. Their patio seating offers a gorgeous canal view that is sure to be memorable.

i Tram #1, 2, 5, 13, 14, or 17 to Dam/Radhuisstraat. Continue along Radhuisstraat and turn right onto Herengracht. Joint €4-6. Weed €8.50-15 per 1g. Hash €10-30 per 1g. ☒ Open daily 10am-1am.

amsterdam

SHOPPING

With shopping, as with pretty much everything else, Amsterdam accommodates both snooty European intellectuals and renegade Rasta men. The Nine Streets just south of Westerkerk are packed with vintage stores and interesting boutiques. Haarlemmerstraat, in Scheepvaartbuurt, is an up-and-coming design district. For more established brands, look to Kalverstraat, with its string of international chains and large department stores. For something really pricey, P. C. Hooftstraat, near Museumplein, is home to all the big-name designers. On the other end of the spectrum, markets like Albert Cuypmarkt and Waterlooplein offer dirt-cheap and, at times, flat-out bizarre clothing and other miscellaneous wares.

COTTONCAKE
DE PIJDAD $$

1e van der Helststraat 76-hs   ☎020 789 58 38   http://cottoncake.nl

Bringing together sweetness and comfort in a way that is unparalleled in Amsterdam, this store allows its guests to browse their collection of designer clothes from all over the world over a cappuccino and slice of walnut banana bread. Both a store and a cafe, this place is dedicated to offering quality products. The clothes are stylish and comfortable and are more suited for music festivals and roaming the city during the day than for parties and night clubs.

i *Tram #3 or 25 to 2e Van der Helstraat. Walk up Sarphatipark with the park on your left. The store is on the right.* ✆ *Open M-F 10am-6:30pm, Sa-Su 10am-5:30pm*

THE BOOK EXCHANGE
OUDE ZIJD

Kloveniersburgwal 58   ☎020 626 62 66   www.bookexchange.nl

Like most of the best book stores, The Book Exchange is just shelf after shelf stocked full of books. Don't let the small size of the first room fool you—this place has a huge selection, and you just have to keep venturing deeper and deeper into its different rooms. The tremendous inventory of secondhand books, ranging from New Age philosophy to a particularly large selection of paperback fiction, is priced extremely well.

i *From Nieuwmarkt, cross to the far side of Kloveniersburgwal and turn left.* ✆ *Open M-Sa 10am-6pm, Su 11:30am-4pm.*

LAURA DOLS
CANAL RING WEST

Wolvenstraat 7   ☎020 624 90 66   www.lauradols.nl

A wonderland for lovers of playing dress up, Laura Dols specializes in vintage gowns, including taffeta prom dresses, fluffy shepherdess numbers, and things you could actually get away with wearing outside the house. It also sells shoes, bags, and old-school lingerie (including some awesome metallic bras). This colorful store is bursting with odds and ends that can help jazz up any wardrobe.

i *Tram #1, 2, or 5 to Spui/Nieuwezijds Voorburgwal. Walk west to the far side of Herengracht, turn right, then left onto Wolvenstraat. Most dresses €35-60. Accessories around €15.* ✆ *Open M 1-6pm, Tu-W 11am-6pm, Th 11am-9pm, F-Sa 11am-6pm, Su 1-6pm.*

ALBERT CUYPMARKT
DE PIJP

Albert Cuypstraat

Stretching almost half a mile along the length of Albert Cuypstraat, this is the most famous market in the city. Need a motorcycle helmet, sundress, and cinnamon all in one afternoon? Albert Cuypmarkt is the place to go. The clothes can be hit or miss, but for produce or knickknacks, it's a great option. Rows of stores behind the market stalls sell similar items at slightly higher prices (though the clothes are a bit more wearable). Be sure to come early if you want to see the full display—some vendors start packing up as early as 4pm.

i *Tram #16 or 24 to Albert Cuypstraat.* ✆ *Open M-Sa 9am-6pm.*

Noordermarkt   www.boerenmarktamsterdam.nl

This organic market pops up every Saturday in a picturesque northern corner of the Jordaan to sell produce, cheese, baked goods, herbs, homeopathic remedies, and some hippie-esque clothes. This market is mostly about food and taking in a bit of the culture as you stroll past vendors. Some good deals can be found here, and be sure to take as many samples as you can.

i *Tram #3 to Nieuwe Willemstraat. Cross Lijnbaansgracht, walk up Willemstraat, turn right onto Brouwersgracht, then right onto Prinsengracht. The market is about 1 block down.* ⏰ *Open Sa 9am-4pm.*

ESSENTIALS

Practicalities

For all the hostels, cafes, museums, and bars we list, we know some of the most important places you visit during your trip might actually be more mundane. Whether it's a tourist office, internet cafe, or post office, these practicalities are vital to a successful trip, and you'll find all you need right here.

- **TOURIST OFFICES: VVV** provides information on sights, museums, performances, and accommodations. They also sell the **I Amsterdam card,** which gives you unlimited transport and free admission to many museums for a set number of days. For other transportation information, you're better off going to the GVB office next door. The lines at the office by Centraal Station can be unbearably long, so unless you need information right after you step off the train, try the one in Leidseplein instead. (Stationsplein 10 ☎020 201 88 00 www.iamsterdam.com *i* Across from the eastern part of Centraal Station, near tram stops #1-4. ⏰ Open July-Aug daily 9am-7pm; Sept-June M-Sa 9am-6pm, Su 9am-5pm.) Other locations at Schiphol Airport (Aankomstpassage 40, in Arrival Hall 2 ⏰ Open daily 7am-10pm) and Leidseplein 26. (⏰ Open M-F 10am-7:30pm, Sa 10am-6pm, Su noon-6pm.)

- **GLBT RESOURCES: GAYtic** is a tourist office that specializes in GLBT info and is authorized by the VVV. (Spuistraat 4 ☎020 330 14 61 www.gaytic.nl *i* Tram #1, 2, 5, 13, or 17 to Nieuwezijds Kolk. Walk 1 block west to Spuistraat; the office is inside the Gays and Gadgets store. ⏰ Open M-Sa 11am-8pm, Su noon-8pm.) **Pink Point** provides information on GLBT issues, events, and attractions in the city and sells all kinds of GLBT souvenirs. (Westermarkt, by the Homomonument ☎020 428 10 70 www.pinkpoint.org *i* Tram #13, 14, or 17 to Westermarkt. ⏰ Open daily 10am-6pm; reduced hours in winter.) **Gay and Lesbian Switchboard** provides anonymous assistance for any GLBT-related questions or concerns. (☎020 623 65 65 www.switchboard.nl ⏰ Operates M-F 2-6pm.)

- **INTERNET: Openbare Bibliotheek Amsterdam** provides free Wi-Fi and free use of computers that can be reserved through the information desk. (Oosterdokskade 143 ☎020 523 09 00 www.oba.nl *i* From Centraal Station, walk east, sticking close to the station building. You'll cross a canal, and the street will become Oosterdokskade. ⏰ Open daily 10am-10pm.) The **Mad Processor** is popular with gamers. (Kinkerstraat 11-13 ☎020 612 18 18 www.madprocessor.nl ⏰ Tram #7, 10, or 17 to Elandsgracht. Cross Nassaukade onto Kinkerstraat. Computers with Skype. Fax machines and scanners available. Internet €1 per 30min. Printing €0.20 per page. ⏰ Open daily noon-2am.)

- **POST OFFICES:** The main branch can deal with all of your postal needs and has banking services and sells phone cards. (Singel 250 ☎020 556 33 11 www.tntpost.nl *i* Tram #1, 2, 5, 13, 14, or 17 to Dam. Walk on Raadhuisstraat away from the square and make a left onto Singel. The post office is in the basement. ⏰ Open M-F 7:30am-6:30pm, Sa 7:30am-5pm.) You can also buy stamps and send packages from any store that has the orange and white TNT sign (including many grocery stores and tobacco shops).

- **POSTAL CODES:** Range from 1000 AA to 1099 ZZ. Check http://maps.google.nl or www. tntpost.com to find out the code for a specific address.

Emergency

Practicalities are great, but some things are particularly important, and we present those to you here. Hopefully you never need any of these things, but if you do, it's best to be prepared.

- **EMERGENCY NUMBER:** ☎112.

- **POLICE:** Politie Amsterdam-Amstelland is the Amsterdam police department. Dialing ☎0900 8844 will connect you to the nearest station or rape crisis center. The following stations are located in and around the city center. Lijnbaansgracht. (Lijnbaansgracht 219 *i* Tram #7 or 10 to Raamplein. Walk 1 block south and make a left onto Leidsegracht. Open 24hr.) Nieuwezijds Voorburgwal. (Nieuwezijds Voorburgwal 104-108 *i* Tram #1, 2, 5, 13, or 17 to Nieuwezijds Kolk. Walk 1 block down Nieuwezijds Voorburgwal, away from Centraal Station. ☑ Open 24hr.) Prinsengracht. (Prinsengracht 1109 *i* Tram #4, 7, 10, or 25 to Fredericksplein. Walk north diagonally through the square, up Utrechtsestraat, and make a right onto Prinsengracht. ☑ Open 24hr.) From outside the Netherlands, you can call the Amsterdam police at ☎31 20 559 91 11.

- **CRISIS HOTLINES:** Telephone Helpline provides general counseling services. (☎020 675 75 75 ☑ Operates 24hr.) Amsterdam Tourist Assistance Service provides help for victimized tourists, generally those who have been robbed. They offer assistance with transferring money, replacing documents, and finding temporary accommodations. (Nieuwezijds Voorburgwal 104-08 ☎020 625 32 46 www.stichtingatas.nl *i* Tram #1, 2, 5, 13, or 17 to Nieuwezijds Kolk. Walk 1 block down Nieuwezijds Voorburgwal. It's inside the police station. ☑ Open daily 10am-10pm.) Sexual Abuse Hotline provides information and assistance to victims of domestic violence, abuse, and rape. (☎020 611 60 22 ☑ Operates 24hr.)

- **LATE-NIGHT PHARMACIES:** Afdeling Inlichtingen Apotheken Hotline provides information about which pharmacies are open late on a given day. (☎020 694 87 09 ☑ Operates 24hr.) You can also check posted signs on the doors of closed pharmacies to find the nearest one open in the area. There are no specifically designated 24hr. pharmacies, but there are always a few open at any given time.

- **HOSPITALS/MEDICAL SERVICES:** Academisch Meidisch Centrum is one of two large university hospitals in Amsterdam, located southeast of the city, past the Amsterdam Arena stadium. (Meibergdreef 9 ☎020 566 91 11 www.amc.uva.nl *i* Bus #45, 47, 355 or metro trains #50 or 54 to Holendrecht. The hospital is directly across. ☑ Open 24hr.) Tourist Medical Service provides doctor's visits for guests at registered hotels and runs a 24hr. line to connect tourists to non-emergency medical care. (☎020 592 33 55 www.tmsdoctor.nl ☑ Operates 24hr.)

Getting There

By Plane

Schiphol Airport (AMS) is the main international airport for the Netherlands. (☎020 900 01 41 from the Netherlands, ☎31 207 940 800 from elsewhere; www.schiphol.nl) It's located 18km outside the city center. The easiest way to reach Centraal Station from the airport is by train. (€4.20. ☑ 15-20min.; 4-10 per hr. 6am-1am; 1 per hr. 1am-6am.) The train station is located just below the airport; you can buy tickets at machines with cards or coins, or from the ticket counter with cash. Buses also leave from the airport, which can be useful for travelers who are staying outside the city center. Bus #370 passes by Leidseplein, and other buses travel to Amsterdam and neighboring towns.

By Train

Within the Netherlands, the easiest way to reach Amsterdam is by train. (☎020 900 92 92 www.ns.nl) Trains arrive from The Hague (€10.20. ⏱ 1hr., 3-6 per hr. 4:45am-12:45am), Rotterdam (€13.40. ⏱ 1hr.; 3-8 per hr. 5:30am-12:45am, 1 per hr. 12:45am-5:30am), and Utrecht. (€6.70. ⏱ 30min.; 4 per hr. 6am-midnight, 1 per hr. midnight-6am) International trains from Belgium and Paris are operated by **Thalys** (www.thalys.com), which runs trains from Brussels (€29-69. ⏱ 2hr., 1 per hr. 7:50am-8:50pm) and Paris (€35-120. ⏱ 3hr.).

You'll need to shop around for the best deals on trains to Amsterdam from other major European cities. Check **Rail Europe** (www.raileurope.com) to compare prices for most companies. Like Dutch trains, all international trains run to the glorious potpourri of travelers known as Centraal Station. Train tickets range from €100-300 depending on the destination and rise rapidly as the date of departure approaches.

By Bus

While buses aren't a great way to get around the Netherlands, they can be cheaper for international travel. **Eurolines** (☎020 560 87 88 www.eurolines.com) is the best choice and runs buses from Brussels (€25, under 25 €19. ⏱ 3-4½hr., 7-12 per day) and Bruges (€25, under 25 €19. ⏱ 5hr., 1 per day) to the Amsterdam Amstel station, which is connected to the rest of the city by metro and tram #12.

If you want to travel to Amsterdam by bus from major cities such as London (€42), Munich (€42), and Paris (€84), you will almost definitely have to go through Brussels, Bruges, and the above-mentioned stops on the way. Eurolines often has deals for those who book in advance.

Getting Around

Tram, bus, and metro lines extend out from **Centraal Station,** while more trams and buses cross those routes perpendicularly or circumnavigate the canal rings. **Trams** are generally the fastest and easiest mode of transport in Amsterdam, serving almost all major points within the city center. The Red Light District and Oude Zijd only have stops on their northern or southern ends. **Buses** are good if you are heading outside of the center or to more residential parts of the city, though trams extend to some of these as well. The **metro** is rarely useful for tourists, as it only goes down the eastern side of the city and has few stops within the center.

Tickets and information can be found at **GVB.** (☎020 460 60 60 www.gvb.nl *i* On Stationsplein, across from the eastern end of Centraal Station and next to the VVV tourist office. ⏱ Open M-F 7am-9pm, Sa-Su 10am-6pm.) The lines here can be long, but it's the easiest place to buy transport tickets. The **OV-chipkaart** (www. ov-chipkaart.nl) has replaced the strippenkaart as the only type of ticket used on Amsterdam public transport. Disposable tickets can be purchased when boarding trams and buses. (*i* 1hr. ticket €2.60, 1- to 7-day tickets €7-30.) A personalized OV-chipkaart, featuring the owner's picture and allowing perks like automatically adding value when the balance is low, is a good option if you're staying in Amsterdam for a long time. You're more likely, however, to get an anonymous card, which can be purchased for €7.50 (plus an extra €5 as a starting balance) and can be reloaded at machines located throughout the city (most visibly in major supermarkets, like Albert Heijn).

You must both tap in and tap out with your chipkaart to avoid being charged for more than you actually travel. With the chipkaart, a ride on the bus, tram, or the metro costs €0.79, plus €0.10 per km. Most rides within the city center will cost around €1-2. Most transport runs 5am-midnight; after that, there are 12 night bus lines that run once per hour (twice per hour on weekend nights). An ordinary chipkaart does not work on night buses; you must buy special tickets (€4; 12 for €30) or one of the one- to seven-day passes.

Bike Rentals

FREDERIC RENT-A-BIKE

Brouwersgracht 78 ☎020 624 55 09 www.frederic.nl

In addition to rooms and general wisdom, come here for bike repairs and rentals.

i From Centraal Station, cross the canal, make a right onto Prins Hendrikkade, cross the Singel, make a left onto Singel, and then a right onto Brouwersgracht. Prices include lock and insurance. No deposit required, just a copy of a credit card or passport. Bike rental €10 per day; €16 per 2 days; €40 per week; €100 per month. ☺ Open daily 9am-5:30pm.

the netherlands essentials

SAFETY AND HEALTH

Drugs and Alcohol

It hardly needs to be stated that attitudes toward conscience-altering substances are quite different in Amsterdam than in other areas of the world, though the city is taking active measures to change this image. The Dutch take a fairly liberal attitude toward alcohol, with the drinking age set at 16 for beer and wine and at 18 for hard liquor. Public drunkenness, however, is frowned upon and is a sure way to mark yourself as a tourist.

When it comes to drugs other than alcohol, things get a little more interesting. Whatever anyone standing outside of a club at 4am might tell you, hard drugs are completely illegal, and possession or consumption of substances like heroin and cocaine will be harshly punished. Soft drugs, such as marijuana, are tolerated, but consumption is confined to certain legalized zones, namely coffeeshops (for marijuana) and smartshops (for herbal drugs). However, the age of the coffeeshop is, in some ways, coming to a close. Under new laws passed by the Dutch government, only Dutch residents over the age of 18 will be allowed to enter coffeeshops. As of 2012, customers will have to sign up for a one-year membership, or "dope pass," in order to use the shops, which have been blamed in recent years for encouraging drug trafficking and criminal activity.

Prostitution

The "world's oldest profession" has flourished in the Netherlands, particularly in Amsterdam's famous Red Light District. Legal prostitution comes in two main forms. Window prostitution, which involves scantily clad women tempting passersby from small chambers fronted by a plate-glass window, is by far the most visible. Another option is legalized brothels. The term usually refers to an establishment centered around a bar. Women, or men, will make your acquaintance—and are then available for hour-long sessions.

The best place to go for information about prostitution in Amsterdam is the Prostitution Information Centre. (Enge Kerksteeg 3, in the Red Light District behind the Oude Kerk ☎020 420 7328 wwww.pic-amsterdam.com ☺ Open Sa 4-7pm. Available at other times for group bookings, call ahead.) Founded in 1994 by Mariska Majoor (once a prostitute herself), the center fills a niche, connecting the Red Light District with its eager visitors.

GLBT Travelers

In terms of sexual diversity, in Amsterdam, anything goes—and goes often. Darkrooms and dungeons rub elbows with saunas and sex clubs, though much more subdued options are the standard. Despite this openness, certain travelers—including drag queens and kings, other cross-dressers, and transgendered visitors more

the netherlands

generally—should take extra caution walking the streets at night, especially in and around the Red Light District. All GLBT visitors to Amsterdam should also be aware that, though the city is a haven of homosexual tolerance, the recent infusion of fundamentalist religiosity into the Dutch political dialogue has created an environment detrimental to complete acceptance of GLBT behaviors and visibility.

Minority Travelers

Despite Amsterdam being known for its openness, there's a lot of hullabaloo about ethnic minorities coming into the Netherlands. Immigrants aren't always welcomed with open arms. Although foreign tourists of all stripes are sometimes treated with suspicion, it's mostly non-white visitors who occasionally encounter hostility. Muslims, or those who appear Muslim, seem to run into the most problems. The city is still generally tolerant, but sadly racism is not unheard of.

the netherlands 101

HISTORY

going dutch (ancient times-1648)

By the 15th century, the Austrian Habsburgs had seized the Dutch crown by that most effective means of conquest: marriage. The various familial complications of the Habsburg family meant that the Netherlands was controlled from Spain. The Netherlands was strongly influenced by the Reformation, and most of the population converted to Protestantism. Religious tension between the Dutch and their Catholic overlords, coupled with the imposition of high taxes, led to a 1568 revolt and the 80 Years' War for independence. The Dutch Republic declared its independence in 1581 and finally rid itself of foreign occupation in 1648.

a brief golden age (1648-1815)

The 17th century is remembered as the Dutch Golden Age, as the Dutch Republic was, briefly, the most powerful, rich, and sophisticated country in the world. The Dutch East India Company (Vereenigde Oost-Indische Compagnie), the world's first publicly traded multinational corporation, sent ships around the world and established outposts from Japan to South Africa. Amsterdam grew from a tiny fishing village to the center of the world's merchant trade. The country's affluence encouraged a renaissance in art and architecture that gave birth to painters like Rembrandt and Vermeer. Fabulous wealth encouraged competition, however, and the Dutch fought a series of wars with rival colonial powers in the 18th century. It turned out the Dutch were much better businessmen than soldiers. They lost many of their overseas colonies to the British and French and entered a period of economic stagnation and political upheaval. In 1795, French forces invaded, reducing the Netherlands to a French satellite. At the end of the Napoleonic Wars, the Netherlands, Belgium, and Luxembourg were reconstituted as a single country, the Kingdom of the United Netherlands.

things fall apart (1815-1945)

The United Netherlands was meant to be a strong buffer state to France, but it wasn't even strong enough to hold itself together. Belgium and Luxembourg split off in 1831, leaving behind the Kingdom of the Netherlands that remains today. The state is a constitutional monarchy under the Orange-Nassau royal family, with a powerful Parliament holding all the legislative power. The Netherlands remained neutral in World War One, though it still suffered from dramatic food shortages. The Dutch didn't get

Although small in size, this little nation can really pack a punch. So head on over to the orange country to explore your interests with a study abroad program, volunteer project, or internship that will get you inspired.

STUDY

Boasting extensive history, innovative design, and a large capacity for the arts, the Netherlands is a fantastic place to learn and grow into a cultured student.

- **CIEE:** Increase your understanding of social, political, and cultural realities in the Netherlands with CIEE's Social Studies program at the University of Amsterdam. Fun excursions include trips to other historical cities, the countryside, and cultural venues. (www.ciee.org/study-abroad)

- **UNIVERSITY OF AMSTERDAM:** Challenge yourself with this intensive summer Dutch language program at the University of Amsterdam. (www.uva.nl)

- **UNLIMITED DELICIOUS:** Learn how to make chocolate bonbons and pastries at Unlimited Delicious's sweet workshops. For groups of eight, it is possible to book a private workshop. (www.unlimiteddelicious.nl)

- **AMSTERDAM CENTRUM VOOR FOTOGRAFIE:** Amsterdam Centrum voor Fotografie hosts workshops for beginner photographers and master classes for those who wish to exhibit their own work at the end. (www.acf-web.nl/workshops)

- **THEATER DE CAMELEON:** On top of offering a wide variety of theater performances, Theater de Cameleon also hosts acting and voice workshops for all ages, some of which are in English. (www.decameleon.nl)

VOLUNTEER

What better place to till the land than in a country famous for its farms and cozy agricultural landscapes? Volunteer to be a friend to the Netherlands and boost the country's international happiness ranking from number four to number one.

- **WWOOF:** The Netherlands does not yet have a national WWOOF group, but there are Dutch farmers who still want to be hosts. View this website for a list of WWOOF Independent farms that are in need of volunteers. (www.wwoofeurope.net)

- **CFA SOCIETY NETHERLANDS:** CFA Institute is a global association of investment professionals. Volunteer at the local level with CFA Society Netherlands to help organize a regional forum for the discussion of investments, economics and finance. (www.cfasociety.org/netherlands/Pages/default.aspx)

- **VRIJWILLIGE HULPDIENST EINDHOVEN:** Everyone needs a buddy. This organization connects volunteers with people who are going through difficult times and are in need of a friend. Dutch proficiency is usually required. (www.vhd-eindhoven.nl)

- **AMSTERDAM CARES:** Don't have the time for a long-term commitment? Amsterdam Cares is a search engine with flexible volunteer opportunities that are as short-term as one-day events. (http://amsterdam.nederlandcares.nl/vrijwilligen/kalender)

WORK

Thanks to its cosmopolitan and cultured capital, Amsterdam, the Netherlands holds internship and job positions ranging from the headquarters of a finance organization to big name publications. Big opportunities abound here for those with big ambitions, so be ready for an experience that will leave you with a more extensive and detailed knowledge of how to navigate the professional world.

- **ING GROUP:** Expand your network and get proactive with an internship with The ING Group, a multinational banking and financial services corporation headquartered in Amsterdam. (www.ing.jobs/Netherlands/Internships.htm)

- **EUROPE INTERNSHIP:** Search these listings of current internship openings for a potential opportunity. (www.europe-internship.com)

- **IKEA:** IKEA goes Dutch! Inquire after internship opportunities at the Swedish furniture company. Also look into their trainee program to see what leadership skills and qualities IKEA is looking for. Dutch proficiency is required. (www.ikea.com)

- **EXPATICA:** Use this expat website as a tool to help you sift through possible job opportunities. (http://jobs.expatica.com/netherlands/home.html)

- **AU PAIR:** Become an au pair in Netherlands. This consists of being a part of a host family while taking up household responsibilities, such as doing chores, helping with childcare, and more. (www.aupair-world.net/index.php/au_pair_program/netherlands)

BEYOND TOURISM

off so easily when World War Two hit Europe. The Nazi occupation shattered the country's tradition of religious tolerance. Though many Jews, including Anne Frank, went into hiding, the majority did not survive the war. Of the 140,000 Jews who lived in the Netherlands at the war's outset, only 40,000 survived.

liberalism, and the retreat from it (1945-present)

After years of steady post-war recovery, the Netherlands found its niche as the most permissive state in Europe. Both prostitution and consumption of soft drugs were legalized. Tourists flocked to Amsterdam to gawk at its Red Light District and get high in its coffeeshops. In recent years, the government has sought to crack down on this liberal culture, pointing to convincing links between the activities and criminal gangs. Brothels have been shut down and, starting in 2012, foreigners have been banned from coffeeshops. For more information on this era-ending legislation, see Drugs and Alcohol above.

The Netherlands's famed liberalism has also been challenged by recent waves of immigration. Many Dutch people worry that migrants from Turkey, North Africa, and former Dutch colonies in the Caribbean do not share their liberal values and will change the character of the country. Paradoxically, this victimization of immigrants has itself served to undermine the country's accepting spirit. Strict social tolerance laws have been imposed to mollify cultural tensions. The Netherlands remains the most liberal country in Europe, but it is questionable whether it will be able to hold onto that title in the decades ahead.

FOOD AND DRINK

The typical Dutch ontbijt (breakfast) consists of bread topped with cold cuts and slices of local cheese, and a dab of appelstroop (syrup made from apple juice). If you're looking to satisfy your morning sweet tooth, top your toast with hagelslag (chocolate, aniseed, or fruit-flavored sprinkles).

Lunch includes rolls, sandwiches, or soup, eaten at one of the city's thousands of cafes. Erwtensoep (pea soup) is a cold-weather favorite and is often made with chunks of smoked sausage. You might also find uitsmijter, or Dutch fried eggs sunny-side-up (for some reason the name translates to "out-thrower" or "bouncer," as in the doorman at a club). A broodje haring (herring sandwich) garnished with onions and pickles is particularly tasty—you'll find one at fish stalls throughout the city. Diner is served in Dutch homes around 5 or 6pm. A meat entree is traditionally accompanied by two vegetable side dishes, though you might encounter a stamppot, which combines meat, vegetables, and gravy in a mash.

The distinction between cafe and bar doesn't exist in the Netherlands. You can order a Heineken on its own turf, or sample some of the other famous Dutch pale lagers. Eet smakelijk (enjoy your meal)!

PORTUGAL

Portugal draws hordes of backpackers by fusing its timeless inland towns and majestic castles with industrialized cities like Lisbon, whose graffiti-covered walls separate bustling bars from posh fado restaurants. The original backpackers, Portuguese patriarchs like Vasco da Gama, pioneered the exploration of Asia, Africa, and South America, and the country continues to foster such discovery within its borders, with wine regions like the Douro Valley, immaculate forests and mountains in its wild northern region, and 2000km of coastline for tourists to traverse and travel.

greatest hits

- **MOMA MIA.** You'll need a lot of energy for Lisbon nights, so spend your days enjoying the tasty fare at **Moma** (p. 694).

- **BAIRRO ALTO NIGHTLIFE.** Don't fear crowd-induced pit stains in this neighborhood—everyone drinks on the sidewalks (p. 696).

- **FADO.** Because you're where this music was born (p. 699).

- **CLUBBIN' BY THE WATER.** **Lisbon** (p. 687) has some of the hottest waterside clubs this side of the Pyrenees.

PORTUGAL

ATLANTIC
OCEAN

Minho
Vila Nova
de Cerveira
Valença
do Minho
Caminha
MINHO
Viana do Castelo
Lima

Parque
Nacional da
Peneda-Gerês

Serra-Do Gerês
Caldas de Gerês

Parque Natural
de Montesinho
Bragança

Cávado
Barcelos
Braga
Guimarães
Costa Verde
Tâmega
TRÁS-OS-MONTES
Mirandela
Parque Natural
do Alvão

Miranda do
Douro

Amarante
DOURO
LITORAL
Vila Real
Serra Do Marão

Parque Natural do
Douro Internacional

Porto
DOURO
ALTO

Espinho
Douro

Ovar

BEIRA ALTA

Aveiro
BEIRA
LITORAL
Viseu

Costa Da Prata
Luso
Buçaco
Mondego
Guarda
Manteigas

Coimbra
Serra Da Estrêla
Parque
Natural da
Serra dá Estrêla
Sabugal
Sortelha

Figueira
da Foz
Conímbriga
Zêzere
Serra Da
Gardunha
Monsanto

BEIRA BAIXA

Leiria
Batalha
Castelo
Branco

Nazaré
São Martinho
do Porto
Fátima
Alcobaça
Tomar

Ilhas
Berlengas
Cabo
Carvoeiro
Caldas da
Rainha
Serra De Aire
Peniche
Óbidos

ESTREMADURA
Tejo
RIBATEJO
Castelo
de Vide
Serra De São Mamede

Ericeira
Vila Franca
de Xira
Santarém
Crato
Marvão
Portalegre

SPAIN

Mafra

Sintra
Queluz
Cascais
Lisboa
ALTO ALENTEJO
Estremoz
Elvas

Estoril

Parque
Natural de
Arrábida
Setúbal
Évora Monte
Évora

Cabo
Espichel
Tróia
Peninsula
Sesimbra
Alcácer do Sal

Baia de
Setúbal
Costa Azul

Santiago
do Cacém
Beja

Sines

BAIXO ALENTEJO
Guadiana

Costa Dourada
Mira
Mértola

Lagos
Silves
ALGARVE
Tavira

Cabo de
São Vicente
Sagres
Portimão
Albufeira
Faro
Olhão
Vila Real de
Santo António
Golfo de Cádiz

0   50 kilometers
0   50 miles

portugal

Students in Lisbon have a lot of nightlife to choose from. The casual and crowded Bairro Alto becomes one big block party in the wee hours, and though you can't wear your swim trunks and flip flops into the clubs, bouncers let pretty much anything else slide. In Porto the area known as Vitoria tends to host the most students—they seem to make up the entire workforce of the neighborhood's restaurants and bars (and most of the clientele, too).

lisbon

Portugal's capital is a mosaic, comprised of different neighborhoods that all come together to form the cohesive metropolis that is Lisbon. Each district has its own indelible character, from the graffiti-covered party that is Bairro Alto to chic Chiado and on to touristy Baixa and the crumbling tiles of Alfama—cross a single street or descend one steep staircase and you're someplace new. As is typical in Europe, the classic-to-the-point-of-cliché juxtaposition of ancient and modern holds here. But the true joy of Lisbon comes in peeling back the different layers of "old" that simultaneously exist. Pre-WWI tram cars run through the streets past buildings reconstructed after the earthquake of 1755. These are mixed in with remnants of the Renaissance, the Moorish invasion, and the Iron Age. Together, all of these layers form Lisbon, a city as full of surprises as it is of history. To experience its character to the fullest, get lost here. Let your nose lead you to *sardinhas assadas;* stumble through an alleyway to find an architectural marvel; talk to the locals at the hole-in-the-wall and take their advice. We promise you won't regret it.

ORIENTATION

Lisbon's historic center has four main neighborhoods: **Baixa,** where accommodations, shopping, and tourists abound; **Chiado,** where the shopping gets a bit ritzier; night-life-rich **Bairro Alto,** still farther west; and ancient **Alfama,** on the east side of Baixa. The narrow, winding streets and stairways of Alfama and Bairro Alto can be confusing and difficult to navigate without a good map. The **Lisboa Mapa da Cidade e Guia Turístico** €3) has nearly every street in these neighborhoods labeled and is a good investment if you're going to be exploring Lisbon for a few days. Even so, expect to spend some time aimlessly wandering, as even the most detailed of maps will have a hard time effectively detailing these neighborhoods. The maps at the tourist offices are reliable but do not show the names of many streets, particularly in Alfama and Bairro Alto. **Tram #28E** runs east-west, parallel to the river, and connects all these neighborhoods, with its eastern terminus in the inexpensive and off-the-beaten-path neighborhood of **Graça.** The palm-tree-lined **Avenida da Liberdade** runs north from Baixa all the way to the business district around the Praça do Marquês de Pombal, and on the far western edge of the city lies **Belém,** a neighborhood full of magnificent sights and delicious treats.

Baixa

Baixa, Lisbon's old business hub, is the city's most centrally located neighborhood, and its streets are lined with accommodations and clothing stores. An oasis of order for travelers weary of getting lost in labyrinthine old cities, the entire neighborhood is flat and on a grid. The main pedestrian thoroughfare is the broad **Rua Augusta,** which runs from the massive riverside **Praça do Comércio** to Pr. de Dom Pedro IV,

lisbon

better known as **Rossio**. Ⓜ**Baixa-Chiado** has an entrance at the western end (to your right as you face the river) of R. da Vitória, which runs east to west and crosses Rua Augusta. Connected to Rossio's northwest corner is **Praça dos Restauradores,** a huge urban transit hub where the Rossio train station (for trains to Sintra) and tourist office can be found; it is also the main drop-off point for airport buses. From Pr. dos Restauradores, **Avenida da Liberdade** runs away from Baixa to the **Praça do Marquês do Pombal** and its surrounding business district.

Bairro Alto and Chiado

Bairro Alto (literally, "High Neighborhood") is a hilly stretch of narrow cobblestone streets with graffiti-covered walls and laundry-lined balconies, best known for its unique nightlife and its *fado* (the Portuguese equivalent of soul music, if soul music made you weep like a little girl). The best way to get there is to take the metro to Baixa-Chiado (Chiado exit), walk straight across Largo do Chiado, between the churches, and right up Rua da Misericórdia (it becomes R. de São Pedro de Alcântara) before heading left into Alto's daytime slumber or nighttime madness.

Chiado, slightly down the hill toward Baixa, is a little more clean-cut and cultured than its raucous neighbor to the west. The **Rua Garrett** cuts through the neighborhood, running between the **Largo do Chiado** and the stores and shopping center on R. do Carmo. The **Praça de Luís de Camões,** right next to Lg. do Chiado, connects the two neighborhoods.

Alfama

Alfama, Lisbon's hilly medieval quarter, was the only district to survive the 1755 earthquake, and those who have spent long, hot hours lost in its confusing maze of alleyways might sometimes wish it hadn't. Many alleys are unmarked and take confusing turns and bends; others are long, winding stairways known as *escadinhas;* still others are dead ends. Expect to get lost repeatedly—with or without a detailed map. The **Castelo de São Jorge** sits at the steep hill's peak, where you will find impressive views of all of Lisbon. The **Sé** (cathedral) is closer to the river and to Baixa. When in doubt, walk downhill to get closer to the river, where there is a flat, open area that will help you get your bearings. The **Mouraria** (the old Moorish quarter, more recently a multicultural neighborhood with immigrants from across the globe) is on the north and west slope of the hill, away from the river; and **Graça,** a slightly less confusing neighborhood, sits to the northeast.

Graça

Graça, a hilly, residential district, is one of Lisbon's oldest neighborhoods. An easy tram ride on **28E** to the end of the line drops you off in **Largo da Graça.** On one side of the square is **Igreja da Graça,** a shady park, and a spectacular *miradouro* (viewpoint); the other side (where the tram stops) is a busy intersection lined with cheap eateries. It's an easy walk downhill from Graça into Alfama, or a less confusing tram ride back.

Around Praça do Marquês de Pombal

The large Praça do Marquês de Pombal sits at the end of **Avenida da Liberdade,** opposite Pr. dos Restauradores. This is Lisbon's modern business district, full of department stores, shopping centers, office buildings, and some accommodations. But what space isn't taken up by commerce is lush and green, with multiple expansive parks. To the north of Praça do Marquês de Pombal is the **Parque Eduardo VII,** and to the northeast of that is the impressive **Museu Calouste Gulbenkian,** which is located in the **São Sebastião** district and has its own green space as well. Behind the shopping malls, the back streets of the area are quiet and contain small mom-and-pop shops where the prices tend to be a bit more reasonable than in more tourist-oriented areas.

SIGHTS

Bairro Alto and Chiado

◙ MUSEU ARQUEOLÓGICO DO CARMO

CHURCH, MUSEUM

Lg. do Carmo ☎213 47 86 29

Sick of those big, boring churches that all look the same? This archaeological museum is housed in a 14th-century Gothic church like any other, except it's missing its roof. The ruins became ruins in the 1755 earthquake and ensuing fire, and today they stand as an open courtyard under empty arches where the roof once stood. After you take in the cinematic setting, head inside to the museum—the collection spans four millennia and includes some pretty gruesome Peruvian mummy children. But even the sight of potentially undead South American kiddies can't trump the view from beneath the vaulted arches of the church.

i Ⓜ*Baixa-Chiado (Chiado exit) or bus #758, or tram 28E. From Rossio, walk (steeply) up Cç. do Carmo to Lg. do Carmo. €3.50, students and seniors €2, under 14 free. ☼ Open M-Sa Jun-Sept 10am-7pm; Oct-May 10am-6pm.*

IGREJA E MUSEU DE SÃO ROQUE

CHURCH, MUSEUM

Lg. Trindade Coelho ☎213 23 54 44 www.museu-saoroque.com

The Plague reached Lisboa in 1505, brought into the city on an infested ship from Venice. King Manuel I was not too happy about this and requested a relic of São Roque from the Venetians in return, as this saint was supposed to have powers that could ward off disease. That didn't work out, and thousands of Portuguese succumbed to the Black Death. Nevertheless, the Jesuits put up this church in the saint's honor in the 16th century. The alms box on the left side of the nave echoes the awestruck words of many who enter: "Jesus, Maria, Jose" ("Jesus, Mary, and Joseph"). The church is truly magnificent, with not a square inch untouched by the ornate decorations, so be sure to look up at the beautifully painted ceiling. The museum houses a collection of art and relics pertaining to the Jesuits as well as a collection of Eastern art that includes a dazzling chest with glimmering inlay from Macau.

i Ⓜ*Baixa-Chiado (Chiado exit). Bus #758 or tram 28. From Lg. do Chiado, head uphill on R. da Misericórdia; the church is at the far side of the plaza on the right. Museum €2.50, students, under 14, and over 65 free; Su before 2pm free. ☼ Church open M 2-6pm, Tu-W 9am-6pm, Th 9am-9pm, F-Su 9am-6pm. Museum open Tu-W 10am-6pm, Th 2-9pm, F-Su 10am-6pm.*

MUSEU DO CHIADO AND MUSEU NACIONAL DE ARTE CONTEMPORÂNEA

ART MUSEUM

R. Serpa Pinto, 4 ☎213 43 21 48 www.museudochiado-ipmuseus.pt

This constantly updated museum has tons and tons of exhibition space but devotes only a small amount of it to its permanent collection (otherwise it wouldn't stay contemporary for very long, now would it?), which means the temporary exhibitions (four per year) get lots of room for full, comprehensive shows. Consequently, this museum is like a box of chocolates—you never know what you're gonna get. You might see abstract paintings or Portuguese photography or something completely different, but even if it's plastic containers (stacked artistically, rest assured), there will be something intriguing for you to ponder.

i Ⓜ*Baixa-Chiado (Chiado exit). Bus #758, or tram 28E. From Lg. do Chiado, head 1 block toward Baixa (behind you as you exit the metro station), then right down R. Serpa Pinto. €4, seniors €2, students €1.60, under 14 free; Su before 2pm free. ☼ Open Tu-Su 10am-6pm.*

Alfama

◙ CASTELO DE SÃO JORGE

CASTLE, HISTORIC SITE, VIEWS

Castelo de São Jorge ☎21 880 06 20 www.castelosaojorge.pt

Built by the Moors in the 11th century on the highest point in Lisbon, this hilltop fortress was captured by Dom Afonso Henriques, Portugal's first king, in 1147.

get a room!

For more Let's Go recommendations, visit **www.letsgo.com.**

🏨 LISBON LOUNGE HOSTEL/LIVING LOUNGE HOSTEL · · · · · · · · · · HOSTEL $
R. do Crucifixo, 116 · · · · · · · · ☎213 46 10 78 · www.lisbonloungehostel.com

These nearby hostels, under joint ownership, have large common spaces and spacious rooms with the best interior design around, hostel or not. While Living Lounge has individually decorated rooms, Lisbon Lounge features bright colors and amazing street art. Both offer breakfast, loads of tours and activities (some free), and a delicious, traditional nightly dinner €10) with endless wine.

i *Lisbon Lounge: From Ⓜ Baixa-Chiado, take R. da Vitória exit, then immediate right onto R. do Crucifixo, then 1st left onto R. de São Nicolau, and walk 4 blocks. Living Lounge: From Ⓜ Baixa-Chiado, take R. da Vitória exit, then immediate left onto R. do Crucifixo. Lisbon Lounge: June 1-Sep 15 dorms €22; doubles €60. Apr 15-May 31 and Sept 16-Oct 14 dorms €20; doubles €60. Oct 15-Apr 14 dorms €18; doubles €50. Living Lounge: dorms and doubles same rates as Lisbon Lounge. Apr 15-Oct 14 singles €35; Oct 15-Apr 14 singles €30. ☑ Reception 24hr.*

🏨 LISBON DESTINATION HOSTEL · HOSTEL $
R. Primeira de Dezembro, 141, 3rd fl. · · · · · ☎213 46 64 57 · www.rossiopatio.com

Set in the top of the stunningly beautiful Neo-Manueline behemoth that is the Rossio train station, Lisbon Destination Hostel takes the cake for best common area in Baixa, if not Lisbon. With astroturf, tropical music, and a soaring ceiling of glass windows, it feels like you are closer to the Caribbean than the Tejo.

i Ⓜ*Restauradores. Walk away from the giant statue as you exit. The Rossio train station will be on your right. On the 3rd fl. Dorms €18-23; singles €35-40; doubles €30-35. ☑ Reception 24hr.*

🏨 LISBON POETS HOSTEL · HOSTEL $
R. Nova da Trindade, 2, 5th fl. · · · · · · · ☎213 46 10 58 · www.lisbonpoetshostel.com

Not just for the literary snob, this cultured hostel is luxurious enough to satisfy even the least poetic of travelers. The dorm rooms, named for famous poets, are large and clean, and the common room has space for you to write your own couplets in comfort. Activities ranging from city tours to fado nights to cafe crawls take place daily and are free for guests.

i Ⓜ*Baixa-Chiado; take the Pr. do Chiado exit, and turn right up R. Nova da Trindade. Credit card min. €50. Dorms €18-22; private doubles €45-60. Discount with stay in Oporto Poets Hostel (min. 5 nights between the two). ☑ Reception 24hr.*

🏨 THE INDEPENDENTE HOSTEL AND SUITES · · · · · · · · · · · · · · HOSTEL $
R. São Pedro de Alcântara, 81 · · · · · · · · ☎213 46 13 81 · www.theindependente.pt

In an opulent white building right across from the gorgeous Miradouro de São Pedro, The Independente is quite luxurious for the price. A large staircase leads up to the generous common room looking out over the miradouro. Rooms are sizable and many have small balconies.

i Ⓜ*Baixa-Chiado (Chiado exit). Take R. da Misericórdia until it becomes R. São Pedro de Alcântara. The hostel is on your left and shares a building with a cafe. Breakfast and linens included. Towels €1.50. Lock and keycard €5 deposit. June-Sept dorms €17-20; suites €110. Oct-May dorms €13-18; suites €95. ☑ Reception 24hr.*

portugal

With one of the best views in Lisbon, the castle also acts as a one-stop shop for the entire historical Lisbon experience. Walk along the ramparts, see live images of Lisbon fed from an ancient periscope, feel like Indiana Jones at archaeological ruins dating from the Iron Age to the Renaissance (whip optional), and gawk at the seemingly random, yet stunningly beautiful, peacocks that strut about. At night, "Lisboa Who Are You?," a show exclusively comprised of images and Portuguese music, tells the story of Lisbon from beginning to end (€15).

i Bus #737, or trams #12E and 28E; follow signs to Castelo €7, students and seniors €3.50, under 10 free. 🕓 Open daily Mar-Oct 9am-9pm, Nov-Feb 9am-6pm. Last entry 30min. before close. Museum has guided tours daily at noon and 4pm. Periscope 10am-5pm.

🏛 SÉ CATEDRAL DE LISBOA
Lg. da Sé

CHURCH, MUSEUM
☎21 886 67 52

Lisbon's 12th-century cathedral is massive and intimidating, built to double as a fortress, if needed. Its austere Romanesque style makes the few brightly-colored stained glass windows leap out of the walls, where the same ornamentation would be lost in a busy Gothic or Baroque church. The cloisters, an archaeological site perpetually under scaffolding, are well worth the cash, giving visitors a glimpse of the remains of Moorish houses, Roman sewers, and more. The treasury boasts relics, manuscripts, and lots of other shiny valuables.

i Bus #737, or tram #28E. From Baixa, follow R. Conceição east (to the left as you face the river) up past the church, then turn right onto R. Santo António da Sé and follow the tram tracks; it's the large, building that looks like a fortress. Free. Cloister €2.50. Treasury €2.50. 🕓 Church open M 9am-5pm, Tu-Sa 9am-7pm, Su 9am-5pm. Treasury open M-Sa 10am-5pm. Cloister open May-Sept M 10am-5pm, Tu-Sa 10am-6pm; Oct-Apr M-Sa 10am-5pm. Mass Tu-Sa 6:30pm, Su 11:30am.

Graça

PANTEÃO NACIONAL
Campo de Santa Clara

TOMBS, HISTORIC SITE
☎21 885 48 39 www.igespar.pt

The Igreja de Santa Engrácia was started in the late 17th century, but once the architect died the king lost interest in the project and the funding dried up, leaving the church unfinished for some 250 years. The dictator Salazar rededicated the building as the National Pantheon, although it now, ironically, houses the remains of some of his staunchest opponents. Start at the ground level and see the tomb of the much beloved Amália Rodrigues, queen of fado, among others, then take the stairs leading all the way up to the top of the dome, a distinctive feature of the Lisbon skyline.

i Ⓜ Santa Apolónia, bus #34, or tram #28E. Get off tram 28E at Voz do Operário stop in front of Igreja e Mosteiro de São Vicente de Fora, then follow Arco Grande de Cima (to the left of church), then take the 1st right, 1st left, and then another right. €3, students and under 14 free, seniors €1.50. Su before 2pm free for all. 🕓 Open Tu-Su 10am-5pm.

IGREJA E MOSTEIRO DE SÃO VICENTE DE FORA
Lg. de São Vicente

CHURCH, MONASTERY
☎21 885 56 52

The Church and Monastery of St. Vincent is grandiose, with impressive architecture, vaulted ceilings, and an extremely intricate altar. However, the recorded classical music (to make sure you experience the proper amount of reverence) is a bit much. The attached monastery—a beautiful site in its own right—has a small museum dedicated to the church's history, as well as lots of great features, such as a tiny Baroque chapel, an extremely old cloister, and access to the roof with a magnificent view of the surrounding area.

i Ⓜ Santa Apolónia, bus #34 or tram #28E. Get off tram 28E in front of the massive white church at the Voz do Operário stop. €4, students and seniors €2. 🕓 Open Tu-Su 10am-6pm. Last entry 1hr. before close.

MUSEU NACIONAL DO AZULEJO   MUSEUM
R. da Madre de Deus, 4   ☎21 810 03 40 mnazulejo.imc-ip.pt

Enter this museum via its tranquil courtyard, passing by the incredible Manueline doorway of the Convento da Madre de Deus. The museum is devoted to the
art of the azulejo (glazed and painted tile), one of Portugal's most famous and
most ubiquitous forms of art. Some of the tiles are whimsical, others saucy, and
others just impressive: the early 18th-century (pre-earthquake) panorama of the
city of Lisbon is one of the world's largest works of azulejo. Ignore the tacky
faux-azulejo boards with cut-outs to stick your face in for a photo-op, and move
on to the incredible sanctuary to lift your spirits.

*i Take bus #794 from Santa Apolónia station bus stop (side closest to the river) to Igreja da Madre
de Deus. €5, seniors €2.50, under 14 free. Su before 2pm free for all. ☼ Open Tu 2-6pm, W-Su
10am-6pm. Last entry 30min. before close.*

Belém

The Belém waterfront, a couple of kilometers west of Lisbon's center, is a majestic
tribute to Portugal's Age of Discovery and its legendary seafaring spirit. This is where
history-changing explorers Vasco da Gama and Prince Henry the Navigator left for
distant lands, and the opulence of the new worlds they opened up can be seen today
just a short tram ride from Baixa, in Belém. Equally as famous and almost as important as the historic sights is ⧉Pasteis de Belém, a pastry shop with a reputation as rich
as its pastries. (R. Belém, 84-92 21 363 74 23 Pastries €1.05 Open daily 9am-11pm.)
The easiest way to get to Belém is to take tram 15E from Pr. do Comércio (dir.: Algés)
to the Mosteiro dos Jerónimos stop, which is one stop beyond the one labeled Belém.

⧉ **MOSTEIRO DOS JERÓNIMOS**   CHURCH, MUSEUM
Pr. do Império   ☎21 362 00 34 www.mosteirojeronimos.pt

The Hieronymite Monastery was established in 1502 to honor Vasco da Gama's
expedition to India. We're guessing the explorer's spirit is pleased with this
ornate tribute. The Manueline building has the detail of its Gothic predecessors
and the sweeping elegance of the oncoming Renaissance. In the 1980s, the
monastery was granted World Heritage Site status by UNESCO and remains in
pristine condition, both inside and out. The church contains tombs (both symbolic and actual) of Portuguese kings and bishops. Symbolic tombs (cenotaphs)
include areas of tribute to Vasco da Gama and Luís de Camões, Portugal's most
celebrated poet. Entrance to the cloister is not cheap (€7), but free Su before
2pm), but it's worth it to see one of Lisbon's most beautiful spaces, which somehow retains its charm despite being filled with hordes of tourists. Those on a
shoestring budget can see the massive chapel for free, but the cloister is the real
sight here.

*i Tram #15E or bus #28, 714, 727, 729, 743, 749, 751 to Mosteiro dos Jerónimos. Free. Cloister
and museum €7, over 65 €3.50, under 14 free; Su before 2pm free. Combined ticket with Torre
de Belém €10. ☼ Open May-Sept Tu-Su 10am-6:30pm; Oct-Apr Tu-Su 10am-5:30pm. Last entry
30min. before close.*

⧉ **TORRE DE BELÉM**   DEFENSE TOWER, VIEWS
Torre de Belém   ☎21 362 00 34

Portugal's most famous tower has risen out of the water (except at low tide,
when it's connected to the shore by a narrow, sandy isthmus) from the banks
of the Tejo for nearly 500 years, gracing visitors' memories and souvenir stores'
postcards since its completion in 1519. Be prepared to relive childhood games
(no, not The Floor is Lava) as you pretend to fire cannons on two different
levels. Then head downstairs and check out the prison cells and ammunition
area (hopefully this doesn't also remind you of your childhood). It's worth going
up all the way to the top to see breathtaking panoramic views of Belém and the

Tejo. There is also a rhinoceros carving in homage to the real rhino the king tried to bring back for the pope, because nothing garners favor from the pope like a large, horned animal.

i From Mosteiro dos Jerónimos, take the unmarked underground walkway in front of the monastery (from entrance, head toward the river; it's a small stairway) to other side of road and tracks and walk west along the river (to the right as you face the water) about 15min. Alternatively, walk in the same direction on the monastery's side of the road and take the pedestrian walkway over the road at the tower. €5, over 65 €2.50, students and under 14 free. Su before 2pm free for all. Combined ticket with Mosteiro dos Jerónimos €10. ⚄ Open May-Sept Tu-Su 10am-6:30pm, Oct-Apr Tu-Su 10am-5:30pm. Last entry 30min. before close.

São Sebastião

MUSEU CALOUSTE GULBENKIAN   MUSEUM
Av. de Berna, 45A   ☎21 782 30 00 www.museu.gulbenkian.pt

Want an art history survey course for under €5? This museum has a large and eclectic collection of works from the ancient Mesopotamians and Egyptians to the Impressionists and beyond. The collection belonged to native Armenian and oil tycoon Calouste Gulbenkian, who came to Portugal on vacation in 1942 and never left. When he died, he gave his massive art collection to the state, which, like any good state, decided to charge people to look at it. The building itself is hideous, but the treasures inside are not—in particular the illuminated manuscripts from the Middle East to France seem to have been dunked in molten gold, and the dark, quiet room with a garden view is a lovely place to unwind.

i Ⓜ São Sebastião, or buses #96, 205, 716, 726, 746, 756. Exit Ⓜ São Sebastião at Av. António Augusto de Aguiar (north exit) and go straight uphill along the avenue until you reach the massive Pr. Espanha, then turn right. It is NOT the building that looks like a castle in the park to the right; keep going along the avenue. €4, students under 25 and seniors €2, under 12 free. Temporary exhibits €3-5. ⚄ Open Tu-Su 10am-6pm.

FOOD

Lisbon has some of the best and most reasonably priced restaurants this side of the Rhine, and some of the finest wine to boot. Depending on the neighborhood, an average full dinner will usually run about €10-12 per person, with the *pratos do dia* often only €5-7. Some of the best and least expensive meals can be found in the ubiquitous **pastelarias**. Although the focus of these pastry shops are the counters, which contain mountains of treats, they also serve up tasty and well-priced meals. That said, don't skip the pastries: **pasteis de nata** are generally less than €1 and are the city's most popular sweet. The Portuguese love their coffee, but realize that when you order **café**, you are actually ordering a shot of espresso. You can order a "normal" coffee (*abatanado* or *americano*), but you might get some looks; many Portuguese think of it more as soup than real coffee. Local specialties include summertime *caracois* (small snails; look for a restaurant with a sign that says "Há caracois" in the window), *lombo de porco com amêijoas* (pork with clams, much tastier than it sounds), and the Portuguese staples *alheira* (smoked chicken sausage) and *sardinhas assadas* (grilled sardines). But the ultimate Portuguese food is **bacalhau** (codfish). Prepared in over 1000 different ways, cod is practically a religion here. A source of national pride, it can be found in almost any restaurant you visit. Some of the best deals, in terms of getting a lot for a little, are the *tostas*, large grilled sandwiches topped with melted butter that usually cost €2-3. The local traditional drink is **ginjinha** (pronounced "jee-JEE-nyah," also often called *ginja*), a sour cherry liqueur served ice-cold in a shot glass and meant to be sipped. If it's bad, it tastes like cough syrup, but if it's good, it's delicious and refreshing, particularly on hot Lisbon afternoons. It usually costs €1-1.50 and is sometimes served in a shot glass made of chocolate for a little extra dough.

lisbon

Baixa

☒ MOMA
PORTUGUESE, ITALIAN $$

R. de São Nicolau, 47 ☎914 41 75 36

A white, simple, and clean aesthetic complements this delicious oasis of good food in the desert that is Baixa. Moma's chalk menu tells the story of Portuguese cuisine with an Italian twist. The dishes tend to be cool, light, and creative for the hot summer months, but heavier meals are here for the taking as well (the €9 veal filet is heaven on a plate). Outside is the best place to enjoy your meal; you will find yourself in the middle of the R. de São Nicolau but separated from the touristy madness by umbrellas and bamboo blinds.

i ⓜBaixa-Chiado (Baixa exit). Exit metro station onto R. da Vitória, then right 1 block, and then left onto R. de São Nicolau. Entrees €6-9. ☒ Open M-F noon-6pm.

BONJARDIM
GRILL $$$

Tv. de Santo Antão, 12 ☎213 42 74 24

A little bit past Rossio, this restaurant is just off the food-filled R. de Santo Antão and takes up almost an entire block to serve massive portions for animal lovers (i.e., not the PETA kind) to feast upon. Dine outside and enjoy your meal from the "king of chicken" while watching either crabs and lobsters duke it out in the window aquarium.

i ⓜRestauradores or buses #36, 44, 709, 711, 732, 745, 759. Take Travessa de Santo Antão from the east side of Pr. dos Restauradores. Meals €10-30. ☒ Open Tu 6-11:30pm, W-Su noon-11:30pm. Outdoor seating until 10pm.

Bairro Alto and Chiado

☒ CERVEJARIA TRINDADE
PORTUGUESE $$$

R. Nova da Trindade, 20C ☎213 42 35 06 www.cervejariatrindade.pt

Cervejaria Trindade is famous all over Lisbon for its molhos, beer-based sauces that were invented here. These savory and buttery sauces taste incredible on just about any meat you can think of, and eateries throughout the city will often offer a course"à trindade," named for this establishment. The restaurant is also famous for its history, as it was occupied by a convent as far back as the 13th century (the pulpit is still in the main dining room) and became one of Lisbon's first breweries at the start of the 19th century (don't skip the beer). The enormous dining rooms are covered with azulejos from this period, and the cloister of the convent is used for dining as well.

i From ⓜBaixa-Chiado, exit onto Lg. do Chiado, then take a sharp right up R. Nova da Trindade (to left of A Brasileira). Meat dishes à trindade €9-18. Pratos do dia M-F €7.50. ☒ Open daily 10am-2am.

☒ KAFFEEHAUS
AUSTRIAN $$

R. Anchieta, 3 ☎210 95 68 28 www.kaffeehaus-lisboa.com

It's understandable if you didn't come to Lisbon to order in German, but this neo-Bohemian cafe has outrageously good food at great prices. The outdoor seats are on the narrow (and thus shady and breezy) street outside, while the inside of the cafe is air-conditioned and contemporary, with angular lamps and a single wall covered in posters. There is a comprehensive bar, but the real treats are the several refreshing homemade lemonades with unexpected but tasty additions such as ginger. Come on Sunday morning for their brunch options (€6.50-10).

i From ⓜBaixa-Chiado, exit onto Lg. do Chiado, take a very sharp right down R. Garrett 2 blocks, then head right down R. Anchieta. Sandwiches €4-6. Salads €5-10. Entrees €9-17. Vegetarian options €9-11. Coffees €1-3. ☒ Open Tu-Sa 11am-midnight, Su 11am-8pm.

portugal

O FOGAREIRO   PORTUGUESE $$
R. da Atalaia, 92   ☎213 46 80 59

As a visitor to Lisbon, it can be difficult to get traditional Portuguese food without stooping to the level of insanely touristy or ridiculously expensive. Luckily, O Fogareiro is there for you, with its tasty plates, its many reasonable pratos do dia, and most importantly, its lack of pushy waiters trying to lure you inside or to their sketchy, nondescript van. It really depends on the place. Order a bottle of wine, some olives, and bacalhau (Portuguese cod), and you will finally have the picturesque dinner you have been waiting for.

i Ⓜ*Baixa-Chiado (Chiado exit), tram 28E, or bus #758 to Lg. do Luís Camões. From there, take R. do Loreto and turn right on R. da Atalaia. Entrees €9-12. Pratos do dia €7-9. ☼ M-Sa 8pm-2am.*

Alfama

Alfama's maze of winding streets hides many small, traditional restaurants. The cheapest options tend to gather along Rua dos Bacalhoeiros, with the tastiest options located along Rua de São João da Praça.

🌊 POIS, CAFE   CAFE $$
R. de São João da Praça, 93   ☎21 886 24 97 www.poiscafe.com

This Austrian-run cafe is quite comfortable, with couches, book-lined walls, and even a toy corner. Don't worry if it looks crowded inside; tables are shared. Almost everything on the menu has something inventive in it (e.g. apple and pesto on a veggie sandwich), although some more traditional options are available. Don't skip out on the custom lemonades, even though the coffee is almost as good.

i *Tram #28E to Sé. From plaza in front of cathedral, walk to the right of cathedral; the cafe is on the right. Lunch menu €5. Baked goods €2-7. ☼ Open Tu-Su 11am-8pm.*

🌊 TASCA BELA   TAPAS, PORTUGUESE $$
R. dos Remédios, 190   ☎96 467 09 64

Tasca Bela deals only in petiscos, the Portuguese version of tapas. Come with friends and enjoy a myriad of reasonably priced small dishes for everyone to share. The restaurant is covered with old-time photos and Portuguese guitars, and they have fado multiple times per week. They are also open late, so it's a great place to fill up when you feel those 2am munchies coming on. Order the chorizo assado (€6) and watch it come out flaming. But beware, you might leave without your eyebrows.

i Ⓜ*Santa Apolónia. Head to the right of the Museu Militar, then left onto R. Remédios. Petiscos €1-6. ☼ Open daily 8pm-4am.*

TABERNA MODERNA   MODERN PORTUGUESE $$$
R. dos Bacalhoeiros, 18   ☎21 886 50 39

This restaurant sits close to the water, but that doesn't mean it's the same as all of its traditional Portuguese neighbors. As the name suggests, Taberna Moderna puts modern twists on Portuguese food by bringing in foreign influences, including Japanese and Italian. The dining room is wide open and minimalistic but gains personality from the giant nude painting adorning one of the walls.

i Ⓜ*Terreiro do Paço. From the north end of Pr. Comércio with the river behind you, take a right onto R. da Alfândega, then take a left after 3 blocks. The restaurant is on your right. Entrees €9-14. ☼ Open Tu-W 7:30pm-midnight, Th-Sa 7:30pm-2am.*

ÓH CALDAS   PORTUGUESE $$$
R. de São Mamede, 22   ☎21 887 57 11

This traditional restaurant (with an untraditional honeycomb design on the wall) has favorites like sardinhas assadas (grilled sardines), alheira (smoked chicken sausage), and an ever-changing three-course daily menu (€12). Its location on the scenic route between the Sé (cathedral) and the Castelo de São Jorge makes it a convenient Alfama stop.

i From Baixa, follow R. Conceiçao east toward Alfama (to left as you face the river), just past the Igreja da Madalena. Head left up Tv. Almada for 3 blocks, then left onto R. São Mamede. Daily menu €12. ☼ Open daily noon-4pm and 8pm-midnight.

Graça

◪ HAWELI TANDOORI INDIAN $$
Tv. do Monte, 14 ☎21 886 77 13

A small island in a sea of pastelarias and other Portuguese cheap eats, Haweli Tandoori offers something that isn't found anywhere else in Graça: Indian food. Not only is it Indian, it's also delicious. The chicken tikka masala (€8) is savory, and the garlic naan (€1.50) is buttery and scrumptious. Naturally, plenty of vegetarian options are also available. And most surprisingly, the vast majority of the clientele is comprised of locals (everyone gets tired of codfish, eventually).

i Take tram #28E to end of the line; walk down the street past the big church, and take a left onto Tv. do Monte. Naan €1-2. Entrees €6-10. ☼ Open M noon-3pm and 7-10:30pm; W-Su noon-3pm, 7-10:30pm.

O VICENTINHO PORTUGUESE $
R. da Voz do Operário, 1A

With a strikingly orange interior, O Vicentinho offers a comfortable place to sit down and enjoy a meal. Nice wooden tables give the ambience of a real restaurant at the prices of a pastelaria. Finally, you can enjoy your Sande Mista (ham and cheese sandwich; €2) without having to stand at a counter, staring at a blank, white, tile wall or pretending to text someone in order to avoid making awkward eye contact.

i Ⓜ Santa Apolonia, bus #34 or tram #28E. Get off tram 28E in front of the massive white church at the Voz do Operário stop. Sandwiches €2. Pratos do dia €6. ☼ Open M-Sa 9am-7pm.

TASCA DO MANEL PORTUGUESE $$
R. de São Tomé, 20 ☎21 886 20 21

Black-and-white photographs line the walls of this traditional restaurant. The typical fare is on display, as are omelettes, so you can get your brunch on whenever the time is right. It's just down the road from Lg. da Graça toward Alfama, which makes it a very convenient stop. Expect a wait, as it's a local favorite.

i From Lg. Graça, go to the small park in front of the church, next to the lookout point, then follow Cç. Graça straight; it becomes R. São Tomé after a small plaza (stay to the right of the kebab place). Pratos do dia €6-9. Entrees €8-12. ☼ Open M-Sa noon-3:30pm and 6:30-10:30pm.

NIGHTLIFE

Bairro Alto

◪ ASSOCIAÇÃO LOUCOS & SONHADORES BAR
Tv. do Conde do Soure, 2 ☎213 47 82 50

A few minutes away from the craziness of the Bairro Alto scene, the Crazies' and Dreamers' Association sits quietly in a nondescript building, with only a small, mysterious yet welcoming wooden sign on the door. Once inside, you will be glad that this gem is a well-kept secret. Dimly lit, this smoky bar is filled with clutter, paintings, and books. The chatter of friends and the smooth sounds of jazz somehow allow it to be simultaneously gritty, sophisticated, and sincere. Beer is cheap, bar snacks are on the table, and cigs are available at the bar.

i Ⓜ Restauradores. Cross the square and take a left onto Cç. da Gloria in the northwest corner, then take a right on R. São Pedro de Alcântara. Take a left onto R. Luisa Todi, which becomes Tv. do Conde do Soure. Beer €1.10. ☼ Open Tu-Su 10pm-3am.

PAVILHÃO CHINÊS

LOUNGE

R. de Dom Pedro V, 89   ☎213 42 47 29

A little north of the main Bairro Alto scene, this nightlife spot is a bit more laid-back (and indoors) than its raucous neighbors, but it's hardly boring. A massive labyrinth, Pavilhão Chinês feels like a clash of the Victorian and the absurd, with thousands of figurines and odd paintings covering the place from floor to ceiling, while men in fancy blue vests tend the ornate wooden bars. There is a huge menu of teas and classic drinks, like the Sidecar (they're bringin' it back, baby) presented in a 50-page menu-cum-graphic novel.

i Bus #758. From Pr. de Luís de Camões, follow R. da Misericórdia up toward the miradouro, and keep following the same street as it bends to the left and becomes R. de Dom Pedro V. Beer €3. Tea €4. Drinks €6-9. ☒ Open M-Sa 6pm-2am, Su 9pm-2am.

PORTAS LARGAS

BAR, MUSIC

R. da Atalaia, 105   ☎213 46 63 79

This staple of the Bairro Alto scene has live music every night (sometimes really good, other times unfortunate covers of '80s songs that are so bad they're good) and some of the biggest, strongest caipirinhas (the national cocktail of Brazil, made from sugar cane rum, sugar, and lime) and mojitos (around €5-7). True to its name, the large doors allow a good deal of traffic to make its way inside, but you can enjoy the music and drinks just outside if things get too crowded. Just don't expect to be able to loiter inside and enjoy the music without buying a drink.

i Ⓜ Baixa-Chiado (Chiado exit). Bus #758 or tram 28E. Walk up R. da Misericórdia 3 blocks from Pr. de Luís de Camões, then left for 5 blocks. Beer €4. Cocktails €5-7. ☒ Open Jul-Sept M-Th 7pm-2am, F-Sa 7pm-3am, Su 7pm-2am; Oct-Jun M-Th 8pm-2am, F-Sa 8pm-3am, Su 8pm-2am.

BICA ABAIXO

BAR

R. da Bica de Duarte Belo, 62   ☎213 47 70 14 www.bicaabaixo.blogspot.pt

This bar is located on the steep slope of the shiny, silver Elevador da Bica funicular, just to the south of the center of Bairro Alto. It's perfect for those making the trek down to the river or for those sick of Bairro Alto's cheaply made drinks—the native Brazilians who own and run this small bar make the best caipirinhas €3.50) in town, crushed, mashed and mixed together right in front of you.

i Ⓜ Baixa-Chiado (Chiado exit). Or tram 28E to Calhariz-Bica. From Pr. de Luís de Camões, follow R. do Loreto (far-right corner of plaza, with your back to the metro station) 3 blocks, then turn left down R. da Bica de Duarte Belo; the bar is on the left. Beer €1.50. Mixed drinks €3-4. ☒ Open daily 9pm-2am.

Alfama

LUX

CLUB

Av. do Infante Dom Henrique   ☎21 882 08 www.luxfragil.com

This club is known far and wide as one of the best clubs in Western Europe; Lisboans abroad will tell you that if you visit one discoteca in Lisbon, it has to be this one. The enormous riverside complex has three stories of debauchery, though you'll leave with a few more of your own Chill on the calm rooftop with amazing views, start to get schwasty at a slightly more intense bar on the floor below that, then descend into the maelstrom on the lowest level to find a raging disco, howling and shrieking with electronic music. Drinks are pricey (cocktails €8-12) and everything is cutting edge. "We cannot escape from each other" is written all around the main bar, giving creepy single guys a great segue into awful pickup lines. The bouncers tend to be very selective, so just act cool and try to get on their good side by being polite and speaking Portuguese.

Dress well—only wear jeans or sneakers if the jeans are super-skinny and the sneakers are canvas high-tops, since the stylin' hipster look tends to play well.

i ⓜSanta Apolónia, bus #28, 34, 706, 712, 735, 759, 781, 782, 794. Just east of Santa Apolónia train station, on the side of the tracks closest to the river. Cover usually €12. ☑ Open Tu-Sa midnight-6am.

🍸 GINJA D'ALFAMA
GINJINHA

R. de São Pedro, 12

Hidden in the heart of Alfama, this tiny hole-in-the-ancient-wall bar specializes in ginjinha, Lisbon's native wild-cherry liqueur, and serves it up cheap and ice cold (€1). You can take it outside to the small tables around the corner, which are much cooler than the stifling bar itself. It's a great place to start the night, serving sandwiches for a good carbo-load before moving on to more raucous nightlife.

i Bus #28, 34, 706, 712, 735, 759, 781, 782, 794. Walk down R. São João da Praça, to the right of Sé Cathedral as you're facing it, and follow the same street (bear left at the fork 1 block past the cathedral) as it becomes R. São Pedro; it's a small store on the left side. Ginjinha €1. Sandwiches €1.50-2.50. ☑ Open M 9:30am-midnight, W-Su 9:30am-midnight.

RESTÔ
BAR, CIRCUS

Costa do Castelo, 7 ☎21 886 73 34 www.chapito.org

This bar has amazing views over Alfama and the Tejo, though they are best enjoyed during the daytime. At night, the outside patio comes alive with a carnival feel, and not without reason—it's on the grounds of Chapitô, a government-funded clown school. On most evenings, there are circus shows, with tightrope walkers and trapeze artists practicing aerial acrobatics over the party below. Go downstairs to enjoy the separate, dark and smoky bar that usually has live music, albeit fewer clowns.

i Bus #737 to Costa do Castelo. From Baixa, it's a long walk uphill: follow R. da Conceição east toward Alfama (left as you face the river), past Igreja da Madalena, and up Tv. Almada to the left to R. São Mamede. Go up the steep and windy Tv. Mata, then left up Cç. Conde de Penafiel to Costa do Castelo, then right. Beer €2. Cocktails €5-7. ☑ Open M-F noon-3pm and 7:30pm-1am, Sa-Su noon-1:30am.

Riverfront: Cais do Sodré, Santos, Alcântara, Docas

OP ART
CLUB

Doca de Santo Amaro ☎21 395 67 87 www.opartcafe.com

During the daytime, this is a pleasant spot to sit by the water and watch the waves while listening to the hum of the cars passing over the bridge. On Friday and Saturday nights, it's a completely different story. Guest DJs rattle the panes of the all-glass structure, pumping hip hop, house beats, and more until the sun starts to rise over the Tejo. Stay all night and see the 25 de Abril Bridge (modeled after the Golden Gate Bridge) light up in the morning for the full experience.

i Buses #28, 201, 714, 720, 732, 738 or trams #15E and 18E. Head toward the bridge along the waterfront. Cove €5-10; includes 1 drink. Beer €2.50. Cocktails €5-7. ☑ Open Tu-Th 3pm-2am, F-Sa 3pm-6am, and Su 3pm-2am.

DOCK'S CLUB
CLUB

R. da Cintura do Porto de Lisboa, 226 ☎21 395 08 56

This disco near the bridge is famous for its Ladies' Nights on Tuesday (well, Wednesday morning), when women not only get in free but also get €14 in free drinks. Spare your friends the social commentary on this potentially sexist practice and enjoy the music blasting from the two different bars inside or the fresh air on the patio in back.

i Buses #28, 201, 714, 720, 732, 738 or trams #15E and 18E. Cove €10-15. Beer €3. Cocktails €6. ☑ Open Tu midnight-6am, Th-Sa midnight-6am.

portugal

MUSICBOX
R. Nova do Carvalho, 24

☎21 343 01 07 www.musicboxlisboa.com

This venue gets great indie and punk bands to play early in the night (sets usually start at 11pm), and the best local DJs spin from 2am until closing, which is shortly after dawn. The line is often so long you'll be surprised there's not a roller coaster waiting when you finally get to the door, but it's worth the wait. The space is small enough that 100 people will feel like a great crowd, but there will likely be even more than that.

i Ⓜ*Cais do Sodré or bus #28, 35, 36, 44, 706, 714, 735, 758, 760, 781, 782, 794 to C. Sodré. From Pr. Luís de Camões, walk all the way down R. Alecrim, then take a sharp right once you get to the bottom to double back under the bridge. Cover €6-10; usually includes 1 drink.* ⏰ *Open W-Sa 11pm-7am.*

ARTS AND CULTURE

Fado

A mandatory experience for visitors, Lisbon's trademark form of entertainment is traditional fado, an art form combining music, song, and narrative poetry. Its roots lie in the Alfama neighborhood, where women whose husbands had gone to sea would lament their fado (fate). Singers of fado traditionally dress in black and sing mournful tunes of lost love, uncertainty, and the famous feelings of saudade (to translate saudade as "loneliness" would be a gruesome understatement). However, many fado venues will have less melancholic songs and even some comical crowd pleasers (if you understand Portuguese, at least). Many fado houses are located in Bairro Alto and in Alfama between the cathedral and the water, and finding one is not difficult, as you can hear snippets of songs drifting into the streets as you pass by (fadistas don't use microphones, but that doesn't mean you won't hear them). Almost all fado houses are rather touristy, but locals—especially older folk—still crowd in amongst the hordes of tourists. Expensive fado houses with mournfully high minimums include Café Luso (Tv. Queimada, 10 213 42 22 81 www.cafeluso.pt €16 min. Open daily 7:30pm-2am) and Adega Machado (R. Norte, 91 213 22 46 40 www. adegamachado.pt €16 min. Open Tu-Su 8pm-3am). There are also some well-marked and easy-to-find places on Rua de São João da Praça in Alfama, including Clube de Fado, with road signs pointing you in that direction all the way from Baixa. The places listed below are either free or truly worth the money.

📷 A TASCA DO CHICO

R. do Diário de Notícias, 39

BARRIO ALTO

☎965 05 96 70

This Bairro Alto fado location is popular with locals and has no cover charge or drink minimum. You're going to want a cold drink, however, as everyone is packed in like sardinhas by the time the fado starts. Many choose to grab a spot at the open window and watch from the cool(er) street outside. Pretty much any amateur fadista who wants to take a turn can sing, so on any given night you can hear something you'd rather forget followed by the next big thing in fado.

i Ⓜ*Baixa-Chiado (Chiado exit). From Pr. Luís de Camões, head up R. Norte (to the right near the far side of the plaza if your back is to the metro station) for 1 block, then take a quick left. Next, turn right up R. Diário de Notícias. Beer €1.50.* ⏰ *Open M-Sa 6pm-3:30am. Fado starts around 9:30pm, but arrive much earlier to get a seat.*

VOSSEMECÊ

R. de Santo António da Sé, 18

ALFAMA

☎218 88 30 56 www.vossemece.com

This fado joint, conveniently located near Baixa, is housed in a beautiful, if oddly shaped, stable; arched ceilings and heavy stone columns run farther than the eye can see into the darkness of the surprisingly spacious restaurant. The fadistas rotate, each singing a couple of songs ranging from lively and funny to mournful and heart-wrenching. There's no cover charge or drink minimum, and the drinks are reasonably priced (€3.50-6.50) and quite good; however, the environment lends itself more toward sitting down for a nice meal with a bottle of wine (you will need it to cope).

i Ⓜ*Baixa-Chiado (Baixa exit), or tram #28E. Follow R. Conceiçao east toward Alfama (to the left as you face the river) past Igreja da Madalena; it's on the corner across the street to the left. Drinks €3.50-6.50. Entrees €10-15.* ☒ *Open M-Tu noon-4pm and 8:30pm-midnight, Th-Su noon-4pm and 8:30pm-midnight. Fado performances 9pm-midnight.*

Feiras Markets

🏴 FEIRA DA LADRA   GRAÇA
Campo de Santa Clara

Held in Graça near the edge of Alfama, the so-called "thief's market" is Lisbon's best known feira. The stalls at this market, which takes place every Tuesday and Saturday, stretch from the Mosteiro de São Vicente da Fora to the Panteão Nacional, with vendors selling treasures (ornate antique silverware), junk (used tennis balls), and everything in between (bootlegged kung-fu action movies). Prices are flexible, and bargaining is encouraged, but initially posing too low of an offer can be taken as an insult. Hawk-like vision may be necessary to spot the diamonds in the rough, but if you want anything worth having, get there early before the tour groups pick the place clean.

i *Take tram #28E to Igreja e Mosteiro de São Vicente de Fora, then walk to the left of the big white church.* ☒ *Open Tu and Sa 7am-2pm.*

ESSENTIALS
Practicalities

- **TOURIST OFFICE: Main Tourist Office.** (Pr. Restauradores, 1250 ☎21 347 56 60 www.visitlisboa.com *i* Ⓜ Restauradores, or bus #36, 44, 91, 709, 711, 732, 745, or 759. On west side of Pr. Restauradores, in Palácio da Foz. ☒ Open daily 9am-8pm.) The **Welcome Center** is the city's main tourist office where you can buy tickets for sightseeing buses and the **Lisboa Card,** which includes transportation and discounted admission to most sights for a flat fee. (R. Arsenal, 15 ☎21 031 28 10) The **airport branch** is located near the terminal exit. (☎21 845 06 60 ☒ Open daily 7am-midnight.) There are also information kiosks in Santa Apolónia, Belém, and on R. Augusta in Baixa.

- **CURRENCY EXCHANGE: NovaCâmbios** in Rossio. (Pr. Dom Pedro IV, 42 ☎21 324 25 53 www.novacambios.com Ⓜ Rossio. Bus #36, 44, 91, 709, 711, 732, 745, or 759. On west side of Rossio plaza. ☒ Open M-F 8:30am-3pm.)

- **INTERNET: Biblioteca Municipal Camões** has free internet access. (Lg. Calhariz, 17 ☎21 342 21 57 www.blx.cm-lisboa.pt *i* Ⓜ Baixa-Chiado, tram 28E, or bus #58 or 100. From Pr. Luís de Camões, follow R. Loreto for 4 blocks. ☒ Open Jul 16-Sept 15 M-F 11am-6pm; Sept 16-Jul 15 Tu-F 10:30am-6pm.)

- **POST OFFICE: Correios** main office is on Pr. Restauradores. (Pr. Restauradores, 58 ☎213 23 89 71 www.ctt.pt *i* Ⓜ Restauradores. Bus #336, 44, 91, 709, 711, 732, 745, or 759. ☒ Open M-F 8am-10pm, Sa-Su 9am-6pm.)

Emergency

- **POLICE: Tourism Police Station** provides police service for foreigners. (Pr. Restauradores, 1250 ☎21 342 16 24 *i* Ⓜ Restauradores. Bus #36, 44, 91, 709, 711, 732, 745, or 759. On west side of Pr. Restauradores, in Palácio da Foz next to the tourist office.)

- **PHARMACY: Farmácia Azevedo and Filhos** in Rossio posts a schedule of pharmacies open late at night, as do most other pharmacies; or just look for a lighted, green cross. (Pr. Dom

Pedro IV, 31 ☎21 343 04 82 *i* ⓂRossio. Bus #36, 44, 91, 709, 711, 732, 745, or 759. In front of metro stop at the side of Rossio closest to river. ⌚ Open daily 8:30am-7:30pm.)

- **HOSPITAL/MEDICAL SERVICES:** Lisbon's main hospital is **Hospital de São José.** (R. José António Serrano ☎21 884 10 00 *i* ⓂMartim Moniz. Bus #34, 708, or 760. ⌚ Open 24hr.) **Hospital de São Luis** is in Bairro Alto. (R. Luz Soriano, 182 *i* ⓂBaixa-Chiado. From Pr. Luís de Camões, follow R. Loreto 4 blocks, then turn right onto R. Luz Soriano. ⌚ Open daily 9am-8pm.)

Getting There

BY PLANE

All flights land at **Aeroporto de Lisboa** (LIS; ☎21 841 35 00), near the northern edge of the city. The cheapest way to get to town from the airport is by **bus.** To get to the bus stop, walk out of the terminal, turn right, and cross the street to the bus stop, marked by yellow metal posts with arrival times of incoming buses. Buses #44 and 745 (€1.75. ⌚ 15-20min., daily every 25min., 6am-12:15am) run to Pr. Restauradores, where they stop in front of the tourist office. The express AeroBus #1 runs to the same locations (€3.50 ⌚ 15min., daily every 20min., 7am-11pm) and is a much faster option during rush hours. A **taxi** downtown costs €10-15, but fares are billed by time, not distance, so watch out for drivers trying to take a longer route.

BY TRAIN

Those traveling in and out of Lisbon by train are regularly confused, as there are multiple major train stations in Lisbon, all serving different destinations. The express and inexpensive **Alfa Pendular** line runs between Braga, Porto, Coimbra, and Lisbon. Regional trains are slow and can be crowded; buses are slightly more expensive but faster and more comfortable. **Urbanos** trains run from Lisbon to Sintra and to Cascais, with stops along the way, and are very cheap and reliable. Contact **Comboios de Portugal** for more information (☎80 820 82 08 www.cp.pt). Those who want to head south should go to the **Entrecampos** station. **Estação Cais do Sodré** is right at the river, a 5min. walk west from Baixa or a quick metro ride to the end of the green line. **Estação Rossio** is the gorgeous neo-Manueline building between Rossio and Pr. Restauradores and services almost all Lisbon suburbs, with lines ending in Sintra, Cascais, Azambuja, and Sado. **Estação Santa Apolónia** is one of the main international and inter-city train stations in Lisbon, running trains to the north and east. It is located on the river to the east of Baixa; to get there, take the blue metro line to the end of the line. Trains run between Santa Apolónia and: Aveiro (€26 ⌚ 2½hr., 16 per day 6am-9:30pm); Braga (€32.50 ⌚ 3½hr., 4 per day 7am-7pm); Coimbra (€22.50 ⌚ 2hr., 20 per day 6am-10pm); and Porto (€24-30 ⌚ 3hr., 16 per day 6am-11pm). **Estação Oriente** runs southbound trains. The station is near the Parque das Nações, up the river to the east of the center; take the red metro line to the end of the line. Trains run between Oriente and Faro (€21-22 ⌚ 3½-4hr., 5 per day 8am-8pm) with connections to other destinations in the Algarve.

BY BUS

Lisbon's bus station is close to ⓂJardim Zoológico but can be hard to find. Once at the metro stop, follow exit signs to Av. C. Bordalo Pinheiro. Exit the metro, go around the corner, and walk straight ahead 100m; then cross left in front of Sete Rios station. The stairs to the bus station are on the left. **Rede Expressos** (☎70 722 33 44 www.rede-expressos.pt) runs buses between Lisbon and: Braga (€20 ⌚ 4-5hr., 14-16 per day 7am-12:15am); Coimbra (€14 ⌚ 2hr., 24-30 per day 7am-12:15am); and Lagos (€19.50 ⌚ 5hr., 14-16 per day 7:30am-1am).

lisbon

Getting Around

Carris (☎21 361 30 00 www.carris.pt) is Lisbon's extensive, efficient, and relatively inexpensive transportation system and is the easiest way to get around the city, which is covered by an elaborate grid of subways, buses, trams, and *elevadores* (funiculars, useful for getting up the steep hills). Fares purchased on board buses, trams, or *elevadores* cost €1.75; the subway costs €1.15, but you must first purchase a rechargeable *viva viagem* card (€0.50). The easiest and most cost- and time-effective option for those who will use a lot of public transportation is the unlimited 24hr. **bilhete combinado** (€5), which can be used on any Carris transport and means you don't have to go into a metro station to recharge your card before getting on a bus or tram. You can buy the *bilhete combinado* in any metro station, and you can fill it with up to seven days' worth of unlimited travel.

BY BUS

Carris buses (€1.75, €1.15 with *viva viagem* card) go to just about any place in the city, including those not served by the metro.

BY METRO

The metro (with €1.15 *viva viagem* card) has four lines that cross the center of Lisbon and go to the major train stations. metro stations are marked with a red "M" logo. Trains run daily 6:30am-1am.

BY TRAM

Trams (€1.75, €1.15 with *viva viagem* card) are used by tourists and locals alike to get around. Many vehicles predate WWI. Line 28E runs through Graça, Alfama, Baixa, Chiado, and Bairro Alto; line 15E goes from the Pr. Comércio to Belém, passing the clubs of Santos and Alcântara.

BY TAXI

Taxis in Lisbon can be hailed on the street throughout the center of town. Good places to find cabs include the train stations and main plazas. Bouncers will be happy to call you a cab after dark. **Rádio Táxis de Lisboa** (☎21 811 90 00) and **Teletáxis** (☎21 811 11 00) are the main companies.

cascais

A quick train ride (or really long swim) from Lisbon takes you away from the frenzied metropolis, past the historic sites of Belém and ritzier resort of Estoril, and into the beach town of Cascais. Once a strategic outpost for sea trade and defense, Cascais became popular with the Portuguese aristocracy at the end of the 19th century, and their palatial homes still dot the coastline. Changing times and multiple beaches mean there is now room on the sand for everyone, whether you came from 19th-century money or have only $19 to your name. Here in Cascais, locals and day-trippers alike seamlessly intermingle along the coast.

ORIENTATION

The Cascais **train station** is at the eastern edge of town; the **bus terminal** is beneath the large blue shopping center to the right as you exit the station. From here, head along Av. Valbom (just to the right of the McDonald's) to the end of the street to reach the **tourism office,** a yellow building with a sign reading *"turismo."* Facing the tourist office, head left down **Avenida dos Combatentes da Grande Guerra** to reach the beaches; **Praia da Ribeira** is the small one to the right, **Praia da Rainha** and **Praia da Conceiçao** are to the left. **Praça 5 de Outubro** and **Largo de Luís de Camões** are the town's main plazas (most of the restaurants are located here), both just west of Av. Combatentes da

portugal

Grande Guerra. The streets around the beaches are full of tourists and shops selling schlock to them; those farther west and north tend to be quieter and are lovely to explore and get lost in.

SIGHTS

▨ BOCA DO INFERNO
CAVE

At this massive open cave, you can supposedly hear the devil's whisper resounding from the crashing surf. If you record the sound and isolate the correct wavelength, then play it backward, you'll hear the Satanic message, "You have way too much free time on your hands." (Idle hands are the devil's playthings, as they say.)

i Follow the road along the water west (to the right as you face the water) about 1km. Free.

THE GREAT OUTDOORS

Cascais has a few beaches more suitable for surfing than sunbathing. Guincho, a 25min. bus ride away, is located on the Atlantic coast. To call this beach windswept or even wind-battered would be an understatement: Guincho is wind-beaten-to-within-an-inch-of-its-life-and-left-for-dead. Gnarly waves and gale-force winds make it a major destination for all kinds of surfers: wind, kite, and regular. Lessons and rentals are available for all levels of experience. To get to Guincho, take ScottURB bus #405 (1 per hr.; M-Sa 6:50am-7:50pm, Su 6:50am-6:50pm) or #415 €3.20 1 per hr.; M-Sa 6:30am-8:30pm, Su 6:30am-7:20pm), which run from the Cascais bus terminal (below shopping center next to train station). From the Guincho bus stop, head to the right as you face the water to get to the beach.

Beaches

There are three main beaches in Cascais, all side by side near the city center. Praia da Ribeira, the westernmost of the three, is small but the most centrally located (right next to the Pr. 5 de Outubro) and tends to get packed. ▨Praia da Rainha is also small, but it has interesting and beautiful rock formations that make it seem like a wild, undiscovered coastline, with hidden nooks and coves behind every boulder. It tends to attract a younger crowd and is better for socializing than swimming. Praia da Conceição, the easternmost of the three, is much larger and looks like any other beachgoer-filled shoreline. A stroll past the final beach will reveal even more beaches as visitors pass over into ritzier Estoril.

FOOD

O VIRIATO
PORTUGUESE $$$

Av. de Vasco da Gama, 34   ☎21 486 81 98

This locals-only joint in an otherwise tourists-only town is refreshing if you can endure the leering glances and whispered comments from the regulars. The food is traditional, which means you'll have to skin, gut, and bone your fish yourself unless you request otherwise—but everything's delicious. An interesting wooden wall with windows divides the patio seating area from the rest of the dining room, so if you get bored, you can always pretend that the people on the other side are in an aquarium.

i From the tourist office, follow R. Alexandre Herculano (to the right of the office as you face it), which becomes Beco das Terras, then turn left onto Av. Vasco da Gama. Entree €7.80-16. ☼ Open M-Tu noon-3:30pm and 7pm-midnight, Th-Su noon-3:30pm and 7pm-midnight.

SHABU SHABU
JAPANESE $$$

Edificio Baía Center, Loja 26, 2nd fl.; R. do Regimento da Infantria, 19   ☎21 483 68 17

It may not be a traditional Portuguese meal (servers wear full Japanese garb), but for a raw taste of what's swimming just a couple of blocks away, try this

get a room!

Inexpensive accommodations are hard to come by in Cascais; it's far more practical to stay in Lisbon, a short and cheap train ride away. If you do want to spend the night, though, there are a few good options. For more information, visit **www.letsgo.com**.

AGARRE O MOMENTO   GUEST HOUSE $$

R. Joaquim Ereira, 458   ☎21 406 45 32 www.agarreomomento.com

Quite affordable and high in quality, Agarre o Momento is more like (brace yourself), home. The cliché is warranted, since you really are just staying in a nice house with a few other people. While Christina is the woman of the house and takes care of the logistics, the true overlord is Senhor Brownie, the Siamese cat who is watching your every move, so don't pull anything funny while you're here.

i From the train station, head left onto Av. Marginal and continue onto Av. 25 de Abril. Turn right at Cidadela Hotel and continue until you see the guest house on the right. Breakfas €4. Linens included. Kitchen. Dorms €25-35; doubles €50-70. ☼ Reception 24hr.

PARSI   HOTEL $$$

R. Afonso Sanches, 8   ☎91 236 35 22

Large colorful rooms with walls covered in freshly painted designs overlook the Pr. 5 de Outubre and the beach. It can get a bit noisy in the evening when the pub downstairs fills up, but with a one-minute walk to the beach, the location can't be beat. The rooms are all different in terms of size and layout (one triple involves a kind of skewed bunk bed affixed to the wall), so ask to see all your options before choosing.

i Just off Pr. 5 de Outubro, in the far left corner with your back to the beach. Singles with shared bat €30; doubles €40, with ensuite bath €50-80; triples with ensuite bath €60. ☼ Reception 24hr.

restaurant's all-you-can-eat buffet—always a good deal for hungry travelers on a budget. In what is probably the most ingenious all-you-can-eat scheme ever, Shabu Shabu has you order a few dishes at a time, allowing them to prepare your sushi fresh as you stuff your face with more. Dessert is also included.

i Upstairs on the side of Lg. Luís de Camões closest to the beach. All-you-can-eat lunch buffet €12.90, dinner buffet €15.90. ☼ Open daily 12:30-3pm and 7-11pm.

RESTAURANTE DOM PEDRO I   PORTUGUESE $$

Beco dos Inválidos, 32   ☎21 483 37 34

Sick of all the tourists and sunbathers on the beach and surrounding streets? Take a hidden alleyway off the Pr. do 5 de Outubre, and have a quiet lunch under the shade of a short but broad tree to escape the maddening crowds. Order some kind of dead animal (you're in Portugal after all), and wait for it to be brought out to your peaceful nook.

i Take narrow Beco dos Inválidos from left side of Pr. 5 de Outubro, with your back to the beach. Entrees €8.50-11.50. ☼ Open M-Sa noon-3pm and 7-10pm.

NIGHTLIFE

Nightlife in Cascais is simple: around 10:30pm, the bars along Largo de Luís de Camões fill up with partygoers, and the few establishments compete with each other to be the loudest. If they're too crowded and you can't get in, try the back entrances on Av. dos Combatentes da Grande Guerra. Praça 5 de Outubro also has some action.

portugal

At 2am, the party migrates down to the waterfront, where there are a couple of clubs along and just off Avenida de Dom Carlos I. These establishments are poppin' until 3 or 4am, but once these close, head back to Largo de Luís de Camões, where a couple of places are open until 6am—it will be obvious which ones.

ESSENTIALS
Practicalities

- **TOURIST OFFICE: Informação Turística** has maps and information. (R. Visconde da Luz, 14 ☎21 482 23 27 *i* From train station, take Av. Valbom—to the right side of the McDonald's—straight to the end of the street. ☼ Open daily 10am-1pm and 2-6pm.)

- **POST OFFICE: Correios** is a full-service post office. (Av. Marginal, 9302 ☎21 482 72 73 www. ctt.pt *i* While exiting the tourist office, look to the left. ☼ Open M-F 8:30am-6pm.)

Emergency

- **PHARMACIES: Farmácia da Misericórdia** posts a schedule of pharmacies open late. (R. do Regimento da Infantria 19, 69 ☎21 483 01 41 *i* From Pr. 5 de Outubro, with your back to the beach, take the street from the far right corner straight 2 blocks; the pharmacy is on the left. *i* Wheelchair accessible. ☼ Open M-F 8am-7pm, Sa 9am-2pm.)

- **POLICE STATION: Polícia de Segurança Pública** (R. Afonso Sanches, 29 ☎21 483 91 00 *i* Take a right at the fork before the train station. The police station is on the right.)

Getting There

Trains run to Cascais from **Lisbon's Cais do Sodré Station.** (€2.05. ☼ 30-40min., daily every 15-30min. 5:30am-1:30am.) Scott URB **buses** run from **Sintra.** (€4. ☼ 40min.-1hr.; M-F 11 per day 6:30am-7:25pm, Sa 12 per day 6:30am-8:35pm, Su 10 per day 7:45am-8:35pm.)

Getting Around

Cascais is a small town, and it's easy to get around on foot, but there are **free bike rental stands** (ID and hotel information required) that are available for the day in front of the train station and at the Cidadela Fortress's parking lot, along Av. de Dom Carlos I from Pr. do 5 de Outubro (get there early if you want a bike). (☼ Apr-Sept daily 8am-7pm; Oct-Mar M-F 9am-4pm, Sa-Su 9am-5pm.) There is also a **taxi stand** outside the train station (☎21 466 01 01). **Buses** are necessary to get to Praia do Guincho.

sintra

The tiny town of Sintra sits at the foot of the mountains, a 45min. train ride west of Lisbon. Quirky romantic castles and ancient fortresses look down on the small city from the surrounding hillsides, with more palatial residences a couple kilometers away. The entire town is encompassed by a breathtaking national park, which, when combined with the fairy-tale castles, makes for a surreal experience. Although most visitors only come for the day, a longer stay in Sintra is both relaxing and rewarding, as the quaint town and natural landscape have a rejuvenating property that can't be found in nearby Lisbon. Sintra and the stretch of mountains just west of it are classified as a World Heritage Cultural Landscape by UNESCO, and castle-hopping visitors will surely understand why.

sintra

ORIENTATION

Sintra has three main neighborhoods: **Estefânia**, where the train station, bus stop, and several inexpensive restaurants and accommodations can be found; **São Pedro**, which is located a bit farther uphill and has some shops and government offices; and the **historic center**, where you'll discover most of the town's sights. To get to the historic center, take a left out of the train station onto **Avenida do Doutor Miguel Bombarda** and follow it 150m to the intersection, at which point the curving **Volta do Duche** veers to the left. This statue-lined road hooks around the valley between Estefânia and is about a 15min. walk to the center. Stay to the right for the **Palácio Nacional de Sintra** or keep straight to get to the **tourist office**. Sintra itself is small and easy to get around, but several sights lie outside of town and are best reached by bus or taxi.

SIGHTS

▣ PALÁCIO E QUINTA DA REGALEIRA   PALACE, GARDENS $$
Quinta da Regaleira   ☎21 910 66 56 www.cultursintra.pt

This UNESCO World Heritage Site was built in the first years of the 20th century for its eccentric owner, wealthy Brazilian capitalist António Augusto de Carvalho Monteiro, who wanted to create a magical and mysterious castle home. Italian architect Luigi Manini was certainly up to the task, and the finished product looks nothing short of fictional. Hidden mythological and occult motifs abound, and the library upstairs is possibly the world's trippiest room. The surrounding gardens are amazing enough to stand alone and are intended to be a transcendent microcosm of the universe—or something like that. You can explore an extensive tunnel system that goes below the castle and gardens or descend the spiral staircase 100ft. into the ground in the Poço Iniciatico (Initiation Well), which was inspired by the rituals of the Knights Templar and has alchemical references.

i Bus #435 €2.50) runs daily every 30min. and stops at the train station and historic center. On foot, turn right out of the tourist office and follow R. Consiglieri Pedroso as it turns into R. MEF Navarro; about a 15-20min. walk. €6, students and seniors €4, ages 9-14 €3, under 9 free. Guided visits €10, students and seniors €8, ages 9-14 €5, under 9 free. ☼ Open daily Apr-Sept 10am-8pm (last entry 7pm); Oct 10am-6:30pm (last entry 6pm); Nov-Jan 10am-5:30pm (last entry 5pm); Feb-Mar 10am-6:30pm (last entry 6pm).

▣ CASTELO DOS MOUROS   CASTLE $$
Parque de Sintra   ☎21 923 73 00 www.parquesdesintra.pt

Not far downhill from the Palácio da Pena is this eighth-century Moorish castle, which looms over Sintra and offers fantastic views of the city and many of the nearby sights. The castle was abandoned and fell into ruin when the Moors were driven out in the 12th century, but Dom Fernando II fixed it up a bit and tore down some of the already decrepit Romanesque church to make a nice garden—very Victorian. The surprisingly large castle stretches along the ridge and looks like Portugal's own Great Wall from a vantage point along the ramparts. There are so many great views of the surrounding area that it is tempting to spread out your arms in an attempt at a cheeky Titanic reference, but do be careful—it's a long fall down the hill.

i Bus #434 €3.50) runs from the tourist office to the castle daily every 15min., 9:15am-7:50pm. €7, students and seniors €6. ☼ Open daily Apr-Sept 9:30am-8pm; Oct-Mar 10am-6pm.

▣ PALÁCIO DA PENA   PALACE $$$
Parque da Pena   ☎21 910 53 40 www.parquesdesintra.pt

Built during the 1840s on what was left of a medieval monastery by Prince Ferdinand of Bavaria and his wife Dona Maria II, this colorful royal retreat is one funky castle. It has Neo-just-about-any-style-you-can-think-of architecture, and the Neo-Mudejar entrance gate has alligator gargoyles at the top. On hot

portugal

For more recommendations, visit **www.letsgo.com**

NICE WAY SINTRA PALACE   HOSTEL $

R. Sotto Mayor, 22   ☎21 924 98 00 · www.nicewaysintrahostel.com

Although it isn't the size of a palace, this hostel sure has the feel of one, even if it is just a bunch of people sharing huge rooms in a very nice house. The mood is extremely laid-back, and no one here bothers to lock up their belongings. The common area has big doors that open onto a giant yard, which plays host to the occasional party. This hostel has relaxed vibes spilling out of the windows and doors.

i From Palácio Nacional, walk away from all of the restaurants, staying alongside the palace. After passing a large hotel, go down a hill and you'll see the hostel on the right. Breakfast, linens, and towels included. Dorms €16-21; doubles €25-35. ☒ Reception 24hr.

ALMÁA SINTRA HOSTEL   HOSTEL $$

Caminho dos Frades   ☎21 924 00 08 www.almaasintrahostel.com

Nestled in a secluded area, this hostel acts as a retreat from the outside world. Much of the seating inside includes simple pillows placed on the floor. Daily yoga takes place in a large tent outside, and an old water tank that sits in the garden is now used as a pool. Stop here to get away from it all and feel rejuvenated.

i From Quinta da Regaleira, go through the car park to the right and simply keep walking for about 500 yards. The hostel is on the left. Breakfast, linens, and towels included. Dorm €22-30; doubles €30-34. ☒ Reception 24hr.

---

days, the fittingly strange "water room," which has holes in the walls that spit out water at seemingly random times, is a great place to be. The archway over the entrance to the purple building (not really purple; get a close look at the tiles) is spectacular in the weirdest, most ornate way, and views from the various terraces (the Queen's Terrace has the best) stretch all the way to Lisbon.

i Bus #434 €3.50) runs from the tourist office to the palace daily every 15min., 9:15am-7:50pm; from entrance, either walk up to the palace or take shuttle bus. €13.50, before 11am €12.50, students and seniors €11. Guided tours additional €5. ☒ Palace open daily Apr-Sept 9:45am-7pm (last entry 6:30pm); Oct-Mar 10am-6pm (last entry 5pm). Surrounding Parque da Pena open daily Apr-Sept 9:30am-8pm; Oct-Mar 10am-6pm.

MONSERRATE   VILLA, GARDENS $$

Parque de Monserrate   ☎21 923 73 00 www.parquesdesintra.pt

This palace looks like something Palladio would have come up with had he traveled extensively in India and had a little more flair for the flamboyant. Moghul-style arches clash wonderfully with Italian Renaissance-inspired domes and Far-Eastern eaves, which are all surrounded by lush gardens filled with exotic vegetation and enormous goldfish. Eclecticism meets Romanticism in a site visited by Lord Byron, who called Sintra a "glorious Eden." Keep an eye out for the arch that was brought over from India following the quelling of the colony's rebellion—because what's the point of subjugating people if you can't bring something nice home for the kids?

i Bus #435 €2.50) runs daily every 30min., 9:45am-6:45pm, and stops at the train station and historic center. €5, students and seniors €4. ☒ Open daily Apr-Sept 9:30am-8pm; Oct-Mar 10am-6pm.

sintra

PALÁCIO NACIONAL DE SINTRA

PALACE $$

Lg. da Rainha Dona Amélia   ☎21 910 68 40   pnsintra.imc-ip.pt

Once a summer residence for Moorish sultans and their harems, the Palácio da Vila was later taken over by the Portuguese; paintings of Portuguese noblemen gunning down Moorish soldiers stand as a testament inside. The palace and gardens were built in two stages: Dom João I built the main structure in the 15th century, and Dom Manuel I made it home to the world's best collection of azulejos (glazed tiles) a century later. The palace includes the gilded Sala dos Brasões, which houses some of the palace's greatest treasures—look up at the ceiling to see the royal coat of arms surrounded by the armorial bearings of 72 noble families, elaborately painted animals, and various other artistic flourishes. The palace is marked by an avian theme: doves symbolizing the Holy Spirit line the walls of the Capela, swans grace the Sala dos Cisnes, and on the ceiling of the Sala das Pegas, magpies represent ladies-in-waiting and hold a piece of paper proclaiming D. João I's motto, "por bem" ("for good").

i *Exit the tourist office, go straight, and find the palace on the left €7, students €3, seniors €4, under 14 free; Su before 2pm free. ☼ Open M-Tu 9:30am-5:30pm, Th-Su 9:30am-5pm. Last entry 30min. before close.*

FOOD

APEADEIRO

CAFE, BAR $

Av. do Doutor Miguel Bombarda, 3A   ☎21 923 18 04

This cafe offers a blend of tasty Portuguese food, low prices, and an interesting atmosphere (which can be hard to come by in Sintra). The faux-roof, with its traditional Portuguese red shingles, hangs over the bar acts as a reminder that the restaurant doesn't take itself too seriously but is still proud of its heritage. The creepy, animatronic little girl dressed as a moustached chef standing on the bar acts as a reminder that—well, that's still a little unclear.

i *Left out of the train station and slightly down the hill. Entree €6-14. ☼ Open M-W and F-Su noon-midnight.*

PANISINTRA

CAFE $

Av. de Dom Francisco de Almeida, 12   ☎21 923 30 00

Planning on getting to Sintra first thing in the morning to get an early start on your hike up to the Palácio da Pena? Or did you catch the early train without realizing that nothing opens before 9:30am? This cafe opens early and has delicious coffee as well as a huge selection of sugary pastries filled with energy. The best deal for a snack is an espresso plus a pastel de nata for only €1.20. Between the sugar and the caffeine, you will feel invincible—or at least ready to take on those dastardly hills. Don't order the fresh orange juice (€1.50) if you're in a hurry or if you advocate against the inhumane treatment of fruit, as you'll have to watch each orange get slowly and painfully juiced.

i *Just across from Palácio Nacional de Sintra. Coffee €0.60-1.50. Pastries €1-2. ☼ Open M-Sa 7am-8pm, Su 8am-8pm.*

CAFÉ DA VILLA

RESTAURANT $$

Cç. do Pelourinho, 8   ☎96 709 13 96

This restaurant, which attempts to feature an Eastern theme but instead winds up with dimly lit acrylic-on-velvet paintings of the Dalai Lama, offers ample three-course meals at low prices. No such charming touches exist outside, but the food here is delicious, so let the discontinuity of the theme slide. The surprisingly large and very filling tostas (grilled sandwiches) are only €5 and come with a heaping plate of chips and a drink.

i *Entering the center from the train station, turn right just before the Palácio Nacional. 3-course meals €8-15. Tostas combo €5. ☼ Open daily noon-2am.*

ESSENTIALS

Practicalities

- **TOURIST OFFICE: Posta de Turismo** is in the historic center, just up the street from the Palácio Nacional de Sintra. (Pr. República, 23 ☎21 923 11 57 www.cm-sintra.pt ☑ Open daily 9:30am-6pm.) There is also a branch in the train station. (☎21 924 16 23 ☑ Open daily 11am-6pm.)

- **INTERNET ACCESS: Sabot** offers Wi-Fi and has luggage storage and pizza. (R. Dr. Miguel Bombarda, 57 ☎219 23 08 02 *i* Just across from the train station, to the right. (€1 per 15min., €1.60 per 30min., €2.50 per hr. ☑ Open M-Sa 1pm-midnight, Su 7pm-midnight.)

- **POST OFFICE: Correios** is on the way to the tourist office. (Pr. República, 26 ☎21 924 61 29 ☑ Open M-F 9:30am-12:30pm and 2:30-6pm.)

Emergency

- **POLICE: Guardia Nacional Republicana:** (R. João de Deus, 6 ☎21 924 78 50 *i* Exit the train station and keep left around the station; the Guardia Nacional building is across the street.)

- **PHARMACY: Pharmazul** is right across from the train station. (Av. Dr. Miguel Bombarda, 37 ☎21 924 38 77 ☑ Open M-F 9:30am-7pm, Sa 10:30am-7:30pm.)

- **MEDICAL SERVICES: Centro de Saúde** (R. Dr. Alfredo Costa, 34, 1st fl. ☎21 924 77 70 *i* Just across from the train station, to the left. ☑ Open M-F 8am-8pm, Sa-Su 10am-6pm.)

Getting There

The easiest way to get to Sintra from Lisbon is by **train.** Trains run from Lisbon's **Rossio Station** in Baixa. €2. ☑ M-F every 15min. 6:08am-8:21pm, every 30min. 8:38pm-1:08am; Sa-Su every 30min. 6:08am-1:06am.) ScottURB runs **buses** from Cascais. (Bus #417 *i* €4. ☑ 40min.; every hr. M-F 6am-9pm, Sa 7am-8pm, Su 8am-8pm.)

Getting Around

The best way to get around within Sintra is by foot. To get to the sights, take a **bus** (#434, 435) from either the tourist office or train station. You can also take a **horse-drawn carriage** from the Palácio Nacional de Sintra. (Sintratur, R. de João de Deus, 82 ☎219 24 12 38 www.sintratur.com *i* Fixed rates of €30-70 depending on time and distance.) **Taxis** are also relatively inexpensive. (☎219 23 02 05 *i* Stands in historic center across from Palácio Nacional and at train station.)

portugal essentials

MONEY

Tipping and Bargaining

Native Portuguese rarely tip more than their spare change, even at expensive restaurants. However, if you make it clear that you're a tourist, they might expect you to tip more. Don't feel obligated to tip; the servers' pay is almost never based on tips. No one will refuse your money, but you're a poor student so don't play the fool.

Bargaining is common and necessary in open-air and street markets. Haggling is also most effective when buying several items or in bulk. However, do not barter in malls or established shops.

Taxes

Portugal has a 13% **value added tax** (*imposto sobre* or *valor acrescentado*; IVA) on all meals and accommodations. The prices listed in *Let's Go* include IVA unless otherwise mentioned. Retail goods bear a much higher 23% IVA, although the listed prices generally include this tax. Non-EU citizens who have stayed in the EU fewer than 180 days can claim back the tax paid on purchases at the airport. Ask the shop where you have made the purchase to supply you with a tax return form, but stores will only provide them for purchases of more than €50-100. **Taxes,** presently 23%, are included in all prices in Portugal. Request a refund form, an *Insenção de IVA*, and present it to customs upon departure.

SAFETY AND HEALTH

Local Laws and Police

You should feel comfortable approaching the police in Portugal, although few officers speak English. The **Polícia de Segurança Pública** is the police force in all major cities and towns. The **Guarda Nacional Republicana** polices more rural areas, while the **Brigada de Trânsito** is the traffic police, who sport red armbands. All three branches wear light blue uniforms.

Drugs and Alcohol

Recreational drugs are illegal in Portugal, and police take these laws seriously. However, recreational drug use has been decriminalized, so instead of jail time and fines, perpetrators face community service and government-imposed therapy. The legal minimum drinking age is 18. Portugal has one of the highest road mortality rates in Europe. Do not drive while intoxicated, and be cautious on the road.

portugal 101

HISTORY

Long, Long Ago (Big Bang-1138 CE)

The first six or seven centuries BCE saw quintessential Mediterranean civilizations like the Carthaginians, the Phoenicians, and the Greeks come and go. Wearing bedsheets and wielding pointed sticks, the Romans invaded during the second and third centuries and (surprise!) quickly took over the whole region. By the early fifth century, Rome had made the classic mistake of empires, spreading its forces too thin and wide, and began to succumb to Germanic tribes. After a relatively brief stint by the Visigoths, the Moors stole the spotlight and took center stage in Portugal. Who were the Moors? As Islam spread from the Arabian Peninsula, Muslim forces moved through North Africa and up into Iberia, settling in Portugal and establishing a thriving culture there. While their name lends itself to bad puns, the Moors left a rich tradition of agricultural infrastructure and architecture—look for colorful ceramic tiles and ornaments that decorate buildings even today.

It's a Boy: A Nation Is Born (1139-1415)

From the 12th to the early 15th century CE, the inhabitants of Portugal fought simultaneously for both their independence and for their religion. The *Reconquista* ultimately drove the Moors out of Iberia, and after a series of power grabs typical of early monarchies, single rule of Portugal fell into the hands of Afonso I. Afonso and his successors slowly began to reclaim and consolidate lands previously controlled by the Muslims. The gleaming, shiny, final product emerged in 1250—a unified and independent nation. A series of territorial scuffles with Spain under João I set the framework for a future soccer rivalry between the two nations.

Sugar and Spice and, er...Some Things Nice (1415-1755)

Portugal's Age of Discovery began in the 15th century with advances in sailing technology and the reign of Prince Henry the Navigator. While their Iberian kingdom may have been small, the Portuguese expanded their overseas empire massively over the next two centuries, gaining control of a large and wealthy empire that spanned the New World and extended into Asia. Countless famed explorers like Vasco da Gama, Bartolomeu Dias, and Ferdinand Magellan discovered and claimed huge chunks of territory for their nation and brought back shiploads of spices, gold, and other bling. This Golden Age peaked with the reign of Manuel I the Fortunate, and while he was indeed fortunate, his successors would not be.

French Fried (1755-1910)

Portugal ran into a string of bad luck in the 1700s, climaxing in 1755 with the great Earthquake of Lisbon. The quake, the accompanying fires, and a tsunami destroyed much of the city, but remarkably, it was rebuilt fairly quickly and successfully under the guidance of the Marquês de Pombal. After this brief stint of optimism, the Portuguese found themselves in a world of trouble as European foreign policy went south. Before they knew it, the nation was on the defensive once again as Napoleon's forces invaded and pillaged the country Viking-style. It was only with the help of the Brits that Portuguese leaders were able to drive out the petit Frenchman and re-establish some semblance of order for the following decades.

A Political Potluck (1910-1986)

Portugal was to have its fair share of radicalism, as the monarchical regime was overthrown early in the 20th century for a weak republic. This was indeed too good to be true, and the republic quickly degenerated into an incredibly unstable political climate. With a turnover rate approaching that of a fast food restaurant, Portugal saw 45 (yes, 45) different regimes from 1910-1945. Eventually, this power vacuum sucked up the powerful dictator Antonio Salazar, who would rule the country with an iron fist and a ruthless secret police for almost 40 years. With his death in 1968, the Portuguese people let out a sigh of relief, only to find themselves increasingly strained and drained by unpopular colonial wars. The pot boiled over in April of 1974 with the **Carnation Revolution,** sending the dictatorial dynasty out the window and ushering in an era of Marxist reforms and release of colonial possessions. In the following decade, Portugal would slowly stabilize economically and politically, joining a proto-EU in 1986.

A Mixed Modernity (1986-present)

With monetary assistance from the EU, Portugal's economy progressed and its democracy solidified after nearly a century of instability. The last of the former empire was finally pried from Portugal's rusty colonial grip in 1999 with the cession of Macau and its slot machines as well as East Timor in 2002. Though politically more stable, the current economic situation in Portugal is not very good, to say the least.

CUSTOMS AND ETIQUETTE

Do You Expect Me to Talk?

In general, the Portuguese are very open to foreigners, and, unlike the French, they appreciate attempts to speak the native language. Although the person you're addressing probably speaks Spanish, don't assume they do: this might be taken offensively and mark you as culturally insensitive. Portuguese often speak loudly

STUDY

As a participant in a study abroad program, you will get to enjoy the Mediterranean lifestyle while also learning more about the Portuguese people and language. Most study abroad programs focus on Portuguese history, the impact of the once enormous Portuguese kingdom, and the contemporary Lusophone world.

- **CIEE LISBON: LANGUAGE AND CULTURE:** Learn Portuguese and enroll in exciting courses such as "Portuguese Cinema" and "Lisbon: City and Architecture" at Universidade Nova de Lisboa. (www.ciee.org ☎1-800-407-8839)

- **UNIVERSITY OF WISCONSIN-MADISON:** Coimbra, Portugal: All undergraduates are welcome to study on the "Silver Coast," learning Portuguese or directly enrolling at the Universidade de Coimbra. (www.studyabroad.wisc.edu ☎1-608-265-6329)

- **UNIVERSITY OF TEXAS AT AUSTIN: THE BAGUNTE PROJECT:** Discover the secrets of the past through the archaeological field school or learn to create ceramic vessels in the museology "Maymester." (www.utexas.edu ☎1-512-475-7348)

- **AFS: GAP YEAR IN PORTUGAL:** Younger travelers can attend a local high school and live with a host family for an entire school year. AFS also organizes field trips and parties throughout the year. (www.afsusa.org ☎1-800-237-4636)

- **CSA:** Porto Language Institute: Improve your Portuguese skills in small classes while staying with local residents. Indulge in the joys of life at Solar do Vinho, the best place to taste the delicious port wine. (www.centerforstudyabroad.com ☎1-206-583-8191)

- **IPSA:** The Portuguese Language School offers eight different sub-levels of instruction in the forms of group, private, and culture classes. (www.studyabroadinternational.com)

- **CESA:** Another Portuguese language school close to the center of Lisbon, CESA offers courses such as the "Portuguese & Surf Course." (www.cesalanguages.com ☎44-1209-211-800)

VOLUNTEER

The shoreline and warm climate of Portugal are enough to make the country a perfect volunteer destination. But in case that's not enough to convince you, think gorgeous, sweaty Mediterranean men and women working together for a better future.

- **GLOBAL VOLUNTEERS:** Help local children and adults in Beja by teaching them conversational English for one or two weeks. You will stay at a family-run hotel located on one of the main streets of the city. (www.globalvolunteers.org ☎1-800-487-1074)

- **QUERCUS:** Quercus is a non-profit environmental organization. If you are proficient in Portuguese, you can volunteer for one of their many projects. (www.quercus.pt ☎217-788-474)

- **WORLD WIDE OPPORTUNITIES ON ORGANIC FARMS:** You can find daily updates on the hundreds of organic farms ready to welcome travelers. Almost all WWOOF hosts speak English, and lots of them speak a variety of other European languages. (www.wwoof.pt)

- **HABITAT FOR HUMANITY:** Habitat for Humanity works mostly in the northern region of Braga. Join the expanding forces in building and rebuilding houses and give families their basic right to a home. (www.habitat.pt ☎00351-253-204-280)

- **VOLUNTEERS FOR PEACE:** Volunteers for Peace lists hundreds of volunteer camps and projects in dozens of countries, including Portugal. (www.vfp.org ☎1-802-540-3060)

WORK

If you don't speak Portuguese but are eager to find some way to pay for all that sweet port wine, you will have to look for teaching jobs. Although there now more English teachers in the area, teaching jobs are still easy to find with a TEFL certification.

- **NIKITAS LANGUAGE SCHOOLS: WORK AND STUDY:** Prefect your Portuguese skills before you begin working at a hotel on the coastline of Algarve, Madeira, or Lisbon. This program consists of a Portuguese language course followed by a work placement for at least two months. (www.nik-las.com)

- **ESL BASE:** ESL Base is a database of English teaching jobs. The website also has information on TEFL teacher training courses in many different countries. (www.eslbase.com)

- **TEACH IN PORTUGAL:** If you have the right teaching qualifications, you can find TEFL, middle school, and high school job opportunities. (www.teachanywhere.com; www.teachaway.com)

- **EMPREGO:** Although only useful for those fluent in Portuguese, this website is a comprehensive job search engine. (http://emprego.sapo.pt)

- **AU PAIR JOBS:** Many busy Portuguese parents and children will welcome your help and valuable English skills. Search these websites for host families. (www.findaupair.com; www.greataupair.com)

and quickly—don't be intimidated; this is normal and doesn't indicate any anger or irritation (usually).

Please, Sir, Can I Have Some More?

Probably not, unless you want to pay for it. Portuguese restaurants often charge for what might seem to be freebies—for example, the cheese, bread, and olives served at the beginning of the meal. Expect to pay a few euros for these small appetizers. Don't forget a five to 10% tip if the service charge is not already included.

FOOD AND DRINK

Something is Fishy

The Portuguese take their food seriously—especially fish. Easily the most prevalent dish throughout the country is *bacalhau*, a salted cod with origins in the sea voyages of the 15th and 16th centuries. While you may be sick of it after a few days, the Portuguese won't be—it is said that a different recipe exists for each day of the year.

Terrestrial Treats

Meat and pastries are also staples of Portuguese cuisine. For a manly meal, head inland to ranching regions like Alentejo, where hearty meat stews (*cozida*) are standard fare. More adventurous travelers should ask for *cabidela*, a dish made with the blood of pigs or chickens. Portuguese foods are not without their delicacy, though, as evidenced by the ever-popular croissant. While one might not normally associate croissants and the Catholic church, the rich tradition of pastries in Portugal dates back to the monasteries of the Middle Ages—explaining today's *barriga de freira* (nun's belly) and *papos de anjo* (angel's chins).

No Wining

Portuguese wine is the famous grandfather of all alcoholic beverages, known for its quality since ancient Roman times. Most well known, especially nowadays, is port—a sweet wine grown in the Douro valley often served as an appetizer drink or as a dessert wine. Your high school Spanish may be good, but don't get caught looking like a tourist—vinho verde isn't green wine but a young white wine often served sparkling. For other drinks, try Tginjinha, a sour cherry liqueur native to Lisbon.

MUSIC

During your travels in Portugal, you are almost guaranteed to encounter *fado*, a traditional genre of music generally characterized by mournful tunes and haunting lyrics. This may sound a bit depressing for your riotous Eurotrip, but in Portugal you're bound to run into it either in restaurants or on the street. The two main centers for *fado* are the capital city, Lisbon, and Coimbra, a small university city in the center of the country. Despite some regional differences, the two styles share much in common: all *fado* is meant to embody a sense of *saudade*, translated into English as a feeling of permanent loss and the emotional damage it causes (cheery, no?). The origins of *fado* are unclear—some trace it back to the early 1800s as the music of the urban poor, while others claim that the genre arose in the 15th century among the lonely wives of men at sea.

SPAIN

Spain is a single, unified nation—but you wouldn't know it from traveling there. Each region's culture is as distinct from that of the rest as another country's. Just as the landscape varies from sun-soaked olive orchards in Andalucía to rainy and verdant hills in Galicia to windswept plains along the Camino de Santiago to Europe's best beaches all along the Mediterranean coast, so, too, do the languages and cuisines and attitudes change. And, of course, the fierce identities of Spain's unique cities can hardly be ignored. Quirky Barcelona, bureaucratic Madrid, sunny and southern Sevilla, and up-and-coming Bilbao will all claim to be the country's best; decide for yourself whether you prefer Madrid's stuffy museums to Barcelona's beaches, or tour Andalucía to figure out which city has the best mosque-turned-cathedral.

Where are you going? Make sure you have the right language, cuisine, and culture going in (don't try to order a pintxo in Granada or a pa amb tomàquet in Santiago), and enjoy the best Spain has to offer.

greatest hits

- **PICASSO, SHMICASSO.** See his works at the **Reina Sofía** in Madrid (p. 726) and the **Museu Picasso** in Barcelona (p. 762).

- **CITY AT YOUR FEET.** Climb the **Columbus Monument** at the end of Las Ramblas and gaze out over all Barcelona (p. 761).

- **THE LONG AND WINDING ROAD.** Finish your pilgrimage at the **Catedral de Santiago de Compostela,** the terminus of the Camino de Santiago (p. 823). Then go out and go hard in the hot nightlife spots next door (p. 825).

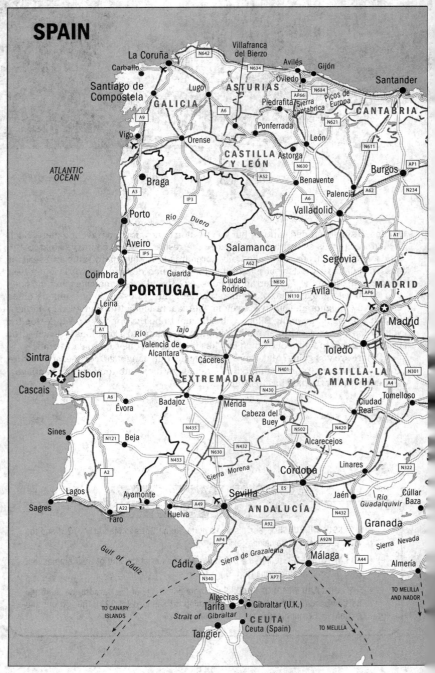

SPAIN

Villafranca del Bierzo

La Coruña

Carballo

Santiago de Compostela

Avilés   Gijón

Santander

Oviedo

Lugo   ASTURIAS

GALICIA   Piedrafita   Sierra   Picos de   CANTABRIA
Cantabrica   Europa

Vigo   Ponferrada   León

Orense   N621

CASTILLA   N611

Y LEÓN   Astorga   Burgos

ATLANTIC   Braga   Benavente   Palencia

OCEAN   Valladolid

Porto   Río   Duero

Aveiro   Salamanca

Segovia

Coimbra   Guarda   Ciudad   MADRID

PORTUGAL   Rodrigo   Ávila

N110   Madrid

Leiria   Río   Tajo

Valencia de   Toledo

Sintra   Alcantara   Cáceres   CASTILLA-LA

Lisbon   MANCHA

Cascais   EXTREMADURA   Tomelloso

Évora   Badajoz   Mérida   Ciudad
Real

Sines   Cabeza del
Buey

Beja   Alcarecejos

Sierra Morena   Linares

Lagos   Córdoba   Cúllar
Baza

Ayamonte   Jaén   Río

Sagres   Faro   Sevilla   Guadalquivir

Huelva   ANDALUCÍA   Granada

Sierra Nevada

Almería

Gulf of Cádiz   Sierra de Grazalema   Málaga

TO MELILLA
AND NADOR

Cádiz

TO CANARY   Algeciras   Gibraltar (U.K.)
ISLANDS   Tarifa

Strait of   CEUTA

Tangier   Gibraltar   Ceuta (Spain)   TO MELILLA

spain

While in Madrid, try low-budget live music bars such as **Club Tempo** or the multi-purpose **El Círculo de Bellas Artes** to get your fix of youth partying. In Barcelona, kids these days tend to hang around L'Eixample: check out **Le Cyrano** for the biggest, strongest drinks and the youngest crowd (no, not like grade-school, you creep) around. El Raval just south of Universitat tends to be a good bet, too. In Sevilla, **Calle Betis** is best for bars and clubs that will be full of students, even if they are all study-abroad students.

madrid

Welcome to Madrid, where the days starts late, the nights ends later, and the locals look like Javier Bardem. Sound good? Well, there's more. Much more. Madrid is home to some of the biggest and baddest sights in the world, from museums filled with iconic art to *discotheques* packed with Spain's most beautiful. From Goya's *The Naked Maya* by day to the (almost) naked *madrileños* at night, Madrid insists that you stay on the move—in only the most laid-back style, of course. When it's time to recuperate, slow down, savor some of the best in Spanish cuisine, and lounge in one of the city's immaculate parks or gardens under the warm Spanish sun.

Madrid's plazas, gardens, and monuments tell of the city's rich history. After Philip II made it the capital of his empire in 1561, Madrid enjoyed centuries of being on top. It served as Spain's artistic hub during the Golden Age, becoming a seat of wealth, culture, and imperial glory, the legacy of which can still be felt in literary neighborhoods like Huertas, in the sumptuous interiors of royal estates like the Palacio Real, and in the badass collections of the museums along the Avenida del Arte. So get some rest on the plane, because from here on out, it's all dinners at midnight, parties at three in the morning, marathon treks through museums the size of small countries by day, and chasing down Javier at high noon.

ORIENTATION

El Centro

Bordered by the beautiful Palacio Real in the west and the relaxing Parque del Retiro in the east, El Centro, the heart of Madrid, encompasses the city's most famous historic sites and modern venues. Churches, plazas, and winding cobblestone streets are set beside clubs and countless tapas restaurants. In the middle is **Puerta del Sol,** the "soul of Madrid," where thousands descend to ring in each New Year. By day, the area around Puerta del Sol is a commercial hub with plenty of name brand stores and fast food chains. The eight streets branching off Puerta del Sol include **Calle Mayor,** which leads west to **Plaza Mayor,** a vibrant square bordered by restaurants and filled with street performers and vendors. On the western side of Pl. Mayor is **Calle Bailen.** Here you will find El Centro's most famous sights, including **El Palacio Real,** and Madrid's most picturesque formal gardens in **Plaza de Oriente.** Finally, **Plaza Santa Ana,** to the south of Puerta del Sol, provides a popular meeting place where locals and tourists escape for drinks and tapas. While El Centro can be a bit chaotic, it is home to the city's most essential landmarks. El Centro is easily walkable, and the Metro provides convenient and reliable access to the rest of the city. The main sights are deceptively close to one another. When in doubt, stick to the main streets of **Calle**

spain

de Alcalá, **Calle Mayor, Calle del Arsenal,** and **Calle de Atocha** for restaurants, nightlife, hostels, and cafes.

La Latina and Lavapiés

La Latina and Lavapiés lie just across the southern border of El Centro. These areas are young, hip, and distinctively *madrileño*. While accommodations here are limited, these areas provide some of the finest dining and nightlife options in the city. Many unadventurous tourists will stick to the obvious food and drink options surrounding Puerta del Sol and Pl. Mayor, but the *tabernas* of **Calle Cava Baja** and **Calle Alemendro** serve some of the city's best traditional Spanish cuisine. These narrow streets are packed with meal options, and one rule is universal: quality matters. While Lavapiés is less active at night, it remains one the best neighborhoods for international cuisine, particularly along **Calle Lavapiés,** where you'll find many Indian restaurants. If you have time, try to make it to the **El Rastro** Sunday flea market (p. 750).

Las Huertas

Las Huertas' streets are lined with quotes from writers like Cervantes and Calderón de la Barca, who lived in this literary neighborhood during its Golden Age. But don't tell that to the other tourists. Most travelers are content with the commercialism of El Centro and miss out on the countless cafes, bars, pubs, and clubs lining the narrow streets of Huertas. Las Huertas feels like a playground for 20-somethings, with small independent shops, cafes, *cervecerías*, bars, and clubs in every direction. **Plaza Santa Ana** and **Plaza del Ángel** are the vital centers of the area, but you will find a greater diversity of food and drink venues as you move outward, especially east down **Calle de las Huertas** and to the north up **Calle de la Cruz.** Huertas is bounded in the north by C. Alcalá, in the south by C. Atocha, and in the east by Paseo del Prado. Despite being only a five minute walk from Sol, Huertas is very much its own world, particularly when Madrid's best nightlife scene (headlined by superclub **Kapital**) gets going.

Avenida del Arte

Avenida del Arte is a beautiful, canopied street that holds all of Madrid's world-class museums. While the city center is largely commercial (save for the odd cathedral or convent), Avenida del Arte protects Spain's most prized cultural artifacts, from Picasso's *Guernica* to Goya's *Second* and *Third of May.* While the **Museo Nacional del Prado,** the **Reina Sofía,** and the **Museo Thyssen** have become famous individually, it is their totality that makes the Avenida del Arte such a powerful showing of Spain's culture. The walk along the tree-lined **Paseo del Prado** has become a cultural phenomenon of its own, a celebration of the beauty and sophistication of this city. The avenue is also conveniently located next to the **Parque del Buen Retiro,** Madrid's Central Park, which borders the eastern edge of the city. This is where the fast pace of cosmopolitan life breaks down, where *madrileño* families come to spend time together, and where tourists can escape their hostel bunk beds.

Gran Vía

Calle Gran Vía is filled with all the stuff that tourists don't need to come to Europe to see: fast-food restaurants, chain stores, and traffic jams. It's like the Broadway of every big city in America. While the main avenue tends to be crowded and commercial, the greater Gran Vía area should not be discounted. Spanning east to west from **Plaza de Cibeles** to **Plaza de España,** Gran Vía has a number of up-and-coming restaurants, bars, clubs, and live music venues—you just have to look hard (and be blessed with the handy guidance of *Let's Go*). On the southeastern boundary with Chueca, you will find the highest concentration of small restaurants, bars, and boutiques, particularly on **Calle de la Reina** and **Calle de las Infantas.** So get off the main road and discover local

madrid

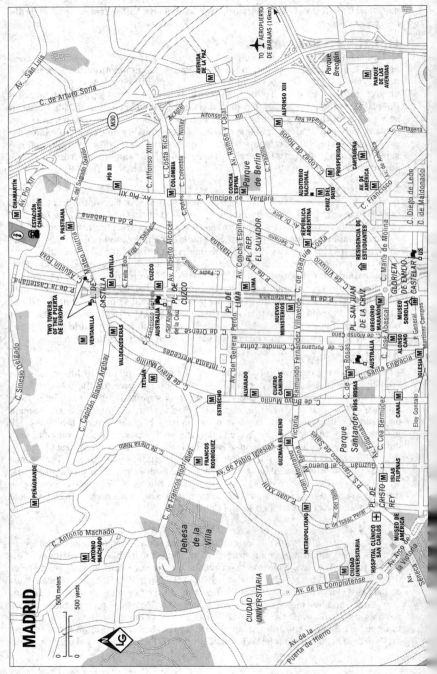

spain

MADRID

TO AEROPUERTO DE BARAJAS (16km)

500 meters
500 yards

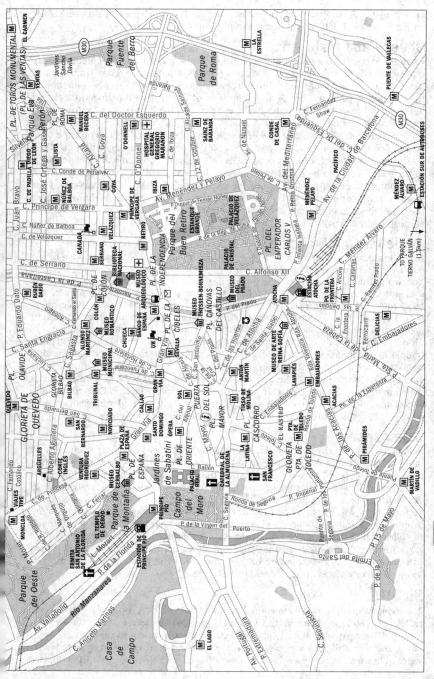

madrid

favorites, like the always-packed Spanish dive bar **El Tigre,** where a single beer comes with a free pile of deliciously greasy, doughy tapas.

Chueca and Malasaña

Once the center of bohemian life in Madrid and the birthplace of a counterculture movement (La Movida) in the 1970s and early'80s, Malasaña is today somewhat of a caricature of its former self. Within a few decades, Malasaña has become one of the most expensive and image-driven *barrios* of the city, with high-end cafes and international novelty restaurants like creperies and fresh juice stands. Art supply stores can be found on every other block, meaning that there are either a lot of artists in this neighborhood or a lot of people who like to spend money on expensive paints. For the traveler, Malasaña is a total playground, with the city's best nightlife, live music, and dining. Chueca is no different. Malasaña's historically gay neighbor to the east (bordered by C. Fuencarral) is today a high-end *barrio* with great food and nightlife in every direction. In Chueca, you will find plenty of art galleries, yoga studios, and boutique shops, but you will also run into the more insidious signs of the bourgeoisie, such as yoga studios that rent movies and movie rental places where you can practice yoga. Oh yeah, and a lot of sex shops.

Argüelles and Moncloa

Argüelles and Moncloa are quiet residential areas spanning the western edge of the city from the north of Plaza de Espana to the city's northwest corner at Moncloa. You won't find many tourists here; instead, these are great areas to get a feel for authentic, everyday *madrileño* life. **Caso de Campo** and **Parque del Oeste** provide the city's most expansive green spaces on the west side of Madrid, which function as both sites of recreation and centers of culture. Outside the major parks, you'll find quiet streets with little bookstores, shops, and cafes. From Argüelles, you can explore the oddly captivating **Templo de Debod** to the west (it's a 2000-year-old Egyptian temple in the middle of a Spanish park) , as well as the restaurants and nightlife options in the popular-with-college-kids Malasaña area to the south. Monocloa is anchored by the presence of Franco's **Arco de la Victoria,** and it is the best outpost from which to explore Parque del Oeste or journey by bus to the Palacio El Pardo . While accommodations are limited in this area, some tourists might find refuge staying in a quiet neighborhood a few stops removed from the chaotic city center.

Salamanca

Salamanca is primarily a high-end residential district filled with luxury shopping and fancy restaurants on the side streets of C. Castellano and C. de Serrano. While this area may seem posh, buried beneath all of the Gucci and Prada is a neighborhood that is very accessible to budget travelers. Salamanca is also deceptively close to city center, just a 5min. walk north up Paseo de la Castellana from el Arco de la Victoria. Here you will find one of Madrid's most beautiful avenues, with a tree lined promenade running through the center. As you make your way north you will reach the **Biblioteca Nacional,** and, making your way further north, you will find two of the city's terrific, less visited art museums: the **Museo Sorrola** and the **Museo de Lazaro Galdiano** (p. 731). A visit to either of these museums will inevitably take you down some of the city's most beautiful residential streets.

SIGHTS

The Avenida del Arte is reason enough to come to Madrid. A trip down this historic path takes you along Madrid's most picturesque, tree-lined avenue and through the canon of Western art. Other neighborhoods may not have world-class art on every block, but they still pack a punch. El Centro contains some of the city's most iconic sights, like the 18th-century Plaza Mayor. Chueca and Malasaña, Madrid's former bohemian centers, provide ample people watching opportunities, with streets lined with high-end cafes and shops. Argüelles and Moncloa, crucial fighting grounds during the Spanish Civil War, are marked by the Arco de la Victoria, erected by General Franco and perhaps the most visible remnant of his haunting legacy. The palace El Pardo, just north of Moncloa, offers a view into the dictator's private bunker. Argüelles and Moncloa are also home to the city's most anomalous historical sight, the Egyptian Templo de Debod.

El Centro

⬛ PALACIO REAL   PALACE
C. de Baillén   ☎91 454 88 00 www.patrimonionacional.es

Before seeing the Palacio Real, it's hard to grasp just how powerful and rich the Spanish Empire was at its peak. And it's only one of six royal palaces in Madrid—the royal family actually resides in the comparatively more modest Palace of Zarzuela on the outskirts of the city (they come to Palacio Real only for special events). The palace was constructed by King Philip V between 1738 and 1755 on the site of a ninth-century Muslim fortress, and one thing is quite clear: the dude had a thing for marble. And gold. And porcelain. For a meager entrance fee of €5 (student rate), members of the peasant class are allowed to view the orgy of artistry and craftsmanship of the palace that was held behind closed doors for 275 years. The self-guided palace tour (1hr.) takes you through 15 rooms, each of which is distinctly curated by a different Spanish royal. For example, the porcelain room contains almost solely porcelain decorations and seems like something out of *Alice and Wonderland*. The result is an eclectic mix of Flemish tapestries, exotic Oriental frescoes, and Persian carpets. Our guess is that some king was trying really hard to overcompensate for something small. The only constant is gorgeous, ceiling-wide vault frescoes, each representing the apotheosis of something or another; look up and find yourself underneath a floating landscape of angels, royals, and beautiful women. If you're in town on the first Wednesday of the month between September and May, check out the changing of the guard ceremony, which takes place at noon.

i Ⓜ*Opera. Walk west down C. de Arrieta. Palacio Real is at the end of the road. Come early to avoid long lines €10, with tour €17; ages 5-16, students, and seniors €5. ⏰ Open daily Apr-Sept 10am-8pm; Oct-Mar 10am-6pm.*

PLAZA MAYOR   PLAZA
Pl. Mayor

Today Plaza Mayor is something of a vestigial structure in the bustling cosmopolitan center of Madrid. It's all been downhill for the plaza ever since they stopped using it as the site of public executions during the Spanish Inquisition. Just kidding, but it's mainly just a tourist hub now (there's even a tourist information center which offers free maps). A costumed Elvis and Spider-Man wander the plaza daily, looking like they may have both had a few too many *cervezas* as they harass you for money. Nowadays, the plaza is notable among locals for the week-long **Fiesta de San Isidor** (starts May 15), during which the city celebrates its patron saint. Looking around, it's just an expansive stony public plaza, with an indistinct statue in the middle, some restaurants scattered around the periphery, and surprisingly few places to sit. The buildings around the plaza have also become entirely residential; now, 237 apartment balconies overlook one of the single most important sites in the city's history. Be on the lookout for little kids playing soccer, for whom the new fad appears to be kicking the ball as hard as they can at tourists' crotches. Seriously, guys, wear a cup.

i Ⓜ*Sol or* Ⓜ*Opera. From Puerta del Sol, walk 2min. down C. Mayor toward the Palacio Real. Pl. Mayor is on the left.*

madrid

PUERTA DEL SOL
Puerta del Sol

Spain's *Kilometre Zero*, the point from which all distances in Spain are measured, is located in Puerta del Sol. You certainly can't get more *"el centro"* than the center of the Spanish kingdom itself, but unfortunately, that's pretty much the most distinctive part about "Sol." It's a geographic reference point, but there's not much to see here other than two statues (the one depicting a bear climbing up a tree is supposed to be famous, but it's hard to see why), chain stores, and hordes of tourists. It's like Times Square, minus the pretty lights and cool stores. In fact, the huge space it spans is actually where locals gather to ring in the New Year. The tradition is to drunkenly eat 12 grapes at midnight and make 12 wishes for each of the upcoming 12 months. The plaza, memorialized in Goya's *The Third* and *Second of May*, is today overrun by newsstands, billboards, scam artists, and street performers dressed like Mickey Mouse and Spongebob. You're better off walking either north, south, east, or west of *Kilometre Zero* if you're looking for a more authentic Madrid. With the regional government situated on the southern end of the plaza, the Puerta del Sol has also been the site of major protests and political rallies.

i Ⓜ*Sol.*

CATEDRAL DE LA ALMUDENA
C. Bailen ☎91 542 22 00

Catedral de la Almudena is an anomaly. Big cathedral in major European city—must be hundreds of years old, right? Nope. While Madrid became the official capital of the Spanish Kingdom during the reign of Philip II, it took many years for the Spanish Catholic Church to recognize the city as a worthy religious center, preferring the former capital of Toledo. Because of this, the Church was resistant to the idea of building a new central cathedral in Spain. While Catedral de la Almudena was conceived in the 16th century, construction did not begin until 1879 and was only just completed in 1999 (meaning this towering European cathedral is younger than you are). Located next to El Palacio Real, this monumental cathedral is a happy accident: the Catholic Church's love child with the city of Madrid. The architectural style reflects this precarious past: the roof is painted in bright,bold patterns that resemble the work of Henri Matisse, while the panes of stained glass recall Picasso and the Cubist tradition. In this way, Catedral de la Almudena separates itself from run-of-the-mill European cathedrals in which you walk into a cavernous space, note that it looks cool, feels impressive, makes you feel insignificant, and then you leave. If you look hard, you'll find little hints of Modernism that you won't find in any other cathedral.

i *Right next to Palacio Real. Free.* 🕐 *Open daily 10am-2pm and 5-8pm.*

CONVENTO DE LA ENCARNACIÓN
Pl. de la Encarnación, 1 ☎91 454 88 00

Every July 27, it is said that the blood of St. Panthalon, held in a crystal orb, visibly liquefies. It is not entirely clear that St. Panthalon was in fact a living, breathing (and bleeding) person, but a crystal orb containing his alleged blood is on display at the Convento de la Encarnación. Convents are normally incredibly exclusive: it doesn't matter how hot your friends are, you still aren't getting in (that bouncer, Sister Martha, is such a witch!). This convent is a little different. While it was founded as an exclusive center of monastic life nearly 400 years ago, today it is accessible to the general public for a small entrance fee. Self-guided tours aren't allowed; the only way into the chapel is to pay for the group tour, which generally runs every 30min. The tour takes you through the formerly secluded chapel, filled with artwork by European masters, and into the famous reliquary, which contains thousands of Christian relics, most notably

spain *(sidebar)*

get a room!

Madrid has a range of affordable housing options, from cheap hostels to boutique hotels, in almost every neighborhood. For more listings, visit **www. letsgo.com**

WAY HOSTEL
HOSTEL $

C. Relatores 17 ☎91 420 05 83 www.wayhostel.com

Cat's, Mad, and Way Hostels form a trifecta of hostels for English-speaking backpackers, each one offering free walking tours of the city during the day and pub/club crawls at night. Way is probably the best choice out of the three thanks to its more modern, decorated rooms. The huge communal kitchen and large TV room feel like upscale college common rooms—perfect for your next beer. This place is very popular and often booked to capacity: make sure to book in advance on their funky website.

i Ⓜ*Tirso de Molina. Walk toward the museum district and make a left up C. Relatores. Laundry service €8 at sister hostel. Towels €1. The hostel is on the right. Free Wi-Fi. Breakfast included. Reserve online. Rooms €18-24.* ☼ *Reception 24hr.*

HOSTAL ASTORIA
HOSTAL $$$

Carrera de San Jeronimo, 32, 5th fl. ☎91 429 11 88 www.hostal-astoria.com

Hostal Astoria's rooms are quieter, brighter, and more carefully decorated (i.e., there's a new-ish coat of paint on walls) than those of Hostal Aguilar, which is located in the same building. All rooms come with modern en-suite bathrooms, flat screen TVs, and Wi-Fi. As an added bonus, Astoria is on the fifth floor of the building, meaning you will be that much more removed from the stammering drunkards below.

i *From Puerta del Sol, walk 100m east along Carrera de San Jeronimo toward Paseo del Prado. Free Wi-Fi. Reserve in advance online. Single €35-45; doubles €45-65; triples €75-85.* ☼ *Reception 24hr.*

ALBERGUE JUVENIL MUNICIPAL
HOSTEL $

C. Meija Lequerica, 21 ☎91 593 96 88 www.ajmadrid.es

This hostel is in another league. Albergue Juvenil Municipal is a state-of-the-art youth hostel built by the city government in 2007. The decor is more like that of a four-star city hotel, with frosted glass, dark wood floors, and IKEA-style furniture. Add the spacious bedrooms, pool tables, cafeteria, laundry room, exercise room with stationary bikes, and media room with a computer lab, and you have a heaven for budget travelers used to dinky hostels.

i *From* Ⓜ*Bilbao, follow C. de Sagasta 3 blocks west to C. Meija Lequerica; the hostel is on the right. Breakfast included. Laundry €3. Towels €3. 4- to 6-bed co-ed dorms. Book at least 5 days in advance. Under 25 €20, age 25 €22, over 25 €27.* ☼ *Reception 24hr.*

madrid

those blood-filled crystal orbs. It's 5min. away from the Catedral de Almudena, and while Almudena is bigger and prettier, the convent has more history and authenticity behind it. And some mean nuns, if getting yelled at by old ladies is your thing.

i Ⓜ*Opera. Take Pl. de Isabel II northwest to C. de Arietta and turn right onto Pl. de la Encarnación. Tours conducted in Spanish every 30min. €3.60.* ☼ *Open Tu-Sa 10am-2pm, Su 10am-3pm.*

Avenida del Arte

🏛 MUSEO NACIONAL CENTRO DE ARTE REINA SOFÍA
MUSEUM

C. Santa Isabel, 52   ☎91 774 10 00 www.museoreinasofia.es

Dedicated by Juan Carlos I to his wife in 1988, the Reina Sofía is itself a master-work of art, metamorphosing what was once Madrid's 18th-century general into a towering temple of 20th-century art. Four stories, two connected buildings (the Sabatini and Nouvel buildings), and a classical courtyard provide the structure for an impressive architectural display of glass and steel. This is a huge museum; give yourself an entire afternoon to do its vast collection justice. The second and fourth floors are mazes of permanent exhibits that chart the avant-garde of Spanish art and include galleries dedicated to Juan Gris, Joan Miró, and Salvador Dalí. The museum's centerpiece is undoubtedly Picasso's *Guernica* in Gallery 206. The best way to make the most of your visit is to invest in an audio tour (€3), which sheds light on what can be some relatively esoteric exhibitions steeped in Spanish history and the intricacies of art history. Try to come in the mornings or on a weekday; Reina Sofía has by far the most cumbersome crowds of all of Madrid's museums.

i Ⓜ Atocha €6; 17 and under, over 65, and students free. Temporary exhibits €3. Audio tour €4. ☼ Open M 10am-9pm, W-Sa 10am-9pm, Su 10am-3pm.

🏛 MUSEO NACIONAL DEL PRADO
MUSEUM

C. Ruiz de Alarcón, 23   ☎91 330 28 00 www.museodelprado.es

The free museum maps offered at the information kiosk will help guide you to the most historically important pieces, while the English audio tour (€3.50) is an invaluable resource for those who wish to learn the history of the 1500-plus works on display. Evenings are free at the museum, but be prepared for large crowds.

i Ⓜ Banco de España and Ⓜ Atocha. From Ⓜ Atocha, walk north up Paseo del Prado; the museum is on the right, just past the gardens. Free entry Tu-Sa 6-8pm, Su 5-8pm. Check the website for an up-to-date schedule. €8; students, under 18, and over 65 free. ☼ Open Tu-Su 9am-8pm.

🏛 MUSEO THYSSEN-BORNEMISZA
MUSEUM

Paseo del Prado, 8   ☎91 369 01 51 www.museothyssen.org

It's easy to forget about the Thyssen-Bornemisza when hopping between the juggernaut that is the Reina Sofía and Prado museums. But that's good news for you—the crowds for this world-class museum are short and sweet. The museum is housed in the 19th-century Palacio de Villahermosa and contains the donated collection of the late Baron Henrich Thyssen-Bornemisza. Today, the museum is the world's most extensive private showcase, with items ranging from 14th-century Flemish altarpieces to an impressive collection of German avant-garde canvases from the early 20th century. This museum is particularly sweet for tourists; whereas Prado and Reina Sofía have exhibits focusing on very particular Spanish art, there's a more diverse selection of art here, including the likes of Edward Hopper.

i From the Prado, walk north up the Paseo del Prado. The museum is at the corner of Carrera de San Jeronimo and Paseo del Prado €7, children under 12 free. ☼ Open Tu-Su 10am-7pm.

🏛 CAIXAFORUM
MUSEUM

Paseo del Prado, 36   ☎91 389 65 45

The most striking feature of the Caixaforum is the vertical garden on the exterior of the building—it looks like someone planted a forest on the side of a modern building. Other than that, this museum is surprisingly uninspiring for having been designed by the same architects as London's legendary Tate Modern. There's not much of a focus at Caixaforum; there are only two floors of monochromatic, tinny gallery space for various art, design, and architecture exhibits. The basement auditorium hosts miscellaneous events, from architecture lectures to film screenings.

i Ⓜ*Atocha. From the metro, walk north up Paseo del Prado; the Caixaforum is on the left €4.* 🕐 *Open daily 10am-8pm. Closed Dec 25, Jan 1, and Jan 6.*

PARQUE DEL BUEN RETIRO
PARK

C. Alfonso XII, 48   ☎91 429 82 40 www.parquedelretiro.es

When a run-of-the-mill millionaire needs a break, he goes to a spa. When a Spanish monarch needs some time off, he just builds his own retreat. A former hunting ground, the Parque del Buen Retiro was reconstructed by Felipe IV in the 1630s as his lavish, personal retreat. *Madrileños* appreciate its more modern additions, including a running track and a sports complex. On weekends, the promenades fill with musicians, families, and young lovers (this is without a doubt the best place to make out in Madrid). Amateur rowers venture out onto the Estanque Grande, and exhibits and performances are showcased at the palaces. No surprise, but try to avoid the park after dark, especially if you're alone (you don't want to get mugged by the pigeon lady!).

i Ⓜ*Retiro. Or, from* Ⓜ*Atocha, pass the roundabout north onto Calle de Alfonso XII. The park is on the right. Free. Row boats M-F until 2pm; €1.40, Sa-Su and holidays €4.55.* 🕐 *Open in summer daily 6am-midnight; in winter 6am-10pm. Estanque pier open 10am to 45min. before sunset; Jul-Aug 10am-11pm.*

Las Huertas

REAL ACADEMIA DE BELLAS ARTES DE SAN FERNANDO
MUSEUM

C. de Alcalá, 13 rabasf.insde.es   ☎91 524 08 64

The oldest permanent art institute in Madrid, the Royal Academy of Fine Arts of San Fernando was created in 1752 and was the premier center for Spanish arts up until the mid-20th century. Since then, it has been transformed into a low-key, badass museum, often forgotten among the museum titans of the Prado and Reina Sofia. This place is great because there are little to no tourists or crowds, it's free all the time for students (and only €5 for everyone else), and it's located in an amazing Baroque palace, where you can imagine 19th-century Spanish students once chilled while making art and other hipster stuff. The museum contains three main floors and features a permanent collection of Spanish, Italian, and Flemish art—particularly notable are the Goya paintings in Room 13, including two rare self-portraits. The third floor is primarily 20th-century contemporary art, which follows the trajectory of post-Cubism Spanish art. Even if you don't like art at all, you get free entry to a baller palace.

i *From Puerta del Sol, walk east down C. de Alcalá. Real Academia de Bellas Artes is on the left. €5; groups of 15-25, university students, teachers, under 18 and over 65 free. Free for everyone on W.* 🕐 *Open Tu-Su 10am-3pm.*

La Latina and Lavapiés

BASILICA DE SAN FRANCISCO EL GRANDE
CATHEDRAL

C. de San Buenaventura   ☎91 365 38 00

One of the grandest and most distinctive structures in Madrid is often overlooked by most tourists. While everyone visits the Catedral Almudena just up the road, many end up missing out on this basilica, which comes to life in stunning fashion when lit up at night. The cathedral has three chapels, including the Chapel of San Bernardino de Siena, where Goya's magnificent painting of the chapel's namesake rests. Pay close attention to the picture, and you will see that the figure looking down on the right is Goya himself. Don't forget to check out the adjacent gardens, which have spectacular views of the rolling edges of Madrid.

i *From* Ⓜ*La Latina, walk straight west down Carrera San Francisco. Free. Guided tour €3.* 🕐 *Open Tu-Su 10:30am-1pm and 4-6:30pm.*

madrid

LA IGLESIA DE SAN ANDRÉS

Pl. de San Andrés

CHURCH

One of the oldest parishes in Madrid, La Iglesia de San Andrés used to be *the* go-to church for La Latina local and patron saint of Madrid, San Isidro Labrador. Much of the original interior was destroyed during the Spanish Civil War, but the structure still showcases a Baroque style crafted by designer José de Villarreal. The large domed ceiling and colorful stained glass make for a pretty, if not particularly daring, aesthetic. It's not a must-see, but it's definitely worth stopping by if you're in the area.

i Ⓜ*La Latina. Make a left onto C. de la Cava. Free.*

Chueca and Malasaña

PALACIO LONGORIA

C. de Fernando VI, 6

BUILDING

This just might be the ugliest building in the city. Depending on who you are, you will either find Palacio Longoria to be an eyesore or a beautiful relic of Neoclassical revivalist architecture. Whether you like it or not, you will probably run into this monochromatic, bombastic building during your time in Chueca—it is worth noting its peculiarity as the only true example of Catalan *modernismo* (à la Gaudí) in Madrid. Palacio Longoria was built in the early 20th century as a private residence for banker Javiar González Longoria. In 1950 it was converted into a private office building for the General Society of Spanish Authors and Editors. As such, the building is rarely open to the public, but its intricately embellished façade is a sight to behold as you make your way through Chueca.

i *From* Ⓜ*Chueca, take C. Gravina 1 block west to C. Pelayo and continue 2 blocks north. The building is on the left. The interior is only open to the public during National Architecture Week (2nd week of Oct).*

CONVENTO DE LAS SALESAS REALES

C. Barbara de Braganza, 1   ☎91 319 48 11 www.parroquiadesantabarbara.es

CATHEDRAL

Conceived in 1748 by Barbara of Portugal, this monastery continues to function as a church, but it's a great place to get away from the irony and trendiness of Malasaña and Chueca and experience some Centro-esque tourism. Right next to the Supreme Court of Spain and some lovely green Spanish plazas, this area has a surprisingly small tourist crowd (tourists' greatest fear seems to be hipsters). The interior of the church is pretty standard, but the clean and peaceful exterior area is a must-see.

i Ⓜ*Colon. From Pl. Colon, go down Paseode Recoletos and take a right onto C. de Barbara de Braganza. Free.* ⏲ *Open M-F 9:30am-1pm and 5:30-8pm, Sa 9:30am-2pm and 5-9pm, Su 9:30am-2pm and 6-9pm. Closed to tourists during mass.*

MUSEO DE HISTORIA

C. Fuencarral, 78   ☎91 701 18 63 www.munimadrid.es/museodehistoria

MUSEUM

This renovated 18th-century building constructed under Philip V now holds small collection of models, illustrations, and documents that showcase the history of Madrid. While it's mildly interesting to see how Gran Vía and Pl. Mayor looked back in the day, it's quite a small exhibit and doesn't justify going out of your way to visit this museum. The building itself is a historical relic, one of Madrid's few lasting examples of Baroque architecture. The facade is currently being renovated, and upon completion, the museum will have a totally new state-of-the-art facility.

i Ⓜ*Tribunal. Walk straight north up C. Fuencarral. The large pink building is on the right. Free.* ⏲ *Open Tu-Sa 10am-9pm, Su 11am-2:30pm.*

spain

Gran Vía

⚑ PLAZA DE ESPAÑA   PLAZA

In a city filled with statues of Spanish royalty and Roman deities, Pl. de España is something of an anomaly. Located on the western edge of Gran Vía, Pl. de España is a monument to the father of Spanish literature, **Miguel de Cervantes.** The stone statue of Cervantes at the center of the plaza is surrounded by characters from his most celebrated work, *Don Quixote.* The bronze statues immediately below Cervantes depict the hero Alonso Quixano and his chubby and slightly less heroic sidekick, Sancho Panza. To the right and left are Quixano's two love interests, the peasant lady Aldonza Lorenzo and the woman of his dreams, Dulcinea Del Toboso. Plazade España is less touristy and more lively than other plazas (like Pl. Mayor). More than just a place to gawk at a statue, this plaza also has a fountain that shoots up "Old Faithful"-style on the hour, with lots of seating around it for people who want to read or make out. In addition, there are hordes of vendors selling items like jewelry, souvenirs, and sunflower seeds. Also, it seems to be the only plaza with park-like grassy lawns for lounging (and fine—for making out).

i *The western end of C. Gran Vía, also accessible by* Ⓜ*Plaza de Espana. Free.*

Argüelles and Moncloa

⚑ TEMPLO DE DEBOD   TEMPLE, PARK

Paseo del Pintor Rosales, 2   ☎91 366 74 15 www.munimadrid.es/templodebod

The Templo de Debod is the centerpiece of the Jardinez Ferraz, a favorite park among locals. It's a 10min. walk north from the Palacio Real, and you'll be hard-pressed to find many tourists among the sun-lounging park goers. It looks out of place, and that's because it is. It's an Egyptian temple, originally built in the second century BCE, but it was donated to Madrid by Egypt in 1968 for the Spanish government's role in saving the temples of Abu Simbel. So there's literally a 2000-year-old Egyptian temple in the heart of Madrid. On top of that, the park is on high ground, offering a great view of Madrid landmarks (such as Palacio Real) as well as the rolling green countryside. Good luck finding a better place to watch the sunset.

i Ⓜ*Plaza de España. Walk to the far side of Pl. de España, cross the street, and walk a couple of blocks right; the temple is on the left. Free.* ⏲ *Open Apr-Sept Tu-F 10am-2pm and 6-8pm, Sa-Su 10am-2pm; Oct-Mar Tu-F 9:45am-1:45pm and 4:15-6:15pm, Sa-Su 10am-2pm. Rose garden open daily 10am-8pm.*

⚑ EL PARDO   PALACE

C. de Manuel Alonso s/n   ☎91 376 15 00

A 20min. bus ride out of Moncloa, El Pardo is Palacio Real's more rural, less tourist-packed, and less grandiose little brother. Originally built in the 15th century as a hunting lodge for Henry IV, El Pardo is now most famous as the private residence of General Franco during his military dictatorship. The mandatory guided tour (45min.) takes you through regal rooms covered with frescoes of royal figures and hunts as well as Franco's private quarters, which have remained largely untouched since his death in 1975. His wardrobe, prayer room, personal study, and bedroom (where he kept his most treasured personal possession, a relic of St. Teresa's silver-encrusted petrified arm) are all on display. The tour even takes you into Franco's bathroom, and yes—he had a bidet. Nowadays, in addition to its function as a tourist attraction, El Pardo is used to host state galas and functions and is the official hotel for foreign dignitaries.

i Ⓜ*Moncloa. Take bus #601 from the underground bus station (terminal 3) adjacent to Moncloa. Mandatory 45min. guided tour in Spanish/English; last tour leaves 1hr. before close €9, students and over 65 €4* ⏲ *Open Oct-Mar M-Sa 10:30am-4:45pm, Su 10am-1:30pm; Apr-Sept M-Sa 10:30am-5:45pm, Su 9:30am-1:30pm.*

madrid

CASA DE CAMPO
PARK

Zoo Madrid   ☎91 512 37 70 www.zoomadrid.com

If Parque del Oeste or Retiro Park are too tame for you, Casa de Campo offers a more sprawling experience. You won't find well-kept, lawn-ready grass to lounge on here; the fauna of Casa de Campo is more wild, rough, and untamed. For a pedestrian traveler, it's easy to get lost in the vast winding paths, so make sure you have a nice map, a good sense of direction, and a love of walking. Bike trails crisscross the park, and kayaks and canoes are available for rent at the park lagoon. If you are looking for something more than a tranquil afternoon in the park, **Parque de Atracciones** (an amusement park) has rides that will jack your heart rate up without fail. No need to commit yourself to the all-day pass (€24); single- and double-ride tickets can be purchased on the cheap (single €7; double €12). The park also has Madrid's only zoo and aquarium, but be prepared to shell out for an entrance pass (€19), and don't expect any particular Castillian flair from the monkeys; they're just regular monkeys. Make sure you know what metro station to get off at to avoid walking long distances: Lago for the lagoon, Batan for the amusement park, and Casa de Campo for the zoo/aquarium.

i Ⓜ*Lago, Batan, and Casa de Campo are all within the park. To get there from the city center:* Ⓜ*Batan or bus #33 or 65. Let's Go does not advise walking here after dark. Entrance to the park is free; venues and rentals are ticketed.* ☼ *Parque de Atracciones open M-Sa 9am-7pm. Zoo Madrid open daily, but check website for hours and schedule changes.*

MUSEO DE AMÉRICA
MUSEUM

Av. de los Reyes Catolicos, 6   ☎91 549 26 41 www.museodeamerica.mcu.es

Gotta love Spain; they know what's up and have created a whole museum dedicated to the greatness of (as the Spanish say) "'Murica!" Just kidding. In 1771, Carlos III started a collection that brought together ethnographic objects from scientific expeditions and pieces from the first archaeological excavations carried out in the Americas. So instead of seeing bald eagles, monster trucks, and Big Macs, you can see old maps and conquistador memorabilia. Today, the modern Museo de América holds a collection that encompasses mainly South American cultures. Some of the most interesting artifacts are treasures from the pre-Columbian cultures conquered by Spain, including some Mayan hieroglyphic documents. This museum isn't nearly as popular as the Prado, so you don't have to worry about crowds. Be warned that all the exhibit descriptions are in Spanish, with no English translation.

i Ⓜ*Moncloa. Cross the street, make a left, and walk straight €3; reduced €1.50; under 18, over 65, and students free.* ☼ *Open M-Sa 9:30am-6:30pm, Su 10am-3pm.*

Salamanca

▧ MUSEO SOROLLA
MUSEUM

C. General Martinez Campos, 47 http://museosorolla.mcu.es/   ☎91 310 15 84

Museo Sorolla is a must-see for art lovers prior knowledge of Joaquim Sorolla not necessary. It's an important counterpoint to the impersonal big museums like Prado or Reina Sofia - where we often forget that there's a human being behind each painting. Focusing on a single artist and inhabiting Sorolla's former residence and studio, Museo Sorolla gives you a sense of the deeply personal nature of art. It helps that Sorolla is also one of Spain's most talented painters. You get a sense of the story of Sorolla's artistic career - starting with the realism of his teachers, turning to impressionism, and then finally pioneering the beautiful luminist movement. The beach scenes are gorgeous: broad swaths of blue-green paint that boldly reflect the play of light on the water. More importantly, you get a sense of the Sorolla the family man, who captured his love in countless portraits such as *Mi Mujer y Mis Hijos*("My Wife and Kids). Come to Museo Sorolla and witness the power of art to immortalize love.

i Ⓜ*Iglesia. Turn right on C. General Martinez Campos €3. Free on Su.* Ⓩ *Open Tu-Sa 9:30am-8pm, Su 10am-3pm.*

MUSEO LAZARO GALDIANO   MUSEUM
C. Serrano, 122   ☎91 561 60 84 www.fig.es

Mueso Lazaro Galdiano calls itself "probably the best private art collection". It puts the word "probably" in there because we all know that title actually belongs to Museo Thyssen in Avenida del Arte. Don't be mistaken, Jose Lazaro Galdiano - one of Spain's most influential patron of arts and literature in the early twentieth century - amassed quite an impressive collection (13,000 pieces on display). But it lacks the breadth of the Thyssen collection. While it includes a number of significant works, such as Goya's *Witch's Sabbath*, and *El Greco's Portrait of St. Francis of Assis*, the vast majority of his collection consists of stiff sixteenth to eighteenth century religious portraits and scenes. If you loved Prado and Palacio Real, you'll probably enjoy this too. Much like the Royal Palace, each room is decked out in fancy woodwork and usually an impossibly intricate ceiling fresco. Worth checking out is the top fifth floor, which includes the miscellaneous items of his collection, such as ivory-coated muskets and fancy sabers.

i Ⓜ*Gregorio Maranon €4, students €3, EU citizens free.* Ⓩ *Open Su 10am-3pm Tu-Sa 10am-4:30pm*

FOOD
El Centro

🖾 EL SOBRINO DE BOTIN   TAPAS $$
C. de Cuchilleros, 17   ☎91 366 42 17 www.botin.es

The world's oldest restaurant according to *The Guinness Book of World Records*, El Sobrino de Botin reeks of roasted pig and illustrious history (it was founded in 1620). Goya was a waiter here, and it was one of Hemingway's favorite haunts thanks to its suckling pig (€24). He writes in *The Sun Also Rises*, "We lunched upstairs at Botin's. It is one of the best restaurants in the world. We had roast young suckling pig and drank rioja alta." This is a truly authentic historic landmark and protector of the *madrileño* culinary tradition, although there is a large crowd of tourists. From the *guildedoil* still life paintings, antique revolvers, and porcelain-tiled walls, El Sobrino is what so many restaurants in the barren El Centro restaurant scene artificially aspire to be. As you approach the winding wooden staircase surrounded by craggy stone walls, you will notice *"el horno,"* the nearly 300-year-old wood-fired oven that continues to roast the same traditional dishes. While the food isn't cheap, even their simple dishes like the *sopa de oja* (garlic soup with egg; €7.90) are all premium authentic quality and far better than what you can expect from neighboring El Centro restaurants. Delicious food and an authentic time capsule of history: Botin is a must-eat in Madrid.

i *From* Ⓜ*Sol, walk 6 blocks west down C. Mayor to C. Cava de San Miguel to C. de Cuchilleros. Prices rang €6-30.* Ⓩ *Open daily 1-4pm and 8pm-midnight.*

🖾 CAFÉ DE CÍRCULO DE BELLAS ARTES   CAFE $$$
C. de Alcalá 42   ☎91 521 69 42 www.circulobellasartes.com

The 10min. walk out of Puerta del Sol to get to this cafe is worth it just to get away from the tourists. It's also good for a nice stroll through Madrid's more modern, Manhattan-esque side. This is a classic European sidewalk cafe, although the emphasis during lunch is more on a sit-down restaurant experience than grab-and-go tapas and coffee à la carte. The interior is decked-out

madrid

with crystal chandeliers, columns stamped with Picasso-like figure drawings, and frescoed ceilings. The wicker chairs on the street side terrace make for a comfortable place to relax and people-watch amid the bustle of C. de Alcala. The lunch menu focuses on a two-course meal; €16 can get you Valencia-style *paella* and Iberian meat with potatoes. Included in all meals is an alcoholic beverage to begin with and a coffee as dessert. Consider it the Spanish version of a Four Loko. Dinner is a cheaper, more traditional tapas experience. After eating, pay €2 (student price) to see the sweeping city view at the top of the connected seven-story Circulo de Bellas building (there's restaurant seating up there during the non-scorching months).

i From ⓂSevilla, walk 2 blocks west down C. Alcala. Coffee €3-6. Wine €3-6. Sandwiches €5-8. Lunch 2-course meal €16. ⏰ Open M-Th 9:30am-1am, F-Sa 9:30am-3am, Su 9:30am-1am.

▓ TABERNA MALASPINA
C. Cadiz, 9

RESTAURANT $
☎34 915 234 024

It's hard to believe that just a block south of the Sol and all its overpriced, tour-ist-trap restaurants is Taberna Malaspina, an authentic, value-priced gem. The house special, *malaspina*, is a generous serving of melted cheese, oregano, to-mato, and ham on an open-faced piece of toasted bread. This place also features a wide selection of wines for around €2 a glass (or €9 a bottle), and the friendly staff is quick to offer suggestions to help you navigate the menu. A few drinks with your meal enhances the restaurant's warm ambiance. It's easy to imagine yourself as Hemingway during his time in Madrid while you sip your wine at the bar, surrounded by conversing locals at this cozy establishment. Good food, drink, and conversation: what else is there to want in life?

i From ⓂSol, walk south down Calle de Carretas. Turn left onto Calle Cadiz, Malaspina is on the left. Tapa €4-10. Beer and wine €2. ⏰ Open daily 10:30am-2am.

MERCADO DE SAN MIGUEL
Pl. de San Miguel, 2

MARKET $
☎91 542 73 64 www.mercadodesanmiguel.es

This isn't your average, bazaar-like open air market, where vendors shout at you as they hock overripe goods. Mercada de San Miguel is a market representative of the modern, hip Madrid. The market is contained in a clean, glass building. While some fresh produce, fish, and meats are sold, Mercada de San Miguel is focused on its specialty: ready-made food boutiques. Full of wildly diverse op-tions, you can get fine meats, cheeses, flowers, *paella*, pastries, and wine within feet of each other. Prices here are quite reasonable, especially compared to the expensive sit-down dining options in nearby Pl. Mayor. Not hungry? Come here just to wander among the Pinterest-ready displays of colorful food porn, such as yogurt shots, delicately crafted sandwiches, and cute pastries. The partial air-conditioning makes it the locals' pit stop for a glass of wine (€2-3), a fresh oyster (€1.50-3), or more traditional tapas (€2-4). Just a few years old, this rein-vention of the open market has already become hugely popular with locals and tourists.

i At the Pl. de San Miguel, off the northwest corner of Pl. Mayor right beside the Cerveceria. Prices vary. ⏰ Open M-W 10am-midnight, Th-Sa 10am-2am, Su 10am-midnight.

CHOCOLATERÍA SAN GINÉS
Pl. de San Ginés, 5

CHOCOLATERÍA $
☎91 366 54 31

After spending all day looking at 500-year-old buildings and pretending to care, it's okay to let loose. Sometimes this means treating yourself to a good dinner; sometimes it means ingesting unconscionable amounts of deep-fried batter and melted dark chocolate. Popular among locals and tourists alike, the famous Chocolatería San Ginés has been serving the world's must gluttonous treat, *churros con chocolate* (churros dipped in warm melted chocolate, (€4), since it was founded in 1894. San Ginés has the neat decor and service (waiters

spain

serve your churros and chocolate) of a fancy, date-ready cafe but is also open 24hr. for all your late-night, post-clubbing needs. Get the best of both worlds: find a hot date at the club, put a pair of churros on your tab, and then have some wicked, chocolate-fueled hostel sex afterward.

i *From Puerta Del Sol, walk down C. Arenal until you get to Joy nightclub. Chocolatería San Ginés is tucked in the tiny Pl. de San Ginés. Chocolates from €4. ☼ Open daily 24hr.*

MUSEO DEL JAMÓN
TAPAS $$

C. Mayor, 7 ☎91 542 26 32 www.museodeljamon.com

You never forget the day you lose your *bocadillo* virginity in Madrid. The *bocadillo* is the simplest but most satisfying meal you will have in the city, and Museo Del Jamón (literally, "Museum of Ham") does right by this tradition: crispy Spanish baguettes, freshly sliced *jamón*, rich Manchego cheese, and dirt cheap prices (€1-2). Vegetarians beware: there is meat everywhere. Cured pig legs dangle from the ceiling, and the window display brims with sausages. Museo del Jamón is reliably packed with tourists drawn in by the hanging meats and the promise of authentic Spanish tapas. Fanny packs and cameras are plentiful, but nothing can take away from the satisfaction of an authentic and criminally cheap meal. The upstairs dining room also offers more substantial entrees like *paella* (€12) and full *raciones* (€10-15) of *jamón* and *queso*. However, as one local put it, "A sandwich for one euro, it's good. But a whole meal, you can find better elsewhere".

i *From ⓂSol, walk 2 blocks west down C. Mayor. Several locations throughout El Centro. Sandwiches €1-3. Sit-down menu €10-20. ☼ Open daily 9am-midnight.*

EL ANCIANO REY DE LOS VINOS
SPANISH $$

C. de Bailén, 19 ☎91 559 53 32 www.elancianoreydelosvinos.es

Right across the street from the Catedral de la Almudena, this is a pit stop for an afternoon drink and snack. Founded in 1909, El Anciano Rey de los Vinos is a granddaddy in the world of tapas bars in El Centro (maybe not a great-granddaddy, but a granddaddy nonetheless). There's noise and bustle from C. de Bailén, but the big draw of this place is its straight-shot view of the cathedral. So as people across the street enter to confess and pray away their sins, you can sit easy and comfortably drink away your own. It helps that the vermouth goes down cold and smooth and comes with a Spanish-style potato salad. While the menu is not particularly inventive, at a certain point, beer is beer and chairs are awesome—especially after a long day of museum-going.

i *From the Catedral de la Almudena, walk across C. de Bailén. Tapas €6-13. Beer €2. Wine €3. ☼ Open daily 8:30am-midnight.*

La Latina and Lavapiés

🏅 ALMENDRO 13
SPANISH $$

C. Almendro, 13 ☎91 365 42 52

The simple, woody interior of Almendro belies the fact that this is not your average Spanish restaurant. While many *madrileño* restaurants serve pre-made tapas at an uncomfortably lukewarm temperature, everything at Almendro 13 is made hot and fresh to order. The specialty here is definitely the *huevos rotos*—fried eggs served on top of a heaping pile of fries with a variety of toppings (€6-9.50). It's so gluttonous and guiltily delicious that it feels like it should belong in America (or on an episode of *Man v. Food*).

i *ⓂLatina. Walk west on C. Plaza Cebada 1 block, take a right onto C. del Humilladero, walk 1 block to C. Almendro, and walk up 1 block. Sandwiches, tortillas, and salad €6-8. Entrees €6-9. Beer, wine, and vermouth €3. ☼ Open daily 1-4pm and 7:30pm-12:30am.*

madrid

CAFE BAR MELO'S

BAR $

C. Ave María, 44   ☎91 527 50 54

Bread, cheese, and meat, cooked together to simple perfection. And for cheap. What else could you want? A Bentley? A fur coat? All you backpackers want all the same things, but Cafe Bar Melo's has mastered the art of the grilled *zapatilla* (grilled pork and cheese sandwich; €3). Don't expect glamorous decor: Cafe Bar Melo's looks something like a hot dog stand at a major league baseball park after seven innings of play, but that's all part of the magic.

i ⓂLavapiés. Walk up C. Ave María 1 block. Sandwiches €2-5. Beer €1-3. ☼ Open Tu-Sa 9pm-2am.

TABERNA DE ANTONIO SANCHEZ

TAPAS $$

C. del Mesón de Paredes, 13   ☎91 539 78 26

Founded in 1830 by legendary bullfighter Antonio Sanchez, this *taberna* is as traditional as it gets. The *taberna* features traditional, matador-worthy favorites like morcilla *a las pasas* (black pudding and raisins; €9), as well as gazpacho €4), *sopa de ajo* (garlic soup; €4), and plenty of Manchego cheese and *jamón ibérico* to keep you happy. If you squint your eyes through the darkness, you can see that the walls are covered with original murals by the 19th-century Spanish painter Ignacio Zuloaga and victory trophies from bullfights of centuries past.

i From ⓂTirso de Molina, walk past Pl. de Tirso de Molina until you get to C. del Mesón de Paredes. Take a left (south) onto C. del Mesón de Paredes. The taberna is on the left. Entrees €3-15. ☼ Open M-Sa noon-4pm and 8pm-midnight, Su noon-4pm.

NUEVO CAFE BARBIERI

CAFE $

C. Ave María, 45   ☎91 527 36 58

With high, molded ceilings and large windows, Nuevo Cafe Barbieri has a much more open and breezy feel than other cramped cafes. While this may be Lavapiés's finest traditional cafe during the late afternoon, it's also a buzzing nightlife hub on weekends. Although you won't find much of a food selection here, they have a Cadillac-sized espresso machine and a Jeep-size mixed drink menu to match. Barbieri specializes in mixed drinks like the Barbieri (coffee, Bailey's, cream; €4.50) and the Haitiano (coffee, rum, cream; €4.50).

i ⓂLavapiés. Walk up C. Ave María 1 block. Desserts €4-7. Coffee drinks €2-5. Tea €2.50. ☼ Open M-W 4pm-12:30am, Th 4pm-1:30am, F-Su 4pm-2:30am.

Las Huertas

CERVECERÍA LOS GATOS

TAPAS $$

C. Jesús, 2   ☎91 429 30 62

If you took one of the grandfather tapas bars of Las Huertas and gave it a healthy dose of Viagra, it would look and feel something like Cervecería Los Gatos. Sandwiched between the madness of Las Huertas and the more quiet museum district, Los Gatos is a local hangout that most tourists haven't yet discovered. At first glance, Los Gatos seems like a pretty typical Spanish tapas bar, but a closer look reveals that it actually has an oddball sense of humor. The decorations are a grab-bag of eclectic items: signed football jerseys, a painting of skeletons drinking at a bar, an antique motorcycle, mounted bull heads, and an actual gas pump. The *pièce de résistance* is the fresco: a version of Leonardo da Vinci's *The Creation of Man*, in which Adam gracefully holds beer. If ever there's a place to snack on traditional tapas, this is it.

i ⓂAntón Martín. Take C. Atocha southeast ½ block to C. de Moratín. Take C. de Moratin 4 blocks east to C. Jesús. Turn left (heading north) onto C. Jesús and walk 2 blocks. Pinchos €2-4. Racciones €8-18. Cash only. ☼ Open daily 1:30pm-2am.

spain

LA BARDEMCILLA DE SANTA ANA
C. de Augusto Figueroa, 47

TRADITIONAL $$
☎91 521 42 56

If you're wondering what made Javier Bardem the tall, strapping, dazzling Spanish beauty he is today, look no further than La Bardemcilla. Unfortunately, this Bardem family restaurant is actually unrelated to everyone's favorite, creepily handsome (fictional) killer. Fortunately, they serve Spanish family recipes like *huevos de oro estrellados* (eggs scrambled with *jamón iberico* and onions; €8.70). With two Madrid locations, Grandma and Grandpa Bardem are getting some long overdue street cred. This place sets itself apart from other traditional tapas bar in the same area with its more homey, less touristy vibe. It almost feels like your aunt's dining room, complete with warm orange paint, framed black and white pictures, and a piano.

i From Pl. Santa Ana, take C. Núñez de Arce, on the west side of the plaza, north toward Puerta del Sol. Follow C. Núñez de Arce 1 block. The restaurant is on the right just before C. de la Cruz. Pinchos €2-4. Entrees €8-10. ② Open Tu-F noon-5:30pm and 7pm-2am, Sa 8pm-2am, Su noon-5:30pm and 7pm-2am.

LATERAL
Pl. Santa Ana

TAPAS $$
☎91 420 15 82 www.cadenalateral.es

Lateral stands apart form the other slightly boring, traditional Spanish cervecerias on Pl. Santa Ana. If the curators of the Reina Sofía were to make a modern tapas restaurant, it would look something like this, with a spacious interior, marble bar, and white leather bar stools. Menu items like the lamb crepe (€4.50), raspberry mango foam (€4), and the salmon sashimi with wasabi (€6.50) are a nice break from the traditional ox tails and butcher-meats of similar establishments. Bring one of your hostel friends to share the €16 sampler. And don't forget to try a hand-crafted berry mojito (€7)—it's so good, you'll be shaken from your everyday hellish malaise and learn to love again. One last thing: they don't offer substantial entrees, so either order a lot of tapas or have your mother pack you a mayonnaise sandwich to eat on the curb.

i Facing the ME Madrid Reina Victoria Hotel in Pl. Santa Ana, Lateral is on the left. Tapas €3-8. Mixed drinks €7. Combination platters €16. ② Open daily noon-midnight.

CASA ALBERTO
C. de las Huertas, 18

TRADITIONAL $$
☎91 429 93 56 www.casaalberto.es

Founded in 1827, Casa Alberto is one of Madrid's oldest taverns. Once upon a time, bullfighters came here for a "cup of courage" before they entered the bullring. Today it's a tourist favorite, and with good reason. The walls are lined with photographs of famous matadors and celebrities who have visited, and the charm hasn't entirely faded. Enter your own bullring of fear by trying tripe: what could be more carnivorous than putting another animal's stomach inside your own? Feeling even more daring? Eat a pig's ear. Damn, still hungry? How about snails and lamb hands? Your insatiable hunger howls for more. Have some beef cheek. Congratulations, you are a winner. If you're not feeling it, you can try less adventurous dishes like the Madrid-style veal meatballs or *huevos fritos* served with garlic lamb sweetbreads and roasted potatoes.

i From Pl. del Ángel, walk down C. de las Huertas toward the Prado. Casa Alberto is on the right. Entrees €5-20. ② Open daily noon-1:30am.

FATIGAS DEL QUERER
C. de la Cruz, 17

TRADITIONAL $$
☎91 523 21 31 www.fatigasdelquerer.es

While it doesn't have the "history" or institutional status of some of Las Huertas' other tapas bars, Fatigas del Querer still serves great traditional fare in a more central location. The spacious interior is a refreshing change-up from the many cramped taverns Madrid offers. Enjoy fairly standard (but still tasty) tapas beneath a fading fresco and mounted racks of wine bottles. The waitstaff is particularly attentive and keeps the turnaround quick.

i From Pl. delÁngel, go north up C. Espoz y Mina and bear right. The street becomes C. de la Cruz. Tapas €4-12. Cash only. ☑ Open M-F 11am-1:30am, Sa-Su 11am-2:30am. Kitchen open until 1am.

LA FINCA DE SUSANA RESTAURANT   MEDITERRANEAN $$
C. de Arlabán, 4   ☎91 429 76 78 www.lafinca-restaurant.com

Despite its proximity to Sol, La Finca de Susana is largely untouched by the tourist hordes. Located down a smaller street, this restaurant is popular among locals for offering a gourmet, sit-down dining experience (think white table-cloths set with silverware and wine glasses) at a surprisingly reasonable price. Though the look and feel is relatively classy (don't worry, your T-shirt is fine), a meal here will only set you back around €10. The Mediterranean-inspired menu offers greater variety than the traditional *taberna*, with popular dishes like *arroz negro con sepia* (stewed rice with cuttlefish; €11) and *cordera al horno* (roasted lamb; €12). Come early or make a reservation.

i ⓂSol. Follow C. de Alcalá east and take a right (south) onto C. de Seville. Follow C. de Seville to C. de Arabal and take a left (east). Entrees €7-16. ☑ Open M-W 1-3:45pm and 8:30-11:30pm, F-Sa 1-3:45pm and 8:30pm-midnight, Su 1-3:45pm and 8:30-11:30pm.

Avenida del Arte and Retiro

EL BRILLANTE   TAPAS $
Pl. Emperador Carlos V, 8   ☎91 539 28 06

El Brillante provides quality budget eating in the pricey Avenida del Arte. There's nothing flashy about the interior—the focus is on the wide selection of affordable Spanish food. While its claims that its *bocadillo de calamares* (fried calamari sandwich; €6) are the best in Madrid have not been substantiated by any awards or reviews, patrons don't seem to care, and they order the sandwich in abundance. Don't like the idea of putting suction cups in your mouth? There's something here for everyone (even Italian food, with pizzas and pasta for €6). The restaurant has indoor bar seating and outdoor terrace seating with a prime view of Reina Sofia's towering glass architecture.

i ⓂAtocha. Sandwiches €4-8. ☑ Open daily 7am-1am.

LA PLATERIA DEL MUSEO   TAPAS $$
C. Huertas, 82   ☎91 429 17 22

Roughly equidistant from the Prado, Reina Sofia, and Thyssen, La Plateria is in prime museum territory. And they know what customers want after a long day of pretending to appreciate art: booze, but in a sophisticated sense. You'll find a more middle-aged clientele sitting outside on the large terrace sipping sangria (€3.50), wine (€4), and mixed drinks (€7). Although they don't have a huge selection of meal-sized entrees, they do offer traditional tapas, with staples like *patatas bravas* (€6), *gazpacho andaluz* (€4.50), and *croqueta de jamon* (€3). More than anything,La Plateria del Museo stands out for its exceptional terrace seating and proximity to the three museums of Avenida del Arte.

i From ⓂAtocha, follow Paseo del Prado 2 blocks to Las Huertas and turn left. Appetizer €2.50-8. Drinks €2-6. ☑ Open daily 7am-1am.

Gran Vía

▨ [H]ARINA   CAFE $$
Pl. de la Independencia, 10   ☎91 522 87 85 www.harinamadrid.com

[H]arina is one of the best cafes in Madrid; it has a prime location, affordable prices, and delectable cafe fare. Its refreshingly modern, whitewashed decor (think Crate&Barrel) stands out among the many cafes that feel old and tired. Outside seating will give you an unobscured view of **Puerta de Alcala**, a Neoclassical arch built in 1778. Lots of restaurants exploit their prime location by offering expensive, mediocre food to compensate for the views. Harina, however, offers surprisingly affordable and delicious salads, pastries, sandwiches, and paper-thin pizzas (all looking like they've been pulled straight out of a food magazine). Indoor and outdoor seating are both generally packed, particularly on weekends, and many patrons take their food to go from the bakery.

i Ⓜ*Banco de España, walk 1 block east to Pl. de la Independencia; the restaurant is on the southwest corner. Coffee €2-4. Salads €8. Sandwiches €6. Pizzas €9-11. Terrace seating requires a €1 additional charge.* ⚂ *Open daily 9am-9pm.*

PIZZERÍA CASAVOSTRA
ITALIAN $$

C. Infantas, 13   ☎91 523 22 07 www.pizzacasavostra.com

Pizzeria Casavostra was first opened five years ago, but it looks like it's here to stay. Locals dig the fact that everything on Casavostra's menu is fresh, from the brick-oven pizzas to the traditional appetizers. While many of the restaurants between Gran Vía and Chueca try hard to break out of the tapas mold, Casovostra keeps things simple with a traditional Italian menu. The pizzas (€8.50-14) are fired in the brick oven and topped with ingredients like arugula, fresh mozzarella, and cherry tomatoes. The appetizer salads come in huge portions and are great to share for a first round (€5-10). They also offer a full selection of *burrata* (unpasteurized mozzarella) appetizers that are so good, you'll never think twice about Louis Pasteur again. The atmosphere is clean and modern, with smooth wooden tables and bulbous, overhanging lamps that make the color of the food really pop.

i *From* Ⓜ*Gran Vía, walk east 1 block to C. Hortaleza, then 2 blocks north to C. de la Infantas. Follow C. de las Infantas. Drinks €2-4. Appetizers €4-12. Entrees €7-15.* ⚂ *Open daily noon-1am.*

EL BOCAITO
TAPAS $$

C. de la Libertad, 6   ☎91 521 31 98 www.bocaito.com

Ever since Spain's most well-known filmmaker, Pedro Almodóvar, cited El Bocaito as one of his favorites in Madrid, it has been all the rage. Founded in 1966, El Bocaito is as traditional as tapas bars get, from the matador paraphernalia on the walls to the platters of *pinchos*. El Bocaito sticks to tradition and does it well, and its back-to-back bars and four small dining rooms are packed nightly with locals. While drinks (€2-4) and tapas (€2-5) won't cost much, a full sit-down dinner with a bottle of wine and entrees (€12-20) is decently expensive.

i *From* Ⓜ*Gran Vía, walk E 1 block to C. Hortaleza, 2 blocks N to C. de la Infantas, and then follow C. de las Infantas 4 blocks west to C. de la Libertad. Drinks €2-4. Appetizers €2-5. Entrees €10-20.* ⚂ *Open M-F 1-4pm and 8:30pm-midnight, Sa 8:30pm-midnight, Su 1-4pm and 8:30pm-midnight.*

Chueca

▧ MERCADO DE SAN ANTON
MARKET $$

C. Augusto Figueroa, 24   ☎91 330 07 30 www.mercadosananton.com

This is Europe's fierce rebuttal to Whole Foods. What was once an open-air market in the middle of Chueca is now a modern glass building filled with fresh produce vendors, *charcuteriás*, *bodegas*, and a rooftop restaurant. It's the bigger, four-story version of Centro's Mercado de San Miguel, a place to get a sweeping tour of Spain's culinary landscape, from tapas to sushi to burger sliders. Prices might be a bit steep, but it's free to just gape and drool over the gorgeous displays of food.

i Ⓜ*Chueca. On the southern end of Pl. de Chueca. For the rooftop restaurant, make reservations in advance at 91 330 02 94. Visit www.lacocinadesananton.com for more on the restaurant. Varies greatly, but a full meal at the market costs around €10. Cash only.* ⚂ *1st fl. market open M-Sa 10am-10pm. 2nd fl. restaurants and bars open Tu-Su 10am-midnight. Rooftop restaurant open M-Th 10am-midnight, F-Sa 10am-1:30am, Su 10am-midnight.*

madrid

⚋ SAN WISH
BURGERS $

C. de Hortaleza, 78   ☎91 319 17 76 www.san-wish.com

The motto of this modern burger joint is "Because a good sandwich is right and necessary." From their language, these guys know that a perfect burger can be a religious experience. Luckily, they're doing God's work here, making juicy, affordable, one-of-a-kind burgers. Go for the *hamburguesa voladora* (chicken, tomato, lettuce, grilled cucumbers, melon chutney; €6.50), or, if you're feeling safe, the *clásica* (sweet pickle, tomato, and lettuce; €6.50). The young and hungry *madrileño* crowd can't seem to get enough of this place; the limited seats are nearly impossible to snag, especially during peak weekend hours.

i From ⓂGravina, take C. Gravina 2 blocks east to C. de Hortaleza, then take a right onto C. de Hortaleza. The restaurant is on the right. Sandwiches €5.50-8.90. Beer €1.50-3.50. Wine €2.50. ⌚ Open M 8pm-midnight, Tu-Sa 1-4pm and 8pm-midnight, Su 2-4pm.

BAZAAR
MEDITERRANEAN $$

C. de la Libertad, 21   ☎91 523 39 05 www.restaurantbazaar.com

You're going on a date with that cute girl from the hostel, but you're trying not to break the bank (after all, who knows if you'll see this chica again after next week). Luckily, Bazaar offers an impressive, classy dining experience at a shockingly reasonable price. This expansive two-story restaurant has the look and feel of a high-end place, with white tablecloths and wine glasses waiting on the table, and they offer a full menu of fresh pasta, salads, and meat dishes. The upstairs and downstairs dining rooms are quite large but partitioned into smaller, more intimate seated spaces by shelves filled with artisanal food displays.

i ⓂChueca. Make a left onto C. Augusto Figuroa and a right onto C. de la Libertad. Entree €7-10. ⌚ Open M-W 1:15-4pm and 8:30-11:30pm, Th-Sa 1:15-4pm and 8:30-midnight, Su 1:15-4pm and 8:30-11:30pm.

LO SIGUIENTE
TAPAS $$

C. Fernando VI, 11   ☎91 319 52 61 www.losiguiente.es

With high bar tables, metal stools, and silver columns, Lo Siguiente is a balance between a traditional tapas bar and a *nouveau* Chueca restaurant. While it may have a cool, polished aesthetic, Lo Siguiente is still an informal restaurant that *madrileños* come to for traditional Spanish staples (after all, all those Chueca sushi-burger fusion restaurants can get tiring and confusing). You can get all of the staples, like the classic *huevos rotos* (a fried egg over pan-fried potatoes, garlic, and chorizo; €9.50), but don't be afraid to try the lighter Mediterranean items, like tomato and avocado salad and ceviche served atop grilled vegetables.

i From ⓂChueca, head 2 blocks northeast on C. San Gregario and take a left onto C. Fernando VI. Lo Siguiente is on the right. Meal €10-15. ⌚ Open M-Th 8:30am-1am, F-Sa 8:30am-2:30am, Su 8:30am-1:30am.

Malasaña

⚋ LA DOMINGA
TABERNA $$

C. del Espíritu Santo, 15   ☎91 523 38 09 www.ladominga.com

Now with two locations (one in Chueca, one in Malasaña), La Dominga is quietly making a name for itself as a *taberna* that balances tradition with modernity. Although it offers traditional dishes like *rabo de toro* (oxtail stew; €14), it also caters to a younger Malasaña clientele with plenty of contemporary dishes. Dishes like the beef carpaccio (served with parmesan and arugula; €13) are more refined than the heavier stewed and grilled meats that dominate traditional Spanish cuisine. That said, the specialty here is still the very traditional *croquettas* (fried stuffed bread; €9.70) that Madrid publication *La Razon* calls the best in the city.

i ⓂTribunal. Go west on C. de San Vincente Ferrer, make a left onto C. del Barco, then a right onto C. del Espíritu Santo. Entrees €10-15. ⌚ Open daily 1-4:30pm and 8:30pm-midnight.

spain (side margin)

LAMUCCA
Pl. Carlos Carbonero, 4 ☎91 521 00 00 www.lamucca.es

Start with an appetizer of Mexican quesadillas (€9.50). Enjoy a pizza "*la de pulpo gallega*" (octopus, potatoes, paprika; €15). Finish with a dessert of sticky rice with mango (€5). Lamucca has possibly the most eclectic, globe-trotting menu in Madrid. Dishes like Thai curried chicken with jasmine rice (€11) share the menu with Italian pizza and pasta, as well as contemporary Spanish dishes like beef carpaccio (€13). This is a hugely popular local favorite. There's not much seating inside, but the outside terrace offers a wide spread of tables on the cozy Pl. Carlos Carbonero.

i ⓂTribunal. *From the pack of restaurants on east C. del Espiritu, head south on C. de la Madera 2 blocks, turn left onto Calle el Escorial, then right onto Calle Molino de Viento. Appetizer €5-12. Entrees €12-20. Pizza €10-15.* 🕐 *Open daily 1pm-1am.*

HOME BURGER BAR
Other locations: C. San Marcos, 25 and C. Silva, 25 ☎91 522 97 28

Home Burger Bar pays its respects to the classic 1950s American diner look but doesn't hit you over the head with it (looking at you, Johnny Rockets). For example, instead of overstated, cherry-red booths, you get plush, wine-colored stools. In addition to classic burgers (with the option of add-ons like thick cut bacon), they offer a number of vegetarian options, like the falafel burger (€11.25). All burgers are made from organic meat and come with a side of Caesar salad.

i ⓂTribunal. *Go west on C. de San Vincente Ferrer, make a left onto C. del Barco, and take a right onto C. del Espíritu Santo. Burgers €10-13. Sandwiches €8-15.* 🕐 *Open M-Sa 1:30-4pm and 8:30pm-midnight, Su 2-4:30pm and 8:30-11pm.*

CAFÉ MAHÓN
Pl. del 2 de Mayo, 4 ☎91 448 90 02

With a combination of international favorites, Mediterranean-inspired salads, and traditional Spanish entrees, Café Mahón has something for everyone—at a budget price. Located on the edge of one of Malasaña's most tranquil plazas, this cafe uses bright open space and simple kitchen furniture to create a casual vibe. International comfort foods spice up the menu next to traditional Spanish tapas. Try the nachos with cheese and guacamole (€7), the hummus appetizer (€6), or the moussaka (€8). A menu of specialty teas (€2-3.50) and coffees keeps people coming throughout the day to enjoy the terrace seating and watch little kids play on the local jungle gym.

i From ⓂTribunal, *head west on C. de la Palma 2 blocks west to C. San Andres, take a right, and continue until you reach the plaza. Cafe Mahon is at the northwest corner. Appetizer €6-9. Salads €7. Entrees €7-12.* 🕐 *Open daily Jul-Aug 3pm-2am; Sept-Jun noon-2am. Terrace open daily Jul-Aug 3pm-1am; Sept-Jun noon-1am.*

EL RINCÓN
C. del Espíritu Santo, 26 ☎91 522 19 86

If you're looking for a classic, bohemian Malasaña cafe experience, look no further than El Rincón, which perfectly balances hip personality with accessibility. With its simple wooden tables, small Asian prints on the walls, and chalkboard menu, it's a thoughtful little cafe. For those consistently overwhelmed by the options at restaurants, El Rincón offers a refreshingly simple five-item entree menu, featuring dishes like rigatoni with truffles.

i ⓂTribunal. *Go west on C. de San Vincente Ferrer, make a left onto C. del Barco, and take a right onto C. del Espíritu Santo. Sandwiches €5. Entrees €10. Cocktails €5-7. Wine €2.50. Coffee €2-3.* 🕐 *Open daily 11am-2am*

madrid

LOLINA VINTAGE CAFÉ

C. del Espíritu Santo, 9

CAFE $

☎66 720 11 69 www.lolinacafe.com

Lolina looks like it was assembled from a shopping spree at a Brooklyn thrift store. Literally nothing matches—from the mismatched armchairs to the vintage lamps to the '60s green and white wallpaper. But in the context of trendy Malasaña, it all somehow works. The cozy space's bright natural light attracts people at all times of the day, whether for morning tea or late-night cocktails. The food options are simple but tasty, with a selection of salads (€8), bratwurst sandwiches (€5), and open-faced *tostas* (€4). Surprisingly one of the only places on C. del Espiritu Santo with Wi-Fi, this is the perfect place to hang out and soak in the hip Malasaña vibe without breaking the bank.

i Ⓜ*Tribunal. Go west on C. de San Vincente Ferrer, make a left onto C. del Barco, then make a right onto C. del Espíritu Santo. Free Wi-Fi. Salads €8. Cocktails €6. Coffee and tea €2-5. ☼ Open M-Tu 9:30am-1am, W-Th 9:30am-2am, F-Sa 9:30am-2:30am, Su 9:30am-1am.*

OLOKUN

C. Fuencarral, 105

CUBAN $$

☎91 445 69 16

Olokun is an authentic Cuban restaurant that doesn't take itself too seriously. While in some senses a classic Cuban bar with a very tropical vibe (melon mojitos and kiwi daiquiris (€5), Olokun's dark walls are covered in the scribbles and signatures of all of its past customers. It also features a foosball table in the basement, just for kicks. Olokun takes its menu of hearty Cuban dishes seriously, from the dark mojito (made with black rum; (€7) to the traditional platters like *Mi Vieja Havana* (pork, fried plantains, black beans; €14) and *soroa* (chili, fried plantains, rice; €15).

i From Ⓜ*Tribunal, walk straight north up C. Fuencarral. The restaurant is on the left. Entree €10-15. ☼ Open daily noon-5pm and 9pm-2am.*

Argüelles and Moncloa

🔲 LA TABERNA DE LIRIA

C. del Duque de Liria, 9

SPANISH $$$

☎91 541 45 19 www.latabernadeliria.com

You're in Spain, and you've already saved a lot of money staying at dirt-cheap hostels and eating €1 *bocadillos*—you owe yourself at least one nice, authentic Spanish meal. Look no further than La Taberna de Liria. Head Chef Miguel Lopez Castanier has led Taberna de Liria through a very successful 22 years in Madrid (and published a cookbook), establishing it as a local favorite for gourmet Spanish cuisine. The dishes aren't particularly experimental, which is good for us travelers who are just looking for authentic Spanish food. The unassuming, simple decor and atmosphere keeps the emphasis on the food. Try the foie gras appetizers (€11-14), and be sure to call ahead to make reservations, particularly on weekends.

i Ⓜ*Ventura Rodriguez. Walk forward, take the left fork in the road (C. San Bernardino), and walk straight forward. Appetizer €8-15. Entrees €17-25. Full tasting menu €50. ☼ Open M-Sa 2-4pm and 9-11:45pm.*

EL JARDÍN SECRETO

C. de Conde Duque, 2

CAFE $

☎91 541 80 23

Tucked away in a tiny street close to C. de la Princesa, El Jardín Secreto takes its secret garden theme very seriously. Even the entrance is hard to find (it literally looks like a normal wall with a window), but that doesn't seem to deter the locals from coming here. Enjoy a selection of affordable, classic cafe fare in a dark, lush, fairy tale environment, filled with beaded window coverings, wooden ceiling canopies, and crystal ball table lamps. For a real taste of what Secreto has to offer, try the chocolate El Jardín, served with chocolate Teddy Grahams and dark chocolate that pools at the bottom of your cup (€6) ,or the George

Clooney cocktail with *horchata*, crème de cacao, and Cointreau (€7.25). Maybe it's a magical potion that makes you as pretty as George Clooney. More likely, you'll just get buzzed.

i Ⓜ*Ventura Rodriguez. Head left at the fork in the road (C. San Bernardino). Coffee and tea €3-6. Cocktails €7.25. Desserts €4.20.* Ⓩ *Open M-W 4:30pm-12:30am, Th-Sa 5:30pm-1:30am, Su 4:30pm-12:30am*

LAS CUEVAS DEL DUQUE   SPANISH $$$
C. de la Princesa, 16   ☎91 559 50 37 www.cuevasdelduque.galeon.com
Eating at this restaurant is kind of like eating in a Neanderthal's den. The restaurant is located partially underground, in a cave-like interior that goes for the same kind of historic Spanish appeal as Sobrino de Botin. Food-wise, Cuevas emulates Botin as well, focusing on big-game dishes like the suckling pig with potatoes (€19). They offer a great selection of steaks and grilled fish; the filet mignon (€20) is particularly popular.

i Ⓜ*Ventura Rodriguez. Take the left fork in the road onto C. San Bernardino; the restaurant is on a tiny street to the right. Entree €15-30.* Ⓩ *Open daily 7-11pm.*

Salamanca

LA ÚRSULA   TAPAS $$
C. López de Hoyos, 17   ☎91 564 23 79 www.laursula.com
Across the street from the Museo Lazaro Galdiano, La Úrsula is an upscale tapas bar with terrace seating on a quiet side street off C. Serrano. The setting is fantastic (although limited), and like most places in Salamanca, it attracts a steady crowd of wealthy, well-dressed *madrileños*. La Úrsula offers particularly great lunch deals, including one of the city's best hamburger specials (€8)—a large burger with three tasty toppings of your choice (fried egg, manchego, sauteed peppers, etc.) and served with fries, a drink, and coffee or dessert. For the early-risers out there, Ursula offers an affordable breakfast menu (€2-5) until 12:30pm.

i Ⓜ*Gregorio Marañon. Cross C. Castella on C. de Maria de Molina. Follow C. de Maria de Molina for 3 blocks until you reach C. Serrano. Menú del día €7-11. Meals €14-20. Cash only.* Ⓩ *Open daily 8am-noon.*

NIGHTLIFE

El Centro y Gran Vía

PALACIO GAVIRIA   CLUB
C. del Arenal, 9   ☎91 526 60 69 www.palaciogaviria.com
Built in 1850 and inspired by the Italian Renaissance, Palacio Gaviria is a beautiful palace turned hot nightlife joint. Make your royal entrance by heading down the grand marble staircase to the dance floor, which is powered by techno beats and electric dance moves. Be on the lookout for promoters of Palacio Gaviria in Puerta del Sol, as they will often have vouchers for free entry or drinks.

i *From Puerta del Sol, walk straight down C. del Arenal. Cover M-Th €10, F-Sa €15, Su €10.* Ⓩ *Open daily 11pm-late.*

CAFE DEL PRÍNCIPE   BAR
Pl. de Canalejas, 5   ☎91 531 81 83
As the name would suggest, this place is more of a restaurant with a large selection of drinks than a designated nightlife bar (no events or bands play here). However, they do advertise the"best mojitos in Madrid" (they're good, but that claim might be a stretch) as well as a variety of entrees and beverages. Only a block away from Sol, come here to take a tranquil break from the noise without

madrid

venturing too far from all the clubs. This place is old-fashioned classy, with dark oak and a gold-trimmed bar that attracts an older clientele.

i Right at the corner of C. de la Cruz and C. de Príncipe. Mixed drinks €5-15. ☼ Open M-Th 9:30am-2am, F-Sa 9:30am-2:30am, Su 9:30am-2am. Kitchen open M-Th 9:30am-4pm and 8pm-2am, F-Sa 9:30am-4pm and 8pm-2am, Su 9:30am-4pm and 8pm-2am.

JOY ESLAVA
CLUB

C. del Arenal, 11 ☎91 366 37 33 www.joy-eslava.com

Joy is a permanent fixture in the ever-changing Madrid nightlife scene. Located just two blocks west from Sol, Joy is an incredibly popular superclub, second in size only to the seven-story Kapital in the art district. Number one among study-abroad students and travelers, Joy Eslava plays an eclectic mix of music and features scantily clad models (of both genders) dancing on the theater stage. Balloons and confetti periodically fall New-Year's-Eve-style from the ceiling onto Joy's famously attractive clientele. Ask your hostel receptionist or promoter during the day for coupons for discounted admission or free drinks.

i Cover M- €12, Th €15, F-Su €18. ☼ Open M-Th 11:30pm-5:30am, F-Sa 11:30pm-6am, Su 11:30pm-5:30am.

REINA BRUJA
CLUB

C. Jacometrezo, 6 ☎91 542 81 93 www.reinabruja.com

Reina Bruja is not just a club; it's a futuristic fantasy land. In Reina Bruja, the internationally renowned industrial designer Tomas Alia has created a world of endless light and sound. Every surface of this club, including the toilet seats, change color using cutting-edge LED technology. Reina Bruja is Madrid nightlife at its most creative and over-the-top. This subterranean world of phosphorescent lighting and stenciled pillars is popular with tourists (although less popular than Joy) but hasn't lost its edge in the *madrileño* scene. It's an edgier, more alternative club than the mainstream, super popular nightlife juggernauts of Joy and Kapital.

i Next to Ⓜ Callao. Cover €12; includes 1 drink. Wine €7. Mixed drinks €9. ☼ Open Th-Sa 11pm-6am.

EL TIGRE
BAR

C. de Hortaleza 23 ☎91 532 00 72

El Tigre doesn't give a flying French fry about hip, frilly foodie trends. On a block with fusion restaurants, contemporary cuisine, and fancy cocktail lounges, El Tigre is refreshing because it's simple, Spanish *machismo*: beer, mojitos, and sangria in towering glasses; bull heads on the rough stone walls; and taxidermied animals. We can only imagine the interior decorator's philosophy was "hold my beer, let's make this place aggressively masculine." Don't worry guys: women seem to dig this vibe, and there's a nice ratio here. It can be hard to make your way through the door of this Spanish dive bar, which is already packed with local and tourist 20-somethings alike by 10:30pm (and if you keep in mind Spain's late nightlife schedule, that's saying something). Drinks are served with a free plate of greasy fries, pork loin, and chorizo. While the noise and crowds may be a turn-off for some, this is definitely a place where you can start your night off cheap, drunk, and greasy.

i From Ⓜ Gran Vía, walk north up C. de Hortaleza, then turn right onto C. de las Infantas. Drinks €2-5. ☼ Open daily 10:30am-1:30am.

POUSSE
BAR

C. de las Infantas, 19 ☎91 521 63 01

With refurbished antique furniture alongside sleek leather loveseats and music from every decade, the ambiance at Pousse is self-consciously eclectic. The cardboard and finger paint art on the walls was made by either avant-garde artists or kindergartners (you never know—there are some pretty pretentious kindergartners out there who really dig Abstract Expressionism). The drink menu is every bit as mixed as the decor, with everything from all-natural fresh fruit milkshakes (€6) to gourmet cocktails made with premium liqueurs (€9-13). Each cocktail has its own full-page entry in the lengthy drink menu and specials like Meet Johnny Black (Black Label whiskey, fresh OJ, sugar, and lemon; €12) are all made with fresh juices and top-dollar booze. Pousse attracts a loyal crowd of locals, but the tourists have caught on, too.

i From Ⓜ Gran Vía, walk north up C. de Hortaleza, then make a right onto C. de las Infantas. Drinks €6-13. ☑ Open M-Sa 10pm-2am.

MUSEO CHICOTE   BAR
C. Gran Vía, 12   ☎ 91 532 67 37 www.museo-chicote.com

After a cursory glance, Museo Chicote seems like an unadventurous, standard bar. But inside, once you see the walls covered in black-and-white photos of all the famous people who have come here since its creation in 1931, you'll realize this is one of Madrid's most historic bars. A longtime favorite of artists and writers (one of the many places Hemingway got drunk), this retro-chic cocktail bar maintains its original design. During the Spanish Civil War, the foreign press came here to wait out the various battles, and during the late Franco era, it became a haven for prostitutes. Today, it's a lounge with lots of dark leather seating for a diverse clientele. Museo Chicote offers one of the best happy hours on Gran Vía (cocktails €5; 5-11pm), but things shift pretty quickly at midnight, when the nightly DJ set starts. Well-known DJs playing everything from '80s American pop to European house.

i From Ⓜ Gran Vía, walk east. Museo Chicote is on the left. Cocktails €10-15. ☑ Open daily 8am-3am.

La Latina and Lavapiés

▣ CASA LUCAS   BAR
C. Cava Baja, 30   ☎ 91 365 08 04 www.casalucas.es

Props to Casa Lucas for making life seem simple and delicious. On a long block of successful restaurants, bars, and *tabernas* that thrive on gimmicks, Casa Lucas stands out by sticking to the basics: freshly prepared tapas and a premium, ever-changing wine list. With no gimmicks or hipness here, this no-frills spot attracts an older crowd. The tapas here are a notch above what you will find elsewhere, if slightly more expensive (starting around €5).

i Ⓜ La Latina. Walk west down Pl. de la Cebada. Make a right onto C. de Humilladero and continue right onto C. Cava Baja. Wine by the glass €2-4, by the bottle €16-25. Raciones €7-15. ☑ Open M-Th 8pm-midnight, F-Sa 8pm-1am, Su 8pm-midnight.

LA PEREJILA   TAPAS, BAR
C. Cava Baja, 25   ☎ 91 364 28 55

La Perejila is filled with beautiful antiques from the golden age of flamenco, vintage photographs, gold-leafed paintings, and vases of flowers that make this place come alive. Live parakeets greet you at the door, and finding a seat in this popular place is hard but well worth the effort. Come here for the titular *"La Perejila"* (veal meatballs served in a clay pot; €9). The wine selection changes daily, but their advertised "exquisite vermouth" is a favorite.

i Ⓜ La Latina. Walk west down Pl. de la Cebada. Make a right onto C. de Humilladero and continue right onto C. Cava Baja. Cocktails €5-10. Tostados €5-7. Entrees €9-12. ☑ Open Tu-Sa 1-4pm and 8:15pm-12:30am, Su 1-4pm.

ANGELIKA COCKTAIL BAR   BAR
C. Cava Baja, 24   ☎ 91 364 55 31 www.angelika.es

Angelika is notable for two things: the mojitos and the movies. You won't find a curated wine list here; instead, you'll find simple and well-don €5 mojitos and daiquiris. In addition to that, the walls are lined with DVDs available for rental. Angelika has over 3000 titles and charges just €10 for 25 movies. We can't decide if this is the most cinema-friendly bar in Madrid or the world's bougiest Blockbuster.

i Ⓜ*La Latina. Walk west down Pl. de la Cebada. Make a right onto C. de Humilladero and continue right onto C. Cava Baja. Cocktails €5-10.* ⏰ *Open M-W 9am-1pm and 3pm-1am, Th-Sa 6pm-2:30am, Su 5pm-1am.*

EL BONANNO
BAR

Pl. del Humilladero, 4 ☎91 366 68 86 www.elbonanno.com

Located at the southern end of the bustling C. Cava Baja, El Bonanno makes a great place for the first stop of the evening or a last-minute drink before you hit the club. Plaza del Humilladero is pure, delightful mayhem on popular nights, with tipsy Spaniards packing into every corner of the plaza. Unfortunately, El Bonanno doesn't have any terrace seating, which limits you to the nice but cramped interior and tempers your ability to partake in the mayhem.

i Ⓜ*La Latina. Walk 1 block west down Pl. de la Cabeza. Take a left onto Plaza del Humilladero. Beer and wine €1.50-3. Cocktails €3-10.* ⏰ *Open daily 12:30pm-2:30am.*

SHOKO
DISCOTECA

C. de Toledo, 86 ☎91 354 16 91 www.shokomadrid.com

Shoko has one of the most distinctive club interiors in Madrid. It features bamboo shoots that reach to the ceiling, a spacious main floor for dancing, and a raised section that doubles as a stage for internationally acclaimed acts or as a swanky VIP section. It feels like a club out of *Kill Bill*. This place has killer feng-shui, but it's also a farther walk from Centro than other clubs (around 20min. south).

i Ⓜ*La Latina. Head south down C. de Toledo. Cover €10-15.* ⏰ *Open daily 11:30pm-late.*

Las Huertas

KAPITAL
CLUB

C. de Atocha, 125 ☎91 420 29 06 www.grupo-kapital.com/kapital

This is the nucleus—nay, the Kanye West—of Madrid nightlife. Built in a gutted theater, Kapital is a **seven-story** temple of trashy superclub fun. The first floor, which blasts house music, features dancing women on stage and periodic euphoric bursts of cooling fog—this where most of the action happens. As you climb higher up the beanstalk, you'll find separate dance floors for hip hop, reggae, and Spanish pop. There is a little bit for everybody here: the third floor has a karaoke bar; the sixth floor screens movies; the seventh floor terrace has hookahs, pool tables, and killer views; and, finally, on the yet-to-be-completed eighth floor, they hold live reenactments of the American Civil War (bring your own beard). Like the Tower of Babel, Kapital is rumored to be expanding upward at a rapid pace, all the way to Heaven itself. If you plan on making the pilgrimage, dress to impress—no sneakers or shorts. While Kapital doesn't get busy until around 2am, arriving early dressed in something nice will help you avoid the long wait. Be sure to grab a readily available coupon, good for €15 entrance and two drinks, from your hostel or the guy on the street next to the club.

i *2min. walk up C. de Atocha from* Ⓜ*Atocha. Cover €15, includes 1 drink. Drinks €10-15.* ⏰ *Open Th-Su 11:30pm-sunrise*

SOL Y SOMBRA
CLUB

C. de Echegaray, 18 ☎91 542 81 93 www.solysombra.name

With thousands of LED lights on every last surface, Sol y Sombra might be the closest you're going to get to *Tron* while clubbing in Madrid. Unlike the warehouse-style *discotecas* around the city, Sol y Sombra is surprisingly intimate, with the size and set-up of a typical bar. The walls shift in color to accent the

spain

bold patterns of the club, while the music shifts between techno, jazz, funk, and hip hop. This is not a sloppy Eurotrash *discoteca;* instead, it's a cool and innovative club. While you should expect a line out the door during prime weekend hours (midnight-3am), you won't be endlessly stranded: people tend to move in and out pretty quickly on their way to bigger *discotecas.* Find a mate on the dance floor and take advantage of the two for €12 mixed drink special.

i ⓜSol. From the metro, walk toward the museum district on Carrera de San Jeronimo and make a right onto C. de Echegaray. Cover €8 on weekend, includes 1 drink. Beer €5. Cocktails €7. ⏲ Open Tu-Sa 1pm-3am.

EL IMPERFECTO   BAR
Pl. de Matute, 2   ☎91 366 72 11

El Imperfecto is rocking the alternative vibe pretty hard (almost to the point of kitschy-ness). An orgasm of colors, hippie slogans, and American film and music icons, El Imperfecto has the feel of a counterculture bar from a decade you can't quite place your finger on. This shoebox interior is always fun and upbeat, with people sipping cocktails (€6-10) and milkshakes (€4-6). The special here is the two for €10 mojito special. While Imperfecto doesn't offer live music or a clubby dance floor, you should expect a crowd—and, on weekend nights, plenty of American study-abroaders, some friendly German accents, and fellas that might smell like cannabis. El Imperfecto is packed during weekend dinner hours (11pm-1am), so expect to stand at the bar.

i ⓜAntón Martín. Walk uphill until you reach Pl. de Matute. Make a right toward C. de las Huertas. El Imperfecto is on the right. Drinks €4-10. Sangria €2 per glass, €11 per pitcher. ⏲ Open M-Th 2:30pm-2am, F-Sa 2:30pm-2:30am, Su 2:30pm-2am.

Chueca

🏷 BOGUI JAZZ CLUB   JAZZ   CLUB
C. Barquillo, 29   ☎91 521 15 68 www.boguijazz.com

Bogui is Chueca's premier jazz venue and one of its most happening weekend clubs. Nightly sets of live jazz (9 and 11pm) are a fantastic way to get plugged into the local music scene. During weekend DJ sets (Th-Sa 1am), Bogui brings in some of Madrid's best-known jazz, funk, and soul DJs from Sala Barco. Bogui also caters to a Chueca crowd that likes to dance. The Wednesday midnight set (otherwise known as *La Descarga,* or "The Dump") is when musicians from around the city convene for a late-night jam session after a long night of gigs.

i From ⓜChueca, take C. Gravina 2 blocks west to C. Barquillo. The club is on the left. DJ sets Th-Sa free; concert €10. Beer €4. Cocktails €7. €1 surcharge on all beverages Th-Su. ⏲ Open Tu-Sa 10pm-5:30am.

AREIA   BAR, TAPAS
C. de Hortaleza, 92   ☎91 310 03 07 www.areiachillout.com

Areia calls itself a "chillout zone," which must sound *so* cool to native Spanish speakers but a little lame to us Anglophones. Luckily, names aside, this is one of the coolest spots in Chueca thanks to its unbeatable beach theme. This bar and lounge is like a huge sandbox. In addition, it has a crimson-draped ceiling, low-lying tables, candles, and large cushion seats where people snack on international tapas. Relive your spring break glory (or infamy) with €5 daiquiris.

i ⓜChueca. Make a right onto C. Augusto Figuroa, then a right onto C. de Hortaleza. Cocktails €5-9. ⏲ Open daily 1pm-3am.

DAME UN MOTIVO   BAR
C. Pelayo, 58   ☎91 319 74 98

The idea here is to do away with all of the excess of Chueca nightlife—cover charges, overpriced sugary drinks, flashing lights, and loud music—and offer an alternative environment for people who just want to hang out and converse.

madrid

Locals seem to dig this minimalist take on nightlife in the otherwise maximalist Chueca scene. It's a popular destination at the start of the night. During the week, people come here to enjoy the film and book library.

i From Ⓜ Chueca, take C. Gravina 1 block west to C. Pelayo and continue north½ a block. The bar is on the right. Check out Dame un Motivo's Facebook page for event listings. Beer €1.30-2.50. Cocktails €5.50. ⏰ Open W-Th 6pm-2am, F-Sa 4pm-2:30am, Su 4pm-2am.

STUDIO 54 DISCOTECA

C. Barbieri, 7 ☎61 512 68 07 www.studio54madrid.com

You're going to see a lot of six packs at Studio 54, and we're not talking about beer. With pulsing Spanish pop and sculpted bartenders wearing nothing but bow ties, Studio 54 tends to attract a crowd of predominantly gay *madrileños* and American and European tourists. This is one of the most popular young gay clubs in Chueca. If you haven't yet spent a night dancing to ridiculous pop music (think One Direction), this is the place to do it, with crystal chandeliers and disco balls hanging above a violet dance floor.

i Ⓜ Chueca. Walk straight south down C. Barbieri toward Gran Vía. The discoteca is on the right. Cover €10 after 1am. Cocktails €8. ⏰ Open Th-Sa 11:30pm-3:30am.

EL 51 COCKTAILS

C. de Hortaleza, 51 ☎91 521 25 64

If you're still stuck on a non-Spanish schedule (that is, getting drunk and going out before midnight), you should take advantage of El 51's happy hour, which runs until 11pm on Friday and Saturday. El 51 is a posh, single-room cocktail lounge with white leather chairs, crystal chandeliers, and mirrors lit with violet bulbs. Just steps from the center of Chueca's nightlife, this place tends to pack people in during prime hours (midnight-2am). Spanish pop plays in the background, but, they keep the volume low enough that you can still hold a conversation.

i Ⓜ Chueca. Make a right onto C. Augusto Figueroa, then a right onto C. de Hortaleza. Cocktails €8-10. ⏰ Open Tu-Su daily 6pm-3am.

LONG PLAY DISCOTECA

Pl. de Vázquez de Mella, 2 ☎91 532 20 66

Clubs in Chueca come and go, but Long Play has been around for a long time. Once a venue of the early 1970s *madrileño* counterculture, today Long Play is the veteran of Chueca's gay clubs. While the younger locals prefer newer clubs to Long Play, it still manages to attract a solid crowd of older gay *madrileños*, European tourists, and American study abroaders. The downstairs DJ plays a variety of international pop, and things get pretty sweaty on the upstairs dance floor, which plays strictly European house.

i Ⓜ Gran Vía. Head north up C. de Hortaleza, make a right onto C. de las Infantas, then a left into Pl. de Vázquez de Mella. Cover €10 Th-F after 1:30am (includes 1 drink), €10 Sa all night. Drinks €8. ⏰ Open daily midnight-7am.

Malasaña

🏅 **LA VÍA LÁCTEA** BAR

C. Velarde, 18 ☎91 446 75 81 www.lavialactea.net

This is a Spanish temple dedicated to rock, grunge, and everything '70s counterculture. La Vía Láctea was founded in the early years of Movida Madrileña, a youth-propelled revolution of art, music, fashion, and literature. Today, it's more a relic of this past than a continuing force of change, with pop music memorabilia covering the walls from floor to ceiling and a fine perfume of stale beer lingering in the air. Every night, locals and tourists gather here to shoot pool and hang out under the warm neon glow.

i Ⓜ Tribunal. Walk north up C. Fuencarral and make a left onto C. Velarde. Cover €10 after 1am, includes 1 drink. Beer €3-5. Cocktails €5-7. ⏰ Open daily 7:30pm-3:30am.

CLUB NASTI DISCOTECA

C. de San Vicente Ferrer, 33 ☎91 521 76 05 www.nasti.es

Club Nasti is the polar opposite of big, touristy nightclubs that you'll find else-where in the city. This is the club of choice for Malasaña hipsters and club rats, who enjoy Club Nasti's curated repertoire of synth pop, electro beats, and punk jams. For a lighter touch, try Friday nights, when house DJs spin indie rock like the Strokes and the Arctic Monkeys. The small dance floor gets packed as the night progresses.

i ⓂTribunal. Walk south down C. de Fuencarral and make a right onto C. de San Vicen-te Ferrer. Cover €10 after 2am, includes 1 drink. Beer €4-5. Cocktails €8-9. ⌚ Open Th-Sa 1-5:30am.

BARCO MUSIC, DISCOTECA

C. del Barco, 34 ☎91 521 24 47 www.barcobar.com

With a jam-packed program of nightly concerts, late-night DJ sets, and weekly jam sessions, this small venue covers a wide spread of musical terrain. BarCo has made itself a name as a stalwart venue for local acts, with most bands drawing heavily on funk, soul, rock, and jazz. While the concert schedule is con-tinually changing, the nightly DJ sets are given to a handful of veteran European DJs who have been spinning in Madrid for years. The Sunday night jam session brings in some of the city's best contemporary jazz musicians. This is the nucleus of Malasaña's eclectic live music scene, and the bar's clientele changes nightly depending on who's playing.

i ⓂTribunal. Head south on C. de Fuencarral 3 blocks. Take a right onto C. Corredara Baja de San Pablo, walk 2 blocks, and take a left (south) onto C. del Barco. The bar is on the right. Cover €5-10. Beer €5. Cocktails €7. €1 drink surcharge F-Sa. Cash only. ⌚ Open M-Th 10pm-5:30am, F-Sa 10pm-6am, Su 10pm-5:30am.

Argüelles and Moncloa

▨ TEMPO CLUB MUSIC

C. Duque de Osuna 8 ☎91 547 75 18 www.tempoclub.net

Tempo Club proclaims that it focuses on *"música negra"*: funk, Afro, Latin, jazz, soul, and beats. Decorated with unorthodox dome chairs and bold, clean streaks of warm reds and oranges, Tempo's decor represents its mission statement: a modern take on '70's-style grooves. Even when the DJ takes over for the late night set, the rhythm section often sticks around. While Tempo thrives on rich instrumentals, most of the acts also involve talented vocalists. The venue is divided between a street-level cafe and cocktail area and the downstairs concert hall. This is a refreshing alternative to the hordes of countless clubs that all feel the same.

i ⓂVentura Rodriguez. From C. Princesa, follow C. del Duque de Liria south to the intersec-tion with C. Duque de Osuna. Turn left onto C. Duque. Live performances Th-Sa. Cocktails €5-8. Cash only. ⌚ Open daily 6pm-late.

CAFE LA PALMA MUSIC

C. de la Palma 62 ☎91 522 50 31 www.cafelapalma.com

Cafe la Palma is in many ways a typical Malasaña rock club even though it's just outside the *barrio*. Like many clubs in the area, La Palma has a clean, versatile open space that strives to be a lot of different things—a cafe that people can enjoy during the day, a cocktail lounge at night, a concert venue in the late night, and a full club with a live DJ set in the early morning. The music acts La Palma attracts are every bit as eclectic as the venue itself, ranging from trance to heavy rock to open mic nights. While this place tries to accomplish a lot within the three small rooms of the cafe, it doesn't spread itself too thin. There is a drink

madrid

minimum €6) for some live sets, but this is a great alternative to forking over a fat cover charge.

i Ⓜ*Pl. de España, follow C. de Los Reyes northeast 2 blocks, take a left onto C. Amaniel, and walk 2 blocks to C. de La Palma. Drink min. for some events €6; check website for more info. Cocktails €6. Cash only. ⓩ Open daily 5pm-3am.*

ORANGE CAFÉ
BAR, CLUB

Serrano Jover, 5 ☎91 542 28 17 www.soyorangecafe.com

Orange Café is a venue for local rock acts in the evening and a packed dance club later at night. This is a pretty standard club, designed for easy consumption by college-age kids and American tourists. Orange Café isn't as popular as similar mainstream clubs Joy Eslava and Kapital because of its not-as-central location. Women should take advantage of free drinks and free entry on Wednesday nights until 1:30am. Check the website for a list of concerts and cover charges.

i Ⓜ*Argüelles. Cover €10-15 depending on the night. ⓩ Open M-Th midnight-5am, F-Sa 11pm-6am.*

EL CHAPANDAZ
BAR

C. de Fernando, 77 ☎91 549 29 68 www.chapandaz.com

Ever wonder to yourself how you would spice up a typical night out at the bar? How about by adding some panther's milk and cave decorations? If that's your idea of fun, El Chapandaz is the place for you. During the day, it's just a funky-looking restaurant, but at night it transforms into the most ridiculous bar in Madrid. It is a fully functional, lactating cave with stalactites hanging from the ceiling that periodically drip milk into glass pitchers. The house milk, *Leche de Pantera* (panther's milk), is a combination of rum, cinnamon, and that special milk. If you are suspicious (for perfectly good reasons), it also offers standard fare and a full menu of sweet, fruity, and colorful drinks. The bar is generally quiet until 11pm but fills up with a mostly international, study-abroad crowd that stops in for the novelty before heading out to the clubs.

i *From* Ⓜ*Moncloa, head to the intersection of C. de Fernando and C. de la Princesa and walk east down C. de Fernando. International night Tu. Drink €10. ⓩ Open daily 1pm-3am.*

ARTS AND CULTURE

With some of the best art museums, public festivals, and performing arts groups in the world, Madrid's arts and culture scene is thriving. From street performers in Parque del Buen Retiro to Broadway musicals, you can find anything you're looking for in this metropolis.

Corridas (Bullfights)

Whether you view it as animal cruelty or national sport, the spectacle of *la corrida* (bullfighting) is a cherished Spanish tradition. Although it has its origins in Roman gladiator practices, bullfighting is now a distinctly Spanish sport. The sport has been subject to continuing animal rights protest in recent years, in addition to suffering fading popularity with the younger generations. More a form of performance art than a sport (every bullfight has the same outcome of the bull "losing"), bullfighting draws hordes of tourists (in addition to lots of old Spanish men) who flock to see the tradition that Hemingway celebrated as "the only art in which the artist is in danger of death and in which the degree of brilliance in the performance is left to the fighter's honor." It's not for the faint of heart, of course—be prepared to see a bull suffer for 20-30min. before being killed.

If you choose to go, it is important to know a little bit about the rituals of the sport. The bullfight has three stages. First, the *picadores* (lancers on horseback), pierce the bull's neck muscles. Then, assistants thrust decorated darts called *banderillas* into the bull's back to injure and fatigue it. Finally, the *matador* kills his large opponent with a sword thrust between the bull's shoulder blades, killing it instantly.

Animal rights activists call the rituals savage and cruel, but aficionados call it an art that requires quick thinking and skill.

The best place to see bullfighting in Madrid is at the country's biggest arena, **Plaza de las Ventas,** where you can buy tickets in *sol* (sun) or *sombra* (shade) sections. Get your tickets at the arena the Friday or Saturday leading up to the bullfight. (C. de Alcalá 237913 56 22 00 www.las-ventas.com Ventas ticket office open 10am-2pm and 5-8pm.) You'll pay more to sit out of the sun, but either way, you'll have a good view of the feverish crowds that cheer on the matador and wave white handkerchiefs, called *pañuelos,* after a particularly good fight. Tickets range from €5 for nosebleeds to €80 for front-row seats. Each ticket includes usually around three bullfights, each of which lasts 20-30min. Rent a seat cushion at the stadium or bring your own for the stone seats. Bullfights are held Sundays and holidays throughout most of the year. During the **Fiesta de San Isidro** in May, fights are held almost every day, and the top bullfighters come face to face with the fiercest bulls. People across Spain are bitterly divided about the future of the sport, so visitors should approach the topic with sensitivity.

Flamenco

Flamenco is a gypsy art that dates back to 18th-century Andalucia and has become a 21st-century business in Madrid. Many flamenco clubs offer overpriced dinners combined with overdone music and dance spectaculars geared toward tourists. There are some clubs in Madrid that offer more traditional and soulful flamenco. You'll still pay a decent amount to see it, but it's a great way to learn about the art form that is often described as Europe's counterpart to the blues.

✇ CASA PATAS
C. de los Cañizares, 10   LAS HUERTAS
☎91 369 04 96 www.casapatas.com

Casa Patas is like the Sobrino de Botin of flamenco venues. It's the place to be if you want the authentic, traditional experience—but it's pricey and attracts a large tourist crowd. Throughout most of the day, it functions as a normal Spanish restaurant, but at night, Madrid's finest dancers perform the art of flamenco on the stage in the back of the restaurant. Tickets aren't cheap, but they're worth every penny if you're looking for a proper flamenco show. Shows sell out frequently, particularly in the summer months, so be sure to get your tickets in advance. The restaurant and tapas bar up front serves the usual suspects: platters of *jamón y queso* (€19), fried squid (€13), and *albondigas de la abuela.*

i ⓂAntón Martín. From the metro, walk up C. de Atocha and turn left onto C. del Olivar. Casa Patas is on the right. Tickets €32; includes 1 drink. Entrees €10-25. ⓄOpen M-Th 1-4pm and 8pm-midnight, F-Sa 7:30pm-2am. Flamenco M-Th 8:30pm, F-Sa 9pm and midnight.

CARDAMOMO
C. de Echegaray, 15   LAS HUERTAS
☎91 369 07 57 www.cardamomo.es

Cardamomo advertises itself as the "only tablao flamenco recommended by *The New York Times.*" More importantly, Let's Go recommends Cardamomo for showcasing less touristy flamenco that features a raw, improvisational quality to it. The focus is more on rhythm and movement and less on the kitschy costumes that are usually synonymous with flamenco. You can expect syncopated guitars, soulful old men crooning flamenco verse, and swift choreography—all in an intimate space, with spectators packed table to table in the narrow interior. The nightly sets are short (50min.) but intense and a good way of seeing flamenco without dedicating an entire evening to it.

i ⓂSol. Walk east toward Pl. de las Cortes and make a right onto C. de Echegaray. Ticket €25; includes 1 drink. Check with your hostel for discounts. ⓄShows daily 10:30pm.

madrid

Fútbol

You might see churches in every city you visit in Spain, but the official national religion is *fútbol*. Matches are a beloved spectacle everywhere in Spain, but particularly in Madrid, which is home to **Real Madrid,** arguably the greatest soccer club the world has ever known (at least that's what the locals will tell you). On game days, which start around the end of August and run through the end of May, locals line the streets and pack bars to watch the matches. Celebrations after games are common in public plazas and squares, helped by the fact that most matches fall on Saturdays. For Real Madrid, the victory party always takes place in **Plaza Cibeles,** just outside the town hall. *Fútbol* doesn't just happen on the field in Spain—it takes over city life, particularly on big game days. The other two major teams in Madrid are **Atlético** and **Getafe.**

Seeing a game live with 80,000 other fans can be an incredible experience but is often logistically difficult to arrange. Tickets are expensive and hard to come by. All teams sell a number of tickets through their stadium box offices and release a limited number online through their club website. If you are intent on going to a game, research ticket availability at least two weeks in advance. Tickets are also available from vendors outside the stadium, but these are often counterfeited or marked up well above face value. Tickets for Atlético and Getafe tend to be cheaper and more available than tickets for Real Madrid. Regardless of whether you make it to the stadium or not, it's worth going to a local tapas bar to watch.

ESTADIO SANTIAGO BERNABEU   NORTH OF CITY CENTER

Av. Cochina Espina, 1   ☎91 464 22 34 www.santiagobernabeu.com, www.realmadrid.com
Site of the 2010 European Final Cup, Estadio Santiago Bernabeu is also home to Real Madrid, named the greatest club of the 20th century by FIFA. Tours are a bit pricey (€19) but a must-do for soccer fans; they take you through the club's most hallowed grounds, from the trophy room to the visitors' dressing room to the pitch itself. If you can, try to see an actual game at the stadium, as tickets can start as low as €25. Advance tickets can be purchased at **www.servicaixa.com,** and remaining tickets are released on the club website at 11am the Monday before each game.

i ⓂSantiago Bernabeu. *The stadium is across the street from the metro. Ticket €30-300. Tours €19, under 14 €13.* 🕑 *Season runs Sept-May. Check online for game schedules and tour times.*

ESTADIO VICENTE CALDERÓN   SOUTH OF CITY CENTER

Paseo de la Virgen del Puerto, 67   ☎91 364 22 34 www.clubatleticodemadrid.com
Estadio Vicente Calderón is home to the Atlético Madrid *fútbol* club. With a storied past that includes European Cups and international recognition, this Madrid-based club participates in the esteemed Primera División of La Liga. While they've had some big wins in the past, Atlético Madrid is the perennial underdog in the city rivalry with Real Madrid. While this stadium may not be the city's biggest stage for football, tickets for games are more readily available and cheaper. Tickets can be purchased at www.servicaixa.com or on the club website.

i ⓂPirámides. *From the metro, head west 1 block to C. de Toledo, follow 1 block south to Paseo de los Melancolicos. The stadium is on the left. Prices vary. Tours €10.* 🕑 *Check the website for schedule. Tours Tu-Su 11am-8pm.*

SHOPPING

El Rastro

El Rastro is the place to be in Madrid on Sundays. This open-air flea market takes over La Latina beginning at **Plaza de Cascorro,** off C. de Toledo, and ending at the bottom of **Calle Ribera de Curtidores,** with rows of stalls set in the middle of the road between the city's infamous streetside pawn shops. There's not a huge variety of wares;

most stalls sell cheap clothes, sunglasses, or small decorative trinkets. The best part of El Rastro is just the bustling vibe—Madrid is transformed every Sunday into a sprawling Moroccan bazaar. While prices are initially reasonable, you can almost always practice your Spanish negotiating skills and haggle them down even lower. While El Rastro is hugely popular with tourists, it's still typical for local families to head to the market together and go out to brunch afterward in La Latina or Lavapiés. El Rastro starts at 9am sharp and ends at 3pm, with many of the better shops closing earlier. While El Rastro is perfectly safe, the large crowds tend to attract pickpockets, so use common sense and be aware of your surroundings.

ESSENTIALS
Practicalities

- **TOURIST OFFICES:** The **Madrid Tourism Centre** in Pl. Mayor (☎91 588 16 36 www.esmadrid.com) is a good place to start; this is where you'll find city and transit maps as well as suggestions for activities, food, and accommodations. English is spoken at most tourist offices throughout the city. There are additional tourist offices and stands around town; look for large orange stands with exclamation marks. **Calle del Duque de Medinaceli 2.** (☎91 429 49 51 ☒ Open M-Sa 9:30am-8:30pm, Su and holidays 9:30am-2pm.) **Estacion de Atocha.** (☎91 528 46 30 ☒ Open M-Sa 9:30am-8:30pm, Su and holidays 9:30am-2pm) **Madrid-Barajas Airport Terminal 1.** (☎91 305 86 56) **Terminal 4.** (]90 210 00 07 ☒ Open daily 9:30am-8:30pm.) There is also a tourist office at the **airport train station.** (☎91 315 99 76 ☒ Open M-Sa 8am-8pm, Su 9am-2pm.)

- **TOURS:** Different themed tours leave regularly from the **Madrid Tourism Centre.** For dates, times, and more info, visit www.esmadrid.com. Many youth hostels host tapas tours, pub crawls, and walking tours for reasonable prices. Check out www.toursnonstop.com. **LeTango Tours** is run by a Spanish-American husband-wife team, with tours that take you to local bars, provide fun city facts, and explain Spanish traditions. (☎91 369 47 52 www.letango.com). Run by historian and writer Stephen Drake-Jones, the **Wellington Society** (☎60 914 32 03 www.wellsoc.org) offers different themed tours of Madrid and daytrips to Toledo and Segovia. Another option is **Madrid Vision** (☎91 779 18 88 www.madridvision.es), which runs the double-decker red buses that you see throughout the city. Choose between the *historicó* and *moderno* routes. Each route makes 15-20 stops around the city. (*i* €17; discounts online.)

- **CURRENCY EXCHANGE:** The most convenient (although not always the cheapest) place to change your money is at the airport. There are also currency exchanges in Puerta Del Sol and Gran Vía (look for booths that say "change"), but try to use these as a last resort, as rates are bad and commission charges are high. Most *hostales* and hotels will also be able to change your money; rates vary by location. Another option is **Banco Santander Central Hispano**, which charges €12-15 commission on non-American Express Travelers Cheques (max. exchange €300). Wherever you go, be sure to bring your passport as identification.

- **LUGGAGE STORAGE:** Store your luggage at the **Aeropuerto Internacional de Barajas.** (☎91 393 68 05 *i* 1-day €3.70; 2-15 days €4.78 per day. ☒ Open 24hr.) or at the **bus station.** (*i* €1.40 per bag per day. ☒ Open M-F 6:30am-10:30pm, Sa 6:30am-3pm.)

- **POST OFFICES:** Buy **stamps** (*sellos*) from a post office or tobacco stand. Madrid's **central post office** is at Pl. de Cibeles. (☎91 523 06 94;90 219 71 97 ☒ Open M-F 8:30am-9:30pm.) Mailboxes are usually yellow, with one slot for "Madrid" and another for everywhere else.

- **POSTAL CODE:** 28008.

Emergency

- **EMERGENCY NUMBERS: Medical emergency:** ☎061 or ☎112. For non-emergency medical concerns, go to **Unidad Medica Angloamericana,** which has English-speaking personnel on duty by appointment. (C. del Conde de Aranda, 1, 1st fl. ☎91 435 18 23 ☼ Open M-F 9am-8pm, Sa 10am-1pm.)

- **POLICE: Servicio de Atención al Turista Extranjero (SATE)** are police who deal exclusively with tourists and help with contacting embassies, reporting crimes, and canceling credit cards. (C. Legantos, 19 ☎91 548 85 27; ☎90 210 21 12 ☼ Open daily 9am-midnight.)

Getting There

By Plane

All flights come in through the **Aeropuerto Internacional de Barajas** (☎902 404 704 www. aena.es). The **Barajas** metro stop connects the airport to the rest of Madrid (€2). To take the subway into the city center, take the #8 toward Nuevo Ministerios, transfer to the #10 toward Puerta del Sur, get off at Tribunal (3 stops), transfer to the #1 toward Valdecarros, and get off at Sol. The journey should take 45-60min. By bus, the **Bus-Aeropeurto 200** leaves from the national terminal (T2) and runs to the city center through Ⓜ️Avenida de America. (☎90 250 78 50 ☼ Every 15min., 5:20am-11:30pm.) **Taxis** (€35. 30min.) are readily available outside of the airport. For more info on ground transport, visit **www.metromadrid.es.**

By Train

Trains (☎90 224 02 02 www.renfe.es) from northern Europe and France arrive on the north side of the city at **Chamartin.** (C. Augustin de Foxa ☎91 300 69 69, ☎91 506 63 29.) Trains to and from the south of Spain and Portugal use **Atocha;** buy tickets at the station or online. There is a **RENFE** information office at the main terminal. (☎90 224 02 02 ☼ Open daily 7am-7pm.) **AVE** trains offer high-speed service throughout Spain, including Barcelona, Salamanca, Segovia, Sevilla, and Toledo. Be sure to keep your ticket, or you won't be able to pass through the turnstiles. Call **RENFE** for both international destinations and domestic travel. (☎902 24 34 02 for international destinations; ☎90 224 02 02 for domestic.) Ticket windows are open daily 6:30am-9pm; when they're closed, you can buy tickets at vending machines.

By Bus

If you prefer four wheels, many private bus companies run through Madrid, and most pass through **Estación Sur de Autobuses.** (C. Mendez Alvaro (☎91 468 42 00 www. estacionautobusesmadrid.com ☼ Info booth open daily 6:30am-1am.) National destinations include Algeciras, Alicante, Oviedo, and Toledo, among others. Inquire at the station, online, or by phone for specific information on routes and schedules.

Getting Around

By Metro

The Madrid metro system is by far the easiest, cheapest way to get you almost anywhere you need to go in the city. It is clean, safe, and recently renovated. Service begins M-Sa at 6am, Su at 7am, and ends daily around 1:30am. Try to avoid rush hours (daily 8-10am, 1-2pm, and 4-6pm). You can buy either a one-way ticket (€1), or, if you're making multiple trips, you can save by purchasing a combined **10-trip metrobus ticket** (€9.30). Trains run frequently, and green timers above most platforms show the next approaching train times. Be sure to grab a free metro map (available at any ticket booth or tourist office). **Abonos mensuales,** or monthly passes, grant unlimited travel within the city proper for €47.60, while **abonos turísticos** (tourist passes) come in various increments (1, 2, 3, 4, or 7 days) and sell for €6-25 at the metro stations or online. For metro information, visit www.metromadrid.es or call ☎90 244 44 03.

spain

By Bus

Buses cover areas that are inaccessible by the metro and are a great way to see the city. The pamphlet "Visiting the Downtown on Public Transport" lists routes and stops. (Free at any tourist office or downloadable at **www.madrid.org**.) Tickets for the bus and metro are interchangeable. The *Búho* (owl), or night bus, travels from Pl. de Cibeles and other marked routes along the outskirts of the city. (🕿 M-Th every 30min. midnight-3am, every hr. 3-6am; F-Sa every 20min. midnight-6am; Su every 30 min. midnight-3am.) These buses, marked on the essential **Red de Autobuses Nocturnos** (available at any tourist office) run along 26 lines covering regular daytime routes. For info, call **Empresa Municipal de Transportes** (🕿90 250 78 50 www.emtmadrid.es). **Estacion Sur** (C. Mendez Alvaro 🕿91 468 42 00) covers mainly southern and southeastern destinations outside Madrid, such as **Granada, Malaga, Sevilla,** and **Valencia.** Visit www.avanzabus.com for timetables and routes.

By Taxi

Registered Madrid taxis are black or white and have red bands and small insignias of a bear and *madroño* tree (symbols of Madrid). Hail them on the street or at taxi stands all over the city. A green light means they're available. The fare starts at €1.75 and increases by €1 every kilometer thereafter. To call a city taxi, dial 🕿91 447 51 80.

By Moped And Bike

Biking in the city is ill-advised, but Casa de Campo and Dehesa de la Villa both have easily navigable bike trails. You can rent a bike from **Karacol Sport.** (C. Tortosa 8 🕿91 539 96 33 www.karacol.com *i* Cash deposit or €50 and photocopy of your passport required. (€18 per day. 🕿 Open M-W 10:30am-3pm and 5-8pm, Th 10:30am-3pm and 5-9:30pm, F-Su 10:30am-3pm and 5-8pm.) **Motocicletas Antonio Castro** rents mopeds for €23-95 per day, including unlimited mileage and insurance, but you'll need your own lock and helmet. You must be at least 25 years old and have a driver's license for motorcycles. (C. Clara del Rey, 17 🕿91 413 00 47 www.blafermotos.com 🕿 Open M-F 8am-6pm, Sa 10am-1:30pm.)

barcelona

Benvolgut a Barcelona! Welcome to a city more exquisite, more idiosyncratic, more bold, and more fun than you ever thought a city could be. There's a whole lot more to Barcelona than Gaudí's architecture and the incredible clubs, and *Let's Go* will show you the way. You'll find that the locals consider themselves Catalan first and Spanish a distant second. Barcelona is quite proud of its Catalan culture and language, which you'll probably hear much more frequently than *castellano.* Everybody in Catalonia speaks Spanish—they just generally prefer not to—and even if your Spanish-language skills don't extend beyond *hola* and *cerveza*, you'll get by just fine. Whether you're strolling through the broad, tree- and modernista building-lined avenues of l'Eixample by day, bar-hopping beneath the walls of the Gothic churches of the Ciutat Vella at night, or napping off that hangover in one of Gràcia's shady plazas, if you take a second to look around, you'll be mesmerized by the city's ubiquitous charm. Oh, and did we mention there's also a beach? Save it for last—once you head there, you'll never see anything else.

ORIENTATION

Though a large and complex city, Barcelona's *barris* (neighborhoods) are fairly well-defined. The **Ciutat Vella** (old city) is the city's heart, comprised of **El Raval** (west of Las Ramblas), **Barri Gòtic** (between **Las Ramblas** and Via Laietana), **El Born** (between Via Laietana and Parc de la Ciutadella), and **La Barceloneta** (the peninsula south of El

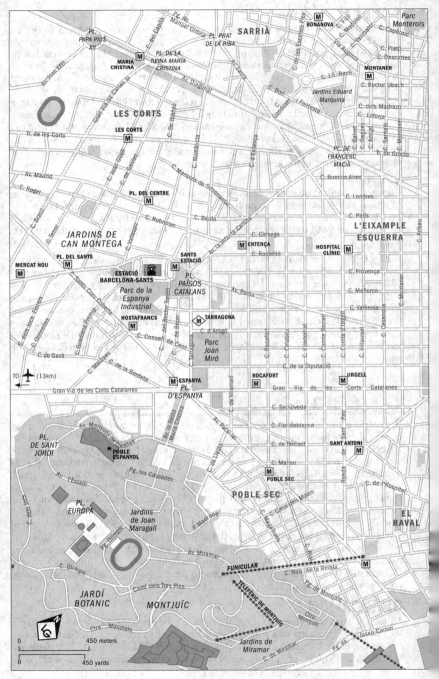

PL. PAPA PIUS XII

MARIA CRISTINA Ⓜ

PL. DE LA REINA MARÍA CRISTINA

Pg. de Manuel Girona

PL. PRAT DE LA RIBA

SARRIA

BONANOVA Ⓜ

C. Vitxi
C. Modhel
Via Augusta
C. Vallmaiò

Parc Monterols

C. Copèrnic

C. Piató
C. Descartes

MUNTANER Ⓜ

C. Rector Ubach

Av. Joan XXIII

Gran Via de Carles III

Av. Diagonal

C. Sarria

C. Bori i Fontestà

Jardins Eduard Marquina

C. dels Madrazo

C. Calvet
C. Sagues
C. Amigo
C. de Santaló
C. Muntaner
Tr. de Gracia

LES CORTS

LES CORTS Ⓜ

Tr. de les Corts

C. Joan Güell
C. de Cartilers
C. Dr. Ibàñez
C. Numància

C. Marquès de Sentmenat

C. d'Entença

PL. DE FRANCESC MACIÀ

C. Buenos Aires

Av. Madrid

C. Roger

C. Brasil

C. Tenor

PL. DEL CENTRE Ⓜ

C. Robrenyo

C. Berlin

C. de l'Infanta Carlota

C. Còrsega

C. Rosselló

ENTENÇA Ⓜ

C. Londres

C. París

L'EIXAMPLE ESQUERRA

C. Aribau

JARDINS DE CAN MONTEGA

PL. DEL SANTS

MERCAT NOU Ⓜ

ESTACIÓ BARCELONA-SANTS

Parc de la Espanya Industrial

HOSTAFRANCS Ⓜ

SANTS ESTACIÓ Ⓜ

PL. PAÏSOS CATALANS

Av. Roma

HOSPITAL CLÍNIC Ⓜ

C. Provença

C. Mallorca

C. València

C. Muntaner

C. Casanova

C. Santa Creu Coberta

C. dels Jocs Florals

C. Olzinelles

C. Guadiana
C. Premià

C. Moianès

C. del Rector Triadó

C. de Sant Roc

TARRAGONA Ⓜ

C. d'Aragó

C. de la Bordeta

C. Consell de Cent

C. de Gava

Parc Joan Miró

C. de la Diputació

C. Rocafort
C. Calàbria
C. Viladomat
C. Comte Borrell
C. Comte d'Urgell
C. Villarroel

TO ✈ (13km)

Gran Via de les Corts Catalanes

ESPANYA Ⓜ PL. D'ESPANYA

ROCAFORT Ⓜ

Gran Via de les Corts Catalanes

URGELL Ⓜ

C. Sepúlveda

C. Floridablanca

SANT ANTONI Ⓜ

C. de Tamarit

EL RAVAL

PL. DE SANT JORDI

Av. Marquès de Comillas

POBLE ESPANYOL ★

Av. l'Estadi

Av. la Reina Maria Cristina

Av. Parallel

C. Tarros

C. de Manso

POBLE SEC Ⓜ

Ronda de Sant Pau

C. de l'Hospital

Pg. los Cascades

PL. EUROPA

Jardins de Joan Maragall

Pg. Olímpic

C. Olímpic

C. dels Jocs

P. Madrona

C. Nou de la Rambla

C. Cesc dels Molers

C. Margallades

FUNICULAR

C. Nou de la Rmbla

Pg. de Montjuïc

JARDÍ BOTÀNIC

MONTJUÏC

Camí dels Tres Pins

Av. Miramar

TELEFÈRIC DE MONTJUÏC

Ctra. Mundials

Ctra. Montjuïc

Pg. de Josep Carner

Av. de Miramar

Jardins de Miramar

0 ⌐———⌐ 450 meters
0 ⌐———⌐ 450 yards

spain

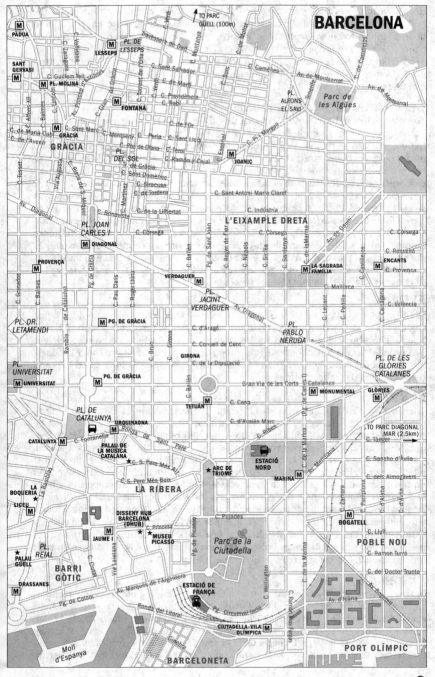

BARCELONA

TO PARC
GÜELL (100m)

PÀDUA Ⓜ

SANT
GERVASI
Ⓜ

PL MOLINA Ⓜ

C. Guillem Tell

PL. DE
LESSEPS

LESSEPS Ⓜ

Travessera de Dalt

C. Sant Salvador

C. de Martí

C. Providència

C. Robí

C. Camèlies

Av. de Montserrat

Av. de Montserrat

PL.
ALFONS
EL SAVI

Parc de
les Aigües

FONTANA Ⓜ

GRÀCIA Ⓜ
C. de Maria Cubí
C. de l'Avenir

GRÀCIA

C. Sant Marc

C. Montseny
C. Ros de Olano

C. de l'Or

C. Perla
PL.
DEL SOL

C. Sant Lluís

C. Terol

C. Ramon y Cajal

C. Sant Antoni Maria Claret

C. Indústria

C. de Gràcia
C. Sant Domènec
C. Siracusa
C. de Tordera

IOANIC Ⓜ

C. de la Llibertat

C. Bonavista
C. Martínez

PL. JOAN
CARLES I

C. Còrsega

L'EIXAMPLE DRETA

C. Còrsega

C. Còrsega

Av. Diagonal

DIAGONAL Ⓜ

C. Rosselló

ENCANTS

C. Provença

PROVENÇA
Ⓜ

VERDAGUER
Ⓜ

LA SAGRADA
FAMÍLIA Ⓜ

C. Mallorca

C. València

PL.
JACINT
VERDAGUER

Av. Diagonal

PL.
PABLO
NERUDA

PL. DR.
LETAMENDI

PG. DE GRÀCIA Ⓜ

C. d'Aragó

C. Consell de Cent

GIRONA

C. de la Diputació

PL.
UNIVERSITAT

Ⓜ UNIVERSITAT

PG. DE GRÀCIA Ⓜ

Gran Via de les Corts Catalanes

Ⓜ MONUMENTAL

PL. DE LES
GLÒRIES
CATALANES

GLÒRIES Ⓜ

PL. DE
CATALUNYA

TETUÁN Ⓜ

C. Casp

TO PARC DIAGONAL
MAR (2.5km)

C. Tànger

URQUINAONA Ⓜ

Ronda de Sant Pere

C. d'Ausiàs Marc

C. Sancho d'Àvila

CATALUNYA Ⓜ

C. Fontanella

PALAU DE
LA MÚSICA
CATALANA ★

C. Ribes

ESTACIÓ
NORD

C. dels Almogàvers

MARINA Ⓜ

LA
BOQUERIA ★

★ C. S. Pere Més Alt

★ ARC DE
TRIOMF

LICEU ★

C. S. Pere Més Baix

LA RIBERA

BOGATELL Ⓜ

DISSENY HUB
BARCELONA
(DHUB) ★

C. Princesa

C. de Pujades

C. Llull

POBLE NOU

JAUME I Ⓜ

★ MUSEU
PICASSO

Parc de la
Ciutadella

C. Ramon Turró

PL.
REIAL

PALAU
GÜELL ★

BARRI
GÒTIC

C. del Doctor Trueta

DRASSANES Ⓜ

Pg. de Colom

ESTACIÓ DE
FRANÇA

Ronda del Litoral

Pg. Circumval·lació

CIUTADELLA-VILA
OLÍMPICA Ⓜ

Moll
d'Espanya

BARCELONETA

PORT OLÍMPIC

barcelona

Born). Farther down the coast (to the left as you look at a map with the sea at the bottom) from the *Ciutat Vella* is the park-mountain **Montjuïc** and the small neighborhood of **Poble Sec** between Montjuïc and Avinguda Paral·lel. Farther inland from the *Ciutat Vella* is the large, central, rigidly gridded zone of **l'Eixample**, and still farther away from the sea is **Gràcia**. The **Plaça de Catalunya** is one of the city's most central points, located where Las Ramblas meets the Passeig de Gràcia; it is essentially the meeting point of El Raval, Barri Gòtic, and l'Eixample.

Barri Gòtic and Las Ramblas

You will get lost in Barri Gòtic. Knowing this, the best way to properly orient yourself in the confusing neighborhood, where streets still follow their medieval routes, is to take a day to learn your way around. **Las Ramblas** provides the western boundary of the neighborhood, stretching from the waterfront to **Plaça de Catalunya. Via Laietana** marks the eastern border, running nearly parallel to Las Ramblas. The primary east-west artery running between Las Ramblas and V. Laietana is known as **Carrer de Ferran** between Las Ramblas and the central **Plaça de Sant Jaume** and as **Carrer de Jaume I** between Pl. Sant Jaume and V. Laietana. Of the many plazas hiding in the Barri Gòtic, **Plaça Reial** (take the tiny C. de Colom off Las Ramblas) and Plaça de Sant Jaume are the grandest. The neighborhood is better known, though, for its more cramped spaces, like the narrow alleys covered with arches or miniature *placetas* in the shadows of parish churches. The **L3** and **L4** metro lines serve this neighborhood, with Ⓜ**Drassanes,** Ⓜ**Liceu,** and Ⓜ**Catalunya** along Las Ramblas (L3) and Ⓜ**Jaume I** at the intersection of C. Jaume I and V. Laietana.

El Born

El Born, which makes up the eastern third of the **Ciutat Vella,** is celebrated for being slightly less touristy than the Barri Gòtic and slightly less prostitute-y than El Raval. The neighborhood is renowned for its confusing medieval streets, whose ancient bends hide fashionable boutiques and restaurants both traditional and modern. The **Passeig del Born,** the lively hub of this quirky *barri*, makes for a good bar- and restaurant-lined starting point.

El Raval

There's no point beating around the bush: El Raval is one of Barcelona's more dangerous neighborhoods. But this doesn't mean that you should avoid it. Just be careful and aware—even during the day—and be prepared to deal with persistent drug dealers and aggressive prostitutes. In particular, avoid **Carrer de Sant Ramon.** Clearly, El Raval does not lack character, and it is actually one of the city's most interesting neighborhoods. Everything tends to be significantly less expensive than on the other side of Las Ramblas, and a large student population supports a bevy of quirky restaurants and bars. Areas around the **Rambla del Raval** and the **Carrer de Joaquim Costa** hide small, unique bars and late-night cafes frequented by Barcelona's alternative crowd. For daytime shopping, check out **Riera Baixa,** a street lined entirely with secondhand shops that also hosts a flea market on Saturdays, or the ritzier neighborhood around **Carrer del Doctor Dou, Carrer del Pintor Fortuny,** and **Carrer Elisabets** for higher-end (though still reasonably priced) shops.

L'Eixample

In this posh neighborhood (pronounced leh-SHAM-plah), big blocks, wide avenues, and dazzling architecture mean lots of walking and lots of exciting storefronts. *Modernista* buildings line **Passeig de Gràcia** (first word pronounced pah-SAYCH), which runs from north to south through the neighborhood's center (Ⓜ Diagonal, Ⓜ Passeig de Gràcia, Ⓜ Catalunya). **L'Eixample Dreta** encompasses the area to the east around the **Sagrada Família,** and **Eixample Esquerra** comprises the area closer to the **University,** uphill from **Plaça de la Universitat.** Though the former contains some surprisingly cheap accommodations for those willing to make the hike, the Eixample Esquerra is somewhat more pedestrian-friendly and more interesting to walk around. While this neighborhood is notoriously expensive, there are some cheaper and more interesting options as you get closer to Pl. Universitat. The stretch of **Carrer del Consell de Cent** west of Pg. de Gràcia boasts vibrant nightlife, where many "hetero-friendly" bars, clubs, and hotels give it the nickname **Gaixample.**

Barceloneta

Barceloneta, the triangular peninsula that juts out into the Mediterranean, is a former mariners' and fishermen's neighborhood, built on a sandbank at the beginning of the 18th century to replace the homes destroyed by the construction of the *ciutadella*. The grid plan, a consequence of Enlightenment city planning, gives the neighborhood's narrow streets a distinct character, seasoned by the salty sea breezes that whip through the urban canyons. Tourists and locals are drawn to the unconventional Barceloneta by the restaurants and views along the **Passeig Joan de Borbó,** the renowned beaches along the **Passeig Marítim de la Barceloneta,** and the *discotecas* at the **Port Olímpic.**

Gràcia

Gràcia is hard to navigate by metro. While this may at first seem like a negative, the poor municipal planning is actually a bonus. Filled with artsy locals, quirky shops, and a few lost travelers, Gràcia is a quieter, more out-of-the-way neighborhood, best approached by foot. Ⓜ**Diagonal** will drop you off at the northern end of the Pg. de Gràcia; follow it across Avda. Diagonal as it becomes **Carrer Gran de Gràcia,** one of the neighborhood's main thoroughfares. ⓂFontana lies farther up on C. Gran de Gràcia. If you're heading uphill on C. Grande Gràcia, any right turn will take you into the charmingly confusing grid of Gràcia's small streets, of which **Carrer de Verdi,** running parallel to C. Gran de Gràcia several blocks away, is probably the most scenic. For bustling *plaças* both day and night, your best bets are **Plaça de la Vila de Gràcia** (more commonly known as Pl. Rius i Taulet), **Plaça del Sol,** and **Plaça de la Revolució de Setembre de 1868,** off of C. de Ros de Olano.

Montjuïc and Poble Sec

Montjuïc, the mountain just down the coast from the old center of Barcelona, is one of the city's chief cultural centers. Its slopes are home to **public parks,** some of the city's best museums, theaters that host everything from classical music to pop, and a kick-ass **castle** on its peak. Montjuïc (old Catalan for "mountain of the Jews," possibly for the Jewish cemetery once located here) also has some of the most incredible views of the city. Many approach the mountain from the **Plaça de Espanya,** passing between the two towers to ascend toward the museums and other sights; others take the funicular from ⓂParal·lel.

The small neighborhood of Poble **Sec** (Catalan for "dry village") lies at the foot of Montjuïc, between the mountain and **Avinguda del Paral·lel.** Tree-lined, sloping streets characterize the largely residential neighborhood, with the **Plaça del Sortidor** as its heart and the pedestrian-friendly, restaurant-lined **Carrer de Blai** as its commercial artery.

SIGHTS

Sights in Barcelona run the gamut from cathedrals to casas to museums and more. Here's a brief overview of what each neighborhood has to offer. El Gòtic is Barcelona's most tourist-ridden neighborhood; despite the crowds of foreigners, however, the Gothic Quarter is filled with alley after alley of medieval charm. Beginning along the sea and cutting straight through to Pl. de Catalunya, Las Ramblas is Barcelona's

barcelona

You can find accommodations in any of the neighborhoods that *Let's Go* lists, and they will all have their pros and cons. For more recommendations visit, **www.letsgo.com.**

HOSTAL MALDÀ
HOSTAL $

C. Pi, 5 ☎933 17 30 02 www.hostalmalda.jimdo.com

Hostal Maldà provides a dirt-cheap home away from home, complete with kitschy clocks, ceramics, confusing knickknacks, and a kick-ass manager who could probably be your grandmother. She ensures that the multiple door keys, specific doorman procedures, and 24hr. reception will keep you and your valuables safe.

i Ⓜ️Liceu. Begin walking away from Las Ramblas in front of the house with the **dragon** and take an immediate left onto C. Casañas. Stay on this road as it passes in front of the church and through the Pl. del Pi. Enter the Galerias Maldà (interior shopping mall) and follow the signs to the hostel. Singles €15, with shower €20; doubles €30; triples €45; quads €60. Cash only. ⓩ Reception 24hr.

SANT JORDI: SAGRADA FAMÍLIA
HOSTEL $$

C. Freser, 5 ☎934 46 05 17 www.santjordihostels.com/apt-sagrada-familia/

From the fun staff to the hostel's apartment-style setup (and even a communal guitar in the main lobby), this place knows how to cater to the backpacking crowd. With rooms for one, two, or four people, you can pick your privacy without the isolation of a *pensión*. If closer quarters are more your style, they also have air-conditioned eight-, 10-, and 12-person dorms in the next building, whose common areas include Seussian wall niches and a small half-pipe on the terrace.

i Ⓜ️Sant Pau/Dos de Maig. Walk downhill on C. Dos de Maig toward C. Còrsega. Turn left onto C. Rosselló and stay left as the road splits to C. Freser. 4-bed dorms €16-28; 4-bed hostel rooms €16-28; 6-, 8-, 10-, and 12-bed hostel dorms €16-35 (triples are scarce); singles €18-40; doubles €30-45. ⓩ Reception 24hr. Quiet hours after 10pm.

ALBERGUE-RESIDENCIA LA CIUTAT
HOSTEL $

C. ca l'Alegre de Dalt, 66 ☎932 13 03 00 www.laciutat.com

This hostel crams 180 beds into a quiet location that's still close to some popular pubs and bars. Relax between the large lobby decorated with some funky cartoon wall art or the common room. The dorms are simple and brightly painted. Consider asking for a discount rate that skips breakfast to save you a few bucks.

i Ⓜ️Joanic. Walk along C. l'Escorial for 5-10min., passing through the plaza. Take a right onto C. Marti before the Clinic and take the 1st left onto C. ca l'Alegre de Dalt. 1- to 10-bed dorms €17-20; singles €35-50; doubles €52-60. 1st night deposit required for online booking. Visitors allowed only from 10am-11pm. ⓩ Reception 24hr.

HELLO BCN HOSTEL
HOSTEL $$

C. Lafont, 8-10 ☎934 42 83 92 www.hellobcnhostel.com

Finally, a place where exercise junkies can pump some iron while on vacation. This hostel boasts a gym, a large, spacious common room where dozens of college kids congregate on nightly basis, and late-night excursions. There are several opportunities to go on daytrips, from tanning on Barceloneta's beaches to trekking at the towering Mt. Monserrat.

i Ⓜ️Paral·lel. Follow C. Nou de la Rambla up into Poble Sec past Apolo Theater and turn left onto C. Vilà i Vilà, then right onto C. Lafont. Dorms €13-30; doubles €90-100; triples €110-120; quads €100-130. ⓩ Reception 24hr.

spain

world-famous tree-lined pedestrian thoroughfare that attracts thousands of visitors daily. El Born is a sight in itself, with ancient streets surrounded by sloping buildings or crumbling arches suddenly opening onto secluded *placetes*. El Raval has its own beauties, from the medieval Hospital de la Santa Creu i Sant Pau to the present-day artwork housed in the modern buildings of MACBA and CCCB. L'Eixample's sights are mostly composed of marvelous examples of modernista architecture; the Sagrada Família, in particular, is a must-see. Barceloneta is filled with Catalan pride, from the red-and-yellow flags hanging on apartment balconies to the museum devoted to Catalonia and its history. Gràcia contains the epic mountain/modernista retreat, Parc Güell, as well as a few independent examples of this historic Barcelonan style. Finally, Montjuïc—you know, that big hill with the castle on it that you can see from just about anywhere in Barcelona—is home to some phenomenal museums, a model Spanish village, and, of course, that castle.

Barri Gòtic and Las Ramblas

Beginning along the famous seaside, tree-lined pedestrian thoroughfare that attracts thousands of visitors daily, the walkway demarcated as La Rambla funnels thousands of tourists every year through its course. Marked by shady trees, cafes galore, tourist traps, and a multifarious array of street performers, gorgeous edifices, animal vendors, and extremely adroit pickpockets, the five distinct promenades seamlessly mesh to create the most lively and exciting pedestrian bustle in Barcelona (and perhaps in all of Europe). The *ramblas*, in order from Pl. de Catalunya to the Columbus Monument are: **La Rambla des Canaletes, La Rambla dels Estudis, La Rambla de Sant Josep, La Rambla dels Caputxins,** and **La Rambla de Santa Mònica.**

🏛 MUSEU D'HISTORIA DE LA CIUTAT   ROMAN RUINS
Pl. del Rei   ☎932 56 21 00 www.museuhistoria.bcn.es

If you thought the winding streets of the Barri Gòtic were old school, check out the Museu d'Història de la Ciutat's Roman ruins, hidden 20m underneath Pl. del Rei. Beneath the medieval plaza lies the excavation site of the long-gone predecessor of Barcelona: the Roman city of Barcino. Raised walkways allow passage through the site of the ruins beneath the plaza; regardless, watch your step, as some parts can be dark and uneven. You'll probably catch sight of huge ceramic wine flasks dotting the intricate ancient mosaics—surefire proof of Barcelona's revelrous ancestry. The second part of the museum features the (comparatively) newer Palacio **Real Major,** a 14th-century palace for Catalan-Aragonese monarchs. Inside the palace, the glorious and impressively empty **Saló de Tinell** (Throne Room) is the iconic seat where Ferdinand and Isabella welcomed Columbus after his journey to the New World. The **Capilla de Santa Àgata** uses its rotating exhibits to delve into the intricacies of the modern Catalonian's way of life.

i Ⓜ *Jaume I. Free multilingual audio tours. Museum and exhibition €7, students and ages 16-25 €5, under 16 free.* ☒ *Open Apr-Oct Tu-Sa 10am-7pm, Su 10am-8pm; Nov-Mar Tu-Sa 10am-5pm, Su 10am-8pm.*

🏛 AJUNTAMENT DE BARCELONA (CITY HALL)   GOVERNMENT
Pl. de Sant Jaume, enter on C. Font de Sant Miquel   ☎934 02 70 00 www.bcn.es

The stolid, 18th-century Neoclassical façade facing the Pl. de Sant Jaume hides a more interesting, 15th-century one, located at the old entrance to the left of the building (where the tourist office is on C. Ciutat). You can only get into the City Hall building on Sundays or if you get voted in, but once you're inside, it's marvelous. The lower level of this bureaucratic palace is home to many pieces of sculpture from modern Catalan masters, while the upper level showcases elaborate architecture, vivid stained glass, and lavish rooms like the *Saló de*

barcelona

Cent, from which the *Consell de Cent* (Council of One Hundred) ruled the city from 1372-1714.

i Ⓜ*Jaume I. Follow C. de Jaume I to Pl. de Sant Jaume; City Hall is on the left. Tourist info available at entrance. To enter, take alley to the left of City Hall and take a right onto C. Font de Sant Miquel. Free.* 🕒 *Open Su 10am-1:30pm. Tours every 30min. in Spanish or Catalan.*

CATEDRAL DE BARCELONA   CATHEDRAL

Pl. de la Seu   ☎933 15 15 54 www.catedralbcn.org

If you're ever around during Corpus Cristi, be sure to catch of a glimpse of the dancing egg celebration, or *l'ou com balla.*

i Ⓜ*Jaume I. From the metro, turn left onto V. Laietana, then left onto Av. de la Catedral. Cathedral free. Museu €3. Elevator to terrace €3. Inquire about guided visit to museum, choir, rooftop terraces, and towers, as hours vary.* 🕒 *Catedral open M-Sa 8am-12:45pm and 5:15-7:30pm, Su 8am-1:45pm and 5:15-7:30pm. Entry with donation M-Sa 1pm-5pm, Su 2pm-5pm.*

PALAU DE LA GENERALITAT   GOVERNMENT

Pl. de Sant Jaume   ☎934 02 46 00 www.gencat.cat/generalitat/eng

Facing the Pl. de Sant Jaume and the Ajuntament, the Palau dela Generalitat is a big player in the plaza's popularity with protesters and petitioners. The 17th-century exterior conceals a Gothic structure that was obtained by the Catalan government in 1400. Although the majority of visitors will be stuck admiring its wonderfully authoritative feel from the exterior, with a bit of magic (i.e., good timing and advance planning), it's possible to see the interior. There, visitors will find a Gothic gallery, an orange tree courtyard, St. George's Chapel, a bridge to the house of the President of the Generalitat, many historic sculptures and paintings, and the **Palau's carillon,** a 4898kg instrument consisting of 49 bells that is played on holidays and during special events.

i Ⓜ*Jaume I. Take C. de Jaume I after exiting the station. Once in Pl. de Sant Jaume; Palau is on the right. Free. Make reservations online at least 2 weeks in advance.* 🕒 *Open to the public on Apr 23, Sept 11, and Sept 24, and on the 2nd and 4th Su of each month from 10am-1:30pm.*

GRAN TEATRE DEL LICEU   THEATER

Las Ramblas, 51-59   ☎934 85 99 00 www.liceubarcelona.cat

Though La Rambla itself is one of Europe's grandest stages (tourists being the main performers), the highbrow Liceu is known for its operatic and classical presentations. The Baroque interior of the auditorium will leave you gawking at the fact that it only dates to 1999. It was reconstructed following a 1995 fire, and you can't say they don't make 'em like they used to. A 20min. tour provides a glimpse of the ornate *Sala de Espejos* (Room of Mirrors), where Apollo and the Muses look down with their divine gazes and judge theater patrons during intermission. If you're lucky, you may just catch a glimpse of authentic Spanish ardor in the form of a director yelling furiously during a rehearsal. For a more in-depth tour that won't leave you spending half of your time looking at the stackable chairs in the foyer or being told about benefactors (always a pleasure, Plácido Domingo), arrange a behind-the-scenes tour with the box office or attend a performance in person (highly recommended—just check out schedules online first).

i Ⓜ*Liceu. Discounted tickets available. Tours start every 20min.* 🕒 *Box office open M-F 1:30pm-8pm.*

PLAÇA DE L'ÀNGEL   LANDMARK

Corner of Via Laietana and C. de la Princesa

The square immediately surrounding the Ⓜ Jaume I metro stop may now seem like nothing but a place to catch the train or grab a pastry and a lame tourist T-shirt, but the days of Roman Barcino saw this spot as the main gate allowing passage into the city. To revel in some of this seemingly absent history, simply walk parallel to **Via Laietana,** the ever-bustling street forming one side of the square's border. For a more contemporary piece of history (though it still dates from the triple digits CE), look no further than the statue of an angel pointing to her toe. This sculpture commemorates the event for which the plaza was named—according to legend, the caravan carrying the remains of St. Eulàlia from the church of Santa Maria del Mar stopped here; suddenly, the urn containing remains became too heavy to carry, and when the caravan members set them down, an angel appeared and pointed to her own toe, alerting the carriers that one of the procession's officials had stolen St. Eulàlia's pedal digit. With a shame equivalent to being published with a thumbs down symbol in a *Let's Go* travel guide, the church member returned the toe to its brethren and the remains miraculously reverted to their original weight.

i Ⓜ*Jaume I. Free.*

COLUMBUS MONUMENT   TOWER
Portal de la Pau   ☎933 02 52 24
The *Mirador de Colom* at the coastal tip of La Rambla offers a phenomenal view of the city and an absolutely killer sunrise/sunset just a smidge farther down the coastline (sometimes also called the extra *Rambla del Mar*). This area features a 60m statue, constructed in the 1880s for Barcelona's World's Fair in order to commemorate Christopher Columbus meeting King Ferd and Queen Izzy in Barcelona upon his return from America. Though some say the 7.2m statue at the top of the tower points west to the Americas, it actually points east (fail, right?), supposedly to his hometown of Genoa. Reliefs around the base of the column depict the journey, as do bronze lions that are guaranteed to be mounted by tourists at any given moment. Just don't try to mount them if you're stumbling back home up Las Ramblas at dawn, especially if you don't have a buddy's camera documenting the whole incident.

i Ⓜ*Drassanes. Entrance located in base facing water €4, seniors and children €3.* 🕐 *Open daily May-Oct 9am-7:30pm; Nov-Apr 9am-6:30pm.*

El Born

This part of the *ciutat vella* (ancient city) is a sight in itself, with ancient streets surrounded by sloping buildings and crumbling arches suddenly opening onto secluded *placetes*. In addition to the joys of just walking through the neighborhood, there are certain sights you just can't miss.

🔲 **PALAU DE LA MÚSICA CATALANA**   MUSIC HALL
C. Palau de la Música, 4-6   ☎902 44 28 82 www.palaumusica.org
Home to both Barcelona's Orfeó Choir and the Catalan musical spirit, the Palau is Barcelona's most spectacular music venue (it became a UNESCO World Heritage Site in 1997). Lluís Domènech i Montaner, contemporary of Gaudí and architect of the **Hospital de Sant Pau, Casa Fuster,** and the Castell **dels Tres Dragons,** crafted this awe-inspiring *modernista* masterpiece from humble materials such as brick, ceramic, stone, iron, and glass in just a short three years. True to the *Art Nou* movement's principles, the building (1905-08) is covered inside and out with organic motifs. The breathtaking inverted dome of the stained glass ceiling and the tall stained glass windows make the luminous interior shimmer. Columns pose as abstract trees, while intricate ceramic flowers decorate the ceiling. In fact, the concert hall's designer packed the floral motif in just about every nook and cranny of the theater—see for yourself, it's rather eye-opening. Behind the stage, angelic muses emerge from the walls, which are part flat ceramic tiles, part stone sculpture. Above and around the stage, angels interact with trees, the riding Valkyries, and musicians such as Wagner and Beethoven. Back in commission after a 30-year hiatus, the Palau's glorious 3772-pipe organ stands front and center in the upper portion of the hall. Below it hangs the coat of arms of Catalunya in all its splendor, comprised of the cross of St. George (patron saint

of Spain) along with four stripes. The Palau offers reduced-admission concerts regularly, which is a nice break from the typical €17 price tag. After touring, you'll officially be able to declare how artsy and Euro-knowledgeable you are.

i ⓂJaume I. *On Via Laietana, walk toward the cathedral for about 5min., then take a right onto C. Sant Pere Mas Alt. Palau de la Música Catalana is on the left. Schedule of events and ticketing info on website. Guided tours €17, students €11, under 10 free. 55min. tours daily 10am-3:30pm, in English every hr. and Catalan and Spanish every 30min.* ⓏGuided tour schedules vary by season. Aug tours daily 9am-6pm, Easter week 10am-6pm. Box office open daily 9:30am-3:30pm; Jul and Aug 9am-8pm.*

▨ MUSEU PICASSO   MUSEUM
C. de Montcada, 15-23   ☎932 19 63 10 www.museupicasso.bcn.cat/en

Safely tucked away between the cobblestone streets of La Ribera is one of the Catalonian government's many treasured art oases. Namely, the assortment of a multitude of paintings by the one and only Pablo Picasso are proudly displayed in white, modern, Guggenheim-esque hallways. They will neither put on fancy airs against neophytic tourists nor will they snap at picture-savvy travelers despite the no photography rule. The museum's trifecta of Spanish, Catalan, and English language options for most anything displayed reflects the international attraction it receives. Granted, the echoey nature of the establishment would merely require a faint whisper to grab one's attention. A conglomeration of five small Gothic castles comprises the showcase of Picasso's entire career, not just the funkily fragmented scenes with misallocated eyeballs. A chronological presentation of his oil paintings demonstrate his time in Paris and afterward show the French influence, while several works from his Blue and Rose periods help to paint a picture of his past. Spectators can feast their eyes upon Picasso's first works (otherwise known as depictions of his friends) among oil canvas, sketches, and still life oeuvres. The museum also contains a work whose title (unclear whether it was Picasso's or added later) represents the greatest disjunction between image and description yet encountered by *Let's Go:* a small but graphic depiction of two women *in flagrante*—and in ecstasy—is dubbed *Two Women and A Cat.* The collection of 58 paintings spanning two rooms comprises the artist's renditions of Velázquez's *Las Meninas*, where the iconic works are spiked and contorted into a nightmarish landscape of Picasso-typic forms. Temporary exhibits highlight the work of Picasso's contemporaries, providing some context for the permanent collection. Also be ready to stare at any random ceiling, given that some former dance parlor rooms encrusted in gold now house artifacts covered by what seems like Michelangelo's side projects aside. Expect a long wait along the crowded Carrer de Montcada any day of the week but especially on Sundays, when the museum is free after 3pm. To beat the throngs, try hitting up the museum early or waiting until the later hours.

i ⓂJaume I. *Walk down C. de la Princesa and turn right onto Carrer de Montcada. Admission €11; ages 16-24 and over 65 €6; under 16, teachers, PinkCard cardholders, and ICOM members free. Audio tour €3. Accepts Mastercard and Visa. 1st Su of each month free, other Su free after 3pm.* ⓏOpen Tu-Su 10am-8pm. Last entry 30min. before close.*

PARC DE LA CIUTADELLA   PARK, MUSEUMS
Between Pg. de Picasso, C. Pujades, and C. Wellington

Once the site of a Spanish fortress built by King Philip V in the 18th century, this park was transformed into its current state after the citadel was leveled in preparation for the Universal Exhibition of 1888. This sprawling complex includes plenty of green space as well as various *modernista* buildings. Points of architectural interest are located in two areas: the old fort holds the governor's palace (now a medical school), the arsenal (today home of the **Parlament de Catalunya**), and the chapel. The 1888 Exhibition area showcases century-old gems.

Many of these are still in use today: the steel and glass **Hivernacle,** a greenhouse-turned-civic-space near the Pujades entrance, maintains its original function as well as its newer one as a concert venue. The **Natural History Museum** (Museu de Ciències Naturals 933 196 912) educates crowds, the **Museu Martorell** functions as a geology museum, and the **Castell dels Tres Dragons** houses the **Zoological Museum** and the entrance to the **Barcelona Zoo** (902 457 545 www.zoobarcelona.cat). Now for the fun stuff! The extravagant **Cascada Monumental** fountain, designed in part by Antoni Gaudí, provides every Kodak moment possibly imaginable. The **mastodon** near the entrance of the zoo isn't bad for a photo op either. For those just looking to use the park as, well, a park, bike trails run around the exterior walls, and dirt pedestrian paths break up the lush grass and tree-shaded pockets. Take your lover out on a light paddle boat ride in the central pond or get lost among the gardens! Expect to see nearly every corner covered in picnickers during the summer months, and be sure to stop by and join the locals for a bath in the fountain (that's your inner Shakira!).

i Ⓜ*Arc de Triomf. Walk through the arch and down the boulevard to enter the park. Free Wi-Fi available at the Geological Museum, Parliament building, and Zoological Museum. Park free. Museum €4.10-7, Su 3-8pm free. Zoo €17. Ⓩ Park open daily 10am-dusk. Natural History Museum open Tu-F 10am-7pm, Sa-Su 10am-8pm. Zoo open daily May 16-Sept 15 10am-7pm; Sept 16-Oct 29 10am-6pm; Oct 30-Mar 26 10am-5pm; Mar 27-May 15 10am-6pm.*

CHURCH OF SANTA MARIA DEL MAR
CHURCH

C. Canvis Vells, 1　　　　　　　　　　　　　☎933 10 23 90 933 10 23 90

El Born is dominated by this church's stoic presence, but it's nearly impossible to get a good glimpse from the outside. Nearby streets allow remotely satisfactory views of the exterior from the Fossar de les Moreres at the end of Pg. del Born. The Pl. de Santa Maria, located at the west entrance of the church, holds the best outside views of the church's impressive rose window (which dates to 1459) and the intricate relief and sculptural work of the main entrance. The best view of the stained glass, of course, is from inside on a sunny day. Constructed between 1329 and 1383, this church exemplifies the Catalan Gothic style—tough on the outside, light and airy on the inside. The inside is spacious and open, with tall, slim, octagonal pillars lining the main nave and no constructed boundaries between the nave and the altar. Despite the beautiful architecture, the interior has limited decoration (apart from the stained glass, of course) due to a fire that gutted the church in 1936 during the Spanish Civil War. Be sure to check the secret, miracle-holding treasure room of eternal light in the back—okay, it's just the chapel, but it goes largely unvisited and grants a close-up of some amazing artistry and friezes of God near the ceiling.

i Ⓜ*Jaume I. Walk down Carrer del'Argenteria to enter the plaça. Santa Maria del Mar is on the right. Free. Ⓩ Open M-Sa 9am-1:30pm and 5:30-8:30pm, Su 10am-1:30pm and 5:30-8:30pm.*

ARC DE TRIOMF
ARCHITECTURE

Between Pg. de Lluís Companys and Pg. de Sant Joan

For a proper greeting from the city of Barcelona, be sure to get off the metro at the **Arc de Triomf Station. At** first glance, you'll notice that this is most definitely not Paris's Arc de Triomphe (this one is actually reachable and not swimming in an ocean of tourists); the slight differences between the two encapsulate why Paris is Paris and Barcelona is awesome. Where else can you find such a relatively unoccupied attraction? People don't really come to Spain to see this, so it's pretty much as private as a massive, open historic site can be. Situated at the beginning of a wide, cinematic-like boulevard leading to the **Parc de la Ciutadella,** the arch not only frames the palm tree- and *modernista*-building-lined road and its incredible terminus but also literally embraces visitors with a sculptural frieze by Josep Reynés inscribed with the phrase *"Barcelona rep les nacions,"* or "Barcelona welcomes the nations." This declaration was made along with the arch's construction for the 1888 Universal Exhibition, when it served as the main entrance to the fair grounds in the Parc. Today, the arch serves as little more than a historical artifact, but it's worth a look if you're in the area. The triumphant bricks-on-bricks of the arch was designed by Josep Jilaseca i Cassanovas in the Moorish revival style. Its exterior is decked out with sculptures of 12 women representing fame and a relief by Josep Lllimona that depicts the award ceremony. Much the opposite of gargoyles atop the structure are several white angel sculptures and eight massive. The whole thing graces the surrounding area with its architectural superiority.

i Ⓜ*Arc de Triomf. Free.*

El Raval

◪ PALAU GÜELL   PALACE

C. Nou de la Rambla, 3-5   ☎934 72 57 75 www.palauguell.cat

Commissioned by Eusebi Güell, the wealthy industrialist of Parc Güell fame, Güell Palace has stood tall since its 1888 completion as the master creation of none other than Antoni Gaudí. Being the only project that Gaudí himself directed until its debut, Palau Güell represents one of the artist's early works. Its roots in the Islamic-Hispanic architectural tradition are visible in the Moorish arched windows that have been elongated and smoothed out with a typical Gaudí twist. Be sure to look up in the Saló Central to see another example of this: tiny holes in the conical ceiling allow in rays of light, reminiscent of a combination of God's light piercing clouds and a nicely constructed Indian harem. You'll probably have someone snicker at you as you stare with your mouth agape at the ceiling's rainbow, typically Gaudían ceramic-tiled chimney, and impressive geometric conglomerations dotting the inside. Check the website before going to check events and exhibits.

i Ⓜ*Liceu. Walk toward the water on Las Ramblas and take a right onto C. Nou de la Rambla. Rooftop closed when raining. Group reservations need 48hr. advance call €12, reduced €8. Free 1st Su of month. Audio tour included in admission.* 🕐 *Open Apr-Oct Tu-Su 10am-8pm; Nov-Mar Tu-Su 10am-5:30pm. Last entry 1hr. before close.*

◪ MUSEU D'ART CONTEMPORANI DE BARCELONA (MACBA)   MUSEUM

Pl.Àngels, 1   ☎934 12 08 10 www.macba.cat

Bursting out of the narrow streets and into its own spacious plaza, American architect Richard Meier's bright white edifice has sought to bring artistic enlightenment to the masses. The stark, simple interior displays an impressive collection of contemporary art, with particular emphasis on Spanish and Catalan artists, including a world-renowned collection of the interwar avant-garde and a selection of works by Miró and Tàpies. Found very near the CCCB, the Universitat, and a host of other sights around El Raval, MACBA is a must-see attraction for travelers, locals, and students alike. Be sure to check the website, as events, exhibitions, and even small concerts may occur within a week's notice. The museum completely transforms during Barcelona's Sónar music festival every year, converting into the Sónar Complex stage.

i Ⓜ*Universitat. Walk down C. Pelai, take the 1st right, and turn left onto C. Tallers. Take a right onto C. Valldonzella and a left onto C. Montalegre. Admission includes English-language tour. Entrance to all exhibit €9; children under 14, Tarjeta Rosa, over 65, the unemployed, teachers, members of the AAVC, and ICOM members free.* 🕐 *Open M-F 11am-7:30pm, Sa 10am-9pm, Su and holidays 10am-7pm. Library open M-Th 10am-7pm. Last entry 30min. before close.*

CENTRE DE CULTURA CONTEMPORÀNIA DE BARCELONA (CCCB)   EXHIBITION CENTER
C. Montalegre, 5   ☎933 06 41 00 www.cccb.org

The Centre de Cultura Contemporània de Barcelona boasts everything from art exhibits of old African sculptures to Shakespearean theater to Roman literature to open-air beer expos—the best potpourri of culture you'll ever see. Three exhibition galleries host large and involved temporary exhibits that vary in quality and quantity by month. Two lecture halls, an auditorium, and a bookstore fill out the architecturally wonderful (and award winning!) complex comprised of several upright glass and mirror structures. Paired with the thought-provoking collections of the nearby MACBA, the CCCB offers everything to help one become the epitome of a cultured character.

i ⓂUniversitat. Walk down C. Pelai, take the 1st right, and then turn left onto C. Tallers. Turn right onto C. Valldonzella and left onto C. Montalegre. General admission €6; seniors, under 25, large families, group visits, and single-parent households €4; 2 or more exhibitions €8/6. Ⓓ Exhibits open daily 11am-8pm. CCCB Archives open Tu-F 3-8pm, Sa-Su 11am-8pm. Guided tours in Spanish Sa 11:30am. Last entry 30min. before close.

L'ANTIC HOSPITAL DE LA SANTA CREU I SANT PAU   HOSPITAL
C. l'Hospital, 54-56

Now the site of the Institue d'Estudis Catalans, the Escola Massana, and the 1.5 million volume Bibilioteca de Catalunya, l'Antic Hospital de la Santa Creu i Sant Peu (or the Old Hospital of the Holy Cross and St. Paul) is a 15th-century Gothic building located in the middle of El Raval. Although it no longer functions as the neighborhood hospital, the interior courtyard, complete with an orangery and romantic perching spots, will nicely pad your collection of Facebook pictures. The operating theater has a rotating marble dissection table for the non-squeamish, and the archives hold records of the admittance of famous Catalan architect Antoni Gaudí to the hospital before his death in 1926. At that time, the hospital was used to treat the poor, and Gaudí was mistaken for a homeless man and brought to the premises after a tram struck him. Try to stop by the Gothic chapel art museum, La Capella, as well—it hosts multiple monthly exhibitions.

i ⓂLiceu. Walk down C. l'Hospital. Free Wi-Fi in courtyard. Biblioteca (932 02 07 97 www.bnc. cat). La Capella(932 42 71 71 www.bcn.cat/lacapella). Ⓓ Open M-F 9am-8pm, Sa 9am-2pm. Biblioteca open M-F 9am-8pm, Sa 9am-2pm. La Capella open Tu-Sa noon-2pm and 4-8pm, Su 11am-2pm.

L'Eixample

🖾 **CASA BATLLÓ**   ARCHITECTURE
Pg. de Gràcia, 43   ☎934 88 06 66 www.casabatllo.es

Built sometime between 1875 and 1877, the Casa Batlló was originally designed for a middle class family in the luxurious center l'Eixample. Take a peek at yet another of Gaudí's creations in all its visceral, organo-skeletal design sprinkled with the ever-present hints of Nouveau Art. From the spinal-column stairwell that holds together the scaly building's interior to the undulating **dragon's** back curve of the ceramic rooftop to the skull-like balconies on the facade, the Casa Batlló will have you wondering what kinds of drugs Gaudí was on and where one might go about acquiring them if they lead to such remarkable renovations (it was originally built by Emilio Salas Cortés). Much of the inside is lined with *trancadís*, or scatters of broken tile that lend to gorgeous color transitions and contrasts. The building has hardly a right angle inside or out; every surface—stone, wood, glass, anything—is soft and molten. This architectural wonderland was once an apartment complex for the fantastically rich and is now the busiest of the three *modernista* marvels in the **Manzana de la Discòrdia** on Pg. de Gràcia. A free audio tour lets you navigate the dream-like space at your own pace, so be sure to spend some time with the doors of wood and stained glass, the soft scaled pattern of the softly bowed walls, and the swirly light fixture that pulls at the entire ceiling, rippling into its center. Gaudí's design ranges from the incredibly rational to the seemingly insane, including a blue light well that passes from deep navy at the top to sky blue below in order to distribute light more evenly. Be sure to visit the rooftop where you can get a great view of Barcelona below.

i ⓂPasseig de Gràcia. Walk away from Pl. Catalunya on Pg. de Gràcia; Casa Batlló is on the left. Tickets available at box office or through TelEntrada. Admission includes audio tour. €20.35, students and BCN cardholders €16.30. ⌚ Open daily 9am-9pm. Last entry 40min. before close.

🏛 SAGRADA FAMÍLIA   ARCHITECTURE
C. Mallorca, 401   ☎932 08 04 14 www.sagradafamilia.cat

If all goes well, the overall projected completion date is 2030, but we wouldn't bet on it. Until that glorious and perhaps apocryphal day arrives, drawings and projections of the completed building can be seen in the adjacent museum, and an exhibit dedicated to the mathematical models lets you imagine the completed building some are already calling God's Crown.

i ⓂSagrada Família. Towers closed during rain. Basilica €13.50, with audio tour €21.50; students €11.50; under 10 free. Elevator €4.50. Combined ticket with Casa-Museu Gaudí (in Parc Güell) €17. Online ticketing strongly recommended. ⌚ Open Apr-Sept daily 9am-8pm; Oct-Mar 9am-6pm; Dec 25-Jan 6 9am-2pm. Visitors must leave by 30min. past ticket office closing. Last elevator to the tower Nativity Lift 15min. before close. Passion Lift 30min. before close. Guided tours in English May-Jun M-F 11am, noon, and 1pm; Jul-Aug M 5pm; Sept-Oct M-F 11am, noon, and 1pm; Nov-Apr M-F 11am, 1, and 3pm.

CASA MILÀ (LA PEDRERA)   ARCHITECTURE
Pg. de Gràcia, 92 C. Provença, 261-265   ☎902 202 138 http://www.lapedrera.com/en/visitor-information

La Pedrera still functions as a home for the rich, famous, and patient—the waitlist for an apartment is over three decades long—as well as the offices of the Caixa Catalunya bank. Many portions of the building are open to the public, including an apartment decorated with period furniture (contemporary to the house, not designed by Gaudí) and the main floor. The attic, a space known as **Espai Gaudí,** boasts a mini-museum to the man himself, including helpful exhibits explaining the science behind his beloved caternary arches and what exactly it means for the architect to be "inspired by natural structures." It is complete with all his jargonistic models and Einsteinian mathematical formulas working behind the scenes to create his living oeuvres. Up top, a rooftop terrace gives light to what many a critic has called the perfect European Kodak moment, whether it be with the desert-like sculptural outcroppings part of the building or of the panorama overlooking Barcelona to the Sagrada Família. During the summer, the terrace lights up with jazz performances on Friday and Saturday nights in a series known as *Nits d'Estiu a La Pedrera.*

i ⓂDiagonal. Walk down Pg. de Gràcia away from Avda. Diagonal; La Pedrera is on the right. Purchase tickets to Nits d'Estiu a La Pedrera online via TelEntrada at www.telentrada.com. €16.50, students and seniors €14.85, under 6 free. Audio tour €4. Nits d'Estiu a La Pedrera €30; includes access to Espai Gaudí. 10 language options available for tours. ⌚ Open daily Mar-Oct 9am-8pm; Nov-Feb 9am-6:30pm. Last entry 30min. before close. Concerts mid-Jun-late-Aug, some F and Sa 8:30pm.

CASA AMATLLER   ARCHITECTURE
Pg. de Gràcia, 41   ☎932 160 175 www.amatller.org

Finally another whimsical place that can rival some of Pg. de Gracia's other creations. Casa Amatller stands as the counterpart to Gaudí's neighboring acid-trip Casa Batlló, and it was the first in the trio of buildings now known as the **Manzana de la Discòrdia.** In 1898, chocolate industrialist Antoni Amatller became the rich hipster of his time by veering form the Gaudí-dominated expert architectural sweets and instead commissioned **Josep Puig i Cadafalch** to build his palatial home along Pg. de Gràcia, and out popped a mix of Catalan, Neo-Gothic, Islamic, and even Dutch architectural motifs all expertly overlapping on a strict gridline. A carving of Sant Jordi battling that pesky dragon appears over the front door, accompanied by four divinely artsy figures engaged in painting, sculpting, and architecture. Also at the foot of the principal entrance is a tile on the ground marking 0km of the **European Route de Modernisme**. The start of this invisible path is Barcelona's age-old endeavor to spread the *moderniste* movement throughout Spain as well as the rest of Europe. The building's entrance is free to see—note the ornate lamps and amazing stained-glass ceiling in the stairwell, created by the same artist that did the ceiling of the Palau de la Música Catalana. The rest of the building is even more spectacular and is well worth the €10 tour.

i ⓂPasseig de Gràcia. Walk away from Pl. Catalunya on Pg. de Gràcia; Casa Amatller is a couple of blocks up on the left. Reservation by phone or email required for tour. Tours €10. Kid workshops €6 daily 10am-8pm. ⓧ Guided tours M-F 10, 11am, noon, 1, 3, 4, 5, and 6pm.

HOSPITAL DE LA SANTA CREU I SANT PAU   ARCHITECTURE
C. Sant Antoni Maria Claret, 167   ☎933 177 652; guided visits 902 076 621

Considered one of the most important pieces of *modernista* public architecture, this hospital's practice challenges the meaning of "neouveau." Dating back to 1401 when six smaller hospitals merged, the Hospital de la Santa Creu i Sant Pau is the newer embodiment of the medical practice formerly housed in the **Antic Hospital de la Santa Creu** in El Raval. Wealthy benefactor Pau Gil bequested funds for the building with strict instructions, including the name appendage. Construction then began in 1902 under the direction of Lluís Domènech i Montaner (designer of the godly **Palau de Musica Catalana** in El Born), who in Gaudían fashion, died before its completion. His son saw the work to fruition, giving the hospital 48 large pavilions connected by underground tunnels and bedazzled with luxurious modern sculptures and paintings. Although the hospital ceased to function as a hospital in 2009, it has been named a UNESCO World Heritage Sight and ironically now welcomes even more visitors than it did as a hospital. Much of the complex is currently closed for renovation, but the little bits open around back are neat spots for a few selfies and snapchats (or 15).

i 8, over 65, and unemployed €5. Modernisme Route 50% discount. Bus Turístic 20% discount. Barcelona City Tour 20% discount. ⓧ Tours in English M-Su 10, 11am, noon, and 1pm. Tours in French M-Su 10:30am. Tours in Spanish M-Su 11:30am. Tours in Catalan M-Su 12:30pm. Follow the information boards for updated information.

FUNDACIÓ ANTONI TÀPIES   ART, ARCHITECTURE
C. Aragó, 255   ☎934 87 03 15 www.fundaciotapies.org

Housed in a building by *modernista* architect Lluís Domènech i Montaner, the Fundació Antoni Tàpies is unmissable thanks to the giant mess ball of wire and steel atop the low brick roofline. Made by the museum's namesake, Antoni Tàpies, it's actually a sculpture entitled *Núvol i Cadira* (Cloud and Chair; 1990) that supposedly shows a chair jutting out of a large cloud. Once inside, the lowest and highest levels are dedicated to temporary exhibitions on modern and contemporary artists and themes—recent shows have included work by Eva Hesse and Steve McQueen—while the middle floors hold Tàpies' own work. Start upstairs and work your way down, watching the descent from surrealist-symbolist beauty into a misshapen chaos of not so well-seeming forms.

i ⓂPasseig de Gràcia. Walk uphill on Pg. de Gràcia and turn left onto C. Aragó. €7; reduced entrance €5.60. Articket free. ⓧ Open Tu-Su 10am-7pm. Closed Dec 25, Jan 1, and Jan 6. Last entry 15min. before closing. Museum shop open Tu-F 10am-7pm, Sa-Su 10am-2:30pm and 3:30-7pm. Library open Tu-F 10am-2pm and 4-7pm. Admission to library by appointment.

FUNDACIÓ FRANCISCO GODIA
C. Diputació, 250   **ART**

☎932 72 31 80   www.fundacionfgodia.org

The next time you start making NASCAR the butt of a redneck joke, consider the Fundació Francisco Godia. Though Godia was a successful businessman by trade, his two true loves are the focus of this museum: art collecting and Formula One racing. The museum reflects these disparate interests—a front room filled with racing trophies and riding goggles amongst other racing paraphernalia. A man of exquisite taste and great artistic sensitivity, Francisco Godia gathered together an exceptional collection of paintings, medieval sculptures, and ceramics. Some of his favorite works are on display at the Francisco Godia Foundation, including many of his favorite 20th-century artifacts. Due to Godia's broad collecting interests, the permanent collection features everything from stunning 12th- and 13th-century wooden sculptures to medieval paintings to modern works by Santiago Rusiñol, Joaquím Mir, and Gutiérrez Solana. In fact, the foundation continues to acquire contemporary pieces, and temporary exhibits attempt to fit somewhere into the framework of the diverse collection.

i Ⓜ*Passeig de Gràcia. Walk away from Pl. Catalunya on Pg. de Gràcia and take the 1st left onto C. Diputació. Guided tours in Spanish and Catalan free Sa-Su at noon. €6.50, students €3.50. Temporary exhibits €5-10.* Ⓩ *Open M-Sa 10am-8pm, Su 10am-3pm.*

Gràcia

Some of the most defining features of Gràcia's cityscape are the cafe-lined **plaças** that seem to appear out of nowhere around every corner. The **Plaça de la Vila de Gràcia** (also known as Plaça de Rius i Taulet) is one of the largest and most beautiful, with a massive 19th-century clock tower (Ⓜ**Fontana**; take a left down C. Gran de Gràcia, then a left onto C. Sant Domènec). With your back to the powder-blue municipal building, head up the street running along the right side of the plaza, and in a few blocks you'll get to the **Plaça del Sol**, the neighborhood's most lively square, especially at night. Two blocks east of that (follow C. Ramon i Cajal) is the **Plaça de la Revolució de Setembre de 1868**, a long, open square with the word "Revolució" engraved in the pavement. Head up C. Verdifrom Pl. Revolució de Setembre 1868 and take a left at the third intersection, which will bring you to the shady **Plaça del Diamant,** while a right will bring you to the true gem that is the **Plaça de la Virreina.**

PARC GÜELL
Main entrance on C. Clot   **PARK, ARCHITECTURE**

Although the main areas of the park are regularly full during the days of summer, it's possible to escape the toddlers and fanny packs by showing up at or before the park's opening—chances are they won't turn you away, and, even if you have to wait, at least there's an incredible view to enjoy while you do so. Otherwise, it's usually busy until closing most every day.

i Ⓜ*Lesseps. Walk uphill on Travessera Dalt and take a left to ride escalators. Or* Ⓜ*Vallcarca. Walk down Avda. República Argentina and take a right onto C. Agramunt, which becomes the partially be-escalatored Baixada Glòria. Bus #24 from Pl. Catalunya stops just downhill from the park. Free. Guardhouse €2, students €1.50. Free Su after 3pm and 1st Su of each month. Casa-Museu Gaudí €5.50, students €4.50.* Ⓩ *Park open daily May-Aug 10am-9pm; Sept 10am-8pm; Oct 10am-7pm; Nov-Feb 10am-6pm; Mar 10am-7pm; Apr 10am-8pm. Guardhouse open daily Apr-Oct 10am-8pm; Nov-Mar 10am-4pm. Casa-Museu Gaudí open daily Apr-Sept 10am-8pm; Oct-Mar 10am-6pm.*

Montjuïc and Poble Sec

FUNDACIÓ MIRÓ
Parc de Montjuïc   **MUSEUM**

☎934 43 94 70   www.fundaciomiro-bcn.org

It's time to visit Fundació Miró. From the outside in, the museum serves as both a shrine to and a celebration of the life and work of Joan Miró, one of Catalonia and Spain's most beloved contemporary artists. The bright white angles and curves of the Lego-esque building were designed by Josep Lluís Sert, a close friend of Joan Miró. Since it first opened, the museum has expanded beyond Miró's original collection to include pieces inspired by the artist. A collection of over 14,000 works now fills the open galleries, which have views of the grassy exterior and adjacent **Sculpture Park.** The collection includes whimsical sculptures, epic paintings, and gargantuan *sobreteixims* (paintings on tapestry) by Miró, as well as works by Calder, Duchamp, Oldenburg, and Léger. Have fun gazing at Calder's politically charged **mercury fountain,** which was exhibited alongside Picasso's *Guernica* at the 1937 World's Fair in Paris. Like much of Barcelona, the foundation refuses to be stuck in its past—although an impressive relic of a previous era, Fundació Miró continues to support contemporary art. Temporary exhibitions have recently featured names such as Olafur Eliasson, Pipllotti Rist, and Kiki Smith, while the more experimental **Espai 13** houses exhibits by emerging artists selected by freelance curators. Overwhelmed? You should be. This is one of the few times we recommend paying for the audio tour (€4).

i ⓂParal·lel. *From the metro, take the funicular to the museum. €11, students €6, under 14 free. Temporary exhibits €4, students €3. Espai 13 €2.50. Sculpture garden free.* Ⓞ *Open Jul-Sept Tu-W 10am-8pm, Th 10am-9:30pm, F-Sa 10am-8pm, Su 10am-2:30pm; Oct-Jun Tu-W 10am-7pm, Th 10am-9:30pm, F-Sa 10am-7pm, Su 10am-2:30pm. Last entry 30min. before close.*

MUSEU NACIONAL D'ART DE CATALUNYA (MNAC) MUSEUM

Palau Nacional, Parc de Montjuïc ☎936 22 03 76 www.mnac.cat

This majestic building perched atop Montjuïc isn't quite as royal as it first appears. Designed by Enric Català and Pedro Cendoya for the 1929 International Exhibition, the Palau Nacional has housed the Museu Nacional d'art de Catalunya (MNAC) since 1934. The sculpture-framed view over Barcelona from outside the museum can't be beat,and more treasures await on the inside. Upon entrance, you'll be dumped into the gargantuan, colonnaded **Oval Hall,** which, though empty, gets your jaw appropriately loose to prepare for its drop in the galleries. The wing to the right houses a collection of Catalan Gothic art, complete with paintings on wood panels and sculptures that Pier 1 would kill to replicate. To the left in the main hall is the museum's impressive collection of Catalan Romanesque art and frescoes, removed from their original settings in the 1920s and installed in the museum—a move that was probably for the best, considering the number of churches devastated in the civil war just a decade later. More modern attractions grace the upstairs, with modern art to the left and drawings, prints, and posters to the far right. For those intoxicated by the quirky architecture of the city, Catalan *modernisme* and *noucentisme* works dot the galleries, from Gaudí-designed furniture to Picasso's Cubist *Woman in Fur Hat and Collar.* The collection, which spans the 19th and early 20th century, includes an impressive selection from the under-appreciated Joaquim Mir and a couple of large, fascinating works by the more renowned José Gutiérrez Solana. If art isn't your thing, check out the currency collection—though beauty may be in the eye of the beholder, this 140,000-piece brief in the history of Catalan coins will have hardly any detractors.

i ⓂEspanya. *Walk through the towers and ride the escalators to the top; the museum is the palace-like structure. Permanent exhibit €12, students €6, under 16 and over 65 free. Annual subscription (permanent and temporary exhibits) €18. Combined ticket with Poble Espanyol €15. Articket €30. Audio tour €3.10. 1st Su of each month free.* Ⓞ *Open Tu-Sa 10am-7pm, Su 10am-2:30pm. Last entry 30min. before close.*

barcelona

POBLE ESPANYOL

Av. Francesc Ferrer i Guàrdia, 13   ☎935 08 63 00 www.poble-espanyol.com

One of the few original relics from the 1929 International Exhibition that still dots the mountain, the Poble Espanyol originally aimed to present a unified Spanish village. Inspired by *modernista* celebrity Josep Puig i Cadafalch, the four architects and artists in charge of its design visited over 1600 villages and towns throughout the country to find models to copy in constructing the village's 117 full-scale buildings, streets,and squares. Though intended simply as a temporary arts pavilion, the outdoor architectural museum was so popular that it was kept open as a shrine (or challenge) to the ideal of a united Spain that never was. It's perfect for those traveling only to Barcelona who want to get some idea of what the rest of the country looks like—the "Barri Andaluz" feels like a Sevilla street, with whitewashed walls and arches. Nowadays, artists' workshops peddle goods along the winding roads, spectacles take place during the day, and parties rage at night.

i Ⓜ*Espanya. Walk through the towers, ride the escalators, and take a right €11, students €7.40, at night €6.50 (valid after 8pm); combined visit with National Art Museum of Catalonia €18. Audio tour €3. ☒ Open M 9am-8pm, Tu-Th 9am-midnight, F 9am-3am, Sa 9am-4am, Su 9am-midnight. Last entry 1hr. before close. Workshops and shops open daily in summer 10am-8pm; in fall 10am-7pm; in winter 10am-6pm; in spring 10am-7pm.*

BARCELONA PAVILION

Av. Francesc Ferrer i Guàrdia, 7   ☎934 23 40 16 www.miesbcn.com

Though the original Barcelona Pavilion was dismantled when the International Exhibition ended in 1930, this faithful 1986 reconstruction recreates the original feel perfectly. **Ludwig Mies van der Rohe's** iconic 1929 structure of glass, steel, and marble reminds us that "less is more." The open interior is populated solely by the famous Barcelona chair and a reflecting pool with a bronze reproduction of Georg Kolbe's *Alba*. This pavilion—simple, tranquil, sleek—changed modern architecture, modern design, and the way we look at both, whether we realize it or not.

i Ⓜ*Espanya. Walk through the towers and take the escalators up Montjuïc. Barcelona Pavilion is on the 1st landing to the right; follow the signs. €5, students €2.60, under 16 free. Free 30min. guide service Sa 10am, English 11am, Spanish noon. Catalan Bus Turístic, Barcelona Card, Barcelona City Tour reduction 20%. Cash only at front entrance. ☒ Open daily 10am-8pm.*

CASTLE OF MONTJUÏC

Carretera Montjuïc, 66   ☎932 56 44 45 www.bcn.cat/castelldemontjuic

Built in 1640 during the revolt against Philip IV, this former fort and castle has been involved in its fair share of both Catalan and Spanish struggles. The fortress first saw action in 1641 against Castilian forces and continued its function as a military post until 1960, when it was ceded to the city and refurbished as a military museum by Franco (incidentally, this is the only place in Catalunya where one can find a statue of the narcissist). Despite being handed to the city, the fort was controlled by the army until 2007, when its direction was finally handed to the Barcelona City Council. The inside walkways offer mazes, incredible views of the harbor and city, as well as a moat-turned-beautifully-manicured-garden for those that make the hike (or shell out for the rather expensive, €11 cable car ride to the top). Once there, try to mount those massive steel juggernauts!

i Ⓜ*Espanya. Montjuïc telefèric on Avda. Miramar. Free. ☒ Open daily Apr 1-Sept 30 9am-9pm; Oct 1-Mar 31 9am-7pm.*

spain

FOOD

Given the cosmopolitan character of Barcelona, you can find just about any food you crave in this city. The cheapest options are chain supermarkets (Dia, Caprabo, and Spar, to name a few) and local groceries that tend to run a few cents cheaper still; in terms of prepared food, kebab restaurants are some of the cheapest and most plentiful. Local Catalan cuisine is varied and includes food from land and sea: some of the most traditional dishes are *botifarra amb mongetes* (Catalan pork sausage with beans), *esqueixada* (cod with tomato and onion), *llonganissa* (a kind of salami), and *coques* (somewhere between a pizza and an open-faced sandwich; singular *coca*). The simplest and most prevalent dish is *pa amb tomàquet* (bread smeared with tomato, garlic, olive oil, salt, and pepper). Note also that the Catalan for "salad" is *amanida;* this bears no relation to the word in English or Spanish, which confuses some travelers poring over a menu in search of *ensalada*.

Barri Gòtic and Las Ramblas

⬛ LA BOQUERIA (MERCAT DE SANT JOSEP)   MARKET
Las Ramblas, 89

If you're looking for ruby red tomatoes, leeks the size of a well-fed child's arm, or maybe just some nuts and a zumo smoothie, the Boqueria has you covered in the most beautiful way—quite literally. Just look for the stained-glass archway facing Las Ramblas that marks the entrance of this expansive tented open market. Though each neighborhood in Barcelona has its own *mercat*, the Mercat de Sant Josep is not only the biggest and most impressive in the city, it's the largest market in all of Spain. If filling your stomach from the glowing rows of perfectly arranged, perfectly ripened produce doesn't satisfy your gut, restaurants surrounding the market and dotting La Rambla offer meals made from produce directly from the nearby vendors.

i Ⓜ*Liceu. Walk on Las Ramblas toward Pl. de Catalunya and take a left onto Pl. de Sant Josep.* Ⓩ *Open M-Sa 8am-8pm, though certain vendors stay open later.*

⬛ ATTIC   RESTAURANT $$$$
Las Ramblas, 120   ☎933 02 48 66 www.angrup.com

After a long day along Las Ramblas, Attic provides a soothing world away from the performers, pickpockets, and fanny-packing crowds. Attic has no dress code, but you should really consider changing out of that pit-stained T-shirt and cargo shorts. With over 10 menus of varied price tags to choose from, Attic provides its customers with everything from €29.95 *Ocells* and *Flors* menus to the hefty €65 *Festa* menu. Perch yourself on the rooftop terrace floor overlooking Las Ramblas at dinner for a truly memorable experience.

i Ⓜ*Liceu. On Las Ramblas, toward Pl. Catalonia. Appetizer €4.50-12. Meat entrees €8-14. Fish €10-13.* Ⓩ *Open M-Th 1-4:30pm and 7-11:30pm, F-Sa 1-4:30pm and 7pm-12:30am, Su 1-4:30pm and 7-11:30pm.*

ESCRIBÀ   DESSERT $
Las Ramblas, 83   ☎933 01 60 27 www.escriba.es

Grab a coffee and feast your eyes on any of the colorful and sugary oeuvres patiently awaiting passage to some lucky customer's mouth. With beckoning tarts, croissants, cakes, and rings made of caramel, Escribà tempts even the most devout sugar-avoiders from all four corners of its beautiful *modernista*-style store. If you're not in the mood for sweets or a mug of their killer raspberry hot chocolate, try a savory dish, such as the croissant with blue cheese, caramelized apple, and walnuts (€4.50) or the "bikini" bread mold with ham and brie (€4).

i Ⓜ*Liceu. Walk toward Pl. Catalonia. Escribà is on the left. Sandwiches €3.50. Menú €5.90. Sweets €3-5.* Ⓩ *Open M-Th 1-4pm and 8-11pm, F-Su 1-5pm and 8-11:30pm.*

L'ANTIC BOCOI DEL GÒTIC
CATALAN $$$

Baixada de Viladecols, 3 ☎933 10 50 67 www.bocoi.net

Enter the lair of L'Antic Bocoi del Gòtic, where walls of stone and exposed brick surround patrons with cave-like intimacy. The restaurant specializes in Catalan cuisine, with fresh, seasonal ingredients, and prides itself on bringing new ideas to traditional food. The amicable staff recommends the selection of cheeses and their own take on the *coques de recapte*, a regional dish made of a thin dough with fresh produce and thickly layered meats (€8.50-9).

i Ⓜ*Jaume I. Follow C. Jaume I toward Pl. Sant Jaume, then turn left onto C. Dagueria, which becomes C. dels Lledó, then Baixada de Viladecols. Reservations recommended. Appetizers €7-10. Entrees €10-21.* ⏰ *Open M-Sa 7:30pm-midnight.*

CAFÉ VIENA
SANDWICHES, CAFE $

Las Ramblas, 115 ☎933 17 14 92 www.viena.es

This cafe has earned much renown for a fulsome 2006 *New York Times* article whose author raved for several paragraphs about Viena's *flauta ibèric* (Iberian ham sandwich; €6.60), calling it "the best sandwich I've ever had." The sandwich's secret, which the article's author almost figured out but couldn't quite discern, is that the *flauta* comes on *pa amb tomàquet*, the staple of the Catalan kitchen that involves smearing tomato on bread before seasoning it with salt, pepper, olive oil, and garlic. And it is a damn good sandwich, the sort that melts in your mouth with each bite. Munch away while the piano echoes its tunes from the veranda at this grandiose establishment.

i Ⓜ*Catalunya. Follow Las Ramblas toward the sea. Sandwiches €2.40-9.30 (most under €4). Coffee €1.30-2.40.* ⏰ *Open M-Th 8am-11:30pm, F-Sa 8am-12:30am, Su 8am-11:30pm.*

LA CLANDESTINA
TEA $

Baixada de Viladecols, 2bis ☎933 19 05 33

This is a hidden—dare we say, clandestine?—tea house with the most relaxed atmosphere in all the Barri Gòtic. With an interior of clutter and many-colored walls, this establishment will envelop you in its thick air, fragrant with freshly brewed tea and hookah. The cavernous *teteria* makes for a great place to take a short (or long, if you're feeling real Spanish) reprieve from the frenetic pace of the Gothic Quarter. Everyone from the neighborhood book club to young'uns in their 20s will meet you here.

i Ⓜ*Jaume I. Follow C. Jaume I toward Pl. Sant Jaume, then turn left onto C. Dagueria, which becomes C. dels Lledó, then Baixada de Viladecols. Free Wi-Fi. Sandwiches €4.20-4.40. Tea €2.50-6; pots €10-15. Juices €2.80-3.60. Cash only.* ⏰ *Open M-Th 9am-10pm, F 9am-midnight, Sa 10am-midnight, Su 11am-10pm.*

VEGETALIA
ORGANIC, VEGETARIAN $$

C. dels Escudellers, 54 ☎933 17 33 31 www.restaurantesvegetalia.com

Vegetalia delivers delicious, organic, natural, and environmentally conscious food at reasonable prices. Relax at the bar and chat with the easygoing staff about the ironic history of the Pl. de George Orwell or experience the square for yourself after ordering at the walk-up window. Try the popular bowl of nachos (€5.50) and wash it down a glass of fresh-squeezed lemonade or a soy drink (€2.20).

i Ⓜ*Liceu. Walk down Las Ramblas toward the sea and take a left onto C. dels Escudellers. Organic store in the rear. Free Wi-Fi. Appetizer €5.50-12. Entrees €4-8.80. Desserts €2.50-4.50.* ⏰ *Open daily 11am-11:30pm.*

El Born

EL XAMPANYET
C. de Montcada, 22

TAPAS $$

☎933 19 70 03

Since its founding in 1929, El Xampanyet is as authentic as it gets, with sheep-skin wine bags, an overwhelming selection of *cava*, and old locals spilling out the door and onto the street. Four generations of family ownership has lead to the museum of casks, blackened bottles, and kitschy bottle openers displayed against hand-painted ceramic tiles and topped by large, century-old barrels filled with vintage beer. We recommend that you try the cask-fresh *cerveza* (€3.50) or the house wine *xampanyet* (€2), and pad your stomach with some of the delicious tapas.

i Ⓜ Jaume I. Walk down C. de la Princesa and take a right onto C. de Montcada, toward the Museu Picasso. Xampanyet is on the right before the Placeta Montcada. Tapa €1-13. Beer €3.50. Wine and cava from €2. ⌚ Open daily noon-3:30pm and 7-11pm.

PETRA
C. dels Sombrerers, 13

RESTAURANT $$

☎933 19 99 99

With dark wood, stained glass, Art Nouveau prints, menus pasted onto wine bottles, and chandeliers made of silverware, Petra's eccentric decor will have you expecting any meal to give your wallet liposuction. Luckily, the lively bohemian feel is matched by bohemian prices. Pasta dishes like the rich gnocchi with mushrooms and hazelnut oil (€5.20) and entrees such as the duck with lentils (€7.90) are easy on the wallet, as is the midday *menú* of a main course (varies daily), salad, and wine for €6.60—a true steal and a local favorite.

i Ⓜ Jaume I. Walk down C. de la Princesa and take a right onto C. del Pou de la Cadena. Take an immediate left onto C. de la Barra de Ferro and a right onto C. dels Banys Vells. Petra is located where C. dels Banys Vells ends at C. dels Sombrerers. Menú €6.50. Appetizers €5-7. Entrees €8. ⌚ Open Tu-Sa 1:30-4pm and 9-11:30pm, Su 1:30pm-4pm.

LA BÁSCULA
C. dels Flassaders, 30

CAFE, VEGETARIAN $$

☎933 19 98 66

This working cooperative serves vegetarian sandwiches, *empanadas*, salads, and more—the menu changes daily. Doors laid flat serve as communal tables, and a mixture of art, environmentally-friendly sodas, and protest flyers set this restaurant apart. Though robed in the same antique exterior (complete with a large, warehouse-like entrance) as more expensive places, Báscula provides a more reasonably priced alternative to the upscale eateries. Hours and seating availability may change as the restaurant fights for its right to serve in-house, but takeout is available no matter the outcome. Try the daily special (€8-10) or one of their recommended plates, like the vegetable curry couscous with coconut milk (€8.50).

i Ⓜ Jaume I. Walk down Carrer de la Princesa and take a right onto Carrer dels Flassaders. Entrees and salad €7-9. Sandwiches and soups €4-5. Piadinas €6. Cash only. ⌚ Open W-Sa 1pm-11pm, Su 1-8pm.

LA PARADETA
C. Comercial, 7

SEAFOOD $$$

☎932 68 19 39 www.laparadeta.com

For the highest quality seafood, this hybrid fish market/restaurant is where Barcelona goes. The line often stretches down the ever-under-construction Carrer Comercial, but it's worth the wait to pick out a fresh fish to be cooked to your liking. When they call your number, head up and grab your meal, then sit back down and dig in. The authentic seaworthy feel of this establishment is worth of an ahoy or two, so drop by if you're feeling fresh (fish, that is).

i Ⓜ Jaume I. Follow Carrer Princesa all the way to Carrer del Comerç, then turn right, then left at Carrer Fusina (just before the market). Turn right onto Carrer Comercial. Market prices fluctuate. ⌚ Open Tu-Su 1pm-4pm and 8pm-11:30pm.

barcelona

El Raval

CAN LLUÍS
CATALAN $$$

C. Cera, 49
☎934 41 11 87

Can Lluís? Yes he can! This crowded restaurant has been an El Raval staple since its founding in the 1920s, when this neighborhood was Barcelona's Chinatown. Don't be intimidated by the fact that everyone already knows each other or that you'll almost certainly be spoken to in traditional Catalan. Just remember: *"Què vols?"* ("What do you want?") is your cue to order. Respond with an order of tiny faba beans with cuttlefish (definitely worth the €13.90) for an appetizer and the Monkfish Rounds with Spanish ham (€18.90) for your main dish.

i Ⓜ*Sant Antoni. Follow Ronda Sant Antoni toward Mercat de Sant Antoni, bear left onto Ronda Sant Pau, and then head left onto C. Cera. Appetizers €7.40-16. Entrees €7.90-27. Desserts €3.20-5.50.* 🕐 *Open M-Sa 1:30-4pm and 8:30-11:30pm.*

SOHO
PITA, HOOKAH $

C. Ramelleres, 26

A welcome recent addition to the neighborhood, Soho might be confused for an average eatery given it's lack of flashy interior design. No matter—try the €2 Moroccan tea or the cheap and simple meat and vegetarian options (€2). The whole place feels very impromptu, with menu items written by hand and plenty of exposed plywood, but at prices this low, you can't really complain. There are smaller, more intimate rooms which are perfect for test-driving a hookah (€10) from the set available on the counter at the entrance.

i Ⓜ*Universitat. Walk down C. Tallers and take a right onto C. Ramelleres. Pita and drink €3.50. Cash only.* 🕐 *Open M-Sa 1-10pm.*

JUICY JONES
VEGETARIAN $$

C. l'Hospital, 74
☎934 43 90 82 www.juicyjones.com

Very similar to the kindred Juicy Jones down in the Barri Gotic, this place will give you some great Indian *thali dahl* and curry options as well as an ever present assortment of zumos and smoothies. The liquid landscape of the menu offers one kickin' Banana GoGo smoothie you would be a fool not to try (cacao, banana, soy milk, cane sugar, ice, and coconut shavings (€3.95). If you've ever wondered what M.C. Escher's art would have looked like if he used more color and took more shrooms, the interior will satisfy your curiosity.

i Ⓜ*Liceu. Walk down C. l'Hospital. Juicy Jones is on the right at the corner of C. l'Hospital and C. En Roig, before Rambla del Raval. Tapas €2-4. Sandwiches €3-5. Daily thali plate €6. Menú €8.50.* 🕐 *Open daily 1-11:30pm.*

NARIN
MEDITERRANEAN $

C. Tallers, 80
☎933 01 90 04

Sitting discreetly among the shops and cafes of C. Tallers, Narin is hiding the best baklava (€1) in Barcelona as well as equally scrumptious falafel, shawarma, kebabs, and pita bread combinations. You have to try the chicken and falafel pita, the perfect snack for a hot afternoon. Luckily, beers come cold and cheap (€1.80) for those looking to brave the bar. A tiled dining room provides a reprieve from the buzz of the electric shawarma shaver.

i Ⓜ*Universitat. Walk down C. Tallers. Pita €2.50-4. Durums €3.50-6.50. Main dishes €6-8.* 🕐 *Open M-Sa 1pm-midnight, Su 6pm-midnight.*

L'Eixample

LA RITA
CATALAN $$

C. Aragó, 279
☎934 87 23 76 http://www.grupandilana.com/es/restaurantes/la-rita-restaurantm

La Rita serves traditional Catalan dishes with a twist; the duck with apples, raspberry *coulis*, and mango chutney—you will surely find—go great with just about everything. Though the price is dirt-cheap given the quality and quantity of food off the pricey C. Aragó, the interior is anything but—expect an upscale but relaxed ambience that will make you appreciate the dressy casual clothes you brought instead of the traveler's reusable T-shirt. Try an order of the exquisitely steamed black sausage croquettes with apple sauce (€3.95) or the veal meatballs with cuttlefish (€8.55).

i Ⓜ*Passeig de Gràcia. Walk up Pg. de Gràcia away from Pl. Catalunya and turn right onto C. Aragó. Appetizers €4.70-8.80. Entrees €7-12. Menu (two main courses and dessert) €19.* Ⓓ *Open daily 1-3:45pm and 8:30-11:30pm.*

🏠 **OMEÍA** SYRIAN $$

C. Aragó, 211 ☎934 52 31 79 www.omeia.es

When you're tired of cheap shawarma stands, stop into Omeía for some authentic Middle Eastern fare. Devour an order of their lamb tagines with prunes and almonds (€13) or fill up with one of the traditional Jordanian dishes (€11-13). Pick something you haven't got a chance of pronouncing correctly and hope for the best! And remember that you can't ever go wrong by ordering yogurt with honey (€2.50).

i Ⓜ*Universitat. Walk up C. Aribau to the left of the University building and turn right onto C. Aragó. Appetizers €6-7. Salads €6-6.50. Entrees €7.50-18. Traditional specialties €11-13. Lunch menú €7.50. Coffee €1.10. Wine €1.80-2.* Ⓓ *Open daily 12:30pm-4:30pm and 8pm-midnight.*

Barceloneta

🏠 **BOMBETA** TAPAS $$

C. de la Maquinista, 3 ☎933 19 94 45

A hardy, good old-fashioned tapas bar is personified in this local, nearly oceanfront establishment. Take heed of the warning scrawled above the bar, "*No hablamos inglés, pero hacemos unas bombas cojonudas*"—or, "We don't speak English, but we make ballsy *bombas*." The TV-aggrandized persona of the typical rough 'n' tough Spaniard finds its incarnation in the bar staff. Ask any question, and they will respond with rough Catalan accents and a trusty smile while doggedly assembling your order. Treat yourself to the house *pièce de résistance* known as *bombas* (scrumptious fried potato balls reminiscent of light garlic and onion scents stuffed with perfectly-seasoned, spicy ground beef and topped with an exquisite house sauce; €3.90 for 2).

i Ⓜ*Barceloneta. Walk down Pg. Juan de Borbó (toward the beach) and take a left onto C. Maquinista. Appetizers €3-9.50. Entrees €5-18. Cash only.* Ⓓ *Open daily M-Tu 11am-midnight, Th-Su 11am-midnight.*

🏠 **SOMORROSTRO** SEAFOOD $$$

C. Sant Carles, 11 ☎932 25 00 10 www.restaurantesomorrostro.com

This extraordinary restaurant assembles a new menu every day based on selections from the catch of the day that the young chefs, Jordi Limón and Andrés Gaspar, have selected. Somorrostro is not cheap—its rotating menu of seafood dishes, *paella*, curries, and other dishes runs about €13-20 per entree—but the nighttime *menú* (€15-17) of the chefs' gastronomical experiments is the real treat. Try to beat the lunch and dinner rush by showing up more near the start of each serving session. The *Mostaca Synera* (€5.40) is the perfect starting drink and can be enjoyed as one wistfully gazes at and interprets the old black-and-white French photographs spanning the back wall.

i Ⓜ*Barceloneta. Walk down Plà del Palau over Ronda Litoral, following the harbor. After crossing Litoral, take the 5th left onto C. Sant Carles. Free Wi-Fi. Appetizers €6-14. Entrees €13-20. Weekday lunch buffet €13 per kg. Dinner menu €15-17. Wine €3-6.* Ⓓ *Open M-Sa 8-11:30pm, Su 2-4pm and 8-11:30pm.*

L'ARRÒS *Paella* $$$
Pg. Joan de Borbó, 12 ☎932 21 26 46 www.larros.es

At first glance, L'Arròs ("Rice") appears to be a typical tourist trap, complete with a striped, blue and white canopy beckoning weary travelers into the pleasant shade. Although it may be found along Barceloneta's main beach drag, don't let the uninspired decor and multilingual menu of this *arrocería* fool you. What the restaurant lacks in atmosphere, it wholeheartedly makes up for with its Spanish *paella*, which Barcelona natives claim is some of the best in town. Top if off with soothing Tahiti vanilla ice cream (€5.90) or Syrian Rose Cake with custard, raspberries, and mango sauce (€7.20). Even more reason to smile is the special-diet-friendly menu, which offers mindful options for those lactose/gluten/nut-allergy intolerant.

i ⓂBarceloneta. Walk on Plà del Palau over Ronda Litoral and follow Pg. Joan de Borbó. Appetizers €8.75-19.50. Entrees €8.60-18.50. 🕐 Open daily noon-11:30pm.

BAR BITÁCORA TAPAS $
C. Balboa, 1 ☎933 19 11 10

During the summer months, the seemingly quaint, relaxed aura of this establishment's main room peers into a vibrantly painted, terrace-like back room crammed full of young people who flock from the beach like pigeons for a crunchy chunk of bread. The 10% surcharge to sit amid the Rubik's-cube assortment of colors in the courtyard terrace will give you a more memorable experience. Your respite from the heat and bustle of Barceloneta will be made much more enjoyable by the groovy atmosphere of the terrace room. A cheap but filling daily *menú* (entree with salad and *patatas bravas*, bread, a drink, and dessert; €5) offers travelers a nice cash-saving option; however, should the heat make you super adventurous, you can order a tangy house *Mojito* or *Caipirinha* €5 each) and an order of refreshing and not too heavy *fresas con nata* (strawberries and cream; €3). Kick back with friends and listen to the varied music from all places international echoing throughout the bar's sound system.

i ⓂBarceloneta. Walk down Pg. Joan de Borbó (toward the beach) and take the 1st left after Ronda del Litoral onto Carrer Balboa. Tapas €2.50-8. Sangria €3. Menú del día €5-7. 🕐 Open M-W 10am-midnight, Th-F 10am-2am, Sa noon-2am, Su noon-5pm.

Gràcia

🔲 **UN LUGAR DE GRÀCIA** CATALAN $$
C. Providència, 88 ☎932 19 32 89

Un Lugar de Gràcia has the best-priced and most ample lunch special in the neighborhood by far: any two dishes from the midday *menú*—no distinction between first and second courses, so the very hungry may essentially order two main courses at no extra cost—bread, water or wine, and pudding/dessert for €11.20. The food may be a bit generic, with your typical assortment of pastas, meats, some fish options, and of course tapas; however, they come in great quantity for a steal of a price. For an ultra hearty meal, try the *bife ancho a la parilla de origen argentino*—that's grilled Argentinian flank steak.

i ⓂJoanic. From the metro, follow C. Escorial uphill and take a left onto C. Providència. Entrees €6-11. 🕐 Open M-Th noon-4pm, F-Sa noon-4pm and 8-11pm. Also open for F.C. Barcelona matches.

🔲 **SAMSARA** TAPAS $$
C. Terol, 6 ☎932 85 36 88

Samsara has a long regular menu with some of the best tapas in the neighborhood as well as about a half dozen "*novetats,*" which are daily tapas specials with international twists on customary Catalonian dishes. This restaurant also offers

spain

comfy cushions for its local and foreign customers; low rising communal tables and even lower cushioned ottomans will help you make new, hungry friends.

i ⓜ*Fontana. Head downhill on C. Gran de Gràcia, then turn left onto C. Ros de Olano, which becomes C. Terol. Tapas €1-7.50. Beer €2.20. Wine €3.30-3.50. ⓩ Open M-W 8:30am-1:30am, Th 8:30pm-3am, F 8:30am-3pm, Su 7:30pm-1am.*

LA NENA
CAFE $
C. Ramón y Cajal, 36 ☎932 85 14 76

Welcome to grandma's house! But this was the cool grandma who used to feed you tons of sweets and spoil you as a kid. La Nena has an extensive menu of gourmet hot chocolate, crepes, *bocadillo* sandwiches, and quiches at unbeatable prices. Watch out, you party people—there's a hilarious banner displaying grandma's "no alcohol served here" declaration. This is a great place to slow down and have a *choco brasil* (hot chocolate with a ball of coffee ice cream inside; €4).

i ⓜ*Fontana. Follow C. d'Astúries away from C. Gran de Gràcia and take a right onto C. Torrent de l'Olla. Walk a few blocks and take a left onto C. Ramón y Cajal. Sandwiches €2.50-6. Quiches €6. Pastries €1.20-4. Cash only. May call to reserve. ⓩ Open daily 9am-10pm.*

GAVINA
PIZZA $$
C. Ros de Olano, 17 ☎934 15 74 50

Gavina is Gràcia's most heavenly pizzeria. The gigantic hand coming out of the wall, or the parade of angels encircling the chandelier, are bound to make you feel super holy (and hopefully hungry). You'll probably forget about the rather bulky figurine watching the tables near the door once you try the strawberry cheesecake tart (€4.50). The big draw, though, is neither the impressive kitsch nor desserts but is instead the gigantic, delicious pizzas (€6.50-14). Try the namesake Gavina (potatoes, ham, onion, and mushrooms; €12) or the pizza of the day—but be sure to bring friends or an otherworldly appetite.

i ⓜ*Fontana. From the metro, walk downhill on C. Gran de Gràcia and take a left onto C. Ros de Olano. Pizza €6.50-14. Midday menú W-F €10, includes pizza, dessert, and a drink. Chupitos €2. ⓩ Open M 1pm-4am and 8pm-1am, Tu 7pm-1am, W-Th 1pm-4am and 8pm-1am.*

Montjuïc and Poble Sec

The neighborhood of **Poble Sec** hides a number of good, inexpensive restaurants and bars—perfect for those who don't feel like breaking the bank to eat at a museum cafe up on Montjuïc, or for those looking to explore a lovely neighborhood a bit off the beaten track.

▨ QUIMET I QUIMET
TAPAS, BAR $$
C. Poeta Cabanyes, 25 ☎934 42 31 42

With five generations and 100-plus years of service under its belt, Quimet i Quimet knows what's up. If you're lucky enough to visit this place when it isn't super busy, take a moment to be mesmerized by the massive liquor bottle display lining the establishment's walls. Try the salmon, yogurt, and truffle honey or the bleu cheese with baked red pepper sandwich.

i ⓜ*Paral·lel. Follow Av. Paral·lel away from the water, past the small plaça on the left, then head left up C. Poeta Cabanyes. Tapas €2.50-3.25. Beer €5.75 per bottle. ⓩ Open M-F noon-4pm and 7-10:30pm, Sa and holidays noon-4pm. Closed Aug.*

NIGHTLIFE
Barri Gòtic and Las Ramblas

▨ BARCELONA PIPA CLUB
BAR, CLUB
Pl. Reial, 3 ☎933 02 47 32 www.bpipaclub.com

With pipes from six continents, smoking paraphernalia decorated by Dalí, and an "ethnological museum dedicated to the smoking accessory," the only pipe-re-

barcelona

lated article missing from this club—albeit somewhat appropriately—is René Magritte's *Ceci n'est pas une pipe* ("This is not a pipe."). Despite its cryptic lack of signage and the furtive ambiance of a secret society, the low-lit, amber-colored bar, pool room, and music lounge has a surprisingly high amount of visitors. Take a few puffs as you listen to the retro blues and ragtime tunes.

i ⓜLiceu. *Walk on Las Ramblas toward the water and turn left onto C. Colom to enter Pl. Reial. Pipa Club is an unmarked door to the right of Glaciar Bar. To enter, ring the bottom bell. Rotating selection of tobacco available for sale. Special smoking events. Jazz jam session Su 8:30pm. Beer €4-5. Wine €4-5. Cocktails €7.50-9. Cash only. ⓩ Open daily 11pm-3am.*

▨ HARLEM JAZZ CLUB
JAZZ CLUB, BAR

C. Comtessa de Sobradiel, 8   ☎933 10 07 55 www.harlemjazzclub.es

With live performances nightly and a drink often included in the cover (check the schedule), this is a budget-conscious music lover's paradise. This sophisticated jazz house posts performance schedules on the door, letting you choose whether you'll drop in to hear lovesick English crooning or a saucier Latin flavor. Acts range from funk and soul to Latin jazz, and the crowd is just as varied.

i ⓜLiceu. *Walk toward the water on Las Ramblas and take a left onto C. Ferran, a right onto C. Avinyó, and a left onto C. Comtessa de Sobradiel. Live music usually begins at 10 or 11pm. Calendar of events available online or at the door. Cover €5-6; sometimes includes 1 drink. Beer €3.80. Cocktails €7.80. Cash only. ⓩ Open M 8pm-1am, Tu 8pm-12:30am, W-Th 8pm-1am, F-Sa 8pm-5am, Su 6pm-1am.*

▨ SINCOPA
BAR

C. Avinyò, 35

At night, this music-themed bar—rumored to have once been owned by none other than Manu Chao—plays host to as many nationalities and performers as it has currencies and secondhand instruments on its walls. Of Barri Gòtic's bars, Sincopa undoubtedly sports some of the most colorful decor and clientele. One night, the crowd might be on a chemically-induced "vacation" and chilling to *Dark Side of the Moon*; the next, everyone will be salsa dancing.

i ⓜLiceu. *Walk on Las Ramblas toward the water and take a left onto C. Ferran and a right onto C. d' Avinyò. Beer €2-4. Cocktails €7. Juices €2.50. Cash only. ⓩ Open M-Th 6pm-2:30am, F-Sa 6pm-3am, Su 6pm-2:30am.*

MANCHESTER
BAR

C. Milans, 5   ☎627 73 30 81 www.manchesterbar.com

The names of the drinks posted on the front door—Joy Division, The Cure, Arcade Fire, and many, many more—set a rockin' mood. After passing the spinning turntable at the entrance, you'll see intimate, perfectly dimmed red seating, and gleefully gabbing young people. The happy hour, with €1 Estrella Damms, will have you singing along to "Friday I'm in Love" before the evening's up.

i ⓜLiceu. *Walk toward the water on Las Ramblas and head left onto C. Ferran, right onto C. d'Avinyó, and left onto C. Milans, before C. Ample. Manchester is at the bend in the street. Beer €2-4. Shots from €2.50. Cocktails €6. Cash only. ⓩ Open M-Th 7pm-2:30am, F-Sa 7pm-3:30am, Su 7pm-2:30am. Happy hour daily 7-10pm.*

LAS CUEVAS DEL SORTE
BAR

C. Gignàs, 2   ☎932 95 40 15

The eponymous caves, with miniature stalactites on the ceiling, are filled with alcohol, partygoers, and a subtle earthy scent. Exquisite mosaics crop up in the most unexpected places, including the bathrooms. Seriously, though, it'll be the most aesthetically pleasing potty break you ever take. Downstairs, small tables and another bar surround a disco-balled dance floor, where revelers party on with cocktail in happy hand.

i ⓜLiceu. *Walk toward the water on Las Ramblas and head left onto C. Ferran, right onto C. d'Avinyó, and left onto C. Gignàs. Cocktails €5-7. ⓩ Open M 7pm-2am, W-Su 7pm-2am*

El Born

🏛 EL CASO BORN
C. de Sant Antoni dels Sombrerers, 7

BAR

☎932 69 11 39

This is a quieter alternative for those too cool to bother with the packed houses and inflated prices of nearby Pg. del Born. Cheap drinks tempt travelers, while relaxed seating, a chill crowd, and a drinks menu with cocktails named for the Bourne movies (the name is a pun on *El Caso Bourne*,the Spanish title of *The Bourne Identity*) provide ample reason to start the night here.

i Ⓜ*Jaume I. Walk down C. de la Princesa and take a right onto C. de Montcada. Upon entering Pg. del Born, take a right onto C. dels Sombrerers and then take a right again onto the 1st street on your the, C. de Sant Antoni dels Sombrerers. Cava €1.80. Beer €2. Cocktails €5-7. ⚑ Open Tu-Th 8pm-2am, F-Sa 8pm-3am.*

🏛 LA LUNA
C. Abaixadors, 10

BAR

☎932 95 55 13 www.lalunabcn.com

Another of Barcelona's most beautiful bars, La Luna sits under timeless vaulted brick arches, with dim lighting and mirrors behind the bar making it seem even larger. Comfortable lounge seating in front makes for a good place to camp out and take in the bar's beauty. The tropical mojito (with coconut rum for €7) and the *mojito de fresa* (€7.30), which replaces the lime with strawberries, are both quite popular. Leather upholstery exudes class, so do your best not to show up in basketball shorts and flip-flops.

i Open M-W 6pm-1:30am, Th-F 6pm-2:30am, Sa 1pm-2:30am, Su 1pm-1:30am.

LA FIANNA
C. Manressa, 4

BAR

☎933 15 18 10 www.lafianna.com

A glass partition divides the restaurant and bar, but be prepared to push your way through on weekend nights no matter where you choose to wine or dine. Unlike at other places in the area, finding a seat at the bar is a distinct possibility; getting a spot on one of the comfy couches is another story altogether. Patience pays off with large mojitos (€7) made with special bitters as you gaze upon the Euro-rockin' interior design, super chic furniture, and just the right amount of dim lighting.

i Ⓜ*Jaume I. Walk down Via Laietana and take a left onto C. Manresa. The restaurant is on the right after passing C. de la Nau. All cocktails €4.50 M-Th 6-9pm. Discounted tapas M-Th 7pm-12:30am, F-Sa 7pm-11:30pm, Su 7pm-12:30am. Tapas €2-4.80. Beer €2.50-3.40. Shots €4. Cocktails €6-7. ⚑ Open daily 6pm-midnight.*

EL BORN
Pg. del Born, 26

BAR

☎933 19 53 33

Shed the themes and pretense and stop at El Born for a straight-up bar—no more, no less. Marble tables and green decor provide a simple, no games interior that nonetheless attracts burly jocks, retired dads, and everyone in between attempting who come here to watch the Champions League finals or the French Open (really, whatever's big in Euro sports at the time of your visit). With cheap beer (€2-2.50) and ambient music, it's no wonder this place is always full. Usual patrons are more of the male variety, so ladies should bear that in mind. Some filling options include the *empandas* (€2) or a *sandwich de Milanesa* (€2.90).

i Ⓜ*Jaume I. Walk down C. de la Princesa and take a right onto C. de Montcada. Follow until you hit Pg. del Born and take a left. Free Wi-Fi. Beer €2-2.50. Mixed drinks €6. ⚑ Open Tu-Su 10am-2:30am.*

EL COPETÍN
Pg. del Born, 19

LATIN BAR

☎607 20 21 76

This dance floor just won't quit: Latin beats blare all night long, attracting a laid-back, fun-loving crowd that knows how to move like Shakira. A narrow, tightly

barcelona

packed bar up front provides little reprieve for those who need a drink, as the waitstaff will probably be too busy shakin' anyway to tend to your every beck and call. Most people who come here come prepared to dance.

i Ⓜ*Jaume I. Walk down C. de la Princesa and take a right onto C. de Montcada. Follow to Pg. del Born. Mixed drink €7. 🕐 Open M-Th 6pm-2:30am, F-Sa 6pm-3am, Su 6pm-2:30am.*

BERIMBAU
Pg. del Born, 17

BRAZILIAN BAR
☎646 00 55 40

This *copas* bar, reportedly the oldest Brazilian bar in Spain (founded 1978), offers a range of drinks you won't easily find this side of the Atlantic. Try the *guaraná* with whiskey (€8), an orange and banana juice with vodka (€9.50), or the tried and true (and damn good) caipirinha (€8). Samba and Brazilian electronic music fill the room with a *brasileiro* feel as the wicker furniture and stifling heat complete the scene.

i Ⓜ*Jaume I. Walk down C. de la Princesa and take a right onto C. de Montcada. Follow to Pg. del Born, then turn left. Beer €2.50-3. Cocktails €7-10. 🕐 Open daily 6pm-2:30am.*

CACTUS BAR
Pg. del Born, 30

BAR
☎933 10 63 54 www.cactusbar.cat

Cactus Bar is renowned along Pg. del Born for its big, tasty, and potent mojitos (€8). If you can get a bartender's attention over the clamor, you generally don't need to specify which drink you want; just use your fingers to indicate how many mojitos it'll be. The constant stream—or devastating flood—of customers means the bartenders work as a team, creating a mojito assembly line that churns out over a dozen of the minty beverages at a time. Get your drink in a plastic cup to go instead of the weighty tall glasses and enjoy it on the (slightly) less crowded Pg. del Born right out front. If mainstream doesn't float your boat, try the house gin and tonic—it'll definitely wake you up (€7.50)

i Ⓜ*Jaume I. Walk down C. de la Princesa and take a right onto C. de Montcada. Continue until you hit Pg. del Born, then take a left. DJs M and W. Beer €3. Cocktails €8. Breakfast €3.50-4.50. Sandwiches €2.50-3.70. Tapas €1.80-6.50. 🕐 Open M-Sa noon-2am, Su noon-midnight.*

El Raval

The nightlife in El Raval is mostly centered on the bars on and around **Rambla del Raval** and **Carrer de Joaquin Costa,** though there are a few music clubs dotting the neighborhood as well.

🔲 MARSELLA BAR
C. Sant Pau, 65

BAR
☎934 42 72 63

Enter this amber-colored establishment lined with antique mirrors, cabinets, old advertisements, and ancient liquor bottles that have likely been there since the *modernisme* art form was first invented. The easygoing crowd is loyal to Marsella even after a few absinthes (€5). It may be a bit crowded in here, but it'll be well worth your glass of greenish glow (really, everyone orders one) below the ridiculously ornate chandeliers. Maybe you can even catch a glimpse of some long-past customers' phantoms, like Hemingway, Gaudí, or Picasso.

i Ⓜ*Liceu. Follow C. Sant Pau from Las Ramblas. Beer €3. Mixed drinks €5-6.50. Cash only. 🕐 Open M-Th 11pm-2am, F-Sa 11pm-3am.*

🔲 MOOG
C. Arc del Teatre, 3

CLUB
☎933 19 17 89 www.masimas.com/moog

Buried in the heart of Old Chinatown and long changed since its days of flamenco bohemia, Moog still stands as one of Europe's most important dance clubs, renowned for its electronic music. This club has featured several big name DJs like Robert X, John Acquaviva, and many from the Berlin label Tresor-all. Come inside to experience musical flavors favored by everyone from electronica afi-

spain

cionados to lost souls just trying to find a place to dance and shed some Spanish cuisine-induced pounds the fun way.

i Ⓜ*Drassanes. Walk away from the water on Las Ramblas and turn left onto C. Arc del Teatre. Discount flyers often available on Las Ramblas. Cover €10. ☼ Open daily midnight-5am.*

BAR BIG BANG
BAR,
MUSIC CLUB C. Botella, 7   www.bigbangbcn.com

Sitting in the Ciutat Vella for over 20 years now, Big Bang features everything from jazz to blues to funky swing. Stand up and vaudeville-esque theater are other acts that the crowd can drink to. Out front, customers are serenaded by big band favorites—both local and national—from the stereo and projector screen that have entertained patrons for years.

i Ⓜ*Sant Antoni. Walk down C. Sant Antoni Abad and take a right onto C. Botella. Free Wi-Fi. Schedule of performances and special events on website. Shot €3. Beer €3-4. ☼ Open Tu-Th 10pm-2:30am, Su 10pm-2:30am.*

BETTY FORD'S
BAR
C. Joaquin Costa, 56   ☎933 04 13 68

This ain't your dad's antique Ford, honey. During the earlier hours of the evening, this bar and restaurant stuffs local students with its relatively cheap and famously delicious burgers (€6.50). Happy hour (6-9pm) provides cheap drinks, and later in the night, the place gets packed with a young, noisy crowd that will actually overflow onto the street, so get here early!

i Ⓜ*Universitat. Walk down Ronda de Sant Antoni and take a slight left onto C. Joaquin Costa. Burger €6.50. Shakes €3.50. Mixed drinks €5-6; happy hour drinks €4. Cash only. ☼ Open M 6pm-1:30am, Tu-Th 11am-1:30am, F-Sa 11am-2:30am. Happy hour M-Sa 6-9pm.*

LLETRAFERIT
BAR, BOOKSTORE
C. Joaquin Costa, 43   ☎933 17 81 30

A chillax oasis away from the hectic nightlife of C. Joaquin Costa, Lletraferit (Catalan for "bookworm") offers some respite in the form of cute, colorful drinks and a little bit of literature to accompany your liquid journey. Grab a cocktail (€6-8.50) and settle into a comfy leather armchair or head around to the back, where a cozy library and bookstore awaits you.

i Ⓜ*Universitat. Walk down Ronda de Sant Antoni and take a slight left onto C. Joaquin Costa. Cocktails €5-8.50. Cash only. ☼ Open M-Th 4pm-2:30am, F-Sa 5pm-3am.*

VALHALLA CLUB DE ROCK
BAR, MUSIC CLUB
C. Tallers, 68

Words to our metalhead *Let's Go* readers: get ready to bust out your screamo skills, air guitars, and '80s rock-on hand gestures. Step through the front entrance, and you'll see what is a concert hall some nights and an industrial nightclub on others. It's a haven for those who may gotten tired of the techno at Moog or the eccentricity of Sant Pau 68. Free entry on non-show nights means you can use the cash you save to try the entire selection of *chupitos del rock*, specialty shots named after rock bands from Elvis to Whitesnake (€1). It'll make you holla for Valhalla.

i Ⓜ*Universitat. Walk down C. Tallers. Search for Valhalla Club de Rock on Facebook to find a calendar of concerts and special events. Shot €1-2. Beer €1.50-5. Mixed drinks €6-7. Cash only. ☼ Open daily 6:30pm-2:30am.*

L'Eixample

▨ LES GENTS QUE J'AIME
BAR
C. València, 286 bis   ☎932 15 68 79

Start with a little red velvet. Then add in some sultry jazz and an environment redolent of gin and *modernisme*, and you'll be transported back some 100 years to a *fin-de-siècle* fiesta. Black-and-white photographs, cool R&B, and vintage

barcelona

chandeliers set the mood for you to partake in sinful pleasures. Not sure where to head for the rest of the night? Cozy up next to the palm reader or have your tarot cards read to avoid making the decision yourself.

i Ⓜ*Diagonal. Head downhill on Pg. de Gràcia and turn left onto C. València. Les Gents Que J'aime is downstairs, just past Campechano. Palm reading €25-35) and tarot €20-30) M-Sa. Beer €4.50. Wine €5-10. Cocktails €5-10.* ☼ *Open M-Th 6pm-2:30am, F-Sa 7pm-3am, Su 6pm-2:30am.*

🏯 LA FIRA
C. Provença, 171

CLUB

☎933 23 72 71

Decorated entirely with pieces from the old Apolo Amusement Park in Barcelona and featuring a slightly Latin vibe, this club is like that creepy carnival from *Scooby Doo*, but with a bar instead of a g-g-g-ghooooost. Check out the upgraded Scooby Snax (mojitos €10) as you jam out to top 40 and Latin tracks along with happy club goers.

i Ⓜ*Hospital Clínic. Walk away from the engineering school along C. Rossello and take a right onto C. Villarroel. Take the 1st left onto C. Provença; La Fira is a few blocks down. Often hosts shows or parties, sometimes with entrance fee or 1 drink min. Cover sometimes €10, includes 1 drink. Beer €5. Cocktails €10.* ☼ *Open F-Sa 11pm-5am.*

LUZ DE GAS
C. Muntaner, 246

CLUB, BAR

☎932 09 77 11   www.luzdegas.com

This is one of the most renowned clubs in the city, and with good reason. Imagine that George Clooney bought out the casino he and his crew robbed in *Ocean's 11* and then recruited hot, classy Spaniards to run it. That's Luz de Gas. Red velvet walls, gilded mirrors, and sparkling chandeliers will have you wondering how you possibly got past the bouncer, while the massive, purple-lit dance floor surrounded by multi-colored bars will remind you what you're here for. Big name jazz, blues, and soul performers occasionally take the stage during the evening hours, but after 1am, it turns into your typical *discoteca*. Ritzy youths dance to deafening pop in the lower area, while the upstairs lounge provides a much-needed break for both your feet and ears.

i Ⓜ*Diagonal. Take a left onto Avda. Diagonal and a right onto C. Muntaner. For show listings and times, check the Guía del Ocio or the club's website. Cover €18, includes 1 drink. Beer €7. Cocktails €10.* ☼ *Open Th-Sa 11:30pm-5am.*

ANTILLA
C. Aragó, 141

CLUB

☎934 51 45 64   www.antillasalsa.com

Be careful when entering—this Latin bar and dance club is so full of energy that dancers often turn into Shakira and J. Lo when getting down. You can do it, too, by attending salsa lessons from 10-11pm on Wednesdays at the Escuela de Baile Antilla. Enjoy it all between the palm trees painted on the walls and the Cuban *maracas*, bongos, and cowbells littering the sandy bar.

i Ⓜ*Urgell. Walk along Gran Via de les Corts Catalanes and take a right up C. Comte d'Urgell. Walk 3 blocks and take a left onto C. Aragó. Cover €10, includes 1 drink. Beer €5-10. Cocktails €5-12.* ☼ *Open W 9pm-2am, Th 11pm-5am, F-Sa 11pm-6am, Su 7pm-1am.*

ESPIT CHUPITOS (ARIBAU)
C. Aribau, 77

BAR

Shots, shots, shots—you know the rest. You can get your inner circus freak on here, as many shots involve spectacular sparks of pyromaniacal proportions. Try the Harry Potter, which might literally light up the night. For a good laugh, order the Monica Lewinsky for somebody else and thank us later. Crowd in with everyone who loves to test this location's 45 person max. capacity or grab your drinks and go.

i Ⓜ*Universitat. Walk up C. Aribau to the left of the university building; Espit Chupitos is 4 blocks uphill. Shot €2-4. Cocktails €8.50.* ☼ *Open M-Th 10:30pm-2:30am, F-Sa 10:30pm-3am.*

Barceloneta

⬛ ABSENTA
BAR

Carrer de Sant Carles, 36   ☎932 21 36 38 www.kukcomidas.com/absenta.html

Not for the easily spooked, Absenta is like an episode of *The Twilight Zone* if you were inside the TV looking out while also experiencing a touch of the absinthe-induced hallucination this establishment is so famous for. This local hangout spot is the original Spanish speakeasy. With funky light fixtures and vintage proscriptions against the consumption of the vivid green liquor scolding you from above the bar, you will naughtily sip away at the eponymous absinthe (shot for €4, glass for €7). If the overhanging, life-size pirate fairy statue with a glass of absinthe in one hand does not grab your attention, perhaps the static TV sets with flickering art will. If you're in the mood to munch while lounging at any one of the several tables shy of the bar's entrance, try a house panini with ham or *empanadas de carne* (classic meat turnovers). Maybe the country-style blues playing overhead will let you muster up the courage to order the head mixologist's special 50-60% alcohol house-brew of absinthe.

i ⓜBarceloneta. Walk down Pg. Joan de Borbó toward the beach and take a left onto C. Sant Carles. Beer €2.30. Mixed drinks €7. ☒ Open M 11am-3am, Tu 6pm-3am, W-Sa 11am-3am, Su 11am-2am.

¿KÉ?
BAR

Carrer del Baluard, 54   ☎932 24 15 88

This small bar attracts internationals and provides a calm alternative to the crowded beaches and throbbing basses of the *platja* (not to mention ridiculously comfy bar stools). A Spanish sign that reads "Barcelona's most well-known secret" entitles you to be part of the in-crowd should you make it to this establishment. Frequented by celebrities, artists, and production crews for movies, this bar speaks for itself in all its vivacious, colorful splendor. The clementine-colored chandeliers shed only enough light to see bottles of all hues stacked on the wall or the barrage of dangly trinkets poised throughout the locale. Shelves doubling as upside-down tables, fruit decals along the bar, and a playful group of semi-creepy faces peering down from overhead will have you wondering "*¿Ké?*" as well. Sip on an infusion drink (€1.50), sangria (€5), a cocktail (€6), or a cheap beer (€2.50) as you jeer at the running slideshow of past bar events displayed on the main parlor TV screen. Drunk-fest caught on camera, anyone?

i ⓜBarceloneta. Walk down Pg. Joan de Borbó toward the sea and take a left onto Carrer Sant Carles. Take a left onto Carrer del Baluart once you enter the plaça. Free Wi-Fi. ☒ Open M-Th 11am-2:30am, F 11am-3am, Sa noon-3am.

CATWALK
DISCOTECA

C. Ramón Trias Fargas, 2-4   ☎932 24 07 40 www.clubcatwalk.net

One of Barcelona's most famous clubs, Catwalk has two packed floors of *discoteca*. *Downstairs*, bikini-clad dancers gyrate to house and techno in neon-lit cages while a well-dressed crowd floods the dance floor. Upstairs, club-goers attempt to dance to American hip hop and pop in very close quarters. Dress well if you want to get in—really well if you want to try to get in without paying the cover (this mostly applies to the ladies). Don't bother trying to get the attention of a bartender at the first bar upon entering; there are about six others, and they're all less busy. Don't come before midnight or you'll find yourself awkwardly standing around semi-old people with those one or two guys on the dance floor who are always going a bit too ham.

i ⓜCiutadella/Vila Olímpica. No T-shirts, ripped jeans, or sneakers permitted. Events listed on website. Cover €15-20, includes 1 drink. Beer €7. Mixed drinks €12. ☒ Open Th midnight-5am, F-Sa midnight-6am, Su midnight-5am.

barcelona

OPIUM MAR CLUB, RESTAURANT

Pg. Marítim de la Barceloneta, 34 ☎902 26 74 86 www.opiummar.com

Slick restaurant by day and even slicker club by night, this lavish indoor and outdoor party spot is a favorite in the Barça nightlife scene. Renowned guest DJs spin every Wednesday, but the resident DJs every other night of the week keep the dance floor sweaty and packed, while six bars make sure the party maintains a base level of schwasty. Dress classy and be prepared to encounter the super rich, super sloppy, and super foreign internationals.

i Ⓜ*Ciutadella/Vila Olímpica. Events are listed on the website. Cover €20, includes 1 drink.* ☒ *Restaurant open daily 1pm-1am. Club open M-Th midnight-5am, F-Sa 1-6am, Su midnight-5am.*

Gràcia

🌊 EL RAÏM 1886 BAR

C. Progrès, 48 www.raimbcn.com

A few steps through the cluttered entrance reveals a calm buzz of chatting patrons who come here to unwind after a long week of work. This time capsule of an establishment is a mix of a Catalan bodega and '50s Cuban bar. Established in 1886, it is now a shrine to Cuban music and memorabilia that attracts down-to-earth locals with rum drinks like the incredible mojitos (€6).

i Ⓜ*Fontana. Walk downhill on C. Gran de Gràcia and make a left onto C. Ros de Olano. Walk for about 4 blocks and take a right onto C. Torrent de l'Olla. Take the 4th left onto Siracusa; El Raïm is on the corner at the intersection with C. Progrès. Wine €2. Beer €2.30-3. Shots €2-3.50. Mixed drinks €5.50-7.* ☒ *Open daily 8pm-2:30am.*

🌊 VINILO BAR

C. Matilde, 2 ☎626 46 7 59

Join the locals on the comfy couches while you enjoy simple tapas and whatever is being played from the back monitor, whether it be movies, concerts, or F.C. Barcelona matches. Ponder at what would possess the interior designers to place such a big gramophone next to the bar and then marvel at the local works of art that grace the walls.

i Ⓜ*Fontana. Head downhill on C. Gran de Gràcia, turn left onto Travessera Gràcia, and take the 2nd right onto C. Matilde. Beer €2.50-3.50. Mixed drinks €6.50-7.* ☒ *Open in summer M-Th 8pm-3am, F-Sa 8pm-3:30am, Su 8pm-3am; in winter M-Th 8pm-2am, F-Sa 8pm-3am, Su 8pm-2am.*

🌊 EL CHATELET BAR

C. Torrijos, 54 ☎932 84 95 90

El Chatelet features happens to dish out some of the biggest glasses of liquor *Let's Go* has ever seen. A cozy street corner setting with an adjacent room makes this a rather spacious environment that is nevertheless always crowded with chatty patrons. Big windows give you front row people watching seats that look onto C. Torrijos and C. Perla. Try the *sexopata* panini, composed of avocado, mayo, and that iconic Iberian ham.

i Ⓜ*Fontana. Head downhill on C. Gran de Gràcia and turn left onto C. Montseny. Follow it as it turns into C. Perla and turn right onto C. Torrijos. Beer €2-4. Mojitos €3.50, weekends €5.50. Mixed drinks €6. Panini €3.50-4.50.* ☒ *Open M-Th 6pm-2:30am, F-Sa 6pm-3am, Su 6pm-2:30am.*

ASTROLABI BAR, LIVE MUSIC

C. Martínez de la Rosa, 14

You will actually have fun cramming into this 38-person joint, as the live music this place features daily (starting around 9pm) is excellent. The neat, trinket-filled interior is a cozy scene in which to mingle with the happy patrons who

spain

frequent this place. Try the crowd pleasing *Great Estrella Galicia* (€2.80) as you merrily sing along with the mix of locals and internationals.

i ⓂDiagonal. Take a left onto Pg. de Gràcia, cross Avda. Diagonal, and turn right onto C. Bonavista before Pg. de Gràcia becomes C. Gran de Gràcia. Take a left onto C. Martínez de la Rosa. See Facebook group for special events. Beer €2.50-2.80. Wine from €2. Mixed drinks €6. Cash only. ⏰ Open M-F 8pm-2:30am, Sa-Su 8pm-3am. Live music daily 10pm.

LA CERVERSERA ARTESANA   BAR, BREWERY
C. Sant Agustí, 14   ☎932 37 95 94 www.lacervesera.net

We must admit, it's pretty neat to drink in the only pub in Barcelona that brews its own beer on site. With a huge variety of brews—dark, amber, honey, spiced, chocolate, peppermint, fruit-flavored, and more—there's literally something for any beer-lover. Kick back with friends as F.C. takes on the world from any of the flat screen TVs in this never-too-crowded spot.

i ⓂDiagonal. Head uphill on Pg. de Gràcia and take a right onto C. Corsega, at the round-about where Pg. de Gràcia meets Avda. Diagonal. C. Sant Agustí is the 3rd left. Beers €3.15-4.95. ⏰ Open M-Th 5pm-2am, F 5pm-3am, Sa 6pm-3am, Su 5pm-2am.

OTTO ZUTZ   CLUB
C. Lincoln, 15   ☎932 38 07 22 www.ottozutz.com

Like a multilayered rum cake, this place has three levels of boogie throughout its interior. The levels host DJs of varying musical genres, blasted for all of C. Lincoln to feel until dawn. As you might expect, a crowd of young people jostles around this club at all hours of the night, and as a result, it tends to get pretty hot during the summer months.

i ⓂFontana. Walk along Rambla de Prat and take a left as it dead ends into Via Augusta. Take the 1st right onto C. Laforja and the 1st right again onto C. Lincoln. Cover €10-15; includes 1 drink. Beer €6. Mixed drinks €6-12. ⏰ Open M midnight-6am, W-Sa midnight-6am.

THE SUTTON CLUB   CLUB
C. Tuset, 13   ☎934 14 42 17 www.thesuttonclub.com

Don't even think about showing up in your black gym shorts, Converse sneakers, or light-wash jeans—wear as fine of threads as a traveler can manage. Make your z's sound extra Catalonian when talking to the bouncers, and don't make any sudden movements at the door. Once you're in, though, all bets are off: four bars provide mass quantities of alcohol to a dance floor that gets sloppier as the night goes on. Check online for concerts or special events.

i ⓂDiagonal. Turn left onto Avda. Diagonal, walk about 4 blocks, and turn right onto C. Tuset. Cover €12-18; includes 1 drink. Beer €7. Mixed drinks €10-15. ⏰ Open M-Th 11:30pm-5am.

KGB   CLUB
C. ca l'Alegre de Dalt, 55   ☎932 10 59 06

In Soviet Russia, the club hits you! But seriously folks, you'll be stunned by the varying music genres here, ranging from dubsteb and reggae all the way to top 40. It's small, but the overcrowding is what makes this place awesome. Entrance is free with a flyer; otherwise you'll have to pay €10-15 to join this Party.

i ⓂJoanic. Walk along C. Pi i Maragall and take the 1st left. Cover with 1 drink €10-12, with 2 drinks until 3am €12-16, free with flyer. Beer €4. Mixed drinks €7-10. Cash only. Check online for concert listings. ⏰ Open Th 1am-5am, F-Sa 1am-6am.

CAFÉ DEL SOL   CAFE, BAR
Pl. Sol, 16   ☎932 37 14 48

One of the many tapas bars lining the Pl. del Sol, the Cafe del Sol offers cheap and delicious eats. Tune into the English pop rock sheltered by some subtle, dimmed lighting that makes for a fun soiree. Try the house recommended pumpkin ravioli and funghi sauce or the runny eggs with straw potatoes (€4.50).

i ⓂFontana. Walk downhill on C. Gran de Gràcia, turn left onto C. Ros de Olano, and right onto C. Virtut. Beer €2.80. Mixed drinks €6-7. Tapas €3.50-8.50. Entrees €4-8. ⏰ Open daily 11pm-3am.

barcelona

Montjuïc and Poble Sec

BARCELONA ROUGE CAFÉ
BAR

C. Poeta Cabanyes, 21   ☎934 42 49 85

Just imagine walking into the newest chamber of the Playboy Mansion in all its lusty red glow. Throw in neat albums for sale and a kicking Moscow Mule (vodka, pickle, ginger, lime, and ginger ale), and you have Rouge. With a nice arrangement of leather chairs and a parade of vintage decor (like a shoddy copy of Jan van Eyck's *The Arnolfini Wedding*), this bar creates a sexy environment where a crowd of hip and friendly customers will party with you. If nothing else, you must try the signature Barcelona Rouge, comprised of vodka, berry liquor, lime juice, and shaved ice (€6.50).

i Ⓜ*Paral·lel. With Montjuïc to your left, walk along Avda. Paral·lel. Take a left onto C. Poeta Cabanyes. Rouge Café is on the left, before Mambo Tango Youth Hostel. Free Wi-Fi. Beer €1.50-3. Cocktails €5-7. ☺ Open Th-Sa 9pm-3am.*

MAUMAU
BAR

C. Fontrodona, 35   ☎934 41 80 15 www.maumaunderground.com

The epicenter of Barcelona's underground, Mau Mau is best known for its online guide to art, film, and other hip happenings around the city (quick tip for the pro partier), but this is very much worth the hike up C. Fontrodona. The mega loft graciously doles out upwards of 20 gins and dozens and dozens of mixed drinks with all sorts of funky names, from Dark and Stormy (€8) to the proletarian Moscow Mule (€8). At a place where only the suavest go to socialize in a cool, open space, there isn't even a cover charge to keep you out.

i Ⓜ*Paral·lel. Facing Montjuïc, walk right along Av. Paral·lel and take a left onto C. Fontrodona. Follow the street as it zig-zags; Mau Mau is just a few blocks down. 1-year membership (includes discounts at Mau Mau and at various clubs, bars, and cultural destinations around the city) €12. No cover for visitors. Beer €2-3. Mixed drinks from €6-11. Cocktails €6-8. ☺ Open Th-Sa and festivals 9pm-3am. Other days of the week for special events (see website for details).*

LA TERRRAZZA
CLUB

Avda. Marquès de Comillas, 13   ☎687 96 98 25 www.laterrrazza.com

One of the most popular clubs in Barcelona, La Terrrazza lights up the Poble Espanyol after the artisans and sunburned tourists call it a day. The open-air dance floor floods with many colored lights and humans as soon as the sun goes down. Try any of the mixed drinks (€8-12), all made quicker than you can twerk.

i Ⓜ*Espanya. Head through the Venetian towers and ride the escalators. Follow the signs to Poble Espanyol. Free bus from Pl. Catalunya to club every 20min. 12:20am-3:20am; free bus from Terrrazza to Pl. Catalunya nonstop 5:30am-6:45am. Cover €18, with flyer €15; includes 1 drink. Beer €5-10. ☺ Open F-Sa 12:30am-6am.*

TINTA ROJA
BAR

C. Creu dels Molers, 17   ☎934 43 32 43 www.tintaroja.net

Resulting from an inventive and artsy couple who have perfected a mix of eccentric and authentic, this establishment was been named after the 1941 tango, "Tinta Roja." Out front, you can sample any of their fine alcoholic beverages that use Argentinian *legui* as the main mixing agent. Inside the buzzing grotto, you can observe many of the head manager's impressive artistic. Ten paces away is where his wife gives dance lessons on Wednesdays at 8:30pm. See how well you can bust out some Spanish groove while a tad under the influence.

i Ⓜ*Poble Sec. With Montjuïc to the right, walk along Avda. Paral·lel. Take a right onto C. Creu dels Molers; Tinta Roja is on the left. Tango classes W 8:30-10pm, dance from 10pm-1am. Wine €2.70-3.90. Beer €2.50-5.50. Argentine liqueurs €6.60-7.50. Mixed drinks €7.50. ☺ Open W 8:30am-midnight, Th 8:30pm-2am, F-Sa8:30pm-3am. Hours may change to accommodate special events; check online.*

Tibidabo

Tibidabo—the mountain that rises behind Barcelona—is easily reached by a combination of FGC and tram during the day, but a seriously long uphill hike once trams stop running at 10pm. A cab from Pl. Lesseps to Pl. Doctor Andreu is about €8; from Pl. Catalunya, it's about €13. Once you figure out a safe way to get home, head here for a night of incredible views that seem to twinkle more with every drink.

📷 MIRABLAU   BAR,CLUB
Pl. Doctor Andreu, S/N   ☎934 18 56 67 www.mirablaubcn.com

With easily the best view in Tibidabo—and arguably the best in Barcelona—Mirablau is a favorite with posh internationals and the younger crowd, so dress well. It also happens to be near the mountain's peak, so we only recommend walking up here if you prefer to sip your cocktails while drenched in sweat. The glimmering lights of the metropolis and the bar's quivering candles create a dreamlike aura that earns Mirablau a *Let's Go* thumbpick. If the club is more your style, head downstairs where pretty young things spill out onto the terrace to catch their breath from the crowded dance floor.

i L7 to FGC: Avinguda de Tibidabo. Take the Tramvia Blau up Avda. Tibidabo to Pl. Doctor Andreu. Th-Sa credit card min €4.70. Drinks discounted M-Sa before 11pm, Su before 6pm. Beer and wine €1.80-6. Cocktails €7-9.50. 11am-5:30am. ☺ Open M-Th 11am-4:30am, F-Sa 11am-5:30am

MERBEYÉ   BAR
Pl. Doctor Andreu, 2   ☎934 17 92 79 www.merbeye.net

Merbeyé provides a dim, romantic atmosphere on an outdoor terrace along the cliff. With the lights in the lounge so low that seeing your companion may be a problem, Merbeyé is the perfect place to bring an unattractive date. Smooth jazz serenades throughout, and with just one Merbeyé cocktail (cava, cherry brandy, and Cointreau (€9-10), you'll be buzzed real quick.

i L7 to FGC: Avinguda de Tibidabo. Take the Tramvía Blau up Avda. Tibidabo to Pl. Doctor Andreu. Beer €2.50-4. Cocktails €9-10. Food €2-7.60. 11am-2am. ☺ Open Th 5pm-2am, F-Sa 11am-3am.

ARTS AND CULTURE

Music and Dance

For comprehensive guides to large events and information on cultural activities, contact the **Guía del Ocio** (www.guiadelociobcn.com) or the **Institut de Cultura de Barcelona (ICUB).** (Palau de la Virreina, La Rambla, ☎99933 16 10 00 www.bcn.cat/cultura. ☺ Open daily 10am-8pm.) Should you be super wary and wish to make good use of Spain's awful Wi-Fi services (and test your Catalan skills), check out **www.butxaca. com,** a comprehensive bimonthly calendar with film, music, theater, and art listings, or **www.maumaunderground.com,** which lists local music news, reviews, and events. The website **www.infoconcerts.cat/ca** (available in English) provides even more concert listings. For tickets, check out **ServiCaixa** (☎902 33 22 11 www.servicaixa.com. ☺Located at any branch of the Caixa Catalonia bank. ☺Open M-F 8am-2:30pm), **TelEntrada** (☎902 10 12 12 www.telentrada.com), or **Ticketmaster** (www.ticketmaster.es).

Although a music destination year-round, Barcelona especially perks up during the summer with an influx of touring bands and music festivals. The biggest and baddest of these is the three-day electronic music festival **Sónar** (www.sonar.es), which takes place in mid-June. Sónar attracts internationally renowned DJs, electronica fans, and partiers from all over the world. From mid-June to the end of July, the **Grec** summer festival (http://grec.bcn.cat) hosts international music, theater, and dance at multiple venues throughout the city, while the indie-centric **Primavera Sound** (www. primaverasound.com) at the end of May is also a regional must-see. *Mondo Sonoro* (www.mondosonoro.com) has more information and lists musical happenings across the Spanish-speaking world.

barcelona

RAZZMATAZZ   POBLE NOU

C. Pamplona, 88 and Almogàvers, 122   ☎933 20 82 00 www.salarazzmatazz.com

This massive labyrinth of a converted warehouse hosts popular acts, from reggae to electropop and indie to metal. The massive nightclub complex spans multiple stories in two buildings connected by industrial stairwells and a rooftop walkway. The big room thumps with remixes of current and past top 40 hits, while the smaller rooms upstairs provide more intimate dance spaces. The open-air top floor could be mistaken for a low flying cloud due to the all the smokers bro-ing out here. If there isn't a concert going on, you can still find a young crowd doing the twist (read: grindage) to a DJ onstage.

i ⓜBogatell. Walk down C. Pere IV away from the plaza and take the 1st slight left onto C. Pamplona. Razzmatazz is on the right. Tickets available online through website, TelEntrada, or Ticketmaster. Ticket €10-25.

SALA APOLO   POBLE SEC

C. Nou de la Rambla, 113   ☎934 41 40 01 www.sala-apolo.com

Looking to party but lamenting the fact that it's Monday? Sulk no more—for a number of years, Sala Apolo has been drawing locals to start the week off right with Nasty Mondays, featuring a mix of rock, pop, indie, garage, '80s, typical electro, and a special electronica dubbed "fidget house." In fact, the night is so popular that it has spawned Crappy Tuesdays (indie and electropop). Stop by later in the week when just about anybody and everybody is around, and check the website to see which of the latest indie groups may be rolling through. If you pop in on the right Sunday evening, you may even get to partake in Churros con Chocolate night, which is exactly what it sounds like, plus some dancing.

i Open daily midnight-6am, earlier for concerts and events; check website for schedule and special events.

Festivals

Barcelona loves to party. Although *Let's Go* fully supports the city's festive agenda, we still need to include some nitty-gritty things like accommodations and, you know, food, so we can't possibly list all of the fun annual events. For a full list of what's going on during your visit, stop by the tourist information office. As a teaser, here are a few of the biggest, most student-relevant shindigs.

FESTA DE SANT JORDI   LAS RAMBLAS

Las Ramblas

A more intelligent, civil alternative to Valentine's Day, this festival celebrates both St. George (the **dragon**-slayer and patron saint of Barcelona) and commemorates the deaths of Shakespeare and Cervantes. On this day, Barcelona gathers along Las Ramblas in search of flowers and books to give to lovers.

🗓 Apr 23.

FESTA DE SANT JOAN   BARCELONETA, POBLENOU

The beachfront

These days light a special fire in every pyromaniac's heart as **fireworks,** bonfires, and torches light the city and waterfront in celebration of the coming of summer.

🗓 Night of Jun 23-Jun 24.

BARCELONA PRIDE   CITYWIDE, L'EIXAMPLE

Parade ends in Avda. Maria Cristina, behind Pl.Espanya

This week is the biggest GLBT celebration in the Mediterranean, and Catalunya is no exception. Multiple venues throughout the region take active part in the festival, which culminates with a parade through "Geixample" and a festival.

🗓 Last week of Jun.

FESTA MAJOR

GRÀCIA

Pl. Rius i Taulet (Pl. Vila de Gràcia)

Festa Major is a community festival in Gràcia during which artsy intellectuals put on performances and fun events in preparation for the Assumption of the Virgin. Expect parades, concerts, floats, arts and crafts, live music, dancing, and, of course, parties.

🕐 *End of Aug.*

LA DIADA

EL BORN

C. Fossar de les Moreres

Catalunya's national holiday celebrates the end of the Siege of Barcelona in 1714 as well as the reclaiming of national—whoops, we mean regional—identity after the death of Franco. Parties are thrown, flags are waved, and Estrella Damm is imbibed—lots of Estrella Damm.

🕐 *Sept 11.*

FESTA MERCÈ

CITYWIDE, EL BORN

Pl. Sant Jaume

This massive outpouring of joy for one of Barcelona's patron saints (Our Lady of Mercy) is the city's main annual celebration. More than 600 free performances take place in multiple venues. There is also a **castellers** competition in the Pl. Sant Jaume; competitors attempt to build *castells* (literally "castles," but in this case human towers) several humans high, which small children clad in helmets and courage then attempt to climb.

🕐 *Weeks before and after Sept 24.*

Fútbol

Although Barcelona technically has two *fútbol* teams, **Fútbol Club Barcelona (FCB)** and the **Real Club Deportiu Espanyol de Barcelona (RCD),** you can easily go weeks in the city without hearing mention of the latter. It's impossible to miss the former, though, and with good reason. Besides being a really incredible athletic team, FCB lives up to its motto as "more than a club."

During the years of Francisco Franco, FCB was forced to change its name and crest in order to avoid nationalistic references to Catalunya and thereafter became a rallying point for oppressed Catalan separatists. The original name and crest were reinstated after Franco's fall in 1974, and the team retained its symbolic importance; it's still seen as a sign of democracy, Catalan identity, and regional pride.

This passion is not merely patriotic or altruistic, though—FCB has been one of the best teams in the world in recent years. In 2009, they were the first team to win six out of six major competitions in a single year; in 2010, they won Spain's Super Cup trophy; in 2010 and in 2011, FCB took Spain's La Liga trophy; and in 2011, they beat Manchester United to win the UEFA Champion's League, cementing their status as the best club in the world. Their world-class training facilities (a legacy of the 1992 Olympics) supply many World Cup competitors each year, leaving some Barcelonans annoyed that Catalunya is not permitted to compete as its own nation, much like England, Wales, and Scotland do in the United Kingdom. In fact, Spain's 2010 World Cup victory disappointed much of the Catalonian populous and many die-hard FCB fanatics.

Because FCB fervor is so pervasive, you don't need to head to their stadium, the Camp Nou, to join in the festivities—almost every bar off the tourist track boasts a screen dedicated to their games. Kick back with a brew and be sure not to root for the competition.

barcelona

ESSENTIALS
Practicalities

- **TOURIST OFFICES: Plaça de Catalunya** is the main office, offering free maps and brochures, last-minute booking service for accommodations, currency exchange, and box office. (Pl. de Catalunya, 17S. ☎93 285 38 34 www.barcelonaturisme.com *i* ⓂCatalunya, underground, across from El Corte Inglès. Look for the pillars with the letter "i" on top. ✆ Open daily 8:30am-8:30pm.) **Plaça de Sant Jaume.** (C. Ciutat, 2. ☎93 270 24 29 *i* ⓂJaume I. Follow C. Jaume I to Pl. Sant Jaume. Located in the Ajuntament building on the left. ✆ Open M-F 8:30am-8:30pm, Sa 9am-7pm, Su and holidays 9am-2pm.) **Oficina de Turisme de Barcelona** (Palau Robert, Pg. de Gràcia, 107. ☎93 238 80 91, toll-free in Catalunya ☎012 www.gencat.es/probert *i* ⓂDiagonal. ✆ Open M-Sa 10am-7pm, Su 10am-2:30pm.) **Institut de Cultura de Barcelona (ICUB)** (Palau de la Virreina, Las Ramblas, 99. ☎93 316 10 00 www.bcn.cat/cultura *i* ⓂLiceu. ✆ Open daily 10am-8pm.) **Estació Barcelona-Sants.** (Pl. Països Catalans. ☎90 224 02 02 *i* ⓂSants-Estació. ✆ Open Jun 24-Sept 24 daily 8am-8pm; Sept 25-Jun 23 M-F 8am-8pm, Sa-Su 8am-2pm.)
- **LUGGAGE STORAGE: Estació Barcelona-Sants.** (*i* ⓂSants-Estació. Lockers €3-4.50 per day. ✆ Open daily 5:30am-11pm.) **Estació Nord.** (*i* ⓂArc de Triomf. Max 90 days. Lockers €3.50-5 per day.) **El Prat Airport.** (*i* €3.80-4.90 per day.)
- **GLBT RESOURCES: GLBT tourist guide,** available at the Pl. de Catalunya tourist office, includes a section on GLBT bars, clubs, publications, and more. **GayBarcelona** (www.gaybarcelona.net) and **Infogai** (www.colectiugai.org) have up-to-date info. **Barcelona Pride** (www.pridebarcelona.org/en) has annual activities during the last week of June. **Antinous** specializes in gay and lesbian books and films. (C. Josep Anselm Clavé, 6. ☎93 301 90 70 www.antinouslibros.com *i* ⓂDrassanes. ✆ Open M-F 10:30am-2pm and 5-8:30pm, Sa noon-2pm and 5-8:30pm.)
- **INTERNET ACCESS:** The **Barcelona City Government** (www.bcn.es) offers free Wi-Fi at over 500 locations, including museums, parks, and beaches. **Easy Internet Café** has decent rates and around 300 terminals. (Las Ramblas, 31 ☎93 301 75 07 *i* ⓂLiceu. €2.10 per hr., min. €2; day unlimited pass €7, week €15, month €30. ✆ Open daily 8am-2:30am.) **Easy Internet Café.** (Ronda Universitat, 35 *i* €2 per hr.; day pass €3, week €7, month €15. ✆ Open daily 8am-2:30am.) **Navegaweb.** (Las Ramblas, 88-94. ☎93 318 90 26 nevegabarcelona@terra.es *i* ⓂLiceu. Calls to US €0.20 per min. Internet €2 per hr. ✆ Open M-Th 9am-midnight, F 9am-1am, Sa 9am-2am, Su 9am-midnight.) **BCNet (Internet Gallery Café).** (C. Barra de Ferro, 3 ☎93 268 15 07 www.bornet-bcn.com. *i* ⓂJaume I. €1 per 15min., €3 per hr., 10hr. ticket €20. ✆ Open M-F 10am-11pm, Sa-Su noon-11pm.
- **POST OFFICE:** Pl. Antonio López. ☎93 486 83 02 www.correos.es. *i* ⓂJaume I or ⓂBarceloneta. ✆ Open M-F 8:30am-9:30pm, Sa 8:30am-2pm.
- **POSTAL CODE:** 08001.

Emergency

- **EMERGENCY NUMBERS:** ☎112. **Ambulance:** ☎061.
- **POLICE: Local police:** ☎092. **Mossos d'Esquadra (regional police):** ☎088. **National police:** ☎091. **Tourist police:** Las Ramblas, 43 ☎93 256 24 30 *i* ⓂLiceu. ✆ Open 24hr.
- **LATE-NIGHT PHARMACY:** Rotates. Check any pharmacy window for the nearest on duty or call **Informació de Farmàcies de Guàrdia** (☎010 or ☎93 481 00 60 www.farmaciesdeguardia.com).
- **MEDICAL SERVICES: Hospital Clínic i Provincial.** (C. Villarroel, 170. ☎93 227 54 00 *i* ⓂHospital Clínic. Main entrance at C. Roselló and C. Casanova.) **Hospital de la Santa Creu i**

spain

Sant Pau. (☎93 291 90 00; emergency ☎91 91 91 *i* ⓜGuinardó-Hospital de Sant Pau.)
Hospital del Mar. (Pg. Marítim, 25-29. ☎93 248 30 00 *i* ⓜCiutadella-Vila Olímpica.)

Getting There

By Plane

There are two possible airports you may use to reach Barcelona. The first, **Aeroport del Prat de Llobregat** (BCN; Terminal 1 ☎93 478 47 04, Terminal 2 ☎93 478 05 65), is located slightly closer to the city, though both necessitate bus rides. To get to Pl. Catalunya from the airport, take the **Aérobus** in front of terminals 1 or 2. (☎92 415 60 20 www.aerobusbcn.com *i* €5.30, round-trip ticket valid for 9 days €9.15. ☼ 35-40min.; every 5-20min. to Pl. Catalunya daily 6am-1am; to airport 5:30am-12:10am.) To get to the airport, the **A1** bus goes to Terminal 1 and the **A2** goes to Terminal 2. For early morning flights, the NitBus **N17** runs from Pl. Catalunya to all terminals. (*i* €1.45. ☼ From Pl. Catalunya every 20min. daily 11pm-5am, from airport every 20min. 9:50pm-4:40am.) The **RENFE Rodalies** train is cheaper and usually a bit faster than the Aérobus if you're arriving at Terminal 2. (☎90 224 34 02 www.renfe.es *i* €1.45, free with T10 transfer from Metro. ☼ 20-25min. to Estació Sants, 25-30min. to Pg. de Gràcia; every 30min., from airport 5:40am-11:38pm, from Estació Sants to airport 5:10am-11:09pm.) To reach the train from Terminal 2, take the pedestrian overpass in front of the airport (with your back to the entrance, it's to the left). For those arriving at Terminal 1, there's a shuttle bus outside the terminal that goes to the train station.

The **Aeroport de Girona-Costa Brava** (GRO; ☎90 240 47 04 www.barcelona-girona-airport.com) is located just outside of Girona, a city about 85km to Barcelona's northeast. However, **Ryanair** flights arrive at this airport, so it may be your best bet for getting to Barcelona on the cheap. The **Barcelona Bus** goes from the airport in Girona to Estació d'Autobusos Barcelona Nord. (☎90 236 15 50 www.barcelonabus. com *i* Buses from the airport to Barcelona Nord are timed to match flight arrivals. Buses from Barcelona Nord arrive at Girona Airport approximately 3hr. before flight departures. €12, round-trip €21. ☼ 1hr. 10min.)

By Train

Depending on the destination, trains can be an economical choice. **Estació Barcelona-Sants** (Pl. Països Catalans *i* ⓜSants-Estació) serves most domestic and international traffic, while **Estació de França** (Av. Marqués de l'Argentera *i* ⓜBarceloneta) serves regional destinations and a few international locations. Note that trains often stop before the main stations; check the schedule. **RENFE** (reservations and info ☎ 90 224 02 02; international ☎90 224 34 02 www.renfe.es) runs to Bilbao (€65); Madrid (€118); Sevilla (€143); Valencia (€40-45); and many other destinations in Spain. Trains also travel to Milan (€135 via Girona, Figueres, Perpignan, and Turin); Montpellier (€60); Paris (€146); and Zurich (€136.) via Geneva and Bern. There's a 20% discount on roundtrip tickets, and domestic trains usually have discounts for reservations made more than two weeks in advance. Call or check website for schedules.

By Bus

Buses are often considerably cheaper than the train. The city's main bus terminal is **Estació d'Autobusos Barcelona Nord.** (☎90 226 06 06 www.barcelonanord.com *i* ⓜArc de Triomf or #54 bus.) Buses also depart from **Estació Barcelona-Sants** and the airport. **Sarfa** (ticket office at Ronda Sant Pere, 21 ☎90 230 20 25 www.sarfa.es) is the primary line for regional buses in Catalunya, but **Eurolines** (☎93 265 07 88 www.eurolines.es) also goes to Paris, France (€80) via Lyon and offers a 10% discount to travelers under 26 or over 60. **Alsa** (☎90 242 22 42 www.alsa.es) is Spain's main bus line. Buses go to Bilbao (€43); Madrid (€29-34); Sevilla (€79-90); Valencia (€26-31); and many other Spanish cities.

barcelona

By Ferry

Ferries to the Balearic Islands (Ibiza, Mallorca, and Minorca) leave daily from the port of Barcelona at **Terminal Drassanes** (☎93 324 89 80) and **Terminal Ferry de Barcelona** (☎93 295 91 82 *i* Ⓜ️Drassanes). The most popular ferries are run by **Trasmediterránea** (☎90 245 46 45 www.trasmediterrana.es) in Terminal Drassanes. They go to Ibiza (€90 ⌚ 9hr. 30min.) and Mallorca. (€83. ⌚ 8hr.)

Getting Around

By Metro

The most convenient mode of transportation in Barcelona is the **Metro.** The Metro is actually comprised of three main companies: **Transports Metropolitans de Barcelona** (TMB ☎93 318 70 74 www.tmb.cat), whose logo is an M in a red diamond; **Ferrocarrils de la Generalitat de Catalunya** (FGC ☎93 205 15 15 www.fgc.cat), whose logo is an orange square; and **Tramvia de Barcelona** (Tram ☎90 070 11 81 www.trambcn.com), whose logo is a green square with a white T. The TMB lines are likely the ones you will use most. Thankfully, all three companies are united, along with the bus system and Rodalies train system, under the **Autoritat del Transport Metropolità** (www.atm.cat), which means that you only need one card for all forms of transport, and that you get free transfers. Most Metro lines are identified with an L (L1, L2, etc.), though some FGC lines begin with S, and all Tram lines begin with T. (*i* 1 day €6.20, 10 rides €8.25, 50 rides €33.50, 1 month €51. ⌚ Trains run M-Th 5am-midnight, F 5am-2am, Sa 24hr., Su 5am-midnight.)

By Bus

For journeys to more remote places, the bus may be an important complement to the metro. The **NitBus** is the most important: it runs ▪all night long after the Metro closes. Look for bus lines that begin with an N. Barcelona's tourist office also offers a **tourist bus** (http://bcnshop.barcelonaturisme.com *i* 1 day €23, 2 days €30) that hits major sights and allows riders to hop on and off. Depending on how much you plan to use the route (and how much you fear being spotted on a red double-decker labeled "Tourist Bus"), a pass may be a worthwhile investment.

By Bike, Motorcycle, And Scooter

Motocicletas (scooters, and less frequently motorcycles—*motos* for short) are a common sight in Barcelona, and **bicycles** are also becoming more popular. Many institutions rent *motos*, but you need a valid driver's license recognized in Spain (depends on the company, but this sometimes means an international driver's license as well as a license from your home country) in order to rent one. Many places also offer bike rental. If you will be staying in the city for an extended period, it is possible to buy a bike secondhand (try **www.loquo.com**) or register for **Bicing** (☎90 231 55 31 www.bicing.cat), the municipal red and white bikes located throughout the city.

By Taxi

When other cheaper and more exciting options fail, call **Radio Taxi** (☎93 225 00 00). Taxis generally cruise at all hours; when the green light is on, the cab is free.

sevilla

Welcome to Sevilla, capital of Andalucía and hub of culture for the last 1000 years. Flamenco, bullfighting, and great food make Sevilla just as enticing as Madrid and Barcelona, though its smaller size means it probably won't keep you enthralled for as long. Stroll, explore, gawk, and get clapping—it's flamenco time.

ORIENTATION

Sevilla can be divided into a few loosely separated neighborhoods. Apart from the prominent geographic feature of the canal, which divides the city center from Triana, there are few absolute barriers between Santa Cruz, El Centro, and La Macarena. As a general rule, the area immediately surrounding the Alcázar and Catedral is regarded as Santa Cruz, the Alameda de Hércules is the heart of La Macarena, and the dominant shopping trio of Calle Sierpes, Calle Cuna, and Calle de Velázquez hold strong in El Centro. The divisions aren't merely geographic—Santa Cruz is tourist-filled, El Centro is commercial, La Macarena is a mix of the religious and the reckless, and Triana is slow-paced and mellow. Ultimately, Sevilla is a small, walkable city, making it easy to move from one *barrio* to the next.

Santa Cruz

Santa Cruz is the historic center of Sevilla, featuring its two most exceptional historic landmarks, the **Cathedral** and the **Alcázar.** There's an array of narrow streets that radiate outward and are lined with kitschy tourist shops and ice cream stands, but you'll also find many of the city's classic restaurants, bars, and bodegas here. This area can be difficult to navigate, so stop by the tourist office to pick up a free map. Beyond this nucleus of tightly wound and meandering streets, you'll find the **University and Plaza de España** just a 5min. walk south of the *barrio.* Santa Cruz is also close to the **Prado de San Sebastián park,** 5min. east across Av. de Menéndez Pelayo.

El Centro

Sevilla's commercial center, El Centro is crossed by **Calle Cuna, Calle Sierpes,** and **Calle de Velázquez,** all three of which run parallel from north to south and are packed with international chain stores like Zara and H&M. While perhaps not the most charming part of town, these streets are a great way to navigate from Santa Cruz to the northern part of the city. The cultural center of El Centro is the **Plaza de la Encarnación.** If Sevilla had a Pl. Mayor, this would be it, but this is one of the few cities in Spain that seems to have avoided this lazy naming habit. Pl. de la Encarnación is the site of political protests as well as outdoor concerts and cultural programs sponsored by the city. To the west of El Centro, you'll find **Estación de Autobuses Plaza de Armas,** where buses from within the province of Andalucía arrive.

La Macarena

La Macarena's biggest landmark is the **Alameda de Hércules,** a center for eating, drinking, and clubbing. Radiating outward, you'll find a residential neighborhood with simple shops, markets, the occasional bar, and neighborhood tapas joints. **Calle Feria** runs from north to south and is lined with a number of good restaurants and bars. While La Macarena is quite active at night, the neighborhood is best known as a religious center, with a number of small convents, monasteries, and churches. **Avenida Torneo** and **Calle Resolana** border La Macarena at the west and north, respectively.

El Arenal and Triana

These two neighborhoods sandwich the canal between the **Puente de San Telmo** and **Puente de Triana.** On the eastern side of the canal, El Arenal's main street is **Paseo de Cristóbal Colón,** and its main center is the **Plaza de Armas** at the base of the Puente de Triana. Making your way to "the other side of the tracks," you'll find the neighborhood of Triana. While the main streets, **Avenida de la República Argentina** and **Calle San Jacinto,** are useful landmarks, the layout of Triana is generally much less confusing compared to the rest of Sevilla. Along the water, **Calle Betis** is home to some of the best seafood restaurants and bars in Sevilla, and **Calle de Salado** is lined with inexpensive ethnic restaurants.

sevilla

SIGHTS

Santa Cruz

▩ PLAZA DE ESPAÑA   MONUMENT

Av. de Isabel "la Católica"

Constructed for the Ibero-American Exposition of 1929, this is one of the most impressive examples of Neo-Mudéjar architecture anywhere, a tribute to Spain and its architectural history. The plaza was built as an apology to the nations of the world who had fallen to the violence of Spanish colonialism and is thus constructed in the shape of a heart. But the plaza also does feature some requisite celebration of Spanish history: the seating surrounding the main area is decorated with colorful, handmade tiles honoring Spain's principal cities of Spain, and all major Spanish leaders are preserved in statue form. More interestingly, George Lucas filmed part of *Star Wars Episode II: Attack of the Clones* on the bridges here.

i Directly across Av. de Portugal from the Prado de San Sebastián. Free. ② Open daily 7am-11pm.

CATEDRAL DE SEVILLA   CHURCH

Entrance by Pl. de la Virgen de los Reyes   ☎95 421 49 71 www.catedraldesevilla.es

This isn't just any old church—La Catedral happens to be the world's largest Gothic building and the third-largest cathedral, right behind St. Peter's in the Vatican and St. Paul's in London . The city has historically restricted any construction project from exceeding 100m tall to ensure that La Giralda, the cathedral's tower, remains Sevilla's highest point. La Giralda was originally the minaret of the mosque that formerly occupied this site and was the only portion of the building to survive an earthquake in 1365. The stained glass windows and gold-plated religious scenes that line the interior of the cathedral are worth checking out, as they have a Moorish-Catholic flair that traditional Renaissance churches lack. La Catedral is perhaps best known for holding the remains of Christopher Columbus. The bones of the world's most famous explorer traveled the world after his death, moving from Spain to Santo Domingo to Havana before finding their final resting place in Sevilla in 1902. The lines for tickets here can be absurdly long, so be sure to get in line early.

i Located off Av. de la Constitución next to the Alcázar. €8.50, students €2. ② Open Jul-Aug M-Sa 11am-5pm, Su 9:30am-4pm; Sept-Jun M-Sa 11am-5pm, Su 2:30-6pm.

ALCÁZAR DE SEVILLA   FORTRESS

Patio de Bandera   ☎95 450 23 23 www.patronato-alcazarsevilla.es

Don't stress about getting your black tie back from the dry cleaners before visiting the Alcázar. While it does double as the summer palace for Spanish royalty, you aren't likely to run into them. After the Romans originally constructed the walls here to protect the city, the Moors then expanded them into an all-out fortress to protect against enemy advances on Sevilla. Once the Catholics took over, they converted the fortress into a palace and overcame the awkwardness of being Christian monarchs residing in a Muslim palace. The Alcázar palace features intricate Moorish architecture and lush gardens filled with towering banyan, cyprus, and palm trees.

i Located off the back corner of La Catedral, off Pl. Triunfo €8.50, students 17-25 with ID €2. ② Open Apr-Sept M-Sa 9:30am-7pm; Oct-Mar daily 9:30am-5pm.

UNIVERSIDAD DE SEVILLA   UNIVERSITY

C. San Fernando, 4   ☎95 455 10 00 www.us.es

If every college in the world looked like this, we'd probably have far more architecture majors. The Universidad de Sevilla is the second-largest building in all of Spain and uses every square inch to saturate you with impressive architecture. Tourists can only appreciate the building from the outside, but the stone

get a room!

Let's Go has plenty more recommendations! Visit us at **www.letsgo.com**.

SAMAY SEVILLA HOSTEL HOSTEL $
Av. Menéndez Pelayo, 13 ☎95 521 56 68 www.samayhostels.com

One of the nicest hostels in Santa Cruz, Samay provides all the essentials at great rates. While the retro wallpaper and furniture might be a bit loud, the decor is worth overlooking. The shared bedrooms are clean, comfortable, and larger than those at competing hostels. They come equipped with electronically coded security lockers, fresh towels, and clean en-suite bathrooms with large showers, all of which makes life just a little bit easier. The top floor terrace hosts a steady crowd of night owls who lounge on the hammocks. Samay also offers newly renovated common areas, a kitchen with modern appliances, and an overwhelming slew of entertainment, including free walking tours, tapas tours, and flamenco and *discoteca* nights.

i 7min. up Av. Menéndez Pelayo from Prado de San Sebastián. Free Wi-Fi. Lockers and towels included. 8-bed dorm €15; 6-bed €18; 4-bed €20. ⏰ Reception 24hr.

courtyards lined with statues of religious and historic Spanish figures are open to all those who wish to read, write, or take a *siesta* in one of them. If you think you're too cool for school, consider the university's rebellious history. Originally built as a tobacco factory, the establishment once employed the "deadly sexy" Carmen, namesake of the famous opera.

i Down the block from Prado de San Sebastián. Free. ⏰ Open M-Sa 7am-9:45pm.

El Centro

MUSEO DEL BAILE FLAMENCO MUSEUM
C. de Manuel Rojas Marcos, 3 ☎95 434 03 11 www.museoflamenco.com

This museum is the one-stop shop for all things flamenco. Walking through the halls of this high-tech museum, you'll be bombarded with movies, photography, and artifacts explaining the rich history of Sevilla's most famous art form. The focus of the museum is more aimed at capturing the style of flamenco than giving you a factual history of the art. Although the €8 student price is still a little steep for such a small museum (you'll spend at most 30min. here), you'll come out with a sense of the passion and soul of flamenco. The museum also offers live flamenco performances in the evenings.

i From La Catedral, take C. Argote de Molina, turn left onto C. Estrella, then left onto C. de Manuel Rojas Marcos; the museum is on the right. Exhibits in English and Spanish. Performers teach a 20min. class that is open to the public €10, students €8. Flamenco performances M-Th €15, students €12; F-Sa €23/20. Classes €10, students €8. ⏰ Museum open daily 10am-7pm. Flamenco performances M-Sa 7pm. Flamenco classes M-Th 6:30pm.

MUSEO DE BELLAS ARTES MUSEUM
Pl. del Museo, 9 ☎95 478 65 00 www.museodeandalucia.es

The most user-friendly art museum you'll ever encounter, the Museo de Bellas Artes is organized chronologically. Starting in the medieval period and progressing to the 20th century, the museum devotes entire rooms to its favorite artists, including Bartolomé Esteban Murillo, Valdés Leal, and Francisco de Zurbarán. Interesting tidbit: Diego Velazquez (legendary painter of *Las Meninas*) is the LeBron James of the 17th-century art world. Velazquez was originally from Seville but took his talents to Madrid instead. Sevillians were quite bitter about

sevilla

this, and as such, they focused their art history on remembering more "loyal" (but less talented) artists such as Murillo, who has a plaza in town named after him. Sevilla is not quite the art museum superpower that Madrid and Barcelona are, but Museo de Bellas Artes is still a great place to get a taste of Spanish art if the other cities aren't on your itinerary.

i *At the intersection of C. de Alfonso XII and C. San Vicente. Locker €1. €1.50, EU citizens free.* 🕙 *Open Jun-Sept 15 Tu-Sa 9am-3:30pm, Su 10am-5pm; Sept 16-May Tu-Sa 10am-8:30pm, Su 10am-5pm.*

La Macarena

BASÍLICA DE SANTA MARÍA DE LA ESPERANZA MACARENA AND HERMANDAD DE LA MACARENA MUSEUM
CHURCH, MUSEUM

C. Bécquer 1 and 3 ☎95 490 18 00 www.hermandaddelamacarena.es

It's hard being a church in Seville. You'll always pale in comparison to the grandeur of the Cathedral of Seville. But the Basílica de la Macarena does have one thing that makes it stand out: aliens. Just kidding. But almost as cool, this church is the home to a secret society. The Hermandad de la Macarena is a 400-year-old Catholic brotherhood that dresses in ominous black robes and leads an annual procession through the city during Semana Santa (Holy Week), just before Easter. This semi-secret brotherhood has had a fraught history with the Catholic church and was denied legitimacy for centuries. With the popularization of Semana Santa in the 20th century, the brotherhood's procession on the eve of Good Friday has become one of the most anticipated events of the year. While the underwhelming architecture of the basilica itself may not justify the 30min. walk north from the central Santa Cruz neighborhood, the clear attraction here is the museum next door, which gives you a full history of Semana Santa and the peculiar story of this brotherhood.

i *At the intersection of C. San Luis and C. Resolana; the entrance is on C. Resolana. La Macarena should not be confused with "The Macarena," a festive dance that you mastered at the age of 10. Basilica free. Museum €5, under 16 €4.* 🕙 *Basilica open M-Sa 9am-2pm and 5-9pm, Su 9am-2pm and 5-9:30pm. Mass M-F 9am, 11:30am, 8pm, and 8:30pm; Sa 9am and 8pm; Su 10:15am, 12:15om, and 8pm. Museum open daily 9am-1:30pm and 5-8:30pm.*

BASÍLICA DE SAN LORENZO Y JESÚS DEL GRAN PODER
CHURCH

Pl. de San Lorenzo, 13 ☎95 491 56 86 www.gran-poder.es

This church combo is one of the most ornate and impressive around (but second obviously to the Cathedral of Seville). When facing the duo, the Basílica de San Lorenzo is on the left, filled with frescoes, gilded artwork, and glistening altars. On the right, the Basílica de Jesús del Gran Poder stays true to its name—it's one powerful place (*"Gran Poder"* = great power). The entirely marble, circular main room pales in comparison to the massive altar in the center. The tall golden statue of Jesus adorned with purple robes and carrying the cross is the basilica's main attraction. People from all over line up to pass behind the statue, kissing its ankle and saying a quick prayer—just be sure not to leave any lipstick stains.

i *From Alameda de Hércules, take C. Santa Ana and turn left onto C. Santa Clara; the plaza and churches are on the right. Free.* 🕙 *Basilica open M-Th 8am-1:30pm and 6-9pm, F 7:30am-10pm, Sa-Su 8am-2pm and 6-9pm. Mass M-F 9:30am, 10:30am, 7:30pm, and 8:30pm; Sa 9:30am, 10:30am, 1:15pm, 7:30pm, and 8:30pm; Su 9:30am, 11am, 12:30pm, 1:30pm, 7:30pm, and 8:30pm.*

CONVENTO DE SANTA PAULA
MUSEUM, CONVENT

C. Santa Paula, 11 ☎95 453 63 30 www.santapaula.es

While you may feel like you're sneaking into the land of Oz when you ring the bell at the tiny door of this convent, the sight of the nuns instead of munchkins will bring you back to Earth. You can visit the small museum (€3) and browse the meager collection of artifacts stored in this 15th-century establishment. While none of the items are labeled, a nun will guide you on a private tour through the three museum rooms, pointing out all of her favorites. This is the kind of attention you just don't get at that tourist-filled, Gothic beast downtown. Your friendly nun may take you to the gift shop downstairs, where they sell home-made marmalade.

i Located near C. Siete Dolores de Nuestra Señora, beside Pl. Santa Isabel and Iglesia San Marcos. Tour €3. Small marmalade €3; large €4.40. ☒ Museum open Tu-Su 10am-1pm. Shop open Tu-Su 10am-1:30pm and 4:30-7pm.

El Arenal and Triana

PLAZA DE TOROS DE MAESTRANZA

MONUMENT

Paseo de Cristóbal Colón, 12 ☎95 421 03 15 www.realmaestranza.com

Constructed between 1761 and 1881, the Maestranza is one of the oldest bull-fighting rings in the world, older even than Ventas in Madrid. The Maestranza offers a tour of the ring, stables, and museum (conducted in both English and Spanish) that will leave you feeling like a true master of almost three centuries of bullfighting history. The museum, full of 18th- to 20th-century bullfighting paintings, features some surprisingly famous names for a little museum, including Goya and Velazquez (the latter of whom was originally from Seville). The bullfights themselves offer a true taste of Sevillian and Spanish culture. Outside the Feria de Abril, when the best matadors are in town, you should be able to grab a ticket the day of or even hours before a fight.

i Off Paseo de Cristóbal Colón between Pl. de Armas and Torre de Oro. Tours €6.50, students €4. Tickets €15-150. Cash only. Visit www.plazadetorosdelamaestranza.com or buy in person at the stadium ticket window. ☒ Museum open May-Oct daily 9:30am-8pm; Nov-Apr 9:30am-7pm. 40min. tours every 20min. Bullfights Apr-Oct on select Su at 7 and 7:30pm.

TORRE DEL ORO

MUSEUM, VIEW

Paseo de Cristóbal Colón ☎95 422 24 19

While it may no longer be filled with gold (sorry to burst your bubble), the Torre del Oro is still worth a visit. The interior of the tower functions as a modest maritime and naval museum. It's surprisingly interesting, too; you can see cannonballs, old diving suits, and other cool stuff items that will help you imagine the good ol' pirate days. But even if you come for some history, you'll stay for the views. Climb the spiraling marble stairs to the top of the tower, and you'll be able to see all of Triana to one side of the canal and great views of La Catedral and Alcázar toward Santa Cruz. You might be huffing a little bit after the 92 steps; all those *siestas* and *cervezas* don't exactly help you stay fit.

i On the canal side of the street at the intersection of Paseo de Cristóbal Colón and C. Almirante Lobo. €2, students and Tu free. ☒ Open Tu-F 9:30am-1:30pm, Sa-Su 10:30am-1:30pm.

Near Estación Plaza de Armas

CENTRO ANDALUZ DE ARTE CONTEMPORÁNEO

MUSEUM

Av. Américo Vespucio, 2 ☎95 503 70 70 www.caac.es

While most modern art museums are housed in contemporary, sleek cages of light and glass (looking at you, Reina Sofía), this center of modern art is tucked in a historic Moorish monastery. You'll half-expect to be greeted with Alcazar-like Muslim chambers, but instead, you'll find bright white walls and multi-media art collections. The small permanent collection primarily features Andalusian artists of the last 50 years, while the temporary exhibits feature prominent artists from around the world. The museum's aim is to connect local movements in Andalusian art to the international scene. From projected films and slideshows to simple audio installations, the museum features an incredible

sevilla

diversity of artistic mediums. And while the museum looks far away on the map, it's really just a short walk from the city center.

i About 10min. from Estación Pl. de Armas. Cross Puente de la Cartuja and make a right. Alternatively, take bus #C1 or C2. Tours available; reserve a spot in advance by phone (☎95 503 70 96) or email (educ.caac@juntdeandalucia.es). Museum €3; free all day Tu, W-F 7-9pm, all day Sa. Cash only. ☒ Open Tu-Sa 11am-9pm, Su 11am-4pm. Tours Su 12:30pm.

THE GREAT OUTDOORS

PARQUE NACIONAL DE DOÑANA
NATIONAL PARK

A-483, km. 37.5   ☎95 943 04 32 http://reddeparquesnacionales.mma.es

One of the largest national parks in all of Europe, Parque Doñana covers a significant portion of the coastal territory of Andalucía. The park itself is bordered by three cities (Huelva, Cádiz, and Sevilla) and spans multiple ecosystems: forest, marshland, dunes, bush, and beach. The national park offers a sweeping tour of these environments in a 4x4 Jeepthat can be described as "safari lite"—you're probably not going to see that stampede of buffalo get mauled by lions the way you've always wanted to, but you will absolutely see some stunning natural habitats and one of Spain's only stretches of untouched coastland. The tour guides will likely provide the disclaimer that you might not see any animals, but we'd be shocked if you went the whole tour without seeing anything with a heartbeat. Common species include red deer, African migratory birds, and pink flamingos. While few visitors get the chance to see the elusive Iberian lynx or eagle, both of which are endangered, this excursion will take you through the highlight reel of the park. If you're Bear Grylls, they also allow free entry for unguided hiking routes through the park (camera crew not included).

i From Estación Pl. de Armas, take a 1½hr. bus to Matalascañas €6.70), then take a 20min. bus to El Rocío/El Almonte €1.20) and get off at "El Rocío." The visitor center for excursions to the park is to the left of the main church at El Rocío. Tours in Spanish. Advance reservations are required and can be made online (www.donanavisitas.es) or by phone (☎95 942 04 32). Excursion through the park by van and bus €29.50; excursions are 4hr. Cash only. ☒ Open May to mid-Sept M-Sa 8:30am-5pm; mid-Sept to Apr Tu-Su 8:30am-5pm.

FOOD

Santa Cruz

TABERNA COLONIALES
ANDALUSIAN, TAPAS $$

Pl. Cristo de Burgos, 19   ☎95 450 11 37 www.tabernacoloniales.es

Locals love this place because it serves affordable, tasty Andalusian tapas like *pollo con salsa de almendras* (chicken with almond sauce; €2.50) and fried cod (€2), as well as traditional country bread platters called *tablas* (€5.10-11). Each helping is like tapas on steroids, piled onto a slice of toast and topped with traditional cheeses, meats, and spreads. Luckily, Taberna Coloniales has added two new locations toease the congestion, but if you can, it's worth it to check out the original on the beautiful Pl. Cristo de Burgos.

i On the southwest corner of Pl. de Burgos. From Pl. de la Encarnación, head south and turn left onto C. Imagen. Stay on C. Imagen for 3 blocks to Pl. Cristo de Burgos. Other locations at C. Fernández y Gonzáles, 36-38 and C. Chaves Nogales, 7. Plates €1.60-3.60. Tablas €5-11. ☒ Open daily 1:30-4:30pm and 8:30pm-12:15am.

HORNO DE SAN BUENAVENTURA
SPANISH, CAFE $$

Pl. de la Alfalfa, 9   ☎95 422 35 42

Between the heat and the general fatigue of sightseeing in Santa Cruz, Horno de San Buenaventura is a good place to cool off. This restaurant/cafe/bakery claims to have been established in 1385, making it only slightly younger than the world's largest Gothic building across the street. They provide any and all midday refreshments, from gelato (€2-3) to gazpacho (€4.50). While they also have a small tapas menu and €8 combination plates, the focus here is on the standard selection of pastries.

i Across Av. de Constitución from the cathedral. Pastries €1-3. Tapas €2.30-4.50. ✪ Open daily 8am-11pm.

El Centro

EL RINCONCILLO
C. Gerona, 40

ANDALUSIAN, TAPAS $$
☎95 422 31 83 www.elrinconcillo.es

Opened in 1670, El Rinconcillo is the oldest tapas bar in Sevilla, and the tiled walls and warm lighting are clear relics of its historic past. El Rinconcillo's staff are such pros that they manage to keep tabs chalked on the bar without getting a speck of white powder on their uniforms. Ask anyone for the house special, and they'll tell you to try the *pavia*—deep fried *bacalao* (cod) served straight from the fryer. The other clear favorite is the *espinacas con garbanzos* (spinach stewed with chickpeas; €2).

i From Pl. de Ponce de León, C. Gerona is a tiny street behind Iglesia Santa Catalina. Tapas €1.80-2.80. ✪ Open daily 1pm-1:30am.

LA BODEGA DE LA ALFALFA
C. Alfalfa, 4

ANDALUSIAN, TAPAS $$
☎95 422 73 62

La Bodega offers the tastiest traditional tapas around, with a huge selection of Andalusian and Sevillian delicacies. Located just off Pl. de Alfalfa, locals are constantly spilling into the spacious, cafe-like interior. The Andulusian favorite,"grandma-style cod" (€2.20), is as good as any in the city. All the tapas are generously portioned and low-priced; grab two slices of *solomillo* cooked in *moztaza* sauce, served over a bed of fried potatoes for only €2.20.

i Located right off Pl. de Alfalfa at the base of C. Alfalfa. Tapa €2-3. Entrees €7-12. ✪ Open daily 12:30-4pm and 8pm-midnight.

HABANITA
C. Golfo, 3

INTERNATIONAL, VEGETARIAN $$
☎60 671 64 56 www.habanita.es

Sevillan cuisine, with its bread and fried meat, probably isn't loved by vegetarians. Luckily, there's Habanita. This restaurant offers a flurry of health-conscious, vegetarian-friendly options with an international flair. A large portion of the menu is dedicated to Caribbean meals, like fried yucca, honey rum, and fufu with black beans.

i From Pl. Alfalfa, exit the far right corner and follow the L-shaped bend and make a quick left onto C. Pérez Galdós. Follow C. Pérez Galdós for a few meters; C. Golfo is on the right. ½ portions €4.20-8.30. Entrees €6-14. Cocktails €4.50-5.80. ✪ Open daily 12:30-4:30pm and 8pm-12:30am.

La Macarena

ESLAVA
C. Eslava, 5

TAPAS $$
☎95 490 65 68 www.restauranteeslava.es

Though just over 20 years old, Eslava is already a Sevilla institution. Eslava is famous among locals for offering an ever-changing chalkboard menu, updated daily to reflect what's currently most fresh and delicious. The menu is rooted in traditional Andalusian recipes, but the chefs are willing to experiment. Dishes like the over-easy egg (served on top of a mushroom cake, with mushroom emulsion and honey (€2.20) have brought serious accolades to the restaurant, including the 2010 Best Tapa of the Year. Other menu items are wonderfully simple, such as the *costillas a la miel* (pork ribs barbecued in honey; €2.20) and a good selection of market-fresh seafood (€12-17). The sit-down restaurant in

sevilla

back is a bit more pricey, but it is easy to eat on the cheap at the bar or outside on the sidewalk, where all tapas cost €2-3.

i *Take C. Santa Ana from the Alameda de Hércules and turn left onto C. Santa Clara. The restaurant is in back of the church of Santa Clara. Drinks €1-2. Ⓩ Restaurant open daily 1-4pm and 9-11pm. Bar open daily 12:30-4:30pm and 7:30pm-midnight.*

CASA PACO
Alameda de Hércules, 23

ANDALUSIAN $$
☎95 490 01 48

While Casa Paco serves an array of classic Sevillian dishes, from *salmorejo* (a chilled soup similar to gazpacho; €2.50) to *carrillada* (pig's cheek; €3.50), its general ambiance offers a nice break from your typical dive-y tapas bar. The prices are a little higher than the competition, but house specialties are clearly worth it. The best dishes come straight from the oven, such as the *queso de cabra* (goat cheese; €4), *solomillo al mostaza* (pork tenderloin roasted in mustard; €3.50), *revuelto de papas* (scrambled eggs with potatoes; €2.50), and the house specialty, *bacalao gratinado* (cod baked with artichoke, peppers, lemon, and olive oil; €4). The alfresco seating along Alameda de Hércules is fantastic, and the beer selection is impressive.

i *On the southwest corner of Alameda de Hércules. Tapas €2.50-4. Entrees €7-12. Wine and beer €1.50-2.50. Ⓩ Open daily 1-4pm and 8:30pm-midnight.*

El Arenal and Triana

📍 FARO DE TRIANA
Puente Isabel II (Puente de Triana)

ANDALUSIAN, SEAFOOD $$$
☎95 433 61 92

Faro de Triana has prime real estate in Triana. This little, two-story yellow house is located literally right next to the bridge and just a stone's throw from the river. Most of the seating is on the outside terrace or on the rooftop. Either way, you're guaranteed a brilliant view of the river as you chow down on some fresh seafood. The heaping half portions are large enough to fill you up and maybe even take you out of commission for your next meal. While this is unquestionably a seafood restaurant, one of the most popular platters is the *solomillo de cerdo con pimientos* (pork tenderloin grilled with peppers; €15).

i *Immediately to the left once you cross Puente de Triana. Ⓩ Open M-Th 8am-12:30am, Sa 9am-1am, Su 9am-1am.*

BLANCA PALOMA
C. San Jacinto, 49

TAPAS, SEAFOOD $$
☎95 433 36 40

Blanca Paloma is an unassuming locals' bar just a few blocks down San Jacinto from the canal. Seafood is the specialty in Triana, but the traditional Andalucian dishes using fresh market seafood can be a little bit pricey. Still, some dishes, like the platters of *boquerones fritos* (fresh anchovies fried with lemon and olive oil; €6), are cheap and popular.

i *At the intersection of San Jacinto and C. Pagés del Corro. On the far right corner if coming from Puente de Triana. Tapas €1.80-3. ½ portions €5.40-9, full €9-15. Ⓩ Open M-F 8:30am-5:30pm and 7pm-midnight, Sa 12:30-4:30pm and 8:30pm-12:30am, Su 8:30am-4:30pm and 7pm-midnight.*

NIGHTLIFE
Santa Cruz

BAR ALFALFA
C. Candilejo, 1

BAR
☎95 422 23 44 baralfalfa@hotmail.com

The plaza's namesake bar anchors Pl. Alfalfa's popularity as a place for some post-dinner drinks. With the feel of a cozy traditional tavern, Bar Alfalfa continues to attract Sevilla's 20-somethings for early evening drinks and tapas. The

spain

food and drinks here are a joint Spanish and Italian effort, with an extensive list of wines from both countries and tapas that use the best Iberian and Mediterranean ingredients. There's a simple food menu featuring some classic Spanish tapas on bruschetta, but Bar Alfalfa's drink offerings are more numerous and include simple cocktails, beer, and a list of affordable wines by the glass.

i At the tip of Pl. Alfalfa, off C. Alfalfa. Drink €1.60 €2.80. Bruschetta €2.30 €2.90. ☼ Open daily noon-4pm and 8pm-12:30am.

ANTIGÜEDADES

BAR

C. Argote de Molina, 40   www.tapearensevilla.com

Stepping into Antigüedades, you may be a little confused as to whether you're in a bar or a Halloween shop. With mannequins dressed as clowns lining the walls and fake, bloodied hands and feet adorning the ceiling, you'll probably love this bar if your favorite character in *Toy Story* was Sid. And if you're not a creepy weirdo, maybe you'll dig the Spanish covers of '80s American hits (*"Vídeo mató a la estrella de radio,"* anyone?) or the equally scary mashups of classic Spanish songs and American hip hop. And if none of that sounds appealing, you'll probably just scratch your head and wonder why this place exists. In any case, the calm terrace seating just north of La Catedral is a convenient stop for an evening drink.

i Just north of the cathedral. From Pl. Virgen de los Reyes, take C. Placentines to C. Argote de Molina; the bar is on the left. Wine and beer €2. Cocktails €6. Pitchers €12. ☼ Open daily 5pm-3am. Terrace seating closes at 1am.

La Macarena and West

◈ THEATRO ANTIQUE

CLUB

C. Matemáticos Pastor y Castro   ☎95 446 22 07 www.antiquetheatro.com

Floor space that sprawls to 2500 sq. m, a 1400-person capacity, three outdoor bars, and a swimming pool? We don't want to get you all flustered with the math, but the Theatro Antique is definitely the biggest, most over-the-top club in Sevilla. This upscale club is the place to see and be seen, catering to a few famous faces and thousands of trendsters looking for the snazziest evening around. You'll hear the booming music from all the way across the river, putting some of the smaller clubs along the Torneo to shame. In the summer, take relaxation to a whole new level by sitting around the pool on the Aqua Antique patio in your personal cabana while hanging with friends and sipping your caipirinha (€8). This is a high end club, so dress accordingly: lose the muscle tank and throw on some slacks, a going-out shirt, and a good pair of shoes. Without the proper attire, you may have trouble getting in.

i From Alameda de Hércules, take C. Calatrava and cross the bridge; the club is on the left. Call in advance to determine cover. Beer €4. Sangria €6. ☼ Open in summer Tu-Su midnight-7am; in winter Th-Sa midnight-7am.

BODEGA VIZCAÍNO

BAR

C. Feria, 27   ☎95 438 60 57

Bodega Vizcaíno is unapologetic about its dive-bar status. You can expect the tiled floor to be littered with crushed peanut shells and dirty napkins, which is a point of pride for Spanish bars—it marks the popularity of a place to grab some cheap beers. There are only a few spare stools and tables available, so most people just take their drinks and drift out onto the sidewalk to enjoy the cool Sevilla evening. While the place is usually buzzing with a younger crowd come 9:30pm, if you stop by at midday you can expect plenty of scruffy, middle-aged men taking a break from the heat with a cold beer.

i Near the intersection of C. Feria and C. Correduría. Cash only. Beer €1.10. House wine €1.30. ☼ Open M-Sa 8am-11:30pm.

sevilla

BOSQUE ANIMADO   BAR
C. Arias Montano, 5   ☎95 491 68 62

Escape the noisy, crowded patios of the Alameda de Hércules and experience
the relief of this fairytale forest-themed cave. This place is a gay-friendly bar as
much as it is a hetero-friendly bar, filled with both attractive men and women of
all orientations. With your *cubata* (rum or whiskey and Coke; €6) in hand, grab
any seat at the bar (aside from the one at the corner—it's permanently occupied
by a gnome statue, Bosque Animado's signature denizen). Filled with a mix of
20- and 30-something locals, this is a great place to enjoy mellow music in the
early evening before moving on to one of La Macarena's few late-night options.

i On the left-hand side of a small street branching west off the Alameda de Hércules between C.
Recreo and C. Santa Ana. Beer €1.50-2.50. Cocktails €6. ☒ Open daily 4pm-2am.

El Arenal and Triana

▨ KUDÉTA CAFE CHILLOUT DISCOTECA (BUDDHA)   CLUB
Pl. de la Legión   ☎95 408 90 95 www.kudetasevilla.es

Who came up with the name "Kudéta"? Although it's the official name of the
club, most people know this place by the catchier, more appropriate name "Buddha." This place rocks a low-key Asian theme, with plush red couches, hanging
red Chinese lanterns, silky drapes, and pictures of Siddhartha. But make no
mistake: this isn't a place for Zen meditation. Although the first floor is a more
relaxed lounge (offering hookah and drinks), the rest of the spacious Kudéta
is a loud and rowdy, flashing-lights nightclub. Thursday nights are reserved for
enormous study abroad student parties of about 1000 visitors. While the club
is quieter early in the week, the outdoor terrace, which sits directly under the
wrought-iron façade of the Pl. de Armas, is a fantastic place to hang, with white
leather seating and large, shady palms that will make you feel like you're living
in your favorite music video.

i In the Centro Comercial de Pl. de Armas, in the portion closest to Av. de la Expiración. Beer €4.
Cocktails €7.50. ☒ Open in summer daily 3pm-6am; in winter M-W 3pm-4am (lounge only), Th-Sa
3pm-6am, Su 3pm-4am (lounge only).Roof terrace open May-Oct.

ARTS AND CULTURE

Flamenco

TARDES DE FLAMENCO EN LA CASA DE LA MEMORIA   SANTA CRUZ
C. Ximénez de Enciso, 28   ☎95 456 06 70 www.casadelamemoria.es

In general, you need to cross the river to Triana to get a taste of really authentic
flamenco. But Casa de la Memoria is the exception to that rule: this is a pure,
authentic flamenco experience right in the heart of Sevilla. The stage is located
in the central courtyard of an 18th-century house, with beautiful plants hanging
from the skylit ceiling and a few wooden chairs centered around the stage. It's
an intimate, packed venue, which conducive to the natural, visceral emotion of
flamenco. The nightly show is performed by four artists, all of whom couldn't
be older than 25, but try not to scrape your chin on the floor when your jaw
drops—these kids know their stuff. Running through two centuries of flamenco,
they layer on the various components, starting with just a guitar before adding
in the male and female dancers one at a time. This is hands-down the best option
for flamenco in Sevilla if you're on a budget. Just do yourself a favor and come
here. Buy tickets in advance and arrive at least 30min. early, as shows sell out.

i From Pl. de la Virgen de los Reyes, facing the cathedral, take a slight left onto C. Mateos Gago
(passing the bar El Giraldo), follow C. Mateos Gago west a few meters past C.Ángeles, then take a
right onto C. Mesón del Moro and continue 1 block until the street ends at C. Ximénez de Enciso.
€15, students €13. ☒ Daily shows 9 and 10:30pm. Arrive at least 30min. early to get a seat.

TABLAO EL ARENAL   ARENAL

C. Rodo, 7   ☎95 421 64 92 www.tablaoelarenal.com

Tablao el Arenal is the most established, famous place to see flamenco in Sevilla. *The New York Times* called it the best place in the world to experience flamenco, but such an experience requires a pretty hefty investment of time and money. The show is about 1½hr. long, and ticket prices range from €37-72 depending on how much you want to eat and drink with the performance. Keep in mind that if you do buy the expensive dinner with the first performance, dinner is served at 7pm before the first show. Call ahead to make reservations and arrive 30min. early so you snag a good seat close to the performers. This is more popular among middle-aged travelers with money to blow.

i Between the bullring and Hospital de Caridad. Show plus 1 drin €37; with tapas, drink, and dessert €59; with full dinner €72. ☒ Shows daily 8 and 10pm.

Festivals

SEMANA SANTA   CITYWIDE

www.semana-santa.org

Semana Santa, or Holy Week, takes place during the last week of Lent, between Palm Sunday and Easter Sunday. During these seven days, all 57 religious brotherhoods of the city don hooded robes and guide two candlelit floats honoring Jesus and the Virgin Mary along the tiny, winding streets of Sevilla. As they make their way to La Catedral, they grab the attention of around one million spectators year after year. You don't need to be religious to be awed by the history and spectacle of Semana Santa. If you're going to stay for the end of the week, you may also consider extending your trip until Feria de Abril (below)—after this, you may be due for a shift from pious patron to partier. Semana Santais the busiest week for tourism in Sevilla, so reserve rooms well in advance and beware the spike in rates. Also note that accommodations may be slightly less full during the first part of the week, as Semana Santa culminates on Good Friday.

☒ Usually falls in the 1st 2 weeks of April.

FERIA DE ABRIL   SOUTH OF TRIANA

Los Remedios district   www.feriadesevilla.andalunet.com

Following the Holy Week of Semana Santa each year, Feria de Abril is the time when Sevilla lets its hair down and celebrates its rich culture and history. Started in 1847 as a cattle trade expo in the Prado de San Sebastián, this week of festivities has made great strides since then, though hardly less animalistic. The Feria today takes up one million sq. m of Sevillian territory, where celebrations take place in three main parts: the 15-block Real de la Feria, the colorful amusement park at Calle de Infierno, and the main entrance. The Real is the heart of the Feria—the asphalt is covered in golden sand to match the bullring, the sidewalks are lined with *casetas* (canvas houses where you can spend the week drinking and eating with friends and family), and horse-drawn carriages and flamenco dancers pass through the streets. Spanish families will also dress up in traditional Spanish outfits and perform the folk dance known as the *"sevillanas"*. Each day, six bulls are set into the ring at Plaza de Toros de la Maestranza to face off against Spain's most famous matadors. Tickets sell out far in advance, so call the ticket office (95 421 03 15) for reservations.

☒ Usually falls between the last 2 weeks of Apr and 1st week of May.

ESSENTIALS
Practicalities

- **TOURIST INFORMATION:** Centro de Información de Sevilla Laredo. (Pl. de San Francisco, 19 ☎95 459 52 88 www.sevilla.org/turismo ☑ Open M-F 9am-7:30pm, Sa-Su 10am-2pm.) Turismo de la Provincia also has tourist info and gives out special discounts at some of the newer and more popular restaurants in the area. (Pl. del Triunfo, 1-3 ☎95 421 00 05 www. tourismosevilla.org ☑ Open daily 10:30am-2:30pm and 3:30-7:30pm.)

- **LAUNDROMAT:** Vera Tintoreria. (C. Aceituna, 6 ☎95 453 44 95 *i* Self-serve wash and dr €10. ☑ Open M-F 9:30am-2pm and 5:30-8pm, Sa 10am-1:30pm.) 2nd location at C. Menéndez Pelayo, 11. (☎95 454 11 48 *i* Self-serve wash and dry €10. ☑ Open M-F 9:30am-2pm and 5:30-8pm, Sa 10am-1:30pm.)

- **INTERNET:** Internetia. (C. Menéndez Pelayo, 43-45 ☎95 453 40 03 *i* €2.20 per hr.)

- **POSTAL OFFICE:** The main post office has a bank and also helps with international cell phones. (Av. de la Constitución, 32 ☎95 422 47 60 www.correos.es.)

- **POSTAL CODES:** 41001.

Getting There

By Train

The train is the best way to get to Sevilla. The main train station, **Estación Santa Justa** (Av. de Kansas City ☎90 224 02 02) offers luggage storage, car rentals, and an ATM. Trains depart from Madrid's Puerta de Atocha via the high speed service AVE (€84 ☑ 2½hr., every 30min. daily 6:15am-9:45pm) or via the Alvia train. (€66. 2¾hr., 2 per day.) There are also daily services from and to Barcelona via AVE. (€143 ☑ 5½ hr., daily 9am and 4pm) or via ARCO. (€64.30. ☑ 12½hr., daily 8am.) A full list of train times and routes leaving from Estación Santa Justa is available at tourist offices.

If you have a foreign credit card, tickets can be purchased online at www.renfe. com only once you have made a purchase in person from a RENFE office and verified your card with valid ID, like a passport or driver's license. Return tickets can be purchased in Sevilla in person at a RENFE office in the city center just off Pl. Nuevo. (C. Zaragoza, 29 ☎95 421 14 55 ☑ Open M-F 9:30am-2pm and 5:30-8pm, Sa 10am-1:30pm.)

To get to the city from Estación Santa Justa, the best bet is to take a taxi (€10); the station is a 25min. walk from the city center that can be grueling in the Sevilla sun. Bus #32 (€1.70) will take you to Pl. Ponce de León, which is still a considerable walk from many hostels. To catch the #32, exit the bus station and walk to the left of the parking lot 100m to Av. de José Laguillo.

By Bus

There are two regional bus stations in Sevilla: **Estación Plaza de Armas** and **Estación Prado de San Sebastián.** Estación Plaza de Armas (Av. Cristo de la Expiración ☎95 490 77 37 ☑ Open daily 5am-1:30am) serves all destinations outside of Andalucía, including daily routes to Madrid operated by **Socibus** (www.socibus.es *i* €20 ☑ 6hr., 10 per day 8am-1am) and to Granada operated by **Alsa.** (www.alsa.es *i* €20. ☑ 2¾hr., 9 per day 8am-11pm.) Pl. Nueva is a 10min. walk or a 5min. taxi ride (€5).

Estación Prado de San Sebastián serves destinations within the province of Andalucia. (Pl.de San Sebastián, 1 ☎95 441 71 11 ☑ Open daily 5:30am-1:30am.) There are three major lines from which to choose: **Los Amarillos** (☎90 221 03 17 www. touristbuses.es), **Alsina Graells** (☎90 242 22 42 www.alsa.es), and **Transportes Comes** (☎90 219 92 08 www.tgcomes.es). Estación Prado de San Sebastián is also a metro, bus, and tram stop. To get to the city center from Estación Prado de San Sebastián, take the tram T1 (€1.30) or a taxi (€5) to Pl. Nueva.

Getting Around

By Bus

Tussam buses blanket the city and run frequently (www.tussam.es *i* €1.30). The best way to navigate this system is to pick up a transit map from a tourist office. The C3 and C4 buses, running every 10min., are particularly helpful, as they circle the border of the city clockwise and counterclockwise, respectively.

By Metro

The metro is very limited, with only one line running currently, but it can be useful nonetheless. **Metro Line 1** (*i* 1-way €1.30, day pass €4.50 ⊠ Open M-Th 6:30am-11pm, F 6:30am-2am, Sa 7:30am-2am, Su 7:30am-11pm) ends in Ciudad Expo and Olivar de Quintos, making stops in Prado de San Sebastián, San Bernardo, Gran Pl., and Parque de los Príncipes.

By Bike

You'll quickly notice that the locals are all biking. You'll also find lines of **Sevici** (www. sevici.es) bicycles around the city if you want to join in the two-wheeled fun. Set up a week- or year-long subscription (€10/25) at any of the kiosks around the city. The system is convenient but comes with many rules. Once you sign up for the service, you can check out a bike for 30min. for free, after which they charge a fee for additional use (€1 per hr.; €2 per hr. thereafter). There's also a €150 safety deposit at sign up. Consult a tourist office for more information and a map of kiosk locations.

By Taxi

City officials recommend **Radio Taxi** (☎95 458 00 00) and **Tele Taxi** (☎95 462 22 22).

córdoba

Forget it, Rome; wait your turn, Constantinople; get in line, Paris; get outta here, New York. During the Middle Ages, Córdoba was the undisputed center of Western civilization and the most populous city in the world. While it's been 1,000 years since the peak of its glory as the capital of the Umayyad Caliphate (932-1031), this justifiably proud Andalusian city retains an exceptional ability to teach, entertain, and inspire like few other cities in the world. You'll experience thousands of years of history and learn about Islamic, Christian, and Jewish culture (and Córdoba's characteristic combination of the three) as you walk through the narrow streets of the old city. Though the Cordoban summer sends temperatures flying up to feverish levels and beyond, you'll find refuge among the plants and gurgling fountains of the city's traditional patios while feasting on typical dishes like the refreshing *salmorejo*, a cold tomato soup. You'll sip infused teas in an Arab bath before making your way over to the city's modern section to sip decidedly non-Islamic things with a little more punch. Córdoba is no longer the capital of the world, nor even of Andalucía, but its unparalleled mix of fascinating medieval history and thoroughly modern splendor make it one of the most unforgettable cities in Spain.

ORIENTATION

Most travelers arrive in Córdoba at the bus and train stations, located in the modern, easy-to-navigate northern part of the city. As soon as you get off the city bus in the *casco antiguo*, though, you'll be in a spaghetti-like mess of streets courtesy of good old (read: bad old) medieval street planning; pick up a map at the tourist office at the train station if you want to have any hope of finding your hotel. Most of the historic sights are packed in and around the narrow streets of **La Judería,** including the **Mezquita** and the **Alcázar de los Reyes Cristianos.** Behind these monuments flows the **Río Guadalquivir,** crossed by bridges including the Puente Romano, though you're unlikely to find yourself needing to cross the river. From the river, C. San Fernando runs uphill to C. Claudio Marcelo, the street that connects the two main plazas of the *centro,* **Plaza de la Corredera** and **Plaza de las Tendillas.** The former has lots of restaurants and bars, while the latter is full of shopping, banks, and pharmacies, as well as a tourist office. Heading north from Pl. Tendillas leads to ever-more modern areas of the city, plus the nightlife of **Avenida del Gran Capitán** and **Avenida del Brillante.**

get a room!

We know you do your booking online! View more listings at **www.letsgo.com.**

▨ FUNKY CÓRDOBA
HOSTEL $

C. Lucano, 12   ☎95 749 29 66 www.funkycordoba.com

The hostel so nice they named it thrice—depending on who you ask, this place is called Funky Córdoba, Terrace Backpackers, or Pensión El Pilar del Potro. Don't be confused—no matter what you call it, this hostel is the perfect stop for any young traveler on the go. It's impossible not to feel upbeat when entering the lobby and seeing every wall painted a different bold color and covered with fun facts and interesting star-shaped lamps. If you're too exhausted after a long trip to head out to the tourist office, the information posted on the walls will spoon-feed you all the info you need. The chalkboards around the hostel provide the daily weather report, tips for local discounts, and maps pointing out the hottest restaurants and clubs. You'll have to get a little active to climb up to the small rooftop terrace, with a comfy seating area to meet fellow travelers, but you can regain all those lost calories with the help of the breakfast buffet €2) and the shared kitchen.

i *From the bus and train stations, take bus #3 to San Fernando, proceed in the direction of the bus, and take the 3rd left onto C. Lucano. Free Wi-Fi (doesn't reach some rooms) and computers with unlimited free internet access. Female-only dorms available. Kitchen available. Sheets included. Towels €2. Laundry €5. Dorm €12-28; double €26-28. ☼ Reception 24hr.*

SIGHTS

▨ LA MEZQUITA-CATEDRAL DE CÓRDOBA
CHURCH, MUSEUM

C. del Cardenal Herrero   ☎95 747 05 12 www.catedraldecordoba.es

No matter how many times you've seen pictures of its red brick and white stone striped arches stretching away to infinity, the inside of the Mezquita will still take your breath away. Boasting one of the most beautiful interior spaces in the world, the Mezquita is the most dramatic and awe-inspiring witness to—and participant in—the complex centuries-long dance between Christianity and Islam in the Iberian Peninsula. On this site originally stood the Visigoths' Christian Church of San Vicente, but when the Moors came to town in 758 CE they knocked it down and constructed a mosque in its place. When complete, the Mezquita turned Córdoba into the hottest thing this side of Baghdad; it was the most important Islamic structure in the West and the second largest mosque in the world, second only to Mecca's. When Córdoba fell once again to the Christians, King Ferdinand III and his successors set about Christianizing the structure, most dramatically adding the bright, pearly white Renaissance nave

spain

where mass is held every morning. A visit doesn't come cheap (€8), but you can get in for free between 8:30-10am any day except Sunday, though you'll have to do without the audio guide (€3.50); almost all of the cathedral is open during this time except the nave, which opens after Mass concludes at 10am. Beware the gypsies outside, especially on C. Cardenal Herrero and C. Torrijos, yelling "Toma!" (Take!) and thrusting an herb toward you; things quickly devolve into fortune-telling and then begin to involve money—a firm "No, gracias" should help you avoid getting into any situations you want to avoid.

i *From the Pl. Tendillas, with your back to the front of the equestrian statue, turn left onto C. Jesús y María, which becomes C. Ángel de Saavedra and C. Blanco Belmonte, which leads to the Pl. Benavente. Cross the plaza and take a slight left onto C. Céspedes, which leads straight to the main façade of the Mezquita. From the main entrance on C. Cardenal Herrero, the ticket offices are to theright, near the base of the belltower. Audioguide available 10am-5pm in Spanish, English, French, German, and Italian. €8, under 14 €4, under 10 and M-Sa 8:30am-10am free (only individual visits allowed). Audioguide €3.50. El Alma de Córdoba nighttime tour €18; students, seniors, and under10 €9; under 7 free but do not receive audioguide. ☏ Open Mar-Oct M-Sa 8:30am-7pm, Su 8:30am-10:30am and 2-7pm; Nov-Feb M-Sa 8:30am-6pm, Su 8:30-10:30am and 2-6pm. Mass M-Sa 9:30am, Su 11am and 1pm.*

ALCÁZAR DE LOS REYES CRISTIANOS
MUSEUM

C. de las Caballerizas Reales   ☎95 742 01 51 www.alcazardelosreyescristianos.cordoba.es

Originally constructed in 1328 as a palace, the Alcázar has been home to far more interesting things than fussy royal dinners over the years: it served as a planning headquarters for the discovery of America and the reconquest of Granada, as well as the seat of the local Inquisition. Today, it's back to being filled with people wearing funny costumes, except the royal ruffs have been replaced with the fanny packs of the tourists that pour into this castle, museum, and garden complex. Climb one of the towers (some are original, while others were added in the 15th, 18th, and 20th centuries) or explore the collections of second- and third-century Roman mosaics discovered in the Pl. Corredera. Perhaps most impressive are the Jardines del Alcázar, a wide expanse of pools, flowers, and immaculately trimmed hedges. Try to arrive early in the morning: not only is it free during the week from 8:30-10:30am, but after that the sun can get oppressively hot, when instead of appreciating the bubbling fountains you'll just stare at them angrily and curse the water for not being potable.

i *From the main entrance to the Mezquita on C. Cardenal Herrero, with your back to the Mezquita, turn left and proceed straight as the street becomes C. Judería, then curves slightly to the left to become C. Manríquez, then curves slightly to the left again to become C. Tomás Conde; continue past the small park and enter the right-hand side of the large building at the end of the street. €4.50, students €2.25, free Tu-F 8:30-10:30am. ☏ Open Jun 16-Sept 15 Tu-Sa 8:30am-2:30pm, Su and holidays 9:30am-2:30pm; Sept 16-Jun 15 Tu-F 8:30am-7:30pm, Sa 9:30am-4:30pm, Su 9:30am-2:30pm. Last entry 30min. before close.*

SINAGOGA
SYNAGOGUE

C. de los Judíos, 20   ☎95 729 06 42 www.turismodecordoba.org

Built all the way back in 5075 (1315, for all you goyim), this synagogue has come a long way over its 700 years. When the Jews were expelled from Spain in 1492, all but three synagogues in the entire country were destroyed, and just one survived in Andalucía—you guessed it, the Sinagoga de Córdoba. Although it wasn't knocked down, it was repurposed into a hermitage and into a hospital for rabies patients. It wasn't until 1884, when a piece of falling plaster revealed the rich artistic design hidden in the ceiling, that the building was converted into a national monument and the careful restoration began. Visitors can now enjoy the historic beauty of the main prayer room's walls, engraved with Hebrew

córdoba

biblical inscriptions from the Book of Psalms and translated on posters around the museum.

i *From the main entrance to the Mezquita on C. Cardenal Herrero, with your back to the Mezquita, turn left and proceed straight as the street becomes C. Judería and curves slightly to the left to become C. Manríquez. Turn right onto C. Tomás Conde, which leads to the Pl. Maimónides; cross the plaza diagonally and proceed along C. Judíos; the synagogue is on the left. Signs in Spanish and English. Free. ☼ Open Tu-Su 9:30am-2pm and 3:30-5:30pm. Last entry 10min. before close.*

FOOD

■ TABERNA SALINAS
C. de Tundidores, 3

CORDOBAN $$

☎95 748 01 35 www.tabernasalinas.com

This welcoming, traditionally decorated restaurant's menu is a veritable who's who of Cordoban specialties, each more delicious than the last. Start off with the first, cheapest, and most refreshing thing on the menu: a glass of gazpacho served with a single ice cube. After that, it's hard to know what to recommend: the refreshing salmorejo might be the only good reason not to order the pretty similar gazpacho; the flamenquín is as much of a crispy guilty pleasure as fried ham ought to be; and the melt-off-the-bone rabo de toro (oxtail), served with french fries, is tender and flavorful. The plates are big enough that one will fill you up just fine, but you'll probably end up trying more than one during your stay in Córdoba—the food is so cheap and so good that few travelers can resist a return trip.

i *From the Pl. Corredera, with your back to C. Sánchez Peña, cross the plaza diagonally to the left, walk up the hill, and take the 1st left onto C. Tundidores. Menu in Spanish, English, French, German, Italian, and Japanese. Raciones €6.40-6.90. Desserts €2.60. ☼ Open Sept-Jul M-Sa 12:30-4pm and 8-11:30pm. Closed Aug.*

■ CASA MAZAL
C. de Tomás Conde, 3

SEPHARDI $$$

☎95 794 18 88 www.casamazal.com

Let's Go Spain and Portugal 1013, painstakingly handwritten by monks, might not have recommended Casa Mazal, since its traditional Sephardi food wouldn't have stood out in La Judería during medieval times. However, since we're in the 21st century, and the Sephardi Jews are long gone from Córdoba, Spain, and most of Europe, we heartily recommends this unique and delicious cultural experience. Treat yourself to one of the house specialty couscous dishes with chicken and citrus fruits, duck confit, or suckling lamb (€17-19) and a glass of red wine. (Those who've visited the Casa de Sefarad will remember that the latter has been called "the best and most exquisite of foods.") The patio is picturesque, but few of the tourists who make up the bulk of the restaurant's clientele have the willpower to turn down a table in the air-conditioned interior.

i *Just off of the Pl. Maimónides in La Judería. From the main entrance to the Mezquita on C. Cardenal Herrero, with your back to the Mezquita, turn left and proceed straight as the street becomes C. Judería, then curves slightly to the left to become C. Manríquez. Turn right onto C. Tomás Conde; the restaurant is on theright. Menu in English available. Appetizers €5.50-8. Entrees €7.50-19. Desserts €5.70-6.90. ☼ Open daily 12:30-4:30pm and 8-11:30pm.*

RESTAURANTE FEDERACIÓN DE PEÑAS
C. del Conde y Luque, 8

CORDOBAN $$

☎95 747 54 27 www.federaciondepeñas.com

If you really must have a *menú del día* in La Judería, this calm restaurant run by a cultural association is one of the best affordable options. There's better food, lower prices, and prettier patios scattered across the neighborhood, but few places have a better combination of the three. Since most of the customers are tourists too exhausted to talk, you'll be able to appreciate the quiet gurgle of the fountain and the mood-setting recorded guitar music. A handful of different cheap *menús* are offered during lunch (€8-13.50, IVA not included), though be warned that while all but the cheapest include a drink, bread, and dessert, the breadstick-like crackers aren't really bread and fruit isn't really dessert, no matter what Michelle Obama wants us to believe.

i From the main entrance to the Mezquita on C. Cardenal Herrero, proceed straight along C. Céspedes, then turn left at the plaza onto C. Conde y Luque; the restaurant is on the right. €8 menú does not include drinks, bread, or dessert. Menús €8-13.50. Appetizers €4.25-12. Entrees €6-15.40. 8% IVA not included. ⏰ Open daily 12:30-4pm and 7:30-11pm.

LA ESTRELLA
Pl. de la Corredera, 14

SPANISH $$
☎95 747 42 60

Walking into Pl. Corredera on a summer evening, it's impossible to miss the large territory marked by La Estrella's metallic tables and blue chairs emblazoned with spray-painted gold stars. A great place to try Cordoban classics outside once the sun goes down and the city cools down a bit, all the favorites are here, like patatas bravas, flamenquín, and their mouth-watering salmorejo. You can either get a hefty bowl of this seasoned, chilled, honey- and ham-topped soup on its own (€5), or pair it with fried eggplant (€6) or a slice of tortilla española (€4.50). Surrounded by mostly 20-somethings looking for a relaxed evening, you'll also find quite a few couples of any age enjoying a casual, outdoor date.

i From the Pl. Corredera, with your back to C. Sánchez Peña, walk straight across the plaza. Appetizers €3.50-9. Meat and fish entrees €6-12. ⏰ Open daily May-Sept noon-4pm and 7pm-2am; Oct-Apr noon-4pm and 7-11pm.

NIGHTLIFE

❧ BAMBUDDHA
Av. del Gran Capitán, 46

BAR, CLUB
☎957 40 39 62

You've seen the synagogue. You've seen the cathedral-mosque. And while this ain't no Buddhist temple, those down for a good time should pay a visit to this Buddha-themed pub as well. The first thing that will catch your eye as you approach is the exclusive-looking terrace, hidden under low-draped white sheets glowing with green and red lights. On a hot summer evening, though, you'll probably want to head inside to the air-conditioned interior, complete with a few Eastern touches like faux-paper lanterns above the bar. Enjoy the air-conditioning while you can, though, since on weekends the temperature rises sharply around 2am as the bar fills up and the cocktails start coaxing out the dance moves.

i From the Pl. Tendillas, with your back to the front of the equestrian statue, proceed straight ahead along C. Conde de Gondomar, then take the 2nd right onto the wide pedestrian Av. Gran Capitán and walk 10-15min.; it's right after the park, at the intersection with Av. Libertad. Beer €1.50-3. Cocktails €6-7. ⏰ Open Jul-Aug M-W 6pm-3am, Th-Sa 6pm-4am, Su 6pm-3am; Sept-Jun M-W 3pm-3am, Th-Sa 3pm-4am, Su 3pm-3am.

❧ JAZZ CAFÉ CÓRDOBA
C. de la Espartería

BAR, LIVE MUSIC
☎957 48 14 73

The perfect place for a one- or two-drink night out with friends, this centrally located jazz club right off of the Pl. Corredera has less of a smoky back-room vibe than most. It also has a more varied program, including not only jazz but also stand-up, magic shows, blues jam sessions, and even classic disco recordings on Saturdays. If Gloria Gaynor groupies and Woody Allen wannabes can both find a home here, surely so can you.

i From the Pl. Corredera, with your back to C. Sánchez Peña, cross the plaza diagonally to the left and walk up the hill; the bar is on the left. Live music Tu-Th at 10 or 11pm (Tu jazz; W miscellaneous concerts, monologues, or magic shows; Th blues jam sessions). Sa disco after midnight. Free Wi-Fi. Beer €2-3. Cocktails €5.50. All drinks €1 more during concerts. ⏰ Open daily summer 9am-2pm and 10pm-4am; winter 9am-2pm and 5pm-4am.

córdoba

SOJO RIBERA
BAR

Paseo de la Ribera, 1, 3rd fl. ☎957 49 21 92 www.cafesojo.es

Despite sharing a building with a parking garage, Sojo Ribera is one of the swankiest places to have a drink in Córdoba near the major tourist sites of the old city. A crowd of all ages sips surprisingly cheap drinks in the well air-conditioned, vaguely Arabian interior, while couples get cozy around a candle in the romantic outdoor area. Live rock music (often '80s covers) on Thursdays at 10pm draws an especially large crowd, though the Thursday night barbecue probably has something do with that as well.

i From the rear side of the Mezquita on C. Corregidor Luis de la Cerda (across from the Puente Romano), with your back to the Mezquita, walk toward the Puente Romano and turn left onto Ronda de Isasa, which will turn into Paseo de la Ribera; the bar is on the left, through the glass doors with the parking sign. Take the elevator to the 3rd fl. Live rock music Th 10pm. Beer €2.50-3.50. Cocktails €7-18. ☺ Open M-Th 8:30am-3am, F 8:30am-4am, Sa 11am-4am, Su 11am-3am.

AUTOMÁTICO MUZIK BAR
CAFE, BAR, CLUB

C. de Alfaros, 4

Automático can be best described a mullet: business in the front, party in the back. The front of Automático is a cafe area, with a bar equipped with a cappuccino and latte machine that can muster up any caffeinated drink you can think of. As you make your way farther into this late-night hangout, you'll find yourself at the modern bar and elevated dance floor, glistening under the disco ball and jamming to dance beats. Whether these tunes are part of the Thursday night live shows (10pm) or the DJ-produced weekend parties, you'll definitely want to get moving with the young, casual crowd into the early morning.

i From the Pl. Corredera, with your back to C. Sánchez Peña, cross the plaza diagonally to the left and walk up the hill and proceed straight as the street becomes C. Capitulares and then C. Alfaros; it's on the right. Free Wi-Fi. Concerts some Th 10pm. Tea €1.50. Coffee €1.90. Beer €1.20-2.50. Cocktails €5-6. ☺ Open Jul-Aug daily 9pm-4am; Sept-Apr M-Th 5pm-3am, F 5pm-4am, Sa 1pm-4am, Su 1pm-3am; May-Jun M-W 5pm-2am, Th 5pm-3am, F-Sa 5pm-4am, Su 5pm-2am.

ARTS AND CULTURE

▨ TABLAO FLAMENCO CARDENAL

C. de Torrijos, 10 ☎957 48 33 20 www.tablaocardenal.com

In an atmosphere as Cordoban as they come, across the street from the Mezquita, Tablao Flamenco Cardenal puts on six 2hr. shows a week (10:35pm) featuring renowned guitarists, singers, and dancers. You'll get a taste of many different types of flamenco from different time periods and regions of Spain including *sevillanas, alegrías, seguilladas,* and *bulerías.* Whether you're looking for the classic show or some modern variations, Tablao Flamenco Cardenal will give you a taste of everything for €20, with a drink thrown in as well.

i From the main entrance to the Mezquita on C. Cardenal Herrero, with your back to the Mezquita, turn left and then take the 1st left onto C. Torrijos. Sho €20, includes 1 drink. ☺ Open M-Sa 10:35pm-12:20am.

HAMMAM AL-ANDALUS

C. del Corregidor Luis de la Cerda, 51 ☎902 33 33 34 www.hammamalandalus.com

For those willing to pay a little more for a relaxing cultural experience, these medieval-style Arab baths, the biggest in Europe, provide a taste of old-school Andalusian luxury. Visits to the baths (€23) last 90min. and include access to a warm bath, a hot bath, and a cold bath; you can switch between the three at your leisure, perhaps taking a quick break from the water to sip a free mint-infused tea. For those looking to relax even more, a variety of massages are available, ranging from a standard 15min. relaxing massage to an elaborate 30min. "al-Andalus ritual." The exotic architecture and dim lighting make this place pretty

spain

romantic, which is great for couples; individual travelers and "just friends," however, should be warned that they might be sitting next to a spectacle of things even steamier than the hot bath. Bring your bathing suit (or rent one—eek!), but leave your sandals at home—entrance to the baths is barefoot.

i *From the rear side of the Mezquita on C. Corregidor Luis de la Cerda (across from the Puente Romano), with your back to the Mezquita, turn left; the bath is on the right. Spanish and English spoken. Reservations recommended 1-2 days in advance during Apr-May, Jul-Oct, Dec, and on weekends; can usually be made same day otherwise. Bathing suit required; rental €1.50. Bathing caps not required. Sandals permitted in the locker room but not in the bath areas; disposable latex sandals are available upon request. Bath alone €23, with 15min. massages €33. Jan-Mar, Jun, Nov M-F 10am-4pm and midnight bath with 15min. massages €28, students €23. ☼ Bath (and massage, if purchased) lasts 1.5hr. Time slots daily every 2hr. 10am-midnight.*

ESSENTIALS
Practicalities

- **TOURIST OFFICES:** The **Consorcio de Turismo de Córdoba** operates several tourist information points that serve as both municipal and provincial tourist offices (☎95 720 17 74 www. turismodecordoba.org.) The main office is actually the least useful for tourists, since it has the most limited hours and does not make tour bookings (C. Rey Heredia, 22 *i* From the main entrance to the Mezquita on C. Cardenal Herrero, with your back to the Mezquita, turn right, take a slight left onto C. Encarnación and proceed until the end of the street, then turn right onto C. Rey Heredia. ☼ Open M-F 8:30am-2:30pm); more services and longer hours are found at the branches in the **Plaza de las Tendillas** (*i* Spanish, English, and French spoken. ☼ Open daily 9am-2pm and 5:30-8pm), across the street from the **Alcázar de los Reyes Cristianos** (C. Campo Santo de los Mártires *i* From the rear side of the Mezquita on C. Corregidor Luis de la Cerda, with your back to the Mezquita, turn right onto C. Amador de los Ríos; it's in the park on the right. Spanish, English, and French spoken. ☼ Open daily 9am-2pm and 5-7:30pm), and at the **train station.** (Glorieta de las Tres Culturas ☎90 220 17 74 *i* Next to the exit onto Av. Libertad. Spanish, English, and French spoken. ☼ Open daily 9am-2pm and 5-7:30pm.) The **regional tourist office,** in the magnificent Palacio de Congresos, does not make tour bookings but provides a much easier-to-read map than the municipal tourist office. (C. Torrijos, 10 ☎95 735 51 79 www.andalucia.org *i* From the main entrance to the Mezquita on C. Cardenal Herrero, with your back to the Mezquita, turn left and then take the 1st left onto C. Torrijos. ☼ Open M-F 9am-7:30pm, Sa-Su and holidays 9:30am-3pm.)

- **ATMS AND CURRENCY EXCHANGE:** Modern Córdoba is as filled with ATMs as any city, but there are very few ATMs in La Judería. The few **ATMs** are found near the Mezquita; try the Caja Rural ATM on C. Judería (*i* From the main entrance to the Mezquita on C. Cardenal Herrero, with your back to the Mezquita, turn left and proceed straight as the street becomes C. Judería) or one of the Caja Sur ATMs on C. Torrijos, preferably the one inside, since that street can get very crowded and you never know who's out there. (*i* From the main entrance to the Mezquita on C. Cardenal Herrero, with your back to the Mezquita, turn left and then take the 1st left onto C. Torrijos.) The **Caja Sur** branch (C. Medina y Corella ☎95 747 53 01 www.cajasur.es *i* At intersection with C. Torrijos. ☼ Open M-F 8:30am-2:30pm) also exchanges major foreign currencies, as does **Banco Santander** (Pl. Tendillas, 5 ☎95 749 79 00 www.bancosantander. es) and many of the banks along **Avenida Gran Capitán.**

- **LUGGAGE STORAGE:** Lockers are available in the **train station** (Glorieta de las Tres Culturas ☎90 243 23 43 *i* €1.75 per 60min. or less, regardless of size; €3-6 per 24hr., depending on size. ☼ Open daily 9:30am-10:30pm) and the **bus station.** (Av. Libertad ☎95 740 40 40 www.estacionautobusescordoba.es *i* €4 per day. ☼ Open daily 5:30am-1am.)

- **INTERNET ACCESS:** The **Biblioteca Provincial de Córdoba** has free Wi-Fi and computers with 1hr. free internet access. (C. Amador de los Ríos ☎95 735 55 00 *i* From the rear side of the Mezquita on C. Corregidor Luis de la Cerda, with your back to the Mezquita, turn right onto C. Amador de los Ríos; it's on the right. ☑ Open Jun 16-Sept 15 M-F 9am-2pm; Sept 16-Jun 15 M-F 9am-9pm, Sa 9am-2pm.) Outside of the library's limited hours, some travelers report having no trouble using the free Wi-Fi in the lobby of the **Albergue Inturjoven de la Creatividad,** even if they are staying elsewhere. (Pl. Judá Leví ☎95 735 50 40 www.inturjoven. com *i* From the main entrance to the Mezquita on C. Cardenal Herrero, with your back to the Mezquita, turn left and proceed straight as the street becomes C. Judería and curves slightly to the left to become C. Manríquez; it's in a small plaza on the right. ☑ Open 24hr.)

- **POST OFFICE:** The main post office is also the most conveniently located. (C. José Cruz Conde, 15 ☎95 749 63 42 www.correos.es *i* From Pl. Tendillas, with your back to the front of the equestrian statue, turn right onto C. José Cruz Conde and walk 2 blocks; it's on the left. ☑ Open M-F 8:30am-8:30pm, Sa 9:30am-2pm.)

- **POSTAL CODE:** 14001.

Emergency

- **EMERGENCY NUMBERS:** General Emergencies ☎061

- **POLICE: Local Police.** (Av. Custodios ☎092 or 95 745 53 00 *i* From the rear side of the Mezquita on C. Corregidor Luis de la Cerda, walk toward the Puente Romano and turn right onto Av. Alcázar, then turn right at the traffic circle onto Av. Corregidor, then take the 2nd left onto Av. Custodios.) **National Police.** (Av. Doctor Fleming, 2 ☎091 or 95 759 45 00 *i* From the Alcázar de los Reyes Cristianos, proceed along Av. Doctor Fleming, on the left side of the park.)

- **FIRE:** ☎080 or 95 745 54 95

- **HOSPITAL: Hospital Universitario Reina Sofía.** (Av. Menéndez Pidal ☎95 701 00 00 www. juntadeandalucia.es/servicioandaluzdesalud/hrs2 *i* From the rear side of the Mezquita on C. Corregidor Luis de la Cerda, walk toward the Puente Romano and turn right onto Av. Alcázar, then turn right at the traffic circle onto Av. Corregidor, then take the 1st left onto Av. Menéndez Pidal.)

- **PHARMACY:** There are many pharmacies in the Pl. Tendillas, but they all keep regular business hours. The most centrally located of Córdoba's three 24hr. pharmacies is the nearby **Farmacia El Globo.** (C. Mármol de Bañuelos, 4 ☎95 747 40 24 *i* From the Pl. Tendillas, with your back to the rear end of the equestrian statue, turn left onto C. Diego León, then at the fork turn left and then immediately right. ☑ Open 24hr.) Complete information on all pharmacies open outside of regular pharmacy hours is available at www.cofco.org or in the window of any pharmacy.

Getting There

By Bus

The cheapest way to get to Córdoba, from cities near and far, is almost always the bus. Buses arrive at the bus station in the modern part of the city northeast of the *centro histórico* (Av. Libertad ☎95 740 40 40 www.estacionautobusescordoba.es *i* Bus #3 to RENFE-Estación de Autobuses from the Glorieta de la Cruz Roja.) **Secorbús,** a subsidiary of Socibus (☎90 222 92 92 www.socibus.es) provides most long-distance bus service to Córdoba, with buses from: Bilbao (€42 ☑ 10¾hr., at 9:15am and 9:30pm); Burgos (€33 ☑ 8hr., at 12:05pm and 12:30am); Cádiz (€9.40 ☑ 3¾hr., 3 per day 8:40am-9:10pm); Jerez de la Frontera (€8.25 ☑ 3¼hr., 2-3 per day 9:20am-9:50pm); Madrid (€16 ☑ 4¾hr., 6 per day 9am-1am); and San Sebastián (€48 ☑ 12hr., 2 per day 8am and 8pm).

Alsina, a subsidiary of ALSA (☎90 242 22 42 www.alsa.es), runs buses from other cities in Andalucía, including: Granada (€14-16 ☑ 2½-4hr., 8 per day 8:30am-8pm); Málaga (€14 ☑ 2½-3½hr., 4 per day 9am-7:30pm); and Sevilla (€12 ☑ 1¾-2¼hr., 7 per day 8am-10pm). **ALSA** also provides service from Barcelona (€71-82 ☑ 12¾-14¼hr., at

4:30pm and 9:30pm). To get from the bus station to the *centro histórico*, catch the #3 bus (€1.15) to San Fernando, the fifth stop—but grab a map from the tourist office across the street in the train station first.

By Train

Relative to buses, trains to Córdoba are usually either a little faster and a little more expensive (regular trains) or much faster and much more expensive (high-speed trains), though sometimes cheap fares are available on www.renfe.es. Both high-speed and regular trains arrive at the Estación de Córdoba in the modern part of the city northeast of the *centro histórico*, across from the bus station. (Glorieta de las Tres Culturas ☎90 243 23 43 *i* Bus #3 to RENFE-Estación de Autobuses from the Glorieta de la Cruz Roja.) **RENFE** (☎90 232 03 20 www.renfe.es) trains arrive from: Barcelona (€66-138 ☒ 4½-9½hr., 4 per day 8:30am-3:50pm); Cádiz (€24-40 ☒ 2½-3½hr.; M-F 10 per day 5:35am-7:05pm, Sa-Su 8 per day 6:35am-7:05pm); Granada (€22-36 ☒ 2½hr., at 9:10am and 6:05pm); Madrid (€28-69 ☒ 1¾-2hr.; M-F 34 per day 6:30am-9:35pm, Sa 28 per day 8am-9:30pm, Su 29 per day 8:30am-9:35pm); Málaga (€19-46 ☒ 1hr.; M-F 19 per day 6:20am-8:30pm, Sa 14 per day 7:55am-8:30pm, Su 15 per day 7:55am-9:05pm); and Sevilla (€13-34 ☒ 45min.-1½hr.; M-F 40 per day 6:15am-9:35pm, Sa 30 per day 7:15am-9:35pm, Su 32 per day 7:15am-9:35pm). To get from the train station to the *centro histórico*, catch the #3 bus across Av. América from the train station (€1.15) to San Fernando, the fifth stop—but grab a map from the tourist office next to the exit on your way out.

By Plane

There are no passenger flights to Córdoba; the nearest airports are in Sevilla (88mi.) and Málaga (100mi.), both of which have regular bus and train service to Córdoba.

Getting Around

The main way to get around Córdoba, and especially La Judería, is on foot. There is a city **bus** system, operated by **Aucorsa** (www.aucorsa.net); the only bus you'll probably ever need to worry about is bus #3, which will take your tired feet and heavy pack from the train and bus stations to the *centro* and La Judería. (€1.15.)

Bikes are available for rental at **Duribaik** (C. Sevilla, 13 ☎95 778 84 76 www.duribaik.com *i* From the Pl. Tendillas, with your back to the front of the equestrian statue, turn left onto C. Jesús y María, then take the 2nd right onto C. Rodríguez Sánchez; it's at the end of the block, on the left. (€5 per 5hr., €8 per 24hr., €20 for F-Su ☒ Open M-F 10:30am-2pm and 5:30-8pm, Sat 10:30am-2pm) and **SóloBici.** (C. María Cristina, 5 ☎95 748 57 66 or 62 031 83 70 *i* From Pl. Tendillas, with your back to the rear end of the equestrian statue, proceed straight ahead along C. Claudio Marcelo and take the 3rd left onto C. María Cristina. (€6 per 3hr., €10 per 5hr., €15 per 24hr. ☒ Open M-F 9:30am-2pm and 6-9pm, Sa 10am-2:30pm.)

Taking a **taxi** is an expensive way to get to sights outside the city and the only way to get to the clubs of the Polígono Industrial de Chinales; taxi stands are located in Pl. Tendillas and on Av. Gran Capitán at the intersection with Ronda de los Tejares, and near the train station on Av. América. In the unlikely event you find yourself very far from one of these, call **Radio Taxi Córdoba.** (☎95 776 44 44 www.radiotaxicordoba.com.)

córdoba

granada

So it's 15th-century *House Hunters*. You're the queen of Spain, and you can live anywhere in the kingdom. Where do you choose? If you're Isabella, the Spanish queen who, with the help of her far less powerful husband, Ferdinand, gobbled up the Iberian Peninsula for the sake of the kingdom and the Church, then Granada it is. By 1492, Granada had spent centuries under Moorish rule. Boabdil, the last sultan on the peninsula, clung to his city as his brethren fell left and right. With a little persuasion (and a lot of gold), Isabella took control of Granada without a drop of bloodshed and made the Moorish royal settlement of the Alhambra her own. This princely paradise of gardens and palaces was considered the most sophisticated example of Moorish architecture and design. While the Spanish royal family added a number of Renaissance palaces and chapels to the grounds, they largely preserved the original complex, and the additions were designed to complement the Moorish palaces and gardens, making the Alhambra an amusement park of wealth, design, and craftsmanship.

Today, the Alhambra is one of Spain's most visited sites, and it offers visitors a treasure trove of art history, design, and craftsmanship to explore. But Granada is far from a one-stop destination. The city retains strong elements of its cross-cultural history, from the remnants of the original city walls built by Boabdil to the timeless gypsy barrio of Sacromonte to the Arabic neighborhood of El Albaicín.

ORIENTATION

Plaza Nueva and City Center

Plaza Nueva is the tourist and commercial center of the city. Located just before the opening of the **Darro River,** Pl. Nueva is only a short distance from the historically ethnic neighborhoods of El Albaicín and Sacromonte. Just west of Pl. Nueva, Cuesta de Gomérez leads to the **Alhambra.** Calle de los Reyes Católicos runs from Pl. Nueva south to the *ayuntamiento* (city hall) and the tourist office at Pl. del Carmen. Just east of Pl. del Carmen, along CalleNavas, you'll find the city's signature tapas restaurants. West of C. Reyes Católicos, **Calle Cría Nueva** and **Calle Calderería Vieja** are part of a confusing network of narrow streets lined with ethnic bars, restaurants, and clothing shops.

Sacromonte and el Albaicín

El Albaicín and Sacromonte lie to the north of the city center. Immediately north of Pl. Nueva, the ancient Moorish quarter **El Albaicín** is a tangle of streets that snake around churches and plazas. Many sights in this neighborhood, including the **Convento de Santa Isabel la Real** and the **Iglesia de San Nicolás,** were built by the Church on the sites of mosques that once dominated the neighborhood. At the center of the neighborhood, the popular **Plaza de San Nicolás** and **Mirador de San Nicolás** are filled with bars and restaurants, some with incredible views of the Alhambra and the city's tiled roofs.

On the north side of Cuesta del Chapiz, the barrio of Sacromonte is most easily navigated along its namesake **Camino del Sacromonte.** Running north to south through the barrio, this street is considered one of the major sites in the development of flamenco. Small restaurants and bars in traditional white stucco dwellings dot the road. If stray cats and poor lighting at night give you the creeps, you might want to take a friend along.

Find more recommendations over at **www.letsgo.com**.

OASIS GRANADA   HOSTEL **$$**
Placeta Correo Viejo, 3   ☎95 821 58 48 www.oasisgranada.com
With locations all around the country, the Oasis chain is one of the most
popular hostel companies in Spain. This hostel, just a few blocks from
Pl. Nueva, is especially popular amongst the English-speaking crowd
(Australians, Americans, Brits, etc.) and is loaded with all the amenities
you could need, including a communal kitchen, full bar (with happy
hour nightly and a free drink upon arrival), and a rooftop terrace to
soak up the sun. Unfortunately, like many hostels in Granada, there's no
air conditioning in the rooms, which can heat up in a hurry during the
summer months. Check the welcome board in front for a list of daily
activities, such as walking tours, tapas tours, bar crawls, and waterfall
hike excursions. With so many hedonistic, party-obsessed Westerners,
this is definitely the liveliest hostel in the city. Meet people, get drunk, go
clubbing, eat kebabs—lather, rinse, repeat.
i *From Pl. Nueva, take C. de Elvira on the western edge of the plaza 3 blocks north, turn
right onto C. de la Calderería Nueva, and take the 1st left onto C. del Correo Viejo. Towels
€2. Security locks €3. Dorms €12-19.* ☒ *Reception 24hr.*

Cathedral and University

South of Calle Gran Vía, the streets become much more organized. The dominant
feature of this area, in case you couldn't guess, is the **Catedral de Granada,** which is
surrounded by a number of small plazas. **Plaza Trinidad and Plaza Bib-Rambla** are lined
with restaurants and small shops. South of Pl. Trinidad, the student presence is
palpable in the neighborhood's many bookstores and cafes. While the Universidad
de Granada is nearby, it isn't much of a tourist attraction. The greater university
area does contain some of the city's best parks, including the student favorite, **Parque
Fuente Nueva.** Parque Federico García Lorca is located south of Pl. Trinidad, down C.
Tablas.

SIGHTS

Alhambra

In 1238, Sultan Al-Ahmar of the Nasrid Dynasty took a look around Granada and
decided that he wanted to transform the Albaicín, a centuries-old fortress with
foundations constructed by the Romans, into a palace retreat for Moorish royalty
and top government officials. And *voilà:* the Alhambra was created. Over the next
two centuries, the descendants of Sultan Al-Ahmar built up an earthly paradise of
palaces and gardens that exhibited the highest achievements of Islamic architec-
ture and design. By the 15th century, Moorish influence on the Iberian peninsula
was beginning to fade,overtaken by the rise of the newly unified Spanish king-
dom. The Alhambra is most famous for being the last stronghold of Islam in Spain
to finally cede power to the Christians. But it wasn't a dramatic 300-like last stand;
power was exchanged without a major battle.

In 1492, the Spanish army under Ferdinand and Isabella finally seized the Al-
hambra, thereby ending the Reconquista, the 780-year-struggle between Christians
and Muslims for control of Iberia. Despite the religious power shift having taken
place more than 500 years ago, the palaces and gardens of the Alhambra remain

granada

remarkably similar to their original design under the Nasrid sultans. Now a UNES-CO World Heritage Site, the Alhambra is the government's biggest moneymaker—Gaudí's Sagrada Família in Barcelona has a higher income but loses tons of money to ongoing construction (due to be completed in 2036). And the Alhambra is more than just a single sight—it's a fortified city full of gardens, museums, towers, and baths. Be prepared to devote at least 3½hr. to your visit.

There are a few ways to get tickets. It is recommended that you purchase them in advance, particularly for visits in June and July. The official online ticket vendor is Ticketmaster, surprisingly, which sells tickets online at www.ticketmaster.es (€14). Tickets purchased from Ticketmaster can be collected at the automated ticket collection terminals at the Alhambra on the day of your visit or in advance at ServiCaixa ticket terminals, located in many La Caixa banks and ATMs throughout Spain. Tickets can also be purchased in person at the Alhambra Ticket Office. (C. Real ☎90 244 12 21www.alhambra-patronato.es *i* €12. ☒ Open daily from 8am until 1hr. before close.) Many hostels will also book tickets for you for an additional charge of €2. The general daytime tickets (€14) allow access to all sights on the grounds—either in the morning (☒ Daily 8:30am-2pm) or afternoon (☒ Daily Mar 15-Oct 14 2-8pm; Oct 15-Mar 14 2-6pm). There are also limited tickets that give you access to the Generalife and Alcazaba but not to the Nasrid Palaces (€8). An evening ticket includes access to the Generalife or Nasrid Palaces, but not both. (€12. ☒ Open Mar 15-May 31 Th-Sa 10-11:30pm; Sept 1-Oct 14 Th-Sa 10-11:30pm; Oct 16-Nov 14 F-Sa 8-9:30pm.) These later visits allow you to see the Alhambra grounds lit up against the night sky.

Audio tours are available in Spanish, English, French, German, Italian, and Portuguese, but they are quite expensive. (*i* Nasrid Palace €4, entire grounds €6; security deposit €20.) The guide focuses more on the aesthetics and design of the gardens and palaces than on the site's history.

PALACIO DE CARLOS V
PALACE

Museo del Alhambra   ☎90 244 12 21 museo.pag@juntadeandalucia.es

The Palacio de Carlos V is sort of a misnomer: it's not a huge royal palace like the Palacio Real in Madrid. Instead, the center of the building is a huge, open-air amphitheater, where operas, orchestras, and recitals are frequently performed. The interior of this 16th-century Renaissance palace is also home to two museums. The Museo de Bellas Artes is an art museum that seems to ignore the area's Islamic past in favor of focusing on post-1492 Spanish art. The Museo del Alhambra contains objects from—you guessed it!—the Alhambra. The museum, in development since 1940, now houses one of the world's best collections of Spanish-Moorish and Nasrid art.

i Museo de Bellas Arte €1.50, EU students free. Museo del Alhambra free. ☒ Palacio box office open daily Mar-Oct 8am-8pm; Nov-Feb 8am-5pm. Museo de Bellas Artes open Mar-Oct Tu 2:30-8pm, W-Sa 9am-8pm, Su 9am-2:30pm; Nov-Feb Tu 2:30-6pm, W-Sa 9am-6pm, Su 9am-2:30pm. Museo del Alhambra open Tu-Su 8:30am-2pm.

Sacromonte

🏛 MUSEO CUEVAS DE SACROMONTE
MUSEUM, CAVES

Barranco de los Negros   ☎95 821 51 20 www.sacromontegranada.com

This museum doesn't have many visitors—it's a bus ride (or long walk) outside the city walls, then a 5min. uphill hike to the museum. But it's worth checking out if you want to see restored gypsy cave dwellings. It's no Batcave, but you can see simple stables, bedrooms, kitchens, and workplaces here. The museum's other exhibits on history are underwhelming and essentially just descriptive text. But the museum does offer a high view of the Granada valley, and it's particularly striking to see the stark difference between the lush, green Alhambra side and the yellow, desert-like Sacromonte side.

i *Barranco de los Negros is off Camino del Sacromonte. From Pl. Nueva, follow the stream north up Carrera del Darro 5min. Take a left onto Cuesta del Chapiz and the 1st right onto Camino del Sacromonte. Follow Camino del Sacromonte 10min. to Barranco de los Negros. Head straight to the path that leads up the mountain. Take this path and follow signs. Alternatively, you can take bus #35 from Pl. Nueva (every 40min.), but it takes longer than walking, and you'll miss some of the best parts of Sacromonte that are only accessible on foot. €5. ☑ Open daily Apr-Oct 10am-2pm and 5-9pm; Nov-Mar 10am-2pm and 4-7pm.*

ABADÍA DEL SACROMONTE
MUSEUM

On Mt. Valparaiso, 2.5km uphill from Camino del Sacromonte   ☎95 822 14 45

The origin of the name Sacromonte, or"Holy Mountain," has several legends attached to it. The holiest of these myths centers on the appropriately named Holy Cave. In 1594, two men exploring the cave discovered a mysterious pile of ashes alongside a series of lead plates inscribed in Arabic. The tablets suggested that the patron saint of Granada, San Cecilio, was actually of Arabic and not Spanish descent. This caused huge problems for the Church—so much so that the pope condemned the tablets in 1682. We've since learned that the pope was kind of right: the tablets are bogus and were written by a Moorish scholar. Bu t that hasn't kept the Museum of the Abadía del Sacromonte from putting them on display. The museum requires a brief tour that takes you through the abbey's courtyard, museum, church, catacombs, and Holy Cave. It's worth noting that this place is quite far removed from the city: it's either an uphill hike (brutal during the scorching summer months) or long bus ride. The upside is that there aren't many tourists, and you'll be rewarded with a nice view of the valley and Granada in the distance.

i *The abbey and museum are located 2.5km uphill from Camino del Sacromonte. It's a 40min. ride on bus #35 or a 30min. uphill walk from Pl. Nueva. €4 includes mandatory guided tour. ☑ Open Tu-Sa 10am-1pm and 4-6pm, Su 11am-1pm and 4-6pm. Tours (in Spanish; English or French by request) every 45-60min.*

El Albaicín

OLD MUSLIM BARRIO
NEIGHBORHOOD

Carrera del Darro, C. de San Juan de los Reyes, Cuesta del Chapiz

You might have an image of the Old Muslim Barrio (known as El Albaicín) as a bustling Arabic neighborhood full of vendors, restaurants, and stores. That's not the case. Instead, Albaicín is a quieter, mainly residential neighborhood. However, beginning just north of Pl. Nueva, this area is a delight to wander through. With all of the narrow, winding roads, it's easy to get lost in these cobblestone streets. Be sure you hit up the main attractions—grab a map and don't be afraid to ask for directions. On Carrera del Darro 31, you'll find **Los Bañuelos,** the now-dry Arab bathhouse. Take the uphill hike into the center of the barrio for **Mirador de San Nicolás,** a plaza that offers the best panoramic views of the Alhambra and Granada. If you're feeling lazy, you can even take a taxi up to the plaza, where locals and tourists alike hang out and drink at night.

CATEDRAL DE GRANADA
CHURCH

C. Gran Vía, 5   ☎95 822 29 59

Queen Isabella grew up in a convent, so it makes sense that she'd put one heck of a church in her favorite city. The Catedral de Granada, formerly connected to the Royal Chapel where Isabella is actually buried, is a massive circular building lined with 13 golden chapels, all of which are overshadowed by the Capilla Mayor in the center. The interior of this sanctuary is pretty standard, with thick marble pillars (you'd need at least three people to give them a good hug) and a

granada

gold-trimmed dome. It looks kind of like a theater, and two levels of balconies and stained-glass windows are the backdrop for an enormous red-carpeted altar.

i *Entrance on C. Oficios. Information in Spanish only €4. With audio tour €6. ☉ Open M-Sa 10:45am-1:30pm and 4-7:45pm, Su 4-7:45pm. Last entry 15min. before close.*

FOOD

CASA LOPEZ CORREA
C. de los Molinos, 5

TAPAS $$
☎95 822 37 75

Casa Lopez Correa is generally full of people, but they're not tourists or locals. What gives—who are these people? Are they aliens? Are they robots? Are you living in a dream world incepted by Leonardo DiCaprio and Joseph Gordon-Levitt? Well, no. Casa Lopez Correa is the go-to expat bar in Granada, popular with Aussies, Brits, and Americans. The half-Italian, half-British chef and owner has cooked all over Europe and ended up here, packing Italian, Spanish, and British cuisine onto a single menu. Try the delicious beef lasagna (€8.50) or British-style barbecued ribs (€6)—also available in smaller tapas form, free with a drink. The family-run restaurant is busiest and most fragrant at midday, when the expats show up for the *menú del día*. The extensive cocktail selection keeps 'em coming into the night with mojitos, caipirinhas, and margaritas made with fresh fruits and quality booze (€5).

i *From Pl. de Isabel La Católica, take C. Pavaneras (to the left of the fountain) 3 blocks until it becomes Pl. del Realejo. At the intersection with C. de los Molinos, follow the pink street that reads "La Alhambra" down C. de los Molinos for ½ block. The restaurant's bright blue façade is on the left. Appetizers €3.50-7.50. Entrees €7.50-9.50. 2-course menú €10; 3-course €12. Beer €1.70. Wine €2.10. ☉ Open M-Th 1-5pm and 8pm-1am, F-Sa noon-5pm and 8pm-2am*

LOS DIAMANTES
C. Navas, 26

TAPAS $$
☎95 822 70 70

On a block lined with expensive sit-down tourist joints, Los Diamantes (with multiple locations around Granada) is the established local favorite. This one-room bar along C. Navas is unapologetically loud and littered with napkins and olive pits—and it's all the better for it. At night, the simple, stainless steel counter swarms with local patrons drinking cheap beer (€1.70) and enjoying their free tapas. "Each tapa is a gift," they write on their menu, meaning you don't get to choose which tapa you want—it's like a Kinder Egg surprise, but fried and tastier. If you're with a large group, you might want to split a platter of *sesos*, fried calamari, or even chicken nuggets.

i *From C. Reyes Católicos, walk through Pl. Carmen to C. Navas. Beer and sangria €2, with free tapas. ½ platter tapas €6-8, full €10-14. ☉ Open daily 12:30-4pm and 8:30pm-midnight.*

🔳 CASA JUANILLO
Camino del Sacromonte, 81-83

ANDALUSIAN $$
☎95 822 30 94 casajuanillosacramonte@hotmail.com

Casa Juanillo is definitely well-removed from central Granada. But if you've already made the trek out of the city walls on Camino del Sacramonte (to check out Museo Sacromonte, for example), you should eat at Casa Juanillo. The charm of this family-run restaurant is hard to resist—a few chairs and tables grace a traditional dining room with fantastic views of the Darro river valley and Alhambra. The menu is simple, with just a dozen or so family recipes of regional specialties. Casa Juanillo is also in close proximity to many of the city's most authentic flamenco bars, making it a popular after-show destination.

i *From Pl. Nueva, follow the stream up Carrera del Darro (5min.) to Cuesta del Chapiz and turn left. Take the 1st right onto Camino del Sacromonte and follow it until you reach Barranco de los Negros. Casa Juanillo is the one with a small terrace, umbrellas, and chairs. Alternatively, bus #35 runs up Camino del Sacromonte from Pl. Nueva. Make reservations in advance. Entree €7-14. Beer €1.80. Wine €2-3. Free tapa with drink. ☉ Open Tu-Sa noon-4:30pm and 8pm-midnight, Su noon-4:30pm.*

EL HUERTO DE JUAN RANAS
C. de Atarazana, 8

ANDALUSIAN, BAR $$$

☎95 828 69 25 www.restaurantejuanranas.com

Located just next to Mirador de San Nicolás, El Huerto de Juan Ranas offers a killer view of the Alhambra and the Darro river valley. Walk through the little metal gate, and you'll feel like you've entered someone's private villa, with a plethora of terrace seating under shaded umbrellas—perfect for watching the sun set over a beer (€3) or cocktail (€8). If you're feeling hungry, the menu offers traditional Andalusian meals, while the downstairs restaurant experiments with more expensive, contemporary gastro-pub cuisine.

i Located just off of the Mirador de San Nicolás, on the southeast edge of the plaza. Terrace entrees €12-20; downstairs €20-35. Beer €3. Wine €3. Sangria €4.50. ☒ Open daily noon-1am.

POE
C. de Verónica de la Magdalena, 40

TAPAS $

www.barpoe.com

Poe is a traveler's paradise: lots of fellow foreigners, cheap beer, and free, tasty tapas. So pull up a seat at the traditional bar, order a cheap half-pint of beer (€1.50), and let Matt, the gracious bartender and owner, take your tapas order. All drinks come with a free tapa, served piping hot in a small ceramic pot. Matt's wife, Ana, cooks up a menu focused on stewed chicken, pork, and fish dishes, which range from chicken in sweet and spicy Thai sauce to a traditional Brazilian black bean and pork stew. Both Matt and Ana are quick to strike up a conversation with customers from the other side of the bar, so don't be surprised if you stick around for at least two rounds. The price is right, and the environment is far friendlier than what you'll find in the tourist center around Pl. Nueva.

i From Pl. de la Trinidad, take C. de la Alhóndiga and turn right onto C. de la Paz. Vegetarian options available. Wine €1.50-2.70. Beer €1.50-4. Extra tapas €1.50; ½-plate €3.50, full €6.50. Cash only. ☒ Open Tu-Th 8pm-2am, F-Su 8pm-3am.

LA CAMPERERÍA
C. Duquesa, 3

BAR $$

☎95 829 41 73

If the sign outside is in all-bold, uppercase Helvetica, you know that a place is going to be trying hard for the contemporary, Apple-esque aesthetic. Despite the slightly strained modern vibe inside, this place is hugely popular with students and locals at night, with a loud crowd stretching out the front door. Patrons come for the speciality *campero*—round, pressed sandwiches sliced up pizza-style. While you can get a free tapa *campero* with a beer (€2), you're better off paying an extra couple euro for the enormous specialty *camperos*, such as the *Mare* (fried calamari, pureed tomatoes, lettuce, and aioli; (€7) and *Granada* (*jamón serrano*, *queso ibérico*, avocado, and olive oil; €6). Campereria's bright lights and cheap drinks make it a popular late-night destination.

i From Pl. Trinidad, follow C. Duquesa½ block. The restaurant is on the left. Entrees €11-14. Menú €9.50. Camperos €3-7. Beer €2. Sangria €2.50. Mixed drinks €4. ☒ Open M-Th 8am-2am, F-Sa 8am-3am, Su 8am-1am.

NIGHTLIFE

GRANADA 10
C. de la Cárcel Baja, 10

CLUB, THEATER

☎61 021 99 10 www.granada10.com

Granada 10 is like the Alhambra of nightclubs in Granada. It's that one place you gotta check out—big, popular, and prospective dates everywhere (wait, that last part is probably only Granada 10). When Granada 10 is packed (particularly on the weekends), partiers fill up the huge theater space that's been converted into the dance floor. Local films were once screened here during the day, but that tradition has since ended in order to keep the focus on the late-night mayhem. The decadent marble bar and golden couches keep things classy, and a fancy light show gets the energy going. While you can't expect tons of locals, you'll be hanging with an enthusiastic, reckless, college-age crowd every night of the week.

i From C. Gran Vía, turn onto C. de la Cárcel Baja; the club is on the right. Ladies' night on W. Student special on Th. Salsa on Su. Cover varies from €3-10. ☒ Open daily midnight-6am.

🔲 LA BULERÍA
Camino de Sacromonte, 55

BAR, FLAMENCO

☎61 704 88 64

Camino del Sacromonte, a 20min. hike out from Pl. Nueva, is known for its authentic flamenco. In the area, La Bulería is the best of the best—the anointed local favorite and as authentic as you can get in Granada. The owner (and neighborhood legend) performs nightly guitar around 1am, and if you come to the outdoor terrace around midnight, you can usually catch him warming up. The concerts can be quite memorable, but even if you miss them, the setting alone—on top of a hill overlooking the city—makes La Bulería a great watering hole.

i From base of Cuesta del Chapiz, walk up Camino de Sacromonte (5min.); the bar is up a flight of stairs, just past the club El Comborio. Beer €2. Wine €3. Mixed drinks €5. ☒ Open Tu-Sa 11pm-4am.

CLUB AFRODISIA
C. Almona del Boquerón

CLUB

www.afrodisiaclub.com

Each week Club Afrodisia plays enough R&B, funk, and soul music to make James Brown roll over in his grave and shake his bony butt. They mix in a bit of hip hop on Tuesdays and reggae on Wednesdays, but the norm here is music straight from the soundtrack of a 1970s Blaxploitation film. The nightly concerts at 11pm offer a mix of live cover bands, original local acts, and DJs spinning in the leopard-curtained booth—all in a relatively intimate, restaurant-sized space. Go for a simple beer (€3) or take the Afrodisia route and just mix anything with Red Bull (€4.50). If you find your groove at Afrodisia, you might also consider trying Booga Club (C. Santa Bárbara, 3 www.boogaclub.com), which is owned by the same people and plays similar music.

i From C. Reyes Católicos, follow C. Gran Vía 9 blocks northwest. C. Almona del Boquerón branches off to the left, and the bar is just past the small flight of stairs from C. Gran Vía. Shots €2.50. Mixed drinks €5-5.50. ☒ Open Tu-Th 11pm-3am, F-Sa 11pm-4am.

PERRA GORDA
C. Almona del Boquerón

CLUB

www.facebook.com/laperragorda

It feels like Perra Gorda was a bar in old-school America's rock and roll heartland that caught a rift in the space-time continuum and appeared in modern day Granada. There's classic rock on the stereo, cheap brews (three Buds for €5), billiards, darts, and foosball—just like a classic American hangout bar. This is a great place to get drunk for cheap without resorting to sad pre-gaming in your hostel dorm. Mixed drinks are €3 and two-for-one during happy hour. On Wednesday nights at midnight, the bar hosts live acoustic rock sets. For the rowdiest crowd, come around 3am on the weekends.

i From C. Reyes Católicos, follow C. Gran Vía 9 blocks northwest. C. Almona del Boquerón branches off to the left, and the bar is just past the small flight of stairs from C. Gran Vía. Shots €1-2. Beer €1.20-2.50. Mojitos €3. Mixed drinks €4. Cash only. ☒ Open M-Th 10pm-3am, F-Sa 10pm-4am, Su 10pm-3am. Happy hour 10pm-midnight.

ESSENTIALS

Practicalities

- **TOUR OFFICES:** There are over 25 tourist offices in the greater Granada area. The primary offices are in Plaza Nueva, City Hall (el Ayuntamiento) in Pl. del Carmen (☎95 824 82 80 www. granadatur.com), at the airport (☎95 824 52 69 iturismo.aeropuerto@dipgra.es), and in the Alhambra (Av. Generalife ☎95 854 40 02 www.andalucia.org).

- **CURRENCY EXCHANGE:** Interchange is a money-exchange office that provides services for all major credit cards, including American Express. (C. Reyes Católicos, 31 ☎95 822 46 44 ② Open M-Sa 9am-10pm, Su 11am-3pm and 4-9pm.)

- **INTERNET:** Biblioteca de Andalucía has 8 computers that you can use for free for up to 1hr. (C. Profesor Sáinz Cantero, 6 ☎95 857 56 50 www.juntadeandalucia.es/cultura/ba ② Open M-F 9am-2pm.) Idolos and Fans has photocopying, fax, scanning, Wi-Fi, and even a Playstation 3. (Camino de Ronda, 80 ☎95 826 57 25 *i* €1.80 per hr., €9 per 6hr., €12 per 10hr. ② Open daily 10am-midnight.)

- **POST OFFICE:** Puerta Real. (Intersection of C. Reyes Católicos and Acera del Darro ☎95 822 11 38 ② Open M-F 8:30am-8:30pm, Sa 9:30am-2pm.)

- **POSTAL CODE:** 18005.

Emergency

- **EMERGENCY NUMBERS:** Municipal police: ☎092. National police: ☎091.

- **LATE-NIGHT PHARMACIES:** You'll find a few 24hr. pharmacies around the intersection of C. Reyes Católicos and Acera del Darro, including Farmácia Martín Valverde (C. Reyes Católicos, 5 ☎95 826 26 64).

- **HOSPITALS/MEDICAL SERVICES:** Hospital Universitario Vírgen de las Nieves. (Av. de las Fuerzas Armadas, 2 ☎95 802 00 00.) Hospital San Juan de Dios. (C. San Juan de Dios ☎95 802 29 04.) For an ambulance, contact a local emergency team (☎95 828 20 00).

Getting There

By Plane

Aeropuerto Federico García Lorca (GRX ☎95 824 52 69) is located about 15km outside the city in Chauchina. The airport has daily flights to and from Barcelona, Madrid, Mallorca, and Sevilla, as well as weekly flights to and from Paris' Orly and Rome's Fiumicino airports. Air Europa, Iberia, SpainAir, Ryanair, and Vueling Airlines all fly through Granada and offer connecting flights to and from cities across Europe.

A taxi will take you to the city center (€25) or directly to the Alhambra (€28). Call **Radio Taxi** in advance at ☎60 605 29 25 or wait in line at the airport. **Autocares José González** bus company offers a direct service between the airport and the city center. (☎95 839 01 64 www.autocaresjosegonzalez.com *i* €3. ② Every hr. 5:20am-8pm.)

By Train

The main **train station** (☎95 827 12 72) is at Av. de los Andaluces. **RENFE trains** (www. renfe.es) run to and from **Barcelona** (€63 ② 11½hr.; daily 8am and 9:30pm), **Madrid** (€70 ② 4½hr.; daily 9:05am and 6:05pm), **Sevilla** (€24 ② 3hr., 4 per day 8am-9pm), and many other smaller cities. To get from the station to the city center, you can take a short taxi ride or bus #3, 6, 9, or 11 (€1.20), which will take you to C. Gran Vía de Colón in the city center.

granada

By Bus

The bus station is at **Carretera de Jaén** (☎95 818 50 10). **Alsa buses** (www.alsa.es) run within Andalucía (☎95 818 54 80) and connect to the Madrid (☎95 818 54 80) and Valencia-Barcelona (☎90 242 22 42) lines. Buses run to and from **Cádiz** (€31 ◎ 5hr., 4 per day 9am-9pm), **Madrid** (€17 ◎ 5hr., 15per day 1am-11:30pm.), **Málaga** (€10 ◎ 1½hr., 15 per day 7am-9:30pm), **Sevilla** (€20 ◎ 3hr., 10 per day 8am-11pm), and many other destinations. **Autocares Bonal** (☎95 846 50 22) also runs a direct route to and from Sierra Nevada ski resorts in the winter. (◎ 25min.; M-F 3 per day, Sa-Su 4 per day.) City buses #3 and 33 on **Transportes Rober** run regular services between the station and the city center.

Getting Around

Transportes Rober runs almost 40 bus lines around the city, along with smaller direct buses to the Alhambra, the Albaicín, and the Sacromonte. (☎90 071 09 00 www. transportesrober.com *i* €1.20; 7 rides €5.) The tourist lines are #30, 31, 32, and 34. The circular lines (#11, 21, and 23) make full loops around the city. Rober also runs a special Feria line €1.40). When most lines stop running at 11:30pm, the Búho lines pick up the slack. (#111 and 121 *i* €1.30. ◎ Daily midnight-5:15am.)

santiago de compostela

If you've made it to Santiago after finishing the Camino, congratulations. Kick back with some local *tinto* or white *albariño* and give those tired pilgrim's feet a rest. If you flew here, give your stiff neck a rest and *Let's Go* will keep the congratulations. Santiago de Compostela was simply wilderness for centuries, until a monk discovered the remains of St. James in the area. This prompted the building of the Cathedral and the population swelled as thousands of pilgrims and new residents descended on what would become the third most important city in all of Christendom. The Cathedral, which houses the remains of the city's namesake St. James, is the main attraction, and much of the city—from the be-crossed almond cakes to the multilingual *menús*—is geared toward its visitors. Pilgrims are at the core of Santiago's identity, to be sure, but look beyond the surface and you will see it has much more to offer. It is a thriving city in the heart of Galicia, and the Galego lifestyle is everywhere, manifesting itself in nationalist flags, bagpipes, and a unique language (*galego*, for the uninitiated). So whether you are a pilgrim or not, take the time to discover what lies beyond the Cathedral; what you find might surprise you.

ORIENTATION

As soon as you arrive in Santiago, be sure to get a map, since the streets are very poorly marked. The main thoroughfares of the old city are **Rúa do Franco, Rúa do Vilar,** and **Rúa Nova,** which run (with some name changes, at times) from the **Praza do Obradoiro** and the **Catedral de Santiago de Compostela,** the old city's hub, to the **Praza de Galicia,** which sits between the old and new parts of town. The **bus station** (Pr. Camilo Díaz Baliño ☎98 154 24 16 ◎ Open daily 6am-10pm) is to the northeast of the old city. To get to Pr. Galicia, take bus #2 or 5 (€1) or head right on R. Ánxel Casal, then left at the roundabout onto R. Pastoriza. Because this area is a life-size IQ test, this street subsequently turns into R. Basquiños, then R. Santa Clara, and finally R. San Roque. Next, turn left onto R. Rodas which turns into R. Aller Ulloa, R. Virxe da Cerca, R. Ensinanza, and Fonte de Santo Antonio before reaching Pr. Galicia. The **train station** (R. Hórreo ☎90 224 02 02) is on the south end of the city; take bus #6 to get to Pr. Galicia or walk up the stairway across the parking lot from the main entrance and take R. Hórreo uphill about seven blocks.

get a room!

For more recommendations, visit **www.letsgo.com.**

PENSIÓN FONSECA   HOTEL $$

R. de Fonseca, 1, 2nd fl.   ☎64 693 77 65 www.pensionfonseca.com

The modern decor of this pensión's bright, high-ceilinged rooms contrasts with the ancient façade of the Cathedral, a literal stone's throw across the street. So when your Camino is finished and you just want to collapse (try not to do that in the Cathedral), the walk here will only be an extra 10 yards. The rooms aren't anything special, but they come at just about the best prices you're going to find in the old city, and you couldn't dream of a better location.

i Take R. Franco toward Pr. Obradoiro, then turn right just before the Cathedral (1 block past the little plaza) onto R. Fonseca. Pensión Fonseca is on R. Fonseca, NOT Pr. Fonseca or Tv. Fonseca, which are all within 2 blocks of each other. All rooms have shared bath. Jul-Sept singles €20-23; doubles €36. Oct-Jun €15-18 per person. ☼ Reception 8:30am-11pm.

SIGHTS

CATEDRAL DE SANTIAGO DE COMPOSTELA AND MUSEUM   CHURCH, MUSEUM

Pr. das Praterías   ☎98 158 11 55; 98 156 93 27 www.catedraldesantiago.es

Pilgrims have arrived at this site for more than a millennium, walking here by following the well-trodden Camino de Santiago in order to gain personal fulfillment and a healthy feeling of superiority from the Church. The Cathedral's towers, speckled with mosses, lichens, and flowers, rise from the center of the city, making the enormous holy site look as though it is ruled by Poseidon. It has been above water the whole time, though (unless you count the frequent Galician rains), and the site has been a destination for pilgrims since the relics of James the Apostle were discovered here in the ninth century. Work on the ancient Romanesque cathedral began in 1075 and was completed in 1211, though the cloister was added during the Spanish Renaissance and most of the façades are 17th- to 18th-century Baroque. Today, pilgrims and tourists line up to embrace the jewel-encrusted statue of the Apostle and see the silver coffer that contains his remains. Entrance is free, but after walking by multiple signs asking for donations, so is the guilt. The botafumeiro, the massive silver-plated censer (a.k.a. the thing that makes you choke annually at Christmas mass) swung across the altar to disperse thick clouds of incense in the Cathedral's most famous spectacle, is usually used during the noon service, though the schedule varies and is not made public. The Cathedral's bells are older than the Cathedral itself, taken to Córdoba in 997 by invading Moors. However, the reconquering Christians had the last laugh when they took Córdoba in the 13th century and made their prisoners carry the bells all the way back to Santiago. The museum includes the peaceful cloister, the library (the books that line the shelves are ancient, but many of those on display are facsimiles), and the crypt. That funky smell in the crypt is caused by the humidity, not by human remains—or at least that's the official line.

i Enter Cathedral on Pr. Praterías; the museum entrance is inside on the left. Cathedral free. Museum €5; students, seniors, and pilgrims €3. ☼ Cathedral open daily 7am-9pm. Museum open Jun-Sept M-Sa 10am-2pm and 4-8pm, Su 10am-2pm; Oct-May M-Sa 10am-1:30pm and 4-6:30pm, Su 10am-1:30pm.

HOSTAL DOS REIS CATÓLICOS
HOSPITAL, MUSEUM, HOTEL

Pr. do Obradoiro, 1 ☎98 158 22 00 www.paradores-spain.com/spain/pscompostela.html

Making the pilgrimage to Santiago used to be dangerous business, and pilgrims would arrive in the city battered and sick. After picking up one too many dead bodies off the floor of the Cathedral, the Catholic Monarchs ordered a hospital to be built in 1499. Fast forward to today and the building is now a luxury hotel, but the integrity of the original structure is still very much intact, and visitors can walk through all four of the former hospital's courtyards. Plaques posted along the walls give an insightful and surprisingly interesting history of the hospital through the years, and the serene courtyards, with their fountains, wells, and gargoyles, are picturesque spots away from the madness outside of the Cathedral. Hidden gems show the builders' senses of humor: one bent-over human gargoyle is aptly dubbed "the male contortionist."

i *On the left side of Pr. Obradoiro, facing the cathedral €3. ☼ May-Oct M-F, Su noon-2pm and 4-6pm; Nov-Apr open daily noon-2pm and 4-6pm.*

FOOD

O DEZASEIS
GALICIAN $$$

R. de San Pedro, 16 ☎98 156 48 80 www.dezaseis.com

Naming itself after its address, this restaurant isn't banking on winning over any new customers with its cleverness, but if you're willing to shell out (mollusk joke) just a few more euro, you can get a serious step up in quality. This basement restaurant has an earthy feel and delicious regional cuisine at very affordable prices, and to make things even better, it is far enough away from the pilgrim madness to have a mostly local clientele. The classics like tortilla española (€5.80) are superb, and if you want a dish that Santiago himself would approve of, try the vieira a galega (a huge scallop served in its own shell, like the ones that line the Camino; €4.50). If you keep the shell, clean it, paint a cross on it, and sell it to a pilgrim, the dish will nearly pay for itself.

i *Take R. Virxe da Cerca along the edge of the old city, then turn onto R. San Pedro away from old city. Menú del día €12. Raciones €3.50-13.50. Entrees €14-16. ☼ Open M-Sa 2-4pm and 8pm-midnight.*

TAPERÍA BOROA
TAPAS $$

R. dos Bautizados, 5-7 ☎98 157 30 32

The automatic sliding glass door in the front of the restaurant is there to give you a heads up: the theme is modern. If you didn't get it at the door, you will most certainly understand once you see the all-black furnishings, all with straight edges. However, the Spongebob episodes running on the TV in the back let you know they don't take themselves too seriously. There are tapas (naturally), but the best deal is the *menú*, which includes some amazingly high-quality options for a price of €12).

i *From Alameda Park, cross the street and head down R. Bautizados. The restaurant is on the right. Menú del día €12. ☼ Open M-Sa 2pm-midnight.*

CAFE CASINO
CAFE, CAFE-CONCERT $$

R. do Vilar, 35 ☎98 157 75 03

This cafe is located in a grandiose room that looks like it came straight out of turn-of-the-century Paris. The gold gilding of the decor combined with the grand piano (no touching!) will make you feel like a proper aristocrat in no time. Sink into a plush armchair and enjoy a rich coffee (think caramel, whipped cream, alcohol, and a dash of coffee (€2.50-4) and a local tarta de Santiago (a not-sweet almond cake with a cross on it; €3.50).

i *On R. Vilar, toward the Cathedral from Pr. Toural. Coffe €2.50-4. Desserts €3.20-5. ☼ Open M-Th 8:30am-2am, F-Sa 9am-3am, Su 9am-2am. Dinner daily 7:30-11pm.*

spain

BAR RECANTOS
R. de San Miguel dos Agros, 2

TAPAS $$
☎98 157 25 44

Don't let its location in the old city fool you; this bar offers modern decor and tries new takes on old tapas favorites, combining ingredients and flavors you wouldn't even dream of—unless you usually dream about chorizo and raspberry sauce. They also have an impressive list of alcoholic coffees and hot chocolates, although the Irish coffee milkshake (€3.50) is next level.

i Follow R. Preguntoiro through Pr. Cervantes as it becomes R. Algalia de Arriba, then turn left onto R. San Miguel dos Agros; it's across from the Museo das Peregrinacións. Tapas €1.50-3. ⏰ Open M-Th 8am-midnight, F 8am-2am, Sa 9:30am-2am, Su 9:30am-midnight.

NIGHTLIFE

CASA DAS CRECHAS
R. da Via Sacra, 3

BAR, LOUNGE, LIVE MUSIC
☎98 157 61 08 www.casadascrechas.com

Take a quick walk up the steps behind the Cathedral and descend into a Celtic witch's den that provides ample seating and beer. Don't worry, though, no one will cast a spell on you...unless you can't speak galego, in which case all bets are off. If you want to get a feel for Galicia and its unique culture, this is the perfect place to start. There are frequent jazz and Galician folk performances, so call ahead or check the website for the schedule; impromptu foliadas usually pop up on Wednesday evenings, but you generally just have to be there when the right group of enthusiastic musicians comes in.

i From Pr. Quintana with the Cathedral to your left, head up the stairs and to the right, then turn left onto R. Via Sacra. Beer €2.50. ⏰ Open daily in summer noon-4am; in winter 4pm-3am.

CAFE O PARIS
R. dos Bautizados, 11

WINE BAR
☎98 158 59 86

Maybe you feel like sticking your pinky out for a night. Or perhaps you are starting to feel guilty about that beer gut you have developed over the course of your trip. Whatever the reason you decide to go out for wine, this is the best place in the city to do it, hands-down. What at first seems like a narrow, cramped interior with pastel colors opens up in the back to a lounge area where you can chat with friends all night. Finally, you can go into a wine bar without feeling like you've entered Cougartown: the crowd is all young people rather than divorcées in their mid-40s.

i From Alameda Park, cross the street and head down R. Bautizados. The bar is on the right. Wine €1.80-2.40. ⏰ Open M-Sa 9am-1am, Su 11am-1am.

ESSENTIALS
Practicalities

- **TOURIST OFFICE: Oficina Municipal de Turismo** has maps and thorough information on accommodations as well as a 24hr. interactive information screen outside. (R. Vilar, 63 ☎98 155 51 29 www.santiagoturismo.com *i* On R. Vilar 1 block toward Cathedral from Pr. Toural. *i* English, French, German, Portuguese, Italian, Galician, and other languages spoken. ⏰ Open daily 9am-9pm.) **Oficina de Turismo de Galicia** has information on the rest of Galicia, and on festivals. (R. Vilar, 30 ☎98 158 40 81 www.turgalicia.es *i* On R. Vilar between Pr. Toural and Cathedral, on opposite side of street from Municipal Tourism Office but closer to Cathedral. ⏰ Open M-F 10am-8pm, Sa 11am-2pm and 5-7pm, Su 11am-2pm.) **Oficina del Xacobeo,** in the same building, provides information on the Camino de Santiago. (R. Vilar, 30 ☎98 158 40 81 ⏰ Open M-F 10am-8pm.)

- **CURRENCY EXCHANGE:** Banco Santander has **Western Union** services and a 24hr. **ATM** outside, and cashes American Express Travelers Cheques commission-free. (Pl. Galicia, 1 ☎98

158 61 11 *i* On right side of Pl. Galicia with your back to the old town. ☼ Open Apr-Sept M-F 8:30am-2pm; Oct-Mar Sa 8:30am-1pm.)

- **INTERNET ACCESS: Ciber Nova 50** has fast computers and pay phones. (R. Nova, 50 ☎98 156 41 33 *i* On R. Nova 1 block toward the Cathedral from Pr. Toural. €0.45 for 12min., €2 per hr. ☼ Open M-F 9am-midnight, Sa-Su 10am-11pm.)

- **ENGLISH-LANGUAGE BOOKS: Libraria Couceiro** has several shelves of books in English. (Pr. Cervantes, 6 ☎98 156 58 12 *i* From Pl. Galicia, take R. Orfas into old city; it becomes R. Caldeirería, then R. Preguntoiro, and the bookstore is immediately to the left on Pr. Cervantes. ☼ Open M-F 10am-noon and 4-9pm, Sa 10am-noon and 5-9pm.)

- **POST OFFICE: Correos** has a *Lista de Correos* and fax. (R. Orfas ☎98 158 12 52 www. correos.es *i* Take Cantón do Toural from Pr. Toural 2 blocks to R. Orfas. ☼ Open M-F 8:30am-8:30pm, Sa 9am-2pm.)

Emergency

- **POLICE: Policía Local.** (Pr. Obradoiro, 1 ☎98 154 23 23 *i* On Pr. Obradoiro across from Cathedral.)

- **MEDICAL SERVICES: Hospital Clínico Universitario** has a public clinic across from the emergency room. (Tr. Choupana ☎98 195 00 00 *i* Take bus #1 from R. Senra toward Hospital Clínico. ☼ Clinic open M-Sa 3-8pm, Su 8am-8pm.)

- **PHARMACY: Farmacia R. Bescansa** has been around since 1843—stop in to gawk at the classic 19th-century decor, even if you don't need anything. (Pl. Toural, 11 ☎98 158 59 40.)

Getting There

By Bus

ALSA (☎91 327 05 40 www.alsa.es) runs buses from: Astorga (€21-25 ☼ 5hr., 4 per day 4:15am-7:30pm); Barcelona (€72-86 ☼ 17hr., 3 per day 10am-10:50pm); Bilbao (€49 ☼ 9-11hr., 4 per day 10:30am-1:45am); Burgos (€40 ☼ 8½hr., daily at 1:15pm); León (€28 ☼ 6hr., daily at 4:45pm); Madrid (€44-64 ☼ 8-9hr.; M-Th 5 per day 7:30am-12:30am, F-Sa 4 per day 7:30am-12:30am); Salamanca (€26-31 ☼ 6-7hr.; M-F 3pm and 1:10am, Sa 5pm and 1:10am, Su 3pm and 1:10am).

By Train

RENFE (www.renfe.es) trains arrive from: A Coruña (€7-15 ☼ 40min.; M-F 20 per day 5:35am-10:15pm, Sa 18 per day 6:55am-9:55pm, Su 17 per day 6:55am-9:55pm); Bilbao (€48 ☼ 11hr., daily at 9:15am); Burgos (€42 ☼ 8hr., 2 per day at 12:12 and 3:25pm.); Madrid (€47-53 ☼ 7-9hr. 3 per day 3-10:30pm).

By Plane

Ryanair (www.ryanair.com) has flights to Santiago's **Lavacolla Airport** (SCQ; ☼ 30min. bus from bus station or city center) from: Alicante, Barcelona (El Prat), Madrid, Málaga, Reus, Frankfurt (Hahn), London (Stansted), and Rome. **Iberia** (www.iberia. es) flies to Santiago from Bilbao, Sevilla, and Valencia.

Getting Around

Most of the old city is closed off to all but foot traffic, so the easiest way to get around is to walk. For those venturing farther afield, **buses** (€1, with *bono* €0.55) are a good way to get around, though not particularly frequent on weekends. Bus #2 and 5 go to the bus station; bus #6 goes to the train station. **Freire** (☎98 158 81 11) runs buses (€3 ☼ 30min.) from R. Doutor Teixeiro and the bus station to the airport. There are **taxi** stands at the bus and train stations and at Pl. Galicia and Pr. Roxa. Otherwise, call **Radio Taxi** (☎98 156 92 92) or **Eurotaxi** (☎67 053 51 54).

spain

spain essentials

MONEY

Tipping and Bargaining

Native Spaniards rarely tip more than their spare change, even at expensive restaurants. If you make it clear that you're a tourist—especially an American—they might expect you to tip more. Don't feel like you have to tip, as the servers' pay is almost never based on tips.

Bargaining is common and necessary in open-air and street markets. If you are buying a number of things, like produce,you can probably get a better deal if you haggle. Do not barter in malls or established shops.

Taxes

Spain has a 10% value added tax (IVA) on all means and accommodations. The prices listed in Let's Go include IVA unless otherwise mentioned. Retail goods bear a much higher 21% IVA, although the listed prices generally include this tax. Non-EU citizens who have stayed in the EU fewer than 180 days can claim back the tax paid on purchases at the airport. Ask the shop where you have made the purchase to supply you with a tax return form, but stores will only provide them for purchases of around €50-100. Due to the economic crises sweeping Europe, don't be surprised if Spain increases its VAT even more.

SAFETY AND HEALTH

Local Laws and Police

Travelers are not likely to break major laws unintentionally while visiting Spain. You can contact your embassy if arrested, although they often cannot do much to assist you beyond finding legal counsel. You should feel comfortable approaching the police, although few officers speak English. There are several types of police in Spain. The policía nacional wear blue or black uniforms and white shirts; they guard government buildings, protect dignitaries, and deal with criminal investigations (including theft). The policía local wear blue uniforms, deal more with local issues, and report to the mayor or town hall in each municipality. The guardia civil wear olive-green uniforms and are responsible for issues more relevant to travelers: customs, crowd control, and national security. Catalonia also has its own police force, the Mossos d'Esquadra. Officers generally wear blue and occasionally sport berets or other interesting headgear. This police force is often used for crowd control and deals with riots.

Drugs and Alcohol

Recreational drugs are illegal in Spain, and police take these laws seriously. The legal drinking age is 16 in Asturias and 18 elsewhere. In Asturias, however, it is still illegal for stores to sell alcohol to those under age 18. Spain has the highest road mortality rates in Europe, and one of the highest rates of drunk driving deaths in Europe. Recently, Spanish officials have started setting up checkpoints on roads to test drivers' blood alcohol levels. Do not drive while intoxicated and be cautious on the road.

Terrorism

Until very recently, Basque terrorism was a serious concern for all travelers in Spain. A militant wing of Basque separatists called the Euskadi Ta Askatasuna (ETA; Basque Homeland and Freedom) continued to have an active presence well into the 2000s, but has recently taken a more dormant stance. Historically, ETA's attacks have been politically targeted and were not considered random terrorist attacks that endanger regular civilians. In January 2011, ETA declared a "permanent and general cease-fire," and at this point, many of ETA's leaders have been arrested. The group has also announced a "definitive cessation of its armed activity."

LANGUAGE

There are four main languages spoken in Spain, along with a slew of less widely spoken ones. Here are the ones you're likely to come across.

Spanish/Castellano

Castilian or Spanish is the official language of Spain. Spain's Spanish is distinct from its Western Hemisphere counterparts in its hallmark lisp of the z and soft c and its use of the vosotros form (second-person plural).

Catalan/Valenciancatalà/Valencià

Along the Mediterranean coast from Alicante up to the French border, the main language spoken is Catalan, along with its close relative Valencian. Throughout the regions of Catalonia, Valencia, and the Balearic Islands, as well as parts of Aragon, this Romance language sounds to most ears like a combination of Spanish, Italian, and French. It's also the official language of the small principality of Andorra. Never imply that Catalan is a dialect of Spanish—this is untrue and will turn the entire nation of Andorra against you.

Basque/Euskara

Basque looks extraterrestrial—full of z's, x's, and k's—but the Basques don't care how pretty their language looks; they just care about preserving it. After decades of concerted efforts by Franco to wipe euskara out, it is still the official language of about 600,000 people, though you won't need to know a word of it to get by in País Vasco's main cities.

Galician/Galego

Somewhere between Spanish and Portuguese falls Galician, spoken in Galicia, in the northwest corner of the peninsula. As with Basque, you won't need your Spanish-Galician dictionary to get by, though it'll probably help with most menus.

Other Languages

In the British territory of Gibraltar, English is spoken, of course, though the locals also speak a creole known as Llanito. Languages you're less likely to come across in your travels include Asturian, spoken along parts of the northern coast; Leonese, in the area around Astorga; Extremaduran, in Extremadura; Aranese, in the valley around Vielha; Aragonese, in the mountains of Aragon north of Huesca; and Caló, spoken by the Romanior gypsy community across Spain.

spain 101

HISTORY

When in Rome's Empire (300 BCE-711 CE)

Although Spanish history doesn't really get exciting—and by exciting we mean recorded—until the Romans, there is a bit to tell about the early tribes on the Iberian Peninsula. The pre-Roman inhabitants consisted mostly of Greeks in the south along the Mediterranean and Celts in the north, with various Iberian tribes scattered throughout. The Romans rolled into Spain in the third century and conquered the peninsula with just the teensiest bit of difficulty. The Basque tribes in the north-east kept up the fight for a good 200 years after the rest of Iberia was conquered. (Think Braveheart: the Spanish version.) Although the Romans were oppressive and attempted to wipe out most Iberian cultural traditions, they did leave a few positive impressions on the country. Organized government and a powerful economy greatly improved the general living standards of the peninsula's residents, with a lasting effect. Where do you think the term Romance language came from? (Besides Catalan's unquestionably romantic nature, of course.)

When the Roman Empire collapsed in the fifth century Spain was once again up for grabs. Germanic tribes invaded Spain in full force, with the super-Christian Visigoths ultimately taking control; they ruled from the fifth to the eighth century.

Tell Me Moor, Tell Me Moor (711-1492)

The rapid spread of Islam and its empire across northern Africa would bring another change to the Iberian Peninsula. The Moors invaded in 711: once they gained control, Spain experienced one of its least violent and most prosperous periods ever. Though the caliphate's capital lay in Damascus, Al-Andalus, as Spain became known, was one of the most important parts of the empire. Though the Muslim-controlled land was relatively conflict free, they did have to deal with the constant threat of the Christian Reconquista, the gradual reconquest of the peninsula from the north by the Christians who held out in the mountains, never conquered.

A Golden Age of Ignorance (1492-1715)

After eight centuries of war, Ferdinand and Isabella finally succeeded at driving the Muslims from the Iberian Peninsula, capturing the last stronghold of Granada in 1492. And that year Columbus just happened to discover America. All of a sudden, boom! Spain's back on top. The royals' objective was to expand and conquer, and with the best land army in the world and a God-sent armada, expand and conquer they did. They threw huge amounts of manpower and money into acquiring more manpower and money. More specifically, they threw all of their energy into acquiring gold from the Americas. The conquistadors pretty much took care of (and we use "took care of" here in the North Jersey sense of the word) any indigenous peoples who got in their way and sent all their plunder back to Spain. This Golden Age quickly lapsed into decadence, however, as Spain's riches flowed right through the Iberian Peninsula and into the rest of Europe to pay down Spain's massive debts. Facing a serious crisis and clearly unaware of the dangers of circular reasoning, Charles V decided to go to war to get money to pay his soldiers. In a completely expected and predictable twist, this led to the collapse of the his dynasty.

It was at this point that Spain stopped being a player on the world stage and started getting played. The War of Spanish Succession, which lasted from 1700-1715, saw France attempting to place their own ruler on the Spanish throne. While this was clever thinking on France's part, there was no way Austria, the Netherlands, and Britain were going to let France obtain that kind of power. With everyone trying to put their own puppet king in place, Spain became a country to be dominated, not feared. In the end, France got their royal Frenchman, Philip V, on the Spanish throne.

Getting Conquered: the Spain Story (1716-1897)

A relatively peaceful era of postwar lull was short-lived. One Napoleon Bonaparte was on the move, and Spain had to pick a side. Napoleon already had a fair amount of land conquered—all of the rest of continental Europe, basically, plus a bit more elsewhere—and was looking to scoop up Portugal while he was rolling. Spain was on board with this plan. What he didn't tell Spain, as he was moving 100,000 troops through their country "to Portugal," was that he planned to pick up Spain along the way. In April 1808, on his casual conquering trip to Portugal, Napoleon deposed the

Spanish monarch and placed his brother, Joseph Bonaparte, in charge of Spain. While the deposing and re-monarching of Spain was pretty easy, quelling the ensuing Spanish revolution was not. With Britain's support, the Spaniards proceeded to give 'em hell, and in 1814 they successfully drove the French out. However, this sparked yet another war of Spanish succession that raged on and off during the 19th century. This time period saw three different rulers, and, just for a bit of spice, the creation of the First Spanish Republic (1873-74).

The Disaster of 1898

Spain had, over the preceding century, lost most of its American possessions as they became independent nations. Cuba, too, was unhappy with Spain's state of affairs, and the United States was unhappy with Cuba's. Fortunately for Spain, the United States had expressed little interest in going to war with Spain, and the Cuban revolution was an easily fixable situation. Unfortunately for Spain, they messed everything up so badly that most Spaniards still refuse to talk about the "Disaster of 1898." The USS Maine, was "mysteriously" blown up on a friendly trip to Cuba. The United States had been more than willing to stay out of the conflict until that moment. The US takes the whole sinking ships thing seriously (World War I, anyone?), and proceeded to invade and liberate Cuba, Puerto Rico, and the Philippines from Spain.

A Century of Turmoil (1900-2000)

Spain remained neutral in WWI, but was soon to encounter its own share of bloodshed. Political divisions within the country eventually led to riots in 1934 by anarchists and other extreme leftists, quelled by the army and one General Francisco Franco. Two years later, the same leftists made some gains in national elections, and Franco dropped the hammer, initiating a civil war that continues to tear the country apart even today, 74 years after its supposed conclusion.

Though the Republicans were technically in control of the government—we use the term "in control" loosely—and had fairly broad-reaching support, they were fractured in their political ideologies. The anarchists, communists, and socialists just couldn't get along—shocking. Franco's fascist supporters, on the other hand, were disciplined and well organized and had the support of Mussolini's and Hitler's powerful governments. The clash between the Republicans and Franco's fascists led to three years of civil war from 1936-39, which saw the loss of hundreds of thousands of lives, many of them civilians, followed by 50 years of brutal dictatorship under Generalísimo Franco.

Even today, Spain is divided over Franco's rule. Over 150,000—including many civilians—were killed, and local languages and traditions were suppressed. Yet, under Franco's rule, Spain had one of its longest periods of political and economic stability. With Franco's death in 1975, Spain transitioned to a constitutional monarchy, once again lagging far behind its European counterparts. Today, Spain is a flourishing liberal country, though just as culturally divided as it's always been. Though considered something of a Eurozone liability in economic terms, modern-day Spain is nevertheless an integral part of the European Union.

CUSTOMS AND ETIQUETTE

When in Spain...Be Late

It's probably best to fully adapt to "Spanish time," or you might end up missing out on most of what Spain has to offer. Besides the little things, like being 15-20min. late for meetings or events, the Spanish basically overhaul their entire day's schedule to better fit their night-owl lifestyle. A prime example: meals. Lunches don't happen before 1pm; most occur around 2pm and are usually followed by a siesta, during which most businesses will close. As for the evening, Spain is not constrained by any

spain

of the Puritan influences that Americans have to deal with—nothing closes at 2am and you can buy alcohol well after 11pm (looking at you, Boston). How does this work, you might wonder? Let us walk you through a normal day. Wake up around 9am and eat a light breakfast. Work until lunch around 2pm, take a siesta, then head back to work from around 4 or 5pm until 8 or 9pm. Dinner is usually around 10 or 11pm. For the younger crowd, the bars only get interesting around midnight or 1am, and clubs only around 2 or 3am. Dance until 5 or 6am, stumble home to your (or a) bed, and get ready to wake up at 9am to do it all over again.

How to Avoid Getting Punched

You've probably realized by now that Spain is a pretty divided country, meaning that Spaniards have a huge sense of pride in their home neighborhoods and regions. In fact, many of them would probably be pretty insulted that we keep writing "Spaniards." Consider them Catalans/Basques/Andalusians/Romani/Madrileños first and Spaniards second. Another tip? Avoid discussing the Spanish Civil War unless you know for sure which side the family of the person to whom you are speaking was on. Same goes for soccer. Unless you know with certainty that your audience is full of Barça supporters, you might want to hold off on describing Messi's most recent goal in excruciating detail.

FOOD AND DRINK

Food

You've probably been to a tapas bar, but you might not have known that tapas is not a type of food—it simply refers to the way the food is presented. The bite-sized portions served at the bar are not to be mistaken with appetizers. Spaniards eat tapas most commonly after work, well before dinner, or while just out drinking. Pinxtos, the Basque equivalent, are served on toothpicks.

If you're in Spain during the summer, you will most likely end up getting gazpacho, a chilled tomato soup. One thicker variety of gazpacho is salmorejo; think of it as the delicious lovechild of normal tomato soup and traditional gazpacho.

On a budget? Probably, given that you're using Let's Go as a travel guide. No worries, Spanish peasants had years to try and make their measly amount of ingredients taste good—cue *paella*. Common at village festivals, this rice-based dish can be flavored with pork, seafood, veggies, snails, and whatever mystery meat is found in the freezer that week—it really doesn't matter. Just cook up some rice, let it marinade for forever (at least all day) with whatever flavoring suits you best, and you're done!

If you've got cash to blow, your primary goal in Spain should probably to get your hands (and tongue) on some jamón ibérico. In simple terms, it's Spanish ham. But there is so much more to it than that. The ibérico pigs are treated like royalty, allowed to roam the countryside stuffing their fat faces with acorns for two years. After being butchered, the ham is salted and cured for two years, during which time it loses at least 20% of its weight and gains about 400% of its monetary value. Make it your life goal to find some of that thinly sliced piece of heaven.

Drinks

Sangria is Spain's drink much the same way that a vodka Red Bull is America's—it gets you drunk, and most people would never drink it in the light of day. It's made by mixing wine with fruit juice and whatever cheap liquor one can easily acquire. Usually it's rum, bourbon, and whiskey. Yes, we meant to say "and," not "or." Think of it as the Spanish version of frat boy punch. Another way to utilize bad wine? Tinto de verano—"red wine of summer." Just take the old/cheap/bad-tasting wine you have/found/made and mix it with some lemon soda. Mix it with Coke, and you have a kalimotxo. The hotter the day, the more mixer you use, and you've got yourself a refreshing summer drink.

If beer is more your thing, Spain isn't famous for its selection. Most bars will just have one beer on tap, and it will most likely be a Mahou, though Cruzcampo and San Miguel are also popular. In Catalonia the standard is TEstrella Damm, which is by far Let's Go's favorite.

SPORTS

Spain, like any other normal European country, does the usual when it comes to European sports—skiing in the mountains, playing soccer on any flat surface, and ignoring American football. As in France, cycling and handball are popular spectator and recreational sports. Basketball, too, is quite popular: several Spaniards have made their way into the NBA. Yet there are a few sports that are considered quint-essentially Spanish.

Not to Be Confused with the Running of the Bulls

Bullfighting, Spain's oldest sport, has historically been its most controversial. Apologists consider it more of an art and a tradition than a sport. Critics call it a horrid spectacle of bloodsport and violence. Either way, it garners attention. Matadors can achieve the same level of celebrity as actors and soccer stars. So how does bull-fighting work, exactly? It's divided into three stages, with three different players for each stage: the picadores, the bandilleros, and the shiny-panted men, more officially known as matadors. First, the picadores come out on horseback and stab the bull many times with a lance to tire and wound it. Then the bandilleros come out and stab the bull in the back of the neck with colorful spears. Finally, the matador arrives to much fanfare, toys with the bull for a little while, and kills it by stabbing it in the neck. This ritual is then repeated five more times in a corrida. The Canary Islands and Catalonia have banned the practice of the sport.

The Favorite Child

Bullfighting may be Spain's oldest sport, but football (the European kind) is Spain's universally adored younger child. Spaniards live and breathe for their teams, the most famous and successful being Real Madrid and TFC Barcelona. La Liga, the Spanish premier league, is arguably the best in the world, though the argument depends on how British you are. Games run from August until May, with league games generally played on the weekends and Copa del Rey (an open tournament for all Spanish teams) and Champions League (comprised of the best clubs in Europe) games during the week.

The Game of a Thousand Thrills

The Basques, ever fiercely independent, have their own sport, too. Jai alai, or pilota, is sort of like racquetball, only the players wear baskets on their hands and the ball might as well be live ammunition. Called the fastest game in the world, the ball can reach speeds of 180mph. While that may not be as fast as a bullet, it is fast enough to do some serious damage to those who get in its way. Basically, the two players hurl the ball at the wall in an attempt to either score a point or decapitate their opponent. Although the decapitating part is not in the official handbook, from empirical observation one can only assume that it's one of the main objectives of the game.

spain

ART AND ARCHITECTURE

Architecture

Spanish architecture, with just as many influences as the rest of Spanish culture, is all over the place. You'll find traces of Roman, Celtic, Islamic, Romanesque, Gothic, Renaissance, Baroque, Modernist, and postmodern architecture all over the country, in various combinations.

All over Andalusia you'll find remnants of the era of Muslim rule. The most astounding examples that still stand are the Alhambra in Granada (p. 1063), the Alcázar de Sevilla (p. 1040), and the mosque (now Cathedral) of Córdoba (p. 1053)—architecture that all dates from the eighth to 15th century.

Most of the churches you'll come across in your Spanish travels will fit into one of these categories. Romanesque architecture is characterized by semicircular arches, heavy stone walls with small windows, and simple interiors; many of the most austerely beautiful spaces in Spain are in this style. Gothic architecture is probably a bit more familiar—pointed arches, huge stained-glass windows, and the famous flying buttresses. Though there is some overlap, Romanesque architecture generally precedes Gothic, with the transition occurring in around the 13th or 14th centuries in most places.

As conquering Christian forces drove south, the Spanish adopted many aspects of Islamic architecture and incorporated it into a new hybrid style called the mudéjar style. This originated on the Castilian plain, most likely in the town of Sahagún, and spread all across the regions of Castile and Aragon. Some chief characteristics of this style are intricate, patterned brickwork as the chief material, with some Islamic-inspired ornaments and motifs, including glazed tile or azulejo. Prime examples include Sevilla's Plaza de España (p. 1039) and Barcelona's Arc de Triomf (p. 998).

Limited mainly to Barcelona and nearby cities during the final decade of the 19th century and the first of the 20th, the modernista movement threw splashes of color and trippy architectural motifs all over Catalonia. Its most famous innovator is undoubtedly Antoni Gaudí.

Painting

Diego Velázquez: court painter, architect, lady-killer. At least, this is what we gather from his famous self-portrait on the left margin of Las Meninas. It calls attention to his long hair, impressive moustache, and piercing gaze. Influenced by Spanish and Flemish realism, Velazquez is best known for his naturalistic paintings, such as Las Meninas and The Water Carrier of Seville. Also operating in the early 1600s was El Greco, real name Doménikos Theotokópoulos. No wonder they gave him a nickname. For those who haven't guessed yet, his name means the Greek. Less of a lady-killer than Velázquez (he was bald), El Greco made up for it with his vivid and emotional paintings. Said to reflect the Counter-Reformation in Spain, his strong color contrasts and elongated human figures can be pretty creepy, but beautifully vivid.

Moving on to the 18th century, we stumble upon Francisco Goya, affectionately called the Father of Modern Art. Also a court painter, his best work was done outside of his courtly duties. His frank, emotional technique created a whole new style of painting, refreshing to the Spanish people. It was a bit too refreshing for the Spanish Inquisition,however. Goya was detained and questioned for his painting, The Naked Maja, one of the first paintings of a nude woman in Spain. Released relatively unscathed, Goya lived on to do some of his best works exposing the French atrocities during Napoleon's rule of Spain. The most famous of these, The Third of May 1808, depicts the slaughter of Spanish civilians by the French army. His Black Paintings are also seriously weird.

STUDY

For the adventurous yet studious traveler, Spain offers plenty. You can indulge your nerdy side amid medieval buildings, Gaudí masterpieces, or arid mountains.

- **UNIVERSIDAD DE SALAMANCA:** A must-see for tourists, the Universidad de Salamanca outstrips Harvard in age and Oxford in beauty. An ideal study abroad destination, the oldest university in Spain can also boast of world-class faculty and a robust college town. (☎34 923 294 400 informacion@usal.es)

- **UNIVERSITAT DE BARCELONA:** Barcelona has it all: medieval buildings, Roman ruins, modern art museums, chic boutiques, hot nightclubs, and, according to several ranking agencies, *the* best university in Spain to boot. Indeed, the city that gave us Razzmatazz is also home to high-level academics. (☎34 934 02 17 79 entorns.web@ub.edu)

- **SUNSEED DESERT TECHNOLOGY:** Spain might be obsessed with La Roja, but that doesn't mean you have to give up your green to visit. Enjoy the Spanish countryside while conducting a long-term (five weeks or more) research project at this educational non-profit, which seeks to "develop, demonstrate, and communicate low-tech methods of living sustainably in a semi-arid environment." (☎34 950 525 770 sunseed@sunseed.org.uk)

- **ESADE BUSINESS SCHOOL:** If the corporate world beckons you, think about spending some time at ESADE Business School in Barcelona; in recent years, *The Wall Street Journal* has ranked it first on its list because of the school's rep with recruiters. (☎34 91 359 77 14)

- **IESE BUSINESS SCHOOL:** At IESE, you can schmooze with Europe's future business leaders by day and party with soccer-obsessed locals by night (work hard, party hard, right?). Unlike its competitor, ESADE, which is situated in the cosmopolitan city of Barcelona, the world-renowned IESE Business School lies in a more traditionally Spanish area—namely, Navarre, the home of the Pamplona bull run. (☎34 932 53 42 00 mbainfo@iese.edu)

VOLUNTEER

Even if your Spanish skills are not up to snuff, you still have the chance to polish your halo abroad. Spaniards are looking for native English speakers to immerse them in the language and help them hone their skills.

- **VAUGHANTOWN:** Volunteering goes upscale with VaughanTown, the week-long, English immersion program that caters mainly to Spanish businessmen. Vaughan Town has several sites in the bucolic landscape of Central Spain and provides airfare, meals, and four-star accommodations (meaning bathrooms with jacuzzis) for English-speaking volunteers. (☎34 902 68 66 64)

- **ESTACIÓN INGLESA:** A little wary about the time commitment involved in these English-immersion programs? Estación Inglesa is a week-long, English immersion program with a more relaxed schedule, meaning that volunteers have time to explore the local town or relax on the beach. (☎34 968 113 555 anglos@estacioninglesa.es)

- **MY FAMILY ABROAD:** With the My Family Abroad program, you'll pay your way to Spain and then enjoy free room and board with a Spanish family living in Madrid; your job is to talk in English with them for at least 15hr. a week. (info@myfamilyabroad.com)

- **SUNSEED DESERT TECHNOLOGY:** Sunseed Desert Technology accommodates volunteers who are staying between two and five weeks. You'll be in the countryside of southern Spain, analyzing irrigation lines, herb preservation, and waste water management while taking in beautiful mountain views of Los Molinos de Rios Aguas—we dare say, it's a lovely way to address an inconvenient truth. (☎34 950 525 770 sunseed@sunseed.org.uk)

WORK

Luckily for the cash-strapped traveler, these islands have plenty of seasonal, hotel entertainment" jobs that are open to English-speakers who know at least one other European language.

- **ACTTIV:** Becoming a hotel "entertainer" with a company like Acttiv is a way to visit these sites and leave Spain with a net gain in money. (☎34 914 324 363 www.acttiv.net)

- **EUROTUTORS:** Teaching English can earn you not only brownie points but also hard cash. EuroTutors is a Valencia-based tutoring company that pays it TEFL teachers to teach individuals or small groups of students. (info@eurotutors.co.uk)

- **STEM ENGLISH:** Stem English is also looking for TEFL teachers, but their credential requirements are a bit tougher than EuroTutors; they ask for tutors with more extensive teaching experience. (info@stemenglish.com)

- **DIVE AND SEA TENERIFE:** For Spain-bound travelers, the Canary Islands offer some of Europe's best waters for warm water scuba diving, and the Dive and Sea Tenerife in the Canary Islands is often looking to fill diving instructor positions. (phil@diveandseatenerife.com)

From there, we move into more modern styles and the inevitable Pablo Picasso. Volatile, emotional, always in need of a muse, Picasso is everything we expect a painter to be. Picasso is credited with starting the Cubism movement, commonly called the "What the heck is happening in this painting?" movement, and made a tremendous political statement with Guernica in 1937, depicting the bombing of civilians by fascists during the Civil War.

Heavily influenced by Picasso, Joan Miró moved the 20th century into Surrealism. An unsmiling man always dressed in somber suits, he took his work very seriously. Not that one could really tell. His playful colors and simple forms bring to mind children's artwork. Look closely though, and there is a certain dark feeling to his work that stays with you.

There's no way to have a conversation on surrealism without the movement's star: Salvador Dalí. With a moustache to die for, greased back hair, and always in a suit, Dalí was a character whose ultimate goal was to get at the greater reality of man's subconscious. Most famous for his painting The Persistence of Memory, (a dorm room favorite) Dalí did much more than paint. He did everything from sculptures to book illustrations to jewelry design. Judging by all the photos we found of him, he also enjoyed intensely staring people down and walking his pet anteater and his Tocelot, Babou.

Literature

Although not always renowned for its literary genius, Spain does have a few key authors to mention. While Miguel de Cervantes's name might not trigger a memory, his world famous opus, Don Quixote, certainly should. Born in 1547, Cervantes's life is almost more interesting than anything he could ever have written: it involves getting kidnapped by pirates and enslaved in Algiers for two years.

Another groundbreaking work of Spanish literature, The Life of Lazarillo de Tormes and His Fortunes and Adversities, came in quite low in the shortest title competition. In the mystery category, however, it ranked quite high. It was published anonymously in 1554 and then outlawed by the Spanish Inquisition for heresy (hence the anonymity of the author). Then again, what wasn't? One of the first Picaresque novels, Lazarillo de Tormes was highly critical of Spanish society and greatly advanced the genres of the satire and the novel in one blow.

Federico García Lorca wore many hats during his lifetime. As a poet, dramatist, and theater director, Lorca gave the world insight into 20th century Spain. Right smack dab in the middle of corruption and coup, Lorca's work reflects the decades of violence, but also dabbled in themes of love and passion. Considered too liberal by conservative nationalists, Lorca was shot and buried in an unmarked grave in 1936 at the start of the Civil War.

Flamenco

Most likely drawing from Jewish, Muslim, and Roma culture, Flamenco may be Spain's most stereotypically known art form. Most people only think of flamenco as shapely ladies in tight polka-dotted dresses, but it actually originated as a musical genre, with the dancing added on later to complement the pairing of guitar and vocals. Flamenco is violent and emotional; you sort of need to see it to get it.

TURKEY

You've trekked the byways of Europe, camped out in hostels from Barcelona to Bruges. You've made your way east to Budapest, and now you're Hungary for something a little...different. Lucky for you, there's a feast of Turkey waiting, just a short plane ride (or long train trip) away. Straddling two continents, Turkey has long served as Europe's portal to the East. Three percent of the country, including most of Istanbul, sits in Europe; the rest spreads out into Asia. Culturally and politically, Turkey sits squarely between East and West. The population is overwhelmingly Muslim, but thestate is avowedly secular and dedicated to the values of multi-party democracy. Ancient and modern also coexist here with ease. The modern Republic of Turkey is only 90 years old, but it rests on a rich heritage built by Ancient Greeks, Romans, Byzantines, and Ottomans. This is the country that inspired the legends of the Trojan Horse and Santa Claus, and it's home to the world's oldest temple and Europe's fastest-growing economy.

No grand tour of Europe can be complete without a visit to Istanbul, home to some of the greatest buildings and monuments on earth—and with apopulation of more than 10 million, this metropolis dwarfs most European cities. For no extra charge, we even throw a bit of Asia into the mix.

greatest hits

- **MOSQUERCIZE.** Istanbul's mosques are truly incredible sights—and most are free (p. 844).
- **PALACE LIFE.** Experience the life of an Ottoman sultan at **Topkapı Palace** (p. 845) and **Dolmabahçe Palace** (p. 850).
- **RUBBER DUCKY, YOU'RE THE ONE.** Nothing makes bath time as fun as having it in an authentic Turkish *hamam* (p. 860).

istanbul

Byzantium. Constantinople. Istanbul. Welcome to the most envied spot on this planet for over two millennia, a place that has been lusted after, besieged, conquered, and glorified by everyone from Ottoman sultans to German chancellors. The haunting calls to prayer, the sweet smoke of *nargile* pipes, the glow of lamps and dark, seductive eyes, the blue of the Evil Eye, and the sea that sparkles all around—it's impossible not to feel a bit more sphinxy and a touch more sensual just by breathing the air of this ancient city of cities. And what a city! Centuries and religions play political bumper cars in the countless church-turned-mosque-turned-museums, with Mothers and Childs and names of the prophets benevolently glittering side by side in some of the most gorgeous spaces constructed by man. From multiple-orgasmic rounds of kebabs to kilograms of cherries, anyone can dine like a king on gloriously good, awesomely affordable Turkish food (a bountiful repertoire that encompasses Anatolian, Mediterranean, and traditional Ottoman cuisine). Here, the burning needs of shopaholics, walkaholics, and those with chronic and severe museum guilt shall all be met. Istanbul is the sexy child of so many marriages: between East and West; between the thrumming, pounding heart of a modern metropolis and the most ancient of fortresses; between the obscene opulence of Rococo palaces and the pure, simple pleasure of a hot glass of *çay*. Fortunately, you won't feel torn in two in any

turkey

sense, except in choosing which part of this bounteous babe to ravish first. Let's start with a question on a scale as grand as Istanbul deserves: which continent first?

ORIENTATION

Istanbul would be nothing without its waters. Acting as barriers, shipping lanes, and passages, they've come to define the city. The Bosphorus links the Sea of Marmara in the south to the Black Sea in the north, marking the border between Europe and Asia. Meanwhile, the Golden Horn *(Haliç)* divides the European side into north and south. Istanbul is a single city, but its components are vibrant and distinct. European Istanbul, which features most of the historic and cultural sights, is the better-looking half (sorry, Asia!), although that also means it's crammed with tourists(and those trying to make money off them). Walk around Sultanahmet for the most famous sights, but cross over to Beyoğlu to find the soul of modern Istanbul. Heading north on the European side, you'll find bustling Beşiktaş and opulent Ortaköy, where Istanbul's glitterati spend and party. On the Asian side, the mostly residential Üsküdar is bordered in the south by Kadiköy, the unofficial center of this half, while farther south, the quiet and comfortable life of Moda might tempt you to move there. With all these neighborhoods stretched between two continents, you'll have a lot to take in. Thankfully, between the city's buses, trains, and trams, you'll never find yourself far from Istanbul's cheap, convenient public transportation network, and the city's ferry service is the cheapest intercontinental cruise you'll ever take.

Sultanahmet and Environs

Home to the **Hagia Sophia** and the other crown jewels of historical Istanbul (fondly known to *Let's Go* as the Blue, the Hippo, and the Fish Tank), Sultanahmet is the first stop for anyone who wants to explore the city of cities they've read and dreamed about. Sultanahmet proper is the area teeming with tourists (and aggressively flirtatious tourist-trappers) around the **Blue Mosque**, where many budget accommodations and historical sights can be found. To the north, along the coast, are the **Sirkeci** and **Eminönü** neighborhoods, known for the **Spice Bazaar,** transportation hubs, bustling market streets, and finger-licking fast food on every corner. The **Galata Bridge** above Eminönü connects the historic peninsula to Karaköy across the **Golden Horn.** You'll find ferry terminals and tram stops on both sides of the bridge. The eastern tip of the peninsula is occupied by the sprawling **Topkapı Palace** and the peaceful **Gülhane Park.** To the west of Sultanahmet are **Çemberlitaş** and **Beyazıt Square,** the home of some university buildings, tea houses, and a gradual gradient of totally touristy to gone-native restaurants. The tram conveniently connects all of these neighborhoods, though the area is also nice and rigorous to walk. Shopaholics, sparkle-eyed ravens, and hardcore hoarders and hagglers can spend hours in the **Grand Bazaar,** a maze-like warren above Beyazıt. Below Beyazıt is the **Kumkapı** neighborhood, renowned (or infamous) for its overpriced fish restaurants. Come to Sultanahmet for the fabled sights and the full *(full,* we emphasize) tourist experience, but look elsewhere for a more authentic (and *cheaper*) vision of the city.

Western Fatih

You will hear two different Fatihs talked about in Istanbul. The municipality of Fatih covers the entire historical peninsula and includes Sultanahmet, Beyazıt, and all the nearby neighborhoods. Fatih proper (Western Fatih), on the other hand, is a small neighborhood around **Fatih Mosque** where government officials dwell and fun goes to die. It's more conservative than other neighborhoods, in the sense that there are more headscarves and mosques here than anywhere else and almost no establishments that serve alcohol, but there are also a surprising number of slick businessmen (which means Wi-Fi cafes!). Some of the best local restaurants in Istanbul can be hunted down in this quiet, residential district. One of the liveliest roads here is

istanbul

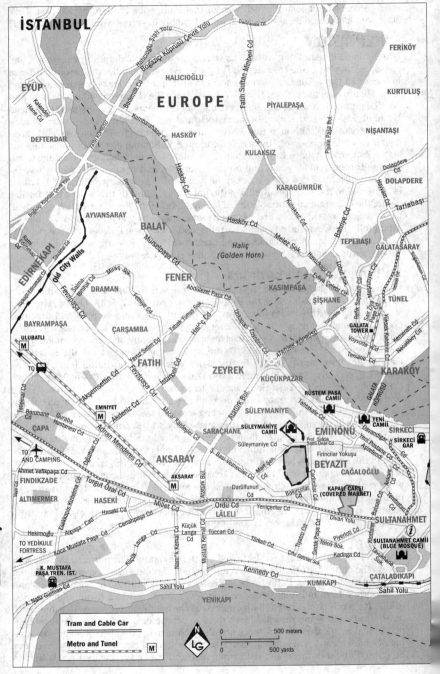

İSTANBUL

FERİKÖY

KURTULUŞ

EYÜP

EUROPE

HALICIOĞLU

PİYALEPAŞA

NİŞANTAŞI

DEFTERDAR

HASKÖY

KULAKSIZ

DOLAPDERE

KARAGÜMRÜK

Tarlabaşı

AYVANSARAY

BALAT

TEPEBAŞI

GALATASARAY

Haliç
(Golden Horn)

EDİRNEKAPI

Old City Walls

FENER

KASIMPAŞA

ŞİŞHANE

TÜNEL

BAYRAMPAŞA

DRAMAN

GALATA
TOWER

ULUBATLI

ÇARŞAMBA

FATİH

ZEYREK

KÜÇÜKPAZAR

KARAKÖY

EMNİYET

SÜLEYMANİYE

RÜSTEM PAŞA
CAMİİ

ÇAPA

SARAÇHANE

SÜLEYMANİYE
CAMİİ

EMİNÖNÜ

YENİ
CAMİİ

SİRKECİ

TO
AND CAMPING

AKSARAY

Süleymaniye Cd

SİRKECİ
GAR

FINDIKZADE

BEYAZIT

CAĞALOĞLU

ALTIMERMER

HASEKİ

AKSARAY

Darülfunun
Cd

KAPALI ÇARŞI
(COVERED MARKET)

LÂLELİ

Millet Cd

Ordu Cd

SULTANAHMET

TO YEDİKULE
FORTRESS

Divan Yolu

SULTANAHMET CAMİİ
(BLUE MOSQUE)

K. MUSTAFA
PAŞA TREN. İST.

ÇATALADIKAPI

KUMKAPI

Kennedy Cd

Sahil Yolu

YENİKAPI

Tram and Cable Car

Metro and Tunel M

N
LG

0   500 meters

0   500 yards

turkey

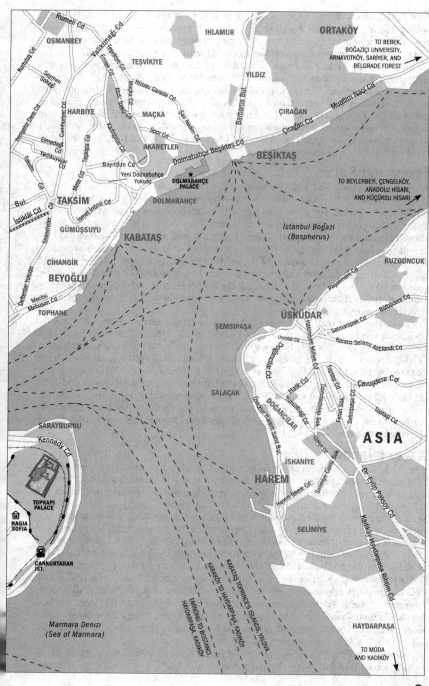

ISTANBUL

Map labels (as shown):

OSMANBEY · Rumeli Cd · Valikonağı Cd · IHLAMUR · ORTAKÖY · TO BEBEK, BOĞAZİÇİ UNIVERSITY, ARNAVUTKÖY, SARIYER, AND BELGRADE FOREST

Kurtuluş Cd · Kırtılaş Cd · Seymen Sokağı · TEŞVİKİYE · YILDIZ · Barbaros Bul

HARBİYE · Cumhuriyet Cd · Ergenekon Cd · Emlak Cd · Maçka Cd · Hüsrev Gerede Cd · ÇIRAĞAN · Muallim Naci Cd

Yenişehir Dere Cd · Elmadağ Cd · Yedikuyular Cd · MAÇKA · Kadırganlar Cd · Şair Nedim Cd · Çırağan Cd

Bayıldım Cd · Spor Cd · AKARETLER · Dolmabahçe Beşiktaş Cd · BEŞİKTAŞ

TAKSİM · Mete Cd · Taşkışla Cd · İsmet İnönü Cd · Yeni Dolmabahçe Yokuşu · DOLMABAHÇE PALACE · TO BEYLERBEYİ, ÇENGELKÖY, ANADOLU HİSARI, AND KÜÇÜKSU HİSARI

İstiklâl Cd · Sıraselviler · GÜMÜŞSUYU · DOLMABAHÇE · İstanbul Boğazi (Bosphorus)

CİHANGİR · KABATAŞ · KUZGUNCUK

BEYOĞLU · Defterdar Yokuşu · Paşalimanı Cd

Meclisi Mebusan Cd · TOPHANE · ŞEMSİPAŞA · ÜSKÜDAR · Bülbüldere Cd

Selmanipak Cd · Karaca Selami Al/Efendi Cd

Hakimiyet Millet Cd · Uncular Cd · Doğancılar Cd · Tonbul Cd · Çavuşdere Cd

SALACAK · Halk Cd · Tunusbağı Cd · Dolmabahçe Cd · Bağlarbaşı Cd · Toptaşı Cd

SARAYBURNU · ÜSküdar Harem Sahil Bul · DOĞANCILAR · Tıbbiye Cd · ASIA

Kennedy Cd · İSHANİYE · Dr. Eyüp Paksoy Cd

TOPKAPI PALACE · HAREM · Selimiye Camiş Sok

HAGIA SOFIA · Harem İskele Cd · Kadıköy Haydarpaşa Rıhtım Cd

CANKURTARAN IST. · SELİMİYE

Marmara Denızı (Sea of Marmara) · KABATAŞ TO PRINCE'S ISLANDS, YALOVA · KARAKÖY TO HAYDARPAŞA, KADIKÖY · EMİNÖNÜ TO BOSTANCI, HAYDARPAŞA, KADIKÖY · HAYDARPAŞA

TO MODA AND KADİKÖY

Fevzi Paşa Caddesi, which runs northwest from Fatih İtfaiye Park and features stores selling the most operatic wedding dresses you'll ever see, along with those long, thin, pretty trench coats that modern Muslim women seem to like wearing around town. If you follow the Valens Aqueduct from its southern end and turn right near the intersection with Atatürk Boulevard, you'll find the Siirt Bazaar, with its pretty, peaceful pedestrian Kadınlar Pazarı—something like Istanbul's "Little Kurdistan," where migrants from southeast Turkey sell the specialties and recipes they've brought with them. You'll have the best lamb of your life here. Atpazarı Meydanı, a cute cluster of cafes and *nargile* joints, lies a few blocks east of the mosque and above the Siirt Bazzar. To the north of the Fatih Mosque is Çarşamba, which makes Fatih look like a hippie commune. Locals advise dressing a touch more conservatively in Fatih (read: no short shorts for women).

Fener and Balat

It's said that Fener and Balat—two districts that sit on each other's laps via an organic spread of tiny, maze-like streets—was where the Ottomans herded all the city's Greek, Jewish, and Armenian minorities, ingenuously counterbalancing every church with a mosque and synagogue. Nowadays, it's mostly a dilapidated residential district that appears to be slowly falling apart, but endearingly so. The buildings are run-down (some built on top of the crumbling walls of Constantinople, "just waiting for the next earthquake," says a local), but they're also well-used and well-worn by giggly children, by laundry hanging on lines stretching across the street, by bearded men sitting on the curb to talk and drink tea for hours, and certainly not by tourists. Unlike in flashy Sultanahmet, each house here looks like a home, and the locals are overwhelmingly kindhearted.

Since the street plan is maddening, bring a good map, use landmarks, and ask old men what you're looking for (unless it's something like "wisdom" or "true love"—and even then they could probably give some advice). Public transportation sticks mainly to the periphery, so get ready for a rigorous walk. Rely on the main roads when going inland (highlighted in yellow on maps), and stick to the coast if covering long distances on foot. Vodina Caddesi runs parallel to the shore between Fener and Balat and is packed with local stores. The hilltop neighborhood of Edirnekapı is a 15min. walk inland, close to the city walls, and home to the mosaic-filled Chora Church. Go further up the Golden Horn to Eyüp to find Eyüp Sultan Mosque, the Pierre Loti Café, and the Istanbul Dolphinarium.

Asian Istanbul

The Asian side of Istanbul tends to be confusing for travelers, since it isn't laid out like most European cities. However, make your way through this part of town to discover a lively, alternative art scene and an abundance of cafes and restaurants, all free from the mobs of tourists that you'll find across the Bosphorus. Window-shoppers might never leave Bağdat Caddesi, İstiklal Cad.'s fancier sibling in Bostancı, where high-end luxury stores compete with sexy cars for the greatest glitz. There are a few streets in the main, historic neighborhood of Kadıköy to keep in mind. Inland from the ferry terminal (where you'll also find the bus and local minibus terminals) runs Söğütlüçeşme Caddesi, which intersects with Kadıköy's important pedestrian street, Bahariye Caddesi. This intersection is home to a well-known statue of a bull, an excellent landmark and meeting point. Parallel to Bahariye Cad. is the neighborhood's "bar street," Kadife Sokak, and tucked away nearby is the "handicrafts street," Ali Suah Sokak, distinguishable by the colored tiling on the ground. Güneşlibahçe Sokak, which intersects with Söğütlüçeşme Cad. near the ferry terminal, is known for Kadıköy Market and streets full of restaurants and live music.

Moda is easily navigated on foot, but if you want you can take the nostalgic, shoe box of a tram that follows a circular route around Kadıköy into suburbia. Üsküdar, home to over 180 mosques, is a rather sleepy, historic neighborhood some kilometers north of Kadıköy; visit the Mihrimah Sultan, Şemsi Pasha, and Çinili mosques for a sampling of the best. For easy travel between Kadıköy and Üsküdar, take public bus #12 or #12A. Farther into Asia, the suburbs have their own charms and personalities.

Beşiktaş and Ortaköy

Beşiktaş is a busy but peaceful residential village a few kilometers up from **Kabataş**. Home to many young professionals, university students, families, and soccer fanatics (Beşiktaş J.K. is a major Turkish team, part of the first established sports club in Turkey), it's well connected to both Taksim to the west and the Bosphorus to the east. Though it's surrounded by extremely upscale, dainty districts like **Nişantaşı** and **Ortaköy**, the heart of Beşiktaş is still thoroughly middle class, with a great fish market, and, for whatever reason, a lot of *kahvaltı* (breakfast) cafes—Beşiktaş is *so* full of breakfast. A small pedestrian and market center is the most popular hub, with a central **eagle statue** as an excellent orientation point. The streets branching out from this center hold lots of cheap food, bakeries, local clothing stores, and cafes. To reach the statue, head inland from the ferry terminal or the bus station onto **Ortabahçe Caddesi** and take the second right.

As you walk or bus it up the **Bosphorus coast,** you'll notice things getting prettier and pricier as you go—the next big village after Beşiktaş is **Ortaköy**, about a 15min. walk north. Ortaköy is the start of the district known as Istanbul's leading site of conspicuous consumption. The city's famous clubs are mostly concentrated on **Muallim Naci Caddesi**, which runs from Ortaköy to **Kuruçeşme**. Muallim Naci is part of the main road (at some points Dolmabahçe and Çirağan) that runs along the beautiful Bosphorus shoreline, connecting Kabataş with these neighborhoods. Although you can take one of the many buses, the frequently bad traffic means that you're better off walking and basking in the opulence of your surroundings. We recommend a day spent walking up and down the 7-mile shoreline between the excellent **Sakıp Sabancı Museum**, way up in **Emirgan** (above both the Bosphorus and the Fatih Sultan Mehmet bridges), and Beşiktaş, or bus-hopping to catch the prettiest waterside villages and their countless ice cream shops. **Rumeli, Arnavutköy,** and **Bebek** (which appropriately means "Baby" in Turkish—the town of Bebek really is an adorable little thing) all offer similarly gorgeous cafes and boutique stores next to areas of the Bosphorus that are so blue and sparkly that anyone can just cannonball off the waterside walkway into the sea and swim (there are also convenient ladders on the sides of the sidewalk). You'll see some of the most stunning, well-dressed girls here, as well as some of the most undressed men and teenage boys.

Beyoğlu

If Fener/Balat is the childhood friend, Asian Istanbul the sweetheart next door, Çanakkale the summer fling, Ortaköy the one out of your league, and Sultanahmet the one you're supposed to marry, Beyoğlu is the Istanbul you want to drunkenly hook up with (and then maybe get a lazy brunch together in the morning). The beating, pounding heart of modern Istanbul, this district is brimming with galleries, stores, cafes, restaurants, bars, and clubs. Many of these establishments are located off **İstiklal Caddesi**, a throbbing promenade that connects the transportation hub of **Taksim Square** in the north with **Tünel Square** in the south. You'll find brand names, consulates, heeled hotties, and a constant flow of people on and around İstiklal. Halfway into İstiklal, you won't miss the ornate gates and columns of Istanbul's most prestigious high school, the **Galatasaray Lisesi**, and two landmark streets that spread like arms out from that point, **Yeni Çarşı Caddesi** and **Meşrutiyet Caddesi**. A bit below Tünel is the **Galata Tower**, the most recognizable point on Istanbul's European skyline. The blocks around it house little designer shops, cafes, and a revitalized creative scene. For a calmer, residential feel, head to **Cihangir**, a drastically gentrified

istanbul

"bohemian" neighborhood that is popular with expats and located south of Taksim Sq., bordered by **Sıraselviler Caddesi** to the west. The Sultanahmet tram doesn't run to İstiklal; to get there, either get off at **Karaköy** and take the **funicular** to Tünel, or go to **Kabataş** and take the funicular to Taksim.

SIGHTS

Historic, beautiful, scenic, artsy, quirky: Istanbul has many personalities. Each sight has a history (often a very long one), and as a rule of thumb, the older the building, the more likely it's had at least one makeover. You'll see many mosques where Muslims covered or destroyed Christian symbols to make way for their own faith. Even contemporary spaces like the Istanbul Modern Art Museum have used the old (in this case, an abandoned warehouse) to create something new (a showcase for the country's contemporary art scene). Sometimes, however, renovation wasn't enough. The sprawling home of the sultans, Topkapı Palace, was abandoned for the more ornate and European-style Dolmabahçe. Go beyond art and architecture, too: you'll find culture and history everywhere. Remember to step back and take in the big picture. Revel in the sensation of crossing between continents like it's no big deal, float into the sky on the Turk Balon for an aerial view, or make your way up Çamlıca Hill for a 360-degree panorama. Whether you have your nose pressed against the glass or your neck craned back to take in the magnificence of the Blue Mosque, Istanbul has an incredible number of things to see.

Sultanahmet and Environs

▨ HAGIA SOPHIA   MUSEUM
Ayasofya Meydanı   ☎0212 522 1750 www.ayasofyamuzesi.gov.tr
The Hagia Sophia (or the more beautiful way of saying it, *Aya Sofya*) is Istanbul in one building. Built by a physicist and a mathematician in the 6th century CE under the Byzantine emperor Justinian I, the Sophia served as a Christian church until the Ottoman conquest of Constantinople in 1453. The Ottomans employed the great architect Mimar Sinan to mosquify it, adding minarets and plastering over much of the Christian art. In the 1930s, religious bumper cars came out again when Atatürk ordered that the Hagia Sophia be turned into a secular museum and opened to all (paying) visitors. Religions and centuries overlap here: Archangel Gabriel watches over the shimmering Mary, baby Jesus, and the *mihrab*, the niche in the wall that points towards Mecca. If you come in the morning, the early light of day will spill in like heaven from the apse windows and climb its way up to engulf the dome in blinding white.
i ⓂSultanahmet. Walk down Caferiye Sok. away from Hotel Sultanahmet; it's the orange-colored building with minarets on the left. Arrive early on weekday mornings for the shortest lines. 25 TL. Audio tour 15 TL. ⓩ Open in summer Tu-Su 9am-7pm; in winter 9am-5pm. Last entry 1hr. before close. Last entry to upper gallery 15min. before close.

BLUE MOSQUE (SULTANAHMET MOSQUE)   MOSQUE
Sultanahmet Camii   ☎0545 577 1899
While people say the Hagia Sophia is less remarkable on the outside than on the inside, the Blue Mosque is often said to be the reverse. Perhaps this is true, but only because the mosque's silvery-blue exterior, shooting minarets, and soaring domes are hard to match. When the Blue Mosque was built in the early 17th century, its six impressive minarets were said to have caused an uproar, as the Haram Mosque in Mecca was the only place of worship with the same number. In an elaborate bit of damage control, the sultan sent his architect to Mecca to build a seventh minaret for their mosque. Intricately decorated with the blue Iznik porcelain tiles responsible for the mosque's name, this mosque feels a bit like being inside a colossal blue china teapot, but filled with light and grace rath-

turkey

844 ⓠ www.letsgo.com

er than hot water. Part of the effect is due to the enormous dome, supported by four "elephant feet," huge pillars 5m in diameter. Unfortunately, the very sacred, old solemnity of this space is broken by the herds of tourists snapping away. Because the Blue Mosque is still in active religious use, tourists have to enter through a separate entrance, keep to a crowded designated area, and remain outside during prayer times. This means no silence at all, of course, and the whole place smells like feet (imagine hundreds of travelers entering the mosque barefoot in summer). If you're not a practicing Muslim but a lover of beauty and sacred space, come early or late for more serenity.

i Ⓜ*Sultanahmet. Walk down Atmeydani Cad., away from the park. The mosque is the big gray building with 6 minarets on the left. Mosque etiquette applies; head coverings, skirts, and scarves distributed at the entrance. Free.* ☼ *Open to non-worshipping visitors M-Th 8:30am-12:15pm, 2-4:45pm, and 5:45-6:30pm; F after 2:30pm; Sa-Su 8:30am-12:15pm, 2-4:45pm, and 5:45-6:30pm.*

TOPKAPI PALACE   PALACE
Topkapı Sarayı   ☎0212 512 0480 www.topkapisarayi.gov.tr

Puppy-guarding its perch on the tip of the European peninsula, Topkapı served as the official residence for Ottoman sultans (and *all* their women—except the daughters who were locked up on tiny nothing-islands to preserve their flowers) for almost 400 years. The views are luxurious, the buildings overwhelmingly crafted, and the treasures outrageous. Once you get through the sweaty trial that is the ticket office, you're mostly left unsupervised in a huge, crowded, sprawling park and on your own to explore with very few signs or directions. You'll need to spend at least a few hours exploring to do justice to this giant of a palace complex.

i Ⓜ*Sultanahmet or Gülhane. Enter the grounds down the hill from behind Hagia Sophia. 25 TL. Entrance to the Harem 15 TL (separate ticket office inside). Audio tour 15 TL. Under 12 free.* ☼ *Open Apr 15-Oct 1 9am-7pm; Oct 1-Apr 15 9am-5pm. Last entry 1hr. before close. Hagia Irene only open to groups of 30+ by request.*

BASILICA CISTERN   CISTERN
Yerebatan Sarayı, Yerebatan Cad. 13   ☎0212 522 1259 www.yerebatan.com

Built more than 1400 years ago under the direction of the Byzantine Emperor Justinian—the same guy responsible for the Hagia Sophia—this underground cistern once stored water for the whole city. Don't read "cistern" and think "ugh, moldy water tank." This is a dark, haunting, almost occult architectural marvel, so strong and beautiful that it was called the "underground palace. "Today, this subterranean sight full of murky water, dripping, eerie music, sensual lighting, and fish as big as your thigh makes for an otherworldly respite from the baking heat and sun. Walk to the back, where two Medusa heads (nobody knows where they came from or why they're there) form the bases of two columns. Supposedly brought here from pagan Roman temples, they're positioned upside down and sideways, presumably to break their killer, petrifying glare.

i Ⓜ*Sultanahmet. The entrance is across the street from Hagia Sophia, near the Million Stone. 10 TL. Audio tour 5 TL.* ☼ *Open daily 9am-6:30pm.*

ISTANBUL ARCHAEOLOGY MUSEUMS   MUSEUM
İstanbul Arkeoloji Müzeleri, Alemdar Cad. Osman Hamdi Bey Yokuşu Sok.   ☎0212 520 7740
                                                        www.istanbularkeoloji.gov.tr

Brace yourself to be dumped on by history. The exhaustive (and exhausting, by the end) collections in Istanbul's Archaeology Museums display millennia of artistic and cultural achievement, from how to embalm a body with Egyptian household products to how to close the Golden Horn with a chain (à la *Game of Thrones*). For a refreshing change of color from ivory and gray, head to the **Tiled Kiosk Museum** across the courtyard from the Archaeology Museum, which

get a room!

Most of Istanbul's budget accommodations are concentrated in Sultanahmet, but Beyoğlu is becoming more and more popular with travelers looking for cheap rooms. Accommodations on the Asian side and in the more conservative districts like Fatih and Fener are sparser, less conveniently located, and generally lacking in English fluency. Beşiktaş is home to mostly upscale hotels. Avoid staying in hotels in the Aksaray area, a seedy district, or Tarlabaşı, the run-down neighborhood close to Taksim. Below are a few of our favorites; you can find the full list of our recommendations on **www.letsgo.com**.

🏨 CHEERS HOSTEL   HOSTEL $

Zeynep Sultan Camii Sok. 21   ☎0212 526 0200 www.cheershostel.com

Ah, Cheers. Cheers gets it—what makes a traveler's day and what makes life good. Created right next to the Hagia Sophia by a group of friends and brothers after seeing "so many bad hostels" in Sultanahmet, Cheers gives you rooms that feel more like living in a spacious loft with friendly strangers than in a cold, bare hostel. The sofa-filled attic terrace is blessedly quiet during the day and lively and inebriated at night, while the hearty breakfast is a joy. Through it all, the staff will treat you like an old friend.

i Ⓜ*Sultanahmet. Follow the tram tracks down toward the Hagia Sophia, and take the 1st left after Donyang Hotel. The hostel is on the right, where the road bends. 10-bed mixed gender dor €16; 8-bed mixed dorm €17; 6-bed female only dorm €20; 4-bed dorm €20; singles €50-60; doubles €60-70; superior rooms (fancier and for 3-5 people) €80. Cash only. ⓩ Reception 24hr.*

🏨 HUSH HOSTEL LOUNGE   HOSTEL $

Iskele Sok. 46, Kadıköy   ☎0216 450 4363 www.hushhostelistanbul.com

HUSH Lounge's sleek, minimalist style—Spartan furniture, cool lounges, alternative music in the lobby, indie art punching up bare walls—creates generous amounts of open living space unheard of in other hostels of this variety. In additions to its kitchen, TV room, and terrace, the staff claims this is the only hostel in town with a garden—and a lovely garden it is. The young backpackers, students, artists, and adventurous tourists who tend to frequent HUSH all create an unusually friendly community of foreigners. Sitting on a quiet, pretty, pastel-colored street, removed from nightlife and on top of a big hill, HUSH Lounge is not meant for those looking for an easy, drunken stumble into bed. Otherwise, it's a pretty sunshiny place to stay.

i *From the Kadıköy ferry terminal, cross the street and head north. Turn right onto Iskele Sok. and continue up the hill. HUSH is on the right. Dorms €13; singles €31-45; doubles €35-55. Rates vary according to A/C and ensuite bathroom availability. Bring your Let's Go book for a 10% discount. ⓩ Reception 24hr.*

is slathered inside and out with blue Ottoman and Seljuk ceramic tiles. By this point, you might want to do as the kitties do and just press your entire body against the cold tiled wall—an appropriately ancient way to cool off.

i Ⓜ*Sultanahmet. From the metro, follow the signs down the tram line, downhill past the Hagia Sophia. It's in the first courtyard of Topkapı Palace. From Topkapı's main entrance behind Hagia Sophia, turn left and go downhill. 10 TL, under 12 free. Audio tour 10 TL. ⓩ Open Tu-Su 9am-7pm. Ticket office open Tu-Su 9am-6pm. Last entry 1hr. before close.*

turkey

GÜLHANE PARK

PARK

Gülhane Parkı

Because Istanbul has everything, of course it has a response to the Hyde Parks of the world. Formerly a royal Ottoman hunting park (imagine exotic captured beasts released as play things for sultans and princes, trapped within the high walls of the park), Gülhane Park is now a beautiful green park with pathways that wind through the many trees and wide swaths of seasonal flowers. Elegant, white-bodied trees gracefully arch and bend to the sky, while old couples hold hands and young couples hold waists. The north end of the park borders the Bosphorus, and the outdoor cafes that line it enjoy spectacular night views of glittery Istanbul on the water. Come here for some green amid the gold, silver, ruby, and diamond that deck out the rest of the city.

i *The park's walls separate it from the Topkapı Palace grounds, and the park itself has 3 gates: 1 near Sultanahmet, on the tram line past the Hagia Sophia toward Sirkeci, where you can also enter Topkapı Palace and the Istanbul Archaeology Museum; 1 right in front of the Sirkeci tram stop; and the last 1 on the avenue lying on the coastline in the north, close to Eminönü. Free entry.* ⏰ *Open daily 7am-11pm.*

SÜLEYMANIYE MOSQUE

MOSQUE

Süleymaniye Camii ☎0212 251 8819

With the highest dome in the city, this mosque represents Ottoman architecture at its innovative best. Much credit to the famous Ottoman architect **Mimar Sinan,** who designed the building's air flow so that the soot from the oil lamps used for heating collected in one small room, rather than making everything sad and dirty. The Süleymaniye Mosque complex is the second largest in Istanbul (after the Fatih Mosque) and looks shower fresh from a recent renovation—though the 19th- and 20th-century repainting makes everything look almost cartoonish, with contours and lines too clear to seem real. More than for its interior, *Let's Go* commends the mosque for excellence in public restroom quality: free, made of marble, and actually equipped withthe main amenities, they're a beacon of hope in the middle of an old city. Come to the complex to use the facilities, to get away from the crowds of tourists, and to enjoy reasonably priced food and *nargile* at the restaurants and cafes along the western wall. When you're done resting, relieving yourself, and religion-gazing, pay your respects at the **Tomb of Mimar Sinan,** located just across the street named after him.

i Ⓜ*Beyazit. Walk north to the gate of Istanbul University, turn right, and follow its walls all the way up. Alternatively,* Ⓜ*Eminönü. Exit the Spice Bazaar on Sabuncuhanı Sok., turn left onto Vasit Çinar Cad., and continue up the hill.* ⏰ *Mosque open daily 9am-7pm, closed during prayer times.*

Western Fatih

▨ FATIH MOSQUE

MOSQUE

Fatih Camii ☎0212 518 2919

A few years after the Ottomans conquered Constantinople ("pulling down" Eastern Rome and "digesting" the base of the Christian world, according to one passionate pamphlet), **Sultan Mehmet the Conqueror** demolished the **Church of the Holy Apostles** (an important Byzantine basilica) and built the Fatih Mosque in its place. Of course, in this city of shifts and tremors, what you'll see today is a very different mosque—the original 15th-century structure was destroyed by an earthquake in 1766 and was completely rebuilt by Sultan Mustafa III. Newly restored, as of 2013, this is another spectacular mosque, with cool gray marble and pistachio-green touches (refreshing in a cucumber-like way). The **tomb of the Conqueror**—whose bio states that he was poisoned by a Jewish doctor in the service of the Venetian kingdom—lies just outside the mosque. Though the sacredness with which Muslim visitors regard his body's resting place is a bit less

istanbul

impressive for non-believers (the unintentionally funny plaque inside describes him as "strong, with a ruddy complexion and a lamb-like nose," among other gems), the tomb is still an ornate affair worth seeing, especially compared to the bareness of his wife's tomb nearby.

i Take the bus to Fatih. The mosque is behind the tall walls near the bus stop. Mosque etiquette applies. Free. ☺ Open daily dawn to dusk, closed for prayer times. Tomb open daily 8:30am-5pm.

▨ MILLET MANUSCRIPT LIBRARY
LIBRARY, MUSEUM

☎0212 631 3607 www.milletkutup.gov.tr

"Treasure at every corner" is usually an exaggeration or a tourist trap, but that's actually what you'll find around the corner of the Fatih Mosque. The modest Millet Manuscript Library houses a beloved collection of rare books, scrolls, and calligraphy gathered by **Ali Emîrî Efendi** (1857-1924), a late-Ottoman government employee who "never married, never had his photograph taken, and never set foot in Beyoğlu" but instead spent his life saving rare books from destruction when he wasn't reading and writing with his cats. You'll find incredibly fine, gold-inlaid manuscripts written by sultans and cartographers in an elegant *medresse* (Arabic school) building, with heavy iron doors and a security guard who enters with you. All this will make you feel like a very important scholar being granted a private look into a treasure vault, so don't wear your "I LOVE OREOS" T-shirt here. And instead of pressing your sweaty nose against the glass to make out all the intricate details, go to the library across the hall to browse the entire collection digitally.

i From Fatih bus stop, head south down Fevzi Paşa Cad. and turn right onto Feyzullah Efendi Sok. The museum is on the left after you enter the complex. No photography allowed. You will need to leave your passport and bag at the entry office and fill out a form stating (any) university affiliation. Free. ☺ Open M-F 8:30am-4pm.

Fener and Balat

EYÜP SULTAN MOSQUE
MOSQUE

Eyüp Sultan Camii

Despite its status as the fourth most sacred Muslim site in the world, you'll see almost no tourists at the Eyüp Sultan Mosque. Little boys in curious white costumes run wild in the courtyard (apparently unaware that it's all part of a circumcision ritual), people get married, and worshipers in headscarves pray reverently in front of Eyüp Sultan's tomb. Even if you're not particularly interested in foreskin theft, marriage, or pilgrimage, this outlying mosque is worth visiting, if only to see how a real mosque is done when there are no lines and loud tourists in the way. Eyüp Sultan—Muhammad's right hand man, and the standard-bearer of Islam until he died in 674 CE during the first Muslim siege of Constantinople—is venerated in a fantastically ornamented tomb (exterior tiling currently under renovation) that is even more beautiful on the inside. Visitors to the mosque are welcome to enter during prayer but may be subject to a friendly slap to the rump if they offend the kindly old Muslim women around them (i.e., by wearing revealing clothes, leaving hair uncovered, keeping shoes on, or snapping photos during the service). After seeing the mosque and tomb, go for a hike up the hill, through the mountainous cemetery, all the way to the scenic **Pierre Loti Café.**

i Bus or ferry to Eyüp. Cross the road and head inland, toward the visible minaret of Eyüp Mosque. You'll have to pass through a long bazaar street and continue past a fountain. Standard mosque etiquette applies. Free. ☺ Mosque open daily 5am-11pm. Tomb open daily 9:30am-4:30pm.

CHORA CHURCH   CHURCH, MUSEUM
Kariye Müzesi, Kariye Camii Sok. 29   ☎0212 631 9241

Chora Church requires some serious ceiling-gazing, cramp-in-the-neck-calming skills—you'll find some of the most beautiful surviving Byzantine art on the domes above your head. The church dates to the fourth century, when Constantinople was so small that this building stood outside the city walls (*Chora* means "countryside" in Old Greek). Notice how the mosaics on your left as you enter are *sooo* much more sumptuous and sparkly than the ones on your right? The story goes that the 14th-century Byzantine statesman, Theodore Metochites, dumped so much money into the first mosaics at the expense of the poor that he was exiled for two years and forced to finish the left side with less "artistic liberty." When your neck starts screaming, finish with the sweeping view of Istanbul from the back of the museum.

i Bus to Edirnekapı. As you get off the bus, turn left, then take the nearest right turn and walk 3 blocks. Just before you reach the city walls, turn right and walk 2 blocks down the slope until you see the museum. 15 TL, under 12 free. ◰ Open in summer M-Tu 9am-6pm, Th-Su 9am-6pm. Last entrance 6pm, church closes at 7pm. Open in winter daily 9am-5pm.

Beyoğlu

▦ ISTANBUL MUSEUM OF MODERN ART   MUSEUM
Meclis-i Mebusan Cad. Limanİşletmeleri Sahası Antrepo 4.
                                     ☎0212 334 7300 wwwistanbulmodern.org

Though almost every corner in Beyoğlu has its own gallery, Istanbul Modern is the place to get a taste (or a filling meal for the soul) of the city's contemporary scene. The upper floor houses a permanent collection called "Past and Future," a chronological record of Turkish contemporary art, from its Western-educated beginnings to the colorful flowering of its own national and individual aesthetic. Don't miss Alaettin Aksoy's *Gardens of My Childhood* (2002, oil on canvas), a gorgeous, "puckish" painting trembling with glowing fragments, leaves, and spots of light (as if there were a million fairies mooning you from all over the surface). Between the first and lower levels is the "Stairway to Hell" staircase, and nearby is the "False Ceiling" installation next to the library (a canopy of books suspended from wires above, forming an artificial ceiling that envelopes you with that wonderful "book smell" when you walk through it). The lower level hosts temporary exhibits by local and international artists, as well as photography and architecture projects, all curated with minimalist cool. Mini dissertations, piece descriptions, and artist biographies accompany each work, making this huge space a joy to both look at and learn from.

i From Ⓜ︎Tophane, walk toward Kabataş. After passing the Nusretiye Mosque, turn right and follow the red, square signs. 15 TL; groups (10+) 12 TL; students and over 65 8 TL; under 12, museum members, and handicapped visitors free. Th free for Turkish residents. ◰ Open Tu-W 10am-6pm, Th 10am-8pm, F-Su 10am-6pm. Check the website for film screenings and special events.

Beşiktaş and Ortaköy

▦ SAKIP SABANCI MUSEUM   MUSEUM
Sakıp Sabancı Cad. 42, Emirgan   ☎0212 277 2200 http://muze.sabanciuniv.edu

Inside a gorgeous white villa, on top of a beautifully landscaped hill, in the middle of a peaceful, pond-filled park, on the edge of the ocean, high up the Bosphorus coast— lies Sakıp Sabancı Museum, one of the most masterfully curated, intelligently presented, forcefully air conditioned museums we've ever visited. Hosting highly Istanbul-appropriate exhibits like "The 1001 Faces of Orientalism" as well as "Turkish Painting, from the Ottoman Reformation to the Republic," this university institution runs a sleek operation, with excellent descriptions and thoughtful insights in perfect English, as well as gorgeous paintings and artifacts from the Louvre to the Istanbul Archaeology Museum. For brains and beauty, come to Sakıp Sabancı.

i Take a bus going along the Bosphorus (22, 25E, and 22RE work), and get off at Çınaraltı. The museum is directly to the left. 15 TL, students and teachers 8 TL, under 14 and over 60 and W free. ☑ Open W 10am-8pm, Th-Su 10am-6pm. Last tickets sold 45min. before close. Museum closed during 1st days of Ramadan.

DOLMABAHÇE PALACE
MUSEUM

Dolmabahçe Sarayı   ☎0212 236 9000 www.millisaraylar.gov.tr

Leading the old, broke, "sick man of Europe" in the latter half of the 1800s, Sultan Abdülmecid I tried to save face and commissioned the building of Dolmabahçe Palace in 1856 to replace Topkapı ("Eh, we've gotten tired of that one") as the sultan's official residence. Borrowing money from the English and scrounging under the couch, they managed to built it using 35 tonnes of gold. Fittingly, this palace is an exercise in architectural vomit and decorative overkill (think uber-Rococo, crystal handrails, polar bear pelts from Russia on the floor, ivory tusks from Africa, man-sized Japanese vases, silver platters on which you could serve elephant ham—that sort of thing). It has 285 rooms, 68 toilets, 44 halls, and six hamams. Be aware that this is a very popular, crowded, slow-moving attraction—come early on a weekday morning, or learn to love baking in the sun and marinating in other people's odors.

i ⓂKabataş. The palace is a short walk northeast, parallel to the shore past the Dolmabahçe Mosque. From Beşiktaş, walk 7min. toward Kabataş down Dolmabahçe Cad. 45min. guided tours in Turkish or English start about every 15min. Separate tour for the Harem 25min. No photos. Selamlık and Harem 40 TL; Selamlık only 30 TL; Harem only 20 TL. Students with ISIC card 5 TL. Under 6 free. Tours mandatory, no individual visits. Museum card does not apply. May also visit Great Palace Collections Museum and Yildiz Şale with palace ticket. ☑ Open Tu-W 9am-4pm, F-Su 9am-4pm. Office may close earlier if they reach their daily quota of visitors.

Asian Istanbul

ISTANBUL TOY MUSEUM
MUSEUM

Dr. Zeki Zeren Sok. 17, Göztepe   ☎0216 359 4550 www.istanbuloyuncakmuzesi.com

It's no Hagia Sophia, but Istanbul's Toy Museum is unlike (read: freakier, more hysterically racist, and sentimental) any other museum you'll visit in the city. This four-story villa houses a collection of antique toys, mostly from the US and Europe, grouped by themes like "The Wild Wild West," "Nazi Germany," "The Space Era," and "The Most Terrifying Miniature Babies You'll Ever See" (okay, that last one is a *Let's Go* grouping). The freaky: shudder at nightmare-inducing German toys from 1900 involving butchers, nurses, and dentists with syringes and pliers as big as their toy patients. The politically incorrect: gotta love 1950s Native American dolls from the US that look like something straight out of the most racist Disney movie of all time. The sad: the first territory Hitler claimed wasn't the battlefield but rather the hearts of German children who once played with manly, heroic soldier figurines—toys whose places the children would naively take in WWII. You might leave the museum with a lot of sloshy feelings.

i Take the Haydarpaşa-Gebze suburban train from Haydarpaşa Train Station to Göztepe (10min.). After you leave the station, cross and walk down the street on the right side of the train tracks. After the street turns right, take the nearest left turn and continue straight. There are giant giraffe statues in front of the museum. 10 TL, students 7 TL. ☑ Open Tu-F 9:30am-6pm, Sa-Su 9:30am-7pm.

FOOD

Contrary to popular belief, food in Istanbul isn't just kebabs and meatballs. Start your day with a generous Turkish breakfast (usually bread, cheese, olives, eggs, tomatoes, cucumbers) or, even better, with *kaymak* (cream) and honey. If you don't have time to sit down for breakfast, grab a street-side *simit* (Turkish bagel with sesame). For lunch, pop into a *lokanta* to choose from the prepared dishes waiting for workers on their lunch breaks, or go to a restaurant and order a thin *pide*, the so-called "Turkish pizza." To combat your afternoon slump, find a patisserie and have some baklava or any one of the many similar, syrup-soaked pastries the Turks love so much. For dinner, try a fish restaurant or order some *mezze* (vegetable or seafood appetizers) to share between friends. When late-night fast-food cravings kick in, look for joints that sell *dürüms* (kebab wraps), *tantuni* (diced meat), or, if you're feeling adventurous, *kokoreç* (chopped lamb intestines). Oh, and let's not forget about *çay* (black tea), without which no Turkish meal would be complete. It's amazing that all these things are just the basics.

Sultanahmet and Environs

Eating in Sultanahmet is a tricky thing. Our default stance? Don't pay for anything within two miles of the Hagia Sophia—if you stay too close to the tourist spots, you'll end up paying twice the price of your dorm room. Then again, no elephant wants to stray too far from the herd (or the hostel) for food. Luckily, there are a few local favorites mixed in with the touristy places, gems in the rough which we've listed below.

🏛 MEŞHUR FILIBE KÖFTECISI   KÖFTE $

Ankara Cad. 112, Sirkeci   ☎0212 519 3976

It's about the size of a dry cleaners in Brooklyn, or whatever the Istanbul equivalent is. No decor to speak of—this is just a small nook on a busy street, with three tables, one waiter, one *usta* (master chef), one cashier. But in this shoebox of an eatery appear the most mouthwatering *köfte* (meatballs), possibly in all the city. Enter and you have no real choices: it's either *köfte* by itself (served with a half loaf of soft white bread, a grilled green pepper, and a small cucumber-tomato salad on the side) or with a larger salad. Sit on the minuscule ground floor next to the tiny grill to hear the sizzle and pop of your meatballs being attentively, lovingly, and masterfully cooked. In 10min., six perfect buttons—small, perfectly plump, round—of *köfte* arrive on your plate, as neighbors and locals poke their heads in to say hello. If you want to eat love on a plate, this is the place.

i Take the tram or follow the tramline to Sirkeci. Take a left (away from the sea) onto Ankara Cad., and walk uphill for a bit until you see Meşhur Filibe Köftecisi's gray sign on the left. Köfte 9 TL. Salad 5 TL. ◌ Open M-Sa 11am-5pm.

🏛 HOCAPAŞA PIDECISI   PIDE $

Hocapaşa Sok. 19, Sirkeci   ☎0212 512 0990 www.hocapasa.com.tr

Unlike its neighbors in the restaurantville that is Hocapaşa Cad., Hocapaşa Pidecisi doesn't have to shove its menu (or its waiter's macho cologne) in your face. The sight of cracklingly fresh *pide* (Turkish boat-shaped pizza) going in and out of the oven in the wall—with the waiter literally running the thing straight to your plate so it arrives popping, crispy, greasy, and hot enough to hurt your mouth—is attraction enough. It lacks the swag and suaveness of Sultanahmet's oily-smooth restaurants, but you'll eat a decidedly more authentic, less expensive meal while sitting in your plastic garden chair and watching real people (like bakers carrying loaves and kids learning how to bike) go by.

i Ⓜ Sirkeci. Go south (up the slope and away from the sea) on Ankara Cad., turn left onto Hocapaşa Sok., and the restaurant is on the left. Free Wi-Fi. Pide 8-14 TL. ◌ Open daily 8am-11:30pm.

🏛 GAZIANTEP BURÇ OCAKBAŞI   KEBAB, DOLMA $

Parçacılar Sok. 12, Grand Bazaar   ☎0212 527 1516

In the hassle and harassment of the Grand Bazaar (honestly, this isn't a harem!), sometimes you need the strength of a stuffed pepper. Gaziantep—a small city in southeast Turkey, one of its great food capitals, and the place after which this restaurant is named—has authentic food that is rich, heartwarming stuff, and

istanbul

the perfect balm for burn-out. Though the generous kebabs will make merry in your mouth, we're personally in love with the *biber dolma*, dried peppers rehydrated, stuffed with seasoned rice and herbs, covered and cooked in red-or-ange olive oil, and served with a wallop of yogurt. And though this little-known, family-run place is warm with the heat of cooking and the bodies of the bazaar, its inconspicuous location will keep you hidden from the salesmen.

i Enter the bazaar from the south side, either through the western Beyazıt Gate or the eastern Nuruosmaniye Gate. Walk along Kalpakçılarbaşı Cad. (jewelry street), then turn onto Sipahi Cad. and walk straight north as it turns into Yağlıkçılar Cad. Pay attention to the signs above your head, and turn immediately right onto the narrow street of Parçacılar Sok., the one right before the bigger Perdahçılar Cad. The entrance to the street has a sign that reads "KUMAŞÇI ATILLA." The restaurant is on the right. Kebabs 10-17 TL. Biber dolma 10 TL. Lamahcun 3 TL. ☼ Open M-Sa 7am-5pm.

▨ AYNEN DÜRÜM   DÜRÜM $
Muhafazacılar Sok. 33, Grand Bazaar   ☎0212 527 4728

It's hot, it's busy, it's carnal. This metal counter, hot enough to fry eggs on, sits in front of a tiny *dürüm* kebab spit just outside the Grand Bazaar and only seats 10 at a time. Like a meaty Last Supper, the diners sit facing and staring each other down while eating, except here, they're stuffing their faces with lamb, chicken, or beef wraps instead of Jesus flesh. While the crowd presses impatiently, wait-ing to steal a seat at the bar, the counter doubles as a self-serve greens buffet, with chokingly hot pickled peppers, red flakes, sour pickles, grilled green pep-pers, lemon juice, and cilantro spread out, fair game for everyone to dump onto the individual plastic sheets set in front of them. Efficient, no-nonsense, brilliant street food of the highest order—you'll feel the madness rise up in you as you devour your soft, spongey, meaty wrap.

i Çemberlitaş. Walk north up Vezirhan Cad., then cut to the right and cross the area in front of the Nuruosmaniye Mosque (Tavuk Pazarı Sok.). Walk north up Nuruosmaniye Cad., pass the Nuruos-maniye Gate into the Grand Bazaar on the left, and take a left at the intersection with Kılıçcılar Sok. Aynen is on the right. Chicken, beef, and lamb dürüm (wrapped kebab) 8 TL. Ayran 1.5 TL. Coke 2 TL. ☼ Open daily 11:30am-6:30pm, but the meat only gets going around 1pm.

Western Fatih

You'll find some of the best food in Istanbul hidden in the conservative corners of Western Fatih. Sultanahmet may have the sights but it's a black hole of eats and has nothing on the local, traditional, and migrant specialties you can find in this residential district. After you've satisfied your eyes and heart with sightseeing, head west to satisfy your stomach.

▨ SUR OCAKBAŞI   TRADITIONAL $$
İtfaiye Cad. 27/1   ☎0212 533 8088 www.surocakbasi.com

We swear to Zeus, God, Allah—whatever deities hold sway over today's Istanbul: if you have one meal in Fatih, it should be this one. A Kurdish kebab restaurant that covers an entire block and sells out seats like Beyoncé, it does meat right. Anthony Bourdain apparently visited this place in 2009, and the food gave him an alleged orgasm. You'll be making sex faces, too, if you try the *sur kebab* plate: a bed of rich, red, slightly spicy, paella-like seasoned rice and chunks of juicy, fatty, grilled lamb, chicken, and beef, plus mini-lahmacuns (crispy, thin-crust Turkish pizzas covered in seasoned meat), plus roasted peppers, tomatoes, and onions on top (1 portion 22 TL). Feeling overwhelmed? Wrap it all up in a pocket of the accompanying bread, and you'll have sensations in your mouth you've never had before. We recommend going all out here: wash it down with the clean, milky homemade *ayran*, and *do not miss out* on their special dessert, *özel sur tatlısı* (a corny, sweet yellow bread, soft as pudding, filled with ice cream and sprinkled with cinnamon and dried cranberries; 8 TL). You won't find

turkey

it anywhere else in the world, as the owner's grandmother invented it. Just trust us on this one.

i From the Fatih Mosque, walk southeast until you reach the aqueduct. Walk along it, then turn left into Siirt Bazaar (1 street west of Atatürk Bulvari) and go straight. The restaurant is on the left. Pide 12 TL. Kebabs 12-22 TL. ☼ Open M-F 8am-2am, Sa-Su 11:30am-2am. Meat ready 1hr. after restaurant opens. This place is always booked, every night, so come early in the day or call ahead to reserve.

▨ FATIH KARADENIZ PIDECISI
PIDE $

Büyük Karaman Cad. 57 ☎0212 635 0509

Snap, crackle, *pide*. This *pideçisi* (the Turkish version of a pizzeria) gets so popular at lunchtime, you'll probably end up sharing a table with the locals and waiting half an hour for your food. That said, the satisfying crack of bread breaking, the astonishing size of the thing (eating the *pide* is like fitting a miniature kayak down your throat), and the perfect cheesy, meaty, greasiness of it all makes it worth the agonizing wait. All of the variations on the menu are delicious and involve combinations of cheese, meat, and egg. Plunge the pile of butter your *pide* arrives with straight into the thick of it all or rub it along the crust—your arteries won't thank you, but your soul will.

i From the Fatih bus stop, walk down Fevzi Paşa Cad. as it turns into Macar Kardeşler Cad. Turn left onto Dülgeroğlu Sok. and take the 1st right. The restaurant is on the left. Free Wi-Fi. Pide 11.50-18 TL. ☼ Open M-F 10:30am-9pm, Sa-Su 9am-9pm.

▨ ÖZ KILIS: KEBAP&LAHMACUN SALONU
KEBAB, LAHMACUN $$

Bedrettin Simavi Sok. No: 5 ☎0212 523 4457

Öz Kilis—a sweet little kebab spot run by a family from Kilis, a small town near the Syrian border—is famous among locals and Turkish celebrities for its awesome baking-pan kebabs. While the only kebabs you've probably seen were skewered at one point or another, the Kilis style gives you *hatay tav* (15 TL): a thin, meatloaf-like layer of sizzling meat on top of a melt-in-your-mouth layer of softened eggplant and ringed by roasted tomatoes, peppers, and onions—all in a pan that's been sitting to perfection in an oven before being served. Why? The story goes that close to the Turkish-Syrian border, you can avoid cooking and making a mess at home by bringing a pan to the butcher, getting some meat off him, spicing it up on the go, then stopping at the bakery next door to cook it. *Let's Go* likes this resourcefulness and also likes the lovely, herby garlic- and parsley-covered *sarımsaklı lahmacun* (think thin-crust Turkish pizza) that is Öz Kilis's second specialty (3 TL).

i From Fatih Camii, walk north up Fevzi Paşa Cad. and take a left into Hirkai Şerif Cad. Take the rightmost fork onto Bedrettin Simavi Sok. The restaurant is on the left. Kebabs 10-20 TL. Lahmacun 3 TL. ☼ Open daily 11am-10:30pm.

▨ SARAY MUHALLEBICISI
SWEETS $

Fevzi Paşa Cad. 1 ☎0212 521 0505 www.saraymuhallebicisi.com

If you want to have a substance-induced state of altered consciousness in dry Fatih, it's gonna have to be a sugar high. Saray Muhallebiçisi is a quality, multi-story dessert edifice, not just a shop. Its menu tells a story of a girl's grandparents having their first date here—it's that sort of place, the nice place where you take your future wife for pudding. And holy cow, what a gorgeous pudding they serve—the *fırın sütlaç* (baked rice pudding, served cold and generous with a tough surface; 6.50 TL) might just change your life. If you don't mind the smell of the entrees fornicating with the smell of the desserts, sit on the first floor and watch the chefs bring out the goods one by one. It's like having multiple orgasms vicariously, through your eyes.

i From the southeastern exit of the Fatih Mosque grounds, turn right and walk to Fevzi Paşa Cad. Saray is on the right, across the road. Breakfast menu 4-8 TL per item. Entrees 5-22 TL. Desserts 6.50-8 TL. Tea 2-4.50 TL. Coffee 5-7 TL. Ask for the English menu. ☼ Open daily 5:30am-1am.

istanbul

Fener and Balat

Like almost everything else in Fener and Balat (and in life), don't expect English-speaking waiters to choo-choo-train your food to you here.

🍴 FINDIK KABUĞU RESTORAN
KÖFTE $

Mürsel Paşa Cad. 89   ☎0212 635 3310 www.findikkofte.com

What happens when a troop of village cops and a local news cameraman arrive at a *köfte* restaurant in Fener, Istanbul? There's no punch line, but you know you've found an authentic neighborhood eatery! Congratulations on discovering Fındık Kabuğu Restoran in particular (the sign outside says "Fındık Kabugunda Köfte"). There's no English on the menu, so point away at the veggie dishes, like the saffron-tinged lentil soup and smoky grilled eggplant (6 TL), or pick between three varieties of meatball *köfte.* Free Wi-Fi downstairs and free Turkish tea on the pretty terrace upstairs seal the already cheap deal. Pro tip: If Hüseyin (the warmhearted owner of the place who also happens to be an English journalism major) is around, *ask for stories.*

i Bus or ferry to Fener. From the ferry jetty, go inland, cross the road, turn right, and walk until you see the Bulgarian St. Stephen Church on the right. The restaurant is opposite the church. Free Wi-Fi. Grill and köftë 13-15 TL. Cold dishes and appetizers 6 TL. Desserts 4-7 TL. ☼ Open daily 9am-11pm.

🍴 UNNAMED (AKA YUSUF'S TEA)
CAFE $

Ayvansaray Mah. Ayan Cad. 85   ☎0537 948 5158

There once was an old, sprightly Turkish man named Yusuf, with warm, crinkly eyes and a great beard, who made the best Turkish tea and coffee in the world. Absolutely everyone in the neighborhood knew Yusuf, and everyone came over for his tea every morning. If they couldn't come to him, Yusuf would hand-deliver little glasses of tea, quivering on their tiny dishes, to the butchers, bakers, and baklava-makers in the area. People called him crazy for selling the best tea in the world for just 0.50 TL and the best coffee in the world for 2 TL. But Yusuf said he didn't care about money—he just really liked making tea for people. This place was so local, it had no name and no words on its front. This place exists, and you are commanded to go to this place.

i Bus or ferry to Fener. From the bus station, cross the street to Mursel Paşa Cad., then turn right and walk up the street past the Bulgarian church. Take the 1st left at Çiçeli Bostan Sok., then the 1st right at Hizir Çavuş Köprü Sok. Walk until the intersection with Ayan Cad. Yusuf's is the 1st white storefront you see. ☼ Open daily 7:30am-10pm

Beyoğlu

🍴 KÖFTECI HÜSEYIN
KÖFTE $

Kurabiye Sok., Akgün ▢ş Hanı 7/A   ☎0212 243 7637

The famous Köfteci Hüseyin: the best *(köfte)* balls you'll ever have in your mouth. Let's not waste space on what the hell the place looks like, whatnot. You sit down and choose: just *köfte* (Turkish meatballs) or *köfte* with salad (chopped carrots, lemon, cilantro, tomatoes, onions, sweet white beans). The meatballs come off the grill hot, juicy, perfectly charred, and nice and fat—one bite, and you're a goner. The grilled tomatoes, hot red paste, onions, salad, soft white bread, and *köfte* roll around like sea otters in your mouth. Best balls ever.

i Ⓜ️Taksim. Walk down İstiklal Cad., then turn right onto Bekâr Sok. Walk to the end, then turn right. Hüseyin is on the left. Köfte 12 TL. Salad 6 TL. Ayran 2 TL. ☼ Open M-Sa 11:30am-3pm.

🍴 ŞIMŞEK PIDE SALONU
PIDE $

Taksim Cad. 2/A, Beyoğlu   ☎0212 249 4642 www.simsekpidesalonu.com

For being wedged in between Taksim Square and İstiklal Cad., this classic *pide*-zzeria is surprisingly local. The waiter speaks no English except his carefully scripted "cheese, salami, beef, mix. . ." while pointing at the all-Turkish menu, and no one seems to understand the concept of "Wi-Fi?" But whatever, this is the best *pide* we've ever had, and this is why: the butter. From a tray holding two huge slabs/bricks/building blocks of butter, the chef slices off a good chunk and floats it on your baking-hot, crispy *pide* as soon as it comes out of the oven. If that's not enough butter for you, ask the waiter for *tereyağı* ("jam," obviously), and he'll smilingly leave two or three more generous pats (more like great slaps) of it on your *pide*, soaking into everything as it melts. On top of a crispy crust, the tangy salami and soft white cheese of the *peynirli sucuklu pide* amorously make gustative babies.

i From Ⓜ️Taksim, go down İstiklal Cad., then turn right with the nostalgic tram tracks onto Taksim Cad. Şimşek Pide is on the right. Pide 9-17 TL. ⏰ Open daily 10am-10pm.

🏅 MANGAL KEYFI
Öğüt Sok. 8

DÜRÜM $

☎0212 245 1534

If the *dürüm* is the burrito's Turkish twin, this place is a great Turkish taqueria. An unpretentious wooden cupboard of a place in a side street off İstiklal, it's filled with locals on their lunch break and makes bigger, better spill-out-of-mouth *dürüm* than any tourist fast-food spit in Taksim. Try the *adana acılı* (spicy) *dürüm*, 6 TL. With extra pickled peppers and red flakes, the thing gets as hot as some of the young studs on İstiklal.

i From Ⓜ️Taksim, walk down İstiklal. Take a right onto Imam Adnan Sok. When you reach Ağa Camii, take the 2nd right onto Öğüt Sok. The restaurant is on the left. Dürüms 6-7.50 TL. Kebabs 11-17 TL. Salads 4 TL. ⏰ Open M-Th 11am-midnight, F-Sa 11am-1am, Su 11am-midnight.

🏅 LADES RESTAURANT
Sadri Alışık Sok. 11/A

MENEMEN $

☎012 251 3203

What do you do when your first restaurant is wildly successful? Build one right across the street, of course—haven't you ever played Monopoly? Lades 1 is a classic *lokanta* serving up all the Turkish appetizers exactly the way its loyal customers have loved them for years—its *mezes* and kebabs are as dependable as dog food and definitely taste better. Lades 2 is a bit more exciting. Come here for a fast, no-frills Turkish breakfast and possibly the best *menemen* (eggs scrambled with butter, sausages, chili, tomatoes, and anything else your stomach might desire) in European Istanbul.

i From Ⓜ️Taksim, go down İstiklal Cad. and turn left at the Ağa Mosque onto Sadri Alısık Sok. The restaurant is a few meters ahead (Lades 2 is on the left, 1 on the right). Menemen 7-9 TL. Yumurta (fried eggs) 4-9 TL. Vegetable appetizers 9 TL. Meat entrees 16-20 TL. Soup 4 TL. Salads 5 TL. Desserts 5-8 TL. ⏰ Open daily 5am-11pm.

Beşiktaş and Ortaköy

🏅 PANDO KAYMAK
Mumcu Bakkal Sok. 5

BREAKFAST $

☎0212 258 2616

What is the food of angels? If your answer is anything but a dreamy-eyed "*Kaymak!*" you clearly haven't seen the sweet, generous, and inexpensive sliver of paradise that Pando offers every morning. *Kaymak* is the Turkish version of clotted cream; made from milk and high in fat (60 percent!), it tastes a bit like breastfeeding from an angel. Seriously. The sweet, elderly Bulgarian couple who have run this place for decades serves a big square of the stuff covered in honey and accompanied by a loaf of soft white bread (7 TL). You'll feel a bit like a newborn while you're gorging and a bit like Winnie the Pooh when you're finished, but who cares? It's angel food.

i From at the eagle statue, walk away from the fish market. Pando Kaymak is on the left (above the door, it says, "Kaymaklı kahvaltı burada"). Kaymak with bread and honey 7 TL. Breakfast omelets 7 TL. Salads 7 TL. Tea 1 TL. Hot milk 2 TL. ⏰ Open daily 8am-5:30pm.

istanbul

🔖 7-8 (YEDI-SEKIZ) HASANPAŞA FIRINI
Şehit Asim Cad. 8

BAKERY $
☎0212 261 9766

If you happen to be living in the area and you're considering a visit to this town-favorite bakery, you're going to have to make a pact with yourself not to eat entire kilograms per day of 7-8's crumbly, sweet, gluey-soft, nutty almond cookies once you've gotten a taste—be stronger than we were. The smell hits you first—sweet, deep, warmth tinged with something like anise, radiating from the piles and piles of baked goods in all shapes and sizes in the window and piled even higher on the tables inside, like a craftsman's workshop for cookies. For many in Beşiktaş, this isn't just a cookie store—it's an institution and a daily habit, as necessary to starting the day as morning coffee. At almost all times, lines of locals brave the grumpy patriarch baker for their cookie crack, and you'll soon feel the urge to have more of the *acı badem kurabiye* (almond cookies) or big paper bags full of multi-flavored *çay kurabiye* (tea cookies).

i From the eagle statue, walk down Şehit Asim Cad.; the store is on the left. Çay kurabiye (tea cookies, all flavors) 16 TL per kg. Acı badem (almond), koko (coconut), and mekik (madeline) cookies 24 TL per kg, around 3 TL per 5 pieces. Savory breads 16 TL per kg. Cakes 14 TL per kg. ☼ Open daily 7:30am-9:30pm.

Asian Istanbul

🔖 ALI USTA
Moda Cad. 176, Moda

ICE CREAM $
☎0216 414 1880

This little shop doesn't look like much, but you'll have to fight through lines of locals for your scoops. Though it's one of the most famous ice cream spots in Istanbul, it stays refreshingly non-touristy (read: you won't be able to understand the flavor labels, so be brave and point by color!). We can safely vouch for the creamy coolness of the milky white "Santa Maria" flavor, dotted with huge chunks of hazelnut. Though slightly pricier, Ali Usta's scoops are bigger than those of most cones on the street. Add chocolate sauce and chopped nuts on top for 1.5 TL more; walk on the nearby beach with sticky fingers afterward for free.

i From Kadıköy, get on the nostalgic tram (near the Osman Ağa Mosque) and get off near Moda Cad. Walk down the street; Ali Usta is on the right, close to where Moda Cad. forks. Scoops 2.5 TL; toppings 1.5 TL. ☼ Open daily 8am-2am.

🔖 PIDE SUN
Moda Cad. 97/1, Kadıköy

PIDE $
☎0216 347 3155 www.pidesun.com

You're in Turkey for God's sake, shame on you for craving pepperoni pizza in the middle of this enriching cultural experience! Lucky for you, Pide Sun hits the same spot Pizza Hut does—cozy, cheap, and satisfying. The *pides* (Turkish "pizzas," but leaf-shaped and without the tomato sauce) are so thin, so greasy, so cheesy, and so meaty that even the most die-hard pizza aficionados will want to eat it the Turkish way (i.e., with a razor-sharp knife). One *pide* will also knock you out for a good two meals, so choose carefully between the toppings of pepperoni, sausages, chicken, turkey, mushrooms, pepper, onions, potato bits, and spices. It's easy to pass by Pide Sun without noticing it, but the food is worth the navigation time!

i From the Kadıköy ferry terminal, go down Söğütlü Çeşme Cad. and turn right just before the Osman Ağa Mosque. Follow the road as it becomes Moda Cad. Pide Sun is on the left, very close to a Migros supermarket. Pides 8-16 TL. ☼ Open daily 11:30am-11pm.

NIGHTLIFE

Istanbul's bars and clubs are concentrated around İstiklal Cad., so if you're staying in Sultanahmet, you should prepare yourself for a good amount of commuting. Sultanahmet does have a few bars, but these are generally looked down upon by the locals—that's why we list a handful of *nargile* cafes instead. Another center of nighttime activity is Muallim Naci Cad., the road running up from Ortaköy. Here you'll find Kuruçeşme, the mecca of the city's most prestigious clubs. Note that during summer, many music venues close down and move to their summer locations. The English-language *Time Out Magazine* lists current performances, as well as a comprehensive list of GLBT-friendly bars and clubs. If you want to drink *rakı*, the anise-flavored Turkish national drink, the best place to do so is at a traditional *meyhane*. Whatever you do, don't fall for the nighttime scams: if a local speaking perfect English approaches you on the street and invites you for a beer after three lines of uninteresting conversation, he's probably planning a scam (which usually involves a traveler, an exorbitant bill, and a dose of coercion).

Sultanahmet and Environs

▨ SETÜSTÜ ÇAY BAHÇESI   CAFE
Gülhane Park

Perched on a ridge along the north end of Gülhane Park may be the most romantic place to have a pot (an entire pot) of tea in Istanbul. With dozens of small wooden tables and chairs everywhere, all oriented toward the sea, it sort of reminds you of sitting at an outdoor movie theater, where the only show is the breathtaking view of Istanbul at night on the Bosphorus—everything glittering and twinkling, ferries and boats slowly passing. As the locals do, bring your loved ones—the pot of tea seems pricey but is meant to be shared. Confused by the two-part teapot they hand you? How to appear culturally pro: pour yourself about half a cup or more of the top pot's brew, then fill the rest with the water from the bottom pot. Don't be surprised if you stay long enough for the moon to disappear behind the trees of the park around you.

i ⓜFrom the tram station, enter the park through the entrance in the high park walls, just ahead and to the right of the tram station, or walk toward Sultanahmet and enter through the main, 3-portal entrance on the left. Walk north through the park until you reach the back gate. Turn right at the gate and walk uphill. The cafe is on the left. Çay for 1 8 TL; for 2 14 TL; for 3 20 TL. Turkish coffee 8 TL. Fruit 6 TL. Ice cream 8 TL. Snacks 3-12 TL. Cash only. ☒ Open daily 8:30am-11pm.

Western Fatih

Ready to rock Western Fatih tonight? Tough luck. Because it's such a conservative area, few places serve alcohol, throw raging parties, or crank out the latest tunes. People stay up late here mostly for *nargile* (hookah pipes) or to chat at cafes.

Fener and Balat

As one of the quieter, more conservative parts of Istanbul, you'll never see the words "nightlife" and "Fener and Balat" in the same sentence—except when the sentence is, "The neighborhoods of Fener and Balat have no nightlife."

Beyoğlu

Beyoğlu is the capital of Istanbul nightlife. It's normal to walk into a building on thudding, flashing **İstiklal Caddesi** any night of the week, find a different bar on each floor, and still have to fight crowds well past midnight. Each small street around **Sofyalı Sokak**, just north of the **Tünel** exit, easily outdoes the proud resident "bar streets" of other districts in the city.

▨ PEYOTE   CONCERT VENUE, BAR
Kameriye Sok. 4, Beyoğlu   ☎0212 251 4398 www.peyote.com.tr

If you're sick of being alone in your hostel room and just want to see a lot of humans having more fun than you, go here. The ground floor is live DJ electronica (come late in the night or you'll be lonely); the second floor is live music (Turkish rock with dashes of jazz, reggae, ska, and folk—Peyote even has its own recording label, so you might catch the next big Turkish thing); and the third floor is a rough and tumble, drinks-all-around, lean back in your chair and laugh until you find yourself lying in someone else's lap-type bar. Though you can barely squeeze in and out of the tables on busy nights, it's all good-natured fun—definitely not a quiet place to nurse a beer all night, unless you're an extroverted, energy vampire.

i Ⓜ*Taksim. Walk to Galatasaray (the big gated thing with Roman columns on the left), then turn right onto Balık Pazarı. (Sahne Sok., the one after Çiçek Pasajı), take the 2nd right, then the 1st left. Peyote is on the left. Beer 7-13 TL. Local drinks 7-16 TL. Cocktails 16-20 TL. Imported drinks 10-23 TL.* 🕐 *Open daily 3pm-3am. Live music, DJ, and dancing usually starts around 9pm-midnight.*

MACHINE
Balo Sok. 31/B
CLUB

This clandestine establishment is sort of the town slut—everyone knows it's there, everyone knows when and where to find it, but there's no official phone number, website, and it's only open for business 10hr. a week. The whole metal warehouse aesthetic sort of screeches in your eyes, metal scraping metal visually—basically, it looks like the inside of a freight truck. With yellow traffic lines painted on the floor, cage bars, crude shipping-container walls, and the width of only about seven grinding couples, it's literally a metal crate plopped down on a back alley. Pressed body to body, the freight in this truck is human cargo. If you're into sucking in toxins and freaking to loud club music until dawn, this one's for you.

i Ⓜ*Taksim. Walk down İstiklal toward Galatasaray, then turn right at Halkbank. Walk downhill to the end of the street. On the left is a small diner called Güzel Kiraathanesi; Machine's entrance is the unmarked black door underneath it. The entrance is to the right of the stairs; look down. Cover 10 TL. Beer 10 TL. Whisky 30 TL. Cocktails 30 TL. Vodka 20 TL. Shots 12-50 TL. Couples and ladies only.* 🕐 *Open W 11pm-5am, F-Sa 11pm-5am.*

TEKYÖN CLUB
Sıraselviler Cad. 63
CLUB, GLBT
☎0533 377 2393 www.clubtekyon.com

Although it's underground, Tekyön (Turkish for "one way only," winky face) is anything but unknown to Istanbul's gay scene. With a large dance floor, 11 disco balls (at last count), and funky neon-lit walls, this is the place to get down with that *hamam* cutie. The music remixes Western and Turkish beats for patrons that include Turkish regulars and eager visitors the world over, from Italy to Saudi Arabia. Special annual events like the International Bear Festival add some heft and hair to the crowd, while every Tuesday hosts a male belly dancing show. A staunch establishment—it's been open every day for the last 12 years (except one day each year for Ramadan)—this place glows with friendly fun.

i *From* Ⓜ*Taksim, walk down Sıraselviler Cad. The club is on the left. Beer 16 TL. Vodka 20 TL. Cocktails 16-25 TL. Whiskey 30 TL. Free entry. Very few women allowed in, close friends and lesbian couples only. No straight, transsexual, or bisexual visitors.* 🕐 *Open M-Th 10pm-4am, F-Sa 10pm-5am, Su 10pm-4am.*

Beşiktaş and Ortaköy

ANJELIQUE
Salhane Sok. 5
CLUB, RESTAURANT
☎0212 327 2844 www.istanbuldoors.com

Sexy and fun, with two indoor lounges (punctuated with columns and tables to snake around) and a waterside deck (with its own private dock for private James Bond water landings), Anjelique is just the right size and has just the right crowd. What does that mean? You won't have room to run laps in your 12in. heels, but you won't want to with the young, beautiful people dancing all around you in the moonlight. Though you might hear big names like "Garanti" being quickly ushered in at the door, you don't have to own a bank to enter. With no cover charge and a beer for 10 TL, you can walk the walk at Anjelique without castrating your budget. It's the cheapest way to experience the beautiful life in Ortaköy.

i From the Ortaköy ferry jetty, head inland and take the 1st left; Anjelique is on the left. It's on a small street in the center of Ortaköy, to the right of the Ortaköy Mosque when facing the sea and near a Hotel Radisson entrance. Men need female company to enter the club. Reservation required for dinner. Dress code (no athletic wear, no shorts) strictly enforced. Beer 10 TL. Vodka 35 TL. Cocktails from 40 TL. Whiskey 40 TL. ☺ Restaurant open daily 6:30pm-midnight. Club open dailymidnight-5am.

REINA   CLUB, RESTAURANT
Muallim Naci Cad. 44   ☎0212 259 5919 www.reina.com.tr
If you're going to indulge, do it properly. Probably the most famous club in the city, Reina is where local and international social elites come to spend obscene amounts of money. The club has six different restaurants (Chinese, sushi, kebabs, Mediterranean, fish, and international) and a dance floor in the middle, all with the Bosphorus Bridge looming as a backdrop. Reina also owns two boats that will transport you here from your hotel, if you happen to be one of the VIP guests. Not sure if you qualify as a VIP or not? Then you probably don't. The actual VIPs vary from college kids to middle-aged couples (as long as they can afford to drink Absolut like water and dance on slabs of marble). But come on a weekday (do dress up) and nurse a beer or two so you can enjoy the atmosphere and people watching without paying like a *paşa*.

i From the Ortaköy bus stop, walk down Muallim Naci Cad. Reina is on the right. Men need female company to enter the club. Reservation required for dinner. Dress code is strictly enforced. Cover F-Sa 70 TL, includes 1 drink. Tequila shots 15 TL. Wine 20 TL. Beer 30 TL. Cocktails 30-40 TL. Vodka 30 TL. Whiskey 30 TL. ☺ Restaurants open daily 6-11pm. Club open daily 11pm-4am.

Asian Istanbul

▨ KARGA   BAR
Kadife Sok. 16, Kadıköy   ☎0216 449 1726 www.kargabar.org
One of the best-known bars this side of the Bosphorus, Karga is so word-of-mouth, it doesn't even need a name on its door. Ducking through the secretive, street-side door is like walking into a system of wooden caves or wandering the hollowed-out niches of a giant mother tree. Sexy, dark corners are easy to find—the wood no doubt rubbed smooth over time by generations of lovers. With four stories, a garden, and numerous balconies, you can choose to eat openly with friends or find a corner for intimacy. The dark interior and rotating playlists of mainly alternative set an edgy mood, but it's easy to leave the volume behind just by climbing higher.

i Walk south on Bahariye Cad. and take the 1st right after (not in front of) the Opera House. Take the 2nd left, walk 1 block, and look for the Hobbit-sized, unmarked wooden door with a raven above it (not the door above the set of stairs) on the right. Free Wi-Fi. Live music Sept-May, but nightly DJs continue through the summer. Tea 4 TL. Beer 7.50-13 TL. Shots 8-13 TL. Cocktails 19-23 TL. ☺ Open M-Th 11am-2am, F-Sa 11am-4am, Su 11am-2am. Closes later in the winter.

ARTS AND CULTURE

In Istanbul, you don't just enjoy arts and culture—you live arts and culture. Music thrums in the city, whether it's jazz, classical, or electronic. Besides large concerts, the city hosts plenty of festivals that showcase local bands and bring in international stars. Cultural centers sponsored by large corporations sometimes offer the cheapest entertainment, with student tickets and frequent programming even in the concert low season (summer). Don't forget the bars, nightclubs, and smaller venues, where you can discover rising talents in the Turkish and European music scenes. While music is for locals and visitors alike, folk and religious dances like the *sema* do great business in the tourist industry. Despite all their marketing and showbiz

istanbul

airs, the dances still offer colorful insights into traditional Turkish culture. Hamams, or bathhouses, are also becoming less of an exclusively local attraction, and there's nothing like a traditional bath to refresh your body after a day of sightseeing.

Theater and Classical Music

GARAJİSTANBUL   BEYOĞLU

Kaymakam Reşat Bey Sokak 11A   ☎0212 244 4499 www.garajistanbul.org

Many performance venues in Istanbul are housed in restored *hamams* or ancient cisterns or some fancy "we got culture" place like that, so a restored parking garage seems fresh. The space is used for contemporary art performances, including theater, music, and dance. You can catch shows ranging from Samuel Beckett's absurdist *Waiting for Godot* to the lighter Istanbul International Puppet Festival. The edgy, dark, ex-parking lot also plays host to promotional parties, "Cult Film Club" events, and unconventional concerts—think hot female violinists in black leather playing in front of a line of parked cars or a counter tenor singing Turkish ballads from the '60s to the '90s. Since Garaj hosts international artists, some of the events are in English or have English subtitles, giving this venue a distinct edge over the small, artsy places.

i Ⓜ*Taksim. Walk down İstiklal and turn left immediately after Yapıkredi, near Yeni Çarşi Cad. Turn right, then left, and you'll see it on the left. Prices vary, but around 40 TL for VIP tickets, 30 TL for bar/table seats, and 20 TL for standing room.* ⌚ *Open Sept-Jun. Consult the online program for performance times.*

Hamams

Steam, sweat, squeeze, and scrub: you can get it all at your local hamam. Once a mainstay of Turkish urban society, the neighborhood *hamam* is losing its share of the bathing scene thanks to the spread of indoor plumbing, adjustable shower nozzles, and the political correctness of not being grappled with by a naked Turk. These days, *hamams* are mostly frequented by older men looking to relive the good ol' days and tourists looking for a taste of tradition. If you can get over the fear of getting pummeled while nearly naked, you're in for an invigorating treat.

Hamams vary: you can either wash yourself or have someone do all the work for you. Everything starts with the shoes—in order to keep the place clean, it's customary to take them off and put on slippers. In the changing rooms, bathers-to-be undress and put on the *peştamal*, a traditional towel that covers those very important parts. Start your journey in the sauna, or *sıcaklık*, where you'll lie on a warm marble slab and feel like every single drop of moisture is being squeezed out of you. When it seems like your body has lost half its weight, cool off by turning on the tap and splashing yourself with the blissfully refreshing water. If you've ordered a massage, the masseur or masseuse will leave almost nowhere on your body untouched. They do leave one or two parts untouched, although it can get uncomfortably close. Next, say *"güle güle"* to your layers of dead skin, as your body is scrubbed, lathered, and washed to baby smoothness. Finally, you'll be handed a towel and dried off before heading to a cool room to lounge and relax with a cup of tea.

And what about those steamy bathhouse fantasies? Forget it—most *hamams* have separate sections or segregated bathing times for men and women, and if they don't, both genders wear bathing suits (all of the *hamams* listed below have separate rooms). *Hamams* in Istanbul, especially the tourist-oriented ones, provide same-gender attendants for men and women. We recommend trying one of these *hamams* first, and if you get hooked, branch out and visit a more authentic (and cheaper) bathhouse. Be aware, though: in the local *hamam* hierarchy, don't be surprised if you, as a tourist, don't outrank the neighborhood grannies who have come every day for the last 15 years; you might be dumping water over yourself with old yogurt buckets, covering yourself with picnic blankets, and getting about half the attention of the staff.

ÇEMBERLİTAŞ HAMAMI
SULTANAHMET

Vezirhan Cad. 8 ☎0212 522 7974 www.cemberlitashamami.com

This is one of best-known *hamams* in Istanbul—which means tourist-land. Everything here corresponds to that fact: it's clean, has a pretty dome you can stare at while sweating like a pig, and is on the expensive side. Built in 1584 and based on plans created by famed Ottoman architect Mimar Sinan, Çemberlitaş Hamamı sneaks out of Ottoman authenticity and gets into spa territory, going beyond the basics of body scrubs and bubble washes to fancy facial masks and Indian head massages. Your experience here depends on the crowds, so try to avoid it during rush hours (4-8pm). If you plan to go to a *hamam* only once, this place should be one of the top contenders, as it's a reassuring (read: clean, not-jerky-to-tourists) first-time *hamam* experience, which is what you want when "authentic" or "local" often means dirty rooms and old yogurt buckets.

i ⓂÇemberlitaş. The hamam is just across the street from the tram stop and the column. Self-service 50 TL. 15min. body scrub and bubble wash 75 TL, with oil massage 127 TL. Facial mask 16 TL. 30min. reflexology 52 TL. 30min. Indian head massage 52 TL. Prices include VAT, unlimited bath time, towel, slippers, bikini underwear, shampoo, soap, and locker with key. You will be asked to tip the attendants in addition. ⏰ Open daily 6am-midnight.

BÜYÜK HAMAM
BEYOĞLU

Potinciler Sok. 22 ☎0212 253 4229

A local place that soap stores will point to, this is one of the biggest *hamams* in town (as you probably figured out by your fourth day in Turkey, *büyük* means "big"). Although this *hamam* isn't full of tourists, it holds historic value similar to that of its more popular brethren—it was built in 1533 and, like Çemberlitaş, was designed by Mimar Sinan. Its walls could use a fresh coat of paint, but the rooftop swimming pool (only for men) and cheap prices make Büyük a decent choice. The catch? It's quite a hike down (and back up) from Taksim, so you'll be sweaty and ready for another bath by the time you hit İstiklal. Try to bring a Turkish friend to avoid any tricks.

i ⓂTünel. Go up İstiklal and turn left onto Asmalı Mescit Cad. Go down the hill, pass the stadium, and follow the road as it turns left onto Çivici Sok. Cross the street, turn right, and walk for 1 block. The hamam is on the left, close to Kasimpaşa Mosque. Self-service 20 TL (women), 23 TL (men). Additional massage 7.50 TL, additional scrub 5 TL. Cash only. ⏰ Open daily 5:30am-10:30pm for men, 8:30am-8pm for women.

Dance

⬛ HODJAPASHA CULTURE CENTER
SULTANAHMET

Hocapaşa Hamamı Sok. 3B ☎0212 511 4626 www.hodjapasha.com

Sema is a religious ceremony that has become a popular tourist attraction—the highlight of the event being that "quintessentially Turkish" element trumpeted by brochures: the **whirling of dervishes**. The dancer's arms, one palm pointing to the sky and the other to the ground, symbolize the channeling of spiritual energy from God to earth in a mystical journey of man's spiritual ascent through mind and love to Perfect Being. The Hodjapasha Center (a former 15th-century hamam) is the easiest, most intimate, and most beautiful place to see a whirling dervishes performance. The ticket price includes water, Turkish coffee, and a booklet along with the performance. Because half of the show is actually a Sufi music concert with no interesting physical movement, this ceremony usually gets a bad rap from unwitting tourists expecting smoke and sparks—we highly suggest you do the research before the show (after all, it's a religious ritual, nota Vegas strip show). More viscerally exciting, perhaps, is the **Turkish Dance Night,**

Istanbul

a mix of almost medieval, elven, fantasy-seeming dancing, jumping, kicking, sword fighting, seducing, twirling, spinning, and, of course, shaking that belly. It may just be the sexiest thing you see in Turkey—from belly dancing to stomp line dancing, you won't be able to stop moving your own body nor keep yourself from ogling the drop-dead gorgeous men and women. For a night of color, music, light, and lots of ass-shaking to remember, do Hodjapasha.

i ⓂSirkeci. *After getting off the tram, walk north away from the water. Take the 1st left after the tram tracks and turn right. There are signs pointing to the venue, which should be on the left. Reserve about 1 week in advance for the best seats. Whirling dervishes show 60 TL, ages 12 and under 40 TL. Turkish Dance Night 70 TL/40 TL. Buy tickets online through the website.* ⓩ *Dervishes show lasts about 45min., every day at 7:30pm. Hodjapasha Dance Night lasts about 90min., every Tu, Th, Sa-Su 9pm.*

Music Festivals

In addition to the **Rock'n Coke**, Turkey's biggest outdoor music festival, check out the **Istanbul Jazz Festival**, the metal **Sonisphere** festival, and the **Club to Club** dance and electronic festival. Keep an eye out for other events advertised on posters, flyers, and billboards across the city.

SHOPPING

Carpets, antiques, clothes, perfumes, Turkish delight, teas, pastries, spices, *nargile*, evil eye beads...we (and you) could go on for days. From weekly street markets to roofed passages, brick-and-mortar stores to covered bazaars, it's not hard to find a place in Istanbul to spend your lire. But since no one wants to overpay, remember the three H's: haggle, haggle, haggle. The prices on the sign are probably too high, and unless you're talented or lucky, the seller will still make good money even when you finally strike a deal. To get a better idea of prices, don't just stop by one shop; similar stores usually cluster around each other, so you should visit more than one to compare. You'll also notice that some things are more expensive in Turkey. Electronics and designer brands are imported, so unless you come from Zimbabwe, you'll probably enjoy a cheaper price for those back home. Also on the do-not-buy list: antiques. If it's more than 100 years old, it's probably illegal to take it out of the country, and you could face fines or a prison sentence. Carpet stores will usually provide a certificate of non-antique-ness, but be extra careful buying in open markets and antique shops. Another antiques-gone-wrong scenario: that calligraphied poem in Sultan Mehmet's own handwriting. It's probably a fake.

Bazaars and Markets

🏛 **GRAND BAZAAR**   SULTANAHMET

Kapalı Çarşı   ☎0212 522 3173 www.kapalicarsi.org.tr

You haven't shopped in Istanbul until you've shopped at the Grand Bazaar. With 21 gates, 66 streets, 3600 shops, and 30,000 employees, you're bound to spend hours in one of the world's oldest and largest covered markets. Arm yourself with your wallet and get ready to haggle. Opened in 1461, the bazaar's streets are named after the trades that were centered there (fez-makers, slipper-manufacturers, goldsmiths, etc.), although much of that doesn't apply anymore. It helps to have a rough idea of the layout in order to navigate and avoid getting lost. There's a central **bedesten** (market hall, also known as *Cehavir*), where jewelry, copperware, silverware, and antiques are sold. Around it, the streets adhere to a grid pattern. If you're hungry, you'll find pretty and overpriced cafes clustered in this area, but there are way better eats hidden like Easter eggs in the narrower streets inside and around the Bazaar (**Gaziantep Burç Ocakbaşı** inside on Parçacılar Sok., **Kara Mehmet Kebap Salonu** out in the İç Cebeci Han courtyard, and **Aynen Dürüm** outside on Muhafazacılar Sok. are great bets for lunch). The

turkey

main gold and jewelry street (a rush and blur of silver and gold and sparkles that goeson for-ev-er) is **Kalpakçılar Caddesi,** which and runs east-west from **Nuruosmaniye Gate (1)** on the eastern side to **Beyazıt Gate (7)** on the western side. Another main street—known part by part as Sipahi, Feraceciler, and **Yağlıkçılar**— connects thesouthern **Çarşı Gate (5)** to the northern **Örücüler Gate (14).** Lined with carpet sellers, **Halıcılar Sokak** runs above the central *bedesten.* Entering from the Nuruosmaniye Gate, you'll find the **Sandal Bedesten** to your right, another place for clothes, souvenirs, and antiques, as well as passionate public auctions. The streets in the bazaar's west end, closer to Beyazıt, are less regular in layout, and you'll find jeans, leather, traditional clothing, and the PTT post and exchange booth there. Try to search online for a map, or pick one up at the director's office near Gate 4, off Kalpakçılar Cad.

i Ⓜ*Beyazıt. Exit the tram station away from Sultanahmet, turn right before the bus stops, and turn right into Beyazıt Gate (7). The Bazaar is a straight shot from the entrance of the Nuruosmaniye Mosque to Gate 1. The police station is 1 block in from Gate 19 (coming in, turn right). Don't be confused by the bedestens, which have their own gate numbers. Currency exchanges are easy to find.* Ⓒ *Open M-Sa 8am-7pm.*

▧ SPICE BAZAAR   SULTANAHMET

Mısır Çarşısı   ☎0212 513 6597 www.misircarsisi.org

Also called the Egyptian Bazaar, this market is much easier to navigate than the Grand one—its layout is brought to you by the letter L (er, just translated 180 degrees counterclockwise). Completed in 1663, the bazaar was built to generate funds for the upkeep of the New Mosque. The bazaar sells what it's named after (that's spices, not Egyptians), as well as tea, caviar, saffron, dried fruits, nuts, Turkish delight, and trinkets—all piled high in a variety of mountains in each shop. By all means, try as many free samples as you like/can get away with! Most merchants will be very open to tasting, though if you're not looking to buy, you should reciprocate by at least feigning vague interest and asking for a business card. This inevitably means stuffing yourself with free Turkish delight: every store here basically sells the same products, offers the same services (vacuum pack, anyone?), and quotes ridiculously high prices (anywhere from 35-85 TL for a kg of delight). Just know that you can get these sweets much cheaper (10-20 TL per kg) in a residential store, although the Spice Bazaar will often have the most variety and the prettiest packaging. Try everything once. Well, almost anything. You'll come across sticky balls of dried figs and walnuts called "Turkish Viagra." *Let's Go* doesn't give medical advice, but after trying one, the only thing that might be hard is trying to win back your friends' respect.

i Ⓜ*Eminönü. After walking out of the station, you'll see Yeni Cami, the New Mosque. The bazaar is right behind the mosque. Its entrance has 3 domes and 3 arches.* Ⓒ *Open M-F 8am-7:30pm, Sa 8am-8pm, Su 9:30am-7:30pm.*

▧ FATIH ÇARŞAMBA PAZARI (WEDNESDAY BAZAAR)

Fatih Çarşamba Pazarı, Fatih Cad.

The biggest open-air bazaar in all of Istanbul, the Fatih Çarşamba Pazarı (or the Wednesday Bazaar) sprawls over 17 avenues and 17 streets, employing 1297 ven- dors and featuring 4811 individual stands, 2500 peddlers, and 16 garbage trucks to deal with the aftermath. It's definitely huge—don't expect to see every potato and pair of panties on sale—but not as dense as the Grand or Spice Bazaars because everything is so spread out through the streets. What you will see is pretty much everything a modest Turkish household might need, from clothing to cheese, ceramics to toilet scrubbers. Pro tip: all the nuts, seeds, spices, and dried fruits of the Spice Bazaar can be bought here, but for real people (read: dirt cheap) prices, rather than tourist (read: in Turkey, still pretty cheap) prices. And you might be the only tourist here! Since you're not the target demographic,

istanbul

you'll be bothered very little, if at all, by vendors who are far more interested in selling eggs to Turkish housewives than in asking you out.

i *Exit the grounds of the Fatih Mosque through the back. The market covers the entire area behind the mosque but doesn't extend west past the main street of Fevzi Paşa Cad. If it's W, you can't miss it. Follow the crowds with shopping bags. Most vendors cash only. Many will claim indirim yok (no discounts), but haggling sometimes works anyway. ☒ Open W 5am-9pm.*

Clothing

Save your money and your consumer greed—Beyoğlu is *the* place in Istanbul to buy things, and you might just find yourself regretting the touristy crap you bought that you thought was cool in Sultanahmet. For cheap new clothes (if you don't feel like braving a Turkish bazaar to get them), hit up the **Atlas** and **Halep** passages (opposite each other, north of Galatasaray). The **Avrupa** ("Europe") passage right next to the **Aslıhan** book passage (on Meşrutiyet Cad., just off İstiklal Cad.) has some good hand-made artisan jewelry hidden among the usual trinkets—remember that in mostlegit jewelry shops, you pay for silver items by their weight, and it's harder to haggle against a scale. **Çukurcuma Caddesi** is the neighborhood "antique street," with some handmade hipster ateliers, pretty coffee shops, and vintage flea shops thrown in. **Yeni Çarsi Caddesi** also has cute, idiosyncratic boutique shop after boutique shop, many buying designs from local artists that won't kill your budget (think along the lines of white canvas heels decorated with hand-drawn illustrations, one-size tutus, and summer dresses that'll fit anyone, and then some used bookstores that are furry with cats lying on the shelves).For your last let's-be-broke splurge, take a *dolmuş* from Taksim to the neighborhood of **Nişantaşi,** which is where the pampered and kitten-heeled go for their frocks and shoes. Death by shopping is a distinct possibility in Beyoğlu—don't trip and roll down any of the San Fran-esque hills, unless you're sure your shopping bags can cushion the fall!

ESSENTIALS
Practicalities

- **TOURIST OFFICES:** There are a number of offices in different districts, including **Sultanahmet** (Meydanı 5 and Divan Yolu Cad. 5 ☎0212 518 1803, 0212 518 1802), **Beyoğlu** (Seyran Apt., Mete Cad. 6 ☎0212 233 0592), **Sirkeci Train Station** (☎0212 511 5888), **Atatürk International Airport** (☎0212 465 3151 ☒ Open daily 9am-10:30pm), **Sabiha Gökçen International Airport** (☎0216 588 8794) and **Karaköy** (Karaköy Limanı Yolcu Sarayı ☎0212 249 5776). All provide free maps, brochures, and information in English. Unless noted otherwise, they are open daily from mid-June to September 9:30am-6pm; from October to mid-June 9am-5:30pm.

- **CURRENCY EXCHANGE:** Exchange bureaus are called *döviz* and can be found on İstiklal and around Divan Yolu. Among the better ones are **Klas Döviz** (Sıraselviler Cad. 6F ☎0212 249 3550 ☒ Open daily 8:30am-10pm) and **Çözüm Döviz** (İstiklal Cad. 53 ☎0212 244 6271 ☒ Open daily 9am-10pm).

- **ATMS:** English-language ATMs *(bankamatik, bankomat)* can be found on almost every corner. If your account is at a foreign bank, cash withdrawal will cost you extra. Most ATMs dispense Turkish lire. If you want to withdraw American dollars or euro, try the banks around Sirkeci Train Station and İstiklal Cad.

- **LUGGAGE STORAGE:** 24hr. luggage storage *(Emanet Bagaj)* is available at **Atatürk International Airport** (☎0212 465 3442 10-20 TL per day) and **Sirkeci Train Station** (☎0539 885 2105 *i* 4-7 TL for 4hr., 0.50 TL per hr. thereafter; max. 4 days).

- **GLBT RESOURCES: Time Out Istanbul** magazine provides a good overview of the city's GLBT establishments. Some other organizations of interest are **Lambda** (Tel Sok. 28/5, 4th fl., Beyoğ-

turkey

lu ☎0212 245 7068, advice line ☎0212 244 5762 www.lambdaistanbul.org ⌂ Open F-Su 3-8pm; hotline open M-Tu 5-7pm and F-Su 5-7pm), trans-focused **Istanbul LGBTT** (Atıf Yılmaz Cad. Öğüt Sok. 18/4, Beyoğlu ☎0212 252 1088 www.istanbul-lgbtt.org), and Ankara-based **Kaos GL** (☎0312 230 0358 http://news.kaosgl.com).

- **LAUNDROMATS:** Most hostels will do your laundry for a small fee. If you'd prefer a laundromat, try **Beybuz** (Topçekerler Sok. 7A ☎0212 249 5900 *i* Wash 3 TL per kg. Dry cleaning 10 TL. ⌂ Open 24hr.) or **Şık Çamaşır Yıkama.** (Güneşli Sok. 1A ☎0212 245 4375 *i* 15 TL per load. ⌂ Open M-Sa 8:30am-8pm.)

- **INTERNET: Sultanahmet Square** offers free Wi-Fi. **İstiklal Caddesi** supposedly has free Wi-Fi as well, but coverage is spotty. One of the best internet cafes in town is **Net Club** (Büyükparmakkapı Sok. 8/6, 3rd fl. *i* Just off Istiklal Cad., a few blocks from Taksim Sq. 1.25 TL per hr. ⌂ Open 24hr.), but there are many others around İstiklal and a few near the Sultanahmet tram stop. In most cafes, expect to pay about 2 TL per hr.

- **POST OFFICES:** You can send letters and make calls at any of the many **PTT booths** around the city. Normal hours are 8:30am-12:30pm and 1:30-5:30pm. There's a central post office in **Eminönü** (Büyük Postahane Cad. 25 ☎0212 511 3818 ⌂ Open daily 8:30am-9pm), while some other offices are in **Taksim** (Cumhuriyet Cad. 2 ☎0212 292 3650 ⌂ Open M-Sa 8:30am-12:30pm and 1:30-5:30pm), **Galatasaray** (Tosbağa Sok. 22 ☎0212 243 3343 ⌂ Open M-Sa 8:30am-7pm, Su 8:30-12:30pm and 1:30-5:30pm), and **Sultanahmet** (Sultanahmet Meydanı ☎0212 517 4966 ⌂ Open in summer Tu-Su 8:30am-12:30pm and 1:30-5:30pm; in winter daily 8:30am-12:30pm and 1:30-5:30pm).

Emergency

- **EMERGENCY NUMBER:** ☎112.

- **POLICE:** ☎155. **Tourism Police,** in Turkish *Turizm Şube Müdürlüğü.* (Yerebatan Cad. 6, Sultanahmet ☎0212 527 4503)

- **LATE-NIGHT PHARMACIES:** Some pharmacies (*eczane*) stay open overnight (*nöbetçi*) on a rotating basis; for a list, go to www.treczane.com. Closed pharmacies will list the nearest open pharmacy on their doors.

- **HOSPITAL/MEDICAL SERVICES:** The best option for international travelers is to use a private hospital. They are clean and efficient, and have 24hr. emergency units and some English-speaking staff. Some of the options are the German Hospital, **Alman Hastanesi** (Sıraselviler Cad. 119 ☎0212 293 2150 www.almanhastanesi.com.tr *i* Consultation 160 TL) and the **American Hospital** (Güzelbahçe Sok. 20 ☎0212 444 3777, ext. 9 www.americanhospitalistanbul. com *i* Consultation 215 TL). Public hospitals are generally crowded, confusing, and lack English-speaking staff, but they are cheaper. The most conveniently located one is **Taksim Hastanesi.** (Sıraselviler Cad. 112 ☎0212 252 4300 www.taksimhastanesi.gov.tr)

Getting There

By Plane

Istanbul is serviced by **Atatürk International Airport** (IST; ☎0212 463 3000 www.ataturkairport.com), which has both international and domestic terminals. The airport serves almost 40 airlines, including Turkish Airlines (☎0212 444 0849), British Airways (☎0212 317 6600), and Air France (☎0212 310 1919). The airport is 28km from central Istanbul. The easiest way to get from the airport to the center is to take the **metro** (M1) and then the **tram.** At the airport, follow the "M" signs, get on the metro (Tokens 1.75 TL), and get off at Zeytinburnu. Here, transfer to the tram going to Ⓜ Kabataş, which passes through Ⓜ Sultanahmet. You'll need to buy another 1.75 TL token for the tram. You can also get off the metro at Ⓜ Aksaray, but the transfer to the tram here isn't as convenient. You can also get to and from the airport via the

istanbul

express **Havaş bus** (☎0212 465 4700 www.havas.net *i* 10 TL ⏰ 40min., every 30min. 4am-1am) and **taxis.** (Around 30 TL to Sultanahmet, 35 TL to Taksim.)

Sabiha Gökçen International Airport (SAW; ☎0216 585 5000 www.sgairport.com) is located on the Asian side, about 40km from Kadıköy and 50km from Taksim. The best way to get from Sabiha Gökçen to central Istanbul is to take the **Havaş bus** (14 TL ⏰ 1hr.; every 30min. from airport 5am-midnight, from Taksim 4am-1am). Alternatively, you can take the **public E10 bus** to Kadıköy (1.75 TL ⏰ 90min., every 10min. or 1hr. depending on time of day) and then transfer to a **ferry** to either Eminönü or Karaköy (1.75 TL ⏰ Around 20min.). **Taxis** are expensive, charging around 80 TL for the trip to Taksim.

By Bus

Buses are concentrated at the **Büyük İstanbul Otogarı** (☎0212 658 0505 www.otogaristanbul.com), known simply as the Otogar. The Aksaray-Havalimanı metro line (M1) has a stop here, so to get to the center from the bus station, take the metro to Aksaray and then walk to the Yusufpaşa tram stop, or take the metro to Zeytinburnu and switch onto the tram. Many bus companies have free shuttle service (*ücretsiz servis*) between the Otogar and Taksim. Among the major bus companies are **metro** (☎0212 444 3455 www.metroturizm.com.tr), **Kamil Koç** (☎0212 444 0562, ☎0212 658 2000 www.kamilkoc.com.tr) and **Ulusoy.** (☎444 1888 www.ulusoy.com.tr) Some of the most frequent bus routes go to: Ankara (From 35 TL ⏰ 6-7hr.); Edirne (From 20 TL ⏰ 2½ hr.); Çanakkale (From 35 TL ⏰ 6hr.); Izmir (From 50 TL ⏰ 9hr.), often via Bursa (From 20 TL ⏰ 4hr.).

By Train

Sirkeci Train Station (☎0212 520 6575) is the final stop for all trains from Europe. The Bosphorus Express connects Istanbul to **Bucharest** (⏰ 20½hr.) while the Balkan Express comes from **Sofia** (⏰ 12½hr.) and **Belgrade.** (⏰ 21½hr.) Trains from the Asian side terminate at **Haydarpaşa Train Station** (☎0216 336 4470). Different trains connect Istanbul with Ankara (Daytime tickets from 16 TL, overnight 90 TL ⏰ 8hr., 5 per day). Information about train schedules and routes can be found on www.tcdd.gov.tr or by calling the **Turkish State Railways** (TCDD) at ☎0212 444 8233.

Getting Around

The public transportation network in Istanbul is reliable and easy to navigate. This applies especially to ferries, trams, and trains, because they don't suffer from Istanbul's traffic congestion. Rides on all of the following (apart from the *dolmuş*es and the Tünel funicular) have a flat rate of 1.75 TL, but it's a bit cheaper if you use **Akbil** or a transit pass like the **Istanbulkart.**

Akbil is a keychain-like transit pass that you can get at major transportation hubs like Taksim (they have signs that say Akbil). Though the passes are useful, they are gradually being phased out. Instead, get the Istanbulkart at the same locations (like Taksim, Kabataş, and ticket booths at metro stops) for 10 TL. The card stores value, and you can add money to it as required. The pass is definitely worth it if you're in the city for a week and don't want to buy individual tickets (*jetons*) for each trip. The card works on buses, ferries (even some to the Princes' Islands), the metro, and trams.

By Tram and Funicular

The tram line that runs from Bağcılar through Zeytinburnu and on to Kabataş is a great option for getting around the European side. It runs from 6am-midnight, stopping in Aksaray, Sultanahmet, and Karaköy. There are two nostalgic tram lines (old streetcar lines dating back to the early 20th century). One runs along İstiklal Cad., connecting Tünel and Taksim, while the other follows a circular route in Kadıköy and Moda, on the Asian side.

turkey

Istanbul is also connected by underground funiculars. Since there is no direct tram connection between Taksim and Sultanahmet, the funicular connecting Kabataş and Taksim is necessary in order to get between the two. Another funicular connects Karaköy and Tünel. (*i* 2.50 TL.)

By metro and Rail
Istanbul's metro (☎0212 568 9970 www.istanbul-ulasim.com.tr) has two lines. The M1 runs from Atatürk International Airport (Havalimanı) through Büyük Otogar to Aksaray. Aksaray is a 5min. walk from the Yusufpaşa tram stop (signs point the way). Another metro line (M2) runs from Şişhane north to Atatürk Oto Sanayi and runs from 6am-midnight. Two suburban trains (www.tcdd.gov.tr) complement the rail service and use the same fare system. One line starts at Sirkeci Train Station and goes west through Kumkapı and Yenikapı (🕐 Around every 20min., 5:45am-midnight.), while the other starts at Haydarpaşa Train Station in Kadıköy and runs east through Göztepe and Bostancı. (🕐 Around every 20min., 5am-midnight.)

By Ferry
Commuter ferries are the best way to get to the Asian side and to access some of the more distant neighborhoods. The most useful lines are **Eminönü-Kadıköy, Karaköy-Haydarpaşa-Kadıköy, Kabataş-Üsküdar, Eminönü-Üsküdar, Kadıköy-Beşiktaş, Kabataş-Kadıköy-Princes' Islands,** and the **Golden Horn line** (stops include Üsküdar, Eminönü, Fener, and Eyüp). Ferries usually run every 20min. or so. The two major intra-city ferry companies are **Şehir Hatları** (☎0212 444 1851 www.sehirhatlari.com.tr) and **Turyol.** (☎0212 251 4421, tourism line ☎0212 512 1287 www.turyol.com)

By Bus
You can get information on the city's many useful bus lines through **IETT** (☎444 1871, Turkish-speaking www.iett.gov.tr). The **dolmuş** is a shared minibus that runs on set routes, stopping every couple of blocks to pick up and drop off passengers. The system is somewhat chaotic, but destinations are always listed on boards visible through the windows. The **Kadıköy-Taksim** *dolmuş* (*i* 5 TL) is especially useful, as it leaves every 20min., even after ferries stop running.

By Taxi
The initial charge for cabs is 2.50 TL and every additional kilometer costs 1.40 TL. If you're taking a cab across the Bosphorus, you'll have to pay the bridge toll as well. Locals round up on the fare for tip. Beware of common taxi scams like a "broken meter" and roundabout routes. While the younger generation in Turkey isn't as hopping as in, say, the Netherlands, you'll be able to find students near the larger city areas. In Istanbul, there is a growing young population, especially in the Beyoğlu area. Beşiktas is also a good option because of its proximity to and popularity with nearby university students. These areas are also where most of Istanbul's worthwhile nightlife is found. Outside of Istanbul, you'll be hard-pressed to find groups of students in European Turkey, besides those on field trips to Troy

turkey essentials

VISAS
Citizens of Australia, Canada, Ireland, the UK, the US, and most other developed countries are required to get three-month, multiple-entry visas in order to enter Turkey. Visas range from €15-45, depending on your nationality, and usually allow you to spend up to 90 days in Turkey. Visas can be purchased at entry points in Turkey: airports, train stations, and bus terminals. Though they are technically called "tourist visas," most travelers report that they are basically a cash grab, and the officials

seem to change the rates at will. Citizens of New Zealand do not need a visa for entrance into Turkey.

MONEY

Currency

Turkey's duality does not end with its continental identity crisis. Both the euro and the Turkish lira (TL) are common currency in the city. It's best to be armed with a little bit of both just in case. We find that travelers will usually use euro to pay for accommodations, and TL for everything else. Many restaurants, non-touristy shops, supermarkets, bars, clubs, sights, and utilities only accept TL. This is not the case with hotels, most of which quote in euro (with the logical exception of those on the Asian side of Turkey). Euro prices tend to be slightly marked up in order to take advantage of lazy tourists. Only tourist-oriented locales bother to list euro prices. In places intended to rip tourists off, such as shopping venues in Sultanahmet, Istanbul, only euro are accepted. Ultimately, it's just cheaper to pay in lire, so the budget traveler should definitely carry many more lire than euro.

Tipping and Bargaining

In Turkey, you should tip around 5-10% in fancier restaurants (but make sure they didn't already include a service fee). Tips aren't expected in inexpensive restaurants. It is not customary to tip taxi drivers, but people will often round up the fare. At hamams, attendants will line up to "bid you goodbye" when you leave, meaning that they expect tips—distribute 10-15% of the total cost among them. Porters expect a few lire, and generally if anyone ever helps you, they are likely to smile kindly (sometimes creepily) and ask for a *baksheesh*, or tip.

The Turks see bargaining in a street market or bazaar as a life skill, but trying to get a cheaper price in an established shop can be disrespectful. If it's unclear whether bargaining is appropriate in a situation, hang back and watch someone else buy first. Be warned, merchants with any pride in their wares will refuse to sell to someone who has offended them in the negotiations, so don't lowball too much.

Taxes

In Turkey, there is an 18% **value added tax (VAT),** known as the KDV, included in the price of most goods and services (including meals, lodging, and car rentals). Before you buy, check if the KDV is included in the price to avoid paying it twice. Theoretically, the KDV that you pay on your trip can be reclaimed at most points of departure, but this requires much persistence and it's a hassle and a half. You may also encounter an airport tax of 15 lira, which is levied only on international travelers, but it is usually included in the cost of plane tickets.

SAFETY AND HEALTH

Unsafe Areas

Suburbs are the least-safe areas of cities, especially at night. Thieves also tend to target known student areas. Nationalist, neo-fascist mobs of students in the Zeytinburnu area have been reported to attack visitors. Another place that locals recommend avoiding at night is Tarlabaşı.

Local Laws and Police

The **General Directorate of Security** (*Emniyet Genel Müdüdlüğü*) is the civilian police force in Turkey. Police officers wear navy-blue uniforms and caps. Police cars are blue and white and have "Polis" written on the side doors and hood. Police violence is a problem in Turkey, especially at protests and demonstrations, so exercise caution when near these events (in fact, try not to be near them at all). According to Human Rights Watch, police routinely use firearms during arrests without exhausting non-violent means and also when there is not an apparent threat of death or injury. Always be respectful and compliant when dealing with the police, and make it clear that you are a tourist.

Drugs and Alcohol

Turkey is a huge locus of drug trafficking coming from Afghanistan and Iran into Europe. It is estimated that as much as 80% of the heroin in Britain comes through Turkey. In recent years, the Interior Ministry has boasted a 149% increase in seizures of opium and opium derivatives, so the government takes drug trafficking very seriously. The Turkish government has adopted a harsh policy (including fines and jail time) for those caught with drugs. If caught, a meek "I didn't know it was illegal" will not suffice. Remember that you are subject to Turkey's laws, not those of your home country, while within its borders.

The official drinking age is 18. **Avoid public drunkenness.** Islam prohibits the consumption of alcohol, even though it is legal in Turkey, so the drinking culture here is very different from what you may be used to. Do not drink during the holy month of Ramadan. At sporting events, the drinking age is 24, but it is not heavily enforced.

Terrorism

Though the threat is lower in Istanbul than elsewhere in the country, terrorism is a persistent problem in Turkey. A number of terrorist groups remain active, mostly in the south east, where the separatist Kurdistan Workers' Party (PKK) regularly attacks national security forces. *Let's Go* does not recommend travel in the southeastern provinces of Hakkari, Sirnak, Siirt, or Tunceli due to the instability and terrorism in these provinces. However, the PKK has in recent years bombed government and civilian targets in Istanbul, Ankara, Izmir, and tourist resorts of the Mediterranean and Aegean. Bombs are normally planted in crowded areas in trash cans, outside banks, or on mini-buses and trains. Bombings occur a few times a year but are generally not deadly and are targeted toward the police and the government. The best thing you can do to be safe is to be aware of your surroundings, especially in crowded areas and tourist sites.

GLBT Travelers

Homosexuality is not illegal in Turkey, but it is recommended that GLBT travelers exercise caution when traveling due to the conservative values embedded in Muslim-majority Turkish society.

Nationalism

The Turks are very proud of all people, items, and history associated with their nation. Do not insult, profane, or ridicule Mustafa Kemal Atatürk. Never. He is a national legend and is practically untouchable. The joke goes that a Turk will flinch if you insult his mother but will kill you if you insult Kemal. So please, don't even try. You should adopt the same reverent attitude toward the Turkish flag. It's everywhere and it symbolizes patriotic pride. It is best to steer clear of discussing politics (especially around election time) or the Kurdish situation.

Contraceptives and Feminine Hygiene

Turkey is much more conservative than other travel destinations. It is almost impossible to find tampons, due to suspicion that they lead to the deflowering of women. Either bring a supply with you, or stock up on sanitary napkins when you get there. The morning-after pill is illegal without a prescription, as is birth control. Pharmacies and some large supermarkets sell condoms, but women should take care to be discreet with these purchases.

turkey essentials

Water

Be wary of the tap water in Turkey. Though Istanbul is fairly modernized, the water throughout the capital and country still isn't safe to drink. Even the locals don't touch it, and there is no need for you to either, since bottled water is pretty cheap.

turkey 101

HISTORY

To Byzantion and Beyond! (667 BCE-324 CE)

Legend has it that a Greek king named Byzas established his own settlement on the European side of the Bosphorus after the Oracle at Delphi told him to set up shop opposite from the "Land of the Blind" (Byzas thought the people on the Asian shore must have been blind not to notice the fabulous land lying across from them). This settlement was called Byzantion, which went on to become Byzantium, then Constantinople, then Istanbul—no matter what you call it, one of world history's most important cities. The region's prime location at the center of various trade routes made it an appealing prize for passing conquerors. Anatolia came under the control of the Persian Empire, before being conquered by Alexander the Great, and then the Romans. In 324 CE, Roman Emperor Constantine I chose to move his capital to Byzantium, which after his death became known as Constantinople.

Capture the Flag (324-1453)

After Rome fell in 476, Constantinople became the capital of the surviving Eastern Roman (or Byzantine) Empire. Byzantine Emperor Justinian expanded the empire's domain to extend from Egypt to Spain, created an organized legal code, and ordered the construction of the magnificent **Hagia Sophia** church—the world's largest building for 1000 years. In the 1100s, the Turks, a nomadic people from Central Asia, began migrating into the fertile lands of Antolia. Described by a historian of the day as "long-haired Turkmen armed with bow and lance on horses which flew like the wind," they were known as much for their fervent Islamic faith as for their military prowess. Constantinople fell to the **Ottoman Turks** in 1453, after a lengthy and tenacious siege led by the aptly named Sultan Mehmed the Conqueror.

Otto-manpower (1453-1923)

For the next 500 years, the Turks ruled a vast empire centered on Constantinople. Architecture and the arts flourished as sultans like Suleiman the Magnificent led campaigns that expanded the empire's borders from the Persian Gulf to the gates of Vienna. After the 17th century though, the Ottomans' fortunes declined, and the empire entered a long period of stagnation and decline, ending with its defeat in **WWI** and collapse in 1923.

Istanbul, not Constantinople (1923-today)

A young Turkish army officer named **Mustafa Kemal** defeated the Western Allies' efforts to colonize the prostrate Turks, creating a secular, modern Republic of Turkey out of the heartland of the old Ottoman Empire. Today, Kemal is better known by his nickname, **Atatürk** (Father of Turks). Atatürk ended Istanbul's 1500-year-run as a capital city and moved the seat of the new Turkey to the more centrally located Ankara. Turkey has continued its balancing act between East and West, as internal tensions between secularism and Islam have manifested themselves in repeated power-struggles between the military and civilian governments. In recent years, Turkey has integrated economically with Europe, even while asserting itself as a regional political power in the Middle East. Today, Turkey exists—as it always has—on the margins of cultures, and at the center of history.

CUSTOMS AND ETIQUETTE

When in Istanbul...

Istanbul is a modern, cosmopolitan city that has adopted many Western social customs, but visitors who've never traveled to a Muslim country before may find certain traditions completely foreign. Public displays of affection are not as common or as widely accepted as in many other European countries, so even if you find yourself a Turkish sweetheart, keep the public canoodling to a minimum. Turks are very proud of their country, and visitors should be aware that insulting the Turkish nation, national flag, or Atatürk is not only rude, but against the law. Steer clear of touchy subjects: Islam and the Armenian Genocide are not acceptable targets for your latest rant or comedy routine. Turkish culture also places a high value on respect for elders. It is considered proper to make your greetings from eldest to youngest, regardless of how well you know each person.

At the Table

Invited to dine at someone's home? Show your gratitude by bringing a small gift, such as flowers or a dessert. Play it safe and don't bring a bottle of wine for your host. Because Turkey is predominately Muslim, many residents don't drink alcohol. Enjoy your meal, and make sure to let your host know how good it tastes. They'll be sure to keep loading up your plate, so bring a hearty appetite and pants loose enough to accommodate an expanding waistline. If you're invited to dine out at a restaurant, bear in mind that the host always pays, although an offer to pay is customary. Leaving a 10% tip in restaurants, cafes, and bars is expected.

Mosque Etiquette

Though some mosques are open only to Muslims, most of Turkey (namely Istanbul's) exquisite mosques welcome all visitors, provided they are courteous and dress appropriately. Remove your shoes before entering and wear modest clothing. Miniskirts, shorts, and tank tops are definite no-nos. Make sure you have your shoulders, upper arms, and thighs completely covered. When entering, women will be provided with a headscarf to cover their hair—though if you want it to match your outfit, you might want to bring your own. Once inside, remember that this is a place of worship, so keep your voice down and be conscientious if you want to snap a picture. When you hear the call for prayer, clear out to make room for worshippers.

Body Language

Remember that body language isn't universal. Even something as simple as shaking your head might not mean what you expect. To say "yes," nod your head downward. "No" is nodding your head upwards, while shaking your head from side to side means that you don't understand. The hand gesture made by forming an "O" with your thumb and index finger, which means "OK" in the US, is considered very offensive in Turkey. It signifies that someone is a homosexual, and if you like your nose unbroken, we don't recommend making it. When you enter someone's home, take off your shoes and accept slippers if offered. Sitting cross-legged on the floor is common, but pay attention: exposing the bottoms of your feet is offensive, no matter how adorable your toe socks are. Blowing your nose in public is considered rude, so take a quick trip to the bathroom to save yourself from awkward stares.

turkey 101

Turkey reminds us of a young Destiny's Child. Replete with Roman and Byzantine ruins and Ottoman palaces, Turkey has its fair share of Beyoncé-style glamour. Meanwhile, scenic landscapes like the cave formations of central Anatolia and small towns full of stray cats, sagging laundry lines, and devout, elderly Muslim women provide the soothing, supporting vocals. If you were working with a five-day itinerary, you might be scrabbling to get a glimpse of all of these facets of Turkey. But with an extended trip, you have the opportunity to survey the country and then dive into your spectacle of choice. Time travel to 330 CE and study the Great Palace of Constantinople, teach English in a small Turkish town, or enjoy Istanbul's high life while tutoring for the TOEFL on the side. Just as that female trio did 20 years ago, Turkey is prepping for its big break on the world stage. It's bound to hit the top of the international charts one of these days, and, when it does, you'll want to say that you discovered it first.

STUDY

If Turkey is Destiny's Child, Istanbul is its Beyoncé—cosmopolitan, vivacious, and just plain sexy. If you're looking for a more authentically Turkish locale, you might consider heading to the capital, Ankara (perhaps the Solange Knowles of Turkey?), which is home to one of Asia's best technical universities.

- **ISTANBUL UNIVERSITY:** Why not study for final exams in a city with world-famous massage houses? Known for both its academics and its historical significance, Istanbul University is the oldest university in Turkey (est. 1453), and its grounds include the former headquarters of the Ottoman Empire's Ministry of War as well as visible Roman and Byzantine ruins.

- **ISLAMIC STUDIES SCHOLARSHIP PROGRAM:** Religion majors might be few and far between, but they get some serious perks. The Turkish government currently provides scholarships (tuition plus pocket money) for undergraduates and post-grads to continue their religious studies in Turkey, the nation that gave us the Blue Mosque and the Haghia Sophia.

- **DUKE IN TURKEY:** If you're looking for a summer introduction to the country, Duke in Turkey (run by—surprise, surprise—Duke University) is a tempting option. The program brings undergraduates to Istanbul to study the rich history of this strategically located city. (☎1 919 660 3151 goknar@duke.edu)

VOLUNTEER

- **KIVA FELLOWS PROGRAM:** Interested in finance but not the Gordon Gekko type? Kiva Fellows Program is an international, microfinance organization that makes loans to low-income women throughout the world, and the organization has an outpost in Istanbul. (☎1 828 479 5482

- **MAVI KALEM:** Mavi Kalem will take you beyond postcard Turkey, whisking you away from Istanbul's surreal Blue Mosque and Topkapi Palace and setting you down in the nearby (and rather poor) neighborhoods of Fener and Balat. As a volunteer, you'll likely assist in teaching some adorable Turkish children English and arts and crafts. (☎90 212 534 41 33 mavikalem@mavikalem.org)

- **BOMONTI FRANSIZ FAKIRHANESI:** If you find yourself in Istanbul for an extended stay, you might consider volunteering at Bomonti Fransiz Farkihanesi. Catholic nuns from the order of "Little Sisters of the Poor"—a name which, admittedly, seems designed to guilt-trip you—run this retirement home for the elderly poor. (☎90 0212 248 09 03 edwenafinn@hotmail.com)

- **HUMAN RIGHTS FOUNDATION OF TURKEY:** For a beautiful country, Turkey has some pretty grim history—most notably, the Armenian Genocide of 1915. The Human Rights Foundation of Turkey documents human rights abuses from both the past and the present and relies on volunteers with expertise in law, medicine, and social services toassist their efforts. (☎90 0 312 310 66 36)

- **EDUCATIONAL VOLUNTEERS FOUNDATION OF TURKEY:** Since its founding in 1995, this group has organized its own corps of volunteers, which it tasks with developing and running after-school programs in underserved areas of Turkey. (☎90 0 216 290 70 00 tegv@tegv.org)

WORK

Just as Destiny's Child did, Turkey has its sights on the top of the charts and has the potential to get there. Unfortunately for foreigners, unlike Destiny's Child (and musical groups, in general), the Turkish government is enforcing a policy of no groupies allowed. The government doesn't want foreigners in positions that Turks could fill, and this attitude makes work visas very hard to come by. Your best bet as a foreigner is to market your skills as a native English speaker and find work as a tutor, hostess, or au pair.

BEYOND TOURISM

www.letsgo.com
Let's GO

FOOD AND DRINK

Fusion Food

With more than 2000 years of culinary history, Turkey has had plenty of opportunity to refine its palate. Modern cuisine is a delicious blend of Balkan, Central Asian, and Middle Eastern specialties. *Doner kebabs* (lamb roasted to perfection on an upright spit) are one of the most popular Turkish dishes. Meat-lovers will also enjoy *kofta*, balls of ground beef or lamb mixed with onions and spices. For lighter fare, there's *dolma*, vine leaves stuffed with anything from spiced rice *(zeytinyagli dolma)* to eggplant *(patlican)* to mussels *(midye)*. Carnivores should try *özbek pilav*, made with diced lamb, onions, tomatoes, and carrots, or *hamsili pilav*, cooked with anchovies. Vegetarians can order *domatesli pilav* (tomato pilaf) or *nohutlu pilav* (rice cooked with seasoned chickpeas). Desserts include *sütlaç*, a fresh rice pudding, and flaky pastries like **baklava** and *kadaif*. Turkish sweets are world-renowned and are sure to sate even the most die-hard sweet tooths.

Drink Up!

Caffeine addicts should try a strong Turkish coffee on for size, then examine the grounds at the bottom to try your hand at kahve fali, or coffee dreg fortune-telling. For less mystery and a stronger kick, sip rakı, an anise-flavored liquor, often served with seafood. Rakı turns milky-white when diluted with water, as it is usually served—hence its nickname, aslan sütü (lion's milk). A common Turkish saying claims that if you want to get to know someone you should either travel or drink rakı together. If you're visiting Istanbul with friends, you can do both, and the effects of this famously strong drink will probably reveal more secrets than the kahve fali did earlier. Teetotalers can try another of Turkey's favorite drinks, ayran. A unique mix of yogurt, water, and salt, ayran is served chilled and is the ideal companion to a steaming kebab. While the younger generation in Turkey isn't as hopping as in, say, the Netherlands, you'll be able to find students near the larger city areas. In Istanbul, there is a growing young population, especially in the Beyoğlu area. Beşiktas is also a good option because of its proximity to and popularity with nearby university students. These areas are also where most of Istanbul's worthwhile nightlife is found. Outside of Istanbul, you'll be hard-pressed to find groups of students in European Turkey, besides those on field trips to Troy.

turkey

ESSENTIALS

You don't have to be a rocket scientist to plan a good trip. (It might help, but it's not required.) You do, however, need to be well prepared, and that's what we can do for you. Essentials is the chapter that gives you all the nitty-gritty you need to know for your trip: the hard information gleaned from 53 years of collective wisdom and several months of furious fact-checking. Planning your trip? Check. Where to find Wi-Fi? Check. The dirt on public transportation? Check. We've also thrown in communications info, safety tips, and a phrasebook, just for good measure. Plus, for overall trip-planning advice from what to pack (money and as little underwear as possible) to how to take a good passport photo (it's physically impossible; consider airbrushing), you can also check out the Essentials section of www.letsgo.com.

greatest hits

- **WE ARE ONE.** Poli Sci majors may think of the EU as a bureaucratic nightmare, but it's awesome for you—the Schengen Agreement allows you to move between most European countries without going through customs (p. 877).

- **WE ARE ONE, PART TWO.** We have mixed feelings about the euro. On one hand, it's awfully convenient to have one currency for most of Europe. On the other hand, the exchange rate is awful (p. 878).

- **ONE-EURO FLIGHTS.** Yes, it's true—budget airlines are a wonderful thing. We've compiled the continent's cheapest and most convenient (p. 879).

- **WE AREN'T REALLY ONE.** As integrated as Europe becomes, they'll always speak some wildly different languages. Enter our handy dandy phrasebook (p. 884). Can you say "Traveling is awesome"? Can you say it in Czech?

planning your trip

DOCUMENTS AND FORMALITIES

We're going to fill you in on visas and work permits, but don't forget the most important one of all: your passport. **Remember to bring your passport!**

Visas

Those lucky enough to be EU citizens do not need a visa to globetrot throughout the
continent. You citizens of Australia, Canada, New Zealand, the US, and most other
non-EU countries do not need a visa for stays of up to 90 days, but this three-month
period begins upon entry into any of the countries that belong to the EU's **freedom of
movement** zone. Those staying longer than 90 days may apply for a longer-term visa;
consult an embassy or consulate for more information.

Double-check entrance requirements at the nearest embassy or consulate for up-
to-date information. US citizens can also consult http://travel.state.gov. Admittance
to a country as a traveler does not include the right to work, which is authorized only
by a **work permit.** You should check online for the process of obtaining a work permit
in the country you are planning to work in.

entrance requirements

- **PASSPORT:** Required for citizens of Australia, Canada, New Zealand, and the US.

- **VISA:** For most EU countries, required for citizens of Australia, Canada, New Zealand,
  and the US only for stays longer than 90 days.

- **WORK PERMIT:** Required for all foreigners planning to work in the EU.

TIME DIFFERENCES

Most of Europe is on Central European Time, which is 1hr. ahead of Greenwich Mean
Time (GMT) and observes Daylight Saving Time during the summer. This means that
it is 6hr. ahead of New York City, 9hr. ahead of Los Angeles, 1hr. ahead of the British
Isles, 8hr. behind Sydney, and 10hr. behind New Zealand. However, the UK, Ireland,
and Portugal are on Western European Time (subtract 1hr. from Central European
Time)—a.k.a. Greenwich Mean Time. In addition, Greece and Turkey (along with
parts of Eastern Europe that *Let's Go* doesn't cover) are on Eastern European Time
(add 1hr. to Central European Time).

money

GETTING MONEY FROM HOME

Stuff happens. When stuff happens, you might need some money. When you need
some money, the easiest and cheapest solution is to have someone back home make
a deposit to your bank account. Otherwise, consider one of the following options.

Wiring Money

Arranging a **bank money transfer** means asking a bank back home to wire money to a bank wherever you are. This is the cheapest way to transfer cash, but it's also the slowest and most agonizing, usually taking several days or more. Note that some banks may only release your funds in local currency, potentially sticking you with a poor exchange rate; inquire about this in advance.

Money transfer services like **Western Union** are faster and more convenient than bank transfers—but also much pricier. Western Union has many locations worldwide. To find one, visit www.westernunion.com or call the appropriate number: in Australia ☎1800 173 833, in Canada 800-235-0000, in the UK 0808 234 9168, in the US 800-325-6000, or in France 08 00 90 04 07. Money transfer services are also available to **American Express** cardholders and at selected **Thomas Cook** offices.

US State Department (US Citizens Only)

In serious emergencies only, the US State Department will help your family or friends forward money within hours to the nearest consular office, which will then disburse it according to instructions for a US$30 fee. If you wish to use this service, you must contact the Overseas Citizens Services division of the US State Department. (☎+1 202-501-4444, from US 888-407-4747)

WITHDRAWING MONEY

ATMs are readily available in most major European destinations. To use a debit or credit card to withdraw money from a cash machine (ATM) in Europe, you must have a four-digit Personal Identification Number (PIN). If your PIN is longer than four digits, ask your bank whether you can just use the first four or whether you'll need a new one. Credit cards don't usually come with PINs, so if you intend to hit

pins and atms

up ATMs in Europe with a credit card to get cash advances, call your credit card company before leaving to request one.

TIPPING

Europe is nowhere near homogenous when it comes to common tipping practices, but suffice it to say that no one tips quite as much as Americans. We sometimes include tipping customs in the **Essentials** section of each chapter. When in doubt, check the bill to make sure tip isn't included, and then see what those around you do. Then hope that those around you aren't overly generous or horribly stingy.

TAXES

Members of the EU have value added tax (VAT) of varying percentages. Non-European Economic Community visitors who are taking goods home may be refunded this tax for certain purchases. To claim a refund, fill out the form you are given at the shop and present it with the goods and receipts at customs upon departure.

the euro

Despite what many dollar-possessing Americans might want to hear, the official currency of 16 members of the European Union—Austria, Belgium, Cyprus, Estonia, Finland, France, Germany, Greece, Ireland, Italy, Luxembourg, Malta, the Netherlands, Portugal, Slovakia, Slovenia, and Spain—is the euro.

Still, the currency has some important—and positive—consequences for travelers hitting more than one eurozone country. For one thing, money-changers across the eurozone are obliged to exchange money at the official, fixed rate and at no commission (though they may still charge a small service fee). Second, euro-denominated traveler's checks allow you to pay for goods and services across the eurozone, again at the official rate and commission-free. For more info, check a currency converter (such as www.xe.com) or www.europa.eu.int.

getting around

BY PLANE

Commercial Airlines

For small-scale travel on the continent, *Let's Go* suggests ✈budget airlines (below) for budget travelers, but more traditional carriers have made efforts to keep up with the revolution. The **Star Alliance Europe Airpass** offers low economy-class fares for travel within Europe to 220 destinations in 45 countries. The pass is available to non-European passengers on Star Alliance (www.staralliance.com) carriers. **EuropebyAir's** snazzy FlightPass also allows you to hop between hundreds of cities in Europe and North Africa. (☎+1 888-321-4737 www.europebyair.com Most flights US$99.)

In addition, a number of European airlines offer discount coupon packets. Most are only available as tack-ons for transatlantic passengers, but some are standalone offers. Most must be purchased before departure, so research in advance. For example, **oneworld** (www.oneworld.com), a coalition of 10 major international airlines, offers deals and cheap connections all over the world, including within Europe.

budget airlines

The recent emergence of no-frills airlines has made hopscotching around Europe by air increasingly affordable. The following resources will be useful not only for crisscrossing countries but also for those ever-popular weekend trips to nearby international destinations.

- **BMIBABY:** To and from most major European cities, and a few less major ones. (www.bmibaby.com)
- **EASYJET:** Who knew London had so many airports? EasyJet did. (www.easyjet.com)
- **RYANAIR:** A budget traveler's dream, Ryanair goes most everywhere, especially in France and Italy. (www.ryanair.com)
- **PEGASUS:** For your inner Bellerophon. (www.flypgs.com)
- **TRANSAVIA:** What every Northern European dreams of: cheap flights to the Mediterranean. (www.transavia.com)
- **WIZZ AIR:** Short hops from Krakow to Paris. (www.wizzair.com)

BY TRAIN

Trains in Europe are generally comfortable, convenient, and reasonably swift. Second-class compartments are great places to meet fellow travelers. Make sure you are on the correct car, as trains sometimes split at crossroads. Towns listed in parentheses on European train schedules require a train switch at the town listed immediately before the parentheses.

You can either buy a **railpass**, which allows you unlimited travel within a particular region for a given period of time, or rely on buying individual **point-to-point** tickets as you go. Almost all countries give students or youths (under 26, usually) direct discounts on regular domestic rail tickets, and many also sell a student or youth card that provides 20-50% off all fares for up to a year.

BY BUS

Though European trains and railpasses are extremely popular, in some cases buses prove a better option. Often cheaper than railpasses, **international bus passes** allow unlimited travel on a hop-on, hop-off basis between major European cities. **Busabout,** for instance, offers three interconnecting bus circuits covering 29 of Europe's best bus hubs. (☎+44 845 026 7514 www.busabout.com. 1 circuit in high season starts at US$559, students US$539.) **Eurolines,** meanwhile, is the largest operator of Europe-wide coach services. We get misty-eyed just thinking about their unlimited 15- and 30-day passes to 41 major European cities. (www.eurolines.com)

rail resources

- **WWW.RAILEUROPE.COM:** Info on rail travel and railpasses.
- **POINT-TO-POINT FARES AND SCHEDULES:** www.raileurope.com/us/rail/fares_schedules/index.htm allows you to calculate whether buying a railpass would save you money.
- **WWW.RAILSAVER.COM:** Uses your itinerary to calculate the best railpass for your trip.
- **WWW.RAILFANEUROPE.NET:** Links to rail servers throughout Europe.

safety and health

In any type of crisis, the most important thing to do is **stay calm.** Your country's embassy abroad is usually your best resource in an emergency; registering with that embassy upon arrival in the country is a good idea. The government offices listed in the **Travel Advisories** feature at the end of this section can provide information on the services they offer their citizens in case of emergencies abroad.

Whenever necessary, *Let's Go* lists specific concerns and local laws in the **Essentials** section of the relevant chapter. Basically, if you want to read about prostitution in Amsterdam, just flip back.

travel advisories

The following government offices provide travel information and advisories:

- **AUSTRALIA: Department of Foreign Affairs and Trade.** (☎+61 2 6261 1111 www. smartraveller.gov.au)
- **CANADA: Department of Foreign Affairs and International Trade.** Call or visit the website for the free booklet *Bon Voyage, But...* (☎+1-800-267-6788 www.international.gc.ca)
- **NEW ZEALAND: Ministry of Foreign Affairs and Trade.** (☎+64 4 439 8000 www. safetravel.govt.nz)
- **UK: Foreign and Commonwealth Office.** (☎+44 845 850 2829 www.fco.gov.uk)
- **US: Department of State.** (☎888-407-4747 from the US, +1-202-501-4444 elsewhere http://travel.state.gov)

PRE-DEPARTURE HEALTH

Matching a prescription to a foreign equivalent is not always easy, safe, or possible, so if you take **prescription drugs,** carry up-to-date prescriptions or a statement from your doctor stating the medications' trade names, manufacturers, chemical names, and dosages. Be sure to keep all medication with you in your carry-on luggage.

Immunizations and Precautions

Travelers over two years old should make sure that the following vaccines are up to date: MMR (for measles, mumps, and rubella); DTaP or Td (for diphtheria, tetanus, and pertussis); IPV (for polio); Hib (for *Haemophilus influenzae* B); and HepB (for Hepatitis B). For recommendations on immunizations and prophylaxis, check with a doctor and consult the **Centers for Disease Control and Prevention (CDC)** in the US (☎+1 800-232-4636 www.cdc.gov/travel) or the equivalent in your home country.

keeping in touch

BY EMAIL AND INTERNET

Hello and welcome to the 21st century, where you're rarely more than a 5min. walk from the nearest Wi-Fi hot spot, even if sometimes you'll have to pay a few bucks or buy a drink for the privilege of using it. **Internet cafes** and the occasional free internet terminal at a public library or university are listed in the **Practicalities** sections of cities that we cover.

Wireless hot spots make internet access possible in public and remote places. Unfortunately, they also pose security risks. Hot spots are public, open networks that use unencrypted, unsecured connections. They are susceptible to hacks and "packet sniffing"—the theft of passwords and other private information. To prevent problems, disable "ad hoc" mode, turn off file sharing and network discovery, encrypt your email, turn on your firewall, beware of phony networks, and watch for over-the-shoulder creeps.

BY TELEPHONE

If you have internet access, your best—i.e., cheapest, most convenient, and most tech-savvy—means of calling home is probably our good friend 🗪**Skype** (www.skype.com). You can even videochat if you have one of those new-fangled webcams. Calls to other Skype users are free; calls to landlines and mobiles worldwide start at US$0.023 per minute, depending on where you're calling.

For those still stuck in the 20th century, **prepaid phone cards** are a common and relatively inexpensive means of calling abroad. Each one comes with a Personal Identification Number (PIN) and a toll-free access number. You call the access number and then follow the directions for dialing your PIN. To purchase prepaid phone cards, check online for the best rates; www.callingcards.com is a good place to start. Online providers generally send your access number and PIN via email, with no actual "card" involved. You can also call home with prepaid phone cards purchased abroad.

Another option is a **calling card,** linked to a major national telecommunications service in your home country. Calls are billed collect or to your account. Cards generally come with instructions for dialing both domestically and internationally. Placing a collect call through an international operator can be expensive but may

international calls

To call Europe from home or to call home from Europe, dial:

1. THE INTERNATIONAL DIALING PREFIX. To call from Australia, dial ☎0011; Canada or the US, ☎011; Ireland, New Zealand, the UK, and most of Europe, ☎00.

2. THE COUNTRY CODE OF THE COUNTRY YOU WANT TO CALL. To call Australia, dial ☎61; Austria, ☎43; Belgium, ☎32; Canada, ☎1; Czech Republic, ☎420; Denmark, ☎45; France, ☎33; Germany, ☎49; Greece, ☎30; Hungary, ☎36; Ireland, ☎353; Italy, ☎39; the Netherlands, ☎31; New Zealand, ☎64; Portugal, ☎351; Spain, ☎34; Turkey, ☎90; the UK, ☎44; the US, ☎1.

3. THE CITY/AREA CODE. *Let's Go* lists the city/area codes for cities and towns in Europe opposite the city or town name, next to a ☎, as well as in every phone number. If the first digit is a zero (e.g., ☎020 for Amsterdam), omit the zero when calling from abroad (e.g., dial ☎20 from Canada to reach Amsterdam).

4. THE LOCAL NUMBER.

be necessary in case of an emergency. You can frequently call collect without even possessing a company's calling card just by calling its access number and following the instructions.

Cellular Phones

The international standard for cell phones is **Global System for Mobile Communication (GSM).** To make and receive calls in Europe, you will need a GSM-compatible phone and a **SIM (Subscriber Identity Module) card,** a country-specific, thumbnail-size chip that gives you a local phone number and plugs you into the local network. Many SIM cards are prepaid, and incoming calls are frequently free. You can buy additional cards or vouchers (usually available at convenience stores) to "top up" your phone. For more information on GSM phones, check out www.telestial.com. Companies like **Cellular Abroad** (www.cellularabroad.com) and **OneSimCard** (www.onesimcard. com) rent cell phones and SIM cards that work in a variety of destinations around the world.

BY SNAIL MAIL

Sending Mail Home from Europe

Airmail is the best way to send mail home from Europe. Write "airmail," *"par avion,"* or the equivalent in the local language on the front. For simple letters or postcards, airmail tends to be surprisingly cheap, but the price will go up sharply for weighty packages. Surface mail is by far the cheapest, slowest, and most antiquated way to send mail. It takes one to two months to cross the Atlantic and one to three to cross the Pacific—good for heavy items you won't need for a while, like souvenirs that you've acquired along the way.

Receiving Mail in Europe

There are several ways to arrange pickup of letters sent to you while you are abroad, even if you do not have an address of your own. Mail can be sent via **Poste Restante** (General Delivery). Address Poste Restante letters like so:

Napoleon BONAPARTE
Poste Restante
City, Country

The mail will go to a special desk in the city's central post office, unless you specify a local post office by street address or postal code. It's best to use the largest post office, since mail may be sent there regardless. Bring your passport (or other photo ID) for pickup; there may be a small fee. If the clerks insist that there is nothing for you, ask them to check under your first name as well. *Let's Go* lists post offices in the **Practicalities** section for each city we cover. It is usually safer and quicker, though more expensive, to send mail express or registered. If you don't want to deal with Poste Restante, consider asking your hostel or accommodation if you can have things mailed to you there. Of course, if you have your own mailing address or a reliable friend to receive mail for you, that will be the easiest solution.

climate

Europe is for lovers, historians, architects, beach bums, and...weather nerds? In fact, the smallest continent has quite the diverse climate. Southern Europe is known for the warm weather surrounding the Mediterranean Sea. This area has warm, wet winters and hot, dry summers. Northern Europe is marked by temperate forests, where cold arctic air in winter contrasts with hot summers. In between sits the exception: the mile-high Alps, where things are generally colder and wetter.

AVG. TEMP. (LOW/HIGH), PRECIP.	JANUARY			APRIL			JULY			OCTOBER		
	°C	°F	mm	°C	°F	mm	°C	°F	mm	°C	°F	mm
Amsterdam	-1/4	30/39	68	4/13	39/55	49	13/22	55/72	77	7/14	45/57	72
Athens	6/13	43/55	62	11/20	52/68	23	23/33	73/91	6	15/24	59/75	51
Barcelona	6/13	43/55	31	11/18	52/64	43	21/28	70/82	27	15/21	59/70	86
Berlin	-3/2	27/36	46	4/13	39/55	42	14/24	57/75	73	6/13	43/55	49
Brussels	-1/4	30/39	66	5/14	41/57	60	12/23	54/73	95	7/15	45/59	83
Budapest	-4/1	25/34	37	7/17	45/63	45	16/28	61/82	56	7/16	45/61	5
Copenhagen	-2/2	28/36	49	3/10	37/50	38	14/22	57/72	71	7/12	45/54	59
Dublin	1/8	34/46	67	4/13	39/55	45	11/20	52/68	70	6/14	43/57	70
Istanbul	3/8	37/46	109	7/16	45/61	46	18/28	64/82	34	13/20	55/68	81
Lisbon	8/14	46/57	111	12/20	54/68	54	17/27	63/81	3	14/22	57/72	62
London	2/6	36/43	54	6/13	43/55	37	14/22	57/72	57	8/14	46/57	57
Madrid	2/9	36/48	39	7/18	45/64	48	17/31	63/88	11	10/19	50/66	53
Marseille	2/10	36/50	43	8/18	46/64	42	17/29	63/84	11	10/20	50/68	76
Paris	1/6	34/43	56	6/16	43/61	42	15/25	59/77	59	8/16	46/61	50
Prague	-5/0	23/32	18	3/12	37/54	27	13/23	55/73	68	5/12	41/54	33
Rome	5/11	41/52	71	10/19	50/66	51	20/30	68/86	15	13/22	55/72	99
Venice	1/6	34/43	37	10/17	50/63	78	19/27	66/81	52	11/19	52/66	77
Vienna	-4/1	25/34	39	6/15	43/59	45	15/25	59/77	84	7/14	45/57	56

To convert from degrees Fahrenheit to degrees Celsius, subtract 32 and multiply by 5/9. To convert from Celsius to Fahrenheit, multiply by 9/5 and add 32. The mathematically challenged may use this handy chart:

°CELSIUS	-5	0	5	10	15	20	25	30	35	40
°FAHRENHEIT	23	32	41	50	59	68	77	86	95	104

measurements

Like the rest of the rational world, Europe uses the metric system. The basic unit of length is the meter (m), which is divided into 100 centimeters (cm) or 1000 millimeters (mm). One thousand meters make up one kilometer (km). Fluids are measured in liters (L), each divided into 1000 milliliters (mL). A liter of pure water weighs one kilogram (kg), the unit of mass that is divided into 1000 grams (g). One metric ton is 1000kg. Gallons in the US and those in Britain are not identical: one US gallon equals 0.83 Imperial gallons. Pub aficionados will note that an Imperial pint (20 oz.) is larger than its US counterpart (16 oz.).

MEASUREMENT CONVERSIONS	
1 inch (in.) = 25.4mm	1 millimeter (mm) = 0.039 in.
1 foot (ft.) = 0.305m	1 meter (m) = 3.28 ft.
1 yard (yd.) = 0.914m	1 meter (m) = 1.094 yd.
1 mile (mi.) = 1.609km	1 kilometer (km) = 0.621 mi.
1 ounce (oz.) = 28.35g	1 gram (g) = 0.035 oz.
1 pound (lb.) = 0.454kg	1 kilogram (kg) = 2.205 lb.
1 fluid ounce (fl. oz.) = 29.57mL	1 milliliter (mL) = 0.034 fl. oz.
1 gallon (gal.) = 3.785L	1 liter (L) = 0.264 gal.

measurements

phrasebook

ENGLISH	ITALIAN	FRENCH	SPANISH	PORTU-GUESE	DANISH	TURKISH
Hello	Buongiorno	Bonjour	Hola	Olá	Hej	Merhaba
Goodbye	Arrivederci	Au revoir	Adiós	Até logo	Farvel	Iyi günler/Iyi akşamlar
Yes	Sì	Oui	Si	Sim	Ja	Evet
No	No	Non	No	Não	Nej	Hayır
Please	Per favore	S'il vous plaît	Por favor	Por favor	Må jeg bede	Lütfen
Thank you	Grazie	Merci	Gracias	Obrigado/a	Tak	Teşekkur ederim
You're welcome	Prego	De rien	De nada	De nada	Selv tak	Bir şey değil
Sorry!	Mi scusi!	Désolé!	¡Perdón!	Desculpe!	Undskyld	Pardon!
My name is...	Mi chiamo...	Je m'appelle...	Me llamo...	O meu nome é...	Jeg hedder...	Ismim...
How are you?	Come sta?	Comment êtes-vous?	¿Cómo estás?	Como você está?	Hvordan har De det?	Sen nasılsın?
I don't know.	Non lo so.	Je ne sais pas.	No sé.	Eu não sei.	Jeg kender ikke	Bilmiyorum.
I don't understand.	Non capisco.	Je ne comprends pas.	No entiendo.	Não entendo.	Jeg forstår jeg ikke	Anlamadım.
Could you repeat that?	Potrebbe ripetere?	Répétez, s'il vous plaît?	¿Puede repetirlo?	Você pode repetir?	En gang til?	Lütfen o tekrarla?
Do you speak English?	Parla inglese?	Parlez-vous anglais?	¿Hablas español?	Fala inglês?	Taler du engelsk?	İngilizce biliyor musun?
I don't speak ____.	Non parlo italiano.	Je ne parle pas français.	No hablo castellano.	Eu não falo português.	Jeg kan ikke tale dansk	Turkçe okuyorum.
Why?	Perché?	Pourquoi?	¿Por qué?	Porque?	Hvorfor	Neden?
Where is...?	Dov'è...?	Où est?	¿Dónde está...?	Onde é...?	Hvor er...?	...nerede?
What time is it?	Che ore sono?	Quelle heure est-il?	¿Qué hora es?	Que horas são?	Hvad er klokken?	Saat kaç?
How much does this cost?	Quanto costa?	Combien ça coûte?	¿Cuánto cuesta esto?	Quanto custa?	Hvad koster det?	Ne kadar bu bedeli do?
I am from the US.	Sono degli Stati Uniti.	Je suis des Etats-Unis.	Soy de los Estados Unidos.	Eu sou de os Estados Unidos.	Jeg er fra de USA.	Ben ABD geliyorum.
I have a visa/ID.	Ho un visto/carta d'identità.	J'ai un visa/identification.	Tengo una visa/identificación.	Eu tenho um visto/identificação.	Jeg har et visum/identifikation.	Benim bir vizem/ID var.
I have nothing to declare.	Non ho nulla da dichiarare.	Je n'ai rien à déclarer.	No tengo nada para declarar.	Não tenho nada a declarar.	Jeg har intet at erklære.	Duyurmak için benim hiçbirşeyim yok.
I will be here for less than three months.	Sarò qui per meno di tré mesi.	Je serai ici pour moins de trois mois.	Estaré aquí por menos de tres meses.	Eu estarei aqui há menos de três meses.	Jeg vil være her i mindre end tre måneder.	Ben üçten az ay için burada olacağım.
One-way	Solo andata	Aller simple	Ida	Ida	En vej	Tek yön
Round-trip	Andata e ritorno	Aller-retour	Ida y vuelta	Ida e volta	Rundtur	Gidiş dönüş
Hotel/hostel	Albergo/ostello	Hôtel/auberge	Hotel/hostel	Hotel/albergue	Hotel/vandrerhjem	Otel/pansiyon
I have a reservation.	Ho una prenotazione.	J'ai une réservation.	Tengo una reserva.	Tenho uma reserva.	Jeg har en reservation.	Benim bir koşulum var.
Single/double room	Camera singola/doppia	Chambre pour un/deux	Habitación simple/doble	Quarto individual/duplo	Enkelt-værelse	Tek/çift kişilik

essentials

ENGLISH	ITALIAN	FRENCH	SPANISH	PORTU-GUESE	DANISH	TURKISH
I'd like...	Vorrei...	Je voudrais...	Me gustaría...	Gostaria...	Jeg vil gerne...	Ben bir ... seveceğim.
Check, please!	Il conto, per favore!	L'addition, s'il vous plaît!	¡La cuenta, por favor!	A conta, por favor!	Må jeg bede om regningen!	Hesap, lütfen!
I feel sick.	Mi sento male.	Je me sens malade.	Me siento mal.	Eu me sinto doente.	Jeg føler mig syg.	Ben hastayım.
Get a doctor!	Telefoni un dottore!	Va chercher un médecin!	¡Llama un médico!	Chamar um doutor!	Ringe til en læge!	Doktor ihtiya-cim!
Hospital	Ospedale	Hôpital	Hospital	Hospital	Hospital	Hastane
I lost my passport/luggage.	Ho perso il mio passapor-to/i miei bagagli.	J'ai perdu mon passeport/baggage.	He perdido mi pasaporte/equipaje.	Eu perdi o meu passaporte/a minha baga-gem.	Jeg har mistet mit pas/min bagage.	Ben benim pasaportumu/bagajımı kaybettim.
Help!	Aiuto!	Au secours!	¡Socorro!	Socorro!	Hjælpe!	Imdat!
Leave me alone!	Lasciami stare!/Mol-lami!	Laissez-moi tranquille!	¡Déjame en paz!	Deixe-me em paz!	Lad mig være i fred!	Beni yalnız bırak!
Go away!	Vattene!	Allez-vous en!	¡Vete!	Vá embora!	Gå!	Git başımdan!
Call the police!	Telefoni alla polizia!	Appelez les flics!	¡Llama la policia!	Chamar a polícia!	Ringede til politiet.	Polis çağırın!

ENGLISH	GERMAN	DUTCH	CZECH	HUNGARIAN	GREEK PRO-NUNCIATION
Hello	Hallo/Tag	Dag/Hallo	Dobrý den	Szervusz	yah sahs
Goodbye	Auf Wiederseh-en/Tschüss	Tot ziens	Nashledanou	Viszontlátásra	yah sahs
Yes	Ja	Ja	Ano	Igen	neh
No	Nein	Nee	Ne	Nem	oh-hee
Please	Bitte	Alstublieft	Prosím	Kérem	pah-rah-kah-LO
Thank you	Danke	Dank u wel	Děkuji	Köszönöm	Ef-hah-ree-STO
You're welcome	Bitte	Alstublieft	Prosím	Kérem	pah-rah-kah-LO
Sorry!	Es tut mir leid!	Sorry!	Promiňte!	Elnézést!	sig-NO-mee
My name is...	Ich bin...	Mijn naam is...	Mé jméno je...	A nevem...	meh LEH-neh
How are you?	Wie geht's (geht es Ihnen)?	Hoe gaat het?	Jak se máš?	Hogy vagy?	tee KAH-neh-teh
I don't know.	Ich weisse nicht/Keine Ahnung.	Ik weet het niet/Geen idee.	Nevím.	Nem tudom.	dthen KSER-o
I don't under-stand.	Ich verstehe nicht.	Ik begrijp het niet.	Nerozumím.	Nem értem.	dthen kah-tah-lah-VEH-no
Could you repeat that?	Können Sie wiederholen?	Kunt u dat herhalen?	Můžete opakovat, že?	Meg tudnád ismételni ezt?	bor-EE-teh na ep-an-a-LAH-vet-eh ahv-TO
Do you speak English?	Sprechen Sie Englisch?	Spreekt u Engels?	Mluví anglicky?	Beszél angolul?	mee-LAH-teh sng-lee-KAH
I don't speak _____.	Ich kann kein Deutsch.	Ik spreek geen Nederlands.	Nemluvím Česky.	Nem tudok (jól) magyarul.	dthen meel-AOH eh-lee-nee-KAH
Why?	Warum?	Waarom?	Proč?	Miért?	gee-ah-TEY
Where is...?	Wo ist...?	Waar is...?	Kde je...?	Hol van...?	poo EE-ne
What time is it?	Wie spät ist es?	Hoe laat is het?	Kolik je hodin?	Hány óra van?	tee O-rah EE-neh
How much does this cost?	Wie viel (kostet das)?	Wat kost het?	Kolik to stojí?	Mennyibe kerül?	PO-so kos-TI-dzeh ahv-TO
I am from the US.	Ich bin von Amerika.	Ik ben uit de VS.	Já jsem ze Spo-jených států.	Én vagyok az Egyesült Államok.	EE-meh ap-OH tiss een-o-MEN-ess pol-ee-TEE-ess
I have a visa/ID.	Ich habe ein Visum/eine ID.	Ik heb een visum/ID.	Mám víza/ID.	Van egy vízumot.	EH-oh mia theh-OH-ray-sey/tahf-TOH-tay-ta
I have nothing to declare.	Ich habe nichts zu verzollen.	Ik heb niets aan te geven.	Nemám nic k proclení.	Nekem van egy azonosítója.	Dthen EH-oh TEE-poh-teh na day-LO-so

phrasebook

ENGLISH	GERMAN	DUTCH	CZECH	HUNGARIAN	GREEK PRO-NUNCIATION
I will be here for less than three months.	Ich reste hier für weniger als drei Monate.	Ik blijf hier minder dan drie maanden.	I tady bude za méně než tři měsíce.	Én itt leszek kevesebb, mint három hónap.	Tha EE-meh eth-OH gee-ah lig-OH-teh-ro ap-OH treess MAY-ness
One-way	Einfache	Enkele reis	Jedním směrem	Csak oda	mon-OH-drom-OSS
Round-trip	Hin und zurück	Rondreis	Zpáteční	Oda-vissza	met ep-eess-tro-FACE
Hotel/hostel	Hotel/Herberge	Hotel/hostel	Hotel/ubytovna	Hotel/szálló	kse-no-dtho-HEE-o/ksen-OH-na
I have a reservation.	Ich habe eine Reservierung.	Ik heb een reservering.	Mám rezervaci.	Foglaltam asztalt.	EH-oh CAHN-ee KRA-tay-say
Single/double room	Einzelzimmer/ Doppelzimmer	Eenpersoons-skamer / Tweep-ersoonskamer	Jednolůžkový/ dvoulůžkový pokoj	Egyágyas / kétágyas szoba	mo-NO-klin-oh/ DIE-klin-oh
I'd like...	Ich möchte...	Ik wil graag...	Prosím...	kérek...	THAH EE-the-lah
Check, please!	Die Rechnung, bitte!	Mag ik de rekening!	Paragon, prosím!	A számlát, kérem!	oh lo-ghah-ree-yah-SMOS, pah-rah-kah-LO
I feel sick.	Ich bin krank.	Ik ben ziek.	Je mi špatně.	Rosszul érzem magam.	EE-meh AH-rose-tose
Get a doctor!	Hol einen Arzt!	Haal een dokter!	Najít lékaře!	Orvost!	PAH-re-te HEN-ah yiah-TROH
Hospital	Krankenhaus	Ziekenhuis	Nemocnice	Orvos	no-so-ko-MEE-o
I lost my passport/luggage.	Ich habe mein Reisepass/Ge-päck verloren.	Ik heb mijn paspoort/bagage verloren.	Ztratil jsem pas/ zavazadla.	Elveszítettem az útlevelemet/ Elfelejtettem a poggyász.	EH-ah-sa toh dthaya-vah-tee-ri-o/vah-LEE-tsah moo
Help!	Hilfe!	Help!	Pomoc!	Segíts nekem!	vo-EE-thee-ah
Leave me alone!	Verloren gehen!	Laat me met rust!	Nech mě být!	Hagyj békén!	a-FIS-te me EE-si-kho (m.)/ EE-si-khee (f.)
Go away!	Geh weg!	Ga weg!	Prosím odejděte!	Távozzék!	FOO-geh
Call the police!	Ruf die Polizei!	Bel de politie!	Zavolejte policii!	Hívja a rendőrséget!	kah-LESS-ee teen ah-stih-noh-MIH-ah

let's go online

Plan your next trip on our spiffy website, **www.letsgo.com.** It features full book content, the latest travel info on your favorite destinations, and tons of interactive features: read blogs from our trusty Researcher-Writers, browse our photo library, watch exclusive videos, check out our newsletter, find travel deals, follow us on Facebook, and buy new guides. Plus, if this Essentials wasn't enough for you, we've got even more online. We're always updating and adding new features, so check back often!

INDEX

index

index

index

index

index

index

index

index

U

V

W

Z

ACKNOWLEDGMENTS

CLAIRE THANKS: Chris, for all the music, screencaps, and laughs and for being the best RM/team mom/pod partner I could have asked for. Never forget that LA is a fortress city. Michael, for being a great Boss Michael and an even greater Friend Michael—there's no one with whom I'd rather spend three hours at Crema. Luis, for all the late-night hours spent watching "8 Out of 10 Cats," "Countdown," and "8 Out of 10 Cats Does Countdown." Mackenzie, for always being game for everything from assassins to weeknight karaoke to too many BeTos. Thanks to all our phenomenal RWs: Andrés, Angie, Anna, Chris, Christine, Kevin, Lynn, Priyanka, Serena, and Uli. Thanks to the third floor for being the best floor; because I know most of you will never pick up this book, I don't feel obligated to recognize any of you by name. Thanks to a vending machine full of Coke Zero for providing me with cheap energy and aspertame. Thanks to Jim, Pat, Andy, and all of HSA for the empowerment and #unity. And thanks to my parents for liking me better than Sam and Jack.

CHRIS THANKS: Claire, for being the best team dad a team mom could ever ask for. Thanks for showing me the ropes, being a great friend, and making me a flipbook in your spare time. Could not have done this summer without you, partner. See you in Khouse. Michael for taking us out for sushi, reminding me to pay our RWs, and for being an all-around incredible boss. All of our RWs, for taking Europe by storm and letting the office gang live vicariously through your ridiculous 8-week summer jobs. You built this: Kevin, for a thoroughly ghetto listing, a thoroughly thick Euro-beard, and for finding a way despite a certain technological disadvantage. Andres, for not letting aggressive prostitutes get the better of him and for tackling one of LG's toughest routes. Serena, for sparing no establishment from the wielding of your opinion, even the Catholic church. Uliana, for toting a lovely little lawn gnome, braving the Italian train system, and surmounting the lands of little Wi-Fi. Angie, for your passion to explore, knack for immersion, poise in the face of political instability, and all-around knock-our-socks-off awesomeness. Christine, for being our rock, pushing your boundaries with UK copy (and nailing it), and keeping us laughing/googling your pop-culture references throughout the summer. Chris, for living the RW life like a true backpacker, for getting lost one time and video blogging about it, and for sending us pictures of food that made us all drool. Lynn, for conquering the beast that is Paris, churning out copious amounts of beautiful copy, and landing free cupcakes along the way. Anna, for undying enthusiasm even with the wettest weather and for being the first RW in a long while to actually stay in a tent. Priyanka, for slaying us with your humor on a daily basis, landing a ticket to see the Pope because why not, and devouring both the old and new sides of Rome like it was a cup of pistachio gelato. Luis, for that hug on my last day. I still get butterflies about it. Mackenzie, for sharing music, cookies, and personal space with a smile and ever-ready water gun. Angela and Nina, for sacrificing your room on multiple occasions. Marketing pod, for being a stellar bunch and a great place to take five (or ten). The market on Brattle, for knowing "the usual" and always being open. Mom, Dad, Luke, and Roman, for planning your summer around my schedule and for being just the greatest. Love you guys.

acknowledgments

THANKS TO OUR SPONSORS

DIRECTOR OF PUBLISHING Michael Goncalves
PRODUCT MANAGER Luis Duarte
EDITORIAL DIRECTOR Claire McLaughlin
RESEARCH MANAGER Christopher Holthouse
MARKETING DIRECTORS Nina Kosaric, Angela Song

DIRECTOR OF IT Bob Bedetti
PRESIDENT Patrick Coats
GENERAL MANAGER Jim McKellar

LET'S GO
masthead

ABOUT LET'S GO

THE STUDENT TRAVEL GUIDE

Let's Go publishes the world's favorite student travel guides, written entirely by Harvard students. Armed with pens, notebooks, and a few changes of clothes stuffed into their backpacks, our student researchers go across continents, through time zones, and above expectations to seek out invaluable travel experiences for our readers. Because we are a completely student-run company, we have a unique perspective on how students travel, where they want to go, and what they're looking to do when they get there. If your dream is to grab a machete and forge through the jungles of Costa Rica, we can take you there. If you'd rather bask in the Riviera sun at a beachside cafe, we'll set you a table. In short, we write for readers who know that there's more to travel than tour buses. To keep up, visit our website, www.letsgo. com, where you can sign up to blog, post photos from your trips, and connect with the Let's Go community.

TRAVELING BEYOND TOURISM

We're on a mission to provide our readers with sharp, fresh coverage packed with socially responsible opportunities to go beyond tourism. Each guide's Beyond Tourism sections share ideas about responsible travel, study abroad, and how to give back to the places you visit while on the road. To help you gain a deeper connection with the places you travel, our fearless researchers scour the globe to give you the heads-up on both world-renowned and off-the-beaten-track opportunities. We've also opened our pages to respected writers and scholars to hear their takes on the countries and regions we cover, and asked travelers who have worked, studied, or volunteered abroad to contribute first-person accounts of their experiences.

FIFTY-FOUR YEARS OF WISDOM

Let's Go has been on the road for 54 years and counting. We've grown a lot since publishing our first 20-page pamphlet to Europe in 1960, but five decades and 75 titles later, our witty, candid guides are still researched and written entirely by students on shoestring budgets who know that train strikes, stolen luggage, food poisoning, and marriage proposals are all part of a day's work. Meanwhile, we're still bringing readers fresh new features, such as a student-life section with advice on how and where to meet students from around the world; a revamped, user-friendly layout for our listings; and greater emphasis on the experiences that make travel abroad a rite of passage for readers of all ages. And, of course, this year's seven titles are still brimming with editorial honesty, a commitment to students, and our irreverent style.

THE LET'S GO COMMUNITY

More than just a travel guide company, Let's Go is a community that reaches from our headquarters in Cambridge, MA, all across the globe. Our small staff of dedicated student editors, writers, and tech nerds comes together because of our shared passion for travel and our desire to help other travelers get the most out of their experience. We love it when our readers become part of the Let's Go community as well—when you travel, drop us a postcard (67 Mt. Auburn St., Cambridge, MA 02138, USA), send us an email (feedback@letsgo.com), or sign up on our website (www.letsgo.com) to tell us about your adventures and discoveries.

For more information, updated travel coverage, and news from our researcher team, visit us online at www.letsgo.com.

HELPING LET'S GO. If you want to share your discoveries, suggestions, or corrections, please drop us a line. We appreciate every piece of correspondence, whether a postcard, a 10-page email, or a coconut. Visit Let's Go at **www.letsgo.com** or send an email to:

feedback@letsgo.com, subject: "Let's Go Europe"

Address mail to:

Let's Go Europe, 67 Mount Auburn St., Cambridge, MA 02138, USA

In addition to the invaluable travel advice our readers share with us, many are kind enough to offer their services as researchers or editors. Unfortunately, our charter enables us to employ only currently enrolled Harvard students.

Maps © Let's Go and Avalon Travel

Distributed by Publishers Group West.
Printed in Canada by Friesens Corp.

ISBN-13: 978-1-61237-042-2
Fifty-fourth edition
10 9 8 7 6 5 4 3 2 1

Let's Go Europe is written by Let's Go Publications, 67 Mt. Auburn St., Cambridge, MA 02138, USA.

Let's Go® and the LG logo are trademarks of Let's Go, Inc.

QUICK REFERENCE

YOUR GUIDE TO LET'S GO ICONS

✎	*Let's Go* recommends	☎	Phone numbers
i	Other hard info	⏰	Hours

IMPORTANT PHONE NUMBERS

EMERGENCY: ☎112			
Austria	☎133	Ireland	☎999
Belgium	☎101	Italy	☎113
Czech Republic	☎158	The Netherlands	☎911
France	☎17	Portugal	☎112
Germany	☎110	Spain	☎092
Great Britain	☎999	Turkey	☎155
Hungary	☎107		

USEFUL PHRASES

ENGLISH	FRENCH	GERMAN	ITALIAN	SPANISH
Hello/Hi	Bonjour/Salut	Hallo/Tag	Ciao	Hola
Goodbye/Bye	Au revoir	Auf Wiedersehen/ Tschüss	Arrivederci/Ciao	Adiós/Chau
Yes	Oui	Ja	Sì	Sí
No	Non	Nein	No	No
Excuse me!	Pardon!	Entschuldigen Sie!	Scusa!	¡Perdón!
Thank you	Merci	Danke	Grazie	Gracias
Go away!	Va t'en!	Geh weg!	Vattene via!	¡Vete!
Help!	Au secours!	Hilfe!	Aiuto!	¡Ayuda!
Call the police!	Appelez la police!	Ruf die Polizei!	Chiamare la polizia!	¡Llame a la policía!
Get a doctor!	Cherchez un médecin!	Hol einen Arzt!	Chiamare un medico!	¡Llame a un médico!
I don't understand	Je ne comprends pas	Ich verstehe nicht	Non capisco	No comprendo
Do you speak English?	Parlez-vous anglais?	Sprechen Sie Englisch?	Lei parla inglese?	¿Habla inglés?
Where is...?	Où est...?	Wo ist...?	Dov' è...?	¿Dónde está...?

TEMPERATURE CONVERSIONS

°CELSIUS	-5	0	5	10	15	20	25	30	35	40
°FAHRENHEIT	23	32	41	50	59	68	77	86	95	104

MEASUREMENT CONVERSIONS

1 inch (in.) = 25.4mm	1 millimeter (mm) = 0.039 in.
1 foot (ft.) = 0.305m	1 meter (m) = 3.28 ft.
1 mile (mi.) = 1.609km	1 kilometer (km) = 0.621 mi.
1 pound (lb.) = 0.454kg	1 kilogram (kg) = 2.205 lb.
1 gallon (gal.) = 3.785L	1 liter (L) = 0.264 gal.